mathematics		
mechanics		
medicine		
military		
music		
noun		
nautical		
negative		negativo
oneself	*o.s.*	se, si mesmo
European Portuguese	*P*	português de Portugal
pejorative	*pej*	pejorativo
philosophy	*phil*	filosofia
plural	*pl*	plural
politics	*pol*	política
European Portuguese	*Port*	português de Portugal
past participle	*pp*	particípio passado
prefix	*pref*	prefixo
preposition	*prep*	preposição
present	*pres*	presente
present participle	*pres p*	particípio presente
pronoun	*pron*	pronome
psychology	*psych/psic*	psicologia
past tense	*pt*	pretérito
relative	*rel*	relativo
religion	*relig*	religião
somebody	*sb*	alguém
singular	*sing*	singular
slang	*sl*	gíria
someone	*s.o.*	alguém
something	*sth*	alguma coisa
subjunctive	*subj*	subjuntivo
technology	*techn/tecn*	tecnologia
theatre	*theat/teat*	teatro
television	*TV*	televisão
university	*univ*	universidade
auxiliary verb	*v aux*	verbo auxiliar
intransitive verb	*vi*	verbo intransitivo
pronominal verb	*vpr*	verbo pronominal
transitive verb	*vt*	verbo transitivo
transitive & intransitive verb	*vt/i*	verbo transitivo e intransitivo

D1047584

Oxford
Portuguese
Minidictionary

SECOND EDITION

Portuguese–English
English–Portuguese

OXFORD
UNIVERSITY PRESS

OXFORD

UNIVERSITY PRESS

Great Clarendon Street, Oxford OX2 6DP

Oxford University Press is a department of the University of Oxford.
It furthers the University's objective of excellence in research, scholarship,
and education by publishing worldwide in

Oxford New York

Auckland Cape Town Dar es Salaam Hong Kong Karachi Kuala Lumpur
Madrid Melbourne Mexico City Nairobi New Delhi Shanghai Taipei
Toronto

With offices in

Argentina Austria Brazil Chile Czech Republic France Greece
Guatemala Hungary Italy Japan Poland Portugal Singapore
South Korea Switzerland Thailand Turkey Ukraine Vietnam

Oxford is a registered trade mark of Oxford University Press
in the UK and in certain other countries

Published in the United States
by Oxford University Press Inc., New York

British Library Cataloguing in Publication Data
Data available

Library of Congress Cataloging in Publication Data
Data available

ISBN 0-19-861456-X   ISBN 978-0-19-861456-2
ISBN 0-19-929998-6   ISBN 978-0-19-929998-0 (SBS edition)

10 9 8 7 6 5 4 3 2

Typeset by SPI Publisher Services, Pondicherry, India
Printed in Italy by
Legoprint S.p.A.

Contents/Índice

Preface/Prefácio iv–v

Introduction/Introdução vi–vii

Proprietary terms/Nomes comerciais viii

Pronunciation/Pronúncia
   Portuguese/Português ix–xiii
   English/Inglês xiv–xvi

European Portuguese xvii

Portuguese–English/Portugues–Inglês **1–261**

Phrasefinder/Acha-frases

English–Portuguese/Inglês–Português **263–626**

Portuguese verbs/Verbos portugueses 627

Verbos irregulares ingleses/English irregular verbs 635

Portuguese-English *compiled by John Whitlam*
English-Portuguese *compiled by Lia Correia Raitt*
Revisions: *Mark Harland, Sarah Bailey*

Preface

The *Oxford Portuguese Minidictionary* has been written for speakers of both Portuguese and English and contains the most useful words and expressions in use today.

The dictionary provides a handy and comprehensive reference work for tourists, students, and business people who require quick and reliable answers to their translation needs.

Thanks are due to: Dr John Sykes, Prof. A. W. Raitt, Commander Virgílio Correia, Marcelo Affonso, Eng. Pedro Carvalho, Eng. Vasco Carvalho, Dr Iva Correia, Dr Ida Reis de Carvalho, Eng. J. Reis de Carvalho, Prof. A. Falcão, Bishop Manuel Falcão, Dr M. Luísa Falcão, Prof. J. Ferraz, Prof. M. de Lourdes Ferraz, Drs Ana and Jorge Fonseca, Mr Robert Howes, Irene Lakhani, Eng. Hugo Pires, Prof. M. Kaura Pires, Dr M. Alexandre Pires, Ambassador L. Pazos Alonso, Dr Teresa Pinto Pereira, Dr Isabel Tully, Carlos Wallenstein, Ligia Xavier, and Dr H. Martins and the members of his Mesa Lusófona at St Anthony's College, Oxford.

Prefácio

O *Oxford Portuguese Minidictionary* foi escrito por pessoas de língua portuguesa e inglesa, e contém as palavras e expressões mais úteis em uso atualmente.

O dicionário constitui uma obra de referência prática e abrangente para turistas, estudantes e pessoas de negócios que necessitam de respostas rápidas e confiáveis para as suas traduções.

Agradecimentos a: Dr John Sykes, Prof. A. W. Raitt, Comandante Virgílio Correia, Marcelo Affonso, Eng. Pedro Carvalho, Eng. Vasco Carvalho, Dr Iva Correia, Dr Ida Reis de Carvalho, Eng. J. Reis de Carvalho, Prof. A. Falcão, Bispo Manuel Falcão, Dr M. Luísa Falcão, Prof. J. Ferraz, Prof. M. de Lourdes Ferraz, Drs Ana e Jorge Fonseca, Mr Robert Howes, Eng. Hugo Pires, Prof. M. Laura Pires, Dr M. Alexandre Pires, Embaixador L. Pazos Alonso, Dr Teresa Pinto Pereira, Dr Isabel Tully, Carlos Wallenstein, e Dr H. Martins e os membros de sua Mesa Lusófona do St Anthony's College, em Oxford.

Introduction

The swung dash (∼) is used to replace a headword, or that part of a headword preceding the vertical bar (|).

In both English and Portuguese, only irregular plural forms are given. Plural forms of Portuguese nouns and adjectives ending in a single vowel are formed by adding an s (e.g. *livro, livros*). Those ending in *n, r, s* where the stress falls on the final syllable, and *z*, add *es* (e.g. *mulher, mulheres, falaz, falazes*). Nouns and adjectives ending in *m* change the final *m* to *ns* (e.g. *homem, homens, bom, bons*). Most of those ending in *ão* change their ending to *ões* (e.g. *estação, estações*).

Portuguese nouns and adjectives ending in an unstressed *o* form the feminine by changing the *o* to *a* (e.g. *belo, bela*). Those ending in *or* become *ora* (e.g. *trabalhador, trabalhadora*). All other masculine-feminine changes are shown at the main headword.

English and Portuguese pronunciation is given by means of the International Phonetic Alphabet. It is shown for all headwords, and for those derived words whose pronunciation is not easily deduced from that of a headword.

Portuguese verb tables will be found in the appendix.

Introdução

O sinal (∼) é usado para substituir o verbete, ou parte deste precedendo a barra vertical (|).

Tanto em inglês como em português, somente as formas irregulares do plural são dadas. As formas regulares do plural dos substantivos ingleses recebem um *s* (ex. *teacher*, *teachers*), ou *es* quando terminarem em *ch*, *sh*, *s*, *ss*, *us*, *x* ou *z* (ex. *sash*, *sashes*). Os substantivos terminados em *y* e precedidos por uma consoante, mudam no plural para *ies* (ex. *baby*, *babies*).

O passado e o particípio passado dos verbos regulares ingleses são formados pelo acréscimo de *ed* à forma infinitiva (ex. *last*, *lasted*). Os verbos terminados em *e* recebem *d* (ex. *move*, *moved*). Aqueles terminados em *y* têm o *y* substituído por *ied* (*carry*, *carried*). As formas irregulares dos verbos aparecem no dicionário em ordem alfabética, remetidas à forma infinitiva, e também, na lista de verbos no apêndice.

As pronúncias inglesa e portuguesa são dadas em acordo com o Alfabeto Fonético Internacional. A pronúncia é dada para todos os verbetes, assim como para aquelas palavras derivadas cuja pronúncia não seja facilmente deduzida a partir do verbete.

Proprietary terms

This dictionary includes some words which are, or are asserted to be, proprietary names or trade marks. Their inclusion does not imply that they have acquired for legal purposes a non-proprietary or general significance, nor is any other judgement implied concerning their legal status. In cases where the editor has some evidence that a word is used as a proprietary name or trade mark this is indicated by the label *propr*, but no judgement concerning the legal status of such words is made or implied thereby.

Nomes comerciais

Este dicionário inclui algumas palavras que são, ou acredita-se ser, nomes comerciais ou marcas registradas. A sua inclusão no dicionário não implica que elas tenham adquirido para fins legais um significado geral ou não-comercial, assim como não afeta em nenhum dos conceitos implícitos o seu status legal.

Nos casos em que o editor tenha prova suficiente de que uma palavra seja usada como um nome comercial ou marca registrada, este emprego é indicado pela etiqueta *propr*, mas nenhuma apreciação relativa ao status legal de tais palavras é feita ou sugerida por esta indicação.

Portuguese Pronunciation

Vowels and Diphthongs

a, à, á, â	/ã/	chamam, ambos, antes	1) before *m* at the end of a word, or before *m* or *n* and another consonant, is nasalized
	/a/	aba, à, acolá, desânimo	2) in other positions is like *a* in English r*a*ther
ã	/ã/	irmã	is nasalized
e	/ẽ/	sem, venda	1) before *m* at the end of a word, or before *m* or *n* and another consonant, is nasalized
	/i/	arte	2) at the end of a word is like *y* in English happ*y*
	/e/	menas	3) in other positions is like *e* in English th*e*y
é	/ɛ/	artéria	is like *e* in English g*e*t
ê	/e/	fêmur	is like *e* in English th*e*y
i	/ĩ/	sím, vindo	1) before *m* at the end of a word, or before *m* or *n* and another consonant, is nasalized
	/i/	fila	2) in other positions is like *ee* in English s*ee*
o	/õ/	com, sombra, onda	1) before *m* at the end of a word, or before *m* or *n* and another consonant, is nasalized
	/u/	muito	2) at the end of a word, unstressed, is like *u* in English r*u*le

	/o/	comover	3) in other positions, unstressed, is like o in English pole
	/o/	bobo	4) stressed, is like o in
	/ɔ/	loja	English pole or o in shop
ó	/o/	ópera	is like o in English shop
ô	/o/	tônica	is like o in English pole
u, ú		guerra, guisado, que, quilo	1) is silent in gue, gui, que, and qui
	/u/	mula, púrpura	2) in other positions is like u in English rule
ü, gü	/gw/	ungüento	in the combinations güe and güi is like g in English got, followed by English w
	/kw/	tranqüilo	in the combinations qüe and qüi is like qu in English queen
ãe	/ãj/	mãe, pães, alemães	is like y in English by, but nasalized
ai	/aj/	vai, pai, sai, caíta	is like y in English by
ao, au	/aw/	aos, autodefesa	is like ow in English how
ão	/ãw/	não	is like ow in English how, but nasalized
ei	/ej/	lei	is like ey in English they
eu	/ew/	deus, fleugma	both vowels pronounced separately
oẽ	/õj/	eleições	is like oi in English coin, but nasalized
oi	/oj/	noíte	is like oi in English coin
ou	/o/	pouco	is like o in English pole

Consonants

b	/b/	*banho*	is like *b* in English *ball*
c	/s/	*cinza, cem*	1) before *e* or *i* is like *s* in English *sit*
	/k/	*casa*	2) in other positions is like *c* in English *cat*
ç	/s/	*estação*	is like *s* in English *sit*
ch	/ʃ/	*chá*	is like *sh* in English *shout*
d	/dʒ/	*dizer, donde*	1) before *i* or final unstressed *e* is like *j* in English *join*
	/d/	*dar*	2) in other positions is like *d* in English *dog*
f	/f/	*falar*	is like *f* in English *fall*
g	/g/	*agente, giro*	1) before *e* or *i* is like *s* in English *vision*
	/g/	*gato*	2) in other positions is like *g* in English *get*
h		*haver*	is silent in Portuguese, but see *ch*, *lh*, *nh*
j	/ʒ/	*junta*	is like *s* in English *vision*
k	/k/	*kit*	is like English *k* in *key*
l	/w/	*falta*	1) between a vowel and a consonant, or following a vowel at the end of a word, is like *w* in English *water*
	/l/	*lata*	2) in other positions is like *l* in English *like*
l	/ʎ/	*calhar*	is like *lli* in English *million*

m		ambas/ˈãbuʃ/ com/kɪ̃/	1) between a vowel and a consonant, or after a vowel at the end of a word, *m* nasalizes the preceding vowel
	/m/	mato, mão	2) in other positions is like *m* in English mother
n		cinza/ˈsĩza/	1) between a vowel and a consonant, *n* nasalizes the preceding vowel
	/n/	benigno	2) in other positions is like *n* in English near
nh	/ɲ/	banho	is like *ni* in English opinion
p	/p/	paz	is like *p* in English poor
q	/k/	que, inquieto	1) *qu* before *e* or *i* is like English *k*
	/kw/	quase, quórum	2) *qu* before *a* or *o*, or *qü* before *e* or *i*, is like *qu* in English queen
r	/r/	aparato, gordo	1) between two vowels, or between a vowel and a consonant, is trilled
	/x/	rato, garra, melro, genro, Israel	2) at the beginning of a word, or in *rr*, or after *l*, *n*, or *s*, is like *ch* in Scottish loch
s	/ʃ/	depois	at the end of a word is like *sh* in English shoot
	/z/	asa, desde, abismo, Israel	2) between two vowels, or before *b, d, g, l, m, n, r, v*, is like *z* in English zebra
	/s/	suave	3) in other positions is like *s* in English sit

t	/tʃ/	tio, antes	1) before *i* or final unstressed *e* is like *ch* in English *cheese*
	/tʃi/	kit	2) at the end of a word is like *chy* in English it*chy*
	/t/	atar	3) in other positions is like *t* in English *tap*
v	/v/	luva	is like *v* in English *vain*
w	/u/	watt	is shorter than English *w*
x	/z/	exato, exemplo	1) in the prefix *ex* before a vowel, is pronounced like *z* in *zero*
	/ʃ/	xícara, baixo, peixe, frouxo	2) at the beginning of a word or after *ai*, *ei* or *ou*, is pronounced like *sh* in *show*
	/s/	explodir, auxiliar	3) is like *s* in English *sit*
	/ks/	axila, fixo	4) is like *x* in English *exit*
			5) in the combination *xce*, *xci*, *x* is not pronounced in Portuguese e.g. *excelente*, *excitar*
z	/s/	falaz	1) at the end of a word, is like *s* in English *sit*
	/z/	dizer	2) in other positions, is like English *z*

Pronúncia Inglesa

Vogais e Ditongos

/iː/	see, tea	como *i* em *giro*
/ɪ/	sit, happy	é um som mais breve do que *i* em *li*
/e/	set	como *e* em *tépido*
/æ/	hat	é um som mais breve do que *a* em *amor*
/ɑː/	arm, calm	como *a* em *cartaz*
/ɒ/	got	como *o* em *exótico*
/ɔː/	saw, more	como *o* em *corte*
/ʊ/	put, look	como *u* em *murro*
/uː/	too, due	como *u* em *duro*
/ʌ/	cup, some	como *a* em *pano*
/ɜː/	firm, fur	como *e* em *enxerto*
/ə/	ago, weather	como *e* no português europeu *parte*
/eɪ/	page, pain, pay	como *ei* em *leite*
/əʊ/	home, roam	é um som mais longo do que *o* em *coma*
/aɪ/	fine, by, guy	como *ai* em *sai*
/aɪə/	fire, tyre	como *ai* em *sai* seguido por /ə/
/aʊ/	now, shout	como *au* em *aula*
/aʊə/	hour, flower	como *au* em *aula* seguido por /ə/
/ɔɪ/	join, boy	como *oi* em *dói*
/ɪə/	dear, here, beer	como *ia* em *dia*
/eə/	hair, care, bear, there	como *e* em *etéreo*
/ʊə/	poor, during	como *ua* em *sua*

Consoantes

/p/	snap	como *p* em *pato*
/b/	bath	como *b* em *bala*

/t/	tap	como *t* em *t*ela
/d/	*d*ip	como *d* em *d*ar
/k/	*c*at, *k*ite, stoma*ch*, pi*que*	como *c* em *c*asa
/ks/	e*x*ercise	como *x* em a*x*ila
/g/	*g*ot	como *g* em *g*ato
/tʃ/	*ch*in	como *t* em *t*io
/dʒ/	*J*une, *g*eneral, *j*u*dg*e	como *d* em *d*izer
/f/	*f*all	como *f* em *f*aca
/v/	*v*ine, o*f*	como *v* em *v*aca
/θ/	*th*in, mo*th*	não tem equivalente, soa como um *s* entre os dentes
/ð/	*th*is	não tem equivalente, soa com um *z* entre os dentes
/s/	*s*o, voi*c*e	como *s* em *s*uave
/z/	*z*oo, ro*s*e	como *z* em fa*z*er
/ʃ/	*sh*e, lun*ch*	como *ch* em *ch*egar
/ʒ/	mea*s*ure, vi*s*ion	como *j* em *j*amais
/h/	*h*ow	*h* aspirado
/m/	*m*an	como *m* em *m*ala
/n/	*n*o*n*e	como *n* em *n*ada
/ŋ/	si*ng*	como *n* em ci*n*to
/l/	*l*eg	como *l* em *l*uva
/r/	*r*ed, w*r*ite	como *r* em ca*r*a
/j/	*y*es, *y*oke	como *i* em *i*oga
/w/	*w*eather, s*w*itch	como *u* em ég*u*a

ˈ indica a sílaba tônica

European Portuguese

Brazilian Portuguese, which is used in this dictionary, differs in a number of respects from that used in Portugal and the rest of the Portuguese-speaking world. These differences affect both spelling and pronunciation. Spelling variations appear on the Portuguese-English side. In so far as they affect pronunciation, the main variants are:

Brazilian Portuguese often omits the letters *b*, *c*, *m*, and *p*, which are retained by European Portuguese:

	Brazilian	**European**
b	sutil	su*b*til
c	ação	a*c*ção
	ato	a*c*to
	elétrico	elé*c*trico
m	indenizar	inde*m*nizar
p	batismo	ba*p*tismo
	exceção	exce*p*ção

Letters *c* and *p* in such variant forms are usually silent, hence acto /'atu/, baptismo/ba'tiʒmu/. However, *c* is pronounced in the combination *ect*, hence eléctrico/i'lektriku/.

The combinations *gü* and *qü* become *gu* and *qu*:

	Brazilian	**European**
	ungüento	ung*u*ento
	tranqüilo	tranq*u*ilo

However, they are still pronounced /gw/ and /kw/ respectively.

The other main differences in pronunciation are:

d	/d/	*dar, dizer, balde, donde*	1) at the beginning of a word, or after *l*, or *n*, is like *d* in English *dog*
	/ð/	*cidade, medroso*	2) in other positions is a sound between *d* in English *dog* and *th* in English *this*
e	/ə/	*arte*	at the end of a word, is like *e* in English *quarrel*
r	/rr/	*rato, garra, melro, genro, Israel, guelra, tenro, israelense*	at the beginning of a word, or in *rr*, or after *l*, *n*, or *s*, is strongly trilled
s	/ʃ/	*depois, asco, raspar, costura*	1) at the end of a word, or before *c*, *f*, *p*, *qu*, or *t*, is like English *sh*
	/ʒ/	*desde, Islã, abismo, Israel*	2) before *b*, *d*, *g*, *l*, *m*, *n*, *r*, or *u* is like *s* in English *vision*
t	/t/	*atar, antes, tio*	is like *t* in English *tap*
z	/ʃ/	*falaz*	at the end of a word, is like *sh* in English *shake*

PORTUGUÊS-INGLÊS
PORTUGUESE-ENGLISH

A

a¹ /a/ *artigo* the □ *pron* (*mulher*) her; (*coisa*) it; (*você*) you

a² /a/ *prep* (*para*) to; (*em*) at; **às 3 horas** at 3 o'clock; **à noite** at night; **a lápis** in pencil; **a mão** by hand

à /a/ **= a² + a¹**

aba /'aba/ *f* (*de chapéu*) brim; (*de camisa*) tail; (*de mesa*) flap

abacate /aba'katʃi/ *m* avocado (pear)

abacaxi /abaka'ʃi/ *m* pineapple; (*fam: problema*) pain, headache

aba|de /a'badʒi/ *m* abbot; **~dia** *f* abbey

aba|fado /aba'fadu/ *a* (*tempo*) humid, close; (*quarto*) stuffy; **~far** *vt* (*asfixiar*) stifle; muffle <*som*>; smother <*fogo*>; suppress <*informação*>; cover up <*escândalo, assunto*>

abagunçar /abagu'sar/ *vt* mess up

abaixar /aba'ʃar/ *vt* lower; turn down <*som, rádio*> □ *vi* **~-se** *vpr* bend down

abaixo /a'baʃu/ *adv* down; **~ de** below; **mais ~** further down; **~-assinado** *m* petition

abajur /aba'ʒur/ *m* (*quebra-luz*) lampshade; (*lâmpada*) (table) lamp

aba|lar /aba'lar/ *vt* shake; (*fig*) shock; **~lar-se** *vpr* be shocked, be shaken; **~lo** *m* shock

abanar /aba'nar/ *vt* shake, wave; wag <*rabo*>; (*com leque*) fan

abando|nar /abãdo'nar/ *vt* abandon; (*deixar*) leave; **~no** *m* abandonment; (*estado*) neglect

abarcar /abar'kar/ *vt* comprise, cover

abarro|tado /abaxo'tadu/ *a* crammed full; (*lotado*) crowded, packed; **~tar** *vt* cram full, stuff

abastado /abas'tadu/ *a* wealthy

abaste|cer /abaste'ser/ *vt* supply; fuel <*motor*>; fill up (with petrol) <*carro*>; refuel <*avião*>; **~cimento** *m* supply; (*de carro, avião*) refuelling

aba|ter /aba'ter/ *vt* knock down; cut down, fell <*árvore*>; shoot down <*avião, ave*>; slaughter <*gado*>; knock down, cut <*preço*>; **~ter alg** <*trabalho*> get s.o. down, wear s.o. out; <*má notícia*> sadden s.o.; <*doença*> lay s.o. low, knock the stuffing out of s.o.; **~tido** *a* dispirited, dejected; <*cara*> haggard, worn; **~timento** *m* dejection; (*de preço*) reduction

abaulado /abaw'ladu/ *a* convex; <*estrada*> cambered

abcesso /ab'sɛsu/ *m* (*Port*) *veja* **abscesso**

abdi|cação /abidʒika'sãw/ *f* abdication; **~car** *vt/i* abdicate

abdômen /abi'domẽ/ *m* abdomen

abecedário /abese'dariu/ *m* alphabet, ABC

abeirar-se /abeˈrarsi/ *vr* draw near

abe|lha /aˈbeʎa/ *f* bee; **~lhudo** *a* inquisitive, nosy

abençoar /abẽsoˈar/ *vt* bless

aber|to /aˈbertu/ *pp de* **abrir** □ *a* open; *<céu>* clear; *<gás, torneira>* on; *<sinal>* green; **~tura** *f* opening; *(foto)* aperture; *(pol)* liberalization

abeto /aˈbetu/ *m* fir (tree)

abis|mado /abizˈmadu/ *a* astonished; **~mo** *m* abyss

abjeto /abiˈʒɛtu/ *a* abject

abóbada /aˈbɔbada/ *f* vault

abobalhado /abobaˈʎadu/ *a* silly

abóbora /aˈbɔbora/ *f* pumpkin

abobrinha /aboˈbriɲa/ *f* courgette, *(Amer)* zucchini

abo|lição /aboliˈsãw/ *f* abolition; **~lir** *vt* abolish

abomi|nação /abominaˈsãw/ *f* abomination; **~nável** (*pl* **~náveis**) *a* abominable

abo|nar /aboˈnar/ *vt* guarantee *<dívida>*; give a bonus to *<empregado>*; **~no** /o/ *m* guarantee; *(no salário)* bonus; *(subsídio)* allowance, benefit; *(reforço)* endorsement

abordar /aborˈdar/ *vt* approach *<pessoa>*; broach, tackle *<assunto>*; *(naut)* board

aborre|cer /aboxeˈser/ *vt* (*irritar*) annoy; *(entediar)* bore; **~cer-se** *vpr* get annoyed; get bored; **~cido** *a* annoyed; bored; **~cimento** *m* annoyance; boredom

abor|tar /aborˈtar/ *vi* miscarry, have a miscarriage □ *vt* abort; **~to** /o/ *m* abortion; *(natural)* miscarriage

aboto|adura /abotoaˈdura/ *f* cufflink; **~ar** *vt* button (up) □ *vi* bud

abra|çar /abraˈsar/ *vt* hug, embrace; embrace *<causa>*; **~ço** *m* hug, embrace

abrandar /abrãˈdar/ *vt* ease *<dor>*; temper *<calor, frio>*; mollify, appease, placate *<povo>*; tone down, smooth over *<escândalo>* □ *vi <dor>* ease; *<calor, frio>* become less extreme; *<tempestade>* die down

abranger /abrãˈʒer/ *vt* cover; *(entender)* take in, grasp; **~ a** extend to

abrasileirar /abrazileˈrar/ *vt* Brazilianize

abre-|garrafas /abrigaˈxafas/ *m invar* (*Port*) bottle-opener; **~latas** *m invar* (*Port*) can-opener

abreugrafia /abrewgraˈfia/ *f* X-ray

abrevi|ar /abreviˈar/ *vt* abbreviate *<palavra>*; abridge *<livro>*; **~atura** *f* abbreviation

abridor /abriˈdor/ *m* **~ de lata** can-opener; **~ de garrafa** bottle-opener

abri|gar /abriˈgar/ *vt* shelter; house *<sem-teto>*; **~gar-se** *vpr* (take) shelter; **~go** *m* shelter

abril /aˈbriw/ *m* April

abrir /aˈbrir/ *vt* open; *(a chave)* unlock; turn on *<gás, torneira>*; make *<buraco, exceção>* □ *vi* open; *<céu, tempo>* clear (up); *<sinal>* turn green; **~-se** *vpr* open up; *(desabafar)* open up

abrupto /aˈbruptu/ *a* abrupt

abrutalhado /abrutaˈʎadu/ *a <sapato>* heavy; *<pessoa>* coarse

abscesso /abiˈsɛsu/ *m* abscess

absolu|tamente /abisolutaˈmẽtʃi/ *adv* absolutely; *(não)* not at all; **~to** *a* absolute; **em ~to** not at all, absolutely not

absol|ver /abisowˈver/ *vt* absolve; *(jurid)* acquit; **~vição** *f* absolution; *(jurid)* acquittal

absor|ção /abisorˈsãw/ *f* absorption; **~to** *a* absorbed; **~vente** *a <tecido>* absorbent; *<livro>* absorbing; **~ver** *vt* absorb; **~ver-se** *vpr* get absorbed

abs|têmio /abisˈtemiu/ *a* abstemious; *(de álcool)* teetotal □ *a* teetotaller; ~**tenção** f abstention; ~**tencionista** a abstaining □ m/f abstainer; ~**ter-se** upr abstain; ~**ter-se de** refrain from; ~**tinência** f abstinence

abstra|ção /abistra'sãw/ f abstraction; (mental) distraction; ~**ir** vt separate; ~**to** a abstract

absurdo /abi'surdu/ a absurd □ m nonsense

abun|dância /abū'dãsia/ f abundance; ~**dante** a abundant; ~**dar** vi abound

abu|sar /abu'zar/ vi go too far; ~**sar de** abuse; (aproveitar-se) take advantage of; ~**so** m abuse

abutre /a'butri/ m vulture

aca|bado /aka'badu/ a finished; (exausto) exhausted; (velho) decrepit; ~**bamento** m finish; ~**bar** vt finish □ vi finish, end; (esgotar-se) run out; ~**bar-se** upr end, be over; (esgotar-se) run out; ~**bar com** put an end to, end; (abolir, matar) do away with; split up with <namorado>; wipe out <adversário>; ~**bou de chegar** he has just arrived; ~**bar fazendo** or **por fazer** end up doing

acabrunhado /akabru'ɲadu/ a dejected

aca|demia /akade'mia/ f academy; (de ginástica etc) gym; ~**dêmico** a & m academic

açafrão /asa'frãw/ m saffron

acalentar /akalē'tar/ vt lull to sleep <bebê>; cherish <esperanças>; have in mind <planos>

acalmar /akaw'mar/ vt calm (down) □ vi <vento> drop; <mar> grow calm; ~**se** upr calm down

acam|pamento /akãpa'mētu/ m camp; (ato) camping; ~**par** vi camp

aca|nhado /aka'ɲadu/ a shy; ~**nhamento** m shyness; ~**nhar-se** upr be shy

ação /a'sãw/ f action; (jurid) lawsuit; (com) share

acariciar /akarisi'ar/ vt (com a mão) caress, stroke; (adular) make a fuss of; cherish <esperanças>

acarretar /akaxe'tar/ vt bring, cause

acasalar /akaza'lar/ vt mate; ~**se** upr mate

acaso /a'kazu/ m chance; **ao** ~ at random; **por** ~ by chance

aca|tamento /akata'mētu/ m respect, deference; ~**tar** vt respect, defer to <pessoa, opinião>; obey, abide by <leis, ordens>; take in <criança>

acc-, acç- (Port) veja **ac-, aç-**

acautelar-se /akawte'larsi/ upr be cautious

acei|tação /asejta'sãw/ f acceptance; ~**tar** vt accept; ~**tável** (pl ~**táveis**) a acceptable

acele|ração /aselera'sãw/ f acceleration; ~**rador** m accelerator; ~**rar** vi accelerate □ vt speed up

acenar /ase'nar/ vi signal; (saudando) wave; ~ **com** promise, offer

acender /asē'der/ vt light <cigarro, fogo, vela>; switch on <luz>; heat up <debate>

aceno /a'senu/ m signal; (de saudação) wave

acen|to /a'sētu/ m accent; ~**tuar** vt accentuate; accent <letra>

acepção /asep'sãw/ f sense

acepipes /ase'pipʃ/ m pl (Port) cocktail snacks

acerca /a'serka/ ~ **de** prep about, concerning

acercar-se /aser'karsi/ upr ~ **de** approach

acertar /aser'tar/ vt find <(com o) caminho, (a) casa>; put right, set <relógio>; get right <pergunta>; guess (correctly) <solução>; hit <alvo>; make <acordo, negócio>; fix, arrange <encontro> □ vi (ter *razão*) be right; (*atingir o alvo*) hit the mark; (*erro*) ~ **com** find, happen upon; ~ **em** hit

acervo /a'servu/ *m* collection; (*jurid*) estate

aceso /a'sezu/ *pp de* **acender** □ *a* <*luz*> on; <*fogo*> alight

aces|sar /ase'sar/ *vt* access; ~**sível** (*pl* ~**síveis**) *a* accessible; (*preço*) affordable <*preço*>; ~**so** /ɛ/ *m* access; (*de raiva, tosse*) fit; (*de febre*) attack; ~**sório** *a* & *m* accessory

acetona /ase'tona/ *f* (*para unhas*) nail varnish remover

achado /a'ʃadu/ *m* find

achaque /a'ʃaki/ *m* ailment

achar /a'ʃar/ *vt* find; (*pensar*) think; ~**-se** *vpr* (*estar*) be; (*considerar-se*) think that one is; **acho que sim/não** I think so/I don't think so

achatar /aʃa'tar/ *vt* flatten; cut <*salário*>

aciden|tado /asidẽ'tadu/ *a* rough <*terreno*>; bumpy <*estrada*>; eventful <*viagem, vida*>; injured <*pessoa*>; ~**tal** (*pl* ~**tais**) *a* accidental; ~**te** *m* accident

acidez /asi'des/ *f* acidity

ácido /'asidu/ *a* & *m* acid

acima /a'sima/ *adv* above; ~ **de** above; **mais** ~ higher up

acio|nar /asio'nar/ *vt* operate; (*jurid*) sue; ~**nista** *m/f* shareholder

acirrado /asi'xadu/ *a* stiff, tough

acla|mação /aklama'sãw/ *f* acclaim; (*de rei*) acclamation; ~**mar** *vt* acclaim

aclarar /akla'rar/ *vt* clarify, clear up □ *vi* clear up; ~**-se** *vpr* become clear

aclimatar /aklima'tar/ *vt* acclimatize, (*Amer*) acclimate; ~**-se** *vpr* get acclimatized, (*Amer*) get acclimated

aço /'asu/ *m* steel; ~ **inoxidável** stainless steel

acocorar-se /akoko'rarsi/ *vpr* squat (down)

acolá /ako'la/ *adv* over there

acolcho|ado /akowʃo'adu/ *m* quilt; ~**ar** *vt* quilt; upholster <*móveis*>

aco|lhedor /akoʎe'dor/ *a* welcoming; ~**lher** *vt* welcome <*hóspede*>; take in <*criança, refugiado*>; accept <*decisão, convite*>; respond to <*pedido*>; ~**lhida** *f*, ~**lhimento** *m* welcome; (*abrigo*) refuge

acomodar /akomo'dar/ *vt* accommodate; (*ordenar*) arrange; (*tornar cômodo*) make comfortable; ~**-se** *vpr* make o.s. comfortable

acompa|nhamento /akõpaɲa'mẽtu/ *m* (*mus*) accompaniment; (*prato*) side dish; (*comitiva*) escort; ~**nhante** *m/f* companion; (*mus*) accompanist; ~**nhar** *vt* accompany, go with; watch <*jogo, progresso*>; keep up with <*eventos, caso*>; keep up with, follow <*aula, conversa*>; share <*política, opinião*>; (*mus*) accompany; **a estrada** ~**nha** o **rio** the road runs alongside the river

aconche|gante /akõʃe'gãtʃi/ *a* cosy, (*Amer*) cozy; ~**gar** *vt* (*chegar* a si) cuddle; (*agasalhar*) wrap up; (*na cama*) tuck up; (*tornar cômodo*) make comfortable; ~**gar-se** *vpr* ensconce o.s.; ~**gar-se com** snuggle up to; ~**go** /e/ *m* cosiness, (*Amer*) coziness; (*abraço*) cuddle

acondicionar /akõdʒisio'nar/ *vt* condition; pack, package <*mercadoria*>

aconse|lhar /akõse'ʎar/ *vt* advise; ~**lhar-se** *vpr* consult; ~**lhar alg a** advise s.o. to; ~**lhar aco a alg** recommend sth to s.o.; ~**lhável** (*pl* ~**lháveis**) *a* advisable

aconte|cer /akõte'ser/ *vi* happen; ~**cimento** *m* event

acordar /akor'dar/ *vt/i* wake up

acorde /a'kordʒi/ *m* chord

acordeão /akordʒi'ãw/ *m* accordion

acordo /a'kordu/ *m* agreement; **de ~ com** in agreement with <*pessoa*>; in accordance with <*lei etc*>; **estar de ~** agree

Açores /a'soris/ *m pl* Azores

açoriano /asori'anu/ *a & m* Azorean

acorrentar /akoxē'tar/ *vt* chain (up)

acossar /ako'sar/ *vt* hound, badger

acos|tamento /akosta'mētu/ *m* hard shoulder, (*Amer*) berm; **~tar-se** *vpr* lean back

acostu|mado /akostu'madu/ *a* usual, customary; **estar ~mado a** be used to; **~mar** *vt* accustom; **~mar-se a** get used to

acotovelar /akotove'lar/ *vt* (*empurrar*) jostle; (*para avisar*) nudge

açou|gue /a'sogi/ *m* butcher's (shop); **~gueiro** *m* butcher

acovardar /akovar'dar/ *vt* cow, intimidate

acre /'akri/ *a* <*gosto*> bitter; <*aroma*> acrid, pungent; <*tom*> harsh

acredi|tar /akredʒi'tar/ *vt* believe; accredit <*representante*>; **~tar em** believe <*pessoa, história*>; believe in <*Deus, fantasmas*>; (*ter confiança*) have faith in; **~tável** (*pl* **~táveis**) *a* believable

acre-doce /akri'dosi/ *a* sweet and sour

acrescentar /akresē'tar/ *vt* add

acres|cer /akre'ser/ *vt* (*juntar*) add; (*aumentar*) increase □ *vi* increase; **~cido de** with the addition of; **~ce que** add to that the fact that

acréscimo /a'kresimu/ *m* addition; (*aumento*) increase

acriançado /akriã'sadu/ *a* childish

acrílico /a'kriliku/ *a* acrylic

acroba|cia /akroba'sia/ *f* acrobatics; **~ta** *m/f* acrobat

act- (*Port*) *veja* **at-**

acuar /aku'ar/ *vt* corner

açúcar /a'sukar/ *m* sugar

açuca|rar /asuka'rar/ *vt* sweeten; sugar <*café, chá*>; **~reiro** *m* sugar bowl

açude /a'sudʒi/ *m* dam

acudir /aku'dʒir/ *vt/i* **~ (a)** come to the rescue (of)

acumular /akumu'lar/ *vt* accumulate; combine <*cargos*>

acupuntura /akupũ'tura/ *f* acupuncture

acu|sação /akuza'sãw/ *f* accusation; **~sar** *vt* accuse; (*jurid*) charge; (*revelar*) reveal, show up; acknowledge <*recebimento*>

acústi|ca /a'kustʃika/ *f* acoustics; **~co** *a* acoustic

adap|tação /adapta'sãw/ *f* adaptation; **~tado** *a* <*criança*> well-adjusted; **~tar** *vt* adapt; (*para encaixar*) tailor; **~tar-se** *vpr* adapt; **~tável** (*pl* **~táveis**) *a* adaptable

adega /a'dɛga/ *f* wine cellar

adentro /a'dētru/ *adv* inside; **selva ~** into the jungle

adepto /a'dɛptu/ *m* follower; (*Port: de equipa*) supporter

ade|quado /ade'kwadu/ *a* appropriate, suitable; **~quar** *vt* adapt, tailor

adereços /ade'resus/ *m pl* props

ade|rente /ade'rētʃi/ *m/f* follower; **~rir** *vi* (*colar*) stick; join <*a partido, causa*>; follow <*a moda*>; **~são** *f* adhesion; (*apoio*) support; **~sivo** *a* sticky, adhesive □ *m* sticker

ades|trado /ades'tradu/ *a* skilled; **~trador** *m* trainer; **~trar** *vt* train; break in <*cavalo*>

adeus /a'dews/ *int* goodbye □ *m* goodbye, farewell

adian|tado /adʒiã'tadu/ *a* advanced; <*relógio*> fast; **chegar ~tado** be early; **~tamento** *m* progress; (*pagamento*) advance; **~tar** *vt* advance <*dinheiro*>; put forward <*relógio*>; bring forward <*data, reunião*>; get ahead with <*trabalho*> □ *vi* <*relógio*> gain; (*ter efeito*) be of use; **~tar-se** *vpr* progress, get ahead; **não ~ta (fazer)** it's no use (doing); **~te** *adv* ahead

adia/r /adʒi'ar/ *vt* postpone; adjourn <*sessão*>; **~mento** *m* postponement, adjournment

adi|ção /adʒi'sãw/ *f* addition; **~cionar** *vt* add; **~do** *m* attaché

adivi|nhação /adʒiviɲa'sãw/ *f* guesswork; (*por adivinho*) fortune-telling; **~nhar** *vt* guess; tell <*futuro, sorte*>; read <*pensamento*>; **~nho** *m* fortune-teller

adjetivo /adʒe'tʃivu/ *m* adjective

adminis|tração /adʒiministra'sãw/ *f* administration; (*de empresas*) management; (*~trador* *m* administrator; manager; **~trar** *vt* administer; manage <*empresa*>

admi|ração /adʒimira'sãw/ *f* admiration; (*assombro*) wonder(ment); **~rado** *a* admired; (*surpreso*) amazed, surprised; **~rador** *m* admirer □ *a* admiring; **~rar** *vt* admire; (*assombrar*) amaze; **~rar-se** *vpr* be amazed; **~rável** (*pl* **~ráveis**) *a* admirable; (*assombroso*) amazing

admis|são /adʒimi'sãw/ *f* admission; (*de escola*) intake; **~sível** (*pl* **~síveis**) *a* admissible

admitir /adʒimi'tʃir/ *vt* admit; (*permitir*) permit, allow; (*contratar*) take on

adoção /ado'sãw/ *f* adoption

ado|çar /ado'sar/ *vt* sweeten; **~cicado** *a* slightly sweet

adoecer /adoe'ser/ *vi* fall ill □ *vt* make ill

adoles|cência /adole'sẽsia/ *f* adolescence; **~cente** *a & m* adolescent

adopt- (*Port*) *veja* **adot-**

adorar /ado'rar/ *vt* (*amar*) adore; worship <*deus*>; (*fam: gostar de*) love

adorme|cer /adorme'ser/ *vi* fall asleep; <*perna*> go to sleep, go numb; **~cido** *a* sleeping; <*perna*> numb

ador|nar /ador'nar/ *vt* adorn; **~no** /o/ *m* adornment

ado|tar /ado'tar/ *vt* adopt; **~tivo** *a* adopted

adquirir /adʒiki'rir/ *vt* acquire

adu|bar /adu'bar/ *vt* fertilize; **~bo** *m* fertilizer

adu|lação /adula'sãw/ *f* flattery; (*do público*) adulation; **~lar** *vt* make a fuss of; (*com palavras*) flatter

adulterar /aduwte'rar/ *vt* adulterate; cook, doctor <*contas*> □ *vi* commit adultery

adúltero /a'duwteru/ *m* adulterer (*f* -ess) □ *a* adulterous

adul|tério /aduw'tεriu/ *m* adultery; **~to** *a & m* adult

advento /adʒi'vẽtu/ *m* advent

advérbio /adʒi'vεrbiu/ *m* adverb

adver|sário /adʒiver'sariu/ *m* opponent; (*inimigo*) adversary; **~sidade** *f* adversity; **~so** *a* adverse; (*adversário*) opposed

adver|tência /adʒiver'tẽsia/ *f* warning; **~tir** *vt* warn

advo|cacia /adʒivoka'sia/ *f* legal practice; **~gado** *m* lawyer; **~gar** *vt* advocate; (*jurid*) plead □ *vi* practise law

aéreo /a'εriu/ *a* air

aero|dinâmica /aerodʒi'namika/ *f* aerodynamics; **~dinâmico** *a* aerodynamic; **~dromo** *m* airfield; **~moça** /o/ *f* air hostess; **~nauta** *m* airman (*f* -woman).

~**náutica** *f* (*força*) air force; (*ciência*) aeronautics; ~**nave** *f* aircraft; ~**porto** /o/ *m* airport
aeros|sol /aero'sɔw/ (*pl* ~**sóis**) *m* aerosol
afabilidade /afabili'dadʒi/ *f* friendliness, kindness
afagar /afa'gar/ *vt* stroke
afamado /afa'madu/ *a* renowned, famed
afas|tado /afas'tadu/ *a* remote; <*parente*> distant; ~**tado** *de* (far) away from; ~**tamento** *m* removal; (*distância*) distance; (*de candidato*) rejection; ~**tar** *vt* move away; (*tirar*) remove; ward off <*perigo, ameaça*>; put out of one's mind <*ideia*>; ~**tar-se** *vpr* move away; (*distanciar-se*) distance o.s.; (*de cargo*) step down
afá|vel /a'favew/ (*pl* ~**veis**) *a* friendly, genial
afazeres /afa'zeris/ *m pl* business; ~ **domésticos** (household) chores
afect- (*Port*) *veja* **afet-**
Afeganistão /afeganis'tãw/ *m* Afghanistan
afe|gão /afe'gãw/ *a & m* (*f* ~**gã**) Afghan
afeição /afej'sãw/ *f* affection, fondness
afeiçoado /afejsu'adu/ *a* (*devoto*) devoted; (*amoroso*) fond
afeminado /afemi'nadu/ *a* effeminate
aferir /afe'rir/ *vt* check, inspect <*pesos, medidas*>; (*avaliar*) assess; (*cotejar*) compare
aferrar /afe'xar/ *vt* grasp; ~**-se a** cling to
afe|tação /afeta'sãw/ *f* affectation; ~**tado** *a* affected; ~**tar** *vt* affect; ~**tivo** *a* (*carinhoso*) affectionate; (*sentimental*) emotional; ~**to** /ɛ/ *m* affection; ~**tuoso** /o/ *a* affectionate
afi|ado /afi'adu/ *a* sharp; skilled <*pessoa*>; ~**ar** *vt* sharpen

aficionado /afisio'nadu/ *m* enthusiast
afilhado /afi'ʎadu/ *m* godson (*f* -daughter)
afili|ação /afilia'sãw/ *f* affiliation; ~**ada** *f* affiliate; ~**ar** *vt* affiliate
afim /a'fĩ/ *a* related, similar
afinado /afi'nadu/ *a* in tune
afinal /afi'naw/ *adv* ~ **(de contas)** (*por fim*) in the end; (*pensando bem*) after all
afinar /afi'nar/ *vt* tune □ *vi* taper
afinco /a'fĩku/ *m* perseverance, determination
afinidade /afini'dadʒi/ *f* affinity
afir|mação /afirma'sãw/ *f* assertion; ~**mar** *vt* claim, assert; ~**mativo** *a* affirmative
afivelar /afive'lar/ *vt* buckle
afixar /afik'sar/ *vt* stick, post
afli|ção /afli'sãw/ *f* (*física*) affliction; (*cuidado*) anxiety; ~**gir** *vt* <*doença*> afflict; (*inquietar*) trouble; ~**gir-se** *vpr* worry; ~**to** *a* troubled, worried
afluente /aflu'ẽtʃi/ *m* tributary
afo|bação /afoba'sãw/ *f* fluster, flap; ~**bado** *a* in a flap, flustered; ~**bar** *vt* fluster; ~**bar-se** *vpr* get flustered, get in a flap
afo|gado /afo'gadu/ *a* drowned; **morrer** ~**gado** drown; ~**gador** *m* choke; ~**gar** *vt/i* drown; (*auto*) flood; ~**gar-se** *vpr* (*matar-se*) drown o.s.
afoito /a'fojtu/ *a* bold, daring
afora /a'fɔra/ *adv* **pelo mundo** ~ throughout the world
afortunado /afortu'nadu/ *a* fortunate
afresco /a'fresku/ *m* fresco
África /'afrika/ *f* Africa; ~ **do Sul South Africa**
africano /afri'kanu/ *a & m* African
afrodisíaco /afrodʒi'ziaku/ *a & m* aphrodisiac
afron|ta /a'frõta/ *f* affront, insult; ~**tar** *vt* affront, insult

afrouxar /afroˈʃar/ *vt/i* loosen; *(de rapidez)* slow down; *(de disciplina)* relax

afta /ˈafta/ *f* (mouth) ulcer

afugentar /afuʒẽˈtar/ *vt* drive away; rout <*inimigo*>

afundar /afũˈdar/ *vt* sink; **~-se** *vpr* sink

agachar /agaˈʃar/ *vi* **~-se** *vpr* bend down

agarrar /agaˈxar/ *vt* grab, snatch; **~-se** *vpr* **~-se a** cling to, hold on to

agasalhar /agazaˈʎar/ *vt* **~-se** *vpr* wrap up (warmly); **~lho** *m* (*casaco*) coat; (*suéter*) sweater

agência /aˈʒẽsia/ *f* agency; **~ de correio** post office; **~ de viagens** travel agency

agenda /aˈʒẽda/ *f* diary

agente /aˈʒẽtʃi/ *m/f* agent

ágil /ˈaʒiw/ (*pl* **ágeis**) *a* <*pessoa*> agile; <*serviço*> quick, efficient

agili|dade /aʒiliˈdadʒi/ *f* agility; (*rapidez*) speed; **~zar** *vt* speed up, streamline

ágio /ˈaʒiu/ *m* premium

agiota /aʒiˈɔta/ *m/f* loan shark

agir /aˈʒir/ *vi* act

agi|tado /aʒiˈtadu/ *a* agitated; <*mar*> rough; **~tar** *vt* wave <*braços*>; wag <*rabo*>; shake <*garrafa*>; (*perturbar*) agitate; **~tar-se** *vpr* get agitated; <*mar*> get rough

aglome|ração /aglomeraˈsãw/ *f* collection; (*de pessoas*) crowd; **~rar** collect; **~rar-se** *vpr* gather

agonia /agoˈnia/ *f* anguish; (*da morte*) death throes

agora /aˈgɔra/ *adv* now; (*há pouco*) just now; **~ mesmo** right now; **de ~ em diante** from now on; **até ~** so far, up till now

agosto /aˈgostu/ *m* August

agouro /aˈgoru/ *m* omen

agraciar /agrasiˈar/ *vt* decorate

agra|dar /agraˈdar/ *vt* please; (*fazer agrados*) be nice to, fuss over

□ *vi* be pleasing, please; (*cair no gosto*) go down well; **~dável** (*pl* **~dáveis**) *a* pleasant

agrade|cer /agradeˈser/ *vt* **~cer aco a alg**, **~cer a alg por aco** thank s.o. for sth □ *vi* say thank you; **~cido** *a* grateful; **~cimento** *m* gratitude; *pl* thanks

agrado /aˈgradu/ *m* **fazer ~s a** be nice to, make a fuss of

agrafar /agraˈfar/ *vt* (*Port*) staple; **~dor** *m* stapler

agrário /aˈgrariu/ *a* land, agrarian

agra|vante /agraˈvãtʃi/ *a* aggravating □ *f* aggravating circumstance; **~var** *vt* aggravate, make worse; **~var-se** *vpr* get worse

agredir /agreˈdʒir/ *vt* attack

agregado /agreˈgadu/ *m* (*em casa*) lodger

agres|são /agreˈsãw/ *f* aggression; (*ataque*) assault; **~sivo** *a* aggressive; **~sor** *m* aggressor

agreste /aˈgrɛstʃi/ *a* rural

agrião /agriˈãw/ *m* watercress

agrícola /aˈgrikola/ *a* agricultural

agricul|tor /agrikuwˈtor/ *m* farmer; **~tura** *f* agriculture, farming

agridoce /agriˈdosi/ *a* bittersweet

agropecuária /agropekuˈaria/ *f* farming; **~rio** *a* agricultural

agru|pamento /agrupaˈmẽtu/ *m* grouping; **~par** *vt* group; **~par-se** *vpr* group (together)

água /ˈagwa/ *f* water; **dar ~ na boca** be mouthwatering; **ir por ~ abaixo** go down the drain; **~ benta** holy water; **~ doce** fresh water; **~ mineral** mineral water; **~ salgada** salt water; **~ sanitária** household bleach

aguaceiro /agwaˈseru/ *m* downpour

água-de-coco /agwadʒiˈkoku/ *f* coconut water; **~-colônia** *f* eau de cologne

aguado /a'gwadu/ a watery

aguardar /agwar'dar/ vt wait for, await □ vi wait

aguardente /agwar'dẽtʃi/ f spirit

aguarrás /agwa'xas/ m turpentine

água-viva /agwa'viva/ f jellyfish

agu|çado /agu'sadu/ a pointed; <sentidos> acute; ~**çar** vt sharpen; ~**deza** f sharpness; (mental) perceptiveness; ~**do** a sharp; <som> shrill; (fig) acute

agüentar /agwẽ'tar/ vt stand, put up with; hold <peso> □ vi <pessoa> hold out; <suporte> hold

águia /'agia/ f eagle

agulha /a'guʎa/ f needle

ai /aj/ m sigh; (de dor) groan □ int ah!; (de dor) ouch!

aí /a'i/ adv there; (então) then

aidético /aj'detʃiku/ a suffering from Aids □ m Aids sufferer

AIDS /'ajdʒis/ f Aids

ainda /a'ĩda/ adv still; **melhor** ~ even better; **não** ... ~ not ... yet; ~ **assim** even so; ~ **bem** just as well; ~ **por cima** moreover, in addition; ~ **que** even if

aipim /aj'pĩ/ m cassava

aipo /'ajpu/ m celery

ajeitar /aʒej'tar/ vt (arrumar) sort out; (arranjar) arrange; (ajustar) adjust; ~**se** vpr adapt; (dar certo) turn out right, sort o.s. out

ajoe|lhado /aʒoe'ʎadu/ a kneeling (down); ~**lhar** vi, ~**lhar-se** vpr kneel (down)

aju|da /a'ʒuda/ f help; ~**dante** m/f helper; ~**dar** vt help

ajuizado /aʒui'zadu/ a sensible

ajus|tar /aʒus'tar/ vt adjust; settle <disputa>; take in <roupa>; ~**tar-se** vpr conform; ~**tável** (pl ~**táveis**) a adjustable; ~**te** m adjustment; (acordo) settlement

ala /'ala/ f wing

ala|gação /alaga'sãw/ f flooding; ~**gadiço** a marshy □ m marsh; ~**gar** vt flood

alameda /ala'meda/ f avenue

álamo /'alamu/ m poplar (tree)

alarde /a'lardʒi/ m **fazer ~ de** flaunt; make a big thing of <notícia>; ~**ar** vt/i flaunt

alargar /alar'gar/ vt widen; (fig) broaden; let out <roupa>

alarido /ala'ridu/ m outcry

alar|ma /a'larma/ m alarm; ~**mante** a alarming; ~**mar** vt alarm; ~**me** m alarm; ~**mista** a & m alarmist

alastrar /alas'trar/ vt scatter; (disseminar) spread □ vi spread

alavanca /ala'vãka/ f lever; ~ **de mudanças** gear lever

alban|ês /awba'nes/ a & m (f ~**esa**) Albanian

Albânia /aw'bania/ f Albania

albergue /aw'bɛrgi/ m hostel

álbum /'awbũ/ m album

alça /'awsa/ f handle; (de roupa) strap; (de fusil) sight

alcachofra /awka'ʃofra/ f artichoke

alçada /aw'sada/ f competence, power

álcali /'awkali/ m alkali

alcan|çar /awkã'sar/ vt reach; (conseguir) attain; (compreender) understand □ vi reach; ~**çável** (pl ~**çáveis**) a reachable; attainable; ~**ce** m reach; (de tiro) range; (importância) consequence; (compreensão) understanding

alcaparra /awka'paxa/ f caper

alcatra /aw'katra/ f rump steak

alcatrão /awka'trãw/ m tar

álcool /'awkow/ m alcohol

alco|latra /awko'ɔlatra/ m/f alcoholic; ~**lico** a & m alcoholic

alcunha /aw'kuɲa/ f nickname

aldeia /aw'deja/ f village

aleatório /alia'tɔriu/ a random, arbitrary

alecrim /ale'krĩ/ m rosemary

ale|gação /alega'sãw/ f allegation; ~**gar** vt allege

alegoria /alego'ria/ f allegory; **~górico** a allegorical

ale|grar /ale'grar/ vt cheer up; brighten up <casa>; **~grar-se** vpr cheer up; **~gre** /ε/ a cheerful; <cores> bright; **~gria** f joy

alei|jado /ale'ʒadu/ a crippled □ m cripple; **~jar** vt cripple

alei|tamento /alejta'mētu/ m breast-feeding; **~tar** vt breastfeed

além /a'lēj/ adv beyond; **~ de** (ao lado de lá de) beyond; (mais de) over; (ademais de) apart from

Alemanha /ale'maɲa/ f Germany

alemão /ale'mãw/ a (pl **~mães**) a & m (f **~mã**) German

alen|tador /alēta'dor/ a encouraging; **~tar** vt encourage; **~tar-se** vpr cheer up; **~to** m courage; (fôlego) breath

alergia /aler'ʒia/ f allergy

alérgico /a'lerʒiku/ a allergic (**a** to)

aler|ta /a'lɛrta/ a & m alert □ adv on the alert; **~tar** vt alert

alfa|bético /awfa'bɛtʃiku/ a alphabetical; **~betização** f literacy; **~betizar** vt teach to read and write; **~beto** m alphabet

alface /aw'fasi/ f lettuce

alfaiate /awfaj'atʃi/ m tailor

al|fândega /aw'fãdʒiga/ f customs; **~fandegário** a customs □ m customs officer

alfine|tada /awfine'tada/ f prick; (dor) stabbing pain; (fig) dig; **~te** /e/ m pin; **~te de segurança** safety pin

alforreca /alfo'xeka/ f (Port) jellyfish

alga /'awga/ f seaweed

algarismo /awga'rizmu/ m numeral

algazarra /awga'zaxa/ f uproar, racket

alge|mar /awʒe'mar/ vt handcuff; **~mas** /e/ f pl handcuffs

algibeira /alʒi'bejra/ f (Port) pocket

algo /'awgu/ pron something; (numa pergunta) anything □ adv somewhat

algodão /awgo'dãw/ m cotton; **~(-doce)** candy floss, (Amer) cotton candy; **~ (hidrófilo)** cotton wool, (Amer) absorbent cotton

alguém /aw'gēj/ pron somebody, someone; (numa pergunta) anybody, anyone

al|gum /aw'gũ/ (f **~guma**) a some; (numa pergunta) any; (nenhum) no, not one □ pron pl some; **~guma coisa** something

algures /aw'guris/ adv somewhere

alheio /a'ʎeju/ a (de outra pessoa) someone else's; (de outras pessoas) other people's; **~ a** foreign to; (impróprio) irrelevant to; (desatento) unaware of; **~ de** removed from

alho /'aʎu/ m garlic; **~-poró** m leek

ali /a'li/ adv (over) there

ali|ado /ali'adu/ a allied □ m ally; **~ança** f alliance; (anel) wedding ring; **~ar** vt, **~ar-se** vpr ally

aliás /a'ljaʃ/ adv (além disso) what's more, furthermore; (no entanto) however; (diga-se de passagem) by the way, incidentally; (senão) otherwise

álibi /'alibi/ m alibi

alicate /ali'katʃi/ m pliers; **~ de unhas** nail clippers

alicerce /ali'sersi/ m foundation; (fig) basis

alie|nado /alie'nadu/ a alienated; (demente) insane; **~nar** vt alienate; transfer <bens>; **~nígena** a & m/f alien

alimen|tação /alimēta'sãw/ f (ato) feeding; (comida) food; (tecn) supply; **~tar** a food; <hábitos> eating □ vt feed; (fig) nurture;

~**tar-se de** live on; ~**tício** *a* gêneros ~**tícios** foodstuffs; ~**to** *m* food

ali**nhado** /ali'ɲadu/ *a* aligned; <*pessoa*> smart, (*Amer*) sharp; ~**nhar** *vt* align

alíquota /a'likwota/ *f (de imposto)* bracket

alisar /ali'zar/ *vt* smooth (out); straighten <*cabelo*>

alistar /alis'tar/ *vt* recruit; ~**-se** *vpr* enlist

aliviar /alivi'ar/ *vt* relieve

alívio /a'liviu/ *m* relief

alma /'awma/ *f* soul

almanaque /awma'naki/ *m* yearbook

almejar /awme'ʒar/ *vt* long for

almirante /awmi'rãtʃi/ *m* admiral

almo|**çar** /awmo'sar/ *vi* have lunch □ *vt* have for lunch; ~**ço** /o/ *m* lunch

almofada /awmo'fada/ *f* cushion; (*Port: de cama*) pillow

almôndega /aw'mõdʒiga/ *f* meatball

almoxarifado /awmoʃari'fadu/ *m* storeroom

alô /a'lo/ *int* hallo

alocar /alo'kar/ *vt* allocate

alo|**jamento** /aloʒa'mẽtu/ *m* accommodation, (*Amer*) accommodations; (*habitação*) housing; ~**jar** *vt* accommodate; house <*sem-teto*>; ~**jar-se** *vpr* stay

alongar /alõ'gar/ *vt* lengthen; extend, stretch out <*braço*>

alpendre /aw'pẽdri/ *m* shed; (*pórtico*) porch

Alpes /'awpis/ *m pl* Alps

alpini|**smo** /awpi'nizmu/ *m* mountaineering; ~**ta** *m/f* mountaineer

alqueire /aw'keri/ *m = 4.84 hectares*, (in *São Paulo* = *2.42 hectares*)

alquimi|**a** /awki'mia/ *f* alchemy; ~**sta** *mf* alchemist

alta /'awta/ *f* rise; **dar** ~ **a** discharge; **ter** ~ be discharged

altar /aw'tar/ *m* altar

alterar /awte'rar/ *vt* alter; (*falsificar*) falsify; ~**-se** *vpr* change; (*zangar-se*) get angry

alter|**nado** /awter'nadu/ *a* alternate; ~**nar** *vt*/*i*, ~**nar-se** *vpr* alternate; ~**nativa** *f* alternative; ~**nativo** *a* alternative; <*corrente*> alternating

al|**teza** /aw'teza/ *f* highness; ~**titude** *f* altitude

alti|**vez** /awtʃi'ves/ *f* arrogance; ~**vo** *a* arrogant; (*elevado*) majestic

alto /'awtu/ *a* high; <*pessoa*> tall; <*barulho*> loud □ *adv* high; <*falar*> loud(ly); <*ler*> aloud □ *m* top; **os** ~**s e baixos** the ups and downs □ *int* halt!; ~**falante** *m* loudspeaker

altura /aw'tura/ *f* height; (*momento*) moment; **ser à** ~ **de** be up to

aluci|**nação** /alusina'sãw/ *f* hallucination; ~**nante** *a* mind-boggling, crazy

aludir /alu'dʒir/ *vi* allude (**a** to)

alu|**gar** /alu'gar/ *vt* rent <*casa*>; hire, rent <*carro*>; <*locador*> let, rent out, hire out; ~**guel** (*Port*), ~**guer** /ɛ/ *m* rent; (*ato*) renting

alumiar /alumi'ar/ *vt* light (up)

alumínio /alu'miniu/ *m* aluminium, (*Amer*) aluminum

aluno /a'lunu/ *m* pupil

alusão /alu'zãw/ *f* allusion (**a** to)

alvará /awva'ra/ *m* permit, licence

alve|**jante** /awve'ʒãtʃi/ *m* bleach; ~**jar** *vt* bleach; (*visar*) aim at

alvenaria /awvena'ria/ *f* masonry

alvo /'awvu/ *m* target

alvorada /awvo'rada/ *f* dawn

alvoro|**çar** /awvoro'sar/ *vt* stir up, agitate; (*entusiasmar*) excite; ~**ço** /o/ *m* (*tumulto*) uproar; (*entusiasmo*) excitement

amabilidade /amabili'dadʒi/ f kindness

amaci|ante /amasi'ãtʃi/ m (de roupa) (fabric) conditioner; **~ar** vt soften; run in <carro>

amador /ama'dor/ a & m amateur; **~ismo** m amateurism; **~ístico** a amateurish

amadurecer /amadure'ser/ vt/i <fruta> ripen; (fig) mature

âmago /'amagu/ m heart, core; (da questão) crux

amaldiçoar /amawdʒiso'ar/ vt curse

amamentar /amamẽ'tar/ vt breast-feed

amanhã /ama'ɲã/ m & adv tomorrow; **depois de ~** the day after tomorrow

amanhecer /amaɲe'ser/ vi & m dawn

amansar /amã'sar/ vt tame; (fig) placate <pessoa>

a|mante /a'mãtʃi/ m/f lover; **~mar** vt/i love

amarelo /ama'rɛlu/ a & m yellow

amar|go /a'margu/ a bitter; **~gura** f bitterness; **~gurar** vt embitter; (sofrer) endure

amarrar /ama'xar/ vt tie (up); (naut) moor; **~ a cara** frown, scowl

amarrotar /amaxo'tar/ vt crease

amassar /ama'sar/ vt crush, squash; screw up <papel>; crease <roupa>; dent <carro>; knead <pão>; mash <batatas>

amá|vel /a'mavew/ (pl **~veis**) a kind

Ama|zonas /ama'zonas/ m Amazon; **~zônia** f Amazonia

âmbar /'ãbar/ m amber

ambi|ção /ãbi'sãw/ f ambition; **~cionar** vt aspire to; **~cioso** /o/ a ambitious

ambien|tal /ãbiẽ'taw/ (pl **~tais**) a environmental; **~tar** vt set <filme, livro>; set up <casa>; **~tar-se** vpr settle in; **~te** m

environment; (atmosfera) atmosphere

am|bigüidade /ãbigwi'dadʒi/ f ambiguity; **~bíguo** a ambiguous

âmbito /'ãbitu/ m scope, range

ambos /'ãbus/ a & pron both

ambu|lância /ãbu'lãsia/ f ambulance; **~lante** a (que anda) walking; <músico> wandering; <venda> mobile; **~latório** m out-patient clinic

amea|ça /ami'asa/ f threat; **~çador** a threatening; **~çar** vt threaten

ameba /a'mɛba/ f amoeba

amedrontar /amedrõ'tar/ vt scare; **~-se** vpr get scared

ameixa /a'meʃa/ f plum; (passa) prune

amém /a'mẽj/ int amen □ m agreement; **dizer ~** a go along with

amêndoa /a'mẽdoa/ f almond

amendoim /amẽdo'ĩ/ m peanut

ame|nidade /ameni'dadʒi/ f pleasantness; pl pleasantries, small talk; **~nizar** vt ease; calm <ânimos>; settle <disputa>; tone down <repreensão>; **~no** /e/ a pleasant; mild <clima>

América /a'mɛrika/ f America; **~ do Norte/Sul** North/South America

america|nizar /amerikani'zar/ vt Americanize; **~no** a & m American

amestrar /ames'trar/ vt train

ametista /ame'tʃista/ f amethyst

amianto /ami'ãtu/ m asbestos

ami|gar-se /ami'garsi/ vpr make friends; **~gável** (pl **~gáveis**) a amicable

amígdala /a'migdala/ f tonsil

amigdalite /amigda'litʃi/ f tonsillitis

amigo /a'migu/ a friendly □ m friend; **~ da onça** false friend

amistoso /amis'tozu/ a & m friendly

amiúde /ami'udʒi/ *adv* often

amizade /ami'zadʒi/ *f* friendship

amnésia /ami'nεzia/ *f* amnesia

amnistia /amnis'tia/ *f* (Port) *veja* **anistia**

amo|lação /amola'sãw/ *f* annoyance; **~lante** *a* annoying; **~lar** *vt* annoy, bother; sharpen <*faca*>; **~lar-se** *vpr* get annoyed

amolecer /amole'ser/ *vt/i* soften

amol|gadura /amowga'dura/ *f* dent; **~gar** *vt* dent

amoníaco /amo'niaku/ *m* ammonia

amontoar /amõto'ar/ *vt* pile up; amass <*riquezas*>; **~-se** *vpr* pile up

amor /a'mor/ *m* love; **~ próprio** self-esteem

amora /a'mɔra/ *f* **~ preta**, (Port) **~ silvestre** blackberry

amordaçar /amorda'sar/ *vt* gag

amoroso /amo'rozu/ *adj* loving

amor-perfeito /amorper'fejtu/ *m* pansy

amorte|cedor /amortese'dor/ *m* shock absorber; **~cer** *vt* deaden; absorb <*impacto*>; break <*queda*> □ *vi* fade

amostra /a'mɔstra/ *f* sample

ampa|rar /ãpa'rar/ *vt* support; (fig) protect; **~rar-se** *vpr* lean; **~ro** *m* (apoio) support; (proteção) protection; (ajuda) aid

ampère /ã'pεri/ *m* amp(ere)

ampli|ação /ãplia'sãw/ *f* (de foto) enlargement; (de casa) extension; **~ar** *vt* enlarge <*foto*>; extend <*casa*>; broaden <*conhecimentos*>

amplifi|cador /ãplifika'dor/ *m* amplifier; **~car** *vt* amplify

amplo /'ãplu/ *a* <*sala*> spacious; <*roupa*> full; <*sentido, conhecimento*> broad

ampola /ã'pola/ *f* ampoule

amputar /ãpu'tar/ *vt* amputate

Amsterdã /amister'dã/, (Port)

Amsterdão /amiʃter'dãw/ *f* Amsterdam

amu|ado /amu'adu/ *a* in a sulk, sulky; **~ar** *vi* sulk

amuleto /amu'leto/ *m* charm

amuo /a'muu/ *m* sulk

ana|crônico /ana'kroniku/ *a* anachronistic; **~cronismo** *m* anachronism

anais /a'najs/ *m pl* annals

analfabeto /anawfa'bεtu/ *a & m* illiterate

analisar /anali'zar/ *vt* analyse

análise /a'nalizi/ *f* analysis

ana|lista /ana'lista/ *m/f* analyst; **~lítico** *a* analytical

analogia /analo'ʒia/ *f* analogy

análogo /a'nalogu/ *a* analogous

ananás /ana'naʃ/ *m invar* (Port) pineapple

anão /a'nãw/ *a & m* (f **anã**) dwarf

anarquia /anar'kia/ *f* anarchy; (fig) chaos

anárquico /a'narkiku/ *a* anarchic

anarquista /anar'kista/ *m/f* anarchist

ana|tomia /anato'mia/ *f* anatomy; **~tômico** *a* anatomical

anca /'ãka/ *f* (de pessoa) hip; (de animal) rump

anchova /ã'ʃova/ *f* anchovy

ancinho /ã'siɲu/ *m* rake

âncora /'ãkora/ *f* anchor

anco|radouro /ãkora'doru/ *m* anchorage; **~rar** *vt/i* anchor

andaime /ã'dajmi/ *m* scaffolding

an|damento /ãda'mẽtu/ *m* (progresso) progress; (rumo) course; **dar ~damento** a set in motion; **~dar** *m* (jeito de andar) gait, walk; (de prédio) floor; (Port: apartamento) flat, (Amer) apartment □ *vi* (ir a pé) walk; (de trem, ônibus) travel; (a cavalo, de bicicleta) ride; (funcionar, progredir) go; **ele anda deprimido** he's been depressed lately

Andes /'ãdʒis/ *m pl* Andes

andorinha /ãdo'riɲa/ *f* swallow

anedota /ane'dæta/ *f* anecdote

anel /a'nɛw/ (*pl* **anéis**) *m* ring; (*no cabelo*) curl; **~ viário** ringroad

anelado /ane'ladu/ *a* curly

anemia /ane'mia/ *f* anaemia

anêmico /a'nemiku/ *a* anaemic

anes|tesia /aneste'zia/ *f* anaesthesia; (*droga*) anaesthetic; **~tesiar** *vt* anaesthetize; **~tésico** *a & m* anaesthetic; **~tesista** *m/f* anaesthetist

ane|xar /anek'sar/ *vt* annex <*terras*>; (*em carta*) enclose; (*juntar*) attach; **~xo** /ɛ/ *a* attached; (*em carta*) enclosed □ *m* annexe; (*em carta*) enclosure

anfíbio /ã'fibiu/ *a* amphibious □ *m* amphibian

anfiteatro /ãfitʃi'atru/ *m* amphitheatre; (*no teatro*) dress circle

anfi|trião /ãfitri'ãw/ *m* (*~triã*) host (*f* -ess)

angariar /ãgari'ar/ *vt* raise <*fundos*>; canvass for <*votos*>; win <*adeptos, simpatia*>

angli|cano /ãgli'kanu/ *a & m* Anglican; **~cismo** *m* Anglicism

anglo-saxônico /ãglusak'soniku/ *a* Anglo-Saxon

Angola /ã'gola/ *f* Angola

angolano /ãgo'lanu/ *a & m* Angolan

angra /'ãgra/ *f* inlet, cove

angular /ãgu'lar/ *a* angular

ângulo /'ãgulu/ *m* angle

angústia /ã'gustʃia/ *f* anguish, anxiety

angustiante /ãgustʃi'ãtʃi/ *a* distressing; <*momento*> anxious

ani|mado /ani'madu/ *a* (*vivo*) lively; (*alegre*) cheerful; (*entusiasmado*) enthusiastic; **~mador** *a* encouraging □ *m* presenter; **~mal** (*pl* **~mais**) *a & m* animal; **~mar** *vt* encourage; liven up <*festa*>; **~mar-se** *vpr* cheer up; <*festa*> liven up

ânimo /'animu/ *m* courage, spirit; *pl* tempers

animosidade /animozi'dadʒi/ *f* animosity

aniquilar /aniki'lar/ *vt* destroy; (*prostrar*) shatter

anis /a'nis/ *m* aniseed

anistia /anis'tʃia/ *f* amnesty

aniver|sariante /aniversari'ãtʃi/ *m/f* birthday boy (*f* girl); **~sário** *m* birthday; (*de casamento etc*) anniversary

anjo /'ãʒu/ *m* angel

ano /'anu/ *m* year; **fazer ~s** have a birthday; **~ bissexto** leap year; **~ letivo** academic year; **~-bom** *m* New Year

anoite|cer /anojte'ser/ *m* nightfall □ *vi* **~ceu** night fell

anomalia /anoma'lia/ *f* anomaly

anonimato /anoni'matu/ *m* anonymity

anônimo /a'nonimu/ *a* anonymous

anor|mal /anor'maw/ (*pl* **~mais**) *a* abnormal

ano|tação /anota'sãw/ *f* note; **~tar** *vt* note down, write down

ânsia /'ãsia/ *f* anxiety; (*desejo*) longing; **~s de vômito** nausea

ansi|ar /ãsi'ar/ *vi* **~ por** long for; **~edade** *f* anxiety; (*desejo*) eagerness; **~oso** /o/ *a* anxious

antártico /ã'tartʃiku/ *a & m* Antarctic

antebraço /ãtʃi'brasu/ *m* forearm

antece|dência /ãtese'dẽsia/ *f* com **~dência** in advance; **~dente** *a* preceding; **~dentes** *m pl* record, past

antecessor /ãtese'sor/ *m* (*f* **~a**) predecessor

anteci|pação /ãtʃisipa'sãw/ *f* anticipation; **com ~pação** in advance; **~padamente** *adv* in advance; **~pado** *a* advance; **~par** *vt* anticipate, forestall; (*adiantar*) bring forward; **~par-se** *vpr* be previous

antena /ã'tena/ *f* aerial, (*Amer*) antenna; (*de inseto*) feeler

anteontem /ãtʃiˈõtʃi/ adv the day before yesterday

antepassado /ãtʃipaˈsadu/ m ancestor

anterior /ãteriˈor/ a previous; (dianteiro) front

antes /ˈãtʃis/ adv before; (ao contrário) rather; ~ de/que before

ante-sala /ãtʃiˈsala/ f ante-room

anti|**biótico** /ãtʃibiˈɔtʃiku/ a & m antibiotic; ~**caspa** a antidandruff; ~**concepcional** (pl ~**concepcionais**) a & m contraceptive; ~**congelante** m antifreeze; ~**corpo** m antibody

antídoto /ãˈtʃidotu/ m antidote

antiético /ãtʃiˈetʃiku/ a unethical

antigamente /ãtʃigaˈmẽtʃi/ adv formerly

anti|**go** /ãˈtʃigu/ a old; (da antiguidade) ancient; <móveis etc> antique; (anterior) former; ~**guidade** f antiquity; (numa firma) seniority; pl (monumentos) antiquities; (móveis etc) antiques

anti-|**higiênico** /ãtʃiʃiˈeniku/ a unhygienic; ~**histamínico** a & m antihistamine; ~**horário** a anticlockwise

antilhano /ãtʃiˈʎanu/ a & m West Indian

Antilhas /ãˈtʃiʎas/ f pl West Indies

anti|**patia** /ãtʃipaˈtʃia/ f dislike; ~**pático** a unpleasant, unfriendly

antiquado /ãtʃiˈkwadu/ a antiquated, out-dated

anti-|**semitismo** /ãtʃisemiˈtʃizmu/ m anti-Semitism; ~**séptico** a & m antiseptic; ~**social** (pl ~**sociais**) a antisocial

antítese /ãˈtʃitezi/ f antithesis

antologia /ãtoloˈʒia/ f anthology

antônimo /ãˈtonimu/ m antonym

antro /ˈãtru/ m cavern; (de animal) lair; (de ladrões) den

antro|**pófago** /ãtroˈpɔfagu/ a man-eating; ~**pologia** f anthropology; ~**pólogo** m anthropologist

anual /anuˈaw/ (pl ~**ais**) a annual, yearly

anu|**lação** /anulaˈsãw/ f cancellation; ~**lar** vt cancel; annul <casamento>; (compensar) cancel out □ m ring finger

anunciar /anũsiˈar/ vt announce; advertise <produto>

anúncio /aˈnũsiu/ m announcement; (propaganda, classificado) advert(isement); (cartaz) notice

ânus /ˈanus/ m invar anus

an|**zol** /ãˈzow/ (pl ~**zóis**) m fishhook

aonde /aˈõdʒi/ adv where

apadrinhar /apadriˈɲar/ vt be godfather to <afilhado>; be best man for <noivo>; (proteger) protect; (patrocinar) support

apa|**gado** /apaˈgadu/ a <fogo> out; <luz, TV> off; (indistinto) faint; <pessoa> dull; ~**gar** vt put out <cigarro, fogo>; blow out <vela>; switch off <luz, TV>; rub out <erro>; clean <quadro-negro>; ~**gar-se** vpr <fogo, luz> go out; <lembrança> fade; (desmaiar) pass out; (fam: dormir) nod off

apaixo|**nado** /apaʃoˈnadu/ a in love (por with); ~**nante** a captivating; ~**nar-se** vpr fall in love (por with)

apalpar /apawˈpar/ vt touch, feel; <médico> examine

apanhar /apaˈɲar/ vt catch; (do chão) pick up; pick <flores, frutas>; (ir buscar) pick up; (alcançar) catch up □ vi be beaten

aparafusar /aparafuˈzar/ vt screw

apa|**ra-lápis** /aparaˈlapiʃ/ m invar (Port) pencil sharpener; ~**rar** vt catch <bola>; parry <golpe>; trim <cabelo>; sharpen <lápis>

aparato /apaˈratu/ m pomp, ceremony

apare|cer /apare'ser/ *vi* appear; ~**ça!** do drop in!; ~**cimento** *m* appearance

apare|lhagem /apare'ʎaʒẽ/ *f* equipment; ~**lhar** *vt* equip; ~**lho** /e/ *m* apparatus; (*máquina*) machine; (*de chá*) set, service; (*fone*) phone

aparência /apa'rēsia/ *f* appearance; **na** ~ apparently

aparen|tado /aparē'tadu/ *a* related; ~**tar** *vt* show; (*fingir*) feign; ~**te** *a* apparent

apar|tamento /aparta'mẽtu/ *m* flat, (*Amer*) apartment; ~**tar** *vt*, ~**tar-se** *vpr* separate; ~**te** *m* aside

apatia /apa'tʃia/ *f* apathy

apático /a'patʃiku/ *a* apathetic

apavo|rante /apavo'rãtʃi/ *a* terrifying; ~**rar** *vt* terrify; ~**rar-se** *vpr* be terrified

apaziguar /apazi'gwar/ *vt* appease

apear-se /api'arsi/ *vpr* (*de cavalo*) dismount; (*de ônibus*) alight

ape|gar-se /ape'garsi/ *vpr* become attached (**a** to); ~**go** /e/ *m* attachment

ape|lação /apela'sãw/ *f* appeal; (*fig*) exhibitionism; ~**lar** *vi* appeal (**de** against); ~**lar para** appeal to; (*fig*) resort to

apeli|dar /apeli'dar/ *vt* nickname; ~**do** *m* nickname

apelo /a'pelu/ *m* appeal

apenas /a'penas/ *adv* only

apêndice /a'pēdʒisi/ *m* appendix

apendicite /apēdʒi'sitʃi/ *f* appendicitis

aperceber-se /aperse'bersi/ *vpr* ~ (**de**) notice, realize

aperfeiçoar /aperfejso'ar/ *vt* perfect

aperitivo /aperi'tʃivu/ *m* aperitif

aper|tado /aper'tadu/ *a* tight; (*sem dinheiro*) hard-up; ~**tar** *vt* (*segurar*) hold tight; tighten <*cinto*>; press <*botão*>; squeeze <*esponja*>; take in <*vestido*>; fasten <*cinto de segurança*>; step up <*vigilância*>; cut down on <*despesas*>; break <*coração*>, (*fig*) pressurize <*pessoa*> □ *vi* <*sapato*> pinch; <*chuva, frio*> get worse; <*estrada*> narrow; ~**tar-se** *vpr* (*gastar menos*) tighten one's belt; (*não ter dinheiro*) feel the pinch; ~**tar** a **mão de alg** shake hands with s.o.; ~**to** /e/ *m* pressure; (*de botão*) press; (*dificuldade*) tight spot, jam; ~**to de mãos** handshake

apesar /ape'zar/ ~ **de** *prep* in spite of

apeti|te /ape'tʃitʃi/ *m* appetite; ~**toso** /o/ *a* appetizing

apetrechos /ape'treʃus/ *m pl* gear; (*de pesca*) tackle

apimentado /apimē'tadu/ *a* spicy, hot

apinhar /api'nar/ *vt* crowd, pack; ~**-se** *vpr* crowd

api|tar /api'tar/ *vi* whistle □ *vt* referee <*jogo*>; ~**to** *m* whistle

aplanar /apla'nar/ *vt* level <*terreno*>; (*fig*) smooth <*caminho*>; smooth over <*problema*>

aplau|dir /aplaw'dʒir/ *vt* applaud; ~**so(s)** *m* (*pl*) applause

apli|cação /aplika'sãw/ *f* application; (*de dinheiro*) investment; (*de lei*) enforcement; ~**car** *vt* apply; invest <*dinheiro*>; enforce <*lei*>; ~**car-se** *vpr* apply (**a** to); (*ao estudo etc*) apply o.s. (**a** to); ~**que** *m* hairpiece

apoderar-se /apode'rarsi/ *vpr* ~ **de** take possession of; <*raiva*> take hold of

apodrecer /apodre'ser/ *vt/i* rot

apoi|ar /apoj'ar/ *vt* lean; (*fig*) support; (*basear*) base; ~**ar-se em** lean on; (*fig*) be based on, rest on; ~**o** *m* support

apólice /a'polisi/ *f* policy; (*ação*) bond

apon|tador /apõta'dor/ *m* pencil sharpener; **~tar** *vt* (*com o dedo*) point at, point to; point out <*erro, caso interessante*>; aim <*arma*>; name <*nomes*>; put forward <*razão*> □ *vi* <*sol, planta*> come up; (*com o dedo*) point (**para** to)

apoquentar /apokẽ'tar/ *vt* annoy

aporrinhar /apoxi'ɲar/ *vt* annoy

após /a'pɔs/ *adv* after; **loção ~- barba** after-shave (lotion)

aposen|tado /apozẽ'tadu/ *a* retired □ *m* pensioner; **~tadoria** *f* retirement; (*pensão*) pension; **~tar** *vt*, **~tar-se** *vpr* retire; **~to** *m* room

após-guerra /apɔz'gɛxa/ *m* postwar period

apos|ta /a'pɔsta/ *f* bet; **~tar** *vt* bet (**em** on); (*fig*) have faith (**em** in)

apostila /apos'tʃila/ *f* revision aid, book of key facts

apóstolo /a'pɔstolu/ *m* apostle

apóstrofo /a'pɔstrofu/ *m* apostrophe

apre|ciação /apresia'sãw/ *f* appreciation; **~ciar** *vt* appreciate; think highly of <*pessoa*>; **~ciativo** *a* appreciative; **~ciável** (*pl* **~ciáveis**) *a* appreciable; **~ço** /e/ *m* regard

apreen|der /apriẽ'der/ *vt* seize <*contrabando*>; apprehend <*criminoso*>; grasp <*sentido*>; **~são** *f* apprehension; (*de contrabando*) seizure; (*percepção*) apprehension; **~sivo** *a* apprehensive

apregoar /aprego'ar/ *vt* proclaim; cry <*mercadoria*>

apren|der /aprẽ'der/ *vt/i* learn; **~diz** *m/f* (*de ofício*) apprentice; (*de direção*) learner; **~dizado** *m*, **~dizagem** *f* (*de ofício*) apprenticeship; (*de profissão*) training; (*escolar*) learning

apresen|tação /aprezẽta'sãw/ *f* presentation; (*teatral etc*) performance; (*de pessoas*) introduc-

tion; **~tador** *m* presenter; **~tar** *vt* present; introduce <*pessoa*>; **~tar-se** *vpr* (*identificar-se*) introduce o.s.; <*ocasião, problema*> present o.s., arise; **~tar-se a** report to <*polícia etc*>; go in for <*exame*>; stand for <*eleição*>; **~tável** (*pl* **~táveis**) *a* presentable

apres|sado /apre'sadu/ *a* hurried; **~sar** *vt* hurry; **~sar-se** *vpr* hurry (**up**)

aprimorar /aprimo'rar/ *vt* perfect, refine

aprofundar /aprofũ'dar/ *vt* deepen; study carefully <*questão*>; **~-se** *vpr* get deeper; **~-se em** go deeper into

aprontar /aprõ'tar/ *vt* get ready; pick <*briga*> □ *vi* act up; **~-se** *vpr* get ready

apropriado /apropri'adu/ *a* appropriate, suitable

apro|vação /aprova'sãw/ *f* approval; (*num exame*) pass; **~var** *vt* approve of; approve <*lei*> □ *vi* make the grade; **ser ~vado** (*num exame*) pass

aprovei|tador /aprovejta'dor/ *m* opportunist; **~tamento** *m* utilization; **~tar** *vt* take advantage of; take <*ocasião*>; (*utilizar*) use □ *vi* make the most of it; (*Port: adiantar*) be of use; **~tar-se** *vpr* take advantage (**de** of); **~te!** (*divirta-se*) have a good time!

aproxi|mação /aprosima'sãw/ *f* (*chegada*) approach; (*estimativa*) approximation; **~mado** *a* <*valor*> approximate; **~mar** *vt* move nearer; (*aliar*) bring together; **~mar-se** *vpr* approach, get nearer (**de** to)

ap|tidão /aptʃi'dãw/ *f* aptitude, suitability; **~to** *a* suitable

apunhalar /apuɲa'lar/ *vt* stab

apu|rado /apu'radu/ *a* refined; **~rar** *vt* (*aprimorar*) refine;

(*descobrir*) ascertain; investigate <*caso*>; collect <*dinheiro*>; count <*votos*>; ~**rar-se** *vpr* (*com a roupa*) dress smartly; ~**ro** *m* refinement; (*no vestir*) elegance; (*dificuldade*) difficulty; *pl* trouble

aquarela /akwa'rɛla/ *f* water-colour

aquariano /akwari'anu/ *a & m* Aquarian

aquário /a'kwariu/ *m* aquarium; **Aquário** Aquarius

aquartelar /akwarte'lar/ *vt* billet

aquático /a'kwatʃiku/ *a* aquatic, water

aque|cedor /akese'dor/ *m* heater; ~**cer** *vt* heat □ *vi*, ~**cer-se** *vpr* heat up; ~**cimento** *m* heating

aqueduto /ake'dutu/ *m* aqueduct

aquele /a'keli/ *a* that; *pl* those □ *pron* that one; *pl* those; ~ **que** the one that

àquele = a² + **aquele**

aqui /a'ki/ *adv* here

aquilo /a'kilu/ *pron* that

àquilo = a² + **aquilo**

aquisi|ção /akizi'sãw/ *f* acquisition; ~**tivo** *a* **poder** ~**tivo** purchasing power

ar /ar/ *m* air; (*aspecto*) look, air; (*Port: no carro*) choke; **ao** ~ **livre** in the open air; **no** ~ (*fig*) up in the air; (*TV*) on air; ~ **condicionado** air conditioning

árabe /'arabi/ *a & m* Arab; (*ling*) Arabic

Arábia /a'rabia/ *f* Arabia; ~ **Saudita** Saudi Arabia

arado /a'radu/ *m* plough, (*Amer*) plow

aragem /a'raʒẽ/ *f* breeze

arame /a'rami/ *m* wire; ~ **farpado** barbed wire

aranha /a'raɲa/ *f* spider

arar /a'rar/ *vt* plough, (*Amer*) plow

arara /a'rara/ *f* parrot

arbi|trar /arbi'trar/ *vt/i* referee <*jogo*>; arbitrate <*disputa*>; ~**trário** *a* arbitrary

arbítrio /ar'bitriu/ *m* judgement; **livre** ~ free will

árbitro /'arbitru/ *m* arbiter <*da moda etc*>; (*jurid*) arbitrator; (*de futebol*) referee; (*de tênis*) umpire

arborizado /arbori'zadu/ *a* wooded, green; <*rua*> tree-lined

arbusto /ar'bustu/ *m* shrub

ar|ca /'arka/ *f* ~**ca de Noé** Noah's Ark; ~**cada** *f* (*galeria*) arcade; (*arco*) arch

arcaico /ar'kajku/ *a* archaic

arcar /ar'kar/ *vi* ~ **com** deal with

arcebispo /arse'bispu/ *m* archbishop

arco /'arku/ *m* (*arquit*) arch; (*arma, mus*) bow; (*eletr, mat*) arc; ~**-da-velha** *m* **coisa do** ~**-da-velha** amazing thing; ~**-íris** *m* *invar* rainbow

ar|dente /ar'dẽtʃi/ *a* burning; (*fig*) ardent; ~**der** *vi* burn; <*olhos, ferida*> sting

ar|dil /ar'dʒiw/ (*pl* ~**dis**) *m* trick, ruse

ardor /ar'dor/ *m* heat; (*fig*) ardour; **com** ~ ardently

árduo /'arduu/ *a* strenuous, arduous

área /'aria/ *f* area; (*grande*) penalty area; ~ (**de serviço**) yard

arear /ari'ar/ *vt* scour <*panela*>

areia /a'reja/ *f* sand

arejar /are'ʒar/ *vt* air □ *vi*, ~**-se** *vpr* get some air; (*descansar*) have a breather

are|na /a'rena/ *f* arena; ~**noso** /o/ *a* sandy

arenque /a'rẽki/ *m* herring

argamassa /arga'masa/ *f* mortar

Argélia /ar'ʒɛlia/ *f* Algeria

argelino /arʒe'linu/ *a & m* Algerian

Argentina /arʒẽ'tʃina/ *f* Argentina

argentino /arʒẽˈtʃinu/ *a & m* Argentinian

argila /arˈʒila/ *f* clay

argola /arˈɡɔla/ *f* ring

argumen|tar /arɡumẽˈtar/ *vt/i* argue; **~to** *m* argument; (*de filme etc*) subject-matter

ariano /ariˈanu/ *a & m* (*do signo Aries*) Arian

árido /ˈaridu/ *a* arid; barren <*serto*>; (*fig*) dull, dry

Aries /ˈaris/ *f* Aries

arisco /aˈrisku/ *a* timid

aristo|cracia /aristokraˈsia/ *f* aristocracy; **~crata** *m/f* aristocrat; **~crático** *a* aristocratic

aritmética /aritʃˈmɛtʃika/ *f* arithmetic

arma /ˈarma/ *f* weapon; *pl* arms; **~ de fogo** firearm

ar|mação /armaˈsãw/ *f* frame; (*de óculos*) frames; (*naut*) rigging; **~madilha** *f* trap; **~madura** *f* suit of armour; (*armação*) framework; **~mar** *vt* (*dar armas a*) arm; (*montar*) put up, assemble; set up <*máquina*>; set, lay <*armadilha*>; fit out <*navio*>; hatch <*plano, complô*>; cause <*briga*>; **~mar-se** *vpr* arm o.s.

armarinho /armaˈriɲu/ *m* haberdashery, (*Amer*) notions

armário /arˈmariu/ *m* cupboard; (*de roupa*) wardrobe

arma|zém /armaˈzẽ/ *m* warehouse; (*loja*) general store; (*depósito*) storeroom; **~zenagem** *f* storage; **~zenamento** *m* storage; **~zenar** *vt* store

Armênia /arˈmenia/ *f* Armenia

armênio /arˈmeniu/ *a & m* Armenian

aro /ˈaru/ *m* (*de roda, óculos*) rim; (*de porta*) frame

aro|ma /aˈroma/ *f* aroma; (*perfume*) fragrance; **~mático** *a* aromatic; fragrant

ar|pão /arˈpãw/ *m* harpoon; **~poar** *vt* harpoon

arquear /arkiˈar/ *vt* arch; **~-se** *vpr* bend, bow

arque|ologia /arkioloˈʒia/ *f* archaeology; **~ológico** *a* archaeological; **~ólogo** *m* archaeologist

arquétipo /arˈkɛtʃipu/ *m* archetype

arquibancada /arkibãˈkada/ *f* terraces, (*Amer*) bleachers

arquipélago /arkiˈpelagu/ *m* archipelago

arquite|tar /arkiteˈtar/ *vt* think up; **~to** /ɛ/ *m* architect; **~tônico** *a* architectural; **~tura** *f* architecture

arqui|var /arkiˈvar/ *vt* file <*papéis*>; shelve <*plano, processo*>; **~vista** *m/f* archivist; **~vo** *m* file; (*conjunto*) files; (*móvel*) filing cabinet; *pl* (*do Estado etc*) archives

arran|cada /axãˈkada/ *f* lurch; (*de atleta, fig*) spurt; **~car** *vt* pull out <*cabelo etc*>; pull off <*botão etc*>; pull up <*erva daninha etc*>; take out <*dente*>; (*das mãos de alg*) wrench, snatch; extract <*confissão, dinheiro*> □ *vi* <*carro*> roar off; <*pessoa*> take off; (*dar solavanco*) lurch forward; **~car-se** *vpr* take off; **~co** *m* pull, tug; *veja* **~cada**

arranha-céu /axaɲaˈsɛw/ *m* skyscraper

arra|nhadura /axaɲaˈdura/ *f* scratch; **~nhão** *m* scratch; **~nhar** *vt* scratch; have a smattering of <*língua*>

arran|jar /axãˈʒar/ *vt* arrange; (*achar*) get, find; (*resolver*) settle, sort out; **~jar-se** *vpr* manage; **~jo** *m* arrangement

arrasar /axaˈzar/ *vt* devastate; raze, flatten <*casa, cidade*>; **~se** *vpr* be devastated

arrastar /axasˈtar/ *vt* drag; <*corrente, avalancha*> sweep away; (*atrair*) draw □ *vi* trail; **~-se** *vpr* crawl; <*tempo*> drag; <*processo*> drag out

arreba|tador /axebata'dor/ *a* entrancing; shocking <*notícia*>; **~tar** *vt* (*enlevar*) entrance, send; (*chocar*) shock

arreben|tação /axebēta'sãw/ *f* surf; **~tar** *vi* (*bomba*) explode; <*corda*> snap, break; <*balão, pessoa*> burst; <*onda*> break; <*guerra, incêndio*> break out □ *vt* snap, break <*corda*>; burst <*balão*>; break down <*porta*>

arrebitar /axebi'tar/ *vt* turn up <*nariz*>; pick up <*orelhas*>

arreca|dação /axekada'sãw/ *f* (*dinheiro*) tax revenue; **~dar** *vt* collect

arredar /axe'dar/ *vt* **não ~ pé** stand one's ground

arredio /axe'dʒiu/ *a* withdrawn

arredondar /axedõ'dar/ *vt* round up <*quantia*>; round off <*ângulo*>

arredores /axe'doris/ *m pl* surroundings; (*de cidade*) outskirts

arrefecer /axefe'ser/ *vt/i* cool

arregaçar /axega'sar/ *vt* roll up

arrega|lado /axega'ladu/ *a* <*olhos*> wide; **~lar** *vt* **~lar os olhos** be wide-eyed with amazement

arreganhar /axega'ɲar/ *vt* bare <*dentes*>; **~se** *vpr* grin

arrema|tar /axema'tar/ *vt* finish off; (*no tricô*) cast off; **~te** *m* conclusion; (*na costura*) finishing off; (*no futebol*) finishing

arremes|sar /axeme'sar/ *vt* hurl; **~so** /e/ *m* throw

arrepen|der-se /axepē'dersi/ *vpr* be sorry; <*pecador*> repent; **~der-se de** regret; **~dido** *a* sorry; <*pecador*> repentant; **~dimento** *m* regret; (*de pecado, crime*) repentance

arrepi|ado /axepi'adu/ *a* <*cabelo*> standing on end; <*pele, pessoa*> covered in goose pimples; **~ar** *vt* (*dar calafrios*) make shudder; make stand on end <*cabelo*>; **me ~a (a pele)** it

gives me goose pimples; **~ar-se** *vpr* (*estremecer*) shudder; <*cabelo*> stand on end; (*na pele*) get goose pimples; **~o** *m* shudder; **me dá ~os** it makes me shudder

arris|cado /axis'kadu/ *a* risky; **~car** *vt* risk; **~car-se** *vpr* take a risk, risk it

arroba /a'xoba/ *m* (*comput*) @, at sign

arro|char /axo'ʃar/ *vt* tighten up □ *vi* be tough; **~cho** /o/ *m* squeeze

arro|gância /axo'gãsia/ *f* arrogance; **~gante** *a* arrogant

arro|jado /axo'ʒadu/ *a* bold; **~jar** *vt* throw

arrombar /axõ'bar/ *vt* break down <*porta*>; break into <*casa*>; crack <*cofre*>

arro|tar /axo'tar/ *vi* burp, belch; **~to** /o/ *m* burp

arroz /a'xoz/ *m* rice; **~ doce** rice pudding; **~al** (*pl* **~ais**) *m* rice field

arrua|ça /axu'asa/ *f* riot; **~ceiro** *m* rioter

arruela /axu'ɛla/ *f* washer

arruinar /axui'nar/ *vt* ruin; **~se** *vpr* be ruined

arru|madeira /axuma'dera/ *f* (*de hotel*) chambermaid; **~mar** *vt* tidy (up) <*casa*>; sort out <*papéis, vida*>; pack <*mala*>; (*achar*) find, get; make up <*desculpa*>; (*vestir*) dress up; **~mar-se** *vpr* (*aprontar-se*) get ready; (*na vida*) sort o.s. out

arse|nal /arse'naw/ (*pl* **~nais**) *m* arsenal

arsênio /ar'seniu/ *m* arsenic

arte /'artʃi/ *f* art; **fazer ~** <*criança*> get up to mischief; **~fato** *m* product, artefact

arteiro /ar'teru/ *a* mischievous

artéria /ar'tɛria/ *f* artery

artesa|nal /arteza'naw/ (*pl* **~nais**) *a* a craft; **~nato** *m* craft-work

arte|são /arte'zãw/ (*pl* ~s) *m* (*f* ~sã) artisan, craftsman (*f* -woman)

ártico /'artʃiku/ *a* & *m* arctic

articu|lação /artʃikula'sãw/ *f* articulation; (*anat*, *tecn*) joint; ~**lar** *vt* articulate

arti|ficial /artʃifisi'aw/ (*pl* ~ficiais) *a* artificial; ~**fício** *m* trick

artigo /ar'tʃigu/ *m* article; (*com*) item

arti|lharia /artʃiʎa'ria/ *f* artillery; ~**lheiro** *m* (*mil*) gunner; (*no futebol*) striker

artimanha /artʃi'maɲa/ *f* trick; (*método*) clever way

ar|tista /ar'tʃista/ *m/f* artist; ~**tístico** *a* artistic

artrite /ar'tritʃi/ *f* arthritis

árvore /'arvori/ *f* tree

arvoredo /arvo'redu/ *m* grove

as /as/ *artigo* & *pron veja* **a¹**

ás /as/ *m* ace

às = **a²** + **as**

asa /'aza/ *f* wing; (*de xícara*) handle; ~**-delta** *f* hang-glider

ascen|dência /asẽ'dẽsia/ *f* ancestry; (*superioridade*) ascendancy; ~**dente** *a* rising; ~**der** *vi* rise; ascend (*ao trono*); ~**são** *f* rise; (*relig*) Ascension; **em** ~**são** rising; (*fig*) up and coming; ~**sor** *m* lift, (*Amer*) elevator; ~**sorista** *m/f* lift operator

asco /'asku/ *m* revulsion, disgust; **dar** ~ be revolting

asfalto /as'fawtu/ *m* asphalt

asfixiar /asfiksi'ar/ *vt/i* asphyxiate

Asia /'azia/ *f* Asia

asiático /azi'atʃiku/ *a* & *m* Asian

asilo /a'zilu/ *m* (*refúgio*) asylum; (*de velhos, crianças*) home

as|ma /'azma/ *f* asthma; ~**mático** *a* & *m* asthmatic

asneira /az'nera/ *f* stupidity; (*uma*) stupid thing

aspas /'aspas/ *f pl* inverted commas

aspargo /as'pargu/ *m* asparagus

aspecto /as'pektu/ *m* appearance, look; (*de um problema*) aspect

aspereza /aspe'reza/ *f* roughness; (*do clima, de um som*) harshness; (*fig*) rudeness

áspero /'asperu/ *a* rough; <*clima, som*> harsh; (*fig*) rude

aspi|ração /aspira'sãw/ *f* aspiration; (*med*) inhalation; ~**rador** *m* vacuum cleaner; ~**rar** *vt* inhale, breathe in <*ar, fumaça*>; suck up <*líquido*>; ~**rar a** aspire to

aspirina /aspi'rina/ *f* aspirin

asqueroso /aske'rozu/ *a* revolting, disgusting

assa|do /a'sadu/ *a* & *m* roast; ~**dura** *f* (*na pele*) sore patch

assalariado /asalari'adu/ *a* salaried □ *m* salaried worker

assal|tante /asaw'tãtʃi/ *m* robber; (*na rua*) mugger; (*de casa*) burglar; ~**tar** *vt* rob; burgle, (*Amer*) burglarize <*casa*>; ~**to** *m* (*roubo*) robbery; (*a uma casa*) burglary; (*ataque*) assault; (*no boxe*) round

assanhado /asa'ɲadu/ *a* worked up; <*criança*> excitable; (*erótico*) amorous

assar /a'sar/ *vt* roast

assassi|nar /asasi'nar/ *vt* murder; (*pol*) assassinate; ~**nato** *m* murder; (*pol*) assassination; ~**no** *m* murderer; (*pol*) assassin

asseado /asi'adu/ *a* well-groomed

as|sediar /asedʒi'ar/ *vt* besiege <*cidade*>; (*fig*) pester; ~**sédio** *m* siege; (*fig*) pestering

assegurar /asegu'rar/ *vt* (*tornar seguro*) secure; (*afirmar*) guarantee; ~ **a alg** assure; ~**se de/ que** make sure of/that

assembléia /asẽ'bleja/ *f* (*pol*) assembly; (*com*) meeting

assemelhar /aseme'λar/ *vt* liken; **~-se** *vpr* be alike; **~-se a** resemble, be like

assen|tar /asẽ'tar/ *vt* (*estabelecer*) establish, define; settle *<povo>*; lay *<tijolo>* □ *vi* *<pó>* settle; **~tar-se** *vpr* settle down; **~tar com** go with; **~tar a** *<roupa>* suit; **~to** *m* seat; (*fig*) basis; **to-mar ~to** take a seat; *<pó>* settle

assen|tir /asẽ'tʃir/ *vi* agree; **~timento** *m* agreement

assessor /ase'sor/ *m* adviser; **~ar** *vt* advise

assexuado /aseksu'adu/ *a* asexual

assiduidade /asidui'dadʒi/ *f* (*à escola*) regular attendance; (*diligência*) diligence

assíduo /a'siduu/ *a* (*que frequenta*) regular; (*diligente*) assiduous

assim /a'sĩ/ *adv* like this, like that; (*portanto*) therefore; **e ~ por diante** and so on; **~ como** as well as; **~ que** as soon as

assimétrico /asi'mεtriku/ *a* asymmetrical

assimilar /asimi'lar/ *vt* assimilate; **~-se** *vpr* be assimilated

assinalar /asina'lar/ *vt* (*marcar*) mark; (*distinguir*) distinguish; (*apontar*) point out

assi|nante /asi'nãtʃi/ *m/f* subscriber; **~nar** *vt/i* sign; **~natura** *f* (*nome*) signature; (*de revista*) subscription

assis|tência /asis'tẽsia/ *f* assistance; (*presença*) attendance; (*público*) audience; **~tente** *a* assistant □ *m/f* assistant; **~tente social** social worker; **~tir (a)** *vt/i* (*ver*) watch; (*presenciar*) attend; assist *<doente>*

assoalho /aso'aλu/ *m* floor

assoar /aso'ar/ *vt* **~ o nariz**, (*Port*) **~-se** blow one's nose

assobi|ar /asobi'ar/ *vt/i* whistle; **~o** *m* whistle

associ|ação /asosia'sãw/ *f* association; **~ado a & m** associate; **~ar** *vt* associate (*a* with); **~ar-se** *vpr* associate; (*com*) go into partnership (a with)

assolar /aso'lar/ *vt* devastate

assom|bração /asõbra'sãw/ *f* ghost; **~brar** *vt* astonish, amaze; **~brar-se** *vpr* be amazed; **~bro** *m* amazement, astonishment; (*coisa*) marvel; **~broso** /o/ *a* astonishing, amazing

assoprar /aso'prar/ *vi* blow □ *vt* blow; blow out *<vela>*

assovi- *veja* **assobi-**

assu|mido /asu'midu/ *a* (*confesso*) confirmed, self-confessed; **~mir** *vt* assume, take on; accept, admit *<defeito>* □ *vi* take office

assunto /a'sũtu/ *m* subject; (*negócio*) matter

assus|tador /asusta'dor/ *a* frightening; **~tar** *vt* frighten, scare; **~tar-se** *vpr* get frightened, get scared

asterisco /aste'risku/ *m* asterisk

as|tral /as'traw/ (*pl* **~trais**) *m* (*fam*) state of mind; **~tro** *m* star; **~trologia** *f* astrology; **~trólogo** *m* astrologer; **~tronauta** *m/f* astronaut; **~tronave** *f* spaceship; **~tronomia** *f* astronomy; **~tronômico** *a* astronomical; **~trônomo** *m* astronomer

as|túcia /as'tusia/ *f* cunning; **~tuto** *a* cunning; *<comerciante>* astute

ata /'ata/ *f* minutes

ataca|dista /ataka'dʒista/ *m/f* wholesaler; **~do** *m* **por ~do** wholesale

ata|cante /ata'kãtʃi/ *a* attacking □ *m/f* attacker; **~car** *vt* attack; tackle *<problema>*

atadura /ata'dura/ *f* bandage

ata|lhar /ata'λar/ *vi* take a shortcut; **~lho** *m* shortcut

ataque /a'taki/ *m* attack; (*de raiva, riso*) fit

atar /a'tar/ *vt* tie

atarantado /atarã'tadu/ *a* flustered, in a flap

atarefado /atare'fadu/ *a* busy

atarracado /ataxa'kadu/ *a* stocky

até /a'tɛ/ *prep* (up) to, as far as; (*tempo*) until □ *adv* even; ~ **logo** goodbye; ~ **que** until

atéia /a'teja/ *a & f veja* **ateu**

ateliê /ateli'e/ *m* studio

atemorizar /atemori'zar/ *vt* frighten

Atenas /a'tenas/ *f* Athens

aten|ção /atẽ'sãw/ *f* attention; *pl* (*bondade*) thoughtfulness; **com ~ção** attentively; ~**cioso** *a* thoughtful, considerate

aten|der /atẽ'der/ *vt/i* ~**der (a)** answer < *telefone, porta* >; answer to < *nome* >; serve < *freguês* >; see < *paciente, visitante* >; grant, meet < *pedido* >; heed < *conselho* >; ~**dimento** *m* service; (*de médico etc*) consultation

aten|tado /atẽ'tadu/ *m* murder attempt; (*pol*) assassination attempt; (*ataque*) attack (*contra* on); ~**tar** *vi* ~**tar contra** make an attempt on

atento /a'tẽtu/ *a* attentive; ~ **a** mindful of

aterrador /atexa'dor/ *a* terrifying

ater|ragem /ate'xaʒẽ/ *f* (*Port*) landing; ~**rar** *vi* (*Port*) land

aterris|sagem /atexi'saʒẽ/ *f* landing; ~**sar** *vi* land

ater-se /a'tersi/ *vpr* ~ **a** keep to, go by

ates|tado /ates'tadu/ *m* certificate; ~**tar** *vt* attest (to)

ateu /a'tew/ *a & m* (*f* **atéia**) atheist

atiçar /ati'sar/ *vt* poke < *fogo* >; stir up < *ódio, discórdia* >; arouse < *pessoa* >

atinar /atʃi'nar/ *vt* work out, guess; ~ **com** find; ~ **em** notice

atingir /atʃĩ'ʒir/ *vt* reach; hit < *alvo* >; (*conseguir*) attain; (*afetar*) affect

atirar /atʃi'rar/ *vt* throw □ *vi* shoot; ~ **em** fire at

atitude /atʃi'tudʒi/ *f* attitude; **tomar uma** ~ take action

ati|va /a'tʃiva/ *f* active service; ~**var** *vt* activate; ~**vidade** *f* activity; ~**vo** *a* active □ *m* (*com*) assets

Atlântico /at'lãtʃiku/ *m* Atlantic

atlas /'atlas/ *m* atlas

at|leta /at'lɛta/ *m/f* athlete; ~**lético** *a* athletic; ~**letismo** *m* athletics

atmosfera /atʃimos'fɛra/ *f* atmosphere

ato /'atu/ *m* act; (*ação*) action; **no** ~ on the spot

ato|lar /ato'lar/ *vt* bog down; ~**lar-se** *vpr* get bogged down; ~**leiro** *m* bog; (*fig*) fix, spot of trouble

atômico /a'tomiku/ *a* atomic

atomizador /atomiza'dor/ *m* atomizer spray

átomo /'atomu/ *m* atom

atônito /a'tonitu/ *a* astonished, stunned

ator /a'tor/ *m* actor

atordoar /atordo'ar/ *vt* < *golpe, notícia* > stun; < *som* > deafen; (*alucinar*) bewilder

atormentar /atormẽ'tar/ *vt* plague, torment

atração /atra'sãw/ *f* attraction

atracar /atra'kar/ *vt/i* (*naut*) moor; ~**-se** *vpr* grapple; (*fam*) neck

atractivo (*Port*) *veja* **atrativo**

atraente /atra'ẽtʃi/ *a* attractive

atraiçoar /atrajso'ar/ *vt* betray

atrair /atra'ir/ *vt* attract

atrapalhar /atrapa'ʎar/ *vt/i* (*confundir*) confuse; (*estorvar*) hinder; (*perturbar*) disturb; ~**-se** *vpr* get mixed up

atrás /a'traʃ/ *adv* behind; (*no fundo*) at the back; ~ **de** behind;

(*depois de, no encalço de*) after; **um mês** ~ a month ago; **ficar** ~ be left behind

atra|sado /atra'zadu/ *a* late; <*país, criança*> backward; <*relógio*> slow; <*pagamento*> overdue; <*idéias*> old-fashioned; **~sar** *vt* delay; put back <*relógio*> □ *vi* be late; (*num trabalho*) get behind; (*no pagar*) get into arrears; **~so** *m* delay; (*de país etc*) backwardness; *pl* (*com*) arrears; **com** ~ **so** late

atrativo /atra'tʃivu/ *m* attraction

através /atra'vɛs/ ~ **de** *prep* through; (*de um lado ao outro*) across

atravessado /atrave'sadu/ *a* <*espinha*> stuck; **estar com** *alg* ~ **na garganta** be fed up with s.o.

atravessar /atrave'sar/ *vt* go through; cross <*rua, rio*>

atre|ver-se /atre'versi/ *vpr* dare; **~ver-se a** dare to; **~vido** *a* daring; (*insolente*) impudent; **~vimento** *m* daring, boldness; (*insolência*) impudence

atribu|ir /atribu'ir/ *vt* attribute (**a** to); confer <*prêmio, poderes*> (**a** on); attach <*importância*> (**a** to); **~to** *m* attribute

atrito /a'tritu/ *m* friction; (*desavença*) disagreement

atriz /a'tris/ *f* actress

atrocidade /atrosi'dadʒi/ *f* atrocity

atrope|lar /atrope'lar/ *vt* run over, knock down <*pedestre*>; (*empurrar*) jostle; miss <*palavras*>; **~lamento** *m* (*de pedestre*) running over; **~lo** /e/ *m* scramble

atroz /a'tros/ *a* awful, terrible; heinous <*crime*>; cruel <*pessoa*>

atuação /atua'sãw/ *f* (*ação*) action; (*desempenho*) performance

atu|al /atu'aw/ (*pl* **~ais**) *a* current, present; <*assunto, interesse*> topical; <*pessoa, carro*> up-to-date; **~alidade** *f* (*presente*) present (time); (*de um livro*) topicality; *pl* current affairs; **~alizado** *a* up-to-date; **~alizar** *vt* update; **~alizar-se** *vpr* bring o.s. up to date; **~almente** *adv* at present, currently

atum /a'tũ/ *m* tuna

aturdir /atur'dʒir/ *vt veja* **atordoar**

audácia /aw'dasia/ *f* boldness; (*insolência*) audacity

audi|ção /awdʒi'sãw/ *f* hearing; (*concerto*) recital; **~ência** *f* audience; (*jurid*) hearing

audiovisu|al /awdʒioviʒu'aw/ (*pl* **~ais**) *a* audiovisual

auditório /awdʒi'toriu/ *m* auditorium; **programa de** ~ variety show

auge /'awʒi/ *m* peak, height

aula /'awla/ *f* class, lesson; **dar** ~ teach

aumen|tar /awmẽ'tar/ *vt* increase; raise <*preço, salário*>; extend <*casa*>; (*com lente*) magnify; (*acrescentar*) add □ *vi* increase; <*preço, salário*> go up; **~to** *m* increase; (*de salário*) rise, (*Amer*) raise

au|sência /aw'zẽsia/ *f* absence; **~sente** *a* absent □ *m/f* absentee

aus|pícios /aws'pisius/ *m pl* auspices; **~picioso** /o/ *a* auspicious

auste|ridade /awsteri'dadʒi/ *f* austerity; **~ro** /ɛ/ *a* austere

Austrália /aws'tralia/ *f* Australia

australiano /awstrali'anu/ *a & m* Australian

Áustria /'awstria/ *f* Austria

austríaco /aws'triaku/ *a & m* Austrian

autarquia /awtar'kia/ *f* public authority

autêntico /aw'tẽtʃiku/ *a* authentic; genuine <*pessoa*>; true <*fato*>

autobio|grafia /awtobiogra'fia/ *f* autobiography; **∼gráfico** *a* autobiographical

autocarro /awto'kaxu/ *m* (*Port*) bus

autocrata /awto'krata/ *a* autocratic

autodefesa /awtode'feza/ *f* self-defence

autodidata /awtodʒi'data/ *a* & *m/f* self-taught (person)

autódromo /aw'tɔdromu/ *m* race track

auto-escola /awtois'kɔla/ *f* driving school

auto-estrada /awtois'trada/ *f* motorway, (*Amer*) expressway

autógrafo /aw'tɔgrafu/ *m* autograph

auto|mação /awtoma'sãw/ *f* automation; **∼mático** *a* automatic; **∼matizar** *vt* automate

auto|mobilismo /awtomobi-'lizmu/ *m* motoring; (*esporte*) motor racing; **∼móvel** (*pl* **∼móveis**) *m* motor car, (*Amer*) automobile

au|tonomia /awtono'mia/ *f* autonomy; **∼tônomo** *a* autonomous; *<trabalhador>* self-employed

autopeça /awto'pεsa/ *f* car spare

autópsia /aw'tɔpsia/ *f* autopsy

autor /aw'tor/ *m* (*f* **∼a**) author; (*de crime*) perpetrator; (*jurid*) plaintiff

auto-retrato /awtoxe'tratu/ *m* self-portrait

autoria /awto'ria/ *f* authorship; (*de crime*) responsibility (**de** for)

autori|dade /awtori'dadʒi/ *f* authority; **∼zação** *f* authorization; **∼zar** *vt* authorize

autuar /awtu'ar/ *vt* sue

au|xiliar /awsili'ar/ *a* auxiliary □ *m/f* assistant □ *vt* assist; **∼xílio** *m* assistance, aid

aval /a'vaw/ (*pl* **avais**) *m* endorsement; (*com*) guarantee

avali|ação /avalia'sãw/ *f* (*de preço*) valuation; (*fig*) evaluation; **∼ar** *vt* value *<quadro etc>* (**em** at); assess *<danos, riscos>*; (*fig*) evaluate

avan|çar /avã'sar/ *vt* move forward □ *vi* move forward; (*mil, fig*) advance; **∼çar a** (*montar*) amount to; **∼ço** *m* advance

avar|eza /ava'reza/ *f* meanness; **∼ento** *a* mean

ava|ria /ava'ria/ *f* damage; (*de máquina*) breakdown; **∼riado** *a* damaged; *<máquina>* out of order; *<carro>* broken down; **∼riar** *vt* damage □ *vi* be damaged; *<máquina>* break down

ave /'avi/ *f* bird; **∼ de rapina** bird of prey

aveia /a'veja/ *f* oats

avelã /ave'lã/ *f* hazelnut

avenida /ave'nida/ *f* avenue

aven|tal /avẽ'taw/ (*pl* **∼tais**) *m* apron

aventu|ra /avẽ'tura/ *f* adventure; (*amorosa*) fling; **∼rar** *vt* venture; **∼rar-se** *vpr* venture (**a** to); **∼reiro** *a* adventurous □ *m* adventurer

averiguar /averi'gwar/ *vt* check (out)

avermelhado /averme'ʎadu/ *a* reddish

aver|são /aver'sãw/ *f* aversion; **∼so** *a* averse (**a** to)

aves|sas /a'vεsas/ **às ∼sas** the wrong way round; (*de cabeça para baixo*) upside down; **∼so** /e/ *m* **ao ∼so** inside out

avestruz /aves'trus/ *m* ostrich

avi|ação /avia'sãw/ *f* aviation; **∼ão** *m* (aero)plane, (*Amer*) (air)plane; **∼ão a jato** jet

avi|dez /avi'des/ *f* (*cobiça*) greediness; **∼do** *a* greedy

avi|sar /avi'zar/ *vt* (*informar*) tell, let know; (*advertir*) warn; **∼so** *m* notice; (*advertência*) warning

avistar /avis'tar/ *vt* catch sight of

avo /'avu/ *m* **um doze ∼s** one twelfth

avó /a'vɔ/ *f* grandmother; **∼s** *m pl* grandparents

avô /a'vo/ *m* grandfather

avoado /avo'adu/ *a* dizzy, scatter-brained

avulso /a'vuwsu/ *a* loose, odd

avultado /avuw'tadu/ *a* bulky

axila /ak'sila/ *f* armpit

azaléia /aza'lɛja/ *f* azalea

azar /a'zar/ *m* bad luck; **ter ∼** be unlucky; **∼ado**, **∼ento** *a* unlucky

aze|dar /aze'dar/ *vt* sour □ *vi* go sour; **∼do** /e/ *a* sour

azei|te /a'zejtʃi/ *m* oil; **∼tona** /o/ *f* olive

azevinho /aze'viɲu/ *m* holly

azia /a'zia/ *f* heartburn

azucrinar /azukri'nar/ *vt* annoy

azul /a'zuw/ (*pl* **azuis**) *a* blue

azulejo /azu'leʒu/ *m* (ceramic) tile

azul-marinho /azuwma'riɲu/ *a invar* navy blue

B

babá /ba'ba/ *f* nanny; **∼ eletrônica** baby alarm

ba|bado /ba'badu/ *m* frill; **∼bador** *m* bib; **∼bar** *vt/i*, **∼bar-se** *vpr* drool (**por ∼er**); < *bebê* > dribble; **∼beiro** (*Port*) *m* bib

baby-sitter /bejbi'siter/ (*pl* **∼s**) *m/f* babysitter

bacalhau /baka'ʎaw/ *m* cod

bacana /ba'kana/ (*fam*) *a* great

bacha|rel /baʃa'rew/ (*pl* **∼réis**) *m* bachelor; **∼relado** *m* bachelor's degree; **∼relar-se** *vpr* graduate

bacia /ba'sia/ *f* basin; (*da privada*) bowl; (*anat*) pelvis

baço /'basu/ *m* spleen

bacon /'bejkõ/ *m* bacon

bactéria /bak'tɛria/ *f* bacterium; *pl* bacteria

ba|dalado /bada'ladu/ *a* (*fam*)

talked about; **∼lar** *vt* ring < *sino* > □ *vi* ring; (*fam*) go out and about; **∼lativo** (*fam*) *a* fun-loving, gadabout

badejo /ba'deʒu/ *m* sea bass

baderna /ba'dɛrna/ *f* (*tumulto*) commotion; (*desordem*) mess

badulaque /badu'laki/ *m* trinket

bafafá /bafa'fa/ (*fam*) *m* to-do, kerfuffle

ba|fo /'bafu/ *m* bad breath; **∼fômetro** *m* Breathalyser; **∼forada** *f* puff

bagaço /ba'gasu/ *m* pulp; (*Port: aguardente*) brandy

baga|geiro /baga'ʒeru/ *m* (*de carro*) roofrack; (*Port: homem*) porter; **∼gem** *f* luggage; (*cultural etc*) baggage

bagatela /baga'tɛla/ *f* trifle

Bagdá /bagi'da/ *f* Baghdad

bago /'bagu/ *m* berry; (*de chumbo*) pellet

bagulho /ba'guʎu/ *m* piece of junk; *pl* junk; **ele é um ∼** he's as ugly as sin

bagun|ça /ba'gũsa/ *f* mess; **∼çar** *vt* mess up; **∼ceiro** *a* messy

baía /ba'ia/ *f* bay

baiano /ba'janu/ *a & m* Bahian

baila /'bajla/ *f* **trazer/vir à ∼** bring/come up

bai|lar /baj'lar/ *vt/i* dance; **∼larino** *m* ballet dancer; **∼le** *m* dance; (*de gala*) ball

bainha /ba'iɲa/ *f* (*de vestido*) hem; (*de arma*) sheath

baioneta /bajo'neta/ *f* bayonet

bairro /'bajxu/ *m* neighbourhood, area

baixa /'baʃa/ *f* drop, fall; (*de guerra*) casualty; (*dispensa*) discharge; **∼-mar** *f* low tide

baixar /ba'ʃar/ *vt* lower; issue < *ordem* >; *m* (*comput*) download □ *vi* drop, fall; (*fam: pintar*) turn up

baixaria /baʃa'ria/ *f* sordidness; (*uma*) sordid thing

baixela /ba'ʃela/ f set of cutlery

baixeza /ba'ʃeza/ f baseness

baixo /'baʃu/ a low; (*pessoa*) short; (*som, voz*) quiet, soft; (*cabeça, olhos*) lowered; (*vil*) sordid □ *adv* low; (*falar*) softly, quietly □ *m* bass; **em ~** underneath; (*em casa*) downstairs; **em ~ de** under; **para ~** down; (*em casa*) downstairs; **por ~ de** under(neath)

baju|lador /baʒula'dor/ a obsequious □ *m* sycophant; **~lar** *vt* fawn on

bala /'bala/ f (*de revólver*) bullet; (*doce*) sweet

balada /ba'lada/ f ballad

balaio /ba'laju/ *m* linen basket

balan|ça /ba'lãsa/ f scales; **Balança** (*signo*) Libra; **~ça de pagamentos** balance of payments; **~çar** *vt/i* (*no ar*) swing; (*numa cadeira etc*) rock; (*carro, avião*) shake; (*navio*) roll; **~çar-se** *vpr* swing; **~cete** /e/ *m* trial balance; **~ço** *m* (*com*) balance sheet; (*brinquedo*) swing; (*movimento no ar*) swinging; (*de carro, avião*) shaking; (*de navio*) rolling; (*de cadeira*) rocking; **fazer um ~ço de** (*fig*) take stock of

balangandã /balãgã'dã/ *m* bauble

balão /ba'lãw/ *m* balloon; **soltar um ~-de-ensaio** (*fig*) put out feelers

balar /ba'lar/ *vi* bleat

balbu|ciar /bawbusi'ar/ *vt/i* babble; **~cio** *m* babble, babbling

balbúrdia /baw'burdʒia/ f hubbub

bal|cão /baw'kãw/ *m* (*em loja*) counter; (*de informações, bilhetes*) desk; (*de cozinha*) worktop, (*Amer*) counter; (*no teatro*) circle; **~conista** *m/f* shop assistant

balde /'bawdʒi/ *m* bucket

baldeação /bawdʒia'sãw/ f fazer ~ change (trains)

baldio /baw'dʒiu/ a fallow; **terreno ~** (piece of) waste ground

balé /ba'le/ *m* ballet

balear /bali'ar/ *vt* shoot

baleia /ba'leja/ f whale

balido /ba'lidu/ *m* bleat, bleating

balísti|ca /ba'listʃika/ f ballistics; **~co** a ballistic

bali|za /ba'liza/ f marker; (*luminosa*) beacon; **~zar** *vt* mark out

balneário /bawni'ariu/ *m* seaside resort

balofo /ba'lofu/ a fat, tubby

baloiço, balouço /ba'lojsu, ba'losu/ (*Port*) *m* (*de criança*) swing

balsa /'bawsa/ f (*de madeira etc*) raft; (*que vai e vem*) ferry

bálsamo /'bawsamu/ *m* balm

báltico /'bawtʃiku/ a *m* Baltic

baluarte /balu'artʃi/ *m* bulwark

bambo /'bãbu/ a loose, slack; (*pernas*) limp; (*mesa*) wobbly

bambo|lê /bãbo'le/ *m* hula hoop; **~lear** *vi* (*pessoa*) sway, totter; (*coisa*) wobble

bambu /bã'bu/ *m* bamboo

ba|nal /ba'naw/ (*pl* **~nais**) a banal; **~nalidade** f banality

bana|na /ba'nana/ f banana □ (*fam*) *m/f* wimp; **~nada** f banana fudge; **~neira** f banana tree; **plantar ~neira** do a handstand

banca /'bãka/ f (*de trabalho*) bench; (*de jornais*) newsstand; **~ examinadora** examining board; **~da** f (*pol*) bench

bancar /bã'kar/ *vt* (*custear*) finance; (*fazer papel de*) play; (*fingir*) pretend

bancário /bã'kariu/ a bank □ *m* bank employee

bancarrota /bãka'xota/ f bankruptcy; **ir à ~** go bankrupt

banco /'bãku/ *m* (*com*) bank; (*no parque*) bench; (*na cozinha, num bar*) stool; (*de bicicleta*) saddle; (*de carro*) seat; **~ de areia** sandbank; **~ de dados** database

banda /'bãda/ f band; (*lado*) side; **de ～** sideways on; **nestas ～s** in these parts; **～ desenhada** (*Port*) cartoon; **～ larga** broad band

bandei|ra /bã'dera/ f flag; (*divisa*) banner; **dar ～ra** (*fam*) give o.s. away; **～rante** m/f pioneer □ f girl guide; **～rinha** m linesman

bandeja /bã'deʒa/ f tray

bandido /bã'dʒidu/ m bandit

bando /'bãdu/ m (*de pessoas*) band; (*de pássaros*) flock

bandolim /bãdo'lĩ/ m mandolin

bangalô /bãga'lo/ m bungalow

Bangcoc /bã'kɔki/ f Bangkok

bangue-bangue /bãgi'bãgi/ (*fam*) m western

banguela /bã'gɛla/ a toothless

banha /'baɲa/ f lard

banhar /ba'ɲar/ vt (*molhar*) bathe; (*lavar*) bath; **～-se** vpr bathe

banhei|ra /ba'ɲera/ f bath, (*Amer*) bathtub; **～ro** m bathroom; (*Port*) lifeguard

banhista /ba'ɲista/ m/f bather

banho /'baɲu/ m bath; (*no mar*) bathe, dip; **tomar ～** have a bath; (*no chuveiro*) have a shower; **～ de loja/cultura** go on a shopping/cultural spree; **～ de espuma** bubble bath; **～ de sol** sunbathing; **～-maria** (*pl* **～s-maria**) m bain marie

ba|nimento /bani'mẽtu/ m banishment; **～nir** vt banish

banjo /'bãʒu/ m banjo

banqueiro /bã'keru/ m banker

banqueta /bã'keta/ f foot-stool

banque|te /bã'ketʃi/ m banquet; **～teiro** m caterer

banzé /bã'zɛ/ (*fam*) m commotion, uproar

bapt- (*Port*) *veja* **bat-**

baque /'baki/ m thud, crash; (*revés*) blow; **～ar** vi topple over □ vt hit hard, knock for six

bar /bar/ m bar

barafunda /bara'fũda/ f jumble; (*barulho*) racket

bara|lhada /bara'ʎada/ f jumble; **～lho** m pack of cards, (*Amer*) deck of cards

barão /ba'rãw/ m baron

barata /ba'rata/ f cockroach

bara|tear /barat'ʃiar/ vt cheapen; **～teiro** a cheap

baratinar /baratʃi'nar/ vt fluster; (*transtornar*) rattle, shake up

barato /ba'ratu/ a cheap □ adv cheaply □ (*fam*) m um ～ great; **que ～!** that's brilliant!

barba /'barba/ f beard; pl (*de gato etc*) whiskers; **fazer a ～** shave; **～da** f walkover; (*cavalo*) favourite; **～do** a bearded

barbante /bar'bãtʃi/ m string

bar|baridade /barbari'dadʒi/ f barbarity; (*fam: muito dinheiro*) fortune; **～bárie** f, **～barismo** m barbarism

bárbaro /'barbaru/ m barbarian □ a barbaric; (*fam: forte, bom*) terrific

barbatana /barba'tana/ f fin

bar|beador /barbia'dor/ m shaver; **～bear** vt shave; **～bear-se** vpr shave; **～bearia** f barber's shop; **～beiragem** (*fam*) f bit of bad driving; **～beiro** m barber; (*fam: motorista*) bad driver

bar|ca /'barka/ f barge; (*balsa*) ferry; **～caça** f barge; **～co** m boat; **～co a motor** motorboat; **～co a remo/vela** rowing/sailing boat, (*Amer*) rowboat/sailboat

barga|nha /bar'gaɲa/ f bargain; **～nhar** vt/i bargain

barítono /ba'ritonu/ m baritone

barômetro /ba'rometru/ m barometer

baronesa /baro'neza/ f baroness

barra /'baxa/ f bar; (*sinal gráfico*) slash, stroke; (*fam: situação*) situation; **segurar a ～** hold out; **forçar a ～** force the issue

barra|ca /ba'xaka/ f (de acampar) tent; (na feira) stall; (casinha) hut; (guarda-sol) sunshade; **~cão** m shed; **~co** m shack, shanty

barragem /ba'xaʒẽ/ f (represa) dam

barra-pesada /baxape'zada/ (fam) a invar < bairro> rough; <pessoa> shady; (difícil) tough

bar|rar /ba'xar/ vt bar; **~reira** f barrier; (em corrida) hurdle; (em futebol) wall

barrento /ba'xẽtu/ a muddy

barricada /baxi'kada/ f barricade

barri|ga /ba'xiga/ f stomach, (Amer) belly; **~ga da perna** calf; **~gudo** a pot-bellied

bar|ril /ba'xiw/ (pl **~ris**) m barrel

barro /'baxu/ m (argila) clay; (lama) mud

barroco /ba'xoku/ a & m baroque

barrote /ba'xɔtʃi/ m beam, joist

baru|lheira /baru'ʎera/ f racket, din; **~lhento** a noisy; **~lho** m noise

base /'bazi/ f base; (fig: fundamento) basis; **com ~ em** on the basis of; **na ~ de** based on; **~ado** a based; (firme) well-founded □ (fam) m joint; **~ar** vt base; **~ar-se em** be based on

básico /'baziku/ a basic

basquete /bas'kɛtʃi/ m, **basquetebol** /basketʃi'bɔw/ m basketball

bas|ta /'basta/ m **dar um ~ta em** call a halt to; **~tante** a (muito) quite a lot of; (suficiente) enough □ adv (com adjetivo, advérbio) quite; (com verbo) quite a lot; (suficientemente) enough

bastão /bas'tãw/ m stick; (num revezamento, de comando) baton

bastar /bas'tar/ vi be enough

bastidores /bastʃi'doris/ m pl (no teatro) wings; **nos ~** (fig) behind the scenes

bata /'bata/ f (de mulher) smock; (de médico etc) overall

bata|lha /ba'taʎa/ f battle; **~lhador** a plucky, feisty □ m fighter; **~lhão** m battalion; **~lhar** vi battle; (esforçar-se) fight hard □ vt fight hard to get

batata /ba'tata/ f potato; **~ doce** sweet potato; **~ frita** chips, (Amer) French fries; (salgadinhos) crisps, (Amer) potato chips

bate-boca /batʃi'boka/ m row, argument

bate|deira /bate'dera/ f whisk; (de manteiga) churn; **~dor** m (policial etc) outrider; (no criquete) batsman; (no beisebol) batter; (de caça) beater; **~dor de carteiras** pickpocket

batelada /bate'lada/ f batch; **~s** de heaps of

batente /ba'tẽtʃi/ m (de porta) doorway; **para o/no ~** (fam: ao trabalho) to/at work

bate-papo /batʃi'papu/ m chat.

bater /ba'ter/ vt beat; stamp <pé>; slam <porta>; strike <horas>; take <foto>; flap <asas>; (datilografar) type; (lavar) wash; (usar muito) wear a lot <roupa>; (fam) pinch <carteira> □ vi <coração> beat; <porta> slam; <janela> bang; <horas> strike; <sino> ring; (à porta) knock; (com o carro) crash; **~-se** vpr (lutar) fight; **~** à máquina type; **~** à ou na porta knock at the door; **~** em hit; harp on <assunto>; <luz, sol> shine on; **~ com o carro** crash one's car, have a crash; **~ com a cabeça** bang one's head; **ele batia os dentes de frio** his teeth were chattering with cold; **ele não bate bem** (fam) he's not all there

bate|ria /bate'ria/ f (eletr) battery; (mus) drums; **~ria de cozinha** kitchen utensils; **~rista** m/f drummer

bati|da /ba'tʃida/ f beat; (à porta) knock; (no carro) crash; (policial) raid; (bebida) cocktail of rum, sugar and fruit juice; ~do a beaten; <roupa> well worn; <assunto> hackneyed □ m ~do de leite (Port) milkshake

batina /ba'tʃina/ f cassock

ba|tismo /ba'tʃizmu/ m baptism; ~tizado m christening; ~tizar vt baptize; (pôr nome) christen

batom /ba'tõ/ m lipstick

batu|cada /batu'kada/ f samba percussion group; ~car vt/i drum in a samba rhythm; ~que m samba rhythm

batuta /ba'tuta/ f baton; sob a ~ de under the direction of

baú /ba'u/ m trunk

baunilha /baw'niʎa/ f vanilla

bazar /ba'zar/ m bazaar; (loja) stationery and haberdashery shop

bê-a-bá /bea'ba/ m ABC

bea|titude /beatʃi'tudʒi/ f (felicidade) bliss; (devoção) piety, devoutness; ~to a (devoto) pious, devout; (feliz) blissful

bêbado /'bebadu/ a & m drunk

bebê /be'be/ m baby; ~ de proveta test-tube baby

bebe|deira /bebe'dera/ f (estado) drunkenness; (ato) drinking bout; ~dor m drinker; ~douro m drinking fountain

beber /be'ber/ vt/i drink

bebericar /beberi'kar/ vt/i sip

bebida /be'bida/ f drink

beca /'bɛka/ f gown

beça /'bɛsa/ f à ~ (fam) (com substantivo) loads of; (com adjetivo) really; (com verbo) a lot

beco /'beku/ m alley; ~ sem saída dead end

bedelho /be'deʎu/ m meter o ~ (em) stick one's oar in(to)

bege /'bɛʒi/ a invar beige

bei|cinho /bej'siɲu/ m fazer ~cinho pout; ~ço m lip; ~çudo a thick-lipped

beija-flor /bejʒa'flor/ m hummingbird

bei|jar /be'ʒar/ vt kiss; ~jo m kiss; ~joca /ɔ/ f peck

bei|ra /'bera/ f edge; (fig: do desastre etc) verge, brink; à ~ra de at the edge of; (fig) on the verge of; ~rada f edge; ~ra-mar f seaside; ~rar vt (ficar) border (on); (andar) skirt; (fig) border on, verge on; ele está ~rando os 30 anos he's nearing thirty

beisebol /bejsi'bɔw/ m baseball

belas-artes /bɛlaʃ'artʃiʃ/ f pl fine arts

beldade /bew'dadʒi/ f, **beleza** /be'leza/ f beauty

belga /'bewga/ a & m Belgian

Bélgica /'bewʒika/ f Belgium

beliche /be'liʃi/ m bunk

bélico /'bɛliku/ a war

belicoso /beli'kozu/ a warlike

belis|cão /belis'kãw/ m pinch; ~car vt pinch; nibble <comida>

Belize /be'lizi/ m Belize

belo /'bɛlu/ a beautiful

beltrano /bew'tranu/ m such-and-such

bem /bẽj/ adv well; (bastante) quite; (muito) very □ m good; pl goods, property; está ~ (it's) fine, OK; fazer ~ a be good for; tudo ~? (fam) how's things?; se ~ que even though; ~ feito (por você) (fam) it serves you right; muito ~! well done!; de ~ com alg on good terms with s.o.; ~ como as well as

bem|-apessoado /bẽjapeso'adu/ a nice-looking; ~-comportado a well-behaved; ~-disposto a keen, willing; ~-estar m wellbeing; ~-humorado a goodhumoured; ~-intencionado a well-intentioned; ~-passado a <carne> well-done; ~-sucedido a successful; ~-vindo a welcome; ~-visto a well thought of

bênção /'bẽsãw/ (pl ~s) f blessing

bendito /bẽ'dʒitu/ a blessed

benefi|cência /benefi'sẽsia/ f (bondade) goodness, kindness; (caridade) charity; **~cente** a <associação> charitable; <concerto, feira> charity; **~ciado** m beneficiary; **~ciar** vt benefit; **~ciar-se** vpr benefit (de from)

benefício /bene'fisiu/ m benefit; **em ~ de** in aid of

benéfico /be'nɛfiku/ a beneficial (a to)

benevolência /benevo'lẽsia/ f benevolence

benévolo /be'nɛvolu/ a benevolent

benfeitor /bẽfej'tor/ m benefactor

bengala /bẽ'gala/ f walking stick; (pão) French stick

benigno /be'niginu/ a benign

ben|to /'bẽtu/ a blessed; <água> holy; **~zer** vt bless; **~zer-se** vpr cross o.s.

berço /'bersu/ m (de embalar) cradle; (caminha) cot; (fig) birthplace; **ter ~** be from a good family

berimbau /berĩ'baw/ m Brazilian percussion instrument shaped like a bow

berinjela /berĩ'ʒela/ f aubergine, (Amer) eggplant

Berlim /ber'lĩ/ f Berlin

berma /'berma/ f (Port) hard shoulder, (Amer) berm

bermuda /ber'muda/ f Bermuda shorts

Berna /'berna/ f Berne

ber|rante /be'xãtʃi/ a loud, flashy; **~rar** vi <pessoa> shout; <criança> bawl; <boi> bellow; **~reiro** m (grito) yelling, shouting; (choro) crying, bawling; **~ro** /ɛ/ m yell, shout; (de boi) bellow; **aos ~ros** shouting

besouro /be'zoru/ m beetle

bes|ta /'besta/ a (idiota) stupid; (cheio de si) full of o.s.; (pedante)

pretentious □ f (pessoa) dimwit, numbskull; **ficar ~ta** (fam) be taken aback; **~teira** f stupidity; (uma) stupid thing; **falar ~teira** talk rubbish; **~tial** (pl ~tiais) a bestial; **~tificar** vt astound, dumbfound

besuntar /bezũ'tar/ vt coat; (sujar) smear

betão /be'tãw/ (Port) m concrete

beterraba /bete'xaba/ f beetroot

betoneira /beto'nera/ f cement mixer

bexiga /be'ʃiga/ f bladder

bezerro /be'zeru/ m calf

bibelô /bibe'lo/ m ornament

Bíblia /'biblia/ f Bible

bíblico /'bibliku/ a biblical

biblio|grafia /bibliogra'fia/ f bibliography; **~teca** /ɛ/ f library; **~tecário** m librarian □ a library

bica /'bika/ f tap; (Port: cafezinho) espresso; **suar em ~s** drip with sweat

bicama /bi'kama/ f truckle bed

bicar /bi'kar/ vt peck

biceps /'biseps/ m invar biceps

bicha /'biʃa/ f (Port: fila) queue; (Bras: fam) queer, fairy

bicheiro /bi'ʃeru/ m organizer of illegal numbers game, racketeer

bicho /'biʃu/ m animal; (inseto) insect, (Amer) bug; **que ~ te mordeu?** what's got into you?; **~-da-seda** (pl ~s-da-seda) m silkworm; **~-de-sete-cabeças** (fam) m big deal, big thing; **~-do-mato** (pl ~s-do-mato) m very shy person

bicicleta /bisi'kleta/ f bicycle, bike

bico /'biku/ m (de ave) beak; (de faca) point; (de sapato) toe; (de bule) spout; (de caneta) nib; (do seio) nipple; (de gás) jet; (fam) (emprego) odd job, sideline; (boca) mouth

bidê /bi'de/ m bidet

bidimensio|nal /bidʒimēsioˈnaw/
(*pl* ~**nais**) *a* two-dimensional

biela /biˈɛla/ *f* connecting rod

Bielo-Rússia /bieloˈxusia/ *f*
Byelorussia

bielo-russo /bieloˈxusu/ *a* & *m*
Byelorussian

bie|nal /bieˈnaw/ (*pl* ~**nais**) *a* bi-
ennial □ *f* biennial art exhibition

bife /ˈbifi/ *m* steak

bifo|cal /bifoˈkaw/ (*pl* ~**cais**) *a*
bifocal

bifur|cação /bifurkaˈsãw/ *f* fork;
~**car-se** *vpr* fork

bigamia /bigaˈmia/ *f* bigamy

bígamo /ˈbigamu/ *a* bigamous □
m bigamist

bigo|de /biˈgodʒi/ *m* moustache;
~**dudo** *a* with a big moustache

bigorna /biˈgorna/ *f* anvil

bijuteria /biʒuteˈria/ *f* costume
jewellery

bilate|ral /bilateˈraw/ (*pl* ~**rais**)
a bilateral

bilhão /biˈʎãw/ *m* thousand million, (*Amer*) billion

bilhar /biˈʎar/ *m* pool, billiards

bilhe|te /biˈʎetʃi/ *m* ticket; (*reca-
do*) note; ~**te de ida e volta** return ticket, (*Amer*) round-trip
ticket; ~**te de identidade** (*Port*)
identity card; **o** ~**te azul** (*fam*)
the sack; ~**teria** *f*, (*Port*) ~**teira**
f (*no cinema, teatro*) box office;
(*na estação*) ticket office

bilíngüe /biˈlĩgwi/ *a* bilingual

bilionário /bilioˈnariu/ *a* & *m* bil-
lionaire

bílis /ˈbilis/ *f* bile

binário /biˈnariu/ *a* binary

bingo /ˈbĩgu/ *m* bingo

binóculo /biˈnɔkulu/ *m* binoculars

biodegradá|vel /biodegraˈdavew/
(*pl* ~**veis**) *a* biodegradable

bio|grafia /biograˈfia/ *f* bio-
graphy; ~**gráfico** *a* biographical

biógrafo /biˈografu/ *m* biographer

bio|logia /bioloˈʒia/ *f* biology;
~**lógico** *a* biological

biólogo /biˈologu/ *m* biologist

biombo /biˈõbu/ *m* screen

biônico /biˈoniku/ *a* bionic; (*pol*)
unelected

biópsia /biˈɔpsia/ *f* biopsy

bioquími|ca /bioˈkimika/ *f* bio-
chemistry; ~**co** *a* biochemical
□ *m* biochemist

biquíni /biˈkini/ *m* bikini

birma|nês /birmaˈnes/ *a* & *m* (*f*
~**nesa**) Burmese

Birmânia /birˈmania/ *f* Burma

birô /biˈro/ *m* bureau

bir|ra /ˈbixa/ *f* wilfulness; **fazer**
~**ra** have a tantrum; ~**rento** *a*
wilful

biruta /biˈruta/ (*fam*) *a* crazy □ *f*
windsock

bis /bis/ *int* encore!, more! □ *m*
invar encore

bisa|vó /bizaˈvɔ/ *f* great-grand-
mother; ~**vós** *m pl* great-
grandparents; ~**vô** *m* great-
grandfather

bisbilho|tar /bizbiʎoˈtar/ *vt* pry
into □ *vi* pry; ~**teiro** *a* prying □ *m* busybody;

bisca|te /bisˈkatʃi/ *m* odd job;
~**teiro** *m* odd-job man

biscoito /bisˈkojtu/ *m* biscuit,
(*Amer*) cookie

bisnaga /bizˈnaga/ *f* (*pão*) bridge
roll; (*tubo*) tube

bisne|ta /bizˈnɛta/ *f* great-grand-
daughter; ~**to** /ɛ/ *m* great-
grandson; *pl* great-grand-
children

bis|pado /bisˈpadu/ *m* bishopric;
~**po** *m* bishop

bissexto /biˈsestu/ *a* occasional;
ano ~ leap year

bissexu|al /biseksuˈaw/ (*pl* ~**ais**)
a & *m/f* bisexual

bisturi /bistuˈri/ *m* scalpel

bito|la /biˈtɔla/ *f* gauge; ~**lado** *a*
narrow-minded

bizarro /biˈzaxu/ *a* bizarre

blablablá /blablaˈbla/ (*fam*) *m*
chitchat

black /'blɛk/ *m* black market; ~-**tie** *m* evening dress

blasfemar /blasfe'mar/ *vi* blaspheme; ~**fêmia** *f* blasphemy; ~**femo** /e/ *a* blasphemous □ *m* blasphemer

blecaute /ble'kawtʃi/ *m* power cut

blefar /ble'far/ *vi* bluff; ~**fe** /ɛ/ *m* bluff

blindado /blĩ'dadu/ *a* armoured; ~**dagem** *f* armour-plating

blitz /blits/ *f invar* police spot-check (on vehicles)

bloco /'bloku/ *m* block; (*pol*) bloc; (*de papel*) pad; (*no carnaval*) section; ~**quear** *vt* block; (*mil*) blockade; ~**queio** *m* blockage; (*psic*) mental block; (*mil*) block-ade

blusa /'bluza/ *f* shirt; (*de mulher*) blouse; (*de lã*) sweater

boa /'boa/ *f de bom*; **numa** ~ (*fam*) well; (*sem problemas*) easily; **estar numa** ~ (*fam*) be doing fine; ~**gente** (*fam*) *a invar* nice; ~**pinta** (*pl* ~**s-pintas**) (*fam*) *a* nice-looking; ~**praça** (*pl* ~**s-praças**) (*fam*) *a* friendly, sociable

boate /bo'atʃi/ *f* nightclub

boato /bo'atu/ *m* rumour

boa|-nova /boa'nɔva/ (*pl* ~**s-novas**) *f* good news; ~**-vida** (*pl* ~**s-vidas**) *m/f* good-for-nothing, waster; ~**zinha** *f* a sweet, kind

bo|bagem /bo'baʒẽ/ *f* silliness; (*uma*) silly thing; ~**beada** *f* slip-up; ~**bear** *vi* slip up; ~**beira** *f veja* bobagem

bobe /'bɔbi/ *m* curler, roller

bobina /bo'bina/ *f* reel; (*eletr*) coil

bobo /'bobu/ *a* silly □ *m* fool; (*da corte*) jester; ~**ca** /ɔ/ (*fam*) *a* stupid □ *m/f* twit

boca /'boka/ *f* mouth; (*no fogão*) ring; ~**ca da noite** nightfall; ~**cado** *m* (*na boca*) mouthful; (*pedaço*) piece, bit; ~**cal** (*pl* ~**cais**) *m* mouthpiece

bocejar /bose'ʒar/ *vi* yawn; ~**jo** /e/ *m* yawn

bochecha /bo'ʃeʃa/ *f* cheek; ~**char** *vi* rinse one's mouth; ~**cho** /e/ *m* mouthwash; ~**chudo** *a* with puffy cheeks

bodas /'bodas/ *f pl* wedding anniversary; ~ **de prata/ouro** silver/golden wedding

bode /'bɔdʒi/ *m* (billy) goat; ~ **expiatório** scapegoat

bodega /bo'dɛga/ *f* (*de bebidas*) off-licence, (*Amer*) liquor store; (*de secos e molhados*) grocer's shop, corner shop

boêmio /bo'emiu/ *a & m* Bohemian

bofe|tada /bofe'tada/ *f*, **bofe|tão** /bofe'tãw/ *m* slap; ~**tear** *vt* slap

boi /boj/ *m* bullock, (*Amer*) steer

bói /bɔj/ *m* office boy

bóia /'bɔja/ *f* (*de balizamento*) buoy; (*de cortiça, isopor etc*) float; (*câmara de borracha*) rubber ring; (*de braço*) armband, water wing; (*na caixa-d'água*) ballcock; (*fam: comida*) grub; ~ **salva-vidas** lifebelt; ~**fria** (*pl* ~**-frias**) *m/f* itinerant farm la-bourer

boiar /bo'jar/ *vt/i* float; (*fam*) be lost

boico|tar /bojko'tar/ *vt* boycott; ~**te** /ɔ/ *m* boycott

boiler /'bɔjler/ (*pl* ~**s**) *m* boiler

boina /'bojna/ *f* beret

bo|jo /'boʒu/ *m* bulge; ~**judo** *a* (*cheio*) bulging; (*arredondado*) bulbous

bola /'bola/ *f* ball; **dar** ~ **para** (*fam*) give attention to <*pessoa*>; care about <*coisa*>; ~ **de gude** marble; ~ **de neve** snowball

bolacha /bo'laʃa/ *f* (*biscoito*) bis-cuit, (*Amer*) cookie; (*descanso*) beermat; (*fam: tapa*) slap

bolada /bo'lada/ *f* large sum of money; ~**lar** *vt* think up, devise

boléia /bo'lɛja/ f cab; (*Port: carona*) lift

boletim /bole'tʃĩ/ m bulletin; (*escolar*) report

bolha /'boʎa/ f bubble; (*na pele*) blister □ (*fam*) m/f pain

boliche /bo'liʃi/ m skittles

Bolívia /bo'livia/ f Bolivia

boliviano /bolivi'anu/ a & m Bolivian

bolo /'bolu/ m cake

bo|lor /bo'lor/ m mould, mildew; **~lorento** a mouldy

bolota /bo'lɔta/ f (*glande*) acorn; (*bolinha*) little ball

bol|sa /'bowsa/ f bag; **~sa** (*de estudo*) scholarship; **~sa** (**de valores**) stock exchange; **~sista** m/f, (*Port*) **~seiro** m scholarship student; **~so** /o/ m pocket

bom /bõ/ a (*f* **boa**) good; (*de saúde*) well; (*comida*) nice; **está ~** that's fine

bomba[1] /'bõba/ f (*explosiva*) bomb; (*doce*) eclair; (*fig*) bombshell; **levar ~** (*fam*) fail

bomba[2] /'bõba/ f (*de bombear*) pump

Bombaim /bõba'ĩ/ f Bombay

bombar|dear /bõbardʒi'ar/ vt bombard; (*do ar*) bomb; **~deio** m bombardment; (*do ar*) bombing

bomba-relógio /bõbaxe'lɔʒiu/ (*pl* **~s-relógio**) f time bomb

bom|bear /bõbi'ar/ vt pump; **~beiro** m fireman; (*encanador*) plumber

bombom /bõ'bõ/ m chocolate

bombordo /bõ'bɔrdu/ m port

bondade /bõ'dadʒi/ f goodness

bonde /'bõdʒi/ m tram; (*teleférico*) cable car

bondoso /bõ'dozu/ a good(-hearted)

boné /bo'nɛ/ m cap

bone|ca /bo'nɛka/ f doll; **~co** /ɛ/ m dummy

bonificação /bonifika'sãw/ f bonus

bonito /bo'nitu/ a (*mulher*) pretty; (*homem*) handsome; (*tempo, casa etc*) lovely

bônus /'bonus/ m invar bonus

boqui|aberto /bokia'bertu/ a open-mouthed, flabbergasted; **~nha** f snack

borboleta /borbo'leta/ f butterfly; (*roleta*) turnstile

borbotão /borbo'tãw/ m spurt

borbu|lha /bor'buʎa/ f bubble; **~lhar** vi bubble

borda /'bɔrda/ f edge; **~do** a edged; (*à linha*) embroidered □ m embroidery

bordão /bor'dãw/ m (*frase*) catchphrase

bordar /bor'dar/ vt (*à linha*) embroider

bor|del /bor'dɛw/ (*pl* **~déis**) m brothel

bordo /'bordu/ m a **~** aboard

borra /'boxa/ f dregs; (*de café*) grounds

borra|cha /bo'xaʃa/ f rubber; **~cheiro** m tyre fitter

bor|rão /bo'xãw/ m (*de tinta*) blot; (*rascunho*) rough draft; **~rar** vt (*sujar*) blot; (*riscar*) cross out; (*pintar*) daub

borrasca /bo'xaska/ f squall

borri|far /boxi'far/ vt sprinkle; **~fo** m sprinkling

bosque /'bɔski/ m wood

bosta /'bɔsta/ f (*de animal*) dung; (*chulo*) crap

bota /'bɔta/ f boot

botâni|ca /bo'tanika/ f botany; **~co** a botanical □ m botanist

bo|tão /bo'tãw/ m button; (*de flor*) bud; **falar com os seus ~tões** say to o.s.

botar /bo'tar/ vt put; put on *<roupa>*; set *<mesa, despertador>*; lay *<ovo>*; find *<defeito>*

bote[1] /'botʃi/ m (*barco*) dinghy; **~ salva-vidas** lifeboat; (*de borracha*) liferaft

bote[2] /'botʃi/ m (*de animal etc*) lunge

botequim /butʃiˈkĩ/ *m* bar

botoeira /botoˈera/ *f* buttonhole

boxe /ˈbɔksi/ *m* boxing; ~**ador** *m* boxer

brabo /ˈbrabu/ *a* <*animal*> ferocious; <*calor*, *sol*> fierce; <*doença*> bad; <*prova*, *experiência*> tough; (*zangado*) angry

braçada /braˈsada/ *f* armful; (*em natação*) stroke; ~**cadeira** (*faixa*) armband; (*ferragem*) bracket; (*de atleta*) sweatband; ~**çal** (*pl* ~**çais**) *a* manual; ~**celete** /e/ *m* bracelet; ~**ço** *m* arm; ~**ço direito** (*fig*: *pessoa*) right-hand man

braçar /braˈdar/ *vt/i* shout; ~**do** *m* shout

braguilha /braˈgiʎa/ *f* fly, flies

braile /ˈbrajli/ *m* Braille

bramido /braˈmidu/ *m* roar; ~**mir** *vi* roar

branco /ˈbrãku/ *a* white □ *m* (*homem*) white man; (*espaço*) blank; **em** ~ <*cheque etc*> blank; **noite em** ~ sleepless night

brandо /ˈbrãdu/ *a* gentle; <*doença*> mild; (*manso*) lenient, soft; ~**dura** *f* gentleness; (*indulgência*) softness, leniency

brasa /ˈbraza/ *f* **em** ~ red-hot; **mandar** ~ (*fam*) go to town

brasão /braˈzãw/ *m* coat of arms

braseiro /braˈzeru/ *m* brasier

Brasil /braˈziw/ *m* Brazil

brasileiro /braziˈleru/ *a* & *m* Brazilian; ~**liense** *a* & *m/f* (*person*) from Brasilia

bravata /braˈvata/ *f* bravado; ~**vio** *a* wild; <*mar*> rough; ~**vo** *a* (*corajoso*) brave; (*zangado*) angry; <*mar*> rough; ~**vura** *f* bravery

breca /ˈbrɛka/ *f* **levado da** ~ very naughty

brecar /breˈkar/ *vt* stop <*carro*>; (*fig*) curb □ *vi* brake

brecha /ˈbrɛʃa/ *f* gap; (*na lei*) loophole

brega /ˈbrɛga/ (*fam*) *a* tacky, naff; ~**guice** (*fam*) *f* tack, tackiness

brejo /ˈbreʒu/ *m* marsh; **ir para o** ~ (*fig*) go down the drain

brenha /ˈbreɲa/ *f* thicket

breque /ˈbrɛki/ *m* brake

breu /brew/ *m* tar, pitch

breve /ˈbrɛvi/ *a* short, brief; **em** ~ soon, shortly; ~**vidade** *f* shortness, brevity

briga /ˈbriga/ *f* fight; (*bate-boca*) argument

brigada /briˈgada/ *f* brigade; ~**deiro** *m* brigadier; (*doce*) chocolate truffle

brigão /briˈgãw/ *a* (*f* ~**gona**) belligerent; (*na fala*) argumentative □ *m* (*f* ~**gona**) troublemaker; ~**gar** *vi* fight; (*com palavras*) argue; <*cores*> clash

brilhante /briˈʎãtʃi/ *a* (*reluzente*) shiny; (*fig*) brilliant; ~**lhar** *vi* shine; ~**lho** *m* (*de sapatos etc*) shine; (*dos olhos, de metais*) gleam; (*das estrelas*) brightness; (*de uma cor*) brilliance; (*fig*: *esplendor*) splendour

brincadeira /brĩkaˈdera/ *f* (*piada*) joke; (*brinquedo, jogo*) game; **de** ~**cadeira** for fun; ~**calhão** (*f* ~**calhona**) *a* playful □ *m* joker; ~**car** *vi* (*divertir-se*) play; (*gracejar*) joke

brinco /ˈbrĩku/ *m* earring

brindar /brĩˈdar/ *vt* (*saudar*) toast, drink to; (*presentear*) give a gift to; ~**dar alg com aco** afford s.o. sth; (*de presente*) give s.o. sth as a gift; ~**de** *m* (*saudação*) toast; (*presente*) free gift

brinquedo /brĩˈkedu/ *m* toy

brio /ˈbriu/ *m* self-esteem, character; ~**so** /o/ *a* self-confident

brisa /ˈbriza/ *f* breeze

britadeira /britaˈdera/ *f* pneumatic drill

britânico /briˈtaniku/ *a* British □ *m* Briton; **os** ~**s** the British

broca /'brɔka/ f drill

broche /'brɔʃi/ m brooch

brochura /broʃura/ f livro de ~ paperback

brócolis /'brɔkulis/ m pl, (Port) **brócolos** /'brɔkuluʃ/ m pl broccoli

bron|ca /'brõka/ (fam) f telling-off; **dar uma ~ca em alg** tell s.o. off; ~**co** a coarse, rough

bronquite /brõ'kitʃi/ f bronchitis

bronze /'brõzi/ m bronze; ~**ado** a tanned, brown □ m (sun)tan; ~**ador** a tanning □ m suntan lotion; ~**amento** m tanning; ~**ar** vt tan; ~**ar-se** vpr go brown, tan

bro|tar /bro'tar/ vt sprout <folhas, flores>; spout <lágrimas, palavras> □ vi <planta> sprout; <água> spout; <idéias> pop up; ~**tinho** (fam) m youngster; ~**to** /o/ m shoot; (fam) youngster

broxa /'brɔʃa/ f (large) paint brush □ (fam) a impotent

bruços /'brusus/ de ~ face down

bru|ma /'bruma/ f mist; ~**moso** /o/ a misty

brusco /'brusku/ a brusque, abrupt

bru|tal /bru'taw/ (pl ~**tais**) a brutal; ~**talidade** f brutality; ~**to** a <feições> coarse; <homem> brutish; <tom, comentário> aggressive; <petróleo> crude; <peso, lucro, salário> gross □ m brute

bruxa /'bruʃa/ f witch; (feia) hag; ~**ria** f witchcraft

Bruxelas /bru'ʃɛlas/ f Brussels

bruxo /'bruʃu/ m wizard

bruxulear /bruʃuli'ar/ vi flicker

bucha /'buʃa/ f (tampão) bung; (para paredes) rawlplug (R); **acertar na ~** (fam) hit the nail on the head

bucho /'buʃu/ m gut; ~ **de boi** tripe

budis|mo /bu'dʒizmu/ m Buddhism; ~**ta** a & m/f Buddhist

bueiro /bu'eru/ m storm drain

búfalo /'bufalu/ m buffalo

bu|fante /bu'fãtʃi/ a full, puffed; ~**far** vi snort; (reclamar) grumble, moan

bufê /bu'fe/ m (refeição) buffet; (serviço) catering service; (móvel) sideboard

bugiganga /buʒi'gãga/ f knick-knack

bujão /bu'ʒãw/ m ~ **de gás** gas cylinder

bula /'bula/ f (de remédio) directions; (do Papa) bull

bulbo /'buwbu/ m bulb

bule /'buli/ m (de chá) teapot; (de café etc) pot

Bulgária /buw'garia/ f Bulgaria

búlgaro /'buwgaru/ a & m Bulgarian

bulhufas /bu'ʎufas/ (fam) pron nothing

bulício /bu'lisiu/ m bustle

bumbum /bũ'bũ/ (fam) m bottom, bum

bunda /'bũda/ f bottom

buquê /bu'ke/ m bouquet

buraco /bu'raku/ m hole; (de agulha) eye; (jogo de cartas) rummy; ~ **da fechadura** keyhole

burburinho /burbu'riɲu/ m (de vozes) hubbub

bur|guês /bur'ges/ a & m (f ~**guesa**) bourgeois; ~**guesia** f bourgeoisie

burlar /bur'lar/ vt get round <lei>; get past <defesas, vigilância>

buro|cracia /burokra'sia/ f bureaucracy; ~**crata** m/f bureaucrat; ~**crático** a bureaucratic; ~**cratizar** vt make bureaucratic

bur|rice /bu'xisi/ f stupidity; (uma) stupid thing; ~**ro** a stupid; (ignorante) dim □ m (animal) donkey; (pessoa) halfwit, dunce; ~**ro de carga** (fig) workhorse

bus|ca /'buska/ *f* search; **dar ~ca em** search; **~ca-pé** *m* banger; **~car** *vt* fetch; (*de carro*) pick up; **mandar ~car** send for

bússola /'busɔla/ *f* compass; (*fig*) guide

busto /'bustu/ *m* bust

butique /bu'tʃiki/ *f* boutique

buzi|na /bu'zina/ *f* horn; **~nada** *f* toot (of the horn); **~nar** *vi* sound the horn, toot the horn

C

cá /ka/ *adv* here; **o lado de ~** this side; **para ~** here; **de ~ para lá** back and forth; **de lá para ~** since then; **~ entre nós** between you and me

ca|bal /ka'baw/ (*pl* **~bais**) *a* complete, full; *<prova>* conclusive

cabana /ka'bana/ *f* hut; (*casinha no campo*) cottage

cabeça /ka'besa/ *f* head; (*de lista*) top; (*pessoa inteligente*) mind □ *m/f* (*chefe*) ringleader; (*integrante mais inteligente*) brains; **de ~** *<saber>* off the top of one's head; *<calcular>* in one's head; **de ~ para baixo** upside down; **deu-lhe na ~ de** he took it into his head to; **esquentar a ~** (*fam*) get worked up about; **fazer a ~ de alg** convince s.o.; **quebrar a ~** rack one's brains; **subir à ~** go to s.o.'s head; **ter a ~ no lugar** have one's head screwed on; **~da** *f* (*no futebol*) header; (*pancada*) head butt; **dar uma ~da no teto** bang one's head on the ceiling; **~-de-porco** (*pl* **~s-de-porco**) *f* tenement; **~-de-vento** (*pl* **~s-de-vento**) *m/f* scatterbrain, airhead; **~lho** *m* heading

cabe|cear /kabesi'ar/ *vt* head

<bola>; **~ceira** *f* head; **~çudo** *a* pigheaded

cabe|dal /kabe'daw/ (*pl* **~dais**) *m* wealth

cabelei|ra /kabe'lera/ *f* head of hair; (*peruca*) wig; **~reiro** *m* hairdresser

cabe|lo /ka'belu/ *m* hair; **cortar o ~lo** have one's hair cut; **~ludo** *a* hairy; (*difícil*) complicated; *<palavra, piada>* dirty

caber /ka'ber/ *vi* fit; (*ter cabimento*) be fitting; **~ a** *<mérito, parte>* be due to; *<tarefa>* fall to; **cabe a você ir** it is up to you to go; **~ em alg** *<roupa>* fit s.o.

cabide /ka'bidʒi/ *m* (*peça de madeira, arame etc*) hanger; (*móvel*) hat stand; (*na parede*) coat rack

cabimento /kabi'mẽtu/ *m* **ter ~** be fitting, be appropriate; **não ter ~** be out of the question

cabine /ka'bini/ *f* cabin; (*de avião*) cockpit; (*de loja*) changing room; **~ telefônica** phone box, (*Amer*) phone booth

cabisbaixo /kabiz'baʃu/ *a* crestfallen

cabí|vel /ka'bivew/ (*pl* **~veis**) *a* appropriate, fitting

cabo[1] /'kabu/ *m* (*militar*) corporal; **ao ~ de** after; **levar a ~** carry out; **~ eleitoral** campaign worker

cabo[2] /'kabu/ *m* (*fio*) cable; (*de panela etc*) handle; **TV por ~** cable TV; **~ de extensão** extension lead; **~ de força** tug of war

caboclo /ka'boklu/ *a & m* mestizo

ca|bra /'kabra/ *f* goat; **~brito** *m* kid

ca|ça /'kasa/ *f* (*atividade*) hunting; (*caçada*) hunt; (*animais*) game □ *m* (*avião*) fighter; **à ~ça de** in pursuit of; **~ça das bruxas** (*fig*) witch hunt; **~çador** *m* hunter; **~ça-minas** *m invar* minesweeper; **~ça-níqueis** *m invar* slot machine; **~çar** *vt* hunt <*animais, criminoso etc*>; (*procurar*) hunt for □ *vi* hunt

cacareco /kaka'rɛku/ *m* piece of junk; *pl* junk

cacare|jar /kakare'ʒar/ *vi* cluck; ~**jo** /e/ *m* clucking

caçarola /kasa'rɔla/ *f* saucepan

cacau /ka'kaw/ *m* cocoa

cace|tada /kase'tada/ *f* blow with a club; (*fig*) annoyance; ~**te** /e/ *m* club □ (*fam*) *int* damn

cachaça /ka'ʃasa/ *f* white rum

cachê /ka'ʃe/ *m* fee

cache|col /kaʃe'kɔw/ (*pl* ~**cóis**) *m* scarf

cachimbo /ka'ʃĩbu/ *m* pipe

cacho /'kaʃu/ *m* (*de banana, uva*) bunch; (*de cabelo*) lock; (*fam: caso*) affair

cachoeira /kaʃo'era/ *f* waterfall

cachor|rinho /kaʃo'xiɲu/ *m* (*nado*) doggy paddle; ~**ro** /o/ *m* dog; (*Port*) puppy; (*pessoa*) scoundrel; ~**ro-quente** (*pl* ~**ros-quentes**) *m* hot dog

cacife /ka'sifi/ *m* (*fig*) pull

caci|que /ka'siki/ *m* (*índio*) chief; (*político*) boss; ~**quia** *f* leadership

caco /'kaku/ *m* shard; (*pessoa*) old crock

cacto /'kaktu/ *m* cactus

caçula /ka'sula/ *m/f* youngest child □ *a* youngest

cada /'kada/ *a* each; ~ **duas horas** every two hours; **custam £5** ~ **(um)** they cost £5 each; ~ **vez mais** more and more; ~ **vez mais fácil** easier and easier; **ele fala** ~ **coisa** (*fam*) he says the most amazing things

cadafalso /kada'fawsu/ *m* gallows

cadarço /ka'darsu/ *m* shoelace

cadas|trar /kadas'trar/ *vt* register; ~**tro** *m* register; (*ato*) registration; (*policial, bancário*) records, files; (*imobiliário*) land register

ca|dáver /ka'daver/ *m* (dead) body, corpse; ~**davérico** *a* cadaverous, corpse-like; <*exame*> post-mortem

cadê /ka'de/ (*fam*) *adv* where is/are...?

cadeado /kadʒi'adu/ *m* padlock

cadeia /ka'deja/ *f* (*de eventos, lojas etc*) chain; (*prisão*) prison; (*rádio, TV*) network

cadeira /ka'dera/ *f* (*móvel*) chair; (*no teatro*) stall; (*de político*) seat; (*função de professor*) chair; (*matéria*) subject; (*pl anat*) hips; ~ **de balanço** rocking chair; ~ **de rodas** wheelchair; ~ **elétrica** electric chair

ca|dência /ka'dẽsia/ *f* (*mus, da voz*) cadence; (*compasso*) rhythm; ~**denciado** *a* rhythmic; <*passos*> measured

cader|neta /kader'neta/ *f* notebook; (*de professor*) register; (*de banco*) passbook; ~**neta de poupança** savings account; ~**no** /ɛ/ *m* exercise book; (*pequeno*) notebook; (*no jornal*) section

cadete /ka'detʃi/ *m* cadet

cadu|car /kadu'kar/ *vi* <*pessoa*> become senile; <*contrato*> lapse; ~**co** *a* <*pessoa*> senile; <*contrato*> lapsed; ~**quice** *f* senility

cafajeste /kafa'ʒestʃi/ *m* swine

ca|fé /ka'fɛ/ *m* coffee; (*botequim*) café; ~**fé da manhã** breakfast; **tomar** ~**fé** have breakfast; ~**fé-com-leite** *a invar* coffee-coloured, light brown □ *m* white coffee; ~**feeiro** *a* coffee □ *m* coffee plant; ~**feicultura** *f* coffee-growing; ~**feína** *f* caffein(e)

cafetã /kafe'tã/ *m* caftan

cafetão /kafe'tãw/ *m* pimp

cafe|teira /kafe'tera/ *f* coffee pot; ~**zal** (*pl* ~**zais**) *m* coffee plantation; ~**zinho** *m* small black coffee

cafo|na /ka'fona/ (*fam*) *a* naff, tacky; ~**nice** *f* tackiness; (*coisa*) tacky thing

cágado /'kagadu/ *m* turtle

caiar /kaj'ar/ *vt* whitewash

cãibra /'kãjbra/ *f* cramp

caí|da /ka'ida/ *f* fall; *veja* **queda**; **~do** *a* <*árvore etc*> fallen; <*beiços etc*> drooping; (*deprimido*) dejected; (*apaixonado*) smitten

caimento /kaj'mẽtu/ *m* fall

caipi|ra /kaj'pira/ *a* <*pessoa*> countrified; <*festa, música*> country; <*sotaque*> rural □ *m/f* country person; (*depreciativo*) country bumpkin; **~rinha** *f* cachaça with limes, sugar and ice

cair /ka'ir/ *vi* fall; <*dente, cabelo*> fall out; <*botão etc*> fall off; <*comércio, trânsito etc*> fall off; <*tecido, cortina*> hang; **~ bem/mal** <*roupa*> go well/badly; <*ato, dito*> go down well, badly; **estou caindo de sono** I'm really sleepy

cais /kajs/ *m* quay; (*Port: na estação*) platform

caixa /'kaʃa/ *f* box; (*de loja etc*) cashdesk □ *m/f* cashier; **~ de correio** letter box; **~ de mudanças**, (*Port*) **~ de velocidades** gear box; **~ postal** post office box, PO Box; **~ (pl ~s-d'água)** *f* water tank; **~-forte** (*pl ~s-fortes*) *f* vault

cai|xão /ka'ʃãw/ *m* coffin; **~xeiro** *m* (*em loja*) assistant; salesman; **~xilho** *m* frame; **~xote** *m* crate

caju /ka'ʒu/ *m* cashew fruit; **~eiro** *m* cashew tree

cal /kaw/ *f* lime

calado /ka'ladu/ *a* quiet

calafrio /kala'friu/ *m* shudder, shiver

calami|dade /kalami'dadʒi/ *f* calamity; **~toso** /o/ *a* calamitous

calar /ka'lar/ *vi* be quiet □ *vt* keep quiet about <*segredo, sentimento*>; silence <*pessoa*>; **~-se** *vpr* go quiet

calça /'kawsa/ *f* trousers, (*Amer*) pants

calça|da /kaw'sada/ *f* pavement, (*Amer*) sidewalk; (*Port: rua*) roadway; **~dão** *m* pedestrian precinct; **~deira** *f* shoe-horn; **~do** *a* paved □ *m* shoe; *pl* footwear

calcanhar /kawka'ɲar/ *m* heel

calção /kaw'sãw/ *m* shorts; **~ de banho** swimming trunks

calcar /kaw'kar/ *vt* (*pisar*) trample; (*comprimir*) press; **~ aco em** (*fig*) base sth on, model sth on

calçar /kaw'sar/ *vt* put on <*sapatos, luvas*>; take <*número*>; pave <*rua*>; (*com calço*) wedge □ *vi* <*sapato*> fit; **~-se** *vpr* put one's shoes on

calcário /kaw'kariu/ *m* limestone □ *a* <*água*> hard

calças /'kawsas/ *f pl veja* **calça**

calcinha /kaw'siɲa/ *f* knickers, (*Amer*) panties

cálcio /'kawsiu/ *m* calcium

calço /'kawsu/ *m* wedge

calcu|ladora /kawkula'dora/ *f* calculator; **~lar** *vt/i* calculate; **~lista** *a* calculating □ *m/f* opportunist

cálculo /'kawkulu/ *m* calculation; (*diferencial*) calculus; (*med*) stone

cal|da /'kawda/ *f* syrup; *pl* hot springs; **~deira** *f* boiler; **~deirão** *m* cauldron; **~do** *m* (*sopa*) broth; (*suco*) juice; **~do de carne/galinha** beef/chicken stock

calefação /kalefa'sãw/ *f* heating

caleidoscópio /kalejdos'kɔpiu/ *m* kaleidoscope

calejado /kale'ʒadu/ *a* <*mãos*> calloused; <*pessoa*> experienced

calendário /kalẽ'dariu/ *m* calendar

calha /'kaʃa/ *f* (*no telhado*) gutter; (*sulco*) gulley

calhamaço /kaʎaˈmasu/ *m* tome

calhambeque /kaʎãˈbɛki/ (*fam*) *m* banger

calhar /kaˈʎar/ *vi* **calhou que it so happened that; calhou pegar em o mesmo trem** they happened to get the same train; **~ de** happen to; **vir a ~** come at the right time

cali|brado /kaliˈbradu/ *a* (*bêbado*) tipsy; **~brar** *vt* calibrate; check (the pressure of) <*pneu*>; **~bre** *m* calibre; **coisas desse ~bre** things of this order

cálice /ˈkalisi/ *m* (*copo*) liqueur glass; (*na missa*) chalice

caligrafia /kaligraˈfia/ *f* (*letra*) handwriting; (*arte*) calligraphy

calista /kaˈlista/ *m/f* chiropodist, (*Amer*) podiatrist

cal|ma /ˈkawma/ *f* calm; **com ~ma** calmly □ *int* calm down; **~mante** *m* tranquilizer; **~mo** *a* calm

calo /ˈkalu/ *m* (*na mão*) callus; (*no pé*) corn

colombo /kaˈlõbu/ *m* bump

calor /kaˈlor/ *m* heat; (*agradável, fig*) warmth; **estar com ~** be hot

calo|rento /kaloˈrẽtu/ *a* <*pessoa*> sensitive to heat; <*lugar*> hot; **~ria** *f* calorie; **~roso** /o/ *a* warm; <*protesto*> lively

calota /kaˈlota/ *f* hubcap

calo|te /kaˈlɔtʃi/ *m* bad debt; **~teiro** *m* bad risk

calouro /kaˈloru/ *m* (*na faculdade*) freshman; (*em outros ramos*) novice

ca|lúnia /kaˈlunia/ *f* slander; **~luniar** *vt* slander; **~lunioso** /o/ *a* slanderous

cal|vície /kawˈvisi/ *f* baldness; **~vo** *a* bald

cama /ˈkama/ *f* bed; **~ de casal/solteiro** double/single bed; **~beliche** (*pl* **~s-beliches**) *f* bunk bed

camada /kaˈmada/ *f* layer; (*de tinta*) coat

câmara /ˈkamara/ *f* chamber; (*fotográfica*) camera; **~ digital** digital camera; **em ~ lenta** in slow motion; **~ municipal** town council; (*Port*) town hall

camarada /kamaˈrada/ *a* friendly □ *m/f* comrade; **~gem** *f* comradeship; (*convivência agradável*) camaraderie

câmara-de-ar /kamaradʒiˈar/ (*pl* **câmaras-de-ar**) *f* inner tube

camarão /kamaˈrãw/ *m* shrimp; (*maior*) prawn

cama|reira /kamaˈrera/ *f* chambermaid; **~rim** *m* dressing room; **~rote** /ɔ/ *m* (*no teatro*) box; (*num navio*) cabin

cambada /kãˈbada/ *f* gang, horde

cambalacho /kãbaˈlaʃu/ *m* scam

camba|lear /kãbaliˈar/ *vi* stagger; **~lhota** *f* somersault

cambi|al /kãbiˈaw/ (*pl* **~ais**) *a* exchange; **~ante** *m* shade; **~ar** *vt* change

câmbio /ˈkãbiu/ *m* exchange; (*taxa*) rate of exchange; **~ oficial/paralelo** official/black market exchange rate

cambista /kãˈbista/ *m/f* (*de entradas*) ticket-tout, (*Amer*) scalper; (*de dinheiro*) money changer

Camboja /kãˈbɔʒa/ *m* Cambodia

cambojano /kãboˈʒanu/ *a* & *m* Cambodian

camburão /kãbuˈrãw/ *m* police van

camelo /kaˈmelu/ *m* camel

camelô /kameˈlo/ *m* street vendor

camião /kamiˈãw/ (*Port*) *m veja* **caminhão**

caminhada /kamiˈɲada/ *f* walk

caminhão /kamiˈɲãw/ *m* lorry, (*Amer*) truck

cami|nhar /kamiˈɲar/ *vi* walk; (*fig*) advance, progress; **~nho** *m* way; (*estrada*) road; (*trilho*) path; **a ~nho** on the way; **a**

meio ~**nho** halfway; ~**nho de ferro** (Port) railway, (Amer) railroad

caminho|neiro /kamiɲo'neru/ m lorry driver, (Amer) truck driver; ~**nete** /ɛ/ m van

camio|neta /kamio'neta/ f van; ~**nista** (Port) m/f veja **caminhoneiro**

cami|sa /ka'miza/ f shirt; ~**sa-de-força** (pl ~**sas-de-força**) f straitjacket; ~**sa-de-vénus** (pl ~**sas-de-vénus**) f condom; ~**seta** /e/ f T-shirt; (de baixo) vest; ~**sinha** (fam) f condom; ~**sola** /ɔ/ f nightdress; (Port) sweater

camomila /kamo'mila/ f camomile

campainha /kãpa'iɲa/ f bell; (da porta) doorbell

campanário /kãpa'nariu/ m belfry

campanha /kã'paɲa/ f campaign

campe|ão /kãpi'ãw/ m (f ~**ã**) champion; ~**onato** m championship

cam|pestre /kã'pɛstri/ a rural; ~**pina** f grassland

cam|ping /'kãpĩ/ m camping; (lugar) campsite; ~**pismo** (Port) m camping

campo /'kãpu/ m field; (interior) country; (de futebol) pitch; (de golfe) course; ~ **de concentração** concentration camp; ~**nês** m (f ~**nesa**) peasant

camu|flagem /kamu'flaʒẽ/ f camouflage; ~**flar** vt camouflage

camundongo /kamũ'dõgu/ m mouse

cana /'kana/ f cane; ~ **de açúcar** sugar cane

Canadá /kana'da/ m Canada

canadense /kana'dẽsi/ a & m Canadian

ca|nal /ka'naw/ (pl ~**nais**) m channel; (hidrovia) canal

canalha /ka'naʎa/ m/f scoundrel

canali|zação /kanaliza'sãw/ f piping; ~**zador** (Port) m plumber; ~**zar** vt channel < líquido, esforço, recursos>; canalize < rio>; pipe for water and drainage <cidade>

canário /ka'nariu/ m canary

canastrão /kanas'trãw/ m (f ~**trona**) ham actor (f actress)

canavi|al /kanavi'aw/ (pl ~**ais**) m cane field; ~**eiro** a sugar cane

canção /kã'sãw/ f song

cance|lamento /kãsela'mẽtu/ m cancellation; ~**lar** vt cancel; (riscar) cross out

câncer /'kãser/ m cancer; **Câncer** (signo) Cancer

cance|riano /kãseri'anu/ a & m Cancerian; ~**rígeno** a carcinogenic; ~**roso** /o/ a cancerous □ m person with cancer

cancro /'kãkru/ m (Port: câncer) cancer; (fig) canker

candango /kã'dãgu/ m person from Brasília

cande|eiro /kãdʒi'eru/ m (oil-) lamp; ~**labro** m candelabra

candida|tar-se /kãdʒida'tarsi/ vpr (a vaga) apply (a for); (à presidência etc) stand, (Amer) run (a for); ~**to m** candidate (a for); (a vaga) applicant (a for); ~**tura** f candidature; (a vaga) application (a for)

cândido /'kãdʒidu/ a innocent

candomblé /kãdõ'blɛ/ m Afro-Brazilian cult; (reunião) candomble meeting

candura /kã'dura/ f innocence

cane|ca /ka'nɛka/ f mug; ~**co** /ɛ/ m tankard

canela[1] /ka'nɛla/ f (condimento) cinnamon

canela[2] /ka'nɛla/ f (da perna) shin; ~**da** f **dar uma** ~**da em alg** kick s.o. in the shins; **dar uma** ~**da em aco** hit one's shins on sth

cane|ta /ka'neta/ f pen; ~ **esferográfica** ball-point pen; ~**ta-**

tinteiro (*pl* **~tas-tinteiro**) *f* fountain pen

cangote /kã'gotʃi/ *m* nape of the neck

canguru /kãgu'ru/ *m* kangaroo

canhão /ka'ɲãw/ *m* (*arma*) cannon; (*vale*) canyon

canhoto /ka'ɲotu/ *a* left-handed □ *m* (*talão*) stub

cani|bal /kani'baw/ (*pl* **~bais**) *m/f* cannibal; **~balismo** *m* cannibalism

caniço /ka'nisu/ *m* reed; (*pessoa*) skinny person

canícula /ka'nikula/ *f* heat wave

ca|nil /ka'niw/ (*pl* **~nis**) *m* kennel

canivete /kani'vetʃi/ *m* penknife

canja /'kãʒa/ *f* chicken soup; (*fam*) piece of cake

canjica /kã'ʒika/ *f* corn porridge

cano /'kanu/ *m* pipe; (*de bota*) top; (*de arma de fogo*) barrel

cano|a /ka'noa/ *f* canoe; **~agem** *f* canoeing; **~ista** *m/f* canoeist

canonizar /kanoni'zar/ *vt* canonize

can|saço /kã'sasu/ *m* tiredness; **~sado** *a* tired; **~sar** *vt* tire; (*aborrecer*) bore □ *vi*, **~sar-se** *vpr* get tired; **~sativo** *a* tiring; (*aborrecido*) boring; **~seira** *f* tiredness; (*lida*) toil

can|tada /kã'tada/ *f* (*fam*) chatup; **~tar** *vt/i* sing; (*fam*) chat up

cântaro /'kãtaru/ *m* **chover a ~s** pour down, bucket down

cantarolar /kãtaro'lar/ *vt/i* hum

cantei|ra /kã'tera/ *f* quarry; **~ro** *m* (*de flores*) flowerbed; (*artífice*) stonemason; **~ro de obras** site office

cantiga /kã'tʃiga/ *f* ballad

can|til /kã'tʃiw/ (*pl* **~tis**) *m* canteen; **~tina** *f* canteen

canto[1] /'kãtu/ *m* (*ângulo*) corner

can|to[2] /'kãtu/ *m* (*cantar*) singing; **~tor** *m* singer; **~toria** *f* singing

canudo /ka'nudu/ *m* (*de beber*) straw; (*tubo*) tube; (*fam: diploma*) diploma

cão /kãw/ (*pl* **cães**) *m* dog

caolho /ka'oʎu/ *a* one-eyed

ca|os /kaws/ *m* chaos; **~ótico** *a* chaotic

capa /'kapa/ *f* (*de livro, revista*) cover; (*roupa sem mangas*) cape; **~ de chuva** raincoat

capacete /kapa'setʃi/ *m* helmet

capacho /ka'paʃu/ *m* doormat

capaci|dade /kapasi'dadʒi/ *f* capacity; (*aptidão*) ability; **~tar** *vt* enable; (*convencer*) convince

capataz /kapa'tas/ *m* foreman

capaz /ka'pas/ *a* capable (**de** of); **ser ~ de** (*poder*) be able to; (*ser provável*) be likely to

cape|la /ka'pɛla/ *f* chapel; **~lão** (*pl* **~lães**) *m* chaplain

capen|ga /ka'pẽga/ *a* doddery; **~gar** *vi* dodder

capeta /ka'peta/ *m* (*diabo*) devil; (*criança*) little devil

capilar /kapi'lar/ *a* hair

ca|pim /ka'pĩ/ *m* grass; **~pinar** *vt/i* weed

capi|tal /kapi'taw/ (*pl* **~tais**) *a* & *m/f* capital; **~talismo** *m* capitalism; **~talista** *a* & *m/f* capitalist; **~talizar** *vt* (*com*) capitalize; (*aproveitar*) capitalize on

capi|tanear /kapitani'ar/ *vt* captain <*navio*>; (*fig*) lead; **~tania** *f* captaincy; **~tania do porto** port authority; **~tão** (*pl* **~tães**) *m* captain

capitulação /kapitula'sãw/ *f* capitulation, surrender

capítulo /ka'pitulu/ *m* chapter; (*de telenovela*) episode

capô /ka'po/ *m* bonnet, (*Amer*) hood

capoeira /kapo'era/ *f* Brazilian kick-boxing

capo|ta /ka'pɔta/ *f* roof; **~tar** *vi* overturn

capote 43 carícia

capote /ka'pɔtʃi/ *m* overcoat

capri|char /kapri'ʃar/ *vi* excel o.s.; **~cho** *m* (*esmero*) care; (*desejo*) whim; (*teimosia*) contrariness; **~choso** /o/ *a* (*cheio de caprichos*) capricious; (*com esmero*) painstaking, meticulous

Capricórnio /kapri'kɔrniu/ *m* Capricorn

capricorniano /kaprikorni'anu/ *a & m* Capricorn

cápsula /'kapsula/ *f* capsule

cap|tar /kap'tar/ *vt* pick up <*emissão, sinais*>; tap <*água*>; catch, grasp <*sentido*>; win <*simpatia, admiração*>; **~tura** *f* capture; **~turar** *vt* capture

capuz /ka'pus/ *m* hood

caquético /ka'kɛtʃiku/ *a* broken-down, on one's last legs

caqui /ka'ki/ *m* persimmon

cáqui /'kaki/ *a invar & m* khaki

cara /'kara/ *f* face; (*aparência*) look; (*ousadia*) cheek □ (*fam*) *m* guy; **~ a** ~ face to face; **de** ~ straightaway; **dar de** ~ **com** run into; **está na** ~ it's obvious; **fechar a** ~ frown; **~ de pau** cheek; **~ de tacho** (*fam*) sheepish look

cara|col /kara'kɔw/ (*pl* **~cóis**) *m* snail

caracte|re /karak'tɛri/ *m* character; **~rística** *f* characteristic, feature; **~rístico** *a* characteristic; **~rizar** *vt* characterize; **~rizar-se** *vpr* be characterized

cara-de-pau /karadʒi'paw/ (*pl* **caras-de-pau**) *a* cheeky, brazen

caramba /ka'rãba/ *int* (*de espanto*) wow; (*de desagrado*) damn

caramelo /kara'mɛlu/ *m* caramel; (*bala*) toffee

caramujo /kara'muʒu/ *m* water snail

caranguejo /karã'geʒu/ *m* crab

caratê /kara'te/ *m* karate

caráter /ka'rater/ *m* character

caravana /kara'vana/ *f* caravan

car|boidrato /karboi'dratu/ *m* carbohydrate; **~bono** /o/ *m* carbon

carbu|rador /karbura'dor/ *m* carburettor, (*Amer*) carburator; **~rante**, (*Amer*) *m* fuel

carcaça /kar'kasa/ *f* carcass; (*de navio etc*) frame

cárcere /'karseri/ *m* jail

carcereiro /karse'reru/ *m* jailer, warder

carcomido /karko'midu/ *a* worm-eaten; <*rosto*> pock-marked

cardápio /kar'dapiu/ *m* menu

carde|al /kardʒi'aw/ (*pl* **~ais**) *a* cardinal

cardíaco /kar'dʒiaku/ *a* cardiac; **ataque** ~ heart attack

cardio|lógico /kardʒio'lɔʒiku/ *a* heart; **~logista** *m/f* heart specialist, cardiologist

cardume /kar'dumi/ *m* shoal

careca /ka'rɛka/ *a* bald □ *f* bald patch

ca|recer /kare'ser/ **~recer de** *vt* lack; **~rência** *f* lack; (*social*) deprivation; (*afetiva*) lack of affection; **~rente** *a* lacking; (*socialmente*) deprived; (*afetivamente*) in need of affection

carestia /kares'tʃia/ *f* high cost; (*geral*) high cost of living; (*escassez*) shortage

careta /ka'reta/ *f* grimace □ *a* (*fam*) straight, square

car|ga /'karga/ *f* load; (*mercadorias*) cargo; (*elétrica*) charge; (*de cavalaria*) charge; (*de caneta*) refill; (*fig*) burden; **~ga horária** workload; **~go** *m* (*função*) post, job; **a ~go de** in the charge of; **~gueiro** *m* (*navio*) cargo ship, freighter

cariar /kari'ar/ *vi* decay

Caribe /ka'ribi/ *m* Caribbean

caricatu|ra /karika'tura/ *f* caricature; **~rar** *vt* caricature; **~rista** *m/f* caricaturist

carícia /ka'risia/ *f* (*com a mão*) stroke, caress; (*carinho*) affection

cari|dade /kari'dadʒi/ f charity;
obra de ~dade charity;
~doso /o/ a charitable

cárie /'kari/ f tooth decay

carim|bar /karĩ'bar/ vt stamp;
postmark <carta>; ~bo m
stamp; (do correio) postmark

cari|nho /ka'riɲu/ m affection;
(um) caress; ~nhoso /o/ a affectionate

carioca /kari'ɔka/ a from Rio de
Janeiro □ m/f person from Rio
de Janeiro □ (Port) m weak coffee

caris|ma /ka'rizma/ m charisma;
~mático a charismatic

carna|val /karna'vaw/ (pl
~vais) a carnival; ~valesco
/e/ a carnival; <roupa> over the
top, overdone □ m carnival organizer

car|ne /'karni/ f (humana etc)
flesh; (comida) meat; ~neiro m
sheep; (macho) ram; (como comida) mutton; ~niça f carrion;
~nificina f slaughter;
~nívoro a carnivorous □ m
carnivore; ~nudo a fleshy

caro /'karu/ a expensive; (querido)
dear □ adv <custar, cobrar> a lot;
<comprar, vender> at a high
price; pagar ~ pay a high price
(for)

caroço /ka'rosu/ m (de pêssego etc)
stone; (de maçã) core; (em sopa,
molho etc) lump

carona /ka'rona/ f lift

carpete /kar'petʃi/ m fitted carpet

carpin|taria /karpĩta'ria/ f
carpentry; ~teiro m carpenter

carran|ca /ka'xãka/ f scowl;
~cudo a <cara> scowling;
<pessoa> sullen

carrapato /kaxa'patu/ m (animal)
tick; (fig) hanger-on

carrasco /ka'xasku/ m executioner; (fig) butcher

carre|gado /kaxe'gadu/ a <céu>
dark, black; <cor> dark; <ambiente> tense; ~gador m porter;
~gamento m loading; (carga)
load; ~gar vt load <navio, arma,
máquina fotográfica>; (levar)
carry; charge <bateria, pilha>;
~gar em overdo; pronounce
strongly <letra>; (Port) press

carreira /ka'xera/ f career

carre|tel /ka'xetɛw/ (pl ~téis) m
reel

car|ril /ka'xiw/ (pl ~ris) (Port)
m rail

carrinho /ka'xiɲu/ m (para bagagem, compras) trolley; (de criança) pram; ~ de mão wheelbarrow

carro /'kaxu/ m car; (de bois) cart;
~ alegórico float; ~ esporte
sports car; ~ fúnebre hearse;
~ça /ɔ/ f cart; ~ceria f
bodywork; ~chefe (pl ~s-
chefes) m (no carnaval) main
float; (fig) centrepiece; ~-forte
(pl ~s-fortes) m security van

carros|sel /kaxo'sɛw/ (pl ~séis)
m merry-go-round

carruagem /kaxu'aʒẽ/ f coach

carta /'karta/ f letter; (mapa)
chart; (do baralho) card; ~
branca (fig) carte blanche; ~
de condução (Port) driving licence, (Amer) driver's license;
~-bomba (pl ~s-bomba) f letter bomb; ~ da f (fig) move

cartão /kar'tãw/ m card; (Port:
papelão) cardboard; ~ de crédito credit card; ~ de visita visiting card; ~ magnético swipe
card; ~-postal (pl cartões-
postais) m postcard

car|taz /kar'tas/ m poster, (Amer)
bill; em ~ showing, (Amer)
playing; ~teira f (para dinheiro) wallet; (cartão) card;
(mesa) desk; ~teira de identidade identity card; ~teira de
motorista driving licence,
(Amer) driver's license; ~teiro
m postman

car|tel /kar'tɛw/ (*pl* **~téis**) *m* cartel

cárter /'karter/ *m* sump

carto|la /kar'tɔla/ *f* top hat □ *m* director; **~lina** *f* card; **~mante** *m/f* tarot reader, fortune-teller

cartório /kar'tɔriu/ *m* registry office

cartucho /kar'tuʃu/ *m* cartridge; (*de dinamite*) stick; (*de amendoim etc*) bag

car|tum /kar'tũ/ *m* cartoon; **~tunista** *m/f* cartoonist

caruncho /ka'rũʃu/ *m* woodworm

carvalho /kar'vaʎu/ *m* oak

car|vão /kar'vãw/ *m* coal; (*de desenho*) charcoal; **~voeiro** *a* coal

casa /'kaza/ *f* house; (*comercial*) firm; (*de tabuleiro*) square; (*de botão*) hole; **em ~** at home; **para ~** home; **na ~ dos 30 anos** in one's thirties; **~ da moeda** mint; **~ de banho** (*Port*) bathroom; **~ de campo** country house; **~ de saúde** private hospital; **~ decimal** decimal place; **~ popular** council house

casaco /ka'zaku/ *m* (*sobretudo*) coat; (*paletó*) jacket; (*de lã*) pullover

ca|sal /ka'zaw/ (*pl* **~sais**) *m* couple; **~samento** *m* marriage; (*cerimônia*) wedding; **~sar** *vt* marry; (*fig*) combine □ *vi* get married; (*fig*) go together; **~sar-se** *vpr* get married; (*fig*) combine; **~sar-se com** marry

casarão /kaza'rãw/ *m* mansion

casca /'kaska/ *f* (*de árvore*) bark; (*de laranja, limão*) peel; (*de banana*) skin; (*de noz, ovo*) shell; (*de milho*) husk; (*de pão*) crust; (*de ferida*) scab

cascalho /kas'kaʎu/ *m* gravel

cascata /kas'kata/ *f* waterfall; (*fam*) fib

casca|vel /kaska'vɛw/ (*pl* **~véis**) *m* (*cobra*) rattlesnake □ *f* (*mulher*) shrew

casco /'kasku/ *m* (*de cavalo etc*) hoof; (*de navio*) hull; (*garrafa vazia*) empty

ca|sebre /ka'zɛbri/ *m* hovel, shack; **~seiro** *a* <*comida*> home-made; <*pessoa*> home-loving; <*vida*> home □ *m* housekeeper

caserna /ka'zɛrna/ *f* barracks

casmurro /kaz'muxu/ *a* sullen

caso /'kazu/ *m* case; (*amoroso*) affair; (*conto*) story □ *conj* in case; **em todo ou qualquer ~** in any case; **fazer ~ de** take notice of; **vir ao ~** be relevant; **~ contrário** otherwise

casório /ka'zɔriu/ *m* (*fam*) wedding

caspa /'kaspa/ *f* dandruff

casquinha /kas'kiɲa/ *f* (*de sorvete*) cone, cornet

cassar /ka'sar/ *vt* revoke, withdraw <*direitos, autorização*>; ban <*político*>

cassete /ka'sɛtʃi/ *m* cassette

cassetete /kase'tɛtʃi/ *m* truncheon, (*Amer*) nightstick

cassino /ka'sinu/ *m* casino; **~ de oficiais** officers' mess

casta|nha /kas'taɲa/ *f* chestnut; **~nha de caju** cashew nut; **~nha-do-pará** (*pl* **~nhas-do-pará**) *f* Brazil nut; **~nheiro** *m* chestnut tree; **~nho** *a* chestnut (-coloured); **~nholas** /ɔ/ *f pl* castanets

castelhano /kaste'ʎanu/ *a* & *m* Castilian

castelo /kas'tɛlu/ *m* castle

casti|çal /kastʃi'saw/ (*pl* **~çais**) *m* candlestick

cas|tidade /kastʃi'dadʒi/ *f* chastity; **~tigar** *vt* punish; **~tigo** *m* punishment; **~to** *a* chaste

castor /kas'tor/ *m* beaver

castrar /kas'trar/ *vt* castrate

casu|al /kazu'aw/ (*pl* **~ais**) *a* chance; (*fortuito*) fortuitous; **~alidade** *f* chance

casulo /ka'zulu/ *m* (*de larva*) cocoon

cata /'kata/ *f* à ~ **de** in search of

cata|lão /kata'lãw/ (*pl* ~**lães**) *a & m* (*f* ~**lã**) Catalan

catalisador /kataliza'dor/ *m* catalyst; (*de carro*) catalytic convertor

catalogar /katalo'gar/ *vt* catalogue

catálogo /ka'talogu/ *m* catalogue; (*de telefones*) phone book

Catalunha /kata'luɲa/ *f* Catalonia

catapora /kata'pɔra/ *f* chicken pox

catar /ka'tar/ *vt* (*procurar*) search for; (*recolher*) gather; (*do chão*) pick up; sort <*arroz, café*>

catarata /kata'rata/ *f* waterfall; (*no olho*) cataract

catarro /ka'taxu/ *m* catarrh

catástrofe /ka'tastrɔfi/ *f* catastrophe

catastrófico /katas'trɔfiku/ *a* catastrophic

catecismo /kate'sizmu/ *m* catechism

cátedra /'katedra/ *f* chair

cate|dral /kate'draw/ (*pl* ~**drais**) *f* cathedral; ~**drático** *m* professor

cate|goria /katego'ria/ *f* category; (*social*) class; (*qualidade*) quality; ~**górico** *a* categorical; ~**gorizar** *vt* categorize

catinga /ka't∫iga/ *f* body odour, stink

cati|vante /kat∫i'vãt∫i/ *a* captivating; ~**var** *vt* captivate; ~**veiro** *m* captivity; ~**vo** *a & m* captive

catolicismo /katoli'sizmu/ *m* Catholicism

católico /ka'toliku/ *a & m* Catholic

catorze /ka'torzi/ *a & m* fourteen

cau|da /'kawda/ *f* tail; ~**dal** (*pl* ~**dais**) *m* torrent

caule /'kawli/ *m* stem

cau|sa /'kawza/ *f* cause; (*jurid*) case; **por** ~**sa de** because of; ~**sar** *vt* cause

caute|la /kaw'tɛla/ *f* caution; (*documento*) ticket; ~**loso** /o/ *a* cautious, careful

cava /'kava/ *f* armhole

cava|do /ka'vadu/ *a* <*vestido*> low-cut; <*olhos*> deep-set; ~**dor** *a* hard-working □ *m* hard worker

cava|laria /kavala'ria/ *f* cavalry; ~**lariça** *f* stable; ~**leiro** *m* horseman; (*na Idade Média*) knight

cavalete /kava'letʃi/ *m* easel

caval|gadura /kavawga'dura/ *f* mount; ~**gar** *vt/i* ride; sit astride <*muro, banco*>; (*saltar*) jump

cavalhei|resco /kavaʎe'resku/ *a* gallant, gentlemanly; ~**ro** *m* gentleman □ *a* gallant, gentlemanly

cavalo /ka'valu/ *m* horse; **a** ~ **on** horseback; ~-**vapor** (*pl* ~**s-vapor**) horsepower

cavanhaque /kava'ɲaki/ *m* goatee

cavaquinho /kava'kiɲu/ *m* ukulele

cavar /ka'var/ *vt* dig; (*fig*) go all out for □ *vi* dig; (*fig*) go all out; ~ **em** (*vascular*) delve into; ~ **a vida** make a living

caveira /ka'vera/ *f* skull

caverna /ka'vɛrna/ *f* cavern

caviar /kavi'ar/ *m* caviar

cavidade /kavi'dadʒi/ *f* cavity

cavilha /ka'viʎa/ *f* peg

cavo /'kavu/ *a* hollow

cavoucar /kavo'kar/ *vt* excavate

caxemira /kaʃe'mira/ *f* cashmere

caxumba /ka'ʃuba/ *f* mumps

cear /si'ar/ *vt* have for supper □ *vi* have supper

cebo|la /se'bola/ *f* onion; ~**linha** *f* spring onion

ceder /se'der/ *vt* give up; (*dar*) give; (*emprestar*) lend □ *vi* (*não resistir*) give way; ~ **a** yield to

cedilha /se'dʒiʎa/ f cedilla

cedo /'sedu/ adv early; **mais ~ ou mais tarde** sooner or later

cedro /'sedru/ m cedar

cédula /'sɛdula/ f (de banco) note, (Amer) bill; (eleitoral) ballot paper

ce|gar /se'gar/ vt blind; blunt <faca>; **~go** /ɛ/ a blind; <faca> blunt □ m blind man; **às ~gas** blindly

cegonha /se'goɲa/ f stork

cegueira /se'gera/ f blindness

ceia /'seja/ f supper

cei|fa /'sejfa/ f harvest; (massacre) slaughter; **~far** vt reap; claim <vidas>; (matar) mow down

cela /'sɛla/ f cell

cele|bração /selebra'sãw/ f celebration; **~brar** vt celebrate

célebre /'sɛlebri/ a celebrated

celebridade /selebri'dadʒi/ f celebrity

celeiro /se'leru/ m granary

célere /'sɛleri/ a swift, fast

celeste /se'lɛstʃi/ a celestial

celeuma /se'lewma/ f uproar

celibato /seli'batu/ m celibacy

celofane /selo'fani/ m cellophane

celta /'sɛwta/ a Celtic □ m/f Celt □ m (língua) Celtic

célula /'sɛlula/ f cell

celu|lar /selu'lar/ a cellular □ m mobile, (Amer.) cell phone **~lite** f cellulite; **~lose** /ɔ/ f cellulose

cem /sẽj/ a & m hundred

cemitério /semi'tɛriu/ m cemetery; (fig) graveyard

cena /'sena/ f scene; (palco) stage; **em ~** on stage

cenário /se'nariu/ m scenery; (de crime etc) scene

cênico /'seniku/ a stage

cenoura /se'nora/ f carrot

cen|so /'sẽsu/ m census; **~sor** m censor; **~sura** f (de jornais etc) censorship; (órgão) censor(s); (condenação) censure; **~surar**

vt censor <jornal, filme etc>; (condenar) censure

centavo /sẽ'tavu/ m cent

centeio /sẽ'teju/ m rye

centelha /sẽ'teʎa/ f spark; (fig: de gênio etc) flash

cente|na /sẽ'tena/ f hundred; **uma ~na de** about a hundred; **às ~nas** in their hundreds; **~nário** m centenary

centésimo /sẽ'tezimu/ a hundredth

centí|grado /sẽ'tʃigradu/ m centigrade; **~litro** m centilitre; **~metro** m centimetre

cento /'sẽtu/ a & m hundred; **por ~** per cent

cen|tral /sẽ'traw/ (pl **~trais**) a central □ f switchboard; (elétrica) **eólica** wind farm; **~tralizar** vt centralize; **~trar** vt centre; **~tro** m centre

cepti- (Port) veja **ceti-**

cera /'sera/ f wax; **fazer ~** waste time, faff about

cerâmi|ca /se'ramika/ f ceramics, pottery; **~co** a ceramic

cer|ca /'sɛrka/ f fence; **~ca viva** hedge □ adv **~ca de** around, about; **~cado** m enclosure; (para criança) playpen; **~car** vt surround; (com muro, cerca) enclose; (assediar) besiege

cercear /sersi'ar/ vt restrict

cerco /'sɛrku/ m (mil) siege; (policial) dragnet

cere|al /seri'aw/ (pl **~ais**) m cereal

cerebral /sere'braw/ a cerebral

cérebro /'sɛrebru/ m brain; (inteligência) intellect

cere|ja /se'reʒa/ f cherry; **~jeira** f cherry tree

cerimônia /seri'monia/ f ceremony; **sem ~** unceremoniously; **fazer ~** stand on ceremony

cerimoni|al /serimoni'aw/ (pl **~ais**) a & m ceremonial; **~oso** /o/ a ceremonious

cer|rado /se'xadu/ *a* <*barba, mata*> thick; <*punho, dentes*> clenched □ *m* scrubland; **~rar** *vt* close; **~rar-se** *vpr* close; <*noites, trevas*> close in

certeiro /ser'teru/ *a* well-aimed, accurate

certeza /ser'teza/ *f* certainty; **com ~** certainly; **ter ~** be sure (**de** of; **de que** that)

certidão /sert∫i'dãw/ *f* certificate; **~ de nascimento** birth certificate

certifi|cado /sert∫ifi'kadu/ *m* certificate; **~car** *vt* certify; **~car-se** *de* make sure of

certo /'sɛrtu/ *a* (*correto*) right; (*seguro*) certain; (*algum*) a certain □ *adv* right; **dar ~** work

cerveja /ser'veʒa/ *f* beer; **~ria** *f* brewery; (*bar*) pub

cervo /'sɛrvu/ *m* deer

cer|zidura /serzi'dura/ *f* darning; **~zir** *vt* darn

cesariana /sezari'ana/ *f* Caesarian

césio /'sɛziu/ *m* caesium

cessar /se'sar/ *vt/i* cease

ces|ta /'sesta/ *f* basket; (*de comida*) hamper; **~to** /e/ *m* basket; **~to de lixo** wastepaper basket

ceticismo /set∫i'sizmu/ *m* scepticism

cético /'sɛt∫iku/ *a* sceptical □ *m* sceptic

cetim /se't∫ĩ/ *m* satin

céu /sɛw/ *m* sky; (*na religião*) heaven; **~ da boca** roof of the mouth

cevada /se'vada/ *f* barley

chá /∫a/ *m* tea

chacal /∫a'kaw/ (*pl* **~cais**) *m* jackal

chácara /'∫akara/ *f* smallholding; (*casa*) country cottage

chaci|na /∫a'sina/ *f* slaughter; **~nar** *vt* slaughter

chá|-de-bar /∫adʒi'bar/ (*pl* **~s-de-bar**) *m* bachelor party; **~-**

de-panela (*pl* **~s-de-panela**) *m* hen night, (*Amer*) wedding shower

chafariz /∫afa'ris/ *m* fountain

chaga /'∫aga/ *f* sore

chaleira /∫a'lera/ *f* kettle

chama /'∫ama/ *f* flame

cha|mada /∫a'mada/ *f* call; (*dos presentes*) roll call; (*dos alunos*) register; **~mado** *m* call □ *a* (*depois do substantivo*) called; (*antes do substantivo*) so-called; **~mar** *vt* call; (*para sair etc*) ask, invite; attract <*atenção*> □ *vi* call; <*telefone*> ring; **~mar-se** *vpr* be called; **~mariz** *m* decoy; **~mativo** *a* showy, flashy

chamejar /∫ame'ʒar/ *vi* flame

chaminé /∫ami'nɛ/ *f* (*de casa, fábrica*) chimney; (*de navio, trem*) funnel

champanhe /∫ã'paɲi/ *m* champagne

champu /∫ã'pu/ (*Port*) *m* shampoo

chamuscar /∫amus'kar/ *vt* singe, scorch

chance /'∫ãsi/ *f* chance

chanceler /∫ãse'ler/ *m* chancellor

chanchada /∫ã'∫ada/ *f* (*peça*) second-rate play; (*filme*) B movie

chanta|gear /∫ãtaʒi'ar/ *vt* blackmail; **~gem** *f* blackmail; **~gista** *m/f* blackmailer

chão /∫ãw/ (*pl* **~s**) *m* ground; (*dentro de casa etc*) floor

chapa /'∫apa/ *f* sheet; (*foto*) plate; **~ eleitoral** electoral list; **~ de matrícula** (*Port*) number plate, (*Amer*) license plate □ (*fam*) *m* mate

chapéu /∫a'pɛw/ *m* hat

charada /∫a'rada/ *f* riddle

char|ge /∫a'rʒi/ *f* (political) cartoon; **~gista** *m/f* cartoonist

charla|tanismo /∫arlata'nizmu/ *m* charlatanism; **~tão** (*pl* **~tães**) *m* (*f* **~tona**) charlatan

char|me /ˈʃarmi/ m charm; **fazer ~me** turn on the charm; **~moso** /o/ a charming

charneca /ʃarˈnɛka/ f moor

charuto /ʃaˈrutu/ m cigar

chassi /ʃaˈsi/ m chassis

chata /ˈʃata/ f (barca) barge

chate|ação /ʃatʃiaˈsãw/ f annoyance; **~ar** vt annoy; **~ar-se** vpr get annoyed

cha|tice /ʃaˈtʃisi/ f nuisance; **~to** a (tedioso) boring; (irritante) annoying; (mal-educado) rude; (plano) flat

chauvinis|mo /ʃoviˈnizmu/ m chauvinism; **~ta** m/f chauvinista □ a chauvinistic

cha|vão /ʃaˈvãw/ m cliché; **~ve** f key; (ferramenta) spanner; **~ve de fenda** screwdriver; **~ve inglesa** wrench; **~veiro** m (aro) keyring; (pessoa) locksmith

chávena /ˈʃavena/ f soup bowl; (Port: xícara) cup

checar /ʃeˈkar/ vt check

che|fe /ˈʃɛfi/ m/f (patrão) boss; (gerente) manager; (dirigente) leader; **~fia** f leadership; (de empresa) management; (sede) headquarters; **~fiar** vt lead; be in charge of <trabalho>

che|gada /ʃeˈgada/ f arrival; **~gado** a <amigo, relação> close; **~gar** vi arrive; (deslocar-se) move up; (ser suficiente) be enough □ vt bring up <prato, cadeira>; **~gar a fazer** go as far as doing; **aonde você quer ~gar?** what are you driving at?; **~gar lá** (fig) make it

cheia /ˈʃeja/ f flood

cheio /ˈʃeju/ a full; (fam: farto) fed up

chei|rar /ʃeˈrar/ vt/i smell **(a** of); **~roso** /o/ a scented

cheque /ˈʃɛki/ m cheque, (Amer) check; **~ de viagem** traveller's cheque; **~ em branco** blank cheque

chi|ado /ʃiˈadu/ m (de pneus, freios) screech; (de porta) squeak; (de vapor, numa fita) hiss; **~ar** vi <porta> squeak; <pneus, freios> screech; <vapor, fita> hiss; <fritura> sizzle; (fam: reclamar) grumble, moan

chiclete /ʃiˈklɛtʃi/ m chewing gum; **~ de bola** bubble gum

chico|tada /ʃikoˈtada/ f lash; **~te** /ɔ/ m whip; **~tear** vt whip

chi|frar /ʃiˈfrar/ (fam) vt cheat on <marido, esposa>; two-time <namorado, namorada>; **~fre** m horn; **~frudo** a horned; (fam) cuckolded □ m cuckold

Chile /ˈʃili/ m Chile

chileno /ʃiˈlenu/ a & m Chilean

chilique /ʃiˈliki/ (fam) m funny turn

chil|rear /ʃiwxiˈar/ vi chirp, twitter; **~reio** m chirping, twittering

chimarrão /ʃimaˈxãw/ m unsweetened maté tea

chimpanzé /ʃĩpãˈzɛ/ m chimpanzee

China /ˈʃina/ f China

chinelo /ʃiˈnɛlu/ m slipper

chi|nês /ʃiˈnes/ a & m (f **~nesa**) Chinese

chinfrim /ʃĩˈfrĩ/ a tatty, shoddy

chio /ˈʃiu/ m squeak; (de pneus) screech; (de vapor) hiss

chique /ˈʃiki/ a <pessoa, aparência, roupa> smart, (Amer) sharp; <hotel, bairro, loja etc> smart, up-market, posh

chiqueiro /ʃiˈkeru/ m pigsty

chis|pa /ˈʃispa/ f flash; **~pada** f dash; **~par** vi (soltar chispas) flash; (correr) dash

choca|lhar /ʃokaˈʎar/ vt/i rattle; **~lho** m rattle

cho|cante /ʃoˈkãtʃi/ a shocking; (fam) incredible; **~car** vt/i hatch <ovos>; (ultrajar) shock; **~car-se** vpr <carros etc> crash; <teorias etc> clash

chocho /ˈʃoʃu/ a dull, insipid

chocolate /ʃokoˈlatʃi/ m chocolate

chofer /ʃoˈfɛr/ m chauffeur

chope /ˈʃopi/ m draught lager

choque /ˈʃɔki/ m shock; (colisão) collision; (conflito) clash

cho|radeira /ʃoraˈdera/ f fit of crying; **~ramingar** vi whine; **~ramingas** m/f invar whiner; **~rão** m (salgueiro) weeping willow □ a (~rona) tearful; **~rar** vi cry; **~ro** /o/ m crying; **~roso** /o/ a tearful

chouriço /ʃoˈrisu/ m black pudding; (Port) sausage

chover /ʃoˈver/ vi rain

chuchu /ʃuˈʃu/ m chayote

chucrute /ʃuˈkrutʃi/ m sauerkraut

chumaço /ʃuˈmasu/ m wad

chum|bado /ʃũˈbadu/ (fam) a knocked out; **~bar** (Port) vt fill <dente>; fail <aluno> □ vi <aluno> fail; **~bo** m lead; (Port: obturação) filling

chu|par /ʃuˈpar/ vt suck; <esponja> suck up; **~peta** /e/ f dummy, (Amer) pacifier

churras|caria /ʃuxaskaˈria/ f barbecue restaurant; **~co** m barbecue; **~queira** f barbecue; **~quinho** m kebab

chu|tar /ʃuˈtar/ vt/i kick; (fam: adivinhar) guess; **~te** m kick; **~teira** f football boot

chu|va /ˈʃuva/ f rain; **~va de pedra** hail; **~varada** f torrential rainstorm; **~veiro** m shower; **~viscar** vi drizzle; **~visco** m drizzle; **~voso** /o/ a rainy

cica|triz /sikaˈtris/ f scar; **~trizar** vt scar □ vi <ferida> heal

cic|lismo /siˈklizmu/ m cycling; **~lista** m/f cyclist; **~lo** m cycle; **~lone** /o/ m cyclone; **~lovia** f cycle lane

cida|dania /sidadaˈnia/ f citizenship; **~dão** (pl **~dãos**) m (f

~dã) citizen; **~de** f town; (grande) city; **~dela** /ɛ/ f citadel

ciência /siˈẽsia/ f science

cien|te /siˈẽtʃi/ a aware; **~tífico** a scientific; **~tista** m/f scientist

ci|fra /ˈsifra/ f figure; (código) cipher; **~frão** m dollar sign; **~frar** vt encode

cigano /siˈganu/ a & m gypsy

cigarra /siˈgaxa/ f cicada; (dispositivo) buzzer

cigar|reira /sigaˈxera/ f cigarette case; **~ro** m cigarette

cilada /siˈlada/ f trap; (estratagema) trick

cilindrada /silĩˈdrada/ f (engine) capacity

cilíndrico /siˈlĩdriku/ a cylindrical

cilindro /siˈlĩdru/ m cylinder; (rolo) roller

cílio /ˈsiliu/ m eyelash

cima /ˈsima/ f em **~** on top; (na casa) upstairs; **em ~ de** on, on top of; **para ~** up; (na casa) upstairs; **por ~** over the top; **por ~ de** over; **de ~** from above; **ainda por ~** moreover

címbalo /ˈsĩbalu/ m cymbal

cimeira /siˈmera/ f crest; (Port: cúpula) summit

cimen|tar /simẽˈtar/ vt cement; **~to** m cement

cinco /ˈsĩku/ a & m five

cine|asta /siniˈasta/ m/f filmmaker; **~ma** /e/ m cinema

Cingapura /sĩgaˈpura/ f Singapore

cínico /ˈsiniku/ a cynical □ m cynic

cinismo /siˈnizmu/ m cynicism

cinquen|ta /sĩˈkwẽta/ a & m fifty; **~tão** a & m (f **~tona**) fifty-year-old

cinti|lante /sĩtʃiˈlãtʃi/ a glittering; **~lar** vi glitter

cin|to /ˈsĩtu/ m belt; **~to de segurança** seatbelt; **~tura** f waist; **~turão** m belt

cin|za /'sĩza/ f ash □ a invar grey; **~zeiro** m ashtray

cin|zel /sĩ'zɛw/ (pl **~zéis**) m chisel; **~zelar** vt carve

cinzento /sĩ'zẽtu/ a grey

cipó /si'pɔ/ m vine, liana; **~poal** (pl **~poais**) m jungle

cipreste /si'prɛstʃi/ m cypress

cipriota /sipri'ɔta/ a & m Cypriot

ciranda /si'rãda/ f (fig) merry-go-round

cir|cense /sir'sẽsi/ a circus; **~co** m circus

circu|ito /sir'kuitu/ m circuit; **~lação** f circulation; **~lar** a & f circular □ vt circulate □ vi <dinheiro, sangue> circulate; <carro> drive; <ônibus> run; <trânsito> move; <pessoa> go round

círculo /'sirkulu/ m circle

circun|dar /sirkũ'dar/ vt circumcise; **~ção** f circumcision

circun|dar /sirkũ'dar/ vt surround; **~ferência** f circumference; **~flexo** /ɛks/ a m circumflex; **~scrição** f district; **~scrição eleitoral** constituency; **~specto** /ɛ/ a circumspect; **~stância** f circumstance; **~stanciado** a detailed; **~stancial** (pl **~stanciais**) a circumstantial; **~stante** m/f bystander

cirrose /si'xɔzi/ f cirrhosis

cirur|gia /sirur'ʒia/ f surgery; **~gião** m (f **~giã**) surgeon

cirúrgico /si'rurʒiku/ a surgical

cisão /si'zãw/ f split, division

cisco /'sisku/ m speck

cisma¹ /'sizma/ m schism

cis|ma² /'sizma/ f (mania) fixation; (devaneio) imagining, daydream; (prevenção) irrational dislike; (de criança) whim; **~mar** vt/i be lost in thought <criança> be insistent; **~mar em** brood over; **~mar de ou em fazer** insist on doing; **~mar que** insist on thinking

that; **~mar com alg** take a dislike to s.o.

cisne /'sizni/ m swan

cistite /sis'tʃitʃi/ f cystitis

ci|tação /sita'sãw/ f quotation; (jurid) summons; **~tar** vt quote; (jurid) summon

ciúme /si'umi/ m jealousy; **ter ~s de** be jealous of

ciu|meira /siu'mera/ f fit of jealousy; **~mento** a jealous

cívico /'siviku/ a civic

ci|vil /si'viw/ (pl **~vis**) a civil □ m civilian; **~vilidade** f civility

civili|zação /siviliza'sãw/ f civilization; **~zado** a civilized; **~zar** vt civilize

civismo /si'vizmu/ m public spirit

cla|mar /kla'mar/ vt/i cry out, clamour (por for); **~mor** m outcry; **~moroso** /o/ a <protesto> loud, noisy; <erro, injustiça> blatant

clandestino /klãdes'tʃinu/ a clandestine

cla|ra /'klara/ f egg white; **~rabóia** f skylight; **~rão** m flash; **~rear** vt brighten; clarify <questão> □ vi brighten up; (fazer-se dia) become light; **~reira** f clearing; **~reza** /e/ f clarity; **~ridade** f brightness; (do dia) daylight

cla|rim /kla'rĩ/ m bugle; **~rinete** /e/ m clarinet

clarividente /klarivi'dẽtʃi/ m/f clairvoyant

claro /'klaru/ a clear; <luz> bright; <cor> light □ adv clearly □ int of course; **ou sim/não** of course! of course not; **às claras** openly; **noite em ~** sleepless night; **já é dia ~** it's already daylight

classe /'klasi/ f class; **~ média** middle class

clássico /'klasiku/ a classical; (famoso, exemplar) classic □ m classic

classifi|cação /klasifika'sãw/ *f* classification; *(numa competição esportiva)* placing, place; **~cado** *a* classified; *<candidato>* successful; *<esportista, time>* qualified; **~car** *vt* classify; *(considerar)* describe (de as); **~car-se** *vpr* *<candidato, esportista>* qualify; *(chamar-se)* describe o.s. (de as); **~catório** *a* qualifying

classudo /kla'sudu/ *(fam)* *a* classy

claustro|fobia /klawstrofo'bia/ *f* claustrophobia; **~fóbico** *a* claustrophobic

cláusula /'klawzula/ *f* clause

cla|ve /'klavi/ *f* clef; **~vícula** *f* collar bone

cle|mência /kle'mẽsia/ *f* clemency; **~mente** *a* *<pessoa>* lenient; *<tempo>* clement

cleptomaníaco /kleptoma'niaku/ *m* kleptomaniac

clérigo /'klɛrigu/ *m* cleric, clergyman

clero /'klɛru/ *m* clergy

clicar /kli'kar/ *vi* *(comput)* click

clien|te /kli'ẽtʃi/ *m/f* *(de loja)* customer; *(de advogado, empresa)* client; **~tela** /ɛ/ *f* *(de loja)* customers; *(de restaurante, empresa)* clientele

cli|ma /'klima/ *m* climate; **~mático** *a* climatic

clímax /'klimaks/ *m invar* climax

clíni|ca /'klinika/ *f* clinic; **~ca geral** general practice; **~co** *a* clinical □ *m* **~co geral** general practitioner, GP

clipe /'klipi/ *m* clip; *(para papéis)* paper clip

clone /'kloni/ *m* clone

cloro /'kloru/ *m* chlorine

close /'klozi/ *m* close-up

clube /'klubi/ *m* club

coação /koa'sãw/ *f* coercion

coadjuvante /koadʒu'vãtʃi/ *a* *<ator>* supporting □ *m/f* *(em peça, filme)* co-star; *(em crime)* accomplice

coador /koa'dor/ *m* strainer; *(de legumes)* colander; *(de café)* filter bag

coadunar /koadu'nar/ *vt* combine

coagir /koa'ʒir/ *vt* compel

coagular /koagu'lar/ *vt/i* clot; **~se** *vpr* clot

coágulo /ko'agulu/ *m* clot

coalhar /koa'ʎar/ *vt/i* curdle; **~se** *vpr* curdle

coalizão /koali'zãw/ *f* coalition

coar /ko'ar/ *vt* strain

coaxar /koa'ʃar/ *vi* croak □ *m* croaking

cobaia /ko'baja/ *f* guinea pig

cober|ta /ko'berta/ *f* *(de cama)* bedcover; *(de navio)* deck; **~to** /ɛ/ *a* covered □ *pp de* **cobrir**; **~tor** *m* blanket; **~tura** *f* *(revestimento)* covering; *(reportagem)* coverage; *(seguro)* cover; *(apartamento)* penthouse

cobi|ça /ko'bisa/ *f* greed, covetousness; **~çar** *vt* covet; **~çoso** /o/ *a* covetous

cobra /'kobra/ *f* snake

co|brador /kobra'dor/ *m* *(no ônibus)* conductor; **~brança** *f* *(de dívida)* collection; *(de preço)* charging; **~brança de pênalti/falta** penalty (kick)/free kick; **~brar** *vt* collect *<dívida>*; ask for *<coisa prometida>*; take *<pênalti>*; **~brar aco a alg** *(em dinheiro)* charge s.o. for sth; *(fig)* make s.o. pay for sth; **~brar uma falta** *(no futebol)* take a free kick

cobre /'kobri/ *m* copper

cobrir /ko'brir/ *vt* cover; **~se** *vpr* *<pessoa>* cover o.s. up; *<coisa>* be covered

cocaína /koka'ina/ *f* cocaine

coçar /ko'sar/ *vt* scratch □ *vi* *(esfregar-se)* scratch; *(comichar)* itch; **~se** *vpr* scratch o.s.

cócegas /'kɔsegas/ *f pl* fazer **~em** tickle; sentir **~** be ticklish

coceira /ko'sera/ *f* itch

cochi|char /koʃi'ʃar/ *vt/i* whisper; **~cho** *m* whisper

cochi|lada /koʃi'lada/ *f* doze; **~lar** *vi* doze; **~lo** *m* snooze

coco /'koku/ *m* coconut

cócoras /'kɔkoras/ *f pl* **de ~** squatting; **ficar de ~** squat

côdea /'kodʒia/ *f* crust

codificar /kodʒifi'kar/ *vt* encode <*mensagem*>; codify <*leis*>

código /'kɔdʒigu/ *m* code; **~ de barras** bar code

codinome /kodʒi'nomi/ *m* code-name

coeficiente /koefisi'ẽtʃi/ *m* coefficient; (*fig: fator*) factor

coelho /ko'eʎu/ *m* rabbit

coentro /ko'ẽtru/ *m* coriander

coe|rência /koe'rẽsia/ *f* (*lógica*) coherence; (*consequência*) consistency; **~rente** *a* (*lógico*) coherent; (*consequente*) consistent

coexis|tência /koezis'tẽsia/ *f* coexistence; **~tir** *vi* coexist

cofre /'kɔfri/ *m* safe; (*de dinheiro público*) coffer

cogi|tação /koʒita'sãw/ *f* contemplation; **fora de ~tação** out of the question; **~tar** *vt/i* contemplate

cogumelo /kogu'mɛlu/ *m* mushroom

coibir /koi'bir/ *vt* restrict; **~-se de** keep o.s. from

coice /'kojsi/ *m* kick

coinci|dência /koĩsi'dẽsia/ *f* coincidence; **~dir** *vi* coincide

coisa /'kojza/ *f* thing

coitado /koj'tadu/ *m* poor thing; **~ do pai** poor father

cola /'kɔla/ *f* glue; (*cópia*) crib

colabo|ração /kolabora'sãw/ *f* collaboration; (*de escritor etc*) contribution; **~rador** *m* collaborator; (*em jornal, livro*) contributor; **~rar** *vi* collabor-

ate; (*em jornal, livro*) contribute (**em** to)

colagem /ko'laʒẽ/ *f* collage

colágeno /ko'laʒenu/ *m* collagen

colapso /ko'lapsu/ *m* collapse

colar[1] /ko'lar/ *m* necklace

colar[2] /ko'lar/ *vt* (*grudar*) stick; (*copiar*) crib □ *vi* stick; (*copiar*) crib; <*desculpa etc*> stand up, stick

colarinho /kola'riɲu/ *m* collar; (*de cerveja*) head

colate|ral /kolate'raw/ (*pl* **~rais**) *a* **efeito ~ral** side effect

col|cha /'kowʃa/ *f* bedspread; **~chão** *m* mattress

colchete /kow'ʃetʃi/ *m* fastener; (*sinal de pontuação*) square bracket; **~ de pressão** press stud, popper

colchonete /kowʃo'nɛtʃi/ *m* (foldaway) mattress

coldre /'kowdri/ *m* holster

cole|ção /kole'sãw/ *f* collection; **~cionador** *m* collector; **~cionar** *vt* collect

colega /ko'lega/ *m/f* (*amigo*) friend; (*de trabalho*) colleague

colegi|al /koleʒi'aw/ (*pl* **~ais**) *a* school □ *m/f* schoolboy (*f* -girl)

colégio /ko'leʒiu/ *m* secondary school, (*Amer*) high school

coleira /ko'lera/ *f* collar

cólera /'kɔlera/ *f* (*doença*) cholera; (*raiva*) fury

colérico /ko'lɛriku/ *a* (*furioso*) furious □ *m* (*doente*) cholera victim

colesterol /koleste'rɔw/ *m* cholesterol

cole|ta /ko'lɛta/ *f* collection; **~tânea** *f* collection; **~tar** *vt* collect

colete /ko'letʃi/ *m* waistcoat, (*Amer*) vest; **~ salva-vidas** lifejacket, (*Amer*) life-preserver

coletivo /kole'tʃivu/ *a* collective; <*transporte*> public □ *m* bus

colheita /ko'ʎejta/ *f* harvest; (*produtos colhidos*) crop

colher[1] /koˈʎɛr/ f spoon

colher[2] /koˈʎer/ vt pick *<flores, frutos>*; gather *<informações>*

colherada /koʎeˈrada/ f spoonful

colibri /koliˈbri/ m hummingbird

cólica /ˈkɔlika/ f colic

colidir /koliˈdʒir/ vi collide

coli|gação /koligaˈsãw/ f (pol) coalition; **~gado** m (pol) coalition partner; **~gar** vt bring together; **~gar-se** vpr join forces; (pol) form a coalition

colina /koˈlina/ f hill

colírio /koˈliriu/ m eyewash

colisão /koliˈzãw/ f collision

collant /koˈlã/ (pl **~s**) m body; (de ginástica) leotard

colmeia /kowˈmeja/ f beehive

colo /ˈkɔlu/ f (regaço) lap; (pescoço) neck

colo|cação /kolokaˈsãw/ f placing; (emprego) position; (exposição de fatos) statement; (de aparelho, pneus, carpete etc) fitting; **~cado** a placed; **o primeiro ~cado** (em ranking) position in first place; **~cador** m fitter; **~car** put; fit *<aparelho, pneus, carpete etc>*; put forward, state *<opinião, idéias>*; (empregar) get a job for

Colômbia /koˈlõbia/ f Colombia

colombiano /kolõbiˈanu/ a & m Colombian

cólon /ˈkɔlõ/ m colon

colônia[1] /koˈlonia/ f (colonos) colony

colônia[2] /koˈlonia/ f (perfume) cologne

coloni|al /koloniˈaw/ (pl **~ais**) a colonial; **~alismo** m colonialism; **~alista** a & m/f colonialist; **~zar** vt colonize

colono /koˈlonu/ m settler, colonist; (lavrador) tenant farmer

coloqui|al /kolokiˈaw/ (pl **~ais**) a colloquial

colóquio /koˈlɔkiu/ m (conversa) conversation; (congresso) conference

colo|rido /koloˈridu/ a colourful □ m colouring; **~rir** vt colour

colu|na /koˈluna/ f column; (vertebral) spine; **~nável** (pl **~náveis**) a famous □ m/f celebrity; **~nista** m/f columnist

com /kõ/ prep with; **o comentário foi comigo** the comment was meant for me; **você está ~ a chave?** have you got the key?; **~ seis anos de idade** at six years of age

coma /ˈkoma/ f coma

comadre /koˈmadri/ f (madrinha) godmother of one's child; (mãe do afilhado) mother of one's god-child; (urinol) bedpan

coman|dante /komãˈdãtʃi/ m commander; **~dar** vt lead; (ordenar) command; (elevar-se acima de) dominate; **~do** m command; (grupo) commando group

comba|te /kõˈbatʃi/ m combat; (a drogas, doença etc) fight (a against); **~ter** vt/i fight; **~ter-se** vpr fight

combi|nação /kõbinaˈsãw/ f combination; (acordo) arrangement; (plano) scheme; (roupa) petticoat; **~nar** vt (juntar) combine; (ajustar) arrange □ vi go together, match; **~nar com** go with, match; **~nar de sair** arrange to go out; **~nar-se** vpr (juntar-se) combine; (harmonizar-se) go together, match

comboio /kõˈboju/ m convoy; (Port: trem) train

combustí|vel /kõbusˈtʃivew/ (pl **~veis**) m fuel

come|çar /komeˈsar/ vt/i start, begin; **~ço** /e/ m beginning, start

comédia /koˈmɛdʒia/ f comedy

comediante /komedʒiˈãtʃi/ m/f comedian (f comedienne)

comemo|ração /komemoraˈsãw/ f (celebração) celebration; (lembrança) commemoration; **~rar** vt (festejar) celebrate; (lembrar) commemorate

comen|tar /komē'tar/ *vt* comment on; (*falar mal de*) make comments about; **~tário** *m* comment; (*de texto, na TV etc*) commentary; **sem ~tários** no comment; **~tarista** *m/f* commentator

comer /ko'mer/ *vt* eat; <*ferrugem etc*> eat away; take <*peça de xadrez*> □ *vi* eat; **~-se** *vpr* (*de raiva etc*) be consumed (**de** with); **dar de ~** a feed

comerci|al /komersi'aw/ (*pl* **~ais**) *a* & *m* commercial; **~alizar** *vt* market; **~ante** *m/f* trader; **~ar** *vi* do business, trade; **~ário** *m* shopworker

comércio /ko'mersiu/ *m* (*atividade*) trade; (*loja etc*) business; (*lojas*) shops: **~ eletrônico** e-commerce

comes /'komis/ *m pl* **~ e bebes** (*fam*) food and drink; **~tíveis** *m pl* foods, food; **~tível** (*pl* **~tíveis**) *a* edible

cometa /ko'meta/ *m* comet

cometer /kome'ter/ *vt* commit <*crime*>; make <*erro*>

comichão /komi'ʃãw/ *f* itch

comício /ko'misiu/ *m* rally

cômico /'komiku/ *a* (*de comédia*) comic; (*engraçado*) comical

comida /ko'mida/ *f* food; (*uma*) meal

comigo = **com** + **mim**

comi|lão /komi'lãw/ *a* (*f* **~lona**) greedy □ *m* (*f* **~lona**) glutton

cominho /ko'miɲu/ *m* cummin

comiserar-se /komize'rarsi/ *vpr* commiserate (**de** with)

comis|são /komi'sãw/ *f* commission; **~sário** *m* commissioner; **~sário de bordo** (*aéreo*) steward; (*de navio*) purser; **~sionar** *vt* commission

comi|tê /komi'te/ *m* committee; **~tiva** *f* group; (*de uma pessoa*) retinue

como /'komu/ *adv* (*na condição de*) as; (*da mesma forma que*) like; (*de que maneira*) how □ *conj* as; **~?** (*pedindo repetição*) pardon?; **~ se** as if; **assim ~** as well as

cômoda /'komoda/ *f* chest of drawers, (*Amer*) bureau

como|didade /komodʒi'dadʒi/ *f* comfort; (*conveniência*) convenience; **~dismo** *m* complacency; **~dista** *a* complacent

cômodo /'komodu/ *a* comfortable; (*conveniente*) convenient □ *m* (*aposento*) room

como|vente /komo'vētʃi/ *a* moving; **~ver** *vt* move □ *vi* be moving; **~ver-se** *vpr* be moved

compacto /kõ'paktu/ *a* compact □ *m* single

compadecer-se /kõpade'sersi/ *vpr* feel pity (**de** for)

compadre /kõ'padri/ *m* (*padrinho*) godfather of one's child; (*pai do afilhado*) father of one's godchild

compaixão /kõpaj'ʃãw/ *f* compassion

companhei|rismo /kõpaɲe'rizmu/ *m* companionship; **~ro** *m* (*de viagem etc*) companion; (*amigo*) friend, mate

companhia /kõpa'ɲia/ *f* company; **fazer ~ a alg** keep s.o. company

compa|ração /kõpara'sãw/ *f* comparison; **~rar** *vt* compare; **~rativo** *a* comparative; **~rável** (*pl* **~ráveis**) *a* comparable

compare|cer /kõpare'ser/ *vi* appear; **~cer a** attend; **~cimento** *m* attendance

comparsa /kõ'parsa/ *m/f* (*ator*) bit player; (*cúmplice*) sidekick

comparti|lhar /kõpartʃi'ʎar/ *vt/i* share (**de** in); **~mento** *m* compartment

compassado /kõpa'sadu/ *a* (*medido*) measured; (*ritmado*) regular

compassivo /kõpaˈsivu/ a compassionate

compasso /kõˈpasu/ m (mus) beat, time; (instrumento) compass, pair of compasses

compatí|vel /kõpaˈtʃivew/ (pl ~veis) a compatible

compatriota /kõpatriˈɔta/ m/f compatriot, fellow countryman (f-woman)

compelir /kõpeˈlir/ vt compel

compene|tração /kõpenetraˈsãw/ f conviction; ~trar vt convince; ~trar-se vpr convince o.s.

compen|sação /kõpẽsaˈsãw/ f compensation; (de cheques) clearing; ~sar vt make up for <defeitos, danos>; offset <peso, gastos>; clear <cheques> □ vi <crime> pay

compe|tência /kõpeˈtẽsia/ f competence; ~tente a competent

compe|tição /kõpetʃiˈsãw/ f competition; ~tidor m competitor; ~tir vi compete; ~tir a be up to; ~tividade f competitiveness; ~titivo a competitive

compla|cência /kõplaˈsẽsia/ f complaisance; ~cente a obliging

complemen|tar /kõplemẽˈtar/ vt complement □ a complementary; ~to m complement

comple|tar /kõpleˈtar/ vt complete; top up <copo, tanque etc>; ~tar 20 anos turn 20; ~to /ɛ/ a complete; (cheio) full up; por ~to completely; escrever por ~to write out in full

comple|xado /kõplekˈsadu/ a with a complex; ~xidade f complexity; ~xo /ɛ/ a & m complex

compli|cação /kõplikaˈsãw/ f complication; ~cado a complicated; ~car vt complicate; ~car-se vpr get complicated

complô /kõˈplo/ m conspiracy, plot

com|ponente /kõpoˈnẽtʃi/ a & m component; ~por vt/i compose;

~por-se vpr (controlar-se) compose o.s.; ~por-se de be composed of

compor|tamento /kõportaˈmẽtu/ m behaviour; ~tar vt hold; bear <dor, prejuízo>; ~tar-se vpr behave

composi|ção /kõpoziˈsãw/ f composition; (acordo) conciliation; ~tor m (de música) composer; (gráfico) compositor

compos|to /kõˈpostu/ pp de compor □ a compound; <pessoa> level-headed □ m compound; ~to de made up of; ~tura f composure

compota /kõˈpɔta/ f fruit in syrup

com|pra /ˈkõpra/ f purchase; pl shopping; fazer ~pras go shopping; ~prador m buyer; ~prar vt buy; bribe <oficial, juiz>; pick <briga>

compreen|der /kõprieˈder/ vt (conter em si) contain; (estender-se a) cover, take in; (entender) understand; ~são f understanding; ~sível (pl ~síveis) a understandable; ~sivo a understanding

compres|sa /kõˈpresa/ f compress; ~são f compression; ~sor m compressor; rolo ~sor steamroller

compri|do /kõˈpridu/ a long; ~mento m length

compri|mido /kõpriˈmidu/ m pill, tablet □ a <ar> compressed; ~mir vt (apertar) press; (reduzir o volume de) compress

comprome|tedor /kõprometeˈdor/ a compromising; ~ter vt (envolver) involve; (prejudicar) compromise; ~ter alg a fazer commit s.o. to doing; ~ter-se vpr (obrigar-se) commit o.s.; (prejudicar-se) compromise o.s.; ~tido a (ocupado) busy; (noivo) spoken for

compromisso /kõpro'misu/ *m* commitment; (*encontro marcado*) appointment; **sem** ~ without obligation

compro|vação /kõprova'sãw/ *f* proof; ~**vante** *m* receipt; ~**var** *vt* prove

compul|são /kõpuw'sãw/ *f* compulsion; ~**sivo** *a* compulsive; ~**sório** *a* compulsory

compu|tação /kõputa'sãw/ *f* computation; (*matéria, ramo*) computing; ~**tador** *m* computer; ~**tadorizar** *vt* computerize; ~**tar** *vt* compute

comum /ko'mũ/ *a* common; (*não especial*) ordinary; **fora do** ~ out of the ordinary; **em** ~ < *trabalho*> joint; (*atuar*) jointly; **ter muito em** ~ have a lot in common

comungar /komũ'gar/ *vi* take communion

comunhão /komu'ɲãw/ *f* communion; (*relig*) (Holy) Communion

comuni|cação /komunika'sãw/ *f* communication; ~**cação social/visual** media studies/graphic design; ~**cado** *m* notice; (*pol*) communiqué; ~**car** *vt vi*, ~**car-se** *vpr* communicate; (*unir*) connect □ *vi*, ~**car-se** *vpr* communicate; ~**cativo** *a* communicative

comu|nidade /komuni'dadʒi/ *f* community; ~**nismo** *m* communism; ~**nista** *a & m/f* communist; ~**nitário** *a* (*da comunidade*) community; (*para todos juntos*) communal

côncavo /'kõkavu/ *a* concave

conce|ber /kõse'ber/ *vt* conceive; (*imaginar*) conceive of □ *vi* conceive; ~**bível** (*pl* ~**bíveis**) *a* conceivable

conceder /kõse'der/ *vt* grant; ~ **em** accede to

concei|to /kõ'sejtu/ *m* concept; (*opinião*) opinion; (*fama*) reputation; ~**tuado** *a* highly thought of; ~**tuar** *vt* (*imaginar*) conceptualize; (*avaliar*) assess

concen|tração /kõsẽtra'sãw/ *f* concentration; (*de jogadores*) training camp; ~**trar** *vt* concentrate; ~**trar-se** *vpr* concentrate

concepção /kõsep'sãw/ *f* conception; (*opinião*) view

concernir /kõser'nir/ *vt* ~ **a** concern

concerto /kõ'sertu/ *m* concert

conces|são /kõse'sãw/ *f* concession; ~**sionária** *f* dealership; ~**sionário** *m* dealer

concha /'kõʃa/ *f* (*de molusco*) shell; (*colher*) ladle

concili|ação /kõsilia'sãw/ *f* conciliation; ~**ador** *a* conciliatory; ~**ar** *vt* reconcile

concílio /kõ'siliu/ *m* council

conci|são /kõsi'zãw/ *f* conciseness; ~**so** *a* concise

conclamar /kõkla'mar/ *vt* call < *eleição, greve*>; call upon < *pessoa*>

conclu|dente /kõklu'dẽtʃi/ *a* conclusive; ~**ir** *vt/i* conclude; ~**são** *f* conclusion; ~**sivo** *a* concluding

concor|dância /kõkor'dãsia/ *f* agreement; ~**dante** *a* consistent; ~**dar** *vi* agree (**em**) □ *vt* bring into line; ~**data** *f* abrir ~**data** go into liquidation

concórdia /kõ'kɔrdʒia/ *f* concord

concor|rência /kõko'xẽsia/ *f* competition (**a** for); ~**rente** *a* competing; ~**rer** *vi* compete (**a** for); ~**rer para** contribute to; ~**rido** *a* popular

concre|tizar /kõkretʃi'zar/ *vt* realize; ~**tizar-se** *vpr* be realized; ~**to** /ɛ/ *a & m* concrete

concurso /kõ'kursu/ *m* contest; (*prova*) competition

con|dado /kõ'dadu/ *m* county; ~**de** *m* count

condeco|ração /kõdekora'sãw/ f
decoration; **~rar** vt decorate
conde|nação /kõdena'sãw/ f con-
demnation; (jurid) conviction;
~nar vt condemn; convict
conden|sação /kõdẽsa'sãw/ f
condensation; **~sar** vt condense; **~sar-se** vpr condense
condescen|dência /kõdesẽ'dẽsia/ f
acquiescence; **~dente** a acquies-
cent; **~der** vi acquiesce; **~der a**
comply with <pedido, desejo>;
~der a ir condescend to go
condessa /kõ'desa/ f countess
condi|ção /kõdʒi'sãw/ f condition;
(qualidade) capacity; **ter ~ção**
ou **~ções para** be able to; **em**
boas ~ções in good condition;
~cionado a conditioned; **~cio-**
nal (pl **~cionais**) a conditional;
~cionamento m conditioning
condimen|tar /kõdʒimẽ'tar/ vt
season; **~to** m seasoning
condoer-se /kõdo'ersi/ vpr **~ de**
feel sorry for
condolência /kõdo'lẽsia/ f sym-
pathy; pl condolences
condomínio /kõdo'miniu/ m
(taxa) service charge
condu|ção /kõdu'sãw/ f (de carro
etc) driving; (transporte) transport; **~cente a conducive (a**
to); **~ta** f conduct; **~to** m
conduit; **~tor** m driver; (eletr)
conductor; **~zir** vt lead; drive
<carro>; (eletr) conduct □ vi (de
carro) drive; (levar) lead (a to)
cone /'koni/ m cone
conecta|r /konek'tar/ vt connect;
~do a connected; (comput) on-
line
cone|xão /konek'sãw/ f con-
nection; **~xo** /ɛ/ a connected
confec|ção /kõfek'sãw/ f (de roupa)
off-the-peg outfit; (loja) clothes
shop, boutique; (fábrica) clothes
manufacturer; **~cionar** vt make
confederação /kõfedera'sãw/ f
confederation

confei|tar /kõfej'tar/ vt ice;
~taria f cake shop; **~teiro** m
confectioner
confe|rência /kõfe'rẽsia/ f confer-
ence; (palestra) lecture; **~ren-**
cista m/f speaker
conferir /kõfe'rir/ vt check (com
against); (conceder) confer (a on)
□ vi (controlar) check; (estar
exato) tally
confes|sar /kõfe'sar/ vt/i confess;
~sar-se vpr confess; **~sio-**
nário m confessional; **~sor** m confessor
confete /kõ'fetʃi/ m confetti
confi|ança /kõfi'ãsa/ f (convicção)
confidence; (fé) trust; **~ante a**
confident (em of); **~ar** (dar)
entrust; **~ar em** trust; **~ável**
(pl **~áveis**) a reliable; **~dência**
f confidence; **~dencial** (pl
~denciais) a confidential;
~denciar vt tell in confidence;
~dente m/f confidant (f con-
fidante)
configu|ração /kõfigura'sãw/ f
configuration; **~rar** vt (representar) represent; (formar)
shape; (comput) configure
confi|nar /kõfi'nar/ vi **~nar**
com border on; **~fins** m pl bor-
ders
confir|mação /kõfirma'sãw/ f con-
firmation; **~mar** vt confirm;
~mar-se vpr be confirmed
confis|car /kõfis'kar/ vt con-
fiscate; **~co** m confiscation
confissão /kõfi'sãw/ f confession
confla|gração /kõflagra'sãw/ f
conflagration; **~grar** vt set
alight; (fig) throw into turmoil
confli|tante /kõfli'tãtʃi/ a con-
flicting; **~to** m conflict
confor|mação /kõforma'sãw/ f
resignation; **~mado** a resigned
(com to); **~mar** vt adapt (a to);
~mar-se com conform to <re-
gra, política>; resign o.s. to, come
to terms with <destino, evento>;

~me /ɔ/ *prep* according to □
conj depending on; ~me it depends; ~**midade** *f* conformity;
~**mismo** *m* conformism; ~**mista** *a* & *m*/*f* conformist

confor|tar /kõfor'tar/ *vt* comfort;
~**tável** (*pl* ~**táveis**) *a* comfortable; ~to /o/ *m* comfort

confraternizar /kõfraterni'zar/ *vi*
fraternize

confron|tação /kõfrõta'sãw/ *f*
confrontation; ~**tar** *vt* confront;
(*comparar*) compare; ~to *m* confrontation; (*comparação*) comparison

con|fundir /kõfũ'dʒir/ *vt* confuse;
~**fundir-se** *vpr* get confused;
~**fusão** *f* confusion; (*desordem*)
mess; (*tumulto*) commotion;
~**fuso** *a* (*confundido*) confused;
(*que confunde*) confusing

conge|lador /kõʒela'dor/ *m*
freezer; ~**lamento** *m* (*de preços
etc*) freeze; ~**lar** *vt* freeze; ~**larse** *vpr* freeze

congênito /kõ'ʒenitu/ *a* congenital

congestão /kõʒes'tãw/ *f* congestion

congestio|nado /kõʒestʃio'nadu/
a <*rua, cidade*> congested; <*pessoa, rosto*> flushed; <*olhos*>
bloodshot; ~**namento** *m* (*de
trânsito*) traffic jam; ~**nar** *vt*
congest; ~**nar-se** *vpr* <*rua*> get
congested; <*rosto*> flush

conglomerado /kõglome'radu/ *m*
conglomerate

congratular /kõgratu'lar/ *vt* congratulate (**por** on)

congre|gação /kõgrega'sãw/ *f* (*na
igreja*) congregation; (*reunião*)
gathering; ~**gar** *vt* bring together; ~**gar-se** *vpr* congregate

congresso /kõ'gresu/ *m* congress

conhaque /ko'ɲaki/ *m* brandy

conhe|cedor /koɲese'dor/ *a* knowing □ *m* connoisseur; ~**cer** *vt*
know; (*ser apresentado a*) get to

know; (*visitar*) go to, visit;
~**cido** *a* known; (*famoso*) well-known □ *m* acquaintance;
~**cimento** *m* knowledge; **tomar**
~**cimento de** learn of; **travar**
~**cimento com alg** make s.o.'s
acquaintance, become acquainted with s.o.

cônico /'koniku/ *a* conical

coni|vência /koni'vẽsia/ *f* connivance; ~**vente** *a* conniving
(**em** at)

conjetu|ra /kõʒe'tura/ *f* conjecture; ~**rar** *vt*/*i* conjecture

conju|gação /kõʒuga'sãw/ *f* (*ling*)
conjugation; ~**gar** *vt* conjugate
<*verbo*>

cônjuge /'kõʒuʒi/ *m*/*f* spouse

conjun|ção /kõʒũ'sãw/ *f* conjunction; ~**tivo** *a* & *m* subjunctive; ~**to** *a* joint □ *m* set;
(*roupa*) outfit; (*musical*) group;
o ~**to de** the body of; **em** ~**to**
jointly; ~**tura** *f* state of affairs;
(*econômica*) state of the economy

conosco = **com** + **nós**

cono|tação /konota'sãw/ *f* connotation; ~**tar** *vt* connote

conquanto /kõ'kwãtu/ *conj* although, even though

conquis|ta /kõ'kista/ *f* conquest;
(*proeza*) achievement; ~**tador**
a conquering □ *m* conqueror; ~**tar** *vt* conquer <*terra, país*>;
win <*riqueza, independência*>;
win over <*pessoa*>

consa|gração /kõsagra'sãw/ *f* (*de
uma igreja*) consecration; (*dedicação*) dedication; ~**grado** *a*
<*artista, expressão*> established;
~**grar** *vt* consecrate <*igreja*>;
establish <*artista, estilo*>; (*dedicar*) dedicate (**a** to); ~**grar-se**
dedicate o.s. to

consci|ência /kõsi'ẽsia/ *f* (*moralidade*) conscience; (*sentidos*) consciousness; (*no trabalho*) conscientiousness; (*de um fato etc*)
awareness; ~**encioso** /o/ *a*

conscientious; ~ente *a* conscious; ~entizar *vt* make aware (de of); ~entizar-se *vpr* become aware (de of)

consecutivo /kõseku'tʃivu/ *a* consecutive

conse|guinte /kõse'gĩtʃi/ *a* por ~guinte consequently; ~guir *vt* get; ~guir fazer manage to do □ *vi* succeed

conse|lheiro /kõse'ʎeru/ *m* counsellor, adviser; ~lho /e/ *m* piece of advice; *pl* advice; (órgão) council

consen|so /kõ'sẽsu/ *m* consensus; ~timento *m* consent; ~tir *vt* allow □ *vi* consent (em to)

conse|qüência /kõse'kwẽsia/ *f* consequence; por ~qüência consequently; ~qüente *a* consequent; (coerente) consistent

conser|tar /kõser'tar/ *vt* repair; ~to /e/ *m* repair

conser|va /kõ'sɛrva/ *f* (em vidro) preserve; (em lata) tinned food; ~vação *f* preservation; ~vador *a* & *m* conservative; ~vadorismo *m* conservatism; ~vante *a* & *m* preservative; ~var *vt* preserve; (manter, guardar) keep; ~var-se *vpr* keep; ~vatório *m* conservatory

conside|ração /kõsidera'sãw/ *f* consideration; (estima) esteem; levar em ~ração take into consideration; ~rar *vt* consider; (estimar) think highly of □ *vi* consider; ~rar-se *vpr* consider o.s.; ~rável (*pl* ~ráveis) *a* considerable

consig|nação /kõsigna'sãw/ *f* consignment; ~nar *vt* consign

consigo = com + si

consis|tência /kõsis'tẽsia/ *f* consistency; ~tente *a* firm; ~tir *vi* consist (em in)

consoante /kõso'ãtʃi/ *f* consonant

conso|lação /kõsola'sãw/ *f* consolation; ~lador *a* consoling;

~lar *vt* console; ~lar-se *vpr* console o.s.

consolidar /kõsoli'dar/ *vt* consolidate; mend <fratura>

consolo /kõ'solu/ *m* consolation

consórcio /kõ'sɔrsiu/ *m* consortium

consorte /kõ'sɔrtʃi/ *m/f* consort

conspícuo /kõs'pikuu/ *a* conspicuous

conspi|ração /kõspira'sãw/ *f* conspiracy; ~rador *m* conspirator; ~rar *vi* conspire

cons|tância /kõs'tãsia/ *f* constancy; ~tante *a* & *f* constant; ~tar *vi* (em lista etc) appear; não me ~ta I am not aware; ~ta que it is said that; ~tar de consist of

consta|tação /kõstata'sãw/ *f* observation; ~tar *vt* note, notice; certify <óbito>

conste|lação /kõstela'sãw/ *f* constellation; ~lado *a* star-studded

conster|nação /kõsterna'sãw/ *f* consternation; ~nar *vt* dismay

consti|pação /kõstʃipa'sãw/ *f* (Port: resfriado) cold; ~pado *a* (resfriado) with a cold; (no intestino) constipated; ~par-se *vpr* (Port: resfriar-se) get a cold

constitu|cional /kõstʃitusio'naw/ (*pl* ~cionais) *a* constitutional; ~ição *f* constitution; ~inte *a* constituent □ *f* Constituinte Constituent Assembly; ~ir *vt* form <governo, sociedade>; (representar) constitute; (nomear) appoint

constran|gedor /kõstrãʒe'dor/ *a* embarrassing; ~ger *vt* embarrass; (coagir) constrain; ~ger-se *vpr* get embarrassed; ~gimento *m* (embaraço) embarrassment; (coação) constraint

constru|ção /kõstru'sãw/ *f* construction; (terreno) building site; ~ir *vt* build <casa, prédio>; (fig) construct; ~tivo *a* constructive; ~**tor** *m* builder; ~**tora** *f* building firm

cônsul /'kõsuw/ (*pl* ~**es**) *m* consul

consulado /kõsu'ladu/ *m* consulate

consul|ta /kõ'suwta/ *f* consultation; ~**tar** *vt* consult; ~**tor** *m* consultant; ~**toria** *f* consultancy; ~**tório** *m* (*médico*) surgery, (*Amer*) office

consu|mação /kõsuma'sãw/ *f* (*taxa*) minimum charge; ~**mado o fato** ~**mado** fait accompli; ~**mar** *vt* accomplish <*projeto*>; carry out <*crime, sacrifício*>; consummate <*casamento*>

consu|midor /kõsumi'dor/ *a & m* consumer; ~**mir** *vt* consume; take up <*tempo*>; ~**mismo** *m* consumerism; ~**mista** *a & m/f* consumerist; ~**mo** *m* consumption

conta /'kõta/ *f* (*a pagar*) bill; (*bancária*) account; (*contagem*) count; (*de vidro etc*) bead; *pl* (*com*) accounts; **em** ~ economical; **por** ~ **de** on account of; **por** ~ **própria** on one's own account; **ajustar** ~**s** settle up; **dar** ~ **de** (*fig*) be up to; **dar** ~ **do recado** (*fam*) deliver the goods; **dar-se** ~ **de** realize; **fazer de** ~ pretend; **ficar por** ~ **de** be left to; **levar** *ou* **ter em** ~ take into account; **prestar** ~**s de** account for; **tomar** ~ **de** take care of; ~**bancária** bank account; ~**rente** current account

contabi|lidade /kõtabili'dadʒi/ *f* accountancy; (*contas*) accounts; (*seção*) accounts department; ~**lista** (*Port*) *m/f* accountant; ~**lizar** *vt* write up <*quantia*>; (*fig*) notch up

contact- (*Port*) *veja* **contat-**

conta|dor /kõta'dor/ *m* (*pessoa*) accountant; (*de luz etc*) meter; ~**gem** *f* counting; (*de pontos*

num jogo) scoring; ~**gem regressiva** countdown

contagi|ante /kõtaʒi'ãtʃi/ *a* infectious; ~**ar** *vt* infect; ~**ar-se** *vpr* become infected

contágio /kõ'taʒiu/ *m* infection

contagioso /kõtaʒi'ozu/ *a* contagious

contami|nação /kõtamina'sãw/ *f* contamination; ~**nar** *vt* contaminate

contanto /kõ'tãtu/ *adv* ~ **que** provided that

contar /kõ'tar/ *vt/i* count; (*narrar*) tell; ~ **com** count on

conta|tar /kõta'tar/ *vt* contact; ~**to** *m* contact; **entrar em** ~**to com** get in touch with; **tomar** ~**to com** come into contact with

contem|plação /kõtẽpla'sãw/ *f* contemplation; ~**plar** *vt* (*considerar*) contemplate; (*dizer respeito a*) concern; ~**plar alg com** treat s.o. to ~ *vi* **ponder**; ~**plativo** *a* contemplative

contemporâneo /kõtẽpo'raniu/ *a & m* contemporary

contenção /kõtẽ'sãw/ *f* containment

conten|cioso /kõtẽsi'ozu/ *a* contentious; ~**da** *f* dispute

conten|tamento /kõtẽta'mẽtu/ *m* contentment; ~**tar** *vt* satisfy; ~**tar-se** *vpr* be content; ~**te** *a* (*feliz*) happy; (*satisfeito*) content; ~**to** *m* **a** ~ **to** satisfactorily

conter /kõ'ter/ *vt* contain; ~**se** *vpr* contain o.s.

conterrâneo /kõte'xaniu/ *m* fellow countryman (*f* -woman)

contestar /kõtes'tar/ *vt* question; (*jurid*) contest

conteúdo /kõte'udu/ *m* (*de recipiente*) contents; (*fig: de carta etc*) content

contexto /kõ'testu/ *m* context

contigo = **com** + **ti**

continência /kõtʃi'nẽsia/ *f* (*mil*) salute

continen|tal /kõtʃinẽ'taw/ (pl ~**tais**) a continental; ~**te** m continent

contin|gência /kõtʃĩ'ʒẽsia/ f contingency; ~**gente** a (eventual) possible; (incerto) contingent □ m contingent

continu|ação /kõtʃinua'sãw/ f continuation; ~**ar** vt/i continue; **eles ~am ricos** they are still rich; ~**idade** f continuity

contínuo /kõ'tʃinuu/ a continuous □ m office junior

con|tista /kõ'tʃista/ m/f (short) story writer; ~**to** m (short) story; ~**to de fadas** fairy tale; ~**to-do-vigário** (pl ~**tos-do-vigário**) m confidence trick, swindle

contorcer /kõtor'ser/ vt twist; ~**se** vpr (de dor) writhe

contor|nar /kõtor'nar/ vt go round; (fig) get round <obstáculo, problema>; (cercar) surround; (delinear) outline; ~**no** /o/ m outline; (da paisagem) contour

contra /'kõtra/ prep against

contra-|atacar /kõtrata'kar/ vt counterattack; ~**ataque** m counterattack

contrabaixo /kõtra'baʃu/ m double bass

contrabalançar /kõtrabalã'sar/ vt counterbalance

contraban|dear /kõtrabãdʒi'ar/ vt smuggle; ~**dista** m/f smuggler; ~**do** m (ato) smuggling; (artigos) contraband

contração /kõtra'sãw/ f contraction

contracenar /kõtrase'nar/ vi ~**com** play up to

contraceptivo /kõtrasep'tʃivu/ a & m contraceptive

contracheque /kõtra'ʃɛki/ m pay slip

contradi|ção /kõtradʒi'sãw/ f contradiction; ~**tório** a contradictory; ~**zer** vt contradict;

~**zer-se** vpr <pessoa> contradict o.s.; <idéias etc> be contradictory

contragosto /kõtra'gostu/ m **a ~** reluctantly

contrair /kõtra'ir/ vt contract; pick up <hábito, vício>; ~**se** vpr contract

contramão /kõtra'mãw/ f opposite direction □ a invar one way

contramestre /kõtra'mɛstri/ m supervisor; (em navio) bosun

contra-ofensiva /kõtraofẽ'siva/ f counter-offensive

contrapartida /kõtrapar'tʃida/ f (fig) compensation; **em ~** on the other hand

contraproducente /kõtraprodu-'sẽtʃi/ a counter-productive

contrari|ar /kõtrari'ar/ vt go against, run counter to; (aborrecer) annoy; ~**edade** f adversity; (aborrecimento) annoyance

contrário /kõ'trariu/ a opposite; (desfavorável) adverse; ~**a** a contrary to; <pessoa> opposed to □ m opposite; **pelo** ou **ao ~** on the contrary; **ao ~ de** contrary to; **em ~** to the contrary

contras|tante /kõtras'tãtʃi/ a contrasting; ~**tar** vt/i contrast; ~**te** m contrast

contra|tante /kõtra'tãtʃi/ m/f contractor; ~**tar** vt employ, take on <operários>

contra|tempo /kõtra'tẽpu/ m hitch; ~**to** /o/ (pl ~**tuais**) a contractual

contraven|ção /kõtravẽ'sãw/ f contravention; ~**tor** m offender

contribu|ição /kõtribui'sãw/ f contribution; ~**inte** m/f contributor; (pagador de impostos) taxpayer; ~**ir** vt contribute □ vi contribute; (pagar impostos) pay tax

contrição /kõtri'sãw/ f contrition

contro|lar /kõtro'lar/ vt control; (fiscalizar) check; ~**le** /o/,

(Port) ~**lo** /o/ m control; (*fiscalização*) check

contro|vérsia /kõtro'vɛrsia/ f controversy; ~**verso** /ɛ/ a controversial

contudo /kõ'tudu/ conj nevertheless

contundir /kõtũ'dʒir/ vt (*dar hematoma em*) bruise; injure <*jogador*>; ~**-se** vpr bruise o.s.; <*jogador*> get injured

conturbado /kõtur'badu/ a troubled

contu|são /kõtu'zãw/ f bruise; (*de jogador*) injury; ~**so** a bruised; <*jogador*> injured

convales|cença /kõvale'sẽsa/ f convalescence; ~**cer** vi convalesce

convenção /kõvẽ'sãw/ f convention

conven|cer /kõvẽ'ser/ vt convince; ~**cido** a (*convicto*) convinced; (*metido*) conceited; ~**cimento** m (*convicção*) conviction; (*imodéstia*) conceitedness

convencio|nal /kõvẽsio'naw/ (pl ~**nais**) a conventional

conveni|ência /kõveni'ẽsia/ f convenience; ~**ente** a convenient; (*cabível*) appropriate

convênio /kõ'veniu/ m agreement

convento /kõ'vẽtu/ m convent

convergir /kõver'ʒir/ vi converge

conver|sa /kõ'vɛrsa/ f conversation; **a** ~**sa dele** the things he says; ~**sa fiada** idle talk; ~**sação** f conversation; ~**sado** a <*pessoa*> talkative; <*assunto*> talked about; ~**sador** a talkative

conversão /kõver'sãw/ f conversion

conversar /kõver'sar/ vi talk

conver|sível /kõver'sivew/ (pl ~**síveis**) a & m convertible; ~**ter** vt convert; ~**ter-se** vpr be converted; ~**tido** m convert

con|vés /kõ'vɛs/ (pl ~**veses**) m deck

convexo /kõ'vɛksu/ a convex

convic|ção /kõvik'sãw/ f conviction; ~**to** a convinced; (*ferrenho*) confirmed; <*criminoso*> convicted

convi|dado /kõvi'dadu/ m guest; ~**dar** vt invite; ~**dativo** a inviting

convincente /kõvĩ'sẽtʃi/ a convincing

convir /kõ'vir/ vi (*ficar bem*) be appropriate; (*concordar*) agree (**em** on); ~ **a** suit, be convenient for; **convém notar que** one should note that

convite /kõ'vitʃi/ m invitation

convi|vência /kõvi'vẽsia/ f coexistence; (*relação*) close contact; ~**ver** vi coexist; (*ter relações*) associate (**com** with)

convívio /kõ'viviu/ m association (**com** with)

convocar /kõvo'kar/ vt call <*eleições, greve*>; call upon <*pessoa*> (**a** to); (*ao serviço militar*) call up

convosco = com + vós

convul|são /kõvuw'sãw/ f (*do corpo*) convulsion; (*da sociedade etc*) upheaval; ~**sionar** vt convulse <*corpo*>; (*fig*) churn up; ~**sivo** a convulsive

cooper /'kuper/ m jogging; **fazer** ~ go jogging

coope|ração /koopera'sãw/ f cooperation; ~**rar** vi cooperate; ~**rativa** f cooperative; ~**rativo** a cooperative

coorde|nação /koordena'sãw/ f co-ordination; ~**nada** f coordinate; ~**nar** vt coordinate

copa /'kɔpa/ f (*de árvore*) top; (*aposento*) breakfast room; (*torneio*) cup; pl (*naipe*) hearts; **a Copa (do Mundo)** the World Cup; ~**cozinha** (pl ~**s-cozinhas**) f kitchen-diner

cópia /'kɔpia/ f copy

copiar /kopi'ar/ vt copy

co-piloto /kopi'lotu/ m co-pilot

copioso /kopi'ozu/ a ample; <*refeição*> substantial

copo /'kɔpu/ m glass

coque /'kɔki/ m (*penteado*) bun

coqueiro /ko'keru/ m coconut palm

coqueluche /koke'luʃi/ f (*doença*) whooping cough; (*mania*) fad

coque|tel /koke'tɛw/ (*pl* ~**téis**) m cocktail; (*reunião*) cocktail party

cor¹ /kɔr/ m **de** ~ by heart

cor² /kor/ f colour; **TV a** ~**es** colour TV; **pessoa de** ~ coloured person

coração /kora'sãw/ m heart

cora|gem /ko'raʒẽ/ f courage; ~**joso** /o/ a courageous

co|ral¹ /ko'raw/ (*pl* ~**rais**) m (*animal*) coral

co|ral² /ko'raw/ (*pl* ~**rais**) m (*de cantores*) choir □ a choral

co|rante /ko'rãtʃi/ a & m colouring; ~**rar** vt colour □ vi blush

cor|da /'kɔrda/ f rope; (*mus*) string; (*para roupa lavada*) clothes line; **dar** ~**da em** wind <*relógio*>; ~**da bamba** tightrope; ~**das vocais** vocal chords; ~**dão** m cord; (*de sapatos*) lace; (*policial*) cordon

cordeiro /kor'deru/ m lamb

cor|del /kor'dɛw/ (*pl* ~**déis**) (*Port*) m string; **literatura de** ~**del** trash

cor-de-rosa /kordʒi'rɔza/ a invar pink

cordi|al /kordʒi'aw/ (*pl* ~**ais**) a & m cordial; ~**alidade** f cordiality

cordilheira /kordʒi'ʎera/ f chain of mountains

coreano /kori'anu/ a & m Korean

Coréia /ko'rɛja/ f Korea

core|ografia /koriogra'fia/ f choreography; ~**ógrafo** m choreographer

coreto /ko'retu/ m bandstand

coriza /ko'riza/ f runny nose

corja /'kɔrʒa/ f pack; (*de pessoas*) rabble

córner /'kɔrner/ m corner

coro /'koru/ m chorus

coro|a /ko'roa/ f crown; (*de flores etc*) wreath □ (*fam*) m/f old man (*f* woman); ~**ação** f coronation; ~**ar** vt crown

coro|nel /koro'nɛw/ (*pl* ~**néis**) m colonel

coronha /ko'roɲa/ f butt

corpete /kor'petʃi/ m bodice

corpo /'korpu/ m body; (*físico de mulher*) figure; (*físico de homem*) physique; ~ **de bombeiros** fire brigade; ~ **diplomático** diplomatic corps; ~ **docente** teaching staff, (*Amer*) faculty; ~**a**- ~ m *invar* pitched battle; ~**ral** (*pl* ~**rais**) a physical; (*pena*) corporal

corpu|lência /korpu'lêsia/ f stoutness; ~**lento** a stout

correção /koxe'sãw/ f correction

corre-corre /kɔxi'kɔxi/ m (*debandada*) stampede; (*correria*) rush

correct- (*Port*) *veja* **corret-**

corre|diço /koxe'dʒisu/ a <*porta*> sliding; ~**dor** m (*atleta*) runner; (*passagem*) corridor

correia /ko'xeja/ f strap; (*peça de máquina*) belt; (*para cachorro*) lead, (*Amer*) leash

correio /ko'xeju/ m post, mail; (*repartição*) post office; **pôr no** ~ post, (*Amer*) mail; ~ **aéreo** air mail; ~ **eletrônico** email

correlação /koxela'sãw/ f correlation

correligionário /koxeliʒio'nariu/ m party colleague

corrente /ko'xẽtʃi/ a <*água*> running; <*mês, conta*> current; <*estilo*> fluid; (*usual*) common □ f (*de água, eletricidade*) current; (*cadeia*) chain; ~ **de ar** draught; ~**za** /e/ f current; (*de ar*) draught

cor|rer /ko'xer/ vi (*à pé*) run; (*de carro*) drive fast, speed; (*fazer* rápido) rush; <*água, sangue*> flow; <*tempo*> elapse; <*boato*> go round □ *vt* draw <*cortina*>; run <*risco*>; ~**reria** *f* rush

correspon|dência /koxespõ'dẽsia/ *f* correspondence; ~**dente** *a* corresponding □ *m/f* correspondent; (*equivalente*) equivalent; ~**der** *vi* ~**der a** correspond to; (*retribuir*) return; ~**der-se** *vpr* correspond (**com** with)

corre|tivo /koxe'tʃivu/ *a* corrective □ *m* punishment; ~**to** /ɛ/ *a* correct

corretor /koxe'tor/ *m* broker; ~ **de imóveis** estate agent, (*Amer*) realtor

corrida /ko'xida/ *f* (*prova*) race; (*ação de correr*) run; (*de taxi*) ride

corrigir /koxi'ʒir/ *vt* correct

corrimão /koxi'mãw/ (*pl* ~**s**) *m* handrail; (*de escada*) banister

corriqueiro /koxi'keru/ *a* ordinary, run-of-the-mill

corroborar /koxobo'rar/ *vt* corroborate

corroer /koxo'er/ *vt* corrode <*metal*>; (*fig*) erode; ~**se** *vpr* corrode; (*fig*) erode

corromper /koxõ'per/ *vt* corrupt; ~**se** *vpr* be corrupted

corro|são /koxo'zãw/ *f* (*de metal*) corrosion; (*fig*) erosion; ~**sivo** *a* corrosive

corrup|ção /koxup'sãw/ *f* corruption; ~**to** *a* corrupt

cor|tada /kor'tada/ *f* (*em tênis*) smash; (*em pessoa*) put-down; ~**tante** *a* cutting; ~**tar** *vt* cut; cut off <*luz, telefone, perna etc*>; cut down <*árvore*>; cut out <*efeito, vício*>; take away <*prazer*>; (*com o carro*) cut up; (*desprezar*) cut dead □ *vi* cut; ~**tar o cabelo** (*no cabeleireiro*) get one's hair cut; ~**te**[1] /ɔ/ *m* cut; (*gume*) blade; (*desenho*) cross-section; **sem** ~**te** <*faca*> blunt; ~**te de cabelo** haircut

cor|te[2] /'kortʃi/ *f* court; ~**tejar** *vt* court; ~**tejo** /e/ *m* (*séquito*) retinue; (*fúnebre*) cortège; ~**tês** *a* (*f* ~**tesa**) courteous, polite; ~**tesão** (*pl* ~**tesãos**) *m* courtier; ~**tesia** *f* courtesy

corti|ça /kor'tʃisa/ *f* cork; ~**ço** *m* (*casa popular*) slum tenement

cortina /kor'tʃina/ *f* curtain

cortisona /kortʃi'zona/ *f* cortisone

coruja /ko'ruʒa/ *f* owl □ *a* <*pai, mãe*> proud, doting

coruscar /korus'kar/ *vi* flash

corvo /'korvu/ *m* crow

cós /kɔs/ *m invar* waistband

coser /ko'zer/ *vt/i* sew

cosmético /koz'mɛtʃiku/ *a* & *m* cosmetic

cósmico /'kɔzmiku/ *a* cosmic

cosmo /'kɔzmu/ *m* cosmos; ~**nauta** *m/f* cosmonaut; ~**polita** *a* cosmopolitan □ *m/f* globetrotter

costa /'kɔsta/ *f* coast; *pl* (*dorso*) back; **Costa do Marfim** Ivory Coast; **Costa Rica** Costa Rica

costarriquenho /kostaxi'keɲu/ *a* & *m* Costa Rican

cos|teiro /kos'teru/ *a* coastal; ~**tela** /ɛ/ *f* rib; ~**teleta** /e/ *f* chop; *pl* (*suíças*) sideburns; ~**telinha** (*de porco*) spare rib

costu|mar /kostu'mar/ *vt* ~**ma fazer** he usually does; ~**mava fazer** he used to do; ~**me** *m* (*uso*) custom; (*traje*) costume; **de** ~**me** usually; **como de** ~**me** as usual; **ter o** ~**me de** have a habit of; ~**meiro** *a* customary

costu|ra /kos'tura/ *f* sewing; ~**rar** *vt/i* sew; ~**reira** *f* (*mulher*) dressmaker; (*caixa*) needlework box

cota /'kɔta/ *f* quota; ~**tação** *f* (*preço*) rate; (*apreço*) rating; ~**tado** *a* <*ação*> quoted; (*conceituado*) highly rated; ~**tar** *vt* rate; quote <*ações*>

cote|jar /kote'ʒar/ *vt* compare; **~jo** /e/ *m* comparison

cotidiano /kotʃidʒi'anu/ *a* everyday □ *m* everyday life

cotonete /koto'netʃi/ *m* cotton bud

cotove|lada /kotove'lada/ *f (para abrir caminho)* shove; *(para chamar atenção)* nudge; **~lo** /e/ *m* elbow

coura|ça /ko'rasa/ *f (armadura)* breastplate; *(de navio, animal)* armour; **~çado** *(Port)* *m* battleship

couro /'koru/ *m* leather; **~ cabeludo** scalp

couve /'kovi/ *f* spring greens; **~-de-bruxelas** *(pl* **~s-de-bruxelas)** *f* Brussels sprout; **~-flor** *(pl* **~s-flores)** *f* cauliflower

couvert /ku'ver/ *(pl* **~s)** *m* cover charge

cova /'kova/ *f (buraco)* pit; *(sepultura)* grave

covar|de /ko'vardʒi/ *m/f* coward □ *a* cowardly; **~dia** *f* cowardice

coveiro /ko'veru/ *m* gravedigger

covil /ko'viw/ *(pl* **~vis)** *m* den, lair

covinha /ko'viɲa/ *f* dimple

co|xa /'koʃa/ *f* thigh; **~xear** *vi* hobble

coxia /ko'ʃia/ *f* aisle

coxo /'koʃu/ *a* hobbling; **ser ~** hobble

co|zer /ko'zer/ *vt/i* cook; **~zido** *m* stew, casserole

cozi|nha /ko'ziɲa/ *f (aposento)* kitchen; *(comida, ação)* cooking; *(arte)* cookery; **~nhar** *vt/i* cook; **~nheiro** *m* cook

crachá /kra'ʃa/ *m* badge, *(Amer)* button

crânio /'kraniu/ *m* skull; *(pessoa)* genius

crápula /'krapula/ *m/f* scoundrel

craque /'kraki/ *m (de futebol)* soccer star; *(fam)* expert

crase /'krazi/ *f* contraction; **a com ~ a** grave (à)

crasso /'krasu/ *a* crass

cratera /kra'tera/ *f* crater

cravar /kra'var/ *vt* drive in *<prego>*; dig *<unha>*; stick *<estaca>*; **~ com os olhos** stare at; **~se** *vpr* stick

cravejar /krave'ʒar/ *vt* nail; *(com balas)* spray, riddle

cravo¹ /'kravu/ *m (flor)* carnation; *(condimento)* clove

cravo² /'kravu/ *m (na pele)* blackhead; *(prego)* nail

cravo³ /'kravu/ *m (instrumento)* harpsichord

creche /'krɛʃi/ *f* crèche

credenci|ais /kredēsi'ajs/ *f pl* credentials; **~ar** *vt* qualify

credi|ário /kredʒi'ariu/ *m* hire purchase agreement, credit plan; **~bilidade** *f* credibility; **~tar** *vt* credit

crédito /'krɛdʒitu/ *m* credit; **a ~** on credit

cre|do /'kredu/ *m* creed □ *int* heavens; **~dor** *m* creditor □ *a* *<saldo>* credit

crédulo /'krɛdulu/ *a* gullible

cre|mação /krema'sãw/ *f* cremation; **~mar** *vt* cremate; **~matório** *m* crematorium

cre|me /'kremi/ *a invar & m* cream; **~me Chantilly** whipped cream; **~me de leite** (sterilized) cream; **~moso** /o/ *a* creamy

cren|ça /'krēsa/ *f* belief; **~dice** *f* superstition; **~te** *m* believer; *(protestante)* Protestant □ *a* religious; *(protestante)* Protestant; **estar ~te que** believe that

crepe /'krɛpi/ *m* crepe

crepitar /krepi'tar/ *vi* crackle

crepom /kre'põ/ *m* crepe; **papel ~** tissue paper

crepúsculo /kre'puskulu/ *m* twilight

crer /krer/ *vt/i* believe (**em** in); **creio que** I think (that); **~se** *vpr* believe o.s. to be

cres|cendo /kre'sẽdu/ *m* crescendo; **~cente** *a* growing □ *m* crescent; **~cer** *vi* grow; <*bolo*> rise; **~cido** *a* grown; **~cimento** *m* growth

crespo /'krespu/ *a* <*cabelo*> frizzy; <*mar*> choppy

cretino /kre'tʃinu/ *m* cretin

cria /'kria/ *f* baby; *pl* young

criação /kria'sãw/ *f* creation; (*educação*) upbringing; (*de animais*) raising; (*gado*) livestock

criado /kri'adu/ *m* servant; **~mudo** (*pl* **~s-mudos**) *m* bedside table

criador /kria'dor/ *m* creator; (*de animais*) farmer, breeder

crian|ça /kri'ãsa/ *f* child □ *a* childish; **~çada** *f* kids; **~cice** *f* childishness; (*uma*) childish thing

criar /kri'ar/ *vt* (*fazer*) create; bring up <*filhos*>; rear <*animais*>; grow <*planta*>; pluck up <*coragem*>; **~-se** *vpr* be brought up, grow up

criati|vidade /kriatʃivi'dadʒi/ *f* creativity; **~vo** *a* creative

criatura /kria'tura/ *f* creature

crime /'krimi/ *m* crime

crimi|nal /krimi'naw/ (*pl* **~nais**) *a* criminal; **~nalidade** *f* crime; **~noso** *m* criminal

crina /'krina/ *f* mane

crioulo /kri'olu/ *a* & *m* creole; (*negro*) black

cripta /'kripta/ *f* crypt

crisálida /kri'zalida/ *f* chrysalis

crisântemo /kri'zãtemu/ *m* chrysanthemum

crise /'krizi/ *f* crisis

cris|ma /'krizma/ *f* confirmation; **~mar** *vt* confirm; **~mar-se** *vpr* get confirmed

crista /'krista/ *f* crest

cris|tal /kris'taw/ (*pl* **~tais**) *m* crystal; (*vidro*) glass; **~talino** *a* crystal-clear; **~talizar** *vt/i* crystallize

cris|tandade /kristã'dadʒi/ *f* Christendom; **~tão** (*pl* **~tãos**) *a* & *m* (*f* **~tã**) Christian; **~tianismo** *m* Christianity

Cristo /'kristu/ *m* Christ

cri|tério /kri'tɛriu/ *m* discretion; (*norma*) criterion; **~terioso** *a* perceptive, discerning

crítica /'kritʃika/ *f* criticism; (*análise*) critique; (*de filme, livro*) review; (*críticos*) critics

criticar /kritʃi'kar/ *vt* criticize; review <*filme, livro*>

crítico /'kritʃiku/ *a* critical □ *m* critic

crivar /kri'var/ *vt* (*furar*) riddle

cri|vel /'krivew/ (*pl* **~veis**) *a* credible

crivo /'krivu/ *m* sieve; (*fig*) scrutiny

crocante /kro'kãtʃi/ *a* crunchy

croché /kro'ʃe/ *m* crochet

crocodilo /kroko'dʒilu/ *m* crocodile

cromo /'kromu/ *m* chrome

cromossomo /kromo'somu/ *m* chromosome

crôni|ca /'kronika/ *f* (*histórica*) chronicle; (*no jornal*) feature; (*conto*) short story; **~co** *a* chronic

cronista /kro'nista/ *m/f* (*de jornal*) feature writer; (*contista*) short story writer; (*historiador*) chronicler

crono|grama /krono'grama/ *m* schedule; **~logia** *f* chronology; **~lógico** *a* chronological; **~metrar** *vt* time

cronômetro /kro'nometru/ *m* stopwatch

croquete /kro'kɛtʃi/ *m* savoury meatball in breadcrumbs

croqui /kro'ki/ *m* sketch

crosta /'krosta/ *f* crust; (*em ferida*) scab

cru /kru/ *a* (*f* **~a**) raw; <*luz, tom, palavra*> harsh; <*linguagem*> crude; <*verdade*> unvarnished, plain

cruci|al /krusi'aw/ (*pl* **~ais**) *a* crucial

crucifi|cação /krusifika'sãw/ *f* crucifixion; **~car** *vt* crucify; **~xo** /ks/ *m* crucifix

cru|el /kru'εw/ (*pl* **~éis**) *a* cruel; **~eldade** *f* cruelty; **~ento** *a* bloody

crupe /'krupi/ *m* croup

crustáceos /krus'tasius/ *m pl* shellfish

cruz /krus/ *f* cross

cruza|da /kru'zada/ *f* crusade; **~do**¹ *m* (*soldado*) crusader

cru|zado² /kru'zadu/ *m* (*moeda*) cruzado; **~zador** *m* cruiser; **~zamento** *m* (*de ruas*) crossroads, junction, (*Amer*) intersection; (*de raças*) cross; **~zar** *vt* cross □ *vi* <*navio*> cruise; **~zar com** pass; **~zar-se** *vpr* cross; <*pessoas*> pass each other; **~zeiro** *m* (*moeda*) cruzeiro; (*viagem*) cruise; (*cruz*) cross

cu /ku/ *m* (*chulo*) arse, (*Amer*) ass

Cuba /'kuba/ *f* Cuba

cubano /ku'banu/ *a & m* Cuban

cúbico /'kubiku/ *a* cubic

cubículo /ku'bikulu/ *m* cubicle

cubis|mo /ku'bizmu/ *m* cubism; **~ta** *a & m/f* cubist

cubo /'kubu/ *m* cube; (*de roda*) hub

cuca /'kuka/ (*fam*) *f* head

cuco /'kuku/ *m* cuckoo; (*relógio*) cuckoo clock

cu|-de-ferro /kudʒi'fεxu/ (*pl* **~s-de-ferro**) (*fam*) *m* swot

cueca /ku'εka/ *f* underpants; *pl* (*Port: de mulher*) knickers

cueiro /ku'eru/ *m* baby wrap

cuia /'kuia/ *f* gourd

cuidado /kui'dadu/ *m* care; **com ~** carefully; **ter** *ou* **tomar ~** be careful; **~so** /o/ *a* careful

cuidar /kui'dar/ *vi* **~ de** take care of; **~-se** *vpr* look after o.s.

cujo /'kuʒu/ *pron* whose

culatra /ku'latra/ *f* breech; **sair pela ~** (*fig*) backfire

culi|nária /kuli'naria/ *f* cookery; **~rio** *a* culinary

culmi|nância /kuwmi'nãsia/ *f* culmination; **~nante** *a* culminating; **~nar** *vi* culminate (**em** in)

cul|pa /'kuwpa/ *f* guilt; **foi ~pa minha** it was my fault; **ter ~pa de** be to blame for; **~pabilidade** *f* guilt; **~pado** *a* guilty □ *m* culprit; **~par** *vt* blame (**de** for); (*na justiça*) find guilty (**de** of); **~par-se** *vpr* take the blame (**de** for); **~pável** (*pl* **~páveis**) *a* culpable, guilty

culti|var /kuwtʃi'var/ *vt* cultivate; grow <*plantas*>; **~vo** *m* cultivation; (*de plantas*) growing

cul|to /'kuwtu/ *a* cultured □ *m* cult; **~tura** *f* culture; (*de terra*) cultivation; **~tural** (*pl* **~turais**) *a* cultural

cumbuca /kũ'buka/ *f* bowl

cume /'kumi/ *m* peak

cúmplice /'kũplisi/ *m/f* accomplice

cumplicidade /kũplisi'dadʒi/ *f* complicity

cumprimen|tar /kũprimẽ'tar/ *vt/i* (*saudar*) greet; (*parabenizar*) compliment; **~to** *m* (*saudação*) greeting; (*elogio*) compliment; (*de lei, ordem*) compliance (**de** with); (*de promessa, palavra*) fulfilment

cumprir /kũ'prir/ *vt* keep <*promessa, palavra*>; comply with <*lei, ordem*>; do <*dever*>; carry out <*obrigações*>; serve <*pena*>; **~ com** keep to □ *vi* **cumpre-nos ir** we should go; **~-se** *vpr* be fulfilled

cúmulo /'kumulu/ *m* height; **é o ~!** that's the limit!

cunha /'kuɲa/ *f* wedge

cunha|da /ku'ɲada/ *f* sister-in-law; **~do** *m* brother-in-law

cunhar /'kuɲar/ vt coin <palavra, expressão>; mint <moedas>

cunho /'kuɲu/ m hallmark

cupim /ku'pĩ/ m termite

cupom /ku'põ/ m coupon

cúpula /'kupula/ f (abóbada) dome; (de abajur) shade; (chefia) leadership; (**reunião de**) ~ summit (meeting)

cura /'kura/ f cure □ m curate, priest

curandeiro /kurã'deru/ m (religioso) faith-healer; (índio) medicine man; (charlatão) quack

curar /ku'rar/ vt cure; dress <ferida>; ~-se vpr be cured

curativo /kura'tʃivu/ m dressing

curá|vel /ku'ravew/ (pl ~veis) a curable

curin|ga /ku'rĩga/ m wild card; ~**gão** m joker

curio|sidade /kuriozi'dadʒi/ f curiosity; ~**so** /o/ a curious □ m (espectador) onlooker

cur|ral /ku'xaw/ (pl ~**rais**) m pen

currículo /ku'xikulu/ m curriculum; (resumo) curriculum vitae, CV

cur|sar /kur'sar/ vt attend <escola, aula>; study <matéria>; ~**so** m course; ~**sor** m cursor

curta-metragem /kurtame'traʒẽ/ (pl ~**s-metragens**) m short (film)

cur|tição /kurtʃi'sãw/ (fam) f enjoyment; ~**tir** vt (fam) enjoy; tan <couro>

curto /'kurtu/ a short; <conhecimento, inteligência> limited; ~-**circuito** (pl ~**s-circuitos**) m short circuit

cur|va /'kurva/ f curve; (de estrada, rio) bend; ~**va fechada** hairpin bend; ~**var** vt bend; ~**var-se** vpr bend; (fig) bow (**a** to); ~**vo** a curved; <estrada> winding

cus|parada /kuspa'rada/ f spit; ~**pe** m spit, spittle; ~**pir** vt/i spit

cus|ta /'kusta/ f **à** ~**ta de** at the expense of; ~**tar** vt cost □ vi (ser difícil) be hard; ~**tar a fazer** (ter dificuldade) find it hard to do; (demorar) take a long time to do; ~**tear** vt finance, fund; ~**teio** m funding; (relação de despesas) costing; ~**to** m cost; **a** ~**to** with difficulty

custódia /kus'tɔdʒia/ f custody

cutelo /ku'telu/ m cleaver

cutícula /ku'tʃikula/ f cuticle

cútis /'kutʃis/ f invar complexion

cutu|car /kutu'kar/ vt (com o cotovelo, joelho) nudge; (com o dedo) poke; (com instrumento) prod

czar /zar/ m tsar

D

da = **de** + **a**

dádiva /'dadʒiva/ f gift; (donativo) donation

dado /'dadu/ m (de jogar) die, dice; (informação) fact, piece of information; pl data

daí /da'i/ adv (no espaço) from there; (no tempo) then; ~ **por diante** from then on; **e** ~? (fam) so what?

dali /da'li/ adv from over there

dália /'dalia/ f dahlia

dal|tônico /daw'toniku/ a colourblind; ~**tonismo** m colourblindness

dama /'dama/ f lady; (em jogos) queen; pl (jogo) draughts, (Amer) checkers; ~ **de honra** bridesmaid

da|nado /da'nadu/ a damned; (zangado) angry; (travesso) naughty; ~**nar-se** vpr be angry; ~**ne-se!** (fam) who cares?

dan|ça /'dãsa/ f dance; ~**çar** vt dance □ vi dance; (fam)

<pessoa> miss out; *<coisa>* go by the board; *<crimonoso>* get caught; **~carino** *m* dancer; **~ceteria** *f* discotheque
da|nificar /danifiˈkar/ *vt* damage; **~ninho** *a* undesirable; **~no** *m* (*pl*) damage; **~noso** /o/ *a* damaging
dantes /ˈdãtʃiʃ/ *adv* formerly
daquela(s), daquele(s) = de + aquela(s), aquele(s)
daqui /daˈki/ *adv* from here; **~ a 2 dias** in 2 days' time); **~ a pouco** in a minute; **~ em diante** from now on
daquilo = de + aquilo
dar /dar/ *vt* give; have *<dormida, lida etc>*; do *<pulo, cambalhota etc>*; cause *<problemas>*; produce *<frutas, leite>*; deal *<cartas>*; (*lecionar*) teach □ *vi* (*ser possível*) be possible; (*ser suficiente*) be enough; **~ com** come across; **~ em** lead to; **ele dá para ator** he'd make a good actor; **~ por** (*considerar como*) consider to be; (*reparar em*) notice; **~-se** *vpr <coisa>* happen; *<pessoa>* get on
dardo /ˈdardu/ *m* dart; (*no atletismo*) javelin
das = de + as
da|ta /ˈdata/ *f* date; **de longa ~** long since; **~tar** *vt/i* date
dati|lografar /datʃilograˈfar/ *vt/i* type; **~lografia** *f* typing; **~lógrafo** *m* typist
de /dʒi/ *prep* of; (*procedência*) from; **~ carro** by car; **trabalho ~ repórter** I work as a reporter
debaixo /dʒiˈbaʃu/ *adv* below; **~ de** under
debalde /dʒiˈbawdʒi/ *adv* in vain
debandada /debãˈdada/ *f* stampede
deba|te /deˈbatʃi/ *m* debate; **~ter** *vt* debate; **~ter-se** *vpr* grapple
debelar /debeˈlar/ *vt* overcome
dé|bil /ˈdɛbiw/ (*pl* **~beis**) *a*

feeble; **~bil mental** retarded (person)
debili|dade /debiliˈdadʒi/ *f* debility; **~tar** *vt* debilitate; **~tar-se** *vpr* become debilitated
debitar /debiˈtar/ *vt* debit
débito /ˈdɛbitu/ *m* debit
debo|chado /deboˈʃadu/ *a* sardonic; **~char** *vt* mock; **~che** /ɔ/ *m* jibe
debruar /debruˈar/ *vt/i* edge
debruçar-se /debruˈsarsi/ *vpr* bend over; **~ sobre** study
debrum /deˈbrũ/ *m* edging
debulhar /debuˈʎar/ *vt* thresh
debu|tante /debuˈtãtʃi/ *f* debutante; **~tar** *vi* debut, make one's debut
década /ˈdɛkada/ *f* decade; **a ~ dos 60** the sixties
deca|dência /dekaˈdẽsia/ *f* decadence; **~dente** *a* decadent
decair /dekaˈir/ *vi* decline; (*degringolar*) go downhill; *<planta>* wilt
decal|car /dekawˈkar/ *vt* trace; **~que** *m* tracing
decapitar /dekapiˈtar/ *vt* decapitate
decatlo /deˈkatlu/ *m* decathlon
de|cência /deˈsẽsia/ *f* decency; **~cente** *a* decent
decepar /deseˈpar/ *vt* cut off
decep|ção /desepˈsãw/ *f* disappointment; **~cionar** *vt* disappoint; **~cionar-se** *vpr* be disappointed
decerto /dʒiˈsɛrtu/ *adv* certainly
deci|dido /desiˈdʒidu/ *a <pessoa>* determined; **~dir** *vt/i* decide; **~dir-se** *vpr* make up one's mind; **~dir-se por** decide on
decíduo /deˈsiduu/ *a* deciduous
decifrar /desiˈfrar/ *vt* decipher
deci|mal /desiˈmaw/ (*pl* **~mais**) *a* decimal
décimo /ˈdɛsimu/ *a & m* tenth; **~ primeiro** eleventh; **~ segundo** twelfth; **~ terceiro** thirteenth;

~ **quarto** fourteenth; ~ **quinto** fifteenth; ~ **sexto** sixteenth; ~ **sétimo** seventeenth; ~ **oitavo** eighteenth; ~ **nono** nineteenth
deci|são /desi'zãw/ *f* decision; ~**sivo** *a* decisive
decla|ração /deklara'sãw/ *f* declaration; ~**rado** *a* <inimigo> sworn; <crente> avowed; <ladrão> self-confessed; ~**rar** *vt* declare
decli|nação /deklina'sãw/ *f* declension; ~**nar** *vt* ~**nar (de)** decline □ *vi* decline; <sol> go down; <chão> slope down
declínio /de'kliniu/ *m* decline
declive /de'klivi/ *m* (downward) slope, incline
decodificar /dekodʒifi'kar/ *vt* decode
deco|lagem /deko'laʒē/ *f* take-off; ~**lar** *vi* take off; (*fig*) get off the ground
decom|por /dekõ'por/ *vt* break down; contort <feições>; ~**por-se** *vpr* break down; <cadáver> decompose; ~**posição** *f* (de cadáver) decomposition
deco|ração /dekora'sãw/ *f* decoration; (aprendizagem) learning by heart; ~**rar** *vt* (adornar) decorate; (aprender) learn by heart, memorize; ~**rativo** *a* decorative; ~**reba** /ɛ/ *f* (fam) *f* rote-learning; ~**ro** /o/ *m* decorum; ~**roso** /o/ *a* decorous
decor|rência /deko'xẽsia/ *f* consequence; ~**rente** *a* resulting (**de** from); ~**rer** *vi* <tempo> elapse; <acontecimento> pass off; (resultar) result (**de** from) □ *m* no ~**rer de** in the course of; **com o** ~**rer do tempo** in time, with the passing of time
deco|tado /deko'tadu/ *a* low-cut; ~**te** /ɔ/ *m* neckline
decrépito /de'krɛpitu/ *a* decrepit
decres|cente /dekre'sẽtʃi/ *a* decreasing; ~**cer** *vi* decrease

decre|tar /dekre'tar/ *vt* decree; declare <estado de sítio>; ~**to** /ɛ/ *m* decree; ~**to-lei** (*pl* ~**tos-leis**) *m* act
decurso /de'kursu/ *m* course
de|dal /de'daw/ (*pl* ~**dais**) *m* thimble; ~**dão** *m* (da mão) thumb; (do pé) big toe
dedetizar /dedetʃi'zar/ *vt* spray with insecticide
dedi|cação /dedʒika'sãw/ *f* dedication; ~**car** *vt* dedicate; devote <tempo>; ~**car-se** *vpr* dedicate o.s. (**a** to); ~**catória** *f* dedication
dedilhar /dedʒi'ʎar/ *vt* pluck
dedo /'dedu/ *m* finger; (do pé) toe; **cheio de** ~**s** all fingers and thumbs; (sem graça) awkward; ~**duro** (*pl* ~**s-duros**) *m* sneak; (político, criminoso) informer
dedução /dedu'sãw/ *f* deduction
dedurar /dedu'rar/ *vt* sneak on; (à polícia) inform on
dedu|tivo /dedu'tʃivu/ *a* deductive; ~**zir** *vt* (descontar) deduct; (concluir) deduce
defa|sado /defa'zadu/ *a* out of step; ~**sagem** *f* gap, lag
defecar /defe'kar/ *vi* defecate
defei|to /de'fejtu/ *m* defect; **botar** ~**to em** find fault with; ~**tuoso** /o/ *a* defective
defen|der /defē'der/ *vt* defend; ~**der-se** *vpr* (virar-se) fend for o.s.; (contra-atacar) defend o.s. (**de** against); ~**siva** *f* **na** ~**siva** on the defensive; ~**sor** *m* defender; (advogado) defence counsel
defe|rência /defe'rẽsia/ *f* deference; ~**rente** *a* deferential
defesa /de'feza/ *f* defence □ *m* defender
defici|ência /defisi'ẽsia/ *f* deficiency; ~**ente** *a* deficient; (física ou mentalmente) handicapped □ *m/f* handicapped person

déficit /'dɛfisitʃi/ (pl **~s**) m deficit

deficitário /defisitʃi'ariu/ a in deficit; <*empresa*> loss-making

definhar /defi'nar/ vi waste away; <*planta*> wither

defi|nição /defini'sãw/ f definition; **~nir** vt define; **~nir-se** vpr (*descrever-se*) define o.s.; (*decidir-se*) come to a decision; (*explicar-se*) make one's position clear; **~nitivo** a definitive; **~nível** (pl **~níveis**) a definable

defla|ção /defla'sãw/ f deflation; **~cionário** a deflationary

deflagrar /defla'grar/ vt set off □ vi break out

defor|mar /defor'mar/ vt misshape; deform <*corpo*>; distort <*imagem*>; **~midade** f deformity

defraudar /defraw'dar/ vt defraud (de of)

defron|tar /defrõ'tar/ vt **~tar com** face; **~te** adv opposite; **~te de** opposite

defumar /defu'mar/ vt smoke

defunto /de'fũtu/ a & m deceased

dege|lar /deʒe'lar/ vt/i thaw; **~lo** /e/ m thaw

degeneração /deʒenera'sãw/ f degeneration

degenerar /deʒene'rar/ vi degenerate (**em** into)

degolar /dego'lar/ vt cut the throat of

degra|dação /degrada'sãw/ f degradation; **~dante** a degrading; **~dar** vt degrade

degrau /de'graw/ m step

degringolar /degrĩgo'lar/ vi deteriorate, go downhill

degustar /degus'tar/ vt taste

dei|tada /dej'tada/ f lie-down; **~tado** a lying down; (*dormindo*) in bed; (*fam: preguiçoso*) idle; **~tar** vt lay down; (*na cama*) put to bed; (*pôr*) put; (*Port: jogar*)

throw □ vi, **~tar-se** vpr lie down; (*ir para cama*) go to bed

dei|xa /'deʃa/ f cue; **~xar** vt leave; (*permitir*) let; **~xar de** (*parar*) stop; (*omitir*) fail; **não pôde ~xar de rir** he couldn't help laughing; **~xar alg nervoso** make s.o. annoyed; **~xar cair** drop; **~xar a desejar** leave a lot to be desired; **~xa (para lá)** (*fam*) never mind, forget it

dela(s) = **de** + **ela(s)**

delatar /dela'tar/ vt report

délavé /dela've/ a invar faded

dele(s) = **de** + **ele(s)**

dele|gação /delega'sãw/ f delegation; **~gacia** f police station; **~gado** m delegate; **~gado de polícia** police chief; **~gar** vt delegate

delei|tar /delej'tar/ vt delight; **~tar-se** vpr delight (**com** in); **~te** m delight; **~toso** /o/ a delightful

delgado /dew'gadu/ a slender

delibe|ração /delibera'sãw/ f deliberation; **~rar** vt/i deliberate

delica|deza /delika'deza/ f delicacy; (*cortesia*) politeness; **~do** a delicate; (*cortês*) polite

delícia /de'lisia/ f delight; **ser uma ~** <*comida*> be delicious; <*sol etc*> be lovely

delici|ar /delisi'ar/ vt delight; **~ar-se** delight (**com** in); **~oso** /o/ a delightful, lovely; <*comida*> delicious

deline|ador /delinia'dor/ m eyeliner; **~ar** vt outline

delin|qüência /delĩ'kwẽsia/ f delinquency; **~qüente** a & m delinquent

deli|rante /deli'rãtʃi/ a rapturous; (*med*) delirious; **~rar** vi go into raptures; <*doente*> be delirious

delírio /de'liriu/ m (*febre*) delirium; (*excitação*) raptures

delito /de'litu/ m crime

delonga /de'lõga/ f delay

delta /'dɛwta/ f delta

dema|gogia /demago'ʒia/ f demagogy; **~gógico** a demagogic; **~gogo** /o/ m demagogue

demais /dʒi'majʃ/ a & adv (muito) very much; (em demasia) too much; **os ~** the rest, the others; **é ~**! (fam) it's great!

deman|da /de'mãda/ f demand; (jurid) action; **~dar** vt sue

demão /de'mãw/ f coat

demar|car /demar'kar/ vt demarcate; **~catório** a demarcation

demasia /dema'zia/ f excess; **em ~** too (much, many)

de|mência /de'mẽsia/ f insanity; (med) dementia; **~mente** a insane; (med) demented

demissão /demi'sãw/ f sacking, dismissal; **pedir ~** resign

demitir /demi't∫ir/ vt sack, dismiss; **~-se** vpr resign

demo|cracia /demokra'sia/ f democracy; **~crata** m/f democrat; **~crático** a democratic; **~cratizar** vt democratize; **~grafia** f demography; **~gráfico** a demographic

demo|lição /demoli'sãw/ f demolition; **~lir** vt demolish

demônio /de'moniu/ m demon

demons|tração /demõstra'sãw/ f demonstration; **~trar** vt demonstrate; **~trativo** a demonstrative

demo|ra /de'mɔra/ f delay; **~rado** a lengthy; **~rar** vi (levar) take; (tardar a voltar, terminar etc) be long; (levar muito tempo) take a long time □ vt delay

dendê /dẽ'de/ m (óleo) palm oil

denegrir /dene'grir/ vt denigrate

dengoso /dẽ'gozu/ a coy

dengue /'dẽgi/ m dengue

denomi|nação /denomina'sãw/ f denomination; **~nar** vt name

denotar /deno'tar/ vt denote

den|sidade /dẽsi'dadʒi/ f density; **~so** a dense

den|tado /dẽ'tadu/ a serrated; **~tadura** f (set of) teeth; (postiça) dentures, false teeth; **~tal** (pl **~tais**) a dental; **~tário** a dental; **~te** m tooth; (de alho) clove; **~te do siso** wisdom tooth; **~tição** f teething; (dentadura) teeth; **~tífrico** m toothpaste; **~tista** m/f dentist

dentre = **de** + **entre**

dentro /'dẽtru/ adv inside; **lá ~** in there; **por ~** on the inside; **~ de** inside; (tempo) within

dentu|ça /dẽ'tusa/ f buck teeth; **~ço** a with buck teeth

denúncia /de'nũsia/ f (à polícia etc) report; (na imprensa etc) disclosure

denunciar /denũsi'ar/ vt (à polícia etc) report; (na imprensa etc) denounce

deparar /depa'rar/ vi **~ com** come across

departamento /departa'mẽtu/ m department

depauperar /depawpe'rar/ vt impoverish

depenar /depe'nar/ vt pluck <aves>; (roubar) fleece

depen|dência /depẽ'dẽsia/ f dependence; pl premises; **~dente** a dependent (**de** on) □ m/f dependant; **~der** vi depend (**de** on)

depi|lação /depila'sãw/ f depilation; **~lar** vt depilate; **~latório** m depilatory cream

deplo|rar /deplo'rar/ vt deplore; **~rável** (pl **~ráveis**) a deplorable

de|poente /depo'ẽt∫i/ m/f witness; **~poimento** /o/ (à polícia) statement; (na justiça, fig) testimony

depois /de'pojs/ adv after(wards); **~ de** after; **~ que** after

depor /de'por/ vi (na polícia) make a statement; (na justiça) give evidence, testify □ *vt* lay down <*armas*>; depose <*rei, presidente*>

depor|tação /deporta'sãw/ *f* deportation; ∼**tar** *vt* deport

deposi|tante /depozi'tãtʃi/ *m/f* depositor; ∼**tar** *vt* deposit; cast <*voto*>; place <*confiança*>

depósito /de'pozitu/ *m* deposit; (*armazém*) warehouse

depra|vação /deprava'sãw/ *f* depravity; ∼**vado** *a* depraved; ∼**var** *vt* deprave

depre|ciação /depresia'sãw/ *f* (*perda de valor*) depreciation; (*menosprezo*) deprecation; ∼**ciar** *vt* (*desvalorizar*) devalue; (*menosprezar*) deprecate; ∼**ciar-se** *vpr* <*bens*> depreciate; <*pessoa*> deprecate o.s.; ∼**ciativo** *a* deprecatory

depre|dação /depreda'sãw/ *f* depredation; ∼**dar** *vt* wreck

depressa /dʒi'prɛsa/ *adv* fast, quickly

depres|são /depre'sãw/ *f* depression; ∼**sivo** *a* depressive

depri|mente /depri'mẽtʃi/ *a* depressing; ∼**mido** *a* depressed; ∼**mir** *vt* depress; ∼**mir-se** *vpr* get depressed

depurar /depu'rar/ *vt* purify

depu|tação /deputa'sãw/ *f* deputation; ∼**tado** *m* deputy, MP, (*Amer*) congressman (*f* -woman); ∼**tar** *vt* delegate

deque /'dɛki/ *m* (sun)deck

deri|va /de'riva/ *f* à ∼**va** adrift; **andar à** ∼**va** drift; ∼**vação** *f* derivation; ∼**var** *vt* derive; (*desviar*) divert □ *vi*, ∼**var-se** *vpr* derive, be derived (**de** from); <*navio*> drift

dermatolo|gia /dermatolo'ʒia/ *f* dermatology; ∼**gista** *m/f* dermatologist

derradeiro /dexa'deru/ *a* last, final

derra|mamento /dexama'mẽtu/

m spill, spillage; ∼**mamento de sangue** bloodshed; ∼**mar** *vt* spill; shed <*lágrimas*>; ∼**mar-se** *vpr* spill; ∼**me** *m* spill, spillage; ∼**me cerebral** stroke

derra|pagem /dexa'paʒẽ/ *f* skidding; (*uma*) skid; ∼**par** *vi* skid

derreter /dexe'ter/ *vt* melt; ∼**-se** *vpr* melt

derro|ta /de'xɔta/ *f* defeat; ∼**tar** *vt* defeat; ∼**tismo** *m* defeatism; ∼**tista** *a & m/f* defeatist

derrubar /dexu'bar/ *vt* knock down; bring down <*governo*>

desaba|far /dʒizaba'far/ *vi* speak one's mind; ∼**fo** *m* outburst

desa|bamento /dʒizaba'mẽtu/ *m* collapse; ∼**bar** *vi* collapse; <*chuva*> pour down

desabotoar /dʒiaboto'ar/ *vt* unbutton

desabri|gado /dʒizabri'gadu/ *a* homeless; ∼**gar** *vt* make homeless

desabrochar /dʒizabro'far/ *vi* blossom, bloom

desaca|tar /dʒizaka'tar/ *vt* defy; ∼**to** *m* (*de pessoa*) disrespect; (*da lei etc*) disregard

desacerto /dʒiza'sertu/ *m* mistake

desacompanhado /dʒizakõpa-'ɲadu/ *a* unaccompanied

desaconse|lhar /dʒizakõse'ʎar/ *vt* advise against; ∼**lhável** (*pl* ∼**lháveis**) *a* inadvisable

desacor|dado /dʒizakor'dadu/ *a* unconscious; ∼**do** /o/ *m* disagreement

desacostu|mado /dʒizakostu-'madu/ *a* unaccustomed; ∼**mar** *vt* ∼**mar alg de** break s.o. of the habit of; ∼**mar-se de** get out of the habit of

desacreditar /dʒizakredʒi'tar/ *vt* discredit

desafeto /dʒiza'fetu/ *m* disaffection

desafi|ador /dʒizafia'dor/ *a* <*tarefa*> challenging; <*pessoa*>

defiant; ～*ar vt* challenge; (*fazer face a*) defy < *perigo, morte*>

desafi|nado /dʒizafi'nadu/ *a* out of tune; ～**nar** *vi* (*cantando*) sing out of tune; (*tocando*) play out of tune □ *vt* put out of tune

desafio /dʒiza'fiu/ *m* challenge

desafivelar /dʒizafive'lar/ *vt* unbuckle

desafo|gar /dʒizafo'gar/ *vt* vent; (*despertar*) relieve; ～**gar-se** *vpr* give vent to one's feelings; ～**go** /o/ *m* (*alívio*) relief

desafo|rado /dʒizafo'radu/ *a* cheeky; ～**ro** /o/ *m* cheek; (*um*) liberty

desafortunado /dʒizafortu'nadu/ *a* unfortunate

desagra|dar /dʒizagra'dar/ *vt* displease; ～**dável** (*pl* ～**dáveis**) *a* unpleasant; ～**do** *m* displeasure

desagravo *m* redress, amends

desagregar /dʒizagre'gar/ *vt* split up; ～**-se** *vpr* split up

desaguar /dʒiza'gwar/ *vt* drain □ *vi* < *rio*> flow (**em** into)

desajeitado /dʒizaʒej'tadu/ *a* clumsy

desajuizado /dʒizaʒui'zadu/ *a* foolish

desajus|tado /dʒizaʒus'tadu/ *a* (*psic*) maladjusted; ～**te** *m* (*psic*) maladjustment

desalen|tar /dʒizalẽ'tar/ *vt* dishearten; ～**tar-se** *vpr* get disheartened; ～**to** *m* discouragement

desali|nhado /dʒizali'nadu/ *a* untidy; ～**nho** *m* untidiness

desalojar /dʒizalo'ʒar/ *vt* turn out < *inquilino*>; flush out < *inimigo, ladrões*>

desamarrar /dʒizama'xar/ *vt* untie □ *vi* cast off

desamarrotar /dʒizamaxo'tar/ *vt* smooth out

desamassar /dʒizama'sar/ *vt* smooth out

desambientado /dʒizãbiẽ'tadu/ *a* unsettled

desampa|rar /dʒizãpa'rar/ *vt* abandon; ～**ro** *m* abandonment

desandar /dʒizã'dar/ *vi* < *molho*> separate; ～ **a** start to

de|sanimar /dʒizani'mar/ *vt* discourage □ *vi* < *pessoa*> lose heart; < *fato*> be discouraging; ～**sânimo** *m* discouragement

desapaixonado /dʒizapajʃo'nadu/ *a* dispassionate

desaparafusar /dʒizaparafu'zar/ *vt* unscrew

desapare|cer /dʒizapare'ser/ *vi* disappear; ～**cimento** *m* disappearance

desapego /dʒiza'pegu/ *m* detachment; (*indiferença*) indifference

desapercebido /dʒizaperse'bidu/ *a* unnoticed

desapertar /dʒizaper'tar/ *vt* loosen

desapon|tamento /dʒizapõta'mẽtu/ *m* disappointment; ～**tar** *vt* disappoint

desapropriar /dʒizapropri'ar/ *vt* expropriate

desapro|vação /dʒizaprova'sãw/ *f* disapproval; ～**var** *vt* disapprove of

desaproveitado /dʒizaprovej'tadu/ *a* wasted

desar|mamento /dʒizarma'mẽtu/ *m* disarmament; ～**mar** *vt* disarm; take down < *barraca*>

desarran|jar /dʒizaxã'ʒar/ *vt* mess up; upset < *estômago*>; ～**jo** *m* mess; (*do estômago*) upset

desarregaçar /dʒizaxega'sar/ *vt* roll down

desarru|mado /dʒizaxu'madu/ *a* untidy; ～**mar** *vt* untidy; unpack < *mala*>

desarticular /dʒizartʃiku'lar/ *vt* dislocate

desarvorado /dʒizarvo'radu/ *a* disoriented, at a loss

desassociar /dʒizasosi'ar/ *vt*

disassociate; ~-se *vpr* disassociate o.s.

desas|trado /dʒizas'tradu/ *a* accident-prone; ~**tre** *m* disaster; ~**troso** /o/ *a* disastrous

desatar /dʒiza'tar/ *vt* untie; ~ **a chorar** dissolve in tears

desatarraxar /dʒizataxa'ʃar/ *vt* unscrew

desaten|cioso /dʒizatẽsi'ozu/ *a* inattentive; ~**to** *a* oblivious (**a** to)

desati|nar /dʒizatʃi'nar/ *vt* bewilder □ *vi* not think straight; ~**no** *m* bewilderment; (*um*) folly

desativar /dʒizatʃi'var/ *vt* deactivate; shut down <*fábrica*>

desatrelar /dʒizatre'lar/ *vt* unhitch

desatualizado /dʒizatuali'zadu/ *a* out-of-date

desavença /dʒiza'vẽsa/ *f* dispute

desavergonhado /dʒizavergo'ɲadu/ *a* shameless

desbancar /dʒizbã'kar/ *vt* outdo

desbaratar /dʒizbara'tar/ *vt* (*desperdiçar*) waste

desbocado /dʒizbo'kadu/ *a* outspoken

desbotar /dʒizbo'tar/ *vt/i* fade

desbra|vador /dʒizbrava'dor/ *m* explorer; ~**var** *vt* explore

desbun|dante /dʒizbũ'dãtʃi/ (*fam*) *a* mind-blowing; ~**dar** (*fam*) *vt* blow the mind of □ *vi* flip, freak out; ~**de** (*fam*) *m* knockout

descabido /dʒiska'bidu/ *a* inappropriate

descafeinado /dʒizkafej'nadu/ *a* decaffeinated

descalabro /dʒiska'labru/ *m* débâcle

descalço /dʒis'kawsu/ *a* barefoot

descambar /dʒiskã'bar/ *vi* deteriorate, degenerate

descan|sar /dʒiskã'sar/ *vt/i* rest; ~**so** *m* rest; (*de prato, copo*) mat

desca|rado /dʒiska'radu/ *a* blatant; ~**ramento** *m* cheek

descarga /dʒis'karga/ *f* (*eletr*) discharge; (*da privada*) flush

descarregar /dʒiskaxe'gar/ *vt* unload <*mercadorias*>; discharge <*poluentes*>; vent <*raiva*> □ *vi* <*bateria*> go flat; ~ **em cima de alg** take it out on s.o.

descarrilhar /dʒiskaxi'ʎar/ *vt/i* derail

descar|tar /dʒiskar'tar/ *vt* discard; ~**tável** (*pl* ~**táveis**) *a* disposable

descascar /dʒiskas'kar/ *vt* peel <*frutas, batatas*>; shell <*nozes*> □ *vi* <*pessoa, pele*> peel

descaso /dʒis'kazu/ *m* indifference

descen|dência /desẽ'dẽsia/ *f* descent; ~**dente** *a* descended □ *m/f* descendant; ~**der** *vi* descend (**de** from)

descentralizar /dʒisẽtrali'zar/ *vt* decentralize

des|cer /de'ser/ *vi* go down; <*avião*> descend; (*do ônibus, trem*) get off; (*do carro*) get out □ *vt* go down <*escada, ladeira*>; scroll down <*página*>; ~**cida** *f* descent

desclassificar /dʒisklasifi'kar/ *vt* disqualify

desco|berta /dʒisko'berta/ *f* discovery; ~**berto** /ɛ/ *a* uncovered; <*conta*> overdrawn; **a** ~**berto** overdrawn; ~**bridor** *m* discoverer; ~**brimento** *m* discovery; ~**brir** *vt* discover; (*expor*) uncover

descolar /dʒisko'lar/ *vt* unstick; (*fam*) (*dar*) give; (*arranjar*) get hold of, rustle up; (*Port*) <*avião*> take off

descom|por /dʒiskõ'por/ *vt* (*censurar*) scold; ~**-se** *vpr* <*pessoa*> lose one's composure; ~**postura** *f* (*estado*) loss of composure; (*censura*) talking-to

descomprometido /dʒiskõpro-me'tʃidu/ a free

descomu|nal /dʒiskomu'naw/ (pl **∼nais**) a extraordinary; (grande) huge

desconcentrar /dʒiskõsẽ'trar/ vt distract

desconcer|tante /dʒiskõser'tãtʃi/ a disconcerting; **∼tar** vt disconcert

desconexo /dʒisko'nɛksu/ a incoherent

desconfi|ado /dʒiskõfi'adu/ a suspicious; **∼ança** f mistrust; **∼ar** vi suspect

desconfor|tável /dʒiskõfor'tavew/ (pl **∼táveis**) a uncomfortable; **∼to** /o/ m discomfort

descongelar /dʒiskõʒe'lar/ vt defrost <geladeira>; thaw <comida>

descongestio|nante /dʒiskõʒest-ʃio'nãtʃi/ a & m decongestant; **∼nar** vt decongest

desconhe|cer /dʒiskoɲe'ser/ vt not know; **∼cido** a unknown □ m stranger

desconsiderar /dʒiskõside'rar/ vt ignore

desconsolado /dʒiskõso'ladu/ a disconsolate

descontar /dʒiskõ'tar/ vt deduct; (não levar em conta) discount

desconten|tamento /dʒiskõtẽta-'mẽtu/ m discontent; **∼te** a discontent

desconto /dʒis'kõtu/ m discount; **dar um ∼** (fig) make allowances

descontra|ção /dʒiskõtra'sãw/ f informality; **∼ído** a informal, casual; **∼ir** vt relax; **∼ir-se** vpr relax

descontro|lar-se /dʒiskõtro'larsi/ vpr <pessoa> lose control; <coisa> go out of control; **∼le** /o/ m lack of control

desconversar /dʒiskõver'sar/ vi change the subject

descortesia /dʒiskorte'zia/ f rudeness

descostu|rar /dʒiskostu'rar/ vt unrip; **∼rar-se** vpr come undone

descrédito /dʒis'krɛdʒitu/ m discredit

descren|ça /dʒis'krẽsa/ f disbelief; **∼te** a sceptical, disbelieving

des|crever /dʒiskre'ver/ vt describe; **∼crição** f description; **∼critivo** a descriptive

descui|dado /dʒiskui'dadu/ a careless; **∼dar** vt neglect; **∼do** m carelessness; (um) oversight

descul|pa /dʒis'kuwpa/ f excuse; **pedir ∼pas** apologize; **∼par** vt excuse; **∼pe!** sorry!; **∼par-se** vpr apologize; **∼pável** (pl **∼páveis**) a excusable

desde /'dezdʒi/ prep since; **∼ que** since

des|dém /dez'dẽj/ m disdain; **∼denhar** vt disdain; **∼nhoso** /o/ a disdainful

desdentado /dʒizdẽ'tadu/ a toothless

desdita /dʒiz'dʒita/ f unhappiness

desdizer /dʒizdʒi'zer/ vt take back, withdraw □ vi take back what one said

desdo|bramento /dʒizdobra-'mẽtu/ m implication; **∼brar** vt (abrir) unfold; break down <dados, contas>; **∼brar-se** vpr unfold; (empenhar-se) go to a lot of trouble, bend over backwards

dese|jar /deze'ʒar/ vt want; (apaixonadamente) desire; **∼jar aco a alg** wish s.o. sth; **∼jável** (pl **∼jáveis**) a desirable; **∼jo** /e/ m wish; (forte) desire; **∼joso** /o/ a desirous

deselegante /dʒizele'gãtʃi/ a inelegant

desemaranhar /dʒizemara'ɲar/ vt untangle

desembaraçado /dʒizībaraˈsadu/ *a* <*pessoa*> confident, nonchalant; ∼**çar-se** *vpr* rid o.s. (**de** of); ∼**ço** *m* confidence, ease

desembarcar /dʒizībarˈkar/ *vt/i* disembark; ∼**que** *m* disembarkation; (*seção do aeroporto*) arrivals

desembocar /dʒizīboˈkar/ *vi* flow

desembolsar /dʒizībowˈsar/ *vt* spend, pay out; ∼**so** /o/ *m* expenditure

desembrulhar /dʒizībruˈʎar/ *vt* unwrap

desembuchar /dʒizībuˈʃar/ (*fam*) *vi* (*desabafar*) get things off one's chest; (*falar logo*) spit it out

desempacotar /dʒizīpakoˈtar/ *vt* unpack

desempatar /dʒizīpaˈtar/ *vt* decide <*jogo*>

desempenhar /dʒizīpeˈɲar/ *vt* perform; play <*papel*>; ∼**nho** *m* performance

desempregado /dʒizīpreˈgadu/ *a* unemployed; ∼**go** /e/ *m* unemployment

desencadear /dʒizīkadʒiˈar/ *vt* set off, trigger

desencaminhar /dʒizīkamiˈɲar/ *vt* lead astray; embezzle <*dinheiro*>

desencantar /dʒizīkãˈtar/ *vt* disenchant

desencontrar-se /dʒizīkõˈtrarsi/ *vpr* miss each other, fail to meet; ∼**tro** *m* failure to meet

desencorajar /dʒizīkoraˈʒar/ *vt* discourage

desenferrujar /dʒizīfexuˈʒar/ *vt* derust <*metal*>; stretch <*pernas*>; brush up <*língua*>

desenfreado /dʒizīfriˈadu/ *a* unbridled

desenganar /dʒizīgaˈnar/ *vt* disabuse; declare incurable <*doente*>

desengonçado /dʒizīgõˈsadu/ *a* <*pessoa*> ungainly

desengrenado /dʒizīgreˈnadu/ *a* <*carro*> in neutral; ∼**nar** *vt* put in neutral <*carro*>; (*tec*) disengage

desenhar /deześˈɲar/ *vt* draw; ∼**nhista** *m/f* drawer; (*industrial*) designer; ∼**nho** /e/ *m* drawing

desenlace /dʒizĩˈlasi/ *m* dénouement, outcome

desenredar /dʒizĩxeˈdar/ *vt* unravel

desenrolar /dʒizĩxoˈlar/ *vt* unroll <*rolo*>

desentender /dʒizĩtẽˈder/ *vt* misunderstand; ∼**der-se** *vpr* (*não se dar bem*) not get on; ∼**dimento** *m* misunderstanding

desenterrar /dʒizĩteˈxar/ *vt* dig up <*cadáver*>; unearth <*informação*>

desentortar /dʒizĩtorˈtar/ *vt* straighten out

desentupir /dʒizĩtuˈpir/ *vt* unblock

desenvolto /dʒizĩˈvowtu/ *a* casual, nonchalant; ∼**tura** *f* casualness, nonchalance; **com** ∼**tura** nonchalantly; ∼**ver** *vt* develop; ∼**ver-se** *vpr* develop; ∼**vimento** *m* development

desequilibrado /dʒizikiliˈbradu/ *a* unbalanced; ∼**librar** *vt* unbalance; ∼**librar-se** *vpr* become unbalanced; ∼**líbrio** *m* imbalance

deserção /dezerˈsãw/ *f* desertion; ∼**tar** *vt/i* desert; ∼**to** /ɛ/ *a* deserted; **ilha** ∼**ta** desert island □ *m* desert; ∼**tor** *m* deserter

desesperado /dʒizispeˈradu/ *a* desperate; ∼**rador** *a* hopeless; ∼**rar** *vt* (*desesperançar*) make despair □ *vi*, ∼**rar-se** *vpr* despair; ∼**ro** /e/ *m* despair

desestabilizar /dʒizistabiliˈzar/ *vt* destabilize

desestimular /dʒizistʃimuˈlar/ *vt* discourage

desfal|car /dʒisfaw'kar/ *vt* embezzle; **~que** *m* embezzlement

desfal|ecer /dʒisfale'ser/ *vt* (*desmaiar*) faint; **~ecimento** *m* faint

desfavor /dʒisfa'vor/ *m* disfavour

desfavo|rável /dʒisfavo'ravew/ (*pl* **~ráveis**) *a* unfavourable; **~recer** *vt* be unfavourable to; treat less favourably <*minorias etc*>

desfazer /dʒisfa'zer/ *vt* undo; unpack <*mala*>; strip <*cama*>; break <*contrato*>; clear up <*mistério*>; **~-se** *vpr* come undone; <*casamento*> break up; <*sonhos*> crumble; **~-se em lágrimas** dissolve into tears

desfe|char /dʒisfe'ʃar/ *vt* throw <*murro, olhar*>; **~cho** /e/ *m* outcome, dénouement

desfeita /dʒis'fejta/ *f* slight, insult

desferir /dʒisfe'rir/ *vt* give <*pontapé*>; launch <*ataque*>; fire <*flecha*>

desfiar /dʒisfi'ar/ *vt* pick the meat off <*frango*>; **~-se** *vpr* <*tecido*> fray

desfigurar /dʒisfigu'rar/ *vt* disfigure; (*fig*) distort

desfi|ladeiro /dʒisfila'deru/ *m* pass; **~lar** *vi* parade; **~le** *m* parade; **~le de modas** fashion show

desflorestamento /dʒisfloresta'mētu/ *m* deforestation

desforra /dʒis'fɔxa/ *f* revenge

desfraldar /dʒisfraw'dar/ *vt* unfurl

desfrutar /dʒisfru'tar/ *vt* enjoy

desgas|tante /dʒizgas'tãtʃi/ *a* wearing, stressful; **~tar** *vt* wear out; **~te** *m* (*de máquina etc*) wear and tear; (*de pessoa*) stress and strain

desgosto /dʒiz'gostu/ *m* sorrow

desgovernar-se /dʒizgover'narsi/ *vpr* go out of control

desgraça /dʒiz'grasa/ *f* misfor-

tune; **~do** *a* wretched □ *m* wretch

desgravar /dʒizgra'var/ *vt* erase

desgrenhado /dʒizgre'ɲadu/ *a* unkempt

desgrudar /dʒizgru'dar/ *vt* unstick; **~-se** *vpr* <*pessoa*> tear o.s. away

desidra|tação /dʒizidrata'sãw/ *f* dehydration; **~tar** *vt* dehydrate

desig|nação /dezigna'sãw/ *f* designation; **~nar** *vt* designate

desi|gual /dʒizi'gwaw/ (*pl* **~guais**) *a* unequal; <*terreno*> uneven; **~gualdade** *f* inequality; (*de terreno*) unevenness

desilu|dir /dʒizilu'dʒir/ *vt* disillusion; **~são** *f* disillusionment

desinfe|tante /dʒizife'tãtʃi/ *a* & *m* disinfectant; **~tar** *vt* disinfect

desinibido /dʒizini'bidu/ *a* uninhibited

desintegrar-se /dʒizĩte'grarsi/ *vpr* disintegrate

desinteres|sado /dʒizĩtere'sadu/ *a* uninterested; **~sante** *a* uninteresting; **~sar-se** *vpr* lose interest (de in); **~se** /e/ *m* disinterest

desis|tência /dezis'tẽsia/ *f* giving up; **~tir** *vt/i* **~tir (de)** give up

desle|al /dʒizle'aw/ (*pl* **~ais**) *a* disloyal; **~aldade** *f* disloyalty

deslei|xado /dʒizle'ʃadu/ *a* sloppy; (*no vestir*) scruffy; **~xo** *m* carelessness; (*no vestir*) scruffiness

desli|gado /dʒizli'gadu/ *a* <*luz, TV*> off; <*pessoa*> absent-minded; **~gar** *vt* turn off <*luz, TV, motor*>; hang up, put down <*telefone*> □ *vi* (*ao telefonar*) hang up, put the phone down

deslindar /dʒizlĩ'dar/ *vt* clear up, solve

desli|zante /dʒizli'zãtʃi/ *a* slippery; <*inflação*> creeping; **~zar** *vi* slip; **~zar-se** *vpr* creep; **~ze** *m* slip; (*fig: erro*) slip-up

deslo|cado a <*membro*> dislocated; (*fig*) out of place; **~car** vt move; (*med*) dislocate; **~carse** vpr move

deslum|brado /dʒizlũ'bradu/ a (*fig*) starry-eyed; **~bramento** m (*fig*) wonderment; **~brante** a dazzling; **~brar** vt dazzle; **~brar-se** vpr (*fig*) be dazzled

desmai|ado /dʒizmaj'adu/ a unconscious; **~ar** vi faint; **~o** m faint

desman|cha-prazeres /dʒizmãʃapra'zeris/ m/f invar spoil-sport; **~char** vt break up; break off <*noivado*>; shatter <*sonhos*>; **~char-se** vpr break up; (*no ar, na água, em lágrimas*) dissolve

desmantelar /dʒizmãte'lar/ vt dismantle

desmarcar /dʒizmar'kar/ vt cancel <*encontro*>

desmascarar /dʒizmaske'rar/ vt unmask

desma|tamento /dʒizmata'mẽtu/ m deforestation; **~tar** vt clear (of forest)

desmedido /dʒizme'didu/ a excessive

desmemoriado /dʒizmemori'adu/ a forgetful

desmen|tido /dʒizmẽ'tʃidu/ m denial; **~tir** vt deny

desmiolado /dʒizmio'ladu/ a brainless

desmontar /dʒizmõ'tar/ vt dismantle

desmorali|zante /dʒizmorali'zãtʃi/ a demoralizing; **~zar** vt demoralize

desmoro|namento /dʒizmorona'mẽtu/ m collapse; **~nar** vt destroy; **~nar-se** vpr collapse

desnatar /dʒizna'tar/ vi skim <*leite*>

desnecessário /dʒiznese'sariu/ a unnecessary

desní|vel /dʒiz'nivew/ (*pl* **~veis**) m difference in height

desnortear /dʒiznortʃi'ar/ vt disorientate, (*Amer*) disorient

desnutrição /dʒiznutri'sãw/ f malnutrition

desobe|decer /dʒizobede'ser/ vt/i **~decer (a)** disobey; **~diência** f disobedience; **~diente** a disobedient

desobrigar /dʒizobri'gar/ vt release (de from)

desobstruir /dʒizobistru'ir/ vt unblock; empty <*casa*>

desocupado /dʒizoku'padu/ a unoccupied

desodorante /dʒizodo'rãtʃi/ m, (*Port*) **desodorizante** /dʒizoduri'zãtʃi/ m deodorant

deso|lação /dezola'sãw/ f desolation; **~lado** a <*lugar*> desolate; <*pessoa*> desolated; **~lar** vt desolate

desones|tidade /dʒizonestʃi'dadʒi/ f dishonesty; **~to** /ɛ/ a dishonest

deson|ra /dʒi'zõxa/ f dishonour; **~rar** vt dishonour; **~roso** /o/ a dishonourable

desor|deiro /dʒizor'deru/ a trouble-making □ m trouble-maker; **~dem** f disorder; **~denado** a disorganized; <*vida*> disordered; **~denar** vt disorganize

desorgani|zação /dʒizorganiza'sãw/ f disorganization; **~zar** vt disorganize; **~zar-se** vpr get disorganized

desorientar /dʒizoriẽ'tar/ vt disorientate, (*Amer*) disorient

desossar /dʒizo'sar/ vt bone

deso|va /dʒi'zɔva/ f roe; **~var** vi spawn

despa|chado /dʒispa'ʃadu/ a efficient; **~chante** m/f (*de mercadorias*) shipping agent; (*de documentos*) documentation agent; **~char** vt deal with; dispatch, forward <*mercadorias*>; **~cho** m dispatch

desparafusar /dʒisparafu'zar/ vt unscrew

despedaçar /dʒispeda'sar/ vt (rasgar) tear to pieces; (quebrar) smash; ~-se vpr <vidro, vaso> smash; <papel, tecido> tear

despe|dida /dʒispe'dʒida/ f farewell; ~dida de solteiro stag night, (Amer) bachelor party; ~dir vt dismiss; sack <empregado>; ~dir-se vpr say goodbye (de to)

despei|tado /dʒispej'tadu/ a spiteful; ~to m spite; a ~to de despite, in spite of

despe|jar /dʒispe'ʒar/ vt pour out <líquido>; empty <recipiente>; evict <inquilino>; ~jo /e/ m (de inquilino) eviction

despencar /dʒispẽ'kar/ vi plummet

despender /dʒispẽ'der/ vt spend <dinheiro>

despensa /dʒis'pẽsa/ f pantry, larder

despentear /dʒispẽtʃi'ar/ vt mess up <cabelo>; mess up the hair of <pessoa>

despercebido /dʒisperse'bidu/ a unnoticed

desper|diçar /dʒisperdʒi'sar/ vt waste; ~dício m waste

desper|tador /dʒisperta'dor/ m alarm clock; ~tar vt rouse <pessoa>; (fig) arouse <interesse, suspeitas etc> □ vi awake

despesa /dʒis'peza/ f expense

des|pido /des'pidu/ a bare, stripped (de of); ~pir vt strip (de of); strip off <roupa>; ~pir-se vpr strip (off), get undressed

despo|jar /dʒispo'ʒar/ vt strip (de of); ~jar-se vpr divest o.s. (de of); ~jo /o/ m spoils, booty; ~jos mortais mortal remains

despontar /dʒispõ'tar/ vi emerge

despor|tista /diʃpur'tiʃta/ (Port) m/f sportsman (f -woman);

~tivo (Port) a sporting; ~to /o/ (Port) m sport; carro de ~to sports car

déspota /'dɛspota/ m/f despot

despótico /des'pɔtʃiku/ a despotic

despovoar /dʒispovo'ar/ vt depopulate

desprender /dʒisprẽ'der/ vt detach; (da parede) take down; ~se vpr come off; (fig) detach o.s.

despreocupado /dʒisprioku'padu/ a unconcerned

despreparado /dʒisprepa'radu/ a unprepared

despretensioso /dʒispretẽsi'ozu/ a unpretentious

desprestigiar /dʒisprestʃiʒi'ar/ vt discredit

desprevenido /dʒispreve'nidu/ a off one's guard, unprepared; apanhar ~ catch unawares

despre|zar /dʒispre'zar/ vt despise; (ignorar) ignore; ~zível (pl ~zíveis) a despicable; ~zo /e/ m contempt

desproporção /dʒispropor'sãw/ f disproportion

desproporcio|nado /dʒispropor-sio'nadu/ a disproportionate; ~nal (pl ~nais) a disproportional

despropositado /dʒispropozi-'tadu/ a (absurdo) preposterous

desprovido /dʒispro'vidu/ a ~ de without

desqualificar /dʒiskwalifi'kar/ vt disqualify

desqui|tar-se /dʒiski'tarsi/ vpr (legally) separate; ~te m (legal) separation

desrespei|tar /dʒizxespej'tar/ vt not respect; (ignorar) disregard; ~to m disrespect; ~toso /o/ a disrespectful

dessa(s), desse(s) = de + essa(s), esse(s)

desta = de + esta

desta|camento /dʒistaka'mẽtu/ m detachment; ~car vt detach;

(*ressaltar*) bring out, make stand out; **~car-se** *vpr* (*desprender-se*) come off; (*corredor*) break away; (*sobressair*) stand out (**sobre** against); **~cável** (*pl* **~cáveis**) *a* detachable; (*cader- no*) pull-out

destam|pado /dʒistãˈpadu/ *a* (*pa- nela*) uncovered; **~par** *vt* re- move the lid of

destapar /dʒistaˈpar/ *vt* uncover

destaque /dʒisˈtaki/ *m* promin- ence; (*coisa, pessoa*) highlight; (*do noticiário*) headline

destas, deste = de + estas, este

destemido /dʒisteˈmidu/ *a* in- trepid, courageous

desterrar /dʒisteˈxar/ *vt* (*exilar*) exile

destes = de + estes

destilar /destiˈlar/ *vt* distil; **~ia** *f* distillery

desti|nado /destʃiˈnadu/ *a* (*fada- do*) destined; **~nar** *vt* intend, mean (**para** for); **~natário** *m* addressee; **~no** *m* (*de viagem*) destination; (*sorte*) fate

destituir /destʃituˈir/ *vt* remove

desto|ante /dʒistoˈãtʃi/ *a* <*sons*> discordant; <*cores*> clashing; **~ar** *vi* **~ar de** clash with

destrancar /dʒistrãˈkar/ *vt* un- lock

destreza /desˈtreza/ *f* skill

destrinchar /dʒistrĩˈʃar/ *vt* (*ex- por*) dissect; (*resolver*) sort out

destro /ˈdestru/ *a* skilful

destro|çar /dʒistroˈsar/ *vt* wreck; **~ços** *m pl* wreckage

destronar /dʒistroˈnar/ *vt* depose

destroncar /dʒistrõˈkar/ *vt* rick

destru|ição /dʒistruiˈsãw/ *f* de- struction; **~idor** *a* destructive ▢ *m* destroyer; **~ir** *vt* destroy

desumano /dʒizuˈmanu/ *a* inhu- man; (*cruel*) inhumane

desunião /dʒizuniˈãw/ *f* disunity

desu|sado /dʒizuˈzadu/ *a* disused; **~so** *m* disuse

desvairado /dʒizvajˈradu/ *a* de- lirious, raving

desvalori|zação /dʒizvaloriza- ˈsãw/ *f* devaluation; **~zar** *vt* de- value

desvanta|gem /dʒizvãˈtaʒẽ/ *f* dis- advantage; **~joso** /o/ *a* disad- vantageous

desve|lar /dʒizveˈlar/ *vt* unveil; uncover <*segredo*>; **~lar-se** *vpr* go to a lot of trouble; **~lo** /e/ *m* great care

desvencilhar /dʒizvẽsiˈʎar/ *vt* ex- tricate, free

desvendar /dʒizvẽˈdar/ *vt* reveal <*segredo*>; solve <*mistério*>

desventura /dʒizvẽˈtura/ *f* misfor- tune; (*infelicidade*) unhappiness

desviar /dʒizviˈar/ *vt* divert <*trânsito, rio, atenção, dinheiro*>; avert <*golpe, suspeitas, olhos*>; **~-se** *vpr* deviate; (*do tema*) di- gress

desvincular /dʒizvĩkuˈlar/ *vt* free

desvio /dʒizˈviu/ *m* diversion; (*do trânsito*) diversion, (*Amer*) de- tour; (*linha ferroviária*) siding

desvirtuar /dʒizvirtuˈar/ *vt* mis- represent <*verdade*>

deta|lhado /detaˈʎadu/ *a* detailed; **~lhar** *vt* detail; **~lhe** *m* detail

detec|tar /detekˈtar/ *vt* detect; **~tive** (*Port*) *m veja* **detetive**; **~tor** *m* detector

de|tenção /detẽˈsãw/ *f* (*prisão*) detention; **~tentor** *m* holder; **~ter** *vt* (*ter*) hold; (*prender*) de- tain

detergente /deterˈʒetʃi/ *m* deter- gent

deterio|ração /deterioraˈsãw/ *f* deterioration; **~rar** *vt* damage; **~rar-se** *vpr* deteriorate

determi|nação /determinaˈsãw/ *f* determination; **~nado** *a* (*certo*) certain; (*resoluto*) determined; **~nar** *vt* determine

detestar /detesˈtar/ *vt* hate

detetive /deteˈtʃivi/ *m* detective

detido /de'tʃidu/ *pp de* **deter** □ *a* thorough □ *m* detainee

detonar /deto'nar/ *vt* detonate; (*fam: criticar*) pull to pieces □ *vi* detonate

detrás /de'traʃ/ *adv* behind □ *prep* ~ **de** behind

detrito /de'tritu/ *m* detritus

deturpar /detur'par/ *vt* misrepresent, distort

deus /dews/ *m* (*f* **deusa**) god (*f* goddess); ~**-dará** *m ao* ~**-dará** at the mercy of chance

devagar /dʒiva'gar/ *adv* slowly

deva|near /devani'ar/ *vi* daydream; ~**neio** *m* daydream

devas|sar /deva'sar/ *vt* expose; ~**sidão** *f* debauchery; ~**so** *a* debauched

devastar /devas'tar/ *vt* devastate

de|vedor /deve'dor/ *a* debit □ *m* debtor; ~**ver** *vt* owe □ *vaux* ~**ve fazer** (*obrigação*) he has to do; ~**ve chegar** (*probabilidade*) he should arrive; ~**ve ser** (*suposição*) he must be; ~**ve ter ido** he must have gone; ~**v(er)ia fazer** he ought to do; ~**v(er)ia ter feito** he ought to have done; ~**vidamente** *adv* duly; ~**vido** *a* due (**a** to)

devoção /devo'sãw/ *f* devotion

de|volução /devolu'sãw/ *f* return; ~**volver** *vt* return

devorar /devo'rar/ *vt* devour

devo|tar /devo'tar/ *vt* devote; ~**tar-se** *vpr* devote o.s. (**a** to); ~**to** /ɔ/ *a* devout

dez /des/ *a & m* ten

dezanove /dza'nɔv/ (*Port*) *a & m* nineteen

dezas|seis /dʒa'sejʃ/ (*Port*) *a & m* sixteen; ~**sete** /ɛ/ (*Port*) *a & m* seventeen

dezembro /de'zẽbru/ *m* December

deze|na /de'zena/ *f* ten; **uma** ~ (**de**) about ten; ~**nove** /ɔ/ *a & m* nineteen

dezes|seis /dʒize'sejʃ/ *a & m* sixteen; ~**sete** /ɛ/ *a & m* seventeen

dezoito /dʒi'zojtu/ *a & m* eighteen

dia /'dʒia/ *m* ~ **a** day; **de** ~ by day; **(no)** ~ **20 de julho** (on) July 20th; ~ **de folga** day off; ~ **útil** working day; **~-a-~** *m* everyday life

dia|bete /dʒia'bɛtʃi/ *f* diabetes; ~**bético** *a & m* diabetic

dia|bo /dʒi'abu/ *m* devil; ~**bólico** *a* diabolical, devilish; ~**brete** /e/ *m* little devil; ~**brura** (*de criança*) bit of mischief; *pl* mischief

diadema /dʒia'dema/ *m* tiara

diafragma /dʒia'fragima/ *m* diaphragm

dia|gnosticar /dʒiagnostʃi'kar/ *vt* diagnose; ~**gnóstico** *m* diagnosis □ *a* diagnostic

diago|nal /dʒiago'naw/ (*pl* ~**nais**) *a & f* diagonal

diagra|ma /dʒia'grama/ *m* diagram; ~**mação** *f* design; ~**mador** *m* designer; ~**mar** *vt* design < *livro, revista*>

dialect- (*Port*) *veja* **dialet-**

dia|lética /dʒia'lɛtʃika/ *f* dialectics; ~**leto** /ɛ/ *m* dialect

dialogar /dʒialo'gar/ *vi* talk; (*pol*) hold talks

diálogo /dʒi'alogu/ *m* dialogue

diamante /dʒia'mãtʃi/ *m* diamond

diâmetro /dʒi'ametru/ *m* diameter

dian|te /dʒi'ãtʃi/ *adv* **de ... em** ~**te** from ... on(wards); ~**te de** (*enfrentando*) faced with; (*perante*) before; ~**teira** *f* lead; ~**teiro** *a* front

diapasão /dʒiapa'zãw/ *m* tuning-fork

diapositivo /dʒiapozi'tʃivu/ *m* transparency

diá|ria /dʒi'aria/ *f* daily rate; ~**rio** *a* daily

diarista /dʒia'rista/ *m/f* day labourer; (*faxineira*) daily (help)

diarréia

diploma

diarréia /dʒiaˈxɛja/ f diarrhoea

dica /ˈdʒika/ f tip, hint

dicção /dʒikˈsãw/ f diction

dicionário /dʒisioˈnariu/ m dictionary

didáti|ca /dʒiˈdatʃika/ f teaching methodology; ~**co** a teaching; <*livro*> educational; <*estilo*> didactic

die|ta /dʒiˈɛta/ f diet; **de** ~**ta** on a diet; ~**tista** m/f dietician

difa|mação /dʒifamaˈsãw/ f defamation; ~**mar** vt defame; ~**matório** a defamatory

diferen|ça /dʒifeˈrẽsa/ f difference; ~**cial** (pl ~**ciais**) a & f differential; ~**ciar** vt differentiate; ~**ciar-se** vpr differ; ~**te** a different

dife|rimento /dʒiferiˈmẽtu/ m deferment; ~**rir** vt defer □ vi differ

difí|cil /dʒiˈfisiw/ (pl ~**ceis**) a difficult; (*improvável*) unlikely

dificilmente /dʒifisiwˈmẽtʃi/ adv ~ **poderá fazê-lo** he's unlikely to be able to do it

dificul|dade /dʒifikuwˈdadʒi/ f difficulty; ~**tar** vt make difficult

difteria /dʒifteˈria/ f diphtheria

difun|dir /dʒifũˈdʒir/ vt spread; (*pela rádio*) broadcast; diffuse <*luz, calor*>; ~**dir-se** vpr spread

difu|são /dʒifuˈzãw/ f diffusion; ~**so** a diffuse

dige|rir /dʒiʒeˈrir/ vt digest; ~**rível** (pl ~**ríveis**) a digestible

diges|tão /dʒiʒesˈtãw/ f digestion; ~**tivo** a digestive

digi|tal /dʒiʒiˈtaw/ (pl ~**tais**) a digital; **impressão** ~ **tal** fingerprint; ~**tar** vt key

dígito /ˈdʒiʒitu/ m digit

digladiar /dʒigladʒiˈar/ vi do battle

dig|nar-se /dʒigˈnarsi/ vpr deign (**de** to); ~**nidade** f dignity; ~**nificar** vt dignify; ~**no** a

worthy (**de** of); (*decoroso*) dignified

dilace|rante /dʒilaseˈratʃi/ a <*dor*> excruciating; ~**rar** vt tear to pieces

dilapidar /dʒilapiˈdar/ vt squander

dilatar /dʒilaˈtar/ vt expand; (*med*) dilate; ~**se** vpr expand; (*med*) dilate

dilema /dʒiˈlema/ m dilemma

diletante /dʒileˈtãtʃi/ a & m/f dilettante

dili|gência /dʒiliˈʒẽsia/ f diligence; (*carruagem*) stagecoach; ~**gente** a diligent, hard-working

diluir /dʒiluˈir/ vt dilute

dilúvio /dʒiˈluviu/ m deluge

dimen|são /dʒimẽˈsãw/ f dimension; ~**sionar** vt size up

diminu|ição /dʒiminuiˈsãw/ f reduction; ~**ir** vt reduce □ vi lessen; <*carro, motorista*> slow down; ~**tivo** a & m diminutive; ~**to** a minute

Dinamarca /dʒinaˈmarka/ f Denmark

dinamar|quês /dʒinamarˈkes/ (f ~**quesa**) a Danish □ m Dane

dinâmi|ca /dʒiˈnamika/ f dynamics; ~**co** a dynamic

dina|mismo /dʒinaˈmizmu/ m dynamism; ~**mite** f dynamite

dínamo /ˈdʒinamu/ m dynamo

dinastia /dʒinasˈtʃia/ f dynasty

dinda /ˈdʒĩda/ (*fam*) f godmother

dinheiro /dʒiˈɲeru/ m money

dinossauro /dʒinoˈsawru/ m dinosaur

diocese /dʒioˈsɛzi/ f diocese

dióxido /dʒiˈɔksidu/ m dioxide; ~ **de carbono** carbon dioxide

diplo|ma /dʒiˈploma/ m diploma; ~**macia** f diplomacy; ~**mar-se** vpr take one's diploma; ~**mata** m/f diplomat □ a diplomatic; ~**mático** a diplomatic

direção /dʒire'sãw/ f (sentido) direction; (de empresa) management; (condução de carro) driving; (manuseio do volante) steering

direct- (Port) veja **diret-**

direi|ta /dʒi'rejta/ f right; **~tinho** adv exactly right; **~tista** a rightwing □ m/f rightwinger, rightist; **~to** a right; (ereto) straight □ adv properly □ m right

direi|tas /dʒi'retas/ f pl direct (presidential) elections; **~to** a direct □ adv directly; **~tor** m director; (de escola) headteacher; (de jornal) editor; **~tor-gerente** managing director; **~toria** f (diretores) board of directors; (sala) boardroom; **~tório** m directory; **~triz** f directive

diri|gente /dʒiri'ʒẽtʃi/ a leading □ m/f leader; **~gir** vt direct; manage <empresa>; drive <carro>; **~gir-se** vpr (ir) make one's way; **~gir-se a** (falar com) address

dis|cagem /dʒis'kaʒe/ f dialling; **~car** vt/i dial

discente /dʒi'sẽtʃi/ a **corpo ~** student body

discer|nimento /dʒiserni'mẽtu/ m discernment; **~nir** vt discern

discipli|na /dʒisi'plina/ f discipline; **~nador** a disciplinary; **~nar** vt discipline

discípulo /dʒi'sipulu/ m disciple

disc-jóquei /dʒisk'ʒokej/ m discjockey

disco /'dʒisku/ m disc; (de música) record; (no atletismo) discus □ (fam) f disco; **~ flexível/rígido** floppy/hard disk; **~ laser** CD, compact disc; **~ voador** flying saucer

discor|dante /dʒiskor'dãtʃi/ a conflicting; **~dar** vi disagree (de with)

discote|ca /dʒisko'tɛka/ f discotheque; **~cário** m DJ

discre|pância /dʒiskre'pãsia/ f discrepancy; **~pante** a inconsistent; **~par** vi diverge (de from)

dis|creto /dʒis'krɛtu/ a discreet; **~crição** f discretion

discrimi|nação /dʒiskrimina-'sãw/ f discrimination; (descrição) description; **~nar** vt discriminate; **~natório** a discriminatory

discur|sar /dʒiskur'sar/ vi speak; **~so** m speech

discussão /dʒisku'sãw/ f discussion; (briga) argument

discu|tir /dʒisku'tʃir/ vt/i discuss; (brigar) argue; **~tível** (pl **~tíveis**) a debatable

disenteria /dʒizẽte'ria/ f dysentery

disfar|çar /dʒisfar'sar/ vt disguise; **~çar-se** vpr disguise o.s.; **~ce** m disguise

dis|léxico /dʒiz'lɛtʃiku/ a & m dyslexic; **~lexia** f dyslexia; **~léxico** a & m dyslexic

dispa|rada /dʒispa'rada/ f bolt; **~rado** adv **o melhor ~rado** the best by a long way; **~rar** vt fire <arma> □ vi (com arma) fire; <preços, inflação> shoot up; <corredor> surge ahead

disparate /dʒispa'ratʃi/ m piece of nonsense; pl nonsense

dis|pêndio /dʒis'pẽdʒiu/ m expenditure; **~pendioso** /o/ a costly

dispen|sa /dʒis'pẽsa/ f exemption; **~sar** vt (distribuir) dispense; (isentar) exempt (de from); (prescindir de) dispense with; **~sável** (pl **~sáveis**) a dispensable

dispersar /dʒisper'sar/ vt disperse; waste <energias> □ vi, **~-se** vpr disperse

disperso /dʒis'persu/ adj scattered

dispo|nibilidade /dʒisponibili-'dadʒi/ *f* availability; **~nível** (*pl* **~níveis**) *a* available

dis|por /dʒis'por/ *vt* arrange □ *vi* **~por de** have at one's disposal; **~por-se** *vpr* form up □ *m* **ao seu ~por** at your disposal; **~posição** *f* (*vontade*) willingness; (*arranjo*) arrangement; (*de espírito*) frame of mind; (*de testamento etc*) provision; **à ~posição de alg** at s.o.'s disposal; **~positivo** *m* device; **~posto** *a* prepared, willing (**a** to)

dispu|ta /dʒis'puta/ *f* dispute; **~tar** *vt* dispute; (*tentar ganhar*) compete for

disquete /dʒis'ketʃi/ *m* diskette, floppy (disk)

dissabores /dʒisa'boris/ *m pl* troubles

disseminar /dʒisemi'nar/ *vt* disseminate

dissertação /dʒiserta'sãw/ *f* dissertation, lecture

dissi|dência /dʒisi'dẽsia/ *f* dissidence; **~dente** *a* & *m* dissident

dissídio /dʒi'sidʒiu/ *m* dispute

dissimular /dʒisimu'lar/ *vt* hide □ *vi* dissimulate

disso = **de** + **isso**

dissipar /dʒisi'par/ *vt* clear <*nevoeiro*>; dispel <*dúvidas, suspeitas, ilusões*>; dissipate <*fortuna*>; **~-se** *vpr* <*nevoeiro*> clear; <*dúvidas etc*> be dispelled

dissolu|ção /dʒisolu'sãw/ *f* dissolution; **~to** *a* dissolute

dissolver /dʒisow'ver/ *vt* dissolve; **~-se** *vpr* dissolve

dissuadir /dʒisua'dʒir/ *vt* dissuade (**de** from)

distância /dʒis'tãsia/ *f* distance

distan|ciar /dʒistãsi'ar/ *vt* distance; **~ciar-se** *vpr* distance o.s.; **~te** *a* distant

disten|der /dʒistẽ'der/ *vt* stretch <*pernas*>; relax <*músculo*>; **~der-se** *vpr* relax; **~são** *f*

(*med*) pull; **~são muscular** pulled muscle

distin|ção /dʒistʃĩ'sãw/ *f* distinction; **~guir** *vt* distinguish (**de** from); **~guir-se** *vpr* distinguish o.s.; **~tivo** *a* distinctive □ *m* badge; **~to** *a* distinct; <*senhor*> distinguished

disto = **de** + **isto**

distor|ção /dʒistor'sãw/ *f* distortion; **~cer** *vt* distort

distra|ção /dʒistra'sãw/ *f* distraction; **~ído** *a* absent-minded; **~ir** *vt* distract; (*divertir*) amuse; **~ir-se** *vpr* be distracted; (*divertir-se*) amuse o.s.

distribu|ição /dʒistribui'sãw/ *f* distribution; **~idor** *m* distributor; **~idora** *f* distributor, distribution company; **~ir** *vt* distribute

distrito /dʒis'tritu/ *m* district

distúrbio /dʒis'turbiu/ *m* trouble

di|tado /dʒi'tadu/ *m* dictation; (*provérbio*) saying; **~tador** *m* dictator; **~tadura** *f* dictatorship; **~tame** *m* dictate; **~tar** *vt* dictate; **~tatorial** (*pl* **~tatoriais**) *a* dictatorial

dito /'dʒitu/ *a* **e feito** no sooner said than done □ *m* remark

ditongo /dʒi'tõgu/ *m* diphthong

DIU /'dʒiu/ *m* IUD, coil

diurno /dʒi'urnu/ *a* day

divã /dʒi'vã/ *m* couch

divagar /dʒiva'gar/ *vi* digress

diver|gência /dʒiver'ʒẽsia/ *a* divergence; **~gente** *a* divergent; **~gir** *vi* diverge (**de** from); **~são** *f* diversion; (*divertimento*) amusement; **~sidade** *f* diversity; **~sificar** *vt/i* diversify; **~so** /ɛ/ *a* (*diferente*) diverse; *pl* (*vários*) several; **~tido** *a* (*engraçado*) funny; (*que se curte*) enjoyable; **~timento** *m* enjoyment, fun; (*um*) amusement; **~tir** *vt* amuse; **~tir-se** *vpr* enjoy o.s., have fun

dívida /'dʒivida/ f debt; ~ **externa** foreign debt

divi|dendo /dʒivi'dẽdu/ m dividend; ~**dido** a <pessoa> torn; ~**dir** vt divide; (compartilhar) share; ~**dir-se** vpr be divided

divindade /dʒivĩ'dadʒi/ f divinity

divino /dʒi'vinu/ a divine

divi|sa /dʒi'viza/ f (lema) motto; (galão) stripes; (fronteira) border; pl foreign currency; ~**são** f division; ~**sória** f partition

divorci|ado /dʒivorsi'adu/ a divorced □ m divorcé (f divorcée); ~**ar** vt divorce; ~**ar-se** vpr get divorced; ~**ar-se de** divorce

divórcio /dʒi'vɔrsiu/ m divorce

divul|gado /dʒivuw'gadu/ a widespread; ~**gar** vt spread; publish <notícia>; divulge <segredo>; ~**gar-se** vpr be spread

dizer /dʒi'zer/ vt say; ~ **a alg que** tell sb that; ~ **para alg fazer** tell s.o. to do □ vi ~ **com** go with; ~**-se** vpr claim to be □ m saying

dizimar /dʒizi'mar/ vt decimate

do = **de** +**o**

dó /dɔ/ m pity; **dar** ~ be pitiful; **ter** ~ **de** feel sorry for

do|ação /doa'sãw/ f donation; ~**ador** m donor; ~**ar** vt donate

do|bra /'dɔbra/ f fold; (de calça) turn-up, (Amer) cuff; ~**bradiça** f hinge; ~**bradiço** a pliable; ~**brado** a (duplo) double; ~**brar** vt (duplicar) double; (fazer dobra em) fold; (curvar) bend; go round <esquina>; ring <sinos>; (Port) dub <filme> □ vi double; <sinos> ring; ~**brar-se** vpr bend; ~**bro** m double

doca /'dɔka/ f dock

doce /'dosi/ a sweet; <água> fresh □ m sweet; ~ **de leite** fudge

docente /do'sẽtʃi/ a teaching; **corpo** ~ teaching staff, (Amer) faculty

dócil /'dɔsiw/ (pl ~**ceis**) a docile

documen|tação /dokumẽta'sãw/ f documentation; ~**tar** vt document; ~**tário** a & m documentary; ~**to** m document

doçura /do'sura/ f sweetness

dodói /do'dɔj/ (fam) m **ter** ~ have a pain □ a poorly, ill

doen|ça /do'ẽsa/ f illness; (infecciosa, fig) disease; ~ **da vaca louca** mad cow disease; ~**te** a ill; ~**tio** a <criança, aspecto> sickly; <interesse, curiosidade> morbid

doer /do'er/ vi hurt; <cabeça, músculo> ache

dog|ma /'dɔgima/ m dogma; ~**mático** a dogmatic

doido /'dojdu/ a crazy

dois /dojs/ a & m (f **duas**) two

dólar /'dɔlar/ m dollar

dolo|rido /dolo'ridu/ a sore; ~**roso** /o/ a painful

dom /dõ/ m gift

do|mador /doma'dor/ m tamer; ~**mar** vt tame

doméstica /do'mɛstʃika/ f housemaid

domesticar /domestʃi'kar/ vt domesticate

doméstico /do'mɛstʃiku/ a domestic

domi|ciliar /domisili'ar/ a home; ~**cílio** m home

domi|nação /domina'sãw/ f domination; ~**nador** a domineering; ~**nante** a dominant; ~**nar** vt dominate; have a command of <língua>; ~**nar-se** vpr control o.s.

domin|go /do'mĩgu/ m Sunday; ~**gueiro** a Sunday

domini|cal /domini'kaw/ (pl ~**cais**) a Sunday; ~**cano** a & m Dominican

domínio /do'miniu/ m command

dona /'dɔna/ f owner; **Dona** (com nome) Miss; ~ **de casa** f housewife

donativo /dona'tʃivu/ m donation

donde /ˈdõdʒi/ *adv* from where; (*motivo*) from whence

dono /ˈdonu/ *m* owner

donzela /dõˈzɛla/ *f* maiden

dopar /doˈpar/ *vt* drug

dor /dor/ *f* pain; (*menos aguda*) ache; **~ de cabeça** headache

dor|mente /dorˈmẽtʃi/ *a* numb □ *m* sleeper; **~mida** *f* sleep; **~minhoco** /o/ *m* sleepyhead; **~mir** *vi* sleep; **~mitar** *vi* doze; **~mitório** *m* bedroom; (*comunitário*) dormitory

dorso /ˈdorsu/ *m* back; (*de livro*) spine

dos = **de** + **os**

do|sagem /doˈzaʒẽ/ *f* dosage; **~sar** *vt* moderate; **~se** /ɔ/ *f* dose; (*de uísque etc*) shot, measure

dossiê /dosiˈe/ *m* file

do|tação /dotaˈsãw/ *f* endowment; **~tado** *a* gifted; **~tado de** endowed with; (*equipado com*) equipped with; **~tar** *vt* endow (*de* with); **~te** /ɔ/ *m* (*de noiva*) dowry; (*dom*) endowment

dou|rado /doˈradu/ *a* (*de cor*) golden; (*revestido de ouro*) gilded, gilt □ *m* gilt; **~rar** *vt* gild

dou|to /ˈdotu/ *a* learned; **~tor** *m* doctor; **~torado** *m* doctorate, PhD; **~trina** *f* doctrine; **~trinar** *vt* indoctrinate

doze /ˈdozi/ *a* & *m* twelve

dragão /draˈgãw/ *m* dragon

dragar /draˈgar/ *vt* dredge

drágea /ˈdraʒia/ *f* lozenge

dra|ma /ˈdrama/ *m* drama; **~malhão** *m* melodrama; **~mático** *a* dramatic; **~matizar** *vt* dramatize; **~maturgo** *m* dramatist, playwright

drapeado /drapiˈadu/ *a* draped

drástico /ˈdrastʃiku/ *a* drastic

dre|nagem /dreˈnaʒẽ/ *f* drainage; **~nar** *vt* drain; **~no** /ɛ/ *m* drain

driblar /driˈblar/ *vt* (*em futebol*) dribble round, beat; (*fig*) get round

drinque /ˈdrĩki/ *m* drink

drive /ˈdrajvi/ *m* disk drive

dro|ga /ˈdrɔga/ *f* drug; (*fam*) (*coisa sem valor*) dead loss; (*coisa chata*) drag □ *int* damn; **~gado** *a* on drugs □ *m* drug addict; **~gar** *vt* drug; **~gar-se** *vpr* take drugs; **~garia** *f* dispensing chemist's, pharmacy

duas /ˈduas/ *veja* **dois**

dúbio /ˈdubiu/ *a* dubious

dub|lagem /duˈblaʒẽ/ *f* dubbing; **~lar** *vt* dub <*filme*>; mime <*música*>; **~lê** *m* double

ducentésimo /dusẽˈtezimu/ *a* two-hundredth

ducha /ˈduʃa/ *f* shower

ducto /ˈduktu/ *m* duct

duelo /duˈɛlu/ *m* duel

duende /duˈẽdʒi/ *m* elf

dueto /duˈetu/ *m* duet

duna /ˈduna/ *f* dune

duodécimo /duoˈdɛsimu/ *a* twelfth

duodeno /duoˈdenu/ *m* duodenum

dupla /ˈdupla/ *f* pair, duo; <*no tênis*> doubles

duplex /duˈpleks/ *a invar* two-floor □ *m invar* two-floor apartment, (*Amer*) duplex

dupli|car /dupliˈkar/ *vt/i* double; **~cidade** *f* duplicity; **~cata** *f* duplicate

duplo /ˈduplu/ *a* double

duque /ˈduki/ *m* duke; **~sa** /e/ *f* duchess

du|ração /duraˈsãw/ *f* duration; **~radouro** *a* lasting; **~rante** *prep* during; **~rar** *vi* last; **~rável** (*pl* **~ráveis**) *a* durable

durex /duˈreks/ *m invar* sellotape

du|reza /duˈreza/ *f* hardness; **~ro** *a* hard; (*fam: sem dinheiro*) hard up, broke

dúvida /ˈduvida/ *f* doubt; (*pergunta*) query

duvi|dar /duviˈdar/ *vt/i* doubt; **~doso** /o/ *a* doubtful

duzentos /duˈzẽtus/ *a* & *m* two hundred

dúzia /ˈduzia/ *f* dozen

E

e /i/ *conj* and

ébano /'ɛbanu/ *m* ebony

ébrio /'ɛbriu/ *a* drunk □ *m* drunkard

ebulição /ebuli'sãw/ *f* boiling

eclesiástico /eklezi'astʃiku/ *a* ecclesiastical

eclético /e'klɛtʃiku/ *a* eclectic

eclip|sar /eklip'sar/ *vt* eclipse; **~se** *m* eclipse

eclodir /eklo'dʒir/ *vi* emerge; (*estourar*) break out; *<flor>* open

eco /'ɛku/ *m* echo; **ter ~** have repercussions; **~ar** *vt/i* echo

eco|logia /ekolo'ʒia/ *f* ecology; **~lógico** *a* ecological; **~logista** *m/f* ecologist

eco|nomia /ekono'mia/ *f* economy; (*ciência*) economics; *pl* (*dinheiro poupado*) savings; **~nômico** *a* economic; (*rentável, barato*) economical; **~nomista** *m/f* economist; **~nomizar** *vt* save □ *vi* economize

écran /ɛ'krã/ (*Port*) *m* screen

eczema /ek'zema/ *m* eczema

edição /edʒi'sãw/ *f* edition; (*de filmes*) editing

edificante /edʒifi'kãtʃi/ *a* edifying

edifício /edʒi'fisiu/ *m* building

Edimburgo /edʒi'burgu/ *f* Edinburgh

edi|tal /edʒi'taw/ (*pl* **~tais**) *m* announcement; **~tar** *vt* publish; (*comput*) edit; **~to** *m* edict; **~tor** *m* publisher; **~tora** *f* publishing company; **~torial** (*pl* **~toriais**) *a* publishing □ *m* editorial

edredom /edre'dõ/, *m*, (*Port*) **edredão** /edre'dãw/ *m* quilt

educa|ção /eduka'sãw/ *f* (*ensino*) education; (*polidez*) good manners; **é falta de ~ção** it's rude; **~cional** (*pl* **~cionais**) *a* education

edu|cado /edu'kadu/ *a* polite; **~car** *vt* educate; **~cativo** *a* educational

EEB /ee'be/ *f* BSE

efeito /e'fejtu/ *m* effect; **fazer ~** have an effect; **para todos os ~s** to all intents and purposes; **~ colateral** side effect; **~ estufa** greenhouse effect

efêmero /e'fêmeru/ *a* ephemeral

efeminado /efemi'nadu/ *a* effeminate

efervescente /eferve'sẽtʃi/ *a* effervescent

efe|tivar /efetʃi'var/ *vt* bring into effect; (*contratar*) make a permanent member of staff; **~tivo** *a* real, effective; *<cargo, empregado>* permanent; **~tuar** *vt* carry out, effect

efi|cácia /efi'kasia/ *f* effectiveness; **~caz** *a* effective

efi|ciência /efisi'ẽsia/ *f* efficiency; **~ente** *a* efficient

efígie /e'fiʒi/ *f* effigy

Egeu /e'ʒew/ *a & m* Aegean

égide /'ɛʒidʒi/ *f* aegis

egípcio /e'ʒipsiu/ *a & m* Egyptian

Egito /e'ʒitu/ *m* Egypt

ego /'ɛgu/ *m* ego; **~cêntrico** *a* self-centred, egocentric; **~ísmo** *m* selfishness; **~ísta** *a* selfish □ *m/f* egoist □ *m* (*de rádio etc*) earplug

égua /'ɛgwa/ *f* mare

eis /ejs/ *adv* (*aqui está*) here is/are; (*isso é*) that is

eixo /'ejʃu/ *m* axle; (*mat, entre cidades*) axis; **pôr nos ~s** set straight

ela /'ɛla/ *pron* she; (*coisa*) it; (*com preposição*) her

elaborar /elabo'rar/ *vt* (*fazer*) make, produce; (*desenvolver*) work out

elasticidade /elastʃisi'dadʒi/ *f* (*de coisa*) elasticity; (*de pessoa*) suppleness

elástico /e'lastʃiku/ a elastic □ m
(de borracha) elastic band; (de
calcinha etc) elastic
ele /'eli/ pron he; (coisa) it; (com
preposição) him; (coisa) it
electr- (Port) veja **eletr-**
eléctrico /i'lɛktriku/ (Port) m
tram; (Amer) streetcar □ a veja
elétrico
elefante /ele'fãtʃi/ m elephant
ele|gância /ele'gãsia/ f elegance;
~**gante** a elegant
eleger /ele'ʒer/ vt elect; ~**-se** vpr
get elected
elegia /ele'ʒia/ f elegy
elei|ção /elej'sãw/ f election; ~**to**
a elected, elect; <povo> chosen;
~**tor** m voter; ~**torado** m
electorate; ~**toral** (pl ~**to-
rais**) a electoral
elemen|tar /eleme'tar/ a ele-
mentary; ~**to** m element
elenco /e'lẽku/ m (de filme, peça)
cast
eletri|cidade /eletrisi'dadʒi/ f
electricity; ~**cista** m/f electrician
elétrico /e'lɛtriku/ a electric
eletri|ficar /eletrifi'kar/ vt elec-
trify; ~**zar** f electrify
eletro /e'lɛtru/ m ECG; ~**cutar** vt
electrocute; ~**do** /ɔ/ m elec-
trode; ~**domésticos** m pl elec-
trical appliances
eletrôni|ca /ele'tronika/ f elec-
tronics; ~**co** a electronic
ele|vação /eleva'sãw/ f elevation;
(aumento) rise; ~**vado** a high;
<sentimento, estilo> elevated;
~**vador** m lift, (Amer) elevator;
~**var** vt raise; (promover)
elevate; ~**var-se** vpr rise
elimi|nar /elimi'nar/ vt eliminate;
~**natória** f heat; ~**natório** a
eliminatory
elipse /e'lipsi/ f ellipse
elíptico /e'liptʃiku/ a elliptical
eli|te /e'litʃi/ f elite; ~**tismo** m
elitism; ~**tista** a & m/f elitist

elmo /'ɛwmu/ m helmet
elo /'ɛlu/ m link
elo|giar /eloʒi'ar/ vt praise; ~**giar
alg por** compliment s.o. on;
~**gio** m (louvor) praise; (um)
compliment; ~**gioso** /o/ a complimentary
elo|qüência /elo'kwẽsia/ f elo-
quence; ~**qüente** a eloquent
eluci|dar /elusi'dar/ vt elucidate;
~**dativo** a elucidatory
em /ẽj/ prep in; (sobre) on; **ela
está no Eduardo** she's at Eduardo's (house); **de casa ~ casa**
from house to house; **aumentar
~ 10%** increase by 10%
emagre|cer /emagre'ser/ vi lose
weight, get thinner □ vt make
thinner; ~**cimento** m slimming
emanar /ema'nar/ vi emanate (**de**
from)
emanci|pação /emãsipa'sãw/ f
emancipation; ~**par** vt emanci-
pate; ~**par-se** vpr become
emancipated
emara|nhado /emara'nadu/ a
tangled □ m tangle; ~**nhar** vt
tangle; (envolver) entangle;
~**nhar-se** vpr get tangled up;
(envolver-se) become entangled
(**em** in)
emba|çar /ĩba'sar/, (Port) **em-
baciar** /ĩbasi'ar/ vt steam up
<vidro> □ vi <vidro> steam up;
<olhos> grow misty
embainhar /ĩbaj'nar/ vt hem
<vestido, calça>
embaixa|da /ĩbaj'ʃada/ f embassy;
~**dor** m ambassador; ~**triz** f
ambassador; (esposa) ambassador's wife
embaixo /ĩ'baʃu/ adv underneath;
(em casa) downstairs; ~ **de** under
emba|lagem /ĩba'laʒẽ/ f pack-
aging; ~**lar**[1] vt pack
emba|lar[2] /ĩba'lar/ vt rock
<criança>; ~**lo** m (fig) excite-
ment, thrill

embalsamar /ĩbawsa'mar/ *vt* embalm

embara|çar /ĩbara'sar/ *vt* embarrass; **~çar-se** *vpr* get embarrassed (**com** by); **~ço** *m* embarrassment; **~çoso** /o/ *a* embarrassing

embaralhar /ĩbara'ʎar/ *vt* muddle up; shuffle <*cartas*>; **~se** *vpr* get muddled up

embar|cação /ĩbarka'sãw/ *f* vessel; **~cadouro** *m* wharf; **~car** *vt/i* board, embark

embar|gado /ĩbar'gadu/ *a* <*voz*> faltering; **~go** *m* embargo

embarque /ĩ'barki/ *m* boarding; (*seção do aeroporto*) departures

embasba|cado /ĩbazba'kadu/ *a* open-mouthed; **~car-se** *vpr* be left open-mouthed

embate /ĩ'batʃi/ *m* (*de carros etc*) crash; (*fig*) clash

embebedar /ĩbebe'dar/ *vt* make drunk; **~se** *vpr* get drunk

embeber /ĩbe'ber/ *vt* soak; **~se de** soak up; **~se em** get absorbed in

embele|zador /ĩbeleza'dor/ *a* <*cirurgia*> cosmetic; **~zar** *vt* embellish; spruce up <*casa*>; **~zar-se** *vpr* make o.s. beautiful

embevecer /ĩbeve'ser/ *vt* captivate, engross; **~se** *vpr* get engrossed, be captivated

emblema /ẽ'blema/ *m* emblem

embocadura /ĩboka'dura/ *f* (*de instrumento*) mouthpiece; (*de freio*) bit; (*de rio*) mouth; (*de rua*) entrance

êmbolo /'ẽbulu/ *m* piston

embolsar /ĩbow'sar/ *vt* pocket; (*reembolsar*) reimburse

embora /ĩ'bora/ *adv* away □ *conj* although

emborcar /ĩbor'kar/ *vi* overturn; <*barco*> capsize

emboscada /ĩbos'kada/ *f* ambush

embrai|agem /ĩbraj'aʒẽ/ (*Port*) *f*

veja **embreagem**; **~ar** (*Port*) *vi veja* **embrear**

embre|agem /ĩbri'aʒẽ/ *f* clutch; **~ar** *vt/i* let in the clutch

embria|gar /ĩbria'gar/ *vt* intoxicate; **~gar-se** *vpr* get drunk, become intoxicated; **~guez** /e/ *f* drunkenness; **~guez no volante** drunken driving

embri|ão /ĩbri'ãw/ *m* embryo; **~onário** *a* embryonic

embro|mação /ĩbroma'sãw/ *f* flannel; **~mar** *vt* flannel, string along; (*enganar*) con □ *vi* stall, drag one's feet

embru|lhada /ĩbru'ʎada/ *f* muddle; **~lhar** *vt* wrap up <*pacote*>; upset <*estômago*>; (*confundir*) muddle up; **~lhar-se** *vpr* <*pessoa*> get muddled up; **~lho** *m* parcel; (*fig*) mix-up

embur|rado /ĩbu'xadu/ *a* sulky; **~rar** *vi* sulk

embuste /ĩ'bustʃi/ *m* hoax, put-up job

embu|tido /ĩbu'tʃidu/ *a* built-in, fitted; **~tir** *vt* build in, fit

emen|da /e'mẽda/ *f* correction, improvement; (*de lei*) amendment; **~dar** *vt* correct; amend <*lei*>; **~dar-se** *vpr* mend one's ways

ementa /i'mẽta/ (*Port*) *f* menu

emer|gência /emer'ʒẽsia/ *f* emergency; **~gente** *a* emergent; **~gir** *vi* surface

emi|gração /emigra'sãw/ *f* emigration; (*de aves etc*) migration; **~grado** *a* & *m* émigré; **~grante** *a* & *m/f* emigrant; **~grar** *vi* emigrate; <*aves, animais*> migrate

emi|nência /emi'nẽsia/ *f* eminence; **~nente** *a* eminent

emis|são /emi'sãw/ *f* (*de ações etc*) issue; (*na rádio, TV*) transmission, broadcast; (*de som, gases*) emission; **~sário** *m* emissary; **~sor** *m* transmitter; **~sora** *f* (*de rádio*) radio station; (*de TV*) TV station

emitir /emi'tʃir/ *vt* issue <*ações, selos etc*>; emit <*sons*>; (*pela rádio, TV*) transmit, broadcast

emoção /emo'sãw/ *f* emotion; (*excitação*) excitement

emocio|nal /emosio'naw/ (*pl* ~**nais**) *a* emotional; ~**nante** *a* (*excitante*) exciting; (*comovente*) touching, emotional; ~**nar** *vt* (*excitar*) excite; (*comover*) move, touch; ~**nar-se** *vpr* get emotional

emoldurar /emowdu'rar/ *vt* frame

emotivo /emo'tʃivu/ *a* emotional

empacar /ĩpa'kar/ *vi* <*cavalo*> baulk; <*negociações etc*> grind to a halt; <*orador*> dry up

empacotar /ĩpako'tar/ *vt* pack up; (*pôr em pacotes*) packet

empa|da /ĩ'pada/ *f* pie; ~**dão** *m* (large) pie

empalhar /ĩpa'ʎar/ *vt* stuff

empalidecer /ĩpalide'ser/ *vi* turn pale

empanar[1] /ĩpa'nar/ *vt* tarnish, dull

empanar[2] /ĩpa'nar/ *vt* cook in batter <*carne etc*>

empantur|rar /ĩpãtu'xar/ *vt* stuff; ~**se** *vpr* stuff o.s. (**de** with)

empapar /ĩpa'par/ *vt* soak

empa|tar /ĩpa'tar/ *vt* draw <*jogo*> □ *vi* <*times*> draw; <*corredores*> tie; ~**te** *m* (*em jogo*) draw; (*em corrida, votação*) tie; (*em xadrez, fig*) stalemate

empatia /ĩpa'tʃia/ *f* empathy

empecilho /ĩpe'siʎu/ *m* hindrance

empenar /ĩpe'nar/ *vt*/*i* warp

empe|nhar /ĩpe'ɲar/ *vt* (*penhorar*) pawn; (*prometer*) pledge; ~**nhar-se** *vpr* do one's utmost (**em** to); ~**nho** /e/ *m* (*compromisso*) pledge; (*diligência*) effort, commitment

emperrar /ĩpe'xar/ *vt* make stick □ *vi* stick

emperti|gado /ĩpertʃi'gadu/ *a* upright; ~**gar-se** *vpr* stand up straight

empilhar /ĩpi'ʎar/ *vt* pile up

empi|nado /ĩpi'nadu/ *a* erect; (*íngreme*) sheer, steep; <*nariz*> turned-up; (*fig*) stuck-up; ~**nar** *vt* stand upright; fly <*pipa*>; tip up <*copo*>

empírico /ĩ'piriku/ *a* empirical

emplacar /ĩpla'kar/ *vt* notch up <*pontos, sucessos, anos*>; license <*carro*>

emplastro /ĩ'plastru/ *m* surgical plaster; ~ **de nicotina** nicotine patch

empobre|cer /ĩpobre'ser/ *vt* impoverish; ~**cimento** *m* impoverishment

empoeirar /ĩpoe'rar/ *vt* perch; ~**se** *vpr* perch

empol|gação /ĩpowga'sãw/ *f* fascination; ~**gante** *a* fascinating; ~**gar** *vt* fascinate

empossar /ĩpo'sar/ *vt* swear in

empreen|dedor /ĩpriẽde'dor/ *a* enterprising □ *m* entrepreneur; ~**der** *vt* undertake; ~**dimento** *m* undertaking

empre|gada /ĩpre'gada/ *f* (*doméstica*) maid; ~**gado** *m* employee; ~**gador** *m* employer; ~**gar** *vt* employ; ~**gar-se** *vpr* get a job; ~**gatício** *a* **vínculo** ~**gatício** contract of employment; ~**go** /e/ *m* (*trabalho*) job; (*uso*) use

emprei|tada /ĩprej'tada/ *f* commission, contract; (*empreendimento*) venture; ~**teira** *f* contractor, firm of contractors; ~**teiro** *m* contractor

empre|sa /ĩ'preza/ *f* company; ~**dot.com** dot-com; ~**sariado** *m* business community; ~**sarial** (*pl* ~**sariais**) *a* business; ~**sário** *m* businessman; (*de cantor etc*) manager

empres|tado /ĩpres'tadu/ *a* on loan; **pedir** ~**tado** (ask to) borrow; **tomar** ~**tado** borrow; ~**tar** vt lend

empréstimo /iˈprɛstʃimu/ m loan

empur|rão /ĩpuˈxãw/ m push; ~**rar** vt push

emular /emuˈlar/ vt emulate

enamorado /enamoˈradu/ a (apaixonado) in love

encabeçar /ĩkabeˈsar/ vt head

encabu|lado /ĩkabuˈladu/ a shy; ~**lar** vt embarrass; ~**lar-se** vpr be shy

encadear /ĩkadeˈar/ vt chain ou link together

encader|nação /ĩkadernaˈsãw/ f binding; ~**nado** a bound; (com capa dura) hardback; ~**nar** vt bind

encai|xar /ĩkaˈʃar/ vt/i fit; ~**xe** m (cavidade) socket; (juntura) joint

encalço /ĩˈkawsu/ m pursuit; no ~ de in pursuit of

encalhar /ĩkaˈʎar/ vi (barco) run aground; (fig) get bogged down; <mercadoria> not sell; (fam: ficar solteiro) be left on the shelf

encaminhar /ĩkamiˈɲar/ vt (dirigir) steer, direct; (remeter) pass on; set in motion <processo>; ~**se** vpr set out

encana|dor /ĩkanaˈdor/ m plumber; ~**mento** m plumbing

encan|tador /ĩkãtaˈdor/ a enchanting; ~**tamento** m enchantment; ~**tar** vt enchant; ~**to** m charm

encaraco|lado /ĩkarakoˈladu/ a curly; ~**lar** vt curl; ~**lar-se** vpr curl up

encarar /ĩkaˈrar/ vt confront, face

encarcerar /ĩkarseˈrar/ vt imprison

encardido /ĩkarˈdʒidu/ a grimy

encarecidamente /ĩkaresidaˈmẽtʃi/ adv insistently

encargo /ĩˈkargu/ m task, responsibility

encar|nação /ĩkarnaˈsãw/ f (do espírito) incarnation; (de um per-

sonagem) embodiment; ~**nar** vt embody; play <papel>

encarre|gado /ĩkaxeˈgadu/ a in charge (de of) □ m person in charge; (de operários) foreman; ~**gado de negócios** chargé d'affaires; ~**gar** vt ~**gar alg de** put s.o. in charge of; ~**gar-se de** undertake to

encarte /ĩˈkartʃi/ m insert

ence|nação /ĩsenaˈsãw/ f (de peça) production; (fingimento) playacting; ~**nar** vt put on □ vi put it on

ence|radeira /ĩseraˈdera/ f floor polisher; ~**rar** vt wax

encer|rado /ĩseˈxadu/ a <assunto> closed; ~**ramento** m close; ~**rar** vt close; ~**rar-se** vpr close

encharcar /ĩʃarˈkar/ vt soak

en|chente /ẽˈʃẽtʃi/ f flood; ~**cher** vt fill; (fam) annoy □ (fam) vi be annoying; ~**cher-se** vpr fill up; (fam: fartar-se) get fed up (with)

enciclopédia /ẽsikloˈpɛdʒia/ f encyclopaedia

enco|berto /ĩkoˈbertu/ a <céu, tempo> overcast; ~**brir** vt cover up □ vi <tempo> become overcast

encolher /ĩkoˈʎer/ vt shrug <ombros>; pull up <pernas>; shrink <roupa> □ vi <roupa> shrink; ~**se** vpr (de medo) shrink; (de frio) huddle; (espremer-se) squeeze up

encomen|da /ĩkoˈmẽda/ f order; **de** ou **sob** ~**da** to order; ~**dar** vt ~**dar** a (from)

encon|trão /ĩkõˈtrãw/ m bump; (empurrão) shove; ~**trar** vt (achar) find; (ver) meet; ~**trar com** meet; ~**trar-se** vpr (ver-se) meet; (estar) be; ~**tro** m meeting; (mil) encounter; - **ir ao** ~**tro de** go to meet; (fig) meet; **ir de** ~**tro a** a run into; (fig) go against

encorajar /ĩkora'ʒar/ *vt* encourage

encor|pado /ĩkor'padu/ *a* stocky; <*vinho*> full-bodied; **~par** *vt/i* fill out

encos|ta /ĩ'kɔsta/ *f* slope; **~car** *vt* (*apoiar*) lean; park <*carro*>; leave on the latch <*porta*>; (*pôr de lado*) put aside □ *vi* <*carro*> pull in; **~tar-se** *vpr* lean; **~to** /o/ *m* back

encra|vado /ĩkra'vadu/ *a* <*unha, pêlo*> ingrowing; **~var** *vt* stick

encren|ca /ĩ'krẽka/ *f* fix, jam; *pl* trouble; **~car** *vt* get into trouble <*pessoa*>; complicate <*situação*> □ *vi* <*situação*> get complicated; <*carro*> break down; **~car-se** *vpr* <*pessoa*> get into trouble; **~queiro** *m* troublemaker

encres|pado /ĩkres'padu/ *a* <*mar*> choppy; **~par** *vt* frizz <*cabelo*>; **~par-se** *vpr* <*cabelo*> go frizzy; <*mar*> get choppy

encruzilhada /ĩkruzi'ʎada/ *f* crossroads

encurralar /ĩkuxa'lar/ *vt* hem in

encurtar /ĩkur'tar/ *vt* shorten

endere|çar /ĩdere'sar/ *vt* address; **~ço** /e/ *m* address; (*comput*) **~ço de e-mail** email address

endinheirado /ĩdʒiɲe'radu/ *a* well-off

endireitar /ĩdʒirej'tar/ *vt* straighten; **~se** *vpr* straighten up

endivi|dado /ĩdʒivi'dadu/ *a* in debt; **~dar** *vt* put into debt; **~dar-se** *vpr* get into debt

endoidecer /ĩdojde'ser/ *vi* get mad

endos|sar /ĩdo'sar/ *vt* endorse; **~so** /o/ *m* endorsement

endurecer /ĩdure'ser/ *vt/i* harden

ener|gético /ener'ʒɛtʃiku/ *a* energy; **~gia** *f* energy

enérgico /e'nɛrʒiku/ *a* vigorous; <*remédio, discurso*> powerful

enevoado /enevu'adu/ *a* (*com*

névoa) misty; (*com nuvens*) cloudy

enfarte /ĩ'fartʃi/ *m* heart attack

ênfase /'ẽfazi/ *f* emphasis; **dar ~ a** emphasize

enfático /ẽ'fatʃiku/ *a* emphatic

enfatizar /ẽfatʃi'zar/ *vt* emphasize

enfei|tar /ĩfej'tar/ *vt* decorate; **~tar-se** *vpr* dress up; **~te** *m* decoration

enfeitiçar /ĩfejtʃi'sar/ *vt* bewitch

enfer|magem /ĩfer'maʒẽ/ *f* nursing; **~maria** *f* ward; **~meira** *f* nurse; **~meiro** *m* male nurse; **~midade** *f* illness; **~mo** *a* sick □ *m* patient

enferru|jado /ĩfexu'ʒadu/ *a* rusty; **~jar** *vt/i* rust

enfezado /ĩfe'zadu/ *a* bad-tempered

enfiar /ẽfi'ar/ *vt* put; slip on <*roupa*>; thread <*agulha*>; string <*pérolas*>

enfileirar /ĩfilej'rar/ *vt* line up; **~se** *vpr* line up

enfim /ẽ'fĩ/ *adv* (*finalmente*) finally; (*resumindo*) anyway

enfo|car /ĩfo'kar/ *vt* tackle; **~que** *m* approach

enfor|camento /ĩforka'mẽtu/ *m* hanging; **~car** *vt* hang; **~car-se** *vpr* hang o.s.

enfraquecer /ĩfrake'ser/ *vt/i* weaken

enfrentar /ĩfrẽ'tar/ *vt* face

enfumaçado /ĩfuma'sadu/ *a* smoky

enfurecer /ĩfure'ser/ *vt* infuriate; **~se** *vpr* get furious

enga|jamento /ĩgaʒa'mẽtu/ *m* commitment; **~jado** *a* committed; **~jar-se** *vpr* get involved (em in)

engalfinhar-se /ĩgawfi'ɲarsi/ *vpr* grapple

enga|nado /ĩga'nadu/ *a* (*errado*) mistaken; **~nar** *vt* deceive; cheat on <*marido, esposa*>; stave off *<fome>*; ~**nar-se** *vpr* be mistaken; ~**no** *m* (*erro*) mistake; (*desonestidade*) deception

engarra|famento /ĩgaxafa'mẽtu/ *m* traffic jam; ~**far** *vt* bottle *<vinho etc>*; block *<trânsito>*

engas|gar /ĩgaz'gar/ *vt* choke □ *vi* choke; *<motor>* backfire; ~**go m** choking

engastar /ĩgaʃ'tar/ *vt* set *<jóias>*

engatar /ĩga'tar/ *vt* hitch *<reboque etc>* (**a** to); engage *<marcha>*

engatinhar /ĩgatʃi'ɲar/ *vi* crawl; (*fig*) start out

engave|tamento /ĩgaveta'mẽtu/ *m* pile-up; ~**tar** *vt* shelve

engelhar /ĩʒe'ʎar/ *vi* (*pele*) wrinkle

enge|nharia /ĩʒeɲa'ria/ *f* engineering; ~**nheiro m** engineer; ~**nho** /e/ *m* (*de pessoa*) ingenuity; (*de açúcar*) sugar mill; (*máquina*) device; ~**nhoca** /ɔ/ *f* gadget; ~**nhoso a** ingenious

engessar /ĩʒe'sar/ *vt* put in plaster

engodo /ĩ'godu/ *m* lure

engolir /ĩgo'lir/ *vt/i* swallow; ~ **em seco** gulp

engomar /ĩgo'mar/ *vt* press; (*com goma*) starch

engordar /ĩgor'dar/ *vt* make fat; fatten *<animais>* □ *vi* *<pessoa>* put on weight; *<comida>* be fattening

engraçado /ĩgra'sadu/ *a* funny

engradado /ĩgra'dadu/ *m* crate

engravidar /ĩgravi'dar/ *vt* make pregnant □ *vi* get pregnant

engraxar /ĩgra'ʃar/ *vt* polish

engre|nado /ĩgre'nadu/ *a* *<carro>* in gear; ~**nagem** *f* gear; (*fig*) mechanism; ~**nar** *vt* put into gear *<carro>*; strike up *<conversa>*; ~**nar-se** *vpr* mesh; (*fig*) *<pessoas>* get on

engrossar /ĩgro'sar/ *vt* thicken; raise *<voz>* □ *vi* thicken; *<pessoa>* turn nasty

enguia /ĩ'gia/ *f* eel

engui|çar /ĩgi'sar/ *vi* break down; ~**ço m** breakdown

enig|ma /e'nigima/ *m* enigma; ~**mático a** enigmatic

enjaular /ĩʒaw'lar/ *vt* cage

enjo|ar /ĩʒo'ar/ *vt* sicken □ *vi*, ~**ar-se** *vpr* get sick (**de** of); ~**ativo a** *<comida>* sickly; *<livro etc>* boring

enjôo /ĩ'ʒou/ *m* sickness

enlameado /ĩlami'adu/ *a* muddy

enlatado /ĩla'tadu/ *a* tinned, canned; ~**s m** *pl* tinned foods

enle|var /ĩle'var/ *vt* enthral; ~**vo** /e/ *m* rapture

enlouquecer /ĩloke'ser/ *vt* drive mad □ *vi* go mad

enluarado /ĩlua'radu/ *a* moonlit

enor|me /e'nɔrmi/ *a* enormous; ~**midade f** enormity

enquadrar /ĩkwa'drar/ *vt* fit □ *vi*, ~**-se** *vpr* fit in

enquanto /ĩ'kwãtu/ *conj* while; ~ **isso** meanwhile; **por** ~ for the time being

enquête /ã'ketʃi/ *f* survey

enraivecer /ĩxajve'ser/ *vt* enrage

enredo /ẽ'redu/ *m* plot

enrijecer /ĩxiʒe'ser/ *vt* stiffen; ~**se** *vpr* stiffen

enrique|cer /ĩxike'ser/ *vt* (*dar dinheiro a*) make rich; (*fig*) enrich □ *vi* get rich; ~**cimento m** enrichment

enro|lado /ĩxo'ladu/ *a* complicated; ~**lar** *vt* (*envolver*) roll up; (*complicar*) complicate; (*enganar*) cheat; ~**lar-se** *vpr* (*envolver-se*) roll up; (*confundir-se*) get mixed up

enroscar /ĩxos'kar/ *vt* twist

enrouquecer /ĩxoke'ser/ *vi* go hoarse

enrugar /ĩxu'gar/ *vt* wrinkle *<pele, tecido>*; furrow *<testa>*

enrustido /ĩxus'tʃidu/ *a* repressed

ensaboar /ĩsabo'ar/ *vt* soap

ensai|ar /ĩsaj'ar/ *vt* (*provar*) try out; (*repetir*) rehearse; ~**o** /i/

(*prova*) test; (*repetição*) re-hearsal; (*escrito*) essay

ensangüentado /ĩsãgwẽ'tadu/ *a* bloody, bloodstained

enseada /ĩsi'ada/ *f* inlet

ensebado /ĩse'badu/ *a* greasy

ensimesmado /ĩsimez'madu/ *a* lost in thought

ensi|nar /ẽsi'nar/ *vt/i* teach (**aco a alg** s.o. sth); ~**nar alg a nadar** teach s.o. to swim; ~**no** *m* teaching; (*em geral*) education

ensolarado /ĩsola'radu/ *a* sunny

enso|pado /ĩso'padu/ *a* soaked □ *m* stew; ~**par** *vt* soak

ensurde|cedor /ĩsurdese'dor/ *a* deafening; ~**cer** *vt* deafen □ *vi* go deaf

entabular /ĩtabu'lar/ *vt* open, start

entalar /ĩta'lar/ *vt* wedge, jam; (*em apertos*) get; ~**se** *vpr* get wedged, get jammed; (*em apertos*) get caught up

entalhar /ĩta'ʎar/ *vt* carve

entanto /ĩ'tãtu/ *m* **no** ~ however

então /ĩ'tãw/ *adv* then; (*nesse caso*) so

entardecer /ĩtarde'ser/ *m* sunset

ente /'ẽtʃi/ *m* being

entea|da /ẽtʃi'ada/ *f* stepdaughter; ~**do** *m* stepson

entedi|ante /ĩtedʒi'ãtʃi/ *a* boring; ~**ar** *vt* bore; ~**ar-se** *vpr* get bored

enten|der /ĩtẽ'der/ *vt* understand; ~**der-se** *vpr* (*dar-se bem*) get on (**com** with); **dar a** ~**der** give to understand; ~**der de futebol** know about football; ~**dimento** *m* understanding

enternecedor /ĩternese'dor/ *a* touching

enter|rar /ĩte'xar/ *vt* bury; ~**ro** /e/ *m* burial; (*cerimónia*) funeral

entidade /ẽtʃi'dadʒi/ *f* entity; (*órgão*) body

entornar /ĩtor'nar/ *vt* tip over, spill

entorpe|cente /ĩtorpe'sẽtʃi/ *m* drug, narcotic; ~**cer** *vt* numb

entortar /ĩtor'tar/ *vt* make crooked

entrada /ĩ'trada/ *f* entry; (*onde se entra*) entrance; (*bilhete*) ticket; (*prato*) starter; (*pagamento*) deposit; *pl* (*no cabelo*) receding hairline; **dar** ~ **a** enter; ~ **proibida** no entry

entranhas /ĩ'traɲas/ *f pl* entrails

entrar /ẽ'trar/ *vi* go/come in; ~ **com** enter <*dados*>; put in <*dinheiro*>; ~ **em detalhes** go into details; ~ **em vigor** come into force

entravar /ẽtra'var/ *vt* hamper

entre /'ẽtri/ *prep* between; (*em meio a*) among

entreaberto /ẽtria'bɛrtu/ *a* half-open

entrecortar /ẽtrikor'tar/ *vt* inter-sperse; (*cruzar*) intersect

entre|ga /ĩ'trega/ *f* delivery; (*rendição*) surrender; ~**ga a domicílio** home delivery; ~**gar** *vt* hand over; deliver <*mercadorias, cartas*>; hand in <*caderno, trabalho escolar*>; ~**gar-se** *vpr* give o.s. up (**a** to); ~**gue** *pp de* **entregar**

entrelaçar /ẽtrela'sar/ *vt* inter-twine; clasp <*mãos*>

entrelinhas /ẽtri'liɲas/ *f pl* **ler nas** ~ read between the lines

entremear /ẽtrimi'ar/ *vt* inter-sperse

entreolhar-se /ẽtrio'ʎarsi/ *vpr* look at one another

entretanto /ẽtre'tãtu/ *conj* how-ever

entre|tenimento /ẽtreteni'mẽtu/ *m* entertainment; ~**ter** *vt* enter-tain

entrever /ẽtre'ver/ *vt* glimpse

entrevis|ta /ẽtre'vista/ *f* inter-view; ~**tador** *m* interviewer; ~**tar** *vt* interview

entristecer /ĩtriste'ser/ *vt* sadden □ *vi* be saddened (**com** by)

entroncamento /ĩtrõka'mẽtu/ *m* junction

entrosar /ĩtro'zar/ *vt/i* integrate

entu|lhar /ĩtu'ʎar/ *vt* cram (de with); **~lho** *m* rubble

entupir /ĩtu'pir/ *vt* block; **~pir-se** *vpr* get blocked; (de comida) stuff o.s. (**de** with)

enturmar-se /ĩtur'marsi/ *vpr* mix in, fit in

entusias|mar /ĩtuziaz'mar/ *vt* fill with enthusiasm; **~mar-se** *vpr* get enthusiastic (**com** about); **~mo** *m* enthusiasm; **~ta** *m/f* enthusiast □ *a* enthusiastic

entusiástico /ĩtuzi'astʃiku/ *a* enthusiastic

enumerar /enume'rar/ *vt* enumerate

envelope /ẽve'lɔpi/ *m* envelope

envelhecer /ẽveʎe'ser/ *vt/i* age

envenenar /ẽvene'nar/ *vt* poison; (fam) soup up <carro>

envergadura /ẽverga'dura/ *f* wingspan; (fig) scale

envergo|nhado /ẽvergo'ɲadu/ *a* ashamed; (constrangido) embarrassed; **~nhar** *vt* disgrace; (constranger) embarrass; **~nhar-se** *vpr* be ashamed; (acanhar-se) get embarrassed

envernizar /ẽverni'zar/ *vt* varnish

en|viado /ẽvi'adu/ *m* envoy; **~viar** *vt* send; **~vio** *m* (ato) sending; (remessa) consignment

envidraçar /ẽvidra'sar/ *vt* glaze

enviesado /ẽvie'zadu/ *a* (não vertical) slanting; (torto) crooked

envol|vente /ẽvow'vẽtʃi/ *a* compelling, gripping; **~ver** *vt* (embrulhar) wrap; (enredar) involve; **~ver-se** *vpr* (enrolar-se) wrap o.s.; (enredar-se) get involved; **~vimento** *m* involvement

enxada /ẽ'ʃada/ *f* hoe

enxaguar /ẽʃa'gwar/ *vt* rinse

enxame /ẽ'ʃami/ *m* swarm

enxaqueca /ẽʃa'keka/ *f* migraine

enxergar /ĩʃer'gar/ *vt/i* see

enxer|tar /ĩʃer'tar/ *vt* graft; **~to** /e/ *m* graft

enxotar /ĩʃo'tar/ *vt* drive away

enxofre /ĩ'ʃofri/ *m* sulphur

enxo|val /ẽʃo'vaw/ (*pl* **~vais**) *m* (de noiva) trousseau; (de bebê) layette

enxugar /ĩʃu'gar/ *vt* dry; **~-se** *vpr* dry o.s.

enxurrada /ĩʃu'xada/ *f* torrent; (fig) flood

enxuto /ĩ'ʃutu/ *a* dry; <corpo> shapely

enzima /ẽ'zima/ *f* enzyme

epicentro /epi'sẽtru/ *m* epicentre

épico /'ɛpiku/ *a* epic

epidemia /epide'mia/ *f* epidemic

epi|lepsia /epilep'sia/ *f* epilepsy; **~léptico** *a* & *m* epileptic

epílogo /e'pilogu/ *m* epilogue

episódio /epi'zɔdʒiu/ *m* episode

epitáfio /epi'tafiu/ *m* epitaph

época /'ɛpoca/ *f* time; (da história) age, period; **fazer ~** make history; **móveis da ~** period furniture

epopéia /epo'pɛja/ *f* epic

equação /ekwa'sãw/ *f* equation

equador /ekwa'dor/ *m* equator; **o Equador** Ecuador

equatori|al /ekwatori'aw/ (*pl* **~ais**) *a* equatorial; **~ano** *a* & *m* Ecuadorian

equilibrar /ekili'brar/ *vt* balance; **~-se** *vpr* balance

equilíbrio /eki'libriu/ *m* balance

equipa /e'kipa/ (Port) *f* team

equi|pamento /ekipa'mẽtu/ *m* equipment; **~par** *vt* equip

equiparar /ekipa'rar/ *vt* equate (**com** with); **~-se** *vpr* compare (**a** with)

equipe /e'kipi/ *f* team

equitação /ekita'sãw/ *f* riding

equiva|lência /ekiva'lẽsia/ *f* equivalence; **~lente** *a* equivalent; **~ler** *vi* be equivalent (**a** to)

equivo|cado /ekivoˈkadu/ *a* mistaken; **~car-se** *vpr* make a mistake

equívoco /eˈkivoku/ *a* equivocal □ *m* mistake

era /ˈɛra/ *f* era

erário /eˈrariu/ *m* exchequer

ereção /ereˈsãw/ *f* erection

eremita /ereˈmita/ *m/f* hermit

ereto /eˈrɛtu/ *a* erect

erguer /erˈger/ *vt* raise; erect <*monumento etc*>; **~-se** *vpr* rise

eri|çado /eriˈsadu/ *a* bristling; **~çar-se** *vpr* bristle

ermo /ˈermu/ *a* deserted □ *m* wilderness

erosão /eroˈzãw/ *f* erosion

erótico /eˈrɔtʃiku/ *a* erotic

erotismo /eroˈtʃizmu/ *m* eroticism

er|rado /eˈxadu/ *a* wrong; **~rante** *a* wandering; **~rar** *vt* (*não fazer certo*) get wrong; miss <*alvo*> □ *vi* (*enganar-se*) be wrong; (*vaguear*) wander; **~ro** /e/ *m* mistake; **fazer um ~ro** make a mistake; **~rôneo** *a* erroneous

erudi|ção /erudʒiˈsãw/ *f* learning; **~to** *a* learned; <*música*> classical □ *m* scholar

erupção /erupˈsãw/ *f* (*vulcânica*) eruption; (*cutânea*) rash

erva /ˈɛrva/ *f* herb; **~ daninha** weed; **~-doce** *f* aniseed

ervilha /erˈviʎa/ *f* pea

esban|jador /izbãʒaˈdor/ *a* extravagant □ *m* spendthrift; **~jar** *vt* squander; burst with <*saúde, imaginação, energia etc*>

esbar|rão /izbaˈxãw/ *m* bump; **~rar** *vi* **~rar com** ou **em** bump into <*pessoa*>; come up against <*problema*>

esbelto /izˈbɛwtu/ *a* svelte

esbo|çar /izboˈsar/ *vt* sketch <*desenho etc*>; outline <*plano etc*>; **~çar um sorriso** give a hint of a smile; **~ço** /o/ *m* (*desenho*)

sketch; (*plano*) outline; (*de um sorriso*) hint

esbofetear /izbofetʃiˈar/ *vt* slap

esborrachar /izboxaˈʃar/ *vt* squash; **~-se** *vpr* crash

esbravejar /izbraveˈʒar/ *vi* rant, rail

esbura|cado /izburaˈkadu/ *a* full of holes; **~car** *vt* make holes in

esbuga|lhado /izbugaˈʎadu/ *a* <*olhos*> bulging; **~lhar-se** *vpr* <*olhos*> pop out

escabroso /iskaˈbrozu/ *a* (*fig*) difficult, tough

escada /isˈkada/ *f* (*dentro de casa*) stairs; (*na rua*) steps; (*de mão*) ladder; **~ de incêndio** fire escape; **~ rolante** escalator; **~ria** *f* staircase

escafan|drista /iskafãˈdrista/ *m/f* diver; **~dro** *m* diving suit

escala /isˈkala/ *f* scale; (*de navio*) port of call; (*de avião*) stopover; **fazer ~** stop over; **sem ~** <*vôo*> non-stop

esca|lada /iskaˈlada/ *f* (*fig*) escalation; **~lão** *m* echelon, level; **~lar** *vt* (*subir a*) scale; (*designar*) select

escaldar /iskawˈdar/ *vt* scald; blanch <*vegetais*>

escalfar /iskawˈfar/ *vt* poach

escalonar /iskaloˈnar/ *vt* schedule <*pagamento*>

escama /isˈkama/ *f* scale

escanca|rado /iskãkaˈradu/ *a* wide open; **~rar** *vt* open wide

escandalizar /iskãdaliˈzar/ *vt* scandalize; **~-se** *vpr* be scandalized

escândalo /isˈkãdalu/ *m* (*vexame*) scandal; (*tumulto*) fuss, uproar; **fazer um ~** make a scene

escandaloso /iskãdaˈlozu/ *a* (*chocante*) scandalous; (*espalhafatoso*) outrageous, loud

Escandinávia /iskãdʒiˈnavia/ *f* Scandinavia

escandinavo /iskãdʒiˈnavu/ *a* & *m* Scandinavian

escanga|lhado /iskãga'ʎadu/ *a* broken; **∼lhar** *vt* break up; **∼lhar-se** *vpr* fall to pieces; **∼lhar-se de rir** split one's sides laughing

escaninho /iska'niɲu/ *m* pigeon-hole

escanteio /iskã'teju/ *m* corner

esca|pada /iska'pada/ *f (fuga)* escape; *(aventura)* escapade; **∼pamento** *m* exhaust; **∼par** *vi* **∼par a** *ou* **de** *(livrar-se)* escape from; *(evitar)* escape; **∼pou-lhe a palavra** the word slipped out; **o copo ∼pou-me das mãos** the glass slipped out of my hands; **o nome me ∼pa** the name escapes me; **∼par de boa** have a narrow escape; **∼patória** *f* way out; *(desculpa)* pretext; **∼pe** *m* escape; *(de carro etc)* exhaust; **∼pulir** *vi* escape (**de** from)

escaramuça /iskara'musa/ *f* skirmish

escaravelho /iskara'veʎu/ *m* beetle

escarcéu /iskar'sɛw/ *m* uproar, fuss

escarlate /iskar'latʃi/ *a* scarlet

escarnecer /iskarne'ser/ *vt* mock

escárnio /is'karniu/ *m* derision

escarpado /iskar'padu/ *a* steep

escarrado /iska'xadu/ *m* **ele é o pai ∼** he's the spitting image of his father

escarro /is'kaxu/ *m* phlegm

escas|sear /iskasi'ar/ *vi* run short; **∼sez** *f* shortage; **∼so** *a* *(raro)* scarce; *(ralo)* scant

esca|vadeira /iskava'dera/ *f* digger; **∼var** *vt* excavate

esclare|cer /isklare'ser/ *vt* explain *<fatos>*; enlighten *<pessoa>*; **∼cer-se** *vpr* *<fato>* be explained; *<pessoa>* find out; **∼cimento** *m* *(de pessoas)* enlightenment; *(de fatos)* explanation

esclerosado /isklero'zadu/ *a* senile

escoar /isko'ar/ *vt/i* drain

esco|cês /isko'ses/ *a (f* **∼cesa)** Scottish □ *m (f* **∼cesa)** Scot

Escócia /is'kɔsia/ *f* Scotland

esco|la /is'kɔla/ *f* school; **∼la de samba** samba school; **∼lar** *a* school □ *m/f* schoolchild; **∼laridade** *f* schooling

esco|lha /is'kɔʎa/ *f* choice; **∼lher** *vt* choose

escol|ta /is'kɔwta/ *f* escort; **∼tar** *vt* escort

escombros /is'kõbrus/ *m pl* debris

escon|de-esconde /iskõdʒis-'kõdʒi/ *m* hide-and-seek; **∼der** *vt* hide; **∼der-se** *vpr* hide; **∼derijo** *m* hiding place; *(de bandidos)* hideout; **∼didas** *f pl* **às ∼didas** secretly

esco|ra /is'kɔra/ *f* prop; **∼rar** *vt* prop up; **∼rar-se** *vpr* *<argumento etc>* be based (**em** on)

escore /is'kɔri/ *m* score

escória /is'kɔria/ *f* scum, dross

escori|ação /iskoria'sãw/ *f* graze, abrasion; **∼ar** *vt* graze

escorpião /iskorpi'ãw/ *m* scorpion; **Escorpião** Scorpio

escorredor /iskoxe'dor/ *m* drainer

escorrega /isko'xega/ *m* slide

escorre|gador /iskoxega'dor/ *m* slide; **∼gão** *m* slip; **∼gar** *vi* slip

escor|rer /isko'xer/ *vt* drain □ *vi* trickle; **∼rido** *a <cabelo>* straight

escoteiro /isko'teru/ *m* boy scout

escotilha /isko'tʃiʎa/ *f* hatch

esco|va /is'kova/ *f* brush; **∼va no cabelo** blow-dry one's hair; **∼va de dentes** toothbrush; **∼var** *vt* brush; **∼vinha** *f* **cabelo à ∼vinha** crew-cut

escra|chado /iskra'ʃadu/ *a* *(fam)* outspoken; **∼char** *(fam)* *vt* tell off

escra|vatura /iskrava'tura/ f slavery; ~**vidão** f slavery; ~**vizar** vt enslave; ~**vo** m slave

escre|vente /iskre'vẽtʃi/ m/f clerk; ~**ver** vt/i write

escri|ta /is'krita/ f writing; ~**to** pp de escrever □ a written; por ~**to** in writing; ~**tor** m writer; ~**tório** m office; (numa casa) study

escritu|ra /iskri'tura/ f (a Bíblia) scripture; (contrato) deed; ~**ração** f bookkeeping; ~**rar** vt keep, write up <contas>; draw up <documento>

escri|vaninha /iskriva'niɲa/ f bureau, writing desk; ~**vão** m (f ~**vã**) registrar

escrúpulo /is'krupulu/ m scruple

escrupuloso /iskrupu'lozu/ a scrupulous

escrutínio /iskru'tʃiniu/ m ballot

escu|dar /isku'dar/ vt shield; ~**deria** f team; ~**do** m shield; (moeda) escudo

escula|chado /iskula'ʃadu/ (fam) a sloppy; ~**char** (fam) vt mess up <coisa>; tell off <pessoa>; ~**cho** (fam) m (bagunça) mess; (bronca) telling-off

escuma /is'kuma/ f scum; ~**deira** f skimmer

escuna /is'kuna/ f schooner

escu|ras /is'kuras/ f pl às ~**ras** in the dark; ~**recer** vt darken □ vi get dark; ~**ridão** f darkness; ~**ro** a & m dark

escuso /is'kuzu/ a shady

escu|ta /is'kuta/ f listening; estar à ~**ta** be listening; ~**ta telefônica** phone tapping; ~**tar** vt (perceber) hear; (prestar atenção a) listen to □ vi (poder ouvir) hear; (prestar atenção) listen

esdrúxulo /iz'druʃulu/ a weird

esfacelar /isfase'lar/ vt wreck

esfalfar /isfaw'far/ vt wear out; ~**-se** vpr get worn out

esfaquear /isfaki'ar/ vt stab

esfarelar /isfare'lar/ vt crumble; ~**-se** vpr crumble

esfarrapado /isfaxa'padu/ a ragged; (desculpa) lame

es|fera /is'fɛra/ f sphere; ~**férico** a spherical

esferográfi|co /isfero'grafiku/ a **caneta** ~**ca** ball-point pen

esfiapar /isfia'par/ vt fray; ~**-se** vpr fray

esfinge /is'fĩʒi/ f sphinx

esfolar /isfo'lar/ vt skin; (fig) overcharge

esfomeado /isfomi'adu/ a starving, famished

esfor|çar-se /isfor'sarsi/ vpr make an effort; ~**ço** /o/ m effort; **fazer** ~**ço** make an effort

esfre|gaço /isfre'gasu/ m smear; ~**gar** vt rub; (para limpar) scrub

esfriar /isfri'ar/ vt cool □ vi cool (down); (sentir frio) get cold

esfumaçado /isfuma'sadu/ a smoky

esfuziante /isfuzi'ãtʃi/ a irrepressible, exuberant

esganar /izga'nar/ vt throttle

esganiçado /izgani'sadu/ a shrill

esgargar /izgar'sar/ vt/i fray

esgo|tado /izgo'tadu/ a exhausted; <estoque, lotação> sold out; ~**tamento** m exhaustion; ~**tamento nervoso** nervous breakdown; ~**tar** vt exhaust; (gastar) use up; ~**tar-se** vpr become exhausted; <estoque, lotação> sell out; <recursos, provisões> run out; ~**to** /o/ m drain; (de detritos) sewer

esgri|ma /iz'grima/ f fencing; ~**mir** vt brandish □ vi fence; ~**mista** m/f fencer

esgrouvinhado /izgrovi'ɲadu/ a tousled, dishevelled

esgueirar-se /izge'rrarsi/ *vpr* slip,
sneak

esguelha /iz'geʎa/ *f* **de ∼** askew;
<olhar> askance

esgui|char /izgi'ʃar/ *vt/i* spurt,
squirt; **∼cho** *m* jet, spurt

esguio /iz'giu/ *a* slender

eslavo /iz'lavu/ *a* Slavic □ *m* Slav

esmaecer /izmaj'ser/ *vi* fade

esma|gador /izmaga'dor/ *a* <*vi-
tória, maioria*> overwhelming;
<*provas*> incontrovertible; **∼-
gar** *vt* crush

esmalte /iz'mawtʃi/ *m* enamel; **∼
de unhas** nail varnish

esmeralda /izme'rawda/ *f* emerald

esme|rar-se /izme'rarsi/ *vpr* take
great care (**em** over); **∼ro** /e/ *m*
great care

esmigalhar /izmiga'ʎar/ *vt* crumble <*pão etc*>; shatter <*vidro,
copo*>; **∼-se** *vpr* <*pão etc*> crumble; <*vidro, copo*> shatter

esmiuçar /izmiu'sar/ *vt* examine
in detail

esmo /'ezmu/ *m* **a ∼** <*escolher*>
at random; <*andar*> aimlessly;
<*falar*> nonsense

esmola /iz'mɔla/ *f* donation; *pl*
charity

esmorecer /izmore'ser/ *vi* flag

esmurrar /izmu'xar/ *vt* punch

esno|bar /izno'bar/ *vt* snub □ *vi*
be snobbish; **∼be** /iz'nɔbi/ *a*
snobbish □ *m/f* snob; **∼bismo**
m snobbishness

esotérico /ezo'teriku/ *a* esoteric

espa|çar /ispa'sar/ *vt* space out;
make less frequent <*visitas,
consultas etc*>; **∼cial** (*pl*
∼ciais) *a* space; <*cosmos etc*>
space; **∼ço** *m* space; (*cultural etc*) venue; **∼çoso** /o/ *a*
spacious

espada /is'pada/ *f* sword; *pl*
(*naipe*) spades; **∼chim** *m*
swordsman

espádua /is'padua/ *f* shoulder
blade

espaguete /ispa'getʃi/ *m* spaghetti

espaire|cer /ispajre'ser/ *vt* amuse
□ *vi* relax; (*dar uma volta*) go for
a walk; **∼cimento** *m* recreation

espaldar /ispaw'dar/ *m* back

espalhafato /ispaʎa'fatu/ *m* (*barulho*) fuss, uproar; (*de roupa etc*)
extravagance; **∼so** /o/ *a* (*ba-
lhento*) noisy, rowdy; (*ostentoso*)
extravagant

espalhar /ispa'ʎar/ *vt* scatter;
spread <*notícia, terror etc*>; shed
<*luz*>; **∼-se** *vpr* spread; <*pes-
soas*> spread out

espa|nador /ispana'dor/ *m*
feather duster; **∼nar** *vt* dust

espan|camento /ispãka'mẽtu/ *m*
beating; **∼car** *vt* beat up

Espanha /is'paɲa/ *f* Spain

espa|nhol /ispa'ɲɔw/ (*pl* **∼
nhóis**) *a* (*f* **∼nhola**) Spanish □
m (*f* **∼nhola**) Spaniard; (*língua*) Spanish; **os ∼nhóis** the
Spanish

espan|talho /ispã'taʎu/ *m* scare-
crow; **∼tar** *vt* (*admirar*) amaze;
(*assustar*) scare; (*afugentar*)
drive away; **∼tar-se** *vpr*
(*admirar-se*) be amazed; (*assustar-se*) get scared; **∼to** *m* (*susto*)
fright; (*admiração*) amazement;
∼toso /o/ *a* amazing

esparadrapo /ispara'drapu/ *m*
sticking plaster

espargo /is'pargu/ (*Port*) *m* asparagus

esparramar /ispaxa'mar/ *vt*
scatter; **∼-se** *vpr* be scattered,
spread

espartano /ispar'tanu/ *a* spartan

espartilho /ispar'tʃiʎu/ *m* corset

espas|mo /is'pazmu/ *m* spasm;
∼módico *a* spasmodic

espatifar /ispatʃi'far/ *vt* smash;
∼-se *vpr* smash; <*carro, avião*>
crash

especi|al /ispesi'aw/ (*pl* **∼ais**) *a*
special; **∼alidade** *f* speciality;
∼alista *m/f* specialist

especializado /ispesiali'zadu/ *a* specialized; ~**zar-se** *vpr* specialize (em in)

especiaria /ispesia'ria/ *f* spice

espécie /is'pɛsi/ *f* sort, kind; (*de animais*) species

especifi|cação /ispesifika'sãw/ *f* specification; ~**car** *vt* specify

específico /ispe'sifiku/ *a* specific

espécime /is'pesimi/ *m* specimen

espectador /ispekta'dor/ *m* (*de TV*) viewer; (*de jogo, espetáculo*) spectator; (*de acidente etc*) onlooker

espectro /is'pɛktru/ *m* (*fantasma*) spectre; (*de cores*) spectrum

especu|lação /ispekula'sãw/ *f* speculation; ~**lador** *m* speculator; ~**lar** *vi* speculate (sobre on); ~**lativo** *a* speculative

espe|lhar /ispe'ʎar/ *vt* mirror; ~**lhar-se** *vpr* be mirrored; ~**lho** /e/ *m* mirror; ~**lho re-trovisor** rear-view mirror

espelunca /ispe'lũka/ *f* (*fam*) dive

espera /is'pɛra/ *f* wait; **à ~ de** waiting for

esperan|ça /ispe'rãsa/ *f* hope; ~**çoso** /o/ *a* hopeful

esperar /ispe'rar/ *vt* (*aguardar*) wait for; (*desejar*) hope for; (*contar com*) expect □ *vi* wait (por for); **fazer alg** ~ keep s.o. waiting; **espero que ele venha** I hope (that) he comes; **espero que sim/não** I hope so/not

esperma /is'pɛrma/ *m* sperm

espernear /isperni'ar/ *vi* kick; (*fig: reclamar*) kick up

esper|talhão /isperta'ʎãw/ *m* (*f* ~**talhona**) wise guy; ~**teza** /e/ *f* cleverness; (*uma*) clever move; ~**to** /e/ *a* clever

espes|so /is'pesu/ *a* thick; ~**sura** *f* thickness

espe|tacular /ispetaku'lar/ *a* spectacular; ~**táculo** *m* (*no teatro etc*) show; (*cena impressio-*

nante) spectacle; ~**taculoso** /o/ *a* spectacular

espe|tar /ispe'tar/ *vt* (*cravar*) stick; (*furar*) skewer; ~**tar-se** *vpr* (*cravar-se*) stick; (*ferir-se*) prick o.s.; ~**tinho** *m* skewer; (*de carne etc*) kebab; ~**to** /e/ *m* spit

espevitado /ispevi'tadu/ *a* cheeky

espezinhar /ispezi'ɲar/ *vt* walk all over

espi|a /is'pia/ *m/f* spy; ~**ão** *m* (*f* ~**ã**) spy; ~**ar** *vt* (*observar*) spy on; (*aguardar*) watch for □ *vi* peer, peep

espicaçar /ispika'sar/ *vt* goad <*pessoa*>; excite <*imaginação, curiosidade*>

espichar /ispi'ʃar/ *vt* stretch □ *vi* shoot up; ~**-se** *vpr* stretch out

espiga /is'piga/ *f* (*de trigo etc*) ear; (*de milho*) cob

espina|fração /ispinafra'sãw/ *f* (*fam*) *f* telling-off; ~**frar** (*fam*) *vt* tell off; ~**fre** *m* spinach

espingarda /ispĩ'garda/ *f* rifle, shotgun

espinha /is'piɲa/ *f* (*de peixe*) bone; (*na pele*) spot; ~ **dorsal** spine

espinho /is'piɲu/ *m* thorn; ~**so** /o/ *a* thorny; (*fig*) difficult, tough

espio|nagem /ispio'naʒẽ/ *f* espionage, spying; ~**nar** *vt* spy on □ *vi* spy

espi|ral /ispi'raw/ (*pl* ~**rais**) *a* & *f* spiral

espírita /is'pirita/ *a* & *m/f* spiritualist

espiritismo /ispiri't∫izmu/ *m* spiritualism

espírito /is'piritu/ *m* spirit; (*graça*) wit

espiritu|al /ispiritu'aw/ (*pl* ~**ais**) *a* spiritual; ~**oso** /o/ *a* witty

espir|rar /ispi'ʃar/ *vt* spurt □ *vi* <*pessoa*> sneeze; <*lama, tinta etc*> spatter; <*fogo, lenha, fritura etc*> spit; ~**ro** *m* sneeze

esplêndido /isˈplẽdʒidu/ a splendid

esplendor /isplẽˈdor/ m splendour

espoleta /ispoˈleta/ f fuse

espoliar /ispoliˈar/ vt plunder, pillage

espólio /isˈpɔliu/ m (herdado) estate; (roubado) spoils

espon|ja /isˈpõʒa/ f sponge; ~**joso** /o/ a spongy

espon|taneidade /ispõtanejˈdadʒi/ f spontaneity; ~**tâneo** a spontaneous

espora /isˈpɔra/ f spur

esporádico /ispoˈradʒiku/ a sporadic

esporear /isporiˈar/ vt spur on

espor|te /isˈpɔrtʃi/ m sport □ a invar <roupa> casual; **carro** ~**te** sports car; ~**tista** m/f sportsman (f -woman); ~**tiva** f sense of humour; ~**tivo** a sporting

espo|sa /isˈpoza/ f wife; ~**so** m husband

espregui|cadeira /ispregizaˈdera/ f (tipo cadeira) deckchair; (tipo cama) sun lounger; ~**car-se** vpr stretch

esprei|ta /isˈprejta/ f ficar à ~**ta** lie in wait; ~**tar** vt stalk <caça, vítima>; spy on <vizinhos, inimigos etc>; look out for <ocasião> □ vi peep, spy

espre|medor /ispremeˈdor/ m squeezer; ~**mer** vt squeeze; wring out <roupa>; squash <pessoa>; ~**mer-se** vpr squeeze up

espu|ma /isˈpuma/ f foam; ~**ma de borracha** foam rubber; ~**mante** a <vinho> sparkling; ~**mar** vi foam, froth

espúrio /isˈpuriu/ a spurious

esqua|dra /isˈkwadra/ f squad; ~**dra de polícia** (Port) police station; ~**drão** m squadron; ~**dria** f doors and windows; ~**drinhar** vt explore; ~**dro** m set square

esqualidez /iskwaliˈdes/ f squalor

esquálido /isˈkwalidu/ a squalid

esquartejar /iskwarteˈʒar/ vt chop up

esque|cer /iskeˈser/ vt/i forget; ~**cer-se de** forget; ~**cido** a forgotten; (com memória fraca) forgetful; ~**cimento** m oblivion; (memória fraca) forgetfulness

esque|lético /iskeˈlɛtʃiku/ a skinny, skeleton-like; ~**leto** /e/ m skeleton

esque|ma /isˈkema/ m outline, draft; (operação) scheme; ~**ma de segurança** security operation; ~**mático** a schematic

esquentar /iskẽˈtar/ vt warm up □ vi warm up; <roupa> be warm; ~**se** vpr get annoyed; ~ **a cabeça** (fam) get worked up

esquer|da /isˈkerda/ f left; à ~**da** (posição) on the left; (direção) to the left; ~**dista** a left-wing □ m/f left-winger; ~**do** /e/ a left

esqui /isˈki/ m ski; (esporte) skiing; ~ **aquático** water skiing; ~**ador** m skier; ~**ar** vi ski

esquilo /isˈkilu/ m squirrel

esquina /isˈkina/ f corner

esquisi|tice /iskiziˈtʃisi/ f strangeness; (uma) strange thing; ~**to** a strange

esqui|var-se /iskiˈvarsi/ vpr dodge out of the way; ~**var-se de** dodge; ~**vo** a elusive; <pessoa> aloof, antisocial

esquizo|frenia /iskizofreˈnia/ f schizophrenia; ~**frênico** a & m schizophrenic

es|sa /ˈɛsa/ pron that one; ~**sa é boa** that's a good one; ~**sa não** come off it; **por** ~**sas e outras** for these and other reasons; ~**se** /e/ a that; pl those; (fam: este) this; pl these □ pron these □ pron that one; pl those; (fam: este) this one; pl these

essência /e'sẽsia/ f essence

essenci|al /esẽsi'aw/ (*pl* ~**ais**) *a* essential; **o** ~**al** what is essential

estabele|cer /istabele'ser/ *vt* establish; ~**cer-se** *vpr* establish o.s.; ~**cimento** *m* establishment

estabili|dade /istabili'dadʒi/ f stability; ~**zar** *vt* stabilize; ~**zar-se** *vpr* stabilize

estábulo /is'tabulu/ *m* cowshed

estaca /is'taka/ f stake; (*de barraca*) peg; **voltar à** ~ **zero** go back to square one

estação /ista'sãw/ f (*do ano*) season; (*ferroviária etc*) station; ~**balneária** seaside resort

estacar /ista'kar/ *vi* stop short

estacio|namento /istasiona'mẽtu/ *m* (*ação*) parking; (*lugar*) car park, (*Amer*) parking lot; ~**nar** *vt/i* park

estada /is'tada/ f, **estadia** /ista-'dʒia/ f stay

estádio /is'tadʒiu/ *m* stadium

esta|dista /ista'dʒista/ *m/f* statesman (f -woman); ~**do** *m* state; ~**do civil** marital status; ~**do de espírito** state of mind; **Estados Unidos da América** United States of America; **Estado-Maior** *m* Staff; ~**dual** (*pl* ~**duais**) *a* state

esta|fa /is'tafa/ f exhaustion; ~**fante** *a* exhausting; ~**far** *vt* tire out; ~**far-se** *vpr* get tired out

estagi|ar /istaʒi'ar/ *vi* do a traineeship; ~**ário** *m* trainee

estágio /is'taʒiu/ *m* traineeship

estag|nado /istag'nadu/ *a* stagnant; ~**nar** *vi* stagnate

estalagem /ista'laʒẽ/ f inn

estalar /ista'lar/ *vt* (*quebrar*) crack; (*fazer barulho com*) click □ *vi* crack

estaleiro /ista'leru/ *m* shipyard

estalo /is'talu/ *m* crack; (*de dedos, língua*) click; **me deu um** ~ it clicked (in my mind)

estam|pa /is'tãpa/ f print; ~**pado** *a* <*tecido*> patterned □ *m* (*desenho*) pattern; (*tecido*) print; ~**par** *vt* print

estampido /istã'pidu/ *m* bang

estancar /istã'kar/ *vt* staunch; ~**se** *vpr* dry up

estância /is'tãsia/ f ~ **hidromineral** spa

estandarte /istã'dartʃi/ *m* banner

estanho /is'taɲu/ *m* tin

estanque /is'tãki/ *a* watertight

estante /is'tãtʃi/ f bookcase

estapafúrdio /istapa'furdʒiu/ *a* weird, odd

estar /is'tar/ *vi* be; (~ **em casa**) be in; **está chovendo**, (*Port*) **está a chover** it's raining; ~ **com** have; ~ **com calor/sono** be hot/sleepy; ~ **para terminar** be about to finish; **ele não está para ninguém** he's not available to see anyone; **o trabalho está por terminar** the work is yet to be finished

estardalhaço /istarda'ʎasu/ *m* (*barulho*) fuss; (*ostentação*) extravagance

estarre|cedor /istaxese'dor/ *a* horrifying; ~**cer** *vt* horrify; ~**cer-se** *vpr* be horrified

esta|tal /ista'taw/ (*pl* ~**tais**) *a* state-owned □ f state company

estate|lado /istate'ladu/ *a* sprawling; ~**lar** *vt* knock down; ~**lar-se** *vpr* go sprawling

estático /is'tatʃiku/ *a* static

estatísti|ca /ista'tʃistʃika/ f statistics; ~**co** *a* statistical

estati|zação /istatʃiza'sãw/ f nationalization; ~**zar** *vt* nationalize

estátua /is'tatua/ f statue

estatueta /istatu'eta/ f statuette

estatura /ista'tura/ f stature

estatuto /ista'tutu/ *m* statute

está|vel /is'tavew/ (*pl* ~**veis**) *a* stable

este¹ /'estʃi/ *m a invar* & *m* east

este² /'estʃi/ *a* this; *pl* these □ *pron* this one; *pl* these; (*mencionado por último*) the latter

esteio /is'teju/ *m* prop; (*fig*) mainstay

esteira /is'tera/ *f* (*tapete*) mat; (*rastro*) wake

estelionato /istelio'natu/ *m* fraud

estender /iste'der/ *vt* (*desdobrar*) spread out; (*alongar*) stretch; (*ampliar*) extend; hold out <*mão*>; hang out <*roupa*>; roll out <*massa*>; draw out <*conversa*>; **~-se** *vpr* (*deitar-se*) stretch out; (*ir longe*) stretch, extend; **~-se sobre** dwell on

esteno|datilógrafo /istenodatʃi'lɔgrafu/ *m* shorthand typist; **~grafia** *f* shorthand

estepe /is'tɛpi/ *m* spare wheel

esterco /is'terku/ *m* dung

estéreo /is'teriu/ *a invar* stereo

estere|otipado /isteriotʃi'padu/ *a* stereotypical; **~ótipo** *m* stereotype

esté|ril /is'teriw/ (*pl* **~reis**) *a* sterile

esterili|dade /isterili'dadʒi/ *f* sterility; **~zar** *vt* sterilize

esterli|no /ister'linu/ *a* **libra ~na** pound sterling

esteróide /iste'rɔjdʒi/ *m* steroid

estética /is'tɛtʃika/ *f* aesthetics

esteticista /istetʃi'sista/ *m/f* beautician

estético /is'tɛtʃiku/ *a* aesthetic

estetoscópio /istetos'kɔpiu/ *m* stethoscope

estiagem /istʃi'aʒẽ/ *f* dry spell

estibordo /istʃi'bɔrdu/ *m* starboard

esti|cada /istʃi'kada/ *f* **dar uma ~cada** go on; **~car** *vt* stretch □ (*fam*) *vi* go on; **~car-se** *vpr* stretch out

estigma /is'tʃigima/ *m* stigma; **~tizar** *vt* brand (de as)

estilha|çar /istʃiʎa'sar/ *vt* shatter;

~çar-se *vpr* shatter; **~ço** *m* shard, fragment

estilingue /istʃi'lĩgi/ *m* catapult

estilis|mo /istʃi'lizmu/ *m* fashion design; **~ta** *m/f* fashion designer

esti|lístico /istʃi'listʃiku/ *a* stylistic; **~lizar** *vt* stylize; **~lo** *m* style; **~lo de vida** lifestyle

esti|ma /es'tʃima/ *f* esteem; **~mação** *f* estimation; **cachorro de ~mação** pet dog; **~mado** *a* esteemed; **Estimado Senhor** Dear Sir; **Estimado Senhor** /value <*bens, jóias etc*> (**em** at); estimate <*valor, preço etc*> (**em** at); think highly of <*pessoa*>; **~mativa** *f* estimate

estimu|lante /istʃimu'lãtʃi/ *a* stimulating □ *m* stimulant; **~lar** *vt* stimulate; (*incentivar*) encourage

estímulo /is'tʃimulu/ *m* stimulus; (*incentivo*) incentive

estio /is'tʃiu/ *m* summer

estipu|lação /istʃipula'sãw/ *f* stipulation; **~lar** *vt* stipulate

estirar /istʃi'rar/ *vt* stretch; **~-se** *vpr* stretch

estirpe /is'tʃirpi/ *f* stock, line

estivador /istʃiva'dor/ *m* docker

estocada /isto'kada/ *f* thrust

estocar /isto'kar/ *vt* stock □ *vi* stock up

Estocolmo /isto'kɔwmu/ *f* Stockholm

esto|far /isto'far/ *vt* upholster <*móveis*>; **~fo** /o/ *m* upholstery

estóico /is'tɔjku/ *a* & *m* stoic

estojo /is'toʒu/ *m* case

estômago /is'tomagu/ *m* stomach

Estônia /is'tonia/ *f* Estonia

estonte|ante /istõtʃi'ãtʃi/ *a* stunning, mind-boggling; **~ar** *vt* stun

estopim /isto'pĩ/ *m* fuse; (*fig*) flashpoint

estoque /is'tɔki/ *m* stock

estore /is'tɔri/ *m* blind

estória /is'tɔria/ f story

estor|var /istor'var/ vt hinder; obstruct <*entrada, trânsito*>; ~**vo** /o/ m hindrance

estourado /isto'radu/ a <*pessoa*> explosive; ~**rar** vi <*bomba, escândalo, pessoa*> blow up; <*pneu*> burst; <*guerra*> break out; <*moda, cantor etc*> make it big; ~**ro** m (*de bomba, moda etc*) explosion; (*de pessoa*) outburst; (*de pneu*) blowout; (*de guerra*) outbreak

estrábico /is'trabiku/ a <*olhos*> squinty; <*pessoa*> squint-eyed

estrabismo /istra'bizmu/ m squint

estraçalhar /istrasa'ʎar/ vt tear to pieces

estrada /is'trada/ f road; ~ **de ferro** railway, (*Amer*) railroad; ~ **de rodagem** highway; ~ **de terra** dirt road

estrado /is'tradu/ m podium; (*de cama*) base

estraga-prazeres /istragapra'zeris/ m/f invar spoilsport

estragão /istra'gãw/ m tarragon

estra|gar /istra'gar/ vt (*tornar desagradável*) spoil; (*acabar com*) ruin □ vi (*quebrar*) break; (*apodrecer*) go off; ~**go** m damage; pl damage; (*da guerra, do tempo*) ravages

estrangeiro /istrã'ʒeru/ a foreign □ m foreigner; **do** ~ from abroad; **para o/no** ~ abroad

estrangular /istrãgu'lar/ vt strangle

estra|nhar /istra'ɲar/ vt (*achar estranho*) find strange; (*não se adaptar a*) find it hard to get used to; (*não se sentir à vontade com*) be shy with; ~**nhar que** find it strange that; **estou te** ~**nhando** that's not like you; **não é de se** ~**nhar** it's not surprising; ~**nheza** /e/ f (*esquisitice*) strangeness; (*surpresa*)

surprise; ~**nho** a strange □ m stranger

estratagema /istrata'ʒema/ m stratagem

estraté|gia /istra'teʒia/ f strategy; ~**gico** a strategic

estrato /is'tratu/ m (*camada*) stratum; (*nuvem*) stratus; ~**sfera** f stratosphere

estre|ante /istri'ãtʃi/ a new □ m/f newcomer; ~**ar** vt première <*peça, filme*>; embark on <*carreira*>; wear for the first time <*roupa*> □ vi <*pessoa*> make one's début; <*filme, peça*> open

estrebaria /istreba'ria/ f stable

estréia /is'treja/ f (*de pessoa*) début; (*de filme, peça*) première

estrei|tar /istrej'tar/ vt narrow; take in <*vestido*>; make closer <*relações, laços*> □ vi narrow; ~**tar-se** vpr <*relações*> become closer; ~**to** a narrow; <*relações, laços*> close; <*saia*> straight □ m strait

estre|la /is'trela/ f star; ~**lado** a <*céu*> starry; <*ovo*> fried; ~**lado por** <*filme etc*> starring; ~**la-do-mar** (pl ~**las-do-mar**) f starfish; ~**lar** vt fry <*ovo*>; star in <*filme, peça*>; ~**lato** m stardom; ~**lismo** m star quality

estreme|cer /istreme'ser/ vt shake; strain <*relações, amizade*> □ vi shudder; <*relações, amizade*> become strained; ~**cimento** m shudder; (*de relações, amizade*) strain

estrepar-se /istre'parsi/ (*fam*) vpr come a cropper

estrépito /is'trepitu/ m noise; **com** ~ noisily

estrepitoso /istrepi'tozu/ a noisy; <*sucesso etc*> resounding

estres|sante /istre'sãtʃi/ a stressful; ~**sar** vt stress; ~**se** /ɛ/ m stress

estria /is'tria/ f streak; (*no corpo*) stretch mark

estribeira /istri'bera/ f stirrup; **perder as ~s** lose control

estribilho /istri'biʎu/ m chorus

estribo /is'tribu/ m stirrup

estridente /istri'dẽtʃi/ a strident

estripulia /istripu'lia/ f antic

estrito /is'tritu/ a strict

estrofe /is'trɔfi/ f stanza, verse

estrogonofe /istrogo'nɔfi/ m stroganoff

estrógeno /is'trɔʒenu/ m oestrogen

estron|do /is'trõdu/ m crash; **~doso** /o/ a loud; (*de aplausos*) thunderous; (*sucesso, fracasso*) resounding

estropiar /istropi'ar/ vt cripple (*pessoa*); mangle (*palavras*)

estrume /is'trumi/ m manure

estrutu|ra /istru'tura/ f structure; **~ral** (pl **~rais**) a structural; **~rar** vt structure

estuário /istu'ariu/ m estuary

estudan|te /istu'dãtʃi/ m/f student; **~til** (pl **~tis**) a student

estudar /istu'dar/ vt/i study

estúdio /is'tudʒiu/ m studio

estu|dioso /istudʒi'ozu/ a studious □ m scholar; **~do** m study

estufa /is'tufa/ f (*para plantas*) greenhouse; (*de aquecimento*) stove; **~do** m stew

estupefato /istupe'fatu/ a dumbfounded

estupendo /iste'pẽdu/ a stupendous

estupi|dez /istupi'des/ f (*grosseria*) rudeness; (*uma*) rude thing; (*burrice*) stupidity; (*uma*) stupid thing

estúpido /is'tupidu/ a (*grosso*) rude, coarse; (*burro*) stupid □ m lout

estupor /istu'por/ m stupor

estu|prador /istupra'dor/ m rapist; **~prar** vt rape; **~pro** m rape

esturricar /istuxi'kar/ vt parch

esvair-se /izva'irsi/ vpr fade; **~ em sangue** bleed to death

esvaziar /izvazi'ar/ vt empty; **~se** vpr empty

esverdeado /izverdʒi'adu/ a greenish

esvoa|çante /izvoa'sãtʃis/ a <*cabelo*> fly-away; **~çar** vi flutter

eta /'eta/ int what a

etapa /e'tapa/ f stage; (*de corrida, turnê etc*) leg

etário /e'tariu/ a age

éter /'ɛter/ m ether

etéreo /e'tɛriu/ a ethereal

eter|nidade /eterni'dadʒi/ f eternity; **~no** /ɛ/ a eternal

éti|ca /'ɛtʃika/ f ethics; **~co** a ethical

etimo|logia /etʃimolo'ʒia/ f etymology; **~lógico** a etymological

etíope /e'tʃiopi/ a & m/f Ethiopian

Etiópia /etʃi'ɔpia/ f Ethiopia

etique|ta /etʃi'keta/ f (*rótulo*) label; (*bons modos*) etiquette; **~tar** vt label

étnico /'ɛtʃniku/ a ethnic

eu /ew/ pron I □ m self; **mais alto do que ~** taller than me; **sou ~** it's me

EUA m pl USA

eucalipto /ewka'liptu/ m eucalyptus

eufemismo /ewfe'mizmu/ m euphemism

euforia /ewfo'ria/ f euphoria

euro /'ewru/ m euro

Europa /ew'rɔpa/ f Europe

euro|peu /ewro'pew/ a & m (f **~péia**) European

eutanásia /ewta'nazia/ f euthanasia

evacu|ação /evakua'sãw/ f evacuation; **~ar** vt evacuate

evadir /eva'dʒir/ vt evade; **~se** vpr escape (de from)

evan|gelho /evã'ʒɛʎu/ m gospel

evaporar /evapo'rar/ vt evaporate; **~se** vpr evaporate

eva|são /eva'zãw/ f escape; (*fiscal etc*) evasion; **~são escolar**

truancy; ~**siva** f excuse; ~**sivo** a evasive

even|to /e'vĕtu/ m event; ~**tual** (pl ~**tuais**) a possible; ~**tualidade** f eventuality

evidência /evi'dẽsia/ f evidence

eviden|ciar /evidẽsi'ar/ vt show up; ~**ciar-se** vpr show up; ~**te** a obvious, evident

evi|tar /evi'tar/ vt avoid; ~**tar de beber** avoid drinking; ~**tável** (pl ~**táveis**) a avoidable

evocar /evo'kar/ vt call to mind, evoke <passado etc>; call up <espíritos etc>

evolu|ção /evolu'sãw/ f evolution; ~**ir** vi evolve

exacerbar /ezaser'bar/ vt exacerbate

exage|rado /ezaʒe'radu/ a over the top; ~**rar** vt (atribuir proporções irreais a) exaggerate; (fazer em excesso) overdo □ vi (ao falar) exaggerate; (exceder-se) overdo it; ~**ro** /e/ m exaggeration

exa|lação /ezala'sãw/ f fume; (agradável) scent; ~**lar** vt give off <perfume etc>

exal|tação /ezawta'sãw/ f (excitação) agitation; (engrandecimento) exaltation; ~**tar** vt (excitar) agitate; (enfurecer) infuriate; (louvar) exalt; ~**tar-se** vpr (excitar-se) get agitated; (enfurecer-se) get furious

exa|me /e'zami/ m examination; (na escola) exam(ination); ~**me de sangue** blood test; ~**minar** vt examine

exaspe|ração /ezaspera'sãw/ f exasperation; ~**rar** vt exasperate; ~**rar-se** vpr get exasperated

exa|tidão /ezatʃi'dãw/ f exactness; ~**to** a exact

exaurir /ezaw'rir/ vt exhaust; ~**se** vpr become exhausted

exaus|tivo /ezaws'tʃivu/ a <estudo> exhaustive; <trabalho> exhausting; ~**to** a exhausted

exce|ção /ese'sãw/ f exception; **abrir** ~ make an exception; **com** ~ **de** with the exception of

exce|dente /ese'dẽtʃi/ a & m excess, surplus; ~**der** vt exceed; ~**der-se** vpr overdo it

exce|lência /ese'lẽsia/ f excellence; (tratamento) excellency; ~**lente** a excellent

excentricidade /esẽtrisi'dadʒi/ f eccentricity

excêntrico /e'sẽtriku/ a & m eccentric

excep|ção /iʃse'sãw/ (Port) f veja **exceção**; ~**cional** (pl ~**cionais**) a exceptional; (deficiente) handicapped

exces|sivo /ese'sivu/ a excessive; ~**so** /ɛ/ m excess; ~**so de bagagem** excess baggage; ~**so de velocidade** speeding

exce|to /e'setu/ prep except; ~**tuar** vt except

exci|tação /esita'sãw/ f excitement; ~**tante** a exciting; ~**tar** vt excite; ~**tar-se** vpr get excited

excla|mação /isklama'sãw/ f exclamation; ~**mar** vt/i exclaim

exclu|ir /isklu'ir/ vt exclude; ~**são** f exclusion; **com** ~**são de** with the exclusion of; ~**sividade** f exclusive rights; **com** ~**sividade** exclusively; ~**sivo** a exclusive; ~**so** a excluded

excomungar /iskomũ'gar/ vt excommunicate

excremento /iskre'mẽtu/ m excrement

excur|são /iskur'sãw/ f excursion; (a pé) hike, walk; ~**sionista** (a pé) day-tripper; (a pé) hiker, walker

execu|ção /ezeku'sãw/ f execution; ~**tante** m/f performer; ~**tar** vt carry out <ordem, plano etc>; perform <papel, música>; execute <preso, criminoso etc>; ~**tivo** a & m executive

exem|plar /ezē'plar/ *a* exemplary □ *m* (*de espécie*) example; (*de livro, jornal etc*) copy; **~plificar** *vt* exemplify

exemplo /e'zēplu/ *m* example; **a ~ de** following the example of; **por ~** for example; **dar o ~** set an example

exeqüí|vel /eze'kwivew/ (*pl* **~veis**) *a* feasible

exer|cer /ezer'ser/ *vt* exercise; exert <*pressão, influência*>; carry on <*profissão*>; **~cício** *m* exercise; (*mil*) drill; (*de profissão*) practice; (*financeiro*) financial year; **~citar** *vt* exercise; practise <*ofício*>; **~citar-se** *vpr* train

exército /e'zersitu/ *m* army

exibição /ezibi'sãw/ *f* (*de filme, passaporte etc*) showing; (*de talento, força, ostentação*) show

exibicionis|mo /ezibisio'nizmu/ *m* exhibitionism; **~ta** *a & m/f* exhibitionist

exi|bido /ezi'bidu/ *a* <*pessoa*> pretentious □ *m* show-off; **~bir** *vt* show; (*ostentar*) show off; **~bir-se** *vpr* (*ostentar-se*) show off

exi|gência /ezi'ʒẽsia/ *f* demand; **~gente** *a* demanding; **~gir** *vt* demand

exíguo /e'zigwu/ *a* (*muito pequeno*) tiny; (*escasso*) minimal

exi|lado /ezi'ladu/ *a* exiled □ *m* exile; **~lar** *vt* exile; **~lar-se** *vpr* go into exile

exílio /e'ziliu/ *m* exile

exímio /e'zimiu/ *a* distinguished

eximir /ezi'mir/ *vt* exempt (**de** from); **~-se** *vpr* get out of

exis|tência /ezis'tẽsia/ *f* existence; **~tencial** (*pl* **~tenciais**) *a* existential; **~tente** *a* existing; **~tir** *vi* exist

êxito /'ezitu/ *m* success; (*música, filme etc*) hit; **ter ~** succeed

êxodo /'ezodu/ *m* exodus

exonerar /ezone'rar/ *vt* (*de cargo*) dismiss, sack; **~-se** *vpr* resign

exorbitante /ezorbi'tãtʃi/ *a* exorbitant

exor|cismo /ezor'sizmu/ *m* exorcism; **~cista** *m/f* exorcist; **~cizar** *vt* exorcize

exótico /e'zotʃiku/ *a* exotic

expan|dir /ispã'dʒir/ *vt* spread; **~dir-se** *vpr* spread; <*pessoa*> open up; **~dir-se sobre** expand upon; **~são** *f* expansion; **~sivo** *a* expansive, open

expatri|ado /ispatri'adu/ *a & m* expatriate; **~ar-se** *vpr* leave one's country

expectativa /ispekta'tʃiva/ *f* expectation; **na ~ de** expecting; **estar na ~** wait to see what happens; **~ de vida** life expectancy

expedição /espedʒi'sãw/ *f* (*de encomendas, cartas*) dispatch; (*de passaporte, diploma etc*) issue; (*viagem*) expedition

expediente /ispedʒi'ẽtʃi/ *a* <*pessoa*> resourceful □ *m* (*horário*) working hours; (*meios*) expedient; **meio ~** part-time

expe|dir /ispe'dʒir/ *vt* dispatch <*encomendas, cartas*>; issue <*passaporte, diploma*>; **~dito** *a* prompt, quick

expelir /ispe'lir/ *vt* expel

experi|ência /isperi'ẽsia/ *f* experience; (*teste, tentativa*) experiment; **~ente** *a* experienced

experimen|tação /isperimẽta'sãw/ *f* experimentation; **~tado** *a* experienced; **~tar** *vt* (*provar*) try out; try on <*roupa*>; (*sentir, viver*) experience; **~to** *m* experiment

expi|ar /espi'ar/ *vt* atone for; **~atório** *a* **bode ~atório** scapegoat

expi|ração /espira'sãw/ *f* (*vencimento*) expiry; (*de ar*) exhalation; **~rar** *vt* exhale □ *vi* (*morrer, vencer*) expire; (*expelir ar*) breath out, exhale

expli|cação /isplika'sãw/ *f* explanation; **~car** *vt* explain; **~car-se** *vpr* explain o.s.; **~cável** (*pl* **~cáveis**) *a* explainable

explicitar /isplisi'tar/ *vt* set out

explícito /is'plisitu/ *a* explicit

explodir /isplo'dʒir/ *vt* explode □ *vi* explode; <*ator etc*> make it big

explo|ração /isplora'sãw/ *f* (*uso, abuso*) exploitation; (*pesquisa*) exploration; **~rar** *vt* (*tirar proveito de*) exploit; (*esquadrinhar*) explore

explo|são /isplo'zãw/ *f* explosion; **~sivo** *a & m* explosive

expor /es'por/ *vt* (*sujeitar, arriscar*) expose (**a** to); display <*mercadorias*>; exhibit <*obras de arte*>; (*explicar*) expound; **~ a vida** risk one's life; **~-se** *vpr* expose o.s. (**a** to)

expor|tação /isporta'sãw/ *f* export; **~tador** *a* exporting □ *m* exporter; (*empresa*) export company; **~tar** *vt* export

exposi|ção /ispozi'sãw/ *f* (*de arte etc*) exhibition; (*de mercadorias*) display; (*de filme fotográfico*) exposure; (*explicação*) exposition; **~tor** *m* exhibitor

exposto /is'postu/ *a* exposed (**a** to); <*mercadoria, obra de arte*> on display

expres|são /ispre'sãw/ *f* expression; **~sar** *vt* express; **~sar-se** *vpr* express o.s.; **~sivo** *a* expressive; <*número, quantia*> significant; **~so** /ɛ/ *a & m* express

exprimir /ispri'mir/ *vt* express; **~-se** *vpr* express o.s.

expropriar /ispropri'ar/ *vt* expropriate

expul|são /ispuw'sãw/ *f* expulsion; (*de jogador*) sending off; **~sar** *vt* (*de escola, partido, país*

etc) expel; (*de clube, bar, festa etc*) throw out; (*de jogo*) send off; **~so** *pp de* **expulsar**

expur|gar /ispur'gar/ *vt* purge; expurgate <*livro*>; **~go** *m* purge

êxtase /'estazi/ *f* ecstasy

extasiado /istazi'adu/ *a* ecstatic

exten|são /istē'sãw/ *f* extension; (*tamanho, alcance, duração*) extent; (*de terreno*) expanse; **~sivo** *a* extensive; **~so** *a* extensive; **por ~so** in full

extenu|ante /istenu'ãtʃi/ *a* wearing, tiring; **~ar** *vt* tire out; **~ar-se** *vpr* tire o.s. out

exterior /isteri'or/ *a* outside, exterior; <*aparência*> outward; <*relações, comércio etc*> foreign □ *m* outside, exterior; (*de pessoa*) exterior; **o ~** (*outros países*) abroad; **para o/no ~** abroad

exter|minar /istermi'nar/ *vt* exterminate; **~mínio** *m* extermination

exter|nar /ister'nar/ *vt* show; **~na** /ɛ/ *f* location shot; **~no** /ɛ/ *a* external; <*dívida etc*> foreign □ *m* day-pupil

extin|ção /istʃĩ'sãw/ *f* extinction; **~guir** *vt* extinguish <*fogo*>; wipe out <*dívida, animal, povo*>; **~guir-se** *vpr* <*fogo, luz*> go out; <*animal, planta*> become extinct; **~to** *a* extinct; <*organização, pessoa*> defunct; **~tor** *m* fire extinguisher

extirpar /istʃir'par/ *vt* remove <*tumor etc*>; uproot <*ervas daninhas*>; eradicate <*abusos*>

extor|quir /istor'kir/ *vt* extort; **~são** /ɛ/ *f* extortion

extra /'estra/ *a & m/f* extra; **horas ~s** overtime

extração /istra'sãw/ *f* extraction; (*da loteria*) draw

extraconju|gal /estrakõʒu'gaw/ (*pl* **~gais**) *a* extramarital

extracurricular /estrakuxiku'lar/ *a* extracurricular

extradi|ção /istradʒi'sãw/ f extradition; **~tar** vt extradite

extrair /istra'ir/ vt extract; draw <*números da loteria*>

extrajudici|al /estraʒudʒisi'aw/ (pl **~ais**) a out-of-court; **~almente** adv out of court

extraordinário /istraordʒi'nariu/ a extraordinary

extrapolar /istrapo'lar/ vt (exceder) overstep; (calcular) extrapolate □ vi overstep the mark, go too far

extra-sensori|al /estrasẽsori'aw/ (pl **~ais**) a extra-sensory

extraterrestre /istrate'xɛstri/ a & m extraterrestrial

extrato /is'tratu/ m extract; (de conta) statement

extrava|gância /istrava'gãsia/ f extravagance; **~gante** a extravagant

extravasar /istrava'zar/ vt release, let out <*emoções, sentimentos*> □ vi overflow

extra|viado /istravi'adu/ a lost; **~viar** vt lose, mislay <*papéis, carta*>; lead astray <*pessoa*>; embezzle <*dinheiro*>; **~viar-se** vpr go astray; <*carta*> get lost; **~vio** m (perda) misplacement; (de dinheiro) embezzlement

extre|midade /estremi'dadʒi/ f end; (do corpo) extremity; **~mismo** m extremism; **~mista** a & m/f extremist; **~mo** (e/ a & m extreme; **o Extremo Oriente** the Far East; **~moso** /o/ a doting

extrovertido /istrover'tʃido/ a & m extrovert

exube|rância /ezube'rãsia/ f exuberance; **~rante** a exuberant

exultar /ezuw'tar/ vi exult

exumar /ezu'mar/ vt exhume <*cadáver*>; dig up <*documentos etc*>

F

fã /fã/ m/f fan

fábrica /'fabrika/ f factory

fabri|cação /fabrika'sãw/ f manufacture; **~cante** m/f manufacturer; **~car** vt manufacture; (inventar) fabricate

fábula /'fabula/ f fable; (fam: dinheirão) fortune

fabuloso /fabu'lozu/ a fabulous

faca /'faka/ f knife; **~da** f knife blow; **dar uma ~da em** (fig) get some money off

façanha /fa'saɲa/ f feat

facção /fak'sãw/ f faction

face /'fasi/ f face; (do rosto) cheek; **~ta** /e/ f facet

fachada /fa'ʃada/ f façade

facho /'faʃu/ m beam

faci|al /fasi'aw/ (pl **~ais**) a facial

fá|cil /'fasiw/ (pl **~ceis**) a easy; <*pessoa*> easy-going

facili|dade /fasili'dadʒi/ f ease; (talento) facility; **~tar** vt facilitate

fã-clube /fã'klubi/ m fan club

fac-símile /fak'simili/ m facsimile; (fax) fax

fact- (Port) veja **fat-**

facul|dade /fakuw'dadʒi/ f (mental etc) faculty; (escola) university, (Amer) college; **fazer ~dade** go to university; **~tativo** a optional

fada /'fada/ f fairy; **~do** a destined, doomed; **~-madrinha** (pl **~s-madrinhas**) f fairy godmother

fadiga /fa'dʒiga/ f fatigue

fa|dista /fa'dʒista/ m/f fado singer; **~do** m fado

fagote /fa'gotʃi/ m bassoon

fagulha /fa'guʎa/ f spark

faia /'faja/ f beech

faisão /faj'zãw/ m pheasant

faísca /fa'iska/ f spark

fais|cante /fajs'kãtʃi/ a sparkling; **~car** vi spark; (cintilar) sparkle

faixa /'fajʃa/ f strip; (cinto) sash; (em karatê, judô) belt; (da estrada) lane; (de ônibus) bus lane; (para pedestres) zebra crossing, (Amer) crosswalk; (atadura) bandage; (de disco) track; **~ etária** age group

fajuto /fa'ʒutu/ (fam) a fake

fala /'fala/ f speech

falácia /fa'lasia/ f fallacy

fa|lado /fa'ladu/ a <língua> spoken; <caso, pessoa> talked about; **~lante** a talkative; **~lar** vt/i speak; (dizer) say; **~lar com** talk to; **~lar de** ou em talk about; por **~lar em** speaking of; sem **~lar** em not to mention; **~lou!** (fam) OK!; **~latório** m (boatos) talk; (som de vozes) talking

falaz /fa'las/ a fallacious

falcão /faw'kãw/ m falcon

falcatrua /fawka'trua/ f swindle

fale|cer /fale'ser/ vi die, pass away; **~cido** a & m deceased; **~cimento** m death

falência /fa'lẽsia/ f bankruptcy; **ir à ~** go bankrupt

falésia /fa'lɛzia/ f cliff

fa|lha /'faʎa/ f fault; (omissão) failure; **~lhar** vi fail; **~lho** a faulty

fálico /'faliku/ a phallic

fa|lido /fa'lidu/ a & m bankrupt; **~lir** vi go bankrupt; **~lível** (pl **~líveis**) a fallible

falo /'falu/ m phallus

fal|sário /faw'sariu/ m forger; **~sear** vt falsify; **~sete** m falsetto; **~sidade** f falseness; (mentira) falsehood

falsifi|cação /fawsifika'sãw/ f forgery; **~cador** m forger; **~car** vt falsify; forge <documentos, notas>

falso /'fawsu/ a false

fal|ta /'fawta/ f lack; (em futebol) foul; em **~ta** at fault; por **~ta**

de for lack of; sem **~ta** without fail; fazer **~ta** be needed; sentir a **~ta de** miss; **~tar** vi be missing; <aluno> be absent; **~tam dois dias para** it's two days until; me **~ta** ... I don't have ...; **~tar a miss** <aula etc>; break <palavra, promessa>; **~to** a short (de of)

fa|ma /'fama/ f reputation; (celebridade) fame; **~migerado** a notorious

família /fa'milia/ f family

famili|ar /famili'ar/ a familiar; (de família) family; **~aridade** f familiarity; **~arizar** vt familiarize; **~arizar-se** vpr familiarize o.s.

faminto /fa'mĩtu/ a starving

famoso /fa'mozu/ a famous

fanático /fa'natʃiku/ a fanatical □ m fanatic

fanatismo /fana'tʃizmu/ m fanaticism

fanfarrão /fãfa'xãw/ m braggart

fanhoso /fa'nozu/ a nasal; ser **~** talk through one's nose

fanta|sia /fãta'zia/ f (faculdade) imagination; (devaneio) fantasy; (roupa) fancy dress; <siar vt dream up □ vi fantasize; **~siar-se** vpr dress up (de as); **~sioso** /o/ a fanciful; <pessoa> imaginative; **~sista** a imaginative

fantasma /fã'tazma/ m ghost; **~górico** a ghostly

fantástico /fã'tastʃiku/ a fantastic

fantoche /fã'tɔʃi/ m puppet

faqueiro /fa'keru/ m canteen of cutlery

fara|ó /fara'ɔ/ m pharaoh; **~ônico** a (fig) of epic proportions

farda /'farda/ f uniform; **~do** a uniformed

fardo /'fardu/ m (fig) burden

fare|jador /fareʒa'dor/ a **cão ~jador** sniffer dog; **~jar** vt sniff out □ vi sniff

farelo /fa'rɛlu/ *m* bran; (*de pão*) crumb; (*de madeira*) sawdust

farfalhar /farfa'ʎar/ *vi* rustle

farináceo /fari'nasiu/ *a* starchy; ~s *m pl* starchy foods

faringe /fa'rĩʒi/ *f* pharynx; ~gite *f* pharyngitis

farinha /fa'riɲa/ *f* flour; ~ **de rosca** breadcrumbs

farmacêutico /farma'sewtʃiku/ *a* pharmaceutical □ *m* (*pessoa*) pharmacist; ~**mácia** *f* (*loja*) chemist's, (*Amer*) pharmacy; (*ciência*) pharmacy

faro /'faru/ *f* sense of smell; (*fig*) nose

faroeste /faro'ɛstʃi/ *m* (*filme*) western; (*região*) wild west

farofa /fa'rɔfa/ *f* fried manioc flour; ~**feiro** *f* (*fam*) day-tripper

farol /fa'rɔw/ (*pl* ~**róis**) *m* (*de carro*) headlight; (*de trânsito*) traffic light; (*à beira-mar*) lighthouse; ~**rol alto** full beam; ~**rol baixo** dipped beam; ~**roleiro** *a* boastful □ bighead; ~**rolete** *e/ m*, (*Port*) ~**rolim** *f* side-light; (*traseiro*) tail-light

farpa /'farpa/ *f* splinter; (*de metal, fig*) barb; ~**do** *a* **arame** □ barbed wire

farra /'faxa/ (*fam*) *f* partying; **cair na** ~ go out and party

farrapo /fa'xapu/ *m* rag

farrear /faxi'ar/ (*fam*) *vi* party; ~**rista** *f* (*fam*) *m/f* raver

farsa /'farsa/ *f* (*peça*) farce; (*fingimento*) pretence; ~**sante** *m/f* (*brincalhão*) joker; (*pessoa sem seriedade*) unreliable character

fartar /far'tar/ *vt* satiate; ~**se** *vpr* (*saciar-se*) gorge o.s. (**de** with); (*cansar*) tire (**de** of); ~**to** *a* (*abundante*) plentiful; (*cansado*) fed up (**de** with); ~**tura** *f* abundance

fascículo /fa'sikulu/ *m* instalment

fascinação /fasina'sãw/ *f* fascination; ~**nante** *a* fascinating; ~**nar** *vt* fascinate

fascínio /fa'siniu/ *m* fascination

fascismo /fa'sizmu/ *m* fascism; ~**cista** *a & m/f* fascist

fase /'fazi/ *f* phase

fatal /fa'taw/ (*pl* ~**tais**) *a* fatal; ~**talismo** *m* fatalism; ~**talista** *a* fatalistic □ *m/f* fatalist; ~**talmente** *adv* inevitably

fatia /fa'tʃia/ *f* slice

fatídico /fa'tʃidʒiku/ *a* fateful

fatigante /fatʃi'gãtʃi/ *a* tiring; ~**gar** *vt* tire, fatigue

fato¹ /'fatu/ *m* fact; **de** ~ as a matter of fact, in fact; ~ **consumado** fait accompli

fato² /'fatu/ (*Port*) *m* suit

fator /fa'tor/ *m* factor

fátuo /'fatuu/ *a* fatuous

fatura /fa'tura/ *f* invoice; ~**ramento** *m* turnover; ~**rar** *vt* invoice for <*encomenda*>; make <*dinheiro*>; (*fig*: *emplacar*) notch up □ *vi* (*fam*) rake it in

fauna /'fawna/ *f* fauna

fava /'fava/ *f* broad bean; **mandar alg às** ~ **s** tell s.o. where to get off

favela /fa'vɛla/ *f* shanty town; ~**do** *m* shanty-dweller

favo /'favu/ *m* honeycomb

favor /fa'vor/ *m* favour; **a** ~ **de** in favour of; **por** ~ please; **faça** ~ please

favorável /favo'ravew/ (*pl* ~**ráveis**) *a* favourable; ~**recer** *vt* favour; ~**ritismo** *m* favouritism; ~**rito** *a & m* favourite

faxina /fa'ʃina/ *f* clean-up; ~**neiro** *m* cleaner

fazenda /fa'zẽda/ *f* (*de café, gado etc*) farm; (*tecido*) fabric, material; (*pública*) treasury; ~**deiro** *m* farmer

fazer /fa'zer/ *vt* do; (*produzir*) make; ask <*pergunta*>; ~**se** *vpr* (*tornar-se*) become; ~**se** *o.s.*

make o.s. out to be; ~ **anos** have a birthday; ~ **20 anos** be twenty; **faz dois dias que ele está aqui** he's been here for two days; **faz dez anos que ele morreu** it's ten years since he died; **tanto faz** it doesn't matter

faz-tudo /fas'tudu/ *m/f invar* jack of all trades

fé /fɛ/ *f* faith

fe|bre /'fɛbri/ *f* fever; ~**bre amarela** yellow fever; ~**bre do feno** hay fever; ~**bril** (*pl* ~**bris**) *a* feverish

fe|chado /fe'ʃadu/ *a* closed; <*curva*> sharp; <*sinal*> red; <*torneira*> off; <*tempo*> overcast; <*cara*> stern; <*pessoa*> reserved; ~**chadura** /f lock; ~**chamento** *m* closure; ~**char** *vt* close, shut; turn off <*torneira*>; do up <*calça, casaco*>; close <*negócio*> □ *vi* close, shut; <*sinal*> go red; <*tempo*> cloud over; ~**char à chave** lock; ~**char a cara** frown; ~**cho** /e/ *m* fastener; ~**cho ecler** zip

fécula /'fɛkula/ *f* starch

fecun|dar /fekũ'dar/ *vt* fertilize; ~**do** *a* fertile

feder /fe'der/ *vi* stink

fede|ração /federa'sãw/ *f* federation; ~**ral** (*pl* ~**rais**) *a* federal; (*fam*) huge; ~**rativo** *a* federal

fedor /fe'dor/ *m* stink, stench; ~**ento** *a* stinking

feérico /feeriku/ *a* magical

feições /fej'sõjs/ *f pl* features

fei|jão /fe'ʒãw/ *m* bean; (*coletivo*) beans; ~**joada** /f bean stew; ~**joeiro** *m* bean plant

feio /'feju/ *a* ugly; <*palavra, situação, tempo*> nasty; <*olhar*> dirty; ~**so** /o/ *a* plain

fei|ra /'fera/ *f* market; (*industrial*) trade fair; ~**rante** *m/f* market trader

feiti|çaria /fejtʃi'sera/ *f* magic; ~**ceira** *f* witch; ~**ceiro** *m*

wizard □ *a* bewitching; ~**ço** *m* spell

fei|tio /fej'tʃiu/ *m* (*de pessoa*) make-up; ~**to** *pp de* **fazer** □ *m* (*ato*) deed; (*proeza*) feat □ *conj* like; **bem** ~**to por ele** (*it*) serves him right; ~**tura** /f making

feiúra /fej'ura/ *f* ugliness

feixe /'feʃi/ *m* bundle

fel /fɛw/ *f* gall; (*fig*) bitterness

felicidade /felisi'dadʒi/ *f* happiness

felici|tações /felisita'sõjs/ *f pl* congratulations; ~**tar** *vt* congratulate (**por** *on*)

felino /fe'linu/ *a* feline

feliz /fe'lis/ *a* happy; ~**ardo** *a* lucky; ~**mente** *adv* fortunately

fel|pa /'fewpa/ *f* (*de pano*) nap; (*penugem*) down, fluff; ~**pudo** *a* fluffy

feltro /'fewtru/ *m* felt

fêmea /'femia/ *a & f* female

femi|nil /femi'niw/ (*pl* ~**nis**) *a* feminine; ~**nilidade** *f* femininity; ~**nino** *a* female; <*palavra*> feminine; ~**nismo** *m* feminism; ~**nista** *a & m/f* feminist

fêmur /'femur/ *m* femur

fen|da /'fẽda/ *f* crack; ~**der** *vt/i* split, crack

feno /'fenu/ *m* hay

fenome|nal /fenome'naw/ (*pl* ~**nais**) *a* phenomenal

fenômeno /fe'nomenu/ *m* phenomenon

fera /'fera/ *f* wild beast; **ficar uma** ~ get really angry; **ser** ~ **em** (*fam*) be brilliant at

féretro /'feretru/ *m* coffin

feriado /feri'adu/ *m* public holiday

férias /'ferias/ *f pl* holiday(s), (*Amer*) vacation; **de** ~ *on* holiday; **tirar** ~ take a holiday

feri|da /fe'rida/ *f* injury; (*com arma*) wound; ~**do** *a* injured; (*mil*) wounded □ *m* injured

person; **os ~dos** the injured;
(*mil*) the wounded; **~r** *vt* injure;
(*com arma*) wound; (*magoar*)
hurt

fermen|tar /fermẽˈtar/ *vt/i* ferment; **~to** *m* yeast; (*fig*)
ferment; **~to em pó** baking
powder

fe|rocidade /ferosiˈdadʒi/ *f* ferocity; **~roz** *a* ferocious

fer|rado /feˈxadu/ *a* **estou ~rado** (*fam*) I've had it; **~rado no sono** fast asleep; **~radura** *f* horseshoe; **~ragem** *f* ironwork; *pl* hardware; **~ramenta** *f* tool; (*coletivo*) tools; **~rão** *m* (*de abelha*) sting; **~rar** *vt* brand <*gado*>; shoe <*cavalo*>; **~rarse** (*fam*) *vpr* come a cropper; **~reiro** *m* blacksmith; **~renho** *a* <*partidário etc*> staunch; <*vontade*> iron

férreo /ˈfɛxiu/ *a* iron

ferro /ˈfɛxu/ *m* iron; **~lho** /o/ *m* bolt; **~-velho** (*pl* **~s-velhos**) *m* (*pessoa*) scrap-metal dealer; (*lugar*) scrap-metal yard; **~via** *f* railway, (*Amer*) railroad; **~viário** *a* railway □ *m* railway worker

ferrugem /feˈxuʒẽ/ *f* rust

fér|til /ˈfɛrtʃiw/ (*pl* **~teis**) *a* fertile

fertili|dade /fertʃiliˈdadʒi/ *f* fertility; **~zante** *m* fertilizer; **~zar** *vt* fertilize

fer|vente /ferˈvẽtʃi/ *a* boiling; **~ver** *vi* boil; (*de raiva*) seethe; **~vilhar** *vi* bubble; **~vilhar de** swarm with; **~vor** *m* fervour; **~vura** *f* boiling

fes|ta /ˈfɛsta/ *f* party; (*religiosa*) festival; **~tejar** *vt/i* celebrate; (*acolher*) fete; **~tejo** /e/ *m* celebration; **~tim** *m* feast; **~tival** (*pl* **~tivais**) *m* festival; **~tividade** *f* festivity; **~tivo** *a* festive

feti|che /feˈtʃiʃi/ *m* fetish; **~**

chismo *m* fetishism; **~chista** *m/f* fetishist □ *a* fetishistic

fétido /ˈfɛtʃidu/ *a* fetid

feto[1] /ˈfɛtu/ *m* (*no útero*) foetus

feto[2] /ˈfɛtu/ (*Port*) *m* (*planta*) fern

feu|dal /few'daw/ (*pl* **~dais**) *a* feudal; **~dalismo** *m* feudalism

fevereiro /feve'reru/ *m* February

fezes /ˈfɛzis/ *f pl* faeces

fia|ção /fiaˈsãw/ *f* (*eletr*) wiring; (*fábrica*) mill

fia|do /fiˈadu/ *a* <*conversa*> idle □ *adv* <*comprar*> on credit; **~dor** *m* guarantor

fiambre /fiˈãbri/ *m* cooked ham

fiança /fiˈãsa/ *f* surety; (*jurid*) bail

fiapo /fiˈapu/ *m* thread

fiar /fiˈar/ *vt* spin <*lã etc*>

fiasco /fiˈasku/ *m* fiasco

fibra /ˈfibra/ *f* fibre

ficar /fiˈkar/ *vi* (*tornar-se*) become; (*estar, ser*) be; (*manter-se*) stay; **~ fazendo** keep (on) doing; **~ com** keep; get <*impressão, vontade*>; **~ com medo** get scared; **~ de fazer** arrange to do; **~ para** be left for; **~ bom** turn out well; (*recuperar-se*) get better; **~ bem** look good

fic|ção /fikˈsãw/ *f* fiction; **~ção científica** science fiction; **~cionista** *m/f* fiction writer

fi|cha /ˈfiʃa/ *f* (*de telefone*) token; (*de jogo*) chip; (*da caixa*) ticket; (*de fichário*) file card; (*na polícia*) record; (*Port: tomada*) plug; **~chário** *m*, (*Port*) **~cheiro** *m* file; (*móvel*) filing cabinet

fictício /fikˈtʃisiu/ *a* fictitious

fidalgo /fiˈdalgu/ *m* nobleman

fide|digno /fideˈdʒignu/ *a* trustworthy; **~lidade** *f* fidelity

fiduciário /fidusiˈariu/ *a* fiduciary □ *m* trustee

fi|el /fiˈew/ (*pl* **~éis**) *a* faithful □ *m* **os ~éis** (*na igreja*) the congregation

figa /ˈfiga/ *f* talisman

fígado /'figadu/ *f* liver

fi|**go** /'figu/ *m* fig; **~gueira** *f* fig tree

figu|**ra** /fi'gura/ *f* figure; (*carta de jogo*) face card; (*fam: pessoa*) character; **fazer** (**má**) **~ra** make a (bad) impression; **~rado** *a* figurative; **~rante** *m*/*f* extra; **~rão** *m* big shot; **~rar** *vi* appear, figure; **~rativo** *a* figurative; **~rinha** *f* sticker; **~rino** *m* fashion plate; (*de filme, peça*) costume design; (*fig*) model; **como manda o ~rino** as it should be

fila /'fila/ *f* line; (*de espera*) queue, (*Amer*) line; (*fileira*) row; **fazer ~** queue up, (*Amer*) stand in line; **~ indiana** single file

filamento /fila'mẽtu/ *m* filament

filante /fi'lãtʃi/ (*fam*) *m*/*f* sponger

filan|**tropia** /filãtro'pia/ *f* philanthropy; **~trópico** *a* philanthropic; **~tropo** /o/ *m* philanthropist

filão /fi'lãw/ *m* (*de ouro*) seam; (*fig*) money-spinner

filar /fi'lar/ (*fam*) *vt* sponge, cadge

filar|**mônica** /filar'monika/ *f* philharmonic (orchestra); **~mônico** *a* philharmonic

filate|**lia** /filate'lia/ *f* philately; **~lista** *m*/*f* philatelist

filé /fi'le/ *m* fillet

fileira /fi'lera/ *f* row

filete /fi'lɛtʃi/ *m* fillet

fi|**lha** /'fiʎa/ *f* daughter; **~lho** *m* son; *pl* (*crianças*) children; **~lho da puta** (*chulo*) bastard, (*Amer*) son of a bitch; **~lho de criação** foster child; **~lhote** *m* (*de cão*) pup; (*de lobo etc*) cub; *pl* young

fili|**ação** /filia'sãw/ *f* affiliation; **~al** (*pl* **~ais**) *a* filial □ *f* branch

Filipinas /fili'pinas/ *f pl* Philippines

filipino /fili'pinu/ *a* & *m* Filipino

fil|**madora** /fiwma'dora/ *f* camcorder; **~magem** *f* filming; **~mar** *vt*/*i* film; **~me** *m* film

fi|**lologia** /filolo'ʒia/ *f* philology; **~lólogo** *m* philologist

filo|**sofar** /filozo'far/ *vi* philosophize; **~sofia** *f* philosophy; **~sófico** *a* philosophical

filósofo /fi'lɔzofu/ *m* philosopher

fil|**trar** /fiw'trar/ *vt* filter; **~tro** *m* filter

fim /fĩ/ *m* end; **a ~ de** (*para*) in order to; **estar a ~ de** fancy; **por ~** finally; **sem ~** endless; **ter ~** come to an end; **~ de semana** weekend

fi|**nado** /fi'nadu/ *a* & *m* deceased, departed; (*pl* **~nal ~nais**) *a* final □ *m* end □ *f* final; **~nalista** *m*/*f* finalist; **~nalizar** *vt*/*i* finish

finan|**ças** /fi'nãsas/ *f pl* finances; **~ceiro** *a* financial □ *m* financier; **~ciamento** *m* financing; (*um*) loan; **~ciar** *vt* finance; **~cista** *m*/*f* financier

fincar /fĩ'kar/ *vt* plant; **~ o pé** (*fig*) dig one's heels in

findar /fĩ'dar/ *vt*/*i* end

fineza /fi'neza/ *f* finesse; (*favor*) kindness

fin|**gido** /fĩ'ʒidu/ *a* feigned; *<pessoa>* insincere; **~gimento** *m* pretence; **~gir** *vt* pretend; feign *<doença etc>* □ *vi* pretend; **~gir-se de** pretend to be

finito /fi'nitu/ *a* finite

finlan|**dês** /fĩlã'des/ *a* (*f* **~desa**) Finnish □ *m* (*f* **~desa**) Finn; (*língua*) Finnish

Finlândia /fĩ'lãdʒia/ *f* Finland

fi|**ninho** /fi'niɲu/ *adv* **sair de ~ninho** slip away; **~no a** (*não grosso*) slip thin; *<areia, pó etc>* fine; (*refinado*) refined; **~nório a** crafty; **~nura** *f* thinness; fineness

fio /'fiu/ *m* thread; (*elétrico*) wire; (*de sangue, água*) trickle; (*de luz,* *esperança*) glimmer; (*de navalha etc*) edge; **horas a** ~ hours on end

fir|ma /'firma/ *f* firm; (*assinatura*) signature; ~**mamento** *m* firmament; ~**mar** *vt* fix; (*basear*) base □ *vi* settle; ~**mar-se** *vpr* be based (**em** on); ~**me** *a* firm; *<tempo>* settled □ *adv* firmly; ~**meza** *f* firmness

fis|cal /fis'kaw/ (*pl* ~**cais**) *m* inspector; ~**calização** *f* inspection; ~**calizar** *vt* inspect; ~**co** *m* inland revenue, (*Amer*) internal revenue service

fis|gada /fiz'gada/ *f* stabbing pain; ~**gar** *vt* hook

físi|ca /'fizika/ *f* physics; ~**co** *a* physical □ *m* (*pessoa*) physicist; (*corpo*) physique

fisio|nomia /fizio'mia/ *f* face; ~**nomista** *m/f* **ser** ~**nomista** have a good memory for faces; ~**terapeuta** *m/f* physiotherapist; ~**terapia** *f* physiotherapy

fissura /fi'sura/ *f* fissure; (*fam*) craving; ~**do** *a* ~**do em** (*fam*) mad about

fita /'fita/ *f* tape; (*fam: encenação*) playacting; **fazer** ~ (*fam*) put on an act; ~ **adesiva** (*Port*) adhesive tape; ~ **métrica** tape measure

fitar /fi'tar/ *vt* stare at

fivela /fi'vɛla/ *f* buckle

fi|xador /fiksa'dor/ *m* (*de cabelo*) setting lotion; (*de fotos*) fixative; ~**xar** *vt* fix; stick up *<cartaz>*; ~**xo** *a* fixed

flácido /'flasidu/ *a* flabby

flagelo /fla'ʒɛlu/ *m* scourge

fla|grante /fla'grãtʃi/ *a* flagrant; **apanhar em** ~**grante** (**delito**) catch in the act; ~**grar** *vt* catch

flame|jante /flame'ʒãtʃi/ *a* blazing; ~**jar** *vi* blaze

flamengo /fla'mẽgu/ *a* Flemish □ *m* Fleming; (*língua*) Flemish

flamingo /fla'mĩgu/ *m* flamingo

flâmula /'flamula/ *f* pennant

flanco /'flãku/ *m* flank

flanela /fla'nɛla/ *f* flannel

flanquear /flãki'ar/ *vt* flank

flash /fleʃ/ *m invar* flash

flau|ta /'flawta/ *f* flute; ~**tista** *m/f* flautist

flecha /'fleʃa/ *f* arrow

fler|tar /fler'tar/ *vi* flirt; ~**te** *m* flirtation

fleuma /flewma/ *f* phlegm

fle|xão /flek'sãw/ *f* press-up, (*Amer*) push-up; (*ling*) inflection; ~**xibilidade** *f* flexibility; ~**xionar** *vt/i* flex *<perna, braço>*; (*ling*) inflect; ~**xível** (*pl* ~**xíveis**) *a* flexible

fliperama /flipe'rama/ *m* pinball machine

floco /'floku/ *m* flake

flor /flor/ *f* flower; **a fina** ~ the cream; **à** ~ **da pele** (*fig*) on edge

flo|ra /'flora/ *f* flora; ~**reado** *a* full of flowers; (*fig*) florid; ~**reio** *m* clever turn of phrase; ~**rescer** *vi* flower; *<perna, /ɛ/ /f* forest; ~**restal** (*pl* ~**restais**) *a* forest; ~**rido** *a* in flower; (*fig*) florid; ~**rir** *vi* flower

flotilha /flo'tʃika/ *f* flotilla

flu|ência /flu'ẽsia/ *f* fluency; ~**ente** *a* fluent

flui|dez /flui'des/ *f* fluidity; ~**do** *a* & *m* fluid

fluir /flu'ir/ *vi* flow

fluminense /flumi'nẽsi/ *a* & *m* (person) from Rio de Janeiro state

fluorescente /fluore'sẽtʃi/ *a* fluorescent

flutu|ação /flutua'sãw/ *f* fluctuation; ~**ante** *a* floating; ~**ar** *vi* float; *<bandeira>* flutter; (*hesitar*) waver

fluvi|al /fluvi'aw/ (*pl* ~**ais**) *a* river

fluxo /'fluksu/ *m* flow; ~**grama** *m* flowchart

fobia /fo'bia/ *f* phobia

foca /'fɔka/ f seal

focalizar /fokali'zar/ vt focus on

focinho /fo'siɲu/ m snout

foco /'fɔku/ m focus; (fig) centre

fofo /'fofu/ a soft; <pessoa> cuddly

fofo|ca /fo'fɔka/ f piece of gossip; pl gossip; ~car vi gossip; ~queiro m gossip □ a gossipy

fo|gão /fo'gãw/ m stove; (de cozinhar) cooker; ~go /o/ m fire; tem ~go? have you got a light?; ser ~go (fam) (ser chato) be a pain in the neck; (ser incrível) be amazing; ~gos de artifício fireworks; ~goso /o/ a fiery; ~gueira f bonfire; ~guete /e/ m rocket

foice /'fojsi/ f scythe

fol|clore /fow'klori/ m folklore; ~clórico a folk

fole /'fɔli/ m bellows

fôlego /'folegu/ m breath; (fig) stamina

fol|ga /'fowga/ f rest, break; (fam: cara-de-pau) cheek; ~gado a <roupa> full, loose; <vida> leisurely; (fam: atrevido) cheeky; ~gar vt loosen □ vi have time off

fo|lha /'foʎa/ f leaf; (de papel) sheet; **novo em ~lha** brand new; ~lha de pagamento payroll; ~lhagem f foliage; ~lhear vt leaf through; ~lheto /e/ m pamphlet; ~lhinha f tear-off calendar; ~lhudo a leafy

foli|a /fo'lia/ f revelry; ~ão m (f ~ona) reveller

folículo /fo'likulu/ m follicle

fome /'fomi/ f hunger; **estar com ~** be hungry

fomentar /fomẽ'tar/ vt foment

fone /'fɔni/ m (do telefone) receiver; (de rádio etc) headphones

fonema /fo'nema/ m phoneme

fonéti|ca /fo'nɛtʃika/ f phonetics; ~co a phonetic

fonologia /fonolo'ʒia/ f phonology

fonte /'fõtʃi/ f (de água) spring; (fig) source

fora /'fɔra/ adv outside; (não em casa) out; (viajando) away □ prep except; **dar um ~** drop a clanger; **dar um ~ em alg** cut s.o. dead; chuck <namorado>; **por ~** on the outside; ~-**de-lei** m/f invar outlaw

foragido /fora'ʒidu/ a at large, on the run □ m fugitive

forasteiro /foras'teru/ m outsider

forca /'fɔrka/ f gallows

for|ça /'fɔrsa/ f (vigor) strength; (violência) force; (elétrica) power; **dar uma ~ça a alg** help s.o. out; **fazer ~ça** make an effort; ~ças armadas armed forces; ~çar vt force; ~ça-tarefa (pl ~ças-tarefa) f task force

fórceps /'fɔrseps/ m invar forceps

forçoso /for'sozu/ a forced

for|ja /'fɔrʒa/ f forge; ~jar vt forge

forma /'fɔrma/ f form; (contorno) shape; (maneira) way; **de qualquer ~** anyway; **manter a ~** keep fit

fôrma /'forma/ f mould; (de cozinha) baking tin

for|mação /forma'sãw/ f formation; (educação) education; (profissionalizante) training; ~mado m graduate; ~mal (pl ~mais) a formal; ~malidade f formality; ~malizar vt formalize; ~mar vt form; (educar) educate; ~mar-se vpr be formed; <estudante> graduate; ~mato m format; ~matura f graduation

formidá|vel /formi'davew/ (pl ~veis) a formidable; (muito bom) tremendous

formi|ga /for'miga/ f ant; ~gamento m pins and needles; ~gar vi swarm (de with); <perna, mão etc> tingle; ~gueiro m ants' nest

formosura /formo'zura/ f beauty

fórmula /'fɔrmula/ f formula

formu|lação /formula'sãw/ f formulation; **~lar** vt formulate; **~lário** m form

fornalha /for'naʎa/ f furnace

forne|cedor /fornese'dor/ m supplier; **~cer** vt supply; **~cer aco a alg** supply s.o. with sth; **~cimento** m supply

forno /'fornu/ m oven; (para louça etc) kiln

foro /'foru/ m forum

forra /'fɔxa/ f **ir à ~** get one's own back

for|ragem /fo'xaʒẽ/ f fodder; **~rar** vt line <roupa, caixa etc>; cover <sofá etc>; carpet <assoalho, sala etc>; **~ro** /o/ m (de roupa, caixa etc) lining; (de sofá etc) cover; (carpete) (fitted) carpet

forró /fo'xɔ/ m type of Brazilian dance

fortale|cer /fortale'ser/ vt strengthen; **~cimento** m strengthening; **~za** /e/ f fortress

for|te /'fɔrtʃi/ a strong; <golpe> hard; <chuva> heavy; <físico> muscular □ adv strongly; <bater, chover> hard □ m (militar) fort; (habilidade) strong point, forte; **~tificação** f fortification; **~tificar** vt fortify

fortu|ito /for'tuitu/ a chance; **~na** f fortune

fosco /'fosku/ a dull; <vidro> frosted

fosfato /fos'fatu/ m phosphate

fósforo /'fɔsforu/ m match; (elemento químico) phosphor

fossa /'fɔsa/ f pit; **na ~** (fig) miserable, depressed

fós|sil /'fɔsiw/ (pl **~seis**) m fossil

fosso /'fosu/ m ditch; (de castelo) moat

foto /'fɔtu/ f photo; **~cópia** f photocopy; **~copiadora** f photo-

copier; **~copiar** vt photocopy; **~gênico** a photogenic; **~grafar** vt photograph; **~grafia** f photography; **~gráfico** a photographic

fotógrafo /fo'tɔgrafu/ m photographer

foz /fɔs/ f mouth

fração /fra'sãw/ f fraction

fracas|sado /fraka'sadu/ a failed □ m failure; **~sar** vi fail; **~so** m failure

fracionar /frasio'nar/ vt break up

fraco /'fraku/ a weak; <luz, som> faint; <medíocre> poor □ m weakness, weak spot

fract- (Port) veja **frat-**

frade /'fradʒi/ m friar

fragata /fra'gata/ f frigate

frá|gil /'fraʒiw/ (pl **~geis**) a fragile; <pessoa> frail

fragilidade /fraʒili'dadʒi/ f fragility; (de pessoa) frailty

fragmen|tar /fragmẽ'tar/ vt fragment; **~tar-se** vpr fragment; **~to** m fragment

fra|grância /fra'grãsia/ f fragrance; **~grante** a fragrant

fralda /'frawda/ f nappy, (Amer) diaper

framboesa /frãbo'eza/ f raspberry

França /'frãsa/ f France

fran|cês /frã'ses/ a (f **~cesa**) French □ m (f **~cesa**) Frenchman (f -woman); (língua) French; **os ~ceses** the French

franco /'frãku/ a (honesto) frank; (óbvio) clear; (gratuito) free □ m franc; **~-atirador** (pl **~-atiradores**) m sniper; (fig) maverick

frangalho /frã'gaʎu/ m tatter

frango /'frãgu/ m chicken

franja /'frãʒa/ f fringe; (do cabelo) fringe, (Amer) bangs

fran|quear /frãki'ar/ vt frank <carta>; **~queza** /e/ f frankness; **~quia** f (de cartas) franking; (jur) franchise

fran|zino /frã'zinu/ *a* skinny; **~zir** *vt* gather <*tecido*>; wrinkle <*testa*>

fraque /'fraki/ *m* morning suit

fraqueza /fra'keza/ *f* weakness; (*de luz, som*) faintness

frasco /'frasku/ *m* bottle

frase /'frazi/ *f* (*oração*) sentence; (*locução*) phrase; **~ado** *m* phrasing

frasqueira /fras'kera/ *f* vanity case

frater|nal /frater'naw/ (*pl* **~nais**) *a* fraternal; **~nidade** *f* fraternity; **~nizar** *vi* fraternize; **~no** *a* fraternal

fratu|ra /fra'tura/ *f* fracture; **~rar** *vt* fracture; **~rar-se** *vpr* fracture

frau|dar /fraw'dar/ *vt* defraud; **~de** *f* fraud; **~dulento** *a* fraudulent

frear /fri'ar/ *vt/i* brake

freezer /'frizer/ *m* freezer

fre|guês /fre'ges/ *m* (*f* **~guesa**) customer; **~guesia** /-'gezia/ (*de loja etc*) clientele; (*paróquia*) parish

frei /frej/ *m* brother

freio /'freju/ *m* brake; (*de cavalo*) bit

freira /'frera/ *f* nun

freixo /'freʃu/ *m* ash

fremir /fre'mir/ *vi* shake

frêmito /'fremitu/ *m* wave

frenesi /frene'zi/ *m* frenzy

frenético /fre'nɛtʃiku/ *a* frantic

frente /'frẽtʃi/ *f* front; **em ~** *a* ou **de** in front of; **para a ~** forward; **pela ~** ahead; fazer **~ a** face

freqüência /fre'kwẽsia/ *f* frequency; (*assiduidade*) attendance; **com muita ~** often

freqüen|tador /frekwẽta'dor/ *m* regular visitor (**de** to); **~tar** *vt* frequent; (*cursar*) attend; **~te** *a* frequent

fres|cão /fres'kãw/ *m* air-conditioned coach; **~co** /e/ *a* <*comida etc*> fresh; <*vento, água, quarto*>

cool; (*fam*) (*afetado*) affected; (*exigente*) fussy; **~cobol** *m* kind of racquetball; **~cor** *m* freshness; **~cura** *f* (*fam*) (*afetação*) affectation; (*ser exigente*) fussiness; (*coisa sem importância*) trifle

fresta /'frɛsta/ *f* slit

fre|tar /fre'tar/ *vt* charter <*avião*>; hire <*caminhão*>; **~te** /ɛ/ *m* freight; (*aluguel de avião*) charter; (*de caminhão*) hire

frevo /'frevu/ *m* type of Brazilian dance

fria /'fria/ (*fam*) *f* difficult situation, spot; **~gem** *f* chill

fric|ção /frik'sãw/ *f* friction; **~cionar** *vt* rub

fri|eira /fri'era/ *f* chilblain; **~eza** /e/ *f* coldness

frigideira /friʒi'dera/ *f* frying pan

frígido /'friʒidu/ *a* frigid

frigorífico /frigo'rifiku/ *m* cold store, refrigerator, fridge

frincha /'friʃa/ *f* chink

frio /'friu/ *a* & *m* cold; **estar com ~** be cold; **~rento** *a* sensitive to the cold

frisar /fri'zar/ *vt* (*enfatizar*) stress; crimp <*cabelo*>

friso /'frizu/ *m* frieze

fri|tada /fri'tada/ *f* fry-up; **~tar** *vt* fry; **~tas** *f pl* chips, (*Amer*) French fries; **~to** *a* fried; **está ~to** (*fam*) he's had it; **~tura** *f* fried food

frivolidade /frivoli'dadʒi/ *f* frivolity; **frívolo** *a* frivolous

fronha /'froɲa/ *f* pillowcase

fronte /'frõtʃi/ *f* forehead, brow

frontei|ra /frõ'tera/ *f* border; **~riço** *a* border

frota /'frota/ *f* fleet

frou|xidão /froʃi'dãw/ *f* looseness; (*moral*) laxity; **~xo** *a* loose; <*regulamento*> lax; <*pessoa*> lackadaisical

fru|gal /fru'gaw/ (*pl* **~gais**) *a* frugal; **~galidade** *f* frugality

frus|tração /frustra'sãw/ f
frustration; **~trante** a frustrat-
ing; **~trar** vt frustrate

fru|ta /'fruta/ f fruit; **~ta-do-**
conde (pl **~tas-do-conde**) f
sweetsop; **~ta-pão** (pl **~tas-**
pão) f breadfruit; **~teira** f
fruitbowl; **~tífero** a (fig)
fruitful; **~to m** fruit

fubá /fu'ba/ m maize flour

fu|car /fu'sar/ vi nose around;
~ças (fam) f pl face, chops

fu|ga /'fuga/ f escape; **~gaz** a
fleeting; **~gida** f escape; **~gir**
vi run away; (soltar-se) escape; **~**
gir a avoid; **~gitivo** a & m fugitive

fulano /fu'lanu/ m whatever his
name is

fuleiro /fu'leru/ a down-market,
cheap and cheerful

fulgor /fuw'gor/ m brightness;
(fig) splendour

fuligem /fu'liʒẽ/ f soot

fulmi|nante /fuwmi'nãtʃi/ a dev-
astating; **~nar** vt strike down;
(fig) devastate; **~nado por um**
raio struck by lightning □ vi (criticar) rail

fu|maça /fu'masa/ f smoke;
~maceira f cloud of smoke;
~mante, (Port) **~mador** m
smoker; **~mar** vt/i smoke; **~**
mê a invar smoked; **~megar** vi
smoke; **~mo m** (tabaco) tobacco;
(Port: fumaça) smoke; (fumar)
smoking

função /fũ'sãw/ f function; **em ~**
de as a result of; **fazer as fun-**
ções de function as

funcho /'fũʃu/ m fennel

funcio|nal /fũsio'naw/ a (pl
~nais) a functional; **~nalismo**
m civil service; **~namento** m
working; **~nar** vi work; **~nário**
m employee; **~nário público**
civil servant

fun|dação /fũda'sãw/ f founda-
tion; **~dador** m founder □ a
founding

fundamen|tal /fũdamẽ'taw/ a (pl
~tais) a fundamental; **~tar** vt
(basear) base; (justificar) substantiate; **~to m** foundation

fun|dar /fũ'dar/ vt (criar) found;
(basear) base; **~dar-se** vpr be
based (em on); **~dear** vi drop
anchor, anchor; **~dilho** m seat

fundir /fũ'dʒir/ vt melt <ouro, ferro>; cast <sino, estátua>; (juntar) merge; **~se** vpr <ouro, ferro> melt; (juntar-se) merge

fundo /'fũdu/ a deep □ m (parte
de baixo) bottom; (parte de trás)
back; (de quadro, foto) background; (de dinheiro) fund; **no ~**
basically; **~s m** pl (da casa
etc) back; (recursos) funds

fúnebre /'funebri/ a funereal

funerário /fune'rariu/ a funeral

funesto /fu'nɛstu/ a fatal

fungar /fũ'gar/ vt/i sniff

fungo /'fũgu/ m fungus

fu|nil /fu'niw/ (pl **~nis**) m
funnel; **~nilaria** f panel-beat-
ing; (oficina) bodyshop

furacão /fura'kãw/ m hurricane

furado /fu'radu/ a **papo ~** (fam)
hot air

furão /fu'rãw/ m (animal) ferret

furar /fu'rar/ vt pierce <orelha
etc>; puncture <pneu>; make a
hole in <roupa etc>; jump <fila>;
break <greve> □ vi <roupa etc>
go into a hole; <pneu> puncture;
(fam) <programa> fall through

fur|gão /fur'gãw/ m van;
~goneta /e/ (Port) f van

fúria /'furia/ f fury

furioso /furi'ozu/ a furious

furo /'furu/ m hole; (de pneu)
puncture; (jornalístico) scoop;
(fam: gafe) blunder, faux pas;
dar um ~ put one's foot in it

furor /fu'ror/ m furore

fur|ta-cor /furta'kor/ a invar
iridescent; **~tar** vt steal; **~**
tivo a furtive; **~to m** theft

furúnculo /fu'rũkulu/ m boil

fusão /fu'zãw/ *f* fusion; (*de empresas*) merger

fusca /'fuska/ *f* VW beetle

fuselagem /fuze'laʒẽ/ *f* fuselage

fusí|vel /fu'zivew/ (*pl* ~**veis**) *m* fuse

fuso /'fuzu/ *m* spindle; ~ **horário** time zone

fustigar /fustʃi'gar/ *vt* lash; (*fig: com palavras*) lash out at

futebol /futʃi'bɔw/ *m* football; ~**ístico** *a* football

fú|til /'futʃiw/ (*pl* ~**teis**) *a* frivolous, inane

futilidade /futʃili'dadʒi/ *f* frivolity, inanity; (*uma*) frivolous thing

futu|rismo /futu'rizmu/ *m* futurism; ~**rista** *a & m* futurist; ~**rístico** *a* futuristic; ~**ro** *a & m* future

fu|zil /fu'ziw/ (*pl* ~**zis**) *m* rifle; ~**zilamento** *m* shooting; ~**zilar** *vt* shoot □ *vi* flash; ~**zileiro** *m* rifleman; ~**zileiro naval** marine

fuzuê /fuzu'e/ *m* commotion

G

gabar-se /ga'barsi/ *vpr* boast (**de** of)

gabarito /gaba'ritu/ *m* calibre

gabinete /gabi'netʃi/ *m* (*em casa*) study; (*escritório*) office; (*ministros*) cabinet

gado /'gadu/ *m* livestock; (*bovino*) cattle

gaélico /ga'ɛliku/ *a & m* Gaelic

gafanhoto /gafa'ɲotu/ *m* (*pequeno*) grasshopper; (*grande*) locust

gafe /'gafi/ *f* faux pas, gaffe

gafieira /gafi'era/ *f* dance; (*salão*) dance hall

gagá /ga'ga/ *a* (*fam*) senile

ga|go /'gagu/ *a* stuttering □ *m* stutterer; ~**gueira** *f* stutter; ~**guejar** *vi* stutter

gaiato /gaj'atu/ *a* funny

gaiola /gaj'ɔla/ *f* cage

gaita /'gajta/ *f* ~ **de foles** bagpipes

gaivota /gaj'vɔta/ *f* seagull

gajo /'gaʒu/ *m* (*Port*) guy, bloke

gala /'gala/ *f* **festa de** ~ gala; **roupa de** ~ formal dress

galã /ga'lã/ *m* leading man

galan|tear /galãtʃi'ar/ *vt* woo; ~**teio** *m* wooing; (*um*) courtesy

galão /ga'lãw/ *m* (*enfeite*) braid; (*mil*) stripe; (*medida*) gallon; (*Port: café*) white coffee

galáxia /ga'laksia/ *f* galaxy

galé /ga'lɛ/ *f* galley

galego /ga'legu/ *a & m* Galician

galera /ga'lɛra/ *f* (*fam*) crowd

galeria /gale'ria/ *f* gallery

Gales /'galis/ *m* **País de** ~ Wales

ga|lês /ga'les/ *a* (*f* ~**lesa**) Welsh □ *m* (*f* ~**lesa**) Welshman (*f* -woman); (*língua*) Welsh

galeto /ga'letu/ *m* spring chicken

galgar /gaw'gar/ *vt* (*transpor*) jump over; climb <*escada*>

galgo /'gawgu/ *m* greyhound

galheteiro /gaʎe'teru/ *m* cruet stand

galho /'gaʎu/ *m* branch; **quebrar um** ~ (*fam*) help out

galináceos /gali'nasius/ *m pl* poultry

gali|nha /ga'liɲa/ *f* chicken; ~**nheiro** *m* chicken coop

galo /'galu/ *m* cock; (*inchação*) bump

galocha /ga'lɔʃa/ *f* Wellington boot

galo|pante /galo'pãtʃi/ *a* galloping; ~**par** *vi* gallop; ~**pe** /ɔ/ *m* gallop

galpão /gaw'pãw/ *m* shed

galvanizar /gawvani'zar/ *vt* galvanize

gama /'gama/ *f* (*musical*) scale; (*fig*) range

gamado /ga'madu/ *a* besotted (**por** with)

gamão /ga'mãw/ *m* backgammon

gamar /ga'mar/ *vi* fall in love (**por** with)

gana /'gana/ *f* desire

ganância /ga'nãsia/ *f* greed

ganancioso /ganãsi'ozu/ *a* greedy

gancho /'gãʃu/ *m* hook

gangorra /gã'goxa/ *f* seesaw

gangrena /gã'grena/ *f* gangrene

gangue /'gãgi/ *m* gang

ga|nhador /gaɲa'dor/ *m* winner □ *a* winning; **~nhar** *vt* win <*corrida, prêmio*>; earn <*salário*>; get <*presente*>; gain <*vantagem, tempo, amigo*> □ *vi* win; **~nhar a vida** earn a living; **~nha-pão** *m* livelihood; **~nho** *m* gain; *pl* (*no jogo*) winnings □ *pp de* **ganhar**

ga|nido *m* squeal; (*de cachorro*) yelp; **~nir** *vi* squeal; <*cachorro*> yelp

ganso /'gãsu/ *m* goose

gara|gem /ga'raʒẽ/ *f* garage; **~gista** *m/f* garage attendant

garanhão /gara'ɲãw/ *m* stallion

garan|tia /garã'tʃia/ *f* guarantee; **~tir** *vt* guarantee

garatujar /garatu'ʒar/ *vt* scribble

gar|bo /'garbu/ *m* grace; **~boso** *a* graceful

garça /'garsa/ *f* heron

gar|com /gar'sõ/ *m* waiter; **~conete** /ɛ/ *f* waitress

gar|fada /gar'fada/ *f* forkful; **~fo** *m* fork

gargalhada /garga'ʎada/ *f* gale of laughter; **rir às ~s** roar with laughter

gargalo /gar'galu/ *m* bottleneck; **tomar no ~** drink out of the bottle

garganta /gar'gãta/ *f* throat

gargare|jar /gargare'ʒar/ *vi* gargle; **~jo** /e/ *m* gargle

gari /ga'ri/ *m/f* (*lixeiro*) dustman, (*Amer*) garbage collector; (*varredor de rua*) roadsweeper, (*Amer*) streetsweeper

garim|par /garĩ'par/ *vi* prospect; **~peiro** *m* prospector; **~po** *m* mine

garo|a /ga'roa/ *f* drizzle; **~ar** *vi* drizzle

garo|ta /ga'rota/ *f* girl; **~to** /o/ *m* boy; (*Port: café*) coffee with milk

garoupa /ga'ropa/ *f* grouper

garra /'gaxa/ *f* claw; (*fig*) drive, determination; *pl* (*poder*) clutches

garra|fa /ga'xafa/ *f* bottle; **~fada** *f* blow with a bottle; **~fão** *m* flagon

garrancho /ga'xãʃu/ *m* scrawl

garrido /ga'xidu/ *a* (*alegre*) lively

garupa /ga'rupa/ *f* (*de animal*) rump; (*de moto*) pillion seat

gás /gas/ *m* gas; *pl* (*intestinais*) wind, (*Amer*) gas; **~ lacrimogêneo** tear gas

gasóleo /ga'zɔliu/ *m* diesel oil

gasolina /gazo'lina/ *f* petrol

gaso|sa /ga'zɔza/ *f*izzy lemonade, (*Amer*) soda; **~so** *a* gaseous; <*bebida*> fizzy

gáspea /gaspia/ *f* upper

gas|tador /gasta'dor/ *a* & *m* spendthrift; **~tar** *vt* spend <*dinheiro, tempo*>; use up <*energia*>; wear out <*roupa, sapatos*>; **~to** *m* expense; *pl* spending, expenditure; **dar para o ~to** do

gastrenterite /gastrēte'ritʃi/ *f* gastroenteritis

gástrico /'gastriku/ *a* gastric

gastrite /gas'tritʃi/ *f* gastritis

gastronomia /gastrono'mia/ *f* gastronomy

ga|ta /'gata/ *f* cat; (*fam*) sexy woman; **~tão** *m* (*fam*) hunk

gatilho /ga'tʃiʎu/ *m* trigger

ga|tinha /ga'tʃiɲa/ *f* (*fam*) sexy woman; **~to** *m* cat; (*fam*) hunk; **fazer alg de ~to-sapato** treat s.o. like a doormat

gatuno /ga'tunu/ *m* crook □ *a* crooked

gaúcho /gaˈuʃu/ *a* & *m* (person) from Rio Grande do Sul

gaveta /gaˈveta/ *f* drawer

gavião /gaviˈãw/ *m* hawk

gaze /ˈgazi/ *f* gauze

gazela /gaˈzɛla/ *f* gazelle

gazeta /gaˈzeta/ *f* gazette

geada /ʒiˈada/ *f* frost

ge|ladeira /ʒelaˈdera/ *f* fridge; **~lado** *a* frozen; (*muito frio*) freezing □ *m* (*Port*) ice cream; **~lar** *vt/i* freeze

gelati|na /ʒelaˈtʃina/ *f* (*sobremesa*) jelly; (*pó*) gelatine; **~noso** /o/ *a* gooey

geléia /ʒeˈlɛja/ *f* jam

ge|leira /ʒeˈlera/ *f* glacier; **~lo** /e/ *m* ice

gema /ˈʒema/ *f* (*de ovo*) yolk; (*pedra*) gem; **carioca da ~** carioca born and bred; **~da** *f* egg yolk whisked with sugar

gêmeo /ˈʒemiu/ *a* & *m* twin; **Gêmeos** (*signo*) Gemini

ge|mer /ʒeˈmer/ *vi* moan, groan; **~mido** *m* moan, groan

gene /ˈʒɛni/ *m* gene; **~alogia** *f* genealogy; **~alógico** *a* a genealogical; **árvore ~alógica** family tree

Genebra /ʒeˈnebra/ *f* Geneva

gene|ral /ʒeneˈraw/ (*pl* **~rais**) *m* general; **~ralidade** *f* generality; **~ralização** *f* generalization; **~ralizar** *vt/i* generalize; **~ralizar-se** *vpr* become generalized

genérico /ʒeˈnɛriku/ *a* generic

gênero /ˈʒeneru/ *m* type, kind; (*gramatical*) gender; (*literário*) genre; *pl* goods; **~s alimentícios** foodstuffs; **ela não faz o meu ~** she's not my type

gene|rosidade /ʒeneroziˈdadʒi/ *f* generosity; **~roso** /o/ *a* generous

genéti|ca /ʒeˈnɛtʃika/ *f* genetics; **~co** *a* genetic

gengibre /ʒẽˈʒibri/ *m* ginger

gengiva /ʒẽˈʒiva/ *f* gum

geni|al /ʒeniˈaw/ (*pl* **~ais**) *a* brilliant

gênio /ˈʒeniu/ *m* genius; (*temperamento*) temperament

genioso /ʒeniˈozu/ *a* temperamental

geni|tal /ʒeniˈtaw/ (*pl* **~tais**) *a* genital

genitivo /ʒeniˈtʃivu/ *a* & *m* genitive

genocídio /ʒenoˈsidʒiu/ *m* genocide

genro /ˈʒẽxu/ *m* son-in-law

gente /ˈʒẽtʃi/ *f* people; (*fam*) folks; **a ~** (*sujeito*) we; (*objeto*) us □ *interj* (*fam*) gosh

gen|til /ʒẽˈtʃiw/ (*pl* **~tis**) *a* kind; **~tileza** /e/ *f* kindness

genuíno /ʒenuˈinu/ *a* genuine

geo|grafia /ʒeograˈfia/ *f* geography; **~gráfico** *a* geographical

geógrafo /ʒeˈɔgrafu/ *m* geographer

geo|logia /ʒeoloˈʒia/ *f* geology; **~lógico** *a* geological

geólogo /ʒeˈɔlogu/ *m* geologist

geo|metria /ʒeomeˈtria/ *f* geometry; **~métrico** *a* geometrical; **~político** *a* geopolitical

Geórgia /ʒiˈɔrʒia/ *f* Georgia

georgiano /ʒiorʒiˈanu/ *a* & *m* Georgian

gera|ção /ʒeraˈsãw/ *f* generation; **~dor** *m* generator

ge|ral /ʒeˈraw/ (*pl* **~rais**) *a* general □ *f* (*limpeza*) spring-clean; **em ~** in general

gerânio /ʒeˈraniu/ *m* geranium

gerar /ʒeˈrar/ *vt* create; generate < *eletricidade* >

gerência /ʒeˈrẽsia/ *f* management

gerenci|ador /ʒerẽsiaˈdor/ *m* manager; **~al** (*pl* **~ais**) *a* management; **~ar** *vt* manage

gerente /ʒeˈrẽtʃi/ *m* manager □ *a* managing

gergelim /ʒerʒeˈli/ *m* sesame

geri|atria /ʒeriaˈtria/ *f* geriatrics; **~átrico** *a* geriatric geringonça /ʒerĩ'gõsɐ/ f contraption

gerir /ʒe'rir/ vt manage

germânico /ʒer'mɐniku/ a Germanic

ger|me /'ʒermi/ m germ; ~me de trigo wheatgerm; ~minar vi germinate

gerúndio /ʒe'rũdʒiu/ m gerund

gesso /'ʒesu/ m plaster

ges|tação /ʒesta'sãw/ f gestation; ~tante f pregnant woman

gestão /ʒes'tãw/ f management

ges|ticular vi gesticulate; ~to /'ʒestu/ m gesture

gibi /ʒi'bi/ m (fam) comic

Gibraltar /ʒibraw'tar/ f Gibraltar

gigan|te /ʒi'gãtʃi/ a & m giant; ~tesco /e/ a gigantic

gilete /ʒi'letʃi/ f razor blade □ a & m/f (fam) bisexual

gim /ʒĩ/ m gin

ginásio /ʒi'naziu/ m (escola) secondary school; (de ginástica) gymnasium

ginasta /ʒi'nasta/ m/f gymnast

ginásti|ca /ʒi'nastʃika/ f gymnastics; (aeróbica) aerobics; ~co a gymnastic

ginecolo|gia /ʒinekolo'ʒia/ f gynaecology; ~gista m/f gynaecologist

gingar /ʒĩ'gar/ vi sway

gira-discos /ʒira'diʃkuʃ/ m invar (Port) record player

girafa /ʒi'rafa/ f giraffe

gi|rar /ʒi'rar/ vt/i spin, revolve; ~rassol (pl ~rassóis) m sunflower; ~ratório a revolving

gíria /'ʒiria/ f slang; (uma ~) slang expression

giro /'ʒiru/ m spin, turn □ a (Port fam) great

giz /ʒis/ m chalk

gla|cê /gla'se/ m icing; ~cial (pl ~ciais) a icy

glamour /gla'mur/ m glamour; ~oso /o/ a glamorous

glândula /'glãdula/ f gland

glandular /glãdu'lar/ a glandular

glicerina /glise'rina/ f glycerine

glicose /gli'kɔzi/ f glucose

glo|bal /glo'baw/ (pl ~bais) a (mundial) global; <preço etc> overall; ~bo /o/ m globe; ~bo ocular eyeball

glóbulo /'globulu/ m globule; (do sangue) corpuscle

glória /'gloria/ f glory

glori|ficar /glorifi'kar/ vt glorify; ~oso /o/ a glorious

glossário /glo'sariu/ m glossary

glu|tão /glu'tãw/ m (f ~tona) glutton □ a (f ~tona) greedy

gnomo /gi'nomu/ m gnome

godê /go'de/ a flared

goela /go'εla/ f gullet

gogó /go'gɔ/ m (fam) Adam's apple

goia|ba /goj'aba/ f guava; ~bada f guava jelly; ~beira f guava tree

gol /gow/ (pl ~s) m goal

gola /'gola/ f collar

gole /'gɔli/ m mouthful

go|lear /goli'ar/ vt thrash; ~leiro m goalkeeper

golfe /'gowfi/ m golf

golfinho /gow'fiɲu/ m dolphin

golfista /gow'fista/ m/f golfer

golo /'golu/ m (Port) goal

golpe /'gɔwpi/ m blow; (manobra) trick; ~ (de estado) coup (d'état); ~ de mestre masterstroke; ~ de vento gust of wind; ~ de vista glance; ~ar vt hit

goma /'goma/ f gum; (para roupa) starch

gomo /'gomu/ m segment

gôndola /'gõdola/ f rack

gongo /'gõgu/ m gong

gonorréia /gono'xeja/ f gonorrhea

gonzo /'gõzu/ m hinge

gorar /go'rar/ vi go wrong, fail

gor|do /'gordu/ a fat; ~ducho a plump

gordu|ra /gor'dura/ f fat; ~rento a greasy; ~roso /u/ a fatty; <pele> greasy, oily

gorgolejar /gorgole'ʒar/ *vi* gurgle

gorila /go'rila/ *m* gorilla

gor|jear /gorʒi'ar/ *vi* twitter; **~jeio** *m* twittering

gorjeta /gor'ʒeta/ *f* tip

gorro /'goxu/ *m* hat

gos|ma /'gɔzma/ *f* slime; **~mento** *a* slimy

gos|tar /gos'tar/ *vi* **~tar de** like; **~to** /o/ *m* taste; (*prazer*) pleasure; **para o meu ~to** for my taste; **ter ~to de** taste of; **~toso** *a* nice; <*comida*> nice, tasty; (*fam*) <*pessoa*> gorgeous

go|ta /'gota/ *f* drop; (*que cai*) drip; (*doença*) gout; **foi a ~ta d'água** (*fig*) it was the last straw; **~teira** *f* (*buraco*) leak; (*cano*) gutter; **~tejar** *vi* drip; <*telhado*> leak □ *vt* drip

gótico /'gɔtʃiku/ *a* Gothic

gotícula /go'tʃikula/ *f* droplet

gover|nador /governa'dor/ *m* governor; **~namental** (*pl* **~namentais**) *a* government; **~nanta** *f* housekeeper; **~nante** *a* ruling □ *m/f* ruler; **~nar** *vt* govern; **~nista** *a* government □ *m/f* government supporter; **~no** /e/ *m* government

go|zação /goza'sãw/ *f* joking; (*uma*) send-up; **~zado** *a* funny; **~zar** *vt* **~zar de** enjoy; (*fam: zombar de*) make fun of □ *vi* (*ter orgasmo*) come; **~zo** *m* (*prazer*) enjoyment; (*posse*) possession; (*orgasmo*) orgasm; **ser um ~zo** be funny

Grã-Bretanha /grãbre'taɲa/ *f* Great Britain

graça /'grasa/ *f* grace; (*piada*) joke; (*humor*) humour, funny side; (*jur*) pardon; **de ~** for nothing; **sem ~** (*enfadonho*) dull; (*não engraçado*) unfunny; (*envergonhado*) embarrassed; **ser uma ~** be lovely; **ter ~** be funny; **não tem ~** sair sozinho

it's no fun to go out alone; **~s a** thanks to

grace|jar /grase'ʒar/ *vi* joke; **~jo** /e/ *m* joke

graci|nha /gra'siɲa/ *f* **ser uma ~nha** be sweet; **~oso** /o/ *a* gracious

grada|ção /grada'sãw/ *f* gradation; **~tivo** *a* gradual

grade /'gradʒi/ *f* grille, grating; (*cerca*) railings; **atrás das ~s** behind bars; **~ado** *a* <*janela*> barred

grado /'gradu/ *m* **de bom/mau ~** willingly/unwillingly

gradu|ação /gradua'sãw/ *f* graduation; (*mil*) rank; (*variação*) gradation; **~ado** *a* <*escala*> graduated; <*estudante*> graduate; <*militar*> high-ranking; (*eminente*) respected; **~al** (*pl* **~ais**) *a* gradual; **~ar** *vt* graduate <*escala*>; (*ordenar*) grade; (*regular*) regulate; **~ar-se** *vpr* <*estudante*> graduate

grafia /gra'fia/ *f* spelling

gráfi|ca /'grafika/ *f* (*arte*) graphics; (*oficina*) print shop; **~co** *a* graphic □ *m* (*pessoa*) printer; (*diagrama*) graph; *pl* (*de computador*) graphics

grã-fino /grã'finu/ (*fam*) *a* posh, upper-class □ *m* posh person

grafite /gra'fitʃi/ *f* (*mineral*) graphite; (*de lápis*) lead; (*pichação*) piece of graffiti

gra|fologia /grafolo'ʒia/ *f* graphology; **~fólogo** *m* graphologist

grama¹ /'grama/ *m* gramme

grama² /'grama/ *f* grass; **~do** *m* lawn; (*campo de futebol*) field

gramática /gra'matʃika/ *f* grammar

gramati|cal /gramatʃi'kaw/ (*pl* **~cais**) *a* grammatical

gram|peador /grãpia'dor/ *m* stapler; **~pear** *vt* staple <*papéis etc*>; tap <*telefone*>; **~po** *m* (*de*

cabelo) hairclip; (para papéis etc)
staple; (ferramenta) clamp

grana /'grana/ f (fam) cash

granada /gra'nada/ f (projétil)
grenade; (pedra) garnet

gran|dalhão /grãda'ʎãw/ a (f
~**dalhona**) enormous; ~**dão** a
(f ~**dona**) huge; ~**de** a big;
(fig) <escritor; amor etc> great;
~**deza** /e/ f greatness; (tamanho) magnitude; ~**dioso** /o/ a
grand

granel /gra'nɛw/ m a ~ in bulk

granito /gra'nitu/ m granite

granizo /gra'nizu/ m hail

gran|ja /'grãʒa/ f farm; ~**jear** vt
win, gain

granulado /granu'ladu/ a granu-
lated

grânulo /'granulu/ m granule

grão /grãw/ (pl ~**s**) m grain; (de
café) bean; ~**de-bico** (pl ~**s-
de-bico**) m chickpea

grasnar /graz'nar/ vi <pato>
quack; <rã> croak; <corvo> caw

grati|dão /grat∫i'dãw/ f gratitude;
~**ficação** f (dinheiro a mais)
gratuity; (recompensa) gratifica-
tion; ~**ficante** a gratifying;
~**ficar** vt (dar dinheiro a) give
a gratuity to; (recompensar) gratify

gratinado /grat∫i'nadu/ a & m
gratin

grátis /'grat∫is/ adv free

grato /'gratu/ a grateful

gratuito /gra'tuitu/ a (de graça)
free; (sem motivo) gratuitous

grau /graw/ m degree; **escola
de 1º/2º** ~ primary/secondary
school

graúdo /gra'udu/ a big; (importante) important

gra|vação /grava'sãw/ f (de som)
recording; (de desenhos etc)
engraving; ~**vador** m (pessoa)
engraver; (máquina) tape recorder; ~**vadora** f record company; ~**var** vt record <música,

disco>; (fixar na memória) memorize; (estampar) engrave

gravata /gra'vata/ f tie; (golpe)
stranglehold; ~ **borboleta** bow-
tie

grave /'gravi/ a serious; <voz,
som> deep; <acento> grave

grávida /'gravida/ f pregnant

gravidade /gravi'dadʒi/ f gravity

gravidez /gravi'des/ f pregnancy

gravura /gra'vura/ f engraving;
(em livro) illustration

graxa /'graʃa/ f (de sapatos) polish; (de lubrificar) grease

Grécia /'grɛsia/ f Greece

grego /'gregu/ a & m Greek

grei /grej/ f flock

gre|lha /'grɛʎa/ f grill; ~**lhado** a
grilled □ m grill; ~**lhar** vt grill

grêmio /'gremiu/ m guild, association

grená /gre'na/ a & m dark red

gre|ta /'greta/ f crack; ~**tar** vt/i
crack

gre|ve /'grevi/ f strike; **entrar em
~ve** go on strike; ~**ve de fome**
hunger strike; ~**vista** m/f
striker

gri|fado /gri'fadu/ a in italics;
~**far** vt italicize

griffe /'grifi/ f label, line

gri|lado /gri'ladu/ a (fam) hung-
up; ~**lar** (fam) vt bug; ~**lar-se**
vpr get hung-up (com about)

grilhão /gri'ʎãw/ m fetter

grilo /'grilu/ m (bicho) cricket;
(fam) (preocupação) hang-up;
(problema) hassle; (barulho)
squeak

grinalda /gri'nawda/ f garland

gringo /'grĩgu/ (fam) a foreign □
m foreigner

gri|pado /gri'padu/ a estar/ficar
~**pado** have/get the flu; ~**par-
se** vpr get the flu; ~**pe** f flu, influenza; ~**pe** das aves bird flu

grisalho /gri'zaʎu/ a gray

gri|tante /gri'tãt∫i/ a <erro> glar-
ing, gross; <cor> loud, garish;

~tar *vt/i* shout; (*de medo*) scream; **~taria** *f* shouting; **~to** *m* shout; (*de medo*) scream; **aos ~tos** in a loud voice; **no ~to** (*fam*) by force

grogue /'grɔgi/ *a* groggy

grosa /'grɔza/ *f* gross

groselha /groˈzɛʎa/ *f* (*vermelha*) redcurrant; (*espinhosa*) gooseberry; **~ negra** blackcurrant

gros|seiro /groˈseru/ *a* rude; (*tosco, malfeito*) rough; (*tosco, malfeito*) rough; **~seria** *f* rudeness; (*uma*) rude thing; **~so** /o/ *a* thick; <*voz*> deep; (*fam*) <*pessoa, atitude*> rude; **~sura** *f* thickness; (*fam: grosseria*) rudeness

grotesco /groˈtesku/ *a* grotesque

grua /'grua/ *f* crane

gru|dado /gruˈdadu/ *a* stuck; (*fig*) very attached (**em** to); **~dar** *vt/i* stick; **~de** *m* glue; **~dento** *a* sticky

gru|nhido /gruˈɲidu/ *m* grunt; **~nhir** *vi* grunt

grupo /'grupu/ *m* group

gruta /'gruta/ *f* cave

guaraná /gwaraˈna/ *m* guarana

guarani /gwaraˈni/ *a* & *m/f* Guarani

guarda /'gwarda/ *f* guard □ *m/f* guard; (*policial*) policeman (*f* -woman); **~ costeira** coastguard; **~-chuva** *m* umbrella; **~-costas** *m invar* bodyguard; **~-dor** *m* parking attendant; **~-florestal** (*pl* **~s-florestais**) *m/f* forest ranger; **~-louça** *m* china cupboard; **~ napo** *m* napkin, serviette; **~-noturno** (*pl* **~s-noturnos**) *m* night watchman

guardar /gwarˈdar/ *vt* (*pôr no lugar*) put away; (*conservar*) keep; (*vigiar*) guard; (*não esquecer*) remember; **~-se** *m* guard against

guarda|-redes /ˈgwarda-ˈxedʒ/ *m invar* (*Port*) goalkeeper; **~-**

roupa *m* wardrobe; **~-sol** (*pl* **~-sóis**) *m* sunshade

guardi|ão /gwardʒiˈãw/ (*pl* **~ães** ou **~ões**) *m* (*f* **~ã**) guardian

guarita /gwaˈrita/ *f* sentry box

guar|necer /gwarneˈser/ *vt* (*fortificar*) garrison; (*munir*) equip; (*enfeitar*) garnish; **~nição** *f* (*mil*) garrison; (*enfeite*) garnish

Guatemala /gwateˈmala/ *f* Guatemala

guatemalteco /gwatemalˈtɛku/ *a* & *m* Guatemalan

gude /'gudʒi/ *m* **bola de ~** marble

guelra /'gɛwxa/ *f* gill

guer|ra /'gɛxa/ *f* war; **~reiro** *m* warrior □ *a* warlike; **~rilha** *f* guerrilla war; **~rilheiro** *a* & *m* guerrilla

gueto /'getu/ *m* ghetto

guia /'gia/ *m/f* guide □ *m* guide(-book) □ *f* delivery note

Guiana /giˈana/ *f* Guyana

guianense /giaˈnẽsi/ *a* & *m/f* Guyanan

guiar /giˈar/ *vt* guide; drive <*veículo*> □ *vi* drive; **~-se** *vpr* be guided

guichê /giˈʃe/ *m* window

guidom /giˈdõ/, (*Port*) **guidão** /giˈdãw/ *m* handlebars

guilhotina /giʎoˈtʃina/ *f* guillotine

guimba /'gĩba/ *f* butt

guinada /giˈnada/ *f* change of direction; **dar uma ~** change direction

guinchar¹ /gĩˈʃar/ *vi* squeal; <*freios*> screech

guinchar² /gĩˈʃar/ *vt* tow <*carro*>; (*içar*) winch

guincho¹ /ˈgĩʃu/ *m* squeal; (*de freios*) screech

guincho² /ˈgĩʃu/ *m* (*máquina*) winch; (*veículo*) tow truck

guin|dar /gĩˈdar/ *vt* hoist; **~daste** *m* crane

Guiné /giˈnɛ/ *f* Guinea

gui|sado /gi'zadu/ *m* stew; **~sar** *vt* stew

guitar|ra /gi'taxa/ *f* (electric) guitar; **~rista** *m/f* guitarist

guizo /'gizu/ *m* bell

gu|la /'gula/ *f* greed; **~lodice** *f* greed; **~loseima** *f* delicacy; **~loso** /o/ *a* greedy

gume /'gumi/ *m* cutting edge

guri /gu'ri/ *m* boy; **~a** *f* girl

guru /gu'ru/ *m* guru

gutu|ral /gutu'raw/ (*pl* **~rais**) *a* guttural

H

há|bil /'abiw/ (*pl* **~beis**) *a* clever, skilful

habili|dade /abili'dadʒi/ *f* skill; **ter ~dade com** be good with; **~doso** /o/ *a* skilful; **~tação** *f* qualification; **~tar** *vt* qualify

habi|tação /abita'sãw/ *f* housing; (*casa*) dwelling; **~tacional** (*pl* **~tacionais**) *a* housing; **~tante** *m/f* inhabitant; **~tar** *vt* inhabit □ *vi* live; **~tável** (*pl* **~táveis**) *a* habitable

hábito /'abitu/ *m* habit

habitu|al /abitu'aw/ (*pl* **~ais**) *a* habitual; **~ar** *vt* accustom (**a** to); **~ar-se** *vpr* get accustomed (**a** to)

hadoque /a'dɔki/ *m* haddock

Haia /'aja/ *f* the Hague

Haiti /aj'tʃi/ *m* Haiti

haitiano /ajtʃi'anu/ *a* & *m* Haitian

hálito /'alitu/ *m* breath

halitose /ali'tɔzi/ *f* halitosis

hall /xɔw/ (*pl* **~s**) *m* hall; (*de hotel*) foyer

halte|re /aw'tɛri/ *m* dumbbell; **~rofilismo** *m* weight lifting; **~rofilista** *m/f* weight lifter

hambúrguer /ã'burger/ *m* hamburger

hangar /ã'gar/ *m* hangar

haras /'aras/ *m invar* stud farm

hardware /'xarduer/ *m* hardware

harmo|nia /armo'nia/ *f* harmony; **~nioso** /o/ *a* harmonious; **~nizar** *vt* harmonize; (*conciliar*) reconcile; **~nizar-se** *vpr* (*combinar*) tone in; (*concordar*) coincide

har|pa /'arpa/ *f* harp; **~pista** *m/f* harpist

haste /'astʃi/ *m* pole; (*de planta*) stem, stalk; **~ar** *vt* hoist, raise

Havaí /ava'i/ *m* Hawaii

havaiano /avaj'anu/ *a* & *m* Hawaiian

haver /a'ver/ *m* credit; *pl* possessions □ *vt* (*auxiliar*) **havia sido** it had been; (*impessoal*) **há** there is/are; **ele trabalha aqui há anos** he's been working here for years; **ela morreu há vinte anos** (*atrás*) she died twenty years ago

haxixe /a'ʃiʃi/ *m* hashish

he|braico /e'brajku/ *a* & *m* Hebrew; **~breu** *a* & *m* (*f* **~bréia**) Hebrew

hectare /ek'tari/ *m* hectare

hediondo /edʒi'õdu/ *a* hideous

hein /ẽj/ *int* eh

hélice /'elisi/ *f* propeller

helicóptero /eli'kɔpteru/ *m* helicopter

hélio /'ɛliu/ *m* helium

heliporto /eli'portu/ *m* heliport

hem /ẽj/ *int* eh

hematoma /ema'tɔma/ *m* bruise

hemisfério /emis'fɛriu/ *m* hemisphere; **Hemisfério Norte/Sul** Northern/Southern Hemisphere

hemo|filia /emofi'lia/ *f* haemophilia; **~fílico** *a* & *m* haemophiliac; **~globina** *f* haemoglobin; **~grama** *m* blood count

hemor|ragia /emoxa'ʒia/ *f* haemorrhage; **~róidas** *f pl* haemorrhoids

henê /e'ne/ *m* henna

hepatite /epa'tʃitʃi/ *f* hepatitis

hera /ˈɛra/ *f* ivy

heráldi|ca /eˈrawdʒika/ *f* heraldry; ~**co** *a* heraldic

herança /eˈrãsa/ *f* inheritance; (*de um povo etc*) heritage

her|bicida /erbiˈsida/ *m* weed-killer; ~**bívoro** *a* herbivorous □ *m* herbivore

her|dar /erˈdar/ *vt* inherit; ~**deiro** *m* heir

hereditário /eredʒiˈtariu/ *a* hereditary

here|ge /eˈrɛʒi/ *m/f* heretic; ~**sia** *f* heresy

herético /eˈrɛtʃiku/ *a* heretical

hermético /erˈmɛtʃiku/ *a* airtight; (*fig*) obscure

hérnia /ˈɛrnia/ *f* hernia

herói /eˈrɔj/ *m* hero; ~**co** *a* heroic

hero|ína /eroˈina/ *f* (*mulher*) heroine; (*droga*) heroin; ~**ismo** *m* heroism

herpes /ˈɛrpis/ *m invar* herpes; ~**-zoster** *m* shingles

hesi|tação /ezitaˈsãw/ *f* hesitation; ~**tante** *a* hesitant; ~**tar** *vi* hesitate

hetero|doxo /eteroˈdɔksu/ *a* unorthodox; ~**gêneo** *a* heterogeneous

heterossexu|al /eteroseksuˈaw/ (*pl* ~**ais**) *a & m* heterosexual

hexago|nal /eksagoˈnaw/ (*pl* ~**nais**) *a* hexagonal

hexágono /ekˈsagonu/ *m* hexagon

hiato /iˈatu/ *m* hiatus

hiber|nação /ibɛrnaˈsãw/ *f* hibernation; ~**nar** *vi* hibernate

híbrido /ˈibridu/ *a & m* hybrid

hidrante /iˈdrãtʃi/ *m* fire hydrant

hidra|tante /idraˈtãtʃi/ *a* moisturising □ *m* moisturizer; ~**tar** *vt* moisturize <*pele*>; ~**to** *m* ~**to de carbono** carbohydrate

hidráuli|ca /iˈdrawlika/ *f* hydraulics; ~**co** *a* hydraulic

hidrelétri|ca /idreˈlɛtrika/ *f* hydroelectric power station; ~**co** *a* hydroelectric

hidro|avião /idroaviˈãw/ *m* seaplane; ~**carboneto** /e/ *m* hydrocarbon

hidrófilo /iˈdrɔfilu/ *a* absorbent; **algodão** ~ cotton wool, (*Amer*) absorbent cotton

hidrofobia /idrofoˈbia/ *f* rabies

hidro|gênio /idroˈʒeniu/ *m* hydrogen; ~**massagem** *f* **banheira de** ~**massagem** jacuzzi; ~**via** *f* waterway

hiena /iˈena/ *f* hyena

hierarquia /ierarˈkia/ *f* hierarchy

hieróglifo /ieˈrɔglifu/ *m* hieroglyphic

hífen /ˈifẽ/ *m* hyphen

higi|ene /iʒiˈeni/ *f* hygiene; ~**ênico** *a* hygienic

hilari|ante /ilariˈãtʃi/ *a* hilarious; ~**dade** *f* hilarity

Himalaia /imaˈlaja/ *m* Himalayas

hin|di /ˈĩdʒi/ *m* Hindi; ~**du** *a & m/f* Hindu; ~**duísmo** *m* Hinduism; ~**duísta** *a & m/f* Hindu

hino /ˈinu/ *m* hymn; ~**nacional** national anthem

hipermercado /ipermɛrˈkadu/ *m* hypermarket

hipersensí|vel /ipersẽˈsivew/ (*pl* ~**veis**) *a* hypersensitive

hipertensão /ipertẽˈsãw/ *f* hypertension

hípico /ˈipiku/ *a* horseriding

hipismo /iˈpizmu/ *m* horseriding; (*corridas*) horseracing

hip|nose /ipiˈnɔzi/ *f* hypnosis; ~**nótico** *a* hypnotic; ~**notismo** *m* hypnotism; ~**notizador** *m* hypnotist; ~**notizar** *vt* hypnotize

hipocondríaco /ipokõˈdriaku/ *a & m* hypochondriac

hipocrisia /ipokriˈzia/ *f* hypocrisy

hipócrita /iˈpɔkrita/ *m/f* hypocrite □ *a* hypocritical

hipódromo /iˈpɔdromu/ *m* race course, (*Amer*) race track

hipopótamo /ipoˈpɔtamu/ *m* hippopotamus

hipote|ca /ipo'tɛka/ f mortgage; **~car** vt mortgage; **~cário** a mortgage

hipotermia /ipoter'mia/ f hypothermia

hipótese /i'potezi/ f hypothesis; **na** ~ **de** in the event of; **na pior das** ~**s** at worst

hipotético /ipo'tɛtʃiku/ a hypothetical

hirto /'irtu/ adj rigid, stiff

hispânico /is'paniku/ a Hispanic

histamina /ista'mina/ f histamine

his|terectomia /isterekto'mia/ f hysterectomy; **~teria** f hysteria; **~térico** a hysterical; **~terismo** m hysteria

his|tória /is'toria/ f (do passado) history; (conto) story; pl (amolação) trouble; **~toriador** m historian; **~tórico** a historical; (marcante) historic □ m history

hoje /'oʒi/ adv today; **~ em dia** nowadays; **~ de manhã** this morning; **~ à noite** tonight

Holanda /o'lãda/ f Holland

holan|dês /olã'des/ a (f ~**desa**) Dutch □ m (f ~**desa**) Dutchman (f -woman); (língua) Dutch; **os** ~**deses** the Dutch

holding /'xowdʒi/ (pl ~**s**) f holding company

holerite /ole'ritʃi/ m pay slip

holo|causto /olo'kawstu/ m holocaust; **~fote** /ɔ/ m spotlight; **~grama** m hologram

homem /'omẽ/ m man; **~ de negócios** businessman; **~-rã** (pl **homens-rã**) m frogman

homena|gear /omenaʒi'ar/ vt pay tribute to; **~gem** f tribute; **em** ~**gem a** in honour of

homeo|pata /omio'pata/ m/f homoeopath; **~patia** f homoeopathy; **~pático** a homoeopathic

homérico /o'mɛriku/ a (estrondoso) booming; (extraordinário) phenomenal

homi|cida /omi'sida/ a homicidal □ m/f murderer; **~cídio** m homicide; **~cídio involuntário** manslaughter

homo|geneizado /omoʒenej'zadu/ a < leite> homogenized; **~gêneo** a homogeneous

homologar /omolo'gar/ vt ratify

homólogo /o'mɔlogu/ m opposite number □ a equivalent

homônimo /o'monimu/ m (xará) namesake; (vocábulo) homonym

homossexu|al /omoseksu'aw/ (pl ~**ais**) a & m homosexual; **~alismo** m homosexuality

Honduras /õ'duras/ f Honduras

hondurenho /õdu'reɲu/ a & m Honduran

hones|tidade /onestʃi'dadʒi/ f honesty; **~to** /ɛ/ a honest

hono|rário /ono'rariu/ a honorary; **~rários** m pl fees; **~rífico** a honorific

hon|ra /'õxa/ f honour; **~radez** f honesty, integrity; **~rado** a honourable; **~rar** vt honour; **~roso** /o/ a honourable

hóquei /'ɔkej/ m (field) hockey; **~ sobre gelo** ice hockey; **~ sobre patins** roller hockey

hora /'ɔra/ f (unidade de tempo) hour; (ocasião) time; **que** ~**s são?** what's the time?; **a que** ~**s?** at what time?; **às três** ~**s** at three o'clock; **dizer as** ~**s** tell the time; **tem** ~**s?** do you have the time?; **de** ~ **em** ~ every hour; **em cima da** ~ at the last minute; **na** ~ (naquele momento) at the time; (no ato) on the spot; (a tempo) on time; **está na** ~ **de ir** it's time to go; **na** ~ **H** (no momento certo) at just the right moment; (no momento crítico) at the crucial moment; **meia** ~ half an hour; **toda** ~ all the time; **fazer** ~ kill time; **marcar** ~ make an appointment; **perder a** ~ lose track of time; **não**

tenho ~ my time is my own; **não vejo a ~ de ir** I can't wait to go; **~s extras** overtime; **~s vagas** spare time

horário /ɔ'rarju/ *a* hourly; **km ~s** km per hour □ *m* (*hora*) time; (*tabela*) timetable; (*de trabalho etc*) hours; **~ nobre** prime time

horda /'ɔrda/ *f* horde

horista /o'rista/ *a* paid by the hour □ *m/f* worker paid by the hour

horizon|tal /orizõ'taw/ (*pl* **~tais**) *a* & *f* horizontal; **~te** *m* horizon

hor|monal /ormo'naw/ (*pl* **~monais**) *a* hormonal; **~mônio** *m* hormone

horóscopo /o'rɔskopu/ *m* horoscope

horrendo /o'xẽdu/ *a* horrid

horri|lante /oxipi'lãtʃi/ *a* horrifying; **~lar** *vt* horrify

horrí|vel /o'xivew/ (*pl* **~veis**) *a* horrible, awful

horror /o'xor/ *m* horror (**a** of); (*coisa horrorosa*) horrible thing; **ser um ~** be awful; **que ~!** how awful!

horro|rizar /oxori'zar/ *vt/i* horrify; **~rizar-se** *vpr* be horrified; **~roso** /o/ *a* horrible

horta /'ɔrta/ *f* vegetable plot; **~ comercial** market garden, (*Amer*) truck farm; **~ liça** *f* vegetable

hortelã /orte'lã/ *f* mint; **~-pimenta** peppermint

horti|cultor /ortʃikuw'tor/ *m* horticulturalist; **~cultura** *f* horticulture; **~frutigranjeiros** *m pl* fruit and vegetables; **~granjeiros** *m pl* vegetables

horto /'ɔrtu/ *m* market garden; (*viveiro*) nursery

hospe|dagem /ospe'daʒẽ/ *f* accommodation; **~dar** *vt* put up; **~dar-se** *vpr* stay

hóspede /'ɔspidʒi/ *m/f* guest

hospedei|ra /ospe'dera/ *f* landlady; **~ra de bordo** (*Port*) stewardess; **~ro** *m* landlord

hospício /os'pisiu/ *m* (*de loucos*) asylum

hospi|tal /ospi'taw/ (*pl* **~tais**) *m* hospital; **~talar** *a* hospital; **~taleiro** *a* hospitable; **~talidade** *f* hospitality; **~talizar** *vt* hospitalize

hóstia /'ɔstʃia/ *f* Host, Communion wafer

hos|til /os'tʃiw/ (*pl* **~tis**) *a* hostile; **~tilidade** *f* hostility; **~tilizar** *vt* antagonize

ho|tel /o'tɛw/ (*pl* **~téis**) *m* hotel; **~teleiro** *a* hotel □ *m* hotelier

huma|nidade /umani'dadʒi/ *f* humanity; **~nismo** *m* humanism; **~nista** *a* & *m/f* humanist; **~nitário** *a* & *m* humanitarian; **~nizar** *vt* humanize; **~no** *a* human; (*compassivo*) humane; **~nos** *m pl* humans

húmido /'umidu/ *adj* (*Port*) humid

humil|dade /umiw'dadʒi/ *f* humility; **~de** *a* humble

humi|lhação /umiʎa'sãw/ *f* humiliation; **~lhante** *a* humiliating; **~lhar** *vt* humiliate

humor /u'mor/ *m* humour; (*disposição do espírito*) mood; **de bom/mau ~** in a good/bad mood

humo|rismo /umo'rizmu/ *m* humour; **~rista** *m/f* (*no palco*) comedian; (*escritor*) humorist; **~rístico** *a* humorous

húngaro /'ũgaru/ *a* & *m* Hungarian

Hungria /ũ'gria/ *f* Hungary

hurra /'uxa/ *int* hurrah □ *m* cheer

I

ia|te /i'atʃi/ *m* yacht; **~tismo** *m* yachting; **~tista** *m/f* yachtsman (*f*-woman)

ibérico /i'bɛriku/ *a & m* Iberian

ibope /i'bɔpi/ *m* **dar ~** (*fam*) be popular

içar /i'sar/ *vt* hoist

iceberg /ajs'bɛrgi/ (*pl* **~s**) *m* iceberg

ícone /'ikoni/ *m* icon

iconoclasta /ikono'klasta/ *m/f* iconoclast □ *a* iconoclastic

icterícia /ikte'risia/ *f* jaundice

ida /'ida/ *f* going; **na ~** on the way there; **~ e volta** return, (*Amer*) round trip

idade /i'dadʒi/ *f* age; **meia ~** middle age; **homem de meia ~** middle-aged man; **senhor de ~** elderly man; **Idade Média** Middle Ages

ideal /ide'aw/ (*pl* **~ais**) *a & m* ideal; **~alismo** *m* idealism; **~alista** *m/f* idealist □ *a* idealistic; **~alizar** *vt* (*criar*) devise; (*sublimar*) idealize; **~ar** *vt* devise; **~ário** *m* ideas

idéia /i'dɛja/ *f* idea; **mudar de ~** change one's mind

idem /'idẽ/ *adv* ditto

idêntico /i'dẽtʃiku/ *a* identical

identidade /idẽtʃi'dadʒi/ *f* identity; **~ficar** *vt* identify; **~ficar-se** *vpr* identify (**com**) with

ideologia /ideolo'ʒia/ *f* ideology; **~lógico** *a* ideological

idílico /i'dʒiliku/ *a* idyllic

idílio /i'dʒiliu/ *m* idyll

idioma /idʒi'oma/ *m* language; **~mático** *a* idiomatic

idiota /idʒi'ɔta/ *m/f* idiot □ *a* idiotic; **~tice** *f* stupidity; (*uma*) stupid thing

idolatrar /idola'trar/ *vt* idolize; **~tria** *f* idolatry

ídolo /'idulu/ *m* idol

idôneo /i'doniu/ *a* suitable

idoso /i'dozu/ *a* elderly

Iêmen /i'emẽ/ *m* Yemen

iemenita /ieme'nita/ *a & m/f* Yemeni

iene /i'ɛni/ *m* yen

iglu /i'glu/ *m* igloo

ignição /igni'sãw/ *f* ignition

ignomínia /igno'minia/ *f* ignominy

ignorância /igno'rãsia/ *f* ignorance; **~rante** *a* ignorant; **~rar** (*desconsiderar*) ignore; (*desconhecer*) not know

igreja /i'greʒa/ *f* church

igual /i'gwaw/ (*pl* **~ais**) *a* equal; (*em aparência*) identical; (*liso*) even □ *m/f* equal; **por ~** equally; **~alar** *vt* equal; twist <*terreno*>; **~alar(-se) a** be equal to; **~aldade** *f* equality; **~alitário** *a* egalitarian; **~almente** *adv* equally; (*como resposta*) the same to you; (*como alzinho* a *z*) **~alzinho** *a* exactly the same (**a as**)

iguaria /igwa'ria/ *f* delicacy

iídiche /i'idiʃi/ *m* Yiddish

ilegal /ile'gaw/ (*pl* **~gais**) *a* illegal; **~galidade** *f* illegality

ilegítimo /ile'ʒitʃimu/ *a* illegitimate

ilegível /ile'ʒivew/ (*pl* **~veis**) *a* illegible

ileso /i'lezu/ *a* unhurt

iletrado /ile'tradu/ *adj & m* illiterate

ilha /'iʎa/ *f* island

ilharga /i'ʎarga/ *f* side

ilhéu /i'ʎɛw/ *m* (*f* **ilhoa**) islander

ilhós /i'ʎɔs/ *m invar* eyelet

ilhota /i'ʎɔta/ *f* small island

ilícito /i'lisitu/ *a* illicit

ilimitado /ilimi'tadu/ *a* unlimited

ilógico /i'lɔʒiku/ *a* illogical

iludir /ilu'dʒir/ *vt* delude; **~-se** *vpr* delude o.s.

iluminação /ilumina'sãw/ *f* lighting; (*inspiração*) enlightenment; **~nar** *vt* light up, illuminate; (*inspirar*) enlighten

ilusão /ilu'zãw/ *f* illusion; (*sonho*) delusion; **~sionista** *m/f* illusionist; **~sório** *a* illusory

ilustração /ilustra'sãw/ *f* illustration; (*erudição*) learning; **~**

trador *m* illustrator; ~trar *vt* illustrate; ~trativo *a* illustrative; ~tre *a* illustrious; ~tríssimo senhor Dear Sir

ímã /ˈimã/ *m* magnet

imaculado /imakuˈladu/ *a* immaculate

imagem /iˈmaʒẽ/ *f* image; (*da TV*) picture

imagi|nação /imaʒinaˈsãw/ *f* imagination; ~nar *vt* imagine; ~nário *a* imaginary; ~nativo *a* imaginative; ~nável *a* (*pl* ~náveis) *a* imaginable; ~noso /o/ *a* imaginative

imatu|ridade /imaturiˈdadʒi/ *f* immaturity; ~ro *a* immature

imbati|vel /ĩbaˈtʃivew/ (*pl* ~veis) *a* unbeatable

imbe|cil /ĩbeˈsiw/ (*pl* ~cis) *a* stupid □ *m/f* imbecile

imberbe /ĩˈberbi/ *adj* (*sem barba*) beardless

imbricar /ĩbriˈkar/ *vt* overlap; ~se *vpr* overlap

imedia|ções /imedʒiaˈsõjs/ *f pl* vicinity; ~tamente *adv* immediately; ~to *a* immediate

imemori|al /imemoriˈaw/ (*pl* ~ais) *a* immemorial

imen|sidão /imẽsiˈdãw/ *f* vastness; ~so *a* immense

imergir /imerˈʒir/ *vt* immerse

imi|gração /imigraˈsãw/ *f* immigration; ~grante *a* & *m/f* immigrant; ~grar *vi* immigrate

imi|nência /imiˈnẽsia/ *f* imminence; ~nente *a* imminent

imiscuir-se /imiskuˈirsi/ *vpr* interfere

imi|tação /imiˈtasãw/ *f* imitation; ~tador *m* imitator; ~tar *vt* imitate

imobili|ária /imobiliˈaria/ *f* estate agent's, (*Amer*) realtor; ~ário *a* property; ~dade *f* immobility; ~zar *vt* immobilize

imo|ral /imoˈraw/ (*pl* ~rais) *a* immoral; ~ralidade *f* immorality

imor|tal /imorˈtaw/ (*pl* ~tais) *a* immortal □ *m/f* member of the Brazilian Academy of Letters; ~talidade *f* immortality; ~talizar *vt* immortalize

imó|vel /iˈmɔvew/ (*pl* ~veis) *a* motionless, immobile □ *m* building, property; *pl* property, real estate

impaci|ência /ĩpasiˈẽsia/ *f* impatience; ~entar-se *vpr* get impatient; ~ente *a* impatient

impacto /ĩˈpaktu/, (*Port*) impacte /ĩˈpaktʃi/ *m* impact

impagá|vel /ĩpaˈgavew/ (*pl* ~veis) *a* priceless

ímpar /ˈĩpar/ *a* unique; <*número*> odd

imparci|al /ĩparsiˈaw/ (*pl* ~ais) *a* impartial; ~alidade *f* impartiality

impasse /ĩˈpasi/ *m* impasse

impassí|vel /ĩpaˈsivew/ (*pl* ~veis) *a* impassive

impecá|vel /ĩpeˈkavew/ (*pl* ~veis) *a* impeccable

impe|dido /ĩpeˈdʒidu/ *a* <*rua*> blocked; (*Port: ocupado*) engaged, (*Amer*) busy; (*no futebol*) offside; ~dimento *m* prevention; (*no futebol*) offside position; ~dir *vt* stop; (*estorvar*) hinder; block <*rua*>; ~dir alg de ir *ou* que alg vá stop s.o. going

impelir /ĩpeˈlir/ *vt* drive

impenetrá|vel /ĩpeneˈtravew/ (*pl* ~veis) *a* impenetrable

impensá|vel /ĩpẽˈsavew/ (*pl* ~veis) *a* unthinkable

impe|rador /ĩperaˈdor/ *m* emperor; ~rar *vi* reign, rule; ~rativo *a* & *m* imperative; ~ratriz *f* empress

impercep|tí|vel /ĩpersepˈtʃivew/ (*pl* ~veis) *a* imperceptible

imperdí|vel /ĩperˈdʒivew/ (*pl* ~veis) *a* unmissable

imperdoá|vel /ĩperdo'avew/ (*pl* ~**veis**) *a* unforgivable

imperfei|ção /ĩperfej'sãw/ *f* imperfection; ~**to** *a* & *m* imperfect

imperi|al /ĩperi'aw/ (*pl* ~**ais**) *a* imperial; ~**alismo** *m* imperialism; ~**alista** *a* & *m/f* imperialist

império /ĩ'periu/ *m* empire

imperioso /ĩperi'ozu/ *a* imperious; <*necessidade*> pressing

imperme|abilizar /ĩpermiabili'zar/ *vt* waterproof; ~**ável** (*pl* ~**áveis**) *a* waterproof; (*fig*) impervious (**a** to) □ *m* raincoat

imperti|nência /ĩpertʃi'nēsia/ *f* impertinence; ~**nente** *a* impertinent

impesso|al /ĩpeso'aw/ (*pl* ~**ais**) *a* impersonal

ímpeto /'ĩpetu/ *m* (*vontade*) urge, impulse; (*de emoção*) surge; (*movimento*) start; (*na física*) impetus

impetu|osidade /ĩpetuozi'dadʒi/ *f* impetuosity; ~**so** /o/ *a* impetuous

impiedoso /ĩpie'dozu/ *a* merciless

impingir /ĩpĩ'ʒir/ *vt* foist (**a** on)

implacá|vel /ĩpla'kavew/ (*pl* ~**veis**) *a* implacable

implan|tar /ĩplã'tar/ *vt* introduce; (*no corpo*) implant; ~**te** *m* implant

implemen|tar /ĩplemē'tar/ *vt* implement; ~**to** *m* implement

impli|cação /ĩplika'sãw/ *f* implication; ~**cância** *f* (*ato*) harassment; (*antipatia*) grudge; **estar de** ~**cância com** have it in for; ~**cante** *a* troublesome □ *m/f* troublemaker; ~**car** (*comprometer*) implicate; ~**car** (**em**) (*dar a entender*) imply; (*acarretar, exigir*) involve; ~**car com** (*provocar*) pick on; (*antipatizar*) not get on with

implícito /ĩ'plisitu/ *a* implicit

implorar /ĩplo'rar/ *vt* plead for (**a** from)

imponente /ĩpo'nētʃi/ *a* imposing

impopular /ĩpopu'lar/ *a* unpopular

impor /ĩ'por/ *vt* impose (**a** on); command <*respeito*>; ~**-se** *vpr* assert o.s.

impor|tação /ĩporta'sãw/ *f* import; ~**tador** *m* importer; ~**tadora** *f* import company; ~**tados** *m pl* imported goods; ~**tância** *f* importance; (*quantia*) amount; **ter** ~**tância** be important; ~**tante** *a* important; ~**tar** *vt* import <*mercadorias*> □ *vi* matter; ~**tar em** (*montar a*) amount to; (*resultar em*) lead to; ~**tar-se** (**com**) mind

importu|nar /ĩportu'nar/ *vt* bother; ~**no** *a* annoying

imposição /ĩpozi'sãw/ *f* imposition

impossibili|dade /ĩposibili'dadʒi/ *f* impossibility; ~**tar** *vt* make impossible; ~**tar alg de ir**, ~**tar a alg** prevent s.o. from going, make it impossible for s.o. to go

impossí|vel /ĩpo'sivew/ (*pl* ~**veis**) *a* impossible

impos|to /ĩ'postu/ *m* tax; ~**to de renda** income tax; ~**to sobre o valor acrescentado** (*Port*) VAT; ~**tor** *m* impostor; ~**tura** *f* deception

impo|tência /ĩpo'tēsia/ *f* impotence; ~**tente** *a* impotent

impreci|são /ĩpresi'zãw/ *f* imprecision; ~**so** *a* imprecise

impregnar /ĩpreg'nar/ *vt* impregnate

imprensa /ĩ'prēsa/ *f* press; ~**marrom** gutter press

imprescindí|vel /ĩpresĩd'ʒivew/ (*pl* ~**veis**) *a* essential

impres|são /ĩpre'sãw/ *f* impression; (*no prelo*) printing; ~**são digital** fingerprint; ~**sionante** *a* (*imponente*) impressive; (*comovente*) striking; ~**sionar** *vt* (*cau-*

sar admiração) impress; (*co-mover*) make an impression on; **~sionar-se** *vpr* be impressed (*com* by); **~sionável** (*pl ~sionáveis*) *a* impressionable; **~sionismo** *m* impressionism; **~sionista** *a & m/f* impressionist; **~so** *a* printed □ *m* printed sheet; *pl* printed matter; **~sor** *m* printer; **~sora** *f* printer

imprestá|vel /ipres'tavew/ (*pl ~veis*) *a* useless

impre|visível /iprevi'zivew/ (*pl ~visíveis*) *a* unpredictable; **~visto** *a* unforeseen □ *m* unforeseen circumstance

imprimir /ipri'mir/ *vt* print

impropério /ipro'periu/ *m* term of abuse; *pl* abuse

impróprio /i'propriu/ *a* improper; (*inadequado*) unsuitable (**para** for)

imprová|vel /ipro'vavew/ (*pl ~veis*) *a* unlikely

improvi|sação /iproviza'sãw/ *f* improvisation; **~sar** *vt/i* improvise; **~so** *m* **de ~so** on the spur of the moment

impru|dência /ipru'dêsia/ *f* recklessness; **~dente** *a* reckless

impul|sionar /ipuwsio'nar/ *vt* drive; **~sivo** *a* impulsive; **~so** *m* impulse

impu|ne /i'puni/ *a* unpunished; **~nidade** *f* impunity

impu|reza /ipu'reza/ *f* impurity; **~ro** *a* impure

imun|dície /imũ'dʒisi/ *f* filth; **~do** *a* filthy

imu|ne /i'muni/ *a* immune (**a** to); **~nidade** *f* immunity; **~nizar** *vt* immunize

inabalá|vel /inaba'lavew/ (*pl ~veis*) *a* unshakeable

ina|bil /i'nabiw/ (*pl ~bis*) *a* (*desafeitado*) clumsy

inabitado /inabi'tadu/ *a* uninhabited

inacabado /inaka'badu/ *a* unfinished

inaceitá|vel /inasej'tavew/ (*pl ~veis*) *a* unacceptable

inacessí|vel /inase'sivew/ (*pl ~veis*) *a* inaccessible

inacreditá|vel /inakredʒi'tavew/ (*pl ~veis*) *a* unbelievable

inadequado /inade'kwadu/ *a* unsuitable

inadmissí|vel /inadʒimi'sivew/ (*pl ~veis*) *a* inadmissible

inadvertência /inadʒiver'têsia/ *f* oversight

inalar /ina'lar/ *vt* inhale

inalcançá|vel /inawkã'savew/ (*pl ~veis*) *a* unattainable

inalterá|vel /inawte'ravew/ (*pl ~veis*) *a* unchangeable

inanição /inani'sãw/ *f* starvation

inanimado /inani'madu/ *a* inanimate

inapto /i'naptu/ *a* (*incapaz*) unfit

inati|vidade /inatʃivi'dadʒi/ *f* inactivity; **~vo** *a* inactive

inato /i'natu/ *a* innate

inaudito /inaw'dʒitu/ *a* unheard of

inaugu|ração /inawgura'sãw/ *f* inauguration; **~ral** (*pl ~rais*) *a* inaugural; **~rar** *vt* inaugurate

incabí|vel /ika'bivew/ (*pl ~veis*) *a* inappropriate

incalculá|vel /ikawku'lavew/ (*pl ~veis*) *a* incalculable

incandescente /ikãde'sêtʃi/ *a* red-hot

incansá|vel /ikã'savew/ (*pl ~veis*) *a* tireless

incapaci|tado /ikapasi'tadu/ *a* <*pessoa*> disabled; **~tar** *vt* incapacitate

incauto /i'kawtu/ *a* reckless

incendi|ar /isêdʒi'ar/ *vt* set alight; **~ar-se** *vpr* catch fire; **~ário** *a* incendiary; (*fig*) <*discurso*> inflammatory □ *m* arsonist; (*fig*) agitator

incêndio /i'sêdʒiu/ *m* fire

incenso /ĩ'sẽsu/ *m* incense

incenti|var /ĩsẽtʃi'var/ *vt* encourage; ~**vo** *m* incentive

incer|teza /ĩser'teza/ *f* uncertainty; ~**to** /ɛ/ *a* uncertain

inces|to /ĩ'sɛstu/ *m* incest; ~**tuoso** /o/ *a* incestuous

in|chação /ĩʃa'sãw/ *f* swelling; ~**char** *vt/i* swell

inci|dência /ĩsi'dẽsia/ *f* incidence; ~**dente** *m* incident; ~**dir** *vi* ~**dir em** <*luz*> shine on; <*imposto*> be payable on

incinerar /ĩsine'rar/ *vt* incinerate

inci|são /ĩsi'zãw/ *f* incision; ~**sivo** *a* incisive

incitar /ĩsi'tar/ *vt* incite

incli|nação /ĩklina'sãw/ *f* (*do chão*) incline; (*da cabeça*) nod; (*propensão*) inclination; ~**nado** *a* <*chão*> sloping; <*edifício*> leaning; (*propenso*) inclined (**a** to); ~**nar** *vt* tilt; nod <*cabeça*> □ *vi* <*chão*> slope; <*edifício*> lean; (*tender*) incline (**para** towards); ~**nar-se** *vpr* lean

inclu|ir /ĩklu'ir/ *vt* include; ~**são** *f* inclusion; ~**sive** *prep* including □ *adv* inclusive; (*até*) even; ~**so** *a* included

incoe|rência /ĩkoe'rẽsia/ *f* (*falta de nexo*) incoherence; (*inconsequência*) inconsistency; ~**rente** *a* (*sem nexo*) incoherent; (*inconsequente*) inconsistent

incógni|ta /ĩ'kɔgnita/ *f* unknown; ~**to** *adv* incognito

incolor /ĩko'lor/ *a* colourless

incólume /ĩ'kɔlumi/ *a* unscathed

incomodar /ĩkomo'dar/ *vt* bother □ *vi* be a nuisance; ~**se** *vpr* (*dar-se ao trabalho*) bother (**em** to); ~**se** (**com**) be bothered (by), mind

incômodo /ĩ'komodu/ *a* (*desagradável*) tiresome; (*sem conforto*) uncomfortable □ *m* nuisance

incompa|rável /ĩkõpa'ravew/ *f* (*pl* ~**ráveis**) *a* incomparable;

~**tível** (*pl* ~**tíveis**) *a* incompatible

incompe|tência /ĩkõpe'tẽsia/ *f* incompetence; ~**tente** *a* incompetent

incompleto /ĩkõ'plɛtu/ *a* incomplete

incompreensí|vel /ĩkõpriẽ'sivew/ (*pl* ~**veis**) *a* incomprehensible

inconcebí|vel /ĩkõse'bivew/ (*pl* ~**veis**) *a* inconceivable

incondicio|nal /ĩkõdʒisio'naw/ (*pl* ~**nais**) *a* unconditional; <*fã, partidário*> firm

inconformado /ĩkõfor'madu/ *a* unreconciled (**com** to)

inconfundí|vel /ĩkõfũ'dʒivew/ (*pl* ~**veis**) *a* unmistakeable

inconsciente /ĩkõsi'ẽtʃi/ *a* & *m* unconscious

inconseqüente /ĩkõse'kwẽtʃi/ *a* inconsistent

incons|tância /ĩkõs'tãsia/ *f* changeability; ~**tante** *a* changeable

inconstitucio|nal /ĩkõstʃitusio'naw/ (*pl* ~**nais**) *a* unconstitutional

incontestá|vel /ĩkõtes'tavew/ (*pl* ~**veis**) *a* indisputable

inconveniente /ĩkõveni'ẽtʃi/ *a* (*difícil*) inconvenient; (*desagradável*) annoying, tiresome; (*indecente*) unseemly □ *m* drawback

incorporar /ĩkorpo'rar/ *vt* incorporate

incorrer /ĩko'xer/ *vi* ~ **em** <*multa etc*> incur

incorrigí|vel /ĩkoxi'ʒivew/ (*pl* ~**veis**) *a* incorrigible

incrédulo /ĩ'krɛdulu/ *a* incredulous

incremen|tado /ĩkremẽ'tadu/ *a* (*fam*) stylish; (*fam*) jazz up; ~**to** *m* development, growth

incriminar /ĩkrimi'nar/ *vt* incriminate

incri|vel /ĩ'krivew/ (*pl* ~**veis**) *a* incredible

incu|bação /ĩkuba'sãw/ f incubation; **~badora** f incubator; **~bar** vt/i incubate

inculto /ĩ'kuwtu/ a <pessoa> uneducated; <terreno> uncultivated

incum|bência /ĩkũ'bẽsia/ f task; **~bir** vi **~bir alg de aco/de ir** assign s.o. sth/to go □ vi **~bir a** be up to; **~bir-se de** take on

incurá|vel /ĩku'ravew/ a (pl **~veis**) a incurable

incursão /ĩkur'sãw/ f incursion

incutir /ĩku'tʃir/ vt instil (**em** in)

indagar /ĩda'gar/ vt/i inquire (into)

inde|cência /ĩde'sẽsia/ f indecency; **~cente** a indecent

indecifrá|vel /ĩdesi'fravew/ (pl **~veis**) a indecipherable

indeciso /ĩde'sizu/ a undecided

indecoroso /ĩdeko'rozu/ a indecorous

indefi|nido /ĩdefi'nidu/ a indefinite; **~nível** (pl **~níveis**) a indefinable

indelé|vel /ĩde'lɛvew/ (pl **~veis**) a indelible

indelica|deza /ĩdelika'deza/ f impoliteness; (uma) impolite thing; **~do** a impolite

indeni|zação /ĩdeniza'sãw/ f compensation; **~zar** vt compensate

indepen|dência /ĩdepẽ'dẽsia/ f independence; **~dente** a independent

indescriti|vel /ĩdʒiskri'tʃivew/ (pl **~veis**) a indescribable

indesculpá|vel /ĩdʒiskuw'pavew/ (pl **~veis**) a inexcusable

indesejá|vel /ĩdʒize'ʒavew/ (pl **~veis**) a undesirable

indestrutí|vel /ĩdʒistru'tʃivew/ (pl **~veis**) a indestructible

indeterminado /ĩdetermi'nadu/ a indeterminate

indevido /ĩde'vidu/ a undue

indexar /ĩdek'sar/ vt index; index-link <salário, preços>

Índia /'ĩdʒia/ f India

indiano /ĩdʒi'anu/ a & m Indian

indi|cação /ĩdʒika'sãw/ f indication; (do caminho) directions; (nomeação) nomination; (recomendação) recommendation; **~cador** m indicator; (dedo) index finger □ a indicative (**de** of); **~car** vt indicate; (para cargo, prêmio) nominate (**para** for); (recomendar) recommend; **~cativo** a & m indicative

índice /'ĩdʒisi/ m (taxa) rate; (em livro etc) index; **~ de audiência** ratings

indiciar /ĩdʒisi'ar/ vt charge

indício /ĩ'dʒisiu/ m sign, indication; (de crime) clue

indife|rença /ĩdʒife'rẽsa/ f indifference; **~rente** a indifferent

indígena /ĩ'dʒiʒena/ a indigenous, native □ m/f native

indiges|tão /ĩdʒiʒes'tãw/ f indigestion; **~to** a indigestible; (fig) heavy-going

indig|nação /ĩdʒigna'sãw/ f indignation; **~nado** a indignant; **~nar** vt make indignant; **~nar-se** vpr get indignant (**com** about)

indig|nidade /ĩdʒigni'dadʒi/ f indignity; **~no** a <pessoa> unworthy; <ato> despicable

índio /'ĩdʒiu/ a & m Indian

indire|ta /ĩdʒi'rɛta/ f hint; **~to** /ɛ/ a indirect

indis|creto /ĩdʒis'krɛtu/ a indiscreet; **~crição** f indiscretion

indiscriminado /ĩdʒiskrimi'nadu/ a indiscriminate

indiscutí|vel /ĩdʒisku'tʃivew/ (pl **~veis**) a unquestionable

indispensá|vel /ĩdʒispẽ'savew/ (pl **~veis**) a indispensable

indisponí|vel /ĩdʒispo'nivew/ (pl **~veis**) a unavailable

indis|por /ĩdʒis'por/ vt upset; **~por alg contra** turn s.o. against; **~por-se** vpr fall out (com with); ~**posição** f indisposition; ~**posto** a (doente) indisposed

indistinto /ĩdʒis'tʃĩtu/ a indistinct

indivídu|al /ĩdʒivídu'aw/ (pl ~ais) a individual; ~**alidade** f individuality; ~**alismo** m individualism; ~**alista** a & m/f individualist

indivíduo /ĩdʒi'viduu/ m individual

indizí|vel /ĩdʒi'zivew/ (pl ~veis) a unspeakable

índole /'ĩdoli/ f nature

indo|lência /ĩdo'lẽsia/ f indolence; ~**lente** a indolent

indolor /ĩdo'lor/ a painless

Indonésia /ĩdo'nezia/ f Indonesia

indonésio /ĩdo'neziu/ a & m Indonesian

indubitá|vel /ĩdubi'tavew/ (pl ~veis) a undoubted

indul|gência /ĩduw'ʒẽsia/ f indulgence; ~**gente** a indulgent

indulto /ĩ'duwtu/ m pardon

indumentária /ĩdumẽ'taria/ f outfit

indústria /ĩ'dustria/ f industry

industri|al /ĩdustri'aw/ (pl ~ais) a industrial □ m/f industrialist; ~**alizado** a <país> industrialized; <mercadoria> manufactured; <comida> processed; ~**alizar** vt industrialize <país, agricultura etc>; process <comida, lixo etc>; ~**oso** /o/ a industrious

induzir /ĩdu'zir/ vt (persuadir) induce; (inferir) infer (**de** from); ~ **em erro** lead astray, mislead s.o.

inebriante /inebri'ãtʃi/ a intoxicating

inédito /i'nedʒitu/ a unheard-of, unprecedented; (não publicado) unpublished

ineficaz /inefi'kas/ a ineffective

inefici|ência /inefisi'ẽsia/ f inefficiency; ~**ente** a inefficient

inegá|vel /ine'gavew/ (pl ~veis) a undeniable

inépcia /i'nepsia/ f ineptitude

inepto /i'neptu/ a inept

inequívoco /ine'kivoku/ a unmistakeable

inércia /i'nersia/ f inertia

inerente /ine'rẽtʃi/ a inherent (**a** in)

inerte /i'nertʃi/ a inert

inesgotá|vel /inezgo'tavew/ (pl ~veis) a inexhaustible

inesperado /inespe'radu/ a unexpected

inesquecí|vel /ineske'sivew/ (pl ~veis) a unforgettable

inevitá|vel /inevi'tavew/ (pl ~veis) a inevitable

inexato /ine'zatu/ a inaccurate

inexis|tência /inezis'tẽsia/ f lack; ~**tente** a non-existent

inexperi|ência /insperi'ẽsia/ f inexperience; ~**ente** a inexperienced

inexpressivo /inespre'sivu/ a expressionless

infalí|vel /ifa'livew/ (pl ~veis) a infallible

infame /ĩ'fami/ a despicable; (péssimo) dreadful

infâmia /ĩ'famia/ f disgrace

infância /ĩ'fãsia/ f childhood

infantaria /ĩfãta'ria/ f infantry

infan|til /ĩfã'tʃiw/ a <roupa, livro> children's; (bobo) childish; ~**tilidade** f childishness; (uma) childish thing

infarto /ĩ'fartu/ m heart attack

infec|ção /ĩfek'sãw/ f infection; ~**cionar** vt infect; ~**cioso** a infectious

infeliz /ife'lis/ a (não contente) unhappy; (inconveniente) unfortunate; (desgraçado) wretched □ m (desgraçado) wretch; ~**mente** adv unfortunately

inferi|or /iferi'or/ a <number> lower; (em qualidade) inferior (**a** to); ~**oridade** f inferiority

inferir /ĩfe'rir/ *vt* infer

infer|nal /ĩfer'naw/ (*pl* ~**nais**) *a* infernal; ~**nizar** *vt* ~**nizar a vida dele** make his life hell; ~**no** /ɛ/ *m* hell

infér|til /ĩ'fertʃiw/ (*pl* ~**teis**) *a* infertile

infertilidade /ĩfertʃili'dadʒi/ *f* infertility

infestar /ĩfes'tar/ *vt* infest

infetar /ĩfe'tar/ *vt* infect

infidelidade /ĩfideli'dadʒi/ *f* infidelity

infi|el /ĩfi'ɛw/ (*pl* ~**éis**) *a* unfaithful

infiltrar /ĩfiw'trar/ *vt* infiltrate; ~**-se em** infiltrate

ínfimo /'ĩfimu/ *a* lowest; (*muito pequeno*) tiny

infindá|vel /ĩfĩ'davew/ (*pl* ~**veis**) *a* unending

infinidade /ĩfini'dadʒi/ *f* infinity; **uma ~ de** an infinite number of

infini|tesimal /ĩfinitezi'maw/ (*pl* ~**tesimais**) *a* infinitesimal; ~**tivo** *a* & *m* infinitive; ~**to a** infinite □ *m* infinity

infla|ção /ĩfla'sãw/ *f* inflation; ~**cionar** *vt* inflate; ~**cionário** *a* inflationary; ~**cionista** *a* & *m/f* inflationist

infla|mação /ĩflama'sãw/ *f* inflammation; ~**mar** *vt* inflame; ~**mar-se** *vpr* become inflamed; ~**matório** *a* inflammatory; ~**mável** (*pl* ~**máveis**) *a* inflammable

in|flar *vt* inflate; ~**flar-se** *vpr* inflate; ~**flável** (*pl* ~**fláveis**) *a* inflatable

infle|xibilidade /ĩfleksibili'dadʒi/ *f* inflexibility; ~**xível** (*pl* ~**xíveis**) *a* inflexible

infligir /ĩfli'ʒir/ *vt* inflict (**a** on)

influência /ĩflu'êsia/ *f* influence

influen|ciar /ĩfluêsi'ar/ *vt* ~**ciar (em)** influence; ~**ciar-se** *vpr* be influenced; ~**ciável** (*pl* ~**ciá-**

veis) *a* open to influence; ~**te** *a* influential

influir /ĩflu'ir/ *vi* ~ **em** *ou* **sobre** influence

informação /ĩforma'sãw/ *f* information; (*uma*) a piece of information; (*mil*) intelligence; *pl* information

infor|mal /ĩfor'maw/ (*pl* ~**mais**) *a* informal; ~**malidade** *f* informality

infor|mar /ĩfor'mar/ *vt* inform; ~**mar-se** *vpr* find out (**de** about); ~**mática** *f* information technology; ~**mativo** *a* informative; ~**matizar** *vt* computerize; ~**me** *m* (*mil*) piece of intelligence

infortúnio /ĩfor'tuniu/ *m* misfortune

infração /ĩfra'sãw/ *f* infringement

infra-estrutura /ĩfraistru'tura/ *f* infrastructure

infrator /ĩfra'tor/ *m* offender

infravermelho /ĩfraver'meʎu/ *a* infrared

infringir /ĩfrĩ'ʒir/ *vt* infringe

infrutífero /ĩfru'tʃiferu/ *a* fruitless

infundado /ĩfũ'dadu/ *a* unfounded

infundir /ĩfũ'dʒir/ *vt* (*insuflar*) infuse; (*incutir*) instil

infusão /ĩfu'zãw/ *f* infusion

ingenuidade /ĩʒenui'dadʒi/ *f* naivety

ingênuo /ĩ'ʒenuu/ *a* naive

Inglaterra /ĩgla'tɛxa/ *f* England

ingerir /ĩʒe'rir/ *vt* ingest; (*engolir*) swallow

in|glês /ĩ'gles/ *a* (*f* ~**glesa**) English □ *m* (*f* ~**glesa**) Englishman (*f* -woman); (*língua*) English; **os** ~**gleses** the English

ingra|tidão /ĩgratʃi'dãw/ *f* ingratitude; ~**to a** ungrateful

ingrediente /ĩgredʒi'etʃi/ *m* ingredient

íngreme /'ĩgrimi/ *a* steep

ingres|sar /ĩgre'sar/ *vi* ~**sar em** join; ~**so** *m* entry; (*bilhete*) ticket

inhame /i'ɲami/ *m* yam

ini|bição /inibi'sãw/ *f* inhibition; ~**bir** *vt* inhibit

inici|ado /inisi'adu/ *m* initiate; ~**al** (*pl* ~**ais**) *a* & *f* initial; ~**ar** *vt* (*começar*) begin; (*em ciência, seita etc*) initiate (**em** into) □ *vi* begin; ~**ativa** *f* initiative

início /i'nisiu/ *m* beginning

igualá|vel /inigwa'lavew/ (*pl* ~**veis**) *a* unparalleled

inimaginá|vel /inimaʒi'navew/ (*pl* ~**veis**) *a* unimaginable

inimi|go /ini'migu/ *a* & *m* enemy; ~**zade** *f* enmity

ininterrupto /inĩte'xuptu/ *a* continuous

inje|ção /ĩʒe'sãw/ *f* injection; ~**tado** *a* <*olhos*> bloodshot; ~**tar** *vt* inject; ~**tável** (*pl* ~**táveis**) *a* <*droga*> intravenous

injúria /ĩ'ʒuria/ *f* insult

injuriar /ĩʒuri'ar/ *vt* insult

injus|tiça /ĩʒus'tʃisa/ *f* injustice; ~**tiçado** *a* wronged; ~**to** *a* unfair, unjust

ino|cência /ino'sẽsia/ *f* innocence; ~**centar** *vt* clear (**de** of); ~**cente** *a* innocent

inocular /inoku'lar/ *vt* inoculate

inócuo /i'nɔkuu/ *a* harmless

inodoro /ino'dɔru/ *a* odourless

inofensivo /inofẽ'sivu/ *a* harmless

inoportuno /inopor'tunu/ *a* inopportune

inorgânico /inor'ganiku/ *a* inorganic

inóspito /i'nɔspitu/ *a* inhospitable

ino|vação /inova'sãw/ *f* innovation; ~**var** *vt/i* innovate

inoxidá|vel /inoksi'davew/ (*pl* ~**veis**) *a* <*aço*> stainless

inquérito /ĩ'kɛritu/ *m* inquiry

inquie|tação /ĩkieta'sãw/ *f* concern; ~**tador,** ~**tante** *a* worry-

ing; ~**tar** *vt* worry; ~**tar-se** *vpr* worry; ~**to** /ɛ/ *a* uneasy

inquili|nato /ĩkili'natu/ *m* tenancy; ~**no** *m* tenant

inquirir /ĩki'rir/ *vt* cross-examine < *testemunha*>

Inquisição /ĩkizi'sãw/ *f a* ~ the Inquisition

insaciá|vel /ĩsasi'avew/ (*pl* ~**veis**) *a* insatiable

insalubre /ĩsa'lubri/ *a* unhealthy

insatis|fação /ĩsatʃisfa'sãw/ *f* dissatisfaction; ~**fatório** *a* unsatisfactory; ~**feito** *a* dissatisfied

ins|crever /ĩskre'ver/ *vt* (*registrar*) register; (*gravar*) inscribe; ~**crever-se** *vpr* register; (*em escola etc*) enrol; ~**crição** *f* (*registro*) registration; (*em clube, escola*) enrolment; (*em monumento etc*) inscription

insegu|rança /ĩsegu'rãsa/ *f* insecurity; ~**ro** *a* insecure

insemi|nação /ĩsemina'sãw/ *f* insemination; ~**nar** *vt* inseminate

insen|satez /ĩsẽsa'tes/ *f* folly; ~**sato** *a* foolish; ~**sibilidade** *f* insensitivity; ~**sível** (*pl* ~**síveis**) *a* insensitive

insepará|vel /ĩsepa'ravew/ (*pl* ~**veis**) *a* inseparable

inserção /ĩser'sãw/ *f* insertion

inserir /ĩse'rir/ *vt* insert; enter < *dados*>

inse|ticida /ĩsetʃi'sida/ *m* insecticide; ~**to** /ɛ/ *m* insect

insígnia /ĩ'signia/ *f* insignia

insignifi|cância /ĩsiɡnifi'kãsia/ *f* insignificance; ~**cante** *a* insignificant

insincero /ĩsĩ'sɛru/ *a* insincere

insinu|ante /ĩsinu'ãtʃi/ *a* suggestive; ~**ar** *vt/i* insinuate

insípido /ĩ'sipidu/ *a* insipid

insis|tência /ĩsis'tẽsia/ *f* insistence; ~**tente** *a* insistent; ~**tir** *vt/i* insist (**em** on)

insolação /ĩsola'sãw/ *f* sunstroke

inso|lência /iso'lẽsia/ f insolence; **~lente** a insolent

insólito /i'sɔlitu/ a unusual

insolú|vel /iso'luvew/ (pl **~veis**) a insoluble

insone /i'sɔni/ a <noite> sleepless; <pessoa> insomniac ▫ m/f insomniac

insônia /i'sonia/ f insomnia

insosso /i'sosu/ a bland; (sem sabor) tasteless; (sem sal) unsalted

inspe|ção /ĩspe'sãw/ f inspection; **~cionar** vt inspect; **~tor** m inspector

inspi|ração /ĩspira'sãw/ f inspiration; **~rar** vt inspire; **~rar-se** vpr take inspiration (em from)

instabilidade /ĩstabili'dadʒi/ f instability

insta|lação /ĩstala'sãw/ f installation; **~lar** vt install; **~lar-se** vpr install o.s.

instan|tâneo /ĩstã'taniu/ a instant; **~te** m instant

instaurar /ĩstaw'rar/ vt set up

instá|vel /i'stavew/ (pl **~veis**) a unstable; <tempo> unsettled

insti|gação /ĩstʃiga'sãw/ f instigation; **~gante** a stimulating; **~gar** vt incite

instin|tivo /ĩstʃĩ'tʃivu/ a instinctive; **~to** m instinct

institu|cional /ĩstʃitusio'naw/ (pl **~cionais**) a institutional; **~ição** f institution; **~ir** vt set up; set <prazo>; **~to** m institute

instru|ção /ĩstru'sãw/ f instruction; **~ir** vt instruct; train <recrutas>; (informar) advise (sobre of)

instrumen|tal /ĩstrumẽ'taw/ (pl **~tais**) a instrumental; **~tista** m/f instrumentalist; **~to** m instrument

instru|tivo /ĩstru'tʃivu/ a instructive; **~tor** m instructor

insubstituí|vel /ĩsubistʃitu'ivew/ (pl **~veis**) a irreplaceable

insucesso /ĩsu'sesu/ m failure

insufici|ência /ĩsufisi'ẽsia/ f insufficiency; (dos órgãos) failure; **~ente** a insufficient

insulina /ĩsu'lina/ f insulin

insul|tar /ĩsuw'tar/ vt insult; **~to** m insult

insuperá|vel /ĩsupe'ravew/ (pl **~veis**) a <problema> insurmountable; <qualidade> unsurpassed

insuportá|vel /ĩsupor'tavew/ (pl **~veis**) a unbearable

insur|gente /ĩsur'ʒẽtʃi/ a & m/f insurgent; **~gir-se** vpr rise up, revolt; **~reição** f insurrection

intato /ĩ'tatu/ a intact

íntegra /'ĩtegra/ f full text; **na ~** in full

inte|gração /ĩtegra'sãw/ f integration; **~gral** (pl **~grais**) a whole; **arroz/pão ~gral** brown rice/bread; **~grante** a integral ▫ m/f member; **~grar** vt make up, form; **~grar-se em** become a part of; **~gridade** f integrity

íntegro /'ĩtegru/ a honest

intei|ramente /ĩtera'mẽtʃi/ adv completely; **~rar** vt (informar) fill in, inform (de about); **~rar-se** vpr find out (de about); **~riço** a in one piece; **~ro** a whole

intelec|to /ĩte'lɛktu/ m intellect; **~tual** (pl **~tuais**) a & m/f intellectual

inteli|gência /ĩteli'ʒẽsia/ f intelligence; **~gente** a clever, intelligent; **~gível** (pl **~gíveis**) a intelligible

intem|périe /ĩte'pɛri/ f bad weather; **~pestivo** a ill-timed

inten|ção /ĩtẽ'sãw/ f intention; **segundas ~ções** ulterior motives

intencio|nado /ĩtẽsio'nadu/ a; **bem ~nado** well-meaning; **~nal** (pl **~nais**) a intentional; **~nar** vt intend

inten|sidade /ĩtẽsi'dadʒi/ f intensity; **~sificar** vt intensify; **~sificar-se** vpr intensify;

~**sivo** a intensive; ~**so** a intense

intento /ĩ'tẽtu/ m intention

intera|ção /ĩtera'sãw/ f interaction; ~**gir** vi interact; ~**tivo** a interactive

inter|calar /ĩterka'lar/ vt insert; ~**câmbio** m exchange; ~**ceptar** vt intercept

intercontinen|tal /ĩterkõtʃinẽ'taw/ (pl ~**tais**) a intercontinental

interdepen|dência /ĩterdepẽ'dẽsia/ f interdependence; ~**dente** a interdependent

interdi|ção /ĩterdʒi'sãw/ f closure; (jurid) injunction; ~**tar** vt close <rua etc>; (proibir) ban

interes|sante /ĩtere'sãtʃi/ a interesting; ~**sar** vt interest □ vi be relevant; ~**sar-se** vpr be interested (**em** ou **por** in); ~**se** /e/ m interest; (próprio) self-interest; ~**seiro** a self-seeking

interestadu|al /ĩteristadu'aw/ (pl ~**ais**) a interstate

interface /ĩter'fasi/ f interface

interfe|rência /ĩterfe'rẽsia/ f interference; ~**rir** vi interfere

interfone /ĩter'foni/ m intercom

ínterim /'ĩteri/ m interim; **nesse ~** in the interim

interino /ĩte'rinu/ a temporary

interior /ĩteri'or/ a inner; (dentro do país) internal, domestic □ m inside; (do país) country, interior

inter|jeição /ĩterʒei'sãw/ f interjection; ~**ligar** vt interconnect; ~**locutor** m interlocutor; ~**mediário** a & m intermediary

intermédio /ĩter'mɛdʒiu/ m **por ~ de** through

intermi|nável /ĩtermi'navew/ (pl ~**veis**) a interminable

internacio|nal /ĩternasio'naw/ (pl ~**nais**) a international

inter|nar /ĩter'nar/ vt intern <preso>; admit to hospital <doente>; ~**-nato** m boarding school

internauta /ĩter'nawta/ m/f

(comput) netsurfer

Internet /ĩter'nɛt/ f Internet

interno /ĩ'tɛrnu/ a internal

interpelar /ĩterpe'lar/ vt question

interpor /ĩter'por/ vt interpose; ~**-se** vpr intervene

interpre|tação /ĩterpreta'sãw/ f interpretation; ~**tar** vt interpret; perform <papel, música>; **intérprete** m/f (de línguas) interpreter; (de teatro etc) performer

interro|gação /ĩtexoga'sãw/ f interrogation; ~**gar** vt interrogate, question; ~**gativo** a interrogative; ~**gatório** m interrogation

inter|romper /ĩtexõ'per/ vt interrupt; ~**rupção** f interruption; ~**ruptor** m switch

interurbano /ĩterur'banu/ a long-distance □ m trunk call

intervalo /ĩter'valu/ m interval

inter|venção /ĩtervẽ'sãw/ f intervention; ~**vir** vi intervene

intesti|nal /ĩtestʃi'naw/ (pl ~**nais**) a intestinal; ~**no** m intestine

inti|mação /ĩtʃima'sãw/ f (da justiça) summons; ~**mar** vt order; (à justiça) summon

intimidade /ĩtʃimi'dadʒi/ f intimacy; (entre amigos) closeness; (vida íntima) private life; **ter ~ com** be close to

intimidar /ĩtʃimi'dar/ vt intimidate; ~**-se** vpr be intimidated

íntimo /'ĩtʃimu/ a intimate; <amigo> close; <vida> private □ m close friend

intitular /ĩtʃitu'lar/ vt entitle

intocável /ĩto'kavew/ (pl ~**veis**) a untouchable

intole|rância /ĩtole'rãsia/ f intolerance; ~**rável** (pl ~**ráveis**) a intolerable

intoxi|cação /ĩtoksika'sãw/ f poisoning; ~**cação alimentar** food poisoning; ~**car** vt poison

intragá|vel /ĩtraˈɡavew/ (*pl* ~**veis**) *a* <*comida*> inedible; <*pessoa*> unbearable

intransigente /ĩtrãziˈʒẽtʃi/ *a* uncompromising

intransi|tável /ĩtrãziˈtavew/ (*pl* ~**táveis**) *a* impassable; ~**tivo** *a* intransitive

intratá|vel /ĩtraˈtavew/ (*pl* ~**veis**) *a* <*pessoa*> difficult

intra-uterino /ĩtrauteˈrinu/ *a* **dispositivo** ~ intra-uterine device, IUD

intrépido /ĩˈtrepidu/ *a* intrepid

intri|ga /ĩˈtriga/ *f* intrigue; (*enredo*) plot; ~**gante** *a* intriguing; ~**gar** *vt* intrigue

intrincado /ĩtrĩˈkadu/ *a* intricate

intrínseco /ĩˈtrĩsiku/ *a* intrinsic

introdu|ção /ĩtroduˈsãw/ *f* introduction; ~**tório** *a* introductory; ~**zir** *vt* introduce

intrometer-se /ĩtromeˈtersi/ *vpr* interfere; ~**tido** *a* interfering □ *m* busybody

introspec|ção /ĩtrospekˈsãw/ *f* introspection; ~**tivo** *a* introspective

introvertido /ĩtroverˈtʃidu/ *a* introverted □ *m* introvert

intruso /ĩˈtruzu/ *a* intrusive □ *m* intruder

intu|ição /ĩtuiˈsãw/ *f* intuition; ~**ir** *vt* intuit; ~**itivo** *a* intuitive; ~**to** *m* purpose

inumano /inuˈmanu/ *a* inhuman

inumerá|vel /inumeˈravew/ (*pl* ~**veis**) *a* innumerable

inúmero /iˈnumeru/ *a* countless

inun|dação /inũdaˈsãw/ *f* flood; ~**dar** *vt/i* flood

inusitado /inuziˈtadu/ *a* unusual

inútil /iˈnutʃiw/ (*pl* ~**teis**) *a* useless

inutilmente /inutʃiwˈmẽtʃi/ *adv* in vain

inutilizar /inutʃiliˈzar/ *vt* render useless; damage <*aparelho*>; thwart <*esforços*>

invadir /ĩvaˈdʒir/ *vt* invade

invali|dar /ĩvaliˈdar/ *vt* invalidate; disable <*pessoa*>; ~**dez** /e/ *f* disability

inválido /ĩˈvalidu/ *a* & *m* invalid

invariá|vel /ĩvariˈavew/ (*pl* ~**veis**) *a* invariable

inva|são /ĩvaˈzãw/ *f* invasion; ~**sor** *m* invader □ *a* invading

inve|ja /ĩˈvɛʒa/ *f* envy; ~**jar** *vt* envy; ~**jável** /a/ (*pl* ~**jáveis**) *a* enviable; ~**joso** /o/ *a* envious

inven|ção /ĩvẽˈsãw/ *f* invention; ~**tar** *vt* invent; ~**tário** *m* inventory; ~**tivo** *a* inventive; ~**tor** *m* inventor

inver|nar /ĩverˈnar/ *vi* winter, spend the winter; ~**no** /ɛ/ *m* winter

inverossímil /ĩveroˈsimiw/ (*pl* ~**meis**) *a* improbable

inver|são /ĩverˈsãw/ *f* inversion; ~**so** *a* inverse; <*ordem*> reverse □ *m* reverse; ~**ter** *vt* reverse; (*colocar de cabeça para baixo*) invert

invertebrado /ĩverteˈbradu/ *a* & *m* invertebrate

invés /ĩˈvɛs/ *m* **ao** ~ **de** instead of

investida /ĩvesˈtʃida/ *f* attack

investidura /ĩvestʃiˈdura/ *f* investiture

investi|gação /ĩvestʃigaˈsãw/ *f* investigation; ~**gar** *vt* investigate

inves|timento /ĩvestʃiˈmẽtu/ *m* investment; ~**tir** *vt/i* invest; ~**tir contra** attack

inveterado /ĩveteˈradu/ *a* inveterate

inviá|vel /ĩviˈavew/ (*pl* ~**veis**) *a* impracticable

invicto /ĩˈviktu/ *a* unbeaten

invisí|vel /ĩviˈzivew/ (*pl* ~**veis**) *a* invisible

invocar /ĩvoˈkar/ *vt* invoke; (*fam*) pester

invólucro /ĩˈvɔlukru/ *m* covering

involuntário /ĩvolũˈtariu/ *a* involuntary

invulnerá|**vel** /ĩvuwne'ravew/ (*pl* ~**veis**) *a* invulnerable

iodo /i'odu/ *m* iodine

ioga /i'ɔga/ *f* yoga

iogurte /io'gurtʃi/ *m* yoghurt

ir /ir/ *vi* go; ~**-se** *vpr* go away; **vou voltar** I will come back; **vou melhorando** I am (gradually) getting better

ira /'ira/ *f* wrath

Irã /i'rã/ *m* Iran

iraniano /irani'anu/ *a* & *m* Iranian

Irão /i'rãw/ *m* (*Port*) Iran

Iraque /i'raki/ *m* Iraq

iraquiano /iraki'anu/ *a* & *m* Iraqui

Irlanda /ir'lãda/ *f* Ireland

irlan|**dês** /irlã'des/ *a* (*f* ~**desa**) Irish □ *m* (*f* ~**desa**) Irishman (*f* -woman); (*língua*) Irish; **os** ~**deses** the Irish

irmã /ir'mã/ *f* sister

irmandade /irmã'dadʒi/ *f* (*associação*) brotherhood

irmão /ir'mãw/ (*pl* ~**s**) *m* brother

ironia /iro'nia/ *f* irony

irônico /i'roniku/ *a* ironic

irracio|**nal** /ixasio'naw/ (*pl* ~**nais**) *a* irrational

irradiar /ixadʒi'ar/ *vt* radiate; (*pelo rádio*) broadcast □ *vi* shine; ~**-se** *vpr* spread, radiate

irre|**al** /ixe'aw/ (*pl* ~**ais**) *a* unreal

irreconheci|**vel** /ixekoɲe'sivew/ (*pl* ~**veis**) *a* unrecognizable

irrecuperá|**vel** /ixekupe'ravew/ (*pl* ~**veis**) *a* irretrievable

irrefletido /ixefle'tʃidu/ *a* rash

irregu|**lar** /ixegu'lar/ *a* irregular; (*inconstante*) erratic; ~**laridade** *f* irregularity

irrelevante /ixele'vãtʃi/ *a* irrelevant

irreparável /ixepa'ravew/ (*pl* ~**veis**) *a* irreparable

irrepreensível /ixeprĩĕ'sivew/ (*pl* ~**veis**) *a* irreproachable

irrequieto /ixeki'ɛtu/ *a* restless

irresistí|**vel** /ixezis'tʃivew/ (*pl* ~**veis**) *a* irresistible

irresoluto /ixezo'lutu/ *a* <*questão*> unresolved; <*pessoa*> indecisive

irresponsá|**vel** /ixespõ'savew/ (*pl* ~**veis**) *a* irresponsible

irreverente /ixeve'rẽtʃi/ *a* irreverent

irri|**gação** /ixiga'sãw/ *f* irrigation; ~**gar** *vt* irrigate

irrisório /ixi'zoriu/ *a* derisory

irri|**tação** /ixita'sãw/ *f* irritation; ~**tadiço** *a* irritable; ~**tante** *a* irritating; ~**tar** *vt* irritate; ~**tar-se** *vpr* get irritated

irromper /ixõ'per/ *vi* ~ **em** burst into

isca /'iska/ *f* bait

isen|**ção** /izẽ'sãw/ *f* exemption; ~**tar** *vt* exempt; ~**to** *a* exempt

Islã /iz'lã/ *m* Islam

islâmico /iz'lamiku/ *a* Islamic

isla|**mismo** /izla'mizmu/ *m* Islam; ~**mita** *a* & *m/f* Muslim

islan|**dês** /izlã'des/ *a* (*f* ~**desa**) Icelandic □ *m* (*f* ~**desa**) Icelander; (*língua*) Icelandic

Islândia /iz'lãdʒia/ *f* Iceland

iso|**lamento** /izola'mẽtu/ *m* isolation; (*eletr*) insulation; ~**lante** *a* insulating; ~**lar** *vt* isolate; (*eletr*) insulate □ *vi* (*contra azar*) touch wood, (*Amer*) knock on wood

isopor /izo'por/ *m* polystyrene

isqueiro /is'keru/ *m* lighter

Israel /izxa'ew/ *m* Israel

israe|**lense** /izraj'lẽsi/ *a* & *m/f* Israeli; ~**lita** *a* & *m/f* Israelite

isso /'isu/ *pron* that; **por** ~ therefore

isto /'istu/ *pron* this; ~ **é** that is

Itália /i'talia/ *f* Italy

italiano /itali'anu/ *a* & *m* Italian

itálico /i'taliku/ *a* & *m* italic

item /'itẽ/ *m* item

itine|**rante** /itʃine'rãtʃi/ *a* itinerant; ~**rário** *m* itinerary

Iugoslávia /iugoz'lavia/ f Yugoslavia

iugoslavo /iugoz'lavu/ a & m Yugoslavian

J

já /ʒa/ adv already; (agora) right away □ conj on the other hand; **desde** ~ from now on; ~ **não** no longer; ~ **que** since; ~, ~ in no time

jabuticaba /ʒabutʃi'kaba/ f jaboticaba

jaca /'ʒaka/ f jack fruit

jacaré /ʒaka'rɛ/ m alligator

jacinto /ʒa'sĩtu/ m hyacinth

jactância /ʒak'tãsia/ f boasting

jade /'ʒadʒi/ m jade

jaguar /ʒagu'ar/ m jaguar

jagunço /ʒa'gũsu/ m hired gunman

jamais /ʒa'majs/ adv never

Jamaica /ʒa'majka/ f Jamaica

jamaicano /ʒamaj'kanu/ a & m Jamaican

jamanta /ʒa'mãta/ f juggernaut

janeiro /ʒa'neru/ m January

janela /ʒa'nɛla/ f window

jangada /ʒã'gada/ f (fishing) raft

janta /'ʒãta/ f (fam) dinner

jantar /ʒã'tar/ m dinner □ vi have dinner □ vt have for dinner

Japão /ʒa'pãw/ m Japan

japo|na /ʒa'pona/ f pea jacket □ m/f (fam) Japanese; ~**nês** a & m (f ~**nesa**) Japanese

jaqueira /ʒa'kera/ f jack-fruit tree

jaqueta /ʒa'keta/ f jacket

jarda /'ʒarda/ f yard

jar|dim /ʒar'dʒĩ/ m garden; ~**dim-de-infância** (pl ~**dins-de-infância**) f kindergarten

jardi|nagem /ʒardʒi'naʒẽ/ f gardening; ~**nar** vi garden; ~**neira** f (calça) dungarees; (vestido) pinafore dress, (Amer)

jumper; (ônibus) open-sided bus; (para flores) flower stand; ~**neiro** m gardener

jargão /ʒar'gãw/ m jargon

jar|ra /'ʒaxa/ f pot; ~**ro** m jug

jasmim /ʒaz'mĩ/ m jasmine

jato /'ʒatu/ m jet

jaula /'ʒawla/ f cage

ja|zer /ʒa'zer/ vi lie; ~**zida** f deposit; ~**zigo** m grave

jazz /dʒaz/ m jazz; ~**ista** m/f jazz artist; ~**ístico** a jazzy

jeca /'ʒɛka/ m/f country bumpkin □ a countrified; (cafona) tacky; ~**-tatu** m/f country bumpkin

jei|tão /ʒej'tãw/ m (fam) individual style; ~**tinho** m knack; ~**to** m way; (de pessoa) manner; (habilidade) skill; de qualquer ~**to** anyway; de ~**to** nenhum no way; pelo ~**to** by the looks of things; sem ~**to** awkward; dar um ~**to** find a way; dar um ~**to em** (arrumar) tidy up; (consertar) fix; (torcer) twist < pé etc>; ter ~**to** de look like; ter ou levar ~**to para** be good at; tomar ~**to** pull one's socks up; ~**toso** /o/ a skilful; (de aparência) elegant

jejuar /ʒeʒu'ar/ vi fast; ~**jum** m fast

Jeová /ʒio'va/ m testemunha de ~ Jehovah's witness

jérsei /'ʒersej/ m jersey

jesuíta /ʒezu'ita/ a & m/f Jesuit

Jesus /ʒe'zus/ m Jesus

jibóia /ʒi'bɔja/ f boa constrictor

jiboiar /ʒiboj'ar/ vi have a rest to let one's dinner go down

jiló /ʒi'lɔ/ m okra

jipe /'ʒipi/ m jeep

jiu-jitsu /ʒiu'ʒitsu/ m jiu-jitsu

joa|lheiro /ʒoa'ʎeru/ m jeweller; ~**lheria** f jeweller's (shop)

joaninha /ʒoa'niɲa/ f ladybird, (Amer) ladybug; (alfinete) safety pin

joão-ninguém /ʒoãwnīˈgẽj/ (*pl* **joões-ninguém**) *m* nobody

jocoso /ʒoˈkozu/ *a* jocular

joe|lhada /ʒoeˈʎada/ *f* blow with the knee; **~lheira** *f* kneepad; **~lho** /e/ *m* knee; **de ~lhos** kneeling

jo|gada /ʒoˈgada/ *f* move; **~gado** *a* <*pessoa*> flat out; <*papéis, roupa etc*> lying around; **~gador** *m* player; (*no cassino etc*) gambler; **~gar** *vt* play; (*atirar*) throw; (*arriscar no jogo*) gamble □ *vi* play; (*no cassino etc*) gamble; (*balançar*) toss; **~gar fora** throw away; **~gatina** *f* gambling

jogging /ˈʒɔgĩ/ *m* (*cooper*) jogging; (*roupa*) track suit

jogo /ˈʒogu/ *m* (*partida*) game; (*ação de jogar*) play; (*jogatina*) gambling; (*conjunto*) set; **em ~** at stake; **~ de cintura** (*fig*) flexibility, room to manoeuvre; **~ de luz** lighting effects; **~ do bicho** illegal numbers game; **Jogos Olímpicos** Olympic Games; **~da-velha** *m* noughts and crosses

joguete /ʒoˈgetʃi/ *m* plaything

jóia /ˈʒɔja/ *f* jewel; (*propina*) entry fee □ *a* (*fam*) great

joio /ˈʒoju/ *m* chaff; **separar o ~ do trigo** separate the wheat from the chaff

jóquei /ˈʒɔkej/ *m* (*pessoa*) jockey; (*lugar*) race course

Jordânia /ʒorˈdania/ *f* Jordan

jordaniano /ʒordaniˈanu/ *a* & *m* Jordanian

jor|nada /ʒorˈnada/ *f* (*viagem*) journey; **~nada de trabalho** working day; **~nal** (*pl* **~nais**) *m* newspaper; (*na TV*) news

jorna|leco /ʒornaˈleku/ *m* rag, scandal sheet; **~leiro** *m* (*vendedor*) newsagent, (*Amer*) newsdealer; (*entregador*) paperboy; **~lismo** *m* journalism; **~lista** *m/f* journalist; **~lístico** *a* journalistic

jor|rar /ʒoˈxar/ *vi* gush, spurt; **~ro** /ˈʒoxu/ *m* spurt

jota /ˈʒɔta/ *m* letter J

jovem /ˈʒɔvẽ/ *a* young; (*criado por jovens*) youth □ *m/f* young man (*f* -woman); *pl* young people

jovi|al /ʒoviˈaw/ (*pl* **~ais**) *a* jovial

juba /ˈʒuba/ *f* mane

jubileu /ʒubiˈlew/ *m* jubilee

júbilo /ˈʒubilu/ *m* joy

ju|daico /ʒuˈdajku/ *a* Jewish; **~daísmo** *m* Judaism; **~deu** *a* (*f* **~dia**) Jewish □ *m* (*f* **~dia**) Jew; **~diação** *f* ill-treatment; (*uma*) terrible thing; **~diar** *vi* (*tribunal*) court; **~diar de** ill-treat

judici|al /ʒudʒisiˈaw/ (*pl* **~ais**) *a* judicial; **~ário** *a* judicial □ *m* judiciary; **~oso** /o/ *a* judicious

judô /ʒuˈdo/ *m* judo

judoca /ʒuˈdɔka/ *m/f* judo player

jugo /ˈʒugu/ *m* yoke

juiz /ʒuˈis/ *m* (*f* **juíza**) judge; (*em jogos*) referee

juizado /ʒuiˈzadu/ *m* court

juízo /ˈʒuizu/ *m* judgement; (*tino*) sense; (*tribunal*) court; **perder o ~** lose one's head; **ter ~** be sensible; **tomar** *ou* **criar ~** come to one's senses

jujuba /ʒuˈʒuba/ *f* (*bala*) fruit jelly

jul|gamento /ʒuwgaˈmẽtu/ *m* judgement; **~gar** *vt* judge; pass judgement on <*réu*>; (*imaginar*) think; **~gar-se** *vpr* consider o.s.

julho /ˈʒuʎu/ *m* July

jumento /ʒuˈmẽtu/ *m* donkey

junção /ʒũˈsãw/ *f* join; (*ação*) joining

junco /ˈʒũku/ *m* reed

junho /ˈʒuɲu/ *m* June

juni|no /ʒuˈninu/ *a* **festa ~na** St John's Day festival

júnior /ˈʒunior/ *a* & *m* junior

jun|ta /ˈʒũta/ *f* board; (*pol*) junta; **~tar** *vt* (*acrescentar*) add; (*uma coisa a outra*) join; (*uma coisa com outra*) combine; save up

<dinheiro>; gather up *<papéis, lixo etc>* □ *vi* gather; **~tar-se** *vpr* join together; *<multidão>* gather; *<casal>* live together; **~tar-se a** join; **~to a** together □ *adv* together; **~to a** next to; **~to com** together with

ju|ra /'ʒura/ *f* vow; **~rado** *m* juror; **~ramentado** *a* accredited; **~ramento** *m* oath; **~rar** *vt/i* swear; **~ra?** (*fam*) really?

júri /'ʒuri/ *m* jury

jurídico /ʒu'ridʒiku/ *a* legal

juris|consulto /ʒuriskõ'suwtu/ *m* legal advisor; **~dição** *f* jurisdiction; **~prudência** *f* jurisprudence; **~ta** *m/f* jurist

juros /'ʒurus/ *m pl* interest

jus /ʒus/ *m* fazer **~** a live up to

jusante /ʒu'zãtʃi/ *f* a **~** downstream

justamente /ʒusta'mẽtʃi/ *adv* exactly; (*com justiça*) fairly

justapor /ʒusta'por/ *vt* juxtapose

justi|ça /ʒus'tʃisa/ *f* (*perante a lei*) justice; (*para com outros*) fairness; (*tribunal*) court; **~ceiro** *a* fair-minded □ *m* vigilante

justi|ficação /ʒustʃifika'sãw/ *f* justification; **~car** *vt* justify; **~cativa** *f* justification; **~cável** (*pl* **~cáveis**) *a* justifiable

justo /'ʒustu/ *a* fair; (*apertado*) tight □ *adv* just

juve|nil /ʒuve'niw/ (*pl* **~nis**) *a* youthful; (*para jovens*) for young people; *<time, torneio>* junior □ *m* junior championship

juventude /ʒuvẽ'tudʒi/ *f* youth

K

karaokê /karao'ke/ *m* karaoke

kart /kartʃi/ (*pl* **~s**) *m* go-kart

ketchup /ke'tʃupi/ *m* ketchup

kit /'kitʃi/ (*pl* **~s**) *m* kit

kitchenette /kitʃe'netʃi/ *f* bedsitter

Kuwait /ku'wajtʃi/ *m* Kuwait

kuwaitiano /kuwajtʃi'anu/ *a & m* Kuwaiti

L

lá /la/ *adv* there; até **~** *<ir>* there; *<esperar etc>* until then; por **~** (*naquela direção*) that way; (*naquele lugar*) around there; **~ fora** outside; sei **~** how should I know?

lã /lã/ *f* wool

labareda /laba'reda/ *f* flame

lábia /'labia/ *f* flannel; ter **~** have the gift of the gab

lábio /'labio/ *m* lip

labirinto /labi'rĩtu/ *m* labyrinth

laboratório /labora'tɔriu/ *m* laboratory

laborioso /labori'ozu/ *a* hardworking

labu|ta /la'buta/ *f* drudgery; **~tar** *vi* slog

laca /'laka/ *f* lacquer

laçada /la'sada/ *f* slipknot

lacaio /la'kaju/ *m* lackey

la|çar /la'sar/ *vt* lasso *<boi>*; **~ço** *m* bow; (*de vaqueiro*) lasso; (*vínculo*) tie

lacônico /la'koniku/ *a* laconic

lacraia /la'kraja/ *f* centipede

la|crar /la'krar/ *vt* seal; **~cre** *m* (*substância*) sealing wax; (*fechamento*) seal

lacri|mejar /lakrime'ʒar/ *vi* water; **~mogêneo** *a <gás>* tear; *<filme>* tearjerking; **~moso** /o/ *a* tearful

lácteo /'laktʃiu/ *a* milk; Via Láctea Milky Way

lacticínio /laktʃi'siniu/ *m veja* laticínio

lacuna /la'kuna/ *f* gap

ladainha /lada'iɲa/ *f* litany

la|dear /ladʒi'ar/ *vt* flank; sidestep <*dificuldade*>; ~**deira** *f* slope

lado /'ladu/ *m* side; **o** ~ **de cá/lá** this/that side; **ao** ~ **de** beside; ~ **a** ~ side by side; **para este** ~ this way; **por outro** ~ on the other hand

la|drão /la'drãw/ *m* (*f* ~**dra**) thief; (*tubo*) overflow pipe □ *a* thieving

ladrar /la'drar/ *vi* bark

ladri|lhar /ladri'ʎar/ *vt* tile; ~**lho** *m* tile

ladroagem /ladro'aʒẽ/ *f* stealing

lagar|ta /la'garta/ *f* caterpillar; (*numa roda*) caterpillar track; ~**tear** *vi* bask in the sun; ~**tixa** *f* gecko; ~**to** *m* lizard

lago /'lagu/ *m* lake

lagoa /la'goa/ *f* lagoon

lagos|ta /la'gosta/ *f* lobster; ~**tim** *m* crayfish; (*Amer*) crawfish

lágrima /'lagrima/ *f* tear

laia /'laja/ *f* kind

laico /'lajku/ *adj* <*pessoa*> lay; <*ensino*> secular

laivos /'lajvus/ *m pl* traces

laje /'laʒi/ *m* flagstone; ~**ar** *vt* pave

lajota /la'ʒɔta/ *f* small paving stone

lama /'lama/ *f* mud; ~**çal** (*pl* ~**çais**) *m* bog; ~**cento** *a* muddy

lamba|da /lã'bada/ *f* lambada; ~**teria** *f* lambada club

lam|ber /lã'ber/ *vt* lick; ~**bida** *f* lick

lambreta /lã'breta/ *f* moped

lambris /lã'bris/ *m pl* panelling

lambuzar /lãbu'zar/ *vt* smear; ~**se** *vpr* get sticky

lamen|tar /lamẽ'tar/ *vt* (*lastimar*) lament; (*sentir*) be sorry; ~**tar-se** *de* lament; ~**tável** (*pl* ~**táveis**) *a* lamentable; ~**to** *m* lament

lâmina /'lamina/ *f* blade; (*de persiana*) slat

laminar /lami'nar/ *vt* laminate

lâmpada /'lãpada/ *f* light bulb; (*abajur*) lamp

lampe|jar /lãpe'ʒar/ *vi* flash; ~**jo** /e/ *m* flash

lampião /lãpi'ãw/ *m* lantern

lamúria /la'muria/ *f* moaning

lamuriar-se /lamuri'arsi/ *vpr* moan (**de** about)

lan|ça /'lãsa/ *f* spear; ~**çamento** *m* (*de navio, foguete, produto*) launch; (*de filme, disco*) release; (*novo produto*) new line; (*novo filme, disco*) release; (*novo livro*) new title; (*em livro comercial*) entry; ~**çar** *vt* (*atirar*) throw; launch <*navio, foguete, novo produto, livro*>; release <*filme, disco*>; (*em livro comercial*) enter; (*em leilão*) bid; ~**çar mão de** make use of; ~**ce** *m* (*num filme, jogo*) bit, moment; (*episódio*) episode; (*questão*) matter; (*jogada*) move; (*em leilão*) bid; (*de escada*) flight; (*de casas*) row

lancha /'lãʃa/ *f* launch

lan|char /lã'ʃar/ *vi* have a snack □ *vt* have a snack of; ~**che** *m* snack; ~**chonete** /ɛ/ *f* snack bar

lancinante /lãsi'nãtʃi/ *a* <*dor*> shooting; <*grito*> piercing

lânguido /'lãgidu/ *a* languid

lantejoula /lãte'ʒola/ *f* sequin

lanter|na /lã'terna/ *f* lantern; (*de bolso*) torch, (*Amer*) flashlight; ~**nagem** *f* panel-beating; (*oficina*) body-shop; ~**ninha** *m/f* usher (*f* usherette)

lanugem /la'nuʒẽ/ *f* down

lapela /la'pɛla/ *f* lapel

lapidar /lapi'dar/ *vt* cut <*pedra preciosa*>; (*fig*) polish

lápide /'lapidʒi/ *f* tombstone

lápis /'lapis/ *m invar* pencil

lapiseira /lapi'zera/ *f* propelling pencil; (*caixa*) pencil box

Lapônia /la'ponia/ *f* Lappland

lapso /'lapsu/ *m* lapse

la|quê /la'ke/ *m* lacquer; ~**quear** *vt* lacquer

lar /lar/ *m* home

laran|ja /la'rãʒa/ *f* orange □ *a invar* orange; ~**jada** *f* orangeade; ~**jeira** *f* orange tree

lareira /la'rera/ *f* hearth, fireplace

lar|gada /lar'gada/ *f* start; **dar a** ~**gada** start off; ~**gar** *vt* (*soltar*) let go of; give up <*estudos, emprego etc*>; ~**gar de fumar** give up smoking; ~**go** *a* wide; <*roupa*> loose □ *m* (*praça*) square; **ao** ~**go** (*no alto-mar*) out at sea; ~**gura** *f* width

larin|ge /la'rĩʒi/ *f* larynx; ~**gite** *f* laryngitis

larva /'larva/ *f* larva

lasanha /la'zaɲa/ *f* lasagna

las|ca /'laska/ *f* chip; ~**car** *vt/i* chip; **de** ~**car** (*fam*) awful

lástima /'lastʃima/ *f* shame

lastro /'lastru/ *m* ballast

la|ta /'lata/ *f* (*material*) tin; (*recipiente*) tin, (*Amer*) can; ~**ta de lixo** dustbin, (*Amer*) trash can; ~**tão** *m* brass

late|jante /late'ʒãtʃi/ *a* throbbing; ~**jar** *vi* throb

latente /la'tẽtʃi/ *a* latent

late|ral /late'raw/ (*pl* ~**rais**) *a* side, lateral

laticínio /latʃi'siniu/ *m* dairy product

latido /la'tʃidu/ *m* bark

lati|fundiário /latʃifũdʒi'ariu/ *a* landowning □ *m* landowner; ~**fúndio** *m* estate

latim /la'tʃĩ/ *m* Latin

latino /la'tʃinu/ *a & m* Latin; ~**americano** *a & m* Latin American

latir /la'tʃir/ *vi* bark

latitude /latʃi'tudʒi/ *f* latitude

lauda /'lawda/ *f* side

laudo /'lawdu/ *m* report, findings

lava /'lava/ *f* lava

lava|bo /la'vabu/ *m* toilet; ~**dora** *f* washing machine; ~**gem** *f* washing; ~**gem a seco** dry cleaning; ~**gem cerebral** brainwashing

lavanda /la'vãda/ *f* lavender

lavanderia /lavãde'ria/ *f* laundry

lavar /la'var/ *vt* wash; ~**a seco** dry-clean; ~**-se** *vpr* wash

lavatório /lava'toriu/ *m* (*Port*) washbasin

lavoura /la'vora/ *f* (*agricultura*) farming; (*terreno*) field

lav|rador /lavra'dor/ *m* farmhand; ~**rar** *vt* work; draw up <*documento*>

laxante /la'ʃãtʃi/ *a & m* laxative

lazer /la'zer/ *m* leisure

le|al /le'aw/ (*pl* ~**ais**) *a* loyal; ~**aldade** *f* loyalty

leão /le'ãw/ *m* lion; **Leão** (*signo*) Leo; ~**-de-chácara** (*pl* **leões-de-chácara**) *m* bouncer

lebre /'lɛbri/ *f* hare

lecionar /lesio'nar/ *vt/i* teach

le|gação /lega'sãw/ *f* legation; ~**gado** *m* (*pessoa*) legate; (*herança*) legacy

le|gal /le'gaw/ (*pl* ~**gais**) *a* legal; (*fam*) good; <*pessoa*> nice; **tá** ~**gal** OK; ~**galidade** *f* legality; ~**galizar** *vt* legalize

legar /le'gar/ *vt* bequeath

legenda /le'ʒẽda/ *f* (*de quadro*) caption; (*de filme*) subtitle; (*inscrição*) inscription

legi|ão /leʒi'ãw/ *f* legion; ~**onário** *m* (*romano*) legionary; (*da legião estrangeira*) legionnaire

legis|lação /leʒizla'sãw/ *f* legislation; ~**lador** *m* legislator; ~**lar** *vi* legislate; ~**lativo** *a* legislative □ *m* legislature; ~**latura** *f* legislature; ~**ta** *m/f* legal expert

legiti|mar /leʒitʃi'mar/ *vt* legitimize; ~**midade** *f* legitimacy

legítimo /le'ʒitʃimu/ *a* legitimate

legí|vel /le'ʒivew/ (*pl* ~**veis**) *a* legible

légua /'lɛgwa/ *f* league

legume /le'gumi/ *m* vegetable

lei /lej/ *f* law

leigo /'lejgu/ *a* lay □ *m* layman

lei|lão /lej'lãw/ *m* auction; **~loar** *vt* auction; **~loeiro** *m* auctioneer

leitão /lej'tãw/ *m* sucking pig

lei|te /'lejtʃi/ *m* milk; **~te condensado/desnatado** condensed/ skimmed milk; **~teira** *f* (*jarro*) milk jug; (*panela*) milk saucepan; **~teiro** *m* milkman □ *a* <*vaca*> dairy

leito /'lejtu/ *m* bed

leitor /lej'tor/ *m* reader

leitoso /lej'tozu/ *a* milky

leitura /lej'tura/ *f* (*ação*) reading; (*material*) reading matter

lema /'lema/ *m* motto

lem|brança /lẽ'brãsa/ *f* memory; (*presente*) souvenir; **~brar** *vt/i* remember; **~brar-se de** remember; **~brar aco a alg** remind s.o. of sth; **~brete** /e/ *m* reminder

leme /'lemi/ *m* rudder

len|ço /'lẽsu/ *m* (*para o nariz*) handkerchief; (*para vestir*) scarf; **~çol** /ɔ/ (*pl* **~çóis**) *m* sheet

len|da /'lẽda/ *f* legend; **~dário** *a* legendary

lenha /'leɲa/ *f* firewood; (*uma*) log; **~dor** *m* woodcutter

lente /'lẽtʃi/ *f* lens; **~ de contato** contact lens

lentidão /lẽtʃi'dãw/ *f* slowness

lentilha /lẽ'tʃiʎa/ *f* lentil

lento /'lẽtu/ *a* slow

leoa /le'oa/ *f* lioness

leopardo /lio'pardu/ *m* leopard

le|pra /'lɛpra/ *f* leprosy; **~proso** /o/ *a* leprous □ *m* leper

leque /'lɛki/ *m* fan; (*fig*) array

ler /ler/ *vt/i* read

ler|deza /ler'deza/ *f* sluggishness; **~do** /e/ *a* sluggish

le|são /le'zãw/ *f* lesion, injury; **~sar** *vt* damage

lésbi|ca /'lɛzbika/ *f* lesbian; **~co** *a* lesbian

lesionar /lezio'nar/ *vt* injure

lesma /'lezma/ *f* slug

leste /'lestʃi/ *m* east

le|tal /le'taw/ (*pl* **~tais**) *a* lethal

le|tão /le'tãw/ *a* & *m* (*f* **~tã**) Latvian

letargia /letar'ʒia/ *f* lethargy

letivo /le'tʃivu/ *a* **ano ~** academic year

Letônia /le'tonia/ *f* Latvia

letra /'letra/ *f* letter; (*de música*) lyrics, words; (*caligrafia*) writing; **Letras** Modern Languages; **ao pé da ~** literally; **com todas as ~s** in no uncertain terms; **tirar de ~** take in one's stride; **~ de fôrma** block letter

letreiro /le'treru/ *m* sign

leucemia /lewse'mia/ *f* leukaemia

leva /e/ *f* batch

levado /le'vadu/ *a* naughty

levan|tamento /levãta'mẽtu/ *m* (*enquete*) survey; (*rebelião*) uprising; **~tamento de pesos** weightlifting; **~tar** *vt* raise; lift <*peso*> □ *vi* get up; **~tar-se** *vpr* get up; (*revoltar-se*) rise up

levante /le'vãtʃi/ *m* east

levar /le'var/ *vt* take; lead <*vida*>; get <*tapa, susto etc*> □ *vi* lead (**a** to)

leve /'levi/ *a* light; (*não grave*) slight; **de ~** lightly

levedura /leve'dura/ *f* yeast

leveza /le'veza/ *f* lightness

levi|andade /leviã'dadʒi/ *f* frivolity; **~ano** *a* frivolous

levitar /levi'tar/ *vi* levitate

lexi|cal /leksi'kaw/ (*pl* **~cais**) *a* lexical

léxico /'lɛksiku/ *m* lexicon

lexicografia /leksikogra'fia/ *f* lexicography

lhe /ʎi/ *pron* (*a ele*) to him; (*a ela*) to her; (*a você*) to you; **~s** *pron* to them; (*a vocês*) to you

liba|nês /liba'nes/ *a* & *m* (*f* **~nesa**) Lebanese

Líbano /'libanu/ *m* Lebanon

libélula /li'belula/ *f* dragonfly

libe|ração /libera'sãw/ *f* release; **∼ral** (*pl* **∼rais**) *a & m* liberal; **∼ralismo** *m* liberalism; **∼ralizar** *vt* liberalize; **∼rar** *vt* release

liberdade /liber'dadʒi/ *f* freedom; **pôr em ∼** set free; **∼ condicional** probation

líbero /'liberu/ *m* sweeper

liber|tação /liberta'sãw/ *f* liberation; **∼tar** *vt* free

Líbia /'libia/ *f* Libya

líbio /'libiu/ *a & m* Libyan

libi|dinoso /libidʒi'nozu/ *a* lecherous; **∼do** *f* libido

li|bra /'libra/ *f* pound; **Libra** (*signo*) Libra; **∼briano** *a & m* Libran

lição /li'sãw/ *f* lesson

licen|ça /li'sẽsa/ *f* leave; (*documento*) licence; **com ∼ça** excuse me; **de ∼ça** on leave; **sob ∼ça** under licence; **∼ciar** *vt* (*autorizar*) license; (*dar férias a*) give leave to; **∼ciar-se** *vpr* (*tirar férias*) take leave; (*formar-se*) graduate; **∼ciatura** *f* degree; **∼cioso** /o/ *a* licentious

liceu /li'sew/ *m* (*Port*) secondary school, (*Amer*) high school

licor /li'kor/ *m* liqueur

lida /'lida/ *f* slog, grind; (*leitura*) read

lidar /li'dar/ *vt/i* **∼ com** deal with

lide /'lidʒi/ *f* (*trabalho*) work

líder /'lider/ *m/f* leader

lide|rança /lide'rãsa/ *f* (*de partido etc*) leadership; (*em corrida, jogo etc*) lead; **∼rar** *vt* lead

lido /'lidu/ *a* well-read

liga /'liga/ *f* (*aliança*) league; (*tira*) garter; (*presilha*) suspender; (*de metais*) alloy

li|gação /liga'sãw/ *f* connection; (*telefónica*) call; (*amorosa*) liaison; **∼gada** *f* call, ring; **∼gado** *a* ⟨*luz, TV*⟩ on; **∼gado em** attached to ⟨*pessoa*⟩; hooked on ⟨*droga*⟩; **∼gamento** *m* ligament; **∼gar** *vt* join, connect;

switch on ⟨*luz, TV etc*⟩; start up ⟨*carro*⟩; bind ⟨*amigos*⟩ □ *vi* ring up, call; **∼gar para** (*telefonar*) ring, call; (*dar importância*) care about; (*dar atenção*) pay attention to; **∼gar-se** *vpr* join

ligeiro /li'ʒeru/ *a* light; ⟨*ferida, melhora*⟩ slight; (*ágil*) nimble

lilás /li'las/ *m* lilac □ *a invar* mauve

lima[1] /'lima/ *f* (*ferramenta*) file

lima[2] /'lima/ *f* (*fruta*) sweet orange

limão /li'mãw/ *m* lime; (*amarelo*) lemon

limar /li'mar/ *vt* file

limeira /li'mera/ *f* sweet orange tree

limiar /limi'ar/ *m* threshold

limi|tação /limita'sãw/ *f* limitation; **∼tar** *vt* limit; **∼tar-se** *vpr* limit o.s.; **∼tar(-se) com** border on; **∼te** *m* limit; (*de terreno*) boundary; **passar dos ∼tes** go too far; **∼te de velocidade** speed limit

limo|eiro /limo'eru/ *m* lime tree; **∼nada** *f* lemonade

lim|pador /lĩpa'dor/ *m* **∼pador de pára-brisas** windscreen wiper; **∼par** *vt* clean; wipe ⟨*lágrimas, suor*⟩; (*fig*) clean up ⟨*cidade, organização*⟩; **∼peza** /e/ *f* (*ato*) cleaning; (*qualidade*) cleanness; (*fig*) clean-up; **∼peza pública** sanitation; **∼po** *a* clean; ⟨*céu, consciência*⟩ clear; ⟨*lucro*⟩ net, clear; (*fig*) pure; **passar a ∼po** write up ⟨*trabalho*⟩; (*fig*) sort out ⟨*vida*⟩; **tirar a ∼po** get to the bottom of ⟨*caso*⟩

limusine /limu'zini/ *f* limousine

lince /'lĩsi/ *m* lynx

lindo /'lĩdu/ *a* beautiful

linear /lini'ar/ *a* linear

lingote /lĩ'gɔtʃi/ *m* ingot

língua /'lĩgwa/ *f* (*na boca*) tongue; (*idioma*) language; **∼ materna** mother tongue linguado /lĩ'gwadu/ *m* sole

lingua|gem /lĩ'gwaʒẽ/ *f* language; **~jar** *m* speech, dialect

lingüeta /lĩ'gweta/ *f* bolt

lingüiça /lĩ'gwisa/ *f* pork sausage

lin|güista /lĩ'gwiʃta/ *m/f* linguist; **~güística** *f* linguistics; **~güístico** *a* linguistic

linha /'liɲa/ *f* line; (*fio*) thread; **perder a ~** lose one's cool; **~ aérea** airline; **~ de fogo** firing line; **~ de montagem** assembly line; **~gem** *f* lineage

linho /'liɲu/ *m* linen; (*planta*) flax

linóleo /li'nɔliu/ *m* lino(leum)

lipoaspiração /lipoaspira'sãw/ *f* liposuction

liqui|dação /likida'sãw/ *f* liquidation; (*de loja*) clearance sale; (*de conta*) settlement; **~dar** *vt* liquidate; settle <*conta*>; pay off <*dívida*>; sell off, clear <*mercadorias*>

liqüidificador /likwidʒifika'dor/ *m* liquidizer

líquido /'likidu/ *a* liquid; <*lucro, salário*> net □ *m* liquid

líri|ca /'lirika/ *f* (*mus*) lyrics; (*poesia*) lyric poetry; **~co** *a* lyrical; <*poesia*> lyric

lírio /'liriu/ *m* lily

Lisboa /liz'boa/ *f* Lisbon

lisboeta /lizbo'eta/ *a & m/f* (person) from Lisbon

liso /'lizu/ *a* smooth; (*sem desenho*) plain; <*cabelo*> straight; (*fam: duro*) broke

lison|ja /li'zõʒa/ *f* flattery; **~jear** *vt* flatter

lista /'liʃta/ *f* list; (*listra*) stripe; **~ telefônica** telephone directory

listra /'liʃtra/ *f* stripe; **~do** *a* striped, stripey

lite|ral /lite'raw/ (*pl* **~rais**) *a* literal; **~rário** *a* literary; **~ratura** *f* literature

litígio /li'tʃiʒiu/ *m* dispute; (*jurid*) lawsuit

lito|ral /lito'raw/ (*pl* **~rais**) *m* coastline; **~râneo** *a* coastal

litro /'litru/ *m* litre

Lituânia /litu'ania/ *f* Lithuania

lituano /litu'anu/ *a & m* Lithuanian

living /'livĩ/ (*pl* **~s**) *m* living room

livrar /li'vrar/ *vt* free; (*salvar*) save; **~-se** *vpr* escape; **~-se de** get rid of

livraria /livra'ria/ *f* bookshop

livre /'livri/ *a* free; **~ de impostos** tax-free; **~-arbítrio** *m* free will

liv|reiro /li'vreru/ *m* bookseller; **~ro** *m* book; **~ro de consulta** reference book; **~ro de cozinha** cookery book; **~ro de texto** text book; **~ro eletrônico** e-book

li|xa /'liʃa/ *f* (*de unhas*) emery board; (*para madeira etc*) sandpaper; **~xar** *vt* sand <*madeira*>; file <*unhas*>; **estou me ~xando** (*fam*) I couldn't care less

li|xeira /li'ʃera/ *f* dustbin, (*Amer*) garbage can; **~xeiro** *m* dustman, (*Amer*) garbage collector; **~xo** *m* rubbish, (*Amer*) garbage; (*atômico*) waste

lobisomem /lobi'zomẽ/ *m* werewolf

lobo /'lobu/ *m* wolf; **~-marinho** (*pl* **~s-marinhos**) *m* sea lion

lóbulo /'lobulu/ *m* lobe

lo|cação /loka'sãw/ *f* (*de imóvel*) lease; (*de carro*) rental; **~cador** *m* (*de casa*) landlord; **~cadora** *f* rental company; (*de vídeos*) video shop

lo|cal /lo'kaw/ (*pl* **~cais**) *a* local □ *m* site; (*de um acidente etc*) scene; **~calidade** *f* locality; **~calização** *f* location; **~calizar** *vt* locate; **~calizar-se** *vpr* (*orientar-se*) get one's bearings

loção /lo'sãw/ *f* lotion; **~ após-barba** aftershave lotion

locatário /loka'tariu/ m (de imóvel) tenant; (de carro etc) hirer

locomo|tiva /lokomo'tʃiva/ f locomotive; ~**ver-se** vpr get around

locu|ção /loku'sãw/ f phrase; ~**tor** m announcer

lodo /'lodu/ m mud; ~**so** /o/ a muddy

logaritmo /loga'ritʃimu/ m logarithm

lógi|ca /'lɔʒika/ f logic; ~**co** a logical

logo /'lɔgu/ adv (em seguida) straightaway; (em breve) soon; (justamente) just; ~ **mais** later; ~ **antes/depois** just before/straight after; ~ **que** as soon as; **até** ~ goodbye

logotipo /logo'tʃipu/ m logo

logradouro /logra'doru/ m public place

loiro /'lojru/ a veja louro

loja /'lɔʒa/ f shop, (Amer) store; ~**ja de departamentos** department store; ~**ja maçônica** masonic lodge; ~**jista** m/f shopkeeper

lom|bada /lõ'bada/ f (de livro) spine; (na rua) speed bump; ~**binho** m tenderloin; ~**bo** m back; (carne) loin

lona /'lona/ f canvas

Londres /'lõdris/ f London

londrino /lõ'drinu/ a London □ m Londoner

longa-metragem /lõga'metraʒẽ/ (pl **longas-metragens**) m feature film

longe /'lõʒi/ adv far, a long way; **de** ~ (de um distance); (por muito) by far; ~ **disso** far from it

longevidade /lõʒevi'dadʒi/ f longevity

longínquo /lõ'ʒĩkwu/ a distant

longitude /lõʒi'tudʒi/ f longitude

longo /'lõgu/ a long □ m long dress; **ao** ~ **de** along; (durante) through, over

lontra /'lõtra/ f otter

lorde /'lɔrdʒi/ m lord

lorota /lo'rota/ (fam) f fib

losango /lo'zãgu/ m diamond

lo|tação /lota'sãw/ f capacity; (ônibus) bus; ~**tação esgotada** full house; ~**tado** a crowded; (teatro, ônibus> full; ~**tar** vt fill □ vi fill up

lote /'lɔtʃi/ m (quinhão) portion; (de terreno) plot, (Amer) lot; (em leilão) lot; (porção de coisas) batch

loteria /lote'ria/ f lottery

louça /'losa/ f china; (pratos de) crockery; **lavar a** ~ wash up, (Amer) do the dishes

lou|co /'loku/ a mad, crazy □ m madman; **estou** ~**co para ir** (fam) I'm dying to go; ~**cura** f madness; (uma) crazy thing

louro /'loru/ a blond □ m laurel; (condimento) bayleaf

lou|var /lo'var/ vt praise; ~**vável** (pl ~**váveis**) a praiseworthy; ~**vor** /o/ m praise

lua /'lua/ f moon; ~**-de-mel** honeymoon

lu|ar /lu'ar/ m moonlight; ~**a-rento** a moonlit

lubrifi|cação /lubrifika'sãw/ f lubrication; ~**cante** a lubricating □ m lubricant; ~**car** vt lubricate

lucidez /lusi'des/ f lucidity

lúcido /'lusidu/ a lucid

lu|crar /lu'krar/ vi profit´ (com by); ~**cratividade** f profitability; ~**crativo** a profitable, lucrative; ~**cro** m profit

ludibriar /ludʒibri'ar/ vt cheat

lúdico /'ludʒiku/ a playful

lugar /lu'gar/ m place; (espaço) room; **em** ~ **de** in place of; **em primeiro** ~ in the first place; **em algum** ~ somewhere; **em todo** ~ everywhere; **dar** ~ **a** give rise to; **ter** ~ take place

lugarejo /luga'reʒu/ m village

lúgubre /'lugubri/ a gloomy, dismal

lula /'lula/ f squid

lume /'lumi/ m fire

luminária /lumi'naria/ f light, lamp; pl illuminations

luminoso /lumi'nozu/ a luminous; <idéia> brilliant

lunar /lu'nar/ a lunar □ m mole

lupa /'lupa/ f magnifying glass

lusco-fusco /lusku'fusku/ m twilight

lusitano /luzi'tanu/, luso /'luzu/ a & m Portuguese

lus|trar /lus'trar/ vt shine, polish; ~tre m shine; (fig) lustre; (luminária) light, lamp; ~troso /o/ a shiny

lu|ta /'luta/ f fight, struggle; ~ta livre wrestling; ~tador m fighter; (de luta livre) wrestler; ~tar vi fight □ vt do <judô etc>

luto /'lutu/ m mourning

luva /'luva/ f glove

luxação /luʃa'sãw/ f dislocation

Luxemburgo /luʃẽ'burgu/ m Luxembourg

luxembur|guês /luʃẽbur'ges/ a (f ~guesa) Luxembourg □ m (f ~guesa) Luxembourger; (língua) Luxembourgish

luxo /'luʃu/ m luxury; hotel de ~ luxury hotel; cheio de ~ (fam) fussy

luxuoso /luʃu'ozu/ a luxurious

luxúria /lu'ʃuria/ f lust

luxuriante /luʃuri'ãtʃi/ a lush

luz /lus/ f light; à ~ de by the light of <velas etc>; in the light of <fatos etc>; dar à ~ give birth to

luzidio /luzi'dʒio/ a shiny

luzir /lu'zir/ vi shine

M

maca /'maka/ f stretcher

maçã /ma'sã/ f apple

macabro /ma'kabru/ a macabre

maca|cão /maka'kãw/ m (de trabalho) overalls, (Amer) coveralls; (tipo de calça) dungarees; (roupa inteiriça) jumpsuit; (para bebê) romper suit; ~co m monkey; (aparelho) jack

maçada /ma'sada/ f bore

maçaneta /masa'neta/ f doorknob

maçante /ma'sãtʃi/ a boring

macar|rão /maka'xãw/ m pasta; (espaguete) spaghetti; ~ronada f pasta with tomato sauce and cheese

macarrônico /maka'xoniku/ a broken

macete /ma'setʃi/ m trick

machado /ma'ʃadu/ m axe

ma|chão /ma'ʃãw/ a tough □ m tough guy; ~chismo m machismo; ~chista a chauvinistic □ m male chauvinist; ~cho /o/ a male; <homem> macho □ m male

machu|cado /maʃu'kadu/ m injury; (na pele) sore patch; ~car vt/i hurt; ~car-se vpr hurt o.s.

maciço /ma'sisu/ a solid; <dose etc> massive □ m massif

macieira /masi'era/ f apple tree

maciez /masi'es/ f softness

macilento /masi'lẽtu/ a haggard

macio /ma'siu/ a soft; <carne> tender

maço /'masu/ m (de cigarros) packet; (de notas) bundle

ma|çom /ma'sõ/ m freemason; ~çonaria f freemasonry

maconha /ma'koɲa/ f marijuana

maçônico /ma'soniku/ a masonic

má-criação /makria'sãw/ f rudeness

macrobiótico /makrobi'ɔtʃiku/ a macrobiotic

macum|ba /ma'kũba/ f Afro-Brazilian cult; (uma) spell; ~beiro m follower of macumba □ a macumba

madame /ma'dami/ f lady

Madeira /ma'dera/ f Madeira

madeira /ma'dera/ f wood □ *m* (*vinho*) Madeira; ~ **de lei** hardwood

madeirense /made'rēsi/ *a* & *m* Madeiran

madeixa /ma'deʃa/ f lock

madrasta /ma'drasta/ f stepmother

madrepérola /madre'pɛrola/ f mother of pearl

madressilva /madre'siwva/ f honeysuckle

Madri /ma'dri/ f Madrid

madrinha /ma'driɲa/ f (*de batismo*) godmother; (*de casamento*) bridesmaid

madrugada /madru'gada/ f early morning; ~**gador** *m* early riser; ~**gar** *vi* get up early

maduro /ma'duru/ *a* <*fruta*> ripe; <*pessoa*> mature

mãe /mãj/ f mother; ~**-de-santo** (*pl* ~**s-de-santo**) f macumba priestess

maestria /majs'tria/ f expertise; ~**tro** *m* conductor

máfia /'mafia/ f mafia

magazine /maga'zini/ *m* department store

magia /ma'ʒia/ f magic

mágica /'maʒika/ f magic; (*uma*) magic trick; ~**co** *a* magic □ *m* magician

magistério /maʒis'teriu/ *m* teaching; (*professores*) teachers; ~**trado** *m* magistrate

magnânimo /mag'nanimu/ *a* magnanimous

magnata /mag'nata/ *m* magnate

magnésio /mag'nɛziu/ *m* magnesium

magnético /mag'nɛtʃiku/ *a* magnetic; ~**netismo** *m* magnetism; ~**netizar** *vt* magnetize; (*fig*) mesmerize

magnificência /magnifi'sẽsia/ f magnificence; ~**nífico** *a* magnificent

magnitude /magni'tudʒi/ f magnitude

mago /'magu/ *m* magician; **os reis** ~**s** the Three Wise Men

mágoa /'magoa/ f sorrow

magoar /mago'ar/ *vt/i* hurt; ~**-se** *vpr* be hurt

magricela /magri'sɛla/ *a* skinny; ~**gro** *a* thin; <*leite*> skimmed; <*carne*> lean; (*fig*) meagre

maio /'maju/ *m* May

maiô /ma'jo/ *m* swimsuit

maionese /majo'nɛzi/ f mayonnaise

maior /ma'jɔr/ *a* bigger; <*escritor, amor etc*> greater; **o** ~ **carro** the biggest car; **o** ~ **escritor** the greatest writer; ~ **de idade** of age

Maiorca /ma'jɔrka/ f Majorca

maioria /majo'ria/ f majority; **a** ~**ria dos brasileiros** most Brazilians; ~**ridade** f majority, adulthood

mais /majs/ *adv* & *pron* more; ~ **dois** two more; **dois dias a** ~ two more days; **não trabalho** ~ I don't work any more; ~ **ou menos** more or less

maisena /maj'zɛna/ f cornflour, (*Amer*) cornstarch

maître /mɛtr/ *m* head waiter

maiúscula /ma'juskula/ *a* capital letter

majestade /maʒes'tadʒi/ f majesty; ~**toso** *a* majestic

major /ma'ʒɔr/ *m* major

majoritário /maʒori'tariu/ *a* majority

mal /maw/ *adv* badly; (*quase não*) hardly □ *conj* hardly □ *m* evil; (*doença*) sickness; **não faz** ~ never mind; **levar a** ~ take offence at; **passar** ~ be sick

mala /'mala/ f suitcase; (*do carro*) boot, (*Amer*) trunk; ~ **aérea** air courier

malabarismo /malaba'rizmu/ *m* juggling act; ~**ta** *m*/f juggler

malagradecido /malagrade'sidu/ *a* ungrateful

malagueta /mala'geta/ *f* chilli pepper

malaio /ma'laju/ *a & m* Malay

Malaísia /mala'izia/ *f* Malaysia

malaísio /mala'iziu/ *a & m* Malaysian

malan|dragem /malã'draʒẽ/ *f* hustling; (*uma*) clever trick; **∼dro** *a* cunning □ *m* hustler

malária /ma'laria/ *f* malaria

mal-assombrado /malasõ'bradu/ *a* haunted

Malavi /mala'vi/ *m* Malawi

malcriado /mawkri'adu/ *a* rude

mal|dade /maw'dadʒi/ *f* wickedness; (*uma*) wicked thing; **por ∼dade** out of spite; **∼dição** *f* curse; **∼dito** *a* cursed, damned; **∼doso** /o/ *a* wicked

maleá|vel /mali'avew/ (*pl* **∼veis**) *a* malleable

maledicência /maledi'sẽsia/ *f* malicious gossip

maléfico /ma'lɛfiku/ *a* evil; (*prejudicial*) harmful

mal-encarado /malĩka'radu/ *a* shady, dubious □ *m* shady character

mal-entendido /malĩtẽ'dʒidu/ *m* misunderstanding

mal-estar /malis'tar/ *m* (*doença*) ailment; (*constrangimento*) discomfort

maleta /ma'leta/ *f* overnight bag

malévolo /ma'lɛvolu/ *a* malevolent

malfei|to /maw'fejtu/ *a* badly done; <*roupa etc*> badly made; (*fig*) wrongful; **∼tor** *m* wrongdoer; **∼toria** *f* wrongdoing

ma|lha /'maʎa/ *f* (*ponto*) stitch; (*tricô*) knitting; (*tecido*) jersey; (*casaco*) jumper, (*Amer*) sweater; (*para ginástica*) leotard; (*de rede*) mesh; **fazer ∼lha** knit; (*de malhado*) **∼lhado** *a* <*animal*> dappled; <*roque*>

heavy; **∼lhar** *vt* beat; thresh <*trigo etc*> □ *vi* (*fam*) work out

mal-humorado /malumo'radu/ *a* in a bad mood, grumpy

malícia /ma'lisia/ *f* (*má índole*) malice; (*astúcia*) guile; (*humor*) innuendo

malicioso /malisi'ozu/ *a* (*mau*) malicious; (*astuto*) crafty; (*que põe malícia*) dirty-minded

maligno /ma'liginu/ *a* malignant

malmequer /mawme'ker/ *m* marigold

maloca /ma'lɔka/ *f* Indian village

malo|grar-se /malo'grarsi/ *vpr* go wrong, fail; **∼gro** /o/ *m* failure

mal-passado /mawpa'sadu/ *a* <*carne*> rare

Malta /'mawta/ *f* Malta

malte /'mawtʃi/ *m* malt

maltrapilho /mawtra'piʎu/ *a* scruffy

maltratar /mawtra'tar/ *vt* illtreat, mistreat

malu|co /ma'luku/ *a* mad, crazy □ *m* madman; **∼quice** *f* madness; (*uma*) crazy thing

malvado /maw'vadu/ *a* wicked

malver|sação /mawversa'sãw/ *f* mismanagement; (*de fundos*) misappropriation; **∼sar** *vt* mismanage; misappropriate <*dinheiro*>

Malvinas /maw'vinas/ *f pl* Falklands

mamadeira /mama'dera/ *f* (baby's) bottle

mamãe /ma'mãj/ *f* mum

mamão /ma'mãw/ *m* papaya

ma|mar /ma'mar/ *vi* suckle; **∼mata** *f* (*fam*) fiddle

mamífero /ma'miferu/ *m* mammal

mamilo /ma'milu/ *m* nipple

mamoeiro /mamo'eru/ *m* papaya tree

manada /ma'nada/ *f* herd

manan|cial /manãsi'aw/ (*pl* **∼ais**) *m* spring; (*fig*) rich source

man|cada /mã'kada/ *f* blunder;
~**car** *vi* limp; ~**car-se** *vpr*
(*fam*) take the hint, get the
message

Mancha /'mãʃa/ *f* **o canal da** ~
the English Channel

man|cha /'mãʃa/ *f* stain; (*na pele*)
mark; ~**char** *vt* stain

manchete /mã'ʃɛtʃi/ *f* headline

manco /'mãku/ *a* lame □ *m* cripple

mandachuva /mãda'ʃuva/ *m*
(*fam*) bigwig; (*chefe*) boss

man|dado /mã'dadu/ *m* order;
~**dado de busca** search
warrant; ~**dado de prisão** arrest warrant; ~**damento** *m*
commandment; ~**dante** *m/f*
person in charge; ~**dão** *a* (*f*
~**dona**) bossy; ~**dar** *vt* (*pedir*)
order; (*enviar*) send □ *vi* be in
charge; ~**dar-se** *vpr* (*fam*) take
off; ~**dar buscar** fetch; ~**dar
dizer** send word; ~**dar alg ir**
tell s.o. to go; ~**dar ver** (*fam*)
go to town; ~**dar em alg** order
s.o. about; ~**dato** *m* mandate

mandíbula /mã'dʒibula/ *f* (lower)
jaw

mandioca /mãdʒi'ɔka/ *f* manioc

maneira /ma'nera/ *f* way; *pl*
(*boas*) manners; **desta** ~ in this
way; **de qualquer** ~ anyway

mane|jar /mane'ʒar/ *vt* handle;
operate <*máquina*>; ~**jável** (*pl*
~**jáveis**) *a* manageable; ~**jo**
/e/ *m* handling

manequim /mane'kĩ/ *m* (*boneco*)
dummy; (*medida*) size □ *m/f*
mannequin, model

maneta /ma'neta/ *a* one-armed □
m/f person with one arm

manga[1] /'mãga/ *f* (*de roupa*)
sleeve

manga[2] /'mãga/ *f* (*fruta*) mango

manganês /mãga'nes/ *m* man-
ganese

mangue /'mãgi/ *m* mangrove
swamp

mangueira[1] /mã'gera/ *f* (*tubo*)
hose

mangueira[2] /mã'gera/ *f* (*árvore*)
mango tree

manha /'maɲa/ *f* tantrum

manhã /ma'ɲã/ *f* morning; **de** ~
in the morning

manhoso /ma'ɲozu/ *a* wilful

mania /ma'nia/ *f* (*moda*) craze;
(*doença*) mania

maníaco /ma'niaku/ *a* a manic □
~**-depressivo** *a* & *m*
manic depressive

manicômio /mani'komiu/ *m* lunatic asylum

manicura /mani'kura/ *f* mani-
cure; (*pessoa*) manicurist

manifes|tação /manifesta'sãw/ *f*
manifestation; (*passeata*) demon-
stration; ~**tante** *m/f* demon-
strator; ~**tar** *vt* manifest,
demonstrate; ~**tar-se** *vpr* (*reve-
lar-se*) manifest o.s.; (*exprimir-se*)
express an opinion; ~**to** /ɛ/ *a*
manifest, clear □ *m* manifesto

manipular /manipu'lar/ *vt* ma-
nipulate

manjedoura /mãʒe'dora/ *f* man-
ger

manjericão /mãʒeri'kãw/ *m* basil

mano|bra /ma'nɔbra/ *f* man-
oeuvre; ~**brar** *vt* manoeuvre;
~**brista** *m/f* parking valet

mansão /mã'sãw/ *f* mansion

man|sidão /mãsi'dãw/ *f* gentle-
ness; (*do mar*) calm; ~**sinho**
adv **de** ~**sinho** (*devagar*)
slowly; (*de leve*) gently; (*de fininho*) stealthily; ~**so** *a* gentle;
<*mar*> calm; <*animal*> tame

manta /'mãta/ *f* blanket; (*casaco*)
cloak

mantei|ga /mã'tejga/ *f* butter;
~**gueira** *f* butter dish

manter /mã'ter/ *vt* keep; ~**se**
vpr keep; (*sustentar-se*) keep o.s.

mantimentos /mãtʃi'mẽtus/ *m pl*
provisions

manto /'mãtu/ *m* mantle

manu|al /manu'aw/ (*pl* **~ais**) *a* & *m* manual; **~fatura** *f* manufacture; (*fábrica*) factory; **~faturar** *vt* manufacture

manuscrito /manus'kritu/ *a* handwritten □ *m* manuscript

manu|sear /manuzi'ar/ *vt* handle; **~seio** *m* handling

manutenção /manute'sãw/ *f* maintenance; (*de prédio*) upkeep

mão /mãw/ (*pl* **~s**) *f* hand; (*do trânsito*) direction; (*de tinta*) coat; **abrir ~ de** give up; **agüentar a ~** hang on; **dar a ~ a alg** hold s.o.'s hand; (*cumprimentando*) shake s.o.'s hand; **deixar alg na ~** let s.o. down; **enfiar ou meter a ~** em hit, slap; **lançar ~ de** make use of; **escrito à ~** written by hand; **ter à ~** have to hand; **de ~s dadas** hand in hand; **em segunda ~** secondhand; **fora de ~** out of the way; **~ única** one way; **~-de-obra** *f* labour

mapa /'mapa/ *m* map

maquete /ma'ketʃi/ *f* model

maqui|agem /maki'aʒē/ *f* makeup; **~ar** *vt* make up; **~ar-se** *vpr* put on make-up

maquiavélico /makia'vɛliku/ *a* Machiavellian

maqui|lagem /maki'laʒē/, (*Port*) **~lhagem, ~lhar** *veja* maqui|agem, **~ar**

máquina /'makina/ *f* machine; (*ferroviária*) engine; **escrever à ~** type; **~ de costura** sewing machine; **~ de escrever** typewriter; **~ de lavar (roupa)** washing machine; **~ de lavar pratos** dishwasher; **~ fotográfica** camera

maqui|nação /makina'sãw/ *f* machination; **~nal**, (*pl* **~nais**) *a* mechanical; **~nar** *vt/i* plot; **~naria** *f* machinery; **~nista** *m/f* (*ferroviária*) engine driver; (*de navio*) engineer

mar /mar/ *m* sea

maracu|já /maraku'ʒa/ *m* passion fruit; **~jazeiro** *m* passion-fruit plant

marasmo /ma'razmu/ *m* stagnation

mara|tona /mara'tona/ *f* marathon; **~nista** *m/f* marathon runner

maravi|lha /mara'viʎa/ *f* marvel; **às mil ~lhas** wonderfully; **~lhar** *vt* amaze; **~lhar-se** marvel (*de* at); **~lhoso** /o/ *a* marvellous

mar|ca /'marka/ *f* (*sinal*) mark; (*de carro, máquina*) make; (*de cigarro, sabão etc*) brand; **~ca registrada** registered trademark; **~cação** *f* marking; (*Port: discagem*) dialling; **~cador** *m* marker; (*em livro*) bookmark; (*placar*) scoreboard; (*jogador*) scorer; **~cante** *a* outstanding; **~capasso** *m* pacemaker; **~car** *vt* mark; arrange <*hora, encontro, jantar etc*>; score <*gol, ponto*>; (*Port: discar*) dial; <*relógio, termómetro*> show; brand <*gado*>; (*observar*) keep a close eye on; (*impressionar*) leave one's mark on □ *vi* make one's mark; **~car época** make history; **~car hora** make an appointment; **~car o compasso** beat time; **~car os pontos** keep the score

marce|naria /marsena'ria/ *f* cabinet-making; (*oficina*) cabinet maker's workshop; **~neiro** *m* cabinet maker

mar|cha /'marʃa/ *f* march; (*de carro*) gear; **pôr-se em ~cha** get going; **~cha à ré**, (*Port*) **~cha atrás** reverse; **~char** *vi* march

marci|al /marsi'aw/ (*pl* **~ais**) *a* martial; **~ano** *a* & *m* Martian

marco¹ /'marku/ *m* (*sinal*) landmark

marco² /'marku/ *m* (*moeda*) mark

março /'marsu/ m March

maré /ma'rɛ/ f tide

mare|chal /mare'ʃaw/ (pl ~chais) m marshal

maresia /mare'zia/ f smell of the sea

marfim /mar'fĩ/ m ivory

margarida /marga'rida/ f daisy; (para impressora) daisywheel

margarina /marga'rina/ f margarine

mar|gem /'marʒẽ/ f (de rio) bank; (de lago) shore; (parte em branco, fig) margin; ~ginal (pl ~ginais) a marginal; (delinqüente) delinquent □ m/f delinquent □ f (rua) riverside road; ~ginalidade f delinquency; ~ginalizar vt marginalize

marido /ma'ridu/ m husband

marimbondo /marĩ'bõdu/ m hornet

marina /ma'rina/ f marina

mari|nha /ma'riɲa/ f navy; ~nha mercante merchant navy; ~nheiro m sailor; ~nho a marine

marionete /mario'netʃi/ f puppet

mariposa /mari'poza/ f moth

mariscos /ma'riskus/ m seafood

mari|tal /mari'taw/ (pl ~tais) a marital

marítimo /ma'ritʃimu/ a sea; <cidade> seaside

marmanjo /mar'mãʒu/ m grown-up

marme|lada /marme'lada/ f (fam) fix; ~lo /ɛ/ m quince

marmita /mar'mita/ f (de soldado) mess tin; (de trabalhador) lunch-box

mármore /'marmori/ m marble

marmóreo /mar'mɔriu/ a marble

marquise /mar'kizi/ f awning

marreco /ma'xeku/ m wild duck

Marrocos /ma'xokus/ m Morocco

marrom /ma'xõ/ a & m brown

marroquino /maxo'kinu/ a & m Moroccan

Marte /'martʃi/ m Mars

marte|lada /marte'lada/ f hammer blow; ~lar vt/i hammer; ~lar em (fig) go on and on about; ~lo /ɛ/ m hammer

mártir /'martʃir/ m/f martyr

mar|tírio /mar'tʃiriu/ m martyrdom; (fig) torture; ~tirizar vt martyr; (fig) torture

marujo /ma'ruʒu/ m sailor

mar|xismo /mark'sizmu/ m Marxism; ~xista a & m/f Marxist

mas /mas/ conj but

mascar /mas'kar/ vt chew

máscara /'maskara/ f mask; (tratamento facial) face-pack

mascarar /maska'rar/ vt mask

mascate /mas'katʃi/ m street vendor

mascavo /mas'kavu/ a açúcar ~ brown sugar

mascote /mas'kɔtʃi/ f mascot

masculino /masku'linu/ a male; (para homens) men's; <palavra> masculine □ m masculine

másculo /'maskulu/ a masculine

masmorra /maz'moxa/ f dungeon

masoquis|mo /mazo'kizmu/ m masochism; ~ta m/f masochist □ a masochistic

massa /'masa/ f mass; (de pão) dough; (de torta, empada) pastry; (macarrão etc) pasta; cultura de ~ mass culture; em ~ en masse; as ~s the masses

massa|crante /masa'krãtʃi/ a gruelling; ~crar vt massacre; (fig: maçar) wear out; ~cre m massacre

massa|gear /masaʒi'ar/ vt massage; ~gem f massage; ~gista m/f masseur (f masseuse)

mastigar /mastʃi'gar/ vt chew; (ponderar) chew over

mastro /'mastru/ m mast; (de bandeira) flagpole

mastur|bação /masturba'sãw/ f masturbation; ~bar-se vpr masturbate

mata /'mata/ f forest

mata-borrão /mataboˈxãw/ m blotting paper

matadouro /mataˈdoru/ m slaughterhouse

mata|gal /mataˈgaw/ (pl ~**gais**) m thicket

mata-moscas /mataˈmoskas/ m invar fly spray

ma|tança /maˈtãsa/ f slaughter; ~**tar** vt kill; satisfy <fome>; quench <sede>; guess <charada>; (fazer nas coxas) dash off; (fam) skive off <aula, serviço> □ vi kill

mata-ratos /mataˈxatus/ m invar rat poison

mate[1] /'matʃi/ m (chá) maté

mate[2] /'matʃi/ a invar matt

matemáti|ca /mateˈmatʃika/ f mathematics; ~**co** a mathematical □ m mathematician

matéria /maˈtɛria/ f (assunto, disciplina) subject; (no jornal) article; (substância) matter; (usada para fazer algo) material; **em ~ de** in the way of

materi|al /materiˈaw/ (pl ~**ais**) m materials □ a material; ~**alismo** m materialism; ~**alista** a materialistic □ m/f materialist; ~**alizar-se** vpr materialize

matéria-prima /maˈtɛriaˈprima/ (pl **matérias-primas**) f raw material

mater|nal /materˈnaw/ (pl ~**nais**) a maternal; ~**nidade** f maternity; (clínica) maternity hospital; ~**no** /ɛ/ a maternal; **língua** ~**na** mother tongue

mati|nal /matʃiˈnaw/ (pl ~**nais**) a morning; ~**nê** f matinée

matiz /maˈtʃis/ m shade; (político) colouring; (pontinha: de ironia etc) tinge

matizar /matʃiˈzar/ vt tinge (**de** with)

mato /'matu/ m scrubland, bush

matraca /maˈtraka/ f rattle; (tagarela) chatterbox

matreiro /maˈtreru/ a cunning

matriar|ca /matriˈarka/ f matriarch; ~**cal** (pl ~**cais**) a matriarchal

matrícula /maˈtrikula/ f enrolment; (taxa) enrolment fee; (Port: de carro) number plate, (Amer) license plate

matricular /matrikuˈlar/ vt enrol; ~**-se** vpr enrol

matri|monial /matrimoniˈaw/ (pl ~**moniais**) a marriage; ~**mônio** m marriage

matriz /maˈtris/ f matrix; (útero) womb; (sede) head office

maturidade /maturiˈdadʒi/ f maturity

matutino /matuˈtʃinu/ a morning □ m morning paper

matuto /maˈtutu/ a countrified □ m country bumpkin

mau /maw/ a (f **má**) bad; ~**caráter** m invar bad lot □ a invar no-good; ~**-olhado** m evil eye

mausoléu /mawzoˈlɛw/ m mausoleum

maus-tratos /mawsˈtratus/ m pl ill-treatment

maxilar /maksiˈlar/ m jaw

máxima /'masima/ f maxim

maximizar /masimiˈzar/ vt maximize; (exagerar) play up

máximo /'masimu/ a (antes do substantivo) utmost, greatest; (depois do substantivo) maximum □ m maximum; **o** ~ (fam: o melhor) really something; **ao** ~ to the maximum; **no** ~ at most

maxixe /maˈʃiʃi/ m gherkin

me /mi/ pron me; (indireto) (to) me; (reflexivo) myself

meada /miˈada/ f skein; **perder o fio da** ~ lose one's thread

meados /miˈadus/ m pl ~ **de maio** mid-May

meandro /miˈadru/ f meander; pl (fig) twists and turns

mecâni|ca /me'kanika/ *f* mechanics; **~co** *a* mechanical □ *m* mechanic

meca|nismo /meka'nizmu/ *m* mechanism; **~nizar** *vt* mechanize

mecenas /me'sɛnas/ *m invar* patron

mecha /'mɛʃa/ *f* (*de vela*) wick; (*de bomba*) fuse; (*porção de cabelos*) lock; (*cabelo tingido*) highlight; **~do** *a* highlighted

meda|lha /me'daʎa/ *f* medal; **~lhão** *m* medallion; (*jóia*) locket

média /'mɛdʒia/ *f* average; (*cafe*) white coffee; **em ~** on average

medi|ação /medʒia'sãw/ *f* mediation; **~ador** *m* mediator; **~ante** *prep* through, by; **~ar** *vi* mediate

medica|ção /medʒika'sãw/ *f* medication; **~mento** *m* medicine

medição /medʒi'sãw/ *f* measurement

medicar /medʒi'kar/ *vt* treat □ *vi* practise medicine; **~-se** *vpr* dose o.s. up

medici|na /medʒi'sina/ *f* medicine; **~na legal** forensic medicine; **~nal** (*pl* **~nais**) *a* medicinal

médico /'mɛdʒiku/ *m* doctor □ *a* medical; **~-legal** (*pl* **~-legais**) *a* forensic; **~-legista** (*pl* **~-legistas**) *m/f* forensic scientist

medi|da /me'dʒida/ *f* measure; (*dimensão*) measurement; **à ~da que** as; **sob ~da** made to measure; **tirar as ~das de alg** take s.o.'s measurements; **~dor** *m* meter

medie|val /medʒie'vaw/ (*pl* **~vais**) *a* medieval

médio /'mɛdʒiu/ *a* (*típico*) average; *<tamanho, prazo>* medium; *<classe, dedo>* middle

mediocre /me'dʒiokri/ *a* mediocre

mediocridade /medʒiokri'dadʒi/ *f* mediocrity

medir /me'dʒir/ *vt* measure; **weigh** *<palavras>* □ *vi* measure; **~-se** *vpr* measure o.s.; **quanto você mede?** how tall are you?

medi|tação /medʒita'sãw/ *f* meditation; **~tar** *vi* meditate

mediterrâneo /medʒite'xaniu/ *a* Mediterranean □ *m* **o Mediterrâneo** the Mediterranean

médium /'mɛdʒiũ/ *m/f* medium

medo /'medu/ *m* fear; **ter ~ de** be afraid of; **com ~** afraid; **~nho** /o/ *a* frightful

medroso /me'drozu/ *a* fearful, timid

medula /me'dula/ *f* marrow

megalomania /megaloma'nia/ *f* megalomania

meia /'meja/ *f* (*comprida*) stocking; (*curta*) sock; (*seis*) six; **~-calça** (*pl* **~s-calças**) *f* tights, (*Amer*) pantihose; **~-idade** *f* middle age; **~-noite** *f* midnight; **~-volta** (*pl* **~s-voltas**) *f* about-turn

mei|go /'mejgu/ *a* sweet; **~guice** *f* sweetness

meio /'meju/ *a* half □ *adv* rather □ *m* (*centro*) middle; (*ambiente*) environment; (*recurso*) means; **~ litro** half a litre; **dois meses e ~** two and a half months; **em ~ a** amid; **por ~ de** through; **o ~ ambiente** the environment; **os ~s de comunicação** the media; **~-dia** *m* midday; **~-fio** *m* kerb; **~-termo** *m* (*acordo*) compromise

mel /mɛw/ *m* honey

mela|ço /me'lasu/ *m* molasses; **~do** *a* sticky □ *m* treacle

melancia /melã'sia/ *f* watermelon

melan|colia /melãko'lia/ *f* melancholy; **~cólico** *a* melancholy

melão /me'lãw/ *m* melon

melar /me'lar/ *vt* make sticky

melhor /me'ʎɔr/ *a* & *adv* better; **o ~** the best

melho|ra /me'ʎɔra/ *f* improvement; **~ras!** get well soon!; **~ramento** m improvement; **~rar** vt improve □ vi improve; <doente> get better

melin|drar /meli'drar/ vt hurt; **~drar-se** vpr be hurt; **~droso** /o/ a delicate; <pessoa> sensitive

melodi|a /melo'dʒia/ f melody; **~oso** /o/ a melodious

melodra|ma /melo'drama/ m melodrama; **~mático** a melodramatic

meloso /me'lozu/ a sickly sweet

melro /'mɛwxu/ m blackbird

membrana /mẽ'brana/ f membrane

membro /'mẽbru/ m member; (braço, perna) limb

memo|rando /memo'rãdu/ m memo; **~rável** (pl **~ráveis**) a memorable

memória /me'mɔria/ f memory; pl (autobiografia) memoirs

men|ção /mẽ'sãw/ f mention; fazer **~ção de** mention; **~cionar** vt mention

mendi|cância /mẽdʒi'kãsia/ f begging; **~gar** vi beg; **~go** m beggar

menina /me'nina/ f girl; **a ~ dos olhos de alg** the apple of s.o.'s eye

meningite /menĩ'ʒitʃi/ f meningitis

meni|nice /meni'nisi/ f (idade) childhood; **~no** m boy

menopausa /meno'pawza/ f menopause

menor /me'nɔr/ a smaller □ m/f minor; **o/a ~** the smallest; (mínimo) the slightest, the least

menos /'menos/ adv & pron less □ prep except; **dois dias a ~** two days less; **a ~ que** unless; **ao ou pelo ~** at least; **o ~ bonito** the least pretty; **~prezar** vt look down upon

mensa|geiro /mẽsa'ʒeru/ m messenger; **~gem** f message;

~gem de texto (telec) text message

men|sal /mẽ'saw/ (pl **~sais**) a monthly; **~salidade** f monthly payment; **~salmente** adv monthly

menstru|ação /mẽstrua'sãw/ f menstruation; **~ada** a **estar ~ada** be having one's period; **~al** (pl **~ais**) a menstrual; **~ar** vi menstruate

menta /'mẽta/ f mint

men|tal /mẽ'taw/ (pl **~tais**) a mental; **~talidade** f mentality; **~te** f mind

men|tir /mẽ'tʃir/ vi lie; **~tira** f lie; **~tiroso** /o/ a lying □ m liar

mentor /mẽ'tor/ m mentor

mercado /mer'kadu/ m market; **~ria** f commodity; pl goods

mercan|te /mer'kãtʃi/ a merchant; **~til** (pl **~tis**) a mercantile

mercê /mer'se/ f **à ~ de** at the mercy of

merce|aria /mersia'ria/ f grocer's; **~eiro** m grocer

mercenário /merse'nariu/ a & m mercenary

mercúrio /mer'kuriu/ m mercury; **Mercúrio** Mercury

merda /'mɛrda/ f (chulo) shit

mere|cedor /merese'dor/ a deserving; **~cer** vt deserve □ vi be deserving; **~cimento** m merit

merenda /me'rẽda/ f packed lunch; **~ escolar** school dinner

mere|trício /mere'trisiu/ m prostitution; **~triz** f prostitute

mergu|lhador /mergu̱ʎa'dor/ m diver; **~lhar** vt dip (em into) □ vi (na água) dive; (no trabalho) bury o.s.; **~lho** m dive; (esporte) diving; (banho de mar) dip

meridi|ano /meridʒi'anu/ m meridian; **~onal** (pl **~onais**) a southern

mérito /'mɛritu/ m merit

merluza /mer'luza/ f hake

mero /'mɛru/ a mere

mês /mes/ (pl **meses**) m month

mesa /'meza/ f table; (de trabalho) desk; ~ **de centro** coffee table; ~ **de jantar** dining table; ~ **telefônica** switchboard

mesada /me'zada/ f monthly allowance

mescla /'mɛskla/ f mixture, blend

mesmice /mez'misi/ f sameness

mesmo /'mezmu/ a same □ adv (até) even; (justamente) right; (de verdade) really; **você** ~ you yourself; **hoje** ~ this very day; ~ **assim** even so; ~ **que** even if; **dá no** ~ it comes to the same thing; **fiquei na mesma** I'm none the wiser

mesqui|nharia /meskiɲa'ria/ f meanness; (uma) mean thing; ~**nho** a mean

mesquita /mes'kita/ f mosque

Messias /me'sias/ m Messiah

mesti|cagem /mestʃi'saʒẽ/ f interbreeding; ~**ço** a <pessoa> of mixed race; <animal> crossbred □ m (pessoa) person of mixed race; (animal) mongrel

mes|trado /mes'tradu/ m master's degree; ~**tre** /ɛ/ m (f ~**tra**) master (f mistress); (de escola) teacher □ a male; <chave> master; ~**tre-de-obras** (pl ~-**tres-de-obras**) m foreman; ~**tre-sala** (pl ~**tres-salas**) m master of ceremonies (in carnival procession); ~**tria** f expertise

meta /'mɛta/ f (de corrida) finishing post; (gol, fig) goal

meta|bólico /meta'bɔliku/ a metabolic; ~**bolismo** m metabolism

metade /me'tadʒi/ f half; **pela** ~ halfway

metafísi|ca /meta'fizika/ f metaphysics; ~**co** a metaphysical

metáfora /me'tafora/ f metaphor

metafórico /meta'fɔriku/ a metaphorical

me|tal /me'taw/ (pl ~**tais**) m metal; pl (numa orquestra) brass; ~**tálico** a metallic

meta|lurgia /metalur'ʒia/ f metallurgy; ~**lúrgica** f metal works; ~**lúrgico** a metallurgical □ m metalworker

metamorfose /metamor'fɔzi/ f metamorphosis

metano /me'tanu/ m methane

meteórico /mete'ɔriku/ a meteoric

meteoro /mete'ɔru/ m meteor; ~**logia** f meteorology; ~**lógico** a meteorological; ~**logista** m/f (cientista) meteorologist; (na TV) weather forecaster

meter /me'ter/ vt put; ~**-se** vpr (envolver-se) get (**em** into); (intrometer-se) meddle (**em** in); ~ **medo** be frightening

meticuloso /metʃiku'lozu/ a meticulous

metido /me'tʃidu/ a snobbish; **ele é** ~ **a perito** he thinks he's an expert

metódico /me'tɔdʒiku/ a methodical

metodista /meto'dʒista/ a & m/f Methodist

método /'mɛtodu/ m method

metra|lhadora /metraʎa'dora/ f machine gun; ~**lhar** vt machine-gun

métri|co /'mɛtriku/ a metric; **fita** ~**ca** tape measure

metro[1] /'mɛtru/ m metre

metro[2] /'mɛtru/ m (Port: metropolitano) underground, (Amer) subway

metrô /me'tro/ m underground, (Amer) subway

metrópole /me'trɔpoli/ f metropolis

metropolitano /metropoli'tanu/ a metropolitan □ m (Port) underground, (Amer) subway

meu /mew/ a (f **minha** /ɲ/) pron (f **minha**) mine; **um amigo** ~ a friend of mine; **fico na**

minha (*fam*) I keep myself to myself

mexer /me'ʃer/ *vt* move; (*com colher etc*) stir □ *vi* move; **~-se** *vpr* move; (*apressar-se*) get a move on; **~ com** (*comover*) affect, get to; (*brincar com*) tease; (*trabalhar com*) work with; **~ em** touch

mexeri|ca /meʃe'rika/ *f* tangerine; **~car** *vi* gossip; **~co** *m* piece of gossip; *pl* gossip; **~queiro** *a* gossiping □ *m* gossip

mexicano /meʃi'kanu/ *a & m* Mexican

México /'mɛʃiku/ *m* Mexico

mexido /me'ʃidu/ *a* **ovos ~s** scrambled eggs

mexilhão /meʃi'ʎãw/ *m* mussel

mi|ado /mi'adu/ *m* miaow; **~ar** *vi* miaow

micreiro /mi'krejru/ *m* pc hacker

micróbio /mi'krɔbiu/ *m* microbe

micro|cosmo /mikro'kɔzmu/ *m* microcosm; **~empresa** /e/ *f* small business; **~empresário** *m* small businessman; **~filme** *m* microfilm; **~fone** *m* micro-phone; **~onda** *f* microwave; **(forno de) ~s** *m* microwave (oven); **~ônibus** *m* *invar* minibus; **~processador** *m* microprocessor

microrganismo /mikrorga-'nizmu/ *m* microorganism

microscó|pico /mikros'kɔpiku/ *a* microscopic; **~pio** *m* microscope

mídia /'midʒia/ *f* media

migalha /mi'gaʎa/ *f* crumb

mi|gração /migra'sãw/ *f* migration; **~grar** *vi* migrate

mijar /mi'ʒar/ *vi* (*fam*) pee; **~jar-se** *vpr* wet o.s.; **~jo** *m* (*fam*) pee

mil /miw/ *a & m invar* thousan **estar a ~** be on top form

mila|gre /mi'lagri/ *m* miracle; **~groso** /o/ *a* miraculous

milênio /mi'leniu/ *m* millennium

milésimo /mi'lɛzimu/ *a* thousandth

milha /'miʎa/ *f* mile

milhão /mi'ʎãw/ *m* million; **um ~ de dólares** a million dollars

milhar /mi'ʎar/ *m* thousand; **~es de vezes** thousands of times; **aos ~es** in their thousands

milho /'miʎo/ *m* maize, (*Amer*) corn

milico /mi'liku/ *m* (*fam*) military man; **os ~s** the military

mili|grama /mili'grama/ *m* milligram; **~litro** *m* millilitre; **~metro** /e/ *m* millimetre

milionário /milio'nariu/ *a & m* millionaire

mili|tante /mili'tãtʃi/ *a & m* militant; **~tar** *a* military □ *m* soldier

mim /mĩ/ *pron* me

mimar /mi'mar/ *vt* spoil

mímica /'mimika/ *f* mime; (*brincadeira*) charades

mi|na /'mina/ *f* mine; **~nar** *vt* mine; (*fig: prejudicar*) under-mine

mindinho /mĩ'dʒiɲu/ *m* little finger, (*Amer*) pinkie

mineiro /mi'neru/ *a* mining; (*de MG*) from Minas Gerais □ *m* miner; (*de MG*) person from Minas Gerais

mine|ração /minera'sãw/ *f* mining; **~ral** (*pl* **~rais**) *a & m* mineral; **~rar** *vt/i* mine

minério /mi'neriu/ *m* ore

mingau /mĩ'gaw/ *m* porridge

míngua /'mĩgwa/ *f* lack

minguante /mĩ'gwãtʃi/ *a* **quarto ~** last quarter

minguar /mĩ'gwar/ *vi* dwindle

minha /'miɲa/ *a & pron veja* **meu**

minhoca /mi'ɲɔka/ *f* worm

miniatura /minia'tura/ *f* miniature

mini|malista /minima'lista/ *a & m/f* minimalist; **~mizar** *vt* minimize; (*subestimar*) play down

mínimo /'minimu/ *a (muito pequeno)* tiny; *(mais baixo)* minimum □ *m* minimum; **a mínima idéia** the slightest idea; **no ~ at** least

minissaia /mini'saja/ *f* miniskirt

minis|terial /ministeri'aw/ *(pl ~teriais) a* ministerial; **~tério** *m* ministry; **Ministério do Interior** Home Office, *(Amer)* Department of the Interior

minis|trar /minis'trar/ *vt* administer; **~tro** *m* minister; **primeiro ~tro** prime minister

Minorca /mi'nɔrka/ *f* Menorca

mino|ritário /minori'tariu/ *a* minority; **~ria** *f* minority

minúcia /mi'nusia/ *f* detail

minucioso /minusi'ozu/ *a* thorough

minúscu|la /mi'nuskula/ *f* small letter; **~lo** *a ‹letra›* small; *(muito pequeno)* minuscule

minuta /mi'nuta/ *f (rascunho)* rough draft

minuto /mi'nutu/ *m* minute

miolo /mi'olu/ *f (de fruta)* flesh; *(de pão)* crumb; *pl* brains

míope /'miopi/ *a* short-sighted

miopia /mio'pia/ *f* myopia

mira /'mira/ *f* sight; **ter em ~** have one's sights on

mirabolante /mirabo'lãtʃi/ *a* amazing; *‹idéias, plano›* grandiose

mi|ragem /mi'raʒẽ/ *f* mirage; **~rante** *m* lookout; **~rar** *vt* look at; **~rar-se** *vpr* look at o.s.

mirim /mi'rĩ/ *a* little

miscelânea /mise'lania/ *f* miscellany

miscigenação /misiʒena'sãw/ *f* interbreeding

mise-en-plis /mizã'pli/ *m* shampoo and set

miserá|vel /mize'ravew/ *(pl ~veis) a* miserable

miséria /mi'zɛria/ *f* misery; *(pobreza)* poverty; **uma ~** *(pouco*

dinheiro) a pittance; **chorar ~** claim poverty

miseri|córdia /mizeri'kɔrdʒia/ *f* mercy; **~cordioso** *a* merciful

misógino /mi'zɔʒinu/ *m* misogynist □ *a* misogynistic

miss /'misi/ *f* beauty queen

missa /'misa/ *f* mass

missão /mi'sãw/ *f* mission

mís|sil /'misiw/ *(pl ~seis) m* missile; **~sil de longo alcance** long-range missile

missionário /misio'nariu/ *m* missionary

missiva /mi'siva/ *f* missive

mis|tério /mis'tɛriu/ *m* mystery; **~terioso** /o/ *a* mysterious; **~ticismo** *m* mysticism

místico /'mistʃiku/ *m* mystic □ *a* mystical

misto /'mistu/ *a* mixed □ *m* mix; **~ quente** toasted ham and cheese sandwich

mistu|ra /mis'tura/ *f* mixture; **~rar** *vt* mix; *(confundir)* mix up; **~rar-se** *vpr* mix (**com** with)

mítico /'mitʃiku/ *a* mythical

mito /'mitu/ *m* myth; **~logia** *f* mythology; **~lógico** *a* mythological

miudezas /miu'dezas/ *f pl* odds and ends

miúdo /mi'udu/ *a* tiny, minute; *‹chuva›* fine; *‹despesas›* minor □ *m (criança)* child, little one; *pl (de galinha)* giblets; **trocar em ~s** go into detail

mixaria /miʃa'ria/ *f (fam) ‹soma irrisória›* pittance

mixórdia /mi'ʃɔrdʒia/ *f* muddle

mnemônico /ne'moniku/ *a* mnemonic

mobilar /mobi'lar/ *vt (Port)* furnish

mobília /mo'bilia/ *f* furniture

mobili|ar /mobili'ar/ *vt* furnish; **~ário** *m* furniture

mobili|dade /mobili'dadʒi/ *f* mobility; **~zar** *vt* mobilize

moça /'mosa/ f girl

moçambicano /mosãbi'kanu/ a & m Mozambican

Moçambique /mosã'biki/ m Mozambique

moção /mo'sãw/ f motion

mochila /mo'ʃila/ f rucksack

moço /'mosu/ a young □ m boy, lad

moda /'mɔda/ f fashion; **na ∼** fashionable

modalidade /modali'dadʒi/ f (esporte) event

mode|lagem /mode'laʒẽ/ f modelling; **∼lar** vt model (a on); **∼lar-se** vpr model o.s. (a on) □ a model; **∼lo** /e/ m model

mode|ração /modera'sãw/ f moderation; **∼rado** a moderate; **∼rar** vt moderate; reduce <velocidade, despesas>; **∼rar-se** vpr restrain oneself

moder|nidade /moderni'dadʒi/ f modernity; **∼nismo** m modernism; **∼nista** a & m/f modernist; **∼nizar** vt modernize; **∼no** /ɛ/ a modern

modess /mo'dɛs/ m invar sanitary towel

modéstia /mo'dɛstʃia/ f modesty

modesto /mo'dɛstu/ a modest

módico /'mɔdʒiku/ a modest

modifi|cação /modʒifika'sãw/ f modification; **∼car** vt modify

mo|dismo /mo'dʒizmu/ m idiom; **∼dista** f dressmaker

modo /'mɔdu/ m way; (ling) mood; pl (maneiras) manners

modular /modu'lar/ vt modulate □ a modular

módulo /'mɔdulu/ m module

moeda /mo'ɛda/ f (peça de metal) coin; (dinheiro) currency

mo|edor /moe'dor/ m **∼edor de café** coffee-grinder; **∼edor de carne** mincer; **∼er** vt grind <café, trigo>; squeeze <cana>; mince <carne>; (bater) beat

mo|fado /mo'fadu/ a mouldy; **∼far** vi moulder; **∼fo** /o/ m mould

mogno /'mɔgnu/ m mahogany

moinho /mo'iɲu/ m mill; **∼ de vento** windmill

moisés /moj'zɛs/ m invar carrycot

moita /'mojta/ f bush

mola /'mɔla/ f spring

mol|dar /mow'dar/ vt mould; cast <metal>; **∼de** /ɔ/ m mould; (para costura etc) pattern

moldu|ra /mow'dura/ f frame; **∼rar** vt frame

mole /'mɔli/ a soft; <pessoa> listless; (fam) (fácil) easy □ adv easily; **é ∼?** (fam) can you believe it?

molécula /mo'lɛkula/ f molecule

moleque /mo'lɛki/ m (menino) lad; (de rua) urchin; (homem) scoundrel

molestar /moles'tar/ vt bother

moléstia /mo'lɛstʃia/ f disease

moletom /mole'tõ/ m (tecido) knitted cotton; (blusa) sweatshirt

moleza /mo'leza/ f softness; (de pessoa) laziness; **viver na ∼** lead a cushy life; **ser ∼** be easy

mo|lhado /mo'ʎadu/ a wet; **∼lhar** vt wet; **∼lhar-se** vpr get wet

molho[1] /'mɔʎu/ m (de chaves) bunch; (de palha) sheaf

molho[2] /'moʎu/ m sauce; (para salada) dressing; **deixar de ∼** leave in soak <roupa>; **∼ inglês** Worcester sauce

molusco /mo'lusku/ m mollusc

momen|tâneo /momẽ'taniu/ a momentary; **∼to** m moment; (força) momentum

Mônaco /'monaku/ m Monaco

monar|ca /mo'narka/ m/f monarch; **∼quia** f monarchy; **∼quista** a & m/f monarchist

monástico /mo'nastʃiku/ a monastic

monção /mõ'sãw/ f monsoon

mone|tário /mone'tariu/ *a* monetary; **~tarismo** *m* monetarism; **~tarista** *a* & *m/f* monetarist

monge /'mõʒi/ *m* monk

monitor /moni'tor/ *m* monitor; **~ de vídeo** VDU

monitorar /monito'rar/ *vt* monitor

mono|cromo /mono'krɔmu/ *a* monochrome; **~gamia** *f* monogamy

monógamo /mo'nɔgamu/ *a* monogamous

monograma /mono'grama/ *m* monogram

monólogo /mo'nɔlogu/ *m* monologue

mononucleose /mononukli'ɔzi/ *f* glandular fever

mono|pólio /mono'pɔliu/ *m* monopoly; **~polizar** *vt* monopolize

monossílabo /mono'silabu/ *a* monosyllabic □ *m* monosyllable

monotonia /monoto'nia/ *f* monotony

monótono /mo'nɔtonu/ *a* monotonous

monóxido /mo'nɔksidu/ *m* **~ de carbono** carbon monoxide

mons|tro /'mõstru/ *m* monster; **~truosidade** *f* monstrosity; **~truoso** /o/ *a* monstrous

monta|dor /mõta'dor/ *m* (*de cinema*) editor; **~dora** *f* assembly company; **~gem** *f* assembly; (*de filme*) editing; (*de peça teatral*) production

monta|nha /mõ'taɲa/ *f* mountain; **~nha-russa** (*pl* **~nhas-russas**) *f* roller coaster; **~nhismo** *m* mountaineering; **~nhoso** /o/ *a* mountainous

mon|tante /mõ'tãtʃi/ *m* amount □ *a* rising; **a ~tante** upstream; (*de cavalo, bicicleta*>; assemble <*peças, máquina*>; put up <*barraca*>; set up <*empresa, escritório*>; mount <*guarda, diamante*>; put on <*espetáculo, peça*>; edit <*filme*>

□ *vi* ride; **~tar a** <*dívidas etc*> amount to; <*valor etc*> mount up to; **~tar em** (*subir em*) mount; **~taria** *f* mount; **~te** *m* heap; **um ~te de coisas** (*fam*) loads of things; **o Monte Branco** Mont Blanc

Montevidéu /mõtʃivi'dɛw/ *f* Montevideo

montra /'mõtra/ *f* (*Port*) shop window

monumen|tal /monumẽ'taw/ (*pl* **~tais**) *a* monumental; **~to** *m* monument

mora|da /mo'rada/ *f* dwelling; (*Port*) address; **~dia** *f* dwelling; **~dor** *m* resident

mo|ral /mo'raw/ (*pl* **~rais**) *a* moral □ *f* (*ética*) morals; (*de uma história*) moral □ *m* (*ânimo*) morale; (*de pessoa*) moral sense; **~ralidade** *f* morality; **~ralista** *a* moralistic □ *m/f* moralist; **~ralizar** *vt* moralize

morango /mo'rãgu/ *m* strawberry

morar /mo'rar/ *vi* live

moratória /mora'tɔria/ *f* moratorium

mórbido /'mɔrbidu/ *a* morbid

morcego /mor'segu/ *m* bat

mor|daça /mor'dasa/ *f* gag; (*para cão*) muzzle; **~daz** *a* scathing; **~der** *vt/i* bite; **~dida** *f* bite

mordo|mia /mordo'mia/ *f* (*no emprego*) perk; (*de casa etc*) comfort; **~mo** /o/ *m* butler

more|na /mo'rena/ *f* brunette; **~no** *a* dark; (*bronzeado*) brown □ *m* dark person

morfina /mor'fina/ *f* morphine

moribundo /mori'bũdu/ *a* dying

moringa /mo'rĩga/ *f* water jug

morma|cento /morma'sẽtu/ *a* sultry; **~ço** *m* sultry weather

morno /'mornu/ *a* lukewarm

moro|sidade /morozi'dadʒi/ *f* slowness; **~so** /o/ *a* slow

morrer /mo'xer/ *vi* die; <*luz, dia, ardor, esperança etc*> fade; <*carro*> stall

morro /'moxu/ *m* hill; (*fig: favela*) slum

mortadela /morta'dɛla/ *f* mortadella, salami

mor|tal /mor'taw/ (*pl* ~**tais**) *a & m* mortal; ~**talha** *f* shroud; ~**talidade** *f* mortality; ~**tandade** *f* slaughter; ~**te** /ɔ/ *f* death; ~**tífero** *a* deadly; ~**tificar** *vt* mortify; ~**to** /o/ *a* dead

mosaico /mo'zajku/ *m* mosaic

mosca /'moska/ *f* fly

Moscou /mos'ku/, (*Port*) **Moscovo** /mof'kovu/ *f* Moscow

mosquito /mos'kitu/ *m* mosquito

mostarda /mos'tarda/ *f* mustard

mosteiro /mos'teru/ *m* monastery

mos|tra /'mɔstra/ *f* display; dar ~**tras de** show signs of; pôr à ~**tra** show up; ~**trador** *m* face, dial; ~**trar** *vt* show; ~**trar-se** *vpr* (*revelar-se*) show o.s. to be; (*exibir-se*) show off; ~**truário** *m* display case

mo|tel /mo'tɛw/ (*pl* ~**téis**) *m* motel

motim /mo'tʃĩ/ *m* riot; (*na marinha*) mutiny

moti|vação /motʃiva'sãw/ *f* motivation; ~**var** *vt* (*incentivar*) motivate; (*provocar*) cause; ~**vo** *m* (*razão*) reason; (*estímulo*) motive; (*na arte, música*) motif; **dar ~vo de** give cause for

moto /'mɔtu/ *f* motorbike; ~**ca** /mo'tɔka/ *f* (*fam*) motorbike

motoci|cleta /motosi'klɛta/ *f* motorcycle; ~**clismo** *m* motorcycling; ~**clista** *m/f* motorcyclist

motoqueiro /moto'keru/ *m* (*fam*) biker

motor /mo'tor/ *m* (*de carro, avião etc*) engine; (*elétrico*) motor □ *a* (*f* **motriz**) <*força*> driving; (*anat*) motor; ~ **de arranque** starter motor; ~ **de popa** outboard motor

moto|rista /moto'rista/ *m/f*

driver; ~**rizado** *a* motorized; ~**rizar** *vt* motorize

movedi|ço /move'dʒisu/ *a* unstable, moving; **areia** ~**ça** quicksand

mó|vel /'mɔvew/ (*pl* ~**veis**) *a* <*peça, parte*> moving; <*tropas*> mobile; <*festa*> movable □ *m* piece of furniture; *pl* furniture

mo|ver /mo'ver/ *vt* move; (*impulsionar, fig*) drive; ~**ver-se** *vpr* move; ~**vido** *a* driven; ~**vido a álcool** alcohol-powered

movimen|tação /movimẽta'sãw/ *f* bustle; ~**tado** *a* <*rua, loja*> busy; <*música*> up-beat, lively; <*pessoa, sessão*> lively; ~**tar** *vt* liven up; ~**tar-se** *vpr* move; ~**to** *m* movement; (*tecn*) motion; (*na rua etc*) activity

muam|ba /mu'ãba/ *f* contraband; ~**beiro** *m* smuggler

muco /'muku/ *m* mucus

muçulmano /musuw'manu/ *a & m* Muslim

mu|da /'muda/ *f* (*planta*) seedling; ~**da de roupa** change of clothes; ~**dança** *f* change; (*de casa*) move; (*de carro*) transmission; ~**dar** *vt/i* change; ~**dar de assunto** change the subject; ~**dar (de casa)** move (house); ~**dar de cor** change colour; ~**dar de idéia** change one's mind; ~**dar de lugar** change places; ~**dar de roupa** change (clothes); ~**dar-se** *vpr* move

mu|dez /mu'des/ *f* silence; ~**do** *a* silent; (*deficiente*) dumb; <*telefone*> dead □ *m* mute

mu|gido /mu'ʒidu/ *m* moo; ~**gir** *vi* moo

muito /'mũitu/ *a* a lot of; *pl* many □ *pron* a lot □ *adv* (*com adjetivo, advérbio*) very; (*com verbo*) a lot; ~ **maior** much bigger; ~ **tempo** a long time

mula /'mula/ *f* mule

mulato /muˈlatu/ a & m mulatto

muleta /muˈleta/ f crutch

mulher /muˈʎer/ f woman; (esposa) wife

mulherengo /muʎeˈrẽgu/ a womanizing □ m womanizer, ladies' man

mul|ta /ˈmuwta/ f fine; **~tar** vt fine

multicolor /muwtʃikoˈlor/ a multicoloured

multidão /muwtʃiˈdãw/ f crowd

multinacio|nal /muwtʃinasioˈnaw/ (pl **~nais**) a & f multinational

multipli|cação /muwtʃiplikaˈsãw/ f multiplication; **~car** vt multiply; **~car-se** vpr multiply; **~cidade** f multiplicity

múltiplo /ˈmuwtʃiplu/ a & m multiple

multirraci|al /muwtʃixasiˈaw/ (pl **~ais**) a multiracial

múmia /ˈmumia/ f mummy

mun|dano /mũˈdanu/ a <prazeres etc> worldly; <vida, mulher> society; **~dial** (pl **~diais**) a world □ m world championship; **~do** m world; **todo (o) ~do** everybody

munição /muniˈsãw/ f ammunition

muni|cipal /munisiˈpaw/ (pl **~cipais**) a municipal; **~cípio** m (lugar) borough, community; (prédio) town hall; (autoridade) local authority

munir /muˈnir/ vt provide (de with); **~-se** vpr equip o.s. (de with)

mu|ral /muˈraw/ (pl **~rais**) a & m mural; **~ralha** f wall

mur|char /murˈʃar/ vi <planta> wither, wilt; <salada> go limp; <beleza> fade □ vt wither, wilt <planta>; **~cho** a <planta> wilting; <pessoa> broken

mur|murar /murmuˈrar/ vi murmur; (queixar-se) mutter □ vt murmur; **~múrio** m murmur

muro /ˈmuru/ m wall

murro /ˈmuxu/ m punch

musa /ˈmuza/ f muse

muscu|lação /muskulaˈsãw/ f weight-training; **~lar** a muscular; **~latura** f musculature

músculo /ˈmuskulu/ m muscle

musculoso /muskuˈlozu/ a muscular

museu /muˈzew/ m museum

musgo /ˈmuzgu/ m moss

música /ˈmuzika/ f music; (uma) song; **~ de câmara** chamber music; **~ de fundo** background music; **~ clássica** ou **erudita** classical music

musi|cal /muziˈkaw/ (pl **~cais**) a & m musical; **~car** vt set to music

músico /ˈmuziku/ m musician □ a musical

musse /ˈmusi/ f mousse

mutilar /mutʃiˈlar/ vt mutilate; maim <pessoa>

mutirão /mutʃiˈrãw/ m joint effort

mútuo /ˈmutuu/ a mutual

muxoxo /muˈʃoʃu/ m **fazer ~** tut

N

na = em + a

nabo /ˈnabu/ m turnip

nação /naˈsãw/ f nation

nacio|nal /nasioˈnaw/ (pl **~nais**) a national; (brasileiro) home-produced; **~nalidade** f nationality; **~nalismo** m nationalism; **~nalista** a & m/f nationalist; **~nalizar** vt nationalize

naco /ˈnaku/ m chunk

nada /ˈnada/ pron nothing □ adv not at all; **de ~** (não há de quê) don't mention it; **que ~!**, **~ disso!** no way!

na|dadeira /nadaˈdera/ f (de peixe) fin; (de mergulhador)

flipper; ~**dador** *m* swimmer;
~**dar** *vi* swim

nádegas /'nadɛgas/ *f pl* buttocks

nado /'nadu/ *m* ~ **borboleta** butterfly stroke; ~ **de costas** backstroke; ~ **de peito** breaststroke;
atravessar a ~ swim across

náilon /'najlõ/ *m* nylon

naipe /'najpi/ *m* (*em jogo de cartas*) suit

namo|rada /namo'rada/ *f* girlfriend; ~**rado** *m* boyfriend; ~**rador** *a* amorous □ *m* ladies' man; ~**rar** *vt* (*ter relação com*) go out with; (*cobiçar*) eye up □ *vi* <*casal*> (*ter relação*) go out together; (*beijar-se etc*) kiss and cuddle; <*homem*> have a girlfriend; <*mulher*> have a boyfriend; ~**ro** /o/ *m* relationship

nanar /na'nar/ *vi* (*col*) sleep

nanico /na'niku/ *a* tiny

não /nãw/ *adv* not; (*resposta*) no □ *m* no; ~**-alinhado** *a* nonaligned; ~**-conformista** *a* & *m/f* non-conformist

naquela, naquele, naquilo = **em** + **aquela, aquele, aquilo**

narci|sismo /narsi'zizmu/ *m* narcissism; ~**sista** *m/f* narcissist □ *a* narcissistic; ~**so** *m* narcissus

narcótico /nar'kɔtʃiku/ *a* □ *m* narcotic

nari|gudo /nari'gudu/ *a* with a big nose; **ser** ~ **gudo** have a big nose; ~**na** /i/ nostril

nariz /na'ris/ *m* nose

nar|ração /naxa'sãw/ *f* narration; ~**rador** *m* narrator; ~**rar** *vt* narrate; ~**rativa** *f* narrative; ~**rativo** *a* narrative

nas = **em** + **as**

na|sal /na'zaw/ (*pl* ~**sais**) *a* nasal; ~**salizar** *vt* nasalize

nas|cença /na'sẽsa/ *f* birth; ~**cente** *a* nascent □ *f* source; ~**cer** *vi* be born; <*dente, espinha*> grow; <*planta*> sprout;

<*sol, lua*> rise; <*dia*> dawn; (*fig*) (*empresa, projeto etc*) come into being □ *m* o ~**cer do sol** sunrise; ~**cimento** *m* birth

nata /'nata/ *f* cream

natação /nata'sãw/ *f* swimming

Natal /na'taw/ *m* Christmas

na|tal /na'taw/ (*pl* ~**tais**) *a* <*país, terra*> native

nata|lício /nata'lisiu/ *a* & *m* birthday; ~**lidade** *f* **índice de** ~**lidade** birth rate; ~**lino** *a* Christmas

nati|vidade /natʃivi'dadʒi/ *f* nativity; ~**vo** *a* & *m* native

nato /'natu/ *a* born

natu|ral /natu'raw/ (*pl* ~**rais**) *a* natural; (*oriundo*) originating (**de** from) □ *m* native (**de** of)

natura|lidade /naturali'dadʒi/ *f* naturalness; **com** ~**lidade** matter-of-factly; **de** ~**lidade carioca** born in Rio de Janeiro; ~**lismo** *m* naturalism; ~**lista** *a* & *m/f* naturalist; ~**lizar** *vt* naturalize; ~**lizar-se** *vpr* become naturalized

natureza /natu'reza/ *f* nature; ~ **morta** still life

naturis|mo /natu'rizmu/ *m* naturism; ~**ta** *m/f* naturist

nau|fragar /nawfra'gar/ *vi* <*navio*> be wrecked; <*tripulação*> be shipwrecked; (*fig*) <*plano, casamento etc*> founder; ~**frágio** *m* shipwreck; (*fig*) failure

náufrago /'nawfragu/ *m* castaway

náusea /'nawzia/ *f* nausea

nauseabundo /nawzia'bũdu/ *a* nauseating

náuti|ca /'nawtʃika/ *f* navigation; ~**co** *a* nautical

na|val /na'vaw/ (*pl* ~**vais**) *a* naval; **construção** ~**val** shipbuilding

navalha /na'vaʎa/ *f* razor; ~**da** *f* cut with a razor

nave /'navi/ *f* nave; ~ **espacial** spaceship

nave|gação /navega'sãw/ *f* navigation; (*tráfego*) shipping; ~**gador** *m* navigator; (comput) browser; ~**gante** *m/f* seafarer; ~**gar** *vt* navigate; sail <*mar*> □ *vi* sail; (*traçar o rumo*) navigate; ~**gável** (*pl* ~**gáveis**) *a* navigable

navio /na'viu/ *m* ship; ~ **car-gueiro** cargo ship; ~ **de guerra** warship; ~ **petroleiro** oil tanker

nazista /na'zista/, (*Port*) **nazi** /na'zi/ *a* & *m/f* Nazi

neblina /ne'blina/ *f* mist

nebulo|sa /nebu'loza/ *f* nebula; ~**sidade** *f* cloud; ~**so** /o/ *a* cloudy; (*fig*) obscure

neces|saire /nese'sɛr/ *m* toilet bag; ~**sário** *a* necessary; ~**sidade** *f* necessity; (*que se impõe*) need; (*pobreza*) need; ~**sitado** *a* needy □ *m* person in need; ~**sitar** *vt* require; (*tornar necessário*) necessitate; ~**sitar de** need

necro|lógio /nekro'lɔʒiu/ *m* obituary column; ~**tério** *m* mortuary, (*Amer*) morgue

nectarina /nekta'rina/ *f* nectarine

nefasto /ne'fastu/ *a* fatal

ne|gação /nega'sãw/ *f* denial; (*ling*) negation; **ser uma** ~**gação em** be hopeless at; ~**gar** *vt* deny; ~**gar-se** a refuse to; ~**gativa** *f* refusal; (*ling*) negative; ~**gativo** *a* & *m* negative

negli|gência /negli'ʒẽsia/ *f* negligence; ~**genciar** *vt* neglect; ~**gente** *a* negligent

negoci|ação /negosia'sãw/ *f* negotiation; ~**ador** *m* negotiator; ~**ante** *m/f* dealer (**de** in); ~**ar** *vt/i* negotiate; ~ **ar em** deal in; ~**ata** *f* shady deal; ~**ável** (*pl* ~**áveis**) *a* negotiable

negócio /ne'gɔsiu/ *m* deal; (*fam: coisa*) thing; *pl* business; **a** *ou* **de** ~**s** <*viajar*> on business

negocista /nego'sista/ *m* wheeler-dealer □ *a* wheeler-dealing

ne|grito /ne'gritu/ *m* bold; ~**gro** /e/ *a* & *m* black; (*de raça*) Negro

nela, nele = **em** + **ela, ele**

nem /nẽj/ *adv* not even □ *conj* ~ ... ~ ... neither ... nor ...; ~ **sempre** not always; ~ **todos** not all; ~ **que** not even if; **que** ~ like; ~ **eu** nor do I

nenê /ne'ne/, **neném** /ne'nẽj/ *m* baby

nenhum /ne'ɲũ/ *a* (*f* **nenhuma**) no □ *pron* (*f* **nenhuma**) not one; ~ **dos dois** neither of them; ~ **erro** no mistakes; **erro** ~ no mistakes at all, not a single mistake; ~ **lugar** nowhere

nenúfar /ne'nufar/ *m* waterlily

neologismo /neolo'ʒizmu/ *m* neologism

néon /'nɛõ/ *m* neon

neozelan|dês /neozelã'des/ *a* (*f* ~**desa**) New Zealand □ *m* (*f* ~**desa**) New Zealander

Nepal /ne'paw/ *m* Nepal

nervo /'nervu/ *m* nerve; ~**sismo** *m* (*chateação*) annoyance; (*medo*) nervousness; ~**so** /o/ *a* <*sistema, doença*> nervous; (*chateado*) annoyed; (*medroso*) nervous; **deixar alg** ~**so** get on s.o.'s nerves

nessa(s), nesse(s) = **em** + **essa(s), esse(s)**

nesta(s), neste(s) = **em** + **esta(s), este(s)**

ne|ta /'nɛta/ *f* granddaughter; ~**to** /ɛ/ *m* grandson; *pl* grandchildren

neuro|logia /newrolo'ʒia/ *f* neurology; ~**lógico** *a* neurological; ~**logista** *m/f* neurologist

neu|rose /new'rɔzi/ *f* neurosis; ~**rótico** *a* neurotic

neutrali|dade /newtrali'dadʒi/ *f* neutrality; ~**zar** *vt* neutralize

neutrão /new'trãw/ *m* (*Port*) *veja* **nêutron**

neutro /'newtru/ *a* neutral

nêutron /'newtrõ/ *m* neutron

ne|vada /ne'vada/ *f* snowfall; **~vado** *a* snow-covered; **~var** *vi* snow; **~vasca** *f* snowstorm; **~ve** /ε/ *f* snow

névoa /'nεvoa/ *f* haze

nevoeiro /nevo'eru/ *m* fog

nexo /'nεksu/ *m* connection; **sem ~** incoherent

Nicarágua /nika'ragwa/ *f* Nicaragua

nicaragüense /nikara'gwẽsi/ *a* & *m/f* Nicaraguan

nicho /'niʃu/ *m* niche

nicotina /niko'tʃina/ *f* nicotine

Níger /'niʒer/ *m* Niger

Nigéria /ni'ʒεria/ *f* Nigeria

nigeriano /niʒeri'anu/ *a* & *m* Nigerian

Nilo /'nilu/ *m* Nile

ninar /ni'nar/ *vt* lull to sleep

ninfa /'nĩfa/ *f* nymph

ninguém /nĩ'gẽj/ *pron* no-one, nobody

ninhada /ni'nada/ *f* brood

ninharia /nina'ria/ *f* trifle

ninho /'ninu/ *m* nest

níquel /'nikew/ *m* nickel

nisei /ni'sej/ *a* & *m/f* Japanese Brazilian

nisso = **em** + **isso**

nisto = **em** + **isto**

nitidez /nitʃi'des/ *f* (*de imagem etc*) sharpness

nítido /'nitʃidu/ *a* < *imagem, foto* > sharp; < *diferença, melhora* > distinct, clear

nitrogênio /nitro'ʒeniu/ *m* nitrogen

ní|vel /'nivew/ (*pl* **~veis**) *m* level; **a ~vel de** in terms of

nivelamento /nivela'mẽtu/ *m* levelling

nivelar /nive'lar/ *vt* level

no = **em** + **o**

nó /nɔ/ *m* knot; **dar um ~** tie a knot; **~ dos dedos** knuckle; **~ na garganta** a lump in one's throat

nobre /'nɔbri/ *a* noble; < *bairro* > exclusive □ *m/f* noble; **~za** /e/ *f* nobility

noção /no'sãw/ *f* notion; *pl* (*rudimentos*) elements

nocaute /no'kawtʃi/ *m* knockout; **pôr alg ~** knock s.o. out; **~ar** *vt* knock out

nocivo /no'sivu/ *a* harmful

nódoa /'nodoa/ *f* (*Port*) stain

nogueira /no'gera/ *f* (*árvore*) walnut tree

noi|tada /noj'tada/ *f* night; **~te** *f* night; (*antes de dormir*) evening; **à ou de ~te** at night; (*antes de dormir*) in the evening; **hoje à ~te** tonight; **ontem à ~te** last night; **boa ~te** (*ao chegar*) good evening; (*ao despedir-se*) good night; **~te em branco ou claro** sleepless night

noi|vado /noj'vadu/ *m* engagement; **~va** *f* fiancée; (*no casamento*) bride; **~vo** *m* fiancé; (*no casamento*) bridegroom; **os ~vos** the engaged couple; (*no casamento*) the bride and groom; **ficar ~vo** get engaged

no|jento /no'ʒẽtu/ *a* disgusting; **~jo** /o/ *m* disgust

nômade /'nomadʒi/ *m/f* nomad □ *a* nomadic

nome /'nomi/ *m* name; **de ~** by name; **em ~ de** in the name of; **~ comercial** trade name; **~ de batismo** Christian name; **~ de guerra** professional name

nome|ação /nomia'sãw/ *f* appointment; **~ar** *vt* (*para cargo*) appoint; (*chamar pelo nome*) name

nomi|nal /nomi'naw/ (*pl* **~nais**) *a* nominal

nonagésimo /nona'ʒεzimu/ *a* ninetieth

nono /'nonu/ *a* & *m* ninth

nora /'nɔra/ *f* daughter-in-law

nordes|te /nor'dεstʃi/ *m* northeast; **~tino** *a* Northeastern □

m person from the Northeast (*of Brazil*)

nórdico /ˈnɔrdʒiku/ *a* Nordic

nor|ma /ˈnɔrma/ *f* norm; **~mal** (*pl* **~mais**) *a* normal

normali|dade /normali'dadʒi/ *f* normality; **~zar** *vt* bring back to normal; normalize <*relações diplomáticas*>; **~zar-se** *vpr* return to normal

noroeste /noro'ɛstʃi/ *a & m* northwest

norte /ˈnɔrtʃi/ *a & m* north; **~africano** *a & m* North African; **~-americano** *a & m* North American; **~-coreano** *a & m* North Korean

nortista /nor'tʃista/ *a* Northern □ *m/f* Northerner

Noruega /noru'ɛga/ *f* Norway

norue|guês /norue'ges/ *a & m* (*f* **~guesa**) Norwegian

nos¹ = **em** + **os**

nos² /nus/ *pron* us; (*indireto*) to us; (*reflexivo*) ourselves

nós /nɔs/ *pron* we; (*depois de preposição*) us

nos|sa /ˈnɔsa/ *int* gosh; **~so** /ɔ/ *a* our □ *pron* ours

nos|talgia /nostaw'ʒia/ *f* nostalgia; **~tálgico** *a* nostalgic

nota /ˈnɔta/ *f* note; (*na escola etc*) mark; (*conta*) bill; **custar uma ~** (*preta*) (*fam*) cost a bomb; **tomar ~** take note (**de** of); **~ fiscal** receipt

no|tação /nota'sãw/ *f* notation; **~tar** *vt* notice, note; **fazer ~tar** point out; **~tável** (*pl* **~táveis**) *a & m/f* notable

notícia /no'tʃisia/ *f* piece of news; *pl* news

notici|ar /notʃi'sjar/ *vt* report; **~ário** *m* (*na TV*) news; (*em jornal*) news section; **~ta** *m/f* (*na TV*) newsreader; (*em jornal*) news reporter; **~oso** /ɔ/ *a* **agência ~osa** news agency

notifi|cação /notʃifika'sãw/ *f* notification; **~car** *vt* notify

notívago /no'tʃivagu/ *a* nocturnal □ *m* night person

notório /no'tɔriu/ *a* well-known

noturno /no'turnu/ *a* night; <*animal*> nocturnal

nova /ˈnɔva/ *f* piece of news; **~mente** *adv* again

novato /no'vatu/ *m* novice

nove /ˈnɔvi/ *a & m* nine; **~centos** *a & m* nine hundred

novela /no'vela/ *f* (*na TV*) soap opera; (*livro*) novella

novembro /no'vẽbru/ *m* November

noventa /no'vẽta/ *a & m* ninety

noviço /no'visu/ *m* novice

novidade /novi'dadʒi/ *f* novelty; (*notícia*) piece of news; *pl* (*notícias*) news

novilho /no'viʎu/ *m* calf

novo /ˈnovu/ *a* new; (*jovem*) young; **de ~** again; **~ em folha** brand new

noz /nɔs/ *f* walnut; **~ moscada** nutmeg

nu /nu/ *a* (*f* **~a**) <*corpo, pessoa*> naked; <*braço, parede, quarto*> bare □ *m* nude; **~ em pêlo** stark naked; **a verdade ~a e crua** the plain truth

nuança /nu'ãsa/ *f* nuance

nu|blado /nu'bladu/ *a* cloudy; **~blar** *vt* cloud; **~blar-se** *vpr* cloud over

nuca /ˈnuka/ *f* nape of the neck

nuclear /nukli'ar/ *a* nuclear

núcleo /ˈnukliu/ *m* nucleus

nu|dez /nu'des/ *f* nakedness; (*na TV etc*) nudity; (*da parede etc*) bareness; **~dismo** *m* nudism; **~dista** *m/f* nudist

nulo /ˈnulu/ *a* void

num, numa(s) = **em** + **um, uma(s)**

nume|ral /nume'raw/ (*pl* **~rais**) *a & m* numeral; **~rar** *vt* number

numérico /nu'mɛriku/ *a* numerical

número /'numeru/ *m* number; (*de jornal, revista*) issue; (*de sapatos*) size; (*espetáculo*) act; **fazer ~** make up the numbers

numeroso /nume'rozu/ *a* numerous

nunca /'nũka/ *adv* never; **~ mais** never again

nuns = **em + uns**

nupci|al /nupsi'aw/ (*pl* **~ais**) *a* bridal

núpcias /'nupsias/ *f pl* marriage

nu|trição /nutri'sãw/ *f* nutrition; **~trir** *vt* nourish; (*fig*) harbour <*ódio, esperança*>; **~tritivo** *a* nourishing; <*valor*> nutritional

nuvem /'nuvẽ/ *f* cloud

O

o /u/ *artigo* the □ *pron* (*homem*) him; (*coisa*) it; (*você*) you; **~ que** (*a coisa que*) what; (*aquele que*) the one that; **~ quê?** what?; **meu livro e ~ do João** my book and John's (one)

ó /ɔ/ *int* (*fam*) look

ô /o/ *int* oh

oásis /o'azis/ *m invar* oasis

oba /'oba/ *int* great

obcecar /obise'kar/ *vt* obsess

obe|decer /obede'ser/ *vt* **~decer** a obey; **~diência** *f* obedience; **~diente** *a* obedient

obe|sidade /obezi'dadʒi/ *f* obesity; **~so** /e/ *a* obese

óbito /'ɔbitu/ *m* death

obituário /obitu'ariu/ *m* obituary

obje|ção /obiʒe'sãw/ *f* objection; **~tar** *vt/i* object (**a** to)

objeti|va /obiʒe'tʃiva/ *f* lens; **~vidade** *f* objectivity; **~vo** *a & m* objective

objeto /obi'ʒetu/ *m* object

oblíquo /o'blikwu/ *a* oblique; <*olhar*> sidelong

obliterar /oblite'rar/ *vt* obliterate

oblongo /o'blõgu/ *a* oblong

obo|é /obo'ɛ/ *m* oboe; **~ísta** *m/f* oboist

obra /'ɔbra/ *f* work; **em ~s** being renovated; **~ de arte** work of art; **~ de caridade** charity; **~-prima** (*pl* **~s-primas**) *f* masterpiece

obri|gação /obriga'sãw/ *f* obligation; (*título*) bond; **~gado** *int* thank you; (*não querendo*) no thank you; **~gar** *vt* force, oblige (**a** to); **~gar-se** *vpr* undertake (**a** to); **~gatório** *a* obligatory, compulsory

obsce|nidade /obiseni'dadʒi/ *f* obscenity; **~no** /e/ *a* obscene

obscu|ridade /obiskuri'dadʒi/ *f* obscurity; **~ro** *a* obscure

obséquio /obi'sɛkiu/ *m* favour

obsequioso /obiseki'ozu/ *a* obsequious

obser|vação /observa'sãw/ *f* observation; **~vador** *a* observant □ *m* observer; **~vância** *f* observance; **~var** *vt* observe; **~vatório** *m* observatory

obses|são /obise'sãw/ *f* obsession; **~sivo** *a* obsessive

obsoleto /obiso'letu/ *a* obsolete

obstáculo /obis'takulu/ *m* obstacle

obstar /obis'tar/ *vt* stand in the way (**a** of)

obs|tetra /obis'tɛtra/ *m/f* obstetrician; **~tetrícia** *f* obstetrics; **~tétrico** *a* obstetric

obsti|nação /obistina'sãw/ *f* obstinacy; **~nado** *a* obstinate; **~nar-se** *vpr* insist (**em** on)

obstru|ção /obistru'sãw/ *f* obstruction; **~ir** *vt* obstruct

ob|tenção /obitẽ'sãw/ *f* obtaining; **~ter** *vt* obtain

obtu|ração /obitura'sãw/ *f* filling; **~rador** *m* shutter; **~rar** *vt* fill <*dente*>

obtuso /obi'tuzu/ a obtuse

óbvio /'ɔbviu/ a obvious

ocasi|ão /okazi'ãw/ f occasion; (*oportunidade*) opportunity; (*compra*) bargain; ~**onal** (*pl* ~**onais**) a chance; ~**onar** vt cause

Oceania /osia'nia/ f Oceania

oce|ânico /osi'aniku/ a ocean; ~**ano** m ocean

ociden|tal /oside'taw/ (*pl* ~**tais**) a western □ m/f Westerner; ~**te** m West

ócio /'ɔsiu/ m (*lazer*) leisure; (*falta de trabalho*) idleness

ocioso /osi'ozu/ a idle □ m idler

oco /'oku/ a hollow; <*cabeça*> empty

ocor|rência /oko'xẽsia/ f occurrence; ~**rer** vi occur (**a** to)

ocu|lar /oku'lar/ a testemunha ~**lar** eye witness; ~**lista** m/f optician

óculos /'ɔkulus/ m pl glasses; ~ **de sol** sunglasses

ocul|tar /okuw'tar/ vt conceal; ~**to** a hidden; (*sobrenatural*) occult

ocu|pação /okupa'sãw/ f occupation; ~**pado** a <*pessoa*> busy; <*cadeira*> taken; <*telefone*> engaged, (*Amer*) busy; ~**par** vt occupy; take up <*tempo, espaço*>; hold <*cargo*>; ~**par-se** vpr keep busy; ~**par-se com** ou **de** be involved with <*política, literatura etc*>; take care of <*cliente, doente, problema*>; occupy one's time with <*leitura, palavras cruzadas etc*>

odiar /odʒi'ar/ vt hate

ódio /'ɔdʒiu/ m hatred, hate; (*raiva*) anger

odioso /odʒi'ozu/ a hateful

odontologia /odõtolo'ʒia/ f dentistry

odor /o'dor/ m odour

oeste /o'ɛstʃi/ a & m west

ofe|gante /ofe'gãtʃi/ a panting;
~**gar** vi pant

ofen|der /ofẽ'der/ vt offend; ~**der-se** vpr take offence; ~**sa** f insult; ~**siva** f offensive; ~**sivo** a offensive

ofere|cer /ofere'ser/ vt offer; ~**cer-se** vpr <*pessoa*> offer o.s. (**como** as); <*ocasião*> arise; ~**cer-se para ajudar** offer to help; ~**cimento** m offer

oferenda /ofe'rẽda/ f offering

oferta /o'fɛrta/ f offer; **em** ~ on offer; **a** ~ **e a demanda** supply and demand

ofici|al /ofisi'aw/ (*pl* ~**ais**) a official □ m officer; ~**alizar** vt make official; ~**ar** vi officiate

oficina /ofi'sina/ f workshop; (*para carros*) garage, (*Amer*) shop

ofício /o'fisiu/ m (*profissão*) trade; (*na igreja*) service

oficioso /ofisi'ozu/ a unofficial

ofus|cante /ofus'kãtʃi/ a dazzling; ~**car** vt dazzle <*pessoa*>; obscure <*sol etc*>; (*fig: eclipsar*) outshine

OGM /oʒe'em/ m (*biol*) GMO

oi /oj/ int (*cumprimento*) hi; (*resposta*) yes?

oi|tavo /oi'tavu/ a & m eighth; ~**tenta** a & m eighty; ~**to** a & m eight; ~**tocentos** a & m eight hundred

olá /o'la/ int hello

olaria /ola'ria/ f pottery

óleo /'ɔliu/ m oil

oleo|duto /oliu'dutu/ m oil pipeline; ~**so** /o/ a oily

olfato /ow'fatu/ m sense of smell

olhada /o'ʎada/ f look; **dar uma** ~ have a look

olhar /o'ʎar/ vt look at; (*assistir*) watch □ vi look □ m look; ~ **para** look at; ~ **por** look after; **olhe lá** (*fam*) and that's pushing it

olheiras /o'ʎeras/ f pl dark rings under one's eyes

olho /'oʎu/ *m* eye; **a ~ nu** with the naked eye; **custar os ~s da cara** cost a fortune; **ficar de ~** keep an eye out; **ficar de ~** keep an eye on; **pôr alg no ~ da rua** throw s.o. out; **não pregar o ~** not sleep a wink; **~ gordo** *ou* **grande** envy; **~ mágico** peephole; **~ roxo** black eye

Olimpíada /oli'piada/ *f* Olympic Games

olímpico /o'lĩpiku/ *a* <*jogos, vila*> Olympic; (*fig*) blithe

oliveira /oli'vera/ *f* olive tree

olmo /'owmu/ *m* elm

om|breira /õ'brera/ *f* (*para roupa*) shoulder pad; **~bro** *m* shoulder; **dar de ~bros** shrug one's shoulders

omelete /ome'lɛtʃi/, (*Port*) **omeleta** /ome'leta/ *f* omelette

omis|são /omi'sãw/ *f* omission; **~so** *a* negligent, remiss

omitir /omi'tʃir/ *vt* omit

omni- (*Port*) *veja* **oni-**

omoplata /omo'plata/ *f* shoulder blade

onça[1] /'õsa/ *f* (*peso*) ounce

onça[2] /'õsa/ *f* (*animal*) jaguar

onda /'õda/ *f* wave; **pegar ~** (*fam*) surf

onde /'õdʒi/ *adv* where; **por ~?** which way?; **~ quer que** wherever

ondu|lação /õdula'sãw/ *f* undulation; (*do cabelo*) wave; **~lado** *a* wavy; **~lante** *a* undulating; **~lar** *vt* wave <*cabelo*> □ *vi* undulate

onerar /one'rar/ *vt* burden

ônibus /'onibus/ *m invar* bus; **~ espacial** space shuttle

onipotente /onipo'tẽtʃi/ *a* omnipotent

onírico /o'niriku/ *a* dreamlike

onisciente /onisi'ẽtʃi/ *a* omniscient

onomatopéia /onomato'pɛja/ *f* onomatopoeia

ontem /'õtẽ/ *adv* yesterday

onze /'õzi/ *a & m* eleven

opaco /o'paku/ *a* opaque

opala /o'pala/ *f* opal

opção /opi'sãw/ *f* option

ópera /'ɔpera/ *f* opera

ope|ração /opera'sãw/ *f* operation; (*bancária etc*) transaction; **~rador** *m* operator; **~rar** *vt* operate; operate on <*doente*>; work <*milagre*> □ *vi* operate; **~rar-se** *vpr* (*acontecer*) come about; (*fazer operação*) have an operation; **~rário** *a* working □ *m* worker

opereta /ope'reta/ *f* operetta

opinar /opi'nar/ *vi* think □ *vi* express one's opinion

opinião /opini'ãw/ *f* opinion; **na minha ~** in my opinion; **~ pública** public opinion

ópio /'ɔpiu/ *m* opium

opor /o'por/ *vt* put up <*resistência, argumento*>; (*pôr em contraste*) contrast (a with); **~-se a** (*não aprovar*) oppose; (*ser diferente*) contrast with

oportu|nidade /oportuni'dadʒi/ *f* opportunity; **~nista** *a & m/f* opportunist; **~no** *a* opportune

oposi|ção /opozi'sãw/ *f* opposition (a to); **~cionista** *a* opposition □ *m/f* opposition politician

oposto /o'postu/ *a & m* opposite

opres|são /opre'sãw/ *f* oppression; (*no peito*) tightness; **~sivo** *a* oppressive; **~sor** *m* oppressor

oprimir /opri'mir/ *vt* oppress; (*com trabalho*) weigh down □ *vi* be oppressive

optar /opi'tar/ *vi* opt (*por* for); **~ por ir** opt to go

óptica, óptico *veja* **ótica, ótico**

opu|lência /opu'lẽsia/ *f* opulence; **~lento** *a* opulent

ora /'ɔra/ *adv & conj* now □ *int* come; **~ essa!** come now!; **~ ..., ~ ...** first ..., then

oração /ora'sãw/ f (prece) prayer; (discurso) oration; (frase) clause

oráculo /o'rakulu/ m oracle

orador /ora'dor/ m orator

oral /o'raw/ (pl **orais**) a & f oral

orar /o'rar/ vi pray

órbita /'ɔrbita/ f orbit; (do olho) socket

orçamen|tário /orsamẽ'tariu/ a budgetary; ~**to** m (plano financeiro) budget; (previsão dos custos) estimate

orçar /or'sar/ vt estimate (**em** at)

ordeiro /or'deru/ a orderly

ordem /'ɔrdẽ/ f order; **por** ~ **alfabética** in alphabetical order; ~ **de pagamento** banker's draft; ~ **do dia** agenda

orde|nação /ordena'sãw/ f ordering; (de padre) ordination; ~**nado** a ordered □ m wages; ~**nar** vt order; put in order <papéis, livros etc>; ordain <padre>

ordenhar /orde'ɲar/ vt milk

ordinário /ordʒi'nariu/ a (normal) ordinary; (grosseiro) vulgar; (de má qualidade) inferior; (sem caráter) rough

ore|lha /o'reʎa/ f ear; ~**lhão** m phone booth; ~**lhudo** a with big ears; **ser** ~**lhudo** have big ears

orfanato /orfa'natu/ m orphanage

ór|fão /'ɔrfãw/ (pl ~**fãos**) a & m (f ~**fã**) orphan

orgânico /or'ganiku/ a organic

orga|nismo /orga'nizmu/ m organism; (do Estado etc) institution; ~ **geneticamente modificado** GMO; ~**nista** m/f organist

organi|zação /organiza'sãw/ f organization; ~**zador** a organizing □ m organizer; ~**zar** vt organize

órgão /'ɔrgãw/ (pl ~**s**) m organ; (do Estado etc) body

orgasmo /or'gazmu/ m orgasm

orgia /or'ʒia/ f orgy

orgu|lhar /orgu'ʎar/ vt make proud; ~**lhar-se** vpr be proud (**de** of); ~**lho** m pride; ~**lhoso** /o/ a proud

orien|tação /oriẽta'sãw/ f orientation; (direção) direction; (vocacional etc) guidance; ~**tador** m advisor; ~**tal** (pl ~**tais**) a eastern; (da Asia) oriental; ~**tar** vt direct; (aconselhar) advise; (situar) position; ~**tar-se** vpr get one's bearings; ~**tar-se por** be guided by; ~**te** m east; **Oriente Médio** Middle East; **Extremo Oriente** Far East

orifício /ori'fisiu/ m opening; (no corpo) orifice

origem /o'riʒẽ/ f origin; **dar** ~ **a** give rise to; **ter** ~ originate

origi|nal /oriʒi'naw/ (pl ~**nais**) a & m original; ~**nalidade** f originality; ~**nar** vt give rise to; ~**nar-se** vpr originate; ~**nário** a <planta, animal> native (**de** to); <pessoa> originating (**de** from)

oriundo /o'rjũdu/ a originating (**de** from)

orla /'ɔrla/ f border; ~ **marítima** seafront

orna|mentação /ornamẽta'sãw/ f ornamentation; ~**tal** (pl ~**tais**) a ornamental; ~**tar** vt decorate; ~**to** m ornament

orques|tra /or'kestra/ f orchestra; ~**tra sinfônica** symphony orchestra; ~**tral** (pl ~**trais**) a orchestral; ~**trar** vt orchestrate

orquídea /or'kidʒia/ f orchid

ortodoxo /orto'doksu/ a orthodox

orto|grafia /ortogra'fia/ f spelling, orthography; ~**gráfico** a orthographic

orto|pedia /ortope'dʒia/ f orthopaedics; ~**pédico** a orthopaedic; ~**pedista** m/f orthopaedic surgeon

orvalho /or'vaʎu/ m dew

os /us/ artigo & pron veja **o**

oscilar /osi'lar/ *vi* oscillate

ósseo /'ɔsiu/ *a* bone

os|so /'osu/ *m* bone; **~sudo** *a* bony

ostensivo /ostẽ'sivu/ *a* ostensible

osten|tação /ostẽta'sãw/ *f* ostentation; **~tar** *vt* show off; **~toso** *a* showy, ostentatious

osteopata /ostfio'pata/ *m/f* osteopath

ostra /'ostra/ *f* oyster

ostracismo /ostra'sizmu/ *m* ostracism

otário /o'tariu/ *m* (*fam*) fool

óti|ca /'ɔtfika/ *f* (*ciência*) optics; (*loja*) optician's; (*ponto de vista*) viewpoint; **~co** *a* optical

otimis|mo /otfi'mizmu/ *m* optimism; **~ta** *m/f* optimist □ *a* optimistic

ótimo /'ɔtfimu/ *a* excellent

otorrino /oto'xinu/ *m* ear, nose and throat specialist

ou /o/ *conj* or; **~ ... ~ ...** either ... or ...; **~ seja** in other words

ouriço /o'risu/ *m* hedgehog; **~do-mar** (*pl* **~s-do-mar**) *m* sea urchin

ouri|ves /o'rivis/ *m/f invar* jeweller; **~vesaria** *f* (*loja*) jeweller's

ouro /'oru/ *m* gold; *pl* (*naipe*) diamonds; **de ~** golden

ou|sadia /oza'dʒia/ *f* daring; (*uma*) daring step; **~sado** *a* daring; **~sar** *vt/i* dare

outdoor /'awtdor/ (*pl* **~s**) *m* billboard

outo|nal /oto'naw/ (*pl* **~nais**) *a* autumnal; **~no** /o'tonu/ *m* autumn, (*Amer*) fall

outorgar /otor'gar/ *vt* grant

ou|trem /o'trẽj/ *pron* (*outro*) someone else; (*outros*) others; **~tro** *a* other □ *pron* (*um*) another (*one*); *pl* others; **~tro copo** another glass; **~tra coisa** something else; **~tro dia** the other day; **no ~tro dia** the next

day; **~tra vez** again; **~trora** *adv* once upon a time; **~trossim** *adv* equally

outubro /o'tubru/ *m* October

ou|vido /o'vidu/ *m* ear; **de ~vido** by ear; **dar ~vidos a** listen to; **~vinte** *m/f* listener; **~vir** *vt* hear; (*atentamente*) listen to □ *vi* hear; **~vir dizer que** hear that; **~vir falar de** hear of

ovação /ova'sãw/ *f* ovation

oval /o'vaw/ (*pl* **ovais**) *a* & *f* oval

ovário /o'variu/ *m* ovary

ovelha /o'veʎa/ *f* sheep

óvni /'ɔvni/ *m* UFO

ovo /'ovu/ *m* egg; **~ cozido/frito/mexido/pochê** boiled/fried/scrambled/poached egg

oxi|genar /oksiʒe'nar/ *vt* bleach <*cabelo*>; **~gênio** *m* oxygen

ozônio /o'zoniu/ *m* ozone

P

pá /pa/ *f* spade; (*de hélice*) blade; (*de moinho*) sail □ *m* (*Port: fam*) mate

pacato /pa'katu/ *a* quiet

paci|ência /pasi'ẽsia/ *f* patience; **~ente** *a* & *m/f* patient

pacificar /pasifi'kar/ *vt* pacify

pacífico /pa'sifiku/ *a* peaceful; **Oceano Pacífico** Pacific Ocean; **ponto ~** undisputed point

pacifis|mo /pasi'fizmu/ *m* pacifism; **~ta** *a* & *m/f* pacifist

paço /'pasu/ *m* palace

pacote /pa'kɔtʃi/ *m* (*de biscoitos etc*) packet; (*mandado pelo correio*) parcel; (*econômico, turístico, software*) package

pacto /'paktu/ *m* pact

padaria /pada'ria/ *f* baker's (shop), bakery

padecer /pade'ser/ *vt/i* suffer

padeiro /pa'deru/ *m* baker

padiola /padʒi'ɔla/ *f* stretcher

padrão /pa'drãw/ *m* standard; (*desenho*) pattern

padrasto /pa'drastu/ *m* stepfather

padre /'padri/ *m* priest

padrinho /pa'driɲu/ *m* (*de batismo*) godfather; (*de casamento*) best man

padroeiro /padro'eru/ *m* patron saint

padronizar /padroni'zar/ *vt* standardize

paga /'paga/ *f* pay; **~mento** *m* payment

pai|gão /pa'gãw/ (*pl* **~gãos**) *a* & *m* (*f* **~gã**) pagan

pagar /pa'gar/ *vt* pay for <*compra, erro etc*>; pay <*dívida, conta, empregado etc*>; pay back <*empréstimo*>; repay <*gentileza etc*> □ *vi* pay; **eu pago para ver** I'll believe it when I see it

página /'paʒina/ *f* page; **~ web** web page

pago /'pagu/ *a* paid □ *pp de* **pagar**

pagode /pa'gɔdʒi/ *m* (*torre*) pagoda; (*fam*) singalong

pai /paj/ *m* father; *pl* (*pai e mãe*) parents; **~-de-santo** (*pl* **~s-de-santo**) *m* macumba priest

pai|nel /paj'nɛw/ (*pl* **~néis**) *m* panel; (*de carro*) dashboard

paio /'paju/ *m* pork sausage

pairar /paj'rar/ *vi* hover

país /pa'is/ *m* country; **País de Gales** Wales; **Países Baixos** Netherlands

paisa|gem /paj'zaʒẽ/ *f* landscape; **~gista** *m*/*f* landscape gardener

paisana /paj'zana/ *f* **à ~** <*policial*> in plain clothes; <*soldado*> in civilian clothes

paixão /pa'ʃãw/ *f* passion

pala /'pala/ *f* (*de boné*) peak; (*de automóvel*) sun visor

palácio /pa'lasiu/ *m* palace

paladar /pala'dar/ *m* palate, taste

palanque /pa'lãki/ *m* stand

palavra /pa'lavra/ *f* word; **pedir a ~** ask to speak; **ter ~** be

reliable; **tomar a ~** start to speak; **sem ~** <*pessoa*> unreliable; **~ de ordem** watchword; **~s cruzadas** crossword

palavrão /pala'vrãw/ *m* swearword

palco /'pawku/ *m* stage

palestino /pales'tʃinu/ *a* & *m* Palestinian

palestra /pa'lɛstra/ *f* lecture

paleta /pa'leta/ *f* palette

paletó /pale'tɔ/ *m* jacket

palha /'paʎa/ *f* straw

palha|cada /paʎa'sada/ *f* joke; **~ço** *m* clown

paliativo /palia'tʃivu/ *a* & *m* palliative

palidez /pali'des/ *f* paleness

pálido /'palidu/ *a* pale

pali|tar /pali'tar/ *vi* pick one's teeth; **~teiro** *m* toothpick holder; **~to** *m* (*para dentes*) toothpick; (*de fósforo*) matchstick; (*pessoa magra*) beanpole

pal|ma /'pawma/ *f* palm; *pl* (*aplauso*) clapping; **bater ~mas** clap; **~meira** *f* palm tree; **~mito** *m* palm heart; **~mo** *m* span; **~mo a ~mo** inch by inch

palpá|vel /paw'pavew/ (*pl* **~veis**) *a* palpable

pálpebra /'pawpebra/ *f* eyelid

palpi|tação /pawpita'sãw/ *f* palpitation; **~tante** *a* (*fig*) thrilling; **~tar** *vi* <*coração*> flutter; <*pessoa*> tremble; (*dar palpite*) stick one's oar in; **~te** *m* (*pressentimento*) hunch; (*no jogo etc*) tip; **dar ~te** stick one's oar in

panacéia /pana'sɛja/ *f* panacea

Panamá /pana'ma/ *m* Panama

panamenho /pana'meɲu/ *a* & *m* Panamanian

pan-americano /panameri'kanu/ *a* Pan-American

pança /'pãsa/ *f* paunch

pancada /pã'kada/ *f* blow; **~ d'água** downpour; **~ria** *f* fight, punch-up

pâncreas /'pãkrias/ *m invar* pancreas

pançudo /pã'sudu/ *a* paunchy

panda /'pãda/ *f* panda

pandarecos /pãda'rɛkus/ *m pl* **aos ou em ~** battered

pandeiro /pã'deru/ *m* tambourine

pandemônio /pãde'moniu/ *m* pandemonium

pane /'pani/ *f* breakdown

panela /pa'nɛla/ *f* saucepan; **~ de pressão** pressure cooker

panfleto /pã'fletu/ *m* pamphlet

pânico /'paniku/ *m* panic; **em ~** in a panic; **entrar em ~** panic

panifica|ção /panifika'sãw/ *f* bakery; **~dora** *f* bakery

pano /'panu/ *m* cloth; **~ de fundo** backdrop; **~ de pó** duster; **~ de pratos** tea towel

pano|rama /pano'rama/ *m* panorama; **~râmico** *a* panoramic

panqueca /pã'kɛka/ *f* pancake

panta|nal /pãta'naw/ (*pl* **~nais**) *m* marshland

pântano /'pãtanu/ *m* marsh

pantanoso /pãta'nozu/ *a* marshy

pantera /pã'tɛra/ *f* panther

pão /pãw/ (*pl* **pães**) *m* bread; **~ de forma** sliced loaf; **~ integral** brown bread; **~-de-ló** *m* sponge cake; **~-duro** (*pl* **pães-duros**) (*fam*) *a* stingy, tight-fisted □ *m/f* skinflint; **~zinho** *m* bread roll

Papa /'papa/ *m* Pope

papa /'papa/ *f* (*de nenem*) food; (*arroz etc*) mush

papagaio /papa'gaju/ *m* parrot

papai /pa'paj/ *m* dad, daddy; **Papai Noël** Father Christmas

papar /pa'par/ *vt/i* (*fam*) eat

papari|car /papari'kar/ *vt* pamper; **~cos** *m pl* pampering

pa|pel /pa'pɛw/ (*pl* **~péis**) *m* (*de escrever etc*) paper; (*um*) piece of paper; (*numa peça, filme*) part; (*fig: função*) role; **de ~pel passado** officially; **~pel de alumínio** aluminium foil; **~pel**

higiênico toilet paper; **~pelada** *f* paperwork; **~pelão** *m* cardboard; **~pelaria** *f* stationer's (shop); **~pelzinho** *m* scrap of paper

papo /'papu/ *f* (*fam: conversa*) talk; (*do rosto*) double chin; **bater um ~** (*fam*) have a chat; **~ furado** idle talk

papoula /pa'pola/ *f* poppy

páprica /'paprika/ *f* paprika

paque|ra /pa'kɛra/ *f* (*fam*) pickup; **~rador** *a* flirtatious □ *m* flirt; **~rar** *vt* flirt with <*pessoa*>; eye up <*vestido, carro etc*> □ *vi* flirt

paquista|nês /pakista'nes/ *a & m* (*f* **~nesa**) Pakistani

Paquistão /pakis'tãw/ *m* Pakistan

par /par/ *a* even □ *m* pair; (*parceiro*) partner; **a ~ de** up to date with <*notícias etc*>; **sem ~** unequalled

para /'para/ *prep* for; (*a*) to; **~ que so that;** (*o*) **quê?** what for?; **~ casa** home; **estar ~ sair** be about to leave; **era ~ eu ir** I was supposed to go

para|benizar /parabeni'zar/ *vt* congratulate (**por** on); **~béns** *m pl* congratulations

parábola /pa'rabola/ *f* (*conto*) parable; (*curva*) parabola

parabóli|co /para'boliku/ *a* **antena ~ca** satellite dish

pára-brisa /para'briza/ *m* windscreen, (*Amer*) windshield; **~choque** *m* bumper

para|da /pa'rada/ *f* stop; (*interrupção*) stoppage; (*militar*) parade; (*fam: coisa difícil*) ordeal, challenge; **~da cardíaca** cardiac arrest; **~deiro** *m* whereabouts

paradisíaco /paradʒi'ziaku/ *a* idyllic

parado /pa'radu/ *a* <*trânsito, carro*> at a standstill, stopped; (*fig*) <*pessoa*> dull; **ficar ~** <*pessoa*>

stand still; <*trânsito*> stop; (*deixar de trabalhar*) stop work
parado|xal /paradok'saw/ (*pl* ~**xais**) *a* paradoxical; ~**xo** /ɔ/ *m* paradox
parafina /para'fina/ *f* paraffin
paráfrase /pa'rafrazi/ *f* paraphrase
parafrasear /parafrazi'ar/ *vt* paraphrase
parafuso /para'fuzu/ *f* screw; **entrar em** ~ get into a state
para|gem /pa'raʒẽ/ *f* (*Port: parada*) stop; **nestas** ~**gens** in these parts
parágrafo /pa'ragrafu/ *m* paragraph
Paraguai /para'gwaj/ *m* Paraguay
paraguaio /para'gwaju/ *a* & *m* Paraguayan
paraíso /para'izu/ *m* paradise
pára-lama /para'lama/ *m* (*de carro*) wing, (*Amer*) fender; (*de bicicleta*) mudguard
parale|la /para'lɛla/ *f* parallel; *pl* (*aparelho*) parallel bars; ~**lepípedo** *m* paving stone; ~**lo** /ɛ/ *a* & *m* parallel
parali|sar /parali'zar/ *vt* paralyse; bring to a halt <*fábrica, produção*>; ~**lisar-se** *vpr* become paralysed; <*fábrica, produção*> grind to a halt; ~**lisia** *f* paralysis; ~**lítico** *a* & *m* paralytic
~**médico** *m* paramedic
paranói|a /para'noja/ *f* paranoia; ~**co** *a* paranoid
parapeito /para'pejtu/ *m* (*muro*) parapet; (*da janela*) window-sill
pára-que|das /para'kedas/ *m invar* parachute; ~**dista** *m/f* parachutist; (*militar*) paratrooper
parar /pa'rar/ *vt/i* stop; ~ **de fumar** stop smoking; **ir** ~ **end up**
pára-raios /para'xajus/ *m invar* lightning conductor
parasita /para'zita/ *a* & *m/f* parasite
parceiro /par'seru/ *m* partner

parce|la /par'sɛla/ *f* (*de terreno*) plot; (*prestação*) instalment; ~**lar** *vt* spread <*pagamento*>
parceria /parse'ria/ *f* partnership
parci|al /parsi'aw/ (*pl* ~**ais**) *a* partial; (*partidário*) biased; ~**alidade** *f* bias
parco /'parku/ *a* frugal; <*recursos*> scant
par|dal /par'daw/ (*pl* ~**dais**) *m* sparrow; ~**do** *a* <*papel*> brown; <*pessoa*> mulatto
pare|cer /pare'ser/ *vi* (*ter aparência de*) seem; (*ter semelhança com*) be like; ~**cer-se com** look like, resemble □ *m* opinion; ~**cido** *a* similar (**com** to)
parede /pa'redʒi/ *f* wall
paren|te /pa'rẽtʃi/ *m/f* relative, relation; ~**tesco** /e/ *m* relationship
parêntese /pa'rẽtʃizi/ *f* parenthesis; *pl* (*sinais*) brackets
paridade /pari'dadʒi/ *f* parity
parir /pa'rir/ *vt* give birth to □ *vi* give birth
parlamen|tar /parlamẽ'tar/ *a* parliamentary □ *m/f* member of parliament; ~**tarismo** *m* parliamentary system; ~**to** *m* parliament
parmesão /parme'zãw/ *a* & *m* (**queijo**) ~ Parmesan (cheese)
paródia /pa'rodʒia/ *f* parody
parodiar /parodʒi'ar/ *vt* parody
paróquia /pa'rɔkia/ *f* parish
parque /'parki/ *m* park; ~ **temático** theme park
parte /'partʃi/ *f* part; (*quinhão*) share; (*num litígio, contrato*) party; **a maior** ~ **de** most of; **à** ~ (*de lado*) aside; (*separadamente*) separately; **um erro da sua** ~ a mistake on your part; **em** ~ in part; **em alguma** ~ somewhere; **por toda** ~ everywhere; **por** ~ **do pai** on one's father's side; **fazer** ~ **de** be part of; **tomar** ~ **em** take part in

parteira /par'tera/ f midwife

partici|pação /partʃisipa'sãw/ f participation; (numa empresa, nos lucros) share; ~**pante** a participating □ m/f participant; ~**par** vi take part (**de** ou **em** in)

particípio /partʃi'sipiu/ m participle

partícula /par'tʃikula/ f particle

particu|lar /partʃiku'lar/ a private; (especial) unusual □ m (pessoa) private individual; pl (detalhes) particulars; **em** ~**lar** (especialmente) in particular; (a sós) in private; ~**laridade** f peculiarity

partida /par'tʃida/ f (saída) departure; (de corrida) start; (de futebol, xadrez etc) match; **dar** ~ **em** start up

par|tidário /partʃi'dariu/ a partisan □ m supporter; ~**tido** a broken □ m (político) party; (casamento, par) match; **tirar** ~**tido de** benefit from; **tomar o** ~**tido de** side with; ~**tilha** f division; ~**tir** vi (sair) depart; <corredor> start □ vt break; ~**tir-se** vpr break; **a** ~**tir de** ... from ... onwards; ~**tir para** (fam) resort to; ~**tir para outra** do something different, change direction; ~**titura** f score

parto /'partu/ m birth

parvo /'parvu/ a (Port) stupid

Páscoa /'paskoa/ f Easter

pas|mar /paz'mar/ vt amaze; ~**mar-se** vpr be amazed (**com** at); ~**mo** a amazed □ m amazement

passa /'pasa/ f raisin

pas|sada /pa'sada/ f **dar uma** ~**sada** em call in at; ~**sadeira** f (mulher) woman who irons; (Port: faixa) zebra crossing, (Amer) crosswalk; ~**sado** a <ano, mês, semana> last; <tem-

po, participio etc> past; <fruta, comida> off □ m past; **são duas horas** ~**sadas** it's gone two o'clock; **bem/mal** ~**sado** <bife> well done/rare

passa|geiro /pasa'ʒeru/ m passenger □ a passing; ~**gem** f passage; (bilhete) ticket; **de** ~**gem** <dizer etc> in passing; **estar de** ~**gem** be passing through; ~**gem de ida e volta** return ticket, (Amer) round trip ticket

passaporte /pasa'portʃi/ m passport

passar /pa'sar/ vt pass; spend <tempo>; cross <ponte, rio>; (a ferro) iron <roupa etc>; (aplicar) put on <creme, batom etc> □ vi pass; <dor, medo, chuva etc> go; (ser aceitável) be passable □ m passing; ~**-se** vpr happen; **passou a beber muito** he started to drink a lot; **passei dos 30 anos** I'm over thirty; **não passa de um boato** it's nothing more than a rumour; ~ **por** go through; go along <rua>; (ser considerado) be taken for; **fazer-se** ~ **por** pass o.s. off as; ~ **por cima de** (fig) overlook; ~ **sem** do without

passarela /pasa'rɛla/ f (sobre rua) footbridge; (para desfile de moda) catwalk

pássaro /'pasaru/ m bird

passatempo /pasa'tẽpu/ m pastime

passe /'pasi/ m pass

pas|sear /pasi'ar/ vi go out and about; (viajar) travel around □ vt take for a walk; ~**seata** f protest march; ~**seio** m outing; (volta a pé) walk; (volta de carro) drive; **dar um** ~**seio** (a pé) go for a walk; (de carro) go for a drive

passio|nal /pasio'naw/ (pl ~**nais**) a **crime** ~**nal** crime of passion

passista /pa'sista/ m/f dancer

passí|vel /pa'sivew/ (*pl* ~**veis**) *a*
~**vel de** subject to

passi|vidade /pasivi'dadʒi/ *f* passivity; ~**vo** *a* passive □ *m* (*com*) liabilities; (*ling*) passive

passo /'pasu/ *m* step; (*velocidade*) pace; (*barulho*) footstep; ~**a** ~ step by step; **a dois** ~**s de a** stone's throw from; **dar um** ~ take a step

pasta /'pasta/ *f* (*matéria*) paste; (*bolsa*) briefcase; (*fichário*) folder; **ministro sem** ~ minister without portfolio; ~ **de dentes** toothpaste

pas|tagem /pas'taʒẽ/ *f* pasture; ~**tar** *vi* graze

pas|tel /pas'tɛw/ (*pl* ~**téis**) *m* (*para comer*) samosa; (*Port: doce*) pastry; (*para desenhar*) pastel; ~**telão** *m* (*comédia*) slapstick; ~**telaria** *f* (*loja*) samosa vendor, (*Port*) pastry shop; (*Port: pastéis*) pastries

pasteurizado /pastewri'zadu/ *a* pasteurized

pastilha /pas'tʃiʎa/ *f* pastille

pas|to /'pastu/ *m* (*erva*) fodder, feed; (*lugar*) pasture; ~**tor** *m* (*de gado*) shepherd; (*clérigo*) vicar; ~**tor alemão** (*cachorro*) Alsatian; ~**toral** (*pl* ~**torais**) *a* pastoral

pata /'pata/ *f* paw; ~**da** *f* kick

patamar /pata'mar/ *m* landing; (*fig*) level

patê /pa'te/ *m* pâté

patente /pa'tẽtʃi/ *a* obvious □ *f* (*mil*) rank; (*de invenção*) patent; ~**ar** *vt* patent <*produto, invenção*>

pater|nal /pater'naw/ (*pl* ~**nais**) *a* paternal; ~**nidade** *f* paternity; ~**no** /ɛ/ *a* paternal

pate|ta /pa'tɛta/ *a* daft, silly □ *m/f* fool; ~**tice** *f* stupidity; (*uma*) silly thing

patético /pa'tɛtʃiku/ *a* pathetic

patíbulo /pa'tʃibulu/ *m* gallows

pati|faria /patʃifa'ria/ *f* roguishness; (*uma*) dirty trick; ~**fe** *m* scoundrel

patim /pa'tʃĩ/ *m* skate; ~ **de rodas** roller skate

pati|nação /patʃina'sãw/ *f* skating; (*rinque*) skating rink; ~**nador** *m* skater; ~**nar** *vi* skate; <*carro*> skid; ~**nete** /ɛ/ *m* skateboard

pátio /'patʃiu/ *m* courtyard; (*de escola*) playground

pato /'patu/ *m* duck

pato|logia /patolo'ʒia/ *f* pathology; ~**lógico** *a* pathological; ~**logista** *m/f* pathologist

patrão /pa'trãw/ *m* boss

pátria /'patria/ *f* homeland

patriar|ca /patri'arka/ *m* patriarch; ~**cal** (*pl* ~**cais**) *a* patriarchal

patrimônio /patri'moniu/ *m* (*bens*) estate, property; (*fig: herança*) heritage

patri|ota /patri'ɔta/ *m/f* patriot; ~**ótico** *a* patriotic; ~**otismo** *m* patriotism

patroa /pa'troa/ *f* boss; (*fam: esposa*) missus, wife

patro|cinador /patrosina'dor/ *m* sponsor; ~**cinar** *vt* sponsor; ~**cínio** *m* sponsorship

patru|lha /pa'truʎa/ *f* patrol; ~**lhar** *vt/i* patrol

pau /paw/ *m* stick; (*fam: cruzeiro*) cruzeiro; (*chulo: pênis*) prick; *pl* (*naipe*) clubs; **a meio** ~ at half mast; **rachar** ~ (*fam: brigar*) row, fight like cat and dog; ~**lada** *f* blow with a stick

paulista /paw'lista/ *a & m/f* (person) from (the state of) São Paulo; ~**no** *a & m* (person) from (the city of) São Paulo

pausa /'pawza/ *f* pause; ~**do** *a* slow

pauta /'pawta/ *f* (*em papel*) lines; (*de música*) stave; (*fig: de discus-*

são etc) agenda; **~do** a <*papel*> lined

pavão /pa'vãw/ m peacock

pavilhão /pavi'ʎãw/ m pavilion; (*no jardim*) summerhouse

pavimen|tar /pavimẽ'tar/ vt pave; **~to** m floor; (*de rua etc*) surface

pavio /pa'viu/ m wick

pavor /pa'vor/ m terror; **ter ~** de be terrified of; **~oso** /o/ a dreadful

paz /pas/ f peace; **fazer as ~es** make up

pé /pɛ/ m foot; (*planta*) plant; (*de móvel*) leg; **a ~** on foot; **ao ~ da letra** literally; **estar de ~** <*festa etc*> be on; **ficar de ~** stand up; **em ~** standing (up); **em ~ de igualdade** on an equal footing

peão /pi'ãw/ m (Port: *pedestre*) pedestrian; (*no xadrez*) pawn

peça /'pɛsa/ f piece; (*de máquina, carro etc*) part; (*teatral*) play; **pregar uma ~** em play a trick on; **~ de reposição** spare part; **~ de vestuário** item of clothing

pe|cado /pe'kadu/ m sin; **~cador** m sinner; **~caminoso** /o/ a sinful; **~car** vi (*contra a religião*) sin; (*fig*) fall down

pechin|cha /pe'ʃiʃa/ f bargain; **~char** vi bargain, haggle

peçonhento /peso'ɲẽtu/ a **animais ~s** vermin

pecu|ária /peku'aria/ f livestock-farming; **~ário** a livestock; **~arista** m/f livestock farmer

peculi|ar /pekuli'ar/ a peculiar; **~aridade** f peculiarity

pecúlio /pe'kuliu/ m savings

pedaço /pe'dasu/ m piece; **aos ~s** in pieces; **cair aos ~s** fall to pieces

pedágio /pe'daʒiu/ m toll; (*cabine*) tollbooth

peda|gogia /pedago'ʒia/ f education; **~gógico** a educational; **~gogo** /o/ m educationalist

pe|dal /pe'daw/ (*pl* **~dais**) m pedal; **~dalar** vt/i pedal

pedante /pe'dãtʃi/ a pretentious □ m/f pseud

pé-de-atleta /pɛdʒiat'lɛta/ m athlete's foot; **~-de-meia** (*pl* **~s-de-meia**) m nest egg; **~-de-pato** (*pl* **~s-de-pato**) m flipper

pederneira /peder'nera/ f flint

pedes|tal /pedes'taw/ (*pl* **~tais**) m pedestal

pedestre /pe'dɛstri/ a & m/f pedestrian

pé-de-vento /pɛdʒi'vẽtu/ (*pl* **~s-de-vento**) m gust of wind

pedia|tra /pedʒi'atra/ m/f paediatrician; **~tria** f paediatrics

pedicuro /pedʒi'kuru/ m chiropodist, (*Amer*) podiatrist

pe|dido /pe'ʒidu/ m request; (*encomenda*) order; **a ~dido de** at the request of; **~dido de demissão** resignation; **~dido de desculpa** apology; **~dir** vt ask for; (*num restaurante etc*) order □ vi ask; (*num restaurante etc*) order; **~dir aco a alg** ask s.o. for sth; **~dir para alg** ir ask s.o. to go; **~dir desculpa** apologize; **~dir em casamento** propose to

pedinte /pe'dʒitʃi/ m/f beggar

pedra /'pɛdra/ f stone; **~ de gelo** ice cube; **chuva de ~** hail; **~ pomes** pumice stone

pedregoso /pedre'gozu/ a stony

pedreiro /pe'dreru/ m builder

pegada /pe'gada/ f footprint; (*de goleiro*) save

pegajoso /pega'ʒozu/ a sticky

pegar /pe'gar/ vt get; catch <*bola, doença, ladrão, ônibus*>; (*segurar*) get hold of; pick up <*emissora, hábito, mania*> □ vi (*aderir*) stick; <*doença*> be catching; <*moda*> catch on; <*carro, motor*> start; <*mentira, desculpa*> stick; **~-se** vpr come to blows; **~ bem/mal** go down well/ badly; **~ fogo** catch fire; **pega**

essa rua take that street; ~ **em**
grab; ~ **no sono** get to sleep

pego /'pegu/ *pp de* **pegar**

pei|dar /pej'dar/ *vi* (*chulo*) fart;
~**do m** (*chulo*) fart

pei|to /'pejtu/ *m* chest; (*seio*)
breast; (*fig: coragem*) guts; ~**to-**
ril (*pl* ~**toris**) *m* window-sill;
~**tudo** *a* <*mulher*> busty; (*fig:*
corajoso) gutsy

pei|xaria /pe∫a'ria/ *f* fishmon-
ger's; ~**xe** *m* fish; **Peixes** (*signo*)
Pisces; ~**xeiro** *m* fishmonger

pela = **por** + **a**

pelado /pe'ladu/ *a* (*nu*) naked, in
the nude

pelan|ca /pe'lãka/ *f* roll of fat; *pl*
flab; ~**cudo** *a* flabby

pelar /pe'lar/ *vt* peel <*fruta, bata-*
ta>; skin <*animal*>; (*fam: tomar*
dinheiro de) fleece

pelas = **por** + **as**

pele /'peli/ *f* skin; (*como roupa*)
fur; ~**teiro** *m* furrier; ~**teria** *f*
furrier's

pelica /pe'lika/ *f* **luvas de** ~ kid
gloves

pelicano /peli'kanu/ *m* pelican

película /pe'likula/ *f* skin

pelo = **por** + **o**

pêlo /'pelu/ *m* hair; (*de animal*)
coat; **nu em** ~ stark naked;
montar em ~ ride bareback

pelos = **por** + **os**

pelotão /pelo'tãw/ *m* platoon

pelúcia /pe'lusia/ *f* **bicho de** ~
soft toy, fluffy animal

peludo /pe'ludu/ *a* hairy

pena¹ /'pena/ *f* (*de ave*) feather; (*de*
caneta) nib

pena² /'pena/ *f* (*castigo*) penalty;
(*de amor etc*) pang; **é uma** ~
que it's a pity that; **que** ~! what
a pity!; **dar** ~ be upsetting; **es-**
tar com ou **ter** ~ **de** feel sorry
for; (**não**) **vale a** ~ it's (not)
worth it; **vale a** ~ **tentar** it's
worth trying; ~ **de morte** death
penalty

penada /pe'nada/ *f* stroke of the
pen

pe|nal /pe'naw/ (*pl* ~**nais**) *a*
penal; ~**nalidade** *f* penalty;
~**nalizar** *vt* penalize

pênalti /'penawt∫i/ *m* penalty

penar /pe'nar/ *vi* suffer

pen|dente /pẽ'dẽt∫i/ *a* hanging;
(*fig: causa*) pending; ~**der** *vi*
hang; (*inclinar-se*) slope; (*tender*)
be inclined (**a** to); ~**dor** *m* inclination

pêndulo /'pẽdulu/ *m* pendulum

pendu|rado /pẽdu'radu/ *a* hang-
ing; (*fam: por fazer, pagar*)
outstanding; ~**rar** *vt* hang (up);
(*fam*) put on the slate <*compra*>
□ *vi* (*fam*) pay later <*compra*>;
~**ricalho**
m pendant

penedo /pe'nedu/ *m* rock

penei|ra /pe'nera/ *f* sieve; ~**rar**
vt sieve, sift □ *vi* drizzle

pene|tra /pe'nεtra/ *m/f* (*fam*)
gatecrasher; ~**tração** *f* penetra-
tion; (*fig*) perspicacity; ~**trante**
a <*som, olhar*> piercing; <*dor*>
sharp; <*ferida*> deep; <*frio*> biting; <*análise, espírito*> incisive,
perceptive; ~**trar** *vt* penetrate
□ *vi* ~**trar em** enter <*casa*>;
(*fig*) penetrate

penhasco /pe'nasku/ *m* cliff

penhoar /peno'ar/ *m* dressing
gown

penhor /pe'nor/ *m* pledge; **casa de**
~**es** pawnshop

penicilina /penisi'lina/ *f* penicillin

penico /pe'niku/ *m* potty

península /pe'nĩsula/ *f* peninsula

pênis /'penis/ *m invar* penis

penitência /peni'tẽsia/ *f* (*arrepen-*
dimento) penitence; (*expiação*)
penance

penitenciá|ria /penitẽsi'aria/ *f*
prison; ~**rio** *a* prison □ *m*
prisoner

penoso /pe'nozu/ *a* <*experiência,*
tarefa, assunto> painful; <*traba-*

lho, viagem> hard, difficult

pensa|dor /pẽsa'dor/ *m* thinker; **~mento** *m* thought

pensão /pẽ'sãw/ *f* (*renda*) pension; (*hotel*) guesthouse; **~ (alimentícia)** (*paga por ex-marido*) alimony; **~ completa** full board

pen|sar /pẽ'sar/ *vt/i* think (**em** *of* **ou** *about*); **~sativo** *a* thoughtful, pensive

pên|sil /'pẽsiw/ (*pl* **~seis**) *a* **ponte ~sil** suspension bridge

penso /'pẽsu/ *m* (*curativo*) dressing

pentágono /pẽ'tagonu/ *m* pentagon

pentatlo /pẽ'tatlu/ *m* pentathlon

pente /'pẽtʃi/ *m* comb; **~adeira** *f* dressing table; **~ado** *m* hairstyle, hairdo; **~ar** *vt* comb; **~ar-se** *vpr* do one's hair; (*com pente*) comb one's hair

Pentecostes /pẽte'kɔstʃis/ *m* Whitsun

pente-fino /pẽtʃi'finu/ *m* **passar a ~** go over with a fine-tooth comb

pente|lhar /pẽte'ʎar/ *vt* (*fam*) bother; **~lho** /e/ *m* pubic hair; (*fam: pessoa inconveniente*) pain (in the neck)

penugem /pe'nuʒẽ/ *f* down

penúltimo /pe'nuwtʃimu/ *a* last but one, penultimate

penumbra /pe'nũbra/ *f* half-light

penúria /pe'nuria/ *f* penury, extreme poverty

pepino /pe'pinu/ *m* cucumber

pepita /pe'pita/ *f* nugget

peque|nez /peke'nes/ *f* smallness; (*fig*) pettiness; **~nininho** *a* tiny; **~no** /e/ *a* small; (*mesquinho*) petty

Pequim /pe'kĩ/ *f* Peking, Beijing

pequinês /peki'nes/ *m* Pekinese

pêra /'pera/ *f* pear

perambular /perãbu'lar/ *vi* wander

perante /pe'rãtʃi/ *prep* before

percalço /per'kawsu/ *m* pitfall

perceber /perse'ber/ *vt* realize; (*Port: entender*) understand; (*psiqu*) perceive

percen|tagem /persẽ'taʒẽ/ *f* percentage; **~tual** (*pl* **~tuais**) *a* & *m* percentage

percep|ção /persep'sãw/ *f* perception; **~tível** (*pl* **~tíveis**) *a* perceptible

percevejo /perse'veʒu/ *m* (*bicho*) bedbug; (*tachinha*) drawing pin, (*Amer*) thumbtack

per|correr /perko'xer/ *vt* cross; cover <*distância*>; (*viajar por*) travel through; **~curso** *m* journey

percus|são /perku'sãw/ *f* percussion; **~sionista** *m/f* percussionist

percutir /perku'tʃir/ *vt* strike

perda /'perda/ *f* loss; **~ de tempo** waste of time

perdão /per'dãw/ *f* pardon

perder /per'der/ *vt* lose; (*não chegar a ver, pegar*) miss <*ônibus, programa na TV etc*>; waste <*tempo*> □ *vi* lose; **~-se** *vpr* get lost; **~-se de alg** lose s.o.; **~ aco de vista** lose sight of sth

perdiz /per'dʒis/ *f* partridge

perdoar /perdo'ar/ *vt* forgive (**aco a alg** s.o. for sth)

perdulário /perdu'lariu/ *a* & *m* spendthrift

perdurar /perdu'rar/ *vi* endure; <*coisa ruim*> persist

pere|cer /pere'ser/ *vi* perish; **~cível** (*pl* **~cíveis**) *a* perishable

peregri|nação /peregrina'sãw/ *f* peregrination; (*romaria*) pilgrimage; **~nar** *vi* roam; (*por motivos religiosos*) go on a pilgrimage; **~no** *m* pilgrim

pereira /pe'rera/ *f* pear tree

peremptório /perẽp'tɔriu/ *a* peremptory

perene /pe'reni/ *a* perennial

perereca /pere'reka/ *f* tree frog

perfazer /perfa'zer/ *vt* make up

perfeccionis|mo /perfeksio'nizmu/ m perfectionism; ~**ta** a & m/f perfectionist

perfei|ção /perfej'sãw/ f perfection; ~**to** a & m perfect

per|fil /per'fiw/ (pl ~**fis**) m profile; ~**filar** vt line up; ~**filar-se** upr line up

perfu|mado /perfu'madu/ a <flor, ar> fragrant; <sabonete etc> scented; <pessoa> with perfume on; ~**mar** vt perfume; ~**mar-se** upr put perfume on; ~**maria** f perfumery; (fam) trimmings, frills; ~**me** m perfume

perfu|rador /perfura'dor/ m punch; ~**rar** vt punch <papel, bilhete>; drill through <chão>; perforate <úlcera, pulmão etc>; ~**ratriz** □ f drill

pergaminho /perga'miɲu/ m parchment

pergun|ta /per'gũta/ f question; **fazer uma** ~ **ta** ask a question; ~**tar** vt/i ask; ~**tar aco a alg** ask s.o. sth; ~**tar por** ask after

perícia /pe'risia/ f (mestria) expertise; (inspeção) investigation; (peritos) experts

perici|al /perisi'aw/ (pl ~**ais**) a expert

pericli|tante /perikli'tãtʃi/ a precarious; ~**tar** vi be at risk

peri|feria /perife'ria/ f periphery; (da cidade) outskirts; ~**férico** a & m peripheral

perigo /pe'rigu/ m danger; ~**so** /o/ a dangerous

perímetro /pe'rimetru/ m perimeter

periódico /peri'ɔdʒiku/ a periodic □ m periodical

período /pe'riodu/ m period; **trabalhar meio** ~ work part-time

peripécias /peri'pɛsias/ f pl ups and downs, vicissitudes

periquito /peri'kitu/ m parakeet; (de estimação) budgerigar

periscópio /peris'kɔpiu/ m periscope

perito /pe'ritu/ a & m expert (**em** at)

per|jurar /perʒu'rar/ vi commit perjury; ~**júrio** m perjury; ~**juro** m perjurer

perma|necer /permane'ser/ vi remain; ~**nência** f permanence; (estadia) stay; ~**nente** a permanent □ f perm

permeá|vel /permi'avew/ (pl ~**veis**) a permeable

permis|são /permi'sãw/ f permission; ~**sível** (pl ~**síveis**) a permissible; ~**sivo** a permissive

permitir /permi'tʃir/ vt allow, permit; ~ **a alg ir** allow s.o. to go

permutar /permu'tar/ vt exchange

perna /'pɛrna/ f leg

pernicioso /pernisi'ozu/ a pernicious

per|nil /per'niw/ (pl ~**nis**) m leg

pernilongo /perni'lõgu/ m (large) mosquito

pernoi|tar /pernoj'tar/ vi spend the night; ~**te** m overnight stay

pérola /'pɛrola/ f pearl

perpendicular /perpẽdʒiku'lar/ a perpendicular

perpetrar /perpe'trar/ vt perpetrate

perpetu|ar /perpetu'ar/ vt perpetuate; ~**idade** f perpetuity

perpétu|o /per'pɛtuu/ a perpetual; **prisão** ~**a** life imprisonment

perple|xidade /perpleksi'dadʒi/ f puzzlement; ~**xo** /ɛ/ a puzzled

persa /'pɛrsa/ a & m/f Persian

perse|guição /persegi'sãw/ f pursuit; (de minorias etc) persecution; ~**guidor** m pursuer; (de minorias etc) persecutor; ~**guir** vt pursue; persecute <minoria, seita etc>

perseve|rança /perseve'rãsa/ f perseverance; ~**rante** a persevering; ~**rar** vi persevere

persiana /persi'ana/ f blind

pérsico /ˈpɛrsiku/ a **Golfo Pérsico** Persian Gulf

persignar-se /persig'narsi/ vt cross o.s.

persis|tência /persis'tẽsia/ f persistence; ~**tente** a persistent; ~**tir** vi persist

perso|nagem /perso'naʒẽ/ m/f (pessoa famosa) personality; (em livro, filme etc) character; ~**nalidade** f personality; ~**nalizar** vt personalize; ~**nificar** vt personify

perspectiva /perspek'tʃiva/ f (na arte, ponto de vista) perspective; (possibilidade) prospect

perspi|cácia /perspi'kasia/ f insight, perceptiveness; ~**caz** a perceptive

persua|dir /persua'dʒir/ vt persuade (**alg** a s.o. to); ~**são** f persuasion; ~**sivo** a persuasive

perten|cente /pertẽ'sẽtʃi/ a belonging (a to); (que tem a ver com) pertaining (a to); ~**cer** vi belong (a to); (referir-se) pertain (a to); ~**ces** m pl belongings

perto /ˈpɛrtu/ adv near (de to); **aqui** ~ near here, nearby; **de** ~ closely; <ver> close up

pertur|bação /perturba'sãw/ f disturbance; (do espírito) anxiety; ~**bado** a <pessoa> unsettled, troubled; ~**bar** vt disturb; ~**bar-se** vpr get upset, be perturbed

Peru /pe'ru/ m Peru

peru /pe'ru/ m turkey

perua /pe'rua/ f (carro grande) estate car, (Amer) station wagon; (caminhonete) van; (para escolares etc) minibus; (fam: mulher) brassy woman

peruano /peru'ano/ a & m Peruvian

peruca /pe'ruka/ f wig

perver|são /perver'sãw/ f perversion; ~**so** a perverse; ~**ter** vt pervert

pesadelo /peza'delu/ m nightmare

pesado /pe'zadu/ a heavy; <estilo, livro> heavy-going □ adv heavily

pêsames /ˈpezamis/ m pl condolences

pesar¹ /pe'zar/ vt weigh; (fig: avaliar) weigh up □ vi weigh; (influir) carry weight; ~ **sobre** <ameaça etc> hang over; ~**-se** vpr weigh o.s.

pesar² /pe'zar/ m sorrow; ~**oso** /o/ a sorry, sorrowful

pes|ca /ˈpeska/ f fishing; **ir à** ~**ca** go fishing; ~**cador** m fisherman; ~**car** vt catch; (retirar da água) fish out □ vi fish; (fam) (entender) understand; (cochilar) nod off; ~**car de** a (fam) know all about

pescoço /pes'kosu/ m neck

peseta /pe'zeta/ f peseta

peso /ˈpezu/ m weight; **de** ~ (fig) <pessoa> influential; <livro, argumento> authoritative

pesqueiro /pes'keru/ a fishing

pesqui|sa /pes'kiza/ f research; (uma) study; pl research; ~**sa de mercado** market research; ~**sador** m researcher; ~**sar** vt/i research

pêssego /ˈpesigu/ m peach

pessegueiro /pesi'geru/ m peach tree

pessi|mismo /pesi'mizmu/ m pessimism; ~**ta** a pessimistic □ m/f pessimist

péssimo /ˈpesimu/ a terrible, awful

pesso|a /pe'soa/ f person; pl people; **em** ~**a** in person; ~**al** (pl ~**ais**) a personal □ m staff; (fam) folks

pesta|na /pes'tana/ f eyelash; **tirar uma** ~**na** (fam) have a nap; ~**nejar** vi blink; **sem** ~**nejar** (fig) without batting an eyelid

peste /'pɛstʃi/ f (doença) plague; (criança etc) pest; **~ticida** m pesticide

pétala /'pɛtala/ f petal

peteca /pe'tɛka/ f kind of shuttle-cock; (jogo) kind of badminton played with the hand

peteleco /pete'lɛku/ m flick

petição /petʃi'sãw/ f petition

petisco /pe'tʃisku/ m savoury, tit-bit

petrificar /petrifi'kar/ vt petrify; (de surpresa) stun; **~-se** vpr be petrified; (de surpresa) be stunned

petroleiro /petro'leru/ a oil □ m oil tanker

petróleo /pe'trɔliu/ m oil, petroleum; **~ bruto** crude oil

petrolífero /petro'liferu/ a oil-producing

petroquími|ca /petro'kimika/ f petrochemicals; **~co** a petro-chemical

petu|lância /petu'lãsia/ f cheek; **~lante** a cheeky

peúga /pi'uga/ f (Port) sock

pevide /pe'vidʒi/ f (Port) pip

pia /'pia/ f (do banheiro) wash-basin; (da cozinha) sink; **~ batismal** font

piada /pi'ada/ f joke

pia|nista /pia'nista/ m/f pianist; **~no** m piano; **~no de cauda** grand piano

piar /pi'ar/ vi <pinto> cheep; <coruja> hoot

picada /pi'kada/ f (de agulha, alfinete etc) prick; (de abelha, vespa) sting; (de mosquito, cobra) bite; (de heroína) shot; (de avião) nosedive; **o fim da ~** (fig) the limit

picadeiro /pika'deru/ m ring

picante /pi'kãtʃi/ a <comida> hot, spicy; <piada> risqué; <filme, livro> raunchy

pica-pau /pika'paw/ m woodpecker

picar /pi'kar/ vt (com agulha, alfinete etc) prick; <abelha, vespa,

urtiga> sting; <mosquito, cobra> bite; <pássaro> peck; chop <carne, alho etc>; shred <papel> □ vi <peixe> bite; <lã, cobertor> prickle

picareta /pika'reta/ f pickaxe

pi|chação /piʃa'sãw/ f piece of graffiti; pl graffiti; **~char** vt spray with graffiti <muro, prédio>; spray <grafite, desenho>; **~che** m pitch

picles /'piklis/ m pl pickles

pico /'piku/ m peak; **20 anos e ~** (Port) just over 20

picolé /piko'lɛ/ m ice lolly

pico|tar /piko'tar/ vt perforate; **~te** /ɔ/ m perforations

pie|dade /pie'dadʒi/ f (religiosidade) piety; (compaixão) pity; **~doso** /o/ a merciful, compas-sionate

pie|gas /pi'egas/ a invar <filme, livro> sentimental, schmaltzy; <pessoa> soppy; **~guice** f senti-mentality

pifar /pi'far/ vi (fam) break down, go wrong

pi|gar|rear /pigaxi'ar/ vi clear one's throat; **~ro** m frog in the throat

pigmento /pig'mẽtu/ m pigment

pig|meu /pig'mew/ a & m (f **~méia**) pygmy

pijama /pi'ʒama/ m pyjamas

pilantra /pi'lãtra/ m/f (fam) crook

pilão /pi'lãw/ m (na cozinha) pestle; (na construção) ram

pilar /pi'lar/ m pillar

pilastra /pi'lastra/ f pillar

pileque /pi'lɛki/ m drinking session; **tomar um ~** get drunk

pilha /'piʎa/ f (monte) pile; (elétrica) battery

pilhar /pi'ʎar/ vt pillage

pilhéria /pi'ʎɛria/ f joke

pilotar /pilo'tar/ vt fly, pilot <avião>; drive <carro>

pilotis /pilo'tʃis/ m pl pillars

piloto /pi'lotu/ *m* pilot; (*de carro*) driver; (*de gás*) pilot light □ *a invar* pilot

pílula /'pilula/ *f* pill

pimen|ta /pi'mẽta/ *f* pepper; **~ta de Caiena** cayenne pepper; **~ta-do-reino** *f* black pepper; **~ta-malagueta** (*pl* **~tas-malagueta**) *f* chilli pepper; **~tão** *m* (bell) pepper; **~teira** *f* pepper pot

pinacoteca /pinako'tɛka/ *f* art gallery

pin|ça /'pĩsa/ (*para tirar pêlos*) tweezers; (*para segurar*) tongs; (*de siri etc*) pincer; **~çar** *vt* pluck < *sobrancelhas*>

pin|cel /pĩ'sɛw/ (*pl* **~céis**) *m* brush; **~celada** *f* brush stroke; **~celar** *vt* paint

pin|ga /'pĩga/ *f* Brazilian rum; **~gado** *a* < *café*> with a dash of milk; **~gar** *vi* drip; (*começar a chover*) spit (with rain) □ *vt* drip; **~gente** *m* pendant; **~go** *m* drop; (*no i*) dot

pingue-pongue /pĩgi'põgi/ *m* table tennis

pingüim /pĩ'gwĩ/ *m* penguin

pi|nha /'pĩɲa/ *f* pine cone; **~nheiro** *f* pine tree; **~nho** *m* pine

pino /'pinu/ *m* pin; (*para trancar carro*) lock; **a** **~** upright; **bater** **~** < *carro*> knock

pin|ta /'pĩta/ *f* (*sinal*) mole; (*fam: aparência*) look; **~tar** *vt* paint; dye < *cabelo*>; put make-up on < *rosto, olhos*> □ *vi* paint; (*fam*) < *pessoa*> show up; < *problema, oportunidade*> crop up; **~tar-se** *vpr* put on make-up

pintarroxo /pĩta'xoʃu/ *m* robin

pinto /'pĩtu/ *m* chick

pin|tor /pĩ'tor/ *m* painter; **~tura** *f* painting

pio[1] /'piu/ *m* (*de pinto*) cheep; (*de coruja*) hoot

pio[2] /'piu/ *a* pious

piolho /pi'oʎu/ *m* louse

pioneiro /pio'neru/ *m* pioneer □ *a* pioneering

pior /pi'or/ *a* & *adv* worse; **o** **~** the worst

pio|ra /pi'ora/ *f* worsening; **~rar** *vt* make worse, worsen □ *vi* get worse, worsen

pipa /'pipa/ *f* (*que voa*) kite; (*de vinho*) cask

pipilar /pipi'lar/ *vi* chirp

pipo|ca /pi'pɔka/ *f* popcorn; **~car** *vi* spring up; **~queiro** *m* popcorn seller

pique /'piki/ *m* (*disposição*) energy; **a** **~** vertically; **ir a** **~** < *navio*> sink

piquenique /piki'niki/ *m* picnic

pique|te /pi'ketʃi/ *m* picket; **~teiro** *m* picket

pirado /pi'radu/ *a* (*fam*) crazy

pirâmide /pi'ramidʒi/ *f* pyramid

piranha /pi'raɲa/ *f* piranha; (*fam: mulher*) maneater

pirar /pi'rar/ (*fam*) *vi* flip out, go mad

pira|ta /pi'rata/ *a* & *m/f* pirate; **~ria** *f* piracy

pires /'piris/ *m invar* saucer

pirilampo /piri'lãpu/ *m* glowworm

Pireneus /piri'news/ *m pl* Pyrenees

pirra|ça /pi'xasa/ *f* spiteful act; **fazer** **~ça** be spiteful; **~cento** *a* spiteful

pirueta /piru'eta/ *f* pirouette

pirulito /piru'litu/ *m* lollipop

pi|sada /pi'zada/ *f* step; (*rastro*) footprint; **~sar** *vt* tread on; tread < *uvas, palco*>; (*esmagar*) trample on □ *vi* step; **~sar em** step on; (*entrar*) set foot in

pis|cadela /piska'dɛla/ *f* wink; **~ca-pisca** *m* indicator; **~car** *vi* (*com o olho*) wink; (*pestanejar*) blink; < *estrela, luz*> twinkle; < *motorista*> indicate □ *m* **num** **~car de olhos** in a flash

piscicultura /pisikuw'tura/ *f* fish farming; (*lugar*) fish farm

piscina /pi'sina/ *f* swimming pool

piso /'pizu/ *m* floor

pisotear /pizotʃi'ar/ *vt* trample

pista /'pista/ *f* track; (*da estrada*) carriageway; (*para aviões*) runway; (*de circo*) ring; (*dica*) clue; **~ de dança** dancefloor

pistache /pis'taʃi/ *m*, **pistacho** /pis'taʃu/ *m* pistachio (nut)

pisto|la /pis'tola/ *f* pistol; (*para pintar*) spray gun; **~lão** *m* influential contact; **~leiro** *m* gunman

pitada /pi'tada/ *f* pinch

piteira /pi'tera/ *f* cigarette-holder

pitoresco /pito'resku/ *a* picturesque

pitu /pi'tu/ *m* crayfish

pivete /pi'vetʃi/ *m/f* child thief

pivô /pi'vo/ *m* pivot

pixaim /piʃa'ĩ/ *a* frizzy

pizza /'pitsa/ *f* pizza; **~ria** *f* pizzeria

placa /'plaka/ *f* plate; (*de carro*) number plate, (*Amer*) license plate; (*comemorativa*) plaque; (*em computador*) board; **~ de sinalização** roadsign

placar /pla'kar/ *m* scoreboard; (*escore*) scoreline

plácido /'plasidu/ *a* placid

plagi|ário /plaʒi'ariu/ *m* plagiarist; **~ar** *vt* plagiarize

plágio /'plaʒiu/ *m* plagiarism

plaina /'plajna/ *f* plane

planador /plana'dor/ *m* glider

planalto /pla'nawtu/ *m* plateau

planar /pla'nar/ *vi* glide

planeamento, planear (*Port*) *veja* **planejamento, planejar**

plane|jamento /planeʒa'mẽtu/ *m* planning; **~jamento familiar** family planning; **~jar** *vt* plan

planeta /pla'neta/ *m* planet

planície /pla'nisi/ *f* plain

planificar /planifi'kar/ *vt* (*programar*) plan (out)

planilha /pla'niʎa/ *f* spreadsheet

plano /'planu/ *a* flat □ *m* plan; (*superfície, nível*) plane; **primeiro ~** foreground

planta /'plãta/ *f* plant; (*do pé*) sole; (*de edifício*) ground plan; **~ção** *f* (*ato*) planting; (*terreno*) plantation; **~do** *a* **deixar alg ~do** (*fam*) keep s.o. waiting around

plantão /plã'tãw/ *m* duty; (*noturno*) night duty; **estar de ~** be on duty

plantar /plã'tar/ *vt* plant

plas|ma /'plazma/ *m* plasma; **~mar** *vt* mould, shape

plásti|ca /'plastʃika/ *f* face-lift; **~co** *a & m* plastic

plataforma /plata'fɔrma/ *f* platform

plátano /'platanu/ *m* plane tree

platéia /pla'teja/ *f* audience; (*parte do teatro*) stalls, (*Amer*) orchestra

platina /pla'tʃina/ *f* platinum; **~dos** *m pl* points

platônico /pla'toniku/ *a* platonic

plausí|vel /plaw'zivew/ (*pl* **~veis**) *a* plausible

ple|be /'plɛbi/ *f* common people; **~beu** *a* (*f* **~béia**) plebeian □ *m* (*f* **~béia**) commoner; **~biscito** *m* plebiscite

plei|tear /plejtʃi'ar/ *vt* contest; **~to** *m* (*litígio*) case; (*eleitoral*) contest

ple|namente /plena'mẽtʃi/ *adv* fully; **~nário** *a* plenary □ *m* plenary assembly; **~no** /e/ *a* full; **em ~no verão** in the middle of summer

plissado /pli'sadu/ *a* pleated

pluma /'pluma/ *f* feather; **~gem** *f* plumage

plu|ral /plu'raw/ (*pl* **~rais**) *a & m* plural

plutônio /plu'toniu/ *m* plutonium

pluvi|al /pluvi'aw/ (*pl* **~ais**) *a* rain

pneu /pi'new/ *m* tyre; ~**mático** *a* pneumatic □ *m* tyre

pneumonia /pineumo'nia/ *f* pneumonia

pó /pɔ/ *f* powder; (*poeira*) dust; **leite em** ~ powdered milk

pobre /'pobri/ *a* poor □ *m*/*f* poor man (*f* woman); **os** ~**s** the poor; ~**za** /e/ *f* poverty

poça /'posa/ *f* pool; (*deixada pela chuva*) puddle

poção /po'sãw/ *f* potion

pocilga /po'siwga/ *f* pigsty

poço /'posu/ *f* (*de água, petróleo*) well; (*de mina, elevador*) shaft

podar /po'dar/ *vt* prune

pó-de-arroz /pɔdʒia'xoz/ *m* (face) powder

poder /po'der/ *m* power □ *v aux* can, be able; (*eventualidade*) may; **ele podia/podía/poderá vir** he can/could/might come; **ele pôde vir** he was able to come; **pode ser que** it may be that; ~ **com** stand up to; **em** ~ **de alg** in sb's possession; **estar no** ~ be in power

poderio /pode'riu/ *m* might; ~**roso** /o/ *a* powerful

pódio /'pɔdʒiu/ *m* podium

podre /'podri/ *a* (*podri*) rotten; (*fam*) (*cansado*) exhausted; (*doente*) grotty; ~ **de rico** filthy rich; ~**s** *m pl* faults

poeira /po'era/ *f* dust; ~**rento** *a* dusty

poema /po'ema/ *m* poem; ~**sia** *f* (*arte*) poetry; (*poema*) poem; ~**ta** *m* poet

poético /po'ɛtʃiku/ *a* poetic

poetisa /poe'tʃiza/ *f* poetess

pois /pojs/ *conj* as, since; ~ **é** that's right; ~ **não** of course; ~ **não?** can I help you?; ~ **sim** certainly not

polaco /pu'laku/ (*Port*) *a* Polish □ *m* Pole; (*língua*) Polish

polar /po'lar/ *a* polar

polarizar /polari'zar/ *vt* polarize; ~**-se** *vpr* polarize

polegada /pole'gada/ *f* inch; ~**gar** *m* thumb

poleiro /po'leru/ *m* perch

polêmica /po'lemika/ *f* controversy, debate; ~**co** *a* controversial

pólen /'pɔlẽ/ *m* pollen

polícia /po'lisia/ *f* police □ *m*/*f* policeman (*f*-woman)

policial /polisi'aw/ (*pl* ~**ais**) *a* <*carro, inquérito etc*> police; <*romance, filme*> detective □ *m*/*f* policeman (*f* -woman); ~**amento** *m* policing; ~**ar** *vt* police

polidez /poli'des/ *f* politeness; ~**do** *a* polite

poligamia /poliga'mia/ *f* polygamy; ~**glota** *a & m*/*f* polyglot

Polinésia /poli'nezia/ *f* Polynesia

polinésio /poli'neziu/ *a & m* Polynesian

pólio /'pɔliu/ *f* polio

polir /po'lir/ *vt* polish

polissílabo /poli'silabu/ *m* polysyllable

política /po'litʃika/ *f* politics; (*uma*) policy; ~**co** *a* political □ *m* politician

pólo[1] /'pɔlu/ *m* pole

pólo[2] /'pɔlu/ *m* (*jogo*) polo; ~ **aquático** water polo

polonês /polo'nes/ *a* (*f* ~**nesa**) Polish □ *m* (*f* ~**nesa**) Pole; (*língua*) Polish

Polônia /po'lonia/ *f* Poland

polpa /'powpa/ *f* pulp

poltrona /pow'trona/ *f* armchair

poluente /polu'ẽtʃi/ *a & m* pollutant; ~**ição** *f* pollution; ~**ir** *vt* pollute

polvilhar /powvi'ʎar/ *vt* sprinkle

polvo /'powvu/ *m* octopus

pólvora /'powvora/ *f* gunpowder

polvorosa /powvo'roza/ *f* uproar; **em** ~ in uproar; <*pessoa*> in a flap

pomada /po'mada/ *f* ointment

pomar /po'mar/ *m* orchard

pom|ba /ˈpõbɐ/ f dove; ~**bo** m pigeon

pomo-de-Adão /pomudʃiaˈdãw/ m Adam's apple

pom|pa /ˈpõpa/ f pomp; ~**poso** /o/ a pompous

ponche /ˈpõʃi/ m punch

ponderar /põdeˈrar/ vt/i ponder

pônei /ˈponej/ m pony

ponta /ˈpõta/ f end; (de faca, prego) point; (de nariz, dedo, língua) tip; (de sapato) toe; (Cin, Teat: papel curto) walk-on part; (no campo de futebol) wing; (jogador) winger; **na ~ dos pés** on tip-toe; **uma ~ de** a touch of <ironia etc>; **agüentar as ~s** (fam) hold on; ~**cabeça** /e/ f **de** ~-**cabeça** upside down

pontada /põˈtada/ f (dor) twinge

pontapé /põtaˈpɛ/ m kick; ~ **inicial** kick-off

pontaria /põtaˈria/ f aim; **fazer ~** take aim

ponte /ˈpõtʃi/ f bridge; ~ **aérea** shuttle; (em tempo de guerra) airlift; ~ **de safena** heart bypass; ~ **pênsil** suspension bridge

ponteiro /põˈteru/ m pointer; (de relógio) hand

pontiagudo /põtʃiaˈgudu/ a sharp

pontilhado /põtʃiˈʎadu/ a dotted

ponto /ˈpõtu/ m point; (de costura, tricô) stitch; (no final de uma frase) full stop, (Amer) period; (sinalzinho, no i) dot; (de ônibus) stop; (no teatro) prompter; **a ~ de** on the point of; **ao ~** <carne> medium; **até certo ~** to a certain extent; **às duas em ~** at exactly two o'clock; **dormir no ~** (fam) miss the boat; **entregar os ~s** (fam) give up; **fazer ~** (fam) hang out; **dois ~s** colon; ~ **de exclamação/interrogação** exclamation/question mark; ~ **de táxi** taxi rank, (Amer) taxi stand; ~ **de vista**

point of view; ~ **morto** neutral; ~**e-vírgula** m semicolon

pontu|ação /põtuaˈsãw/ f punctuation; ~**al** (pl ~**ais**) a punctual; ~**alidade** f punctuality; ~**ar** vt punctuate

pontudo /põˈtudu/ a pointed

popa /ˈpopa/ f stern

popu|lação /populaˈsãw/ f population; ~**lacional** (pl ~**lacionais**) a population; ~**lar** a popular; ~**laridade** f popularity; ~**larizar** vt popularize; ~**larizar-se** vpr become popular

pôquer /ˈpoker/ m poker

por /por/ prep for; (através de) through; (indicando meio, agente) by; (motivo) out of; ~ **ano/mês/** etc per year/month/etc; ~ **cento** per cent; ~ **aqui** (nesta área) around here; (nesta direção) this way; ~ **dentro/fora** on the inside/outside; ~ **isso** for this reason; ~ **sorte** luckily; ~ **que** why; ~ **mais caro que seja** however expensive it may be; **está ~ acontecer/fazer** it is yet to happen/to be done

pôr /por/ vt put; put on <roupa, chapéu, óculos>; lay <mesa, ovos>; **o ~** **do sol** sunset; ~**se** vpr <sol> set; ~**se a** start to; ~**se a caminho** set off

porão /poˈrãw/ m (de prédio) basement; (de casa) cellar; (de navio) hold

porca /ˈporka/ f (de parafuso) nut; (animal) sow

porção /porˈsãw/ f portion; **uma ~ de** (muitos) a lot of

porcaria /porkaˈria/ f (sujeira) filth; (coisa malfeita) piece of trash; pl trash

porcelana /porseˈlana/ f china

porcentagem /porsẽˈtaʒẽ/ f percentage

porco /ˈporku/ a filthy □ m (animal, fig) pig; (carne) pork; ~-

espinho (pl ~s-espinhos) m porcupine

porém /po'rěj/ conj however

pormenor /porme'nor/ m detail

por|nó /por'no/ a porn □ m porn film; **~nografia** f pornography; **~nográfico** a pornographic

poro /'poru/ m pore; **~so** /o/ a porous

por|quanto /por'kwãtu/ conj since; **~que** /por'ki/ conj because; (Port: por quê?) why; **~quê** /por'ke/ adv (Port) why □ m reason why

porquinho|-da-índia /porkiɲu-da'ídʒia/ (pl ~s-da-índia) m guinea pig

porrada /po'xada/ f (fam) beating

porre /'pɔxi/ m (fam) drinking session, booze-up; **de ~** drunk; **tomar um ~** get drunk

porta /'pɔrta/ f door

porta-aviões /portavi'õjs/ m invar aircraft carrier

portador /porta'dor/ m bearer

portagem /por'taʒẽ/ f (Port) toll

porta|chaves /porta'ʃavis/ m invar key-holder ou key-ring; **~jóias** m invar jewellery box; **~lápis** m invar pencil holder; **~-luvas** m invar glove compartment; **~-malas** m invar boot, (Amer) trunk; **~-níqueis** m invar purse

portanto /por'tãtu/ conj therefore

portão /por'tãw/ m gate

portar /por'tar/ vt carry; **~se** vpr behave

porta-retrato /portaxe'tratu/ m photo frame; **~-revistas** m invar magazine rack

portaria /porta'ria/ f (entrada) entrance; (decreto) decree

portá|til (pl ~teis) a portable

porta-toalhas /portato'aʎas/ m invar towel rail; **~-voz** m/f spokesman / f-woman

porte /'pɔrtʃi/ m (frete) carriage; (de cartas etc) postage; (de pessoa)

bearing; (dimensão) scale; **de grande/pequeno ~** large-/small-scale

porteiro /por'teru/ m doorman; **~ eletrónico** entryphone

porto /'portu/ m port; **o Porto** Oporto; **~ de escala** port of call; **Porto Rico** m Puerto Rico; **~-riquenho** /e/ a & m Puerto-rican; **porto USB** m USB port

portuense /portu'ẽsi/ a & m/f (person) from Oporto

Portugal /portu'gaw/ m Portugal

portu|guês /portu'ges/ a & m (f ~guesa) Portuguese

portuário /portu'ariu/ a port □ m dock worker, docker

po|sar /po'zar/ vi pose; **~se** /o/ f pose; (de filme) exposure

pós-datar /pɔzda'tar/ vt postdate

pós-escrito /pɔzis'kritu/ m postscript

pós-gradua|ção /pɔzgradua'sãw/ f postgraduation; **~do** a & m postgraduate

pós-guerra /pɔz'gɛxa/ m post-war period; **a Europa do ~** post-war Europe

posi|ção /pozi'sãw/ f position; **~cionar** vt position; **~tivo** a & m positive

posologia /pozolo'ʒia/ f dosage

pos|sante /po'sãtʃi/ a powerful; **~se** /ɔ/ f (de casa etc) possession, ownership; (do presidente etc) swearing in; pl (pertences) possessions; **tomar ~se** take office; **tomar ~se de** take possession of

posses|são /pose'sãw/ f possession; **~sivo** a possessive; **~so** /ɛ/ a possessed; (com raiva) furious

possibili|dade /posibili'dadʒi/ f possibility; **~tar** vt make possible

possí|vel /po'sivew/ (pl ~veis) a possible; **fazer todo o ~vel** do one's best

possuir /posu'ir/ vt possess; (ser dono de) own

posta /'pɔsta/ f (de peixe) steak

pos|tal /pos'taw/ (pl ~**tais**) a postal □ m postcard

postar /pos'tar/ vt place; ~**-se** vpr position o.s.

poste /'pɔstʃi/ m post

pôster /'poster/ m poster

posteri|dade /posteri'dadʒi/ f posterity; ~**or** a (no tempo) subsequent, later; (no espaço) rear; ~**ormente** adv subsequently

postiço /pos'tʃisu/ a false

posto /'pɔstu/ m post; ~ **de gasolina** petrol station, (Amer) gas station; ~ **de saúde** health centre □ pp de **pôr**; ~ **que** although

póstumo /'pɔstumu/ a posthumous

postura /pos'tura/ f posture

potá|vel /po'tavew/ (pl ~**veis**) a **água** ~**vel** drinking water

pote /'pɔtʃi/ m pot; (de vidro) jar

potência /po'tẽsia/ f power

poten|cial /potẽsi'aw/ (pl ~**ciais**) a & m potential; ~**te** a potent

potro /'potru/ m foal

pouco /'poku/ a & pron little; pl few □ adv not much □ m **um** ~ a little; ~ **a** ~ little by little; **aos** ~**s** gradually; **daqui a** ~ shortly; **por** ~ almost; ~ **tempo** a short time

pou|pança /po'pãsa/ f saving; (conta) savings account; ~**par** vt save; spare <vida>

pouquinho /po'kiɲu/ m **um** ~ (**de**) a little

pou|sada /po'zada/ f inn; ~**sar** vi land; ~**so** m landing

po|vão /po'vãw/ m common people; ~**vo** /o/ m people

povo|ação /povoa'sãw/ f settlement; ~**ar** vt populate

poxa /'pɔʃa/ int gosh

pra /pra/ prep (fam) veja **para**

praça /'prasa/ f (largo) square;

(mercado) market □ m (soldado) private

prado /'pradu/ m meadow

pra-frente /pra'frẽtʃi/ a invar (fam) with it, modern

praga /'praga/ f curse; (inseto, doença, pessoa) pest

prag|mático /prag'matʃiku/ a pragmatic; ~**matismo** m pragmatism

praguejar /prage'ʒar/ vt/i curse

praia /'praja/ f beach

pran|cha /'prãʃa/ f plank; (de surfe) board; ~**cheta** /e/ f drawing board

pranto /'prãtu/ m weeping

pra|ta /'prata/ f silver; ~**taria** f (coisas de prata) silverware; ~**teado** a silver-plated; (cor) silver

prateleira /prate'lera/ f shelf

prática /'pratʃika/ f practice; **na** ~ in practice

prati|cante /pratʃi'kãtʃi/ a practising □ m/f apprentice; (de esporte etc) player; ~**car** vt practise; (cometer, executar) carry out □ vi practise; ~**cável** (pl ~**cáveis**) a practicable

prático /'pratʃiku/ a practical

prato /'pratu/ m (objeto) plate; (comida) dish; (parte de uma refeição) course; (do toca-discos) turntable; pl (instrumento) cymbals; ~ **fundo** dish; ~ **principal** main course

praxe /'praʃi/ f normal practice; **de** ~ usually

prazer /pra'zer/ m pleasure; **muito** ~ (**em conhecê-lo**) pleased to meet you; ~**oso** /o/ a pleasurable

prazo /'prazu/ m term, time; **a** ~ <compra etc> on credit; **a curto/longo** ~ in the short/long term; **último** ~ deadline

preâmbulo /pri'ãbulu/ m preamble

precário /pre'kariu/ a precarious

precaução /prekaw'sãw/ f precaution

preca|ver-se /preka'versi/ vpr take precautions (**de** against); **~vido** a cautious

prece /'prɛsi/ f prayer

prece|dência /prese'dẽsia/ f precedence; **~dente** a preceding □ m precedent; **~der** vt/i precede

preceito /pre'sejtu/ m precept

precioso /presi'ozu/ a precious

precipício /presi'pisiu/ m precipice

precipi|tação /presipita'sãw/ f haste; (chuva etc) precipitation; **~tado** a <fuga> headlong; <decisão, ato> hasty, rash; **~tar** vt (lançar) throw; (antecipar) hasten; **~tar-se** vpr (lançar-se) throw o.s.; (apressar-se) rush; (agir sem pensar) act rashly

precisão /presi'zãw/ f precision, accuracy

precisamente /presiza'mẽtʃi/ adv precisely

preci|sar /presi'zar/ vt (necessitar) need; (indicar com exatidão) specify □ vi be necessary; **~sar de** need; **~so ir** I have to go; **~sa-se** wanted; **~so a** (exato) precise; (necessário) necessary

preço /'presu/ m price; **~ de custo** cost price; **~ fixo** set price

precoce /pre'kɔsi/ a <fruto> early; <velhice, calvície etc> mature; <criança> precocious

precon|cebido /prekõse'bidu/ a preconceived; **~ceito** m prejudice; **~ceituoso** a prejudiced

preconizar /prekoni'zar/ vt advocate

precursor /prekur'sor/ m forerunner

preda|dor /preda'dor/ m predator; **~tório** a predatory

predecessor /predese'sor/ m predecessor

predestinar /predestʃi'nar/ vt predestine

predeterminar /predetermi'nar/ vt predetermine

predição /predʒi'sãw/ f prediction

predile|ção /predʒile'sãw/ f preference; **~to** /ɛ/ a favourite

prédio /'predʒiu/ m building

predis|por /predʒis'por/ vt prepare (**para** for); (tornar parcial) prejudice (**contra** against); **~por-se** vpr prepare o.s.; **~posto** a predisposed; (contra) prejudiced

predizer /predʒi'zer/ vt predict, foretell

predomi|nância /predomi'nãsia/ f predominance; **~nante** a predominant; **~nar** vi predominate

predomínio /predo'miniu/ m predominance

preencher /priẽ'ʃer/ vt fill; fill in, (Amer) fill out <formulário>; meet <requisitos>

pré-escola /prɛis'kɔla/ f infant school, (Amer) preschool; **~escolar** a pre-school; **~estréia** f preview; **~fabricado** a prefabricated

prefácio /pre'fasiu/ m preface

prefei|to /pre'fejtu/ m mayor; **~tura** f prefecture; (prédio) town hall

prefe|rência /prefe'rẽsia/ f preference; (direito no trânsito) right of way; **de ~rência** preferably; **~rencial** (pl **~renciais**) a preferential; <rua> main; **~rido** a favourite; **~rir** vt prefer (**a** to); **~rível** (pl **~ríveis**) a preferable

prefixo /pre'fiksu/ m prefix

prega /'prɛga/ f pleat

pregador[1] /prega'dor/ m (de roupa) peg

pre|gador[2] /prega'dor/ m (quem prega) preacher; **~gão** m (de vendedor) cry; **o ~gão** (na bolsa de valores) trading; (em leilão) bidding

pregar[1] /pre'gar/ *vt* fix; (*com prego*) nail; sew on <*botão*>; **não ∼ olho** not sleep a wink; **∼ uma peça em** play a trick on; **∼ um susto em alg** give s.o. a fright

pregar[2] /pre'gar/ *vt/i* preach

prego /'pregu/ *m* nail

pregui|ça /pre'gisa/ *f* laziness; (*bicho*) sloth; **estou com ∼ça de ir** I can't be bothered to go; **∼çoso** *a* lazy

pré-histórico /prɛjs'tɔriku/ *a* pre-historic

preia-mar /preja'mar/ *f* high tide

prejudi|car /preʒudʒi'kar/ *vt* harm; damage <*saúde*>; **∼car-se** *vpr* harm o.s.; **∼cial** (*pl* ∼**ciais**) *a* harmful, damaging (**a** to)

prejuízo /preʒu'izu/ *m* damage; (*financeiro*) loss; **em ∼ de** to the detriment of

prejulgar /preʒuw'gar/ *vt* pre-judge

preliminar /prelimi'nar/ *a & m/f* preliminary

prelo /'prelu/ *m* printing press; **no ∼** being printed

prelúdio /pre'ludʒiu/ *m* prelude

prematuro /prema'turu/ *a* premature

premeditar /premedʒi'tar/ *vt* premeditate

premente /pre'mẽtʃi/ *a* pressing

premi|ado /premi'adu/ *a* <*romance, atleta etc*> prize-winning; <*bilhete, número etc*> winning □ *m* prize-winner; **∼ar** *vt* award a prize to <*romance, atleta etc*>; reward <*honestidade, mérito*>

prêmio /'premiu/ *m* prize; (*de seguro*) premium; **Grande Prêmio** (*de F1*) Grand Prix

premissa /pre'misa/ *f* premiss

premonição /premoni'sãw/ *f* premonition

pré-na|tal /prɛna'taw/ (*pl* ∼**tais**) *a* antenatal, (*Amer*) prenatal

prenda /'prẽda/ *f* (*Port*) present; **∼s domésticas** household chores; **∼do** *a* domesticated

pren|dedor /prẽde'dor/ *m* clip; **∼dedor de roupa** clothes peg; **∼der** *vt* (*pregar*) fix; (*capturar*) arrest; (*atar*) tie up <*cachorro*>; tie back <*cabelo*>; (*restringir*) restrict; (*ligar afetivamente*) bind; **∼der (a atenção de) alg** grab s.o.('s attention)

prenhe /'preɲi/ *a* pregnant

prenome /pre'nomi/ *m* first name

pren|sa /'prẽsa/ *f* press; **∼sar** *vt* press

preocu|pação /preokupa'sãw/ *f* concern; **∼pante** *a* worrying; **∼par** *vt* worry; **∼par-se** *vpr* worry (**com** about)

prepa|ração /prepara'sãw/ *f* preparation; **∼rado** *m* preparation; **∼rar** *vt* prepare; **∼rar-se** *vpr* prepare, get ready; **∼rativos** *m pl* preparations; **∼ro** *m* preparation; (*competência*) knowledge; **∼ro físico** physical fitness

preponderar /prepõde'rar/ *vi* prevail (**sobre** over)

preposição /prepozi'sãw/ *f* preposition

prerrogativa /prexoga'tʃiva/ *f* prerogative

presa /'preza/ *f* (*de caça*) prey; (*de cobra*) fang; (*de elefante*) tusk; **∼ de guerra** spoils of war

prescin|dir /presĩ'dʒir/ *vi* **∼dir de** dispense with; **∼dível** (*pl* ∼**díveis**) *a* dispensable

pres|crever /preskre'ver/ *vt* prescribe; **∼crição** *f* prescription; (*norma*) rule

presen|ça /pre'zẽsa/ *f* presence; **∼ça de espírito** presence of mind; **∼ciar** *vt* (*estar presente a*) be present at; (*testemunhar*) witness; **∼te** *a & m* present; **∼tear** *vt* **∼tear alg (com aco)** give s.o. (sth as) a present

presépio /prɛˈzɛpiu/ *m* crib

preser|vação /prezervaˈsãw/ *f* preservation; **~var** *vt* preserve, protect; **~vativo** *m* (*em comida*) preservative; (*camisinha*) condom

presi|dência /preziˈdẽsia/ *f* presidency; (*de uma reunião*) chair; **~dencial** (*pl* **~denciais**) *a* presidential; **~dencialismo** *m* presidential system; **~dente** (*f* **~denta**) president; (*de uma reunião*) chairperson

presidiário /preziˈdʒiariu/ *m* convict

presídio /preˈzidʒiu/ *m* prison

presidir /preziˈdʒir/ *vi* preside (**a** over)

presilha /preˈziʎa/ *f* fastener; (*de cabelo*) slide

preso /ˈprezu/ *pp de* **prender** □ *m* prisoner; **ficar ~** get stuck; <*saia, corda etc*> get caught

pressa /ˈprɛsa/ *f* hurry; **às ~** in a hurry, hurriedly; **estar com** *ou* **ter ~** be in a hurry

presságio /preˈsaʒiu/ *m* omen

pressão /preˈsãw/ *f* pressure; **fazer ~ sobre** put pressure on; **~ arterial** blood pressure

pressen|timento /presẽtʃiˈmẽtu/ *m* premonition, feeling; **~tir** *vt* sense

pressionar /presioˈnar/ *vt* press <*botão*>; pressure <*pessoa*>

pressupor /presuˈpor/ *vt* <*pessoa*> presume; <*coisa*> presuppose

pressurizado /presuriˈzadu/ *a* pressurized

pres|tação /prestaˈsãw/ *f* repayment, instalment; **~tar** *vt* render <*contas, serviço*> □ *vi* be of use; **não ~ta** he/it is no good; **~tar atenção** pay attention; **~tar juramento** take an oath; **~tativo** *a* helpful; **~tável** (*pl* **~táveis**) *a* serviceable

prestes /ˈprɛstʃis/ *a invar* **~ a** about to

prestidigita|ção /prestʃidʒiʒitaˈsãw/ *f* conjuring; **~dor** *m* conjurer

pres|tigiar /prestʃiʒiˈar/ *vt* give prestige to; **~tígio** *m* prestige; **~tigioso** /o/ *a* prestigious

préstimo /ˈprɛstʃimu/ *m* merit

presumir /prezuˈmir/ *vt* presume

presun|ção /prezũˈsãw/ *f* presumption; **~çoso** /o/ *a* presumptuous

presunto /preˈzũtu/ *m* ham

pretendente /pretẽˈdẽtʃi/ *m/f* (*candidato*) candidate, applicant

preten|der /pretẽˈder/ *vt* intend; **~são** *f* pretension; **~sioso** /o/ *a* pretentious

preterir /preteˈrir/ *vt* disregard

pretérito /preˈtɛritu/ *m* preterite

pretexto /preˈtestu/ *m* pretext

preto /ˈpretu/ *a & m* black; **~e-branco** *a invar* black and white

prevalecer /prevaleˈser/ *vi* prevail

prevenção /prevẽˈsãw/ *f* (*impedimento*) prevention; (*parcialidade*) bias

prevenir /preveˈnir/ *vt* (*evitar*) prevent; (*avisar*) warn; **~-se** *vpr* take precautions

preventivo /prevẽˈtʃivu/ *a* preventive

prever /preˈver/ *vt* foresee, predict

previdência /previˈdẽsia/ *f* foresight; **~ social** social security

prévio /ˈprɛviu/ *a* prior

previ|são /previˈzãw/ *f* prediction, forecast; **~são do tempo** weather forecast; **~sível** (*pl* **~síveis**) *a* predictable

pre|zado /preˈzadu/ *a* esteemed; **Prezado Senhor** Dear Sir; **~zar** *vt* think highly of; **~zar-se** *vpr* have self-respect

prima /ˈprima/ *f* cousin

primário /priˈmariu/ *a* primary; (*fundamental*) basic

primata /priˈmata/ *m* primate

primave|ra /prima'vera/ *f* spring;
 (*flor*) primrose; **~ril** (*pl* **~ris**)
 a spring

primazia /prima'zia/ *f* primacy

primei|ra /pri'mera/ *f* (*marcha*)
 first (gear); **de ~ra** first-rate;
 <*carne*> prime; **~ra-dama** (*pl*
 ~ras-damas) *f* first lady;
 ~ranista *m/f* first-year
 (student); **~ro** *a & adv* first; **no
 dia ~ro de maio** on the first of
 May; **em ~ro lugar** (*para começar*) in the first place; (*numa
 corrida, competição*) in first
 place; **~ro de tudo** first of all;
 ~ros socorros first aid; **~ro-
 ministro** (*pl* **~ros-ministros**)
 m (*f* **~ra-ministra**) prime-
 minister

primitivo /primi'tʃivu/ *a* primitive

primo /'primu/ *m* cousin □ *a* **número ~** prime number; **~gêni-
 to** *a & m* first-born

primor /pri'mor/ *m* perfection

primordi|al /primordʒi'aw/ (*pl*
 ~ais) *a* (*primitivo*) primordial;
 (*fundamental*) fundamental

primoroso /primo'rozu/ *a* exquisite

princesa /prĩ'seza/ *f* princess

princi|pado /prĩsipi'adu/ *m* prin-
 cipality; **~pal** (*pl* **~pais**) *a*
 main □ *m* principal

príncipe /'prĩsipi/ *m* prince

principiante /prĩsipi'ãtʃi/ *m/f* beginner

princípio /prĩ'sipiu/ *m* (*início*) beginning; (*regra*) principle; **em ~**
 in principle; **por ~** on principle

priori|dade /priori'dadʒi/ *f*
 priority; **~tário** *a* priority

prisão /pri'zãw/ *f* (*ato de prender*)
 arrest; (*cadeia*) prison; (*encarce-
 ramento*) imprisonment; **~ per-
 pétua** life imprisonment; **~ de
 ventre** constipation

prisioneiro /prizio'neru/ *m*
 prisoner

prisma /'prizma/ *m* prism

privação /priva'sãw/ *f* deprivation

privacidade /privasi'dadʒi/ *f* privacy

pri|vada /pri'vada/ *f* toilet;
 ~vado *a* private; **~vado de** de-
 prived of; **~var** *vt* deprive (**de**
 of); **~var-se** *vpr* deprive o.s.
 (**de of**)

privati|vo /priva'tʃivu/ *a* private;
 ~zar *vt* privatize

privi|legiado /privileʒi'adu/ *a*
 privileged; <*tratamento*> prefer-
 ential; **~legiar** *vt* favour; **~-
 légio** *m* privilege

pro (*fam*) = **para + o**

pró /prɔ/ *adv* for □ *m* **os ~s e os
 contras** the pros and cons

proa /'proa/ *f* bow, prow

probabilidade /probabili'dadʒi/ *f*
 probability

proble|ma /pro'blema/ *m* prob-
 lem; **~mático** *a* problematic

proce|dência /prose'dẽsia/ *f* ori-
 gin; **~dente** *a* logical; **~dente
 de** coming from; **~der** *vi* proceed; (*comportar-se*) behave; (*na
 justiça*) take legal action; **~der
 de** come from; **~dimento** *m*
 procedure; (*comportamento*) behaviour; (*na justiça*) proceedings

proces|sador /prosesa'dor/ *m* pro-
 cessor; **~sador de texto** word
 processor; **~samento** *m* processing; (*na justiça*) prosecution;
 ~samento de dados data
 processing; **~sar** *vt* process;
 (*por crime*) prosecute; (*por causa
 civil*) sue; **~so** /ɛ/ *m* process;
 (*criminal*) trial; (*civil*) lawsuit

procla|mação /proklama'sãw/ *f*
 proclamation; **~mar** *vt* proclaim

procri|ação /prokria'sãw/ *f* pro-
 creation; **~ar** *vt/i* procreate

procu|ra /pro'kura/ *f* search; (*de
 produto*) demand; **à ~ra de** in
 search of; **~ração** *f* power of

attorney; ~**rado** *a* sought after, in demand; ~**rado pela polícia** wanted by the police; ~**rador** *m* (*mandatário*) proxy; (*advogado*) public prosecutor; ~**rar** *vt* look for; (*contatar*) get in touch with; (*ir visitar*) look up; ~**rar saber** try to find out

prodígio /pro'dʒiʒiu/ *m* wonder; (*pessoa*) prodigy

prodigioso /prodʒiʒi'ozu/ *a* prodigious

pródigo /'prɔdigu/ *a* lavish, extravagant

produ|ção /produ'sãw/ *f* production; ~**tividade** *f* productivity; ~**tivo** *a* productive; ~**to** *m* product; (*renda*) proceeds; ~**to nacional bruto** gross national product; ~**tos agrícolas** agricultural produce; ~**tor** *m* producer □ *a* **país** ~**tor de trigo** wheat-producing country; ~**zido** *a* (*fam: arrumado*) done up; ~**zir** *vt* produce

proeminente /proemi'nẽtʃi/ *a* prominent

proeza /pro'eza/ *f* achievement

profa|nar /profa'nar/ *vt* desecrate; ~**no** *a* profane

profecia /profe'sia/ *f* prophecy

proferir /profe'rir/ *vt* utter; give <*discurso, palestra*>; pass <*sentença*>

profes|sar /profe'sar/ *vt* profess; ~**so** /ɛ/ *a* professed; <*político etc*> seasoned; ~**sor** *m* teacher; ~**sor catedrático** professor

profeta /pro'fɛta/ *m* prophet; ~**fético** *a* prophetic; ~**fetizar** *vt* prophesy

profissão /profi'sãw/ *f* profession

profissio|nal /profisio'naw/ (*pl* ~**nais**) *a* & *m/f* professional; ~**nalismo** *m* professionalism; ~**nalizante** *a* vocational; ~**nalizar-se** *vpr* <*esportista etc*> turn professional

profun|didade /profũdʒi'dadʒi/ *f*

depth; ~**do** *a* deep; <*sentimento etc*> profound

profusão /profu'zãw/ *f* profusion

prog|nosticar /prognostʃi'kar/ *vt* forecast; ~**nóstico** *m* forecast; (*med*) prognosis

progra|ma /pro'grama/ *m* programme; (*de computador*) program; (*diversão*) thing to do; ~**mação** *f* programming; ~**mador** *m* programmer; ~**mar** *vt* plan; program <*computador etc*>; ~**mável** (*pl* ~**máveis**) *a* programmable

progredir /progre'dʒir/ *vi* progress

progres|são /progre'sãw/ *f* progression; ~**sista** *a* & *m/f* progressive; ~**sivo** *a* progressive; ~**so** /ɛ/ *m* progress

proi|bição /proibi'sãw/ *f* ban (de on); ~**bido** *a* forbidden; ~**bir** *vt* forbid (**alg de** s.o. to); ban <*livro, importações etc*>; ~**bitivo** *a* prohibitive

proje|ção /proʒe'sãw/ *f* projection; ~**tar** *vt* plan <*viagem, estrada etc*>; design <*casa, carro etc*>; project <*filme, luz*>

projétil /pro'ʒɛtʃiw/ (*pl* ~**teis**) *m* projectile

proje|tista /proʒe'tʃista/ *m/f* designer; ~**to** /ɛ/ *m* project; (*de casa, carro*) design; ~**to de lei** bill; ~**tor** *m* projector

prol /prɔw/ *m* **em** ~ **de** on behalf of

prole /'prɔli/ *f* offspring; ~**tariado** *m* proletariat; ~**tário** *a* & *m* proletarian

prolife|ração /prolifera'sãw/ *f* proliferation; ~**rar** *vi* proliferate

prolífico /pro'lifiku/ *a* prolific

prolixo /pro'liksu/ *a* verbose, long-winded

prólogo /'prɔlogu/ *m* prologue

prolon|gado /prolõ'gadu/ *a* prolonged; ~**gar** *vt* prolong; ~**gar-se** *vpr* go on

promessa /pro'mɛsa/ f promise

prome|tedor /promete'dor/ a promising; **~ter** vt promise □ vi (dar esperança) show promise; **~ter voltar** promise to return

promíscuo /pro'miskuu/ a promiscuous

promis|sor /promi'sor/ a promising; **~sória** f promissory note

promoção /promo'sãw/ f promotion

promontório /promõ'tɔriu/ m promontory

promo|tor /promo'tor/ m promoter; (advogado) prosecutor; **~ver** vt promote

promulgar /promuw'gar/ vt promulgate

prono|me /pro'nomi/ m pronoun; **~minal** (pl **~minais**) a pronominal

pron|tidão /prõtʃi'dãw/ f readiness; **com ~tidão** promptly; **estar de ~tidão** be at the ready; **~tificar** vt get ready; **~tificar-se** vpr volunteer (a to; **para** for); **~to** a ready; (rápido) prompt □ int that's that; **~to-socorro** (pl **~tos-socorros**) m casualty department; (Port: reboque) towtruck; **~tuário** m (manual) manual, handbook; (médico) notes; (policial) record, file

pronúncia /pro'nũsia/ f pronunciation

pronunci|ado /pronũsi'adu/ a pronounced; **~amento** m pronouncement; **~ar** vt pronounce

propagar /propa'gar/ vt propagate <espécie>; spread <notícia, idéia, fé>; **~se** vpr spread <espécie> propagate

propen|são /propẽ'sãw/ f propensity; **~so** a inclined (a to)

pro|piciar /propisi'ar/ vt provide; **~pício** a propitious

propina /pro'pina/ f bribe; (Port: escolar) fee

propor /pro'por/ vt propose; **~-se** vpr set o.o. <objetivo>; **~-se a estudar** set out to study

proporção /propor'sãw/ f proportion

proporcio|nado /proporsio'nadu/ a proportionate (a to); **bem ~nado** well proportioned; **~nal** (pl **~nais**) a proportional; **~nar** vt provide

propo|sição /propozi'sãw/ f proposition; **~tado** a, **~tal** (pl **~tais**) a intentional

propósito /pro'pɔzitu/ m intention; **a ~** by the way; **a ~ de** on the subject of; **chegar a ~** arrive at the right time; **de ~** on purpose

proposta /pro'pɔsta/ f proposal

propriamente /propria'mẽtʃi/ adv strictly; **a casa ~ dita** the house proper

proprie|dade /proprie'dadʒi/ f property; (direito sobre bens) ownership; **~tário** m owner; (de casa alugada) landlord

próprio /'propriu/ a (de si) own; <sentido> literal; <nome> proper; **meu ~ carro** my own car; **um carro ~** a car of my own; **o ~ rei** the king himself; **~ a** peculiar to; **~ para** suited to

prorro|gação /proxoga'sãw/ f extension; (de dívida) deferment; (em futebol etc) extra time; **~gar** vt extend <prazo>; defer <pagamento>

pro|sa /'prɔza/ f prose; **~sador** m prose writer; **~saico** a prosaic

proscrever /proskre'ver/ vt proscribe

prospecto /pros'pɛktu/ m (livro) brochure; (folheto) leaflet

prospe|rar /prospe'rar/ vi prosper; **~ridade** f prosperity

próspero /'prɔsperu/ a prosperous

prosse|guimento /prosegi'mẽtu/ m continuation; **~guir** vt continue □ vi proceed, go on

prostitu|ição /prostʃitui'sãw/ *f* prostitution; **~ta** *f* prostitute

pros|tração /prostra'sãw/ *f* debility; **~trado** *a* prostrate; **~trar** *vt* prostrate; (*enfraquecer*) debilitate; **~trar-se** *vpr* prostrate o.s.

protago|nista /protago'nista/ *m/f* protagonist; **~nizar** *vt* to be at the centre of <*acontecimento*>; feature in <*peça, filme*>

prote|ção /prote'sãw/ *f* protection; **~cionismo** *m* protectionism; **~cionista** *a & m/f* protectionist; **~ger** *vt* protect; **~gido** *m* protégé

proteína /prote'ina/ *f* protein

protelar /prote'lar/ *vt* put off

protes|tante /protes'tãtʃi/ *a & m/f* Protestant; **~tar** *vt/i* protest; **~to** /ɛ/ *m* protest

protetor /prote'tor/ *m* protector □ *a* protective

protocolo /proto'kɔlu/ *m* protocol; (*registro*) register

protótipo /pro'tɔtʃipu/ *m* prototype

protuberância /protube'rãsia/ *f* bulge

pro|va /'prɔva/ *f* (*que comprova*) proof; (*teste*) trial; (*exame*) exam; (*esportiva*) competition; (*de livro etc*) proof; *pl* (*na justiça*) evidence; **à ~va de bala** bulletproof; **pôr à ~va** put to the test; **~vado** *a* proven; **~var** *vt* try <*comida*>; try on <*roupa*>; try out <*carro, novo sistema etc*>; (*comprovar*) prove

prová|vel /pro'vavew/ (*pl* **~veis**) *a* probable

proveito /pro'vejtu/ *m* profit, advantage; **tirar ~ de** (*beneficiar-se*) profit from; (*explorar*) take advantage of; **~so** /o/ *a* useful

proveni|ência /proveni'ẽsia/ *f* origin; **~ente** *a* originating (de from)

proventos /pro'vẽtus/ *m pl* proceeds

prover /pro'ver/ *vt* provide (**with**)

provérbio /pro'vɛrbiu/ *m* proverb

proveta /pro'veta/ *f* test tube; **bebê de ~** test-tube baby

provi|dência /provi'dẽsia/ *f* (*medida*) measure, step; (*divina*) providence; **tomar ~dências** take steps, take action; **~denciar** *vt* (*prover*) get hold of, provide; (*resolver*) see to, take care of □ *vi* take action

província /pro'vĩsia/ *f* province; (*longe da cidade*) provinces

provinci|al /provĩsi'aw/ (*pl* **~ais**) *a* provincial; **~ano** *a & m* provincial

provir /pro'vir/ *vi* come (**de** from); (*resultar*) be due (**de** to)

provi|são /provi'zãw/ *f* provision; **~sório** *a* provisional

provo|cação /provoka'sãw/ *f* provocation; **~cador,** **~cante** *a* provocative; **~car** *vt* provoke; (*ocasionar*) cause

proximidade /prosimi'dadʒi/ *f* closeness; *pl* (*imediações*) vicinity

próximo /'prɔsimu/ *a* (*no tempo*) next; (*perto*) near, close (**de** to); <*parente*> close; <*futuro*> near □ *m* neighbour, fellow man

pru|dência /pru'dẽsia/ *f* prudence; **~dente** *a* prudent

prumo /'prumu/ *m* plumb line; **a ~** vertically

prurido /pru'ridu/ *m* itch

pseudônimo /psew'donimu/ *m* pseudonym

psica|nálise /psika'nalizi/ *f* psychoanalysis; **~nalista** *m/f* psychoanalyst

psi|cologia /psikolo'ʒia/ *f* psychology; **~cológico** *a* psychological; **~cólogo** *m* psychologist

psico|pata /psiko'pata/ *m/f* psychopath; **~se** /ɔ/ *f* psychosis;

~terapeuta /m/f/ psycho-therapist; **~terapia** f psychotherapy

psicótico /pisi'kɔtʃiku/ a & m psychotic

psique /pi'siki/ f psyche

psiqui|atra /pisiki'atra/ m/f psychiatrist; **~atria** f psychiatry; **~átrico** a psychiatric

psíquico /pi'sikiku/ a psychological

pua /'pua/ f bit

puberdade /puber'dadʒi/ f puberty

publi|cação /publika'sãw/ f publication; **~car** vt publish

publici|dade /publisi'dadʒi/ f publicity; (reclame) advertising; **~tário** a publicity; (de reclame) advertising □ m advertising executive

público /'publiku/ a public □ m public; (platéia) audience; **em ~** in public; **o grande ~** the general public

pudera /pu'dɛra/ int no wonder!

pudico /pu'dʒiku/ a prudish

pudim /pu'dʒĩ/ m pudding

pudor /pu'dor/ m modesty, shame

pue|ril /pue'riw/ (pl **~ris**) a puerile

pugilis|mo /puʒi'lizmu/ m boxing; **~ta** m boxer

pu|ído /pu'idu/ a worn through; **~ir** vt wear through

pujan|ça /pu'ʒãsa/ f power; **~te** a powerful; (de saúde) robust

pular /pu'lar/ vt jump (over); (omitir) skip □ vi jump; **~ de contente** jump for joy; **~ carnaval** celebrate Carnival; **~ corda** skip

pulga /'puwga/ f flea

pulmão /puw'mãw/ m lung

pulo /'pulu/ m jump; **dar um ~ em** drop by; **dar ~s** jump up and down

pulôver /pu'lover/ m pullover

púlpito /'puwpitu/ m pulpit

pul|sar /puw'sar/ vi pulsate; **~seira** f bracelet; **~so** m (do braço) wrist; (batimento arterial) pulse

pulular /pulu'lar/ vi swarm (de with)

pulveri|zador /puwveriza'dor/ m spray; **~zar** vt spray <líquido>; (reduzir a pó, fig) pulverize

pun|gente /pũ'ʒẽtʃi/ a consuming; **~gir** vt afflict

pu|nhado /pu'ɲadu/ m handful; **~nhal** (pl **~nhais**) m dagger; **~nhalada** f stab wound; **~nho** m fist; (de camisa etc) cuff; (de espada) hilt

pu|nição /puni'sãw/ f punishment; **~nir** vt punish; **~nitivo** a punitive

pupila /pu'pila/ f pupil

purê /pu're/ m purée; **~ de batata** mashed potato

pureza /pu'reza/ f purity

pur|gante /pur'gãtʃi/ a & m purgative; **~gar** vt purge; **~gatório** m purgatory

purificar /purifi'kar/ vt purify

puritano /puri'tanu/ a & m puritan

puro /'puru/ a pure; <aguardente> neat; **~ e simples** pure and simple; **~-sangue** (pl **~s-sangues**) a & m thoroughbred

púrpura /'purpura/ a purple

purpurina /purpu'rina/ f glitter

purulento /puru'lẽtu/ a festering

pus /pus/ m pus

pusilânime /puzi'lanimi/ a faint-hearted

pústula /'pustula/ f pimple

puta /'puta/ f whore □ a invar (fam) **um ~ carro** one hell of a car; **filho da ~** (chulo) bastard; **~ que (o) pariu!** (chulo) fucking hell!

puto /'putu/ a (fam) furious

putrefazer /putrefa'zer/ vi putrefy

puxa /'puʃa/ int gosh

pu|xado /puˈʃadu/ a (fam) <exame> tough; <trabalho> hard; <aluguel, preço> steep; **~xador** m handle; **~xão** m pull, tug; **~xa-puxa** m toffee; **~xar** vt pull; strike up <conversa>; bring up <assunto>; **~xar de uma perna** limp; **~xar para** (parecer com) take after; **~xar por** (exigir muito de) push (hard); **~xa-saco** m (fam) creep

Q

QI /ke i/ m IQ
quadra /ˈkwadra/ f (de tênis etc) court; (quarteirão) block; **~do** a & m square
quadragésimo /kwadraˈʒɛzimu/ a fortieth
qua|dril /kwaˈdriw/ (pl **~dris**) m hip
quadrilha /kwaˈdriʎa/ f (bando) gang; (dança) square dance
quadrinho /kwaˈdriɲu/ m frame; **história em ~s** comic strip
quadro /ˈkwadru/ m picture; (pintado) painting; (tabela) table; (pessoal) staff; (equipe) team; (de uma peça) scene; **~-negro** (pl **~s-negros**) m blackboard
quadruplicar /kwadrupliˈkar/ vt/i quadruple
quádruplo /ˈkwadruplu/ a quadruple; **~s** m pl (crianças) quads
qual /kwaw/ (pl **quais**) pron which (one); **o/a ~** (coisa) that, which; (pessoa) that, who; **~ é o seu nome?** what's your name?; **seja ~ for a decisão** whatever the decision may be
qualidade /kwaliˈdadʒi/ f quality; **na ~ de** in one's capacity as, as
qualifi|cação /kwalifikaˈsãw/ f qualification; **~car** vt qualify; (descrever) describe (**de** as); **~car-se** vpr qualify

qualitativo /kwalitaˈtʃivu/ a qualitative
qualquer /kwawˈkɛr/ (pl **quaisquer**) a any; **um livro ~** any old book; **~ um** any one
quando /ˈkwãdu/ adv & conj when; **~ quer que** whenever; **~ de** at the time of; **~ muito** at most
quantia /kwãˈtʃia/ f amount
quanti|dade /kwãtʃiˈdadʒi/ f quantity; **uma ~dade de** a lot of; **em ~dade** in large amounts; **~ficar** vt quantify; **~tativo** a quantitative
quanto /ˈkwãtu/ adv & pron how much; (pl how many; **~ tempo?** how long?; **~ mais barato melhor** the cheaper the better; **tão alto ~ eu** as tall as me; **~ ri!** how I laughed!; **~ a** as for; **~ antes** as soon as possible
quaren|ta /kwaˈrẽta/ a & m forty; **~tão** a & m (f **~tona**) forty-year-old; **~tena** /e/ f quarantine
quaresma /kwaˈrezma/ f Lent
quarta /ˈkwarta/ f (dia) Wednesday; (marcha) fourth (gear); **~-de-final** (pl **~s-de-final**) f quarter final; **~-feira** (pl **~s-feiras**) f Wednesday
quartanista /kwartaˈnista/ m/f fourth-year (student)
quarteirão /kwarteˈrãw/ m block
quar|tel /kwarˈtɛw/ (pl **~téis**) m barracks; **~tel-general** (pl **~téis-generais**) m headquarters
quarteto /kwarˈtetu/ m quartet; **~ de cordas** string quartet
quarto /ˈkwartu/ a fourth □ m (parte) quarter; (aposento) bedroom; (guarda) watch; **são três e/menos um** (Port) it's quarter past/to three; **~ de banho** (Port) bathroom; **~ de hora** quarter of an hour; **~ de hóspedes** guest room
quartzo /ˈkwartzu/ m quartz

quase /'kwazi/ *adv* almost, nearly; ~ **nada/nunca** hardly anything/ever

quatro /'kwatru/ *a & m* four; **de** ~ *(no chão)* on all fours; ~**centos** *a & m* four hundred

que /ki/ *a* which, what; ~ **dia é hoje!** what's the date today?; ~ **homem!** what a man!; ~ **triste!** how sad! □ *pron* what; ~ **é** ~ **é?** what is it? □ *pron rel (coisa)* which, that; *(pessoa)* who, that; *(interrogativo)* what; **o dia em** ~ ... the day when/that ... □ *conj* that; *(porque)* because; **espero** ~ **sim/não** I hope so/not

quê /ke/ *pron* what □ *m* **um** ~ something; **não tem de** ~ don't mention it

quebra /'kɛbra/ *f* break; *(de empresa, banco)* crash; *(de força)* cut; **de** ~ in addition; ~**cabeça** *m* jigsaw (puzzle); *(fig)* puzzle; ~**diço** *a* breakable; ~**do** *a* broken; <*carro*> broken down; ~**dos** *m pl* small change; ~**galho** *(fam)* *m* stopgap; ~**mar** *m* breakwater; ~**-molas** *m invar* speed bump; ~**-nozes** *m invar* nutcrackers; ~**-pau** *(fam) m* row; ~**-quebra** *m* riot

quebrar /ke'brar/ *vt* break □ *vi* break; <*carro etc*> break down; <*banco, empresa etc*> crash, go bust; ~**-se** *vpr* break

queda /'kɛda/ *f* fall; **ter uma** ~ **por** have a soft spot for; ~**-de-braço** *f* arm wrestling

queijeira /ke'ʒera/ *f* cheese dish; ~**jo** *m* cheese; ~**jo prato** cheddar; ~**jo-de-minas** *m* Cheshire cheese

queima /'kejma/ *f* burning; ~**da** *f* forest fire; ~**do** *a* burnt; *(bronzeado)* tanned, brown; **cheiro de** ~**do** smell of burning

queimar /kej'mar/ *vt* burn; *(bronzear)* tan □ *vi* burn; <*lâmpada*> go; <*fusível*> blow; ~**-se**

vpr burn o.s.; *(bronzear-se)* go brown

queima-roupa /kejma'xopa/ *f* à ~ point-blank

quei|xa /'keʃa/ *f* complaint; ~**xar-se** *vpr* complain *(de* about)

queixo /'keʃu/ *m* chin; **bater o** ~ shiver

queixoso /ke'ʃozu/ *a* plaintive □ *m* plaintiff

quem /kẽj/ *pron* who; *(a pessoa que)* anyone who, he who; **de** ~ **é este livro?** whose is this book?; ~ **quer que** whoever; **seja** ~ for whoever it is; ~ **falou isso fui eu** it was me who said that; ~ **me dera (que)** ... I wish ..., if only

Quênia /'kenia/ *m* Kenya

queniano /keni'anu/ *a & m* Kenyan

quen|tão /kẽ'tãw/ *m* mulled wine; ~**te** *a* hot; *(com calor agradável)* warm; ~**tura** *f* heat

quepe /'kɛpi/ *m* cap

quer /ker/ *conj* ~ ... ~ ... whether ... or ...

querer /ke'rer/ *vt/i* want; **quero ir** I want to go; **quero que você vá** I want you to go; **eu queria falar com o Sr X** I'd like to speak to Mr X; **vai** ~ **vir amanhã?** do you want to come tomorrow?; **vou** ~ **um cafezinho** I'd like a coffee; **se você quiser** if you want; **queira sentar** do sit down; ~ **dizer** mean; **quer dizer** *(isto é)* that is to say, I mean

querido /ke'ridu/ *a* dear □ *m* darling

quermesse /ker'mɛsi/ *f* fête, fair

querosene /kero'zeni/ *m* kerosene

questão /kes'tãw/ *f* question; *(assunto)* matter; **em** ~ in question; **fazer** ~ **de** really want to; **não faço** ~ **de ir** I don't mind not going

questio|nar /kestʃio'nar/ *vt/i* question; ~**nário** *m* questionnaire; ~**nável** (*pl* ~**náveis**) *a* questionable

quiabo /ki'abu/ *m* okra

quibe /'kibi/ *m* savoury meatball

quicar /ki'kar/ *vt/i* bounce

quiche /'kiʃi/ *f* quiche

quie|to /ki'etu/ *a* (*calado*) quiet; (*imóvel*) still; ~**tude** *f* quiet

quilate /ki'latʃi/ *m* carat; (*fig*) calibre

quilha /'kiʎa/ *f* keel

quilo /'kilo/ *m* kilo; ~**grama** *m* kilogram; ~**metragem** *f* mileage; ~**métrico** *a* mile-long

quilômetro /ki'lometru/ *m* kilometre

quimbanda /kĩ'bãda/ *m* Afro-Brazilian cult

qui|mera /ki'mɛra/ *f* fantasy; ~**mérico** *a* fanciful

quími|ca /'kimika/ *f* chemistry; ~**co** *a* chemical □ *m* chemist

quimioterapia /kimiotera'pia/ *f* chemotherapy

quimono /ki'mɔnu/ *m* kimono

quina /'kina/ *f* de ~ edgeways

quindim /kĩ'dʒĩ/ *m* sweet made of coconut, sugar and egg yolks

quinhão /ki'ɲãw/ *m* share

quinhentos /ki'ɲẽtus/ *a & m* five hundred

quinina /ki'nina/ *f* quinine

qüinquagésimo /kwĩkwa'ʒezimu/ *a* fiftieth

quinquilharias /kĩkiʎa'rias/ *f pl* knick-knacks

quinta¹ /'kĩta/ *f* (*fazenda*) farm

quinta² /'kĩta/ *f* (*dia*) Thursday; ~**-feira** (*pl* ~**s-feiras**) *f* Thursday

quin|tal /kĩ'taw/ (*pl* ~**tais**) *m* back yard

quinteiro /kĩ'tajru/ *m* (*Port*) farmer

quinteto /kĩ'tetu/ *m* quintet

quin|to /'kĩtu/ *a & m* fifth; ~**tuplo** *a* fivefold; ~**tuplos** *m pl* (*crianças*) quins

quinze /'kĩzi/ *a & m* fifteen; **às dez e** ~ at quarter past ten; **são** ~ **para as dez** it's quarter to ten; ~**na** /e/ *f* fortnight; ~**nal** (*pl* ~**nais**) *a* fortnightly; ~**nalmente** *adv* fortnightly

quiosque /ki'ɔski/ *m* (*banca*) kiosk; (*no jardim*) gazebo

quiro|mância /kiro'mãsia/ *f* palmistry; ~**mante** *m/f* palmist

quisto /'kistu/ *m* cyst

quitan|da /ki'tãda/ *f* grocer's (shop); ~**deiro** *m* grocer

qui|tar /ki'tar/ *vt* pay off <*dívida*>; ~**te a estar** ~**te** be quits

quociente /kwosi'etʃi/ *m* quotient

quórum /'kwɔrũ/ *m* quorum

R

rã /xã/ *f* frog

rabanete /xaba'netʃi/ *m* radish

rabear /xabi'ar/ *vi* <*caminhão*> jack-knife

rabino /xa'binu/ *m* rabbi

rabis|car /xabis'kar/ *vt* scribble □ *vi* (*escrever mal*) scribble; (*fazer desenhos*) doodle; ~**co** *m* doodle

rabo /'xabu/ *m* (*de animal*) tail; **com o** ~ **do olho** out of the corner of one's eye; ~**-de-cavalo** (*pl* ~**s-de-cavalo**) *m* pony tail

rabugento /xabu'ʒẽtu/ *a* grumpy

raça /'xasa/ *f* (*de homens*) race; (*de animais*) breed

ração /xa'sãw/ *f* (*de comida*) ration; (*para animal*) food

racha /'xaʃa/ *f* crack; ~**dura** *f* crack

rachar /xa'ʃar/ *vt* (*dividir*) split; (*abrir fendas em*) crack; chop <*lenha*>; split <*despesas*> □ *vi* (*dividir-se*) split; (*apresentar fendas*) crack; (*ao pagar*) split the cost

raci|al /xasi'aw/ (*pl* ~**ais**) *a* racial

rácio|cinar /xasiosi'nar/ *vi* reason; **~cínio** *m* reasoning; **~nal** (*pl* **~nais**) *a* rational; **~nalizar** *vt* rationalize

racio|namento /xasiona'mẽtu/ *m* rationing; **~nar** *vt* ration

racismo /xa'sizmu/ *m* racism; **~ta** *a & m/f* racist

radar /xa'dar/ *m* radar; (*na estrada*) speed camera

radia|ção /xadʒia'sãw/ *f* radiation; **~dor** *m* radiator

radialista /xadʒia'lista/ *m/f* radio announcer

radiante /xadʒi'ãtʃi/ *a* (*de alegria*) overjoyed

radi|cal /xadʒi'kaw/ (*pl* **~cais**) *a & m* radical; **~car-se** *vpr* settle

rádio¹ /'xadʒiu/ *m* radio □ *f* radio station

rádio² /'xadʒiu/ *m* (*elemento*) radium

radioati|vidade /xadioatʃivi'dadʒi/ *f* radioactivity; **~vo** *a* radioactive

radiodifusão /xadʒiodʒifu'zãw/ *f* broadcasting

radiogra|far /xadʒiogra'far/ *vt* X-ray <*pulmões, osso etc*>; radio <*mensagem*>; **~fia** *f* X-ray

radiolo|gia /xadʒiolo'ʒia/ *f* radiology; **~gista** *m/f* radiologist

radionovela /xadʒiono'vɛla/ *f* radio serial; **~patrulha** *f* patrol car; **~táxi** *m* radio taxi; **~terapia** *f* radiotherapy

raia /'xaja/ *f* (*em corrida*) lane; (*peixe*) ray

rainha /xa'iɲa/ *f* queen; **~-mãe** *f* queen mother

raio /'xaju/ *m* (*de luz etc*) ray; (*de círculo*) radius; (*de roda*) spoke; (*relâmpago*) bolt of lightning; **~ de ação** range

rai|va /'xajva/ *f* rage; (*doença*) rabies; **estar com ~va** be furious (**de** with); **ter ~va de alg** have it in for s.o.; **~voso** *a* furious; <*cachorro*> rabid

raiz /xa'iz/ *f* root; **~ quadrada/ cúbica** square/cube root

rajada /xa'ʒada/ *f* (*de vento*) gust; (*de tiros*) burst

ra|lador /xala'dor/ *m* grater; **~lar** *vt* grate

ralé /xa'lɛ/ *f* rabble

ralhar /xa'ʎar/ *vi* scold

ralo¹ /'xalu/ *m* (*ralador*) grater; (*de escoamento*) drain

ralo² /'xalu/ *a* <*cabelo*> thinning; <*sopa, tecido*> thin; <*vegetação*> sparse; <*café*> weak

ra|mal /xa'maw/ (*pl* **~mais**) *m* (*telefone*) extension; (*de ferrovia*) branch line

ramalhete /xama'ʎetʃi/ *m* posy, bouquet

ramifi|cação /xamifika'sãw/ *f* branch; **~car-se** *vi* branch off

ramo /'xamu/ *m* branch; (*profissional etc*) field; (*buquê*) bunch; **Domingo de Ramos** Palm Sunday

rampa /'xãpa/ *f* ramp

rancor /xã'kor/ *m* resentment; **~oso** /o/ *a* resentful

rançoso /xã'sozu/ *a* rancid

ran|ger /xã'ʒer/ *vt* grind <*dentes*> □ *vi* creak; **~gido** *m* creak

ranhura /xa'ɲura/ *f* groove; (*para moedas*) slot

ranzinza /xã'zĩza/ *a* cantankerous

rapariga /xapa'riga/ *f* (*Port*) girl

rapaz /xa'pas/ *m* boy

rapé /xa'pɛ/ *m* snuff

rapidez /xapi'des/ *f* speed

rápido /'xapidu/ *a* fast □ *adv* <*fazer*> quickly; <*andar*> fast

rapina /xa'pina/ *f* **ave de ~** bird of prey

rapo|sa /xa'poza/ *f* vixen; **~so** *m* fox

rapsódia /xap'sɔdʒia/ *f* rhapsody

rap|tar /xap'tar/ *vt* abduct, kidnap <*criança*>; **~to** *m* abduction, kidnapping (*de criança*)

raquete /xa'ketʃi/ *f*, (*Port*) **raqueta** /xa'keta/ *f* racquet

raquítico /xa'kitʃiku/ a puny

ra|ramente /xara'mẽtʃi/ adv rarely; **~ridade** f rarity; **~ro** a rare □ adv rarely

rascunho /xas'kuɲu/ m rough version, draft

ras|gado /xaz'gadu/ a torn; (fig) <elogios etc> effusive; **~gão** m tear; **~gar** vt tear; (em pedaços) tear up □ vi, **~gar-se** vpr tear; **~go** m tear; (fig) burst

raso /'xazu/ a <água> shallow; <sapato> flat; <colher etc> level

ras|pão /xas'pãw/ m graze; **atingir de ~pão** graze; **~par** vt shave <cabeça, pêlos etc>; plane <madeira>; (para limpar) scrape; (tocar de leve) graze; **~par em** scrape

ras|teiro /xas'teru/ a <planta> creeping; <animal> crawling; **~tejante** a crawling; <voz> slurred; **~tejar** vi crawl

rasto /'xastu/ m veja **rastro**

ras|trear /xastri'ar/ vt track <satélite etc>; scan <céu, corpo etc>; **~tro** m trail

ratear¹ /xatʃi'ar/ vi <motor> miss

ra|tear² /xatʃi'ar/ vt share; **~teio** m sharing

ratifi|cação /xatʃifika'sãw/ f ratification; **~car** vt ratify

rato /'xatu/ m rat; (camundongo) mouse; **~eira** f mousetrap

ravina /xa'vina/ f ravine

razão /xa'zãw/ f reason; (proporção) ratio □ m ledger; **à ~ de** at the rate of; **em ~ de** on account of; **ter ~** be right; **não ter ~** be wrong

razoá|vel /xazo'avew/ a (pl **~veis**) a reasonable

ré¹ /xɛ/ f (na justiça) defendant

ré² /xɛ/ f (marcha) reverse; **dar ~** reverse

reabastecer /xeabaste'ser/ vt/i refuel

reabilitar /xeabili'tar/ vt rehabilitate

rea|ção /xea'sãw/ f reaction; **~ção em cadeia** chain reaction; **~cionário** a & m reactionary

readmitir /xeadʒimi'tʃir/ vt reinstate <funcionário>

reagir /xea'ʒir/ vi react; <doente> respond

reajus|tar /xeaʒus'tar/ vt readjust; **~te** m adjustment

re|al /xe'aw/ (pl **~ais**) a (verdadeiro) real; (da realeza) royal

real|çar /xeaw'sar/ vt highlight; **~ce** m prominence

realejo /xea'leʒu/ m barrel organ

realeza /xea'leza/ f royalty

realidade /xeali'dadʒi/ f reality

realimentação /xealimẽta'sãw/ f feedback

realis|mo /xea'lizmu/ m realism; **~ta** a realistic □ m/f realist

reali|zado /xeali'zadu/ a <pessoa> fulfilled; **~zar** vt (fazer) carry out; (tornar real) realize <sonho, capital>; **~zar-se** vpr <sonho> come true; <pessoa> fulfil o.s.; <casamento, reunião etc> take place

realmente /xeaw'mẽtʃi/ adv really

reaparecer /xeapare'ser/ vi reappear

reativar /xeatʃi'var/ vt reactivate

reaver /xea'ver/ vt get back

reavivar /xeavi'var/ vt revive

rebai|xar /xebaj'ʃar/ vt lower <preço>; (fig) demean □ vi <preços> drop; **~se** vpr demean o.s.

rebanho /xe'baɲu/ m herd; (fiéis) flock

reba|te /xe'batʃi/ m alarm; **~ter** vt return <bola>; refute <acusação>; (à máquina) retype

rebelar-se /xebe'larsi/ vpr rebel

rebel|de /xe'bewdʒi/ a rebellious □ m/f rebel; **~dia** f rebelliousness

rebelião /xebeli'ãw/ f rebellion

reben|tar /xebẽ'tar/ vt/i veja **arrebentar**; **~to** m (de planta) shoot; (descendente) offspring

rebite /xe'bitʃi/ m rivet

rebobinar /xebobi'nar/ vt rewind

rebo|cador /xeboka'dor/ m tug; **~car** vt (tirar) tow; (cobrir com reboco) plaster; **~co** /o/ m plaster

reboque /xe'bɔki/ m towing; (veículo a ~) trailer; (com guindaste) towtruck; **a ~** on tow

rebuçado /xebu'sadu/ m (Port) sweet, (Amer) candy

rebuliço /xebu'lisu/ m commotion

rebuscado /xebus'kadu/ a récherché

recado /xe'kadu/ m message

reca|ída /xeka'ida/ f relapse; **~ir** vi relapse; <acento, culpa> fall

recal|cado /xekaw'kadu/ a repressed; **~car** vt repress

recanto /xe'kãtu/ m nook, recess

recapitular /xekapitu'lar/ vt review □ vi recap

recarregar /xekare'gar/ vt (bateria) recharge; (crédito) top up

reca|tado /xeka'tadu/ a reserved, withdrawn; **~to** m reserve

recear /xesi'ar/ vt/i fear (por for)

rece|ber /xese'ber/ vt receive; entertain <convidados> □ vi (~ber salário) get paid; (~ber convidados) entertain; **~bimento** m receipt

receio /xe'seju/ m fear

recei|ta /xe'sejta/ f (de cozinha) recipe; (médica) prescription; (dinheiro) revenue; **~tar** vt prescribe

recém-casados /xesẽjka'zadus/ m pl newly-weds; **~-chegado** m newcomer; **~-nascido** a newborn □ m newborn child, baby

recente /xe'sẽtʃi/ a recent; **~mente** adv recently

receoso /xese'ozu/ a (apreensivo) afraid

recep|ção /xesep'sãw/ f reception; (Port: de carta) receipt; **~cionar** vt receive; **~cionista** m/f receptionist; **~táculo** m recept-

acle; **~tivo** a receptive; **~tor** m receiver

reces|são /xese'sãw/ f recession; **~so** /ɛ/ m recess

re|chear /xeʃi'ar/ vt stuff <frango, assado>; fill <empada>; **~cheio** m (para frango etc) stuffing; (de empada etc) filling

rechonchudo /xeʃõ'ʃudu/ a plump

recibo /xe'sibu/ m receipt

reciclar /xesik'lar/ vt recycle

recife /xe'sifi/ m reef

recinto /xe'sĩtu/ m enclosure

recipiente /xesipi'ẽtʃi/ m container

reciprocar /xesipro'kar/ vt reciprocate

recíproco /xe'siproku/ a reciprocal; <sentimento> mutual

reci|tal /xesi'taw/ (pl **~tais**) m recital; **~tar** vt recite

recla|mação /xeklama'sãw/ f complaint; (no seguro) claim; **~mar** vt claim □ vi complain (de about); (no seguro) claim; **~me** m, (Port) **~mo** m advertising

reclinar-se /xekli'narsi/ vpr recline

recluso /xe'kluzu/ a reclusive □ m recluse

recobrar /xeko'brar/ vt recover; **~-se** vpr recover

recolher /xeko'ʎer/ vt collect; (retirar) withdraw; **~-se** vpr retire

recomeçar /xekome'sar/ vt/i start again

recomen|dação /xekomẽda'sãw/ f recommendation; **~dar** vt recommend; **~dável** (pl **~dáveis**) a advisable

recompen|sa /xekõ'pẽsa/ f reward; **~sar** vt reward

reconcili|ação /xekõsilia'sãw/ f reconciliation; **~ar** vt reconcile; **~ar-se** vpr be reconciled

reconhe|cer /xekoɲe'ser/ vt recognize; (admitir) acknowledge;

(*mil*) reconnoitre; identify <*corpo*>; ~**cimento** *m* recognition; (*gratidão*) gratitude; (*mil*) reconnaissance; (*de corpo*) identification; ~**cível** (*pl* ~**cíveis**) *a* recognizable

reconsiderar /xekõside'rar/ *vt/i* reconsider

reconstituinte /xekõstʃitu'ĩtʃi/ *m* tonic

reconstituir /xekõstʃitu'ir/ *vt* reform; reconstruct <*crime, cena*>

reconstruir /xekõstru'ir/ *vt* rebuild

recor|dação /xekorda'sãw/ *f* recollection; (*objeto*) memento; ~**dar** *vt* recollect; ~**dar-se** (**de**) recall

recor|de /xe'kɔrdʒi/ *a invar* & *m* record; ~**dista** *a* record-breaking □ *m/f* record-holder

recorrer /xeko'xer/ *vi* ~ **a** turn to <*médico, amigo*>; resort to <*violência, tática*>; ~ **de** appeal against

recor|tar /xekor'tar/ *vt* cut out; ~**te** /ɔ/ *m* cutting, (*Amer*) clipping

recostar /xekos'tar/ *vt* lean back; ~**-se** *vpr* lean back

recreio /xe'kreju/ *m* recreation; (*na escola*) break

recriar /xekri'ar/ *vt* recreate

recriminação /xekrimina'sãw/ *f* recrimination

recrudescer /xekrude'ser/ *vi* intensify

recru|ta /xe'kruta/ *m/f* recruit; ~**tamento** *m* recruitment; ~**tar** *vt* recruit

recu|ar /xeku'ar/ *vi* move back; <*tropas*> retreat; (*no tempo*) go back; (*ceder*) back down; (*não cumprir*) back out (**de** of) □ *vt* move back; ~**o** *m* retreat; (*fig: de intento*) climbdown

recupe|ração /xekupera'sãw/ *f* recovery; ~**rar** *vt* recover; make up <*atraso, tempo perdido*>; ~**rar-se** *vpr* recover (**de** from)

recurso /xe'kursu/ *m* resort; (*coisa útil*) resource; (*na justiça*) appeal; *pl* resources

recu|sa /xe'kuza/ *f* refusal; ~**sar** *vt* refuse; turn down <*convite, oferta*>; ~**sar-se** *vpr* refuse (**a** to)

reda|ção /xeda'sãw/ *f* (*de livro, contrato*) draft; (*pessoal*) editorial staff; (*seção*) editorial department; (*na escola*) composition; ~**tor** *m* editor

rede /'xedʒi/ *f* net; (*para deitar*) hammock; (*fig: sistema*) network; ~ **corporativa** (*comput*) intranet

rédea /'xedʒia/ *f* rein

redemoinho /xedemo'iɲu/ *m veja* **rodamoinho**

reden|ção /xedẽ'sãw/ *f* redemption; ~**tor** *a* redeeming □ *m* redeemer

redigir /xedʒi'ʒir/ *vt* draw up <*contrato*>; write <*artigo*>; edit <*dicionário*>

redimir /xedʒi'mir/ *vt* redeem

redobrar /xedo'brar/ *vt* redouble

redon|deza /xedõ'deza/ *f* roundness; *pl* vicinity; ~**do** *a* round

redor /xe'dor/ *m* **ao** *ou* **em** ~ **de** around

redução /xedu'sãw/ *f* reduction

redun|dante /xedũ'dãtʃi/ *a* redundant; ~**dar** *vi* ~ **dar em** develop into

redu|zido /xedu'zidu/ *a* limited; (*pequeno*) small; ~**zir** *vt* reduce; ~**zir-se** *vpr* (*ficar reduzido*) be reduced (**a** to); (*resumir-se*) come down (**a** to)

reeleger /xeele'ʒer/ *vt* re-elect

reeleição /xeelej'sãw/ *f* re-election

reembol|sar /xeẽbow'sar/ *vt* reimburse <*pessoa*>; refund <*dinheiro*>; ~**so** /o/ *m* refund; ~**so postal** cash on delivery

reencarnação /xeẽkarna'sãw/ *f* reincarnation

reentrância /xeẽ'trãsia/ *f* recess

reescalonar /xeeskalo'nar/ *vt* reschedule

reescrever /xeeskre'ver/ *vt* re-write

refastelar-se /xefaste'larsi/ *vpr* stretch out

refazer /xefa'zer/ *vt* redo; rebuild <*vida*>; **~-se** *vpr* recover (**de** from)

refei|ção /xefej'sãw/ *f* meal; **~tório** *m* dining hall

refém /xe'fẽj/ *m* hostage

referência /xefe'rẽsia/ *f* reference; **com ~ a** with reference to

referendum /xefe'rẽdū/ *m* referendum

refe|rente /xefe'rẽtʃi/ *a* regarding; **~rir** *vt* report; **~rir-se** *vpr* refer (**a** to)

refestelar-se /xefeste'larsi/ *vpr* (*Port*) veja **refastelar-se**

re|fil /xe'fiw/ (*pl* **~fis**) *m* refill

refi|nado /xefi'nadu/ *a* refined; **~namento** *m* refinement; **~nar** *vt* refine; **~naria** *f* refinery

refle|tido /xefle'tʃidu/ *a* <*decisão*> well-thought-out; <*pessoa*> thoughtful; **~tir** *vt/i* reflect; **~tir-se** *vpr* be reflected; **~xão** /ks/ *f* reflection; **~xivo** /ks/ *a* reflexive; **~xo** /ks/ *a* <*luz*> reflected; <*ação*> reflex □ *m* (*de luz etc*) reflection; (*físico*) reflex; (*no cabelo*) streak

refluxo /xe'fluksu/ *m* ebb

refo|gado /xefo'gadu/ *m* lightly fried mixture of onions and garlic; **~gar** *vt* fry lightly

refor|çar /xefor'sar/ *vt* reinforce; **~ço** /o/ *m* reinforcement

refor|ma /xe'fɔrma/ *f* (*da lei etc*) reform; (*na casa etc*) renovation; (*de militar*) discharge; (*pensão*) pension; **~ma ministerial** cabinet reshuffle; **~mado** *a* reformed; (*Port*: *aposentado*) retired □ *m* (*Port*) pensioner; **~mar** *vt* reform <*lei, sistema etc*>; renovate <*casa, prédio*>; (*Port*: *aposentar*) retire; **~mar-**

se *vpr* (*Port*: *aposentar-se*) retire; <*criminoso*> reform; **~matório** *m* reform school; **~mista** *a & m/f* reformist

refratário /xefra'tariu/ *a* <*tigela etc*> ovenproof, heatproof

refrear /xefri'ar/ *vt* rein in <*cavalo*>; (*fig*) curb, keep in check <*paixões etc*>; **~-se** *vpr* restrain o.s.

refrega /xe'frega/ *f* clash, fight

refres|cante /xefres'kãtʃi/ *a* refreshing; **~car** *vt* freshen, cool <*ar*>; refresh <*pessoa, memória etc*> □ *vi* get cooler; **~car-se** *vpr* refresh o.s.; **~co** /e/ *m* (*bebida*) soft drink; *pl* refreshments

refrige|rado /xefriʒe'radu/ *a* cooled; <*casa etc*> air-conditioned; (*na geladeira*) refrigerated; **~rador** *m* refrigerator; **~rante** *m* soft drink; **~rar** *vt* keep cool; (*na geladeira*) refrigerate

refugi|ado /xefuʒi'adu/ *m* refugee; **~ar-se** *vpr* take refuge

refúgio /xe'fuʒiu/ *m* refuge

refugo /xe'fugu/ *m* waste, refuse

refutar /xefu'tar/ *vt* refute

regaço /xe'gasu/ *m* lap

regador /xega'dor/ *m* watering can

regalia /xega'lia/ *f* privilege

regar /xe'gar/ *vt* water

regata /xe'gata/ *f* regatta

regatear /xegatʃi'ar/ *vi* bargain, haggle

re|gência /xe'ʒẽsia/ *f* (*de verbo etc*) government; **~gente** *m/f* (*de orquestra*) conductor; **~ger** *vt* govern □ *vi* rule

região /xeʒi'ãw/ *f* region; (*de cidade etc*) area

regi|me /xe'ʒimi/ *m* regime; (*dieta*) diet; **fazer ~me** diet; **~mento** *m* (*militar*) regiment; (*regulamento*) regulations

régio /'xeʒiu/ *a* royal

regio|nal /xeʒio'naw/ (*pl* **~nais**) *a* regional

regis|trador /xeʒistra'dor/ *a* **caixa ~tradora** cash register; **~trar** *vt* register; (*anotar*) record; **~tro** *m* (*lista*) register; (*de um fato, em banco de dados*) record; (*ato de ~trar*) registration

rego /'xegu/ *m* (*de arado*) furrow; (*de roda*) rut; (*para escoamento*) ditch

regozi|jar /xegozi'ʒar/ *vt* delight; **~jar-se** *vpr* be delighted; **~jo** *m* delight

regra /'xɛgra/ *f* rule; *pl* (*menstruações*) periods; **em ~** as a rule

regres|sar /xegre'sar/ *vi* return; **~sivo** *a* regressive; **contagem ~siva** countdown; **~so** /ɛ/ *m* return

régua /'xɛgwa/ *f* ruler

regu|lagem /xegu'laʒẽ/ *f* (*de carro*) tuning; **~lamento** *m* regulations; **~lar** *a* regular; <*estatura, qualidade etc*> average □ *vt* regulate; tune <*carro, motor*>; set <*relógio*> □ *vi* work; **~lar-se por** go by, be guided by; **~laridade** *f* regularity; **~larizar** *vt* regularize

regurgitar /xegurʒi'tar/ *vt* bring up

rei /xej/ *m* king; **~nado** *m* reign

reincidir /xeĩsi'dʒir/ *vi* <*criminoso*> reoffend

reino /'xejnu/ *m* kingdom; (*fig: da fantasia etc*) realm; **Reino Unido** United Kingdom

reiterar /xejte'rar/ *vt* reiterate

reitor /xej'tor/ *m* chancellor, (*Amer*) president

reivindi|cação /xejvĩdʒika'sãw/ *f* demand; **~car** *vt* claim, demand

rejei|ção /xeʒej'sãw/ *f* rejection; **~tar** *vt* reject

rejuvenescer /xeʒuvene'ser/ *vt* rejuvenate □ *vi* be rejuvenated

rela|ção /xela'sãw/ *f* relationship; (*relatório*) account; (*lista*) list; *pl* relations; **com** *ou* **em ~ a** in relation to, regarding

relacio|namento /xelasiona'mẽtu/ *m* relationship; **~nar** *vt* relate (**com** to); (*listar*) list; **~nar-se** *vpr* relate (**com** to)

relações-públicas /xelasõjs'publikas/ *m/f invar* public-relations person

relâmpago /xe'lãpagu/ *m* flash of lightning; *pl* lightning □ *a* lightning; **num ~** in a flash

relampejar /xelãpe'ʒar/ *vi* flash; **relampejou** there was a flash of lightning

relance /xe'lãsi/ *m* glance; **olhar de ~** glance (at)

rela|tar /xela'tar/ *vt* relate; **~tivo** *a* relative; **~to** *m* account; **~tório** *m* report

rela|xado /xela'ʃadu/ *a* relaxed; <*disciplina*> lax; <*pessoa*> lazy, complacent; **~xamento** *m* (*físico*) relaxation; (*de pessoa*) complacency; **~xante** *a* relaxing □ *m* tranquillizer; **~xar** *vt* relax □ *vi* (*descansar*) relax; (*tornar-se omisso*) get complacent; **~xar-se** *vpr* relax; **~xe** *m* relaxation

reles /'xɛlis/ *a invar* <*gente*> common; (*ação*) despicable

rele|vância /xele'vãsia/ *f* relevance; **~vante** *a* relevant; **~var** *vt* emphasize; **~vo** /e/ *m* relief; (*importância*) prominence

religi|ão /xeliʒi'ãw/ *f* religion; **~oso** /o/ *a* religious

relin|char /xelĩ'ʃar/ *vi* neigh; **~cho** *m* neighing

relíquia /xe'likia/ *f* relic

relógio /xe'lɔʒiu/ *m* clock; (*de pulso*) watch

relu|tância /xelu'tãsia/ *f* reluctance; **~tante** *a* reluctant; **~tar** *vi* be reluctant (**em** to)

reluzente /xelu'zẽtʃi/ *a* shining, gleaming

relva /'xɛwva/ *f* grass; **~do** *m* lawn

remador /xema'dor/ *m* rower

remanescente /xemane'sĕtʃi/ *a* remaining □ *m* remainder

remar /xe'mar/ *vt/i* row

rema|tar /xema'tar/ *vt* finish off; ~**te** *m* finish; (*adorno*) finishing touch; (*de piada*) punch line

remediar /xemedʒi'ar/ *vt* remedy

remédio /xe'mɛdʒiu/ *m* (*contra doença*) medicine, drug; (*a problema etc*) remedy

remelento /xeme'lẽtu/ *a* bleary

remen|dar /xemẽ'dar/ *vt* mend; (*com pedaço de pano*) patch; ~**do** *m* mend; (*pedaço de pano*) patch

remessa /xe'mɛsa/ *f* (*de mercadorias*) shipment; (*de dinheiro*) remittance

reme|tente /xeme'tẽtʃi/ *m/f* sender; ~**ter** *vt* send <*mercadorias, dinheiro etc*>; refer <*leitor*> (**a** to)

remexer /xeme'ʃer/ *vt* shuffle <*papéis*>; stir up <*poeira, lama*>; wave <*braços*> □ *vi* rummage; ~**se** *vpr* move around

reminiscência /xemini'sĕsia/ *f* reminiscence

remir /xe'mir/ *vt* redeem; ~**se** *vpr* redeem o.s.

remissão /xemi'sãw/ *f* (*de pecados*) redemption; (*de doença, pena*) remission; (*num livro*) cross-reference

remo /'xemu/ *m* oar; (*esporte*) rowing

remoção /xemo'sãw/ *f* removal

remoinho /xemo'iɲu/ *m* (*Port*) *veja* **rodamoinho**

remontar /xemõ'tar/ *vi* ~ **a** <*coisa*> date back to; <*pessoa*> think back to

remorso /xe'mɔrsu/ *m* remorse

remo|to /xe'mɔtu/ *a* remote; ~**ver** *vt* remove

remune|ração /xemunera'sãw/ *f* payment; ~**rador** *a* profitable; ~**rar** *vt* pay

rena /'xena/ *f* reindeer

re|nal /xe'naw/ (*pl* ~**nais**) *a* renal, kidney

Renascença /xena'sẽsa/ *f* Renaissance

renas|cer /xena'ser/ *vi* be reborn; ~**cimento** *m* rebirth

renda[1] /'xẽda/ *f* (*tecido*) lace

ren|da[2] /'xẽda/ *f* income; (*Port: aluguel*) rent; ~**der** bring in, yield <*lucro*>; earn <*juros*>; fetch <*preço*>; bring <*resultado*> □ *vi* <*investimento, trabalho, ação*> pay off; <*comida*> go a long way; <*produto comprado*> give value for money; ~**der-se** *vpr* surrender; ~**dição** *f* surrender; ~**dimento** *m* (*renda*) income; (*de investimento, terreno*) yield; (*de motor etc*) output; (*de produto comprado*) value for money; ~**doso** *a* profitable

rene|gado /xene'gadu/ *a & m* renegade; ~**gar** *vt* renounce

renhido /xe'ɲidu/ *a* hard-fought

Reno /'xenu/ *m* Rhine

reno|mado /xeno'madu/ *a* renowned; ~**me** /o/ *m* renown

reno|vação /xenova'sãw/ *f* renewal; ~**var** *vt* renew

renque /'xẽki/ *m* row

ren|tabilidade /xẽtabili'dadʒi/ *f* profitability; ~**tável** (*pl* ~**táveis**) *a* profitable

rente /'xẽtʃi/ *adv* ~ **a** close to □ *a* <*cabelo*> cropped

renúncia /xe'nũsia/ *f* renunciation (**a** of); (*a cargo*) resignation (**a** from)

renunciar /xenũsi'ar/ *vi* <*presidente etc*> resign; ~ **a** give up; waive <*direito*>

reorganizar /xeorgani'zar/ *vt* reorganize

repa|ração /xepara'sãw/ *f* reparation; (*conserto*) repair; ~**rar** *vt* (*consertar*) repair; make up for <*ofensa, injustiça, erro*>; make good *<danos, prejuízo>* □ *vi* **~rar (em)** notice; **~ro** *m (conserto)* repair

repar|tição /xepartʃiˈsãw/ *f* division; *(seção do governo)* department; **~tir** *vt* divide up

repassar /xepaˈsar/ *vt* revise *<matéria, lição>*

repatriar /xepatriˈar/ *vt* repatriate

repe|lente /xepeˈlẽtʃi/ *a & m* repellent; **~lir** *vt* repel; reject *<ideia, proposta etc>*

repensar /xepẽˈsar/ *vt/i* rethink

repen|te /xeˈpẽtʃi/ *m* **de ~te** suddenly; *(fam: talvez)* maybe; **~tino** *a* sudden

reper|cussão /xeperkuˈsãw/ *f* repercussion; **~cutir** *vi <som>* reverberate; *(fig: ter efeito)* have repercussions

repertório /xeperˈtɔriu/ *m (músico etc)* repertoire; *(lista)* list

repe|tição /xepetʃiˈsãw/ *f* repetition; **~tido** *a* repeated; **~tidas vezes** repeatedly; **~tir** *vt* repeat □ *vi (ao comer)* have seconds; **~tir-se** *vpr <pessoa>* repeat o.s.; *<fato, acontecimento>* recur; **~titivo** *a* repetitive

repi|car /xepiˈkar/ *vt/i* ring; **~que** *m* ring

replay /xeˈplej/ *(pl* **~s)** *m* action replay

repleto /xeˈplɛtu/ *a* full up

réplica /ˈxɛplika/ *f* reply; *(cópia)* replica

replicar /xepliˈkar/ *vt* answer □ *vi* reply

repolho /xeˈpoʎu/ *m* cabbage

repor /xeˈpor/ *vt (num lugar)* put back; *(substituir)* replace

reportagem /xeporˈtaʒẽ/ *f (uma)* report; *(ato)* reporting

repórter /xeˈpɔrter/ *m/f* reporter

reposição /xepoziˈsãw/ *f* replacement

repou|sar /xepoˈsar/ *vt/i* rest; **~so** *m* rest

repreen|der /xepriẽˈder/ *vt* rebuke, reprimand; **~são** *f* rebuke, reprimand; **~sível** *(pl* **~síveis)** *a* reprehensible

represa /xeˈpreza/ *f* dam

represália /xepreˈzalia/ *f* reprisal

represen|tação /xeprezẽtaˈsãw/ *f* representation; *(espetáculo)* performance; *(ofício de ator)* acting; **~tante** *m/f* representative; **~tar** *vt* represent; *(no teatro)* perform *<peça>*; play *<papel, personagem>* □ *vi <ator>* act; **~tativo** *a* representative

repres|são /xepreˈsãw/ *f* repression; **~sivo** *a* repressive

repri|mido /xepriˈmidu/ *a* repressed; **~mir** *vt* repress

reprise /xeˈprizi/ *f (filme)* repeat; *(na TV)* rerun

reprodu|ção /xeproduˈsãw/ *f* reproduction; **~zir** *vt* reproduce; **~zir-se** *vpr (multiplicar-se)* reproduce; *(repetir-se)* recur

repro|vação /xeprovaˈsãw/ *f* disapproval; *(em exame)* failure; **~var** *vt (rejeitar)* disapprove of; *(em exame)* fail; **ser ~vado** *<aluno>* fail

rép|til /ˈxɛptʃiw/ *(pl* **~teis)** *a* reptile

república /xeˈpublika/ *f* republic; *(de estudantes)* hall of residence

republicano /xepubliˈkanu/ *a & m* republican

repudiar /xepudʒiˈar/ *vt* disown; repudiate *<esposa>*

repug|nância /xepugˈnãsia/ *f* repugnance; **~nante** *a* repugnant

repul|sa /xeˈpuwsa/ *f* repulsion; *(recusa)* rejection; **~sivo** *a* repulsive

reputação /xeputaˈsãw/ *f* reputation

requebrar /xekeˈbrar/ *vt* swing; **~-se** *vpr* sway

requeijão /xekeˈʒãw/ *m* cheese spread, cottage cheese

reque|rer /xeke'rer/ *vt* (*pedir*) apply for; (*exigir*) require; ~**rimento** *m* application

requin|tado /xekĩ'tadu/ *a* refined; ~**tar** *vt* refine; ~**te** *m* refinement

requisi|ção /xekizi'sãw/ *f* requisition; ~**tar** *vt* requisition; ~**to** *m* requirement

rês /xes/ (*pl* **reses**) *m* head of cattle; *pl* cattle

rescindir /xesĩ'dʒir/ *vt* rescind

rés-do-chão /xezdu'ʃãw/ *m invar* (*Port*) ground floor, (*Amer*) first floor

rese|nha /xe'zeɲa/ *f* review; ~**nhar** *vt* review

reser|va /xe'zɛrva/ *f* reserve; (*em hotel, avião etc, ressalva*) reservation; ~**var** *vt* reserve; ~**vatório** *m* reservoir; ~**vista** *m/f* reservist

resfri|ado /xesfri'adu/ *a* **estar** ~**ado** have a cold □ *m* cold; ~**ar** *vt* cool □ *vi* get cold; (*tornar-se morno*) cool down; ~**ar-se** *vpr* catch a cold

resga|tar /xezga'tar/ *vt* (*salvar*) rescue; (*remir*) redeem; ~**te** *m* (*salvamento*) rescue; (*pago por refém*) ransom; (*remissão*) redemption

resguardar /xezgwar'dar/ *vt* protect; ~**se** *vpr* protect o.s. (*de* from)

residência /xezi'dẽsia/ *f* residence

residen|cial /xezidẽsi'aw/ (*pl* ~**ciais**) *a* <*bairro*> residential; <*telefone etc*> home; ~**te** *a* & *m/f* resident

residir /xezi'dʒir/ *vi* reside

resíduo /xe'ziduu/ *m* residue

resig|nação /xezigna'sãw/ *f* resignation; ~**nado** *a* resigned; ~**nar-se** *vpr* resign o.s. (**com** to)

resina /xe'zina/ *f* resin

resis|tência /xezis'tẽsia/ *f* resistance; (*de atleta, mental*) endurance; (*de material, objeto*)

toughness; ~**tente** *a* strong, tough; <*tecido, roupa*> hardwearing; <*planta*> hardy; ~**tente** *a* resistant to; ~**tir** *vi* (*opor* ~*tência*) resist; (*aguentar* <*pessoa*> hold out; <*objeto*> hold; ~**tir a** (*combater*) resist; (*aguentar*) withstand; ~**tir ao tempo** stand the test of time

resmun|gar /xezmũ'gar/ *vi* grumble; ~**go** *m* grumbling

resolu|ção /xezolu'sãw/ *f* resolution; (*firmeza*) resolve; (*de problema*) solution; ~**to a** resolute; ~**to a** resolved to

resolver /xezow'ver/ *vt* (*esclarecer*) sort out; solve <*problema, enigma*>; (*decidir*) decide; ~**se** *vpr* make up one's mind (**a** to)

respaldo /xes'pawdu/ *m* (*de cadeira*) back; (*fig: apoio*) backing

respectivo /xespek'tʃivu/ *a* respective

respei|tabilidade /xespejtabili'dadʒi/ *f* respectability; ~**tador** *a* respectful; ~**tar** *vt* respect; ~**tável** (*pl* ~**táveis**) *a* respectable; ~**to** *m* respect (**por** for); **a** ~**to de** about; **a este** ~**to** in this respect; **com** ~**to a** with regard to; **dizer** ~**to a** a concern; ~**toso** /o/ *a* respectful

respin|gar /xespĩ'gar/ *vt/i* splash; ~**go** *m* splash

respi|ração /xespira'sãw/ *f* breathing; ~**rador** *m* respirator; ~**rar** *vt/i* breathe; ~**ratório** *a* respiratory; ~**ro** *m* breath; (*descanso*) break, breather

resplande|cente /xesplãde'sẽtʃi/ *a* resplendent; ~**cer** *vi* shine

resplendor /xesplẽ'dor/ *m* brilliance; (*fig*) glory

respon|dão /xespõ'dãw/ *a* (*f* ~**dona**) cheeky; ~**der** *vt/i* answer; (*com insolência*) answer back; ~**der a** answer; ~**der por** answer for, take responsibility for

responsabili|dade /xespõsabili-'dadʒi/ *f* responsibility; **~zar** *vt* hold responsible (**por** for); **~zar-se** *vpr* take responsibility (**por** for)

responsá|vel /xespõ'savew/ (*pl* **~veis**) *a* responsible (**por** for)

resposta /xes'posta/ *f* answer

resquício /xes'kisiu/ *m* vestige, remnant

ressabiado /xesabi'adu/ *a* wary, suspicious

ressaca /xe'saka/ *f* (*depois de beber*) hangover; (*do mar*) undertow

ressaltar /xesaw'tar/ *vt* emphasize □ *vi* stand out

ressalva /xe'sawva/ *f* reservation, proviso; (*proteção*) safeguard

ressarcir /xesar'sir/ *vt* refund

resse|cado /xese'kadu/ *a* <*terra*> parched; <*pele*> dry; **~car** *vt/i* dry up

ressen|tido /xesẽ'tʃidu/ *a* resentful; **~timento** *m* resentment; **~tir-se de** (*ofender-se*) resent; (*ser influenciado*) show the effects of

ressequido /xese'kidu/ *a veja* **ressecado**

resso|ar /xeso'ar/ *vi* resound; **~nância** *f* resonance; **~nante** *a* resonant; **~nar** *vi* (*Port*) snore

ressurgimento /xesurʒi'mẽtu/ *m* resurgence

ressurreição /xesuxej'sãw/ *f* resurrection

ressuscitar /xesusi'tar/ *vt* revive

restabele|cer /xestabele'ser/ *vt* restore; restore to health <*doente*>; **~cer-se** *vpr* recover; **~cimento** *m* restoration; (*de doente*) recovery

res|tante /xes'tãtʃi/ *a* remaining □ *m* remainder; **~tar** *vi* remain; **~ta-me dizer que ...** it remains for me to say that

restau|ração /xestawra'sãw/ *f* restoration; **~rante** *m* restaurant; **~rar** *vt* restore

restitu|ição /xestʃitui'sãw/ *f* return, restitution; **~ir** *vt* (*devolver*) return; restore <*forma, força etc*>; reinstate <*funcionário*>

resto /'xestu/ *m* rest; *pl* (*de comida*) left-overs; (*de cadáver*) remains; **de ~** besides

restrição /xestri'sãw/ *f* restriction

restringir /xestrĩ'ʒir/ *vt* restrict

restrito /xes'tritu/ *a* restricted

resul|tado /xezuw'tadu/ *m* result; **~tante** *a* resulting (**de** from); **~tar** *vi* result (**de** from; **em** in)

resu|mir /xezu'mir/ *vt* (*abreviar*) summarize; (*conter em poucas palavras*) sum up; **~mir-se** *vpr* (*ser expresso em poucas palavras*) be summed up; **~mir-se em** (*ser apenas*) come down to; **~mo** *m* summary; **em ~mo** briefly

resvalar /xezva'lar/ *vi* (*sem querer*) slip; (*deslizar*) slide

reta /'xeta/ *f* (*linha*) straight line; (*de pista etc*) straight; **~ final** home straight

retaguarda /xeta'gwarda/ *f* rearguard

retalho /xe'taʎu/ *m* scrap; **a ~** (*Port*) retail

retaliação /xetalia'sãw/ *f* retaliation

retangular /xetãgu'lar/ *a* rectangular

retângulo /xe'tãgulu/ *m* rectangle

retar|dado /xetar'dadu/ *a* retarded □ *m* retard; **~dar** *vt* delay; **~datário** *m* latecomer

retenção /xetẽ'sãw/ *f* retention

reter /xe'ter/ *vt* keep <*pessoa*>; hold back <*águas, riso, lágrimas*>; (*na memória*) retain; **~se** *vpr* restrain o.s.

rete|sado /xete'zadu/ *a* taut; **~sar** *vt* pull taut

reticência /xetʃi'sẽsia/ *f* reticence

reti|dão /xetʃi'dãw/ *f* rectitude; **~ficar** *vt* rectify

reti|rada /xetʃiˈrada/ f (de tropas) retreat; (de dinheiro) withdrawal; ~rado a secluded; ~rar vt withdraw; (afastar) move away; ~rar-se vpr <tropas> retreat; (afastar-se) withdraw; (de uma atividade) retire; ~ro m retreat

reto /ˈxɛtu/ a <linha etc> straight; <pessoa> honest

retocar /xetoˈkar/ vt touch up <desenho, maquiagem etc>; alter <texto>

reto|mada /xetoˈmada/ f (continuação) resumption; (reconquista) retaking; ~mar vt (continuar com) resume; (conquistar de novo) retake

retoque /xeˈtɔki/ m finishing touch

retorcer /xetorˈser/ vt twist; ~-se vpr writhe

retóri|ca /xeˈtɔrika/ f rhetoric; ~co a rhetorical

retor|nar /xetorˈnar/ vi return; ~no m return; (na estrada) turning place; dar ~no do a U-turn

retrair /xetraˈir/ vt retract, withdraw; ~-se vpr (recuar) withdraw; (encolher-se) retract

retrasa|do /xetraˈzadu/ a a semana ~da the week before last

retratar[1] /xetraˈtar/ vt (desdizer) retract

retra|tar[2] /xetraˈtar/ vt (em quadro, livro) portray, depict; ~to m portrait; (foto) photo; (representação) portrayal; ~to falado identikit picture

retribuir /xetribuˈir/ vt return <favor, visita>; repay <gentileza>

retroativo /xetroaˈtʃivu/ a retroactive; <pagamento> backdated

retro|ceder /xetroseˈder/ vi retreat; (desistir) back down; ~cesso /ɛ/ m retreat; (ao passado) regression

retrógrado /xeˈtrɔgradu/ a retrograde

retrospec|tiva /xetrospekˈtʃiva/ f retrospective; ~tivo a retrospective; ~to /ɛ/ m look back; em ~to in retrospect

retrovisor /xetroviˈzor/ a & m (espelho) ~ rear-view mirror

retrucar /xetruˈkar/ vt/i retort

retum|bante /xetũˈbãtʃi/ a resounding; ~bar vi resound

réu /ˈxɛw/ m (f ré) defendant

reumatismo /xewmaˈtʃizmu/ m rheumatism

reu|nião /xeuniˈãw/ f meeting; (descontraída) get-together; (de família) reunion; ~nião de cúpula summit meeting; ~nir vt bring together <pessoas>; combine <qualidades>; ~nir-se vpr meet; <amigos, familiares> get together; ~nir-se a join

revanche /xeˈvãʃi/ f revenge; (jogo) return match

reveillon /xeveˈjõ/ (pl ~s) m New Year's Eve

reve|lação /xevelaˈsãw/ f revelation; (de fotos) developing; (novo talento) promising newcomer; ~lar vt reveal; develop <filme, fotos>; ~lar-se vpr (vir a ser) turn out to be

revelia /xeveˈlia/ f à ~ by default; à ~ de without the knowledge of

reven|dedor /xevẽdeˈdor/ m dealer; ~der vt resell

rever /xeˈver/ vt (ver de novo) see again; (revisar) revise; (examinar) check

reve|rência /xeveˈresia/ f reverence; (movimento do busto) bow; (dobrando os joelhos) curtsey; ~rente a reverent

reverso /xeˈversu/ m reverse; o ~ da medalha the other side of the coin

revés /xeˈvɛs/ (pl reveses) m setback

reves|timento /xevestʃiˈmẽtu/ m covering; ~tir vt cover

reve|zamento /xeveza'mẽtu/ *m*
alternation; ~zar *vt/i* alternate; ~zar-se *vpr* alternate

revi|dar /xevi'dar/ *vt* return
<*golpe, insulto*>; refute
<*crítica*>; (*retrucar*) retort □ *vi* hit
back; ~de *m* response

revigorar /xevigo'rar/ *vt*
strengthen □ *vi*, ~-se *vpr* regain
one's strength

revi|rar /xevi'rar/ *vt* turn out
<*bolsos, gavetas*>; turn over <*terra*>; turn inside out <*roupa*>;
roll <*olhos*>; ~rar-se *vpr* toss
and turn; ~ravolta /ʒi'vawta/ *f* (*na política etc*) about-face, about-turn;
(*da situação*) turnabout, dra-
matic change

revi|são /xevi'zãw/ *f* (*de lições etc*) revision; (*de máquina, motor*) overhaul; (*de carro*)
service; ~são de provas proof-
reading; ~sar *vt* revise <*provas, lições*>; service <*carro*>;
~sor *m* (*de bilhetes*) ticket
inspector; ~sor de provas
proofreader

revis|ta /xe'vista/ *f* (*para ler*) ma-
gazine; (*teatral*) revue; (*de tropas etc*) review; passar ~ta a
review; ~tar *vt* search

reviver /xevi'ver/ *vt* relive □ *vi*
revive

revogar /xevo'gar/ *vt* revoke
<*lei*>; cancel <*ordem*>

revol|ta /xe'vowta/ *f* (*rebelião*)
revolt; (*indignação*) disgust;
~tante *a* disgusting; ~tar *vt*
disgust; ~tar-se *vpr* (*rebelar-se*)
revolt; (*indignar-se*) be disgusted;
~to /o/ *a* <*casa, gaveta*> upside
down; <*cabelo*> dishevelled;
<*mar*> rough; <*mundo, região*>
troubled; <*anos*> turbulent

revolu|ção /xevolu'sãw/ *f* re-
volution; ~cionar *vt* revolu-
tionize; ~cionário *a* & *m* re-
volutionary

revolver /xevow'ver/ *vt* turn over

<*terra*>; roll <*olhos*>; go through
<*gavetas, arquivos*>

revólver /xe'vowver/ *m* revolver

re|za /'xeza/ *f* prayer; ~zar *vi*
pray □ *vt* say <*missa, oração*>;
(*dizer*) state

riacho /xi'aʃu/ *m* stream

ribalta /xi'bawta/ *f* footlights

ribanceira /xibã'sera/ *f* embankment

ribombar /xibõ'bar/ *vi* rumble

rico /'xiku/ *a* rich □ *m* rich man;
os ~s the rich

ricochete /xiko'ʃetʃi/ *m* ricochet;
~ar *vi* ricochet

ricota /xi'kota/ *f* curd cheese,
ricotta

ridicularizar /xidʒikulari'zar/ *vt*
ridicule

ridículo /xi'dʒikulu/ *a* ridiculous

ri|fa /'xifa/ *f* raffle; ~far *vt* raffle

rifão /xi'fãw/ *m* saying

rifle /'xifli/ *m* rifle

rigidez /xiʒi'des/ *f* rigidity

rígido /'xiʒidu/ *a* rigid

rigor /xi'gor/ *m* severity; (*meticu-
losidade*) rigour; vestido a ~
evening dress; de ~ essential

rigoroso /xigo'rozu/ *a* strict; <*inverno, pena*> severe, harsh; <*ló-
gica, estudo*> rigorous

rijo /'xiʒu/ *a* stiff; <*músculos*>
firm

rim /xĩ/ *m* kidney; *pl* (*parte das
costas*) small of the back

ri|ma /'xima/ *f* rhyme; ~mar *vt/i*
rhyme

rí|mel /'ximew/ (*pl* ~meis) *m*
mascara

ringue /'xĩgi/ *m* ring

rinoceronte /xinose'rõtʃi/ *m* rhinoceros

rinque /'xĩki/ *m* rink

rio /'xio/ *m* river

riqueza /xi'keza/ *f* wealth; (*qualidade*) richness; *pl* riches

rir /xir/ *vi* laugh (de at)

risada /xi'zada/ *f* laugh, laughter;
dar ~ laugh

ris|ca /'xiska/ f stroke; (*listra*) stripe; (*do cabelo*) parting; **à ~ca** to the letter; **~car** vt (*apagar*) cross out <*erro*>; strike <*fósforo*>; scratch <*mesa, carro etc*>; write off <*amigo etc*>; **~co¹** m (*na parede etc*) scratch; (*no papel*) line; (*esboço*) sketch

risco² /'xisku/ m risk

riso /'xizu/ m laugh; **~nho** /o/ a smiling

ríspido /'xispidu/ a harsh

rítmico /'xitʃmiku/ a rhythmic

ritmo /'xitʃimu/ m rhythm

rito /'xitu/ m rite

ritu|al /xitu'aw/ (*pl* **~ais**) a & m ritual

ri|val /xi'vaw/ (*pl* **~vais**) a & m/f rival; **~validade** f rivalry; **~valizar** vt rival □ vi vie (**com** with)

rixa /'xiʃa/ f fight

robô /xo'bo/ m robot

robusto /xo'bustu/ a robust

roça /'xosa/ f (*campo*) country

rocambole /xokã'bɔli/ m roll

roçar /xo'sar/ vt graze; **~ em** brush against

ro|cha /'xoʃa/ f rock; **~chedo** /e/ m cliff

roda /'xoda/ f (*de carro etc*) wheel; (*de amigos etc*) circle; **~ dentada** f cog; **~da** f round; **~do a saia ~da** full skirt; **~-gigante** (*pl* **~s-gigantes**) f big wheel, (*Amer*) ferris wheel; **~moinho** m (*de vento*) whirlwind; (*na água*) whirlpool; (*fig*) whirl, swirl; **~pé** m skirting board, (*Amer*) baseboard

rodar /xo'dar/ vt (*fazer girar*) spin; (*viajar por*) go round; do <*quilometragem*>; shoot <*filme*>; run <*programa*> □ vi (*girar*) spin; (*de carro*) drive round

rodear /xodʒi'ar/ vt (*circundar*) surround; (*andar ao redor de*) go round

rodeio /xo'deju/ m (*ao falar*) circumlocution; (*de gado*) round-up; **falar sem ~s** talk straight

rodela /xo'dɛla/ f (*de limão etc*) slice; (*peça de metal*) washer

rodízio /xo'dʒiziu/ m rota

rodo /'xodu/ m rake

rodopiar /xodopi'ar/ vi spin round

rodovi|a /xodo'via/ f highway; **~ária** f bus station; **~ário a** road; **polícia ~ária** traffic police

ro|edor /xoe'dor/ m rodent; **~er** vt gnaw; bite <*unhas*>; (*fig*) eat away

rogar /xo'gar/ vi request

rojão /xo'ʒãw/ m rocket

rol /xow/ (*pl* **róis**) m roll

rolar /xo'lar/ vt roll □ vi roll; (*fam*) (*acontecer*) happen

roldana /xow'dana/ f pulley

roleta /xo'leta/ f (*jogo*) roulette; (*borboleta*) turnstile

rolha /'xoʎa/ f cork

roliço /xo'lisu/ a <*objeto*> cylindrical; <*pessoa*> plump

rolo /'xolu/ m (*de filme, tecido etc*) roll; (*máquina, bobe*) roller; **~ compressor** steamroller; **~ de massa** rolling pin

Roma /'xoma/ f Rome

romã /xo'mã/ f pomegranate

roman|ce /xo'mãsi/ m (*livro*) novel; (*caso*) romance; **~cista** m/f novelist

romano /xo'manu/ a & m Roman

romântico /xo'mãtʃiku/ a romantic

romantismo /xomã'tʃizmu/ m (*amor*) romance; (*idealismo*) romanticism

romaria /xoma'ria/ f pilgrimage

rombo /'xõbu/ m hole

Romênia /xo'menia/ f Romania

romeno /xo'menu/ a & m Romanian

rom|per /xõ'per/ vt break; break off <*relações*> □ vi <*dia*> break;

<sol> rise; **~per com** break up with; **~pimento** *m* break; *(de relações)* breaking off

ron|car /xõ'kar/ *vi (ao dormir)* snore; *<estômago>* rumble; **~co** *m* snoring; *(um)* snore; *(de motor)* roar

ron|da /'xõda/ *f* round, patrol; **~dar** *vt (patrulhar)* patrol; *(espreitar)* prowl around □ *vi <vigia etc>* patrol; *<animal, ladrão>* prowl around

ronronar /xõxo'nar/ *vi* purr

roque¹ /'xɔki/ *m (em xadrez)* rook

ro|que² /'xɔki/ *m (música)* rock; **~queiro** *m* rock musician

rosa /'xɔza/ *f* rose □ *a invar* pink; **~do** *a* rosy; *<vinho>* rosé

rosário /xo'zariu/ *m* rosary

rosbife /xoz'bifi/ *m* roast beef

rosca /'xɔska/ *f (de parafuso)* thread; *(biscoito)* rusk; **farinha de ~** breadcrumbs

roseira /xo'zera/ *f* rosebush

roseta /xo'zeta/ *f* rosette

rosnar /xoz'nar/ *vi <cachorro>* growl; *<pessoa>* snarl

rosto /'xostu/ *m* face

rota /'xɔta/ *f* route

rota|ção /xota'sãw/ *f* rotation; **~tividade** *f* turnround; **~tivo** *a* rotating

rotei|rista /xote'rista/ *m/f* scriptwriter; **~ro** *m (de viagem)* itinerary; *(de filme, peça)* script; *(de discussão etc)* outline

roti|na /xo'tʃina/ *f* routine; **~neiro** *a* routine

rótula /'xɔtula/ *f* kneecap

rotular /xotu'lar/ *vt* label *(de* as*)*

rótulo /'xɔtulu/ *m* label

rou|bar /xo'bar/ *vt* steal *<dinheiro, carro etc>*; rob *<pessoa, loja etc>* □ *vi* steal; *(em jogo)* cheat; **~bo** *m* theft, robbery

rouco /'xoku/ *a* hoarse; *<voz>* gravelly

rou|pa /'xopa/ *f* clothes; *(uma)* outfit; **~pa de baixo** under-

wear; **~pa de cama** bedclothes; **~pão** *m* dressing gown

rouquidão /xoki'dãw/ *f* hoarseness

rouxi|nol /xoʃi'nɔw/ *(pl* **~nóis** *)* *m* nightingale

roxo /'xoʃu/ *a* purple

rua /'xua/ *f* street

rubéola /xu'bɛola/ *f* German measles

rubi /xu'bi/ *m* ruby

rude /'xudʒi/ *a* rude

rudimentos /xudʒi'mẽtus/ *m pl* rudiments, basics

ruela /xu'ɛla/ *f* backstreet

rufar /xu'far/ *vi <tambor>* roll □ *m* roll

ruga /'xuga/ *f (na pele)* wrinkle; *(na roupa)* crease

ru|gido /xu'ʒidu/ *m* roar; **~gir** *vi* roar

ruibarbo /xui'barbu/ *m* rhubarb

ruído /xu'idu/ *m* noise

ruidoso /xui'dozu/ *a* noisy

ruim /xu'ĩ/ *a* bad

ruína /xu'ina/ *f* ruin

ruivo /'xuivu/ *a <cabelo>* red; *<pessoa>* red-haired □ *m* redhead

rulê /xu'le/ *a* **gola ~** roll-neck

rum /xũ/ *m* rum

ru|mar /xu'mar/ *vi* head *(para* for*)*; **~mo** *m* course; **~mo a** heading for; **sem ~mo** *<vida>* aimless; *<andar>* aimlessly

rumor /xu'mor/ *m (da rua, de vozes)* hum; *(do trânsito)* rumble; *(boato)* rumour

ru|ral /xu'raw/ *(pl* **~rais** *)* *a* rural

rusga /'xuzga/ *f* quarrel, disagreement

rush /xaʃ/ *m* rush hour

Rússia /'xusia/ *f* Russia

russo /'xusu/ *a & m* Russian

rústico /'xustʃiku/ *a* rustic

S

Saará /saa'ra/ *m* Sahara

sábado /'sabadu/ *m* Saturday

sabão /sa'bãw/ *m* soap; ~ **em pó** soap powder

sabatina /saba't∫ina/ *f* test

sabedoria /sabedo'ria/ *f* wisdom

saber /sa'ber/ *vt/i* know (**de** about); (*descobrir*) find out (**de** about) □ *m* knowledge; **eu sei cantar** I know how to sing, I can sing; **sei lá** I've no idea; **que eu saiba** as far as I know

sabiá /sabi'a/ *m* thrush

sabi|chão /sabi'∫ãw/ *a* & *m* (*f* ~**chona**) know-it-all

sábio /'sabiu/ *a* wise □ *m* wise man

sabone|te /sabo'net∫i/ *m* bar of soap; ~**teira** *f* soapdish

sabor /sa'bor/ *m* flavour; **ao** ~ **de** at the mercy of

sabo|rear /sabori'ar/ *vt* savour; ~**roso** *a* tasty

sabo|tador /sabota'dor/ *m* saboteur; ~**tagem** *f* sabotage; ~**tar** *vt* sabotage

saca /'saka/ *f* sack

sacada /sa'kada/ *f* balcony

sa|cal /sa'kaw/ *a* (*pl* ~**cais**) *a* (*fam*) boring

saca|na /sa'kana/ (*fam*) *a* (*desonesto*) devious; (*lascivo*) dirty-minded, naughty □ *m/f* rogue; ~**nagem** (*fam*) *f* (*esperteza*) trickery; (*sexo*) sex; (*uma*) dirty trick; ~**near** (*fam*) *vt* (*enganar*) do the dirty on; (*amolar*) take the mickey out of

sacar /sa'kar/ *vt/i* withdraw <*dinheiro*>; draw <*arma*>; (*em tênis, vôlei etc*) serve; (*fam*) (*entender*) understand

saçaricar /sasari'kar/ *vi* play around

sacarina /saka'rina/ *f* saccharine

saca-rolhas /saka'xoʎas/ *m invar* corkscrew

sacer|dócio /saser'dɔsiu/ *m* priesthood; ~**dote** /ɔ/ *m* priest; ~**dotisa** *f* priestess

sachê /sa'∫e/ *m* sachet

saciar /sasi'ar/ *vt* satisfy

saco /'saku/ *m* bag; **que** ~! (*fam*) what a pain!; **estar de** ~ **cheio (de)** (*fam*) be fed up (with), be sick (of); **encher o** ~ **de alg** (*fam*) get on s.o.'s nerves; **puxar o** ~ **de alg** (*fam*) suck up to s.o.; ~ **de dormir** sleeping bag; ~**la** /ɔ/ *f* bag; ~**lão** *m* wholesale fruit and vegetable market; ~**lejar** *vt* shake

sacramento /sakra'mẽtu/ *m* sacrament

sacri|ficar /sakrifi'kar/ *vt* sacrifice; have put down <*cachorro etc*>; ~**fício** *m* sacrifice; ~**légio** *m* sacrilege

sacrílego /sa'krilegu/ *a* sacrilegious

sacro /'sakru/ *a* <*música*> religious

sacrossanto /sakro'sãtu/ *a* sacrosanct

sacu|dida /saku'dʒida/ *f* shake; ~**dir** *vt* shake

sádico /'sadʒiku/ *a* sadistic □ *m* sadist

sadio /sa'dʒiu/ *a* healthy

sadismo /sa'dʒizmu/ *m* sadism

safa|deza /safa'deza/ *f* (*desonestidade*) deviousness; (*libertinagem*) indecency; (*uma*) dirty trick; ~**do** *a* (*desonesto*) devious; (*lascivo*) dirty-minded; (*esperto*) quick; <*criança*> naughty

safena /sa'fena/ *f* **ponte de** ~ heart bypass; ~**do** *m* bypass patient

safira /sa'fira/ *f* sapphire

safra /'safra/ *f* crop

sagitariano /saʒitari'anu/ *a* & *m* Sagittarian

Sagitário /saʒi'tariu/ *m* Sagittarius

sagrado /sa'gradu/ *a* sacred

saguão /sa'gwãw/ *m* (*de teatro, hotel*) foyer, (*Amer*) lobby; (*de estação, aeroporto*) concourse

saia /'saja/ *f* skirt; **~-calça** /~s-calças/ *f* culottes

saída /sa'ida/ *f* (*partida*) departure; (*porta, fig*) way out; **de ~** at the outset; **estar de ~** be on one's way out

sair /sa'ir/ *vi* (*de dentro*) go/come out; (*partir*) leave; (*desprender-se*) come off; <*mancha*> come out; (*resultar*) turn out; **~-se** *vpr* fare; **~-se com** (*dizer*) come out with; **~ mais barato** work out cheaper

sal /saw/ *m* (*pl* **sais**) *m* salt; **~ de frutas** Epsom salts

sala /'sala/ *f* (*numa casa*) lounge; (*num lugar público*) hall; (*classe*) class; **fazer ~** a entertain; **~ (de aula)** classroom; **~ de embarque** departure lounge; **~ de espera** waiting room; **~ de jantar** dining room; **~ de operação** operating theatre

sala|da /sa'lada/ *f* salad; (*fig*) jumble, mishmash; **~da de frutas** fruit salad; **~deira** *f* salad bowl

sala-e-quarto /salaj'kwartu/ *m* two-room flat

sala|me /sa'lami/ *m* salami; **~minho** /m pepperoni

salão /sa'lãw/ *m* hall; (*de cabeleireiro*) salon; (*de carros*) show; **~ de beleza** beauty salon

salari|al /salari'aw/ (*pl* **~ais**) *a* wage

salário /sa'lariu/ *m* salary

sal|dar /saw'dar/ *vt* settle; **~do** *m* balance

saleiro /sa'leru/ *m* salt cellar

sal|gadinhos /sawga'dʒinus/ *m pl* snacks; **~gado** *a* salty; <*preço*> exorbitant; **~gar** *vt* salt

salgueiro /saw'geru/ *m* willow; **~ chorão** weeping willow

saliência /sali'ẽsia/ *f* projection

salien|tar /saliẽ'tar/ *vt* (*deixar claro*) point out; (*acentuar*) highlight; **~tar-se** *vpr* distinguish o.s.; **~te** *a* prominent

saliva /sa'liva/ *f* saliva

salmão /saw'mãw/ *m* salmon

salmo /'sawmu/ *m* psalm

salmonela /sawmo'nɛla/ *f* salmonella

salmoura /saw'mora/ *f* brine

salpicar /sawpi'kar/ *vt* sprinkle; (*sem querer*) spatter

salsa /'sawsa/ *f* parsley

salsicha /saw'siʃa/ *f* sausage

saltar /saw'tar/ *vt* (*pular*) jump; (*omitir*) skip □ *vi* jump; **~ à vista** be obvious; **~ do ônibus** get off the bus

saltear /sawtʃi'ar/ *vt* sauté <*batatas etc*>

saltitar /sawtʃi'tar/ *vi* hop

salto /'sawtu/ *m* (*pulo*) jump; (*de sapato*) heel; **~ com vara** pole vault; **~ em altura** high jump; **~ em distância** long jump; **~-mortal** (*pl* **~s-mortais**) *m* somersault

salu|bre /sa'lubri/ *a* healthy; **~taris** *a* salutary

salva[1] /'sawva/ *f* (*de canhões*) salvo; (*bandeja*) salver; **~ de palmas** round of applause

salva[2] /'sawva/ *f* (*erva*) sage

salva|ção /sawva'sãw/ *f* salvation; **~dor** *m* saviour

salvaguar|da /sawva'gwarda/ *f* safeguard; **~dar** *vt* safeguard

sal|vamento /sawva'mẽtu/ *m* rescue; (*de navio*) salvage; **~var** *vt* save; **~var-se** *vpr* escape; **~va-vidas** *m invar* (*bóia*) lifebelt □ *m/f* (*pessoa*) lifeguard □ *a* barco **~va-vidas** lifeboat; **~vo** *a* safe □ *prep* save; **a ~vo** safe

samambaia /samã'baja/ *f* fern

sam|ba /'sãba/ *m* samba; **~ba-canção** (*pl* **~bas-canção**) *m* slow samba □ *a* invar **cueca ~ba-canção** boxer shorts; **~ba-enredo** (*pl* **~bas-enredo**) *m* samba story; **~bar** *vi* samba; **~bista** *m/f* (*dançarino*) samba dancer; (*compositor*) composer of sambas; **~bódromo** *m* Carnival parade ground

samovar /samo'var/ *m* tea urn

sanar /sa'nar/ *vt* cure

san|ção /sã'sãw/ *f* sanction; **~cionar** *vt* sanction

sandália /sã'dalia/ *f* sandal

sandes /'sãdiʃ/ *f invar* (*Port*) sandwich

sanduíche /sãdu'iʃi/ *m* sandwich

sane|amento /sania'mẽtu/ *m* (*esgotos*) sanitation; (*de finanças*) rehabilitation; **~ar** *vt* set straight <*finanças*>

sanfona /sã'fona/ *f* (*instrumento*) accordion; (*tricô*) ribbing; **~do** *a* <*porta*> folding; <*pulôver*> ribbed

san|grar /sã'grar/ *vt/i* bleed; **~grento** *a* bloody; <*carne*> rare; **~gria** *f* bloodshed; (*de dinheiro*) extortion

sangue /'sãgi/ *m* blood; **~ pisado** bruise; **~-frio** *m* cool, coolness

sanguessuga /sãgi'suga/ *f* leech

sanguinário /sãgi'nariu/ *a* bloodthirsty

sanguíneo /sã'giniu/ *a* blood

sanidade /sani'dadʒi/ *f* sanity

sanitário /sani'tariu/ *a* sanitary; **~s** *mpl* toilets

san|tidade /sãtʃi'dadʒi/ *f* sanctity; **~tificar** *vt* sanctify; **~to** *a* holy □ *m* saint; **todo ~to dia** every single day; **~tuário** *m* sanctuary

São /sãw/ *a* Saint

são /sãw/ (*pl* **~s**) *a* (*f* **sã**) healthy; (*mentalmente*) sane; <*conselho*> sound

sapato /sa'pata/ *m* shoe; **~ria** *f* shoe shop

sapate|ado /sapatʃi'adu/ *m* tap dancing; **~ador** *m* tap dancer; **~ar** *vi* tap one's feet; (*dançar*) tap-dance

sapa|teiro /sapa'teru/ *m* shoemaker; **~tilha** *f* pump; **~tilha de balé** ballet shoe; **~to** *m* shoe

sapeca /sa'pɛka/ *a* saucy

sa|pinho /sa'piɲu/ *m* thrush; **~po** *m* toad

saque[1] /'saki/ *m* (*do banco*) withdrawal; (*em tênis, vôlei etc*) serve

saque[2] /'saki/ *m* (*de loja etc*) looting; **~ar** *vt* loot

saraiva /sa'rajva/ *f* hail; **~da** *f* hailstorm; **uma ~da de** a hail of

sarampo /sa'rãpu/ *m* measles

sarar /sa'rar/ *vt* cure □ *vi* get better; <*ferida*> heal

sar|casmo /sar'kazmu/ *m* sarcasm; **~cástico** *a* sarcastic

sarda /'sarda/ *f* freckle

Sardenha /sar'deɲa/ *f* Sardinia

sardento /sar'dẽtu/ *a* freckled

sardinha /sar'dʒiɲa/ *f* sardine

sardônico /sar'doniku/ *a* sardonic

sargento /sar'ʒẽtu/ *m* sergeant

sarjeta /sar'ʒeta/ *f* gutter

Satanás /sata'nas/ *m* Satan

satânico /sa'taniku/ *a* satanic

satélite /sa'tɛlitʃi/ *a & m* satellite

sátira /'satʃira/ *f* satire

satírico /sa'tʃiriku/ *a* satirical

satirizar /satʃiri'zar/ *vt* satirize

satisfa|ção /satʃisfa'sãw/ *f* satisfaction; **dar ~ções** a answer to; **~tório** *a* satisfactory; **~zer** *vt* **~zer (a)** satisfy □ *vi* be satisfactory; **~zer-se** *vpr* be satisfied

satisfeito /satʃis'fejtu/ *a* satisfied; (*contente*) content; (*de comida*) full

saturar /satu'rar/ *vt* saturate

Saturno /sa'turnu/ *m* Saturn

saudação /sawda'sãw/ *f* greeting

saudade /saw'dadʒi/ *f* longing; (*lembrança*) nostalgia; **estar**

com ~s de miss; **matar ~s** catch up

saudar /saw'dar/ *vt* greet

saudá|vel /saw'davew/ (*pl* ~**veis**) *a* healthy

saúde /sa'udʒi/ *f* health □ *int* (*ao beber*) cheers; (*ao espirrar*) bless you

saudo|sismo /sawdo'zizmu/ *m* nostalgia; ~**so** /o/ *a* longing; **estar ~so de** miss; **o nosso ~so amigo** our much-missed friend

sauna /'sawna/ *f* sauna

saxofo|ne /sakso'foni/ *m* saxophone; ~**nista** *m/f* saxophonist

sazo|nado /sazo'nadu/ *a* seasoned; ~**nal** (*pl* ~**nais**) *a* seasonal

se[1] /si/ *conj* if; **não sei ~** ... I don't know if/whether

se[2] /si/ *pron* (*ele mesmo*) himself; (*ela mesma*) herself; (*você mesmo*) yourself; (*eles/elas*) themselves; (*vocês*) yourselves; (*um ao outro*) each other; **dorme~ tarde no Brasil** people go to bed late in Brazil; **aqui ~ fala inglês** English is spoken here

sebo /'sebu/ *m* (*sujeira*) grease; (*livraria*) secondhand bookshop; ~**so** /o/ *a* greasy; <*pessoa*> slimy

seca /'seka/ *f* drought; ~**dor m** ~**dor de cabelo** hairdryer; ~**dora** *f* tumble dryer

seção /se'sãw/ *f* section; (*de loja*) department

secar /se'kar/ *vt/i* dry

sec|ção /sek'sãw/ *f veja* **seção**; ~**cionar** *vt* split up

seco /'seku/ *a* dry; <*resposta, tom*> curt; <*pessoa, caráter*> cold; <*barulho, pancada*> dull; **estar ~ por** I'm dying for

secretaria /sekreta'ria/ *f* (*de empresa*) general office; (*ministério*) department

secretá|ria /sekre'taria/ *f* secretary; ~**ria eletrônica** ansaphone; ~**rio** *m* secretary

secreto /se'krɛtu/ *a* secret

secular /seku'lar/ *a* (*não religioso*) secular; (*antigo*) age-old

século /'sɛkulu/ *m* century; *pl* (*muito tempo*) ages

secundário /sekũ'dariu/ *a* secondary

secura /se'kura/ *f* dryness; **estar com uma ~ de** be longing for/to

seda /'seda/ *f* silk

sedativo /seda'tʃivu/ *a & m* sedative

sede[1] /'sɛdʒi/ *f* headquarters; (*local do governo*) seat

sede[2] /'sedʒi/ *f* thirst (**de** for); **estar com ~** be thirsty

sedentário /sedẽ'tariu/ *a* sedentary

sedento /se'dẽtu/ *a* thirsty (**de** for)

sediar /sedʒi'ar/ *vt* host

sedimen|tar /sedʒimẽ'tar/ *vt* consolidate; ~**to m** sediment

sedoso /se'dozu/ *a* silky

sedu|ção /sedu'sãw/ *f* seduction; ~**tor** *a* seductive; ~**zir** *vt* seduce

segmento /seg'mẽtu/ *m* segment

segredo /se'gredu/ *m* secret; (*de cofre etc*) combination

segregar /segre'gar/ *vt* segregate

segui|da /se'gida/ *f* **em ~da** (*imediatamente*) straight away; (*depois*) next; ~**do a** followed (**de** by); **cinco horas ~das** five hours running; ~**dor m** follower; ~**mento m** continuation; **dar ~mento a** go on with

se|guinte /se'gĩtʃi/ *a* following; (*dia, semana etc*) next; ~**guir** *vt/i* follow; (*continuar*) continue; ~**guir-se** *vpr* follow; ~**guir em frente** (*ir embora*) go; (*indicação na rua*) go straight ahead

segun|da /se'gũda/ *f* (*dia*) Monday; (*marcha*) second; **de ~da** second-rate; ~**da-feira** (*pl* ~**das-feiras**) *f* Monday; ~**do a & m** second □ *adv* secondly □

prep according to □ *conj* according to what; ~**das intenções** ulterior motives; **de** ~**da mão** second-hand

segu|rança /segu'rāsa/ *f* security; (*estado de seguro*) safety; (*certeza*) assurance □ *m//f* security guard; ~**rar** *vt* hold; ~**rar-se** *upr* (*controlar-se*) control o.s.; ~**rar-se em** hold on to; ~**ro** *a* secure; (*fora de perigo*) safe; (*com certeza*) sure □ *m* insurance; **estar no** ~**ro** < *bens* > be insured; **fazer** ~**ro de** insure; ~**ro-desemprego** *m* unemployment benefit

seio /'seju/ *m* breast, bosom; **no** ~ **de** within

seis /sejs/ *a & m* six; ~**centos** *a & m* six hundred

seita /'sejta/ *f* sect

seixo /'sejʃu/ *m* pebble

sela /'sɛla/ *f* saddle

selar¹ /se'lar/ *vt* saddle < *cavalo* >

selar² /se'lar/ *vt* seal; (*franquear*) stamp

sele|ção /sele'sāw/ *f* selection; (*time*) team; ~**cionar** *vt* select; ~**to** /ɛ/ *a* select

selim /se'lĩ/ *m* saddle

selo /'selu/ *m* seal; (*postal*) stamp; (*de discos*) label

selva /'sɛwva/ *f* jungle; ~**gem** *a* wild; ~**geria** *f* savagery

sem /sēj/ *prep* without; ~ **eu saber** without me knowing; **ficar** ~ **dinheiro** run out of money

semáforo /se'maforu/ *m* (*na rua*) traffic lights; (*de ferrovia*) signal

sema|na /se'mana/ *f* week; ~**nal** (*pl* ~**nais**) *a* weekly; ~**nalmente** *adv* weekly; ~**nário** *m* weekly

semear /semi'ar/ *vt* sow

semelhan|ça /seme'ʎāsa/ *f* similarity; ~**te** *a* similar; (*tal*) such

sêmen /'semē/ *m* semen

semente /se'mētʃi/ *f* seed; (*em fruta*) pip

semestre /se'mɛstri/ *m* six months; (*da faculdade etc*) term, (*Amer*) semester

semi|círculo /semi'sirkulu/ *m* semicircle; ~**final** (*pl* ~**finais**) *f* semifinal

seminário /semi'nariu/ *m* (*aula*) seminar; (*colégio religioso*) seminary

sem-número /sē'numeru/ *m* **um** ~ **de** innumerable

sempre /'sēpri/ *adv* always; **como** ~ as usual; **para** ~ for ever; ~ **que** whenever

semi|-terra /semi'tɛʃxa/ *m//f invar* landless labourer; ~**-teto** *a* homeless □ *m//f* homeless person; ~**-vergonha** *a invar* brazen □ *m//f invar* scoundrel

sena|do /se'nadu/ *m* senate; ~**dor** *m* senator

senão /si'nāw/ *conj* otherwise; (*mas antes*) but rather □ *m* snag

senda /'sēda/ *f* path

senha /'sena/ *f* (*palavra*) password; (*número*) code; (*sinal*) signal

senhor /se'nor/ *m* gentleman; (*homem idoso*) older man; (*tratamento*) sir □ *a* (*f* ~**a**) mighty; **Senhor** (*com nome*) Mr; (*Deus*) Lord; **o** ~ (*você*) you

senho|ra /se'nora/ *f* lady; (*mulher idosa*) older woman; (*tratamento*) madam; **Senhora** (*com nome*) Mrs; **a** ~**ra** (*você*) you; **nossa** ~**ra!** (*fam*) gosh; ~**ria** *f* you, (*Vossa* **Senhoria** you; ~**rita** *f* young lady; (*tratamento*) miss; **Senhorita** (*com nome*) Miss

se|nil (*pl* ~**nis**) *a* senile; ~**nilidade** *f* senility

sensação /sēsa'sāw/ *f* sensation

sensacio|nal /sēsasio'naw/ (*pl* ~**nais**) *a* sensational; ~**nalismo** *m* sensationalism; ~**nalista** *a* sensationalist

sen|sato /sē'satu/ *a* sensible; ~**sibilidade** *f* sensitivity; ~**sí-**

vel (*pl* ~**síveis**) *a* sensitive; (*que se pode sentir*) noticeable; ~**so** *m* sense; ~**sual** (*pl* ~**suais**) *a* sensual

sen|**tado** /sẽ'tadu/ *a* sitting; ~**tar** *vt/i* sit; ~**tar-se** *vpr* sit down

sentença /sẽ'tẽsa/ *f* sentence

sentido /sẽ'tʃidu/ *m* sense; (*direção*) direction □ *a* hurt; **fazer** *ou* **ter** ~ make sense

sentimen|**tal** /sẽtʃimẽ'taw/ (*pl* ~**tais**) *a* sentimental; **vida** ~**tal** love life; ~**to** *m* feeling

sentinela /sẽtʃi'nɛla/ *f* sentry

sentir /sẽ'tʃir/ *vt* feel; (*notar*) sense; smell <*cheiro*>; taste <*gosto*>; tell <*diferença*>; (*ficar magoado por*) be hurt by □ *vi* feel; ~**se** *vpr* feel; **sinto muito** I'm very sorry

sepa|**ração** /separa'sãw/ *f* separation; ~**rado** *a* separate; <*casal*> separated; ~**rar** *vt* separate; ~**rar-se** *vpr* separate

séptico /'sɛptʃiku/ *a* septic

sepul|**tar** /sepuw'tar/ *vt* bury; ~**tura** *f* grave

seqüência /se'kwẽsia/ *f* sequence

sequer /se'kɛr/ *adv* nem ~ not even

seqües|**trador** /sekwestra'dor/ *m* kidnapper; (*de avião*) hijacker; ~**trar** *vt* kidnap <*pessoa*>; hijack <*avião*>; ~**tro** /ɛ/ *m* (*de pessoa*) kidnapping; (*de avião*) hijack; (*de bens*) sequestration

ser /ser/ *vi* be □ *m* being; é (*como resposta*) yes; **você gosta, não é?** you like it, don't you?; **ele foi morto** he was killed; **será que ele volta?** I wonder if he's coming back; **ou seja** in other words; **a não** ~ except; **a não** ~ **que** unless; **não sou de fofocar** I'm not one to gossip

sereia /se'reja/ *f* mermaid

serenata /sere'nata/ *f* serenade

sereno /se'renu/ *a* serene; <*tem-*

po> fine

série /'sɛri/ *f* series; (*na escola*) grade; **fora de** ~ incredible

seriedade /serie'dadʒi/ *f* seriousness

serin|**ga** /se'rĩga/ *f* syringe; ~**gueiro** *m* rubber tapper

sério /'sɛriu/ *a* serious; (*responsável*) responsible; ~? really?; **falar** ~ be serious; **levar a** ~ take seriously

sermão /ser'mãw/ *m* sermon

serpen|**te** /ser'pẽtʃi/ *f* serpent; ~**tear** *vi* wind; ~**tina** *f* streamer

serra¹ /'sɛxa/ *f* (*montanhas*) mountain range

serra² /'sɛxa/ *f* (*de serrar*) saw; ~**gem** *f* sawdust; ~**lheiro** *m* locksmith

serrano /se'xanu/ *a* mountain

serrar /se'xar/ *vt* saw

ser|**tanejo** /serta'neʒu/ *a* from the backwoods □ *m* backwoodsman; ~**tão** *m* backwoods

servente /ser'vẽtʃi/ *m/f* labourer

Sérvia /'sɛrvia/ *f* Serbia

servi|**cal** /servi'saw/ (*pl* ~**çais**) *a* helpful □ *m/f* servant; ~**ço** *m* service; (*trabalho*) work; (*tarefa*) job; **estar de** ~**ço** be on duty; ~**dor** *m* servant; (*comput*) server; ~ **público** civil servant

ser|**vil** /ser'viw/ (*pl* ~**vis**) *a* servile

sérvio /'sɛrviu/ *a* & *m* Serbian

servir /ser'vir/ *vt* serve □ *vi* serve; (*ser adequado*) do; (*ser útil*) be of use; <*roupa, sapato etc*> fit; ~**se** *vpr* (*ao comer etc*) help o.s. (**de** to); ~**se de** make use of; ~ **como** *ou* **de** serve as; **para que serve isso?** what is this (used) for?

sessão /se'sãw/ *f* session; (*no cinema*) showing, performance

sessenta /se'sẽta/ *a* & *m* sixty

seta /'sɛta/ *f* arrow; (*de carro*) indicator

sete /'sɛtʃi/ *a* & *m* seven; **~centos** *a* & *m* seven hundred

setembro /se'tẽbru/ *m* September

setenta /se'tẽta/ *a* & *m* seventy

sétimo /'sɛtʃimu/ *a* seventh

setuagésimo /setua'ʒɛzimu/ *a* seventieth

setor /se'tor/ *m* sector

seu /sew/ *a* (*f* **sua**) (*dele*) his; (*dela*) her; (*de coisa*) its; (*deles*) their; (*de você, de vocês*) your □ *pron* (*dele*) his; (*dela*) hers; (*deles*) theirs; (*de você, de vocês*) yours; **~ idiota!** you idiot!; **seu João** Mr John

seve|ridade /severi'dadʒi/ *f* severity; **~ro** /ɛ/ *a* severe

sexagésimo /seksa'ʒɛzimu/ *a* sixtieth

sexo /'sɛksu/ *m* sex; **fazer ~** have sex

sex|ta /'sesta/ *f* Friday; **~ta-feira** (*pl* **~tas-feiras**) *f* Friday; **Sexta-feira Santa** Good Friday; **~to** /e/ *a* & *m* sixth

sexu|al /seksu'aw/ (*pl* **~ais**) *a* sexual; **vida ~al** sex life

sexy /'sɛksi/ *a invar* sexy

shopping /'ʃɔpĩ/ (*pl* **~s**) *m* shopping centre, (*Amer*) mall

short /'ʃɔrtʃi/ *m* (*pl* **~s**) shorts; **um ~** a pair of shorts

show /'ʃow/ (*pl* **~s**) *m* show; (*de música*) concert

si /si/ *pron* (*ele*) himself; (*ela*) herself; (*coisa*) itself; (*você*) yourself; (*eles*) themselves; (*vocês*) yourselves; (*qualquer pessoa*) oneself; **em ~** in itself; **fora de ~** beside o.s.; **cheio de ~** full of o.s.; **voltar a ~** come round

sibilar /sibi'lar/ *vi* hiss

SIDA /'sida/ *f* (*Port*) AIDS

side|ral /side'raw/ (*pl* **~rais**) *a* **espaço ~ral** outer space.

siderurgia /siderur'ʒia/ *f* iron and steel industry

siderúrgi|ca /side'rurʒika/ *f* steel-works; **~co** *a* iron and steel □ *m* steelworker

sifão /si'fãw/ *m* syphon

sífilis /'sifilis/ *f* syphilis

sigilo /si'ʒilu/ *m* secrecy; **~so** /o/ *a* secret

sigla /'sigla/ *f* acronym

signatário /signa'tariu/ *m* signatory

signifi|cação /signifika'sãw/ *f* significance; **~cado** *m* meaning; **~car** *vt* mean; **~cativo** *a* significant

signo /'signu/ *m* sign

sílaba /'silaba/ *f* syllable

silenciar /silẽsi'ar/ *vt* silence

silêncio /si'lẽsiu/ *m* silence

silencioso /silẽsi'ozu/ *a* silent □ *m* silencer, (*Amer*) muffler

silhueta /siʎu'eta/ *f* silhouette

silício /si'lisiu/ *m* silicon

silicone /sili'kɔni/ *m* silicone

silo /'silu/ *m* silo

silvar /siw'var/ *vi* hiss

sil|vestre /siw'vestri/ *a* wild; **~vicultura** /f forestry

sim /sĩ/ *adv* yes; **acho que ~** I think so

simbólico /sĩ'bɔliku/ *a* symbolic

simbo|lismo /sĩbo'lizmu/ *m* symbolism; **~lizar** *vt* symbolize

símbolo /'sĩbolu/ *m* symbol

sime|tria /sime'tria/ *f* symmetry; **~métrico** *a* symmetrical

similar /simi'lar/ *a* similar

sim|patia /sĩpa'tʃia/ *f* (*qualidade*) pleasantness; (*afeto*) fondness (*por* for); (*compreensão, apoio*) sympathy; *pl* sympathies; **ter ~patia por** be fond of; **~pático** *a* nice

simpati|zante /sĩpatʃi'zãtʃi/ *a* sympathetic □ *m/f* sympathizer; **~zar** *vi* **~zar com** take a liking to < *pessoa*>; sympathize with < *idéias, partido etc*>

simples /'sĩplis/ *a invar* simple; (*único*) single □ *f* (*no tênis etc*) singles; **~mente** *adv* simply

simpli|cidade /sĩpliʃi'dadʒi/ f simplicity; **~ficar** vt simplify

simplório /sĩ'plɔriu/ a simple

simpósio /sĩ'pɔziu/ m symposium

simu|lação /simula'sãw/ f simulation; **~lar** vt simulate

simultâneo /simuw'taniu/ a simultaneous

sina /'sina/ f fate

sinagoga /sina'gɔga/ f synagogue

si|nal /si'naw/ (pl **~nais**) m sign; (aviso, de rádio etc) signal; (de trânsito) traffic light; (no telefone) tone; (dinheiro) deposit; (na pele) mole; **por ~nal** as a matter of fact; **~nal de pontuação** punctuation mark; **~naleira** f traffic lights; **~nalização** f (na rua) road signs; **~nalizar** vt signal; signpost < rua, cidade >

since|ridade /sĩseri'dadʒi/ f sincerity; **~ro** /ɛ/ a sincere

sincro|nia /sĩkro'nia/ f synchronization; **~nizar** vt synchronize

sindi|cal /sĩdʒi'kaw/ (pl **~cais**) a trade union; **~calismo** m trade unionism; **~calista** m/f trade unionist; **~calizar** vt unionize; **~cato** m trade union

síndico /'sĩdʒiku/ m house manager

síndrome /'sĩdromi/ f syndrome

sineta /si'neta/ f bell

sin|fonia /sĩfo'nia/ f symphony; **~fônica** f symphony orchestra

singe|leza /sĩʒe'leza/ f simplicity; **~lo** /ɛ/ a simple

singu|lar /sĩgu'lar/ a singular; (estranho) peculiar; **~larizar** vt single out

sinis|trado /sinis'tradu/ a damaged; **~tro** /i/ a sinister □ m accident

sino /'sinu/ m bell

sinônimo /si'nonimu/ a synonymous □ m synonym

sintaxe /sĩ'taksi/ f syntax

síntese /'sĩtezi/ f synthesis

sin|tético /sĩ'tɛtʃiku/ a (artificial) synthetic; (resumido) concise; **~tetizar** vt summarize

sinto|ma /sĩ'toma/ m symptom; **~mático** a symptomatic

sintoni|zador /sĩtoniza'dor/ m tuner; **~zar** vt tune < rádio, TV>; tune in to < emissora > □ vi be in tune (com with)

sinuca /si'nuka/ f snooker

sinuoso /sinu'ozu/ a winding

sinusite /sinu'zitʃi/ f sinusitis

siri /si'ri/ m crab

Síria /'siria/ f Syria

sírio /'siriu/ a & m Syrian

siso /'sizu/ m good sense

siste|ma /sis'tema/ m system; **~mático** a systematic

sisudo /si'zudu/ a serious

site /sajt/ m (comput) website

sítio /'sitʃiu/ m (chácara) farm; (Port: local) place; **estado de ~** state of siege

situ|ação /situa'sãw/ f situation; (no governo) party in power; **~ar** vt situate; **~ar-se** vpr be situated; < pessoa> position o.s.

smoking /iz'mɔki/ (pl **~s**) m dinner jacket, (Amer) tuxedo

só /sɔ/ a alone; (sentindo solidão) lonely □ adv only; **um ~ voto** one single vote; **~ um carro** only one car; **a ~s** alone; **imagina ~** just imagine; **~ que** except (that)

soalho /so'aʎu/ m floor

soar /so'ar/ vt/i sound

sob /sobi/ prep under

sobera|nia /sobera'nia/ f sovereignty; **~no** a & m sovereign

soberbo /so'berbu/ a < pessoa> haughty; (magnífico) splendid

sobra /'sɔbra/ f surplus; pl leftovers; **tempo de ~** (muito) plenty of time; **ficar de ~** be left over; **ter aco de ~** (sobrando) have sth left over

sobraçar /sobra'sar/ vt carry under one's arm

sobrado /so'bradu/ m (casa) house; (andar) upper floor

sobrancelha /sobrã'seʎa/ f eyebrow

so|brar /so'brar/ vi be left; ~**bram-me dois** I have two left

sobre /'sobri/ prep (em cima de) on; (por cima de, acima de) over; (acerca de) about

sobreaviso /sobria'vizu/ m **estar de ~** be on one's guard

sobrecapa /sobri'kapa/ f dust jacket

sobrecarregar /sobrikaxe'gar/ vt overload

sobreloja /sobri'lɔʒa/ f mezzanine

sobremesa /sobri'meza/ f dessert

sobrenatu|ral /sobrinatu'raw/ (pl ~**rais**) a supernatural

sobrenome /sobri'nomi/ m surname

sobrepor /sobri'por/ vt superimpose

sobrepujar /sobripu'ʒar/ vt (em altura) tower over; (em valor, número etc) surpass; (inimigo) overwhelm <adversário>; overcome <problemas>

sobrescritar /sobriskri'tar/ vt address

sobressair /sobrisa'ir/ vi stand out; ~**-se** vpr stand out

sobressalente /sobrisa'lẽtʃi/ a spare

sobressal|tar /sobrisaw'tar/ vt startle; ~**tar-se** vpr be startled; ~**to** m (movimento) start; (susto) fright

sobretaxa /sobri'taʃa/ f surcharge

sobretudo /sobri'tudu/ adv above all □ m overcoat

sobrevir /sobri'vir/ vi happen suddenly; (seguir) ensue; ~**a** follow

sobrevi|vência /sobrivi'vẽsia/ f survival; ~**vente** a surviving □ m/f survivor; ~**ver** vt/i ~**ver (a)** survive

sobrevoar /sobrivo'ar/ vt fly over

sobri|nha /so'briɲa/ f niece; ~**nho** m nephew

sóbrio /'sɔbriu/ a sober

socar /so'kar/ vt (esmurrar) punch; (amassar) crush

soci|al /sosi'aw/ (pl ~**ais**) a social; **camisa ~al** dress shirt; ~**alismo** m socialism; ~**alista** a & m/f socialist; ~**alite** /-a'lajtʃi/ m/f socialite; ~**ável** (pl ~**áveis**) a sociable

sociedade /sosie'dadʒi/ f society; (parceria) partnership; ~ **anônima** limited company

sócio /'sɔsiu/ m (de empresa) partner; (de clube) member

socio-econômico /sosioeko'nomiku/ a socio-economic

soci|ologia /sosiolo'ʒia/ f sociology; ~**ológico** a sociological; ~**ólogo** m sociologist

soco /'soku/ m punch; **dar um ~** em punch

socor|rer /soko'xer/ vt help; ~**ro** m aid □ int help; **primeiros ~ros** first aid

soda /'sɔda/ f (água) soda water; ~ **cáustica** caustic soda

sódio /'sɔdʒiu/ m sodium

sofá /so'fa/ m sofa; ~**-cama** (pl ~**s-camas**) m sofa-bed

sofisticado /sofistʃi'kadu/ a sophisticated

so|fredor /sofre'dor/ a martyred; ~**frer** vt suffer <dor, derrota, danos etc>; have <acidente>; undergo <operação, mudança etc> □ vi suffer; ~**frer de** suffer from <doença>; have trouble with <coração etc>; ~**frido** a long-suffering; ~**frimento** m suffering; ~**frível** (pl ~**fríveis**) a passable

soft /'softʃi/ (pl ~**s**) m software package; ~**ware** m software; (um) software package

so|gra /'sɔgra/ f mother-in-law; ~**gro** /o/ m father-in-law; ~**gros** /ɔ/ m pl in-laws

soja /'sɔʒa/ f soya, (*Amer*) soy

sol /sɔw/ (*pl* **sóis**) *m* sun; **faz ~** it's sunny

sola /'sɔla/ f sole; **~do a <*bolo*>** flat

solapar /sola'par/ *vt* undermine

solar¹ /so'lar/ *a* solar

solar² /so'lar/ *vt* sole <*sapato*> □ *vi <bolo>* go flat

solavanco /sola'vãku/ *m* jolt; **dar ~s** jolt

soldado /sow'dadu/ *m* soldier

solda|dura /sowda'dura/ f weld; **~dar** *vt* weld

soldo /'sowdu/ *m* pay

soleira /so'lera/ f doorstep

sole|ne /so'leni/ *a* solemn; **~nidade** f (*cerimônia*) ceremony; (*qualidade*) solemnity

soletrar /sole'trar/ *vt* spell

solici|tação /solisita'sãw/ f request (**de** for); (*por escrito*) application (**de** for); **~tante** *m/f* applicant; **~tar** *vt* request; (*por escrito*) apply for

solícito /so'lisitu/ *a* helpful

solidão /soli'dãw/ f loneliness

soli|dariedade /solidarie'dadʒi/ f solidarity; **~dário** *a* supportive (**com** of)

soli|dez /soli'des/ f solidity; **~dificar** *vt* solidify; **~dificar-se** *vpr* solidify

sólido /'solidu/ *a* & *m* solid

solista /so'lista/ *m/f* soloist

solitá|ria /soli'taria/ f (*verme*) tapeworm; (*cela*) solitary confinement; **~rio** *a* solitary

solo¹ /'sɔlu/ *m* (*terra*) soil; (*chão*) ground

solo² /'sɔlu/ *m* solo

soltar /sow'tar/ *vt* let go <*prisioneiros, animal etc*>; let loose <*cães*>; (*deixar de segurar*) let go of; (*soltar*) loosen <*gravata, corda etc*>; let down <*cabelo*>; let out <*grito, suspiro etc*>; let off <*foguetes*>; tell <*piada*>; take off <*freio*>; **~-se** *vpr* <*peça, parafuso*> come loose; <*pessoa*> let o.s. go

soltei|ra /sow'tera/ f single woman; **~rão** *m* bachelor; **~ro** *a* single □ *m* single man; **~rona** f spinster

solto /'sowtu/ *a* (*livre*) free; <*cães*> loose; <*cabelo*> down; <*arroz*> fluffy; (*frouxo*) loose; (*à vontade*) relaxed; (*abandonado*) abandoned; **correr ~** run wild

solução /solu'sãw/ f solution

soluçar /solu'sar/ *vi* (*ao chorar*) sob; (*engasgar*) hiccup

solucionar /solusio'nar/ *vt* solve

soluço /so'lusu/ *m* (*ao chorar*) sob; (*engasgo*) hiccup; **estar com ~s** have the hiccups

solú|vel /so'luvew/ (*pl* **~veis**) *a* soluble

solvente /sow'vẽtʃi/ *a* & *m* solvent

som /sõ/ *m* sound; (*aparelho*) stereo; **um ~** (*fam*) (*música*) a bit of music

so|ma /'soma/ f sum; **~mar** *vt* add up <*números etc*>; (*ter como soma*) add up to

sombra /'sõbra/ f shadow; (*área abrigada do sol*) shade; **à ~ de** in the shade of; **sem ~ de dúvida** without a shadow of a doubt

sombre|ado /sõbri'adu/ *a* shady □ *m* shading; **~ar** *vt* shade

sombrinha /sõ'briɲa/ f parasol

sombrio /sõ'briu/ *a* gloomy

somente /sõ'mẽtʃi/ *adv* only

sonâmbulo /so'nãbulu/ *m* sleepwalker

sonante /so'nãtʃi/ *a* **moeda ~** hard cash

sonata /so'nata/ f sonata

son|da /'sõda/ f probe; (*no mar*) sounding; (*de terreno*) survey; **~dagem** f (*de terreno*) survey; **~dagem de opinião** opinion poll; **~dar** *vt* probe; sound <*profundeza*>; (*fig*) sound out <*pessoas, opiniões etc*>

soneca /so'nɛka/ *f* nap; **tirar uma ~** have a nap

sone|gação /sonega'sãw/ *f* (*de impostos*) tax evasion; **~gador** *m* tax dodger; **~gar** *vt* withhold

soneto /so'netu/ *m* sonnet

so|nhador /soɲa'dor/ *a* dreamy □ *m* dreamer; **~nhar** *vt/i* dream (**com** about); **~nho** /'soɲu/ *m* dream; (*doce*) doughnut

sono /'sonu/ *m* sleep; **estar com ~** be sleepy; **pegar no ~** get to sleep; **~lento** *a* sleepy

sono|plastia /sonoplas'tʃia/ *f* sound effects; **~ridade** *f* sound quality; **~ro** /ɔ/ *a* sound; (*voz*) sonorous; <*consoante*> voiced

sonso /'sõsu/ *a* devious

sopa /'sopa/ *f* soup

sopapo /so'papu/ *m* slap; **dar um ~ em** slap

sopé /so'pɛ/ *m* foot

sopeira /so'pera/ *f* soup tureen

soprano /so'pranu/ *m/f* soprano

so|prar /so'prar/ *vt* blow <*folhas etc*>; blow up <*balão*>; blow out <*vela*> □ *vi* blow; **~pro** *m* blow; (*de vento*) puff; **instrumento de ~pro** wind instrument

soquete[1] /so'kɛtʃi/ *f* ankle sock

soquete[2] /so'kɛtʃi/ *m* socket

sordidez /sordʒi'des/ *f* sordidness; (*imundície*) squalor

sórdido /'sordʒidu/ *a* (*reles*) sordid; (*imundo*) squalid

soro /'soru/ *m* (*remédio*) serum; (*de leite*) whey

sorrateiro /soxa'teru/ *a* crafty

sor|ridente /soxi'dẽtʃi/ *a* smiling; **~rir** *vi* smile; **~riso** *m* smile

sorte /'sortʃi/ *f* luck; (*destino*) fate; **pessoa de ~** lucky person; **por ~** luckily; **ter** *ou* **dar ~** be lucky; **tive a ~ de conhecê-lo** I was lucky enough to meet him; **tirar a ~** draw lots; **trazer** *ou* **dar ~** bring good luck

sor|tear /sortʃi'ar/ *vt* draw for <*prêmio*>; select in a draw <*pessoa*>; **~teio** *m* draw

sorti|do /sor'tʃidu/ *a* assorted; **~mento** *m* assortment

sorumbático /sorũ'batʃiku/ *a* sombre, gloomy

sorver /sor'ver/ *vt* sip <*bebida*>

sósia /'sɔzia/ *m/f* double

soslaio /soz'laju/ *m* **de ~** sideways; <*olhar*> askance

sosse|gado /sose'gadu/ *a* <*vida*> quiet; **ficar ~gado** <*pessoa*> rest assured; **~gar** *vt* reassure □ *vi* rest; **~go** /e/ *m* peace

sótão /'sɔtãw/ *m* (*pl* **~s**) *m* attic, loft

sotaque /so'taki/ *m* accent

soterrar /sote'xar/ *vt* bury

soutien /suti'ã/ (*pl* **~s**) *m* (*Port*) bra

sova|co /so'vaku/ *m* armpit; **~queira** *f* BO, body odour

soviético /sovi'etʃiku/ *a & m* Soviet

sovi|na /so'vina/ *a* stingy, mean, (*Amer*) cheap □ *m/f* cheapskate; **~nice** *f* stinginess, meanness, (*Amer*) cheapness

sozinho /so'ziɲu/ *a* (*sem ninguém*) alone, on one's own; (*por si próprio*) by o.s.; **falar ~** talk to o.s.

spray /is'prej/ (*pl* **~s**) *m* spray

squash /is'kwɛʃ/ *m* squash

stand /is'tãdʒi/ (*pl* **~s**) *m* stand

status /is'tatus/ *m* status

stripper /is'triper/ (*pl* **~s**) *m/f* stripper

strip-tease /istripi'tʃizi/ *m* striptease

sua /'sua/ *a & pron veja* **seu**

su|ado /su'adu/ *a* <*pessoa, roupa*> sweaty; (*fig*) hard-earned; **~ar** *vt/i* sweat; **~ar por/para** (*fig*) work hard for/to; **~ar frio** come out in a cold sweat

sua|ve /su'avi/ *a* <*toque, subida*> gentle; <*gosto, cheiro, dor, inverno*> mild; <*música, voz*> soft; <*vinho*> smooth; <*trabalho*> light; <*prestações*> easy;

~vidade *f* gentleness; mildness; softness; smoothness; *veja* suave;

~vizar *vt* soften; soothe *<dor, pessoa>*

subalterno /subaw'tɛrnu/ *a & m* subordinate

subconsciente /subikõsi'ẽtʃi/ *a & m* subconscious

subdesenvolvido /subidʒizĩvow̃'vidu/ *a* underdeveloped

súbdito /'subditu/ *m* (Port) *veja* súdito

subdividir /subidʒivi'dʒir/ *vt* subdivide

subemprego /subĩ'pregu/ *m* menial job

subempreitar /subĩprej'tar/ *vt* subcontract; ~teiro *m* subcontractor

subentender /subĩtẽ'der/ *vt* infer; ~dido *a* implied □ *m* insinuation

subestimar /subestʃi'mar/ *vt* underestimate

su|bida /su'bida/ *f* (*ação*) ascent; (*ladeira*) incline; (*de preços etc, fig*) rise; ~bir *vi* go up; *<água>* rise □ *vt* go up, climb; ~bir em climb *<árvore>*; get up onto *<mesa>*; get on *<ônibus>*

súbito /'subitu/ *a* sudden; (de) ~ suddenly

subjacente /subiʒa'sẽtʃi/ *a* underlying

subjeti|vidade /subiʒetʃivi'dadʒi/ *f* subjectivity; ~vo *a* subjective

subjugar /subiʒu'gar/ *vt* subjugate

subjuntivo /subiʒũ'tʃivu/ *a & m* subjunctive

sublevar-se /suble'varsi/ *vpr* rise up

sublime /su'blimi/ *a* sublime

subli|nhado /subli'ɲadu/ *m* underlining; ~nhar *vt* underline

sublocar /sublo'kar/ *vt/i* sublet

submarino /subima'rinu/ *a* underwater □ *m* submarine

submer|gir /subimer'ʒir/ *vt* submerge; ~gir-se *vpr* submerge; ~so *a* submerged

submeter /subime'ter/ *vt* subject (a to); put down, subdue *<povo, rebeldes etc>*; submit *<projeto>*; ~se *vpr* (*render-se*) submit; ~se a (*sofrer*) undergo

submis|são /submi'sãw/ *f* submission; ~so *a* submissive

submundo /subi'mũdu/ *m* underworld

subnutrição /subinutri'sãw/ *f* malnutrition

subordi|nado /subordʒi'nadu/ *a & m* subordinate; ~nar *vt* subordinate (a to)

subor|nar /subor'nar/ *vt* bribe; ~no /o/ *m* bribe

subproduto /subipro'dutu/ *m* by-product

subs|crever /subiskre'ver/ *vt* sign *<carta etc>*; subscribe to *<opinião>*; subscribe *<dinheiro>* (para to); ~crever-se *vpr* sign one's name; ~crição *f* subscription; ~crito *pp de* ~crever

subseqüente /subise'kwẽtʃi/ *a* subsequent

subserviente /subiservi'ẽtʃi/ *a* subservient

subsidiar /subisidʒi'ar/ *vt* subsidize

subsidi|ária /subisidʒi'aria/ *f* subsidiary; ~rio *a* subsidiary

subsídio /subi'sidʒiu/ *m* subsidy

subsistência /subisis'tẽsia/ *f* subsistence

subsolo /subi'sɔlu/ *m* (*porão*) basement

substância /subis'tãsia/ *f* substance

substan|cial /subistãsi'aw/ (*pl* ~ciais) *a* substantial; ~tivo *m* noun

substitu|ição /subistʃitui'sãw/ *f* replacement; substitution; ~ir *vt* (*pôr B no lugar de A*) replace

(A por B A with B); (*usar B em vez de A*) substitute (**A por B B** for A); **~to** *a* **a** substitute

subterfúgio /subiter'fuʒiu/ *m* subterfuge

subterrâneo /subite'xaniu/ *a* underground

sub|til /sub'til/ (*pl* **~tis**) *a* (*Port*) *veja* **sutil**

subtra|ção /subitra'sãw/ *f* subtraction; **~ir** *vt* subtract <*números*>; (*roubar*) steal

suburbano /subur'banu/ *a* suburban

subúrbio /su'burbiu/ *m* suburbs

subven|ção /subivẽ'sãw/ *f* grant, subsidy; **~cionar** *vt* subsidize

subver|são /subiver'sãw/ *f* subversion; **~sivo** *a* & *m* subversive

suca /su'kata/ *f* scrap metal; **~tear** *vt* scrap

sucção /suk'sãw/ *f* suction

suce|der /suse'der/ *vi* (*acontecer*) happen □ *vt* **~der a** succeed <*rei etc*>; (*vir depois*) follow; **~der-se** *vpr* follow on from one another; **~dido** *a* **bem ~dido** successful

suces|são /suse'sãw/ *f* succession; **~sivo** *a* successive; **~so** /ɛ/ *m* success; (*música*) hit; **fazer ou ter ~so** be successful; **~sor** *m* successor

sucinto /su'sĩtu/ *a* succinct

suco /'suku/ *m* juice

suculento /suku'lẽtu/ *a* juicy

sucumbir /sukũ'bir/ *vi* succumb (**a** to)

sucur|sal /sukur'saw/ (*pl* **~sais**) *f* branch

Sudão /su'dãw/ *m* Sudan

sudário /su'dariu/ *m* shroud

sudeste /su'dɛstʃi/ *a* & *m* south-east; **o Sudeste Asiático** South-east Asia

súdito /'sudʒitu/ *m* subject

sudoeste /sudo'ɛstʃi/ *a* & *m* south-west

Suécia /su'ɛsia/ *f* Sweden

sueco /su'ɛku/ *a* & *m* Swedish

suéter /su'ɛter/ *m/f* sweater

sufici|ência /sufisi'ẽsia/ *f* sufficiency; **~ente** *a* enough, sufficient; **o ~ente** enough

sufixo /su'fiksu/ *m* suffix

suflê /su'fle/ *m* soufflé

sufo|cante /sufo'kãtʃi/ *a* stifling; **~car** *vt* (*asfixiar*) suffocate; (*fig*) stifle □ *vi* suffocate; **~co** /o/ *m* hassle; **estar num ~co** be having a tough time

sufrágio /su'fraʒiu/ *m* suffrage

sugar /su'gar/ *vt* suck

sugerir /suʒe'rir/ *vt* suggest

suges|tão /suʒes'tãw/ *f* suggestion; **dar uma ~tão** make a suggestion; **~tivo** *a* suggestive

Suíça /su'isa/ *f* Switzerland

suíças /su'isas/ *f pl* sideburns

sui|cida /sui'sida/ *a* suicidal □ *m/f* suicide (victim); **~cidar-se** *vpr* commit suicide; **~cídio** *m* suicide

suíço /su'isu/ *a* & *m* Swiss

suíno /su'inu/ *a* & *m* pig

suíte /su'itʃi/ *f* suite

su|jar /su'ʒar/ *vt* dirty; (*fig*) sully <*reputação etc*> □ *vi*, **~jar-se** *vpr* get dirty; **~jar-se com alg** queer one's pitch with s.o.; **~jeira** *f* dirt; (*uma*) dirty trick

sujei|tar /suʒej'tar/ *vt* subject (**a** to); **~tar-se** *vpr* subject o.s. (**a** to); **~to** *a* subject (**a** to) □ *m* (*de oração*) subject; (*pessoa*) person

su|jidade /suʒi'dadʒi/ *f* (*Port*) dirt; **~jo** *a* dirty

sul /suw/ *a invar* & *m* south; **~africano** *a* & *m* South African; **~-americano** *a* & *m* South American; **~-coreano** *a* & *m* South Korean

sul|car /suw'kar/ *vt* furrow <*testa*>; **~co** *m* furrow

sulfúrico /suw'furiku/ *a* sulphuric

sulista /su'lista/ *a* southern □ *m/f* southerner

sultão /suw'tãw/ *m* sultan

sumário /su'mariu/ *a* <*justiça*> summary; <*roupa*> skimpy, brief

su|miço /su'misu/ *m* disappearance; **dar ~miço em** spirit away; **tomar chá de ~miço** disappear; **~mido** *a* <*cor, voz*> faint; **ele anda ~mido** he's disappeared; **~mir** *vi* disappear

sumo /'sumu/ *m* (*Port*) juice

sumptuoso /sũtu'ozu/ *a* (*Port*) *veja* **suntuoso**

sunga /'sũga/ *f* swimming trunks

suntuoso /sũtu'ozu/ *a* sumptuous

suor /su'or/ *m* sweat

superar /supe'rar/ *vt* overcome <*dificuldade etc*>; surpass <*expectativa, pessoa*>

superá|vel /supe'ravew/ (*pl* ~**veis**) *a* surmountable; **~vit** (*pl* ~**vits**) *m* surplus

superestimar /superestʃi'mar/ *vt* overestimate

superestrutura /superistru'tura/ *f* superstructure

superfici|al /superfisi'aw/ (*pl* ~**ais**) *a* superficial

superfície /super'fisi/ *f* surface; (*medida*) area

supérfluo /su'pεrfluu/ *a* superfluous

superintendência /superĩtẽ'dẽsia/ *f* bureau

superi|or /superi'or/ *a* (*de cima*) upper; <*ensino*> higher; <*número, temperatura etc*> greater (**a** than); (*melhor*) superior (**a** to) □ *m* superior; **~oridade** *f* superiority

superlativo /superla'tʃivu/ *a* & *m/f* superlative

superlota|ção /superlota'sãw/ *f* overcrowding; **~do** *a* overcrowded

supermercado /supermer'kadu/ *m* supermarket

superpotência /superpo'tẽsia/ *f* superpower

superpovoado /superpovo'adu/ *a* overpopulated

supersecreto /superse'krεtu/ *a* top secret

supersensí|vel /supersẽ'sivew/ (*pl* ~**veis**) *a* oversensitive

supersônico /super'soniku/ *a* supersonic

supersti|ção /superstʃi'sãw/ *f* superstition; **~cioso** /o/ *a* superstitious

supervi|são /supervi'zãw/ *f* supervision; **~sionar** *vt* supervise; **~sor** *m* supervisor

supetão /supe'tãw/ *m* **de ~** all of a sudden

suplantar /suplã'tar/ *vt* supplant

suplemen|tar /suplemẽ'tar/ *a* supplementary □ *vt* supplement; **~to** *m* supplement

suplente /su'plẽtʃi/ *a* & *m/f* substitute

supletivo /suple'tʃivu/ *a* supplementary; **ensino ~** adult education

súplica /'suplika/ *f* plea; **tom de ~** pleading tone

suplicar /supli'kar/ *vt* plead for; (*em juízo*) petition for

suplício /su'plisiu/ *m* torture; (*fig: aflição*) torment

supor /su'por/ *vt* suppose

supor|tar /supor'tar/ *vt* (*sustentar*) support; (*tolerar*) stand, bear; **~tável** (*pl* ~**táveis**) *a* bearable; **~te** /ɔ/ *m* support

suposição /supozi'sãw/ *f* supposition

supositório /supozi'toriu/ *m* suppository

supos|tamente /suposta'mẽtʃi/ *adv* supposedly; **~to** /o/ *a* supposed; **~to que** supposing that

supre|macia /suprema'sia/ *f* supremacy; **~mo** /e/ *a* supreme

supressão /supre'sãw/ *f* (*de lei, cargo, privilégio*) abolition; (*de jornal, informação, nomes*) suppression; (*de palavras, cláusula*) deletion

suprimento /supri'mẽtu/ *m* supply

suprimir /supri'mir/ *vt* abolish < *lei, cargo, privilégio* >; suppress < *jornal, informação, nomes* >; delete < *palavras, cláusula* >

suprir /su'prir/ *vt* provide for < *família, necessidades* >; make up for < *falta* >; make up < *quantia* >; supply < *o que falta* >; (*substituir*) take the place of; ~ **alg de** provide s.o. with; ~ **A por B** substitute B for A

supurar /supu'rar/ *vi* turn septic

sur|**dez** /sur'des/ *f* deafness; ~**do** *a* deaf; < *consoante* > voiceless □ *m* deaf person; **os** ~**dos** the deaf; ~**do-mudo** (*pl* ~**dos-mudos**) *a* deaf and dumb □ *m* deaf-mute

sur|**fe** /'surfi/ *m* surfing; ~**fista** *m/f* surfer

sur|**gimento** /surʒi'mẽtu/ *m* appearance; ~**gir** *vi* arise; ~**gir à mente** spring to mind

Suriname /suri'nami/ *m* Surinam

surpreen|**dente** /surpriẽ'dẽtʃi/ *a* surprising; ~**der** *vt* surprise □ *vi* be surprising; ~**der-se** *vpr* be surprised (**de** at)

surpre|**sa** /sur'preza/ *f* surprise; **de** ~**sa** by surprise; ~**so** /e/ *a* surprised

sur|**ra** /'suxa/ *f* thrashing; ~**rado** *a* < *roupa* > worn-out; ~**rar** *vt* thrash < *pessoa* >; wear out < *roupa* >

surrealis|**mo** /suxea'lizmu/ *m* surrealism; ~**ta** *a* & *m/f* surrealist

surtir /sur'tʃir/ *vt* produce; ~ **efeito** be effective

surto /'surtu/ *m* outbreak

suscep- (*Port*) *veja* **suscet**-

susce|**tibilidade** /susetʃibili'dadʒi/ *f* (*de pessoa*) sensitivity; ~**tível** (*pl* ~**tíveis**) *a* < *pessoa* > touchy, sensitive; ~**tível de** open to

suscitar /susi'tar/ *vt* cause; raise < *dúvida, suspeita* >

suspei|**ta** /sus'pejta/ *f* suspicion; ~**tar** *vt/i* ~**tar** (**de**) suspect; ~**to** *a* suspicious; (*duvidoso*) suspect □ *m* suspect; ~**toso** /o/ *a* suspicious

suspen|**der** /suspẽ'der/ *vt* suspend; ~**são** *f* suspension; ~**se** *m* suspense; ~**so** *a* suspended; ~**sórios** *m pl* braces, (*Amer*) suspenders

suspi|**rar** /suspi'rar/ *vi* sigh; ~**rar por** long for; ~**ro** *m* sigh; (*doce*) meringue

sussur|**rar** /susu'xar/ *vt/i* whisper; ~**ro** *m* whisper

sustar /sus'tar/ *vt/i* stop

susten|**táculo** /sustẽ'takulu/ *m* mainstay; ~**tar** *vt* support; (*afirmar*) maintain; ~**to** *m* support; (*ganha-pão*) livelihood

susto /'sustu/ *m* fright

sutiã /sutʃi'ã/ *m* bra

su|**til** /su'tʃiw/ (*pl* ~**tis**) *a* subtle; ~**tileza** *f* subtlety

sutu|**ra** /su'tura/ *f* suture; ~**rar** *vt* suture

T

tá /ta/ *int* (*fam*) OK; *veja* **estar**

taba|**caria** /tabaka'ria/ *f* tobacconist's; ~**co** *m* tobacco

tabefe /ta'bɛfi/ *m* slap

tabe|**la** /ta'bɛla/ *f* table; ~**lar** *vt* tabulate

tablado /ta'bladu/ *m* platform

tabu /ta'bu/ *a* & *m* taboo

tábua /'tabua/ *f* board; ~ **de passar roupa** ironing board

tabuleiro /tabu'leru/ *m* (*de xadrez etc*) board

tabuleta /tabu'lɛta/ *f* (*letreiro*) sign

taça /'tasa/ *f* (*prêmio*) cup; (*de champanhe etc*) glass

tacada /ta'kada/ *f* shot; **de uma ~cada** in one go; **~car** *vt* hit <*bola*>; (*fam*) throw

tacha /'taʃa/ *f* tack

tachar /ta'ʃar/ *vt* brand (**de as**)

tachinha /ta'ʃiɲa/ *f* drawing pin, (*Amer*) thumbtack

tácito /'tasitu/ *a* tacit

taciturno /tasi'turnu/ *a* taciturn

taco /'taku/ *m* (*de golfe*) club; (*de bilhar*) cue; (*de hóquei*) stick

tact- (*Port*) *veja* **tat-**

tagare|la /taga'rɛla/ *a* chatty, talkative □ *m/f* chatterbox; **~lar** *vi* chatter

tailan|dês /tajlã'des/ *a & m* (*f* **~desa**) Thai

Tailândia /taj'lãdʒia/ *f* Thailand

tailleur /ta'jer/ (*pl* **~s**) *m* suit

Taiti /taj'tʃi/ *m* Tahiti

tal /taw/ (*pl* **tais**) *a* such; **que ~?** what do you think?; (*Port*) how are you?; **que ~ uma cerveja?** how about a beer?; **~ como** such as; **~ qual** just like; **um ~ de João** someone called John; **e ~** and so on

tala /'tala/ *f* splint

talão /ta'lãw/ *m* stub; **~ de cheques** chequebook

talco /'tawku/ *m* talc

talen|to /ta'lētu/ *m* talent; **~toso** /o/ *a* talented

talhar /ta'ʎar/ *vt* slice <*dedo, carne*>; carve <*pedra, imagem*>

talharim /taʎa'rĩ/ *m* tagliatelle

talher /ta'ʎer/ *m* set of cutlery; *pl* cutlery

talho /'taʎu/ *m* (*Port*) butcher's

talismã /taliz'mã/ *m* charm, talisman

talo /'talu/ *m* stalk

talvez /taw'ves/ *adv* perhaps; **~ ele venha amanhã** he may come tomorrow

tamanco /ta'mãku/ *m* clog

tamanho /ta'maɲu/ *m* size □ *adj* such

tâmara /'tamara/ *f* date

tamarindo /tama'rĩdu/ *m* tamarind

também /tã'bēj/ *adv* also; **~ não** not ... either, neither

tam|bor /tã'bor/ *m* drum; **~borilar** *vi* <*dedos*> drum; <*chuva*> patter; **~borim** *m* tambourine

Tâmisa /'tamiza/ *m* Thames

tam|pa /'tãpa/ *f* lid; **~pão** *m* (*vaginal*) tampon; **~par** *vt* put the lid on <*recipiente*>; (*tapar*) cover; **~pinha** *f* top □ *m/f* (*fam*) shorthouse

tampouco /tã'poku/ *adv* nor, neither

tanga /'tãga/ *f* G-string; (*avental*) loincloth

tangente /tã'ʒētʃi/ *f* tangent; **pela ~** (*fig*) narrowly

tangerina /tãʒe'rina/ *f* tangerine

tango /'tãgu/ *m* tango

tanque /'tãki/ *m* tank; (*para lavar roupa*) sink

tanto /'tãtu/ *a & pron* so much; *pl* so many □ *adv* so much; **~ ... como** ... both ... and ...; **~ ... (...)** **quanto** as much (...) as; **~ melhor** so much the better; **~ tempo** so long; **vinte e ~s anos** twenty odd years; **nem ~** not as much; **um ~ difícil** somewhat difficult; **~ que** to the extent that

Tanzânia /tã'zania/ *f* Tanzania

tão /tãw/ *adv* so; **~ grande quanto** as big as; **~-somente** *adv* solely

tapa /'tapa/ *m ou f* slap; **dar um ~ em** slap

tapar /ta'par/ *vt* (*cobrir*) cover; block <*luz, vista*>; cork <*garrafa*>

tapeçaria /tapesa'ria/ *f* (*pano*) tapestry; (*loja*) carpet shop

tape|tar /tape'tar/ *vt* carpet; **~te** /e/ *m* carpet

tapioca /tapi'ɔka/ *f* tapioca

tapume /ta'pumi/ *m* fence

taquicardia /takikar'dʒia/ f palpitations

taquigra|far /takigra'far/ vt/i write in shorthand; **~fia** f shorthand

tara /'tara/ f fetish; **~do** a sex-crazed □ m sex maniac; **ser ~do por** be crazy about

tar|dar /tar'dar/ vi (atrasar) be late; (demorar muito) be long □ vt delay; **~dar a responder** take a long time to answer, be a long time answering; **o mais ~dar** at the latest; **sem mais ~dar** without further delay; **~de** adv late □ f afternoon; **hoje à ~de** this afternoon; **~de da noite** late at night; **~dinha** f late afternoon; **~dio** a late

tarefa /ta'refa/ f task, job

tarifa /ta'rifa/ f tariff; **~ de embarque** airport tax

tarimbado /tarĩ'badu/ a experienced

tarja /'tarʒa/ f strip

ta|rô /ta'ro/ m tarot; **~rólogo** m tarot reader

tartamu|dear /tartamudʒi'ar/ vi stammer; **~do** a stammering □ m stammerer

tártaro /'tartaru/ m tartar

tartaruga /tarta'ruga/ f (bicho) turtle; (material) tortoiseshell

tatear /tatʃi'ar/ vt feel □ vi feel one's way

táti|ca /'tatʃika/ f tactics; **~co** a tactical

tá|til /'tatʃiw/ (pl **~teis**) a tactile

tato /'tatu/ m (sentido) touch; (diplomacia) tact

tatu /ta'tu/ m armadillo

tatu|ador /tatua'dor/ m tattooist; **~agem** f tattoo; **~ar** vt tattoo

tauromaquia /tawroma'kia/ f bullfighting

taxa /'taʃa/ f (a pagar) charge; (índice) rate; **~ de câmbio** exchange rate; **~ de juros** interest rate; **~ rodoviária** road tax

taxar /ta'ʃar/ vt tax

taxativo /taʃa'tʃivu/ a firm, categorical

táxi /'taksi/ m taxi

taxiar /taksi'ar/ vi taxi

taxímetro /tak'simetru/ m taxi meter

taxista /tak'sista/ m/f taxi driver

tchã /tʃã/ f (fam) special something

tchau /tʃaw/ int goodbye, bye

tcheco /'tʃɛku/ a & m Czech

Tchecoslováquia /tʃekoslo'vakia/ f Czechoslovakia

te /tʃi/ pron you; (a ti) to you

tear /tʃi'ar/ m loom

tea|tral /tʃia'traw/ (pl **~trais**) a theatrical; <grupo> theatre; **~tro** m theatre; **~trólogo** m playwright

tece|lagem /tese'laʒẽ/ f (trabalho) weaving; (fábrica) textile factory; **~lão** m (f **~lã**) weaver

te|cer /te'ser/ vt/i weave; **~cido** m cloth; (no corpo) tissue

te|cla /'tekla/ f key; **~cladista** m/f (músico) keyboard player; (de computador) keyboard operator; **~clado** m keyboard; **~clar** vt key (in)

técni|ca /'teknika/ f technique; **~co** a technical □ m specialist; (de time) manager; (que mexe com máquinas) technician

tecno|crata /tekno'krata/ m/f technocrat; **~logia** f technology; **~lógico** a technological

teco-teco /teku'teku/ m light aircraft

tecto /'tetu/ m (Port) veja **teto**

tédio /'tedʒiu/ m boredom

tedioso /tedʒi'ozu/ a boring, tedious

Teerã /tee'rã/ f Teheran

teia /'teja/ f web

tei|ma /'tejma/ f persistence; **~mar** vi insist; **~mar em ir**

insist on going; **~mosia** *f* stubbornness; **~moso** /o/ *a* stubborn; <*ruido*> insistent

teixo /'tejʃu/ *m* yew

Tejo /'teʒu/ *m* Tagus

tela /'tɛla/ *f* (*de cinema, TV etc*) screen; (*tecido, pintura*) canvas; **~plana** flat screen

telecoman|dado /telekomã'dadu/ *a* remote-controlled; **~do** *m* remote control

telecomunicação /telekomunika-'sãw/ *f* telecommunication

teleférico /tele'fɛriku/ *m* cable car

telefo|nar /telefo'nar/ *vi* telephone; **~nar para alg** phone s.o.; **~ne** /o/ *m* telephone; (*número*) phone number; **~ne celular** cell phone; **~ne sem fio** cordless phone; **~nema** /e/ *m* phone call; **~nia** *f* telephone technology

telefôni|co /tele'foniku/ *a* telephone; **cabine ~ca** phone box, (*Amer*) phone booth; **mesa ~ca** switchboard

telefonista /telefo'nista/ *m/f* (*da companhia telefônica*) operator; (*dentro de empresa etc*) telephonist

tele|grafar /telegra'far/ *vt/i* telegraph; **~gráfico** *a* telegraphic

telégrafo /te'lɛgrafu/ *m* telegraph

tele|grama /tele'grama/ *m* telegram; **~guiado** *a* remote-controlled

telejor|nal /teleʒor'naw/ (*pl* **~nais**) *m* television news

telemóvel /tele'mɔvew/ *m* mobile phone, (*Amer*) cell phone

tele|novela /teleno'vela/ *f* TV soap opera; **~objetiva** *f* telephoto lens

tele|patia /telepa'tʃia/ *f* telepathy; **~pático** *a* telepathic

telescó|pico /teles'kɔpiku/ *a* telescopic; **~pio** *m* telescope

telespectador /telespekta'dor/ *m* television viewer □ *a* viewing

teletrabalho /teletra'baʎu/ *m* teleworking

televi|são /televi'zãw/ *f* television; **~são a cabo** cable television; **~sionar** *vt* televise; **~sivo** *a* television; **~sor** *m* television set

telex /te'lɛks/ *m invar* telex

telha /'teʎa/ *f* tile; **~do** *m* roof

te|ma /'tema/ *m* theme; **~mático** *a* thematic

temer /te'mer/ *vt* fear □ *vi* be afraid; **~ por** fear for

teme|rário /teme'rariu/ *a* reckless; **~ridade** *f* recklessness; **~roso** /o/ *a* fearful

te|mido /te'midu/ *a* feared; **~mível** (*pl* **~míveis**) *a* fearsome; **~mor** *m* fear

tempão /tẽ'pãw/ *m* **um ~** a long time

temperado /tẽpe'radu/ *a* <*clima*> temperate □ *pp* de **temperar**

temperamen|tal /tẽperamẽ'taw/ (*pl* **~tais**) *a* temperamental; **~to** *m* temperament

temperar /tẽpe'rar/ *vt* season <*comida*>; temper <*aço*>

temperatura /tẽpera'tura/ *f* temperature

tempero /tẽ'peru/ *m* seasoning

tempestade /tẽpes'tadʒi/ *f* storm

templo /'tẽplu/ *m* temple

tempo /'tẽpu/ *m* (*período*) time; (*atmosférico*) weather; (*do verbo*) tense; (*de jogo*) half; **ao mesmo ~** at the same time; **nesse meio ~** in the meantime; **o ~ todo** all the time; **de todos os ~s** of all time; **quanto ~** how long; **muito/pouco ~** a long/short time; **~ integral** full time

tempo|rada /tẽpo'rada/ *f* (*sazão*) season; (*tempo*) while; **~ral** (*pl* **~rais**) *a* temporal □ *m* storm; **~rário** *a* temporary

te|nacidade /tenasi'dadʒi/ *f* tenacity; **~naz** *a* tenacious □ *f* tongs

tenção /tẽ'sãw/ *f* intention

tencionar /tẽsio'nar/ *vt* intend

tenda /'tẽda/ f tent

tendão /tẽ'dãw/ m tendon; **~ de Aquiles** Achilles tendon

tendência /tẽ'dẽsia/ f (moda) trend; (propensão) tendency

tendencioso /tẽdẽsi'ozu/ a tendentious

ten|der /tẽ'der/ vi tend (para towards); **~de a engordar** he tends to get fat; **o tempo ~de a ficar bom** the weather is improving

tenebroso /tene'brozu/ a dark; (fig: terrível) dreadful

tenente /te'nẽtʃi/ m/f lieutenant

tênis /'tenis/ m invar (jogo) tennis; (sapato) trainer; **um ~** (par) a pair of trainers; **~ de mesa** table tennis

tenista /te'nista/ m/f tennis player

tenor /te'nor/ m tenor

tenro /'tẽxu/ a tender

ten|são /tẽ'sãw/ f tension; **~são (arterial)** blood pressure; **~so** a tense

tentação /tẽta'sãw/ f temptation

tentáculo /tẽ'takulu/ m tentacle

ten|tador /tẽta'dor/ a tempting; **~tar** vt try; (seduzir) tempt □ vi try; **~tativa** f attempt; **~tativo** a tentative

tênue /'tenui/ a faint

teo|logia /teolo'ʒia/ f theology; **~lógico** a theological

teólogo /te'ɔlogu/ m theologian

teor /te'or/ m (de gordura etc) content; (de carta, discurso) drift

teo|rema /teo'rema/ m theorem; **~ria** f theory

teórico /te'ɔriku/ a theoretical

teorizar /teori'zar/ vt theorize

tépido /'tɛpidu/ a tepid

ter /ter/ vt have; **tenho vinte anos** I am twenty (years old); **~ medo/sede** be afraid/thirsty; **tenho que** ou **de ir** I have to go; **tem** (há) there is/are; **não tem de quê** don't mention it; **~ a ver com** have to do with

tera|peuta /tera'pewta/ m/f therapist; **~pêutico** a therapeutic; **~pia** f therapy

terça /'tersa/ f Tuesday; **~-feira** (pl **~s-feiras**) f Tuesday; **Ter-ça-Feira Gorda** Shrove Tuesday

tercei|ra /ter'sera/ f (marcha) third; **~ranista** m/f third-year; **~ro** a third □ m third party

terço /'tersu/ m third

ter|col (pl **~cóis**) m stye

tergal /ter'gaw/ m Terylene

tér|mico /'tɛrmiku/ a thermal; **garrafa ~ca** Thermos flask

termi|nal /termi'naw/ (pl **~nais**) a & m terminal; **~nal de vídeo** VDU; **~nante** a definite; **~nar** vt finish □ vi <pessoa, coisa> finish; <coisa> end; **~nar com alg** (cortar relação) break up with s.o.

ter|minologia /terminolo'ʒia/ f terminology; **~mo¹** /'termu/ m term; **pôr ~mo a** put an end to; **meio ~mo** compromise

termo² /'termu/ m (Port) Thermos flask

ter|mômetro /ter'mometru/ m thermometer; **~mostato** m thermostat

terno¹ /'tɛrnu/ m suit

ter|no² /'tɛrnu/ a tender; **~nura** f tenderness

terra /'texa/ f land; (solo, elétrico) earth; (chão) ground; **a Terra** Earth; **por ~** on the ground; **~ natal** homeland

terraço /te'xasu/ m terrace

terra|cota /texa'kɔta/ f terracotta; **~moto** /texa'mɔtu/ m (Port) earthquake; **~plenagem** f earth moving

terreiro /te'xeru/ m meeting place for Afro-Brazilian cults

terremoto /texe'mɔtu/ m earthquake

terreno /te'xenu/ a earthly □ m ground; (geog) terrain; (um) piece of land; ~ **baldio** piece of waste ground

térreo /'tɛxiu/ *a* ground-floor; **(andar)** ~ ground floor, (*Amer*) first floor

terrestre /te'xɛstri/ *a* <*animal, batalha, forças*> land; (*da Terra*) of the Earth, the Earth's; <*alegrias etc*> earthly

terrificante /texifi'kãtʃi/ *a* terrifying

terrina /te'xina/ *f* tureen

territori|al /texitori'aw/ (*pl* ~**ais**) *a* territorial

território /texi'tɔriu/ *m* territory

terri|vel /te'xivew/ (*pl* ~**veis**) *a* terrible

terror /te'xor/ *m* terror; **filme de** ~ horror film

terroris|mo /texo'rizmu/ *m* terrorism; ~**ta** *a & m/f* terrorist

tese /'tɛzi/ *f* theory; (*escrita*) thesis

teso /'tɛzu/ *a* (*apertado*) taut; (*rígido*) stiff

tesoura /te'zora/ *f* scissors; **uma** ~ a pair of scissors

tesou|reiro /tezo'reru/ *m* treasurer; ~**ro** *m* treasure; (*do Estado*) treasury

testa /'tɛsta/ *f* forehead; ~**de-ferro** (*pl* ~**s-de-ferro**) *m* frontman

testamento /testa'mẽtu/ *m* will; (*na Bíblia*) testament

tes|tar /tes'tar/ *vt* test; ~**te** /ɛ/ *m* test

testemu|nha /teste'muɲa/ *f* witness; ~**nha ocular** eye witness; ~**nhar** *vt* bear witness to □ *vi* testify; ~**nho** *m* evidence, testimony

testículo /tes'tʃikulu/ *m* testicle

teta /'teta/ *f* teat

tétano /'tɛtanu/ *m* tetanus

teto /'tɛtu/ *m* ceiling; ~ **solar** sun roof

tétrico /'tɛtriku/ *a* (*triste*) dismal; (*medonho*) horrible

teu /tew/ (*f* **tua**) *a* your □ *pron* yours

têx|til /'testʃiw/ (*pl* ~**teis**) *m* textile

tex|to /'testu/ *m* text; ~**tura** *f* texture

texugo /te'ʃugu/ *m* badger

tez /tes/ *f* complexion

ti /tʃi/ *pron* you

tia /'tʃia/ *f* aunt; ~**-avó** (*pl* ~**s-avós**) *f* great aunt

tiara /tʃi'ara/ *f* tiara

tíbia /'tʃibia/ *f* shinbone

ticar /tʃi'kar/ *vt* tick

tico /'tʃiku/ *m* **um** ~ **de** a little bit of

tiete /tʃi'etʃi/ *m/f* fan

tifo /'tʃifu/ *m* typhoid

tigela /tʃi'ʒɛla/ *f* bowl; **de meia** ~ smalltime

tigre /'tʃigri/ *m* tiger; ~**sa** /e/ *f* tigress

tijolo /tʃi'ʒolu/ *m* brick

til /tʃiw/ (*pl* **tis**) *m* tilde

tilintar /tʃili'tar/ *vi* jingle □ *m* jingling

timão /tʃi'mãw/ *m* tiller

timbre /'tʃibri/ *m* (*insígnia*) crest; (*em papel*) heading; (*de som*) tone; (*de vogal*) quality

time /'tʃimi/ *m* team

timidez /tʃimi'des/ *f* shyness

tímido /'tʃimidu/ *a* shy

tímpano /'tʃĩpanu/ *m* (*tambor*) kettledrum; (*no ouvido*) eardrum

tina /'tʃina/ *f* vat

tingir /tʃi'ʒir/ *vt* dye <*tecido, cabelo*>; (*fig*) tinge

ti|nido /tʃi'nidu/ *m* tinkling; ~**nir** *vi* tinkle; <*ouvidos*> ring; (*tremer*) tremble; **estar** ~**nindo** (*fig*) be in peak condition

tino /'tʃinu/ *m* sense, judgement; **ter** ~ **para** have a flair for

tin|ta /'tʃita/ *f* (*para pintar*) paint; (*para escrever*) ink; (*para tingir*) dye; ~**teiro** *m* inkwell

tintim /tʃĩ'tʃĩ/ *m* **contar** ~ **por** ~ give a blow-by-blow account of

tin|to /'tʃĩtu/ a dyed; < *vinho* > red; **~tura** f dye; (*fig*) tinge; **~turaria** f dry cleaner's

tio /'tʃiu/ m uncle; *pl* (**~** e *tia*) uncle and aunt; **~avô** (*pl* **~s-avôs**) m great uncle

típico /'tʃipiku/ a typical

tipo /'tʃipu/ m type

tipóia /tʃi'pɔja/ f sling

tique /'tʃiki/ m (*sinal*) tick; (*do rosto etc*) twitch

tíquete /'tʃiketʃi/ m ticket

tiquinho /tʃi'kiɲu/ m um **~** de a tiny bit of

tira /'tʃira/ f strip □ m/f (*fam*) copper, (*Amer*) cop

tiracolo /tʃira'kɔlu/ m a < *bolsa* > over one's shoulder; < *pessoa* > in tow

tiragem /tʃi'raʒẽ/ f (*de jornal*) circulation

tira|-gosto /tʃira'gostu/ m snack; **~-manchas** m invar stain remover

ti|rania /tʃira'nia/ f tyranny; **~rânico** a tyrannical; **~rano** m tyrant

tirar /tʃi'rar/ vt (*afastar*) take away; (*de dentro*) take out; take off < *roupa, sapato, tampa* >; take < *foto, cópia, férias* >; clear < *mesa* >; get < *nota, diploma, salário* >; get out < *mancha* >

tiritar /tʃiri'tar/ vi shiver

tiro /'tʃiru/ m shot; **~ ao alvo** shooting; **é ~ e queda** (*fam*) it can't fail; **~teio** m shoot-out

titânio /tʃi'taniu/ m titanium

títere /'tʃiteri/ m puppet

ti|tia /tʃi'tʃia/ f auntie; **~tio** m uncle

titi /tʃi'tʃitʃi/ m (*fam*) talk

titubear /tʃitubi'ar/ vi stagger, totter; (*fig: hesitar*) waver

titular /tʃitu'lar/ m/f title holder; (*de time*) captain □ vt title

título /'tʃitulu/ m title; (*obrigação*) bond; **a ~ de** on the basis of; **a ~ pessoal** on a personal basis

toa /'toa/ f à **~** (*sem rumo*) aimlessly; (*ao acaso*) at random; (*sem motivo*) without reason; (*em vão*) for nothing; (*desocupado*) at a loose end; (*de repente*) out of the blue

toada /to'ada/ f melody

toalete /toa'lɛtʃi/ m toilet

toalha /to'aʎa/ f towel; **~ de mesa** tablecloth

tobogã /tobo'gã/ m (*rampa*) slide; (*trenó*) toboggan

toca /'tɔka/ f burrow

toca|-discos /toka'dʒiskus/ m invar record player; **~-fitas** m invar tape player

tocaia /to'kaja/ f ambush

tocante /to'kãtʃi/ a (*enternecedor*) moving

tocar /to'kar/ vt touch; play < *piano, música, disco etc* >; ring < *campainha* > □ vi touch; < *pianista, música, disco etc* > play; < *campainha, telefone, sino* > ring; **~-se** vpr touch; (*mancar-se*) take the hint; **~ a** (*dizer respeito*) concern; **~ em** touch; touch on < *assunto* >

tocha /'tɔʃa/ f torch

toco /'toku/ m (*de árvore*) stump; (*de cigarro*) butt

toda /'toda/ f **a ~** at full speed

todavia /toda'via/ conj however

todo /'todu/ a all; (*cada*) every; *pl* all; **~ o dinheiro** all the money; **~ dia, ~s os dias** every day; **~s os alunos** all the pupils; **o dia ~** all day; **em ~ lugar** everywhere; **~ mundo, ~s everyone; ~s nós** all of us; **ao ~** in all; **~-poderoso** a almighty

tofe /'tofi/ m toffee

toga /'tɔga/ f gown; (*de romano*) toga

toicinho /toj'siɲu/ m bacon

toldo /'towdu/ m awning

tole|rância /tole'rãsia/ f tolerance; **~rante** a tolerant; **~rar**

rar *vt* tolerate; ∼**rável** (*pl* ∼**ráveis**) *a* tolerable

to|lice /to'lisi/ *f* foolishness; (*uma*) foolish thing; ∼**lo** /o/ *a* foolish □ *m* fool

tom /tõ/ *m* tone

to|mada /to'mada/ *f* (*conquista*) capture; (*elétrica*) plughole; (*de filme*) shot; ∼**mar** *vt* take; (*beber*) drink; ∼**mar café** have breakfast

tomara /to'mara/ *int* I hope so; ∼ que let's hope that; ∼**-que-caia** *a invar* <*vestido*> strapless

tomate /to'matʃi/ *m* tomato

tom|bar /tõ'bar/ *vt* (*derrubar*) knock down; list <*edifício*> □ *vi* fall over; ∼**bo** *m* fall; **levar um** ∼**bo** have a fall

tomilho /to'miʎu/ *m* thyme

tomo /'tomu/ *m* volume

tona /'tona/ *f* **trazer à** ∼ bring up; **vir à** ∼ emerge

tonalidade /tonali'dadʒi/ *f* (*de música*) key; (*de cor*) shade

to|nel /to'nɛw/ (*pl* ∼**néis**) *m* cask; ∼**nelada** *f* tonne

tôni|ca /'tonika/ *a* tonic; (*fig: assunto*) keynote; ∼**co** *a* & *m* tonic

tonificar /tonifi'kar/ *vt* tone up

ton|tear /tõtʃi'ar/ *vt* ∼**tear alg** make s.o.'s head spin; ∼**teira** *f* dizziness; ∼**to** *a* (*zonzo*) dizzy; (*bobo*) stupid; (*atrapalhado*) flustered; ∼**tura** *f* dizziness

to|pada /to'pada/ *f* trip; **dar uma** ∼**pada em** stub one's toe on; ∼**par** *vt* agree to, accept; ∼**par com** bump into <*pessoa*>; come across <*coisa*>

topázio /to'paziu/ *m* topaz

topete /to'petʃi/ *m* quiff

tópico /'tɔpiku/ *a* topical □ *m* topic

topless /topi'lɛs/ *a invar* & *adv* topless

topo /'topu/ *m* top

topografia /topogra'fia/ *f* topography

topônimo /to'poɲimu/ *m* place name

toque /'tɔki/ *m* touch; (*da campainha, do telefone*) ring; (*de instrumento*) playing; **dar um** ∼ **em** (*fam*) have a word with

Tóquio /'tɔkiu/ *f* Tokyo

tora /'tɔra/ *f* log

toranja /to'rãʒa/ *f* grapefruit

tórax /'tɔraks/ *m invar* thorax

tor|ção /tor'sãw/ *f* (*do braço etc*) sprain; ∼**cedor** *m* supporter; ∼**cer** *vt* twist; (*machucar*) sprain; (*espremer*) wring <*roupa*>; (*centrifugar*) spin <*roupa*> □ *vi* (*gritar*) cheer (**por** for); (*desejar sucesso*) keep one's fingers crossed (**por** for; **para que** that); ∼**cer-se** *vpr* twist about; ∼**cicolo** /o/ *m* stiff neck; ∼**cida** *f* (*torção*) twist; (*torcedores*) supporters; (*gritaria*) cheering

tor|menta /tor'mẽta/ *f* storm; ∼**to** *m* torment; ∼**toso** /o/ *a* stormy

tornado /tor'nadu/ *m* tornado

tornar /tor'nar/ *vt* make; ∼**-se** *vpr* become

torne|ado /torni'adu/ *a* **bem** ∼**ado** shapely; ∼**ar** *vt* turn

torneio /tor'neju/ *m* tournament

torneira /tor'nera/ *f* tap, (*Amer*) faucet

torniquete /torni'ketʃi/ *m* (*para ferido*) tourniquet; (*Port: de entrada*) turnstile

torno /'tornu/ *m* lathe; (*de ceramista*) wheel; **em** ∼ **de** around

tornozelo /torno'zelu/ *m* ankle

toró /to'rɔ/ *m* downpour

torpe /'tɔrpi/ *a* dirty

torpe|dear /torpedʒi'ar/ *vt* torpedo; ∼**do** /e/ *m* torpedo

torpor /tor'por/ *m* torpor

torra|da /to'xada/ *f* piece of toast; *pl* toast; ∼**deira** *f* toaster

torrão /to'xãw/ *m* (*de terra*) turf; (*de açúcar*) lump

torrar /to'xar/ vt toast <*pão*>; roast <*café*>; blow <*dinheiro*>; sell off <*mercadorias*>

torre /'toxi/ f tower; (em *xadrez*) rook; ~ **de controle** control tower; ~**ão** m turret

torrefação /toxefa'sãw/ f (*ação*) roasting; (*fábrica*) coffee-roasting plant

torren|cial /toxẽsi'aw/ (*pl* ~**ciais**) a torrential; ~**te** f torrent

torresmo /to'xezmu/ m crackling

tórrido /'toxidu/ a torrid

torrone /to'xoni/ m nougat

torso /'torsu/ m torso

torta /'torta/ f pie, tart

tor|to /'tortu/ a crooked; **a ~ e a direito** left, right and centre; ~**tuoso** a winding

tortu|ra /tor'tura/ f torture; ~**rador** m torturer; ~**rar** vt torture

to|sa /'tɔza/ f (*de cachorro*) clipping; (*de ovelhas*) shearing; ~**são** m fleece; ~**sar** vt clip <*cachorro*>; shear <*ovelhas*>; crop <*cabelo*>

tosco /'tosku/ a rough, coarse

tosquiar /toski'ar/ vt shear <*ovelha*>

tos|se /'tɔsi/ f cough; ~**se de cachorro** whooping cough; ~**sir** vi cough

tostão /tos'tãw/ m penny

tostar /tos'tar/ vt brown <*carne*>; tan <*pele, pessoa*>; ~**se** vpr (*ao sol*) go brown

to|tal /to'taw/ (*pl* ~**tais**) a & m total

totali|dade /totali'dadʒi/ f entirety; ~**tário** a totalitarian; ~**zar** vt total

touca /'toka/ f bonnet; (*de freira*) wimple; ~ **de banho** bathing cap; ~**dor** m dressing table

toupeira /to'pera/ f mole

tou|rada /to'rada/ f bullfight; ~**reiro** m bullfighter; ~**ro** m bull; **Touro** (*signo*) Taurus

tóxico /'tɔksiku/ a toxic □ m toxic substance

toxicômano /toksi'komanu/ m drug addict

toxina /tok'sina/ f toxin

traba|lhador /trabaʎa'dor/ a <*pessoa*> hard-working; <*classe*> working □ m worker; ~**lhar** vt work □ vi work; (*numa peça, filme*) act; ~**lheira** f big job; ~**lhista** a labour; ~**lho** m work; (*um*) job; (*na escola*) assignment; **dar-se o ~lho** to go to the trouble of; ~**lho de parto** labour; ~**lhos forçados** hard labour; ~**lhoso** a laborious

traça /'trasa/ f moth

tração /tra'sãw/ f traction

tra|çar /tra'sar/ vt draw; draw up <*plano*>; set out <*ordens*>; ~**ço** m stroke; (*entre frases*) dash; (*vestígio*) trace; (*características*) trait; *pl* (*do rosto*) features

tractor /tra'tor/ m (*Port*) *veja* **trator**

tradi|ção /tradʒi'sãw/ f tradition; ~**cional** (*pl* ~**cionais**) a traditional

tradu|ção /tradu'sãw/ f translation; ~**tor** m translator; ~**zir** vt/i translate (**de** from; **para** into)

trafe|gar /trafe'gar/ vi run; ~**gável** (*pl* ~**gáveis**) a open to traffic

tráfego /'trafegu/ m traffic

trafi|cância /trafi'kãsia/ f trafficking; ~**cante** m/f trafficker; ~**car** vt/i traffic (**com** in)

tráfico /'trafiku/ m traffic

tra|gada /tra'gada/ f (*de bebida*) swallow; (*de cigarro*) drag; ~**gar** vt swallow; inhale <*fumaça*>

tragédia /tra'ʒedʒia/ f tragedy

trágico /'traʒiku/ a tragic

trago /'tragu/ m (*de bebida*) swallow; (*de cigarro*) drag; **de um** ~ in one go trai|ção /traj'sãw/ f (ato) betrayal; (deslealdade) treachery; (da pátria) treason; ~coeiro a treacherous; ~dor a treacherous □ m traitor

trailer /'trejler/ (pl ~s) m (de filme etc) trailer; (casa móvel) caravan, (Amer) trailer

traineira /traj'nera/ f trawler

training /'trejni/ (pl ~s) m track suit

trair /tra'ir/ vt betray; be unfaithful to <marido, mulher>; ~-se vpr give o.s. away

tra|jar /tra'ʒar/ vt wear; ~jar-se vpr dress (de in); ~je m outfit; ~je a rigor evening dress; ~je espacial space suit

traje|to /tra'ʒetu/ m (percurso) journey; (caminho) route; ~tória f trajectory; (fig) course

tralha /'traʎa/ f (trastes) junk

tra|ma /'trama/ f plot; ~mar vt/i plot

trambi|que /trã'biki/ (fam) m con; ~queiro (fam) m con artist

tramitar /trami'tar/ vi be processed

trâmites /'tramitʃis/ m pl channels

tramóia /tra'mɔja/ f scheme

trampolim /trãpo'lĩ/ m (de ginástica) trampoline; (de piscina, fig) springboard

tranca /'trãka/ f bolt; (em carro) lock

trança /'trãsa/ f (de cabelo) plait

tran|cafiar /trãkafi'ar/ vt lock up; ~car vt lock; cancel <matricula>

trançar /trã'sar/ vt plait <cabelo>; weave <palha etc>

tranco /'trãku/ m jolt; aos ~s e barrancos in fits and starts

tranqueira /trã'kera/ f junk

tranqüi|lidade /trãkwili'dadʒi/ f tranquillity; ~lizador a reassuring; ~lizante m tranquil-

lizer □ a reassuring; ~lizar vt reassure; ~lizar-se vpr be reassured; ~lo a <bairro, sono> peaceful; <pessoa, voz, mar> calm; <consciência> clear; <sucesso, lucro> sure-fire □ adv with no trouble

transa /'trãza/ f (fam) (negócio) deal; (caso) affair; ~ção f transaction; ~do a (fam) <roupa, pessoa, casa> stylish; <relação> healthy

Transamazônica /transama'zonika/ f trans-Amazonian highway

transar /trã'zar/ (fam) vt set up; do <drogas> □ vi (negociar) deal; (fazer sexo) have sex

transatlântico /trãzat'lãtʃiku/ a transatlantic □ m liner

transbordar /trãzbor'dar/ vi overflow

transcen|dental /trãsẽdẽ'taw/ (pl ~dentais) a transcendental; ~der vt/i ~der (a) transcend

trans|crever /trãskre'ver/ vt transcribe; ~crição f transcription; ~crito a transcribed □ m transcript

transe /'trãzi/ m trance

transeunte /trãzi'ũtʃi/ m/f passer-by

transfe|rência /trãsfe'rẽsia/ f transfer; ~ridor m protractor; ~rir vt transfer; ~rir-se vpr transfer

transfor|mação /trãsforma'sãw/ f transformation; ~mador m transformer; ~mar vt transform; ~mar-se vpr be transformed

trânsfuga /'trãsfuga/ m/f deserter; (de um país) defector

transfusão /trãsfu'zãw/ f transfusion

trans|gredir /trãzgre'dʒir/ vt infringe; ~gressão f infringement

transi|ção /trãzi'sãw/ f transition; ~cional (pl ~cionais) a transitional

transi|gente /trãzi'ʒẽtʃi/ a open to compromise; **∼gir** vi compromise

transis|tor /trãzis'tor/ m transistor; **∼torizado** a transistorized

transi|tar /trãzi'tar/ vi pass; **∼tável** (pl **∼táveis**) a passable; **∼tivo** a transitive

trânsito /'trãzitu/ m traffic; **em ∼** in transit

transitório /trãzi'tɔriu/ a transitory

translúcido /trãz'lusidu/ a translucent

transmis|são /trãzmi'sãw/ f transmission; **∼sor** m transmitter

transmitir /trãzmi'tʃir/ vt transmit <programa, calor, doença>; convey <notícia, ordens>; transfer <herança, direito>; **∼-se** vpr <doença> be transmitted

transpa|recer /trãspare'ser/ vi be visible; (fig) <emoção, verdade> come out; **∼rência** f transparency; **∼rente** a transparent

transpi|ração /trãspira'sãw/ f perspiration; **∼rar** vt exude □ vi (suar) perspire; <notícia> trickle through; <verdade> come out

transplan|tar /trãsplã'tar/ vt transplant; **∼te** m transplant

transpor /trãs'por/ vt cross <rio, fronteira>; get over <obstáculo, dificuldade>; transpose <letras, música>

transpor|tadora /trãsporta'dora/ f transport company; **∼tar** vt transport; (em contas) carry forward; **∼te** m transport; **∼te coletivo** public transport

transposto /trãs'postu/ pp de transpor

transtor|nar /trãstor'nar/ vt mess up <papéis, casa>; disrupt <rotina, ambiente>; disturb, upset <pessoa>; **∼nar-se** vpr <pessoa> be rattled; **∼no** /o/ m (de

casa, rotina) disruption; (de pessoa) disturbance; (contratempo) upset

transver|sal /trãzver'saw/ (pl **∼sais**) a **(rua) ∼sal** cross street; **∼so** /ɛ/ a transverse

transvi|ado /trãzvi'adu/ a wayward; **∼ar** vt lead astray

trapa|ça /tra'pasa/ f swindle; **∼cear** vi cheat; **∼ceiro** a crooked □ m cheat

trapa|lhada /trapa'ʎada/ f bungle; **∼lhão** a (f **∼lhona**) bungling □ m (f **∼lhona**) bungler

trapézio /tra'pɛziu/ m trapeze

trapezista /trape'zista/ m/f trapeze artist

trapo /'trapu/ m rag

traquéia /tra'keja/ f windpipe, trachea

traquejo /tra'keʒu/ m knack

traquinas /tra'kinas/ a invar mischievous

trás /tras/ adv de **∼** from behind; **a roda de ∼** the back wheel; **de ∼ para frente** back to front; **para ∼** backwards; **deixar para ∼** leave behind; **por ∼ de** behind

traseiro /tra'zeru/ a rear, back □ m bottom

trasladar /trazla'dar/ vt transport

traspas|sado /traspa'sadu/ a <paletó> double-breasted; **∼sar** vt pierce

traste /'trastʃi/ m (pessoa) pain; (coisa) piece of junk

tra|tado /tra'tadu/ m (pacto) treaty; (estudo) treatise; **∼tamento** m treatment; (título) title; **∼tar** vt treat; negotiate <preço, venda> □ vi (manter relações) have dealings (com with); (combinar) negotiate (com with); **∼tar de** deal with; **∼tar alg de** ou **por** address s.o. as; **∼tar de voltar** (tentar) seek to return; (resolver) decide to return; **∼tar-se de** be a matter of; **∼tável**

(*pl* ~**táveis**) *a* <*doença*> treatable; <*pessoa*> accommodating; ~**tos** *m pl* **maus** ~**tos** illtreatment

trator /tra'tor/ *m* tractor

trauma /'trawma/ *m* trauma; ~**tizante** *a* traumatic; ~**tizar** *vt* traumatize

tra|vão /tra'vãw/ *m* (*Port*) brake; ~**var** *vt* lock <*rodas, músculos*>; stop <*carro*>; block <*passagem*>; strike up <*amizade, conversa*>; wage <*luta, combate*> □ *vi* (*Port*) brake

trave /'travi/ *f* beam, joist; (*do gol*) crossbar

traves|sa /tra'vesa/ *f* (*trave*) crossbar; (*rua*) side street; (*prato*) dish; (*pente*) slide; ~**são** *m* dash; ~**seiro** *m* pillow; ~**sia** *f* crossing; ~**so** /e/ *a* <*criança*> naughty; ~**sura** *f* prank; *pl* mischief

travesti /traves'tʃi/ *m* transvestite; (*artista*) drag artist; ~**do** *a* in drag

trazer /tra'zer/ *vt* bring; bear <*nome, ferida*>; wear <*barba, chapéu, cabelo curto*>

trecho /'treʃu/ *m* (*de livro etc*) passage; (*de rua etc*) stretch

treco /'trεku/ *m* (*fam*) (*coisa*) thing; (*ataque*) turn

trégua /'trεgwa/ *f* truce; (*fig*) respite

trei|nador /trejna'dor/ *m* trainer; ~**namento** *m* training; ~**nar** *vt* train <*atleta, animal*>; practise <*língua etc*> □ *vi* <*atleta*> train; <*pianista, principiante*> practise; ~**no** *m* training; (*um*) training session

trejeito /tre'ʒejtu/ *m* grimace

trela /'trεla/ *f* lead, (*Amer*) leash

treliça /tre'lisa/ *f* trellis

trem /trẽj/ *m* train; ~**de aterrissagem** undercarriage; ~**de carga** goods train, (*Amer*) freight train

trema /'trema/ *m* dieresis

treme|deira /treme'dera/ *f* shiver; ~**licar** *vi* tremble; ~**luzir** *vi* glimmer, flicker

tremendo /tre'mẽdu/ *a* tremendous

tre|mer /tre'mer/ *vi* tremble; <*terra*> shake; ~**mor** *m* tremor; (*tremedeira*) shiver; ~**mular** *vi* <*bandeira*> flutter; <*luz, estrela*> glimmer, flicker

trêmulo /'tremulu/ *a* trembling; <*luz*> flickering

trena /'trena/ *f* tape measure

trenó /tre'nɔ/ *m* sledge, (*Amer*) sled; (*puxado a cavalos etc*) sleigh

tre|padeira /trepa'dera/ *f* climbing plant; ~**par** *vt* climb □ *vi* climb; (*chulo*) fuck

três /tres/ *a* & *m* three

tresloucado /trezlo'kadu/ *a* deranged

trevas /'trεvas/ *f pl* darkness

trevo /'trevu/ *m* (*planta*) clover; (*rodoviário*) interchange

treze /'trezi/ *a* & *m* thirteen

trezentos /tre'zẽtus/ *a* & *m* three hundred

triagem /tri'aʒẽ/ *f* (*escolha*) selection; (*separação*) sorting; **fazer uma** ~ **de** sort

tri|angular /triãgu'lar/ *a* triangular; ~**ângulo** *m* triangle

tri|bal /tri'baw/ *a* (*pl* ~**bais**) *a* tribal; ~**bo** *f* tribe

tribuna /tri'buna/ *f* rostrum; ~**nal** (*pl* ~**nais**) *m* court

tribu|tação /tributa'sãw/ *f* taxation; ~**tar** *vt* tax; ~**tário** *a* □ *m* tributary; ~**to** *m* tribute

tri|cô /tri'ko/ *m* knitting; **artigos de** ~**cô** knitwear; ~**cotar** *vt/i* knit

tridimensio|nal /tridʒimẽsio'naw/ (*pl* ~**nais**) *a* three-dimensional

trigêmeo /tri'ʒemiu/ *m* triplet

trigésimo /tri'ʒεzimu/ *a* thirtieth

tri|go /'trigu/ *m* wheat; **~gueiro** *a* dark

trilha /'triʎa/ *f* path; (*pista, de disco*) track; **~ sonora** soundtrack

trilhão /tri'ʎãw/ *m* billion, (*Amer*) trillion

trilho /'triʎu/ *m* track

trilogia /trilo'ʒia/ *f* trilogy

trimes|tral /trimes'traw/ (*pl* **~trais**) *a* quarterly; **~tre** /ɛ/ *m* quarter; (*do ano letivo*) term

trincar /trĩ'kar/ *vt/i* crack

trincheira /trĩ'ʃera/ *f* trench

trinco /'trĩku/ *m* latch

trindade /trĩ'dadʒi/ *f* trinity

trinta /'trĩta/ *a & m* thirty

trio /'triu/ *m* trio; **~ elétrico** music float

tripa /'tripa/ *f* gut

tripé /tri'pɛ/ *m* tripod

tripli|car /tripli'kar/ *vt/i*, **~car-se** *vpr* treble; **~cata** *f* triplicate

triplo /'triplu/ *a & m* treble

tripu|lação /tripula'sãw/ *f* crew; **~lante** *m/f* crew member; **~lar** *vt* man

triste /'tristʃi/ *a* sad; **~za** /e/ *f* sadness; **é uma ~za** (*fam*) it's pathetic

tritu|rador /tritura'dor/ *m* (*de papel*) shredder; **~rador de lixo** waste disposal unit; **~rar** *vt* shred <*legumes, papel*>; grind up <*lixo*>

triun|fal /triũ'faw/ (*pl* **~fais**) *a* triumphal; **~fante** *a* triumphant; **~far** *vi* triumph; **~fo** *m* triumph

trivi|al /trivi'aw/ (*pl* **~ais**) *a* trivial; **~alidade** *f* triviality; *pl* trivia

triz /tris/ *m* **por um ~** narrowly, by a hair's breadth; **não foi atropelado por um ~** he narrowly missed being knocked down

tro|ca /'trɔka/ *f* exchange; **em ~ca de** in exchange for; **~cadilho** *m* pun; **~cado** *m*

change; **~cador** *m* conductor; **~car** *vt* (*dar e receber*) exchange (*por* for); change <*dinheiro, lençóis, lâmpada, lugares etc*>; (*transpor*) change round; (*confundir*) mix up; **~car-se** *vpr* change; **~car de roupa/trem/lugar** change clothes/trains/places; **~ca-troca** *m* swap; **~co** /o/ *m* change; **a ~co de quê?** what for?; **dar o ~co em alg** pay s.o. back

troço /'trɔsu/ (*fam*) *m* (*coisa*) thing; (*ataque*) turn; **me deu um ~** I had a funny turn

troféu /tro'fɛw/ *m* trophy

trólebus /'trɔlebus/ *m invar* trolley bus

trom|ba /'trõba/ *f* (*de elefante*) trunk; (*cara amarrada*) long face; **~bada** *f* crash; **~ba-d'água** (*pl* **~bas-d'água**) *f* downpour; **~badinha** *m* bag snatcher; **~bar** *vi* **~bar com** crash into <*poste, carro*>; bump into <*pessoa*>

trombo|ne /trõ'boni/ *m* trombone; **~nista** *m/f* trombonist

trompa /'trõpa/ *f* French horn; **~ de Falópio** fallopian tube

trompe|te /trõ'petʃi/ *m* trumpet; **~tista** *m/f* trumpeter

tron|co /'trõku/ *m* trunk; **~cudo** *a* stocky

trono /'tronu/ *m* throne

tropa /'trɔpa/ *f* troop; (*exército*) army; *pl* troops; **~ de choque** riot police

trope|ção /trope'sãw/ *m* trip; (*erro*) slip-up; **~çar** *vi* trip; (*errar*) slip up; **~ço** /e/ *m* stumbling block

trôpego /'tropegu/ *a* unsteady

tropi|cal /tropi'kaw/ (*pl* **~cais**) *a* tropical

trópico /'trɔpiku/ *m* tropic

tro|tar /tro'tar/ *vi* trot; **~te** /ɔ/ *m* (*de cavalo*) trot; (*de estudantes*) practical joke; (*mentira*) hoax

trouxa /'troʃa/ f (de roupa etc) bundle □ m/f (fam) sucker □ a (fam) gullible

tro|vão /tro'vãw/ m clap of thunder; pl thunder; ∼**vejar** vi thunder; ∼**voada** f thunderstorm; ∼**voar** vi thunder

trucidar /trusi'dar/ vt slaughter

trucu|lência /truku'lēsia/ f barbarity; ∼**lento** a (cruel) barbaric; (brigão) belligerent

trufa /'trufa/ f truffle

trunfo /'trũfu/ m trump; (fig) trump card

truque /'truki/ m trick

truta /'truta/ f trout

tu /tu/ pron you

tua /'tua/ veja teu

tuba /'tuba/ f tuba

tubarão /tuba'rãw/ m shark

tubá|rio /tu'bariu/ a **gravidez ∼ria** ectopic pregnancy

tuberculose /tuberku'lɔzi/ f tuberculosis

tubo /'tubu/ m tube; (no corpo) duct

tubulação /tubula'sãw/ f ducting

tucano /tu'kanu/ m toucan

tudo /'tudu/ pron everything; ∼ **bem?** (cumprimento) how are things?; ∼ **de bom** all the best; **em ∼ quanto é lugar** all over the place

tufão /tu'fãw/ m typhoon

tulipa /tu'lipa/ f tulip

tumba /'tũba/ f tomb

tumor /tu'mor/ m tumour; ∼ **cerebral** brain tumour

túmulo /'tumulu/ m grave

tumul|to /tu'muwtu/ m commotion; (motim) riot; ∼**tuado** a disorderly, rowdy; ∼**tuar** vt disrupt □ vi cause a commotion; ∼**tuoso** a tumultuous

tú|nel /'tunew/ (pl ∼**neis**) m tunnel

túnica /'tunika/ f tunic

Tunísia /tu'nizia/ f Tunisia

tupiniquim /tupini'kĩ/ a Brazilian

turbante /tur'bãtʃi/ m turban

turbilhão /turbi'ʎãw/ m whirlwind

turbina /tur'bina/ f turbine

turbu|lência /turbu'lēsia/ f turbulence; ∼**lento** a turbulent

turco /'turku/ a & m Turkish

turfa /'turfa/ f peat

turfe /'turfe/ m horse-racing

turis|mo /tu'rizmu/ m tourism; **fazer ∼mo** go sightseeing; ∼**ta** m/f tourist

turístico /tu'ristʃiku/ a <ponto, indústria> tourist; <viagem> sightseeing

turma /'turma/ f group; (na escola) class

turnê /tur'ne/ f tour

turno /'turnu/ m (de trabalho) shift; (de competição, eleição) round

turquesa /tur'keza/ m/f & a invar turquoise

Turquia /tur'kia/ f Turkey

turra /'tuxa/ f **às ∼s com** at loggerheads with

tur|var /tur'var/ vt cloud; ∼**vo** a cloudy

tutano /tu'tanu/ m marrow

tutela /tu'tela/ f guardianship

tutor /tu'tor/ m guardian

tutu /tu'tu/ m (vestido) tutu; (prato) beans with bacon and manioc flour

TV /te've/ f TV

U

ubíquo /u'bikwu/ a ubiquitous

Ucrânia /u'krania/ f Ukraine

ucraniano /ukrani'anu/ a & m Ukrainian

ué /u'ɛ/ int hang on

ufa /'ufa/ int phew

ufanis|mo /ufa'nizmu/ m chauvinism; ∼**ta** a & m/f chauvinist

Uganda /u'gãda/ m Uganda

ui /ui/ *int* (*de dor*) ouch; (*de nojo*) ugh; (*de espanto*) oh

uísque /u'iski/ *m* whisky

ui|var /ui'var/ *vi* howl; **~vo** *m* howl

úlcera /'uwsera/ *f* ulcer

ulterior /uwteri'or/ *a* further

ulti|mamente /uwtʃima'mẽtʃi/ *adv* recently; **~mar** *vt* finalize; **~mato** *m* ultimatum

último /'uwtʃimu/ *a* last; <*moda, notícia etc*> latest; **em ~ caso** as a last resort; **nos ~s anos** in recent years; **por ~** last

ultra|jante /uwtra'ʒãtʃi/ *a* offensive; **~jar** *vt* offend; **~je** *m* outrage

ultraleve /uwtra'lɛvi/ *m* microlite

ultra|mar /uwtra'mar/ *m* overseas; **~marino** *a* overseas

ultrapas|sado /uwtrapa'sadu/ *a* outdated; (*Amer*) passing; **~sagem** *f* overtaking, (*Amer*) passing; **~sar** *vt* (*de carro*) overtake, (*Amer*) pass; (*ser superior a*) surpass; (*exceder*) exceed; (*extrapolar*) go beyond □ *vt* overtake, (*Amer*) pass

ultra-sonografia /uwtrasonogra-'fia/ *f* ultrasound scan

ultravioleta /uwtravio'leta/ *a* ultraviolet

ulu|lante /ulu'lãtʃi/ *a* (*fig*) blatant; **~lar** *vi* wail

um /ũ/ (*f* **uma**; *m pl* **uns**, *f pl* **umas**) *art* a, an; *pl* some □ *a* & *pron* one; **~ ao outro** one another; **vieram umas 20 pessoas** about 20 people came

umbanda /ũ'bãda/ *m* Afro-Brazilian cult

umbigo /ũ'bigu/ *m* navel

umbili|cal /ũbili'kaw/ (*pl* **~cais**) *a* umbilical

umedecer /umede'ser/ *vt* moisten; **~-se** *vpr* moisten

umidade /umi'dadʒi/ *f* moisture; (*desagradável*) damp; (*do ar*) humidity

úmido /'umidu/ *a* moist; <*parede,*

roupa etc> damp; <*ar, clima*> humid

unânime /u'nanimi/ *a* unanimous

unanimidade /unanimi'dadʒi/ *f* unanimity

undécimo /ũ'dɛsimu/ *a* eleventh

ungüento /ũ'gwẽtu/ *m* ointment

unha /'uɲa/ *f* nail; (*de animal, utensílio*) claw

união /uni'ãw/ *f* union; (*concórdia*) unity; (*ato de unir*) joining; **União Européia** European Union, EU

unicamente /unika'mẽtʃi/ *adv* only

único /'uniku/ *a* only; (*ímpar*) unique

uni|dade /uni'dadʒi/ *f* unit; **~do** *a* united; <*família*> close

unifi|cação /unifika'sãw/ *f* unification; **~car** *vt* unify

unifor|me /uni'formi/ *a* uniform; <*superfície*> even □ *m* uniform; **~midade** *f* uniformity; **~mizado** *a* <*policial etc*> uniformed; (*padronizado*) standardized; **~zar** *vt* (*padronizar*) standardize

unilate|ral /unilate'raw/ (*pl* **~rais**) *a* unilateral

unir /u'nir/ *vt* unite <*povo, nações, família etc*>; (*ligar, casar*) join; (*combinar*) combine (**a ou com** with); **~-se** *vpr* (*aliar-se*) unite (**a** with); (*juntar-se*) join together; (*combinar-se*) combine (**a ou com** with)

unissex /uni'sɛks/ *a invar* unisex

uníssono /u'nisonu/ *m* **em ~** in unison

univer|sal /univer'saw/ (*pl* **~sais**) *a* universal

universi|dade /universi'dadʒi/ *f* university; **~tário** *a* university □ *m* university student

universo /uni'vɛrsu/ *m* universe

untar /ũ'tar/ *vt* grease <*fôrma*>; spread <*pão*>; smear <*corpo*>

upa /'upa/ *int* (*incentivação*) up-sadaisy; (*ao cair algo etc*) whoops

urânio /u'raniu/ *m* uranium

Urano /u'ranu/ *m* Uranus

urbanismo /urba'nizmu/ *m* town planning; ~ta *m/f* town planner

urbanizado /urbani'zadu/ *a* built-up; ~zar *vt* urbanize

urbano /ur'banu/ *a* (*da cidade*) urban; (*refinado*) urbane

urdir /ur'dʒir/ *vt* weave; (*maquinar*) hatch

urdu /ur'du/ *m* Urdu

urgência /ur'ʒẽsia/ *f* urgency; ~gente *a* urgent; ~gir *vi* be urgent; <*tempo*> press; ~ge irmos we must go urgently

urina /u'rina/ *f* urine; ~nar *vt* pass □ *vi* urinate; ~nol (*pl* ~nóis*) *m* (*penico*) chamber pot; (*em banheiro*) urinal

urna /'urna/ *f* (*para cinzas*) urn; (*para votos*) ballot box; *pl* (*fig*) polls

urrar /u'xar/ *vt/i* roar; ~ro *m* roar

urso /'ursu/ *m* bear; ~-branco (*pl* ~s-brancos*) *m* polar bear

urticária /urtʃi'karia/ *f* nettle rash; ~ga *f* nettle

urubu /uru'bu/ *m* black vulture

Uruguai /uru'gwaj/ *m* Uruguay

uruguaio /uru'gwaju/ *a & m* Uruguayan

urze /'urzi/ *f* heather

usado /u'zadu/ *a* used; <*roupa*> worn; <*palavra*> common

usar /u'zar/ *vt* wear <*roupa, óculos, barba etc*>; ~ (de) (*utilizar*) use

usina /u'zina/ *f* plant; ~ termonuclear nuclear power station

uso /'uzu/ *m* use; (*de palavras, linguagem*) usage; (*praxe*) practice

usual /uzu'aw/ (*pl* ~ais*) *a* common; ~ário *m* user; ~fruir *vt* enjoy <*coisas boas*>; have the use of <*prédio, jardim etc*>; ~fruto *m* use

usurário /uzu'rariu/ *a* moneygrubbing □ *m* money-lender

usurpar /uzur'par/ *vt* usurp

utensílio /utẽ'siliu/ *m* utensil; ~te *m/f* (*Port*) user

útero /'uteru/ *m* uterus, womb

UTI /ute'i/ *f* intensive care unit

útil /'utʃiw/ (*pl* úteis*) *a* useful; dia ~ workday

utilidade /utʃili'dadʒi/ *f* usefulness; (*uma*) utility; ~tário *a* utilitarian; ~zar *vt* (*empregar*) use; (*tornar útil*) utilize; ~zável (*pl* ~záveis*) *a* usable

utopia /uto'pia/ *f* Utopia

utópico /u'tɔpiku/ *a* Utopian

uva /'uva/ *f* grape

úvula /'uvula/ *f* uvula

V

vaca /'vaka/ *f* cow

vacilante /vasi'lãtʃi/ *a* wavering; <*luz*> flickering; ~lar *vi* waver; <*luz*> flicker; (*fam: bobear*) slip up

vacina /va'sina/ *f* vaccine; ~nação *f* vaccination; ~nar *vt* vaccinate

vácuo /'vakuu/ *m* vacuum

vadiar /vadʒi'ar/ *vi* (*viver ocioso*) laze around; (*fazer cera*) mess about; ~dio *a* idle □ *m* idler

vaga /'vaga/ *f* (*posto*) vacancy; (*para estacionar*) parking place

vagabundear /vagabũdʒi'ar/ *vi* (*perambular*) roam; (*vadiar*) laze around; ~do *a* <*pessoa, vida*> idle; <*produto, objeto*> shoddy □ *m* tramp; (*pessoa vadia*) bum

vaga-lume /vaga'lumi/ *m* glowworm

vagão /va'gãw/ *m* (*de passageiros*) carriage; (*Amer*) car; (*de carga*) wagon; ~gão-leito (*pl* ~gões-leitos*) *m* sleeping car; ~gão-restaurante (*pl* ~gões-restaurantes*) *m* dining car

vagar[1] /va'gar/ *vi* <*pessoa*> wander about; <*barco*> drift

vagar[2] /va'gar/ *vi* <*cargo, apartamento*> become vacant

vagaroso /vaga'rozu/ *a* slow

vagem /'vaʒẽ/ *f* green bean

vagi|na /va'ʒina/ *f* vagina; ~**nal** (*pl* ~**nais**) *a* vaginal

vago[1] /'vagu/ *a* (*indefinido*) vague

vago[2] /'vagu/ *a* (*desocupado*) vacant; <*tempo*> spare

vaguear /vagi'ar/ *vi* roam

vai|a /'vaja/ *f* boo; ~**ar** *vi* boo

vai|dade /vaj'dadʒi/ *f* vanity; ~**doso** *a* vain

vaivém /vaj'vẽj/ *m* comings and goings, toing and froing

vala /'vala/ *f* ditch; ~ **comum** mass grave

vale[1] /'vali/ *m* (*de rio etc*) valley

vale[2] /'vali/ *m* (*ficha*) voucher; ~ **postal** postal order

valen|tão /valẽ'tãw/ *a* (*f* ~**tona**) tough □ *m* tough guy; ~**te** *a* brave; ~**tia** *f* bravery; (*uma*) feat

valer /va'ler/ *vt* be worth □ *vi* be valid; ~ **aco a alg** earn s.o. sth; ~**-se de** avail o.s. of; ~ **a pena** be worth it; **vale a pena tentar** it's worth trying; **mais vale desistir** it's better to give up; **vale tudo** anything goes; **fazer** ~ enforce <*lei*>; stand up for <*direitos*>; **para** ~ (*a sério*) for real; (*muito*) really

vale|-refeição /valirefej'sãw/ (*pl* ~**s-refeição**) *m* luncheon voucher

valeta /va'leta/ *f* gutter

valete /va'letʃi/ *m* jack

valia /va'lia/ *f* value

validar /vali'dar/ *vt* validate

válido /'validu/ *a* valid

valioso /vali'ozu/ *a* valuable

valise /va'lizi/ *f* travelling bag

valor /va'lor/ *m* value; (*valentia*) valour; *pl* (*títulos*) securities; **no** ~ **de** to the value of; **sem** ~

worthless; **objetos de** ~ valuables; ~ **nominal** face value

valori|zação /valoriza'sãw/ *f* (*apreciação*) valuing; (*aumento no valor*) increase in value; ~**zado** *a* highly valued; ~**zar** *vt* (*apreciar*) value; (*aumentar o valor de*) increase the value of; ~**zar-se** *vt* <*coisa*> increase in value; <*pessoa*> value o.s.

val|sa /'vawsa/ *f* waltz; ~**sar** *vi* waltz

válvula /'vawvula/ *f* valve

vampiro /vã'piru/ *m* vampire

vandalismo /vãda'lizmu/ *m* vandalism

vândalo /'vãdalu/ *m* vandal

vangloriar-se /vãglori'arsi/ *vpr* brag (**de** about)

vanguarda /vã'gwarda/ *f* vanguard; (*de arte*) avant-garde

vanta|gem /vã'taʒẽ/ *f* advantage; **contar** ~**gem** boast; **levar** ~**gem** have the advantage (**over**); **tirar** ~**gem de** take advantage of; ~**joso** /o/ *a* advantageous

vão /vãw/ (*pl* ~**s**) *a* (*f* **vã**) vain □ *m* gap; **em** ~ in vain

vapor /va'por/ *m* (*fumaça*) steam; (*gás*) vapour; (*barco*) steamer; **máquina a** ~ steam engine; **a todo** ~ at full blast

vaporizar /vapori'zar/ *vt* vaporize; (*com spray*) spray

vaqueiro /va'keru/ *m* cowboy

vaquinha /va'kina/ *f* collection, whip-round

vara /'vara/ *f* rod; ~ **cívil** civil district; ~ **mágica** *ou* **de condão** magic wand

va|ral /va'raw/ (*pl* ~**rais**) *m* washing line

varanda /va'rãda/ *f* veranda

varão /va'rãw/ *m* male

varar /va'rar/ *vt* (*furar*) pierce; (*passar por*) sweep through

varejão /vare'ʒãw/ *m* wholesale store

varejeira /vare'ʒera/ f bluebottle

vare|jista /vare'ʒista/ a retail
□ m/f retailer; **~jo** /e/ m
retail trade; **vender a ~jo** sell
retail

vari|ação /varia'sãw/ f variation;
~ado a varied; **~ante** a & f
variant; **~ar** vt/i vary; **para
~ar** for a change; **~ável** (pl
~áveis) a variable; <tempo>
changeable

varicela /vari'sɛla/ f chickenpox

variedade /varie'dadʒi/ f variety

vários /'varius/ a pl several

varíola /va'riola/ f smallpox

variz /va'ris/ f varicose vein

varo|nil /varo'niw/ (pl **~nis**) a
manly

var|rer /va'xer/ vt sweep; (fig)
sweep away; **~rido a um doido
~rido** a raving lunatic

Varsóvia /var'sovia/ f Warsaw

vasculhar /vasku'ʎar/ vt search
through

vasectomia /vazekto'mia/ f vas-
ectomy

vaselina /vaze'lina/ f vaseline

vasilha /va'ziʎa/ f jug

vaso /'vazu/ m pot; (para flores)
vase; **~ sanguíneo** blood vessel

vassoura /va'sora/ f broom

vas|tidão /vastʃi'dãw/ f vastness;
~to a vast

vatapá /vata'pa/ m spicy North-
Eastern dish

Vaticano /vatʃi'kanu/ m Vatican

vati|cinar /vatʃisi'nar/ vt proph-
esy; **~cínio** m prophecy

va|zamento /vaza'mẽtu/ m leak;
~zante f ebb tide; **~zão** m
outflow; **dar ~zão a** (fig) give
vent to; **~zar** vt/i leak

vazio /va'ziu/ a empty □ m empti-
ness; (um) void

veado /vi'adu/ m deer

ve|dação /veda'sãw/ f (de casa, ja-
nela) insulation; (em motor etc)
gasket; **~dar** vt seal <recipiente,
abertura>; stanch <sangue>;

seal off <saída, área>; **~dar
aco (a alg)** prohibit sth (for s.o.)

vedete /ve'dɛte/ f star

vee|mência /vee'mẽsia/ f vehe-
mence; **~mente** a vehement

vege|tação /veʒeta'sãw/ f vege-
tation; **~tal** (pl **~tais**) a & m
vegetable; **~tar** vi vegetate;
~tariano a & m vegetarian

veia /'veja/ f vein

veicular /veiku'lar/ vt convey;
place <anúncios>

veículo /ve'ikulu/ m vehicle; (de
comunicação etc) medium

vela¹ /'vɛla/ f (de barco) sail;
(esporte) sailing

vela² /'vɛla/ f candle; (em motor)
spark plug; **segurar a ~** (fam)
play gooseberry

velar¹ /ve'lar/ vt (cobrir) veil

velar² /ve'lar/ vt watch over □ vi
keep vigil

veleidade /velej'dadʒi/ f whim

ve|leiro /ve'leru/ m sailing boat;
~lejar vi sail

velhaco /ve'ʎaku/ a crooked □ m
crook

ve|lharia /veʎa'ria/ f old thing;
~lhice f old age; **~lho** /ɛ/ a
old □ m old man; **~lhote** /ɔ/ m
old man

velocidade /velosi'dadʒi/ f speed;
(Port: marcha) gear; **a toda ~** at
full speed; **~ máxima** speed
limit

velocímetro /velo'simetru/ m
speedometer

velocista /velo'sista/ m/f sprinter

velório /ve'loriu/ m wake

veloz /ve'los/ a fast

veludo /ve'ludu/ m velvet; **~ cotelê** corduroy

ven|cedor /vẽse'dor/ a winning □
m winner; **~cer** vt win over
<adversário etc>; win <partida,
corrida, batalha> □ vi (triunfar)
win; <prestação, aluguel, dívida>
fall due; <contrato, passaporte,
prazo> expire; <apólice> ma-

ture; ~**cido** *a* dar-se por ~**cido** give in; ~**cimento** *m* (*de dívida, aluguel*) due date; (*de contrato, prazo*) expiry date; (*de alimento, remédio etc*) best before date; (*salário*) payment; *pl* earnings

venda[1] /'vẽda/ *f* sale; (*loja*) general store; **à** ~ on sale; **pôr à** ~ put up for sale

ven|**da**[2] /'vẽda/ *f* blindfold; ~**dar** *vt* blindfold

venda|**val** /vẽda'vaw/ (*pl* ~**vais**) *m* gale, storm

ven|**dável** /vẽ'davew/ (*pl* ~**dáveis**) *a* saleable; ~**dedor** *m* (*de loja*) shop assistant; (*em geral*) seller; ~**der** *vt/i* sell; **estar** ~**dendo saúde** be bursting with health

vendeta /vẽ'deta/ *f* vendetta

veneno /ve'nenu/ *m* poison; (*de cobra etc, malignidade*) venom; ~**so** /o/ *a* poisonous; (*maldoso*) venomous

vene|**ração** /venera'sãw/ *f* reverence; (*de Deus etc*) worship; ~**rar** *vt* revere; worship < *Deus etc*>

vené|**reo** /ve'nɛriu/ *a* **doença** ~**rea** venereal disease

Veneza /ve'neza/ *f* Venice

veneziana /venezi'ana/ *f* blind

Venezuela /venezu'ɛla/ *f* Venezuela

venezuelano /venezue'lanu/ *a* & *m* Venezuelan

venta /'vẽta/ *f* nostril

ven|**tania** /vẽta'nia/ *f* gale; ~**tar** *vi* be windy; ~**tarola** /ɔ/ *f* fan

venti|**lação** /vẽtʃila'sãw/ *f* ventilation; ~**lador** *m* fan; ~**lar** *vt* ventilate; air < *sala, roupa*>

ven|**to** /'vẽtu/ *m* wind; **de** ~**to em popa** smoothly; ~**toinha** *f* (*cata-vento*) weather vane; (*Port: ventilador*) fan; ~**tosa** /ɔ/ *f* sucker; ~**toso** /o/ *a* windy

ven|**tre** /'vẽtri/ *m* belly; ~**tríloquo** *m* ventriloquist

Vênus /'venus/ *f* Venus

ver /ver/ *vt* see; watch < *televisão*>; (*resolver*) see to □ *vi* see □ *m* **a meu** ~ in my view; ~**se** *vpr* (*no espelho etc*) see o.s.; (*em estado, condição*) find o.s.; (*um ao outro*) see each other; **ter a** ~ **com** have to do with; **vai** ~ **que ela não sabe** (*fam*) I bet she doesn't know; **vê se você não volta tarde** be sure you don't get back late; **viu?** (*fam*) right?

veracidade /verasi'dadʒi/ *f* truthfulness

vera|**near** /verani'ar/ *vi* spend the summer; ~**neio** *m* summer holiday, (*Amer*) summer vacation; ~**nista** *m/f* holidaymaker, (*Amer*) vacationer

verão /ve'rãw/ *m* summer

veraz /ve'ras/ *a* truthful

verbas /'vɛrbas/ *f pl* funds

ver|**bal** /ver'baw/ (*pl* ~**bais**) *a* verbal; ~**bete** /e/ *m* entry; ~**bo** *m* verb; ~**borragia** *f* waffle; ~**boso** /o/ *a* verbose

verda|**de** /ver'dadʒi/ *f* truth; **de** ~**de** < *coisa*> real; < *fazer*> really; **na** ~**de** actually; **para falar a** ~**de** to tell the truth; ~**deiro** *a* < *declaração, pessoa*> truthful; (*real*) true

verde /'verdʒi/ *a* & *m* green; **jogar** ~ **para colher maduro** fish for information; ~**abacate** *a invar* avocado; ~**amarelo** *a* yellow and green; (*brasileiro*) Brazilian; (*nacionalista*) nationalistic; ~**esmeralda** *a invar* emerald green; ~**jar** *vi* turn green

verdu|**ra** /ver'dura/ *f* (*para comer*) greens; (*da natureza*) greenery; ~**reiro** *m* greengrocer, (*Amer*) produce dealer

vereador /veria'dor/ *m* councillor

vereda /ve'reda/ *f* path

veredito /vere'dʒitu/ *m* verdict

vergar /ver'gar/ *vt/i* bend

vergo|nha /ver'goɲa/ *f* (*pudor*) shame; (*constrangimento*) embarrassment; (*timidez*) shyness; (*uma*) disgrace; **ter ~nha** be ashamed; be embarrassed; be shy; **cria** *ou* **tome ~nha na cara!** you should be ashamed of yourself!; **~nhoso** *a* shameful

verídico /ve'ridʒiku/ *a* true

verificar /verifi'kar/ *vt* check, verify <*fatos, dados etc*>; ~ **que** ascertain that; ~ **se** check that; ~se *vpr* <*previsão etc*> come true; <*acidente etc*> happen

verme /'vɛrmi/ *m* worm

verme|lhidão /vermeʎi'dãw/ *f* redness; ~**lho** /e/ *a* & *m* red; **no ~lho** (*endividado*) in the red

vernáculo /ver'nakulu/ *a* & *m* vernacular

verniz /ver'nis/ *f* varnish; (*couro*) patent leather

veros|símil /vero'simiw/ (*pl* ~**símeis**) *a* plausible; ~**similhança** *f* plausibility

verruga /ve'xuga/ *f* wart

ver|sado /ver'sadu/ *a* well-versed (**em** in); ~**são** *f* version; ~**sar vi** ~**sar sobre** concern; ~**sátil** (*pl* ~**sáteis**) *a* versatile; ~**satilidade** *f* versatility; ~**sículo** *m* (*da Bíblia*) verse; ~**so**[1] /ɛ/ *m* verse

verso[2] /ɛ/ *m* (*de página*) reverse, other side; **vide ~** see over

vértebra /'vɛrtebra/ *f* vertebra

verte|brado /verte'bradu/ *a* & *m* vertebrate; ~**bral** (*pl* ~**brais**) *a* spinal

ver|tente /ver'tẽtʃi/ *f* slope; ~**ter** *vt* (*derramar*) pour; shed <*lágrimas, sangue*>; (*traduzir*) render (**para** into)

verti|cal /vertʃi'kaw/ (*pl* ~**cais**) *a* & *f* vertical; ~**gem** *f* dizziness; ~**ginoso** /o/ *a* dizzy

vesgo /'vezgu/ *a* cross-eyed

vesícula /ve'zikula/ *f* gall bladder

vespa /'vespa/ *f* wasp

véspera /'vɛspera/ *f* **a ~** the day before; **a ~ de** the eve of; **a ~ de Natal** Christmas Eve; **nas ~s** de on the eve of

vespertino /vesper'tʃinu/ *a* evening

ves|te /'vestʃi/ *f* robe; ~**tiário** *m* (*para se trocar*) changing room; (*para guardar roupa*) cloakroom

vestibular /vestʃibu'lar/ *m* university entrance exam

vestíbulo /ves'tʃibulu/ *m* hall(-way); (*do teatro*) foyer

vestido /ves'tʃidu/ *m* dress □ *a* dressed (**de** in)

vestígio /ves'tʃiʒiu/ *m* trace

ves|timenta /vestʃi'mẽta/ *f* (*de sacerdote*) vestments; ~**tir** *vt* (*pôr* put on; (*usar*) wear; (*pôr roupa em*) dress; (*dar roupa a*) clothe; ~**tir-se** *vpr* dress; ~**tir-se de** **branco** *ou* **de padre** dress in white/as a priest; ~**tuário** *m* clothing

vetar /ve'tar/ *vt* veto

veterano /vete'ranu/ *a* & *m* veterano

veterinário /veteri'nariu/ *a* veterinary □ *m* vet

veto /'vɛtu/ *m* veto

véu /vew/ *m* veil

vexa|me /ve'ʃami/ *m* disgrace; **dar um ~me** make a fool of o.s.; ~**minoso** /o/ *a* disgraceful

vexar /ve'ʃar/ *vt* shame; ~**se** *vpr* be ashamed (**de** of)

vez /ves/ *f* (*ocasião*) time; (*turno*) turn; **às ~es** sometimes; **cada ~ mais** more and more; **de ~** for good; **desta ~** this time; **de ~ em quando** now and again, from time to time; **de uma ~** (*ao mesmo tempo*) at once; (*de um golpe*) in one go; **de uma ~ por todas** once and for all; **duas ~es** twice; **em ~ de** instead of; **fazer as ~es de** take the place of; **mais uma ~** again; **muitas ~es** (*com* *muita freqüência*) often; (*repetidamente*) many times; **raras ~es** seldom; **repetidas ~es** repeatedly; **uma ~** once; **uma ~ que** since

via /'via/ *f* (*estrada*) road; (*rumo, meio*) way; (*exemplar*) copy; *pl* (*trâmites*) channels □ *prep* via; **em ~s de** on the point of; **por ~ aérea/marítima** by air/sea; **por ~ das dúvidas** just in case; **por ~ de regra** as a rule; **Via Láctea** Milky Way

viabili|dade /viabili'dadʒi/ *f* feasibility; **~zar** *vt* make feasible

viação /via'sãw/ *f* (*transporte*) road transport; (*estradas*) road network; (*companhia*) bus company

viaduto /via'dutu/ *m* viaduct; (*rodoviário*) flyover, (*Amer*) overpass

via|gem /vi'aʒẽ/ *f* (*uma*) trip, journey; (*em geral*) travelling; *pl* (*de uma pessoa*) travels; (*em geral*) travel; **boa ~gem!** have a good trip!; **~jado** *a* well-travelled; **~jante** *a* travelling □ *m/f* traveller; **~jar** *vi* travel; **estar ~jando** (*fam*) (*com o pensamento longe*) be miles away

viário /vi'ariu/ *a* road; **anel ~** ring road

viatura /via'tura/ *f* vehicle

viá|vel /vi'avew/ *a* (*pl* **~veis**) *a* feasible

víbora /'vibora/ *f* viper

vi|bração /vibra'sãw/ *f* vibration; (*fig*) thrill; **~brante** *a* vibrant; **~brar** *vt* shake □ *vi* vibrate; (*fig*) be thrilled (**com** by)

vice /'visi/ *m/f* deputy

vice-cam|peão /visikãpi'ãw/ *m* (*f* **~peã**) runner-up

vicejar /vise'ʒar/ *vi* flourish

vice-presiden|te /visiprezi'dẽtʃi/ *m* (*f* **~ta**) vice-president

vice-rei /visi'xej/ *m* viceroy

vice-versa /visi'vɛrsa/ *adv* vice-versa

vici|ado /visi'adu/ *a* addicted (**em** to) □ *m* addict; **um ~ado em drogas** a drug addict; **~ar** *vt* (*falsificar*) tamper with; (*estragar*) ruin □ *vi* <*droga*> be addictive; **~ar-se** *vpr* get addicted (**em** to)

vício /'visiu/ *m* vice

vicioso /visi'ozu/ *a* **círculo ~** vicious circle

vicissitudes /visisi'tudʒis/ *f pl* ups and downs

viço /'visu/ *m* (*de plantas*) exuberance; (*de pessoa, pele*) freshness; **~so** /o/ *a* <*planta*> lush; <*pele, pessoa*> fresh

vida /'vida/ *f* life; **sem ~** lifeless; **dar ~ a** a liven up

videira /vi'dera/ *f* vine

vidente /vi'dẽtʃi/ *m/f* clairvoyant

vídeo /'vidʒiu/ *m* video; (*tela*) screen

vídeo|cassete /vidʒiuka'sɛtʃi/ *m* (*fita*) video tape; (*aparelho*) video, (*Amer*) VCR; **~clipe** *m* video; **~clube** *m* video club; **~game** *m* videogame; **~teipe** *m* video tape

vidra|ça /vi'drasa/ *f* window pane; **~çaria** *f* (*fábrica*) glassworks; (*vidraças*) glazing; **~ceiro** *m* glazier

vi|drado /vi'dradu/ *a* glazed; **estar ~drado em** ou *que* (*fam*) love; **~drar** *vt* glaze □ *vi* (*fam*) fall in love (**em** ou *por* with); **~dro** *m* (*material*) glass; (*pote*) jar; (*janela*) window; **~dro fumê** tinted glass

viela /vi'ɛla/ *f* alley

Viena /vi'ena/ *f* Vienna

Vietnã /vietʃi'nã/ *m*, (*Port*) **Vietname** /viet'nam/ *m* Vietnam

vietnamita /vietna'mita/ *a* & *m/f* Vietnamese

viga /'viga/ *f* joist

vigarice /viga'risi/ *f* swindle

vigário /vi'gariu/ *m* vicar

vigarista /viga'rista/ *m/f* swindler, con artist

vi|gência /vi'ʒẽsia/ *f* (*qualidade*) force; (*tempo*) period in force; **~gente** *a* in force

vigésimo /vi'ʒezimu/ *a* twentieth

vigi|a /vi'ʒia/ *f* (*guarda*) watch; (*em navio*) porthole □ *m* night watchman; **~ar** *vt* (*observar*) watch; (*cuidar de*) watch over; (*como sentinela*) guard □ *vi* keep watch

vigi|lância /viʒi'lãsia/ *f* vigilance; **~lante** *a* vigilant

vigília /vi'ʒilia/ *f* vigil

vigor /vi'gor/ *m* vigour; **em ~** in force

vigo|rar /vigo'rar/ *vi* be in force; **~roso** *a* vigorous

vil /viw/ (*pl* **vis**) *a* base, despicable

vila /'vila/ *f* (*cidadezinha*) small town; (*casa elegante*) villa; (*conjunto de casas*) housing estate; **~ olímpica** Olympic village

vi|lania /vila'nia/ *f* villainy; **~lão** *m* (*f* **~lã**) villain

vilarejo /vila'reʒu/ *m* village

vilipendiar /vilipẽdʒi'ar/ *vt* disparage

vime /'vimi/ *m* wicker

vina|gre /vi'nagri/ *m* vinegar; **~grete** /ɛ/ *m* vinaigrette

vin|car /vĩ'kar/ *vt* crease; line <*rosto*>; **~co** *m* crease; (*no rosto*) line

vincular /vĩku'lar/ *vt* bond, tie

vínculo /'vĩkulu/ *m* link, bond; **~ empregatício** contract of employment

vinda /'vĩda/ *f* coming; **dar as boas ~s** a welcome

vindicar /vĩdʒi'kar/ *vt* vindicate

vindima /vĩ'dʒima/ *f* vintage

vin|do /'vĩdu/ *pp* e *pres* de **vir**; **~douro** *a* coming

vin|gança /vĩ'gãsa/ *f* vengeance, revenge; **~gar** *vt* revenge □ *vi*

<*flores*> thrive; <*criança*> survive; <*plano, empreendimento*> be successful; **~gar-se** *vpr* take one's revenge (**de** for; **em** on); **~gativo** *a* vindictive

vinha /'viɲa/ *f* vineyard

vinhedo /vi'ɲedu/ *m* vineyard

vinheta /vi'ɲeta/ *f* (*na TV etc*) sequence

vinho /'viɲu/ *m* wine □ *a invar* maroon; **~ do Porto** port

vinícola /vi'nikola/ *a* wine-growing

vinicul|tor /vinikuw'tor/ *m* wine grower; **~tura** *f* wine growing

vinil /vi'niw/ *m* vinyl

vinte /'vĩtʃi/ *a* & *m* twenty; **~na** /e/ *f* score

viola /vi'ɔla/ *f* viola

violação /viola'sãw/ *f* violation

violão /vio'lãw/ *m* guitar

violar /vio'lar/ *vt* violate

vio|lência /vio'lẽsia/ *f* violence; (*uma*) act of violence; **~lentar** *vt* rape <*mulher*>; **~lento** *a* violent

violeta /vio'leta/ *f* violet □ *a invar* violet

violi|nista /violi'nista/ *m/f* violinist; **~no** *m* violin

violonce|lista /violõse'lista/ *m/f* cellist; **~lo** /ɛ/ *m* cello

vir /vir/ *vi* come; **o ano que vem** next year; **venho lendo os jornais** I have been reading the papers; **vem cá** come here; (*fam*) listen; **isso não vem ao caso** that's irrelevant; **~ a ser** turn out to be; **~ com** give <*argumento etc*>

virabrequim /virabre'kĩ/ *m* crankshaft

viração /vira'sãw/ *f* breeze

vira-casaca /viraka'zaka/ *m/f* turncoat

vira|da /vi'rada/ *f* turn; **~do** *a* <*roupa*> inside out; (*de cabeça para baixo*) upside down; **~do para** facing

vira-lata /vira'lata/ *m* mongrel

virar /vi'rar/ *vt* turn; turn over <*disco, barco etc*>; turn inside out <*roupa*>; turn out <*bolsos*>; tip <*balde, água etc*> □ *vi* turn; <*barco*> turn over; (*tornar-se*) become; ∼**-se** *vpr* turn round; (*na vida*) get by, cope; ∼**-se para** turn to; **vira e mexe** every so often

viravolta /vira'vowta/ *f* about-turn

virgem /'virʒẽ/ *a* <*fita*> blank; <*floresta, noiva etc*> virgin □ *f* virgin; **Virgem** (*signo*) Virgo

virgindade /virʒĩ'dadʒi/ *f* virginity

vírgula /'virgula/ *f* comma; (*decimal*) point

vi|ril /vi'riw/ (*pl* ∼**ris**) *a* virile

virilha /vi'riʎa/ *f* groin

virilidade /virili'dadʒi/ *f* virility

virtu|al /virtu'aw/ (*pl* ∼**ais**) *a* virtual

virtude /vir'tudʒi/ *f* virtue

virtuo|sismo /virtuo'zizmu/ *m* virtuosity; ∼**so** /o/ *a* virtuous □ *m* virtuoso

virulento /viru'lẽtu/ *a* virulent

vírus /'virus/ *m invar* virus

visão /vi'zãw/ *f* vision; (*aspecto, ponto de vista*) view

visar /vi'zar/ *vt* aim at <*caça, alvo*>; ∼ **(a)** aim for <*objetivo*> <*medida, ação*> be aimed at

vísceras /'viseras/ *f pl* innards

viscon|de /vis'kõdʒi/ *m* viscount; ∼**dessa** /e/ *f* viscountess

viscoso /vis'kozu/ *a* viscous

viseira /vi'zera/ *f* visor

visibilidade /vizibili'dadʒi/ *f* visibility

visionário /vizio'nariu/ *a & m* visionary

visi|ta /vi'zita/ *f* visit; (*visitante*) visitor; **fazer uma** ∼**ta a** alg pay s.o. a visit; ∼**tante** *a* visiting □ *m/f* visitor; ∼**tar** *vt* visit

visi|vel /vi'zivew/ (*pl* ∼**veis**) *a* visible

vislum|brar /vizlũ'brar/ *vt* (*entrever*) glimpse; (*imaginar*) envisage; ∼**bre** *m* glimpse

visom /vi'zõ/ *m* mink

visor /vi'zor/ *m* viewfinder

vis|ta /'vista/ *f* sight; (*dos olhos*) eyesight; (*panorama*) view; à ∼**ta** (*visível*) in view; (*em dinheiro*) in cash; à **primeira** ∼**ta** at first sight; **pôr à** ∼**ta** put on show; **de** ∼**ta** <*conhecer*> by sight; **em** ∼**ta de** in view of; **ter em** ∼**ta** have in view; **dar na** ∼**ta** attract attention; **fazer** ∼**ta** look nice; **fazer** ∼**ta grossa** turn a blind eye (**a** to); **perder de** ∼**ta** lose sight of (**a perder de** ∼**ta** as far as the eye can see); **uma** ∼**ta de olhos** a quick look; ∼**to a** seen □ *m* visa; **pelo** ∼**to** by the looks of things; ∼**to que** seeing that

visto|ria /visto'ria/ *f* inspection; ∼**riar** *vt* inspect

vistoso /vis'tozu/ *a* eye-catching

visu|al /vizu'aw/ (*pl* ∼**ais**) *a* visual □ *m* look; ∼**alizar** *vt* visualize

vi|tal /vi'taw/ (*pl* ∼**tais**) *a* vital; ∼**talício** *a* for life; ∼**talidade** *f* vitality

vita|mina /vita'mina/ *f* vitamin; (*bebida*) liquidized fruit drink; ∼**minado** *a* with added vitamins; ∼**mínico** *a* vitamin

vitela /vi'tela/ *f* (*carne*) veal

viticultura /vitʃikuw'tura/ *f* viticulture

vítima /'vitʃima/ *f* victim

viti|mar /vitʃi'mar/ *vt* (*matar*) claim the life of; **ser** ∼**mado por** fall victim to

vitória /vi'tɔria/ *f* victory

vitorioso /vitori'ozu/ *a* victorious

vi|tral /vi'traw/ (*pl* ∼**trais**) *m* stained glass window

vitrine /vi'trini/ *f* shop window

vitrola /vi'trɔla/ *f* jukebox

viú|va /vi'uva/ *f* widow; **~vo** *a* widowed □ *m* widower

viva /'viva/ *f* cheer □ *int* hurray; **~ a rainha** long live the queen

vivacidade /vivasi'dadʒi/ *f* vivacity

vivalma /vi'vawma/ *f* **não há ~ lá fora** there's not a soul outside

vivar /vi'var/ *vt/i* cheer

vivaz /vi'vas/ *a* lively, vivacious; <*planta*> hardy

viveiro /vi'veru/ *m* (*de plantas*) nursery; (*de peixes*) fishpond; (*de aves*) aviary; (*fig*) breeding ground

vivência /vi'vẽsia/ *f* experience

vívido /'vividu/ *a* vivid

viver /vi'ver/ *vt/i* live (**de** on) □ *m* life; **ele vive reclamando** he's always complaining

víveres /'viveris/ *m pl* provisions

vivissecção /vivisek'sãw/ *f* vivisection

vivo /'vivu/ *a* (*que vive*) living; (*animado*) lively; <*cor*> bright □ *m* **os ~s** the living; **ao ~** live; **estar ~** be alive; **dinheiro ~** cash

vizi|nhança /vizi'ɲãsa/ *f* neighbourhood; **~nho** *a* neighbouring □ *m* neighbour

vo|ador /voa'dor/ *a* flying; **~ar** *vi* fly; (*explodir*) blow up; **sair ~ando** rush off

vocabulário /vokabu'lariu/ *m* vocabulary

vocábulo /vo'kabulu/ *m* word

voca|ção /voka'sãw/ *f* vocation; **~cional** (*pl* **~cionais**) *a* vocational; **orientação ~cional** careers guidance

vo|cal /vo'kaw/ (*pl* **~cais**) *a* vocal

você /vo'se/ *pron* you; **~s** *pron* you

vociferar /vosife'rar/ *vi* shout abuse

vodca /'vodʒka/ *f* vodka

voga /'vɔga/ *f* (*moda*) vogue

vo|gal /vo'gaw/ (*pl* **~gais**) *f* vowel

volante /vo'lãtʃi/ *m* (*de carro*) steering wheel

volá|til /vo'latʃiw/ (*pl* **~teis**) *a* volatile

vôlei /'volej/ *m*, **voleibol** /volej'bow/ *m* volleyball

volt /'vɔwtʃi/ (*pl* **~s**) *m* volt

volta /'vɔwta/ *f* (*retorno*) return; (*da pista*) lap; (*resposta*) response; **às ~s com** tied up with; **de ~** back; **em ~ de** around; **na ~** on the way back; **na ~ do correio** by return of post; **por ~ de** around; **dar a ~ ao mundo** go round the world; **dar a ~ por cima** make a comeback; **dar meia ~** turn round; **dar uma ~** (*a pé*) go for a walk; (*de carro*) go for a drive; **dar uma ~ em** turn round; **dar ~s** spin round; **ter ~** get a response; **e meia** every so often; **~do a ~do** para geared towards

voltagem /vow'taʒẽ/ *f* voltage

voltar /vow'tar/ *vi* go/come back, return □ *vt* rewind <*fita*>; **~ se** *vpr* turn round; **~se para/contra** turn to/against; **~ a si** come to; **~ a fazer** do again; **~ atrás** backtrack

volu|me /vo'lumi/ *m* volume; **~moso** *a* sizeable; <*som*> loud

voluntário /volũ'tariu/ *a & m* volunteer

volúpia /vo'lupia/ *f* sensuality, lust

voluptuoso /voluptu'ozu/ *a* sensual; <*mulher*> voluptuous

volú|vel /vo'luvew/ (*pl* **~veis**) *a* fickle

vomitar /vomi'tar/ *vt/i* vomit

vômito /'vomitu/ *m* vomit; *pl* vomiting

vontade /võ'tadʒi/ *f* will; **à ~ (bem)** at ease; (*quanto quiser*) as much as one likes; **fique à ~** make yourself at home; **tem comida à ~** there's plenty of food;

estar com ~ de feel like; **isso
me dá ~ de chorar** it makes
me feel like crying; **fazer a ~
de alg** do what s.o. wants

vôo /'vou/ *m* flight; **levantar ~**
take off; **~ livre** hang-gliding

voraz /vo'ras/ *a* voracious

vos /vus/ *pron* you; *(a vocês)* to you

vós /vɔs/ *pron* you

vosso /'vɔsu/ *a* your □ *pron* yours

vo|tação /vota'sãw/ *f* vote;
~tante *m/f* voter; **~tar** *vt* devote
on *<lei etc>*; *(dedicar)* devote
(prometer) vow □ *vi* vote **(em for)**

voto /'vɔtu/ *m* (*em votação*) vote;
(promessa) vow; *pl (desejos)*
wishes

vo|vó /vo'vɔ/ *f* grandma; **~vô** *m*
grandpa

voz /vɔs/ *f* voice; **dar ~ de prisão
a alg** place s.o. under arrest

vozerio /voze'riu/ *m* shouting

vul|cânico /vuw'kaniku/ *a* vol-
canic; **~cão** *m* volcano

vul|gar /vuw'gar/ *a* ordinary;
(baixo) vulgar; **~garizar** *vt* pop-
ularize; *(tornar baixo)* vulgarize;
~go *adv* commonly known as

vulne|rabilidade /vuwnerabili-
'dadʒi/ *f* vulnerability; **~rável**
(pl **~ráveis)** *a* vulnerable

vul|to /'vuwtu/ *m (figura)* figure;
(tamanho) bulk; *(importância)*
importance; **de ~to** important;
~toso /o/ *a* bulky

W

walkie-talkie /uɔki'tɔki/ *(pl* **~s)**
m walkie-talkie

walkman /uɔk'mɛn/ *m invar*
walkman

WAP /uap/ *a (telec)* WAP

watt /u'ɔtʃi/ *(pl* **~s)** *m* watt

web /uɛb/ *m* web, WWW

windsur|fe /uĩ'surfi/ *m* wind-
surfing; **~fista** *m/f* windsurfer

X

xadrez /ʃa'dres/ *m (jogo)* chess;
(desenho) check; *(fam: prisão)*
prison □ *a invar* check

xale /'ʃali/ *m* shawl

xampu /ʃã'pu/ *m* shampoo

xará /ʃa'ra/ *m/f* namesake

xarope /ʃa'rɔpi/ *m* syrup

xaxim /ʃa'ʃĩ/ *m* plant fibre

xenofobia /ʃenofo'bia/ *f* xenopho-
bia

xenófobo /ʃe'nɔfobu/ *a* xenopho-
bic □ *m* xenophobe

xepa /'ʃepa/ *f* scraps

xeque[1] /'ʃɛki/ *m (árabe)* sheikh

xeque[2] /'ʃɛki/ *m (no xadrez)*
check; **~-mate** *m* checkmate

xere|ta /ʃe'reta/ *(fam)* *a* nosy □
m/f nosy parker; **~tar** *(fam)* *vi*
nose around

xerez /ʃe'res/ *m* sherry

xerife /ʃe'rifi/ *m* sheriff

xerocar /ʃero'kar/ *vt* photocopy

xerox /ʃe'rɔks/ *m invar* photocopy

xexelento /ʃeʃe'lẽtu/ *(fam)* *a*
scruffy □ *m* scruff

xícara /'ʃikara/ *f* cup

xiita /ʃi'ita/ *a* & *m/f* Shiite

xilofone /ʃilo'foni/ *m* xylophone

xingar /ʃi'gar/ *vt* swear at □ *vi*
swear

xis /ʃis/ *m invar* letter X; **o ~ do
problema** the crux of the problem

xixi /ʃi'ʃi/ *(fam)* *m* wee; **fazer ~**
do a wee

xô /ʃo/ *int* shoo

xucro /'ʃukru/ *a* ignorant

Z

zagueiro /za'geru/ *m* fullback

Zaire /'zajri/ *m* Zaire

Zâmbia /ˈzãbia/ f Zambia

zan|gado /zãˈgadu/ a cross, annoyed; **~gar** vt annoy; **~gar-se** vpr get cross, get annoyed (**com** with)

zanzar /zãˈzar/ vi wander

zarpar /zarˈpar/ vi set off; (de navio) set sail

zebra /ˈzebra/ f zebra; (pessoa) fool; (resultado) upset

ze|lador /zelaˈdor/ m caretaker, (Amer) janitor; **~lar** vt **~lar (por)** take care of; **~lo** /e/ m zeal; **~lo por** devotion to; **~loso** /o/ a zealous

zero /ˈzεru/ m zero; (em escores) nil; **~quilômetro** a invar brand new

ziguezague /zigiˈzagi/ m zigzag; **~ar** vi zigzag

Zimbábue /zĩˈbabui/ m Zimbabwe

zinco /ˈzĩku/ m zinc

zíper /ˈziper/ m zip, zipper

zodíaco /zoˈdʒiaku/ m zodiac

zoeira /zoˈera/ f din

zom|bador /zõbaˈdor/ a mocking; **~bar** vi **~bar (de)** mock; **~baria** f mockery

zona /ˈzona/ f (área) zone; (de cidade) district; (desordem) mess; (tumulto) commotion; (bairro do meretrício) red-light district

zonzo /ˈzõzu/ a dizzy

zôo /ˈzou/ m zoo

zoo|logia /zooloˈʒia/ f zoology; **~lógico** a zoological

zoólogo /zoˈɔlogu/ m zoologist

zum /ˈzũ/ m zoom lens

zumbi /zũˈbi/ m zombie

zum|bido /zũˈbidu/ m buzz; (no ouvido) ringing; **~bir** vi buzz

zu|nido /zuˈnidu/ m (de vento, bala) whistle; (de inseto) buzz; **~nir** vi <vento, bala> whistle; <inseto> buzz

zunzum /zũˈzũ/ m rumour

Zurique /zuˈriki/ f Zurich

zurrar /zuˈxar/ vi bray

Phrasefinder

Useful phrases

Frases úteis

yes, please//no, thank you   sim, por favor//não, obrigado/a
sorry   desculpe, perdão
excuse me   com licença
I'm sorry, I don't understand   perdão, não entendo

Meeting people
Conhecendo/encontrando pessoas

Good morning/afternoon/evening   bom dia/boa tarde/boa noite
hello/goodbye   olá/até logo
how are you   como está
nice to meet you   prazer lhe conhecer

Asking questions
Fazendo perguntas

do you speak English/Portuguese?   fala inglês/português?
what's your name?   como se chama?
Where are you from?   você é de onde?
how much is it?   quanto é?/qual é o preço?
where is...?   onde é/onde fica ...?
would you like ...?   (você) queria/aceita ...?

Statements about yourself
Informações pessoais

my name is ...   meu nome é .../eu me chamo ...
I'm American//English   sou americano/a//inglês/inglesa
I don't speak Portuguese/English   não falo português/inglês
I live near Salvador/Chester   moro perto de Salvador/Chester
I'm a student   sou estudante
I work in an office   trabalho num escritório

Emergencies
Emergências

can you help me, please?   poderia me ajudar, por favor
I'm lost   estou perdido/a
I'm ill/feeling ill   estou doente/estou passando mal
call an ambulance   chame a ambulância

Reading signs
Lendo as placas

no entry   não entrar
no smoking   não fumar
fire exit   saída de emergência
for sale   à venda/vende-se

❶ Going Places

On the road	**Na estrada**
where's the nearest service station?	onde fica o posto de gasolina mais perto?
what's the best way to get there?	qual é o melhor caminho para chegar lá?
I've got a puncture	furou o pneu
I'd like to hire a bike/car	eu queria alugar uma bicicleta/um carro
there's been an accident	houve um acidente
my car's broken down	meu carro quebrou/(*Port*) avariou
the car won't start	meu carro não liga

By rail	**De trem, (Port) comboio**
where can I buy a ticket?	onde fica a bilheteria?
what time is the next train to York/Porto?	qual é o horário do próximo trem para York?/comboio para Porto?
do I have to change?	é preciso mudar?
can I take my bike on the train?	posso levar a minha bicicleta no trem/comboio?
which platform for the train to Salvador?	qual é a plataforma do trem/comboio para Salvador ?
there's a train to Porto at 10 o'clock	há um trem/comboio para Porto às 10h/22h?
a single.return to ..., please	um bilhete para ..., por favor
a return ticket to ..., please	uma ida e volta para ..., por favor
I'd like an all-day ticket	eu queria um passe para o dia todo
I'd like to reserve a ticket for ...	eu queria reservar um bilhete para ...

At the airport	**No aeroporto**
when's the next flight to Rome?	quando sai o próximo vôo para Roma?
where do I check in?	onde é o check-in?
I'd like to confirm my flight	eu gostaria de confirmar meu vôo
I'd like a window seat/an aisle seat	eu queria uma janela/corredor
I want to change/cancel my reservation	quero mudar/cancelar a minha reserva

Getting there	**Chegando**
could you tell me the way to the castle?	podia me indicar o caminho para o castelo?
how long will it take to get there?	quanto tempo leva para chegar lá?
how far is it from here?	a que distância fica?
which bus do I take for the cathedral?	qual é o ônibus/(*Port*) autocarro que eu pego para a catedral?
can you tell me where to get off?	podia me dizer onde devo descer?
what time is the last bus?	a que horas sai o último ônibus/(*Port*) autocarro?
how do I get to the airport?	como se vai para o aeroporto?
where's the nearest underground station, (*US*) subway station?	onde é a estação de metrô mais perto?
I'll take a taxi	vou pegar um taxi
can you call me a taxi?	podia chamar um taxi para mim?
take the first turning on the right	pegue a primeira entrada à direita
turn left at the traffic lights	vire à esquerda no semáforo

❷ Keeping in touch

On the phone	No telefone
may I use your phone?	poderia usar seu telefone?
do you have a mobile, (US) cell phone?	você tem um celular/(Port) telemóvel?
what is the code for São Paulo/Cardiff?	qual é o código para São Paulo/Cardiff?
I want to make a phone call	quero fazer um telefonema
I'd like to reverse the charges, (US) call collect	quero ligar a cobrar
I need to top up my mobile, (US) cell phone	preciso colocar crédito no meu celular, (Port) telemóvel
the line's busy	a linha está ocupada
there's no answer	ninguém atende
hello, this is Natalia	alô, fala Natália
is João there, please?	João está?
who's calling?	quem fala/está falando?
sorry, wrong number	desculpe, foi engano
just a moment, please	um momento, por favor
would you like to hold?	poderia aguardar?
please tell him/her I called	por favor diga a ele/ela que telefonei
I'd like to leave a message for him/her	eu queria deixar uma mensagem para ele/ela
... I'll try again later	... vou tentar mais tarde
tell him/her that Maria called	diga a ele/ela que Maria telefonou
can he/she ring me back?	ele/ela poderia me retornar?
my home number is ...	meu telefone de casa é ...
my business number is ...	meu telefone do trabalho é ...
my mobile, (US) cell phone number is...	meu (número) de celular/(Port) telemóvel é ...
we were cut off	caiu a linha

Writing

what's your address?

where is the nearest post office?

could I have a stamp for Angola, please?

I'd like to send a parcel/a fax

Escrevendo

qual é seu endereço

onde fica o correio mais próximo?

podia me dar um selo para Angola por favor?

eu gostaria de enviar um pacote/fax

On line

are you on the Internet?

what's your e-mail address?

we could send it by e-mail

I'll e-mail it to you on Tuesday

I looked it up on the Internet

the information is on their website

On-line

está conectado/a à Internet?

qual é seu e-mail?

poderíamos enviar por e-mail

eu lhe enviarei por e-mail na terça feira

pesquisei na Internet

as informações estão no site deles

Meeting up

what shall we do this evening?

where shall we meet?

I'll be outside the café at 6 o'clock

see you later

I can't today, I'm busy

Encontrando

o que vamos fazer hoje a noite?

onde vamos nos encontrar?

estarei na frente do café às 18 horas

até mais tarde

hoje não posso, estou ocupado/a

❸ Food and Drink

Reservations | Reservas

can you recommend a good restaurant?	podia indicar-me um bom restaurante?
I'd like to reserve a table for four	eu queria reservar uma mesa para quatro
a reservation for tomorrow at eight o'clock	uma reserva para amanhã às 20 horas

Ordering | Fazendo o pedido

the menu/wine list, please?	o cardápio/(Port) menu, por favor?
do you have a children's menu?	tem menu para crianças?
as a starter … and to follow…	como entrada … e para seguir…
could we have some more bread/rice?	poderia nos trazer mais pão/arroz, por favor?
what would you recommend?	o que me sugere?
I'd like a	eu queria um
… white coffee, (US) coffee with cream	… café com leite/creme
… black coffee	… café/cafezinho/expresso
… a decaffeinated coffee	… um descafeinado
… a liqueur	… um licor
could I have the bill, (US) check	a conta, por favor?

You will hear | Escutará

Já está pronto/a para pedir?	Are you ready to order?
Deseja (sing) um aperitivo?	Would you like an aperitif?
Desejam (pl) uma entrada?	Would you like a starter?
O que gostaria(m) como prato principal?	What will you have for the main course?
Queriam café/licores?	Would you like coffee/liqueurs?
Alguma coisa mais?	Anything else?
Bom apetite!	Enjoy your meal!
O serviço não está incluído	Service is not included.

The menu

O cardápio/(Port) menu

starters/entradas		entradas/starters	
hors d'oeuvres	tira-gostos	omelete	omelette
omelette	omelete	sopa	soup
soup	sopa	tira-gostos	hors d'oeuvres

fish/peixe		peixe/fish	
bass	labro	arenque	herring
cod	bacalhau	atún	tuna
eel	enguia	bacalhau	cod
hake	merluza	camarões	prawns, shrimps
herring	arenque	enguia	eel
monk fish	peixe-sapo	labro	bass
mussels	mexilhões	linguado	sole
oyster	ostra	lula	squid
prawns	camarões	merluza	hake
salmon	salmão	mexilhões	mussels
sardines	sardinhas	ostra	oyster
shrimps	camarões	peixe-sapo	monk fish
sole	linguado	rodavalho	turbot
squid	lula	salmão	salmon
trout	truta	saramunete	red mullet
tuna	atún	sardinhas	sardines
turbot	rodavalho	truta	trout

meat/carne		carne/meat	
beef	carne (de vaca, bovina)	bife, filé	steak
chicken	galinha	carne (de vaca, bovina)	beef
duck	pato	carne de porco	pork
goose	ganso	carne de veado	venison
guinea fowl	guiné	carne de vitela	veal
hare	lebre	carneiro	lamb
ham	presunto	coelho	rabbit
kidneys	rins	fígado	liver
lamb	carneiro	galinha	chicken
liver	fígado	ganso	goose
pork	carne de porco	guiné	guinea fowl
rabbit	coelho	javali	wild boar
steak	bife, filé	lebre	hare

❸ Food and Drink

turkey	peru	pato	duck
veal	carne de vitela	peru	turkey
venison	carne de veado	presunto	ham
wild boar	javali	rins	kidneys

vegetables/verduras

		verduras/vegetables	
artichoke	alcachofra	aborbrinha	zuccini
asparagus	aspargo	alcachofra	artichoke
aubergine	berinjela	alface	lettuce
beans	feijão, fava	aspargo (LAm)	asparagus
carrots	cenoura	aipo	celery
cabbage	couve, repolho	batata doce (LAm)	sweet potato
celery	aipo	batata inglesa	potato
endive	endívia	berinjela	aubergine
lettuce	alface	cebola	onion
mushrooms	cogumelo, champignon	cenoura	carrot
peas	ervilha	cogumelo, champignon	mushroom
pepper	pimentão	couve, repolho	cabbage
potatoes	batata inglesa	couveflor	cauliflower
runner bean	vagem	ervilha	peas
tomato	tomate	fava	broad bean
sweet potato	batata doce	feijão	beans
salad	salada	pimenta	chilli
zucchini	aborbrinha	pimentão verde/ vermelho	green/red pepper
		vagem	runner bean

the way it's cooked/como se prepara

		como se prepara/the way it's cooked	
boiled	cozido–da	assado–da	roast
fried	frito–ta	bem passado–da	well done
griddled	na chapa	cozido–da,	boiled
grilled	grelhado–da	fervido–da	
pureed	puré de	ensopado–da	stewed
rare	mal passado–da	frito–ta	fried
roast	assado–da	grelhado–da	grilled
stewed	ensopado–da, guisado–da	mal passado	rare
well done	bem passado–da	na chapa	griddled
		puré de	pureed

desserts/sobremesas

ice cream	sorvete
fruits	fruta
pie	pastel (*Port*), torta (*Braz*)

sobremesas/desserts

fruta	fruit
sorvete	ice cream
pastel (*Port*)	pie
torta (*Braz*)	tart, pie

other/otros

bread	pão
butter	manteiga
cheese	queijo
cheeseboard	mesa de queijos
garlic	alho
mayonnaise	maionese
mustard	mostarda
olive oil	azeite de oliva
pepper (black)	pimenta do reino
rice	arroz
salt	sal
sauce	molho
seasoning	têmpero, condimento
vinegar	vinagre

otros/others

azeite de oliva	olive oil
alho	garlic
arroz	rice
condimento,	seasoning
manteiga	butter
maionese	mayonnaise
mesa de queijos	cheeseboard
molho	sauce
mostarda	mustard
pão	bread
pimenta do reino	(black) pepper
queijo	cheese
sal	salt
tempero	seasoning
vinagre	vinegar

drinks/bebidas

beer	cerveja
bottle	garrafa
carbonated	com gás
half-bottle	méia garrafa
liqueur	licor
mineral water	água mineral
red wine	vinho tinto
rosé	vinho rosado
soft drink	bebida não alcoólica
still	sem gás
house wine	vinho da casa
table wine	vinho de mesa
white wine	vinho branco
wine	vinho

bebidas/drinks

agua mineral	mineral water
bebida não alcoólica	soft drink
cerveja	beer
com gás	carbonated
garrafa	bottle
méia garrafa	half-bottle
licor	liqueur
sem gás	still
vinho	wine
vinho branco	white wine
vinho da casa	house wine
vinho de mesa	table wine
vinho rosado	rosé
vinho tinto	red wine

Camping

can we pitch our tent here?	poderíamos armar nossa barraca aqui?
can we park our caravan here?	poderíamos estacionar nosso trailer/(Port) nossa roulotte aqui?
what are the facilities like?	qual é a infra-estrutura?
how much is it per night?	quanto custa por noite?
where do we park the car?	onde podemos estacionar?
we're looking for a campsite	estamos procurando um *camping*
this is a list of local campsites	aqui tem/isto é um lista de locais para
we go on a camping holiday every year	nós costumamos acampar todo ano

At the hotel — **No hotel**

I'd like a single/double room with bath	eu queria um quarto para uma pessoa/duplo com banheiro/(Port) com casa de banho
we have a reservation in the name of Morris	temos uma reserva no nome de Morris
we'll be staying three nights	queremos passar três noites
how much does the room cost?	quanto custa o quarto?
I'd like to see the room	eu gostaria de ver o quarto
what time is breakfast?	qual é o horário do café da manhã/(Port) pequeno almoço
can I leave this in your safe?	eu poderia deixar isto no seu cofre?
bed and breakfast	pernoite com pequeno almoço/(Port) café da manhã
we'd like to stay another night	gostaríamos de ficar outra noite
please call me at 7:30	por favor me chame às 7.30
are there any messages for me?	tem algum recado para mim?

Hostels	**Albergues**
could you tell me where the youth hostel is?	a senhora/o senhor poderia me informar onde fica o albergue?
what time does the hostel close?	a que horas fecha o albergue?
I'll be staying in a hostel	vou ficar num albergue
the hostel we're staying in is great value	o albergue onde estamos hospedados é muito razoável
I know a really good hostel in Dublin	conheço um albergue ótimo em Dublin
I'd like to go backpacking in Australia	eu queria viajar de mochila na Austrália

Rooms to rent	**Aluga-se quartos/quartos para alugar**
I'm looking for a room with a reasonable rent	estou procurando um quarto com aluguel razoável
I'd like to rent an apartment for a few weeks	eu gostaria de alugar um apartamento por algumas semanas
where do I find out about rooms to rent?	onde posso me informar sobre quartos para alugar?
what's the weekly rent?	quanto é o aluguel por semana?
I'm staying with friends at the moment	estou hospedado(a) com amigos no momento
I rent an apartment on the outskirts of town	alugo um apartamento nos arredores da cidade
the room's fine – I'll take it	o quarto está bom – vou querê-lo
is there a larger room/that has a sea view?	há outro quarto maior/com vista para o mar?
the deposit is one month's rent in advance	há um depósito de um mês adiantado

➎ Shopping and money

banking | No banco

I'd like to change some money	eu gostaria de trocar dinheiro
I want to change some dollars into euros	quero cambiar uns dólares por euros
do you need identification?	precisa de algum documento de identificação?
what's the exchange rate today?	qual é o câmbio de hoje?
Do you accept traveller's cheques, (US) traveler's checks	aceita *traveler*/cheque de viagem?
I'd like to transfer some money from my account	eu gostaria de fazer uma transferência da minha conta
Where is there an ATM?	aonde tem um banco 24 horas?
I'd like high value notes, (US) bills	eu queria notas de valores mais altos
I'm with another bank	sou cliente de outro banco

Finding the right shop | Encontrando a loja certa

where's the main shopping district?	onde é a área comercial principal?
where can I buy batteries/postcards?	onde posso comprar pilhas/cartões postais?
where's the nearest pharmacy/bookshop?	onde fica a farmácia/livraria mais próxima?
is there a good food shop around here?	onde poderia comprar alimentos por aqui?
what time do the shops open/close?	qual é o horário de funcionamento das lojas/do comércio?
where did you get that/these shoes?	onde comprou isso/estes sapatos?
I' looking for presents for my family	estou buscando lembranças para minha família?
we'll do our shopping on Saturday	faremos nossas compras sábado
I love shopping	adoro fazer compras

Are you being served?	**Já foi atendido/a?**
how much does that cost?	quanto custa aquilo
can I try it on?	posso experimentar?
could you wrap it for me, please?	pode embrulhar (para presente) para mim por favor
can I pay by credit card?	posso pagar com cartão (de crédito)?
do you have this in another colour?	tem isto em outra cor?
could I have a bag, please?	poderia me dar um sacola, por favor?
I'm just looking	só estou olhando
I'll think about it	vou pensar
I'd like a receipt, please	poderia me dar um recibo, por favor
I need a bigger/smaller size	preciso de um tamanho maior/menor
I take a size 10/a S/M/Large	uso tamanho 10/Pequeno/Médio/Grande
it doesn't suit me	não ficou bem em mim
I'm sorry, I don't have any change	lamento, mas não tenho trocado
that's all, thank you	é só isto, obrigado/obrigada

Changing things	**Trocando compras**
I'd like to change this shirt, please	eu queria trocar esta camisa, por favor
I bought this here yesterday	comprei isto aqui ontem
can I have a refund?	eu poderia ter um reembolso?
can you mend it for me?	poderia consertar isto para mim?
it doesn't work	não funciona
can I speak to the manager?	eu poderia falar com o gerente?

❻ Sport and leisure

Keeping fit

where can we play football/squash?

where is the sports centre, (US) center?

What's the charge per day?

is there a reduction for children/ students?

I'm looking for a swimming pool/ tennis court

you have to be a member

I play tennis on Mondays

I would like to go fishing/riding

I want to do aerobics

I love swimming/rollerblading/walking

we want to hire skis/snowboards

Mantendo a forma

onde podemos jogar futebol/squash

onde fica o centro de esportes/ desportos?

quanto custa a diária?

tem desconto para crianças/ estudantes?

estou procurando uma piscina/quadra de tênis

tem de ser sócio

jogo tênis nas segundas (feiras)

gostaria de pescar/andar a cavalo

quero fazer aeróbica

adoro nadar/patinar/caminhar

queremos alugar esquis/snowboards

Watching sport

is there a football match on Saturday?

which teams are playing?

where can I get tickets?

I'd like to see a rugby/football match

my favourite, (US) favorite team is...

let's watch the game on TV

Assistir esportes/(Port) desportos (Port)

tem jogo de futebol no sábado?

quais times/(Port) clubes estão jogando

onde posso comprar ingressos/(Port) bilhetes?

eu queria ver um jogo de rúgby/ futebol

meu time/(Port) clube predileto é ...

vamos assistir o jogo na TV

Going to the cinema/theatre/club

What film/show is on?	qual é o filme/o show que está passando
when does the box office open/close?	a que horas abre/fecha a bilheteria?
what time does the concert/performance start?	a que horas começa o concerto/Espetáculo/(*Port*) espectáculo?
when does it finish?	a que horas termina?
are there any seats left for tonight?	ainda tem lugares para hoje à noite?
how much are the tickets?	quanto custam os ingressos/(*Port*) bilhetes?
where can I get a programme, (*US*) program?	onde tem programas?
I want tickets for tonight's performance	quero fazer uma reserva para o espetáculo/(*Port*) espectáculo de hoje à noite
I'll book seats in the circle	vou reservar lugares no balcão
I'd rather have seats in the stalls	prefiro poltronas na platéia, no térreo
a seat in the middle, but not too far back	um lugar no meio, mas não muito para trás
four, please	quatro, por favor
for Saturday	para sábado
we'd like to go to a club	gostaríamos de ir para uma boate
I go clubbing every weekend	vou para uma boate todo final de semana

Hobbies

what do you do at the weekend?	o que você faz nos finais de semana?
I like yoga/listening to music	eu gosto de ioga/escutar música
I spend a lot of time surfing the Net	passo muito tempo surfando/(*Port*) a navegar na Internet
I read a lot	leio muito
I collect instruments	coleciono instrumentos musicais

Indo ao cinema/teátro/boate...

(qual é o filme/o show que está passando)

Passatempos prediletos

❼ Good timing

Telling the time

what time is it?

it's 2 o'clock

at about 8 o'clock (am/pm)

from 10 o'clock onwards

at 5 o'clock in the morning/afternoon

it's five past/quarter past one

it's half past one

it's twenty to/quarter to three

in a quarter/three quarters of an hour

Vendo a hora

que horas são?

são duas horas

às oito/vinte horas aproximadamente

a partir das dez horas

às cinco da manhã/tarde

é uma e cinco/quinze/(Port) um quarto

é uma e meia

são vinte/quinze para as três/(Port) são três menos vinte/um quarto

em quinze/quarenta e cinco minutos

Days and dates

Sunday, Monday, Tuesday, Wednesday, Thursday, Friday, Saturday

January, February, March, April, May, June, July, August, September, October, November, December

what's the date?

it's the second of June

we meet up every Monday

we're going away in August

on November 8th

Dias e datas

Domingo, Segunda-feira, Terça-feira, Quarta-feira, Quinta-feira, Sexta-feira, Sábado

janeiro, fevereiro, março, abril maio, junho, julho, agosto, setembro, outubro, novembro, dezembro

qual é a data?

é dois de junho

nós nos encontramos toda Segunda-feira

vamos viajar em agosto

no dia oito de novembro

Public holidays and special days	Feriados e dias especiais
Bank holiday (UK)	feriado nacional
New Year's Day (Jan 1)	Dia de Ano Novo
Epiphany (Jan 6)	Dia de Reis
St Valentine's Day (Feb 14)	Dia de São Valentino (= Dia dos Namorados)
Shrove Tuesday	Terça-feira de carnaval
Ash Wednesday	Quarta-feira de Cinzas
St Anthony's Day (June 13) (similar to Valentines Day)	Dia de Santo Antônio/Dia dos Namorados
Independence Day (July 4, USA)	Dia da Independência
Good Friday	Sexta-feira da Paixão
May Day (May 1)	Dia do Trabalhador
Brazilian Independence Day (Sept 7)	Dia da Independência do Brasil
Portuguese Republic Day (Oct 5)	Dia da República
Halloween (Oct 31)	Noite das Bruxas
All Saints' Day	Dia de Todos os Santos
All Souls' Day	Dia de Finados, Dia dos Mortos
Bonfire Night (Nov 5) (UK)	*tentativa de incendiar o parlamento inglês em 1605*
Thanksgiving (Nov, US)	*primeiros colonos ingleses na América do Norte*
Remembrance Sunday (Nov, UK)	*os mortos nas guerras*
Immaculate Conception (Dec 8)	Imaculada Conceição
Christmas Eve (Dec 24)	Véspera de Natal
Christmas Day (Dec 25)	Dia de Natal
New Year's Eve (Dec 31)	Véspera de Ano Novo, Reveillon

❽ Weights & measures/Pesos e medidas

Length/Comprimento

inches/polegadas	0.39	3.9	7.8	11.7	15.6	19.7	39
cm/centímetros	1	10	20	30	40	50	100

Distance/Distância

miles/milhas	0.62	6.2	12.4	18.6	24.9	31	62
km/quilómetros	1	10	20	30	40	50	100

Weight/Peso

pounds/libras	2.2	22	44	66	88	110	220
kilos/quilos	1	10	20	30	40	50	100

Capacity/Capacidade

US gallons/galões	0.26	2.64	5.28	7.92	10.56	13.2	26.4
litres/litros	1	10	20	30	40	50	100

Temperature/Temperatura

°C	0	5	10	15	20	25	30	37	38	40
°F	32	41	50	59	68	77	86	98.4	100	104

Clothing and shoe sizes/Roupas e número calçado

Women's clothing sizes/Tamanhos de roupa feminina

UK	8	10	12	14	16	18
US	6	8	10	12	14	16
Europa	36	38	40	42	44	46

Men's clothing sizes/Tamanhos de roupa masculina

UK/US	36	38	40	42	44	46
Europa	46	48	50	52	54	56

Men's and women's shoes/Sapatos masculinos e femininos

UK women	4	5	6	7	7.5	8				
UK men				6	7	8	9	10	11
US	6.5	7.5	8.5	9.5	10.5	11.5	12.5	13.5	14.5
Europa	37	38	39	40	41	42	43	44	45

ENGLISH-PORTUGUESE
INGLÊS-PORTUGUÊS

A

a /ə/; *emphatic* /eɪ/ (*before vowel* **an** /ən/; *emphatic* /æn/) *a* um. **two pounds a metre** duas libras o metro. **sixty miles an hour** sessenta milhas por hora, (P) à hora. **once a year** uma vez por ano

aback /ə'bæk/ *adv* **taken ~** desconcertado, (P) surpreendido

abandon /ə'bændən/ *vt* abandonar □ *n* abandono *m*. **~ed** *a* abandonado *m*. (*behaviour*) livre, dissoluto. **~ment** *n* abandono *m*, diminuição *f*

abashed /ə'bæʃt/ *a* confuso, (P) atrapalhado

abate /ə'beɪt/ *vt/i* abater, abrandar, diminuir. **~ment** *n* abrandamento *m*, diminuição *f*

abattoir /'æbətwɑː(r)/ *n* matadouro *m*

abbey /'æbɪ/ *n* abadia *f*, mosteiro *m*

abbreviat|e /ə'briːvɪeɪt/ *vt* abreviar. **~ion** /-'eɪʃn/ *n* abreviação *f*; (*short form*) abreviatura *f*

abdicat|e /'æbdɪkeɪt/ *vt/i* abdicar. **~ion** /-'keɪʃn/ *n* abdicação *f*

abdom|en /'æbdəmən/ *n* abdômen *m*, (P) abdómen *m*. **~inal** /'dɒmnl/ *a* abdominal

abduct /æb'dʌkt/ *vt* raptar. **~ion** /-ʃn/ *n* rapto *m*. **~or** *n* raptor, -a *mf*

aberration /æbə'reɪʃn/ *n* aberração *f*

abet /ə'bet/ *vt* (*pt* **abetted**) (*jur*) instigar; (*aid*) auxiliar

abeyance /ə'beɪəns/ *n* **in ~** (*matter*) em suspenso; (*custom*) em desuso

abhor /əb'hɔː(r)/ *vt* (*pt* **abhorred**) abominar, ter horror a. **~rence** /-'hɒrəns/ *n* horror *m*. **~rent** /-'hɒrənt/ *a* abominável, execrável

abide /ə'baɪd/ *vt* (*pt* **abided**) suportar, tolerar. **~ by** (*promise*) manter; (*rules*) acatar

abiding /ə'baɪdɪŋ/ *a* eterno, perpétuo

ability /ə'bɪlətɪ/ *n* capacidade *f* (**to do** para or de fazer); (*cleverness*) habilidade *f*, esperteza *f*

abject /'æbdʒekt/ *a* abjeto, (P) abjecto

ablaze /ə'bleɪz/ *a* em chamas; (*fig*) aceso, (P) excitado

abl|e /'eɪbl/ *a* (**~er**, **~est**) capaz (**to** de). **be ~e to** (*have power, opportunity*) ser capaz de, poder; (*know how to*) ser capaz de, saber. **~y** *adv* habilmente

ablutions /ə'bluːʃnz/ *npl* ablução *f*, abluções *fpl*

abnormal /æb'nɔːml/ *a* anormal. **~ity** /-'mælətɪ/ *n* anormalidade *f*. **~ly** *adv* (*unusually*) excepcionalmente

aboard /ə'bɔːd/ *adv* a bordo □ *prep* a bordo de

abode /ə'bəʊd/ *n* (*old use*) habitação *f*. **place of ~** domicílio *m*

aboli|sh /ə'bɒlɪʃ/ vt abolir, extinguir. **~tion** /æbə'lɪʃn/ n abolição f, extinção f

abominable /ə'bɒmɪnəbl/ a abominável, detestável

abominat|e /ə'bɒmɪneɪt/ vt abominar, detestar. **~ion** /-'neɪʃn/ n abominação f

abort /ə'bɔːt/ vt/i (fazer) abortar. **~ive** a (attempt etc) abortado, malogrado

abortion /ə'bɔːʃn/ n aborto m. **have an ~** fazer um aborto, ter um aborto. **~ist** n abortad/or, -eira mf

abound /ə'baʊnd/ vi abundar (**in** em)

about /ə'baʊt/ adv (approximately) aproximadamente, cerca de; (here and there) aqui e ali; (all round) por todos os lados, em roda, em volta; (in existence) por aí □ prep acerca de, sobre; (round) em torno de; (somewhere in) em, por. **~-face**, **~-turn** n reviravolta f. **~ here** por aqui. **be ~ to** estar prestes a. **he was ~ to eat** ia comer. **how or what were you ~ leaving?** e se nós fôssemos embora? **know/talk ~** saber/falar sobre

above /ə'bʌv/ adv acima, por cima □ prep sobre. **he's not ~ lying** ele não é de mentir. **~ all** sobretudo. **~-board** a franco, honesto □ adv com lisura. **~-mentioned** a acima, supracitado

abrasion /ə'breɪʒn/ n atrito m; (injury) escoriação f, esfoladura f

abrasive /ə'breɪsɪv/ a abrasivo; (fig) agressivo □ n abrasivo m

abreast /ə'brest/ adv lado a lado. **keep ~ of** manter-se a par de

abridge /ə'brɪdʒ/ vt abreviar. **~ment** n abreviação f, abreviatura f, redução f; (abridged text) resumo m

abroad /ə'brɔːd/ adv no estran-

geiro; (far and wide) por todo o lado. **go ~** ir para o estrangeiro

abrupt /ə'brʌpt/ a (sudden, curt) brusco; (steep) abrupto. **~ly** adv (suddenly) bruscamente; (curtly) com brusquidão. **~ness** n brusquidão f; (steepness) declive m

abscess /'æbsɪs/ n abscesso m, (P) abcesso m

abscond /əb'skɒnd/ vi evadir-se, andar fugido

absen|t[1] /'æbsənt/ a ausente; (look etc) distraído. **~ce** n ausência f; (lack) falta f. **~t-minded** a distraído. **~t-mindedness** n distração f, (P) distracção f

absent[2] /əb'sent/ v refl **~ o.s.** ausentar-se

absentee /æbsən'tiː/ n ausente m, (P) absentista mf. **~ism** n absenteísmo m, (P) absentismo m

absolute /'æbsəluːt/ a absoluto; (colloq: coward etc) autêntico, (P) verdadeiro. **~ly** adv absolutamente

absolution /æbsə'luːʃn/ n absolvição f

absolve /əb'zɒlv/ vt (from sin) absolver (**from** de); (from vow) desligar (**from** de)

absor|b /əb'sɔːb/ vt absorver. **~ption** n absorção f

absorbent /əb'sɔːbənt/ a absorvente. **~ cotton** (Amer) algodão hidrófilo m

abst|ain /əb'stem/ vi abster-se (**from** de). **~ention** /-'stenʃn/ n abstenção f

abstemious /əb'stiːmɪəs/ a abstêmio, (P) abstémio, sóbrio

abstinen|ce /'æbstɪnəns/ n abstinência f. **~t** a abstinente

abstract[1] /'æbstrækt/ a abstrato, (P) abstracto

abstract[2] /əb'strækt/ vt (take out) extrair; (separate) abstrair. **~ed** a distraído. **~ion** /-ʃn/ n (of mind) distração f, (P) distracção f; (idea) abstração f, (P) abstracção f

absurd /əb'sɜːd/ a absurdo. **~ity** n absurdo m

abundan|t /ə'bʌndənt/ a abundante. **~ce** n abundância f

abuse[1] /ə'bjuːz/ vt (misuse) abusar de; (ill-treat) maltratar; (insult) injuriar, insultar

abus|e[2] /ə'bjuːs/ n (wrong use) abuso m (of de); (insults) insultos m pl. **~ive** a injurioso, ofensivo

abysmal /ə'bɪzməl/ a abismal; (colloq: bad) abissal

abyss /ə'bɪs/ n abismo m

academic /ækə'demɪk/ a académico, (P) académico, universitário; (scholarly) intelectual; (pej) académico, (P) teórico □ n universitário

academy /ə'kædəmɪ/ n academia f

accede /ək'siːd/ vi **~ to** (request) aceder a; (post) assumir; (throne) ascender a, subir a

accelerat|e /ək'seləreɪt/ vt acelerar □ vi acelerar-se; (auto) acelerar. **~ion** /-'reɪʃn/ n aceleração f

accelerator /ək'seləreɪtə(r)/ n (auto) acelerador m

accent[1] /'æksənt/ n acento m; (local pronunciation) sotaque m

accent[2] /æk'sent/ vt acentuar

accentuate /æk'sentʃʊeɪt/ vt acentuar

accept /ək'sept/ vt aceitar. **~able** a aceitável. **~ance** n aceitação f; (approval) aprovação f

access /'ækses/ n acesso m (to a). **~ible** /ək'sesəbl/ a acessível

accessory /ək'sesərɪ/ a acessório □ n acessório m; (jur: person) cúmplice m

accident /'æksɪdənt/ n acidente m, desastre m; (chance) acaso m. **~al** /-'dentl/ a acidental, fortuito. **~ally** /-'dentəlɪ/ adv acidentalmente, por acaso

acclaim /ə'kleɪm/ vt aclamar □ n aplauso m, aclamações fpl

acclimatiz|e /ə'klaɪmətaɪz/ vt/i

acclimatar(-se). **~ation** /-'zeɪʃn/ n aclimatação f

accommodat|e /ə'kɒmədeɪt/ vt acomodar; (lodge) alojar; (adapt) adaptar; (supply) fornecer; (oblige) fazer a vontade de. **~ing** a obsequioso, amigo de fazer vontades. **~ion** /-'deɪʃn/ n acomodação f; (rooms) alojamento m, quarto m

accompan|y /ə'kʌmpənɪ/ vt acompanhar. **~iment** n acompanhamento m. **~ist** n (mus) acompanhad|or, (B) -eira mf

accomplice /ə'kʌmplɪs/ n cúmplice mf

accomplish /ə'kʌmplɪʃ/ vt (perform) executar, realizar; (achieve) realizar, conseguir fazer. **~ed** a acabado. **~ment** n realização f; (ability) talento m, dote m

accord /ə'kɔːd/ vi concordar □ vt conceder □ n acordo m. **of one's own ~** por vontade própria, espontaneamente. **~ance** n **in ~ance with** em conformidade com, de acordo com

according /ə'kɔːdɪŋ/ adv **~ to** conforme. **~ly** adv (therefore) por conseguinte, por consequência; (appropriately) conformemente

accordion /ə'kɔːdɪən/ n acordeão m

accost /ə'kɒst/ vt abordar, abeirar-se de

account /ə'kaʊnt/ n (comm) conta f; (description) relato m; (importance) importância f □ vt considerar. **~ for** dar contas de, explicar. **on ~ of** por causa de. **on no ~** em caso algum. **take into ~** ter ou levar em conta. **~able** /-əbl/ a responsável (for por). **~ability** /-ə'bɪlətɪ/ n responsabilidade f

accountant /ə'kaʊntənt/ n conta- dor(a) m/f, (P) contabilista m

accrue /ə'kruː/ vi acumular-se. **~ to** reverter em favor de

accumulat|e /əˈkjuːmjʊleɪt/ *vt/i* acumular(-se). **~ion** /-ˈleɪʃn/ *n* acumulação *f*, acréscimo *m*

accumulator /əˈkjuːmjʊleɪtə(r)/ *n* (*electr*) acumulador *m*

accura|te /ˈækjərət/ *a* exato, (P) exacto, preciso. **~cy** *n* exatidão *f*, (P) exactidão *f*, precisão *f*. **~tely** *adv* com exatidão, (P) exactidão

accus|e /əˈkjuːz/ *vt* acusar. **the ~ed** o acusado. **~ation** /ækjuːˈzeɪʃn/ *n* acusação *f*

accustom /əˈkʌstəm/ *vt* acostumar, habituar. **~ed** *a* acostumado, habituado. **get ~ed to** acostumar-se a, habituar-se a

ace /eɪs/ *n* ás *m*

ache /eɪk/ *n* dor *f* □ *vi* doer. **my leg ~s** dói-me a perna, tenho dores na perna

achieve /əˈtʃiːv/ *vt* realizar, efetuar; (*success*) alcançar. **~ment** *n* realização *f*; (*feat*) feito *m*, façanha *f*, sucesso *m*

acid /ˈæsɪd/ *a* ácido; (*wine*) azedo; (*words*) áspero □ *n* ácido *m*. **~ity** /əˈsɪdəti/ *n* acidez *f*

acknowledge /əkˈnɒlɪdʒ/ *vt* reconhecer. **~ (receipt of)** acusar a recepção de. **~ment** *n* reconhecimento *m*; (*letter etc*) acusação *f* de recebimento, (P) aviso *m* de recepção

acne /ˈækni/ *n* acne *mf*

acorn /ˈeɪkɔːn/ *n* bolota *f*, glande *f*

acoustic /əˈkuːstɪk/ *a* acústico. **~s** *npl* acústica *f*

acquaint /əˈkweɪnt/ *vt* **~ s.o. with sth** pôr alg a par de algo coisa. **be ~ed with** (*person, fact*) conhecer. **~ance** *n* (*knowledge, person*) conhecimento *m*; (*person*) conhecido *m*

acquiesce /ækwɪˈes/ *vi* consentir. **~nce** *n* aquiescência *f*, consentimento *m*

acqui|re /əˈkwaɪə(r)/ *vt* adquirir. **~sition** /ækwɪˈzɪʃn/ *n* aquisição *f*

acquit /əˈkwɪt/ *vt* (*pt* **acquitted**) absolver. **~ o.s. well** sair-se bem. **~tal** *n* absolvição *f*

acrid /ˈækrɪd/ *a* acre

acrimon|ious /ækrɪˈməʊnɪəs/ *a* acrimonioso. **~y** /ˈækrɪmənɪ/ *n* acrimónia *f*

acrobat /ˈækrəbæt/ *n* acrobata *mf*. **~ic** /-ˈbætɪk/ *a* acrobático. **~ics** /-ˈbætɪks/ *npl* acrobacia *f*

acronym /ˈækrənɪm/ *n* sigla *f*

across /əˈkrɒs/ *adv & prep* (*side to side*) de lado a lado (de), de um lado para o outro (de); (*on the other side*) do outro lado (de); (*crosswise*) através (de), de través. **go** *or* **walk ~** atravessar. **swim ~** atravessar a nado

act /ækt/ *n* (*deed, theatr*) ato *m*, (P) acto *m*; (*in variety show*) número *m*; (*decree*) lei *f* □ *vi* agir, atuar; (P) actuar; (*theatr*) representar; (*function*) funcionar; (*pretend*) fingir □ *vt* (*part, role*) desempenhar. **~ as** servir de. **~ing** *a* interino □ *n* (*theatr*) desempenho *m*

action /ˈækʃn/ *n* ação *f*, (P) acção *f*; (*mil*) combate *m*. **out of ~** fora de combate; (*techn*) avariado. **take ~** agir, atuar, (P) actuar

activ|e /ˈæktɪv/ *a* ativo, (P) activo; (*interest*) vivo; (*volcano*) em atividade, (P) actividade. **~ity** /-ˈtɪvətɪ/ *n* atividade *f*, (P) actividade *f*

ac|tor /ˈæktə(r)/ *n* ator *m*, (P) actor *m*. **~tress** *n* atriz *f*, (P) actriz *f*

actual /ˈæktʃʊəl/ *a* real, verdadeiro; (*example*) concreto. **the ~ pen which** a própria caneta que. **~ity** /-ˈælətɪ/ *n* realidade *f*. **~ly** *adv* (*in fact*) na realidade

acumen /əˈkjuːmen/ *n* agudeza *f*, perspicácia *f*

acupunctur|e /ˈækjʊpʌŋktʃə(r)/ *n* acupuntura *f*, (P) acupunctura *f*.

~ist n acupunturador m, (P) acupuncturista mf

acute /ə'kju:t/ a agudo; (mind) perspicaz; (emotion) intenso, vivo; (shortage) grande. **~ly** adv vivamente

ad /æd/ n (colloq) anúncio m

AD abbr dC

adamant /'ædəmənt/ a inflexível

adapt /ə'dæpt/ vt/i adaptar(-se). **~ation** /ædæp'teɪʃn/ n adaptação f. **~or** (electr) adaptador m

adaptab|le /ə'dæptəbl/ a adaptável. **~ility** /-'bɪlətɪ/ n adaptabilidade f

add /æd/ vt/i acrescentar. **~ (up)** somar. **~ up to** (total) elevar-se a

adder /'ædə(r)/ n víbora f

addict /'ædɪkt/ n viciado m. **drug ~** (B) viciado em droga, viciado da droga, (P) toxicodependente mf

addict|ed /ə'dɪktɪd/ a **be ~ed to** (drink, drugs; fig) ter o vício de. **~ion** /-ʃn/ n (med) dependência f; (fig) vício m. **~ive** a que produz dependência

addition /ə'dɪʃn/ n adição f. **in ~** além disso. **in ~ to** além de. **~al** /-ʃənl/ a adicional, suplementar

address /ə'dres/ n endereço m; (speech) discurso m □ vt endereçar; (speak to) dirigir-se a

adenoids /'ædɪnoɪdz/ npl adenóides mpl

adept /'ædept/ a & n especialista (mf), perito (m) (at em)

adequa|te /'ædɪkwət/ a adequado; (satisfactory) satisfatório. **~cy** n adequação f; (of person) competência f. **~tely** adv adequadamente

adhere /əd'hɪə(r)/ vi aderir (**to** a)

adhesive /əd'hi:sɪv/ a & n adesivo (m). **~ plaster** esparadrapo m, (P) adesivo m

adjacent /ə'dʒeɪsnt/ a adjacente, contíguo (**to** a)

adjective /'ædʒektɪv/ n adjetivo m, (P) adjectivo m

adjoin /ə'dʒɔɪn/ vt confinar com, ficar contíguo a

adjourn /ə'dʒɜ:n/ vt adiar □ vi suspender a sessão. **~ to** (go) passar a, ir para

adjudicate /ə'dʒu:dɪkeɪt/ vt/i julgar; (award) adjudicar

adjust /ə'dʒʌst/ vt/i (alter) ajustar, regular; (arrange) arranjar. **~ (o.s.) to** adaptar-se a. **~able** a regulável. **~ment** n (techn) regulação f, afinação f; (of person) adaptação f

ad lib /æd'lɪb/ vi (pt **ad libbed**) (colloq) improvisar □ adv à vontade

administer /əd'mɪnɪstə(r)/ vt administrar

administrat|e /əd'mɪnɪstreɪt/ vt administrar, gerir. **~ion** /-'streɪʃn/ n administração f. **~or** n administrador m

administrative /əd'mɪnɪstrətɪv/ a administrativo

admirable /'ædmərəbl/ a admirável

admiral /'ædmərəl/ n almirante m

admir|e /əd'maɪə(r)/ vt admirar. **~ation** /-'reɪʃn/ n admiração f. **~er** /-'maɪərə(r)/ n admirador m

admission /əd'mɪʃn/ n admissão f; (to museum, theatre, etc) ingresso m, (P) entrada f; (confession) confissão f

admit /əd'mɪt/ vt (pt **admitted**) (let in) admitir, permitir a entrada a; (acknowledge) reconhecer, admitir. **~ to** confessar. **~tance** n admissão f

admoni|sh /əd'mɒnɪʃ/ vt admoestar. **~tion** /-nɪʃn/ n admoestação f

adolescen|t /ædə'lesnt/ a & n adolescente (mf). **~ce** n adolescência f

adopt /ə'dɒpt/ vt adotar, (P) adoptar. ~ed child filho adotivo, (P) adoptivo. ~ion /-ʃn/ n adoção f, (P) adopção f

ador|e /ə'dɔː(r)/ vt adorar. ~able a adorável. ~ation /ædə'reɪʃn/ n adoração f

adorn /ə'dɔːn/ vt adornar, enfeitar

adrenalin /ə'drenəlɪn/ n adrenalina f

adrift /ə'drɪft/ a & adv à deriva

adult /'ædʌlt/ a & n adulto (m). ~hood n idade f adulta, (P) maioridade f

adulterat|e /ə'dʌltəreɪt/ vt adulterar. ~ion /-'reɪʃn/ n adulteração f

adulter|y /ə'dʌltərɪ/ n adultério m. ~er, ~ess n adúlter/o, -a mf. ~ous a adúltero

advance /əd'vɑːns/ vt/i avançar □ n avanço m; (payment) adiantamento m □ a (payment, booking) adiantado. in □ com antecedência. ~d a avançado. ~ment n promoção f, ascensão f

advantage /əd'vɑːntɪdʒ/ n vantagem f. take ~ of aproveitar-se de, tirar partido de; (person) explorar. ~ous /ædvən'teɪdʒəs/ a vantajoso

adventur|e /əd'ventʃə(r)/ n aventura f. ~er n aventureiro m, explorador m. ~ous a aventuroso

adverb /'ædvɜːb/ n advérbio m

adversary /'ædvəsərɪ/ n adversário m, antagonista f

advers|e /'ædvɜːs/ a (contrary) adverso; (unfavourable) desfavorável. ~ity /əd'vɜːsətɪ/ n adversidade f

advert /'ædvɜːt/ n (colloq) anúncio m

advertise /'ædvətaɪz/ vt/i anunciar, fazer publicidade (de); (sell) pôr um anúncio (para). ~ for procurar. ~r /-ə(r)/ n anunciante mf

advertisement /əd'vɜːtɪsmənt/ n anúncio m; (advertising) publicidade f

advice /əd'vaɪs/ n conselho(s) mpl; (comm) aviso m

advis|e /əd'vaɪz/ vt aconselhar; (inform) avisar, informar. ~e against desaconselhar. ~able a aconselhável. ~er n conselheiro m; (in business) consultor m. ~ory a consultivo

advocate[1] /'ædvəkət/ n (jur) advogado m; (supporter) defensor(a) m/f

advocate[2] /'ædvəkeɪt/ vt advogar, defender

aerial /'eərɪəl/ a aéreo □ n antena f

aerobatics /eərə'bætɪks/ npl acrobacia f aérea

aerobics /eə'rəʊbɪks/ n ginástica f aeróbica

aerodynamic /eərəʊdaɪ'næmɪk/ a aerodinâmico

aeroplane /'eərəpleɪn/ n avião m

aerosol /'eərəsɒl/ n aerossol m

aesthetic /iːs'θetɪk/ a estético

affair /ə'feə(r)/ n (business) negócio m; (romance) ligação f, aventura f; (matter) assunto m. love ~ paixão f

affect /ə'fekt/ vt afetar, (P) afectar. ~ation /æfek'teɪʃn/ n afetação f, (P) afectação f. ~ed a afetado, (P) afectado, pretencioso

affection /ə'fekʃn/ n afeição f, afeto m, (P) afecto m

affectionate /ə'fekʃənət/ a afetuoso, (P) afectuoso, carinhoso

affiliat|e /ə'fɪlɪeɪt/ vt afiliar. ~ed company filial f. ~ion /-'eɪʃn/ n afiliação f

affirm /ə'fɜːm/ vt afirmar. ~ation /æfə'meɪʃn/ n afirmação f

affirmative /ə'fɜːmətɪv/ a afirmativo □ n afirmativa f

afflict /ə'flɪkt/ vt afligir. ~ion /-ʃn/ n aflição f

affluen|t /'æfluənt/ a rico, afluente. ~ce n riqueza f, afluência f

afford /ə'fɔːd/ vt (have money for) permitir-se, ter meios (para). **can you afford the time?** você teria tempo? **I can't afford a car** eu não posso comprar um carro. **we can't afford to lose** não podemos perder

affront /ə'frʌnt/ n afronta f □ vt insultar

afield /ə'fiːld/ adv **far ~** longe

afloat /ə'fləʊt/ adv & a à tona, a flutuar; (at sea) no mar; (business) lançado, (P) sem dívidas

afraid /ə'freɪd/ a **be ~** ter medo (of, to de; that que); (be sorry) lamentar, ter muita pena. **I'm ~ (that)** (regret to say) lamento or tenho muita pena de dizer que

afresh /ə'freʃ/ adv de novo

Africa /'æfrɪkə/ n África f. **~n** a & n africano (m)

after /'ɑːftə(r)/ adv depois □ prep depois de □ conj depois que. **~ all** afinal de contas. **~ doing**, depois de fazer. **be ~** (seek) querer,pretender. **~-effect** n sequela f, (P) sequela f, efeito m retardado; (of drug) efeito m secundário

aftermath /'ɑːftəmæθ/ n consequências fpl

afternoon /ɑːftə'nuːn/ n tarde f

aftershave /'ɑːftəʃeɪv/ n loção f após-barba, (P) loção f para a barba

afterthought /'ɑːftəθɔːt/ n reflexão f posterior. **as an ~** pensando melhor

afterwards /'ɑːftəwədz/ adv depois, mais tarde

again /ə'gen/ adv de novo, outra vez; (on the other hand) por outro lado. **then ~** além disso

against /ə'genst/ prep contra

age /eɪdʒ/ n idade f; (period) época f, idade f □ vt/i (pres p ageing) envelhecer. **~s** (colloq: very long time) há séculos mpl. **of ~** (jur) maior. **ten years of ~** com/de dez anos. **under ~**

menor. **~-group** n faixa etária f. **~less** a sempre jovem de idade

aged[1] /eɪdʒd/ a **~ six** de seis anos

aged[2] /'eɪdʒɪd/ a idoso, velho

agen|cy /'eɪdʒənsɪ/ n agência f; (means) intermédio m. **~t** n agente mf

agenda /ə'dʒendə/ n ordem f do dia

aggravat|e /'ægrəveɪt/ vt agravar; (colloq: annoy) irritar. **~ion** /-'veɪʃn/ n (worsening) agravamento m; (exasperation) irritação f, (colloq: trouble) aborrecimentos mpl

aggregate /'ægrɪgeɪt/ vt/i agregar (-se) □ a /'ægrɪgət/ total, global □ n (total, mass, materials) agregado m. **in the ~** no todo

aggress|ive /ə'gresɪv/ a agressivo; (weapons) ofensivo. **~ion** /-ʃn/ n agressão f. **~iveness** n agressividade f. **~or** n agressor m

aggrieved /ə'griːvd/ a (having a grievance) lesado

agil|e /'ædʒaɪl/ a ágil. **~ity** /ə'dʒɪlətɪ/ n agilidade f

agitat|e /'ædʒɪteɪt/ vt agitar. **~ion** /-'teɪʃn/ n agitação f. **~or** n agitador m

agnostic /æg'nɒstɪk/ a & n agnóstico (m)

ago /ə'gəʊ/ adv há. **a month ~** há um mês. **long ~** há muito tempo

agon|y /'ægənɪ/ n agonia f; (mental) angústia f. **~ize** vi atormentar-se, torturar-se. **~izing** a angustiante, (P) doloroso

agree /ə'griː/ vt/i concordar; (of figures) acertar. **~ that** reconhecer que. **~ to do** concordar em or aceitar fazer. **~ to sth** concordar com alguma coisa. **seafood doesn't ~ with me** não me dou bem com mariscos. **~d** a (time, place) combinado. **be ~d** estar de acordo

agreeable /əˈgriːəbl/ a agradável. **be ~ to** estar de acordo com

agreement /əˈgriːmənt/ n acordo m; (*gramm*) concordância f; (*contract*) contrato m. **in ~** de acordo

agricultur|e /ˈægrɪkʌltʃə(r)/ n agricultura f. **~al** /-ˈkʌltʃərəl/ a agrícola

aground /əˈɡraʊnd/ adv **run ~** (*of ship*) encalhar

ahead /əˈhed/ adv à frente, adiante; (*in advance*) adiantado. **~ of sb** diante de alguém, à frente de alguém. **~ of time** antes da hora, adiantado. **straight ~** sempre em frente

aid /eɪd/ vt ajudar □ n ajuda f. **~ and abet** ser cúmplice de. **in ~ of** em auxílio de, a favor de

AIDS /eɪdz/ n (*med*) AIDS f, (P) sida m

ail /eɪl/ vt **what ~s you?** o que é que você tem? **~ing** a doente. **~ment** n doença f, achaque m

aim /eɪm/ vt (*gun*) apontar; (*efforts*) dirigir; (*send*) atirar (**at** para) □ vi visar □ n alvo m. **~ at** visar. **~ to** aspirar a, tencionar. **take ~** fazer pontaria. **~less** a, **~lessly** adv sem objectivo, (P) objectivo

air /eə(r)/ n ar m □ vt arejar; (*views*) expor □ a (*base etc*) aéreo. **in the ~** (*rumour*) espalhado; (*plans*) no ar. **on the ~** (*radio*) no ar. **~-conditioned** a com ar condicionado. **~-conditioning** n condicionamento m do ar, (P) ar m condicionado. **~ force** Força f Aérea. **~ hostess** aeromoça f, (P) hospedeira f de bordo. **~ raid** ataque m aéreo

airborne /ˈeəbɔːn/ a (*aviat: in flight*) no ar; (*diseases*) levado pelo ar; (*freight*) por transporte aéreo

aircraft /ˈeəkrɑːft/ n (*pl invar*)

avião m. **~-carrier** n porta-aviões m

airfield /ˈeəfiːld/ n campo m de aviação

airgun /ˈeəɡʌn/ n espingarda f de pressão

airlift /ˈeəlɪft/ n ponte f aérea □ vt transportar em ponte aérea

airline /ˈeəlaɪn/ n linha f aérea

airlock /ˈeəlɒk/ n câmara f de vácuo; (*in pipe*) bolha f de ar

airmail /ˈeəmeɪl/ n correio m aéreo. **by ~** por avião

airport /ˈeəpɔːt/ n aeroporto m

airsick /ˈeəsɪk/ a enjoado. **~ness** /-nɪs/ n enjôo m, (P) enjoo m

airstrip /ˈeəstrɪp/ n pista f de aterrissagem, (P) pista f de aterragem

airtight /ˈeətaɪt/ a hermético

airy /ˈeərɪ/ a (-ier, -iest) arejado; (*manner*) desenvolto

aisle /aɪl/ n (*of church*) nave f lateral; (*gangway*) coxia f

ajar /əˈdʒɑː(r)/ adv & a entreaberto

alabaster /ˈæləbɑːstə(r)/ n alabastro m

à la carte /ɑːlɑːˈkɑːt/ adv & a à la carte, (P) à lista

alarm /əˈlɑːm/ n alarme m; (*clock*) campainha f □ vt alarmar. **~-clock** n despertador m. **~-bell** n campainha f de alarme. **~ing** a alarmante. **~ist** n alarmista mf

alas /əˈlæs/ int ai! ai de mim!

albatross /ˈælbətrɒs/ n albatroz m

album /ˈælbəm/ n álbum m

alcohol /ˈælkəhɒl/ n álcool m. **~ic** /-ˈhɒlɪk/ a (*person, drink*) alcoólico □ n alcoólico m. **~ism** n alcoolismo m

alcove /ˈælkəʊv/ n recesso m, alcova f

ale /eɪl/ n cerveja f inglesa

alert /əˈlɜːt/ a (*lively*) vivo; (*watchful*) vigilante □ n alerta m □ vt alertar. **be on the ~** estar alerta

algebra /'ældʒɪbrə/ n álgebra f.
~ic /-'breɪk/ a algébrico

Algeria /æl'dʒɪərɪə/ n Argélia f.
~n a & n argelino (m)

alias /'eɪlɪəs/ n (pl -ases) outro
nome m, nome falso m, (P) pseudónimo m ☐ adv aliás

alibi /'ælɪbaɪ/ n (pl -is) álibi m, (P)
alibi m

alien /'eɪlɪən/ n & a estrangeiro
(m). **~ to** (contrary) contrário a;
(differing) alheio a, estranho a

alienat|e /'eɪlɪəneɪt/ vt alienar.
~ion /-'neɪʃn/ n alienação f

alight¹ /ə'laɪt/ vi descer; (bird)
pousar

alight² /ə'laɪt/ a (on fire) em chamas; (lit up) aceso

align /ə'laɪn/ vt alinhar. **~ment** n
alinhamento m

alike /ə'laɪk/ a semelhante, parecido ☐ adv da mesma maneira.
look or **be ~** parecer-se

alimony /'ælɪmənɪ/ n pensão f alimentar, (P) de alimentos

alive /ə'laɪv/ a vivo. **~ to** sensível
a. **~ with** fervilhando de, (P) a
fervilhar de

alkali /'ælkəlaɪ/ n (pl -is) álcali
m, (P) alcali m

all /ɔːl/ a & pron todo (f & pl -a,
-os, -as) ☐ pron (everything) tudo
☐ adv completamente, de todo ☐
n tudo m. **~ the better/less/
more/worse** etc tanto melhor/
menos/mais/pior etc. **~ (the)
men** todos os homens. **~ of us**
todos nós. **~ but** quase, todos
menos. **~ in** (colloq: exhausted)
estafado. **~-in** a tudo incluído.
~ out a fundo, (P) completamente. **~-out** a (effort)
máximo. **~ over** (in one's body)
todo; (finished) acabado; (in all
parts of) por todo. **~ right** bem;
(as a response) está bem. **~
round** em tudo; (for all) para
todos. **~-round** a geral. **~ the
same** apesar de tudo. **it's ~**

the same to me (para mim) tanto faz

allay /ə'leɪ/ vt acalmar

allegation /ælɪ'geɪʃn/ n alegação f

alleg|e /ə'ledʒ/ vt alegar. **~dly**
/-ɪdlɪ/ adv segundo dizem, alega-
damente

allegiance /ə'liːdʒəns/ n fidelidade f, lealdade f

allegor|y /'ælɪgərɪ/ n alegoria f.
~ical /-'gɒrɪkl/ a alegórico

allerg|y /'ælədʒɪ/ n alergia f. **~ic**
/ə'lɜːdʒɪk/ a alérgico

alleviate /ə'liːvɪeɪt/ vt aliviar

alley /'ælɪ/ n (pl -eys) (street) viela f; (for bowling) pista f

alliance /ə'laɪəns/ n aliança f

allied /'ælaɪd/ a aliado

alligator /'ælɪgeɪtə(r)/ n jacaré m

allocat|e /'æləkeɪt/ vt (share out)
distribuir; (assign) destinar.
~ion /-'keɪʃn/ n atribuição f

allot /ə'lɒt/ vt (pt allotted)
atribuir. **~ment** n atribuição f;
(share) distribuição f; (land) horta f alugada

allow /ə'laʊ/ vt permitir; (grant)
conceder, dar; (reckon on) contar
com; (agree) admitir, reconhecer.
~ sb to (+ inf) permitir a alg (+
inf or que + subj). **~ for** levar
em conta

allowance /ə'laʊəns/ n (for em-
ployees) ajudas fpl de custo;
(monthly, for wife, child) benefício m; (tax) desconto m. **make
~s for** (person) levar em consideração, ser indulgente para
com; (take into account) atender
a, levar em consideração

alloy /'ælɔɪ/ n liga f

allude /ə'luːd/ vi **~ to** aludir a

allure /ə'lʊə(r)/ vt seduzir, atrair

allusion /ə'luːʒn/ n alusão f

ally¹ /'ælaɪ/ n (pl -lies) aliado m

ally² /ə'laɪ/ vt aliar. **~ oneself
with/to** aliar-se com/a

almanac /'ɔːlmənæk/ n almanaque m

almighty /ɔːlˈmaɪtɪ/ *a* todopoderoso; (*colloq*) grande, formidável

almond /ˈɑːmənd/ *n* amêndoa *f*. ~ **paste** maçapão *m*

almost /ˈɔːlməʊst/ *adv* quase

alone /əˈləʊn/ *a* & *adv* só. leave ~ (*abstain from interfering with*) deixar em paz. let ~ (*without considering*) sem *or* para não falar de

along /əˈlɒŋ/ *prep* ao longo de □ *adv* (*onward*) para diante. all ~ durante todo o tempo. ~ with com. come ~, please ande, por favor

alongside /əlɒŋˈsaɪd/ *adv* (*naut*) atracado. come ~ acostar □ *prep* ao lado de

aloof /əˈluːf/ *adv* à parte □ *a* distante. ~ness *n* reserva *f*

aloud /əˈlaʊd/ *adv* em voz alta

alphabet /ˈælfəbet/ *n* alfabeto *m*. ~ical /-ˈbetɪkl/ *a* alfabético

alpine /ˈælpaɪn/ *a* alpino, alpestre

Alps /ælps/ *npl* the ~ os Alpes *mpl*

already /ɔːlˈredɪ/ *adv* já

also /ˈɔːlsəʊ/ *adv* também

altar /ˈɔːltə(r)/ *n* altar *m*

alter /ˈɔːltə(r)/ *vt/i* alterar(-se), modificar(-se). ~ation /-ˈreɪʃn/ *n* alteração *f*; (*to garment*) modificação *f*

alternate[1] /ɔːlˈtɜːnət/ *a* alternado. ~ly *adv* alternadamente

alternate[2] /ˈɔːltəneɪt/ *vt/i* alternar(-se). ~ing current (*elect*) corrente *f* alterna. ~or (*elect*) alternador *m*

alternative /ɔːlˈtɜːnətɪv/ *a* alternativo □ *n* alternativa *f*. ~ly *adv* em alternativa. or ~ly ou então

although /ɔːlˈðəʊ/ *conj* embora, conquanto

altitude /ˈæltɪtjuːd/ *n* altitude *f*

altogether /ɔːltəˈgeðə(r)/ *adv* (*completely*) completamente; (*in total*) ao todo; (*on the whole*) de modo geral

aluminium /æljʊˈmɪnɪəm/ (*Amer* **aluminum** /əˈluːmɪnəm/) *n* alumínio *m*

always /ˈɔːlweɪz/ *adv* sempre

am /æm/ *see* be

a.m. /eɪˈem/ *adv* da manhã

amalgamate /əˈmælgəmeɪt/ *vt/i* amalgamar(-se); (*comm*) fundir

amass /əˈmæs/ *vt* amontoar, juntar

amateur /ˈæmətə(r)/ *n* & *a* amador (*m*). ~ish *a* (*pej*) de amador, (*P*) amadorístico

amaze /əˈmeɪz/ *vt* assombrar, espantar. ~ed *a* assombrado. ~ement *n* assombro *m*. ~ingly *adv* espantosamente

Amazon /ˈæməzən/ *n* the ~ o Amazonas

ambassador /æmˈbæsədə(r)/ *n* embaixador *m*

amber /ˈæmbə(r)/ *n* âmbar *m*; (*traffic light*) luz *f* amarela

ambiguous /æmˈbɪgjʊəs/ *a* ambíguo. ~ity /-ˈgjuːətɪ/ *n* ambigüidade *f*, (*P*) ambiguidade *f*

ambition /æmˈbɪʃn/ *n* ambição *f*. ~ous *a* ambicioso

ambivalent /æmˈbɪvələnt/ *a* ambivalente. ~ce *n* ambivalência *f*

amble /ˈæmbl/ *vi* caminhar sem pressa

ambulance /ˈæmbjʊləns/ *n* ambulância *f*

ambush /ˈæmbʊʃ/ *n* emboscada *f* □ *vt* fazer uma emboscada para, (*P*) fazer uma emboscada a

amenable /əˈmiːnəbl/ *a* ~ **to** (*responsive*) sensível a

amend /əˈmend/ *vt* emendar, corrigir. ~ment *n* (*to rule*) emenda *f*. ~s *n* make ~s for reparar, compensar

amenities /əˈmiːnətɪz/ *npl* (*pleasant features*) atrativos *mpl*, (*P*) atractivos *mpl*; (*facilities*) confortos *mpl*, comodidades *fpl*

America /ə'merɪkə/ *n* América *f.*
~n *a* & *n* americano (*m*).
~nism /-nɪzəm/ *n* americanismo *m.* **~nize** *vt* americanizar

amiable /'eɪmɪəbl/ *a* amável

amicable /'æmɪkəbl/ *a* amigável, amigo

amid(st) /ə'mɪd(st)/ *prep* entre, no meio de

amiss /ə'mɪs/ *a* & *adv* mal. **sth ~** qq coisa que não está bem. **take sth ~** levar qq coisa a mal

ammonia /ə'məʊnɪə/ *n* amoníaco *m*

ammunition /æmjʊ'nɪʃn/ *n* munições *fpl*

amnesia /æm'niːzɪə/ *n* amnésia *f.*

amnesty /'æmnəstɪ/ *n* anistia *f,* (*P*) amnistia *f*

amok /ə'mɒk/ *adv* **run ~** enlouquecer; (*crowd*) correr desordenadamente

among(st) /ə'mʌŋ(st)/ *prep* entre, no meio de. **~ ourselves** (aqui) entre nós

amoral /eɪ'mɒrəl/ *a* amoral

amorous /'æmərəs/ *a* amoroso

amount /ə'maʊnt/ *n* quantidade *f*; (*total*) montante *m*; (*sum of money*) quantia *f* □ *vi* **~ to** elevar-se a; (*fig*) equivaler a

amp /æmp/ *n* (*colloq*) ampère *m*

amphibi|**an** /æm'fɪbɪən/ *n* anfíbio *m.* **~ous** *a* anfíbio

ampl|**e** /'æmpl/ *a* (**-er, -est**) (*large, roomy*) amplo; (*enough*) suficiente, bastante. **~y** *adv* amplamente

amplif|**y** /'æmplɪfaɪ/ *vt* ampliar, amplificar. **~ier** *n* amplificador *m*

amputat|**e** /'æmpjʊteɪt/ *vt* amputar. **~ion** /-'teɪʃn/ *n* amputação *f*

amus|**e** /ə'mjuːz/ *vt* divertir. **~ement** *n* divertimento *m.* **~ing** *a* divertido

an /ən, æn/ *see* **a**

anachronism /ə'nækrənɪzəm/ *n* anacronismo *m*

anaem|**ia** /ə'niːmɪə/ *n* anemia *f.* **~ic** *a* anémico, (*P*) anémico

anaesthetic /ænɪs'θetɪk/ *n* anestético *m,* (*P*) anestésico *m.* **give an ~ to** anestesiar

anaesthetist /ə'niːsθətɪst/ *n* anestesista *mf*

anagram /'ænəgræm/ *n* anagrama *m*

analog(ue) /'ænəlɒg/ *n* análogo *m*

analogy /ə'nælədʒɪ/ *n* analogia *f*

analys|**e** /'ænəlaɪz/ *vt* analisar. **~t** /-ɪst/ *n* analista *mf*

analysis /ə'næləsɪs/ *n* (*pl* **-yses** /-əsiːz/) análise *f*

analytic(al) /ænə'lɪtɪk(l)/ *a* analítico

anarch|**y** /'ænəkɪ/ *n* anarquia *f.* **~ist** *n* anarquista *mf*

anatom|**y** /ə'nætəmɪ/ *n* anatomia *f.* **~ical** /ænə'tɒmɪkl/ *a* anatómico, (*P*) anatómico

ancest|**or** /'ænsestə(r)/ *n* antepassado *m.* **~ral** /-'sestrəl/ *a* ancestral (*pl* -ais)

ancestry /'ænsestrɪ/ *n* ascendência *f,* estirpe *f*

anchor /'æŋkə(r)/ *n* âncora *f* □ *vt/ i* ancorar. **~age** /-rɪdʒ/ *n* ancoradouro *m*

anchovy /'æntʃəvɪ/ *n* enchova *f,* (*P*) anchova *f*

ancient /'eɪnʃənt/ *a* antigo

ancillary /æn'sɪlərɪ/ *a* ancilar, (*P*) subordinado

and /ənd/; *emphatic* /ænd/ *conj* e. **go ~ see** vá ver. **better ~ better/less ~ less** cada vez melhor/menos *etc*

anecdote /'ænɪkdəʊt/ *n* anedota *f*

angel /'eɪndʒl/ *n* anjo *m.* **~ic** /æn'dʒelɪk/ *a* angélico, angelical

anger /'æŋgə(r)/ *n* cólera *f,* zanga *f* □ *vt* irritar

angle¹ /'æŋgl/ *n* ângulo *m*

angle² /'æŋgl/ *vi* (*fish*) pescar (à linha). **~ for** (*fig*: *compliments*) *information*) andar à procura de. ~r /-ə(r)/ *n* pescador *m*

anglicism /'æŋɡlɪsɪzəm/ *n* anglicismo *m*

Anglo- /'æŋɡləʊ/ *pref* anglo-

Anglo-Saxon /'æŋɡləʊ'sæksn/ *a* & *n* anglo-saxão (*m*)

angr|y /'æŋɡrɪ/ *a* (-ier, -iest) zangado. **get ~y** zangar-se (**with** com). ~**ily** *adv* furiosamente

anguish /'æŋɡwɪʃ/ *n* angústia *f*

angular /'æŋɡjʊlə(r)/ *a* angular; (*features*) anguloso

animal /'ænɪml/ *a* & *n* animal (*m*)

animate[1] /'ænɪmət/ *a* animado

animat|e[2] /'ænɪmeɪt/ *vt* animar. ~**ion** /-'meɪʃn/ *n* animação *f*. ~**ed cartoon** filme *m* de bonecos animados, (*P*) de desenhos animados

animosity /ænɪ'mɒsətɪ/ *n* animosidade *f*

aniseed /'ænɪsiːd/ *n* semente *f* de anis

ankle /'æŋkl/ *n* tornozelo *m*. ~ **sock** meia *f* soquete

annex /ə'neks/ *vt* anexar. ~**ation** /ænek'seɪʃn/ *n* anexação *f*

annexe /'æneks/ *n* anexo *m*

annihilate /ə'naɪəleɪt/ *vt* aniquilar

anniversary /ænɪ'vɜːsərɪ/ *n* aniversário *m*

announce /ə'naʊns/ *vt* anunciar. ~**ment** *n* anúncio *m*. ~**r** /-ə(r)/ *n* (*radio, TV*) locutor *m*

annoy /ə'nɔɪ/ *vt* irritar, aborrecer. ~**ance** *n* aborrecimento *m*. ~**ed** *a* aborrecido (**with** com). **get ~ed** aborrecer-se. ~**ing** *a* irritante

annual /'ænjʊəl/ *a* anual □ *n* (*bot*) planta *f* anual; (*book*) anuário *m*. ~**ly** *adv* anualmente

annuity /ə'njuːətɪ/ *n* anuidade *f*

annul /ə'nʌl/ *vt* (*pt* **annulled**) anular. ~**ment** *n* anulação *f*

anomal|y /ə'nɒməlɪ/ *n* anomalia *f*. ~**ous** *a* anómalo, (*P*) anómalo

anonym|ous /ə'nɒnɪməs/ *a* anónimo, (*P*) anónimo. ~**ity** /ænə'nɪmətɪ/ *n* anonimato *m*

anorak /'ænəræk/ *n* anoraque *m*, anorak *M*

another /ə'nʌðə(r)/ *a* & *pron* (um) outro. ~ **ten minutes** mais dez minutos. **to one ~** um ao outro, uns aos outros

answer /'aːnsə(r)/ *n* resposta *f*; (*solution*) solução *f* □ *vt* responder a; (*prayer*) atender □ *vi* responder. ~ **the door** atender à porta. ~ **back** retrucar, (*P*) responder torto. ~ **for** responder por. ~**able** *a* responsável (**for** por; **to** perante). ~**ing machine** *n* secretária *f* eletrónica

ant /ænt/ *n* formiga *f*

antagonis|m /æn'tæɡənɪzəm/ *n* antagonismo *m*. ~**t** *n* antagonista *mf*. ~**tic** /-'nɪstɪk/ *a* antagónico, (*P*) antagónico, hostil

antagonize /æn'tæɡənaɪz/ *vt* antagonizar, hostilizar

Antarctic /æn'taːktɪk/ *n* Antártico, (*P*) Antárctico *m* □ *a* antártico, (*P*) antárctico

ante- /'æntɪ/ *pref* ante-

antecedent /æntɪ'siːdnt/ *a* & *n* antecedente (*m*)

antelope /'æntɪləʊp/ *n* antílope *m*

antenatal /æntɪ'neɪtl/ *a* pré-natal

antenna /æn'tenə/ *n* (*pl* **-ae** /-iː/) antena *f*

anthem /'ænθəm/ *n* cântico *m*. **national ~** hino *m* nacional

anthology /æn'θɒlədʒɪ/ *n* antologia *f*

anthropolog|y /ænθrə'pɒlədʒɪ/ *n* antropologia *f*. ~**ist** *n* antropólogo *m*

anti- /ænti/ *pref* anti-. ~**aircraft** /-eəkraːft/ *a* antiaéreo

antibiotic /æntɪbaɪ'ɒtɪk/ *n* antibiótico *m*

antibody /'æntɪbɒdɪ/ *n* anticorpo *m*

anticipat|e /æn'tɪsɪpeɪt/ vt (foresee, expect) prever; (forestall) antecipar-se a. **~ion** /-'peɪʃn/ n antecipação f; (expectation) expectativa f. **in ~ion of** na previsão or expectativa de

anticlimax /æntr'klaɪmæks/ n anticlímax m; (let-down) decepção f. **it was an ~** (coll) não correspondeu à expectativa

anticlockwise /æntr'klɒkwaɪz/ adv & a no sentido contrário ao dos ponteiros dum relógio

antics /'æntɪks/ fpl (of clown) palhaçadas fpl; (behaviour) comportamento m bizarro

anticyclone /æntɪ'saɪkləʊn/ n anticiclone m

antidote /'æntɪdəʊt/ n antídoto m

antifreeze /'æntɪfriːz/ n anticongelante m

antihistamine /æntɪ'hɪstəmiːn/ a & n anti-histamínico (m)

antipathy /æn'tɪpəθɪ/ n antipatia f

antiquated /'æntɪkweɪtɪd/ a antiquado

antique /æn'tiːk/ a antigo □ n antiguidade f. **~ dealer** antiquário m. **~ shop** loja f de antiguidades, (P) antiquário m

antiquity /æn'tɪkwətɪ/ n antiguidade f

antiseptic /æntɪ'septɪk/ a & n antiséptico (m)

antisocial /æntɪ'səʊʃl/ a antisocial; (unsociable) insociável

antithesis /æn'tɪθəsɪs/ n (pl -eses) /-siːz/ antítese f.

antlers /'æntləz/ npl chifres mpl, esgalhos mpl

antonym /'æntənɪm/ n antónimo m, (P) antónimo m

anus /'eɪnəs/ n ânus m

anvil /'ænvɪl/ n bigorna f

anxiety /æŋ'zaɪətɪ/ n ansiedade f; (eagerness) ânsia f

anxious /'æŋkʃəs/ a (worried, eager) ansioso (**to** de, por). **~ly**

adv ansiosamente; (eagerly) impacientemente

any /'enɪ/ a & pron qualquer, quaisquer; (in neg and interr sentences) algum, alguns; (in neg sentences) nenhum, nenhuns; (every) todo. **at ~ moment** a qualquer momento. **at ~ rate** de qualquer modo, em todo o caso. **in ~ case** em todo o caso. **have you ~ money/friends?** você tem (algum) dinheiro/(alguns) amigos? **I don't have ~ time** não tenho nenhum tempo or tempo nenhum or tempo algum. **has she ~?** ela tem algum? **she doesn't have ~** ela não tem nenhum □ adv (at all) de modo algum or nenhum; (a little) um pouco. **~ the less/the worse** etc menos/pior etc

anybody /'enɪbɒdɪ/ pron qualquer pessoa; (somebody) alguém; (after negative) ninguém. **he didn't see ~** ele não viu ninguém

anyhow /'enɪhaʊ/ adv (no matter how) de qualquer maneira, ao acaso; (in any case) em todo o caso. **you can try, ~** em todo o caso, você pode tentar

anyone /'enɪwʌn/ pron = anybody

anything /'enɪθɪŋ/ pron (something) alguma coisa; (no matter what) qualquer coisa; (after negative) nada. **he didn't say ~** não disse nada. **it is ~ but cheap** é tudo menos barato. **~ you do** tudo o que você fizer

anyway /'enɪweɪ/ adv de qualquer modo; (in any case) em todo o caso

anywhere /'enɪweə(r)/ adv (somewhere) em qualquer parte; (after negative) em parte alguma/nenhuma. **~ else** em qualquer outro lado. **~ you go** onde quer que você vá. **he doesn't go ~ else** ele não vai a lado nenhum

apart /ə'pɑːt/ adv à parte; (*separated*) separado; (*into pieces*) aos bocados. **~ from** à parte, além de. **ten metres ~** a dez metros de distância entre si. **come ~** desfazer-se. **keep ~** manter separado. **take ~** desmontar

apartment /ə'pɑːtmənt/ n (*Amer*) apartamento m. **~s** aposentos mpl

apath|y /'æpəθɪ/ n apatia f. **~etic** /-'θetɪk/ a apático

ape /eɪp/ n macaco m □ vt macaquear

aperitif /ə'perətɪf/ n aperitivo m

aperture /'æpətʃə(r)/ n abertura f

apex /'eɪpeks/ n ápice m, cume m

apiece /ə'piːs/ adv cada, por cabeça

apologetic /əplə'dʒetɪk/ a (*tone etc*) apologético, de desculpas. **be ~** desculpar-se. **~ally** /-lɪ/ adv desculpando-se

apologize /ə'pɒlədʒaɪz/ vi desculpar-se (**for** de, por; **to** junto de, perante), pedir desculpa (**for**, por; **to**, a)

apology /ə'pɒlədʒɪ/ n desculpa f; (*defence of belief*) apologia f

apostle /ə'pɒsl/ n apóstolo m

apostrophe /ə'pɒstrəfɪ/ n apóstrofe f

appal /ə'pɔːl/ vt (*pt* **appalled**) estarrecer. **~ling** a estarrecedor

apparatus /æpə'reɪtəs/ n aparelho m

apparent /ə'pærənt/ a aparente. **~ly** adv aparentemente

apparition /æpə'rɪʃn/ n aparição f

appeal /ə'piːl/ vi (*jur*) apelar (**to** para); (*attract*) atrair (**to** a); (*for funds*) angariar □ n apelo m; (*attractiveness*) atrativo m; (*P*) atractivo m; (*for funds*) angariação f. **~ to sb for sth** pedir uma coisa a alg. **~ing** a (*attractive*) atraente

appear /ə'pɪə(r)/ vi aparecer; (*seem*) parecer; (*in court, theatre*)

apresentar-se. **~ance** n aparição f; (*aspect*) aparência f; (*in court*) comparecimento m, (*P*) comparência f

appease /ə'piːz/ vt apaziguar

appendage /ə'pendɪdʒ/ n apêndice m

appendicitis /əpendɪ'saɪtɪs/ n apendicite f

appendix /ə'pendɪks/ n (*pl* **-ices** /-siːz/) (*of book*) apêndice m; (*pl* **-ixes** /-ksɪz/) (*anat*) apêndice m

appetite /'æpɪtaɪt/ n apetite m

appetizer /'æpɪtaɪzə(r)/ n (*snack*) tira-gosto m; (*drink*) aperitivo m

appetizing /'æpɪtaɪzɪŋ/ a apetitoso

applau|d /ə'plɔːd/ vt/i aplaudir. **~se** n aplauso(s) m(pl)

apple /'æpl/ n maçã f. **~ tree** macieira f

appliance /ə'plaɪəns/ n aparelho m, instrumento m, utensílio m. **household ~s** utensílios mpl domésticos

applicable /'æplɪkəbl/ a aplicável

applicant /'æplɪkənt/ n candidato m (**for** a)

application /æplɪ'keɪʃn/ n aplicação f; (*request*) pedido m; (*form*) formulário m; (*for job*) candidatura f

appl|y /ə'plaɪ/ vt aplicar □ vi **~y to** (*refer*) aplicar-se a; (*ask*) dirigir-se a. **~y for** (*job, grant*) candidatar-se a. **~y o.s. to** aplicar-se a. **~ied** a aplicado

appoint /ə'pɔɪnt/ vt (*to post*) nomear; (*time, date*) marcar. **well-~ed** a bem equipado, bem provido. **~ment** n nomeação f; (*meeting*) entrevista f; (*with friends*) encontro m; (*with doctor etc*) consulta f, (*P*) marcação f; (*job*) posto m

apprais|e /ə'preɪz/ vt avaliar. **~al** n avaliação f

appreciable /ə'priːʃəbl/ a apreciável

appreciat|e /ə'pri:ʃɪeɪt/ *vt* (*value*) apreciar; (*understand*) compreender; (*be grateful for*) estar-ficar grato por □ *vi* encarecer. **~ion** /-'eɪʃn/ *n* apreciação *f*, (*rise in value*) encarecimento *m*; (*gratitude*) reconhecimento *m*, **~ive** /ə'priːʃɪətɪv/ *a* apreciador; (*grateful*) reconhecido

apprehen|d /æprɪ'hend/ *vt* (*seize, understand*) apreender; (*dread*) recear. **~sion** *n* apreensão *f*

apprehensive /æprɪ'hensɪv/ *a* apreensivo

apprentice /ə'prentɪs/ *n* aprendiz, -a *mf* □ *vt* pôr como aprendiz (**to** de). **~ship** *n* aprendizagem *f*

approach /ə'prəʊtʃ/ *vt* aproximar; (*with request or offer*) abordar □ *vi* aproximar-se □ *n* aproximação *f*. **~ to** (*problem*) abordagem *f* de; (*place*) acesso *m* a; (*person*) diligência junto de. **~able** *a* acessível

appropriate[1] /ə'prəʊprɪət/ *a* apropriado, próprio. **~ly** *adv* apropriadamente, a propósito

appropriate[2] /ə'prəʊprɪeɪt/ *vt* apropriar-se de

approval /ə'pruːvl/ *n* aprovação *f*. **on ~** (*comm*) sob condição, à aprovação

approv|e /ə'pruːv/ *vt/i* aprovar. **~e of** aprovar. **~ingly** *adv* com ar de aprovação

approximate[1] /ə'prɒksɪmət/ *a* aproximado. **~ly** *adv* aproximadamente

approximat|e[2] /ə'prɒksɪmeɪt/ *vt/i* aproximar(-se) de. **~ion** /-'meɪʃn/ *n* aproximação *f*

apricot /'eɪprɪkɒt/ *n* damasco *m*

April /'eɪprəl/ *n* Abril *m*. **~ Fool's Day** o primeiro de Abril, o dia das mentiras. **make an ~ fool of** pregar uma mentira em, (*P*) pregar uma mentira a

apron /'eɪprən/ *n* avental *m*

apt /æpt/ *a* apto; (*pupil*) dotado.

be ~ to ser propenso a. **~ly** *adv* apropriadamente

aptitude /'æptɪtjuːd/ *n* aptidão *f*, (*P*) aptitude *f*

aqualung /'ækwəlʌŋ/ *n* escafandro autónomo, (*P*) autónomo *m*

aquarium /ə'kweərɪəm/ *n* (*pl* **-ums**) aquário *m*

Aquarius /ə'kweərɪəs/ *n* (*astr*) Aquário *m*

aquatic /ə'kwætɪk/ *a* aquático; (*sport*) náutico, aquático

aqueduct /'ækwɪdʌkt/ *n* aqueduto *m*

Arab /'ærəb/ *a* & *n* árabe (*mf*). **~ic** *a* & *n* (*lang*) árabe (*m*), arábico (*m*). **a~ic numerals** algarismos *mpl* árabes or arábicos

Arabian /ə'reɪbɪən/ *a* árabe

arable /'ærəbl/ *a* arável

arbitrary /'ɑːbɪtrərɪ/ *a* arbitrário

arbitrat|e /'ɑːbɪtreɪt/ *vi* arbitrar. **~ion** /-'treɪʃn/ *n* arbitragem *f*. **~or** *n* árbitro *m*

arc /ɑːk/ *n* arco *m*. **~ lamp** lâmpada *f* de arco. **~ welding** soldadura *f* a arco

arcade /ɑː'keɪd/ *n* (*shop*) arcada *f*. **amusement ~** fliperama *m*

arch /ɑːtʃ/ *n* arco *m*; (*vault*) abóbada *f* □ *vt/i* arquear(-se)

arch- /ɑːtʃ/ *pref* arqui-.

archaeolog|y /ɑːkɪ'ɒlədʒɪ/ *n* arqueologia *f*. **~ical** /-ə'lɒdʒɪkl/ *a* arqueológico. **~ist** *n* arqueólogo *m*

archaic /ɑː'keɪɪk/ *a* arcaico

archbishop /ɑːtʃ'bɪʃəp/ *n* arcebispo *m*

arch-enemy /ɑːtʃ'enəmɪ/ *n* inimigo *m* número um

archer /'ɑːtʃə(r)/ *n* arqueiro *m*. **~y** *n* tiro *m* ao arco

archetype /'ɑːkɪtaɪp/ *n* arquétipo *m*

architect /'ɑːkɪtekt/ *n* arquiteto *m*, (*P*) arquitecto *m*

architectur|e /'ɑːkɪtektʃə(r)/ *n* arquitetura *f*, (*P*) arquitectura *f*

~al /-'tektʃərəl/ *a* arquitetônico, (P) arquitectónico

archiv|es /'a:kaɪvz/ *npl* arquivo *m*. **~ist** /-ɪvɪst/ *n* arquivista *mf*

archway /'a:tʃweɪ/ *n* arcada *f*

Arctic /'a:ktɪk/ *n* the **~** o Árctico *m* □ *a* Ártico, (P) árctico. **~ weather** tempo *m* glacial

ardent /'a:dnt/ *a* ardente. **~ly** *adv* ardentemente

ardour /'a:də(r)/ *n* ardor *m*

arduous /'a:djʊəs/ *a* árduo

are /ə(r)/; *emphatic* /a:(r)/ *see* **be**

area /'eərɪə/ *n* área *f*

arena /ə'ri:nə/ *n* arena *f*

aren't /a:nt/ = **are not**

Argentin|a /a:dʒən'ti:nə/ *n* Argentina *f*. **~ian** /-'tɪnɪən/ *a & n* argentino (*m*)

argue /'a:gju:/ *vi* discutir; (*reason*) argumentar, arguir □ *vt* (*debate*) discutir. **~ e** that alegar que. **~able** *a* alegável. **it's ~able that** pode-se sustentar que

argument /'a:gjʊmənt/ *n* (*dispute*) disputa *f*; (*reasoning*) argumento *m*. **~ative** /-'mentətɪv/ *a* que gosta de discutir, argumentativo

arid /'ærɪd/ *a* árido

Aries /'eəri:z/ *n* (*astr*) Áries *m*, Carneiro *m*

arise /ə'raɪz/ *vi* (*pt* **arose**, *pp* **arisen**) surgir. **~ from** resultar de

aristocracy /ærɪ'stɒkrəsɪ/ *n* aristocracia *f*

aristocrat /'ærɪstəkræt/ *n* aristocrata *mf*. **~ic** /-'krætɪk/ *a* aristocrático

arithmetic /ə'rɪθmətɪk/ *n* aritmética *f*

ark /a:k/ *n* Noah's **~** arca *f* de Noé

arm¹ /a:m/ *n* braço *m*. **~ in ~** de braço dado

arm² /a:m/ *vt* armar □ *n* (*mil*) arma *f*. **~ed robbery** assalto *m* à mão armada

armament /'a:məmənt/ *n* armamento *m*

armchair /'a:mtʃeə(r)/ *n* cadeira *f* de braços, poltrona *f*

armistice /'a:mɪstɪs/ *n* armistício *m*

armour /'a:mə(r)/ *n* armadura *f*; (*on tanks etc*) blindagem *f*. **~ed** *a* blindado

armoury /'a:mərɪ/ *n* arsenal *m*

armpit /'a:mpɪt/ *n* axila *f*, sovaco *m*

arms /a:mz/ *npl* armas *fpl*. **coat of ~** brasão *m*

army /'a:mɪ/ *n* exército *m*

aroma /ə'rəʊmə/ *n* aroma *m*. **~tic** /ærə'mætɪk/ *a* aromático

arose /ə'rəʊz/ *see* **arise**

around /ə'raʊnd/ *adv* em redor, em volta; (*here and there*) por aí □ *prep* em redor de, em torno de, em volta de; (*approximately*) aproximadamente. **~ here** por aqui

arouse /ə'raʊz/ *vt* despertar; (*excite*) excitar

arrange /ə'reɪndʒ/ *vt* arranjar; (*time, date*) combinar. **~ to do sth** combinar fazer alg coisa. **~ment** *n* arranjo *m*; (*agreement*) acordo *m*. **make ~ments (for)** (*plans*) tomar disposições (para); (*preparations*) fazer preparativos (para)

array /ə'reɪ/ *vt* revestir □ *n* **an ~ of** (*display*) um leque de, uma série de

arrears /ə'rɪəz/ *npl* dívidas *fpl* em atraso, atrasos *mpl*. **in ~** em atraso

arrest /ə'rest/ *vt* (*by law*) deter, prender; (*process, movement*) deter □ *n* captura *f*. **under ~** sob prisão

arrival /ə'raɪvl/ *n* chegada *f*. **new ~** recém-chegado *m*

arrive /ə'raɪv/ *vi* chegar

arrogan|t /'ærəgənt/ *a* arrogante. **~ce** *n* arrogância *f*. **~tly** *adv* com arrogância

arrow /ˈærəʊ/ n flecha f, seta f

arsenal /ˈɑːsənl/ n arsenal m

arsenic /ˈɑːsnɪk/ n arsénico m, (P) arsénico m

arson /ˈɑːsn/ n fogo m posto. **~ist** n incendiário m

art[1] /ɑːt/ n arte f. **the ~s** (univ) letras fpl. **fine ~** as belas-artes fpl. **~ gallery** museu m (de arte); (private) galeria f de arte

artery /ˈɑːtərɪ/ n artéria f

artful /ˈɑːtfl/ a manhoso. **~ness** n manha f

arthritis /ɑːˈθraɪtɪs/ n artrite f

artichoke /ˈɑːtɪtʃəʊk/ n alcachofra f. **Jerusalem ~** topinambo m

article /ˈɑːtɪkl/ n artigo m. **~d a** (jur) em estágio, (P) a estagiar

articulate[1] /ɑːˈtɪkjʊlət/ a que se exprime com clareza; (speech) bem articulado

articulat|**e**[2] /ɑːˈtɪkjʊleɪt/ vt/i articular. **~ed lorry** camião m articulado. **~ion** /-ˈleɪʃn/ n articulação f

artifice /ˈɑːtɪfɪs/ n artifício m

artificial /ɑːtɪˈfɪʃl/ a artificial

artillery /ɑːˈtɪlərɪ/ n artilharia f

artisan /ɑːtɪˈzæn/ n artífice mf, artesão m, artesã f

artist /ˈɑːtɪst/ n artista mf. **~ic** /-ˈtɪstɪk/ a artístico. **~ry** n arte f

artiste /ɑːˈtiːst/ n artista mf

artless /ˈɑːtlɪs/ a ingênuo, (P) ingénuo, simples

as /əz/; emphatic /æz/ adv & conj como; (while) enquanto; (when) quando. **~ a gift** de presente. **~ tall as** tão alto quanto, (P) tão alto como □ pron que. **I ate the same ~** he comi o mesmo que ele. **~ for, ~** to quanto a. **~ from** a partir de. **~ if** como se. **~ much** tanto, tantos. **~ many** quanto, quantos. **~ soon as** logo que. **~ well** (also) também. **~ well as** (in addition to) assim como

asbestos /æzˈbestəs/ n asbesto m, amianto m

ascend /əˈsend/ vt/i subir. **~ the throne** ascender or subir ao trono

ascent /əˈsent/ n ascensão f; (slope) subida f, rampa f

ascertain /æsəˈteɪn/ vt certificar-se de. **~ that** certificar-se de que

ascribe /əˈskraɪb/ vt atribuir

ash[1] /æʃ/ n (~-tree) freixo m

ash[2] /æʃ/ n cinza f. **A~ Wednesday** Quarta-feira f de Cinzas. **~en a** pálido

ashamed /əˈʃeɪmd/ a **be ~** ter vergonha, ficar envergonhado (of de, por)

ashore /əˈʃɔː(r)/ adv em terra. **go ~** desembarcar

ashtray /ˈæʃtreɪ/ n cinzeiro m

Asia /ˈeɪʃə/ n Ásia f. **~n a & n** asiático (m)

aside /əˈsaɪd/ adv de lado, de parte □ n (theat) aparte m. **~ from** (Amer) à parte

ask /ɑːsk/ vt/i pedir; (a question) perguntar; (invite) convidar. **~ sb sth** pedir uma coisa a alguém. **~ about** informar-se de. **~ after sb** pedir noticias de alg, perguntar por alg. **~ for** pedir. **~ sb in** mandar entrar alg. **~ sb to do sth** pedir alguém para fazer alguma coisa

askew /əˈskjuː/ adv & a de través, de esguelha

asleep /əˈsliːp/ adv & a adormecido; (numb) dormente. **fall ~** adormecer

asparagus /əˈspærəgəs/ n (plant) espargo m, (P) espargo m; (culin) aspargos mpl, (P) espargo m

aspect /ˈæspekt/ n aspecto m; (direction) exposição f

aspersions /əˈspɜːʃnz/ npl **cast ~ on** caluniar

asphalt /ˈæsfælt/ n asfalto m □ vt asfaltar

asphyxiat|**e** /əsˈfɪksɪeɪt/ vt/i asfixiar. **~ion** /-ˈeɪʃn/ n asfixia f

aspir|**e** /əsˈpaɪə(r)/ vi **~e to** aspirar a. **~ation** /æspəˈreɪʃn/ n aspiração f

aspirin /ˈæsprɪn/ n aspirina f

ass /æs/ n burro m. **make an ~ of o.s.** fazer papel de palhaço, (P) fazer figura de parvo

assail /əˈseɪl/ vt assaltar, agredir. **~ant** n assaltante mf, agressor m

assassin /əˈsæsɪn/ n assassino m

assassinat|**e** /əˈsæsɪneɪt/ vt assassinar. **~ion** /-ˈeɪʃn/ n assassinato m

assault /əˈsɔːlt/ n assalto m □ vt assaltar, atacar

assemble /əˈsembl/ vt (people) reunir; (fit together) montar □ vi reunir-se

assembly /əˈsemblɪ/ n assembléia f, (P) assembleia f. **~ line** linha f de montagem

assent /əˈsent/ n assentimento m □ vi **~ to** consentir em

assert /əˈsɜːt/ vt afirmar; (one's rights) reivindicar. **~ o.s.** impor-se. **~ion** /-ʃn/ n asserção f. **~ive** a dogmático, peremptório. **~iveness** n assertividade f, (P) firmeza f

assess /əˈses/ vt avaliar; (payment) estabelecer o montante de. **~ment** n avaliação f. **~or** n (valuer) avaliador m

asset /ˈæset/ n (advantage) vantagem f. **~s** (comm) ativo m, (P) activo m; (possessions) bens mpl

assiduous /əˈsɪdjʊəs/ a assíduo

assign /əˈsaɪn/ vt atribuir, destinar; (jur) transmitir. **~ sb to** designar alg para

assignation /æsɪɡˈneɪʃn/ n combinação f (de hora e local) de encontro

assignment /əˈsaɪnmənt/ n tarefa f, missão f; (jur) transmissão f

assimilat|**e** /əˈsɪmɪleɪt/ vt/i assimilar(-se). **~ion** /-ˈeɪʃn/ n assimilação f

assist /əˈsɪst/ vt/i ajudar. **~ance** n ajuda f, assistência f

assistant /əˈsɪstənt/ n (helper) assistente mf, auxiliar mf; (in shop) ajudante mf, empregado m □ a adjunto

associat|**e**[1] /əˈsəʊʃɪeɪt/ vt associar □ vi **~e with** conviver com. **~ion** /-ˈeɪʃn/ n associação f.

associate[2] /əˈsəʊʃɪət/ a & n associado (m)

assort|**ed** /əˈsɔːtɪd/ a variados; (foods) sortidos. **~ment** n sortimento m, (P) sortido m

assume /əˈsjuːm/ vt assumir; (presume) supor, presumir

assumption /əˈsʌmpʃn/ n suposição f

assurance /əˈʃʊərəns/ n certeza f, garantia f; (insurance) seguro m; (self-confidence) segurança f, confiança f

assure /əˈʃʊə(r)/ vt assegurar. **~d** a certo, garantido. **rest ~d that** ficar certo que

asterisk /ˈæstərɪsk/ n asterisco m

asthma /ˈæsmə/ n asma f. **~tic** /-ˈmætɪk/ a & n asmático (m)

astonish /əˈstɒnɪʃ/ vt espantar. **~ingly** adv espantosamente. **~ment** n espanto m

astound /əˈstaʊnd/ vt espantar

astray /əˈstreɪ/ adv & a **go ~** perder-se, extraviar-se. **lead ~** desencaminhar

astride /əˈstraɪd/ adv & prep escarranchado (em)

astringent /əˈstrɪndʒənt/ a & n adstringente (m)

astrolog|**y** /əˈstrɒlədʒɪ/ n astrologia f. **~er** n astrólogo m

astronaut /ˈæstrənɔːt/ n astronauta mf

astronom|**y** /əˈstrɒnəmɪ/ n astronomia f. **~er** n astrônomo m, (P) astrónomo m. **~ical** /æstrəˈnɒmɪkl/ a astronômico, (P) astronómico

astute /ə'stju:t/ *a* astuto, astucioso. **~ness** *n* astúcia *f*

asylum /ə'saɪləm/ *n* asilo *m*

at /ət/; *emphatic* /æt/ *prep* a, em. **~ sign** *m* arroba. **~ home** em casa. **~ night** à noite. **~ once** imediatamente; (*simultaneously*) ao mesmo tempo; (*at*) **school** na escola. **~ sea** no mar. **~ the door** na porta. **~ times** às vezes. **angry/ surprised ~** zangado/ surpreendido com. **not ~ all** de nada. **no wind ~ all** nenhum vento

ate /et/ *see* eat

atheist /'eɪθɪɪst/ *n* ateu *m*. **~m** /-zəm/ *n* ateísmo *m*

athlet|e /'æθli:t/ *n* atleta *mf*. **~ic** /-'letɪk/ *a* atlético. **~ics** /-'letɪks/ *n(pl)* atletismo *m*

Atlantic /ət'læntɪk/ *a* atlântico □ *n* **~ (Ocean)** Atlântico *m*

atlas /'ætləs/ *n* atlas *m*

atmospher|e /'ætməsfɪə(r)/ *n* atmosfera *f*. **~ic** /-'ferɪk/ *a* atmosférico

atom /'ætəm/ *n* átomo *m*. **~ic** /ə'tɒmɪk/ *a* atómico, (*P*) atómico. **~(ic) bomb** bomba *f* atómica

atomize /'ætəmaɪz/ *vt* atomizar, vaporizar, pulverizar. **~r** /-ə(r)/ *n* pulverizador *m*, vaporizador *m*

atone /ə'təʊn/ *vi* **~ for** expiar. **~ment** *n* expiação *f*

atrocious /ə'trəʊʃəs/ *a* atroz

atrocity /ə'trɒsətɪ/ *n* atrocidade *f*

atrophy /'ætrəfɪ/ *n* atrofia *f* □ *vt/i* atrofiar(-se)

attach /ə'tætʃ/ *vt/i* (*affix*) ligar (-se), prender(-se); (*join*) juntar (-se). **~ed** *a* (*document*) junto, anexo. **be ~ed to** (*like*) estar apegado a. **~ment** *n* ligação *f*; (*affection*) apego *m*; (*accessory*) acessório *m*

attaché /ə'tæʃeɪ/ *n* (*pol*) adido *m*. **~ case** pasta *f*

attack /ə'tæk/ *n* ataque *m* □ *vt/i* atacar. **~er** *n* atacante *mf*

attain /ə'tem/ *vt* atingir. **~able** *a* atingível. **~ment** *n* consecução *f*. **~ments** *npl* conhecimentos *mpl*, talentos *mpl* adquiridos

attempt /ə'tempt/ *vt* tentar □ *n* tentativa *f*

attend /ə'tend/ *vt/i* atender (**to** a); (*escort*) acompanhar; (*look after*) tratar; (*meeting*) comparecer a; (*school*) frequentar, (*P*) frequentar. **~ance** *n* comparecimento *m*; (*times present*) frequência *f*, (*P*) frequência *f*; (*people*) assistência *f*

attendant /ə'tendənt/ *a* concomitante, que acompanha □ *n* empregado *m*; (*servant*) servidor *m*

attention /ə'tenʃn/ *n* atenção *f*. **~!** (*mil*) sentido! **pay ~** prestar atenção (**to** a)

attentive /ə'tentɪv/ *a* atento; (*considerate*) atencioso

attest /ə'test/ *vt/i* **~ (to)** atestar. **~ a signature** reconhecer uma assinatura. **~ation** /ætə'steɪʃn/ *n* atestação *f*, prova *f*

attic /'ætɪk/ *n* sótão *m*, águafurtada *f*

attitude /'ætɪtju:d/ *n* atitude *f*

attorney /ə'tɜ:nɪ/ *n* (*pl* **-eys**) procurador *m*; (*Amer*) advogado *m*

attract /ə'trækt/ *vt* atrair. **~ion** /-ʃn/ *n* atração *f*, (*P*) atracção *f*; (*charm*) atrativo *m*, (*P*) atractivo *m*

attractive /ə'træktɪv/ *a* atraente. **~ly** *adv* atraentemente, agradavelmente

attribute¹ /ə'trɪbju:t/ *vt* **~ to** atribuir a

attribute² /'ætrɪbju:t/ *n* atributo *m*

attrition /ə'trɪʃn/ *n* **war of ~** guerra *f* de desgaste

aubergine /'əʊbəʒi:n/ *n* berinjela *f*

auburn /'ɔ:bən/ *a* cor de acaju, castanho-avermelhado

auction /'ɔ:kʃn/ *n* leilão *m* □ *vt* leiloar. **~eer** /-ə'nɪə(r)/ *n* leiloeiro *m*, (*P*) pregoeiro *m*

audacious /ɔ:'deɪʃəs/ a audacioso, audaz. **~ty** /-æsɪtɪ/ n audácia f

audible /'ɔ:dəbl/ a audível

audience /'ɔ:dɪəns/ n auditório m; (theat, radio; interview) audiência f

audiovisual /ɔ:dɪəʊ'vɪʒʊəl/ a audio-visual

audit /'ɔ:dɪt/ n auditoria f □ vt fazer uma auditoria

audition /ɔ:'dɪʃn/ n audição f □ vt dar/fazer uma audição

auditor /'ɔ:dɪtə(r)/ n perito-contador m, (P) perito-contabilista m

auditorium /ɔ:dɪ'tɔ:rɪəm/ n auditório m

augment /ɔ:g'ment/ vt/i aumentar(-se)

augur /'ɔ:gə(r)/ vi ~ **well/ill** ser de bom ou mau agouro

August /'ɔ:gəst/ n Agosto m

aunt /ɑ:nt/ n tia f

au pair /əʊ'peə(r)/ n au pair f

aura /'ɔ:rə/ n aura f, emanação f

auspices /'ɔ:spɪsɪz/ npl **under the ~ of** sob os auspícios or o patrocínio de

auspicious /ɔ:'spɪʃəs/ a auspicioso

austere /ɒ'stɪə(r)/ a austero. **~ity** /-erətɪ/ n austeridade f

Australia /ɒ'streɪlɪə/ n Austrália f. **~n** a & n australiano (m)

Austria /'ɒstrɪə/ n Áustria f. **~n** a & n austríaco (m)

authentic /ɔ:'θentɪk/ a autêntico. **~ity** /-ən'tɪsətɪ/ n autenticidade f

authenticate /ɔ:'θentɪkeɪt/ vt autenticar

author /'ɔ:θə(r)/ n autor m, autora f. **~ship** n (origin) autoria f

authoritarian /ɔ:θɒrɪ'teərɪən/ a autoritário

authority /ɔ:'θɒrətɪ/ n autoridade f; (permission) autorização f. **~ative** /-ɪtətɪv/ a (trusted) autorizado; (manner) autoritário

authorize /'ɔ:θəraɪz/ vt autorizar. **~ation** /-'zeɪʃn/ n autorização f

autistic /ɔ:'tɪstɪk/ a autista, autístico

autobiography /ɔ:təˈbaɪɒɡrəfɪ/ n autobiografia f

autocrat /'ɔ:təkræt/ n autocrata mf. **~ic** /-'krætɪk/ a autocrático

autograph /'ɔ:təgrɑ:f/ n autógrafo m □ vt autografar

automate /'ɔ:təmeɪt/ vt automatizar. **~ion** /-'meɪʃn/ n automação f

automatic /ɔ:tə'mætɪk/ a automático □ n (car) automático m. **~ally** /-klɪ/ adv automaticamente

automobile /'ɔ:təməbi:l/ n (Amer) automóvel m

autonom|y /ɔ:'tɒnəmɪ/ n autonomia f. **~ous** a autônomo, (P) autónomo

autopsy /'ɔ:tɒpsɪ/ n autópsia f

autumn /'ɔ:təm/ n outono m. **~al** /-'tʌmnəl/ a outonal

auxiliary /ɔ:g'zɪlɪərɪ/ a & n auxiliar (mf). **~ verb** verbo m auxiliar

avail /ə'veɪl/ vt ~ **o.s.** of servir-se de □ vi (be of use) valer □ n of no ~ inútil. to no ~ sem resultado, em vão

available /ə'veɪləbl/ a disponível. **~ility** /-'bɪlətɪ/ n disponibilidade f

avalanche /'ævəlɑ:nʃ/ n avalanche f

avaric|e /'ævərɪs/ n avareza f. **~ious** /-'rɪʃəs/ a avarento

avenge /ə'vendʒ/ vt vingar

avenue /'ævənju:/ n avenida f; (fig: line of approach) via f

average /'ævərɪdʒ/ n média f □ a médio □ vt tirar a média de; (produce, do) fazer em média □ vi ~ **out at** dar de média, dar uma média de. **on ~** em média

avers|e /ə'vɜ:s/ a be **~e to** ser avesso a. **~ion** /-ʃn/ n aversão f, repugnância f

avert /ə'vɜːt/ vt (turn away) desviar; (ward off) evitar

aviary /'eɪvɪərɪ/ n aviário m

aviation /eɪvɪ'eɪʃn/ n aviação f

avid /'ævɪd/ a ávido

avocado /ævə'kɑːdəʊ/ n (pl -s) abacate m

avoid /ə'vɔɪd/ vt evitar. **~able** a que se pode evitar, evitável. **~ance** n evitação f

await /ə'weɪt/ vt aguardar

awake /ə'weɪk/ vt/i (pt **awoke**, pp **awoken**) acordar □ a **be ~** estar acordado

awaken /ə'weɪkən/ vt/i despertar.

~ing n despertar m

award /ə'wɔːd/ vt atribuir, conferir; (jur) adjudicar □ n recompensa f, prêmio m, (P) prémio m; (scholarship) bolsa f

aware /ə'weə(r)/ a ciente, cônscio. **be ~ of** estar consciente de or ter consciência de. **become ~ of** tomar consciência de. **make sb ~ of** sensibilizar alg para. **~ness** n consciência f

away /ə'weɪ/ adv (at a distance) longe; (to a distance) para longe; (absent) fora; (persistently) sem parar; (entirely) completamente. **eight miles ~** a oito milhas (de distância). **four days ~** daí a quatro dias □ a & n **~ (match)** jogo m fora de casa

awe /ɔː/ n assombro m, admiração f reverente, terror m respeitoso. **~some** a assombroso. **~struck** a assombrado, aterrado

awful /'ɔːfl/ a terrível. **~ly** adv muito, terrivelmente

awhile /ə'waɪl/ adv por algum tempo

awkward /'ɔːkwəd/ a difícil; (clumsy, difficult to use) desajeitado, maljeitoso; (inconvenient) inconveniente; (embarrassing) embaraçoso; (embarrassed) embaraça-do. **an ~ customer** (colloq) um pregueso perigoso or intratável

awning /'ɔːnɪŋ/ n toldo m

awoke, awoken /ə'wəʊk, ə'wəʊkən/ see **awake**

awry /ə'raɪ/ adv torto. **go ~** dar errado. **be ~** estar torto

axe /æks/ n machado m □ vt (pres p **axing**) (reduce) cortar; (dismiss) despedir

axiom /'æksɪəm/ n axioma m

axis /'æksɪs/ n (pl **axes** /-iːz/) eixo m

axle /'æksl/ n eixo (de roda) m

Azores /ə'zɔːz/ n Açores mpl

B

BA abbr see **Bachelor of Arts**

babble /'bæbl/ vi balbuciar; (baby) palrar; (stream) murmurar □ n balbucio m; (of baby) palrice f; (of stream) murmúrio m

baboon /bə'buːn/ n babuíno m

baby /'beɪbɪ/ n bebê m, (P) bebé m. **~ carriage** (Amer) carrinho m de bebê, (P) bebé. **~-sit** vi tomar conta de crianças. **~-sitter** n baby-sitter mf, babá f

babyish /'beɪbɪɪʃ/ a infantil

bachelor /'bætʃələ(r)/ n solteiro m. **B~ of Arts/Science** Bacharel m em Letras/Ciências

back /bæk/ n (of person, hand, chair) costas fpl; (of animal) dorso m; (of car, train) parte f traseira; (of house, room) fundo m; (of coin) reverso m; (of page) verso m; (football) beque m; zagueiro m, (P) defesa m □ a traseiro, posterior; (taxes) em atraso □ adv atrás, para trás; (returned) de volta □ vt (support) apoiar; (horse) apostar em; (car) (fazer) recuar □ vi recuar. **at the ~ of beyond** em casa do diabo, no fim do mundo. **~-bencher** n (pol) deputado m sem pasta. **~ down** desistir (from de). **~**

number número *m* atrasado. ~
out (*of an undertaking etc*) fugir
(ao combinado *etc*). ~ **up** (*auto*)
fazer marcha à ré, (*P*) atrás;
(*comput*) tirar um back-up de.
~**-up** *n* apoio *m*; (*comput*) back-
up *m*; (*Amer: traffic-jam*) engarrafamento *m* □ *a* de reserva;
(*comput*) back-up

backache /'bækeɪk/ *n* dor *f* nas
costas

backbiting /'bækbaɪtɪŋ/ *n* maledicência *f*

backbone /'bækbəʊn/ *n* espinha *f*
dorsal

backdate /bæk'deɪt/ *vt* antedatar

backer /'bækə(r)/ *n* (*of horse*)
apostador *m*, (*of cause*) partidário *m*, apoiante *mf*; (*comm*) patrocinador *m*, financiador *m*

backfire /bæk'faɪə(r)/ *vi* (*auto*)
dar explosões no tubo de escape;
(*fig*) sair o tiro pela culatra

background /'bækɡraʊnd/ *n* (*of
picture*) fundo *m*, segundo-plano
m; (*context*) contexto *m*; (*environment*) meio *m*; (*experience*) formação *f*

backhand /'bækhænd/ *n* (*tennis*)
esquerda *f*. ~**ed** *a* com as costas
da mão. ~**ed compliment** cumprimento *m* ambíguo. ~**er**
/-'hændə(r)/ *n* (*sl: bribe*) suborno
m, (*P*) luvas *fpl* (*colloq*)

backing /'bækɪŋ/ *n* apoio *m*;
(*comm*) patrocínio *m*

backlash /'bæklæʃ/ *n* (*fig*) reação
f violenta, repercussões *fpl*

backlog /'bæklɒɡ/ *n* acúmulo *m*
(de trabalho *etc*)

backside /'bæksaɪd/ *n* (*colloq: buttocks*) traseiro *m*

backstage /bæk'steɪdʒ/ *a & adv*
por detrás dos bastidores

backstroke /'bækstrəʊk/ *n* nado
m de costas

backtrack /'bæktræk/ *vi* (*fig*) voltar atrás

backward /'bækwəd/ *a* retrógra-

do; (*retarded*) atrasado; (*step,
look, etc*) para trás

backwards /'bækwədz/ *adv* para
trás; (*walk*) para trás; (*fall*) de
costas, para trás; (*in reverse
order*) de trás para diante, às
avessas. **go** ~ **and forwards** ir
e vir, andar para trás e para a
frente. **know sth** ~ saber alg
coisa de trás para a frente

backwater /'bækwɔːtə(r)/ *n* (*pej:
place*) lugar *m* atrasado

bacon /'beɪkən/ *n* toucinho *m*
defumado; (*in rashers*) bacon *m*

bacteria /bæk'tɪərɪə/ *npl* bacté-
rias *fpl*. ~**l** *a* bacteriano

bad /bæd/ *a* (**worse, worst**) mau;
(*accident*) grave; (*food*) estragado; (*ill*) doente. **feel** ~ sentir-se
mal. ~ **language** palavrões *mpl*.
~**-mannered** *a* mal educado.
~**-tempered** *a* mal humorado.
~**ly** *adv* mal; (*seriously*) gravemente. **want** ~**ly** (*desire*) desejar imensamente, ter grande
vontade de; (*need*) precisar muito de

badge /bædʒ/ *n* emblema *m*;
(*policeman's*) crachá *m*, (*P*) distintivo *m*

badger /'bædʒə(r)/ *n* texugo *m* □
vt atormentar; (*pester*) importu-
nar

badminton /'bædmɪntən/ *n* badminton *m*

baffle /'bæfl/ *vt* atrapalhar, desconcertar

bag /bæɡ/ *n* saco *m*; (*handbag*) bolsa *f*, carteira *f*. ~**s**
(*luggage*) malas *fpl* □ *vt* (*pt
bagged*) ensacar; (*colloq: take*)
embolsar

baggage /'bæɡɪdʒ/ *n* bagagem *f*

baggy /'bæɡɪ/ *a* (*clothes*) muito
largo, bufante

bagpipes /'bæɡpaɪps/ *npl* gaita *f*
de foles

Bahamas /bə'hɑːməz/ *npl* **the** ~
as Bahamas *fpl*

bail[1] /beɪl/ n fiança f □ vt pôr em liberdade sob fiança. **be out on ~** estar solto sob fiança

bail[2] /beɪl/ vt ~ **(out)** (naut) esgotar, tirar água de

bailiff /'beɪlɪf/ n (officer) oficial m de diligências; (of estate) feitor m

bait /beɪt/ n isca f □ vt pôr isca; (fig) atormentar (com insultos), atazanar

bak|e /beɪk/ vt/i cozer (no forno); (bread, cakes, etc) assar; (in the sun) torrar. **~er** n padeiro m; (of cakes) doceiro m. **~ing** n cozedura f; (batch) fornada f. **~ing-powder** n fermento m em pó. **~ing tin** forma f

bakery /'beɪkərɪ/ n padaria f; (cakes) confeitaria f

balance /'bæləns/ n equilíbrio m; (scales) balança f; (sum) saldo m; (comm) balanço m. **~ of power** equilíbrio m político. **~ of trade** balança f comercial. **~-sheet** n balanço m □ vt equilibrar; (weigh up) pesar; (budget) equilibrar □ vi equilibrar-se. **~d** a equilibrado

balcony /'bælkənɪ/ n balcão m; (in a house) varanda f

bald /bɔːld/ a (-er, -est) calvo, careca; (tyre) careca. **~ing** a **be ~ing** ficar calvo. **~ly** adv a nu e cru, (P) secamente. **~ness** n calvície f

bale[1] /beɪl/ n (of straw) fardo m; (of cotton) balote m □ vt enfardar

bale[2] /beɪl/ vi ~ **out** saltar em páraquedas

balk /bɔːk/ vt frustrar, contrariar □ vi ~ **at** assustar-se com, recuar perante

ball[1] /bɔːl/ n bola f. **~-bearing** n rolamento m de esferas. **~-cock** n válvula f de depósito de água. **~-point** n esferográfica f

ball[2] /bɔːl/ n (dance) baile m

ballad /'bæləd/ n balada f

ballast /'bæləst/ n lastro m

ballerina /bælə'riːnə/ n bailarina f

ballet /'bæleɪ/ n balé m, (P) ballet m, bailado m

balloon /bə'luːn/ n balão m

ballot /'bælət/ n escrutínio m. **~(-paper)** n cédula f eleitoral, (P) boletim m de voto. **~-box** n urna f □ vi (pt balloted) (pol) votar □ vt (members) consultar por voto secreto

ballroom /'bɔːlruːm/ n salão m de baile

balm /baːm/ n bálsamo m. **~y** a balsâmico; (mild) suave

balustrade /bælə'streɪd/ n balaustrada f

bamboo /bæm'buː/ n bambu m

ban /bæn/ vt (pt **banned**) banir. **~ from** proibir de □ n proibição f

banal /bə'naːl/ a banal. **~ity** /-æləti/ n banalidade f

banana /bə'naːnə/ n banana f

band /bænd/ n (for fastening) cinta f, faixa f; (strip) tira f, banda f; (mus: mil) banda f; (mus: dance, jazz) conjunto m; (group) bando m □ vi ~ **together** juntar-se

bandage /'bændɪdʒ/ n atadura f, (P) ligadura f □ vt ligar

bandit /'bændɪt/ n bandido m

bandstand /'bændstænd/ n coreto m

bandwagon /'bændwægən/ n **climb on the ~** (fig) apanhar o trem

bandy[1] /'bændɪ/ vt trocar. **~ a story about** espalhar uma história

bandy-legged /'bændɪlegd/ a cambaio, de pernas tortas

bang /bæŋ/ n (blow) pancada f; (loud noise) estouro m, estrondo m; (of gun) detonação f □ vt/i (hit, shut) bater □ vi explodir □ int pum. **~ in the middle** jogar no meio. **shut the door with a ~** bater (com) a porta

banger /'bæŋə(r)/ n (*firework*) bomba f; (*sl: sausage*) salsicha f. **(old)** ~ (*sl: car*) calhambeque m (*colloq*)

bangle /'bæŋgl/ n pulseira f, bracelete m

banish /'bænɪʃ/ vt banir, desterrar

banisters /'bænɪstəz/ npl corrimão m

banjo /'bændʒəʊ/ pl (**-os**) banjo m

bank[1] /bæŋk/ n (*of river*) margem f; (*of earth*) talude m; (*of sand*) banco m □ vt amontoar □ vi (*aviat*) inclinar-se numa curva

bank[2] /bæŋk/ n (*comm*) banco m □ vt depositar no banco. ~ account conta f bancária. ~ holiday feriado m nacional. ~ on contar com. ~ rate taxa f bancária. ~ with ter conta em

bank|er /'bæŋkə(r)/ n banqueiro m. ~ing /-ɪŋ/ n operações fpl bancárias; (*career*) carreira f bancária, banca f

banknote /'bæŋknəʊt/ n nota f de banco

bankrupt /'bæŋkrʌpt/ a & n falido (m). **go** ~ falir □ vt levar à falência. ~cy n falência f, bancarrota f

banner /'bænə(r)/ n bandeira f, estandarte m

banns /bænz/ npl proclamas mpl, (*P*) banhos mpl

banquet /'bæŋkwɪt/ n banquete m

banter /'bæntə(r)/ n gracejo m, brincadeira f □ vi gracejar, brincar

baptism /'bæptɪzəm/ n batismo m, (*P*) baptismo m

Baptist /'bæptɪst/ n batista mf, (*P*) baptista mf

baptize /bæp'taɪz/ vt batizar, (*P*) baptizar

bar /ba:(r)/ n (*of chocolate*) tablete f, barra f; (*of metal, soap, sand etc*) barra f; (*of door, window*) tranca f; (*in pub*) bar m; (*counter*)

balcão m, bar m; (*mus*) barra f de compasso; (*fig: obstacle*) barreira f; (*in lawcourt*) teia f. **the B**~ a advocacia f □ vt (*pt* **barred**) (*obstruct*) barrar; (*prohibit*) proibir (**from** de); (*exclude*) excluir; (*door, window*) trancar □ *prep* salvo, exceto, (*P*) excepto. ~ **none** sem exceção, (*P*) excepção. ~ **code** código m de barra. **behind** ~**s** na cadeia

Barbados /ba:'beɪdɒs/ n Barbados mpl

barbarian /ba:'beərɪən/ n bárbaro m

barbari|c /ba:'bærɪk/ a bárbaro. ~**ty** /-əti/ n barbaridade f

barbarous /'ba:bərəs/ a bárbaro

barbecue /'ba:bɪkju:/ n (*grill*) churrasqueira f; (*occasion, food*) churrasco m □ vt assar

barbed /ba:bd/ a ~ **wire** arame m farpado

barber /'ba:bə(r)/ n barbeiro m

barbiturate /ba:'bɪtjʊrət/ n barbitúrico m

bare /beə(r)/ a (**-er, -est**) nu; (*room*) vazio; (*mere*) mero □ vt pôr à mostra, pôr a nu, descobrir

bareback /'beəbæk/ adv em pêlo

barefaced /'beəfeɪst/ a descarado

barefoot /'beə(r)fʊt/ adv descalço

barely /'beəlɪ/ adv apenas, mal

bargain /'ba:gɪn/ n (*deal*) negócio m; (*good buy*) pechincha f □ vi negociar; (*haggle*) regatear. ~ **for** esperar

barge /ba:dʒ/ n barcaça f □ vi ~ **in** interromper (despropositadamente); (*into room*) irromper

bark[1] /ba:k/ n (*of tree*) casca f

bark[2] /ba:k/ n (*of dog*) latido m □ vi latir. **his** ~ **is worse than his bite** cão que ladra não morde

barley /'ba:lɪ/ n cevada f. ~ **sugar** n açúcar m de cevada. ~ **water** n água f de cevada

barmaid /'ba:meɪd/ n empregada f de bar

barman /'ba:mən/ *n* (*pl* **-men**) barman *m*, empregado *m* de bar

barmy /'ba:mɪ/ *a* (*sl*) maluco

barn /ba:n/ *n* celeiro *m*

barometer /bə'rɒmɪtə(r)/ *n* barómetro *m*, (*P*) barómetro *m*

baron /'bærən/ *n* barão *m*. **~ess** *n* baronesa *f*

baroque /bə'rɒk/ *a* & *n* barroco (*m*)

barracks /'bærəks/ *n* quartel *m*, caserna *f*

barrage /'bæra:ʒ/ *n* barragem *f*; (*fig*) enxurrada *f*; (*mil*) fogo *m* de barragem

barrel /'bærəl/ *n* (*of oil, wine*) barril *m*; (*of gun*) cano *m*. **~-organ** *n* realejo *m*

barren /'bærən/ *a* estéril; (*soil*) árido, estéril

barricade /bærɪ'keɪd/ *n* barricada *f* □ *vt* barricar

barrier /'bærɪə(r)/ *n* barreira *f*; (*hindrance*) entrave *m*, barreira *f*

barring /'ba:rɪŋ/ *prep* salvo, exceto, (*P*) excepto

barrister /'bærɪstə(r)/ *n* advogado *m*

barrow /'bærəʊ/ *n* carrinho *m* de mão

barter /'ba:tə(r)/ *n* troca *f* □ *vt* trocar

base /beɪs/ *n* base *f* □ *vt* basear (**on** em) □ *a* baixo, ignóbil. **~less** *a* infundado

baseball /'beɪsbɔ:l/ *n* beisebol *m*

basement /'beɪsmənt/ *n* porão *m*, (*P*) cave *f*

bash /bæʃ/ *vt* bater com violência □ *n* pancada *f* forte. **have a ~ at** (*sl*) experimentar

bashful /'bæʃfl/ *a* tímido

basic /'beɪsɪk/ *a* básico, elementar, fundamental. **~ally** *adv* basicamente, no fundo

basil /'bæzl/ *n* mangericão *m*

basin /'beɪsn/ *n* bacia *f*; (*for food*) tigela *f*; (*naut*) ante-doca *f*; (*for washing*) pia *f*

basis /'beɪsɪs/ *n* (*pl* **bases** /-si:z/) base *f*

bask /ba:sk/ *vi* **~ in the sun** apanhar sol

basket /'ba:skɪt/ *n* cesto *m*

basketball /'ba:skɪtbɔ:l/ *n* basquete(bol) *m*

Basque /ba:sk/ *a* & *n* basco (*m*)

bass[1] /bæs/ *n* (*pl* **bass**) (*fish*) perca *f*

bass[2] /beɪs/ *a* (*mus*) grave □ *n* (*pl* **basses**) (*mus*) baixo *m*

bassoon /bə'su:n/ *n* fagote *m*

bastard /'ba:stəd/ *n* (*illegitimate child*) bastardo *m*; (*sl: pej*) safado (*sl*) *m*; (*colloq: not pej*) cara *m*

baste /beɪst/ *vt* (*culin*) regar (com molho)

bastion /'bæstɪən/ *n* bastião *m*, baluarte *m*

bat[1] /bæt/ *n* (*cricket*) pá *f*; (*baseball*) bastão *m*; (*table tennis*) rafuete *f* □ *vt/i* (*pt* **batted**) bater (em). **without ~ting an eyelid** sem pestanejar

bat[2] /bæt/ *n* (*zool*) morcego *m*

batch /bætʃ/ *n* (*loaves*) fornada *f*; (*people*) monte *m*; (*goods*) remessa *f*; (*papers, letters etc*) batelada *f*, monte *m*

bated /'beɪtɪd/ *a* **with ~ breath** com a respiração em suspenso, com a respiração suspensa

bath /ba:θ/ *n* (*pl* **-s** /ba:ðz/) banho *m*; (*tub*) banheira *f*. **~s** (*washing*) banho *m* público; (*swimming*) piscina *f* □ *vt* dar banho a □ *vi* tomar banho

bathe /beɪð/ *vt* dar banho em; (*wound*) limpar □ *vi* tomar banho (de mar) □ *n* banho *m* (de mar). **~r** /-ə(r)/ *n* banhista *mf*

bathing /'beɪðɪŋ/ *n* banho *m* de mar. **~-costume/-suit** *n* traje *m* de banho, (*P*) fato *m* de banho

bathrobe /'ba:θrəʊb/ *n* (*Amer*) roupão *m*

bathroom /'baːθruːm/ n banheiro m, (P) casa f de banho

baton /'bætən/ n (mus) batuta f; (policeman's) cassetete m; (mil) bastão m

battalion /bə'tæljən/ n batalhão m

batter /'bætə(r)/ vt bater, espancar, maltratar □ n (culin: for cakes) massa f de bolos; (culin: for frying) massa f de empanar. ~ed a (car, pan) amassado; (child, wife) maltratado, espancado. ~ing n take a ~ing levar pancada or uma surra

battery /'bætərɪ/ n (mil, auto) bateria f; (electr) pilha f

battle /'bætl/ n batalha f; (fig) luta f □ vi combater, batalhar, lutar

battlefield /'bætlfiːld/ n campo m de batalha

battlements /'bætlmənts/ npl ameias fpl

battleship /'bætlʃɪp/ n couraçado m

baulk /bɔːlk/ vt/i = balk

bawdy /'bɔːdɪ/ a (-ier, -iest) obsceno, indecente

bawl /bɔːl/ vt/i berrar

bay¹ /beɪ/ n (bot) loureiro m

bay² /beɪ/ n (geog) baía f. ~ window janela f saliente

bay³ /beɪ/ n (bark) latido m □ vi latir. at ~ (animal; fig) cercado, (P) em apuros. keep at ~ manter à distância

bayonet /'beɪənɪt/ n baioneta f

bazaar /bə'zɑː(r)/ n bazar m

BC abbr (before Christ) a C

be /biː/ vi (pres am, are, is; pt was, were; pp been) (permanent quality/place) ser; (temporary place/state) estar; (become) ficar. ~ hot/right etc ter calor/razão etc. he's 30 (age) ele tem 30 anos. it's fine/cold etc (weather) faz bom tempo/frio etc. how are you? (health) como está? I'm a doctor

— are you? eu sou médico — é mesmo? it's pretty, isn't it? é bonito, não é? he is to come (must) ele deve vir. how much is it? (cost) quanto é? ~ reading eating etc estar lendo/comendo etc. the money was found o dinheiro foi encontrado. have been to ter ido a, ter estado em

beach /biːtʃ/ n praia f

beacon /'biːkən/ n farol m; (marker) baliza f

bead /biːd/ n conta f. ~ of sweat gota f de suor

beak /biːk/ n bico m

beaker /'biːkə(r)/ n copo m de plástico com bico; (in lab) proveta f

beam /biːm/ n (of wood) trave f, viga f; (of light) raio m; (of torch) feixe m de luz □ vt/i (radiate) irradiar; (fig) sorrir radiante. ~ing a radiante

bean /biːn/ n feijão m. broad ~ fava f; **coffee** ~ s café m em grão. **runner** ~ feijão m verde

bear¹ /beə(r)/ n urso m

bear² /beə(r)/ vt/i (pt bore, pp borne) sustentar, suportar; (endure) aguentar, (P) aguentar, suportar; (child) dar à luz. ~ in mind ter em mente, lembrar. ~ left virar à esquerda. ~ on relacionar-se com, ter a ver com. ~ out confirmar. ~ up! coragem! ~able a tolerável, suportável. ~er n portador m

beard /bɪəd/ n barba f. ~ed a barbado, com barba

bearing /'beərɪŋ/ n (manner) porte m; (relevance) relação f; (naut) marcação f. get one's ~s orientar-se

beast /biːst/ n (animal, person) besta f, animal m; (in fables) fera f. ~ of burden besta f de carga

beat /biːt/ vt/i (pt beat, pp beaten) bater □ n (med) batimento m; (mus) compasso m, ritmo *m*; (*of drum*) toque *m*; (*of policeman*) ronda *f*, (P) giro *m*. ~ **about the bush** estar com rodeios. ~ **a retreat** bater em retirada. ~ **it** (*sl: go away*) pôr-se a andar. ~s **me** (*colloq*) não consigo entender. ~ **up** espancar. ~**er** *n* (*culin*) batedeira *f*. ~**ing** *n* sova *f*

beautician /bju:'tɪʃn/ *n* esteticista *mf*

beautiful /'bju:tɪfl/ *a* belo, lindo. ~**ly** *adv* lindamente

beautify /'bju:tɪfaɪ/ *vt* embelezar

beauty /'bju:tɪ/ *n* beleza *f*. ~ **parlour** instituto *m* de beleza. ~ **spot** sinal *m* no rosto, mosca *f*; (*place*) local *m* pitoresco

beaver /'bi:və(r)/ *n* castor *m*

became /bɪ'keɪm/ *see* **become**

because /bɪ'kɒz/ *conj* porque □ *adv* ~ **of** por causa de

beckon /'bekən/ *vt/i* ~ **(to)** fazer sinal (para)

become /bɪ'kʌm/ *vt/i* (*pt* **became**, *pp* **become**) tornar-se; (*befit*) ficar bem a. **what has** ~ **of her?** que é feito dela?

becoming /bɪ'kʌmɪŋ/ *a* que fica bem, apropriado

bed /bed/ *n* cama *f*; (*layer*) camada *f*; (*of sea*) fundo *m*; (*of river*) leito *m*; (*of flowers*) canteiro *m* □ *vt/i* (*pt* **bedded**) ~ **down** ir deitar-se. ~ **in** plantar. ~ **and breakfast (b & b)** quarto *m* com café da manhã. ~**sit(ter)** *n* (*colloq*) mixto *m* de quarto e sala. **go to** ~ ir para cama. **in** ~ na cama. ~**ding** *n* roupa *f* de cama

bedclothes /'bedkləʊðz/ *n* roupa *f* de cama

bedlam /'bedləm/ *n* confusão *f*, balbúrdia *f*

bedraggled /bɪ'drægld/ *a* (*wet*) molhado; (*untidy*) desarrumado; (*dishevelled*) desgrenhado

bedridden /'bedrɪdn/ *a* preso ao leito, doente de cama

bedroom /'bedru:m/ *n* quarto *m* de dormir

bedside /'bedsaɪd/ *n* cabeceira *f*. ~ **manner** (*doctor's*) modos *mpl* que inspiram confiança

bedspread /'bedspred/ *n* colcha *f*

bedtime /'bedtaɪm/ *n* hora *f* de deitar, hora *f* de ir para a cama

bee /bi:/ *n* abelha *f*. **make a** ~-**line for** ir direto a

beech /bi:tʃ/ *n* faia *f*

beef /bi:f/ *n* carne *f* de vaca

beefburger /'bi:fbɜ:gə(r)/ *n* hambúrguer *m*

beehive /'bi:haɪv/ *n* colméia *f*

been /bi:n/ *see* **be**

beer /bɪə(r)/ *n* cerveja *f*

beet /bi:t/ *n* beterraba *f*

beetle /'bi:tl/ *n* escaravelho *m*

beetroot /'bi:tru:t/ *n* (raiz de) beterraba *f*

before /bɪ'fɔ:(r)/ *prep* (*time*) antes de; (*place*) em frente de □ *adv* antes; (*already*) já □ *conj* antes que. ~ **leaving** antes de partir. ~ **he leaves** antes que ele parta, antes de ele partir

beforehand /bɪ'fɔ:hænd/ *adv* de antemão, antecipadamente

befriend /bɪ'frend/ *vt* tornar-se amigo de; (*be helpful to*) auxiliar

beg /beg/ *vt/i* (*pt* **begged**) mendigar; (*entreat*) suplicar. ~ **sb's pardon** pedir desculpa a alg. ~ **the question** fazer uma petição de princípio. **it's going** ~**ging** está sobrando

began /bɪ'gæn/ *see* **begin**

beggar /'begə(r)/ *n* mendigo *m*, pedinte *mf*; (*colloq: person*) cara (*colloq*) *m*

begin /bɪ'gɪn/ *vt/i* (*pt* **began**, *pp* **begun**, *pres p* **beginning**) começar, principiar. ~**ner** *n* principiante *mf*. ~**ning** *n* começo *m*, princípio *m*

begrudge /bɪ'grʌdʒ/ *vt* ter inveja de; (*give*) dar de má vontade.

doing fazer de má vontade *or* a contragosto

beguile /br'gaıl/ *vt* enganar

begun /br'gʌn/ *see* **begin**

behalf /br'ha:f/ *n* **on ~ of** em nome de; (*in the interest of*) em favor de

behave /br'heıv/ *vi* portar-se. **~ (o.s.)** portar-se bem

behaviour /br'heıvjə(r)/ *n* conduta *f*, comportamento *m*

behead /br'hed/ *vt* decapitar

behind /br'haınd/ *prep* atrás de □ *adv* atrás; (*late*) com atraso □ *n* (*colloq: buttocks*) traseiro (*colloq*) *m*. **~ the times** antiquado, retrógrado. **leave ~** deixar para trás

behold /br'həʊld/ *vt* (*pt* **beheld**) (*old use*) ver

beholden /br'həʊldən/ *a* em dívida (**to** para com)

beige /beıʒ/ *a* & *n* bege (*m*), (*P*) beige (*m*)

being /'bi:ıŋ/ *n* ser *m*. **bring into ~** criar. **come into ~** nascer, originar-se

belated /br'leıtıd/ *a* tardio, atrasado

belch /beltʃ/ *vi* arrotar □ *vt* **~ out** (*smoke*) vomitar, lançar □ *n* arroto *m*

belfry /'belfrı/ *n* campanário *m*

Belgi|um /'beldʒəm/ *n* Bélgica *f*. **~an** *a* & *n* belga (*mf*)

belief /br'li:f/ *n* crença *f*; (*trust*) confiança *f*; (*opinion*) convicção *f*

believ|e /br'li:v/ *vt/i* acreditar. **~e in** acreditar em. **~able** *a* crível. **~er** /-ə(r)/ *n* crente *mf*

belittle /br'lıtl/ *vt* depreciar

bell /bel/ *n* sino *m*; (*small*) sineta *f*; (*on door, of phone*) campainha *f*; (*on cat, toy*) guizo *m*

belligerent /br'lıdʒərənt/ *a* & *n* beligerante (*mf*)

bellow /'beləʊ/ *vt/i* berrar, bramir. **~ out** rugir

bellows /'beləʊz/ *npl* fole *m*

belly /'belı/ *n* barriga *f*, ventre *m*. **~-ache** *n* dor *f* de barriga

bellyful /'belıfʊl/ *n* **have a ~** estar com a barriga cheia

belong /br'lɒŋ/ *vi* **~ (to)** pertencer (a); (*club*) ser sócio de

belongings /br'lɒŋıŋz/ *npl* pertences *mpl*. **personal ~** objetos *mpl* de uso pessoal

beloved /br'lʌvıd/ *a* & *n* amado (*m*)

below /br'ləʊ/ *prep* abaixo de, debaixo de □ *adv* abaixo, em baixo; (*on page*) abaixo

belt /belt/ *n* cinto *m*; (*techn*) correia *f*; (*fig*) zona *f* □ *vt* (*sl: hit*) zurzir □ *vi* (*sl: rush*) safar-se

bemused /br'mju:zd/ *a* estonteado, confuso; (*thoughtful*) pensativo

bench /bentʃ/ *n* banco *m*; (*seat, working-table*) bancada *f*. **the ~** (*jur*) os magistrados (*no tribunal*)

bend /bend/ *vt/i* (*pt* & *pp* **bent**) curvar(-se); (*arm, leg*) dobrar; (*road, river*) fazer uma curva, virar □ *n* curva *f*. **~ over** debruçar-se *or* inclinar-se sobre

beneath /br'ni:θ/ *prep* abaixo de, debaixo de; (*fig*) abaixo de □ *adv* debaixo, em baixo

benediction /benı'dıkʃn/ *n* benção *f*

benefactor /'benıfæktə(r)/ *n* benfeitor *m*

beneficial /benı'fıʃl/ *a* benéfico, proveitoso

benefit /'benıfıt/ *n* (*advantage, performance*) benefício *m*; (*profit*) proveito *m*; (*allowance*) subsídio *m* □ *vt/i* (*pt* **benefited**, *pres p* **benefiting**) (*be useful to*) beneficiar (**by** de); (*do good to*) beneficiar, fazer bem a; (*receive benefit*) lucrar, ganhar (**by, from** com)

beneficiary /benı'fıʃərı/ *n* beneficiário *m*

benevolen|t /br'nevələnt/ a benevolente. ~**ce** n benevolência f

benign /br'nam/ a (incl med) benigno

bent /bent/ see bend □ n (for para) (skill) aptidão f, jeito m; (liking) queda f □ a curvado; (twisted) torcido; (sl: dishonest) desonesto. ~ **on** decidido a

bequeath /br'kwi:ð/ vt legar

bequest /br'kwest/ n legado m

bereave|d /br'ri:vd/ a the ~**d wife**/etc a esposa/etc do falecido. the ~**d family** a família enlutada. ~**ment** n luto m

bereft /br'reft/ a ~ **of** privado de

beret /'bereɪ/ n boina f

Bermuda /bə'mju:də/ n Bermudas fpl

berry /'berɪ/ n baga f

berserk /bə'sɜ:k/ a ~ **go** ficar louco de raiva, perder a cabeça

berth /bɜ:θ/ n (in ship) beliche m; (in train) couchette f; (anchorage) ancoradouro m □ vi atracar. **give a wide** ~ **to** passar ao largo, (P) de largo

beside /br'saɪd/ prep ao lado de, junto de. ~ **o.s.** fora de si. **be** ~ **the point** não ter nada a ver com o assunto, não vir ao caso

besides /br'saɪdz/ prep além de; (except) fora, salvo □ adv além disso

besiege /br'si:dʒ/ vt sitiar, cercar. ~ **with** assediar

best /best/ a & n (the) ~ (o/a) melhor (mf) □ adv melhor. ~ **man** padrinho m de casamento. **at (the)** ~ na melhor das hipóteses. **do one's** ~ fazer o (melhor) que se pode. **make the** ~ **of** tirar o melhor partido de. **the** ~ **part of** a maior parte de. **to the** ~ **of my knowledge** que eu saiba

bestow /br'stəʊ/ vt conferir. ~ **praise** fazer or tecer elogios

best-seller /best'selə(r)/ n best-seller m

bet /bet/ n aposta f □ vt/i (pt bet or betted) apostar (on em)

betray /br'treɪ/ vt trair. ~**al** n traição f

better /'betə(r)/ a & adv melhor □ vt melhorar □ n our ~**s** os nossos superiores mpl. **all the** ~ tanto melhor. ~ **off** (richer) mais rico. **he's** ~ **off at home** é melhor para ele ficar em casa. **I'd** ~ **go** é melhor ir-me embora. **the** ~ **part of it** a maior parte disso. **get** ~ melhorar. **get the** ~ **of sb** levar a melhor em relação a alg

betting-shop /'betɪnʃɒp/ n agência f de apostas

between /br'twi:n/ prep entre □ adv in ~ no meio, no intervalo. ~ **you and me** aqui entre nós

beverage /'bevərɪdʒ/ n bebida f

beware /br'weə(r)/ vi acautelar-se (of com), tomar cuidado (of com)

bewilder /br'wɪldə(r)/ vt desorientar. ~**ment** n desorientação f, confusão f

bewitch /br'wɪtʃ/ vt encantar, cativar

beyond /br'jɒnd/ prep além de; (doubt, reach) fora de □ adv além. **it's** ~ **me** isso ultrapassa-me. **he lives** ~ **his means** ele vive acima dos seus meios

bias /'baɪəs/ n parcialidade f; (pej: prejudice) preconceito m; (sewing) viés m □ vt (pt biased) influenciar. ~**ed** a parcial. ~**ed against** de prevenção contra, (P) de pé atrás contra

bib /bib/ n babeiro m, babette m

Bible /'baɪbl/ n Bíblia f

biblical /'bɪblɪkl/ a bíblico

bibliography /bɪblɪ'ɒgrəfɪ/ n bibliografia f

bicarbonate /baɪ'ka:bənət/ n ~ **of soda** bicarbonato m de soda

biceps /'baɪseps/ n bíceps m

bicker /'bɪkə(r)/ *vi* questionar, discutir

bicycle /'baɪsɪkl/ *n* bicicleta *f* □ *vi* andar de bicicleta

bid /bɪd/ *n* oferta *f*, lance *m*; (*attempt*) tentativa *f* □ *vt/i* (*pt* **bid**, *pres p* **bidding**) fazer uma oferta, lançar, oferecer como lance. **~der** *n* licitante *mf*. **the highest ~der** quem dá *or* oferece mais

bide /baɪd/ *vt* **~ one's time** esperar pelo bom momento

bidet /'biːdeɪ/ *n* bidé *m*, (*P*) bidé *m*

biennial /baɪ'enɪəl/ *a* bienal

bifocals /baɪ'fəʊklz/ *npl* óculos *mpl* bifocais

big /bɪg/ *a* (**bigger**, **biggest**) grande; (*sl: generous*) generoso □ *adv* (*colloq*) em grande. **~headed** *a* pretensioso, convencido. **~ shot** (*sl*) manda-chuva *m*. **talk ~** gabar-se (*colloq*). **think ~** (*colloq*) ter grandes planos

bigam|y /'bɪgəmɪ/ *n* bigamia *f*. **~ist** *n* bígamo *m*. **~ous** *a* bígamo

bigot /'bɪgət/ *n* fanático *m*, intolerante *mf*. **~ed** *a* fanático, intolerante. **~ry** *n* fanatismo *m*, intolerância *f*

bigwig /'bɪgwɪg/ *n* (*colloq*) manda-chuva *m*

bike /baɪk/ *n* (*colloq*) bicicleta *f*

bikini /bɪ'kiːnɪ/ *n* (*pl* **-is**) biquíni *m*

bilberry /'bɪlbərɪ/ *n* arando *m*

bile /baɪl/ *n* bílis *f*

bilingual /baɪ'lɪŋgwəl/ *a* bilíngüe

bilious /'bɪlɪəs/ *a* bilioso

bill[1] /bɪl/ *n* (*invoice*) fatura *f*, (*P*) factura *f*; (*in restaurant*) conta *f*; (*pol*) projeto *m*, (*P*) projecto *m* de lei; (*Amer: banknote*) nota *f* de banco; (*poster*) cartaz *m* □ *vt* facturar, (*P*) facturar; (*theatre*) anunciar, pôr no programa. **~ of exchange** letra *f* de câmbio

~ sb for apresentar a alg a conta de

bill[2] /bɪl/ *n* (*of bird*) bico *m*

billiards /'bɪlɪədz/ *n* bilhar *m*

billion /'bɪlɪən/ *n* (10⁹) mil milhões; (10¹²) um milhão de milhões

bin /bɪn/ *n* (*for storage*) caixa *f*, lata *f*; (*for rubbish*) lata *f* do lixo, (*P*) caixote *m*

bind /baɪnd/ *vt* (*pt* **bound**) (*tie*) atar; (*book*) encadernar; (*jur*) obrigar; (*cover the edge of*) debruar □ *n* (*sl: bore*) chatice *f* (*sl*). **be ~ing on** ser obrigatório para

binding /'baɪndɪŋ/ *n* encadernação *f*; (*braid*) debrum *m*

binge /bɪndʒ/ *n* (*sl*) **go on a ~** cair na farra; (*overeat*) empanturrar-se

bingo /'bɪŋgəʊ/ *n* bingo *m* □ *int* acertei!

binoculars /bɪ'nɒkjʊləz/ *npl* binóculo *m*

biochemistry /baɪəʊ'kemɪstrɪ/ *n* bioquímica *f*

biodegradable /baɪəʊdɪ'greɪdəbl/ *a* biodegradável

biograph|y /baɪ'ɒgrəfɪ/ *n* biografia *f*. **~er** *n* biógrafo *m*

biolog|y /baɪ'ɒlədʒɪ/ *n* biologia *f*. **~ical** /-ə'lɒdʒɪkl/ *a* biológico. **~ist** *n* biólogo *m*

biopsy /'baɪɒpsɪ/ *n* biópsia *f*

birch /bɜːtʃ/ *n* (*tree*) bétula *f*

bird /bɜːd/ *n* ave *f*, pássaro *m*; (*sl: girl*) garota *f* (*colloq*). **~ flu** gripe *f* das aves. **~ sanctuary** refúgio *m* ornitológico. **~ watcher** *n* ornitófilo *m*

Biro /'baɪərəʊ/ *n* (*pl* **-os**) (caneta) esferográfica *f*, Bic *f*

birth /bɜːθ/ *n* nascimento *m*. **~ certificate** certidão *f* de nascimento. **~ control/rate** controle *m*/índice *m* de natalidade. **~-place** *n* lugar *m* de nascimento. **give ~ to** dar à luz

birthday /'bɜ:θdeɪ/ n aniversário m, (P) dia m de anos. **his ∼ is on 9 July** ele faz anos no dia 9 de julho

birthmark /'bɜ:θma:k/ n sinal m

biscuit /'bɪskɪt/ n biscoito m, bolacha f

bisect /baɪ'sekt/ vt dividir ao meio

bishop /'bɪʃəp/ n bispo m

bit¹ /bɪt/ n (small piece, short time) pedaço m, bocado m; (of bridle) freio m; (of tool) broca f. **a ∼** um pouco

bit² /bɪt/ see **bite**

bitch /bɪtʃ/ n cadela f; (sl: woman) peste f (fig), cadela f (sl) □ vt/i (colloq: criticize) malhar, (P) cortar (em) (colloq); (colloq: grumble) resmungar. **∼y** a (colloq) maldoso

bite /baɪt/ vt/i (pt bit, pp bitten) morder; (insect) picar □ n mordida f; (sting) picada f. **have a ∼ (to eat)** comer qualquer coisa

biting /'baɪtɪŋ/ a cortante

bitter /'bɪtə(r)/ a amargo; (weather) glacial. **∼ly** adv amargamente. **it's ∼ly cold** está um frio de rachar. **∼ness** n amargura f; (resentment) ressentimento m

bizarre /bɪ'za:(r)/ a bizarro

black /blæk/ a (-er, -est) negro, preto □ n negro m, preto m. **a B∼** (person) um preto, um negro □ vt enegrecer; (goods) boicotar. **∼ and blue** coberto de nódoas negras. **∼ coffee** café m (sem leite). **∼ eye** olho m negro. **∼ ice** gelo m negro sobre o asfalto. **∼ market** mercado m negro. **∼ spot** n (place) local m perigoso, ponto m negro

blackberry /'blækbərɪ/ n amora f silvestre

blackbird /'blækbɜ:d/ n melro m

blackboard /'blækbɔ:d/ n quadro m preto

blackcurrant /'blækkʌrənt/ n groselha f negra

blacken /'blækən/ vt/i escurecer. **∼ sb's name** difamar, denegrir

blackleg /'blækleg/ n fura-greves m

blacklist /'blæklɪst/ n lista f negra □ vt pôr na lista negra

blackmail /'blækmeɪl/ n chantagem f □ vt fazer chantagem. **∼er** n chantagista mf

blackout /'blækaʊt/ n (wartime) blecaute m; (med) desmaio m; (electr) falta f de corrente; (theatr) apagar m de luzes

blacksmith /'blæksmɪθ/ n ferreiro m

bladder /'blædə(r)/ n bexiga f

blade /bleɪd/ n lâmina f; (of oar, propeller) pá f; (of grass) ervinha f, folhinha f de erva

blame /bleɪm/ vt culpar □ n culpa f. **be to ∼** ser o culpado. **∼less** a irrepreensível; (innocent) inocente

bland /blænd/ a (-er, -est) (of manner) suave; (mild) brando; (insipid) insípido

blank /blæŋk/ a (space, cheque) em branco; (look) vago; (wall) nu □ n espaço m em branco; (cartridge) cartucho m sem bala

blanket /'blæŋkɪt/ n cobertor m; (fig) manto m □ vt (pt blanketed) cobrir com cobertor; (cover thickly) encobrir, recobrir. **wet ∼** desmancha-prazeres mf

blare /bleə(r)/ vt/i ressoar, atroar □ n clangor m; (of horn) buzinar m

blasé /'bla:zeɪ/ a blasé

blaspheme /blæs'fi:m/ vt/i blasfemar

blasphem|y /'blæsfəmɪ/ n blasfêmia f, (P) blasfémia f. **∼ous** a blasfemo

blast /bla:st/ n (gust) rajada f; (sound) som m; (explosion) explosão f □ vt dinamitar. **∼!** droga!

~**ed** *a* maldito. ~**-furnace** *n* alto forno *m*. ~**-off** *n* (*of missile*) lançamento *m*, início *m* de combustão

blatant /'bleɪtnt/ *a* flagrante; (*shameless*) descarado

blaze /bleɪz/ *n* chamas *fpl*; (*light*) clarão *m*; (*outburst*) explosão *f* □ *vi* arder; (*shine*) resplandecer, brilhar. ~ **a trail** abrir o caminho, ser pioneiro

blazer /'bleɪzə(r)/ *n* blazer *m*

bleach /bliːtʃ/ *n* descolorante, descorante *m*; (*household*) água *f* sanitária □ *vt/i* branquear; (*hair*) oxigenar

bleak /bliːk/ *a* (-er, -est) (*place*) desolado; (*chilly*) frio; (*fig*) desanimador

bleary-eyed /'blɪəraɪd/ *a* com olhos injetados

bleat /bliːt/ *n* balido *m* □ *vi* balir

bleed /bliːd/ *vt/i* (*pt* **bled**) sangrar

bleep /bliːp/ *n* bip *m*. ~ **er** *n* bip *m*

blemish /'blemɪʃ/ *n* defeito *m*; (*on reputation*) mancha *f* □ *vt* manchar

blend /blend/ *vt/i* misturar(-se); (*go well together*) combinar-se □ *n* mistura *f*. ~**er** *n* (*culin*) liquidificador *m*

bless /bles/ *vt* abençoar. **be** ~**ed with** ter a felicidade de ter. ~**ing** *n* benção *f*; (*thing one is glad of*) felicidade *f*. **it's a** ~**ing in disguise** há males que vêm para bem

blessed /'blesɪd/ *a* bem-aventurado; (*colloq: cursed*) maldito

blew /bluː/ *see* **blow**

blight /blaɪt/ *n* doença *f* de plantas; (*fig*) influência *f* maligna □ *vt* arruinar, frustrar

blind /blaɪnd/ *a* cego □ *vt* cegar □ *n* (*on window*) persiana *f*; (*deception*) ardil *m*. ~ **alley** (*incl fig*) beco *m* sem saída. ~ **man/woman** cego *m*/cega *f*. **be** ~ **to** não ver. **turn a** ~ **eye to** fingir não

ver, fechar os olhos a. ~**ly** *adv* às cegas. ~**ness** *n* cegueira *f*

blindfold /'blaɪndfəʊld/ *a & adv* de olhos vendados □ *n* venda *f* □ *vt* vendar os olhos a

blink /blɪŋk/ *vi* piscar

blinkers /'blɪŋkəz/ *npl* antolhos *mpl*

bliss /blɪs/ *n* felicidade *f*, beatitude *f*. ~**ful** *a* felicíssimo. ~**fully** *adv* maravilhosamente

blister /'blɪstə(r)/ *n* bolha *f*, empola *f* □ *vi* empolar

blizzard /'blɪzəd/ *n* tempestade *f* de neve, nevasca *f*

bloated /'bləʊtɪd/ *a* inchado

bloater /'bləʊtə(r)/ *n* arenque *m* salgado e defumado

blob /blɒb/ *n* pingo *m* grosso; (*stain*) mancha *f*

bloc /blɒk/ *n* bloco *m*

block /blɒk/ *n* bloco *m*; (*buildings*) quarteirão *m*; (*in pipe*) entupimento *m*. ~ **(of flats)** prédio *m* (de andares) □ *vt* bloquear, obstruir; (*pipe*) entupir. ~ **letters** maiúsculas *fpl*. ~**age** *n* obstrução *f*

blockade /blɒ'keɪd/ *n* bloqueio *m* □ *vt* bloquear

bloke /bləʊk/ *n* (*colloq*) sujeito *m* (*colloq*), cara *m* (*colloq*)

blond /blɒnd/ *a & n* louro (*m*)

blonde /blɒnd/ *a & n* loura (*f*)

blood /blʌd/ *n* sangue *m* □ *a* (*bank, donor, transfusion, etc*) de sangue; (*poisoning*) do sangue; (*group, vessel*) sangüíneo. ~**curdling** *a* horrendo. ~ **pressure** tensão *f* arterial. ~ **test** exame *m* de sangue. ~**less** *a* (*fig*) pacífico

bloodhound /'blʌdhaʊnd/ *n* sabujo *m*

bloodshed /'blʌdʃed/ *n* derramamento *m* de sangue, carnificina *f*

bloodshot /'blʌdʃɒt/ *a* injetado *or* (*P*) injectado de sangue

bloodstream /'blʌdstri:m/ *n* sangue *m*, fluxo *m* sanguíneo

bloodthirsty /'blʌdθɜ:stɪ/ *a* sanguinário

bloody /'blʌdɪ/ *a* (**-ier**, **-iest**) ensanguentado; (*with much bloodshed*) sangrento; (*sl*) grande, maldito □ *adv* (*sl*) pra burro. **~-minded** *a* (*colloq*) do contra (*colloq*), chato (*sl*)

bloom /blu:m/ *n* flor *f*; (*beauty*) frescura *f*, viço *m* □ *vi* florir; (*fig*) vicejar. **in ~** em flor

blossom /'blɒsəm/ *n* flor *f*. **in ~** em flor □ *vi* (*flower*) florir, desabrochar; (*develop, flourish*) florescer, desabrochar

blot /blɒt/ *n* mancha *f* □ *vt* (*pt* **blotted**) manchar; (*dry*) secar. **~ out** apagar; (*hide*) tapar, toldar. **~ter**, **~ting-paper** *n* (papel) mata-borrão *m*

blotch /blɒtʃ/ *n* mancha *f*. **~y** *a* manchado

blouse /blaʊz/ *n* blusa *f*; (*in uniform*) blusão *m*

blow[1] /bləʊ/ *vt/i* (*pt* **blew**, *pp* **blown**) soprar; (*fuse*) fundir-se, queimar; (*sl: squander*) esbanjar; (*trumpet etc*) tocar. **~ a whistle** apitar. **~ away** *or* **off** *vt* levar, soprar □ *vi* roar, ir pelos ares (fora). **~-dry** *vt* (*hair*) fazer um brushing □ *n* brushing *m*. **~ one's nose** assoar o nariz. **~ out** (*candle*) apagar, soprar. **~-out** *n* (*colloq: of tyre*) rebentar *m*; (*colloq: large meal*) comilança *f* (*colloq*). **~ over** passar. **~ up** *vt* (*explode*) explodir; (*tyre*) encher; (*photograph*) ampliar □ *vi* (*explode*) explodir

blow[2] /bləʊ/ *n* pancada *f*; (*slap*) bofetada *f*; (*punch*) murro *m*; (*fig*) golpe *m*

blowlamp /'bləʊlæmp/ *n* maçarico *m*

blown /bləʊn/ *see* **blow**[1]

bludgeon /'blʌdʒən/ *n* moca *f* □ *vt*

malhar em. **~ to death** matar à pancada

blue /blu:/ *a* (**-er**, **-est**) azul; (*indecent*) indecente □ *n* azul *m*. **come out of the ~** ser inesperado. **~s** *n* (*mus*) blues. **have the ~s** estar deprimido (*colloq*)

bluebell /'blu:bel/ *n* jacinto *m* dos bosques

bluebottle /'blu:bɒtl/ *n* mosca *f* varejeira

blueprint /'blu:prɪnt/ *n* cópia *f* fotográfica de planta; (*fig*) projeto *m*, (*P*) projecto *m*

bluff /blʌf/ *vi* blefar, (*P*) fazer bluff □ *vt* enganar (fingindo), blefar □ *n* blefe *m*, (*P*) bluff *m*

blunder /'blʌndə(r)/ *vi* cometer um erro crasso; (*move*) avançar às cegas *or* tateando □ *n* erro *m* crasso, (*P*) bronca *f*

blunt /blʌnt/ *a* (**-er**, **-est**) embotado; (*person*) direto, (*P*) directo □ *vt* embotar. **~ly** *adv* sem rodeios. **~ness** *n* franqueza *f* rude

blur /blɜ:(r)/ *n* mancha *f* □ *vt* (*pt* **blurred**) (*smear*) manchar; (*make indistinct*) toldar

blurb /blɜ:b/ *n* contracapa *f*, sinopse *f* de um livro

blurt /blɜ:t/ *vt* **~ out** deixar escapar

blush /blʌʃ/ *vi* corar □ *n* rubor *m*, vermelhidão *f*

bluster /'blʌstə(r)/ *vi* (*wind*) soprar em rajadas; (*swagger*) andar com ar fanfarrão. **~y** *a* borrascoso

boar /bɔ:(r)/ *n* varrão *m*. **wild ~** javali *m*

board /bɔ:d/ *n* tábua *f*; (*for notices*) quadro *m*, (*P*) placard *m*; (*food*) pensão *f*; (*admin*) conselho *m* □ *vt/i* cobrir com tábuas; (*aircraft, ship, train*) embarcar (em); (*bus, train*) subir (em). **full ~** pensão *f* completa. **half ~** meia-pensão *f*. **on ~** a bordo.

up entaipar. ~ with ser pensionista em casa de. ~er n pensionista mf; (at school) interno m. ~ing-card n cartão m de embarque. ~ing-house n pensão f. ~ing-school n internato m

boast /bəʊst/ vi gabar-se □ vt orgulhar-se de □ n gabarolice f. ~er n gabola mf. ~ful a vaidoso. ~fully adv com vaidade, gabando-se

boat /bəʊt/ n barco m. in the same ~ nas mesmas circunstâncias. ~ing n passear de barco

bob /bɒb/ vt/i (pt bobbed) (curtsy) inclinar-se; (hair) cortar pelos ombros, (P) cortar à Joãozinho. ~ (up and down) andar para cima e para baixo

bobbin /'bɒbɪn/ n bobina f; (sewing-machine) canela f, bobina f

bob-sleigh /'bɒbsleɪ/ n trenó m

bode /bəʊd/ vi ~ well/ill ser de bom/mau agouro

bodice /'bɒdɪs/ n corpete m

bodily /'bɒdɪlɪ/ a corporal, físico. □ adv (in person) fisicamente, em pessoa; (lift) em peso

body /'bɒdɪ/ n corpo m; (organization) organismo m. ~(work) n (of car) carroçaria f. in a ~ em massa. the main ~ of o grosso de. ~-building n body building m

bodyguard /'bɒdɪgɑːd/ n guarda-costas m; (escort) escolta f

bog /bɒg/ n pântano m □ vt get ~ged down atolar-se; (fig) ficar emperrado

boggle /'bɒgl/ vi the mind ~s não da para imaginar

bogus /'bəʊgəs/ a falso

boil¹ /bɔɪl/ n (med) furúnculo m

boil² /bɔɪl/ vt/i ferver. come to the ~ ferver. ~ down to resumir-se a. ~ over transbordar.

~ing hot fervendo. ~ing point ponto m de ebulição

boiler /'bɔɪlə(r)/ n caldeira f. ~suit n macacão m, (P) fato m de macaco

boisterous /'bɔɪstərəs/ a turbulento; (noisy and cheerful) animado

bold /bəʊld/ a (-er, -est) ousado; (of colours) vivo. ~ness n ousadia f

Bolivia /bə'lɪvɪə/ n Bolívia f. ~n a & n boliviano (m)

bollard /'bɒləd/ n (ship) abita f; (road) poste m

bolster /'bəʊlstə(r)/ n travesseiro m □ vt sustentar; ajudar. ~ one's spirits levantar o moral

bolt /bəʊlt/ n (on door etc) ferrolho m; (for nut) parafuso m; (lightning) relâmpago m □ vt aferrolhar; (food) engolir □ vi fugir, disparar. ~ upright reto como um fuso

bomb /bɒm/ n bomba f □ vt bombardear. ~er n (aircraft) bombardeiro m; (person) bombista mf

bombard /bɒm'bɑːd/ vt bombardear. ~ment n bombardeamento m

bombastic /bɒm'bæstɪk/ a bombástico

bombshell /'bɒmʃel/ n granada f; (fig) bomba f

bond /bɒnd/ n (agreement) compromisso m; (link) laço m, vínculo m; (comm) obrigação f. in ~ em depósito na alfândega

bondage /'bɒndɪdʒ/ n escravidão f, servidão f

bone /bəʊn/ n osso m; (of fish) espinha f □ vt desossar. ~-dry a completamente seco, ressecado. ~ idle preguiçoso

bonfire /'bɒnfaɪə(r)/ n fogueira f

bonnet /'bɒnɪt/ n chapéu m; (auto) capô m do motor, (P) capot m

bonus /'bəʊnəs/ n bônus m, (P) bónus m

bony /'bəʊnɪ/ a (-ier, -iest) ossudo; (meat, fish) cheio de ossos/de espinhas

boo /buː/ int fora □ vt/i vaiar □ n vaia f

boob /buːb/ n (sl: mistake) asneira f, disparate m □ vi (sl) fazer asneira(s)

booby /'buːbɪ/ n ~ prize prêmio m de consolação. ~ trap bomba f armadilhada

book /bʊk/ n livro m. ~s (comm) contas fpl, escrita f □ vt (enter) averbar, registrar; (comm) escriturar; (reserve) marcar, reservar. ~ of matches carteira f de fósforos. ~ of tickets (bus, tube) caderneta f de módulos. be fully ~ed ter a lotação esgotada. ~ing office bilheteria f, (P) bilheteira f

bookcase /'bʊkkeɪs/ n estante f

bookkeep|er /'bʊkiːpə(r)/ n guarda-livros m. ~ing n contabilidade f, escrituração f

booklet /'bʊklɪt/ n brochura f

bookmaker /'bʊkmeɪkə(r)/ n book (maker) m

bookmark /'bʊkmɑːk/ n marca f de livro, marcador m de página

bookseller /'bʊkselə(r)/ n livreiro m

bookshop /'bʊkʃɒp/ n livraria f

bookstall /'bʊkstɔːl/ n quiosque m

boom /buːm/ vi ribombar; (of trade) prosperar □ n (sound) ribombo m; (comm) boom m, prosperidade f

boon /buːn/ n benção f, vantagem f

boost /buːst/ vt desenvolver, promover; (morale) levantar; (price) aumentar □ n força f (colloq). ~er n (med) dose suplementar f; (vaccine) revacinação f, (P) reforço m

boot /buːt/ n bota f; (auto) portamala f □ vt ~ (up) (comput) dar

cargaem. to ~ (in addition) ainda por cima

booth /buːð/ n barraca f; (telephone, voting) cabine f

booty /'buːtɪ/ n saque m, pilhagem f

booze /buːz/ vi (colloq) embebedar-se (colloq), encharcar-se (colloq) □ n (colloq) pinga f (colloq)

border /'bɔːdə(r)/ n borda f, margem f; (frontier) fronteira f; (garden bed) canteiro m □ vi ~ on confinar com; (be almost the same as) atingir as raias de

borderline /'bɔːdəlaɪn/ n linha f divisória. ~ case caso m limite

bore[1] /bɔː(r)/ see **bear**[2]

bore[2] /bɔː(r)/ vt/i (techn) furar, perfurar □ n (of gun barrel) calibre m

bore[3] /bɔː(r)/ vt aborrecer, entediar □ n maçante m; (thing) chatice f. **be ~d** aborrecer-se, maçar-se. ~dom n tédio m. boring a tedioso, maçante

born /bɔːn/ a nascido. **be ~** nascer

borne /bɔːn/ see **bear**[2]

borough /'bʌrə/ n município m

borrow /'bɒrəʊ/ vt pedir emprestado (from a)

bosom /'bʊzəm/ n peito m; (woman's; fig: midst) seio m. ~ friend amigo m íntimo

boss /bɒs/ n (colloq) patrão m, patroa f, manda-chuva (colloq) m □ vt mandar. ~ sb about (colloq) mandar em alg

bossy /'bɒsɪ/ a mandão, autoritário

botan|y /'bɒtənɪ/ n botânica f. ~ical /bə'tænɪkl/ a botânico. ~ist /-ɪst/ n botânico m

botch /bɒtʃ/ vt atamancar; (spoil) estragar, escangalhar

both /bəʊθ/ a & pron ambos, os dois □ adv ~ ... and não só ... mas também, tanto ... como ...

of us nós dois. ~ the books ambos os livros

bother /'bɒðə(r)/ *vt/i* incomodar (-se) □ *n* (*inconvenience*) incómodo *m*, (*P*) incómodo *m*, trabalho *m*; (*effort*) custo *m*, trabalho *m*; (*worry*) preocupação *f*. **don't** ~ não se incomode. **I can't be** ~**ed** não posso me dar o trabalho

bottle /'bɒtl/ *n* garrafa *f*; (*small*) frasco *m*; (*for baby*) mamadeira *f*, (*P*) biberão *m* □ *vt* engarrafar. ~**-opener** *n* saca-rolhas *m*. ~ **up** reprimir

bottleneck /'bɒtlnek/ *n* (*obstruction*) entrave *m*; (*traffic-jam*) engarrafamento *m*

bottom /'bɒtəm/ *n* fundo *m*; (*of hill*) sopé *m*; (*buttocks*) traseiro *m* □ *a* inferior; (*last*) último. **from top to** ~ de alto a baixo. ~**less** *a* sem fundo

bough /baʊ/ *n* ramo *m*

bought /bɔːt/ *see* **buy**

boulder /'bəʊldə(r)/ *n* pedregulho *m*

bounce /baʊns/ *vi* saltar; (*of person*) pular, dar pulos; (*sl: of cheque*) ser devolvido □ *vt* fazer saltar □ *n* (*of ball*) salto *m*, (*P*) ressalto *m*

bound¹ /baʊnd/ *vi* pular; (*move by jumping*) ir aos pulos □ *n* pulo *m*

bound² /baʊnd/ *see* **bind** □ *a* **be** ~ **for** ir com destino a, ir para. **be** ~ **to** (*obliged*) ser obrigado a; (*certain*) haver de. **she's** ~ **to like it** ela há de gostar disso

boundary /'baʊndrɪ/ *n* limite *m*

bound|s /baʊndz/ *npl* limites *mpl*. **out of** ~**s** interdito. ~**ed by** limitado por, ~**less** *a* sem limites

bouquet /bʊ'keɪ/ *n* ramo *m* de flores; (*wine*) aroma *m*

bout /baʊt/ *n* período *m*; (*med*) ataque *m*; (*boxing*) combate *m*

boutique /buː'tiːk/ *n* boutique *f*

bow¹ /bəʊ/ *n* (*weapon, mus*) arco *m*; (*knot*) laço *m*. ~**-tie** *n* gravata borboleta *f*, (*P*) laço *m*

bow² /baʊ/ *n* vênia *f*, (*P*) vénia *f* □ *vt/i* inclinar(-se), curvar-se

bow³ /baʊ/ *n* (*naut*) proa *f*

bowels /'baʊəlz/ *npl* intestinos *mpl*; (*fig*) entranhas *fpl*

bowl¹ /bəʊl/ *n* (*basin*) bacia *f*; (*for food*) tigela *f*; (*of pipe*) fornilho *m*

bowl² /bəʊl/ *n* (*ball*) boliche *m*, (*P*) bola *f* de madeira. ~**s** *npl* boliche *m*, (*P*) jogo *m* com bolas de madeira □ *vt* (*cricket*) lançar. ~ **over** siderar, varar. ~**ing** *n* boliche *m*, (*P*) bowling *m*. ~**ing-alley** *n* pista *f*

bowler¹ /'bəʊlə(r)/ *n* (*cricket*) lançador *m*

bowler² /'bəʊlə(r)/ *n* ~ (*hat*) (chapéu de) coco *m*

box¹ /bɒks/ *n* caixa *f*; (*theatr*) camarote *m* □ *vt* pôr dentro duma caixa. ~ **in** fechar. ~ **office** *n* bilheteria *f*, (*P*) bilheteira *f*. **Boxing Day** feriado *m* no primeiro dia útil depois do Natal

box² /bɒks/ *vt/i* (*sport*) lutar boxe. ~ **the ears of** esbofetear. ~**er** *n* pugilista *m*, boxeur *m*. ~**ing** *n* boxe *m*, pugilismo *m*

boy /bɔɪ/ *n* rapaz *m*. ~**-friend** *n* namorado *m*. ~**-hood** *n* infância *f*. ~**ish** *a* de menino

boycott /'bɔɪkɒt/ *vt* boicotar □ *n* boicote *m*

bra /brɑː/ *n* soutien *m*

brace /breɪs/ *n* braçadeira *f*; (*dental*) aparelho *m*; (*tool*) berbequim *m*; (*of birds*) par *m*. ~**s** *npl* (*for trousers*) suspensórios *mpl* □ *vt* apoiar, firmar. ~ **o.s.** concentrar as energias, fazer força; (*for blow*) preparar-se

bracelet /'breɪslɪt/ *n* bracelete *m*, pulseira *f*

bracing /'breɪsɪŋ/ *a* tonificante, estimulante

bracken /'brækən/ n (bot) samambaia f, (P) feto m

bracket /'brækɪt/ n suporte m; (group) grupo m □ vt (pt **bracketed**) pôr entre parênteses; (put together) pôr em pé de igualdade, agrupar. **age/income** ~s parênteses mpl. **square** ~s parênteses mpl, colchetes mpl

brag /bræg/ vi (pt **bragged**) gabar-se (**about** de)

braid /breɪd/ n galão m; (of hair) trança f

Braille /breɪl/ n braile m

brain /breɪn/ n cérebro m, miolos mpl (colloq); (fig) inteligência f. ~s (culin) miolos mpl. ~**child** n invenção f. ~**less** a estúpido

brainwash /'breɪnwɒʃ/ vt fazer uma lavagem cerebral

brainwave /'breɪnweɪv/ n idéia f, (P) ideia f genial

brainy /'breɪnɪ/ a (-ier, -iest) inteligente, esperto

braise /breɪz/ vt (culin) estufar

brake /breɪk/ n travão m □ vt/i travar. ~ **light** farol m do freio

bran /bræn/ n (husks) farelo m

branch /brɑːntʃ/ n ramo m; (of road) ramificação f, (of railway line) ramal m; (comm) sucursal f; (of bank) balcão m □ vi ~ (**off**) bifurcar-se, ramificar-se

brand /brænd/ n marca f □ vt marcar. ~ **name** marca f de fábrica. ~**new** a novo em folha. ~ **sb as** tachar alg de, (P) rotular alg de

brandish /'brændɪʃ/ vt brandir

brandy /'brændɪ/ n aguardente f, conhaque m

brass /brɑːs/ n latão m. **the** ~ (mus) os metais mpl □ a de cobre, de latão. **get down to** ~ **tacks** tratar das coisas sérias. **top** ~ (sl) os chefões (colloq)

brassière /'bræsɪə(r)/ n soutien m

brat /bræt/ n (pej) fedelho m

bravado /brə'vɑːdəʊ/ n bravata f

brave /breɪv/ a (-er, -est) bravo, valente □ vt arrostar. ~**ry** /-ərɪ/ n bravura f

brawl /brɔːl/ n briga f, rixa f, desordem f □ vi brigar

brawn /brɔːn/ n força f muscular, músculo m. ~**y** a musculoso

bray /breɪ/ n zurro m □ vi zurrar

brazen /'breɪzn/ a descarado

brazier /'breɪzɪə(r)/ n braseiro m

Brazil /brə'zɪl/ n Brasil m. ~**ian** a & n brasileiro (m). ~ **nut** castanha f do Pará

breach /briːtʃ/ n brecha f; (gap) brecha f □ vt abrir uma brecha em. ~ **of contract** quebra f de contrato. ~ **of the peace** perturbação f da ordem pública. ~ **of trust** abuso m de confiança

bread /bred/ n pão m. ~-**winner** n ganha-pão m

breadcrumbs /'bredkrʌmz/ npl migalhas fpl; (culin) farinha f de rosca

breadline /'bredlaɪn/ n **on the** ~ na miséria

breadth /bredθ/ n largura f; (of mind, view) abertura f

break /breɪk/ vt (pt **broke**, pp **broken**) partir, quebrar; (vow, silence, etc) quebrar; (law) transgredir; (journey) interromper; (news) dar; (a record) bater □ vi partir-se, quebrar-se; (voice, weather) mudar □ n quebra f, ruptura f; (interval) intervalo m; (colloq: opportunity) oportunidade f, chance f. ~ **one's arm/ leg** quebrar o braço/a perna ~ **down** vt analisar □ vi (of person) ir-se abaixo; (of machine) avariarse. ~ **in** forçar uma entrada. ~ **off** vt quebrar □ vi desligar-se. ~ **out** rebentar. ~ **up** vt/i terminar □ vi (of schools) entrar em férias. ~**able** a quebrável. ~**age** n quebra f

breakdown /'breɪkdaʊn/

breaker /'breɪkə(r)/ *n* vaga *f* de rebentação

(*techn*) avaria *f*, pane *f*; (*med*) esgotamento *m* nervoso; (*of figures*) análise *f* □ *a* (*auto*) de pronto-socorro. ~ **van** pronto-socorro *n*

breakfast /'brekfəst/ *n* café *m* da manhã

breakthrough /'breɪkθru:/ *n* descoberta *f* decisiva, avanço *m*

breakwater /'breɪkwɔ:tə(r)/ *n* quebra-mar *m*

breast /brest/ *n* peito *m*. ~**-feed** *vt* (*pt* **-fed**) amamentar. ~**-stroke** *n* estilo *m* bruços

breath /breθ/ *n* respiração *f*. **bad** ~ mau hálito *m*. **out of** ~ sem fôlego. **under one's** ~ num murmúrio, baixo. ~**less** *a* ofegante

breathalyser /'breθəlaɪzə(r)/ *n* aparelho *m* para medir o nível de álcool no sangue, bafômetro *m* (*colloq*)

breath|e /bri:ð/ *vt/i* respirar. ~**e in** inspirar. ~ **out** expirar. ~**ing** *n* respiração *f*. ~**ing-space** *n* pausa *f*

breather /'bri:ðə(r)/ *n* pausa *f* de descanso, momento *m* para respirar

breathtaking /'breθteɪkɪŋ/ *a* assombroso, arrebatador

bred /bred/ *see* **breed**

breed /bri:d/ *vt* (*pt* **bred**) criar □ *vi* reproduzir-se □ *n* raça *f*. ~**er** *n* criador *m*. ~**ing** *n* criação *f*; (*fig*) educação *f*

breez|e /bri:z/ *n* brisa *f*. ~**y** *a* fresco

brevity /'brevətɪ/ *n* brevidade *f*

brew /bru:/ *vt* (*beer*) fabricar; (*tea*) fazer; (*fig*) armar, tramar □ *vi* fermentar; (*tea*) preparar; (*fig*) armar-se, preparar-se □ *n* decocção *f*; (*tea*) infusão *f*. ~**er** *n* cervejeiro *m*. ~**ery** *n* cervejaria *f*

bribe /braɪb/ *n* suborno *m*, (*P*) peita *f* □ *vt* subornar. ~**ry** /-ərɪ/ *n* suborno *m*, corrupção *f*

brick /brɪk/ *n* tijolo *m*

bricklayer /'brɪkleɪə(r)/ *n* pedreiro *m*

bridal /'braɪdl/ *a* nupcial

bride /braɪd/ *n* noiva *f*

bridegroom /'braɪdgrom/ *n* noivo *m*

bridesmaid /'braɪdzmeɪd/ *n* dama *f* de honra, (*P*) honor

bridge[1] /brɪdʒ/ *n* ponte *f*; (*of nose*) cana *f* □ *vt* ~ **a gap** preencher uma lacuna

bridge[2] /brɪdʒ/ *n* (*cards*) bridge *m*

bridle /'braɪdl/ *n* cabeçada *f*, freio *m* □ *vt* refrear. ~**-path** *n* atalho *m*, carreiro *m*

brief[1] /bri:f/ *a* (**-er**, **-est**) breve. ~**s** *n pl* (*men's*) cueca *f*, (*P*) slip *m*; (*women's*) calcinhas *fpl*, (*P*) cuecas *fpl*. ~**ly** *adv* brevemente

brief[2] /bri:f/ *n* (*jur*) sumário *m*; (*case*) causa *f*; (*instructions*) instruções *fpl* □ *vt* dar instruções a

briefcase /'bri:fkeɪs/ *n* pasta *f*

brigad|e /brɪ'geɪd/ *n* brigada *f*. ~**ier** /-ə'dɪə(r)/ *n* brigadeiro *m*

bright /braɪt/ *a* (**-er**, **-est**) brilhante; (*of colour*) vivo; (*of light*) forte; (*room*) claro; (*cheerful*) alegre; (*clever*) inteligente. ~**ness** *n* (*sheen*) brilho *m*; (*clarity*) claridade *f*, (*intelligence*) inteligência *f*

brighten /'braɪtn/ *vt* alegrar □ *vi* (*of weather*) clarear; (*of face*) animar-se, iluminar-se

brillian|t /'brɪljənt/ *a* brilhante. ~**ce** *n* brilho *m*

brim /brɪm/ *n* borda *f*; (*of hat*) aba *f* □ *vi* (*pt* **brimmed**) ~ **over** transbordar, cair por fora

brine /braɪn/ *n* salmoura *f*

bring /brɪŋ/ *vt* (*pt* **brought**) trazer. ~ **about** causar. ~ **back** trazer (de volta); (*call to mind*) relembrar. ~ **down** trazer para baixo; (*bird*, *plane*) abater; (*prices*) baixar. **~ forward** adiantar, apresentar. **~ it off** ser bem sucedido (em alg coisa). **~ out** (*take out*) tirar; (*show*) revelar; (*book*) publicar. **~ round** *or* to reanimar, fazer voltar a si. **~ to bear** (*pressure etc*) exercer. **~ up** educar; (*med*) vomitar; (*question*) levantar

brink /brɪŋk/ *n* beira *f*, borda *f*

brisk /brɪsk/ *a* (-er, -est) (*pace, movement*) vivo, rápido; (*business, demand*) grande

bristle /ˈbrɪsl/ *n* pêlo *m*.

Britain /ˈbrɪtən/ *n* Grã-Bretanha *f*

British /ˈbrɪtɪʃ/ *a* britânico. the **~** o povo *m* britânico, os britânicos *mpl*

brittle /ˈbrɪtl/ *a* frágil

broach /brəʊtʃ/ *vt* abordar, entabular, encetar

broad /brɔːd/ *a* (-er, -est) largo; (*daylight*) pleno. **~band** banda *f* larga **~ bean** fava *f*. **~-minded** *a* tolerante, liberal. **~ly** *adv* de modo geral

broadcast /ˈbrɔːdkɑːst/ *vt/i* (*pt* **broadcast**) transmitir, fazer uma transmissão; (*person*) cantar, falar *etc* na rádio ou na TV □ *n* emissão *f*. **~ing** *a* de rádiodifusão □ *f*

broaden /ˈbrɔːdn/ *vt/i* alargar(-se)

broccoli /ˈbrɒkəlɪ/ *n* brócolis *mpl*, (*P*) brócolos *mpl*

brochure /ˈbrəʊʃə(r)/ *n* brochura *f*

broke /brəʊk/ *see* **break** □ *a* (*sl*) depenado (*sl*), liso (*sl*), (*P*) teso (*sl*)

broken /ˈbrəʊkən/ *see* **break** □ *a* **~ English** inglês *m* estropeado. **~-hearted** *a* com o coração despedaçado

broker /ˈbrəʊkə(r)/ *n* corretor *m*, broker *m*

bronchitis /brɒŋˈkaɪtɪs/ *n* bronquite *f*

bronze /brɒnz/ *n* bronze *m*

brooch /brəʊtʃ/ *n* broche *m*

brood /bruːd/ *n* ninhada *f* □ *vi* chocar; (*fig*) cismar. **~y** *a* (*hen*) choca; (*fig*) sorumbático

brook /brʊk/ *n* regato *m*, ribeiro *m*

broom /bruːm/ *n* vassoura *f*; (*bot*) giesta *f*

broth /brɒθ/ *n* caldo *m*

brothel /ˈbrɒθl/ *n* bordel *m*

brother /ˈbrʌðə(r)/ *n* irmão *m*. **~-in-law** (*pl* **~s-in-law**) cunhado *m*. **~hood** *n* irmandade *f*, fraternidade *f*. **~ly** *a* fraternal

brought /brɔːt/ *see* **bring**

brow /braʊ/ *n* (*forehead*) testa *f*; (*of hill*) cume *m*; (*eyebrow*) sobrancelha *f*

browbeat /ˈbraʊbiːt/ *vt* (*pt* **-beat**, *pp* **-beaten**) intimidar

brown /braʊn/ *a* (-er, -est) castanho □ *n* castanho *m* □ *vt/i* acastanhar; (*in the sun*) bronzear, tostar; (*meat*) alourar

browse /braʊz/ *vi* (*through book*) folhear; (*of animal*) pastar; (*in a shop*) olhar sem comprar. **~r** (*comput*) navegador *m*

bruise /bruːz/ *n* hematoma *m*, contusão *f* □ *vt* causar um hematoma. **~d** *a* coberto de hematomas, contuso; (*fruit*) machucado

brunette /bruːˈnet/ *n* morena *f*

brunt /brʌnt/ *n* the **~ of** o maior peso de, o pior de

brush /brʌʃ/ *n* escova *f*; (*painter's*) pincel *m*; (*skirmish*) escaramuça *f*. **~ against** roçar. **~ aside** não fazer caso de. **~ off** (*colloq*: *reject*) mandar passear (*colloq*). **~ up (on)** aperfeiçoar

brusque /bruːsk/ *a* brusco

Brussels /ˈbrʌslz/ *n* Bruxelas *f*. **~ sprouts** couve-de-Bruxelas *f*

brutal /ˈbruːtl/ *a* brutal. **~ity** /-ˈtælətɪ/ *n* brutalidade *f*

brute /bruːt/ *n* & *a* (*animal*, *person*) bruto (*m*). **by ~ force** por força bruta

BSc *abbr see* **Bachelor of Science**

BSE /'biːɛsˈiː/ *n* EEB, encefalopatia espongiforme bovina

bubb|le /'bʌbl/ *n* bolha *f*; (*of soap*) bola *f* de sabão □ *vi* borbulhar. ~**le gum** *n* chiclete *m*, (*P*) pastilha *f* elástica. ~**le over** transbordar. ~**ly** *a* efervescente

buck[1] /bʌk/ *n* macho *m* □ *vi* dar galões, (*P*) corcovear. ~ **up** *vt/i* (*sl*) animar(-se); (*sl: rush*) apressar-se, despachar-se

buck[2] /bʌk/ *n* (*Amer sl*) dólar *m*

buck[3] /bʌk/ *n* **pass the** ~ (*sl*) fazer o jogo do empurra

bucket /'bʌkɪt/ *n* balde *m*

buckle /'bʌkl/ *n* fivela *f* □ *vt/i* afivelar(-se); (*bend*) torcer(-se), vergar. ~ **down to** empenhar-se

bud /bʌd/ *n* botão *m*, rebento *m* □ *vi* (*pt* budded) rebentar. **in** ~ em botão

Buddhis|t /'bʊdɪst/ *a* & *n* budista (*mf*). ~**m** /-zəm/ *n* budismo *m*

budding /'bʌdɪŋ/ *a* nascente, em botão, incipiente

budge /bʌdʒ/ *vt/i* mexer(-se)

budgerigar /'bʌdʒərɪɡɑː(r)/ *n* periquito *m*

budget /'bʌdʒɪt/ *n* orçamento *m* □ *vi* (*pt* budgeted) ~ **for** prever no orçamento *m*

buff /bʌf/ *n* (*colour*) côr *f* de camurça; (*colloq*) fanático *m*, entusiasta *mf* □ *vt* polir

buffalo /'bʌfələʊ/ *n* (*pl* -oes) búfalo *m*; (*Amer*) bisão *m*

buffer /'bʌfə(r)/ *n* pára-choque *m*

buffet[1] /'bʊfeɪ/ *n* (*meal, counter*) bufê *m*, (*P*) bufete *m*

buffet[2] /'bʌfɪt/ *vt* (*pt* buffeted) esbofetear

buffoon /bə'fuːn/ *n* palhaço *m*

bug /bʌg/ *n* (*insect*) bicho *m*; (*bedbug*) percevejo *m*; (*sl: germ*) vírus *m*; (*sl: device*) microfone *m* de escuta; (*sl: defect*) defeito *m* □ *vt* (*pt* bugged) grampear; (*Amer sl: an-*

noy) chatear (*sl*)

bugbear /'bʌgbeə(r)/ *n* papão *m*

buggy /'bʌgɪ/ *n* (*for baby*) carrinho *m*

bugle /'bjuːgl/ *n* clarim *m*

build /bɪld/ *vt/i* (*pt* built) construir, edificar □ *n* físico *m*, compleição *f*. ~ **up** *vt/i* criar; (*increase*) aumentar; (*accumulate*) acumular(-se). ~-**up** *n* acumulação *f*; (*fig*) publicidade *f*. ~**er** *n* construtor *m*; empreiteiro *m*; (*workman*) operário *m*

building /'bɪldɪŋ/ *n* edifício *m*, prédio *m*. ~ **site** canteiro *m* de obras. ~ **society** sociedade *f* de investimentos imobiliários

built /bɪlt/ *see* **build**. ~-**in** *a* incorporado. ~-**in wardrobe** armário *m* embutido na parede. ~-**up** *a* urbanizado

bulb /bʌlb/ *n* bolbo *m*; (*electr*) lâmpada *f*. ~**ous** *a* bolboso

Bulgaria /bʌl'geəriə/ *n* Bulgária *f*. ~**n** *a* & *n* búlgaro (*m*)

bulge /bʌldʒ/ *n* bojo *m*, saliência *f* □ *vi* inchar; (*jut out*) fazer uma saliência. ~**ing** *a* inchado; (*pocket etc*) cheio

bulk /bʌlk/ *n* quantidade *f*, volume *m*. **in** ~ por grosso; (*loose*) a granel. **the** ~ **of** a maior parte de. ~**y** *a* volumoso

bull /bʊl/ *n* touro *m*. ~'**s-eye** *n* (*of target*) centro *m* do alvo, mosca *f*

bulldog /'bʊldɒg/ *n* buldogue *m*

bulldoze /'bʊldəʊz/ *vt* terraplanar. ~**r** /-ə(r)/ *n* bulldozer *m*

bullet /'bʊlɪt/ *n* bala *f*. ~-**proof** *a* à prova de balas; (*vehicle*) blindado

bulletin /'bʊlətɪn/ *n* boletim *m*

bullfight /'bʊlfaɪt/ *n* tourada *f*, corrida *f* de touros. ~**er** *n* toureiro *m*. ~**ing** *n* tauromaquia *f*

bullring /'bʊlrɪŋ/ *n* arena *f*, (*P*) praça *f* de touros

bully /'bʊlɪ/ *n* mandão *m*, pessoa *f* prepotente; (*schol*) terror *m*, o mau □ *vt* intimidar; (*treat badly*) atormentar; (*coerce*) forçar (**into** a)

bum[1] /bʌm/ *n* (*sl: buttocks*) traseiro *m*, bunda *f* (*sl*)

bum[2] /bʌm/ *n* (*Amer sl*) vagabundo *m*

bump /bʌmp/ *n* choque *m*, embate *m*; (*swelling*) inchaço *m*; (*on head*) galo *m* □ *vt/i* bater, chocar. **~ into** bater em, chocar com; (*meet*) esbarrar com, encontrar. **~y** *a* (*surface*) irregular; (*ride*) aos solavancos

bumper /ˈbʌmpə(r)/ *n* párachoques *m inv* □ *a* excepcional

bun /bʌn/ *n* pãozinho *m* doce com passas; (*hair*) coque *m*

bunch /bʌntʃ/ *n* (*of flowers*) ramo *m*; (*of keys*) molho *m*; (*of people*) grupo *m*; (*of grapes*) cacho *m*

bundle /ˈbʌndl/ *n* molho *m* □ *vt* atar num molho; (*push*) despachar

bung /bʌŋ/ *n* batoque *m*, rolha *f* □ *vt* rolhar; (*sl: throw*) atirar, deitar. **~ up** entupir

bungalow /ˈbʌŋɡələʊ/ *n* chalé *m*; (*outside Europe*) bungalô *m*, (*P*) bungalow *m*

bungle /ˈbʌŋɡl/ *vt* fazer mal feito, estragar

bunion /ˈbʌnjən/ *n* (*med*) joanete *m*

bunk /bʌŋk/ *n* (*in train*) couchette *f*; (*in ship*) beliche *m*. **~-beds** *npl* beliches *mpl*

bunker /ˈbʌŋkə(r)/ *n* (*mil*) abrigo *m*, casamata *f*, bunker *m*; (*golf*) obstáculo *m* em cova de areia

buoy /bɔɪ/ *n* bóia *f* □ *vt* **~ up** animar

buoyant /ˈbɔɪənt/ *a* flutuante; (*fig*) alegre. **~cy** *n* (*fig*) alegria *f*, exuberância *f*

burden /ˈbɜːdn/ *n* fardo *m* □ *vt* collegar, sobrecarregar. **~some** *a* pesado

bureau /ˈbjʊərəʊ/ *n* (*pl* **-eaux**) /-əʊz/ (*desk*) secretária *f*; (*office*) seção *f*, (*P*) secção *f*

bureaucracy /bjʊəˈrɒkrəsɪ/ *n* burocracia *f*

bureaucrat /ˈbjʊərəkræt/ *n* burocrata *mf*. **~ic** /-ˈkrætɪk/ *a* burocrático

burger /ˈbɜːɡə(r)/ *n*

burglar /ˈbɜːɡlə(r)/ *n* ladrão *m*, assaltante *mf*. **~ alarm** *n* alarme *m* contra ladrões. **~ize** *vt* (*Amer*) assaltar. **~y** *n* assalto *m*

burgle /ˈbɜːɡl/ *vt* assaltar

burial /ˈberɪəl/ *n* enterro *m*

burly /ˈbɜːlɪ/ *a* (**-ier, -iest**) robusto e corpulento, forte

Burm|a /ˈbɜːmə/ *n* Birmânia *f*. **~ese** /-ˈmiːz/ *a* & *n* birmanês (*m*)

burn /bɜːn/ *vt* (*pt* **burned** *or* **burnt**) queimar □ *vi* queimar (-se), arder □ *n* queimadura *f*. **~ down** reduzir a cinzas. **~er** *n* (*of stove*) bico *m* de gás. **~ing** *a* (*thirst, desire*) ardente; (*topic*) candente

burnt /bɜːnt/ *see* **burn**

burp /bɜːp/ *n* (*colloq*) arroto *m* □ *vi* (*colloq*) arrotar

burrow /ˈbʌrəʊ/ *n* toca *f* □ *vi* cavar, fazer uma toca

burst /bɜːst/ *vt/i* (*pt* **burst**) arrebentar □ *n* estouro *m*, rebentar *m*; (*of anger, laughter*) explosão *f*; (*of firing*) rajada *f*, (*of energy*) acesso *m*. **~ into** (*flames, room, etc*) irromper em. **~ into tears** desatar num choro, desfazer-se em lágrimas. **~ out laughing** desatar a rir

bury /ˈberɪ/ *vt* sepultar, enterrar; (*hide*) esconder; (*engross, thrust*) mergulhar

bus /bʌs/ *n* (*pl* **buses**) ônibus *m*, (*P*) autocarro *m*. **~-lane** faixa *f* de ônibus, de autocarro (*p*). **~-stop** *n* paragem *f*

bush /bʊʃ/ *n* arbusto *m*; (*land*) mato *m*. **~y** *a* espesso

business /'bɪznɪs/ n (*trade, shop, affair*) negócio m; (*task*) função f; (*occupation*) ocupação f. **have no ~ to** não ter o direito de. **it's no ~ of yours** não é da sua conta. **mind your own ~** cuide da sua vida. **that's my ~** isso é meu problema. **~like** a eficiente, sistemático. **~man** n homem m de negócios, comerciante m

busker /'bʌskə(r)/ n músico m ambulante

bust[1] /bʌst/ n busto m

bust[2] /bʌst/ vt/i (*pt* **busted** or **bust**) (*sl*) = **burst**, **break** □ a falido. **~-up** n (*sl*) discussão f, (*P*) bulha f. **go ~** (*sl*) falir

bustl|e /'bʌsl/ vi andar numa azáfama; (*hurry*) apressar-se □ n azáfama f. **~ing** a animado, movimentado

bus|y /'bɪzɪ/ a (*-ier, -iest*) ocupado; (*street*) movimentado; (*day*) atarefado □ vt **~y o.s. with** ocupar-se com. **~ily** adv ativamente, atarefadamente

busybody /'bɪzɪbɒdɪ/ n intrometido m, pessoa f abelhuda

but /bʌt/ conj mas □ prep exceto, (*P*) excepto, senão □ adv apenas, só. **all ~** todos menos; (*nearly*) quaze, por pouco não. **~ for** sem, se não fosse. **last ~ one/two** penúltimo/antepenúltimo. **nobody ~** ninguém a não ser

butcher /'bʊtʃə(r)/ n açougueiro m, (*P*) homem m do talho; (*fig*) carrasco m □ vt chacinar. **the ~'s** açougue m, (*P*) talho m. **~y** n chacina f

butler /'bʌtlə(r)/ n mordomo m

butt /bʌt/ n (*of gun*) coronha f; (*of cigarette*) ponta f; (*target*) alvo m de troça, de ridículo etc; (*cask*) barril m □ vt/i dar cabeçada em. **~ in** interromper

butter /'bʌtə(r)/ n manteiga f □ vt

pôr manteiga em. **~-bean** n feijão m branco

buttercup /'bʌtəkʌp/ n botão-de-ouro m

butterfly /'bʌtəflaɪ/ n borboleta f

buttock /'bʌtək/ n nádega f

button /'bʌtn/ n botão m □ vt/i abotoar(-se)

buttonhole /'bʌtnhəʊl/ n casa f de botão; (*in lapel*) botoeira f □ vt (*fig*) obrigar a ouvir

buttress /'bʌtrɪs/ n contraforte m; (*fig*) esteio m □ vt sustentar

buxom /'bʌksəm/ a roliço, rechonchudo

buy /baɪ/ vt (*pt* **bought**) comprar (**from** a); (*sl: believe*) engolir (*colloq*) □ n compra f. **~er** n comprador m

buzz /bʌz/ n zumbido m □ vi zumbir. **~ off** (*sl*) pôr-se a andar. **~er** n campainha f

by /baɪ/ prep (*near*) junto de, perto de; (*along, past, means*) por; (*according to*) conforme; (*before*) antes de. **~ land/sea/air** por terra/mar/ar. **~ bike/car** etc de bicicleta/carro etc. **~ day/night** de dia/noite. **~ the kilo** por quilo. **~ now** a esta hora. **~ accident/mistake** sem querer. **~ oneself** sozinho □ adv (*near*) perto. **~ and ~** muito em breve. **~ and large** no conjunto. **~-election** n eleição f suplementar. **~-law** n regulamento m. **~-product** n derivado m

bye(-bye) /'baɪ(baɪ)/ int (*colloq*) adeus, adeusinho

bygone /'baɪgɒn/ a passado. **let ~s be ~s** o que passou, passou

bypass /'baɪpɑːs/ n (*estrada*) secundária f, desvio m; (*med*) bypass m, ponte f de safena □ vt fazer um desvio, (*fig*) contornar

bystander /'baɪstændə(r)/ n circumstante mf, espectador m

byte /baɪt/ n byte m

C

cab /kæb/ n táxi m; (of lorry, train) cabina f, cabine f

cabaret /'kæbəreɪ/ n variedades fpl, cabaré m

cabbage /'kæbɪdʒ/ n couve f, repolho m

cabin /'kæbɪn/ n cabana f; (in plane) cabina f; (in ship) camarote m

cabinet /'kæbɪnɪt/ n armário m. **C~** (pol) gabinete m

cable /'keɪbl/ n cabo m. ~-car n funicular m, teleférico m. ~ **railway** funicular m. ~ **television** televisão f a cabo

cache /kæʃ/ n (esconderijo m de) tesouro m, armas fpl, provisões f pl

cackle /'kækl/ n cacarejo m □ vi cacarejar

cactus /'kæktəs/ n (pl ~es or cacti /-taɪ/) cacto m

caddie /'kædɪ/ n (golf) caddie m

caddy /'kædɪ/ n lata f para o chá

cadet /kə'det/ n cadete m

cadge /kædʒ/ vt/i filar, (P) cravar

Caesarean /sɪ'zeərɪən/ a ~ (section) cesariana f

café /'kæfeɪ/ n café m

cafeteria /kæfɪ'tɪərɪə/ n cafeteria f, restaurante m self-service

caffeine /'kæfiːn/ n cafeína f

cage /keɪdʒ/ n gaiola f

cagey /'keɪdʒɪ/ a (colloq: secretive) misterioso, reservado

cajole /kə'dʒəʊl/ vt ~ **sb into doing sth** convencer alguém (com lábia ou lisonjas) a fazer alg coisa

cake /keɪk/ n bolo m. ~**d** a empastado. **his shoes were ~d with mud** tinha os sapatos cobertos de lama. **a piece of ~** (sl) canja f (sl)

calamity /kə'læmətɪ/ n calamidade f

calcium /'kælsɪəm/ n cálcio m

calculat|e /'kælkjʊleɪt/ vt/i calcular; (Amer: suppose) supor. ~**ed** a (action) deliberado, calculado. ~**ing** a calculista. ~**ion** /-'leɪʃn/ n cálculo m. ~**or** n calculador m, (P) maquina f de calcular

calendar /'kælɪndə(r)/ n calendário m

calf[1] /kɑːf/ n (pl **calves**) (young cow or bull) vitelo m, bezerro m; (of other animals) cria f

calf[2] /kɑːf/ n (pl **calves**) (of leg) barriga f da perna

calibrat|e /'kælɪbreɪt/ vt calibrar. ~**ion** /-'breɪʃn/ n calibragem f

calibre /'kælɪbə(r)/ n calibre m

calico /'kælɪkəʊ/ n pano m de algodão; (printed) chita f, algodão m

call /kɔːl/ vt/i chamar; (summon) convocar; (phone) telefonar. ~ (**in or round**) (visit) passar por casa de □ n chamada f; (bird's cry) canto m; (shout) brado m, grito m. **be ~ed** (named) chamar-se. **be on ~** estar de serviço. ~ **back** (phone) tornar a telefonar; (visit) voltar. ~ **for** (demand) pedir, requerer; (fetch) ir buscar. ~ **off** cancelar. ~ **on** (visit) visitar, fazer uma visita a. ~ **out (to)** chamar. ~ **up** (mil) mobilizar, recrutar; (phone) telefonar. ~**-box** n cabina f telefónica, (P) telefónica. ~**-centre** n central f tele fónica ~ er n visitante f, visita f; (phone) chamador m, (P) pessoa f que faz a chamada. ~**ing** n vocação f

callous /'kæləs/ a insensível. ~**ly** adv sem piedade.

callow /'kæləʊ/ a (-er, -est) inexperiente, verde

calm /kɑːm/ a (-er, -est) calmo □ n calma f □ vt/i ~ (**down**) acalmar(-se). ~**ness** n calma f

calorie /'kælərɪ/ n caloria f

camber /'kæmbə(r)/ *n* (*of road*) abaulamento *m*

camcorder /'kæmkɔːdə(r)/ *n* câmera *f* de filmar

came /keɪm/ *see* **come**

camel /'kæml/ *n* camelo *m*

camera /'kæmərə/ *n* máquina *f* fotográfica; (*cine, TV*) câmera *f*. **∼man** *n* (*pl* **-men**) operador *m*

camouflage /'kæməflɑːʒ/ *n* camuflagem *f* □ *vt* camuflar

camp[1] /kæmp/ *n* acampamento *m* □ *vi* acampar. **∼bed** *n* cama *f* de campanha. **∼er** *n* campista *mf*; (*car*) auto-caravana *f*. **∼ing** *n* campismo *m*

camp[2] /kæmp/ *a* afetado, efeminado

campaign /kæm'peɪn/ *n* campanha *f* □ *vi* fazer campanha

campsite /'kæmpsaɪt/ *n* área *f* de camping, parque *m* de campismo

campus /'kæmpəs/ *n* (*pl* **-puses** /-pəsɪz/) campus *m*, (*P*) cidade *f* universitária

can[1] /kæn/ *n* vasilha *f* de lata; (*for food*) lata *f* (de conserva) □ *vt* (*pt* **canned**) enlatar. **∼ned music** música *f* em fita para locais públicos. **∼-opener** *n* abridor *m* de latas, (*P*) abrelatas *m*

can[2] /kæn/ *v aux* (*be able to*) poder, ser capaz de; (*know how to*) saber. **I ∼not**/**∼'t go** não posso ir

Canada /'kænədə/ *n* Canadá *m*. **∼ian** /kə'neɪdɪən/ *a* & *n* canadense (*mf*), (*P*) canadiano (*m*)

canal /kə'næl/ *n* canal *m*

canary /kə'neərɪ/ *n* canário *m*. **C∼ Islands** *npl* as (Ilhas) Canárias

cancel /'kænsl/ *vt* (*pt* **cancelled**) cancelar; (*cross out*) riscar; (*stamps*) inutilizar. **∼ out** *vi* (*fig*) neutralizar-se mutuamente. **∼lation** /-'leɪʃn/ *n* cancelamento *m*

cancer /'kænsə(r)/ *n* câncer *m*, cancro *m*. **C∼** (*astrol*) Caranguejo *m*, Câncer *m*. **∼ous** *a* canceroso

candid /'kændɪd/ *a* franco. **∼ly** *adv* francamente

candidate /'kændɪdeɪt/ *n* candidato *m*. **∼cy** /-əsɪ/ *n* candidatura *f*

candle /'kændl/ *n* vela *f*; (*in church*) vela *f*, círio *m*. **∼-light** *n* luz *f* de velas

candlestick /'kændlstɪk/ *n* castiçal *m*

candour /'kændə(r)/ *n* franqueza *f*, candura *f*

candy /'kændɪ/ *n* bala *f*, (*P*) açúcar cândi; (*Amer: sweet, sweets*) doce(s) *m* (*pl*). **∼-floss** *n* algodão-doce *m*

cane /keɪn/ *n* cana *f*; (*walking-stick*) bengala *f*; (*for baskets*) verga *f*; (*school: for punishment*) vergasta *f* □ *vt* vergastar

canine /'keɪnaɪn/ *a* & *n* canino (*m*)

canister /'kænɪstə(r)/ *n* lata *f*

cannabis /'kænəbɪs/ *n* cânhamo *m*, maconha *f*

cannibal /'kænɪbl/ *n* canibal *mf*. **∼ism** /-zəm/ *n* canibalismo *m*

cannon /'kænən/ *n inv* canhão *m*. **∼-ball** *n* bala *f* de canhão

cannot /'kænət/ = **can not**

canny /'kænɪ/ *a* (**-ier, -iest**) astuto, manhoso

canoe /kə'nuː/ *n* canoa *f* □ *vi* andar de canoa. **∼ing** *n* (*sport*) canoagem *f*. **∼ist** *n* canoeiro *m*, (*P*) canoísta *mf*

canon /'kænən/ *n* cônego *m*, (*P*) cónego *m*; (*rule*) cânone *m*

canonize /'kænənaɪz/ *vt* canonizar

canopy /'kænəpɪ/ *n* dossel *m*; (*over doorway*) toldo *m*, marquise *f*; (*fig*) abóbada *f*

can't /kɑːnt/ = **can not**

cantankerous /kæn'tæŋkərəs/ *a* irascível, intratável

canteen /kæn'ti:n/ *n* cantina *f*; (*flask*) cantil *m*; (*for cutlery*) estojo *m*

canter /'kæntə(r)/ *n* meio galope *m*, cânter *m* □ *vi* andar a meio galope

canton /'kæntɒn/ *n* cantão *m*

canvas /'kænvəs/ *n* lona *f*; (*for painting or tapestry*) tela *f*

canvass /'kænvəs/ *vt/i* angariar votos *or* fregueses

canyon /'kænjən/ *n* canhão *m*, (P) desfiladeiro *m*

cap /kæp/ *n* (*with peak*) boné *m*; (*without peak*) barrete *m*; (*of nurse*) touca *f*; (*of bottle, pen, tube, etc*) tampa *f*; (*mech*) tampa *f*, tampão *m* □ *vt* (*pt* **capped**) (*bottle, pen, tube, etc*) tapar, tampar; (*rates*) impor um limite a; (*outdo*) suplantar; (*sport*) seleccionar, (P) seleccionar. **~ped with** encimado de, coroado de

capab|**le** /'keɪpəbl/ *a* (*a person*) capaz (**of** de); (*things, situations*) susceptível, (P) susceptível (**of** de). **~ility** /-'bɪlətɪ/ *n* capacidade *f*. **~ly** *adv* capazmente

capacity /kə'pæsətɪ/ *n* capacidade *f*. **in one's ~ as** na (sua) qualidade de

cape[1] /keɪp/ *n* (*cloak*) capa *f*

cape[2] /keɪp/ *n* (*geog*) cabo *m*

caper[1] /'keɪpə(r)/ *vi* andar aos pinotes

caper[2] /'keɪpə(r)/ *n* (*culin*) alcaparra *f*

capillary /kə'pɪlərɪ/ *n* (*pl* -ies) vaso *m* capilar

capital /'kæpɪtl/ *a* capital □ *n* (*town*) capital *f*; (*money*) capital *m*. **~ (letter)** maiúscula *f*. **~ punishment** pena *f* de morte

capitalis|**t** /'kæpɪtəlɪst/ *a* & *n* capitalista (*mf*). **~m** /-zəm/ *n* capitalismo *m*

capitalize /'kæpɪtəlaɪz/ *vi* capitalizar; (*finance*) financiar; (*writ-*

ing) escrever com maiúscula. **~ on** tirar partido de

capitulat|**e** /kə'pɪtʃʊleɪt/ *vi* capitular. **~ion** *n* capitulação *f*

capricious /kə'prɪʃəs/ *a* caprichoso

Capricorn /'kæprɪkɔ:n/ *n* (*astrol*) Capricórnio *m*

capsicum /'kæpsɪkəm/ *n* pimento *m*

capsize /kæp'saɪz/ *vt/i* virar(-se)

capsule /'kæpsju:l/ *n* cápsula *f*

captain /'kæptɪn/ *n* capitão *m*; (*navy*) capitão-de-mar-e-guerra *m* □ *vt* capitanear, comandar

caption /'kæpʃn/ *n* legenda *f*; (*heading*) título *m*

captivate /'kæptɪveɪt/ *vt* cativar

captiv|**e** /'kæptɪv/ *a* & *n* cativo (*m*), prisioneiro (*m*). **~ity** /-'tɪvətɪ/ *n* cativeiro *m*

captor /'kæptə(r)/ *n* captor *m*

capture /'kæptʃə(r)/ *vt* capturar; (*attention*) prender □ *n* captura *f*

car /ka:(r)/ *n* carro *m*. **~ ferry** barca *f* para carros. **~-park** *n* (parque *m* para) estacionamento (*m*). **~ phone** telefone *m* de carro. **~-wash** *n* estação *f* de lavagem

carafe /kə'ræf/ *n* garrafa *f* para água ou vinho

caramel /'kærəmel/ *n* caramelo *m*

carat /'kærət/ *n* quilate *m*

caravan /'kærəvæn/ *n* caravana *f*, reboque *m*

caraway /'kærəweɪ/ *n* **~ seed** cariz *f*

carbohydrate /ka:bəʊ'haɪdreɪt/ *n* hidrato *m* de carbono

carbon /'ka:bən/ *n* carbono *m*. **~ copy** cópia *f* em papel carbono, (P) químico. **~ monoxide** óxido *m* de carbono. **~ paper** papel *m* carbono, (P) químico

carburettor /ka:bjʊ'retə(r)/ *n* carburador *m*

carcass /'ka:kəs/ n carcaça f

card /ka:d/ n cartão m; (postcard) postal m; (playing-card) carta f. **~-game(s)** n(pl) jogo(s) m(pl) de cartas. **~ index** n fichário m, (P) ficheiro m

cardboard /'ka:dbɔ:d/ n cartão m, papelão m

cardiac /'ka:diæk/ a cardíaco

cardigan /'ka:dɪgən/ n casaco m de lã

cardinal /'ka:dɪnl/ a cardeal, principal. **~ number** numeral m cardinal □ n (relig) cardeal m

care /keə(r)/ n cuidado m; (concern) interesse m □ vi ~ **about** (be interested) estar interessado por; (be worried) estar preocupado com. ~ **for** (like) gostar de; (look after) tomar conta de. **take** ~ tomar cuidado. **take** ~ **of** cuidar de; (deal with) tratar de. **he couldn't** ~ **less** ele está pouco ligando, ele não dá a menor (colloq)

career /kə'rɪə(r)/ n carreira f □ vi ir a toda a velocidade, ir numa carreira

carefree /'keəfri:/ a despreocupado

careful /'keəfl/ a cuidadoso; (cautious) cauteloso. ~! cuidado! **~ly** adv cuidadosamente; (cautiously) cautelosamente

careless /'keəlɪs/ a descuidado (about com). **~ly** adv descuidadamente. **~ness** n descuido m, negligência f

caress /kə'res/ n carícia f □ vt acariciar

caretaker /'keəteɪkə(r)/ n zelador m duma casa vizia; (janitor) zelador m, (P) porteiro m

cargo /'ka:gəʊ/ n (pl -oes) carregamento m, carga f

Caribbean /kærɪ'bi:ən/ a caraíba. **the** ~ as Caraíbas fpl

caricature /'kærɪkətjʊə(r)/ n caricatura f □ vt caricaturar

caring /'keərɪŋ/ a carinhoso, afetuoso, (P) afectuoso

carnage /'ka:nɪdʒ/ n carnificina f

carnation /ka:'neɪʃn/ n cravo m

carnival /'ka:nɪvl/ n carnaval m

carol /'kærəl/ n cântico m or canto m de Natal

carp¹ /ka:p/ n inv carpa f

carp² /ka:p/ vi ~ (at) criticar

carpenter /'ka:pɪntə(r)/ n carpinteiro m. **~ry** n carpintaria f

carpet /'ka:pɪt/ n tapete m □ vt (pt carpeted) atapetar. **with fitted** ~s (estar) atapetado. **be on the** ~ (colloq) ser chamado à ordem. **~-sweeper** n limpador m de tapetes

carport /'ka:pɔ:t/ n abrigo m, (P) telheiro m para automóveis

carriage /'kærɪdʒ/ n carruagem f; (of goods) frete m, transporte m; (cost, bearing) porte m

carriageway /'kærɪdʒweɪ/ n faixa f de rodagem, pista f

carrier /'kærɪə(r)/ n transportador m; (company) transportadora f; (med) portador m. ~ **(bag)** saco m de plástico

carrot /'kærət/ n cenoura f

carry /'kærɪ/ vt/i levar; (goods) transportar; (involve) acarretar; (have for sale) ter à venda. **be carried away** entusiasmar-se, deixar-se levar. **~-cot** n moisés m. ~ **off** levar à força; (prize) incluir. ~ **it off** sair-se bem (de). ~ **on** continuar; (colloq: flirt) flertar; (colloq: behave) portar-se (mal). ~ **out** executar; (duty) cumprir. ~ **through** levar a cabo

cart /ka:t/ n carroça f; carro m □ vt acarretar; (colloq) carregar com

cartilage /'ka:tɪlɪdʒ/ n cartilagem f

carton /'ka:tn/ n embalagem f de cartão or de plástico; (of yogurt) embalagem f, pote m; (of milk) pacote m

cartoon /ka:'tu:n/ n desenho m humorístico, caricatura f; (strip) estória f em quadrinhos, (P) banda f desenhada; (film) desenhos mpl animados. ~ist n caricaturista mf; (of strip, film) desenhador m

cartridge /'ka:trɪdʒ/ n cartucho m

carve /ka:v/ vt esculpir, talhar; (meat) trinchar. ~d n obra f de talha; (on tree-trunk) incisão f. ~ing knife faca f de trinchar, trinchante m

cascade /kæs'keɪd/ n cascata f □ vi cair em cascata

case¹ /keɪs/ n caso m; (jur) causa f, processo m; (phil) argumentos mpl. in any ~ em todo caso. in ~ (of) no caso de. in that ~ nesse caso

case² /keɪs/ n caixa f, (crate) caixa f, caixote m; (for camera, jewels, spectacles, etc) estojo m; (suitcase) mala f; (for cigarettes) cigarreira f

cash /kæʃ/ n dinheiro m, numerário m, cash m □ vt (obtain money for) cobrar, receber; (give money for) pagar. **be short of** ~ ter pouco dinheiro. ~ a cheque (receive/give) cobrar/descontar um cheque. ~ in receber. ~ in (on) aproveitar-se de. in ~ em dinheiro. **pay** ~ pagar em dinheiro. ~ **desk** caixa f. ~ **dispenser** caixa f electrónica. ~-**flow** n cash-flow m. ~ **register** caixa f registadora, (P) registadora f

cashew /kæ'ʃu:/ n caju m

cashier /kæ'ʃɪə(r)/ n caixa mf

cashmere /kæʃ'mɪə(r)/ n caxemira f

casino /kə'si:nəʊ/ n (pl -os) casino m

cask /ka:sk/ n casco m, barril m

casket /'ka:skɪt/ n pequeno cofre m; (Amer: coffin) caixão m

casserole /'kæsərəʊl/ n caçarola f; (stew) estufado m

cassette /kə'set/ n cassette f. ~ **player** gravador m. ~ **recorder** n gravador m

cast /ka:st/ vt (pt cast) lançar, arremessar; (shed) despojar-se de; (vote) dar; (metal) fundir; (shadow) projetar, (P) projectar □ n (theatr) elenco m; (mould) molde m; (med) aparelho m de gesso. ~ **iron** n ferro m fundido. ~-**iron** a de ferro fundido; (fig) muito forte. ~-**offs** npl roupa f velha

castanets /kæstə'nets/ npl castanholas fpl

castaway /'ka:stəweɪ/ n náufrago m

caste /ka:st/ n casta f

castigate /'kæstɪgeɪt/ vt castigar

castle /'ka:sl/ n castelo m; (chess) torre f

castor /'ka:stə(r)/ n roda f de pé de móvel. ~ **sugar** açúcar m em pó

castrate /kæ'streɪt/ vt castrar. ~**ion** /-ʃn/ n castração f

casual /'kæʒʊəl/ a (chance: meeting) casual; (careless, unmethodical) descuidado; (informal) informal. ~ **clothes** roupa f prática or de lazer. ~ **work** trabalho m ocasional. ~**ly** adv casualmente; (carelessly) sem cuidado

casualty /'kæʒʊəltɪ/ n (dead) morto m; (death) morte f; (injured) ferido m; (victim) vítima f; (mil) baixa f

cat /kæt/ n gato m. ~'s-**eyes** npl (P) reflectores mpl

Catalonia /kætə'ləʊnɪə/ n Catalunha f

catalogue /'kætəlɒg/ n catálogo m □ vt catalogar

catalyst /'kætəlɪst/ n catalisador m

catapult /'kætəpʌlt/ n (child's) atiradeira f, (P) fisga f □ vt catapultar

cataract /'kætərækt/ f (waterfall & med) catarata f

catarrh /kə'ta:(r)/ n catarro m

catastroph|e /kə'tæstrəfi/ *n* catástrofe *f*. **∼ic** /kætəs'trɒfik/ *a* catastrófico

catch /kætʃ/ *vt* (*pt* **caught**) apanhar; (*grasp*) agarrar; (*hear*) perceber □ *vi* prender-se (**in** em); (*get stuck*) ficar preso □ *n* apanha *f*; (*of fish*) pesca *f*; (*trick*) ratoeira *f*; (*snag*) problema *m*; (*on door*) trinco *m*; (*fastener*) fecho *m*. **∼ fire** pegar fogo, (*P*) incendiar-se. **∼ on** (*colloq*) pegar, tornar-se popular. **∼ sb's eye** atrair a atenção de alg. **∼ sight of** avistar. **∼ up (with)** pôr-se a par (com); (*work*) pôr em dia. **∼-phrase** *n* clichê *m*

catching /'kætʃɪŋ/ *a* contagioso, infeccioso

catchment /'kætʃmənt/ *n* **∼ area** (*geog*) bacia *f* de captação; (*fig: of school, hospital*) área *f*

catchy /'kætʃɪ/ *a* que pega fácil

categorical /kætɪ'gɒrɪkl/ *a* categórico

category /'kætɪgərɪ/ *n* categoria *f*

cater /'keɪtə(r)/ *vi* fornecer comida (para clubes, casamentos, etc). **∼ for** (*pander to*) satisfazer; (*consumers*) dirigir-se a. **∼er** *n* fornecedor *m*. **∼ing** *n* catering *m*

caterpillar /'kætəpɪlə(r)/ *n* lagarta *f*

cathedral /kə'θi:drəl/ *n* catedral *f*

catholic /'kæθəlɪk/ *a* universal; (*eclectic*) ecléctico, (*P*) eclético. **C∼** *a & n* católico (*m*). **C∼ism** /kə'θɒlɪsɪzəm/ *n* catolicismo *m*

cattle /'kætl/ *npl* gado *m*

catty /'kætɪ/ *a* (dissimuladamente) maldoso, com perfídia

caught /kɔ:t/ *see* **catch**

cauldron /'kɔ:ldrən/ *n* caldeirão *m*

cauliflower /'kɒlɪflaʊə(r)/ *n* couve-flor *f*

cause /kɔ:z/ *n* causa *f* □ *vt* causar. **∼ sth to grow/move** *etc* fazer crescer/mexer *etc* alg coisa

causeway /'kɔ:zweɪ/ *n* estrada *f* elevada, caminho *m* elevado

caustic /'kɔ:stɪk/ *a* cáustico

caution /'kɔ:ʃn/ *n* cautela *f*; (*warning*) aviso *m* □ *vt* avisar. **∼ous** /'kɔ:ʃəs/ *a* cauteloso. **∼ously** *adv* cautelosamente

cavalry /'kævəlrɪ/ *n* cavalaria *f*

cave /keɪv/ *n* caverna *f*, gruta *f* □ *vi* **∼ in** desabar, dar de si

caveman /'keɪvmæn/ *n* (*pl* **-men**) troglodita *m*, homem *m* das cavernas; (*fig*) (tipo) primário *m*

cavern /'kævən/ *n* caverna *f*. **∼ous** *a* cavernoso

caviare /'kævɪɑ:(r)/ *n* caviar *m*

caving /'keɪvɪŋ/ *n* espeleologia *f*

cavity /'kævətɪ/ *n* cavidade *f*

cavort /kə'vɔ:t/ *vi* curvetear; (*person*) andar aos pinotes

CD /si:'di:/ *see* **compact disc**

cease /si:s/ *vt/i* cessar. **∼-fire** *n* cessar-fogo *m*. **∼less** *a* incessante

cedar /'si:də(r)/ *n* cedro *m*

cedilla /sɪ'dɪlə/ *n* cedilha *f*

ceiling /'si:lɪŋ/ *n* (*lit & fig*) teto *m*, (*P*) tecto *m*

celebrat|e /'selɪbreɪt/ *vt/i* celebrar, festejar. **∼ion** /-'breɪʃn/ *n* celebração *f*, festejo *m*

celebrated /'selɪbreɪtɪd/ *a* célebre

celebrity /sɪ'lebrətɪ/ *n* celebridade *f*

celery /'selərɪ/ *n* aipo *m*

celiba|te /'selɪbət/ *a* celibatário. **∼cy** *n* celibato *m*

cell /sel/ *n* (*of prison, convent*) cela *f*; (*biol, pol, electr*) célula *f* **∼phone** (*B*) celular *m*, (*p*) telemóvel

cellar /'selə(r)/ *n* porão *m*, cave *f* (*for wine*) adega *f*, cave *f*

cell|o /'tʃeləʊ/ *n* (*pl* **-os**) violoncelo *m*. **∼ist** *n* violoncelista *m/f*

Cellophane /'seləfeɪn/ *n* (*P*) celofane *m*

cellular /'seljʊlə(r)/ *a* celular

Celt /kelt/ n celta mf. ～**ic** a celta, céltico

cement /sɪ'ment/ n cimento m □ vt cimentar. ～**mixer** n betoneira f

cemetery /'semətrɪ/ n cemitério m

censor /'sensə(r)/ n censor m □ vt censurar. ～**ship** n censura f

censure /'senʃə(r)/ n censura f, crítica f □ vt censurar, criticar

census /'sensəs/ n recenseamento m, censo m

cent /sent/ n cêntimo m

centenary /sen'ti:nərɪ/ n centenário m

centigrade /'sentɪgreɪd/ a centígrado

centilitre /'sentɪli:tə(r)/ n centilitro m

centimetre /'sentɪmi:tə(r)/ n centímetro m

centipede /'sentɪpi:d/ n centópeia f, (P) centopeia f

central /'sentrəl/ a central. ～ **heating** aquecimento m central. ～**ize** vt centralizar. ～**ly** adv no centro

centre /'sentə(r)/ n centro m □ vt (pt **centred**) centrar □ vi ～ **on** concentrar-se em, fixar-se em

centrifugal /sen'trɪfjʊgl/ a centrífugo

century /'sentʃərɪ/ n século m

ceramic /sɪ'ræmɪk/ a (object) em cerâmica. ～**s** n cerâmica f

cereal /'sɪərɪəl/ n cereal m

cerebral /'serɪbrəl/ a cerebral

ceremonial /serɪ'məʊnɪəl/ a de cerimónia □ n cerimonial m

ceremon|**y** /'serɪmənɪ/ n cerimónia f, (P) cerimónia f. ～**ious** /-'məʊnɪəs/ a cerimonioso

certain /'sɜ:tn/ a certo. **be** ～ ter a certeza. **for** ～ com certeza, ao certo. **make** ～ confirmar, verificar. ～**ly** adv com certeza, certamente. ～**ty** n certeza f

certificate /sə'tɪfɪkət/ n certificado m; (birth, marriage) certidão f; (health) atestado m

certif|**y** /'sɜ:tɪfaɪ/ vt/i certificar. ～**ied** a (as insane) declarado

cervical /sɜ:'vaɪkl/ a cervical; (of cervix) do útero

cesspit, cesspool /'sespɪt, 'sespu:l/ ns fossa f sanitária

chafe /tʃeɪf/ vt/i esfregar; (make become sore) esfolar/ficar esfolado; (fig) irritar(-se)

chaff /tʃa:f/ vt brincar com □ n brincadeira f; (husk) casca f

chaffinch /'tʃæfɪntʃ/ n tentilhão m

chagrin /'ʃægrɪn/ n decepção f, desgosto m, aborrecimento m

chain /tʃeɪn/ n corrente f, cadeia f; (series) cadeia f □ vt acorrentar. ～ **reaction** reacção f, (P) reacção f em cadeia. ～**-smoke** vi fumar cigarros um atrás do outro. ～**store** loja f pertencente a uma cadeia

chair /tʃeə(r)/ n cadeira f; (position of chairman) presidência f; (univ) cátedra f □ vt presidir

chairman /'tʃeəmən/ n (pl -men) presidente mf

chalet /'ʃæleɪ/ n chalé m

chalk /tʃɔ:k/ n greda f, cal f; (for writing) giz m □ vt traçar com giz

challenge /'tʃælɪndʒ/ n desafio m; (by sentry) interpelação f □ vt desafiar; (question truth of) contestar. ～**er** n (sport) pretendente mf (ao título). ～**ing** a estimulante, que constitui um desafio

chamber /'tʃeɪmbə(r)/ n (old use) aposento m. ～**-maid** n arrumadeira f. ～ **music** música f de câmara. **C～ of Commerce** Câmara f de Comércio

chamois /'ʃæmɪ/ n. ～ **(-leather)** camurça f

champagne /ʃæm'peɪn/ n champanhe m

champion /'tʃæmpɪən/ n campeão m, campeã f □ vt defender. **~ship** n campeonato m

chance /tʃɑːns/ n acaso m; (luck) sorte f; (opportunity) oportunidade f, chance f; (likelihood) hipótese f, probabilidade f; (risk) risco m □ a casual, fortuito □ vt calhar □ vt arriscar. **by ~** por acaso

chancellor /'tʃɑːnsələ(r)/ n chanceler m. **C~ of the Exchequer** Ministro m das Finanças

chancy /'tʃɑːnsɪ/ a arriscado

chandelier /ʃændə'lɪə(r)/ n lustre m

change /tʃeɪndʒ/ vt mudar; (exchange) trocar (for por); (clothes, house, trains, etc) mudar de □ vi mudar; (clothes) mudar-se, mudar de roupa □ n mudança f; (money) troco m. **a ~ of clothes** uma muda de roupa. **~ hands** (ownership) mudar de dono. **~ into** (a butterfly etc) transformar-se em; (evening dress etc) pôr. **~ one's mind** mudar de ideia. **~ over** passar, mudar (**to** para). **~ over** n mudança f. **~able** a variável

channel /'tʃænl/ n canal m □ vt (pt channelled) canalizar. **the C~ Islands** as Ilhas do Canal da Mancha. **the (English) C~** o Canal da Mancha

chant /tʃɑːnt/ n cântico m; (of crowd etc) vt/i cantar, entoar

chaos /'keɪɒs/ n caos m. **~tic** /-'ɒtɪk/ a caótico

chap /tʃæp/ n (colloq) sujeito m, (B) cara m, (P) tipo m

chapel /'tʃæpl/ n capela f

chaperon /'ʃæpərəʊn/ n pau-de-cabeleira m, chaperon m □ vt servir de pau-de-cabeleira or de chaperon

chaplain /'tʃæplɪn/ n capelão m. **~cy** n capelania f

chapter /'tʃæptə(r)/ n capítulo m

char /tʃɑː(r)/ vt (pt charred) carbonizar

character /'kærəktə(r)/ n caráter m, (P) carácter m; (in novel, play) personagem m; (reputation) fama f; (eccentric person) excêntrico m; (letter) caractere m, (P) carácter m. **~ize** vt caracterizar

characteristic /kærəktə'rɪstɪk/ a característico □ n característica f. **~ally** adv tipicamente

charade /ʃə'rɑːd/ n charada f

charcoal /'tʃɑːkəʊl/ n carvão m de lenha

charge /tʃɑːdʒ/ n preço m; (electr, mil) carga f; (jur) acusação f; (task, custody) cargo m □ vt/i (price) cobrar; (enemy) atacar; (jur) incriminar. **be in ~ of** ter a cargo. **take ~ of** encarregar-se de

chariot /'tʃærɪət/ n carro m de guerra or triunfal

charisma /kə'rɪzmə/ n carisma m. **~tic** /kærɪz'mætɪk/ a carismático

charit|y /'tʃærətɪ/ n caridade f; (society) instituição f de caridade. **~able** a caridoso

charlatan /'ʃɑːlətən/ n charlatão m

charm /tʃɑːm/ n encanto m, charme m; (spell) feitiço m; (talisman) amuleto m □ vt encantar. **~ing** a encantador

chart /tʃɑːt/ n (naut) carta f; (table) mapa m, gráfico m, tabela f □ vt fazer o mapa de

charter /'tʃɑːtə(r)/ n carta f. **~** (flight) (voo) charter m □ vt fretar. **~ed accountant** n perito m contador, (P) perito m de contabilidade

charwoman /'tʃɑːwʊmən/ n (pl -women) faxineira f, (P) mulher f a dias

chase /tʃeɪs/ vt perseguir □ vi (colloq) correr (**after** atrás de) □ n caça *f*, perseguição *f*. **~ away** *or* **off** afugentar, expulsar

chasm /'kæzm/ *n* abismo *m*

chassis /'ʃæsɪ/ *n* chassi *m*

chaste /tʃeɪst/ *a* casto

chastise /tʃæs'taɪz/ *vt* castigar

chastity /'tʃæstətɪ/ *n* castidade *f*

chat /tʃæt/ *n* conversa *f* □ *vi* (*pt* chatted) conversar, cavaquear. **have a ~** bater um papo, *(P)* dar dois dedos de conversa. **~ty** *a* conversador

chatter /'tʃætə(r)/ *vi* tagarelar. **his teeth are ~ing** seus dentes estão tiritando □ *n* tagarelice *f*

chauffeur /'ʃəʊfə(r)/ *n* motorista *m*, chofer (*particular*) *m*, chauffeur *m*

chauvinis|t /'ʃəʊvɪnɪst/ *n* chauvinista *mf*. **male ~t** (*pej*) machista *m*. **~m** /-zəm/ *n* chauvinismo *m*

cheap /tʃiːp/ *a* (-er, -est) barato; (*fare, rate*) reduzido. **~(ly)** *adv* barato. **~ness** *n* barateza *f*

cheapen /'tʃiːpən/ *vt* depreciar

cheat /tʃiːt/ *vt* enganar, trapacear □ *vi* (*at games*) roubar, *(P)* fazer batota; (*in exams*) copiar □ *n* intrujão *m*; (*at games*) trapaceiro *m*, *(P)* batoteiro *m*

check[1] /tʃek/ *vt*/*i* (*examine*) verificar; (*tickets*) revisar; (*restrain*) controlar, refrear □ *n* verificação *f*; (*tickets*) controle *m*; (*curb*) freio *m*; (*chess*) xeque *m*; (*Amer: bill*) conta *f*; (*Amer: cheque*) cheque *m*. **~ in** assinar o registro; (*at airport*) fazer o check-in. **~-in** *n* check-in *m*. **~ out** pagar a conta. **~-out** *n* caixa *f*. **~-up** *n* exame *m* médico, check-up *m*

check[2] /tʃek/ *n* (*pattern*) xadrez *m*. **~ed** *a* de xadrez

checkmate /'tʃekmeɪt/ *n* xeque-mate *m*

cheek /tʃiːk/ *n* face *f*; (*fig*) descaramento *m*. **~y** *a* descarado

cheer /tʃɪə(r)/ *n* alegria *f*; (*shout*)

viva *m* □ *vt*/*i* aclamar, aplaudir. **~s!** à sua, *(P)* vossa (saúde)!; (*thank you*) obrigadinho. **~(up)** animar(-se). **~ful** *a* bem disposto; alegre

cheerio /tʃɪərɪ'əʊ/ *int* (*colloq*) até logo, *(P)* adeusinho

cheese /tʃiːz/ *n* queijo *m*

cheetah /'tʃiːtə/ *n* chita *f*, lobotigre *m*

chef /ʃef/ *n* cozinheiro-chefe *m*

chemical /'kemɪkl/ *a* químico □ *n* produto *m* químico

chemist /'kemɪst/ *n* farmacêutico *m*; (*scientist*) químico *m*. **~'s (shop)** *n* farmácia *f*. **~ry** *n* química *f*

cheque /tʃek/ *n* cheque *m*. **~book** *n* talão *m* de cheques. **~card** *n* cartão *m* de banco

cherish /'tʃerɪʃ/ *vt* estimar, querer; (*hope*) acalentar

cherry /'tʃerɪ/ *n* cereja *f*. **~-tree** *n* cerejeira *f*

chess /tʃes/ *n* jogo *m* de xadrez. **~-board** *n* tabuleiro *m* de xadrez

chest /tʃest/ *n* peito *m*; (*for money, jewels*) cofre *m*. **~ of drawers** cômoda *f*, *(P)* cômoda *f*

chestnut /'tʃesnʌt/ *n* castanha *f*. **~-tree** *n* castanheiro *m*

chew /tʃuː/ *vt* mastigar. **~ing-gum** *n* chiclete *m*, *(P)* pastilha *f* elástica

chic /ʃiːk/ *a* chique

chick /tʃɪk/ *n* pinto *m*

chicken /'tʃɪkɪn/ *n* galinha *f* □ *vi* **~ out** (*sl*) acovardar-se. **~-pox** *n* catapora *f*, *(P)* varicela *f*

chicory /'tʃɪkərɪ/ *n* (*for coffee*) chicória *f*; (*for salad*) endívia *f*

chief /tʃiːf/ *n* chefe *m* □ *a* principal. **~ly** *adv* principalmente

chilblain /'tʃɪlbleɪn/ *n* frieira *f*

child /tʃaɪld/ *n* (*pl* children /'tʃɪldrən/) criança *f*; (*son*) filho *m*; (*daughter*) filha *f*. **~hood**

infância *f*, meninice *f*. **~ish** *a* infantil; (*immature*) acriançado, pueril. **~less** *a* sem filhos. **~like** *a* infantil. **~-minder** *n* babá *f* que cuida de crianças em sua própria casa

childbirth /'tʃaɪldbɜːθ/ *n* parto *m*

Chile /'tʃɪlɪ/ *n* Chile *m*. **~an** *a* & *n* chileno (*m*)

chill /tʃɪl/ *n* frio *m*; (*med*) resfriado *m*, (*P*) constipação *f* □ *vt/i* arrefecer; (*culin*) refrigerar. **~y** *a* frio. be *or* feel **~y** ter frio

chilli /'tʃɪlɪ/ *n* (*pl* **-ies**) malagueta *f*

chime /tʃaɪm/ *n* carrilhão *m*; (*sound*) música *m* de carrilhão □ *vt/i* tocar

chimney /'tʃɪmnɪ/ *n* (*pl* **-eys**) chaminé *f*. **~-sweep** *n* limpador *m* de chaminés, (*P*) limpa-chaminés *m*

chimpanzee /tʃɪmpæn'ziː/ *n* chimpanzé *m*

chin /tʃɪn/ *n* queixo *m*

china /'tʃaɪnə/ *n* porcelana *f*, (*crockery*) louça *f*

Chin|a /'tʃaɪnə/ *n* China *f*. **~ese** /-'niːz/ *a* & *n* chinês (*m*)

chink[1] /tʃɪŋk/ *n* (*crack*) fenda *f*, fresta *f*

chink[2] /tʃɪŋk/ *n* tinir *m* □ *vt/i* (fazer) tinir

chip /tʃɪp/ *n* (*broken piece*) bocado *m*; (*culin*) batata *f* frita em palitos; (*gambling*) ficha *f*; (*electronic*) chip *m*, circuito *m* integrado □ *vt/i* (*pt* **chipped**) lascar(-se)

chipboard /'tʃɪpbɔːd/ *n* compensado *m* (de madeira)

chiropodist /kɪ'rɒpədɪst/ *n* calista *mf*

chirp /tʃɜːp/ *n* pipilar *m*; (*of cricket*) cricri *m* □ *vi* pipilar; (*cricket*) cantar, fazer cricri

chisel /'tʃɪzl/ *n* cinzel *m*, escopro *m* □ *vt* (*pt* **chiselled**) talhar

chivalr|y /'ʃɪvlrɪ/ *n* cavalheirismo *m*. **~ous** *a* cavalheiresco

chive /tʃaɪv/ *n* cebolinho *m*

chlorine /'klɔːriːn/ *n* cloro *m*

chocolate /'tʃɒklɪt/ *n* chocolate *m*

choice /tʃɔɪs/ *n* escolha *f* □ *a* escolhido, seleto, (*P*) seleccionado

choir /'kwaɪə(r)/ *n* coro *m*

choirboy /'kwaɪəbɔɪ/ *n* menino *m* de coro, corista *m*, (*P*) coralista *m*

choke /tʃəʊk/ *vt/i* sufocar; (*on food*) engasgar(-se) □ *n* (*auto*) afogador *m*, (*P*) botão *m* de ar (*colloq*)

cholesterol /kə'lestərɒl/ *n* colesterol *m*

choose /tʃuːz/ *vt/i* (*pt* **chose**, *pp* **chosen**) escolher; (*prefer*) preferir. **~ to do** decidir fazer

choosy /'tʃuːzɪ/ *a* (*colloq*) exigente, difícil de contentar

chop /tʃɒp/ *vt/i* (*pt* **chopped**) cortar □ *n* (*wood*) machadada *f*; (*culin*) costeleta *f*. **~ down** abater. **~per** *n* cutelo *m*; (*sl: helicopter*) helicóptero *m*

choppy /'tʃɒpɪ/ *a* (*sea*) picado

chopstick /'tʃɒpstɪk/ *n* fachi *m*, pauzinho *m*

choral /'kɔːrəl/ *a* coral

chord /kɔːd/ *n* (*mus*) acorde *m*

chore /tʃɔː(r)/ *n* trabalho *m*; (*unpleasant task*) tarefa *f* maçante. **household~s** afazeres *mpl* domésticos

choreograph|er /kɒrɪ'ɒgrəfə(r)/ *n* coreógrafo *m*. **~y** *n* coreografia *f*

chortle /'tʃɔːtl/ *n* risada *f* □ *vi* rir alto

chorus /'kɔːrəs/ *n* coro *m*; (*of song*) refrão *m*, estribilho *m*

chose, chosen /tʃəʊz, 'tʃəʊzn/ *see* **choose**

Christ /kraɪst/ *n* Cristo *m*

christen /'krɪsn/ *vt* batizar, (*P*) baptizar. **~ing** *n* batismo *m*, (*P*) baptismo *m*

Christian /'krɪstʃən/ *a* & *n* cristão (*m*). **~ name** nome *m* de batismo, (*P*) baptismo. **~ity** /-strˈænətɪ/ *n* cristandade *f*

Christmas /ˈkrɪsməs/ n Natal m □ a do Natal. **~ card** cartão m de Boas Festas. **~ Day/Eve** dia m/ véspera f de Natal. **~ tree** árvore f de Natal

chrome /krəʊm/ n cromo m

chromosome /ˈkrəʊməsəʊm/ n cromossoma m

chronic /ˈkrɒnɪk/ a crônico, (P) crónico

chronicle /ˈkrɒnɪkl/ n crônica f

chronological /krɒnəˈlɒdʒɪkl/ a cronológico

chrysanthemum /krɪˈsænθəməm/ n crisântemo m

chubby /ˈtʃʌbɪ/ a (**-ier, -iest**) gorducho, rechonchudo

chuck /tʃʌk/ vt (colloq) deitar, atirar. **~ out** (person) expulsar; (thing) jogar fora. **~ out** (P) deitar fora

chuckle /ˈtʃʌkl/ n riso m abafado □ vi rir sozinho

chum /tʃʌm/ n (colloq) amigo m íntimo, camarada mf. **~my** a amigável

chunk /tʃʌŋk/ n (grande) bocado m, naco m

church /tʃɜːtʃ/ n igreja f

churchyard /ˈtʃɜːtʃjɑːd/ n cemitério m

churlish /ˈtʃɜːlɪʃ/ a grosseiro, indelicado

churn /tʃɜːn/ n batedeira f; (milkcan) vasilha f de leite □ vt bater. **~ out** produzir em série

chute /ʃuːt/ n calha f; (for rubbish) conduta f de lixo

chutney /ˈtʃʌtnɪ/ n (pl **-eys**) chutney m

cider /ˈsaɪdə(r)/ n sidra f, (P) cidra f

cigar /sɪˈɡɑː(r)/ n charuto m

cigarette /sɪɡəˈret/ n cigarro m. **~-case** n cigarreira f

cinder /ˈsɪndə(r)/ n brasa f. **burnt to a ~** estorricado

cinema /ˈsɪnəmə/ n cinema m

cinnamon /ˈsɪnəmən/ n canela f

cipher /ˈsaɪfə(r)/ n cifra f

circle /ˈsɜːkl/ n círculo m; (theat) balcão m □ vt dar a volta a □ vi descrever círculos, voltear

circuit /ˈsɜːkɪt/ n circuito m

circuitous /sɜːˈkjuːɪtəs/ a indireto, tortuoso

circular /ˈsɜːkjʊlə(r)/ a circular

circulat|e /ˈsɜːkjʊleɪt/ vt/i (fazer) circular. **~ion** /-ˈleɪʃn/ n circulação f; (sales of newspaper) tiragem f

circumcis|e /ˈsɜːkəmsaɪz/ vt circuncidar. **~ion** /-ˈsɪʒn/ n circuncisão f

circumference /səˈkʌmfərəns/ n circunferência f

circumflex /ˈsɜːkəmfleks/ n circunflexo m

circumstance /ˈsɜːkəmstəns/ n circunstância f. **~s** (means) situação f econômica, (P) económica

circus /ˈsɜːkəs/ n circo m

cistern /ˈsɪstən/ n reservatório m; (of WC) autoclismo m

cit|e /saɪt/ vt citar. **~ation** /-ˈteɪʃn/ n citação f

citizen /ˈsɪtɪzn/ n cidadão m, cidadã f; (of town) habitante mf. **~ship** n cidadania f

citrus /ˈsɪtrəs/ n **~ fruit** citrino m

city /ˈsɪtɪ/ n cidade f

civic /ˈsɪvɪk/ a cívico

civil /ˈsɪvl/ a civil; (rights) cívico; (polite) delicado. **~ servant** funcionário m público. **C~ Service** Administração f Pública. **~ war** guerra f civil. **~ity** /-ˈvɪlətɪ/ n civilidade f, cortesia f

civilian /sɪˈvɪlɪən/ a & n civil (mf), paisano m

civiliz|e /ˈsɪvəlaɪz/ vt civilizar. **~ation** /-ˈzeɪʃn/ n civilização f

claim /kleɪm/ vt reclamar; (assert) pretender □ vi (from insurance) reclamar □ n reivindicação f; (assertion) afirmação f; (right) direito m; (from insurance) reclamação f

clairvoyant /kleə'vɔɪənt/ n vidente *mf* □ *a* clarividente
clam /klæm/ n molusco *m*
clamber /'klæmbə(r)/ *vi* trepar
clammy /'klæmɪ/ *a* (-ier, -iest) úmido, (*P*) húmido e pegajoso
clamour /'klæmə(r)/ n clamor *m*, vociferação *f* □ *vi* ~ **for** exigir aos gritos
clamp /klæmp/ n grampo *m*; (*for car*) bloqueador *m* □ *vt* prender com grampo; (*a car*) bloquear. ~ **down on** apertar, suprimir; (*colloq*) cair em cima de (*colloq*)
clan /klæn/ n clã *m*
clandestine /klæn'destɪn/ *a* clandestino
clang /klæŋ/ n tinir *m*
clap /klæp/ *vt/i* (*pt* **clapped**) aplaudir; (*put*) meter □ *n* aplauso *m*; (*of thunder*) ribombo *m*. ~ **one's hands** bater palmas
claptrap /'klæptræp/ n parlapatice *f*
claret /'klærət/ n clarete *m*
clarify /'klærɪfaɪ/ *vt* esclarecer. ~**ication** /-ɪ'keɪʃn/ n esclarecimento *m*
clarinet /klærɪ'net/ n clarinete *m*
clarity /'klærətɪ/ n claridade *f*
clash /klæʃ/ n choque *m*; (*sound*) estridor *m*; (*fig*) conflito *m* □ *vt/i* entrechocar(-se); (*of colours*) destoar
clasp /klɑːsp/ n (*fastener*) fecho *m*; (*hold, grip*) aperto *m* de mão □ *vt* apertar, serrar
class /klɑːs/ n classe *f* □ *vt* classificar
classic /'klæsɪk/ *a* & *n* clássico (*m*). ~**s** *npl* letras *fpl* clássicas, (*P*) estudos *mpl* clássicos. ~**al** *a* clássico
classify /'klæsɪfaɪ/ *vt* classificar. ~**ication** /-ɪ'keɪʃn/ n classificação *f*. ~**ied advertisement** (*anúncio m*) classificado (*m*)
classroom /'klɑːsruːm/ n sala *f* de aulas

clatter /'klætə(r)/ n estardalhaço *m* □ *vi* fazer barulho
clause /klɔːz/ n cláusula *f*; (*gram*) oração *f*
claustrophobia /klɔːstrə'fəʊbɪə/ n claustrofobia *f*. ~**ic** *a* claustrofóbico
claw /klɔː/ n garra *f*; (*of lobster*) tenaz *f*, pinça *f* □ *vt* (*seize*) agarrar; (*scratch*) arranhar; (*tear*) rasgar
clay /kleɪ/ n argila *f*, barro *m*
clean /kliːn/ *a* (-er, -est) limpo □ *adv* completamente □ *vt* limpar □ *vi* ~ **up** fazer a limpeza. ~-**shaven** *a* de cara rapada. ~**er** n faxineira *f*, (*P*) mulher *f* da limpeza; (*of clothes*) empregado *m* da tinturaria. ~**ly** *adv* com limpeza, como deve ser
cleanse /klenz/ *vt* limpar; (*fig*) purificar. ~**ing cream** creme *m* de limpeza
clear /klɪə(r)/ *a* (-er, -est) claro; (*glass*) transparente; (*without obstacles*) livre; (*profit*) líquido; (*sky*) limpo □ *adv* claramente □ *vt* (*snow, one's name, etc*) limpar; (*the table*) tirar; (*jump*) transpor; (*debt*) saldar; (*jur*) absolver; (*through customs*) despachar □ *vi* (*fog*) dissipar-se; (*sky*) clarear. ~ **of** (*away from*) afastado de. ~ **off** *or* **out** (*sl*) sair andando, zarpar. ~ **out** (*clean*) fazer a limpeza. ~ **up** (*tidy*) arrumar; (*mystery*) desvendar; (*of weather*) clarear, limpar. ~**ly** *adv* claramente
clearance /'klɪərəns/ n autorização *f*; (*for ship*) despacho *m*; (*space*) espaço *m* livre. ~ **sale** liquidação *f*, saldos *mpl*
clearing /'klɪərɪŋ/ n clareira *f*
clearway /'klɪəweɪ/ n rodovia *f* de estacionamento proibido
cleavage /'kliːvɪdʒ/ n divisão *f*; (*between breasts*) rego *m*; (*of dress*) decote *m*

cleaver /'kli:və(r)/ *n* cutelo *m*

clef /klef/ *n* (mus) clave *f*

cleft /kleft/ *n* fenda *f*

clench /klentʃ/ *vt* (teeth, fists) cerrar; (grasp) agarrar

clergy /'klɜ:dʒɪ/ *n* clero *m*. **~man** *n* (pl **-men**) clérigo *m*, sacerdote *m*

cleric /'klerɪk/ *n* clérigo *m*. **~al** *a* (relig) clerical; (of clerks) de escritório

clerk /kla:k/ *n* auxiliar *m* de escritório

clever /'klevə(r)/ *a* (-er, -est) esperto, inteligente; (skilful) hábil, habilidoso. **~ly** *adv* inteligentemente; (skilfully) habilmente, habilidosamente. **~ness** *n* esperteza *f*, inteligência *f*

cliché /'kli:ʃeɪ/ *n* chavão *m*, lugar-comum *m*, clichê *m*

click /klɪk/ *n* estalido *m*, clique *m* □ *vi* dar um estalido; (comput) clicar

client /'klaɪənt/ *n* cliente *mf*

clientele /kli:ɑn'tel/ *n* clientela *f*

cliff /klɪf/ *n* penhasco *m*. **~s** *npl* falésia *f*

climat|e /'klaɪmɪt/ *n* clima *m*. **~ic** /-'mætɪk/ *a* climático

climax /'klaɪmæks/ *n* clímax *m*, ponto *m* culminante

climb /klaɪm/ *vt* (stairs) subir; (tree, wall) subir em, trepar em; (mountain) escalar □ *vi* subir, trepar □ *n* subida *f*; (mountain) escalada *f*. **~ down** descer; (fig) dar a mão à palmatória (fig). **~er** *n* (sport) alpinista *mf*; (plant) trepadeira *f*

clinch /klɪntʃ/ *vt* (deal) fechar; (argument) resolver

cling /klɪŋ/ *vi* (pt **clung**) **~ (to)** agarrar-se a (a); (stick) colar-se a (a)

clinic /'klɪnɪk/ *n* clínica *f*

clinical /'klɪnɪkl/ *a* clínico

clink /klɪŋk/ *n* tinido *m* □ *vt/i* (fazer) tilintar

clip¹ /klɪp/ *n* (for paper) clipe *m*;

(for hair) grampo *m*, (P) gancho *m*; (for tube) braçadeira *f* □ *vt* (pt **clipped**) prender

clip² /klɪp/ *vt* (pt **clipped**) cortar; (trim) aparar □ *n* tosquia *f*; (colloq: blow) murro *m*. **~ping** *n* recorte *m*

clique /kli:k/ *n* panelinha *f*, facção *f*, conventículo *m*

cloak /kləʊk/ *n* capa *f*, manto *m*

cloakroom /'kləʊkru:m/ *n* vestiário *m*; (toilet) toalete *m*, (P) lavabo *m*

clock /klɒk/ *n* relógio *m* □ *vi* **~in/out** marcar o ponto (à entrada/à saída). **~ up** (colloq: miles etc) fazer

clockwise /'klɒkwaɪz/ *a & adv* no sentido dos ponteiros do relógio

clockwork /'klɒkwɜ:k/ *n* mecanismo *m*. **go like ~** ir às mil maravilhas

clog /klɒg/ *n* tamanco *m*, soco *m* □ *vt/i* (pt **clogged**) entupir(-se)

cloister /'klɔɪstə(r)/ *n* claustro *m*

close¹ /kləʊs/ *a* (-er, -est) próximo (to de); (link, collaboration) estreito; (friend) íntimo; (weather) abafado □ *adv* perto. **~ at hand, ~ by** muito perto. **~ together** (crowded) espremido. **have a ~ shave** (fig) escapar por um triz. **~-up** *n* grande plano *m*. **~ly** *adv* de perto. **~ness** *n* proximidade *f*

close² /kləʊz/ *vt/i* fechar(-se); (end) terminar; (of shop etc) fechar □ *n* fim *m*. **~d shop** organização *f* que só admite trabalhadores sindicalizados

closet /'klɒzɪt/ *n* armário *m*

closure /'kləʊʒə(r)/ *n* encerramento *m*

clot /klɒt/ *n* coágulo *m* □ *vi* (pt **clotted**) coagular

cloth /klɒθ/ *n* pano *m*; (tablecloth) toalha *f* de mesa

cloth|e /kləʊð/ *vt* vestir. **~ing** *n* vestuário *m*, roupa *f*

clothes /kləʊðz/ *npl* roupa *f*, vestuário *m*. **~-line** *n* varal *m* para roupa

cloud /klaʊd/ *n* núvem *f* □ *vt/i* toldar(-se). **~y** *a* nublado, toldado; (*liquid*) turvo

clout /klaʊt/ *n* cascudo *m*, (P) carolo *m*; (*colloq: power*) poder *m* efectivo □ *vt* (*colloq*) bater

clove /kləʊv/ *n* cravo *m*. **~ of garlic** dente *m* de alho

clover /'kləʊvə(r)/ *n* trevo *m*

clown /klaʊn/ *n* palhaço *m* □ *vi* fazer palhaçadas

club /klʌb/ *n* clube *m*; (*weapon*) cacete *m*. **~s** (*cards*) paus *mpl* □ *vt/i* (*pt* **clubbed**) dar bordoadas *or* cacetadas (em). **~ together** (*share costs*) cotizar-se

cluck /klʌk/ *vi* cacarejar

clue /klu:/ *n* indício *m*, pista *f*; (*in crossword*) definição *f*. **not have a ~** (*colloq*) não fazer a menor idéia

clump /klʌmp/ *n* maciço *m*, tufo *m*

clumsy /'klʌmzɪ/ *a* (-ier, -iest) desajeitado

clung /klʌŋ/ *see* **cling**

cluster /'klʌstə(r)/ *n* (pequeno) grupo *m*; (*bot*). cacho *m* □ *vt/i* agrupar(-se)

clutch /klʌtʃ/ *vt* agarrar (em), apertar □ *vi* agarrar-se (**at a** □ *n* (*auto*) embreagem *f*, (P) embraiagem *f*. **~es** *npl* garras *fpl*

clutter /'klʌtə(r)/ *n* barafunda *f*, desordem *f* □ *vt* atravancar

coach /kəʊtʃ/ *n* ônibus *m*, (P) camioneta *f*; (*of train*) carruagem *f*; (*sport*) treinador *m* □ *vt* (*tutor*) dar aulas a; (*sport*) treinar

coagulate /kəʊ'ægjʊleɪt/ *vt/i* coagular(-se)

coal /kəʊl/ *n* carvão *m*

coalfield /'kəʊlfi:ld/ *n* região *f* carbonífera

coalition /kəʊə'lɪʃn/ *n* coligação *f*

coarse /kɔ:s/ *a* (-er, -est) grosseiro

coast /kəʊst/ *n* costa *f* □ *vi* costear; (*cycle*) descer em roda-livre; (*car*) ir em ponto morto. **~al** *a* costeiro

coastguard /'kəʊstgɑ:d/ *n* polícia *f* marítima

coastline /'kəʊstlaɪn/ *n* litoral *m*

coat /kəʊt/ *n* casaco *m*; (*of animal*) pêlo *m*; (*of paint*) camada *f*, demão *f* □ *vt* cobrir. **~ of arms** brasão *m*. **~ing** *n* camada *f*

coax /kəʊks/ *vt* levar com afagos ou lisonjas, convencer

cobble /'kɒbl/ *n* **~(-stone)** *n* pedra *f* de calçada

cobweb /'kɒbweb/ *n* teia *f* de aranha

cocaine /kəʊ'keɪn/ *n* cocaína *f*

cock /kɒk/ *n* (*male bird*) macho *m*; (*rooster*) galo *m* □ *vt* (*gun*) engatilhar; (*ears*) fitar. **~-eyed** *a* (*sl: askew*) de esguelha

cockerel /'kɒkərəl/ *n* frango *m*, galo *m* novo

cockle /'kɒkl/ *n* berbigão *m*

cockney /'kɒknɪ/ *n* (*pl* -eys) (*person*) londrino *m*; (*dialect*) dialeto *m* do leste de Londres

cockpit /'kɒkpɪt/ *n* cabine *f*

cockroach /'kɒkrəʊtʃ/ *n* barata *f*

cocktail /'kɒkteɪl/ *n* cocktail *m*, coquetel *m*. **fruit ~** salada *f* de fruta

cocky /'kɒkɪ/ *a* (-ier, -iest) convencido (*colloq*)

cocoa /'kəʊkəʊ/ *n* cacau *m*

coconut /'kəʊkənʌt/ *n* coco *m*

cocoon /kə'ku:n/ *n* casulo *m*

cod /kɒd/ *n* (*pl invar*) bacalhau *m*. **~-liver oil** óleo *m* de fígado de bacalhau

code /kəʊd/ *n* código *m* □ *vt* codificar

coeducational /kəʊedʒʊ'keɪʃənl/ *a* misto

coerc|e /kəʊ'ɜ:s/ *vt* coagir. **~ion** /-ʃn/ *n* coação *f*, (P) coacção *f*

coexist /kəʊɪg'zɪst/ *vi* coexistir. **~ence** *n* coexistência *f*

coffee /'kɒfɪ/ n café m. ~ bar café m. ~-pot n cafeteira f. ~-table n mesa f baixa

coffin /'kɒfɪn/ n caixão m

cog /kɒg/ n dente m de roda. a ~ in the machine (fig) uma rodinha numa engrenagem

cogent /'kəʊdʒənt/ a convincente; (relevant) pertinente

cognac /'kɒnjæk/ n conhaque m

cohabit /kəʊ'hæbɪt/ vi coabitar

coherent /kəʊ'hɪərənt/ a coerente

coil /kɔɪl/ vt/i enrolar(-se) □ n rolo m; (electr) bobina f; (one ring) espiral f; (contraceptive) dispositivo m intra-uterino, DIU

coin /kɔɪn/ n moeda f □ vt cunhar

coincide /kəʊɪn'saɪd/ vi coincidir

coinciden|ce /kəʊ'ɪnsɪdəns/ n coincidência f. ~tal /-'dentl/ a que acontece por coincidência

colander /'kʌləndə(r)/ n peneira f, (P) coador m

cold /kəʊld/ a (-er, -est) frio □ n frio m; (med) resfriado m, constipação f. be or feel ~ estar com frio. it's ~ está frio. ~-blooded a (person) insensível; (deed) a sangue frio. ~ cream creme m para a pele. ~ness n frio m; (of feeling) frieza f

coleslaw /'kəʊlslɔː/ n salada f de repolho cru

colic /'kɒlɪk/ n cólica(s) f (pl)

collaborat|e /kə'læbəreɪt/ vi colaborar. ~ion /-'reɪʃn/ n colaboração f. ~or n colaborador m

collapse /kə'læps/ vi desabar; (med) ter um colapso □ n colapso m

collapsible /kə'læpsəbl/ a desmontável, dobrável

collar /'kɒlə(r)/ n gola f; (of shirt) colarinho m; (of dog) coleira f □ vt (colloq) pôr a mão a. ~-bone n clavícula f

colleague /'kɒliːg/ n colega mf

collect /kə'lekt/ vt (gather) jun-

tar; (fetch) ir/vir buscar; (money, rent) cobrar; (as hobby) coleccionar, (P) colecionar □ vi juntar-se. call ~ (Amer) chamar a cobrar. ~ion /-ʃn/ n coleção f, (P) colecção f; (in church) coleta f, (P) colecta f; (of mail) tiragem f, coleta f, (P) abertura f. ~or n (as hobby) colecionador m, (P) coleccionador m

collective /kə'lektɪv/ a coletivo, (P) colectivo

college /'kɒlɪdʒ/ n colégio m

collide /kə'laɪd/ vi colidir

colliery /'kɒlɪərɪ/ n mina f de carvão

collision /kə'lɪʒn/ n colisão f, choque m; (fig) conflito m

colloquial /kə'ləʊkwɪəl/ a coloquial. ~ism n expressão f coloquial

collusion /kə'luːʒn/ n conluio m

colon /'kəʊlən/ n (gram) dois pontos mpl; (anat) cólon m

colonel /'kɜːnl/ n coronel m

colonize /'kɒlənaɪz/ vt colonizar

colon|y /'kɒlənɪ/ n colônia f, (P) colónia f. ~ial /kə'ləʊnɪəl/ a & n colonial (mf)

colossal /kə'lɒsl/ a colossal

colour /'kʌlə(r)/ n cor f □ a (photo, TV, etc) a cores; (film) colorido □ vt colorir, dar cor a □ vi (blush) corar. ~-blind a daltónico, (P) daltónico. ~ful a colorido. ~ing n (of skin) cor f; (in food) corante m. ~less a descolorido

coloured /'kʌləd/ a (pencil, person) de cor □ n pessoa f de cor

column /'kɒləm/ n coluna f

columnist /'kɒləmnɪst/ n colunista mf

coma /'kəʊmə/ n coma m

comb /kəʊm/ n pente m □ vt pentear; (search) vasculhar. ~ one's hair pentear-se

combat /'kɒmbæt/ n combate m □ vt (pt combated) combater

combination /kɒmbɪˈneɪʃn/ *n* combinação *f*

combine /kəmˈbaɪn/ *vt/i* combinar(-se), juntar(-se), reunir(-se)

combustion /kəmˈbʌstʃən/ *n* combustão *f*

come /kʌm/ *vi* (*pt* **came**, *pp* **come**) vir; (*arrive*) chegar; (*occur*) suceder. ∼ **about** acontecer. ∼ **across** encontrar, dar com. ∼ **away** *or* **off** soltar-se. ∼ **back** voltar. ∼**-back** *n* regresso *m*; (*retort*) réplica *f*. ∼ **by** obter. ∼ **down** descer; (*price*) baixar. ∼**down** *n* humilhação *f*. ∼ **from** vir de. ∼ **in** entrar. ∼ **into** (*money*) herdar. ∼ **off** (*succeed*) ter êxito; (*fare*) sair-se. ∼ **on**! vamos! ∼ **out** sair. ∼ **round** (*after fainting*) voltar a si; (*be converted*) deixar-se convencer. ∼ **to** (*amount to*) montar a. ∼ **up** subir; (*seeds*) despontar; (*fig*) surgir. ∼ **up with** (*idea*) vir com, propor. ∼**-uppance** *n* castigo *m* merecido

comedian /kəˈmiːdɪən/ *n* comediante *mf*

comedy /ˈkɒmədɪ/ *n* comédia *f*

comet /ˈkɒmɪt/ *n* cometa *m*

comfort /ˈkʌmfət/ *n* conforto *m* □ *vt* confortar, consolar. ∼**able** *a* confortável

comic /ˈkɒmɪk/ *a* cómico, (*P*) cómico □ *n* cómico *m*, (*P*) cómico *m*; (*periodical*) estórias *fpl* em quadrinhos, (*P*) revista *f* de banda desenhada. ∼ **strip** estória *f* em quadrinhos, (*P*) banda *f* desenhada. ∼**al** *a* cómico, (*P*) cómico

coming /ˈkʌmɪŋ/ *n* vinda *f* □ *a* próximo. ∼**s and goings** idas e vindas *fpl*

comma /ˈkɒmə/ *n* vírgula *f*

command /kəˈmɑːnd/ *n* (*mil*) comando *m*; (*order*) ordem *f*; (*mastery*) domínio *m* □ *vt* comandar; (*respect*) inspirar, impor. ∼**er** *n*

comandante *m*. ∼**ing** *a* imponente

commandeer /kɒmənˈdɪə(r)/ *vt* requisitar

commandment /kəˈmɑːndmənt/ *n* mandamento *m*

commemorat|e /kəˈmeməreɪt/ *vt* comemorar. ∼**ion** /-ˈreɪʃn/ *n* comemoração *f*. ∼**ive** *a* comemorativo

commence /kəˈmens/ *vt/i* começar. ∼**ment** *n* começo *m*

commend /kəˈmend/ *vt* louvar; (*entrust*) confiar. ∼**able** *a* louvável. ∼**ation** /kɒmenˈdeɪʃn/ *n* louvor *m*

comment /ˈkɒment/ *n* comentário *m* □ *vi* comentar. ∼ **on** comentar, fazer comentários

commentary /ˈkɒməntrɪ/ *n* comentário *m*; (*radio, TV*) relato *m*

commentat|e /ˈkɒməntert/ *vi* fazer um relato. ∼**or** *n* (*radio, TV*) comentarista *mf*, (*P*) comentador *m*

commerce /ˈkɒmɜːs/ *n* comércio *m*

commercial /kəˈmɜːʃl/ *a* comercial □ *n* publicidade (comercial) *f*. ∼**ize** *vt* comercializar

commiserat|e /kəˈmɪzəreɪt/ *vi* ∼ **with** compadecer-se de. ∼**ion** /-ˈreɪʃn/ *n* comiseração *f*, pesar *m*

commission /kəˈmɪʃn/ *n* comissão *f*; (*order for work*) encomenda *f* □ *vt* encomendar; (*mil*) nomear. ∼ **to do** encarregar de fazer. **out of** ∼ fora de serviço activo, (*P*) activo. ∼**er** *n* comissário *m*; (*police*) chefe *m*

commit /kəˈmɪt/ *vt* (*pt* **committed**) cometer; (*entrust*) confiar. ∼ **o.s.** comprometer-se, empenhar-se. ∼ **suicide** suicidar-se. ∼ **to memory** decorar. ∼**ment** *n* compromisso *m*

committee /kəˈmɪtɪ/ *n* comissão *f*, comité *m*, (*P*) comité *m*

commodity /kəˈmɒdətɪ/ *n* artigo *m*, mercadoria *f*

common /'kɒmən/ a (-er, -est) comum; (usual) usual, corrente; (pej: ill-bred) ordinario □ n prado m público, (P) baldio m. ~ **law** direito m consuetudinário. **C~ Market** Mercado m Comum. ~-**room** n sala f dos professores. ~ **sense** bom senso m, senso m comum. **House of C~s** Câmara f dos Comuns. **in** ~ em comum. ~**ly** adv mais comum

commoner /'kɒmənə(r)/ n plebeu m

commonplace /'kɒmənpleɪs/ a banal □ n lugar-comum m

commotion /kə'məʊʃn/ n agitação f, confusão f, barulheira f

communal /'kɒmjunl/ a (of a commune) comunal; (shared) comum

commune /'kɒmju:n/ n comuna f

communicat|e /kə'mju:nɪkeɪt/ vt/i comunicar. ~**ion** n comunicação f. ~**ion cord** sinal m de alarme. ~**ive** /-ətɪv/ a comunicativo

communion /kə'mju:nɪən/ n comunhão f

communis|t /'kɒmjunɪst/ n comunista mf □ a comunista. ~**m** /-zəm/ n comunismo m

community /kə'mju:nəti/ n comunidade f. ~ **centre** centro m comunitário

commute /kə'mju:t/ vi viajar diariamente para o trabalho. ~**r** /-ə(r)/ n pessoa f que viaja diariamente para o trabalho

compact[1] /kəm'pækt/ a compacto. ~ **disc** /'kɒmpækt/ cd m

compact[2] /'kɒmpækt/ n estojo m de pó-de-arroz, (P) caixa f

companion /kəm'pænɪən/ n companheiro m. ~**ship** n companhia f, convívio m

company /'kʌmpəni/ n companhia f, (guests) visitas fpl. **keep sb** ~ fazer companhia a alg

comparable /'kɒmpərəbl/ a comparável

compar|e /kəm'peə(r)/ vt/i parar(-se) **(to, with** com). ~**ative** /-'pærətɪv/ a comparativo; (comfort etc) relativo

comparison /kəm'pærɪsn/ n comparação f

compartment /kəm'pa:tmənt/ n compartimento m

compass /'kʌmpəs/ n bússola f. ~**es** compasso m

compassion /kəm'pæʃn/ n compaixão f. ~**ate** a compassivo

compatib|le /kəm'pætəbl/ a compatível. ~**ility** /-'bɪlətɪ/ n compatibilidade f

compel /kəm'pel/ vt (pt **compelled**) compelir, forçar. ~**ling** a irresistível, convincente

compensat|e /'kɒmpənseɪt/ vt/i compensar. ~**ion** /-'seɪʃn/ n compensação f; (financial) indemnização f, (P) indemnização f

compete /kəm'pi:t/ vi competir. ~ **with** rivalizar com

competen|t /'kɒmpɪtənt/ a competente. ~**ce** n competência f

competition /kɒmpə'tɪʃn/ n competição f; (comm) concorrência f

competitive /kəm'petɪtɪv/ a (sport, prices) competitivo. ~ **examination** concurso m

competitor /kəm'petɪtə(r)/ n competidor m, concorrente mf

compile /kəm'paɪl/ vt compilar, coligir. ~**r** /-ə(r)/ n compilador m

complacen|t /kəm'pleɪsnt/ a satisfeito consigo mesmo, (P) complacente. ~**cy** n (auto)-satisfação f, (P) complacência f

complain /kəm'pleɪn/ vi queixar-se (about, of de)

complaint /kəm'pleɪnt/ n queixa f; (in shop) reclamação f, (med) doença f, achaque m

complement /'kɒmplɪmənt/ n complemento m □ vt completar, complementar. ~**ary** /-'mentrɪ/ a complementar

complet|e /kəm'pli:t/ a completo; (*finished*) acabado; (*downright*) perfeito □ vt completar; (*a form*) preencher. **~ely** adv completamente. **~ion** /-ʃn/ n conclusão f, feitura f, realização f

complex /'kɒmpleks/ a complexo □ n complexo m. **~ity** /kəm'pleksəti/ n complexidade f

complexion /kəm'plekʃn/ n cor f da tez; (*fig*) caráter m, (*P*) carácter m, aspecto m

compliance /kəm'plaɪəns/ n docilidade f; (*agreement*) conformidade f. **in ~ with** em conformidade com

complicat|e /'kɒmplɪkeɪt/ vt complicar. **~ed** a complicado. **~ion** /-'keɪʃn/ n complicação f

compliment /'kɒmplɪmənt/ n cumprimento m □ vt /'kɒmplɪment/ cumprimentar

complimentary /kɒmplɪ'mentrɪ/ a amável, elogioso. **~ copy** oferta f. **~ ticket** bilhete m grátis

comply /kəm'plaɪ/ vi **~ with** agir em conformidade com

component /kəm'pəʊnənt/ n componente m; (*of machine*) peça f □ a componente, constituinte

compose /kəm'pəʊz/ vt compor. **~ o.s.** acalmar-se, dominar-se. **~d** a calmo, senhor de si. **~r** /-ə(r)/ n compositor m

composition /kɒmpə'zɪʃn/ n composição f

compost /'kɒmpɒst/ n húmus m, adubo m

composure /kəm'pəʊʒə(r)/ n calma f, domínio m de si mesmo

compound /'kɒmpaʊnd/ n composto m; (*enclosure*) cercado m, recinto m □ a (*P*) composto. **~ fracture** fratura f, (*P*) fractura f exposta

comprehen|d /kɒmprɪ'hend/ vt compreender. **~sion** n compreensão f

comprehensive /kɒmprɪ'hensɪv/

a compreensivo, vasto; (*insurance*) contra todos os riscos. **~ school** escola f de ensino secundário técnico e acadêmico, (*P*) académico

compress /kəm'pres/ vt comprimir. **~ion** /-ʃn/ n compressão f

comprise /kəm'praɪz/ vt compreender, abranger

compromise /'kɒmprəmaɪz/ n compromisso m □ vt comprometer □ vi chegar a um meio-termo

compulsion /kəm'pʌlʃn/ n (*constraint*) coação f; (*psych*) desejo m irresistível

compulsive /kəm'pʌlsɪv/ a (*psych*) compulsivo; (*liar, smoker etc*) inveterado

compulsory /kəm'pʌlsərɪ/ a obrigatório, compulsório

computer /kəm'pju:tə(r)/ n computador m. **~ science** informática f. **~ize** vt computerizar

comrade /'kɒmreɪd/ n camarada mf. **~ship** n camaradagem f

con¹ /kɒn/ vt (*pt* conned) (*sl*) enganar □ n (*sl*) intrujice f, vigarice f, burla f. **~ man** (*sl*) intrujão m, vigarista m, burlão m

con² /kɒn/ *see* pro

concave /'kɒŋkeɪv/ a côncavo

conceal /kən'si:l/ vt ocultar, esconder. **~ment** n encobrimento m

concede /kən'si:d/ vt conceder, admitir; (*in a game etc*) ceder

conceit /kən'si:t/ n presunção f. **~ed** a presunçoso, presumido, cheio de si

conceivable /kən'si:vəbl/ a concebível. **~y** adv possivelmente

conceive /kən'si:v/ vt/i conceber

concentrat|e /'kɒnsntreɪt/ vt/i concentrar(-se). **~ion** /-'treɪʃn/ n concentração f

concept /'kɒnsept/ n conceito m

conception /kən'sepʃn/ n concepção f

concern /kən'sɜːn/ n (worry) preocupação f; (business) negócio m □ vt dizer respeito a, respeitar. **~ o.s. with, be ~ed with** interessar-se por, ocupar-se de; (regard) dizer respeito a. **it's no ~ of mine** não me diz respeito. **~ing** prep sobre, respeitante a

concerned /kən'sɜːnd/ a inquieto, preocupado (**about** com)

concert /'kɒnsət/ n concerto m

concerted /kən'sɜːtɪd/ a concertado

concession /kən'seʃn/ n concessão f

concise /kən'saɪs/ a conciso. **~ly** adv concisamente

conclu|de /kən'kluːd/ vt concluir □ vi terminar. **~ding** a final. **~sion** n conclusão f

conclusive /kən'kluːsɪv/ a conclusivo. **~ly** adv de forma conclusiva

concoct /kən'kɒkt/ vt preparar por mistura; (fig: invent) fabricar. **~ion** /-ʃn/ n mistura f; (fig) invenção f, mentira f

concrete /'kɒnkriːt/ n concreto m, (P) cimento m □ a concreto □ vt concretar, (P) cimentar

concur /kən'kɜː(r)/ vi (pt concurred) concordar; (of circumstances) concorrer

concussion /kən'kʌʃn/ n comoção f cerebral

condemn /kən'dem/ vt condenar. **~ation** /kɒndem'neɪʃn/ n condenação f

condens|e /kən'dens/ vt/i condensar(-se). **~ation** /kɒnden'seɪʃn/ n condensação f

condescend /kɒndɪ'send/ vi condescender; (lower o.s.) rebaixar-se

condition /kən'dɪʃn/ n condição f □ vt condicionar. **on ~ that** com a condição de que. **~al** a condicional. **~er** n (for hair) condicionador m, creme m rinse

condolences /kən'dəʊlənsɪz/ npl condolências fpl, pêsames mpl, sentimentos mpl

condom /'kɒndəm/ n preservativo m

condone /kən'dəʊn/ vt desculpar, fechar os olhos a

conducive /kən'djuːsɪv/ a **be ~ to** contribuir para, ser propício a

conduct¹ /kən'dʌkt/ vt conduzir, dirigir; (orchestra) reger

conduct² /'kɒndʌkt/ n conduta f

conductor /kən'dʌktə(r)/ n maestro m; (electr; of bus) condutor m

cone /kəʊn/ n cone m; (bot) pinha f; (for ice-cream) casquinha f, (P) cone m

confectioner /kən'fekʃnə(r)/ n confeiteiro m, (P) pasteleiro m. **~y** n confeitaria f, (P) pastelaria f

confederation /kənfedə'reɪʃn/ n confederação f

confer /kən'fɜː(r)/ (pt conferred) vt conferir, outorgar □ vi conferenciar

conference /'kɒnfərəns/ n conferência f. **in ~** em reunião f

confess /kən'fes/ vt/i confessar; (relig) confessar(-se). **~ion** /-ʃn/ n confissão f. **~ional** n confessionário m. **~or** n confessor m

confetti /kən'fetɪ/ n confetes mpl, (P) confeti mpl

confide /kən'faɪd/ vt confiar □ vi **~ in** confiar em

confiden|t /'kɒnfɪdənt/ a confiante, confiado. **~ce** n confiança f; (boldness) confiança f em si; (secret) confidência f. **~ce trick** vigarice f. **in ~ce** em confidência

confidential /kɒnfɪ'denʃl/ a confidencial

confine /kən'faɪn/ vt fechar; (limit) limitar (**to** a). **~ment** n detenção f; (med) parto m

confirm /kən'fɜːm/ vt confirmar. **~ation** /kɒnfə'meɪʃn/

confirmação *f.* **~ed** *a* (*bachelor*) inveterado

confiscat|e /'kɒnfɪskeɪt/ *vt* confiscar. **~ion** /-'ʃn/ *n* confiscação *f*

conflict[1] /'kɒnflɪkt/ *n* conflito *m*

conflict[2] /kən'flɪkt/ *vi* estar em contradição. **~ing** *a* contraditório

conform /kən'fɔ:m/ *vt/i* conformar(-se)

confound /kən'faʊnd/ *vt* confundir. **~ed** *a* (*collog*) maldito

confront /kən'frʌnt/ *vt* confrontar, defrontar, enfrentar. **~** with confrontar-se com. **~ation** /kɒnfrʌn'teɪʃn/ *n* confrontação *f*

confus|e /kən'fju:z/ *vt* confundir. **~ed** *a* confuso. **~ing** *a* que faz confusão. **~ion** /-ʒn/ *n* confusão *f*

congeal /kən'dʒi:l/ *vt/i* congelar, solidificar

congenial /kən'dʒi:nɪəl/ *a* (*agreeable*) simpático

congenital /kən'dʒenɪtl/ *a* congênito, (*P*) congénito

congest|ed /kən'dʒestɪd/ *a* congestionado. **~ion** /-tʃn/ *n* (*traffic*) congestionamento *m*; (*med*) congestão *f*

congratulat|e /kən'grætjʊleɪt/ *vt* felicitar, dar os parabéns (**on** por). **~ions** /-'leɪʃnz/ *npl* felicitações *fpl*, parabéns *mpl*

congregat|e /'kɒŋgrɪgeɪt/ *vi* reunir-se. **~ion** /-'geɪʃn/ *n* (*in church*) congregação *f*, fiéis *mpl*

congress /'kɒŋgres/ *n* congresso *m*. **C~** (*Amer*) Congresso *m*

conjecture /kən'dʒektʃə(r)/ *n* conjetura *f*, (*P*) conjectura *f* □ *vt/i* conjeturar, (*P*) conjecturar

conjugal /'kɒndʒʊgl/ *a* conjugal

conjugat|e /'kɒndʒʊgeɪt/ *vt* conjugar. **~ion** /-'geɪʃn/ *n* conjugação *f*

conjunction /kən'dʒʌŋkʃn/ *n* conjunção *f*

conjur|e /'kʌndʒə(r)/ *vi* fazer truques mágicos □ *vt* **~** up fazer aparecer. **~or** *n* mágico *m*, prestidigitador *m*

connect /kə'nekt/ *vt/i* ligar(-se); (*of train*) fazer ligação. **~** *a* ligado. **be ~ed with** estar relacionado com

connection /kə'nekʃn/ *n* relação *f*; (*rail; phone call*) ligação *f*; (*electr*) contacto *m*

connoisseur /kɒnə'sɜ:(r)/ *n* conhecedor *m*, apreciador *m*

connotation /kɒnə'teɪʃn/ *n* conotação *f*

conquer /'kɒŋkə(r)/ *vt* vencer; (*country*) conquistar. **~or** *n* conquistador *m*

conquest /'kɒŋkwest/ *n* conquista *f*

conscience /'kɒnʃəns/ *n* consciência *f*

conscientious /kɒnʃɪ'enʃəs/ *a* consciencioso

conscious /'kɒnʃəs/ *a* consciente. **~ly** *adv* conscientemente. **~ness** *n* consciência *f*

conscript[1] /'kɒnskrɪpt/ *vt* recrutar. **~ion** /-ʃn/ *n* serviço *m* militar obrigatório

conscript[2] /'kɒnskrɪpt/ *n* recruta *m*

consecrate /'kɒnsɪkreɪt/ *vt* consagrar

consecutive /kən'sekjʊtɪv/ *a* consecutivo, seguido

consensus /kən'sensəs/ *n* consenso *m*

consent /kən'sent/ *vi* consentir (**to em**) □ *n* consentimento *m*

consequence /'kɒnsɪkwəns/ *n* conseqüência *f*, (*P*) consequência *f*

consequent /'kɒnsɪkwənt/ *a* resultante (**on, upon** de). **~ly** *adv* por consequência, (*P*) consequência, por conseguinte

conservation /kɒnsə'veɪʃn/ *n* conservação *f*

conservative /kən'sɜːvətɪv/ a conservador; (*estimate*) moderado. **C~** a & n conservador (m)

conservatory /kən'sɜːvətrɪ/ n (*greenhouse*) estufa f; (*house extension*) jardim m de inverno

conserve /kən'sɜːv/ vt conservar

consider /kən'sɪdə(r)/ vt considerar; (*allow for*) levar em consideração. **~ation** /-'reɪʃn/ n consideração f. **~ing** prep em vista de, tendo em conta

considerabl|e /kən'sɪdərəbl/ a considerável; (*much*) muito. **~y** adv consideravelmente

considerate /kən'sɪdərət/ a atencioso, delicado

consign /kən'saɪn/ vt consignar. **~ment** n consignação f

consist /kən'sɪst/ vi consistir (of, in, em)

consisten|t /kən'sɪstənt/ a (*unchanging*) constante; (*not contradictory*) coerente. **~t with** conforme com. **~cy** n consistência f; (*fig*) coerência f. **~tly** adv regularmente

consol|e /kən'səʊl/ vt consolar. **~ation** /kɒnsə'leɪʃn/ n consolação f. **~ation prize** prêmio m de consolação

consolidat|e /kən'sɒlɪdeɪt/ vt/i consolidar(-se). **~ion** /-'deɪʃn/ n consolidação f

consonant /'kɒnsənənt/ n consoante f

consortium /kən'sɔːtɪəm/ n (pl -tia) consórcio m

conspicuous /kən'spɪkjʊəs/ a conspícuo, visível; (*striking*) notável. **make o.s. ~** fazer-se notar, chamar a atenção

conspira|cy /kən'spɪrəsɪ/ n conspiração f. **~tor** n conspirador m

conspire /kən'spaɪə(r)/ vi conspirar

constable /'kʌnstəbl/ n polícia m

constant /'kɒnstənt/ a constante. **~ly** adv constantemente

constellation /kɒnstə'leɪʃn/ n constelação f

consternation /kɒnstə'neɪʃn/ n consternação f

constipation /kɒnstɪ'peɪʃn/ n prisão f de ventre

constituency /kən'stɪtjʊənsɪ/ n (pl -cies) círculo m eleitoral

constituent /kən'stɪtjʊənt/ a & n constituinte (m)

constitut|e /'kɒnstɪtjuːt/ vt constituir. **~ion** /-'tjuːʃn/ n constituição f. **~ional** /-'tjuːʃənl/ a constitucional

constrain /kən'streɪn/ vt constranger

constraint /kən'streɪnt/ n constrangimento m

constrict /kən'strɪkt/ vt constringir, apertar. **~ion** /-ʃn/ n constrição f

construct /kən'strʌkt/ vt construir. **~ion** /-ʃn/ n construção f. **under ~ion** em construção

constructive /kən'strʌktɪv/ a construtivo

consul /'kɒnsl/ n cônsul m

consulate /'kɒnsjʊlət/ n consulado m

consult /kən'sʌlt/ vt consultar. **~ation** /kɒnsl'teɪʃn/ n consulta f

consultant /kən'sʌltənt/ n consultor m; (*med*) especialista mf

consum|e /kən'sjuːm/ vt consumir. **~r** /-ə(r)/ n consumidor m

consumption /kən'sʌmpʃn/ n consumo m

contact /'kɒntækt/ n contacto m; (*person*) relação f. **~ lenses** lentes fpl de contacto □ vt contactar

contagious /kən'teɪdʒəs/ a contagioso

contain /kən'teɪn/ vt conter. **~ o.s.** conter-se. **~er** n recipiente m; (for transport) contentor m

contaminat|e /kən'tæmɪneɪt/ vt contaminar. **~ion** /-'neɪʃn/ n contaminação f

contemplat|e /'kɒntempleɪt/ vt contemplar; (*intend*) ter em vista; (*consider*) esperar, pensar em. **~ion** /-'pleɪʃn/ n contemplação f

contemporary /kən'temprərɪ/ a & n contemporâneo (m)

contempt /kən'tempt/ n desprezo m. **~ible** a desprezível. **~uous** /-tʃʊəs/ a desdenhoso

contend /kən'tend/ vt afirmar, sustentar □ vi **~ with** lutar contra. **~er** n adversário m, contendor m

content[1] /kən'tent/ a satisfeito, contente □ vt contentar. **~ed** a satisfeito, contente. **~ment** n contentamento m, satisfação f

content[2] /'kɒntent/ n conteúdo m. **(table of) ~s** índice m

contention /kən'tenʃn/ n disputa f, contenda f; (*assertion*) argumento m

contest[1] /'kɒntest/ n competição f; (*struggle*) luta f

contest[2] /kən'test/ vt contestar; (*compete for*) disputar. **~ant** n concorrente mf

context /'kɒntekst/ n contexto m

continent /'kɒntɪnənt/ n continente m. **the C~** a Europa (continental) f. **~al** /-'nentl/ a continental; (*of mainland Europe*) europeu **~al breakfast** café m da manhã europeu (P) pequeno almoço m europeu. **~al quilt** edredom m, (P) edredão m

contingen|t /kən'tɪndʒənt/ a & n contingente (m). **~cy** n contingência f. **~cy plan** plano m de emergência

continual /kən'tɪnjʊəl/ a contínuo. **~ly** adv continuamente

continu|e /kən'tɪnjuː/ vt/i continuar. **~ation** /-tɪnjʊ'eɪʃn/ n continuação f

continuity /kɒntɪ'njuːətɪ/ n continuidade f

continuous /kən'tɪnjʊəs/ a contínuo. **~ly** adv continuamente

contort /kən'tɔːt/ vt contorcer; (*fig*) distorcer. **~ion** /-ʃn/ n torção f

contour /'kɒntʊə(r)/ n contorno m

contraband /'kɒntrəbænd/ n contrabando m

contraception /kɒntrə'sepʃn/ n contracepção f

contraceptive /kɒntrə'septɪv/ a & n contraceptivo (m)

contract[1] /'kɒntrækt/ n contrato m

contract[2] /kən'trækt/ vt/i contrair(-se); (*make a contract*) contratar. **~ion** /-ʃn/ n contração f, (P) contracção f

contractor /kən'træktə(r)/ n empreiteiro m; (*firm*) firma f empreiteira de serviços, (P) recrutadora f de mão de obra temporária

contradict /kɒntrə'dɪkt/ vt contradizer. **~ion** /-ʃn/ n contradição f. **~ory** a contraditório

contraflow /'kɒntrəfləʊ/ n fluxo m em sentido contrário

contrary[1] /'kɒntrərɪ/ a & n (*opposite*) contrário (m) □ adv **~ to** contrariamente a. **on the ~** ao ou pelo contrário

contrary[2] /kən'treərɪ/ a (*perverse*) do contra, embirrento

contrast[1] /'kɒntrɑːst/ n contraste m

contrast[2] /kən'trɑːst/ vt/i contrastar. **~ing** a contrastante

contraven|e /kɒntrə'viːn/ vt infringir. **~tion** /-'venʃn/ n contravenção f

contribut|e /kən'trɪbjuːt/ vt/i contribuir (**to** para); (*to newspaper etc*) colaborar (**to** em). **~ion** /kɒntrɪ'bjuːʃn/ n contribuição f. **~or** /-'trɪbjʊtə(r)/ n contribuinte mf; (*to newspaper*) colaborador m

contrivance /kən'traɪvəns/ n (*invention*) engenho m; (*device*) engenhoca f; (*trick*) maquinação f

contrive /kən'traɪv/ vt imaginar, inventar. **~ to do** conseguir fazer

control /kən'trəʊl/ vt (pt **controlled**) (check, restrain) controlar; (firm etc) dirigir □ n controle m; (management) direção f, (P) direcção f. **~s** (of car, plane) comandos mpl; (knobs) botões mpl. **be in ~ of** dirigir. **under ~** sob controle

controversial /kɒntrə'vɜːʃl/ a controverso, discutível

controversy /'kɒntrəvɜːsɪ/ n controvérsia f

convalesce /kɒnvə'les/ vi convalescer. **~nce** n convalescença f. **~nt** /-nt/ a & n convalescente (mf). **~nt home** casa f de repouso

convene /kən'viːn/ vt convocar □ vi reunir-se

convenience /kən'viːnɪəns/ n conveniência f. **~s** (appliances) comodidades fpl; (lavatory) privada f, (P) casa f de banho. **at your ~** quando (e como) lhe convier. **~ foods** alimentos mpl semiprontos

convenient /kən'viːnɪənt/ a conveniente. **be ~ for** convir a. **~ly** adv sem inconveniente; (situated) bem; (arrive) a propósito

convent /'kɒnvənt/ n convento m. **~ school** colégio m de freiras

convention /kən'venʃn/ n convenção f; (custom) uso m, costume m. **~al** a convencional

converge /kən'vɜːdʒ/ vi convergir

conversant /kən'vɜːsnt/ a **be ~ with** conhecer; (fact) saber; (machinery) estar familiarizado com

conversation /kɒnvə'seɪʃn/ n conversa f. **~al** a de conversa, coloquial

converse[1] /kən'vɜːs/ vi conversar

converse[2] /'kɒnvɜːs/ a & n inverso (m). **~ly** /kən'vɜːslɪ/ adv ao invés, inversamente

conver|t[1] /kən'vɜːt/ vt converter;

(house) transformar. **~sion** /-ʃn/ n conversão f; (house) transformação f. **~tible** a convertível, conversível □ n (auto) conversível m

convert[2] /'kɒnvɜːt/ n convertido m, converso m

convex /'kɒnveks/ a convexo

convey /kən'veɪ/ vt transmitir; (goods) transportar; (idea, feeling) comunicar. **~ance** n transporte m. **~or belt** tapete m rolante, correia f transportadora

convict[1] /kən'vɪkt/ vt declarar culpado. **~ion** /-ʃn/ n condenação f; (opinion) convicção f

convict[2] /'kɒnvɪkt/ n condenado m

convinc|e /kən'vɪns/ vt convencer. **~ing** a convincente

convoluted /kɒnvə'luːtɪd/ a retorcido; (fig) complicado; (bot) convoluto

convoy /'kɒnvɔɪ/ n escolta f

convuls|e /kən'vʌls/ vt convulsionar; (fig) abalar. **be ~ed with laughter** torcer-se de riso. **~ion** /-ʃn/ n convulsão f

coo /kuː/ vi (pt cooed) arrulhar □ n arrulho m

cook /kʊk/ vt/i cozinhar □ n cozinheira f, cozinheiro m. **~ up** (collog) cozinhar (fig), fabricar

cooker /'kʊkə(r)/ n fogão m

cookery /'kʊkərɪ/ n cozinha f. **~ book** livro m de culinária

cookie /'kʊkɪ/ n (Amer) biscoito m

cool /kuːl/ a (-er, -est) fresco; (calm) calmo; (fig) frio □ n frescura f; (sl: composure) sangue-frio m □ vt/i arrefecer. **~box** n geladeira f portátil. **in the ~** no fresco. **~ly** /kuːllɪ/ adv calmamente; (fig) friamente. **~ness** n frescura f; (fig) frieza f

coop /kuːp/ n galinheiro m □ vt **~ up** engaislar, fechar

co-operate /kəʊ'ɒpəreɪt/ vi cooperar. **~ion** /-'reɪʃn/ n cooperação f

cooperative /kəʊˈɒpərətɪv/ a cooperativo □ n cooperativa f

coordinat|e /kəʊˈɔːdmeɪt/ vt coordenar. **~ion** /-ˈneɪʃn/ n coordenação f

cop /kɒp/ n (sl) guarda m (sl), (P) xui m (sl)

cope /kəʊp/ vi aguentar-se, arranjar-se. **~ with** poder com, dar conta de

copious /ˈkəʊpɪəs/ a copioso

copper[1] /ˈkɒpə(r)/ n cobre m □ a de cobre

copper[2] /ˈkɒpə(r)/ n (sl) porco m (sl), (P) xui m (sl)

coppice /ˈkɒpɪs/, **copse** /kɒps/ ns mata f de corte

copulat|e /ˈkɒpjʊleɪt/ vi copular. **~ion** /-ˈleɪʃn/ n cópula f

copy /ˈkɒpɪ/ n cópia f; (of book) exemplar m; (of newspaper) número m □ vt/i copiar

copyright /ˈkɒpɪraɪt/ n direitos mpl autorais

coral /ˈkɒrəl/ n coral m

cord /kɔːd/ n cordão m; (electr) fio m

cordial /ˈkɔːdɪəl/ a & n cordial (m)

cordon /ˈkɔːdn/ n cordão m □ vt **~ off** fechar (com um cordão de isolamento)

corduroy /ˈkɔːdərɔɪ/ n veludo m cotelê

core /kɔː(r)/ n âmago m; (of apple, pear) coração m

cork /kɔːk/ n cortiça f; (for bottle) rolha f □ vt rolhar

corkscrew /ˈkɔːkskruː/ n saca-rolhas m

corn[1] /kɔːn/ n trigo m; (Amer: maize) milho m; (seed) grão m. **~ on the cob** espiga f de milho

corn[2] /kɔːn/ n (hard skin) calo m

corned /kɔːnd/ a **~ beef** carne f de vaca enlatada

corner /ˈkɔːnə(r)/ n canto m; (of street) esquina f; (bend in road) curva f □ vt encurralar; (market)

monopolizar □ vi dar uma curva, virar

cornet /ˈkɔːnɪt/ n (mus) cornetim m; (for ice-cream) casquinha f, (P) cone m

cornflakes /ˈkɔːnfleɪks/ npl cornflakes mpl, cereais mpl

cornflour /ˈkɔːnflaʊə(r)/ n fécula f de milho, maisena f

Corn|wall /ˈkɔːnwəl/ n Cornualha f. **~ish** a da Cornualha

corny /ˈkɔːnɪ/ a (colloq) batido, (P) estafado

coronary /ˈkɒrənrɪ/ n **~ (thrombosis)** infarto m, enfarte m

coronation /kɒrəˈneɪʃn/ n coroação f

coroner /ˈkɒrənə(r)/ n magistrado m que investiga os casos de morte suspeita

corporal[1] /ˈkɔːpərəl/ n (mil) cabo m

corporal[2] /ˈkɔːpərəl/ a **~ punishment** castigo m corporal

corporate /ˈkɔːpərət/ a coletivo, (P) colectivo; (body) corporativo

corporation /kɔːpəˈreɪʃn/ n corporação f; (of town) municipalidade f

corps /kɔː(r)/ n (pl corps /kɔːz/) corpo m

corpse /kɔːps/ n cadáver m

corpuscle /ˈkɔːpʌsl/ n corpúsculo m

correct /kəˈrekt/ a correto, (P) correcto. the **~ time** a hora certa. you are **~** você tem razão □ vt corrigir. **~ion** /-ʃn/ n correção f, (P) correcção f, emenda f

correlat|e /ˈkɒrəleɪt/ vt/i correlacionar(-se). **~ion** /-ˈleɪʃn/ n correlação f

correspond /kɒrɪˈspɒnd/ vi corresponder (to, with, a); (write letters) corresponder-se (with, com). **~ence** n correspondência f. **~ent** n correspondente mf. **~ing** a correspondente

corridor /ˈkɒrɪdɔː(r)/ n corredor m

corroborate /kəˈrɒbəreɪt/ vt corroborar

corro|de /kəˈrəʊd/ vt/i corroer (-se). **~sion** n corrosão f

corrugated /ˈkɒrəgeɪtɪd/ a corrugado. **~ cardboard** cartão m canelado. **~ iron** chapa f de ondulada

corrupt /kəˈrʌpt/ a corrupto □ vt corromper. **~ion** /-ʃn/ n corrupção f

corset /ˈkɔːsɪt/ n espartilho m; (elasticated) cinta f elástica

Corsica /ˈkɔːsɪkə/ n Córsega f

cosmetic /kɒzˈmetɪk/ n cosmético m □ a cosmético; (fig) superficial

cosmonaut /ˈkɒzmənɔːt/ n cosmonauta mf

cosmopolitan /kɒzməˈpɒlɪtən/ a & n cosmopolita (mf)

cosset /ˈkɒsɪt/ vt (pt cosseted) proteger

cost /kɒst/ vt (pt cost) custar; (pt costed) fixar o preço de □ n custo m. **~s** (jur) custos mpl. **at all ~s** custe o que custar. **to one's ~** à sua custa. **~ of living** custo m de vida

costly /ˈkɒstlɪ/ a (-ier, -iest) a caro; (valuable) precioso

costume /ˈkɒstjuːm/ n traje m

cos|y /ˈkəʊzɪ/ a (-ier, -iest) confortável, íntimo □ n abafador m (do bule do chá). **~iness** n conforto m

cot /kɒt/ n cama f de bêbé, berço m

cottage /ˈkɒtɪdʒ/ n pequena casa f de campo. **~ cheese** requeijão m, ricota f. **~ industry** artesanato m. **~ pie** empada f de carne picada

cotton /ˈkɒtn/ n algodão m; (thread) fio m, linha f. **~ wool** algodão m hidrófilo

couch /kaʊtʃ/ n divã m

couchette /kuːˈʃet/ n couchette f

cough /kɒf/ vi tossir □ n tosse f

could /kʊd, kəd/ pt of can²

couldn't /ˈkʊdnt/ = **could not**

council /ˈkaʊnsl/ n conselho m. **~ house** casa f de bairro popular

councillor /ˈkaʊnsələ(r)/ n vereador m

counsel /ˈkaʊnsl/ n conselho m; (pl invar) (jur) advogado m. **~lor** n conselheiro m

count¹ /kaʊnt/ vt/i contar □ n conta f. **~down** n (rocket) contagem f regressiva. **~ on** contar com

count² /kaʊnt/ n (nobleman) conde m

counter¹ /ˈkaʊntə(r)/ n (in shop) balcão m; (in game) ficha f, (P) tento m

counter² /ˈkaʊntə(r)/ adv **~ to** contrário a; (in the opposite direction) em sentido contrário a □ a oposto □ vt opor; (blow) aparar □ vi ripostar

counter- /ˈkaʊntə(r)/ pref contra-

counteract /kaʊntərˈækt/ vt neutralizar, frustrar

counter-attack /ˈkaʊntərətæk/ n contra-ataque m □ vt/i contra-atacar

counterbalance /ˈkaʊntəbæləns/ n contrapeso m □ vt contrabalançar

counterfeit /ˈkaʊntəfɪt/ a falsificado, falso □ n falsificação f □ vt falsificar

counterfoil /ˈkaʊntəfɔɪl/ n talão m, canhoto m

counterpart /ˈkaʊntəpɑːt/ n equivalente m; (person) homólogo m

counter-productive /ˈkaʊntəprədʌktɪv/ a contraproducente

countersign /ˈkaʊntəsaɪn/ vt subscrever documento já assinado; (cheque) contrassinar

countess /ˈkaʊntɪs/ n condessa f

countless /ˈkaʊntlɪs/ a sem conta, incontável, inúmero

country /'kʌntrɪ/ n país m; (*homeland*) pátria f; (*countryside*) campo m

countryside /'kʌntrɪsaɪd/ n campo m

county /'kaʊntɪ/ n condado m

coup /ku:/ n ~ (**d'état**) golpe m (de estado)

couple /'kʌpl/ n par m, casal m ☐ vt/i unir(-se), ligar(-se); (*techn*) acoplar. **a** ~ **of** um par de

coupon /'ku:pɒn/ n cupão m

courage /'kʌrɪdʒ/ n coragem f. ~**ous** /kə'reɪdʒəs/ a corajoso

courgette /kʊə'ʒet/ n abobrinha f

courier /'kʊrɪə(r)/ n correio m; (*for tourists*) guia mf; (*for parcels, mail*) estafeta m

course /kɔːs/ n curso m; (*series*) série f; (*culin*) prato m; (*for golf*) campo m; (*fig*) caminho m. **in due** ~ na altura devida, oportunamente. **in the** ~ **of** durante. **of** ~ está claro, com certeza

court /kɔːt/ n (*of monarch*) corte f; (*courtyard*) pátio m; (*tennis*) court m, quadra f, (P) campo m; (*jur*) tribunal m ☐ vt cortejar; (*danger*) provocar. ~ **martial** (*pl* **courts martial**) conselho m de guerra

courteous /'kɜːtɪəs/ a cortês, delicado

courtesy /'kɜːtəsɪ/ n cortesia f

courtship /'kɔːtʃɪp/ n namoro m, corte f

courtyard /'kɔːtjɑːd/ n pátio m

cousin /'kʌzn/ n primo m. **first/second** ~ primo m em primeiro/segundo grau

cove /kəʊv/ n angra f, enseada f

covenant /'kʌvənənt/ n convenção f, convénio m; (*jur*) contrato m; (*relig*) aliança f

cover /'kʌvə(r)/ vt cobrir ☐ n cobertura f; (*for bed*) colcha f; (*for book, furniture*) capa f; (*lid*) tampa f; (*shelter*) abrigo m. ~

charge serviço m. ~ **up** tapar; (*fig*) encobrir. ~**-up** n (*fig*) encobrimento m. **take** ~ abrigar-se. **under separate** ~ em separado. ~**ing** n cobertura f. ~**ing letter** carta f (que acompanha um documento)

coverage /'kʌvərɪdʒ/ n (*of events*) reportagem f, cobertura f

covet /'kʌvɪt/ vt cobiçar

cow /kaʊ/ n vaca f

coward /'kaʊəd/ n covarde mf. ~**ly** a covarde

cowardice /'kaʊədɪs/ n covardia f

cowboy /'kaʊbɔɪ/ n cowboy m, vaqueiro m

cower /'kaʊə(r)/ vi encolher-se (de medo)

cowshed /'kaʊʃed/ n estábulo m

coy /kɔɪ/ a (-**er**, -**est**) (falsamente) tímido

crab /kræb/ n caranguejo m

crack /kræk/ n fenda f; (*in glass*) rachadura f; (*noise*) estalo m; (*sl: joke*) piada f; (*drug*) crack m ☐ a (*colloq*) de élite ☐ vt/i estalar; (*nut*) quebrar; (*joke*) contar; (*problem*) resolver; (*voice*) mudar. ~ **down on** (*colloq*) cair em cima de, arrochar. **get** ~ (*colloq*) pôr mãos à obra

cracker /'krækə(r)/ n busca-pé m, bomba f de estalo; (*culin*) bolacha f de água e sal

crackers /'krækəz/ a (*sl*) desmiolado, maluco

crackle /'krækl/ vi crepitar ☐ n crepitação f

crackpot /'krækpɒt/ n (*sl*) desmiolado, maluco

cradle /'kreɪdl/ n berço m ☐ vt embalar

craft[1] /krɑːft/ n ofício m; (*technique*) arte f; (*cunning*) manha f, astúcia f

craft[2] /krɑːft/ n (*invar*) (*boat*) embarcação f

craftsman /'krɑːftsmən/ n (*pl* -**men**) artífice mf. ~**ship** n arte f

crafty /'kra:ftɪ/ a (**-ier, -iest**) manhoso, astucioso

crag /kræg/ n penhasco m. **~gy** a escarpado, íngreme

cram /kræm/ vt (pt **crammed**) **~ (for an exam)** decorar, (P) empinar. **~ into/with** entulhar com

cramp /kræmp/ n cãimbra f □ vt restringir, tolher. **~ed** a apertado

crane /kreɪn/ n grua f; (bird) grou m □ vt (neck) esticar

crank[1] /kræŋk/ n (techn) manivela f. **~-shaft** n (techn) cambota f

crank[2] /kræŋk/ n excêntrico m. **~y** a excêntrico

crash /kræʃ/ n acidente m; (noise) estrondo m; (comm) falência f, (financial) colapso m, crash m □ vt/i (fall/strike) cair/bater com estrondo; (two cars) chocar, bater; (comm) abrir falência; (plane) cair □ a (course, programme) intensivo. **~-helmet** n capacete m. **~-land** vi fazer uma aterrissagem forçada

crate /kreɪt/ n engradado m

crater /'kreɪtə(r)/ n cratera f

crav|e /kreɪv/ vt/i **~e (for)** ansiar por. **~ing** n desejo m irresistível, ânsia f

crawl /krɔːl/ vi rastejar; (of baby) engatinhar, (P) andar de gatas; (of car) mover-se lentamente □ n rastejo m; (swimming) crawl m. **be ~ing** with fervilhar de, estar cheio de

crayfish /'kreɪfɪʃ/ n (pl invar) lagostim m

crayon /'kreɪən/ n crayon m, lápis m de pastel

craze /kreɪz/ n moda f, febre f

craz|y /'kreɪzɪ/ a (**-ier, -iest**) doido, louco (**about** por). **~iness** n loucura f

creak /kriːk/ n rangido m □ vi ranger

cream /kriːm/ n (milk fat; fig)

nata f; (cosmetic; culin) creme m □ a creme invar □ vt desnatar. **~ cheese** queijo-creme m. **~y** a cremoso

crease /kriːs/ n vinco m □ vt/i amarrotar(-se)

creat|e /kriː'eɪt/ vt criar. **~ion** /-ʃn/ n criação f. **~ive** a criador. **~or** n criador m

creature /'kriːtʃə(r)/ n criatura f

crèche /kreɪʃ/ n creche f

credentials /krɪ'denʃlz/ npl credenciais fpl; (of competence etc) referências f

credib|le /'kredəbl/ a crível, verosímil, (P) verossímil. **~ility** /-'bɪlətɪ/ n credibilidade f

credit /'kredɪt/ n crédito m; (honour) honra f. **~s** (cinema) créditos mpl □ vt (pt **credited**) acreditar em; (comm) creditar. **~ card** cartão m de crédito. **~ sb with** atribuir a alg. **~or** n credor m

creditable /'kredɪtəbl/ a louvável, honroso

credulous /'kredjʊləs/ a crédulo

creed /kriːd/ n credo m

creek /kriːk/ n enseada f estreita. **be up the ~** (sl) estar frito (sl)

creep /kriːp/ vi (pt **crept**) rastejar; (move stealthily) mover-se furtivamente □ n (sl) cara m nojento. **give sb the ~s** dar arrepios a alg. **~er** n (planta f) trepadeira (f). **~y** a arrepiante

cremat|e /krɪ'meɪt/ vt cremar. **~ion** /-ʃn/ n cremação f

crematorium /kremə'tɔːrɪəm/ n (pl **-ia**) crematório m

crêpe /kreɪp/ n crepe m. **~ paper** papel m crepom, (P) plissado

crept /krept/ see **creep**

crescent /'kresnt/ n crescente m; (street) rua f em semicírculo

cress /kres/ n agrião m

crest /krest/ n (of bird, hill) crista f; (on coat of arms) timbre m

Crete /kriːt/ n Creta f

crevasse /krɪ'væs/ n fenda f (em geleira)

crevice /'krevɪs/ n racha f, fenda f

crew[1] /kru:/ see **crow**

crew[2] /kru:/ n tripulação f; (gang) bando m. ~-**cut** n corte m à escovinha. ~-**neck** n gola f redonda e un pouco subida

crib[1] /krɪb/ n berço m; (Christmas) presépio m

crib[2] /krɪb/ vt/i (pt **cribbed**) (colloq) colar (sl), (P) cabular (sl) □ n cópia f, plágio m; (translation) burro m (sl)

cricket[1] /'krɪkɪt/ n críquete m. ~**er** n jogador m de críquete

cricket[2] /'krɪkɪt/ n (insect) grilo m

crime /kraɪm/ n crime m; (minor) delito m; (collectively) criminalidade f

criminal /'krɪmɪnl/ a & n criminoso (m)

crimp /krɪmp/ vt preguear; (hair) frisar

crimson /'krɪmzn/ a & n carmesim (m)

cringe /krɪndʒ/ vi encolher-se. ~**ing** a servil

crinkle /'krɪŋkl/ vt/i enrugar(-se) □ n vinco m, ruga f

cripple /'krɪpl/ n aleijado m, coxo m □ vt estropiar; (fig) paralisar

crisis /'kraɪsɪs/ n (pl **crises** /-si:z/) crise f

crisp /krɪsp/ a (-**er**, **est**) (culin) crocante; (air) fresco; (manners, reply) decidido. ~**s** npl batatas fpl fritas redondas

criterion /kraɪ'tɪərɪən/ n (pl -**ia**) critério m

critic /'krɪtɪk/ n crítico m. ~**al** a crítico. ~**ally** adv de forma crítica; (ill) gravemente

criticism /'krɪtɪsɪzm/ n crítica f

criticize /'krɪtɪsaɪz/ vt/i criticar

croak /krəʊk/ n (frog) coaxar m; (raven) crocitar m, crocito m □ vi (frog) coaxar; (raven) crocitar

crochet /'krəʊʃeɪ/ n crochê m □ vt fazer em crochê

crockery /'krɒkərɪ/ n louça f

crocodile /'krɒkədaɪl/ n crocodilo m

crocus /'krəʊkəs/ n (pl -**uses** /-sɪz/) croco m

crony /'krəʊnɪ/ n camarada mf, amigão m, parceiro m

crook /krʊk/ n (colloq: criminal) vigarista mf; (stick) cajado m

crooked /'krʊkɪd/ a torcido; (winding) tortuoso; (askew) torto; (colloq: dishonest) desonesto. ~**ly** adv de través

crop /krɒp/ n colheita f; (fig) quantidade f; (haircut) corte m rente □ vt (pt **cropped**) cortar □ vi ~ **up** aparecer, surgir

croquet /'krəʊkeɪ/ n croquet m, croquê m

cross /krɒs/ n cruz f □ vt/i cruzar; (cheque) cruzar, (P) barrar; (oppose) contrariar; (of paths) cruzar-se □ a zangado. ~ **off** or **out** riscar. ~ **o.s.** benzer-se. ~ **sb's mind** passar pela cabeça or pelo espírito de alg, ocorrer a alg. **talk at** ~ **purposes** falar sem se entender. ~-**country** a a corta-mato. ~-**examine** vt fazer o contra-interrogatório de (testemunhas). ~-**eyed** a vesgo, estrábico. ~-**fire** n fogo m cruzado. ~-**reference** n nota f remissiva. ~-**section** n corte m transversal; (fig) grupo m or sector m representativo. ~**ly** adv irritadamente

crossbar /'krɒsbɑ:(r)/ n barra f transversal f; (of bicycle) travessão m

crossing /'krɒsɪŋ/ n cruzamento m; (by boat) travessia f; (on road) passagem f

crossroads /'krɒsrəʊdz/ n encruzilhada f, cruzamento m

crossword /'krɒswɜ:d/ n palavras fpl cruzadas

crotch /krɒtʃ/ n entrepernas fpl

crotchet /'krɒtʃɪt/ n (mus) semínima f

crouch /krautʃ/ vi agachar-se

crow /krəʊ/ n corvo m □ vi (cock). (pt crew) cantar; (fig) rejubilar-se (over com). as the ~ flies em linha reta, (P) recta

crowbar /'krəʊbɑː(r)/ n alavanca f, pé-de-cabra m

crowd /kraʊd/ n multidão f □ vi afluir □ vt encher. ~ into apinhar-se em. ~ed a cheio, apinhado

crown /kraʊn/ n coroa f; (of hill) topo m, cume m □ vt coroar; (tooth) pôr uma coroa em

crucial /'kruːʃl/ a crucial

crucifix /'kruːsɪfɪks/ n crucifixo m

crucif|y /'kruːsɪfaɪ/ vt crucificar. ~ixion /-'fɪkʃn/ n crucificação f

crude /kruːd/ a (-er, -est) (raw) bruto; (rough, vulgar) grosseiro. ~ oil petróleo m bruto

cruel /krʊəl/ a (crueller, cruellest) cruel. ~ty n crueldade f

cruis|e /kruːz/ n cruzeiro m □ vi cruzar; (of tourists) fazer um cruzeiro; (of car) ir a velocidade de cruzeiro. ~er n cruzador m. ~ing speed velocidade f de cruzeiro

crumb /krʌm/ n migalha f, farelo m

crumble /'krʌmbl/ vt/i desfazer (-se); (bread) esmigalhar(-se); (collapse) desmoronar-se

crumple /'krʌmpl/ vt/i amarrotar (-se)

crunch /krʌntʃ/ vt trincar; (under one's feet) fazer ranger

crusade /kruː'seɪd/ n cruzada f. ~r /-ə(r)/ n cruzado m; (fig) militante mf

crush /krʌʃ/ vt esmagar; (clothes, papers) amassar, amarrotar □ n aperto m. a ~ on (sl) uma paixonite, (P) paixoneta por.

crust /krʌst/ n côdea f, crosta f. ~y a crocante

crutch /krʌtʃ/ n muleta f; (crotch) entrepernas fpl

crux /krʌks/ n (pl cruxes) o ponto crucial

cry /kraɪ/ n grito m □ vi (weep) chorar; (call out) gritar. a far ~ from muito diferente de.

crying /'kraɪɪŋ/ a a ~ shame uma grande vergonha

crypt /krɪpt/ n cripta f

cryptic /'krɪptɪk/ a críptico, enigmático

crystal /'krɪstl/ n cristal m. ~lize vt/i cristalizar(-se)

cub /kʌb/ n cria f, filhote m. C~ (Scout) lobito m

Cuba /'kjuːbə/ n Cuba f. ~n a e n cubano (m)

cubby-hole /'kʌbɪhəʊl/ n cochicho m; (snug place) cantinho m

cub|e /kjuːb/ n cubo m. ~ic a cúbico

cubicle /'kjuːbɪkl/ n cubículo m, compartimento m; (at swimming-pool) cabine f

cuckoo /'kʊkuː/ n cuco m

cucumber /'kjuːkʌmbə(r)/ n pepino m

cuddle /'kʌdl/ vt/i abraçar com carinho; (nestle) aninhar(-se) □ n abracinho m, festinha f. ~y a fofo, aconchegante

cudgel /'kʌdʒl/ n cacete m, moca f □ vt (pt cudgelled) dar cacetadas em

cue¹ /kjuː/ n (theat) deixa f; (hint) sugestão f, sinal m

cue² /kjuː/ n (billiards) taco m

cuff /kʌf/ n punho m; (blow) sopapo m □ vt dar um sopapo. ~-link n botão m de punho. off the ~ de improviso

cul-de-sac /'kʌldəsæk/ n (pl culs-de-sac) beco m sem saída

culinary /'kʌlɪnərɪ/ a culinário

cull /kʌl/ vt (select) escolher; (kill)

abater seletivamente, (P) selecti-vamente □ n abate m

culminat|e /'kʌlmɪnet/ vi ~**e in** acabar em. ~**ion** /-'neɪʃn/ n auge m, ponto m culminante

culprit /'kʌlprɪt/ n culpado m

cult /kʌlt/ n culto m

cultivat|e /'kʌltɪvet/ vt cultivar. ~**ion** /-'veɪʃn/ n cultivo m, culti-vação f

cultural /'kʌltʃərəl/ a cultural

culture /'kʌltʃə(r)/ n cultura f. ~**d** a culto

cumbersome /'kʌmbəsəm/ a (un-wieldy) pesado, incômodo, in-cômodo

cumulative /'kju:mjʊlətɪv/ a cu-mulativo

cunning /'kʌnɪŋ/ a astuto, ma-nhoso □ n astúcia f, manha f

cup /kʌp/ n xícara f, (P) chávena f, (prize) taça f. **C~ Final** Final de Campeonato f

cupboard /'kʌbəd/ n armário m

cupful /'kʌpfʊl/ n xícara f cheia, (P) chávena f (cheia)

curable /'kjʊərəbl/ a curável

curator /kjʊə'reɪtə(r)/ n (museum) conservador m, (jur) curador m

curb /kɜ:b/ n freio m □ vt refrear; (price increase etc) sustar

curdle /'kɜ:dl/ vt/i coalhar

cure /kjʊə(r)/ vt curar □ n cura f

curfew /'kɜ:fju:/ n toque m de recolher

curio /'kjʊərɪəʊ/ n (pl -os) curio-sidade f

curi|ous /'kjʊərɪəs/ a curioso. ~**osity** /-'ɒsətɪ/ n curiosidade f

curl /kɜ:l/ vt/i encaracolar(-se) □ n caracol m. ~ **up** enroscar(-se)

curler /'kɜ:lə(r)/ n rolo m

curly /'kɜ:lɪ/ a (-ier, -iest) encara-colado, crespo

currant /'kʌrənt/ n passa f de Corinto

currency /'kʌrənsɪ/ n moeda f cor-rente; (general use) circulação f. **foreign ~** moeda f estrangeira

current /'kʌrənt/ a (common) cor-rente; (event, price, etc) atual, (P) actual □ n corrente f. ~ **account** conta f corrente. ~ **affairs** atua-lidades fpl, (P) actualidades fpl. ~**ly** adv atualmente, (P) actual-mente

curriculum /kə'rɪkjʊləm/ n (pl -la) currículo m, programa m de estudos. ~ **vitae** n curriculum vitae m

curry¹ /'kʌrɪ/ n caril m

curry² /'kʌrɪ/ vt ~ **favour with** procurar agradar a

curse /kɜ:s/ n maldição f, praga f; (bad language) palavrão m □ vt amaldiçoar, praguejar contra □ vi praguejar; (swear) dizer pala-vrões

cursor /'kɜ:sə(r)/ n cursor m

cursory /'kɜ:sərɪ/ a apressado, superficial. **a ~ look** uma olha-da superficial

curt /kɜ:t/ a brusco

curtail /kɜ:'teɪl/ vt abreviar; (ex-penses etc) reduzir

curtain /'kɜ:tn/ n cortina f; (theat) pano m

curtsy /'kɜ:tsɪ/ n reverência f □ vi fazer uma reverência

curve /kɜ:v/ n curva f □ vt/i cur-var(-se); (of road) fazer uma cur-va

cushion /'kʊʃn/ n almofada f □ vt (a blow) amortecer; (fig) proteger

cushy /'kʊʃɪ/ a (-ier, -iest) (colloq) fácil, agradável. ~ **job** sinecura f, boca f (fig)

custard /'kʌstəd/ n creme m

custodian /kʌ'stəʊdɪən/ n guarda m

custody /'kʌstədɪ/ n (safe keeping) custódia f; (jur) detenção f; (of child) tutela f

custom /'kʌstəm/ n costume m; (comm) freguesia f, clientela f. ~**ary** a habitual

customer /'kʌstəmə(r)/ n freguês m, cliente mf

customs /'kʌstəmz/ *npl* alfândega *f* □ *a* alfandegário. **~ clearance** desembaraço *m* alfandegário. **~ officer** funcionário *m* da alfândega

cut /kʌt/ *vt/i* (*pt* **cut**, *pres p* **cutting**) cortar; (*prices etc*) reduzir □ *n* corte *m*, golpe *m*; (*of clothes, hair*) corte *m*; (*piece*) pedaço *m*; (*prices etc*) redução *f*, corte *m*; (*sl: share*) comissão *f*, (*P*) talhada *f* (*sl*). **~ back** or **down** (**on**) reduzir. **~-back** *n* corte *m*. **~ in** intrometer-se; (*auto*) cortar. **~ off** cortar; (*fig*) isolar. **~ out** recortar; (*leave out*) suprimir. **~-out** *n* figura *f* para recortar. **~-price** *a* a preço(s) reduzido(s). **~ short** encurtar, (*P*) atalhar

cute /kjuːt/ *a* (**-er, -est**) (*colloq: clever*) esperto; (*attractive*) bonito, (*P*) giro (*colloq*)

cuticle /'kjuːtɪkl/ *n* cutícula *f*

cutlery /'kʌtlərɪ/ *n* talheres *mpl*

cutlet /'kʌtlɪt/ *n* costeleta *f*

cutting /'kʌtɪŋ/ *a* cortante □ *n* (*from newspaper*) recorte *m*; (*plant*) estaca *f*. **~ edge** gume *m*

CV *abbr see* **curriculum vitae**

cyanide /'saɪənaɪd/ *n* cianeto *m*

cycl|e /'saɪkl/ *n* ciclo *m*; (*bicycle*) bicicleta *f* □ *vi* andar de bicicleta. **~lane** cicloria *f*. **~ing** *n* ciclismo *m*. **~ist** *n* ciclista *mf*

cyclone /'saɪkləʊn/ *n* ciclone *m*

cylind|er /'sɪlɪndə(r)/ *n* cilindro *m*. **~rical** *a* cilíndrico

cymbals /'sɪmblz/ *npl* (*mus*) pratos *mpl*

cynic /'sɪnɪk/ *n* cínico *m*. **~al** *a* cínico. **~ism** /-sɪzəm/ *n* cinismo *m*

Cypr|us /'saɪprəs/ *n* Chipre *m*. **~iot** /'sɪprɪət/ *a & n* cipriota (*mf*)

cyst /sɪst/ *n* quisto *m*

Czech /tʃek/ *a & n* tcheco (*m*), (*P*) checo

D

dab /dæb/ *vt* (*pt* **dabbed**) levemente □ *n* **a ~ of** um caçãozinha de. **~ sth on a** qq coisa em gestos leves

dabble /'dæbl/ *vi* **~ in** inte sar-se por, fazer um pouco (como amador). **~r** /-ə(r)/ amador *m*

dad /dæd/ *n* (*colloq*) paizinho **~dy** *n* (*children's use*) papai *m* (*P*) papá *m*. **~dy-long-legs** *n* pernilongo *m*

daffodil /'dæfədɪl/ *n* narciso *m*

daft /dɑːft/ *a* (**-er, -est**) doido, maluco

dagger /'dægə(r)/ *n* punhal *m*. **at ~s drawn** prestes a lutar (**with** com)

daily /'deɪlɪ/ *a* diário, quotidiano □ *adv* diariamente, todos os dias □ *n* (*newspaper*) diário *m*; (*colloq: charwoman*) faxineira *f*, (*P*) mulher *f* a dias

dainty /'deɪntɪ/ *a* (**-ier, -iest**) delicado; (*pretty, neat*) gracioso

dairy /'deərɪ/ *n* leiteria *f*. **~ products** laticínios *mpl*

daisy /'deɪzɪ/ *n* margarida *f*

dam /dæm/ *n* barragem *f*, represa *f* □ *vt* (*pt* **dammed**) represar

damag|e /'dæmɪdʒ/ *n* estrago(s) *mpl*. **~es** (*jur*) perdas *fpl* e danos *mpl* □ *vt* estragar, danificar; (*fig*) prejudicar. **~ing** *a* prejudicial

dame /deɪm/ *n* (*old use*) dama *f*; (*Amer sl*) mulher *f*

damn /dæm/ *vt* (*relig*) condenar ao inferno; (*swear at*) amaldiçoar, maldizer; (*fig: condemn*) condenar □ *int* raios!, bolas! □ *n* **not care a ~** (*colloq*) estar pouco ligando (*colloq*), (*P*) estar-se marimbando (*colloq*) □ *a*

damn

□ *adv*

... be **~ed**

...ja se.

...ado *f*,

...mpro-

...apu...

...dicar

...t umedecer, (P)

...**en** *vt* = **damp**

...res.

...nidade *f*, (P) humi-

.../ *vt/i* dançar □ n dan-

...**all** sala *f* de baile. **~r**

... dançarino *m*; (*profes-*

...bailarino *m*

...**ion** /'dændɪlaɪən/ n dente-

...**ruff** /'dændrʌf/ n caspa *f*

...**e** /dem/ n dinamarquês *m*

...**nger** /'deɪndʒə(r)/ n perigo *m*.

be in ~ (*lang*) dinamarquês *m*

dangle /'dæŋgl/ *vi* oscilar, pender □ *vt* ter *or* trazer dependurado; (*hold*) balançar; (*fig:* hopes, *etc*) acenar com

Danish /'deɪnɪʃ/ *a* dinamarquês □ n (*lang*) dinamarquês *m*

dank /dæŋk/ *a* (**-er**, **-est**) frio e úmido, (P) húmido

dare /deə(r)/ *vt* **~ to do** ousar fazer. **~ sb to do** desafiar alg a fazer □ n desafio *m*. **I ~ say** creio

daredevil /'deədevl/ n louco *m*, temerário *m*

daring /'deərɪŋ/ *a* audacioso □ n audácia *f*

dark /dɑːk/ *a* (**-er**, **-est**) escuro, sombrio; (*gloomy*) sombrio; (of *colour*) escuro; (of *skin*) moreno □ n escuridão *f*, escuro *m*; (*nightfall*) anoitecer *m*, cair *m* da noite. **~ horse** concorrente *mf* que é uma incógnita. **~-room** n câmara *f* escura. **be in the ~ about** (*fig*) ignorar. **~ness** n escuridão *f*

darken /'dɑːkən/ *vt/i* escurecer

darling /'dɑːlɪŋ/ *a & n* querido (*m*)

darn /dɑːn/ *vt* serzir, remendar

dart /dɑːt/ n dardo *m*, flecha *f*. **~s** (*game*) jogo *m* de dardos □ *vi* lançar-se

dartboard /'dɑːtbɔːd/ n alvo *m*

dash /dæʃ/ *vi* precipitar-se □ *vt* arremessar; (*hopes*) destruir □ n corrida *f*; (*stroke*) travessão *m*; (*Morse*) traço *m*. **a ~ of** um pouco de. **~ off** partir a toda a velocidade; (*letter*) escrever às pressas

dashboard /'dæʃbɔːd/ n painel *m* de instrumentos, quadro *m* de bordo

data /'deɪtə/ *npl* dados *mpl*. **~ capture** aquisição *f* de informações, recolha *f* de dados. **~ base** n base *f* de dados. **~ processing** processamento *m* or tratamento *m* de dados

date[1] /deɪt/ n data *f*; (*colloq*) encontro *m* marcado □ *vt/i* datar; (*colloq*) andar com. **out of ~** dessatualizado, (P) desactualizado. **to ~** até à data. **up to ~** (*style*) moderno; (*information etc*) em dia. **~d** *a* antiquado

date[2] /deɪt/ n (*fruit*) tâmara *f*

daub /dɔːb/ *vt* borrar, pintar toscamente

daughter /'dɔːtə(r)/ n filha *f*. **~-in-law** n (*pl* **~s-in-law**) nora *f*

daunt /dɔːnt/ *vt* assustar, intimidar, desencorajar

dawdle /'dɔːdl/ *vi* perder tempo

dawn /dɔːn/ n madrugada *f* □ *vi* madrugar, amanhecer. **~ on** (*fig*) fazer-se luz no espírito de, começar a perceber

day /deɪ/ n dia *m*; (*period*) época *f*, tempo *m*. **~-dream** n devaneio *m* □ *vi* devanear. **the ~ before** a véspera

daybreak /'deɪbreɪk/ n romper *m* do dia, aurora *f*, amanhecer *m*

daylight /'deɪlaɪt/ n luz *f* do dia. **~ robbery** roubar descaradamente

daytime /'deɪtaɪm/ n dia m, dia m claro

daze /deɪz/ vt aturdir □ n in a ~ aturdido

dazzle /'dæzl/ vt deslumbrar; (with headlights) ofuscar

dead /ded/ a o morto; (numb) dormente □ adv completamente, de todo □ n in the ~ of the night a horas mortas, na calada da noite. the ~ os mortos. in the ~ centre bem no meio. stop ~ estacar. ~ beat a (colloq) morto de cansaço. ~ end beco m sem saída. ~-pan a inexpressivo

deaden /'dedn/ vt (sound, blow) amortecer; (pain) aliviar

deadline /'dedlaɪn/ n prazo m final

deadlock /'dedlɒk/ n impasse m

deadly /'dedlɪ/ a (-ier, -iest) mortal; (weapon) mortífero

deaf /def/ a (-er, -est) surdo. turn a ~ ear fingir que não ouve. ~-mute surdo-mudo m. ~ness n surdez f

deafen /'defn/ vt ensurdecer. ~ing a ensurdecedor

deal /di:l/ vt (pt dealt) distribuir; (a blow, cards) dar □ vi negociar □ n negócio m; (cards) vez de dar f. a great ~ muito (of de). ~ in negociar em. ~ with (person) tratar (com); (affair) tratar de. ~er n comerciante m; (agent) concessionário m; representante m

dealings /'di:lɪŋz/ npl relações fpl; (comm) negócios mpl

dealt /delt/ see deal

dean /di:n/ n decano m

dear /dɪə(r)/ a (-er, -est) (cherished) caro, querido; (expensive) caro □ n amor m □ adv caro □ int oh ~! meu Deus! □ ~ly adv (very much) muito; (pay) caro

dearth /dɜ:θ/ n escassez f

death /deθ/ n morte f. ~ certificate certidão f de óbito. ~ pen-

alty pena f de morte. ~ rate taxa f de mortalidade. ~-trap n lugar m perigoso, ratoeira f. ~ly a de morte, mortal

debase /dɪ'beɪs/ vt degradar

debat|e /dɪ'beɪt/ n debate m □ vt debater. ~able a discutível

debauchery /dɪ'bɔ:tʃərɪ/ n deboche m, devassidão f

debility /dɪ'bɪlətɪ/ n debilidade f

debit /'debɪt/ n débito m □ vt (pt debited) debitar

debris /'debri:/ n destroços mpl

debt /det/ n dívida f. in ~ endividado. ~or n devedor m

debunk /di:'bʌŋk/ vt (colloq) desmitificar

début /'deɪbju:/ n (of actor, play etc) estréia f

decade /'dekeɪd/ n década f

decaden|t /'dekədənt/ a decadente. ~ce n decadência f

decaffeinated /di:'kæfɪmeɪtɪd/ a sem cafeína

decanter /dɪ'kæntə(r)/ n garrafa f para vinho, de vidro ou cristal

decapitate /dɪ'kæpɪteɪt/ vt decapitar

decay /dɪ'keɪ/ vi apodrecer, estragar-se; (food, fig) deteriorar-se; (building) degradar-se □ n apodrecimento m; (of tooth) cárie f; (fig) declínio m, decadência f

deceased /dɪ'si:st/ a & n falecido (m), defunto (m)

deceit /dɪ'si:t/ n engano m. ~ful a enganador

deceive /dɪ'si:v/ vt enganar, iludir

December /dɪ'sembə(r)/ n dezembro m

decen|t /'di:snt/ a decente; (colloq: good) (bastante) bom; (colloq: likeable) simpático. ~cy n decência f

decentralize /di:'sentrəlaɪz/ vt descentralizar

decept|ive /dɪ'septɪv/ a enganador, ilusório. ~ion /-ʃn/ n engano m

decibel /'desɪbel/ n decibel m

decide /dɪˈsaɪd/ vt/i decidir. ~ **on** decidir-se por. ~ **to do** decidir fazer. ~**d** /-ɪd/ a decidido; (clear) definido, nítido. ~**dly** /-ɪdlɪ/ adv decididamente

decimal /ˈdesɪml/ a decimal □ n (fração f, (P) fracção f) decimal m. ~ **point** vírgula f decimal

decipher /dɪˈsaɪfə(r)/ vt decifrar

decision /dɪˈsɪʒn/ n decisão f

decisive /dɪˈsaɪsɪv/ a decisivo; (manner) decidido. ~**ly** adv decisivamente

deck /dek/ n convés m; (of cards) baralho m. ~**chair** n espreguiçadeira f

declare /dɪˈkleə(r)/ vt declarar. ~**ation** /dekləˈreɪʃn/ n declaração f

decline /dɪˈklaɪn/ vt (refuse) declinar, recusar delicadamente; (gram) declinar □ vi (deteriorate) declinar; (fall) baixar □ n declínio m; (fall) abaixamento m

decode /diːˈkəʊd/ vt descodificar

decompose /diːkəmˈpəʊz/ vt/i decompor(-se). ~**ition** /-ɒmpəˈzɪʃn/ n decomposição f

décor /ˈdeɪkɔː(r)/ n decoração f

decorat|e /ˈdekəreɪt/ vt decorar, enfeitar; (paint) pintar; (paper) pôr papel em. ~**ion** /-ˈreɪʃn/ n decoração f; (medal etc) condecoração f. ~**ive** /-ətɪv/ a decorativo

decorum /dɪˈkɔːrəm/ n decoro m

decoy¹ /ˈdiːkɔɪ/ n chamariz m, engodo m; (trap) armadilha f

decoy² /dɪˈkɔɪ/ vt atrair, apanhar

decrease¹ /dɪˈkriːs/ vt/i diminuir

decrease² /ˈdiːkriːs/ n diminuição f

decree /dɪˈkriː/ n decreto m; (jur) decisão f judicial □ vt decretar

decrepit /dɪˈkrepɪt/ a decrépito

dedicat|e /ˈdedɪkeɪt/ vt dedicar. ~**ed** a dedicado. ~**ion** /-ˈkeɪʃn/ n dedicação f; (in book) dedicatória f

deduce /dɪˈdjuːs/ vt deduzir

deduct /dɪˈdʌkt/ vt deduzir; (from pay) descontar

deduction /dɪˈdʌkʃn/ n dedução f; (from pay) desconto m

deed /diːd/ n ato m; (jur) contrato m

deem /diːm/ vt julgar, considerar

deep /diːp/ a (-er, -est) profundo □ adv profundamente. ~**freeze** n congelador m □ vt congelar. **take a** ~ **breath** respirar fundo. ~**ly** adv profundamente

deepen /ˈdiːpən/ vt/i aprofundar (-se); (mystery, night) adensar-se

deer /dɪə(r)/ n (pl invar) veado m

deface /dɪˈfeɪs/ vt danificar, degradar

defamation /defəˈmeɪʃn/ n difamação f

default /dɪˈfɔːlt/ vi faltar □ n **by** ~ à revelia. **win by** ~ (sport) ganhar por não comparecimento, (P) comparência □ n (comput) default m

defeat /dɪˈfiːt/ vt derrotar; (thwart) malograr □ n derrota f; (of plan, etc) malogro m

defect¹ /ˈdiːfekt/ n defeito m. ~**ive** /dɪˈfektɪv/ a defeituoso

defect² /dɪˈfekt/ vi desertar. ~**ion** n defecção m. ~**or** n tránsfuga mf, dissidente mf; (political) asilado m político

defence /dɪˈfens/ n defesa f. ~**less** a indefeso

defend /dɪˈfend/ vt defender. ~**ant** n (jur) réu m, acusado m. ~**er** n advogado m de defesa, defensor m

defensive /dɪˈfensɪv/ a defensivo □ n **on the** ~ na defensiva f; (person, sport) na retranca f (collog)

defer /dɪˈfɜː(r)/ vt (pt deferred) adiar, diferir □ vi ~ **to** ceder, deferir

deferen|ce /ˈdefərəns/ n deferência f. ~**tial** /-ˈrenʃl/ a deferente

defian|ce /dɪˈfaɪəns/ n desafio m. **in ~ of** sem respeito por. **~t** a de desafio. **~tly** adv com ar de desafio

deficien|t /dɪˈfɪʃnt/ a deficiente. **be ~t in** ter falta de. **~cy** n deficiência f

deficit /ˈdefɪsɪt/ n déficit m

define /dɪˈfaɪn/ vt definir

definite /ˈdefɪnɪt/ a definido; (clear) categórico, claro; (certain) certo. **~ly** adv decididamente; (clearly) claramente

definition /defɪˈnɪʃn/ n definição f

definitive /dɪˈfɪnətɪv/ a definitivo

deflat|e /dɪˈfleɪt/ vt esvaziar; (person) desemproar, desinchar. **~ion** /-ʃn/ n esvaziamento m; (econ) deflação f

deflect /dɪˈflekt/ vt/i desviar(-se)

deform /dɪˈfɔːm/ vt deformar. **~ed** a deformado, disforme. **~ity** n deformidade f

defraud /dɪˈfrɔːd/ vt defraudar

defrost /diːˈfrɒst/ vt descongelar

deft /deft/ a (-er, -est) hábil

defunct /dɪˈfʌŋkt/ a (law etc) caduco, extinto

defuse /diːˈfjuːz/ vt (a bomb) desativar, (P) desactivar; (a situation) acalmar

defy /dɪˈfaɪ/ vt desafiar; (attempts) resistir a; (the law) desobedecer a; (public opinion) opor-se a

degenerate /dɪˈdʒenəreɪt/ vi degenerar (into em)

degrade /dɪˈɡreɪd/ vt degradar. **~ation** /degrəˈdeɪʃn/ n degradação f

degree /dɪˈɡriː/ n grau m; (univ) diploma m. **to a ~** ao mais alto grau, muito

dehydrate /diːˈhaɪdreɪt/ vt/i desidratar(-se)

de-ice /diːˈaɪs/ vt descongelar, degelar; (windscreen) tirar o gelo de

deign /deɪn/ vt **~ to do** dignar-se (a) fazer

deity /ˈdiːɪtɪ/ n divindade f

dejected /dɪˈdʒektɪd/ a abatido

delay /dɪˈleɪ/ vt atrasar; (postpone) retardar □ vi atrasar-se □ n atraso m, demora f

delegate[1] /ˈdelɪɡət/ n delegado m

delegat|e[2] /ˈdelɪɡeɪt/ vt delegar. **~ion** /-ˈɡeɪʃn/ n delegação f

delet|e /dɪˈliːt/ vt riscar. **~ion** /-ʃn/ n rasura f

deliberate[1] /dɪˈlɪbərət/ a deliberado; (steps etc) compassado. **~ly** adv deliberadamente, de propósito

deliberat|e[2] /dɪˈlɪbəreɪt/ vt/i deliberar. **~ion** /-ˈreɪʃn/ n deliberação f

delica|te /ˈdelɪkət/ a delicado. **~cy** n delicadeza f; (food) gulo-seima f, iguaria f, (P) acepipe m

delicatessen /delɪkəˈtesn/ n (shop) mercearia fpl finas

delicious /dɪˈlɪʃəs/ a delicioso

delight /dɪˈlaɪt/ n grande prazer m, delícia f; (thing) delícia f, encanto m □ vt deliciar □ vi **~ in** deliciar-se com. **~ed** a deliciado, encantado. **~ful** a delicioso, encantador

delinquen|t /dɪˈlɪŋkwənt/ a & n delinquente mf, (P) delinquente mf. **~cy** n delinquência f, (P) delinquência f

deliri|ous /dɪˈlɪrɪəs/ a delirante. **be ~ous** delirar. **~um** /-əm/ n delírio m

deliver /dɪˈlɪvə(r)/ vt entregar; (letters) distribuir; (free) libertar; (med) fazer o parto. **~ance** n libertação f. **~y** n entrega f; (letters) distribuição f; (med) parto m

delu|de /dɪˈluːd/ vt enganar. **~de o.s.** ter ilusões. **~sion** /-ʒn/ n ilusão f

deluge /ˈdeljuːdʒ/ n dilúvio m □ vt inundar

de luxe /dɪˈlʌks/ a de luxo

delve /delv/ vi **~ into** pesquisar, rebuscar

demand /dɪ'maːnd/ *vt* exigir; (*ask to be told*) perguntar □ *n* exigência *f*; (*comm*) procura *f*; (*claim*) reivindicação *f*. **in ~** procurado. **~ing** *a* exigente; (*work*) puxado, custoso

demean /dɪ'miːn/ *vt* **~ o.s.** rebaixar-se

demeanour /dɪ'miːnə(r)/ *n* comportamento *m*, conduta *f*

demented /dɪ'mentɪd/ *a* louco, demente. **become ~** enlouquecer

demo /'deməʊ/ *n* (*pl* **-os**) (*colloq*) manifestação *f*, (*P*) manif *f*

democracy /dɪ'mɒkrəsɪ/ *n* democracia *f*

democrat /'deməkræt/ *n* democrata *mf*. **~ic** /-'krætɪk/ *a* democrático

demolish /dɪ'mɒlɪʃ/ *vt* demolir. **~tion** /demə'lɪʃn/ *n* demolição *f*

demon /'diːmən/ *n* demónio *m*

demonstrat|e /'demənstreɪt/ *vt* demonstrar □ *vi* (*pol*) fazer uma manifestação,   manifestar-se. **~ion** /-'streɪʃn/ *n* demonstração *f*; (*pol*) manifestação *f*. **~or** *n* (*pol*) manifestante *mf*

demonstrative /dɪ'mɒnstrətɪv/ *a* demonstrativo

demoralize /dɪ'mɒrəlaɪz/ *vt* desmoralizar

demote /dɪ'məʊt/ *vt* fazer baixar de posto, rebaixar

demure /dɪ'mjʊə(r)/ *a* recatado, modesto

den /den/ *n* antro *m*, covil *m*; (*room*) cantinho *m*, recanto *m*

denial /dɪ'naɪəl/ *n* negação *f*; (*refusal*) recusa *f*; (*statement*) desmentido *m*

denigrate /'denɪgreɪt/ *vt* denegrir

denim /'denɪm/ *n* brim *m*. **~s** (*jeans*) blue-jeans *mpl*

Denmark /'denmaːk/ *n* Dinamarca *f*

denomination /dɪnɒmɪ'neɪʃn/ *n* denominação *f*; (*relig*) confissão *f*, seita *f*; (*money*) valor *m*

denote /dɪ'nəʊt/ *vt* denotar

denounce /dɪ'naʊns/ *vt* denunciar

dens|e /dens/ *a* (**-er, -est**) denso; (*colloq: person*) obtuso. **~ely** *adv* (*packed etc*) muito. **~ity** *n* densidade *f*

dent /dent/ *n* mossa *f*, depressão *f* □ *vt* dentear

dental /'dentl/ *a* dentário, dental

dentist /'dentɪst/ *n* dentista *mf*. **~ry** *n* odontologia *f*

denture /'dentʃə(r)/ *n* dentadura *f* (postiça)

denunciation /dɪnʌnsɪ'eɪʃn/ *n* denúncia *f*

deny /dɪ'naɪ/ *vt* negar; (*rumour*) desmentir; (*disown*) renegar; (*refuse*) recusar

deodorant /diː'əʊdərənt/ *n* & *a* desodorante (*m*), (*P*) desodorizante (*m*)

depart /dɪ'paːt/ *vi* partir. **~ from** (*deviate*) afastar-se de, desviar-se de

department /dɪ'paːtmənt/ *n* departamento *m*; (*in shop, office*) secção *f*; (*government*) repartição *f*. **~ store** loja *f* de departamentos, (*P*) grande armazém *m*

departure /dɪ'paːtʃə(r)/ *n* partida *f*. **a ~ from** (*custom, diet etc*) uma mudança de. **a new ~** uma nova orientação

depend /dɪ'pend/ *vi* **~ on** depender de; (*trust*) contar com. **~able** *a* de confiança. **~ence** *n* dependência *f*. **~ent (on)** *a* dependente (de)

dependant /dɪ'pendənt/ *n* dependente *mf*

depict /dɪ'pɪkt/ *vt* descrever; (*in pictures*) representar

deplete /dɪ'pliːt/ *vt* reduzir; (*use up*) esgotar

deplor|e /dɪ'plɔː(r)/ *vt* deplorar. **~able** *a* deplorável

deport /dɪ'pɔːt/ *vt* deportar. **~ation** /diːpɔː'teɪʃn/ *n* deportação *f*

depose /dɪˈpəʊz/ vt depor

deposit /dɪˈpɒzɪt/ vt (pt **deposited**) depositar □ n depósito m. ~ **account** conta f de prazo. ~**or** n depositante mf

depot /ˈdepəʊ/ n (mil) depósito m; (buses) garagem f, (Amer: station) rodoviária f, estação f de trem, (P) de comboio

deprave /dɪˈpreɪv/ vt depravar. ~**ity** /-ˈprævətɪ/ n depravação f

depreciat|e /dɪˈpriːʃɪeɪt/ vt/i depreciar(-se). ~**ion** /-ˈeɪʃn/ n depreciação f

depress /dɪˈpres/ vt deprimir; (press down) carregar em. ~**ion** /-ʃn/ n depressão f

deprivation /deprɪˈveɪʃn/ n privação f

deprive /dɪˈpraɪv/ vt ~ **of** privar de. ~**d** a privado; (underprivileged) desperdado (da sorte), destituído; (child) carente

depth /depθ/ n profundidade f. **be out of one's** ~ perder pé, (P) não ter pé; (fig) ficar desnorteado, estar perdido. **in the** ~(**s**) **of** no mais fundo de, nas profundezas de

deputation /depjʊˈteɪʃn/ n delegação f

deputy /ˈdepjʊtɪ/ n (pl **-ies**) delegado m □ a adjunto. ~ **chairman** vice-presidente m

derail /dɪˈreɪl/ vt descarrilhar. **be** ~**ed** descarrilhar. ~**ment** n descarrilhamento m

deranged /dɪˈreɪndʒd/ a (mind) transtornado, louco

derelict /ˈderəlɪkt/ a abandonado

deri|**de** /dɪˈraɪd/ vt escarnecer de. ~**sion** /-ˈrɪʒn/ n escárnio m. ~**sive** a escarninho; (offer etc) irrisório. ~**sory** a escarninho; (offer etc) irrisório

derivative /dɪˈrɪvətɪv/ a derivado; (work) pouco original □ n derivado m

deriv|**e** /dɪˈraɪv/ vt ~**e from** tirar de □ vi ~**e from** derivar de.

~**ation** /derɪˈveɪʃn/ n derivação f

derogatory /dɪˈrɒgətrɪ/ a pejorativo; (remark) depreciativo

derv /dɜːv/ n gasóleo m

descend /dɪˈsend/ vt/i descer, descender. **be** ~**ed from** descender de. ~**ant** n descendente mf

descent /dɪˈsent/ n descida f; (lineage) descendência f, origem f

descri|**be** /dɪsˈkraɪb/ vt descrever. ~**ption** /-ˈkrɪpʃn/ n descrição f; ~**ptive** /-ˈkrɪptɪv/ a descritivo

desecrat|**e** /ˈdesɪkreɪt/ vt profanar. ~**ion** /-ˈkreɪʃn/ n profanação f

desert[1] /ˈdezət/ a, n deserto (m). ~ **island** ilha f deserta

desert[2] /dɪˈzɜːt/ vt/i desertar. ~**ed** a abandonado. ~**er** n desertor m. ~**ion** /-ʃn/ n deserção f

deserv|**e** /dɪˈzɜːv/ vt merecer. ~**edly** /dɪˈzɜːvɪdlɪ/ adv merecidamente, a justo título. ~**ing** a (person) merecedor; (action) meritório

design /dɪˈzaɪn/ n desenho m; (artistic) design m; (style of dress) modelo m; (pattern) padrão m, motivo m □ vt desenhar; (devise) conceber. ~**er** n desenhador m; (of dresses) costureiro m; (of machine) inventor m

designat|**e** /ˈdezɪgneɪt/ vt designar. ~**ion** /-ˈneɪʃn/ n designação f

desir|**e** /dɪˈzaɪə(r)/ n desejo m □ vt desejar. ~**able** a desejável, atraente

desk /desk/ n secretária f, (of pupil) carteira f, (in hotel) recepção f; (in bank) caixa f

desolat|**e** /ˈdesələt/ a desolado. ~**ion** /-ˈleɪʃn/ n desolação f

despair /dɪˈspeə(r)/ n desespero m □ vi desesperar (**of** de)

desperat|**e** /ˈdespərət/ a desesperado; (criminal) capaz de tudo. ~ **for** ter uma vontade doida de. ~**ly** adv desesperadamente

desperation /despə'reɪʃn/ n desespero m

despicable /dɪ'spɪkəbl/ a desprezível

despise /dɪ'spaɪz/ vt desprezar

despite /dɪ'spaɪt/ prep apesar de, a despeito de, mau grado

despondent /dɪ'spɒndənt/ a desanimado. **~cy** n desânimo m

despot /'despɒt/ n déspota mf

dessert /dɪ'zɜːt/ n sobremesa f. **~spoon** n colher f de sobremesa

destination /destɪ'neɪʃn/ n destino m, destinação f

destine /'destɪn/ vt destinar

destiny /'destɪnɪ/ n destino m

destitute /'destɪtjuːt/ a destituído, indigente

destroy /dɪ'strɔɪ/ vt destruir. **~uction** /-'strʌkʃn/ n destruição f. **~uctive** a destrutivo, destruidor

detach /dɪ'tætʃ/ vt separar, arrancar. **~able** a separável; (lining etc) solto. **~ed** a separado; (impartial) imparcial; (unemotional) desprendido. **~ed house** casa f sem parede-meia com outra

detachment /dɪ'tætʃmənt/ n separação f; (indifference) desprendimento m; (mil) destacamento m; (impartiality) imparcialidade f

detail /'diːteɪl/ n pormenor m, detalhe m ⬜ vt detalhar; (troops) destacar. **~ed** a detalhado

detain /dɪ'teɪn/ vt reter; (in prison) deter. **~ee** /diːteɪ'niː/ n detido m

detect /dɪ'tekt/ vt detectar. **~ion** /-ʃn/ n detecção f. **~or** n detector m

detective /dɪ'tektɪv/ n detective m. **~ story** romance m policial

detention /dɪ'tenʃn/ n detenção f. **be given a ~** (school) ficar de castigo na escola

deter /dɪ'tɜː(r)/ vt (pt deterred) dissuadir; (hinder) impedir

detergent /dɪ'tɜːdʒənt/ a & n detergente (m)

deteriorate /dɪ'tɪərɪəreɪt/ vi deteriorar(-se). **~ion** /-'reɪʃn/ n deterioração f

determin|e /dɪ'tɜːmɪn/ vt determinar. **~e to do** decidir fazer. **~ation** /-'neɪʃn/ n determinação f. **~ed** a determinado. **~ed to do** decidido a fazer

deterrent /dɪ'terənt/ n dissuasivo m

detest /dɪ'test/ vt detestar. **~able** a detestável

detonat|e /'detəneɪt/ vt/i detonar. **~ion** /-'neɪʃn/ n detonação f. **~or** n espoleta f, detonador m

detour /'diːtʊə(r)/ n desvio m

detract /dɪ'trækt/ vi **~ from** depreciar, menosprezar

detriment /'detrɪmənt/ n detrimento m. **~al** /-'mentl/ a prejudicial

devalu|e /diː'væljuː/ vt desvalorizar. **~ation** /-'eɪʃn/ n desvalorização f

devastat|e /'devəsteɪt/ vt devastar; (fig: overwhelm) arrasar. **~ing** a devastador; (criticism) arrasador

develop /dɪ'veləp/ vt/i (pt developed) desenvolver(-se); (get) contrair; (build on) urbanizar; (film) revelar. **~ into** tornar-se. **~ing country** país m subdesenvolvido. **~ment** n desenvolvimento m; (film) revelação f; (of land) urbanização f

deviat|e /'diːvɪeɪt/ vi desviar-se. **~ion** /-'eɪʃn/ n desvio m

device /dɪ'vaɪs/ n dispositivo m, (scheme) processo m. **left to one's own ~s** entregue a si mesmo

devil /'devl/ n diabo m

devious /'diːvɪəs/ a tortuoso; (fig: means) escuso; (fig: person) pouco franco

devise /dɪ'vaɪz/ vt imaginar, inventar

devoid /dɪˈvɔɪd/ a ~ of desprovido de, destituído de

devote /dɪˈvəʊt/ vt dedicar, devotar. ~ed a dedicado, devotado. ~ion /-ʃn/ n devoção f

devotee /devəˈtiː/ n ~ of adepto m de, entusiasta mf de

devour /dɪˈvaʊə(r)/ vt devorar

devout /dɪˈvaʊt/ a devota; (prayer) fervoroso

dew /djuː/ n orvalho m

dext|erity /dekˈsterɪtɪ/ n destreza f, jeito m. ~rous /ˈdekstrəs/ a destro, hábil

diabet|es /daɪəˈbiːtiːz/ n diabetes f. ~ic /-ˈbetɪk/ a diabético

diabolical /daɪəˈbɒlɪkl/ a diabólico

diagnose /ˈdaɪəɡnəʊz/ vt diagnosticar

diagnosis /daɪəɡˈnəʊsɪs/ n (pl -oses /-siːz/) diagnóstico m

diagonal /daɪˈæɡənl/ a & n diagonal (f)

diagram /ˈdaɪəɡræm/ n diagrama m, esquema m

dial /ˈdaɪəl/ n mostrador m □ vt (pt dialled) (number) marcar, discar. ~ling code código m de discagem. ~ling tone sinal m de discar

dialect /ˈdaɪəlekt/ n dialeto m, (P) dialecto m

dialogue /ˈdaɪəlɒɡ/ n diálogo m

diameter /daɪˈæmɪtə(r)/ n diâmetro m

diamond /ˈdaɪəmənd/ n diamante m, brilhante m; (shape) losango m. ~s (cards) ouros mpl

diaper /ˈdaɪəpə(r)/ n (Amer) fralda f

diaphragm /ˈdaɪəfræm/ n diafragma m

diarrhoea /daɪəˈrɪə/ n diarréia f, (P) diarreia f

diary /ˈdaɪərɪ/ n agenda f; (record) diário m

dice /daɪs/ n (pl invar) dado m

dictat|e /dɪkˈteɪt/ vt/i ditar. ~ion /-ʃn/ n ditado m

dictator /dɪkˈteɪtə(r)/ n ditador m. ~ship n ditadura f

diction /ˈdɪkʃn/ n dicção f

dictionary /ˈdɪkʃənrɪ/ n dicionário m

did /dɪd/ see **do**

diddle /ˈdɪdl/ vt (colloq) trapacear, enganar

didn't /ˈdɪdnt/ = **did not**

die /daɪ/ vi (pres p dying) morrer. **be dying to** estar doido para. ~ **down** diminuir, baixar. ~ **out** desaparecer, extinguir-se

diesel /ˈdiːzl/ n diesel m. ~ **engine** motor m diesel

diet /ˈdaɪət/ n dieta f □ vi fazer dieta, estar de dieta

differ /ˈdɪfə(r)/ vi diferir; (disagree) discordar

differen|t /ˈdɪfrənt/ a diferente. ~**ce** n diferença f; (disagreement) desacordo m. ~**ly** adv diferentemente

differentiate /dɪfəˈrenʃɪeɪt/ vt/i diferençar(-se), diferenciar(-se)

difficult /ˈdɪfɪkəlt/ a difícil. ~**y** n dificuldade f

diffiden|t /ˈdɪfɪdənt/ a acanhado, inseguro. ~**ce** n acanhamento m, insegurança f

diffuse[1] /dɪˈfjuːs/ a difuso

diffuse[2] /dɪˈfjuːz/ vt difundir. ~**ion** /-ʒn/ n difusão f

dig /dɪɡ/ vt/i (pt dug, pres p digging) cavar; (thrust) espetar □ n (with elbow) cotovelada f; (with finger) cutucada f, (P) espetadela f; (remark) ferroada f; (archaeol) escavação f. ~**s** (colloq) quarto m alugado. ~ **up** desenterrar

digest /dɪˈdʒest/ vt/i digerir. ~**ible** a digerível, digestível. ~**ion** /-ʃn/ n digestão f

digestive /dɪˈdʒestɪv/ a digestivo

digit /ˈdɪdʒɪt/ n dígito m

digital /ˈdɪdʒɪtl/ a digital. ~ **camera** câmara f digital. ~ **clock** relógio m digital

dignify /'dɪgnɪfaɪ/ *vt* dignificar.
~ied *a* digno

dignitary /'dɪgnɪtərɪ/ *n* dignitário *m*

dignity /'dɪgnətɪ/ *n* dignidade *f*

digress /daɪ'gres/ *vi* digressar, divagar. **~ from** desviar-se de. **~ion** /-ʃn/ *n* digressão *f*

dike /daɪk/ *n* dique *m*

dilapidated /dɪ'læpɪdeɪtɪd/ *a* (*house*) arruinado, degradado; (*car*) estragado

dilate /daɪ'leɪt/ *vt/i* dilatar(-se). **~ion** /-ʃn/ *n* dilatação *f*

dilemma /dɪ'lemə/ *n* dilema *m*

diligen|t /'dɪlɪdʒənt/ *a* diligente, aplicado. **~ce** *n* diligência *f*, aplicação *f*

dilute /daɪ'ljuːt/ *vt* diluir □ *a* diluído

dim /dɪm/ *a* (**dimmer, dimmest**) (*weak*) fraco; (*dark*) sombrio; (*indistinct*) vago; (*colloq: stupid*) burro (*colloq*) □ *vt/i* (*pt* **dimmed**) (*light*) baixar. **~ly** *adv* (*shine*) fracamente; (*remember*) vagamente

dime /daɪm/ *n* (*Amer*) moeda *f* de dez centavos

dimension /daɪ'menʃn/ *n* dimensão *f*

diminish /dɪ'mɪnɪʃ/ *vt/i* diminuir

diminutive /dɪ'mɪnjutɪv/ *a* diminuto □ *n* diminutivo *m*

dimple /'dɪmpl/ *n* covinha *f*

din /dɪn/ *n* barulheira *f*, (*P*) chinfrim *m*

dine /daɪn/ *vi* jantar. **~r** /-ə(r)/ *n* (*person*) comensal *m*; (*rail*) vagão-restaurante *m*; (*Amer: restaurant*) lanchonete *f*

dinghy /'dɪŋgɪ/ *n* (*pl* **-ghies**) bote *m*; (*inflatable*) bote *m* de borracha, (*P*) barco *m* de borracha

dingy /'dɪndʒɪ/ *a* (**-ier, -iest**) com ar sujo, esquálido

dining-room /'daɪnɪŋruːm/ *n* sala *f* de jantar

dinner /'dɪnə(r)/ *n* jantar *m*;

(*lunch*) almoço *m*. **~-jacket** *n* smoking *m*

dinosaur /'daɪnəsɔː(r)/ *n* dinossauro *m*

dip /dɪp/ *vt/i* (*pt* **dipped**) mergulhar; (*lower*) baixar □ *n* mergulho *m*; (*bathe*) banho *m* rápido, mergulho *m*; (*slope*) descida *f*; (*culin*) molho *m*. **~ into** (*book*) folhear. **~ one's headlights** baixar para médios

diphtheria /dɪf'θɪərɪə/ *n* difteria *f*

diphthong /'dɪfθɒŋ/ *n* ditongo *m*

diploma /dɪ'pləumə/ *n* diploma *m*

diplomacy /dɪ'pləuməsɪ/ *n* diplomacia *f*

diplomat /'dɪpləmæt/ *n* diplomata *mf*. **~ic** /-'mætɪk/ *a* diplomático

dire /daɪə(r)/ *a* (**-er, -est**) terrível; (*need, poverty*) extremo

direct /dɪ'rekt/ *a* direto, (*P*) directo □ *adv* diretamente, (*P*) directamente □ *vt* dirigir. **~ sb** to indicar a alg o caminho para

direction /dɪ'rekʃn/ *n* direção *f*, (*P*) direcção *f*, sentido *m*. **~s** instruções *fpl*. **~s for use** modo *m* de emprego

directly /dɪ'rektlɪ/ *adv* diretamente, (*P*) directamente; (*at once*) imediatamente, logo

director /dɪ'rektə(r)/ *n* diretor *m*, (*P*) director *m*

directory /dɪ'rektərɪ/ *n* (**telephone**) **~** lista *f* telefônica, (*P*) telefónica

dirt /dɜːt/ *n* sujeira *f*. **~ cheap** (*colloq*) baratíssimo

dirty /'dɜːtɪ/ *a* (**-ier, -iest**) sujo; (*word*) obsceno □ *vt/i* sujar(-se). **~ trick** golpe *m* baixo, (*P*) boa partida *f*

disability /dɪsə'bɪlətɪ/ *n* deficiência *f*

disable /dɪs'eɪbl/ *vt* incapacitar. **~d** *a* inválido, deficiente

disadvantage /dɪsəd'vaːntɪdʒ/ *n* desvantagem *f*

disagree /dɪsəˈgriː/ *vi* discordar
(**with** de). ~ **with** (*food, climate*) não fazer bem. ~**ment** *n*
desacordo *m*; (*quarrel*) desintendimento *m*

disagreeable /dɪsəˈgriːəbl/ *a* desagradável

disappear /dɪsəˈpɪə(r)/ *vi* desaparecer. ~**ance** *n* desaparecimento *m*

disappoint /dɪsəˈpɔɪnt/ *vt* desapontar, decepcionar. ~**ment** *n*
desapontamento *m*, decepção *f*

disapprove /dɪsəˈpruːv/ *vi* ~**e**
(**of**) desaprovar. ~**al** *n* desaprovação *f*

disarm /dɪˈsɑːm/ *vt/i* desarmar.
~**ament** *n* desarmamento *m*

disaster /dɪˈzɑːstə(r)/ *n* desastre
m. ~**rous** *a* desastroso

disband /dɪsˈbænd/ *vt/i* debandar;
(*troops*) dispersar

disbelief /dɪsbɪˈliːf/ *n* incredulidade *f*

disc /dɪsk/ *n* disco *m*. ~ **jockey**
disc(o) jockey *m*

discard /dɪsˈkɑːd/ *vt* pôr de lado,
descartar(-se) de; (*old clothes etc*)
desfazer-se de

discern /dɪˈsɜːn/ *vt* discernir.
~**ible** *a* perceptível. ~**ing** *a*
perspicaz. ~**ment** *n* discernimento *m*, perspicácia *f*

discharge[1] /dɪsˈtʃɑːdʒ/ *vt* descarregar; (*dismiss*) despedir, mandar
embora; (*duty*) cumprir; (*liquid*)
vazar, (*P*) deitar; (*patient*) dar
alta a; (*prisoner*) absolver, pôr
em liberdade; (*pus*) purgar, (*P*)
deitar

discharge[2] /ˈdɪstʃɑːdʒ/ *n* descarga
f; (*dismissal*) despedimento *m*;
(*of patient*) alta *f*; (*of prisoner*) absolvição *f*; (*med*) secreção *f*

disciple /dɪˈsaɪpl/ *n* discípulo *m*

disciplin|**e** /ˈdɪsɪplɪn/ *n* disciplina
f □ *vt* disciplinar; (*punish*)
castigar. ~**ary** *a* disciplinar

disclaim /dɪsˈkleɪm/ *vt* (*jur*) repu-

diar; (*deny*) negar. ~**er** *n* desmentido *m*

disclos|**e** /dɪsˈkləʊz/ *vt* revelar.
~**ure** /-ʒə(r)/ *n* revelação *f*

disco /ˈdɪskəʊ/ *n* (*pl* -**os**) (*colloq*)
discoteca *f*

discolour /dɪsˈkʌlə(r)/ *vt/i* descolorir(-se); (*in sunlight*) desbotar
(-se)

discomfort /dɪsˈkʌmfət/ *n* mal-
estar *m*; (*lack of comfort*) desconforto *m*

disconcert /dɪskənˈsɜːt/ *vt* desconcertar. ~**ing** *a* desconcertante

disconnect /dɪskəˈnekt/ *vt* desligar

discontent /dɪskənˈtent/ *n* descontentamento *m*. ~**ed** *a* descontente

discontinue /dɪskənˈtɪnjuː/ *vt* descontinuar, suspender

discord /ˈdɪskɔːd/ *n* discórdia *f*.
~**ant** /-ˈskɔːdənt/ *a* discordante

discothèque /ˈdɪskətek/ *n* discoteca *f*

discount[1] /ˈdɪskaʊnt/ *n* desconto
m

discount[2] /dɪsˈkaʊnt/ *vt* descontar; (*disregard*) dar o desconto a

discourage /dɪsˈkʌrɪdʒ/ *vt* desencorajar

discourte|**ous** /dɪsˈkɜːtɪəs/ *a* indelicado. ~**sy** /-sɪ/ *n* indelicadeza *f*

discover /dɪsˈkʌvə(r)/ *vt* descobrir.
~**y** *n* descoberta *f*; (*of island etc*)
descobrimento *m*

discredit /dɪsˈkredɪt/ *vt* (*pt* **discredited**) desacreditar □ *n* descrédito *m*

discreet /dɪˈskriːt/ *a* discreto

discrepancy /dɪˈskrepənsɪ/ *n* discrepância *f*

discretion /dɪˈskreʃn/ *n* discrição
f; (*prudence*) prudência *f*

discriminat|**e** /dɪsˈkrɪmɪneɪt/ *vt/i*
discriminar. ~**e against** tomar
partido contra, fazer discriminação contra. ~**ing** *a* discrimina-

dor; (*having good taste*) com discernimento. **~ion** /-'neɪʃn/ *n* discernimento *m*; (*bias*) discriminação *f*

discus /'dɪskəs/ *n* disco *m*

discuss /dɪ'skʌs/ *vt* discutir. **~ion** /-ʃn/ *n* discussão *f*

disdain /dɪs'deɪn/ *n* desdém *m* □ *vt* desdenhar. **~ful** *a* desdenhoso

disease /dɪ'ziːz/ *n* doença *f*. **~d** *a* (*plant*) atacado por doença; (*person, animal*) doente

disembark /dɪsɪm'baːk/ *vt/i* desembarcar

disembodied /dɪsɪm'bɒdɪd/ *a* desencarnado

disenchant /dɪsɪn'tʃaːnt/ *vt* desencantar. **~ment** *n* desencantamento *m*

disengage /dɪsɪn'geɪdʒ/ *vt* desprender, soltar; (*mech*) desengatar

disentangle /dɪsɪn'tæŋgl/ *vt* desembaraçar, desenredar

disfavour /dɪs'feɪvə(r)/ *n* desfavor *m*, desgraça *f*

disfigure /dɪs'fɪgə(r)/ *vt* desfigurar

disgrace /dɪs'greɪs/ *n* vergonha *f*, (*disfavour*) desgraça *f* □ *vt* desonrar. **~ful** *a* vergonhoso

disgruntled /dɪs'grʌntld/ *a* descontente

disguise /dɪs'gaɪz/ *vt* disfarçar □ *n* disfarce *m*. **in ~** disfarçado

disgust /dɪs'gʌst/ *n* repugnância *f* □ *vt* repugnar. **~ing** *a* repugnante

dish /dɪʃ/ *n* prato *m* □ *vt* (*colloq*) distribuir. **~ up** servir. **the ~es** (*crockery*) a louça *f*

dishcloth /'dɪʃklɒθ/ *n* pano *m* de prato

dishearten /dɪs'haːtn/ *vt* desencorajar, desalentar

dishevelled /dɪ'ʃevld/ *a* desgrenhado

dishonest /dɪs'ɒnɪst/ *a* desonesto. **~y** *n* desonestidade *f*

dishonour /dɪs'ɒnə(r)/ *n* desonra *f*

□ *vt* desonrar. **~able** *a* desonroso

dishwasher /'dɪʃwɒʃə(r)/ *n* lavadora *f* de pratos, (*P*) máquina *f* de lavar a louça

disillusion /dɪsɪ'luːʒn/ *vt* desiludir. **~ment** *n* desilusão *f*

disinfect /dɪsɪn'fekt/ *vt* desinfetar, (*P*) desinfectar. **~ant** *n* desinfetante *m*, (*P*) desinfectante *m*

disinherit /dɪsɪn'herɪt/ *vt* deserdar

disintegrate /dɪs'ɪntɪgreɪt/ *vt/i* desintegrar(-se)

disinterested /dɪs'ɪntrəstɪd/ *a* desinteressado

disjointed /dɪs'dʒɔɪntɪd/ *a* (*talk*) descosido, desconexo

disk /dɪsk/ *n* (*comput*) disco *m*; (*Amer*) = disc. **~ drive** unidade *f* de disco

dislike /dɪs'laɪk/ *n* aversão *f*, antipatia *f* □ *vt* não gostar de, antipatizar com

dislocat|e /dɪs'ləkeɪt/ *vt* (*limb*) deslocar. **~ion** /-'keɪʃn/ *n* deslocação *f*

dislodge /dɪs'lɒdʒ/ *vt* desalojar

disloyal /dɪs'lɔɪəl/ *a* desleal. **~ty** *n* deslealdade *f*

dismal /'dɪzməl/ *a* tristonho

dismantle /dɪs'mæntl/ *vt* desmantelar

dismay /dɪs'meɪ/ *n* consternação *f* □ *vt* consternar

dismiss /dɪs'mɪs/ *vt* despedir; (*from mind*) afastar, pôr de lado. **~al** *n* despedimento *m*

dismount /dɪs'maʊnt/ *vi* desmontar

disobedien|t /dɪsə'biːdɪənt/ *a* desobediente. **~ce** *n* desobediência *f*

disobey /dɪsə'beɪ/ *vt/i* desobedecer (a)

disorder /dɪs'ɔːdə(r)/ *n* desordem *f*; (*med*) perturbações *fpl*, disfunção *f*. **~ly** *a* desordenado; (*riotous*) desordeiro

disorganize /dɪsˈɔːgənaɪz/ *vt* desorganizar

disorientate /dɪsˈɔːrɪənteɪt/ *vt* desorientar

disown /dɪsˈəʊn/ *vt* repudiar

disparaging /dɪˈspærɪdʒɪŋ/ *a* depreciativo

disparity /dɪˈspærətɪ/ *n* disparidade *f*

dispatch /dɪˈspætʃ/ *vt* despachar □ *n* despacho *m*

dispel /dɪsˈpel/ *vt* (*pt* **dispelled**) dissipar

dispensary /dɪˈspensərɪ/ *n* dispensário *m*, farmácia *f*

dispense /dɪˈspens/ *vt* dispensar □ *vi* ~ **with** dispensar, passar sem. ~**r** /-ə(r)/ *n* (*container*) distribuidor *m*

dispers|e /dɪˈspɜːs/ *vt/i* dispersar (-se). ~**al** *n* dispersão *f*

dispirited /dɪˈspɪrɪtɪd/ *a* desanimado

displace /dɪsˈpleɪs/ *vt* deslocar; (*take the place of*) substituir. ~**d person** deslocado *m* de guerra

display /dɪˈspleɪ/ *vt* exibir, mostrar; (*feeling*) manifestar, dar mostras de □ *n* exposição *f*; (*of computer*) apresentação *f* visual; (*comm*) objetos *mpl* expostos

displeas|e /dɪsˈpliːz/ *vt* desagradar a. ~**ed with** descontente com. ~**ure** /-ˈpleʒə(r)/ *n* desagrado *m*

disposable /dɪˈspəʊzəbl/ *a* descartável

dispos|e /dɪˈspəʊz/ *vt* dispor □ *vi* ~**e of** desfazer-se de. **well** ~**ed towards** bem disposto para. ~**al** *n* (*of waste*) eliminação *f*. **at sb's** ~**al** à disposição de alg

disposition /dɪspəˈzɪʃn/ *n* disposição *f*; (*character*) índole *f*

disproportionate /dɪsprəˈpɔːʃənət/ *a* desproporcionado

disprove /dɪsˈpruːv/ *vt* refutar

dispute /dɪˈspjuːt/ *vt* contestar; (*fight for, quarrel*) disputar □ *n*

disputa *f*; (*industrial, pol*) conflito *m*. **in** ~ em questão

disqualif|y /dɪsˈkwɒlɪfaɪ/ *vt* tornar inapto; (*sport*) desqualificar. ~**y from driving** apreender a carteira de motorista. ~**ication** /-ˈkeɪʃn/ *n* desqualificação *f*

disregard /dɪsrɪˈgɑːd/ *vt* não fazer caso de □ *n* indiferença *f* (**for** por)

disrepair /dɪsrɪˈpeə(r)/ *n* mau estado *m*, abandono *m*, degradação *f*

disreputable /dɪsˈrepjʊtəbl/ *a* pouco recomendável; (*in appearance*) com mau aspecto; (*in reputation*) vergonhoso, de má fama

disrepute /dɪsrɪˈpjuːt/ *n* descrédito *m*

disrespect /dɪsrɪˈspekt/ *n* falta *f* de respeito. ~**ful** *a* desrespeitoso, irreverente

disrupt /dɪsˈrʌpt/ *vt* perturbar; (*plans*) transtornar; (*break up*) dividir. ~**ion** /-ʃn/ *n* perturbação *f*. ~**ive** *a* perturbador

dissatisf|ied /dɪˈsætɪsfaɪd/ *a* descontente. ~**action** /dɪsætɪsˈfækʃn/ *n* descontentamento *m*

dissect /dɪˈsekt/ *vt* dissecar. ~**ion** /-ʃn/ *n* dissecação *f*

dissent /dɪˈsent/ *vi* dissentir, discordar □ *n* dissensão *f*, desacordo *m*

dissertation /dɪsəˈteɪʃn/ *n* dissertação *f*

disservice /dɪsˈsɜːvɪs/ *n* **do sb a** ~ prejudicar alg

dissident /ˈdɪsɪdənt/ *a* & *n* dissidente (*mf*)

dissimilar /dɪˈsɪmɪlə(r)/ *a* diferente

dissipate /ˈdɪsɪpeɪt/ *vt* dissipar; (*efforts, time*) desperdiçar. ~**d** *a* dissoluto

dissociate /dɪˈsəʊʃɪeɪt/ *vt* dissociar, desassociar

dissolution /dɪsəˈluːʃn/ *n* dissolução *f*

dissolve /dɪ'zɒlv/ vt/i dissolver (-se)

dissuade /dɪ'sweɪd/ vt dissuadir

distance /'dɪstəns/ n distância f. **from a ~** de longe. **in the ~** ao longe, à distância

distant /'dɪstənt/ a distante; (relative) afastado

distaste /dɪs'teɪst/ n aversão f. **~ful** a desagradável

distemper /dɪ'stempə(r)/ n pintura f a têmpera; (animal disease) cinomose f □ vt pintar a têmpera

distend /dɪ'stend/ vt/i distender (-se)

distil /dɪ'stɪl/ vt (pt distilled) destilar. **~lation** /-'leɪʃn/ n destilação f

distillery /dɪ'stɪlərɪ/ n destilaria f

distinct /dɪ'stɪŋkt/ a distinto; (marked) claro, nítido. **~ion** /-ʃn/ n distinção f. **~ive** a distintivo, característico. **~ly** adv distintamente; (markedly) claramente

distinguish /dɪ'stɪŋgwɪʃ/ vt/i distinguir. **~ed** a distinto

distort /dɪ'stɔ:t/ vt distorcer; (misrepresent) deturpar. **~ion** /-ʃn/ n distorção f; (misrepresentation) deturpação f

distract /dɪ'strækt/ vt distrair. **~ed** a (distraught) desesperado, fora de si. **~ing** a enlouquecedor. **~ion** /-ʃn/ n distração f, (P) distracção f

distraught /dɪ'strɔ:t/ a desesperado, fora de si

distress /dɪ'stres/ n (physical) dor f; (anguish) aflição f; (poverty) miséria f; (danger) perigo m □ vt afligir. **~ing** a aflitivo, doloroso

distribute /dɪ'strɪbju:t/ vt distribuir. **~ion** /-'bju:ʃn/ n distribuição f. **~or** n distribuidor m

district /'dɪstrɪkt/ n região f; (of town) zona f

distrust /dɪs'trʌst/ n desconfiança f □ vt desconfiar de

disturb /dɪ'stɜ:b/ vt perturbar; (move) desarrumar; (bother) incomodar. **~ance** n (noise, disorder) distúrbio m. **~ed** a perturbado. **~ing** a perturbador

disused /dɪs'ju:zd/ a fora de uso, desusado, em desuso

ditch /dɪtʃ/ n fosso m □ vt (sl: abandon) abandonar, largar

dither /'dɪðə(r)/ vi hesitar

ditto /'dɪtəʊ/ adv idem

div|**e** /daɪv/ vi mergulhar; (rush) precipitar-se □ n mergulho m; (of plane) picada f; (sl: place) espelunca f. **~er** n mergulhador m. **~ing-board** n prancha f de saltos. **~ing-suit** n escafandro m

diverge /daɪ'vɜ:dʒ/ vi divergir

divergent /daɪ'vɜ:dʒənt/ a divergente

diverse /daɪ'vɜ:s/ a diverso

diversify /daɪ'vɜ:sɪfaɪ/ vt diversificar

diversity /daɪ'vɜ:sətɪ/ n diversidade f

diver|**t** /daɪ'vɜ:t/ vt desviar; (entertain) divertir. **~sion** /-ʃn/ n diversão f; (traffic) desvio m

divide /dɪ'vaɪd/ vt/i dividir(-se). **~ in two** (branch, river, road) bifurcar-se

dividend /'dɪvɪdend/ n dividendo m

divine /dɪ'vaɪn/ a divino

divinity /dɪ'vɪnətɪ/ n divindade f; (theology) teologia f

division /dɪ'vɪʒn/ n divisão f

divorce /dɪ'vɔ:s/ n divórcio m □ vt/i divorciar(-se) de. **~d** a divorciado

divorcee /dɪvɔ:'si:/ n divorciado m

divulge /daɪ'vʌldʒ/ vt divulgar

DIY abbr see **do-it-yourself**

dizz|**y** /'dɪzɪ/ a (-ier, -iest) tonto. **be** or **feel ~y** ter tonturas, sentir-se tonto. **~iness** n tontura f, vertigem f

do /duː/ *vt/i* (3 *sing pres* **does**, *pt* **did**, *pp* **done**) fazer; (*be suitable*) servir; (*be enough*) bastar (a); (*sl: swindle*) enganar, levar (*colloq*). **how ~ you ~?** como vai? **well done** muito bem!, (P) bravo!; (*culin*) bem passado. **done for** (*colloq*) liquidado (*colloq*), (P) anumado (*colloq*) □ *v aux* ~ **you see?** vê?; **I ~ not smoke** não fumo. **don't you?, doesn't he?** *etc* não é? □ *n* (*pl* **dos** *or* **do's**) festa *f*. **~-it-yourself** a faça-você-mesmo. **~ away with** eliminar, suprimir. **~ in** (*sl*) matar, liquidar (*colloq*). **~ out** limpar. **~ up** (*fasten*) fechar; (*house*) renovar. **I could ~ with a cup of tea** apetece-me uma xícara de chá. **it could ~ with a wash** precisa de uma lavagem

docile /ˈdəʊsaɪl/ a dócil

dock[1] /dɒk/ *n* doca *f* □ *vt* levar à doca □ *vi* entrar na doca. **~er** *n* estivador *m*

dock[2] /dɒk/ *n* (*jur*) banco *m* dos réus

dockyard /ˈdɒkjɑːd/ *n* estaleiro *m*

doctor /ˈdɒktə(r)/ *n* médico *m*, doutor *m*; (*univ*) doutor *m* □ *vt* (*cat*) capar; (*fig*) adulterar, falsificar

doctorate /ˈdɒktərət/ *n* doutorado *m*, (P) doutoramento *m*

doctrine /ˈdɒktrɪn/ *n* doutrina *f*

document /ˈdɒkjʊmənt/ *n* documento *m* □ *vt* documentar. **~ary** /-ˈmentrɪ/ a documental □ *n* documentário *m*

dodge /dɒdʒ/ *vt/i* esquivar(-se), furtar(-se) a □ *n* (*colloq*) truque *m*

dodgy /ˈdɒdʒɪ/ a (-**ier**, -**iest**) (*colloq*) delicado, difícil, embaraçoso

does /dʌz/ *see* **do**

doesn't /ˈdʌznt/ = **does not**

dog /dɒg/ *n* cão *m* □ *vt* (*pt* **dogged**) ir no encalço de, perseguir. **~-eared** a com os cantos dobrados

dogged /ˈdɒgɪd/ a obstinado, persistente

dogma /ˈdɒgmə/ *n* dogma *m*. **~tic** /-ˈmætɪk/ a dogmático

dogsbody /ˈdɒgzbɒdɪ/ *n* (*colloq*) pau-para-toda-obra *m* (*colloq*), factótum *m*

doldrums /ˈdɒldrəmz/ *npl* **be in the ~** estar com a neura; (*business*) estar parado

dole /dəʊl/ *vt* **~ out** distribuir □ *n* (*colloq*) auxílio *m* desemprego. **on the ~** (*colloq*) desempregado (titular de auxílio)

doleful /ˈdəʊlfl/ a tristonho, melancólico

doll /dɒl/ *n* boneca *f* □ *vt/i* **~ up** (*colloq*) embonecar(-se)

dollar /ˈdɒlə(r)/ *n* dólar *m*

dolphin /ˈdɒlfɪn/ *n* golfinho *m*

domain /dəʊˈmeɪn/ *n* domínio *m*

dome /dəʊm/ *n* cúpula *f*; (*vault*) abóbada *f*

domestic /dəˈmestɪk/ a (*of home, animal, flights*) doméstico; (*trade*) interno; (*news*) nacional. **~ated** /-ɪketɪd/ a (*animal*) domesticado; (*person*) que gosta de trabalhos caseiros

dominant /ˈdɒmɪnənt/ a dominante

dominat|e /ˈdɒmɪneɪt/ *vt/i* dominar. **~ion** /-ˈneɪʃn/ *n* dominação *f*, domínio *m*

domineer /dɒmɪˈnɪə(r)/ *vi* **~ over** mandar (em), ser autocrático (para com). **~ing** a mandão, autocrático

dominion /dəˈmɪnjən/ *n* domínio *m*

domino /ˈdɒmɪnəʊ/ *n* (*pl* -**oes**) dominó *m*

donat|e /dəʊˈneɪt/ *vt* fazer doação de, doar, dar. **~ion** /-ʃn/ *n* donativo *m*

done /dʌn/ *see* **do**

donkey /ˈdɒŋkɪ/ *n* burro *m*

donor /ˈdəʊnə(r)/ *n* (*of blood*) doador *m*, (P) dador *m*

don't /dəʊnt/ = **do not**

doodle /'duːdl/ *vi* rabiscar

doom /duːm/ *n* ruína *f*; (*fate*) destino *m*. **be ~ed to** ser/estar condenado a. **~ed (to failure)** condenado ao fracasso

door /dɔː(r)/ *n* porta *f*

doorman /'dɔːmən/ *n* (*pl* **-men**) porteiro *m*

doormat /'dɔːmæt/ *n* capacho *m*

doorstep /'dɔːstep/ *n* degrau *m* da porta

doorway /'dɔːweɪ/ *n* vão *m* da porta, (*P*) entrada *f*

dope /dəʊp/ *n* (*colloq*) droga *f*; (*sl: idiot*) imbecil *mf* □ *vt* dopar, drogar

dormant /'dɔːmənt/ *a* dormente; (*inactive*) inativo, (*P*) inactivo; (*latent*) latente

dormitory /'dɔːmɪtrɪ/ *n* dormitório *m*; (*Amer univ*) residência *f*

dos|e /dəʊs/ *n* dose *f* □ *vt* medicar. **~age** *n* dosagem *f*; (*on label*) posologia *f*

doss /dɒs/ *vi* **~ (down)** dormir sem conforto. **~-house** *n* pensão *f* miserável, asilo *m* noturno, (*P*) nocturno. **~er** *n* vagabundo *m*

dot /dɒt/ *n* ponto *m*. **on the ~** no momento preciso □ *vt* **be ~ted with** estar semeado de. **~ted line** linha *f* pontilhada

dot-com /dɒt'kɒm/ *n* empresa *f* dot.com

dote /dəʊt/ *vi* **~ on** ser louco por

double /'dʌbl/ *a* duplo; (*room, bed*) de casal □ *adv* duas vezes mais □ *n* dobro *m*. **~s** (*tennis*) dupla *f*, (*P*) pares *mpl* □ *vt/i* dobrar, duplicar; (*fold*) dobrar em dois. **at the ~** a passo acelerado. **~-bass** *n* contrabaixo *m*. **~-chin** papada *f*. **~-cross** *vt* enganar. **~-dealing** *n* jogo *m* duplo. **~-decker** *n* ônibus *m*, (*P*) autocarro *m* de dois andares. **~ Dutch** algaraviada *f*, fala *f* incompreensível. **~ glazing**

(*janela f* de) vidro (*m*) duplo.

doubly *adv* duplamente

doubt /daʊt/ *n* dúvida *f* □ *vt* duvidar de. **~ if** *or* **that** duvidar que. **~ful** *a* duvidoso; (*hesitant*) que tem dúvidas. **~less** *adv* sem dúvida, indubitavelmente

dough /dəʊ/ *n* massa *f*

doughnut /'dəʊnʌt/ *n* sonho *n*, (*P*) bola *f* de Berlim

dove /dʌv/ *n* pomba *f*

dowdy /'daʊdɪ/ *a* (**-ier, -iest**) sem graça, sem gosto

down[1] /daʊn/ *n* (*feathers, hair*) penugem *f*

down[2] /daʊn/ *adv* (*to lower place*) abaixo, para baixo; (*in lower place*) em baixo. **be ~** (*level, price*) descer; (*sun*) estar posto □ *prep* (*or* (+*n*) (*n*+) abaixo. **~ the hill/street** *etc* pelo monte/pela rua *etc* abaixo □ *vt* (*colloq: knock down*) jogar abaixo; (*colloq: drink*) esvaziar. **come** *or* **go ~** descer. **~-and-out** *n* marginal *m*. **~-hearted** *a* desencorajado, desanimado. **~-to-earth** *a* terra-a-terra *invar*. **~ under** na Austrália. **with** abaixo

downcast /'daʊnkɑːst/ *a* abatido, deprimido, desmoralizado

downfall /'daʊnfɔːl/ *n* queda *f*, ruína *f*

downhill /daʊn'hɪl/ *adv* **go ~** descer; (*fig*) ir abaixo □ *a* /'daʊnhɪl/ *a* descer, descendente

download /daʊn'ləʊd/ *vt.*(*comput*) baixar

downpour /'daʊnpɔː(r)/ *n* aguaceiro *m* forte, (*P*) chuvada *f*

downright /'daʊnraɪt/ *a* franco; (*utter*) autêntico, verdadeiro □ *adv* positivamente

downstairs /daʊn'steəz/ *adv* (*at/to*) em/para baixo, no/para o andar de baixo □ *a* /'daʊnsteəz/ (*flat etc*) de baixo, do andar de baixo

downstream /'daʊnstriːm/ *adv* rio abaixo

downtown /'dauntaun/ a & adv (de, em, para) o centro da cidade. ~ **Boston** o centro de Boston

downtrodden /'dauntrodn/ a espezinhado, oprimido

downward /'daunwəd/ a descendente. ~**(s)** adv para baixo

dowry /'dauərɪ/ n dote m

doze /dəuz/ vi dormitar. ~ **off** cochilar □ n soneca f, cochilo m

dozen /'dʌzn/ n dúzia f. ~**s of** (colloq) dezenas de, dúzias de

Dr abbr (Doctor) Dr

drab /dræb/ a insípido; (of colour) morto, apagado

draft[1] /dra:ft/ n rascunho m; (comm) ordem f de pagamento □ vt fazer o rascunho de; (draw up) redigir. **the** ~ (Amer: mil) recrutamento m

draft[2] /dra:ft/ n (Amer) = **draught**

drag /dræg/ vt/i (pt **dragged**) arrastar(-se); (river) dragar; (pull away) arrancar □ n (colloq: task) chatice f (sl); (colloq: person) estorvo m; (sl: clothes) travesti m

dragon /'drægən/ n dragão m

dragonfly /'drægənflaɪ/ n libélula f

drain /dreɪn/ vt drenar; (vegetables) escorrer; (glass, tank) esvaziar; (use up) esgotar □ vi ~ **(off)** escoar-se □ n cano m. ~**s** npl (sewers) esgotos mpl. ~**age** n drenagem f. ~**(-pipe)** cano m de esgoto. ~**ing-board** n escorredouro m

drama /'dra:mə/ n arte f dramática; (play, event) drama m. ~**tic** /drə'mætɪk/ a dramático. ~**tist** /'dræmətɪst/ n dramaturgo m. ~**tize** /'dræmətaɪz/ vt dramatizar

drank /dræŋk/ see **drink**

drape /dreɪp/ vt ~ **round/over** dispor (tecido) em pregas à volta de or sobre. ~**s** npl (Amer) cortinas fpl

drastic /'dræstɪk/ a drástico, violento

draught /dra:ft/ n corrente f de ar; (naut) calado m. ~**s** (game) (jogo m das) damas fpl. ~ **beer** chope m, (P) cerveja f à caneca, imperial f (colloq). ~**y** a com correntes de ar, ventoso

draughtsman /'dra:ftsmən/ n (pl -men) desenhista m, (P) desenhador m

draw /drɔ:/ vt (pt **drew**, pp **drawn**) puxar; (attract) atrair; (picture) desenhar; (in lottery) tirar à sorte; (line) traçar; (open curtains) abrir; (close curtains) fechar □ vi desenhar; (sport) empatar; (come) vir □ n (sport) empate m; (lottery) sorteio m. ~ **back** recuar. ~ **in** (of days) diminuir. ~ **near** aproximar-se. ~ **out** (money) levantar. ~ **up** deter-se, parar; (document) redigir; (chair) aproximar, chegar

drawback /'drɔ:bæk/ n inconveniente m, desvantagem f

drawer /drɔ:(r)/ n gaveta f

drawing /'drɔ:ɪŋ/ n desenho m. ~**-board** n prancheta f. ~**-pin** n percevejo m

drawl /drɔ:l/ n fala f arrastada

drawn /drɔ:n/ see **draw**

dread /dred/ n terror m □ vt temer

dreadful /'dredfl/ a medonho, terrível. ~**ly** adv terrivelmente

dream /dri:m/ n sonho m □ vt/i (pt **dreamed** or **dreamt**) sonhar (**of** com) □ a (ideal) dos seus sonhos. ~ **up** imaginar. ~**er** n sonhador m. ~**y** a sonhador; (music) romântico

dreary /'drɪərɪ/ a (-ier, -iest) tristonho; (boring) aborrecido

dredge /dredʒ/ n draga f □ vt/i dragar. ~**r** n draga f; (for sugar) polvilhador m

dregs /dregz/ npl depósito m, sedimento m; (fig) escória f

drench /drentʃ/ vt encharcar

dress /dres/ n vestido m; (clothing) roupa f □ vt/i vestir(-se); (food) temperar; (wound) fazer curativo, (P) pensar, (P) tratar. ~ rehearsal ensaio m geral. ~ up as fantasiar-se de. get ~ed vestir-se

dresser /'dresə(r)/ n (furniture) guarda-louça m

dressing /'dresɪŋ/ n (sauce) tempero m; (bandage) curativo m, (P) penso m. ~-gown n roupão m. ~-room n (sport) vestiário m; (theat) camarim m. ~-table n toucador m

dressmak|er /'dresmeɪkə(r)/ n costureira f, modista f. ~ing n costura f

dressy /'dresɪ/ a (-ier, -iest) elegante, chique invar

drew /dru:/ see draw

dribble /'drɪbl/ vi pingar; (person) babar-se; (football) driblar

dried /draɪd/ a (fruit etc) seco

drier /'draɪə(r)/ n secador m

drift /drɪft/ vi ir à deriva; (pile up) amontoar-se □ n força f da corrente; (pile) monte m; (of events) rumo m; (meaning) sentido m. ~er n pessoa f sem rumo

drill /drɪl/ n (tool) broca f; (training) exercício m, treino m; (routine procedure) exercícios mpl □ vt furar, perfurar; (train) treinar; (tooth) abrir □ vi treinar-se

drink /drɪŋk/ vt/i (pt drank, pp drunk) beber □ n bebida f. a ~ of water um copo de água. ~able a potável; (palatable) bebível. ~er n bebedor m. ~ing water água f potável

drip /drɪp/ vi (pt dripped) pingar □ n pingar m; (sl: person) banana mf (colloq). ~-dry vt deixar escorrer □ a que não precisa passar

dripping /'drɪpɪŋ/ n gordura f do assado

drive /draɪv/ vt (pt drove, pp driven) /'drɪvn/ empurrar, impelir, levar; (car, animal) dirigir, conduzir, (P) guiar; (machine) acionar, (P) accionar □ vi dirigir, conduzir, (P) guiar □ n passeio m de carro; (private road) entrada f para veículos; (fig) energia f; (psych) drive m, compulsão f, impulso m; (campaign) campanha f. ~ at chegar a. ~ away (car) partir. ~ in (force in) enterrar. ~-in n (bank, cinema etc) banco m, cinema m etc em que se é atendido no carro, drive-in m. ~ mad (fazer) enlouquecer, pôr fora de si

drivel /'drɪvl/ n baboseira f, bobagem f

driver /'draɪvə(r)/ n condutor m; (of taxi, bus) chofer m, motorista mf

driving /'draɪvɪŋ/ n condução f. ~-licence n carteira f de motorista, (P) carta f de condução. ~ school auto-escola f; (P) escola f de condução. ~ test exame m de motorista, (P) de condução

drizzle /'drɪzl/ n chuvisco m □ vi chuviscar

drone /drəʊn/ n zumbido m; (male bee) zangão m □ vi zumbir; (fig) falar monotonamente

drool /dru:l/ vi babar(-se)

droop /dru:p/ vi pender, curvar-se

drop /drɒp/ n gota f; (fall) queda f; (distance) altura f de queda □ vt/i (pt dropped) (deixar) cair; (fall, lower) baixar. ~ (off) (person from car) deixar, largar. ~ a line escrever duas linhas (to a). ~ in passar por (on em casa de). ~ off (doze) adormecer. ~ out (withdraw) retirar-se; (of student) abandonar. ~-out n marginal mf, marginalizado m

droppings /'drɒpɪŋz/ npl excrementos mpl de animal; (of birds) cocô m (colloq), porcaria f (colloq)

dross /drɒs/ *n* escória *f*; (*refuse*) lixo *m*

drought /draʊt/ *n* seca *f*

drove /drəʊv/ *see* **drive**

drown /draʊn/ *vt/i* afogar(-se)

drowsy /'draʊzɪ/ *a* sonolento. be *or* feel ~ ter vontade de dormir

drudge /drʌdʒ/ *n* mouro *m* de trabalho. ~ry /-ərɪ/ *n* trabalho *m* penoso e monótono, estafa *f*

drug /drʌg/ *n* droga *f*; (*med*) medicamento *m*, remédio *m* □ *vt* (*pt* **drugged**) drogar. ~ addict drogado *m*, tóxico-dependente *m*

drugstore /'drʌgstɔ:(r)/ *n* (*Amer*) farmácia *f* que vende também sorvetes etc

drum /drʌm/ *n* (*mus*) tambor *m*; (*for oil*) barril *m*, tambor *m*. ~s (*mus*) bateria *f* □ *vi* (*pt* **drummed**) tocar tambor; (*with one's fingers*) tamborilar □ *vt* ~ into sb fazer entrar na cabeça de alg. ~ up (*support*) conseguir obter; (*business*) criar. ~mer *n* tambor *m*; (*in pop group etc*) baterista *m*, (*P*) bateria *m*

drunk /drʌŋk/ *see* **drink** □ *a* embriagado, bêbedo. get ~ embebedar-se, embriagar-se □ *n* bêbedo *m*. ~ard *n* alcoólico *m*, bêbedo *m*. ~en *a* embriagado, bêbedo; (*habitually*) bêbedo

dry /draɪ/ *a* (**drier**, **driest**) seco; (*day*) sem chuva □ *vt/i* secar. be *or* feel ~ ter sede. ~-clean *vt* limpar a seco. ~-cleaner's *n* (loja de) lavagem *f* a seco, lavanderia *f*. ~ up (*dishes*) secar a louça *f*; (*of supplies*) esgotar-se. ~ness *n* secura *f*

dual /'dju:əl/ *a* duplo. ~ carriageway estrada *f* dividida por faixa central. ~-purpose *a* com fim duplo

dub /dʌb/ *vt* (*pt* **dubbed**) (*film*) dobrar; (*nickname*) apelidar de

dubious /'dju:bɪəs/ *a* duvidoso; (*character*, *compliment*) dúbio

feel ~ about ter dúvidas quanto a

duchess /'dʌtʃɪs/ *n* duquesa *f*

duck /dʌk/ *n* pato *m* □ *vi* abaixar-se rapidamente □ *vt* (*head*) baixar; (*person*) batizar, pregar uma amona em. ~ling *n* patinho *m*

duct /dʌkt/ *n* canal *m*, tubo *m*

dud /dʌd/ *a* (*sl: thing*) que não presta ou não funciona; (*sl: coin*) falso; (*sl: cheque*) sem fundos, (*P*) careca (*sl*)

due /dju:/ *a* devido; (*expected*) esperado □ *adv* ~ east/*etc* exatamente, (*P*) exactamente a leste/*etc* □ *n* devido *m*. ~s direitos *mpl*; (*of club*) cota *f*. ~ to devido a, por causa de. in ~ course no tempo devido

duel /'dju:əl/ *n* duelo *m*

duet /dju:'et/ *n* dueto *m*

duffel /'dʌfl/ *a* ~ bag saco *m* de lona. ~-coat *n* casaco *m* de tecido de lã

dug /dʌg/ *see* **dig**

duke /dju:k/ *n* duque *m*

dull /dʌl/ *a* (-**er**, -**est**) (*boring*) enfadonho; (*colour*) morto; (*mirror*) embaçado; (*weather*) encoberto; (*sound*) surdo; (*stupid*) burro

duly /'dju:lɪ/ *adv* devidamente; (*in due time*) no tempo devido

dumb /dʌm/ *a* (-**er**, -**est**) mudo; (*colloq: stupid*) bronco, burro

dumbfound /dʌm'faʊnd/ *vt* pasmar

dummy /'dʌmɪ/ *n* imitação *f*, coisa *f* simulada; (*of tailor*) manequim *m*; (*of baby*) chupeta *f*

dump /dʌmp/ *vt* (*-er, -est*) jogar fora; (*put down*) deixar cair; (*colloq: abandon*) largar □ *n* monte *m* de lixo; (*tip*) lixeira *f*, (*mil*) depósito *m*; (*colloq*) buraco *m*

dunce /dʌns/ *n* burro *m*. ~'s cap orelhas *fpl* de burro

dune /dju:n/ *n* duna *f*

dung /dʌŋ/ *n* esterco *m*; (*manure*) estrume *m*

dungarees /ˌdʌŋgəˈriːz/ npl macacão m, (P) fato m de macaco

dungeon /ˈdʌndʒən/ n calabouço m, masmorra f

dupe /djuːp/ vt enganar □ n trouxa m

duplicate[1] /ˈdjuːplɪkət/ n duplicado m □ a idêntico

duplicate[2] /ˈdjuːplɪkeɪt/ vt duplicar, fazer em duplicado; (on machine) fotocopiar

duplicity /djuːˈplɪsətɪ/ n duplicidade f

durable /ˈdjʊərəbl/ a resistente; (enduring) duradouro, durável

duration /djʊˈreɪʃn/ n duração f

duress /djʊˈres/ n under ~ sob coação f, (P) coacção f

during /ˈdjʊərɪŋ/ prep durante

dusk /dʌsk/ n crepúsculo m, anoitecer m

dusky /ˈdʌskɪ/ a (-ier, -iest) escuro, sombrio

dust /dʌst/ n pó m, poeira f □ vt limpar o pó de; (sprinkle) polvilhar. ~-jacket n sobrecapa f de livro

dustbin /ˈdʌstbɪn/ n lata f do lixo, (P) caixote m

duster /ˈdʌstə(r)/ n pano m do pó

dustman /ˈdʌstmən/ n (pl -men) lixeiro m, (P) homem m do lixo

dusty /ˈdʌstɪ/ a (-ier, -iest) poeirento, empoeirado

Dutch /dʌtʃ/ a holandês □ n (lang) holandês m. ~man n holandês m. ~woman n holandesa f. go ~ pagar cada um a sua despesa

dutiful /ˈdjuːtɪfl/ a cumpridor; (showing respect) respeitador

dut|**y** /ˈdjuːtɪ/ n dever m; (tax) impostos mpl. ~ies (of official etc) funções fpl. off ~ de folga. on ~y de serviço. ~y-free a isento de impostos. ~y-free shop free shop m

duvet /ˈdjuːveɪ/ n edredom m, (P) edredão m de penas

dwarf /dwɔːf/ n (pl -fs) anão m

dwell /dwel/ vi (pt dwelt) morar. ~ on alongar-se sobre. ~er n habitante. ~ing n habitação f

dwindle /ˈdwɪndl/ vi diminuir, reduzir-se

dye /daɪ/ vt (pres p dyeing) tingir □ n tinta f

dying /ˈdaɪɪŋ/ see **die**

dynamic /daɪˈnæmɪk/ a dinâmico

dynamite /ˈdaɪnəmaɪt/ n dinamite f □ vt dinamitar

dynamo /ˈdaɪnəməʊ/ n (pl -os) dínamo m

dynasty /ˈdɪnəstɪ/ n dinastia f

dysentery /ˈdɪsəntrɪ/ n disenteria f

dyslex|**ia** /dɪsˈleksɪə/ n dislexia f. ~ic a disléxico

E

each /iːtʃ/ a & pron cada. ~ one cada um. ~ other um ao outro, uns aos outros. they like ~ other gostam um do outro/uns dos outros. know/love/etc ~ other conhecer-se/amar-se/etc

eager /ˈiːgə(r)/ a ansioso (for); (supporter) entusiástico. be ~ to ter vontade de. ~ly adv com impaciência, ansiosamente; (keenly) com entusiasmo. ~ness n ansiedade f, desejo m; (keenness) entusiasmo m

eagle /ˈiːgl/ n águia f

ear[1] /ɪə(r)/ n ouvido m; (external part) orelha f. ~-drum n tímpano m. ~-ring n brinco m

earache /ˈɪəreɪk/ n dor f de ouvidos

earl /ɜːl/ n conde m

early /ˈɜːlɪ/ (-ier, -iest) adv cedo □ a primeiro; (hour) matinal; (fruit) temporão; (retirement) antecipado. have an ~ dinner jantar cedo. **in ~ summer** no princípio do verão

earmark /'ɪəmaːk/ vt destinar, reservar (**for** para)

earn /ɜːn/ vt ganhar; (*deserve*) merecer

earnest /'ɜːnɪst/ a sério. **in ~** a sério

earnings /'ɜːnɪŋz/ npl salário m; (*profits*) ganhos mpl, lucros mpl

earshot /'ɪəʃɒt/ n **within ~** ao alcance da voz

earth /ɜːθ/ n terra f □ vt (*electr*) ligar à terra. **why on ~?** por que diabo?, por que cargas d'água? **~ly** a terrestre, terreno

earthenware /'ɜːθənweə(r)/ n louça f de barro, faiança f

earthquake /'ɜːθkweɪk/ n tremor m de terra, terremoto m

earthy /'ɜːθɪ/ a terroso, térreo; (*coarse*) grosseiro

earwig /'ɪəwɪg/ n lacrainha f, (P) bicha-cadela f

ease /iːz/ n facilidade f; (*comfort*) bem-estar m □ vt/i (*from pain, anxiety*) acalmar(-se); (*slide down*) afrouxar; (*slide*) deslizar. **at ~** à vontade; (*mil*) descansar. **ill at ~** pouco à vontade. **with ~** facilmente. **in/out** fazer entrar/sair com cuidado

easel /'iːzl/ n cavalete m

east /iːst/ n este m, leste m, nascente m, oriente m. **the E~** o Oriente □ a este, (de) leste, oriental □ adv a/para leste. **~ of** para o leste de **~erly** a oriental, leste, a/de leste. **~ward** a, **~ward(s)** adv para leste

Easter /'iːstə(r)/ n Páscoa f. **~ egg** ovo m de Páscoa

eastern /'iːstən/ a oriental, leste

easy /'iːzɪ/ a (-**ier**, -**iest**) fácil; (*relaxed*) natural, descontraído. **take it ~** levar as coisas com calma. **~ chair** poltrona f. **~going** a bonacheirão. **easily** adv facilmente

eat /iːt/ vt/i (pt **ate**, pp **eaten**) comer. **~ into** corroer. **~able** a comestível

eaves /iːvz/ npl beiral m

eavesdrop /'iːvzdrɒp/ vi (pt -**dropped**) escutar por detrás da porta

e-book /'iːbʊk/ n livro m eletrônico

ebb /eb/ n vazante f, baixa-mar m □ vi vazar; (*fig*) declinar

EC /iː'siː/ n (abbr of *European Commission*) CE f

eccentric /ɪk'sentrɪk/ a & n excêntrico (m). **~ity** /eksen'trɪsətɪ/ n excentricidade f

ecclesiastical /ɪkliːzɪ'æstɪkl/ a eclesiástico

echo /'ekəʊ/ n (pl -**oes**) eco m □ vt/i (pt **echoed**, pres p **echoing**) ecoar; (*fig*) repetir

eclipse /ɪ'klɪps/ n eclipse m □ vt eclipsar

ecology /iː'kɒlədʒɪ/ n ecologia f. **~ical** /iːkə'lɒdʒɪkl/ a ecológico

e-commerce /'iːkɒmɜːs/ n comércio m eletrônico

economic /iːkə'nɒmɪk/ a econômico; (*profitable*) rentável. **~al** a econômico. **~s** n economia f política

economist /ɪ'kɒnəmɪst/ n economista mf

econom|y /ɪ'kɒnəmɪ/ n economia f. **~ize** vt/i economizar

ecstasy /'ekstəsɪ/ n êxtase m

ecstatic /ɪk'stætɪk/ a extático

ecu /'eɪkjuː/ n unidade f monetária européia

eczema /'eksɪmə/ n eczema m

edge /edʒ/ n borda f, beira f; (*of town*) periferia f, limite m; (*of knife*) fio m □ vt debruar □ vi(*move*) avançar pouco a pouco

edging /'edʒɪŋ/ n borda f, (P) bordadura f

edgy /'edʒɪ/ a irritadiço, nervoso

edible /'edɪbl/ a comestível

edict /'iːdɪkt/ n édito m

edifice /'edɪfɪs/ n edifício m

edit /'edɪt/ vt (pt **edited**) (newspaper) dirigir; (text) editar

edition /ɪ'dɪʃn/ n edição f

editor /'edɪtə(r)/ n (of newspaper) diretor m, (P) director m, editor m responsável; (of text) organizador m de texto. **the ~ (in chief)** redator-chefe m, (P) redactor-chefe m. **~ial** /edɪ'tɔːrɪəl/ a & n editorial (m)

educate /'edʒʊkeɪt/ vt instruir; (mind, public) educar. **~ed** a instruído; educado. **~ion** /-'keɪʃn/ n educação f; (schooling) ensino m. **~ional** /-'keɪʃənl/ a educativo, pedagógico

EEC /iːiː'siː/ n (abbr of European Economic Community) CEE f

eel /iːl/ n enguia f

eerie /'ɪərɪ/ a (-ier, -iest) arrepiante, misterioso

effect /ɪ'fekt/ n efeito m □ vt efetuar, (P) efectuar. **come into ~** entrar em vigor. **in ~** na realidade. **take ~** ter efeito

effective /ɪ'fektɪv/ a eficaz, eficiente; (striking) sensacional; (actual) efetivo, (P) efectivo. **~ly** adv (efficiently) eficazmente; (strikingly) de forma sensacional; (actually) efetivamente, (P) efectivamente. **~ness** n eficácia f

effeminate /ɪ'femɪnət/ a efeminado, afeminado

effervescent /efə'vesnt/ a efervescente

efficien|**t** /ɪ'fɪʃnt/ a eficiente, eficaz. **~cy** n eficiência f. **~tly** adv eficientemente

effigy /'efɪdʒɪ/ n efígie f

effort /'efət/ n esforço m. **~less** a fácil, sem esforço

effrontery /ɪ'frʌntərɪ/ n desfaçatez f

effusive /ɪ'fjuːsɪv/ a efusivo, expansivo

e.g. /iː'dʒiː/ abbr por ex

egg[1] /eg/ n ovo m. **~-cup** n copinho m para ovo quente, oveiro m. **~-plant** n beringela f

egg[2] /eg/ vt **~ on** (colloq) incitar

eggshell /'egʃel/ n casca f de ovo

ego /'egəʊ/ n (pl **-os**) ego m, eu m. **~ism** n egoísmo m. **~ist** n egoísta mf. **~tism** n egotismo m. **~tist** n egotista mf

Egypt /'iːdʒɪpt/ n Egito m, (P) Egipto m. **~ian** /ɪ'dʒɪpʃn/ a & n egípcio (m)

eh /eɪ/ int (colloq) hã?

eiderdown /'aɪdədaʊn/ n edredão m, edredom m

eight /eɪt/ a & n oito (m). **eighth** /eɪtθ/ a & n oitavo (m)

eighteen /eɪ'tiːn/ a & n dezoito (m). **~th** a & n décimo-oitavo (m)

eight|**y** /'eɪtɪ/ a & n oitenta (m). **~ieth** a & n octogésimo (m)

either /'aɪðə(r)/ a & pron um e outro; (with negative) nem um nem outro; (each) cada □ adv também não □ conj ~ ... or ou ... ou; (with negative) nem ... nem

ejaculate /ɪ'dʒækjʊleɪt/ vt/i ejacular; (exclaim) exclamar

eject /ɪ'dʒekt/ vt expelir; (expel) expulsar, despejar

elaborate[1] /ɪ'læbərət/ a elaborado, rebuscado, minucioso

elaborate[2] /ɪ'læbəreɪt/ vt elaborar □ vi entrar em pormenores. **~ on** estender-se sobre

elapse /ɪ'læps/ vi decorrer

elastic /ɪ'læstɪk/ a & n elástico (m). **~ band** elástico m

elated /ɪ'leɪtɪd/ a radiante, exultante. **~ion** n exultação f

elbow /'elbəʊ/ n cotovelo m

elder[1] /'eldə(r)/ a mais velho. **~s** npl pessoas fpl mais velhas

elder[2] /'eldə(r)/ n (tree) sabugueiro m

elderly /'eldəlɪ/ a idoso. **the ~** as pessoas de idade

eldest /'eldɪst/ a & n o mais velho (m)

elect /ɪˈlekt/ vt eleger □ a eleito. **~ion** /-kʃn/ n eleição f

electric /ɪˈlektrɪk/ a elétrico, (P) eléctrico.

electrician /ɪlekˈtrɪʃn/ n eletricista m, (P) electricista m

electricity /ɪlekˈtrɪsətɪ/ n eletricidade f, (P) electricidade f

electrify /ɪˈlektrɪfaɪ/ vt eletrificar, (P) electrificar; (fig: excite) eletrizar, (P) electrizar

electrocute /ɪˈlektrəkjuːt/ vt eletrocutar, (P) electrocutar

electronic /ɪlekˈtrɒnɪk/ a eletrônico, (P) electrónico. **~s** n eletrônica f, (P) electrónica f

elegan|t /ˈelɪɡənt/ a elegante. **~ce** n elegância f. **~tly** adv elegantemente, com elegância

element /ˈelɪmənt/ n elemento m; (of heater etc) resistência f. **~ary** /-ˈmentrɪ/ a elementar; (school) primário

elephant /ˈelɪfənt/ n elefante m

elevat|e /ˈelɪveɪt/ vt elevar. **~ion** /-ˈveɪʃn/ n elevação f

elevator /ˈelɪveɪtə(r)/ n (Amer: lift) elevador m, ascensor m

eleven /ɪˈlevn/ a & n onze (m). **~th** a & n décimo primeiro (m). at the **~th hour** à última hora

elicit /ɪˈlɪsɪt/ vt extrair, obter

eligible /ˈelɪdʒəbl/ a (for office) idôneo, (P) idóneo (for para); (desirable) aceitável. be **~ for** (entitled to) ter direito a

eliminat|e /ɪˈlɪmɪneɪt/ vt eliminar. **~ion** /-ˈneɪʃn/ n eliminação f

élite /eɪˈliːt/ n elite f

ellip|se /ɪˈlɪps/ n elipse f. **~tical** a elíptico

elm /elm/ n olmo m, ulmeiro m

elocution /eləˈkjuːʃn/ n elocução f

elongate /ˈiːlɒŋɡeɪt/ vt alongar

elope /ɪˈləʊp/ vi fugir. **~ment** n fuga f (de amantes), (P) (de amorosos)

eloquen|t /ˈeləkwənt/ a eloquente, (P) eloquente. **~ce** n eloquência f, (P) eloquência f

else /els/ adv mais. **everybody ~** todos os outros. **nobody ~** mais ninguém. **nothing ~** nada mais. **or ~** ou então, senão. **somewhere ~** noutro lado qualquer. **~where** adv noutro lado

elude /ɪˈluːd/ vt escapar a; (a question) evadir

elusive /ɪˈluːsɪv/ a (person) esquivo, difícil de apanhar; (answer) evasivo

emaciated /ɪˈmeɪʃɪeɪtɪd/ a emaciado, macilento

email /ˈiːmeɪl/ n correio m eletrônico, e-mail m; **~ address** endereço m de e-mail

emancipat|e /ɪˈmænsɪpeɪt/ vt emancipar. **~ion** /-ˈpeɪʃn/ n emancipação f

embalm /ɪmˈbɑːm/ vt embalsamar

embankment /ɪmˈbæŋkmənt/ n (of river) dique m, (of railway) terrapleno m, talude m, (P) aterro m

embargo /ɪmˈbɑːɡəʊ/ n (pl -oes) embargo m

embark /ɪmˈbɑːk/ vt/i embarcar. **~ on** (business etc) embarcar em, meter-se em (colloq); (journey) começar

embarrass /ɪmˈbærəs/ vt embaraçar, confundir. **~ment** n embaraço m, atrapalhação f

embassy /ˈembəsɪ/ n embaixada f

embellish /ɪmˈbelɪʃ/ vt embelezar, enfeitar. **~ment** n embelezamento m, enfeite m

embezzle /ɪmˈbezl/ vt desviar (fundos). **~ment** n desfalque m

embitter /ɪmˈbɪtə(r)/ vt (person) amargurar; (situation) azedar

emblem /ˈembləm/ n emblema m

embod|y /ɪmˈbɒdɪ/ vt encarnar; (include) incorporar, incluir. **~iment** n personificação f

emboss /ɪmˈbɒs/ vt (metal) gravar em relevo; (paper) gofrar

embrace /ɪm'breɪs/ vt/i abraçar (-se); (offer, opportunity) acolher □ n abraço m

embroider /ɪm'brɔɪdə(r)/ vt bordar. **~y** n bordado m

embryo /'embrɪəʊ/ n (pl -os) embrião m. **~nic** /-'ɒnɪk/ a embrionário

emerald /'emərəld/ n esmeralda f

emerge /ɪ'mɜːdʒ/ vi emergir, surgir

emergency /ɪ'mɜːdʒənsɪ/ n emergência f; (urgent case) urgência f. **~ exit** saída f de emergência. **in an ~** em caso de urgência

emigrant /'emɪɡrənt/ n emigrante mf

emigrat|e /'emɪɡreɪt/ vi emigrar. **~ion** /-'ɡreɪʃn/ n emigração f

eminen|t /'emɪnənt/ a eminente. **~tly** adv eminentemente

emi|t /ɪ'mɪt/ vt (pt emitted) emitir. **~ssion** /-ʃn/ n emissão f

emotion /ɪ'məʊʃn/ n emoção f. **~al** a (person, shock) emotivo; (speech, scene) emocionante

emperor /'empərə(r)/ n imperador m

emphasis /'emfəsɪs/ n ênfase f. **lay ~ on** pôr em relevo

emphasize /'emfəsaɪz/ vt enfatizar, sublinhar; (syllable, word) acentuar

emphatic /ɪm'fætɪk/ a enfático; (manner) enérgico. **~ally** adv enfaticamente

empire /'empaɪə(r)/ n império m

employ /ɪm'plɔɪ/ vt empregar. **~ee** /emplɔɪ'iː/ n empregado m. **~er** n patrão m. **~ment** n emprego m. **~ment agency** agência f de empregos

empower /ɪm'paʊə(r)/ vt autorizar (**to do** a fazer)

empress /'emprɪs/ n imperatriz f

empt|y /'emptɪ/ a vazio; (promise) falso □ vt/i esvaziar(-se). **on an ~y stomach** com o estômago vazio, em jejum. **~ies** npl

garrafas fpl vazias. **~iness** n vazio m

emulate /'emjʊleɪt/ vt imitar, rivalizar com, emular com

emulsion /ɪ'mʌlʃn/ n emulsão f

enable /ɪ'neɪbl/ vt **~ sb to do** permitir a alg fazer

enact /ɪ'nækt/ vt (jur) decretar; (theat) representar

enamel /ɪ'næml/ n esmalte m □ vt (pt enamelled) esmaltar

enamoured /ɪ'næməd/ a **~ of** enamorado de, apaixonado por

encase /ɪn'keɪs/ vt encerrar (**in** em); (cover) revestir (**in** de)

enchant /ɪn'tʃɑːnt/ vt encantar. **~ing** a encantador. **~ment** n encantamento m

encircle /ɪn'sɜːkl/ vt cercar, rodear

enclose /ɪn'kləʊz/ vt (land) cercar; (with letter) enviar incluso/junto. **~d** a (space) fechado; (with letter) anexo, incluso, junto

enclosure /ɪn'kləʊʒə(r)/ n cercado m, recinto m; (with letter) documento m anexo

encompass /ɪn'kʌmpəs/ vt abranger

encore /ɒŋ'kɔː(r)/ int & n bis (m)

encounter /ɪn'kaʊntə(r)/ vt encontrar, deparar com □ n encontro m

encourage /ɪn'kʌrɪdʒ/ vt encorajar. **~ment** n encorajamento m

encroach /ɪn'krəʊtʃ/ vi **~ on** (land) invadir; (time) abusar de

encumb|er /ɪn'kʌmbə(r)/ vt estorvar; (burden) sobrecarregar. **~rance** n estorvo m, empecilho m; (burden) ônus m, (P) ónus m, encargo m

encyclop|edia /ɪnsaɪklə'piːdɪə/ n enciclopédia f. **~ic** a enciclopédico

end /end/ n fim m; (farthest part) extremo m, ponta f □ vt/i acabar, terminar. **~ up** (arrive finally) ir parar (**in** a/em). **~ up doing**

acabar por fazer. **in the** ～ **por fim. no** ～ **of** (*colloq*) muito, enorme, imenso. **on** ～ (*upright*) em pé; (*consecutive*) a fio, de seguida

endanger /ɪn'deɪndʒə(r)/ *vt* pôr em perigo

endear|ing /ɪn'dɪərɪŋ/ *a* cativante. ～**ment** *n* palavra *f* meiga; (*act*) carinho *m*

endeavour /ɪn'devə(r)/ *n* esforço *m* □ *vi* esforçar-se (**to** por)

ending /'endɪŋ/ *n* fim *m*; (*of word*) terminação *f*

endless /'endlɪs/ *a* interminável; (*times*) sem conta; (*patience*) infinito

endorse /ɪn'dɔ:s/ *vt* (*document*) endossar; (*action*) aprovar. ～**ment** *n* (*auto*) averbamento *m*

endow /ɪn'daʊ/ *vt* doar. ～**ment** *n* doação *f*

endur|e /ɪn'djʊə(r)/ *vt* suportar □ *vi* durar. ～**able** *a* suportável. ～**ance** *n* resistência *f*

enemy /'enəmɪ/ *n* & *a* inimigo *m*

energetic /enə'dʒetɪk/ *a* enérgico

energy /'enədʒɪ/ *n* energia *f*

enforce /ɪn'fɔ:s/ *vt* aplicar

engage /ɪn'geɪdʒ/ *vt* (*staff*) contratar; (*mech*) engrenar □ *vi* ～ **in** envolver-se em, lançar-se em. ～**d** *a* noivo; (*busy*) ocupado. ～**ment** *n* noivado *m*; (*undertaking, appointment*) compromisso *m*; (*mil*) combate *m*

engender /ɪn'dʒendə(r)/ *vt* engendrar, produzir, causar

engine /'endʒɪn/ *n* motor *m*; (*of train*) locomotiva *f*

engineer /endʒɪ'nɪə(r)/ *n* engenheiro *m* □ *vt* engenhar. ～**ing** *n* engenharia *f*

England /'ɪŋglənd/ *n* Inglaterra *f*

English /'ɪŋglɪʃ/ *a* inglês □ *n* (*lang*) inglês *m*. **the** ～ os ingleses *mpl*. ～**man** *n* inglês *m*. ～**-speaking** *a* de língua inglesa *f*. ～**woman** *n* inglesa *f*

engrav|e /ɪn'greɪv/ *vt* gravar. ～**ing** *n* gravura *f*

engrossed /ɪn'grəʊst/ *a* absorto (**in** em)

engulf /ɪn'gʌlf/ *vt* engolfar, tragar

enhance /ɪn'hɑ:ns/ *vt* aumentar; (*heighten*) realçar

enigma /ɪ'nɪgmə/ *n* enigma *m*. ～**tic** /enɪg'mætɪk/ *a* enigmático

enjoy /ɪn'dʒɔɪ/ *vt* gostar de; (*benefit from*) gozar de. ～ **o.s.** divertir-se. ～**able** *a* agradável. ～**ment** *n* prazer *m*

enlarge /ɪn'lɑ:dʒ/ *vt/i* aumentar. ～ **upon** alargar-se sobre. ～**ment** *n* ampliação *f*

enlighten /ɪn'laɪtn/ *vt* esclarecer. ～**ment** *n* esclarecimento *m*, elucidação *f*

enlist /ɪn'lɪst/ *vt* recrutar; (*fig*) aliciar, granjear □ *vi* alistar-se

enliven /ɪn'laɪvn/ *vt* animar

enmity /'enmətɪ/ *n* inimizade *f*

enormous /ɪ'nɔ:məs/ *a* enorme

enough /ɪ'nʌf/ *a*, *adv* & *n* bastante (*m*), suficiente (*m*) □ *int* basta!, chega! **have** ～ **of** estar farto de

enquir|e /ɪn'kwaɪə(r)/ *vt/i* perguntar, indagar. ～**e about** informar-se de, pedir informações sobre. ～**y** *n* pedido *m* de informações *f*

enrage /ɪn'reɪdʒ/ *vt* enfurecer, enraivecer

enrich /ɪn'rɪtʃ/ *vt* enriquecer

enrol /ɪn'rəʊl/ *vt/i* (*pt* **enrolled**) inscrever(-se); (*schol*) matricular(-se). ～**ment** *n* inscrição *f*; (*schol*) matrícula *f*

ensemble /ɒn'sɒmbl/ *n* conjunto *m*

ensign /'ensən/ *n* pavilhão *m*; (*officer*) guarda-marinha *m*

ensu|e /ɪn'sju:/ *vi* seguir-se. ～**ing** *a* decorrente

ensure /ɪn'ʃʊə(r)/ *vt* assegurar. ～ **that** assegurar-se de que

entail /ɪn'teɪl/ *vt* acarretar

entangle /ɪn'tæŋgl/ *vt* emaranhar, enredar

enter /'entə(r)/ vt (*room, club etc*) entrar em; (*register*) registar; (*data*) entrar com □ vi entrar (into em). ~ **for** inscrever-se em

enterprise /'entəpraɪz/ n empresa f, empreendimento m; (*fig*) iniciativa f

enterprising /'entəpraɪzɪŋ/ a empreendedor

entertain /entə'teɪn/ vt entreter; (*guests*) receber; (*ideas*) alimentar, nutrir. ~**er** n artista mf. ~**ment** n entretenimento m; (*performance*) espetáculo m, (P) espectáculo m

enthral /ɪn'θrɔːl/ vt (*pt* **enthralled**) fascinar

enthuse /ɪn'θjuːz/ vi ~ **over** entusiasmar-se por

enthusiasm /ɪn'θjuːzɪæzm/ n entusiasmo m. ~**t** n entusiasta mf. ~**tic** /-'æstɪk/ a entusiástico. ~**tically** /-'æstɪkəli/ adv entusiasticamente

entice /ɪn'taɪs/ vt atrair. ~ **to do** induzir a fazer. ~**ment** n tentação f, engodo m

entire /ɪn'taɪə(r)/ a inteiro. ~**ly** adv inteiramente

entirety /ɪn'taɪərəti/ n in its ~ por inteiro, na (sua) totalidade

entitle /ɪn'taɪtl/ vt dar direito. ~**d** a (*book*) intitulado. **be ~d to** sth ter direito a alg coisa. ~**ment** n direito m

entity /'entəti/ n entidade f

entrance /'entrəns/ n entrada f (to para); (*right to enter*) admissão f

entrant /'entrənt/ n (*sport*) concorrente mf; (*in exam*) candidato m

entreat /ɪn'triːt/ vt rogar, suplicar. ~**y** n rogo m, súplica f

entrench /ɪn'trentʃ/ vt (*mil*) entrincheirar; (*fig*) fincar

entrust /ɪn'trʌst/ vt confiar

entry /'entri/ n entrada f; (*on list*) item m; (*in dictionary*) verbete m.

~ **form** ficha f de inscrição, (P) boletim m de inscrição. **no ~** entrada proibida

enumerate /ɪ'njuːməreɪt/ vt enumerar

envelop /ɪn'veləp/ vt (*pt* **enveloped**) envolver

envelope /'envələʊp/ n envelope m, sobrescrito m

enviable /'envɪəbl/ a invejável

envious /'envɪəs/ a invejoso. **be ~ of** ter inveja de. ~**ly** adv invejosamente, com inveja

environment /ɪn'vaɪərənmənt/ n meio m; (*ecological*) meio-ambiente m. ~**al** /-'mentl/ a do meio; (*ecological*) do ambiente

envisage /ɪn'vɪzɪdʒ/ vt encarar; (*foresee*) prever

envoy /'envɔɪ/ n enviado m

envy /'envɪ/ n inveja f □ vt invejar, ter inveja de

enzyme /'enzaɪm/ n enzima f

epic /'epɪk/ n epopéia f □ a épico

epidemic /epɪ'demɪk/ n epidemia f

epilepsy /'epɪlepsɪ/ n epilepsia f. ~**tic** /-'leptɪk/ a & n epiléptico (m)

episode /'epɪsəʊd/ n episódio m

epitaph /'epɪtɑːf/ n epitáfio m

epithet /'epɪθet/ n epíteto m

epitome /ɪ'pɪtəmɪ/ n (*summary*) epítome m; (*embodiment*) modelo m. ~**ize** vt (*fig*) representar, encarnar; (*summarize*) resumir

epoch /'iːpɒk/ n época f. ~**making** a que marca uma época

equal /'iːkwəl/ a & n igual (m) □ vt (*pt* **equalled**) igualar, ser igual a. ~ **to** (*task*) à altura de. ~**ity** /iː'kwɒlətɪ/ n igualdade f. ~**ly** adv igualmente; (*similarly*) de igual modo

equalize /'iːkwəlaɪz/ vt/i igualar; (*sport*) empatar

equanimity /ekwə'nɪmətɪ/ n equanimidade f, serenidade f

equate /ɪ'kweɪt/ vt equacionar (with com); (*treat as equal*) equiparar (with a)

equation 361 **estimate**

equation /ɪˈkweɪʒn/ n equação f
equator /ɪˈkweɪtə(r)/ n equador m.
~**ial** /ekwəˈtɔːrɪəl/ a equatorial
equilibrium /iːkwɪˈlɪbrɪəm/ n
equilíbrio m
equip /ɪˈkwɪp/ vt (pt **equipped**)
equipar (**with** com), munir (**with**
de). ~**ment** n equipamento m
equitable /ˈekwɪtəbl/ a eqüitativo,
(P) equitativo
equity /ˈekwətɪ/ n eqüidade f, (P)
equidade f
equivalent /ɪˈkwɪvələnt/ a & n
eqüivalente (m), (P) equivalente
(m)
equivocal /ɪˈkwɪvəkl/ a equívoco
era /ˈɪərə/ n era f, época f
eradicate /ɪˈrædɪkeɪt/ vt erradicar, suprimir
erase /ɪˈreɪz/ vt apagar. ~**r** /-ə(r)/
n borracha f (de apagar)
erect /ɪˈrekt/ a ereto, (P) erecto □
vt erigir. ~**ion** /-ʃn/ n ereção f,
(P) erecção f; (building) construção f, edifício m
ero|de /ɪˈrəʊd/ vt corroer. ~**sion**
/ɪˈrəʊʒn/ n erosão f
erotic /ɪˈrɒtɪk/ a erótico
err /ɜː(r)/ vi (pt **erred**) errar
errand /ˈerənd/ n recado m
erratic /ɪˈrætɪk/ a errático, irregular; (person) variável, impre-
vísível
erroneous /ɪˈrəʊnɪəs/ a errôneo,
(P) erróneo, errado
error /ˈerə(r)/ n erro m
erudit|e /ˈeruːdaɪt/ a erudito.
~**ion** /-dɪʃn/ n erudição f
erupt /ɪˈrʌpt/ vi (war, fire) irromper; (volcano) entrar em erupção.
~**ion** /-ʃn/ n erupção f
escalat|e /ˈeskəleɪt/ vt/i intensi-
ficar(-se); (of prices) subir em
espiral. ~**ion** /-ˈleɪʃn/ n escalada
f
escalator /ˈeskəleɪtə(r)/ n escada f
rolante
escapade /eskəˈpeɪd/ n peripécia
f

escape /ɪˈskeɪp/ vi escapar-se □ vt
escapar a □ n fuga f; (of prisoner)
evasão f, fuga f. ~ **from sb** escapar de alguém. ~ **to** fugir para.
have a lucky or **narrow** ~ escapar por um tris
escapism /ɪˈskeɪpɪzəm/ n escapis-
mo m
escort[1] /ˈeskɔːt/ n escolta f; (of woman) cavalheiro m, acompa-
nhante m
escort[2] /ɪˈskɔːt/ vt escoltar; (accompany) acompanhar
escudo /esˈkjuːdəʊ/ n (pl -os) escudo m
Eskimo /ˈeskɪməʊ/ n (pl -os) es-
quimó mf
especial /ɪˈspeʃl/ a especial. ~**ly**
adv especialmente
espionage /ˈespɪənaːʒ/ n espionagem f
espouse /ɪˈspaʊz/ vt (a cause etc)
abraçar
espresso /eˈspresəʊ/ n (pl -os)
(coffee) expresso m
essay /ˈeseɪ/ n ensaio m; (schol)
redação f, (P) redacção f
essence /ˈesns/ n essência f
essential /ɪˈsenʃl/ a essencial □ n
the ~**s** o essencial m. ~**ly** adv
essencialmente
establish /ɪˈstæblɪʃ/ vt estabelecer; (business, state) fundar;
(prove) provar, apurar. ~**ment**
n estabelecimento m; (institution)
instituição f. **the E**~**ment** o Es-
tablishment m, a classe f dirigente
estate /ɪˈsteɪt/ n propriedade f;
(possessions) bens mpl; (inheritance) herança f. ~ **agent** agente
m imobiliário. (**housing**) ~ conjunto m habitacional. ~ **car** per-
rua f
esteem /ɪˈstiːm/ vt estimar □ n estima f
estimate[1] /ˈestɪmət/ n cálculo m,
avaliação f; (comm) orçamento
m, estimativa f

estimate|e² /'estɪmeɪt/ vt calcular, estimar. **~ion** /-'meɪʃn/ n opinião f

estuary /'estʃʊərɪ/ n estuário m

etc abbr = **et cetera** /ɪt'setərə/ etc

etching /'etʃɪŋ/ n água-forte f

eternal /ɪ'tɜːnl/ a eterno

eternity /ɪ'tɜːnətɪ/ n eternidade f

ethic /'eθɪk/ n ética f. **~s** ética f. **~al** a ético

ethnic /'eθnɪk/ a étnico

etiquette /'etɪket/ n etiqueta f

etymology /etɪ'mɒlədʒɪ/ n etimologia f

eulogy /'juːlədʒɪ/ n elogio m

euphemism /'juːfəmɪzəm/ n eufemismo m

euphoria /juː'fɔːrɪə/ n euforia f

euro /'jʊərəʊ/ n euro m

Europe /'jʊərəp/ n Europa f. **~an** /-'pɪən/ a & n europeu (m). **~an Union** União f Européia

euthanasia /juːθə'neɪzɪə/ n eutanásia f

evacuat|e /ɪ'vækjʊeɪt/ vt evacuar. **~ion** /-'eɪʃn/ n evacuação f

evade /ɪ'veɪd/ vt evadir

evaluate /ɪ'væljʊeɪt/ vt avaliar

evangelical /iːvæn'dʒelɪkl/ a evangélico

evaporat|e /ɪ'væpəreɪt/ vt/i evaporar(-se). **~ed milk** leite m evaporado. **~ion** /-'reɪʃn/ n evaporação f

evasion /ɪ'veɪʒn/ n evasão f

evasive /ɪ'veɪsɪv/ a evasivo

eve /iːv/ n véspera f

even /'iːvn/ a regular; (surface) liso, plano; (amounts) igual; (number) par □ vt/i **~ up** igualar(-se), acertar □ adv mesmo. **better** ainda melhor. **get ~ with** ajustar contas com. **~ly** adv uniformemente

evening /'iːvnɪŋ/ n entardecer m, anoitecer m, (whole evening) serão m. **~ class** aula f à noite (para adultos). **~ dress** traje m de cerimônia, (P) trajo m de ce-

rimónia or de rigor; (woman's) vestido m de noite

event /ɪ'vent/ n acontecimento m. **in the ~ of** no caso de. **~ful** a movimentado, memorável

eventual /ɪ'ventʃʊəl/ a final. **~ity** /-'ælətɪ/ n eventualidade f. **~ly** adv por fim; (in future) eventualmente

ever /'evə(r)/ adv jamais; (at all times) sempre. **do you ~ go?** você já foi alguma vez?, vais alguma vez? **the best I ~ saw** o melhor que já vi. **~ since** adv desde então □ prep desde □ conj desde que. **~ so** (colloq) muitíssimo, tão. **hardly ~** quase nunca

evergreen /'evəɡriːn/ n sempreverde f, planta f de folhas persistentes □ a persistente

everlasting /evəˈlɑːstɪŋ/ a eterno

every /'evrɪ/ a cada. **~ now and then** de vez em quando, volta e meia. **~ one** cada um. **~ other day** dia sim dia não, de dois em dois dias. **~ three days** de três em três dias

everybody /'evrɪbɒdɪ/ pron todo mundo, todos

everyday /'evrɪdeɪ/ a cotidiano, (P) quotidiano, diário; (common) do dia a dia, vulgar

everyone /'evrɪwʌn/ pron todo mundo, todos

everything /'evrɪθɪŋ/ pron tudo

everywhere /'evrɪweə(r)/ adv (position) em todo lugar, em toda parte; (direction) a todo lugar, a toda parte

evict /ɪ'vɪkt/ vt expulsar, despejar. **~ion** /-ʃn/ n despejo m

evidence /'evɪdəns/ n evidência f; (proof) prova f; (testimony) testemunho m, depoimento m. **~ of** sinal de. **give ~** testemunhar. **in ~** em evidência

evident /'evɪdənt/ a evidente. **~ly** adv evidentemente

evil /ˈiːvl/ a mau □ n mal m

evo|ke /ɪˈvəʊk/ vt evocar. ~**cative** /ɪˈvɒkətɪv/ a evocativo

evolution /iːvəˈluːʃn/ n evolução f

evolve /ɪˈvɒlv/ vi evolucionar, evoluir □ vt desenvolver, produzir

ex- /eks/ pref ex-

exacerbate /ɪɡˈzæsəbeɪt/ vt exacerbar

exact /ɪɡˈzækt/ a exato, (P) exacto □ vt exigir (**from** de). ~**ing** a exigente; (task) difícil. ~**ly** adv exatamente, (P) exactamente

exaggerat|e /ɪɡˈzædʒəreɪt/ vt/i exagerar. ~**ion** /-ˈreɪʃn/ n exagero m

exam /ɪɡˈzæm/ n (colloq) exame m

examination /ɪɡzæmɪˈneɪʃn/ n exame m; (jur) interrogatório m

examine /ɪɡˈzæmɪn/ vt examinar; (witness etc) interrogar. ~**r** /-ə(r)/ n examinador m

example /ɪɡˈzɑːmpl/ n exemplo m. **for** ~ por exemplo. **make an** ~ **of** castigar para servir de exemplo

exasperat|e /ɪɡˈzæspəreɪt/ vt exasperar. ~**ion** /-ˈreɪʃn/ n exaspero m

excavat|e /ˈekskəveɪt/ vt escavar; (uncover) desenterrar. ~**ion** /-ˈveɪʃn/ n escavação f

exceed /ɪkˈsiːd/ vt exceder; (speed limit) ultrapassar, exceder

excel /ɪkˈsel/ vi (pt **excelled**) distinguir-se □ vt superar, ultrapassar

excellen|t /ˈeksələnt/ a excelente. ~**ce** n excelência f. ~**tly** adv excelentemente

except /ɪkˈsept/ prep exceto, (P) excepto, fora □ vt excetuar, (P) exceptuar. ~ **for** a não ser, menos, salvo. ~**ing** prep à exceção de, (P) à excepção de. ~**ion** /-ʃn/ n exceção f, (P) excepção f. **take** ~**ion to** (object to) achar inaceitável; (be offended by) achar ofensivo

exceptional /ɪkˈsepʃənl/ a excepcional. ~**ly** adv excepcionalmente

excerpt /ˈeksɜːpt/ n trecho m, excerto m

excess¹ /ɪkˈses/ n excesso m

excess² /ˈekses/ a excedente, em excesso. ~ **fare** excesso m, suplemento m. ~ **luggage** excesso m de peso

excessive /ɪkˈsesɪv/ a excessivo. ~**ly** adv excessivamente

exchange /ɪksˈtʃeɪndʒ/ vt trocar □ n troca f; (of currency) câmbio m. (**telephone**) ~ central f telefônica, (P) telefónica. ~ **rate** taxa f de câmbio

excise /ˈeksaɪz/ n imposto m (indireto, (P) indirecto)

excit|e /ɪkˈsaɪt/ vt excitar; (rouse) despertar; (enthuse) entusiasmar. ~**able** a excitável. ~**ed** a excitado. **get** ~**ed** excitar-se, entusiasmar-se. ~**ement** n excitação f. ~**ing** a excitante, emocionante

exclaim /ɪkˈskleɪm/ vi exclamar

exclamation /ekskləˈmeɪʃn/ n exclamação f. ~ **mark** ponto m de exclamação

exclu|de /ɪkˈskluːd/ vt excluir. ~**ding** prep excluído. ~**sion** /ɪkˈskluːʒn/ n exclusão f

exclusive /ɪkˈskluːsɪv/ a (rights etc) exclusivo; (club etc) seleto, (P) selecto; (news item) (em) exclusivo. ~ **of** sem incluir. ~**ly** adv exclusivamente

excruciating /ɪkˈskruːʃɪeɪtɪŋ/ a excruciante, atroz

excursion /ɪkˈskɜːʃn/ n excursão f

excus|e¹ /ɪkˈskjuːz/ vt desculpar. ~ **e me!** desculpe!, com licença! ~ **e from** (exempt) dispensar de. ~**able** a desculpável

excuse² /ɪkˈskjuːs/ n desculpa f

ex-directory /eksdɪˈrektərɪ/ a que não vem no anuário, (P) na lista

execute /ˈeksɪkjuːt/ vt executar

execution /eksɪˈkjuːʃn/ *n* execução *f*

executive /ɪgˈzekjʊtɪv/ *a* & *n* executivo (*m*)

exemplary /ɪgˈzemplərɪ/ *a* exemplar

exemplify /ɪgˈzemplɪfaɪ/ *vt* exemplificar, ilustrar

exempt /ɪgˈzempt/ *a* isento (**from** de) □ *vt* dispensar, eximir. **~ion** /-ʃn/ *n* isenção *f*

exercise /ˈeksəsaɪz/ *n* exercício *m* □ *vt* (*powers, restraint etc*) exercer; (*dog*) levar para passear □ *vi* fazer exercício. **~ book** caderno *m*

exert /ɪgˈzɜːt/ *vt* empregar, exercer. **~ o.s.** esforçar-se, fazer um esforço. **~ion** /-ʃn/ *n* esforço *m*

exhaust /ɪgˈzɔːst/ *vt* esgotar □ *n* (*auto*) (tubo de) escape *m*. **~ed** *a* esgotado, exausto. **~ion** /-stʃən/ *n* esgotamento *m*, exaustão *f*

exhaustive /ɪgˈzɔːstɪv/ *a* exaustivo, completo

exhibit /ɪgˈzɪbɪt/ *vt* exibir, mostrar; (*thing, collection*) expor □ *n* objecto *m*, (*P*) objeto *m* exposto

exhibition /eksɪˈbɪʃn/ *n* exposição *f*; (*act of showing*) demonstração *f*

exhilarat|e /ɪgˈzɪləreɪt/ *vt* regozijar; (*invigorate*) animar, estimular. **~ion** /-ˈreɪʃn/ *n* animação *f*, alegria *f*

exhort /ɪgˈzɔːt/ *vt* exortar

exile /ˈeksaɪl/ *n* exílio *m*; (*person*) exilado *m* □ *vt* exilar, desterrar

exist /ɪgˈzɪst/ *vi* existir. **~ence** *n* existência *f*. **be in ~ence** existir

exit /ˈeksɪt/ *n* saída *f*

exonerate /ɪgˈzɒnəreɪt/ *vt* exonerar

exorbitant /ɪgˈzɔːbɪtənt/ *a* exorbitante

exorcize /ˈeksɔːsaɪz/ *vt* esconjurar, exorcisar

exotic /ɪgˈzɒtɪk/ *a* exótico

expan|d /ɪkˈspænd/ *vt/i* expandir (-se); (*extend*) estender(-se), alargar(-se); (*gas, liquid, metal*) dilatar(-se). **~sion** /ɪkˈspænʃn/ *n* expansão *f*; (*extension*) alargamento *m*; (*of gas etc*) dilatação *f*

expanse /ɪkˈspæns/ *n* extensão *f*

expatriate /eksˈpætrɪət/ *a* & *n* expatriado (*m*)

expect /ɪkˈspekt/ *vt* esperar; (*suppose*) crer, supor; (*require*) contar com, esperar; (*baby*) esperar. **~ to do** contar fazer. **~ation** /ekspekˈteɪʃn/ *n* esperança *f*

expectan|t /ɪkˈspektənt/ *a* **~t mother** gestante *f*. **~cy** *n* expectativa *f*

expedient /ɪkˈspiːdɪənt/ *a* oportuno □ *n* expediente *m*

expedition /ekspɪˈdɪʃn/ *n* expedição *f*

expel /ɪkˈspel/ *vt* (*pt* **expelled**) expulsar; (*gas, poison etc*) expelir

expend /ɪkˈspend/ *vt* despender. **~able** *a* descartável

expenditure /ɪkˈspendɪtʃə(r)/ *n* despesa *f*, gasto *m*

expense /ɪkˈspens/ *n* despesa *f*; (*cost*) custo *m*. **at sb's ~** à custa de alg. **at the ~ of** (*fig*) à custa de

expensive /ɪkˈspensɪv/ *a* caro, dispendioso; (*tastes, habits*) de luxo

experience /ɪkˈspɪərɪəns/ *n* experiência *f* □ *vt* experimentar; (*feel*) sentir. **~d** *a* experiente

experiment /ɪkˈsperɪmənt/ *n* experiência *f* □ *vi* /ɪkˈsperɪment/ fazer uma experiência. **~al** /-ˈmentl/ *a* experimental

expert /ˈekspɜːt/ *a* & *n* perito (*m*). **~ly** *adv* com perícia, habilmente

expertise /ekspɜːˈtiːz/ *n* perícia *f*, competência *f*

expire /ɪkˈspaɪə(r)/ *vi* expirar. **~y** *n* fim *m* de prazo, expiração *f*

expl|ain /ɪkˈspleɪn/ *vt* explicar. **~anation** /ekspləˈneɪʃn/ *n* explicação f. **~anatory** /ɪkˈsplæ-nətrɪ/ a explicativo

expletive /ɪkˈspliːtɪv/ n impreca-ção f, praga f

explicit /ɪkˈsplɪsɪt/ a explícito

explo|de /ɪkˈspləʊd/ vt/i (fazer) explodir. **~sion** /ɪkˈspləʊʒn/ n explosão f. **~sive** a & n explosi-vo (m)

exploit[1] /ˈeksplɔɪt/ n façanha f

exploit[2] /ɪkˈsplɔɪt/ vt explorar. **~ation** /eksplɔɪˈteɪʃn/ n explo-ração f

exploratory /ɪkˈsplɒrətrɪ/ a ex-ploratório; (talks) preliminar

explor|e /ɪkˈsplɔː(r)/ vt explorar; (fig) examinar. **~ation** /eks-pləˈreɪʃn/ n exploração f. **~er** n explorador m

exponent /ɪkˈspəʊnənt/ n (person) expoente mf; (math) expoente m

export[1] /ɪkˈspɔːt/ vt exportar. **~er** n exportador m

export[2] /ˈekspɔːt/ n exportação f. **~s** npl exportações fpl

expos|e /ɪkˈspəʊz/ vt expor; (dis-close) revelar; (unmask) desmas-carar. **~ure** /-ʒə(r)/ n exposição f; (cold) frio m

expound /ɪkˈspaʊnd/ vt explanar, expor

express[1] /ɪkˈspres/ a expresso, ca-tegórico □ adv (por) expresso □ n (train) rápido m, expresso m. **~ly** adv expressamente

express[2] /ɪkˈspres/ vt exprimir. **~ion** /-ʃn/ n expressão f. **~ive** a expressivo

expulsion /ɪkˈspʌlʃn/ n expulsão f

exquisite /ˈekskwɪzɪt/ a requintado

extempore /ekˈstempərɪ/ a impro-visado □ adv de improviso, sem preparação prévia

exten|d /ɪkˈstend/ vt (stretch) es-tender; (enlarge) aumentar, ampliar; (prolong) prolongar; (grant) oferecer □ vi (stretch) es-tender-se; (in time) prolongar-se. **~sion** /ɪkˈstenʃn/ n (incl phone)

extensão f; (of deadline) prorro-gação f; (building) anexo m

extensive /ɪkˈstensɪv/ a extenso; (damage, study) vasto. **~ly** adv muito

extent /ɪkˈstent/ n extensão f; (de-gree) medida f. **to some ~** até certo ponto, em certa medida. **to such an ~ that** a tal ponto que

exterior /ɪkˈstɪərɪə(r)/ a & n exte-rior (m)

exterminat|e /ɪkˈstɜːmɪneɪt/ vt exterminar. **~ion** /-ˈneɪʃn/ n ex-terminação f, extermínio m

external /ɪkˈstɜːnl/ a externo. **~ly** adv exteriormente

extinct /ɪkˈstɪŋkt/ a extinto. **~ion** /-ʃn/ n extinção f

extinguish /ɪkˈstɪŋgwɪʃ/ vt extin-guir, apagar. **~er** n extintor m

extol /ɪkˈstəʊl/ vt (pt extolled) exaltar, elogiar, louvar

extort /ɪkˈstɔːt/ vt extorquir (from a). **~ion** /-ʃn/ n extorsão f

extortionate /ɪkˈstɔːʃənət/ a exor-bitante

extra /ˈekstrə/ a extra, adicional □ adv extra, excepcionalmente. **~ strong** extra-forte □ n extra m; (cine, theat) extra mf, figu-rante mf. **~ time** (football) prorrogação f

extra- /ˈekstrə/ pref extra-

extract[1] /ɪkˈstrækt/ vt extrair; (promise, tooth) arrancar; (fig) obter. **~ion** /-ʃn/ n extração f, (P) extracção f; (descent) origem f

extract[2] /ˈekstrækt/ n extrato m, (P) extracto m

extradit|e /ˈekstrədaɪt/ vt extradi-tar. **~ion** /-ˈdɪʃn/ n extradição f

extramarital /ekstrəˈmærɪtl/ a extraconjugal, extramatrimonial

extraordinary /ɪkˈstrɔːdnrɪ/ a ex-traordinário

extravagan|t /ɪkˈstrævəgənt/ a extravagante; (wasteful) esban-jador. **~ce** n extravagância f; (wastefulness) esbanjamento m

extreme /ɪk'striːm/ *a* & *n* extremo (*m*). **~ely** *adv* extremamente. **~ist** *n* extremista *mf*

extremity /ɪk'stremətɪ/ *n* extremidade *f*

extricate /'ekstrɪkeɪt/ *vt* desembaraçar, livrar

extrovert /'ekstrəvɜːt/ *n* extrovertido *m*

exuberan|t /ɪg'zjuːbərənt/ *a* exuberante. **~ce** *n* exuberância *f*

exude /ɪg'zjuːd/ *vt* (*charm etc*) destilar, ressumar, (*P*) transpirar

exult /ɪg'zʌlt/ *vi* exultar

eye /aɪ/ *n* olho *m* □ *vt* (*pt* eyed, *pres p* eyeing) olhar. keep an ~ on vigiar. see ~ to ~ concordar inteiramente. **~-opener** *n* revelação *f*. **~-shadow** *n* sombra *f*

eyeball /'aɪbɔːl/ *n* globo *m* ocular

eyebrow /'aɪbraʊ/ *n* sobrancelha *f*

eyelash /'aɪlæʃ/ *n* pestana *f*

eyelid /'aɪlɪd/ *n* pálpebra *f*

eyesight /'aɪsaɪt/ *n* vista *f*

eyesore /'aɪsɔː(r)/ *n* monstruosidade *f*, horror *m*

eyewitness /'aɪwɪtnɪs/ *n* testemunha *f* ocular

F

fable /'feɪbl/ *n* fábula *f*

fabric /'fæbrɪk/ *n* tecido *m*; (*structure*) edifício *m*

fabricat|e /'fæbrɪkeɪt/ *vt* fabricar; (*invent*) urdir, inventar. **~ion** /-'keɪʃn/ *n* fabrico *m*; (*invention*) invenção *f*

fabulous /'fæbjʊləs/ *a* fabuloso

façade /fə'saːd/ *n* fachada *f*

face /feɪs/ *n* face *f*, cara *f*, rosto *m*; (*expression*) face *f*; (*grimace*) careta *f*; (*of clock*) mostrador *m* □ *vt* (*look towards*) encarar; (*confront*) enfrentar □ *vi* (*be opposite*)

estar de frente para. **~ up to** enfrentar. **~ to face** cara a cara, frente a frente. in the **~ of** em vista de. on the **~ of it** a julgar pelas aparências. pull **~s** fazer caretas. **~-cloth** *n* toalha *f* de rosto, (*P*) toalhete *m* de rosto. **~-lift** *n* cirurgia *f* plástica do rosto. **~-pack** *n* máscara de beleza *f*

faceless /'feɪslɪs/ *a* (*fig*) anónimo, (*P*) anónimo

facet /'fæsɪt/ *n* faceta *f*

facetious /fə'siːʃəs/ *a* faceto; (*pej*) engraçadinho (*colloq pej*)

facial /'feɪʃl/ *a* facial

facile /'fæsaɪl/ *a* fácil; (*superficial*) superficial

facilitate /fə'sɪlɪteɪt/ *vt* facilitar

facilit|y /fə'sɪlətɪ/ *n* facilidade *f*. **~ies** (*means*) facilidades *fpl*; (*installations*) instalações *fpl*

facing /'feɪsɪŋ/ *n* revestimento *m*

facsimile /fæk'sɪməlɪ/ *n* fac-símile *m*

fact /fækt/ *n* fato *m*, (*P*) facto. in **~, as a matter of ~** na realidade

faction /'fækʃn/ *n* facção *f*

factor /'fæktə(r)/ *n* fator *m*, (*P*) factor *m*

factory /'fæktərɪ/ *n* fábrica *f*

factual /'fæktʃʊəl/ *a* concreto, real

faculty /'fækltɪ/ *n* faculdade *f*

fad /fæd/ *n* capricho *m*, mania *f*, (*craze*) moda *f*

fade /feɪd/ *vt/i* (*colour*) desbotar; (*sound*) diminuir; (*disappear*) apagar(-se)

fag /fæg/ *n* (*colloq: chore*) estafa *f*; (*sl: cigarette*) cigarro *m*. **~ged** *a* estafado

fail /feɪl/ *vt/i* falhar; (*in an examination*) reprovar; (*omit, neglect*) deixar de; (*comm*) falir □ *n* **without ~** sem falta

failing /'feɪlɪŋ/ *n* deficiência *f* □ *prep* na falta de, à falta de

failure /ˈfeɪljə(r)/ n fracasso m, (P) falhanço m; (of engine) falha f; (of electricity) falta f; (person) fracassado m.

faint /feɪnt/ a (-er, -est) (indistinct) apagado; (weak) fraco; (giddy) tonto □ vi desmaiar □ n desmaio m. **~-hearted** a tímido. **~ly** adv vagamente. **~ness** n debilidade f; (indistinctness) apagado m

fair[1] /feə(r)/ n feira f. **~-ground** n parque m de diversões, (P) largo m de feira

fair[2] /feə(r)/ a (-er, -est) (hair) louro; (weather) bom; (of moderate quality) razoável; (just) justo. **~ play** jogo m limpo, fair-play m. **~ly** adv razoavelmente. **~ness** n justiça f

fairy /ˈfeərɪ/ n fada f. **~ story, ~ tale** conto m de fadas

faith /feɪθ/ n fé f; (religion) religião f; (loyalty) lealdade f. **in good ~** de boa fé, (P) à boa fé. **~-healer** n curandeiro m

faithful /ˈfeɪθfl/ a fiel. **~ly** adv fielmente. **yours ~ly** atenciosamente. **~ness** n fidelidade f

fake /feɪk/ n (thing) imitação f; (person) impostor m □ a falsificado □ vt falsificar; (pretend) simular, fingir

falcon /ˈfɔːlkən/ n falcão m

fall /fɔːl/ vi (pt fell, pp fallen) cair □ n quedas f; (Amer. autumn) outono m. **~s** npl (waterfall) queda d'água f. **~ back on** recorrer a. **~ behind** atrasar-se (with em). **~ down** or **off** cair. **~ flat** falhar, não resultar. **~ flat on one's face** estatelar-se. **~ for** (a trick) cair em, deixar-se levar por; (colloq: a person) apaixonar-se por, ficar caído por (colloq). **~ in** (roof) ruir; (mil) alinhar-se, pôr-se em forma. **~ out** brigar, (P) zangar-se (with com). **~-out** n poeira f radioativa, (P) radioactiva. **~ through** (of plans) falhar

fallacy /ˈfæləsɪ/ n falácia f, engano m. **~ious** /fəˈleɪʃəs/ a errôneo

fallen /ˈfɔːlən/ see **fall**

fallible /ˈfæləbl/ a falível

fallow /ˈfæləʊ/ a (of ground) de pousio; (uncultivated) inculto

false /fɔːls/ a falso. **~ teeth** dentadwa f. **~ly** adv falsamente. **~ness** n falsidade f

falsehood /ˈfɔːlshʊd/ n falsidade f, mentira f

falsify /ˈfɔːlsɪfaɪ/ vt (pt -fied) falsificar; (a story) deturpar

falter /ˈfɔːltə(r)/ vi vacilar; (of the voice) hesitar

fame /feɪm/ n fama f. **~d** a afamado

familiar /fəˈmɪliə(r)/ a familiar; (intimate) íntimo. **be ~ with** estar familiarizado com

familiarity /fəmɪlɪˈærɪtɪ/ n familiaridade f

familiarize /fəˈmɪliəraɪz/ vt familiarizar (with/to com); (make well known) tornar conhecido

family /ˈfæməlɪ/ n família f. **~ doctor** médico m da família. **~ tree** árvore f genealógica

famine /ˈfæmɪn/ n fome f

famished /ˈfæmɪʃt/ a esfomeado, faminto. **be ~** (colloq) estar morrendo de fome, (P) estar a morrer de fome

famous /ˈfeɪməs/ a famoso

fan[1] /fæn/ n (in the hand) leque m; (mechanical) ventilador m, (P) ventoínha f □ vt (pt fanned) abanar; (a fire; fig) atiçar □ vi **~ out** abrir-se um leque. **~ belt** correia f da ventoínha

fan[2] /fæn/ n (colloq) fã mf. **~ mail** correio m de fãs

fanatic /fəˈnætɪk/ n fanático m. **~al** a fanático. **~ism** /-sɪzəm/ n fanatismo m

fanciful /'fænsɪfl/ a fantasioso, fantasista

fancy /'fænsɪ/ n fantasia f, (liking) gosto m □ a extravagante, fantástico; (of buttons etc) de fantasia; (of prices) exorbitante □ vt imaginar; (colloq: like) gostar de; (colloq: want) apetecer. **it took my ~** gostei disso, (P) deu-me no gosto. **a passing ~** um entusiasmo passageiro. **~ dress** traje m fantasia, (P) trajo m de fantasia

fanfare /'fænfeə(r)/ n fanfarra f

fang /fæŋ/ n presa f, dente m canino

fantastic /fæn'tæstɪk/ a fantástico

fantas|y /'fæntəsɪ/ n fantasia f. **~ize** vt fantasiar, imaginar

far /fa:(r)/ adv longe; (much, very) muito □ a distante, longínquo; (end, side) outro. **~ away**, **~ off** ao longe. **as ~ as** (up to) até. **as ~ as I know** tanto quanto saiba. **the F~ East** o Extremo-Oriente m. **~-away** a distante, longínquo. **~-fetched** a forçado; (unconvincing) pouco plausível. **~-reaching** a de grande alcance

farc|e /fa:s/ n farsa f. **~ical** a de farsa; ridículo

fare /feə(r)/ n preço m da passagem; (in taxi) tarifa f, preço m da corrida; (passenger) passageiro m; (food) comida f □ vi (get on) dar-se

farewell /feə'wel/ int & n adeus (m)

farm /fa:m/ n quinta f, fazenda f □ vt cultivar □ vi ser (fazendeiro), (P) lavrador. **~ out** (of work) delegar a tarefeiros. **~-hand** n trabalhador m rural. **~er** n fazendeiro m, (P) lavrador m. **~ing** n agricultura f, lavoura f

farmhouse /'fa:mhaʊs/ n casa f da fazenda, (P) quinta

farmyard /'fa:mja:d/ n quintal de fazenda m, (P) pátio m de quinta

farth|er /'fa:ðə(r)/ adv mais longe □ a mais distante. **~est** adv mais longe □ a o mais distante

fascinat|e /'fæsɪneɪt/ vt fascinar. **~ion** /-'neɪʃn/ n fascínio m, fascinação f

fascis|t /'fæʃɪst/ n fascista mf. **~m** /-zəm/ n fascismo m

fashion /'fæʃn/ n moda f; (manner) maneira f □ vt amoldar, (P) moldar. **~able** a na moda, (P) à moda. **~ably** adv na moda, (P) à moda

fast¹ /fa:st/ a (-er, -est) rápido; (colour) fixo, que não desbota □ adv depressa; (firmly) firmemente. **be ~** (of clock) adiantar-se, estar adiantado. **~ asleep** profundamente adormecido, ferrado no sono. **~ food** n fast-food f

fast² /fa:st/ vi jejuar □ n jejum m

fasten /'fa:sn/ vt/i prender; (door, window) fechar(-se); (seat-belt) apertar. **~er**, **~ing** ns fecho m

fastidious /fə'stɪdɪəs/ a exigente

fat /fæt/ n gordura f □ a (fatter, fattest) gordo. **~ness** n gordura f

fatal /'feɪtl/ a fatal. **~ injuries** ferimentos mpl mortais. **~ity** /fə'tælətɪ/ n fatalidade f. **~ly** adv fatalmente, mortalmente

fate /feɪt/ n (destiny) destino m; (one's lot) destino m, sorte f. **~ful** a fatídico

fated /'feɪtɪd/ a predestinado; (doomed) condenado (to, a)

father /'fa:ðə(r)/ n pai m □ vt gerar. **~-in-law** (pl **~s-in-law**) sogro m. **~ly** a paternal

fathom /'fæðəm/ n braça f □ vt ~ (out) (comprehend) compreender

fatigue /fə'ti:g/ n fadiga f □ vt fatigar

fatten /'fætn/ vt/i engordar. **~ing** a que engorda

fatty /'fætɪ/ a (-ier, -iest) gorduroso; (tissue) adiposo

fault /fɔːlt/ n defeito m, falha f; (blame) falta f, culpa f; (geol) falha f. **at** ~ culpado. **it's your** ~ é culpa sua. ~**less** a impecável. ~**y** a defeituoso

favour /'feɪvə(r)/ n favor m □ vt favorecer; (prefer) preferir. **do sb a** ~ fazer um favor a alg. ~**able** a favorável. ~**ably** adv favoravelmente

favourit|e /'feɪvərɪt/ a & n favorito (m). ~**ism** /-ɪzəm/ n favoritismo m

fawn[1] /fɔːn/ n cervo m novo □ a (colour) castanho claro

fawn[2] /fɔːn/ vi ~ **on** adular, bajular

fax /fæks/ n fax m, fac-símile m □ vt mandar um fax. ~ **machine** fax m

fear /fɪə(r)/ n medo m, receio m, temor m; (likelihood) perigo m □ vt recear, ter medo de. **for** ~ **of**/ **that** com medo de/que. ~**ful** a (terrible) medonho; (timid) medroso, receoso. ~**less** a destemido, intrépido

feasib|le /'fiːzəbl/ a factível, praticável; (likely) plausível. ~**ility** /-'bɪlɪtɪ/ n possibilidade f; (plausibility) plausibilidade f

feast /fiːst/ n festim m; (relig; fig) festa f □ vt/i festejar; (eat and drink) banquetear-se. ~ **on** regalar-se com

feat /fiːt/ n feito m, façanha f

feather /'feðə(r)/ n pena f, pluma f

feature /'fiːtʃə(r)/ n feição f, traço m; (quality) característica f; (film) longa metragem f; (article) artigo m em destaque □ vt representar; (film) ter como protagonista □ vi figurar

February /'februərɪ/ n Fevereiro m

fed /fed/ see **feed**. **be** ~ **up** estar farto (colloq) (**with** de)

federal /'fedərəl/ a federal. ~**tion** /-'reɪʃn/ n federação f

fee /fiː/ n preço m. ~(**s**) (of doctor,

lawyer etc) honorários mpl; (member's subscription) quota f; (univ) (P) propinas fpl; (enrolment/registration) matrícula f; (school) ~**s** mensalidades fpl escolares, (P) mensalidades fpl

feeble /'fiːbl/ a (-er, -est) débil, fraco. ~**-minded** a débil mental, (P) deficiente

feed /fiːd/ vt (pt **fed**) alimentar, dar de comer a; (suckle) alimentar; (supply) alimentar, abastecer □ vi alimentar-se □ n comida f; (breast-feeding) mamada f; (mech) alimentação f

feedback /'fiːdbæk/ n reação f, (P) reacção f; (electr) regeneração f

feel /fiːl/ vt (pt **felt**) sentir; (touch) apalpar, tatear □ vi (tired, lonely etc) sentir-se. ~ **hot/thirsty** ter calor/sede. ~ **as if** ter a impressão de que. ~ **like** ter vontade de

feeler /'fiːlə(r)/ n antena f

feeling /'fiːlɪŋ/ n sentimento m; (physical) sensação f

feet /fiːt/ see **foot**

feign /feɪn/ vt fingir

feline /'fiːlaɪn/ a felino

fell[1] /fel/ vt abater, derrubar

fell[2] /fel/ see **fall**

fellow /'feləʊ/ n companheiro m, camarada m; (of society, college) membro m; (colloq) cara m, (P) tipo m (colloq). ~**-traveller** n companheiro m de viagem. ~**-ship** n companheirismo m, camaradagem f; (group) associação f

felt[1] /felt/ n feltro m

felt[2] /felt/ see **feel**

female /'fiːmeɪl/ a (animal etc) fêmea f; (voice, sex etc) feminino □ n mulher f, (animal) fêmea f

feminin|e /'femənɪn/ a & n feminino (m). ~**ity** /-'nɪnɪtɪ/ n feminilidade f

feminist /'femɪnɪst/ n feminista mf

fenc|e /fens/ *n* tapume *m*, cerca *f* □ *vt* cercar □ *vi* esgrimir. **~er** *n* esgrimista *mf*. **~ing** *n* esgrima *f*; (*fences*) tapume *m*

fend /fend/ *vi* **~ for o.s.** defender-se, virar-se (*colloq*), governar-se □ *vt* **~ off** defender-se de

fender /'fendə(r)/ *n* guarda-fogo *m*; (*Amer: mudguard*) pára-lama *m*, guarda-lama *m*, (*P*) pára-choques *m*

fennel /'fenl/ *n* (*herb*) funcho *m*, erva-doce *f*

ferment[1] /fə'ment/ *vt/i* fermentar; (*excite*) excitar. **~ation** /fɜ:men'teɪʃn/ *n* fermentação *f*

ferment[2] /'fɜ:ment/ *n* fermento *m*; (*fig*) efervescência *f*

fern /fɜ:n/ *n* feto *m*

feroc|ious /fə'rəʊʃəs/ *a* feroz. **~ity** /-'rɒsəti/ *n* ferocidade *f*

ferret /'ferɪt/ *n* furão *m* □ *vi* (*pt* ferreted) caçar com furões □ *vt* **~ out** desenterrar

ferry /'ferɪ/ *n* barco *m* de travessia, ferry(-boat) *m* □ *vt* transportar

fertil|e /'fɜ:taɪl/ *a* fértil, fecundo. **~ity** /fə'tɪləti/ *n* fertilidade *f*, fecundidade *f*. **~ize** /-əlaɪz/ *vt* fertilizar, fecundar

fertilizer /'fɜ:təlaɪzə(r)/ *n* adubo *m*, fertilizante *m*

fervent /'fɜ:vənt/ *a* fervoroso

fervour /'fɜ:və(r)/ *n* fervor *m*, ardor *m*

fester /'festə(r)/ *vt/i* infectar; (*fig*) envenenar

festival /'festɪvl/ *n* festival *m*; (*relig*) festa *f*

festiv|e /'festɪv/ *a* festivo. **~e season** periodo *m* das festas. **~ity** /fes'tɪvətɪ/ *n* festividade *f*, regozijo *m*. **~ities** festas *fpl*, festividades *fpl*

festoon /fe'stu:n/ *vt* engrinaldar

fetch /fetʃ/ *vt* (*go for*) ir buscar; (*bring*) trazer; (*be sold for*) vender-se por, render

fetching /'fetʃɪŋ/ *a* atraente

fête /feɪt/ *n* festa *f* or feira *f* de caridade ao ar livre □ *vt* festejar

fetish /'fetɪʃ/ *n* fetiche *m*, idolo *m*; (*obsession*) mania *f*

fetter /'fetə(r)/ *vt* agrilhoar. **~s** *npl* ferros *mpl*, grilhões *mpl*, grilhetas *fpl*

feud /fju:d/ *n* discórdia *f*, inimizade *f*. **~al** *a* feudal

fever /'fi:və(r)/ *n* febre *f*. **~ish** *a* febril

few /fju:/ *a* & *n* poucos (*mpl*). **~ books** poucos livros. **they are ~** são poucos. **a ~** *a* & *n* alguns (*mpl*). **a good ~, quite a ~** bastantes. **~er** *a* & *n* menos (de). **they were ~er** eram menos numerosos. **~est** *a* & *n* o menor número (de)

fiancé /fɪ'ɒnseɪ/ *n* noivo *m*. **~e** *n* noiva *f*

fiasco /fɪ'æskəʊ/ *n* (*pl* -os) fiasco *m*

fib /fɪb/ *n* lorota *f*, cascata *f*, peta *f*, (*P*) mentira *f* □ *vi* (*pt* fibbed) mentir

fibre /'faɪbə(r)/ *n* fibra *f*

fibreglass /'faɪbəglɑ:s/ *n* fibra *f* de vidro

fickle /'fɪkl/ *a* leviano, inconstante

fiction /'fɪkʃn/ *n* ficção *f*. **(works of) ~** romances *mpl*, obras *fpl* de ficção. **~al** *a* de ficção, ficticio

fictitious /fɪk'tɪʃəs/ *a* ficticio

fiddle /'fɪdl/ *n* (*colloq*) violino *m*; (*sl: swindle*) trapaça *f* □ *vi* (*sl*) trapacear (*sl*) □ *vt* (*sl: falsify*) falsificar, cozinhar (*sl*). **~ with** (*colloq*) brincar com, remexer em, (*P*) estar a brincar com, estar a (re)mexer em. **~r** /-ə(r)/ *n* (*colloq*) violinista *m/f*

fidelity /fɪ'delətɪ/ *n* fidelidade *f*

fidget /'fɪdʒɪt/ *vi* (*pt* fidgeted) estar irrequieto, remexer-se. **~ with** remexer em. **~y** *a* irrequieto; (*impatient*) impaciente

field /fiːld/ n campo m □ vt/i (cricket) (estar pronto para) apanhar ou interceptar a bola. **~-day** n grande dia m. **~-glasses** npl binóculo m. **F~-Marshal** marechal-de-campo m

fieldwork /ˈfiːldwɜːk/ n trabalho m de campo; (mil) fortificação f de campanha

fiend /fiːnd/ n diabo m, demónio m, (P) demónio m. **~ish** a diabólico

fierce /fɪəs/ a (-er, -est) feroz; (storm, attack) violento; (heat) intenso, abrasador. **~ness** n ferocidade f; (of storm, attack) violência f; (of heat) intensidade f

fiery /ˈfaɪərɪ/ a (-ier, -iest) ardente; (temper, speech) inflamado

fifteen /fɪfˈtiːn/ a & n quinze (m). **~th** a & n décimo quinto (m)

fifth /fɪfθ/ a & n quinto (m)

fifty /ˈfɪftɪ/ a & n cinquenta (m), (P) cinquenta (m). **~y-~y** a meias. **~ieth** a & n quinquagésimo (m), (P) quinquagésimo (m)

fig /fɪɡ/ n figo m. **~-tree** n figueira f

fight /faɪt/ vi (pt **fought**) lutar, combater □ vt lutar contra, combater □ n briga f, (quarrel, brawl) briga f. **~ over sth** lutar por algo coisa. **~ shy of** esquivar-se de, fugir de. **~er** n lutador m; (mil) combatente mf; (plane) caça m. **~ing** n combate m

figment /ˈfɪɡmənt/ n **~ of the imagination** fruto m or produto m da imaginação

figurative /ˈfɪɡərətɪv/ a figurado. **~ly** adv em sentido figurado

figure /ˈfɪɡə(r)/ n (number) algarismo m; (diagram, body) figura f. **~s** npl (arithmetic) contas fpl, aritmética f □ vt imaginar, supor □ vi (appear) figurar (in em). **~ of speech** figura f de retórica. **~ out** compreender. **~-head** n fi-

gura f de proa; (pej: person) testa-de-ferro m, chefe m nominal

filament /ˈfɪləmənt/ n filamento m

file[1] /faɪl/ n (tool) lixa f, lima f □ vt lixar, limar. **~ings** npl limalha f

file[2] /faɪl/ n fichário m, (P) dossier m; (box, drawer) fichário m, (P) ficheiro m; (comput) arquivo m; (line) fila f □ vt arquivar □ vi **~e** (past) desfilar, marchar em fila. **~e in/out** entrar/sair em fila. **(in) single ~e** (em) fila indiana. **~ing cabinet** fichário m, (P) ficheiro m

fill /fɪl/ vt/i encher(-se); (vacancy) preencher □ n **eat one's ~** comer o que quiser. **have one's ~** estar farto. **~ in** (form) preencher. **~ out** (get fat) engordar. **~ up** encher até cima; (auto) encher o tanque

fillet /ˈfɪlɪt/ n (meat, fish) filé m, (P) filete m □ vt (pt **filleted**) (meat, fish) cortar em filés, (P) filetes

filling /ˈfɪlɪŋ/ n recheio m; (of tooth) obturação f, (P) chumbo m. **~ station** posto m de gasolina

film /fɪlm/ n filme m □ vt/i filmar. **~ star** estrela f or vedete f or (P) vedeta f de cinema, astro m

filter /ˈfɪltə(r)/ n filtro m □ vt/i filtrar(-se). **~ coffee** café m filtro. **~-tip** n cigarro m com filtro

filth /fɪlθ/ n imundície f; (fig) obscenidade f. **~y** a imundo; (fig) obsceno

fin /fɪn/ n barbatana f

final /ˈfaɪnl/ a final; (conclusive) decisivo □ n (sport) final f. **~s** npl (exams) finais fpl. **~ist** n finalista mf. **~ly** adv finalmente, por fim; (once and for all) definitivamente

finale /fɪˈnɑːlɪ/ n final m

finalize /ˈfaɪnəlaɪz/ vt finalizar

financ|e /'fainæns/ n finança(s) f
(pl) □ a financeiro □ vt financiar. **~ier** /-'nænsiə(r)/ n financeiro m

financial /fai'nænʃl/ a financeiro.
~ly adv financeiramente

find /faind/ vt (pt **found** (sth lost))
achar, encontrar; (think) achar;
(discover) descobrir; (jur) declarar □ n achado m. **~ out** vt
apurar, descobrir □ vi informar-
se (about sobre)

fine[1] /fain/ n multa f □ vt multar

fine[2] /fain/ a (-er, -est) fino; (splendid) belo, lindo □ adv (muito)
bem; (small) fino, fininho. **~
arts** belas artes fpl. **~ weather**
bom tempo. **~ly** adv lindamente; (cut) fininho, aos bocadinhos

finesse /fi'nes/ n finura f, sutileza
f

finger /'fiŋgə(r)/ n dedo m □ vt
apalpar. **~mark** n dedada f.
~nail n unha f

fingerprint /'fiŋgəprint/ n impressão f digital

fingertip /'fiŋgətip/ n ponta f do
dedo

finicky /'finiki/ a meticuloso, miu-
dinho

finish /'finiʃ/ vt/i acabar, terminar □ n fim m; (of race) chegada
f; (on wood, clothes) acabamento
m. **~ doing** acabar de fazer. **~
up doing** acabar por fazer. **~ up**
in ir parar a, acabar em

finite /'fainait/ a finito

Fin|land /'finlənd/ n Finlândia f.
~n n finlandês m. **~nish** a & n
(lang) finlandês (m)

fir /fɜː(r)/ n abeto m

fire /'faiə(r)/ n fogo m; (conflagration) incêndio m; (heater) aquecedor m □ vt (bullet, gun, etc)
disparar; (dismiss) despedir;
(fig: stimulate) inflamar □ vi
atirar, fazer fogo (at sobre). **on
~** em chamas. **set ~ to** pôr fogo

em. **~-alarm** n alarme m de
incêndio. **~ brigade** bombeiros
mpl. **~-engine** n carro m de
bombeiro, (P) da bomba. **~-
escape** n saída f de incêndio. **~-
extinguisher** n extintor m de
incêndio. **~ station** quartel m
dos bombeiros

firearm /'faiəraːm/ n arma f de
fogo

fireman /'faiəmən/ n (pl -men)
bombeiro m

fireplace /'faiəpleis/ n chaminé f,
lareira f

firewood /'faiəwʊd/ n lenha f

firework /'faiəwɜːk/ n fogo m de
artifício

firing-squad /'faiəriŋskwɒd/ n pelotão m de execução

firm[1] /fɜːm/ n firma f comercial

firm[2] /fɜːm/ a (-er, -est) firme;
(belief) firme, inabalável. **~ly**
adv firmemente. **~ness** n firmeza f

first /fɜːst/ a & n primeiro (m);
(auto) primeira (f) □ adv primeiro, em primeiro lugar. **at ~**
a princípio, no início. **~ of all**
antes de mais nada. **for the ~
time** pela primeira vez. **~ aid**
primeiros socorros mpl. **~-
class** a de primeira classe. **~
name** nome de batismo m,
(P) baptismo m. **~-rate** a
excelente. **~ly** adv primeira-
mente, em primeiro lugar

fiscal /'fiskl/ a fiscal

fish /fiʃ/ n (pl usually invar) peixe
m □ vt/i pescar. **~ out** (colloq)
tirar. **~ing** n pesca f, ato de
ir pescar, (P) ir à pesca. **~ing-
rod** n vara f de pescar. **~y** a de
peixe; (fig: dubious) suspeito

fisherman /'fiʃəmən/ n (pl -men)
pescador m

fishmonger /'fiʃmʌŋgə(r)/ n dono
m/empregado m de peixaria.
~'s (shop) peixaria f

fission /'fiʃn/ n fissão f, cisão f

fist /fɪst/ n punho m, mão f fechada, (P) punho m

fit¹ /fɪt/ n acesso m, ataque m; (of generosity) rasgo m

fit² /fɪt/ a (fitter, fittest) de boa saúde, em forma; (proper) próprio; (good enough) em condições; (able) capaz □ vt/i (pt fitted) (clothes) assentar, ficar bem (a); (into space) caber; (match) ajustar(-se) (a); (install) instalar □ n be a good ~ assentar bem. be a tight ~ estar justo. ~ out equipar. ~ted carpet carpete m, (P) alcatifa f. ~ness n saúde f, (P) condição f física

fitful /fɪtfl/ a intermitente

fitment /fɪtmənt/ n móvel m de parede

fitting /fɪtɪŋ/ a apropriado □ n (clothes) prova f. ~s (fixtures) instalações fpl; (fitments) mobiliário m. ~ room cabine f

five /faɪv/ a & n cinco (m)

fix /fɪks/ vt fixar; (mend, prepare) arranjar □ n in a ~ em apuros, (P) numa alhada. ~ up with sth conseguir alg coisa para alguém. ~ed a fixo

fixation /fɪkˈseɪʃn/ n fixação f; (obsession) obsessão f

fixture /fɪkstʃə(r)/ n equipamento m, instalação f; (sport) (data f marcada para) competição f

fizz /fɪz/ vi efervescer, borbulhar □ n efervescência f. ~y a gasoso

fizzle /fɪzl/ vi ~ out (plan etc) acabar em nada or (P) em águas de bacalhau (colloq)

flab /flæb/ n (colloq) gordura f, banha f (colloq). ~by a flácido

flabbergasted /flæbəgɑːstɪd/ a (colloq) espantado, pasmado (colloq)

flag¹ /flæg/ n bandeira f. ~ down fazer sinal para parar. ~-pole n mastro m (de bandeira)

flag² /flæg/ vi (pt flagged) (droop) cair, pender, tombar; (of person) esmorecer

flagrant /fleɪgrənt/ a flagrante

flagstone /flægstəʊn/ n laje f

flair /fleə(r)/ n jeito m, habilidade f

flak|**e** /fleɪk/ n floco m; (paint) lasca f □ vi descamar-se, lascar-se. ~y a (paint) descamado, lascado

flamboyant /flæmˈbɔɪənt/ a flamejante; (showy) flamante, vistoso; (of manner) extravagante

flame /fleɪm/ n chama f, labareda f □ vi flamejar. burst into ~s incendiar-se

flamingo /fləˈmɪŋgəʊ/ n (pl -os) flamingo m

flammable /flæməbl/ a inflamável

flan /flæn/ n torta f, (P) tarte f

flank /flæŋk/ n flanco m □ vt flanquear

flannel /flænl/ n flanela f; (for face) toalha f, (P) toalhete m de rosto

flap /flæp/ vi (pt flapped) bater □ vt ~ its wings bater as asas □ n (of table, pocket) aba f; (sl: panic) pânico m

flare /fleə(r)/ vi ~ up irromper em chamas; (of war) rebentar; (fig: of person) enfurecer-se □ n chamejar m; (dazzling light) clarão m; (signal) foguete m de sinalização. ~d a (skirt) évasé

flash /flæʃ/ vi brilhar subitamente; (on and off) piscar; (auto) fazer sinal com o pisca-pisca □ vt fazer brilhar; (send) lançar, dardejar; (flaunt) fazer alarde de, ostentar □ n clarão m, lampejo m; (photo) flash m. ~ past passar como uma bala, (P) passar como um bólide

flashback /flæʃbæk/ n cena f retrospectiva, flashback m

flashlight /flæʃlaɪt/ n lanterna f eléctrica, (P) eléctrica

flashy /'flæʃɪ/ a espalhafatoso, que dá na vista

flask /flɑːsk/ n frasco m; (*vacuum flask*) garrafa f térmica, (P) garrafa f termos

flat /flæt/ a (**flatter, flattest**) plano, chato; (*tyre*) arriado, vazio; (*battery*) fraco; (*refusal*) categórico; (*fare, rate*) fixo; (*monotonous*) monótono; (*mus*) bemol; (*out of tune*) desafinado □ n apartamento m; (*colloq: tyre*) furo m no pneu; (*mus*) bemol m. ~ **out** (*drive*) em alta velocidade; (*work*) a dar tudo por tudo. ~ **ly** adv categoricamente

flatter /'flætə(r)/ vt lisonjear, adular. ~ **er** n lisonjeiro m, adulador m. ~ **ing** a lisonjeiro, adulador. ~ **y** n lisonja f

flatulence /'flætjʊləns/ n flatulência f

flaunt /flɔːnt/ vt/i pavonear(-se), ostentar

flavour /'fleɪvə(r)/ n sabor m (*of*) □ vt dar sabor a, temperar. ~ **ing** n aroma m sintético; (*seasoning*) tempero m

flaw /flɔː/ n falha f, imperfeição f. ~ **ed** a imperfeito. ~ **less** a perfeito

flea /fliː/ n pulga f

fled /fled/ see **flee**

fledged /fledʒd/ a **fully-~** (*fig*) treinado, experiente

flee /fliː/ vi (*pt* fled) fugir □ vt fugir de

fleece /fliːs/ n lã f de carneiro, velo m □ vt (*fig*) esfolar, roubar

fleet /fliːt/ n (*of warships*) esquadra f; (*of merchant ships, vehicles*) frota f

fleeting /'fliːtɪŋ/ a curto, fugaz

Flemish /'flemɪʃ/ a & n (*lang*) flamengo (m)

flesh /fleʃ/ n carne f; (*of fruit*) polpa f. ~ **y** a carnudo

flew /fluː/ see **fly**²

flex¹ /fleks/ vt flexionar

flex² /fleks/ n (*electr*) fio f flexível

flexib|**le** /'fleksəbl/ a flexível. ~ **ility** /-'bɪlətɪ/ n flexibilidade f

flexitime /'fleksɪtaɪm/ n horário m flexível

flick /flɪk/ n (*light blow*) safanão m; (*with fingertip*) piparote m □ vt dar um safanão em; (*with fingertip*) dar um piparote a. ~ **knife** n navalha f de ponta e mola. ~ **through** folhear

flicker /'flɪkə(r)/ vi vacilar, oscilar, tremular □ n oscilação f, tremular m; (*light*) luz f oscilante

flier /'flaɪə(r)/ n = **flyer**

flies /flaɪz/ npl (*of trousers*) braguilha f

flight¹ /flaɪt/ n (*flying*) voo m. ~ **of stairs** lance m, (P) lanço m de escada. ~ **deck** n cabine f, (P) cabina f

flight² /flaɪt/ n (*fleeing*) fuga f. **put to ~** pôr em fuga. **take ~** pôr-se em fuga

flimsy /'flɪmzɪ/ a (**-ier, -iest**) (*material*) fino; (*object*) frágil; (*excuse etc*) fraco, esfarrapado

flinch /flɪntʃ/ vi (*wince*) retrair-se; (*draw back*) recuar; (*hesitate*) hesitar

fling /flɪŋ/ vt/i (*pt* flung) atirar(-se), arremessar(-se); (*rush*) precipitar-se

flint /flɪnt/ n sílex m; (*for lighter*) pedra f

flip /flɪp/ vt (*pt* flipped) fazer girar com o dedo e o polegar □ n pancadinha f. ~ **through** folhear

flippant /'flɪpənt/ a irreverente, petulante

flipper /'flɪpə(r)/ n (*of seal*) nadadeira f; (*of swimmer*) pé-de-pato m

flirt /flɜːt/ vt namoriscar, flertar, (P) flartar □ n namorador m, namoradeira f. ~ **ation** /-'teɪʃn/ n namorico m, flerte m, (P) flirt m. ~ **atious** a namorador m, namoradeira f

flit /flɪt/ vi (pt **flitted**) esvoaçar

float /fləʊt/ vt/i (fazer) flutuar; (company) lançar □ n bóia f; (low cart) carro m de alegórico

flock /flɒk/ n (of sheep; congregation) rebanho m; (of birds) bando m; (crowd) multidão f □ vi afluir, juntar-se

flog /flɒg/ vt (pt **flogged**) açoitar; (sl: sell) vender

flood /flʌd/ n inundação f, cheia f; (of tears) dilúvio m □ vt inundar, alagar □ vi estar inundado; (river) transbordar; (fig: people) afluir

floodlight /flʌdlaɪt/ n projetor m, (P) projector m, holofote m □ vt (pt **floodlit**) iluminar

floor /flɔ:(r)/ n chão m, soalho m; (for dancing) pista f; (storey) andar m □ vt assoalhar; (baffle) desconcertar, embatucar

flop /flɒp/ vi (pt **flopped**) (drop) (deixar-se) cair; (move helplessly) debater-se; (sl: fail) ser um fiasco □ n (sl) fiasco m. **~py** n mole, tombado. **~py (disk)** disquete m

floral /flɔ:rəl/ a floral

florid /flɒrɪd/ a florido

florist /flɒrɪst/ n florista mf

flounce /flaʊns/ n babado m, debrum m

flounder /flaʊndə(r)/ vi esbracejar, debater-se; (fig) meter os pés pelas mãos

flour /flaʊə(r)/ n farinha f. **~y** a farinhento

flourish /flʌrɪʃ/ vi florescer, prosperar □ vt brandir □ n floreado m; (movement) gesto m elegante. **~ing** a próspero

flout /flaʊt/ vt escarnecer (de)

flow /fləʊ/ vi correr, fluir; (traffic) mover-se; (hang loosely) flutuar; (gush) jorrar □ n corrente f; (of tide; fig) enchente f. **~ into** (of river) desaguar em. **~ chart** organograma m, (P) organigrama m

flower /flaʊə(r)/ n flor f □ vi flo-

rir, florescer. **~-bed** n canteiro m. **~ed** a de flores, (P) florido, às flores. **~y** a florido

flown /fləʊn/ see **fly**[2]

flu /flu:/ n (colloq) gripe f

fluctuat|e /flʌktʃʊeɪt/ vi flutuar, oscilar. **~ion** /-'eɪʃn/ n flutuação f, oscilação f

flue /flu:/ n cano m de chaminé

fluen|t /flu:ənt/ a fluente. **be ~t (in a language)** falar correntemente (uma língua). **~cy** n fluência f. **~tly** adv fluentemente

fluff /flʌf/ n cotão m; (down) penugem f □ vt (colloq: bungle) estender-se em (sl), executar mal. **~y** a penugento, fofo

fluid /flu:ɪd/ a & n fluido (m)

fluke /flu:k/ n bambúrrio (colloq) m, golpe m de sorte

flung /flʌŋ/ see **fling**

flunk /flʌŋk/ vt/i (Amer colloq) levar pau (colloq), (P) chumbar (colloq)

fluorescent /flʊə'resnt/ a fluorescente

fluoride /flʊəraɪd/ n flúor m, fluor m

flurry /flʌrɪ/ n rajada f, rabanada f, lufada f; (fig) atrapalhação f, agitação f

flush[1] /flʌʃ/ vi corar, ruborizar-se □ vt lavar com água, (P) lavar a jorros de água □ n rubor m, vermelhidão f; (fig) excitação f; (of water) jorro m □ a ~ with ao nível de, rente a. **~ the toilet** dar descarga

flush[2] /flʌʃ/ vt ~ out desalojar

fluster /flʌstə(r)/ vt atarantar, perturbar, enervar

flute /flu:t/ n flauta f

flutter /flʌtə(r)/ vi esvoaçar; (wings) bater; (heart) palpitar □ vt bater. **~ one's eyelashes** pestanejar □ n (of wings) batimento m; (fig) agitação f

flux /flʌks/ n **in a state of ~** em mudança f contínua

fly[1] /flaɪ/ n mosca f

fly[2] /flaɪ/ vi (pt **flew**, pp **flown**) voar; (passengers) ir de/viajar de avião; (rush) correr □ vt pilotar; (passengers, goods) transportar por avião; (flag) hastear, (P) arvorar □ n (of trousers) braguilha f

flyer /'flaɪə(r)/ n aviador m; (Amer: circular) prospecto m

flying /'flaɪɪŋ/ a voador. **with ~ colours** com grande êxito, esplendidamente. **~ saucer** disco m voador. **~ start** bom arranque m. **~ visit** visita f de médico

flyleaf /'flaɪliːf/ n (pl **-leaves**) guarda f, folha f em branco

flyover /'flaɪəʊvə(r)/ n viaduto m

foal /fəʊl/ n potro m

foam /fəʊm/ n espuma f □ vi espumar. **~ (rubber)** n espuma f de borracha

fob /fɒb/ vt (pt **fobbed**) **~ off** iludir, entreter com artifícios. **~ off on** impingir a

focus /'fəʊkəs/ n (pl **-cuses** or **-ci** /-saɪ/) foco m □ vt/i (pt **focused**) focar; (fig) concentrar(-se). **in ~** focado, em foco. **out of ~** desfocado

fodder /'fɒdə(r)/ n forragem f

foetus /'fiːtəs/ n (pl **-tuses**) feto m

fog /fɒg/ n nevoeiro m □ vt/i (pt **fogged**) enevoar(-se). **~-horn** n sereia f de nevoeiro. **~gy** a enevoado, brumoso. **it is ~gy** está nevoento

foible /'fɔɪbl/ n fraqueza f, ponto m fraco

foil[1] /fɔɪl/ n papel m de alumínio; (fig) contraste m

foil[2] /fɔɪl/ vt frustrar

foist /fɔɪst/ vt impingir (on a)

fold /fəʊld/ vt/i dobrar(-se); (arms) cruzar; (colloq: fail) falir □ n dobra f. **~er** n pasta f; (leaflet) prospecto m (desdobrável). **~ing** a dobrável, dobradiço

foliage /'fəʊlɪɪdʒ/ n folhagem f

folk /fəʊk/ n povo m. **~s** (family, people) gente f (colloq) □ a folclórico, popular. **~-lore** n folclore m

follow /'fɒləʊ/ vt/i seguir. **it ~s that** quer dizer que. **~ suit** (cards) servir o naipe jogado; (fig) seguir o exemplo, fazer o mesmo. **~ up** (letter etc) dar seguimento a. **~er** n partidário m, seguidor m. **~ing** n partidários mpl □ a seguinte □ prep em seguimento a

folly /'fɒlɪ/ n loucura f

fond /fɒnd/ a (-er -est) carinhoso; (hope) caro. **be ~ of** gostar de, ser amigo de. **~ness** n (for people) afeição f; (for thing) gosto m

fondle /'fɒndl/ vt acariciar

font /fɒnt/ n pia f batismal, (P) baptismal

food /fuːd/ n alimentação f, comida f; (nutrient) alimento m □ a alimentar. **~ poisoning** envenenamento m alimentar

fool /fuːl/ n idiota mf, parvo m □ vt enganar □ vi **~ around** andar sem fazer nada

foolhardy /'fuːlhɑːdɪ/ a imprudente, atrevido

foolish /'fuːlɪʃ/ a idiota, parvo. **~ly** adv parvamente. **~ness** n idiotice f, parvoíce f

foolproof /'fuːlpruːf/ a infalível

foot /fʊt/ n (pl **feet**) (of person, bed, stairs) pé m; (of animal) pata f; (measure) pé m (= 30,48 cm) □ vt **~ the bill** pagar a conta. **on ~** a pé. **on** or **to one's feet** de pé. **put one's ~ in it** fazer uma gafe. **to be under sb's feet** atrapalhar alg. **~-bridge** n passarela f

football /'fʊtbɔːl/ n bola f de futebol; (game) futebol m. **~ pools** loteria f esportiva, (P) totobola m. **~er** n futebolista mf, jogador m de futebol

foothills /'fʊthɪlz/ npl contrafortes mpl

foothold /'fʊthəʊld/ n ponto m de apoio

footing /'fʊtɪŋ/ n: **firm** ~ apois seguro **on an equal** ~ em pé de igualdade

footlights /'fʊtlaɪts/ npl ribalta f

footnote /'fʊtnəʊt/ n nota f de rodapé

footpath /'fʊtpɑːθ/ n (pavement) calçada f, (P) passeio m; (in open country) atalho m, caminho m

footprint /'fʊtprɪnt/ n pegada f

footstep /'fʊtstep/ n passo m

footwear /'fʊtweə(r)/ n calçado m

for /fə(r)/; emphatic /fɔː(r)/ prep para; (in favour of; in place of) por; (during) durante □ conj porque, visto que. **a liking** ~ gosto por. **he has been away** ~ **two years** há dois anos que ele está fora. ~ **ever** para sempre

forage /'fɒrɪdʒ/ vi forragear; (rummage) remexer à procura de (de) □ n forragem f

forbade /fə'bæd/ see **forbid**

forbear /fɔː'beə(r)/ vt/i (pt forbore, pp forborne) abster-se (from de). ~ance n paciência f, tolerância f

forbid /fə'bɪd/ vt (pt forbade, pp forbidden) proibir. **you are** ~**den to smoke** você está proibido de fumar, (P) estás proibido de fumar. ~**ding** a severo, intimidante

force /fɔːs/ n força f □ vt forçar. ~ **into** fazer entrar à força. ~ **on** impor a. **come into** ~ entrar em vigor. **the** ~**s as** Forças Armadas. ~**d** a forçado. ~**ful** a enérgico

force-feed /'fɔːsfiːd/ vt (pt -fed) alimentar à força

forceps /'fɔːseps/ n (pl invar) fórceps m

forcibl|e /'fɔːsəbl/ a convincente; (done by force) à força. ~**y** adv à força

ford /fɔːd/ n vau m □ vt passar a vau, vadear

fore /fɔː(r)/ a dianteiro □ n **to the** ~ em evidência

forearm /'fɔːrɑːm/ n antebraço m

foreboding /fɔː'bəʊdɪŋ/ n pressentimento m

forecast /'fɔːkɑːst/ vt (pt forecast) prever □ n previsão f. **weather** ~ boletim m meteorológico, previsão f do tempo

forecourt /'fɔːkɔːt/ n pátio m de entrada; (of garage) área f das bombas de gasolina

forefinger /'fɔːfɪŋɡə(r)/ n (dedo) indicador m

forefront /'fɔːfrʌnt/ n vanguarda f

foregone /'fɔːɡɒn/ a ~ **conclusion** resultado m previsto

foreground /'fɔːɡraʊnd/ n primeiro plano m

forehead /'fɒrɪd/ n testa f

foreign /'fɒrən/ a estrangeiro; (trade) externo; (travel) ao/no estrangeiro. **F**~ **Office** Ministério m dos Negócios Estrangeiros. ~**er** n estrangeiro m

foreman /'fɔːmən/ n (pl foremen) contramestre m; (of jury) primeiro jurado m

foremost /'fɔːməʊst/ a principal, primeiro □ adv **first and** ~ antes de mais nada, em primeiro lugar

forename /'fɔːneɪm/ n prenome m

forensic /fə'rensɪk/ a forense. ~ **medicine** medicina f legal

forerunner /'fɔːrʌnə(r)/ n precursor m

foresee /fɔː'siː/ vt (pt -saw, pp -seen) prever. ~**able** a previsível

foreshadow /fɔː'ʃædəʊ/ vt prefigurar, pressagiar

foresight /'fɔːsaɪt/ n previsão f, previdência f

forest /'fɒrɪst/ n floresta f

forestall /fɔː'stɔːl/ vt (do first) antecipar-se a; (prevent) prevenir; (anticipate) antecipar

forestry /'fɒrɪstrɪ/ n silvicultura f

foretell /fɔːˈtel/ vt (pt **foretold**) predizer, profetizar

forever /fəˈrevə(r)/ adv (endlessly) constantemente

foreword /ˈfɔːwɜːd/ n prefácio m

forfeit /ˈfɔːfɪt/ n penalidade f, preço m; (in game) prenda f □ vt perder

forgave /fəˈɡeɪv/ see **forgive**

forge¹ /fɔːdʒ/ vi ~ **ahead** tomar a dianteira, avançar

forge² /fɔːdʒ/ n forja f □ vt (metal, friendship) forjar; (counterfeit) falsificar, forjar. ~**r** /-ə(r)/ n falsificador m, forjador m. ~**ry** /-ərɪ/ n falsificação f

forget /fəˈɡet/ vt/i (pt **forgot**, pp **forgotten**) esquecer. ~ **o.s.** portar-se com menos dignidade, esquecer-se de quem é. ~**-me-not** n miosótis m. ~**ful** a esquecido. ~**fulness** n esquecimento m

forgive /fəˈɡɪv/ vt (pt **forgave**, pp **forgiven**) perdoar (**sb for sth** alg coisa a alg). ~**ness** n perdão m

forgo /fɔːˈɡəʊ/ vt (pt **forwent**, pp **forgone**) renunciar a

fork /fɔːk/ n garfo m; (for digging etc) forquilha f; (in road) bifurcação f □ vi bifurcar. ~ **out** (sl) desembolsar. ~**-lift truck** empilhadeira f. ~**ed** a bifurcado; (lightning) em ziguezague

forlorn /fəˈlɔːn/ a abandonado, desolado

form /fɔːm/ n forma f; (document) impresso m, formulário m; (schol) classe f □ vt/i formar(-se)

formal /ˈfɔːml/ a formal; (dress) de cerimónia, (P) cerimónia. ~**ity** /-ˈmælətɪ/ n formalidade f. ~**ly** adv formalmente

format /ˈfɔːmæt/ n formato m □ vt (pt **formatted**) (disk) formatar

formation /fɔːˈmeɪʃn/ n formação f

former /ˈfɔːmə(r)/ a antigo; (first of two) primeiro. **the** ~ aquele. ~**ly** adv antigamente

formidable /ˈfɔːmɪdəbl/ a formidável, tremendo

formula /ˈfɔːmjʊlə/ n (pl **-ae** /-iː/ or **-as**) fórmula f

formulate /ˈfɔːmjʊleɪt/ vt formular

forsake /fəˈseɪk/ vt (pt **forsook**, pp **forsaken**) abandonar

fort /fɔːt/ n (mil) forte m

forth /fɔːθ/ adv adiante, para a frente. **and so** ~ e assim por diante, etcetera. **go back and** ~ andar de trás para diante.

forthcoming /fɔːθˈkʌmɪŋ/ a que está para vir, próximo; (communicative) comunicativo, receptivo; (book) no prelo

forthright /ˈfɔːθraɪt/ a franco, direto, (P) directo

fortify /ˈfɔːtɪfaɪ/ vt fortificar. ~**ication** /-ɪˈkeɪʃn/ n fortificação f

fortitude /ˈfɔːtɪtjuːd/ n fortitude f, fortaleza f

fortnight /ˈfɔːtnaɪt/ n quinze dias mpl, (P) quinzena f. ~**ly** a quinzenal □ adv de quinze em quinze dias

fortress /ˈfɔːtrɪs/ n fortaleza f

fortuitous /fɔːˈtjuːɪtəs/ a fortuito, acidental

fortunate /ˈfɔːtʃənət/ a feliz, afortunado. **be** ~ ter sorte. ~**ly** adv felizmente

fortune /ˈfɔːtʃən/ n sorte f; (wealth) fortuna f. **have the good** ~ **to** ter a sorte de. ~**-teller** n cartomante mf

fort|y /ˈfɔːtɪ/ a & n quarenta (m). ~**ieth** a & n quadragésimo (m)

forum /ˈfɔːrəm/ n fórum m, foro m

forward /ˈfɔːwəd/ a (in front) dianteiro; (towards the front) para a frente; (advanced) adiantado; (pert) atrevido □ n (sport) atacante m, (P) avançado m □ adv ~(**s**) para a frente, para diante □ vt (letter) remeter; (goods) expedir; (fig: help) favorecer.

come ~ apresentar-se. go ~
avançar. **~ness** n adiantamento
m; (pertness) atrevimento m.

fossil /'fɒsl/ a & n fóssil (m)

foster /'fɒstə(r)/ vt fomentar;
(child) criar. **~-child** n filho m
adotivo, (P) adoptivo. **~-mother**
n mãe f adotiva, (P) adoptiva

fought /fɔ:t/ see **fight**

foul /faʊl/ a (-er, -est) infecto;
(language) obsceno; (weather)
mau □ n. (football) falta f □ vt
sujar, emporcalhar. **~-mouthed**
a de linguagem obscena. **~ play**
jogo m desleal; (crime) crime m

found[1] /faʊnd/ see **find**

found[2] /faʊnd/ vt fundar. **~ation**
/-'deɪʃn/ n fundação f; (basis) fundamento m. **~ations** npl (of
building) alicerces mpl

founder[1] /'faʊndə(r)/ n fundador
m

founder[2] /'faʊndə(r)/ vi afundar-se

foundry /'faʊndrɪ/ n fundição f

fountain /'faʊntɪn/ n fonte f. **~-
pen** n caneta-tinteiro f, (P) caneta f de tinta permanente

four /fɔ:(r)/ a & n quatro (m).
~fold a quádruplo □ adv qua-
druplamente. **~th** a & n quarto
(m)

foursome /'fɔ:səm/ n grupo m de
quatro pessoas

fourteen /fɔ:'ti:n/ a & n catorze
(m). **~th** a & n décimo quarto
(m)

fowl /faʊl/ n ave f de capoeira

fox /fɒks/ n raposa f □ vt (colloq)
mistificar, enganar. **be ~ed** ficar
perplexo

foyer /'fɔɪeɪ/ n foyer m

fraction /'frækʃn/ n fracção f, (P)
fracção f; (small bit) bocadinho
m, partícula f

fracture /'fræktʃə(r)/ n fratura f,
(P) fractura f □ vt/i fraturar(-se),
(P) fracturar(-se)

fragile /'frædʒaɪl/ a frágil

fragment /'frægmənt/ n fragmen-

to m. **~ary** /'frægməntrɪ/ a fragmentário

fragran|t /'freɪgrənt/ a fragrante,
perfumado. **~ce** n fragrância f,
perfume m

frail /freɪl/ a (-er, -est) frágil

frame /freɪm/ n (techn; of spectacles) armação f; (of picture) moldura f; (of window) caixilho m;
(body) corpo m, (P) estrutura f □
vt colocar a armação em; (picture) emoldurar; (fig) formular;
(sl) incriminar falsamente, tramar. **~ of mind** estado m de
espírito

framework /'freɪmwɜ:k/ n estrutura f; (context) quadro m, esquema m

France /fra:ns/ n França f

franchise /'fræntʃaɪz/ n (pol) direito m de voto; (comm) concessão f, franchise f

frank[1] /fræŋk/ a franco. **~ly** adv
francamente. **~ness** n franqueza f

frank[2] /fræŋk/ vt franquear

frantic /'fræntɪk/ a frenético

fraternal /frə'tɜ:nl/ a fraternal

fraternize /'frætənaɪz/ vi confraternizar

fraud /frɔ:d/ n fraude f; (person)
impostor m. **~ulent** /'frɔ:djʊ-
lənt/ a fraudulento

fraught /frɔ:t/ a **~ with** cheio de

fray[1] /freɪ/ n rixa f

fray[2] /freɪ/ vt/i desfiar(-se), puir,
esgarçar(-se)

freak /fri:k/ n aberração f, anomalia f □ a anormal. **~ of
nature** aborto m da natureza.
~ish a anormal

freckle /'frekl/ n sarda f. **~d** a
sardento

free /fri:/ a (**freer**, **freest**) livre;
(gratis) grátis; (lavish) liberal □
vt (pt **freed**) libertar (**from** de);
(rid) livrar (**of** de). **~ of charge**
grátis, de graça. **a ~ hand** carta
f branca. **~-lance** a indepen-

dente, free-lance. **~-range** *a*
(*egg*) de galinha criada em
galinheiro. **~ly** *adv* livremente
freedom /fríːdəm/ *n* liberdade *f*
freez|e /friːz/ *vt/i* (*pt* **froze**, *pp*
frozen) gelar; (*culin; finance*)
congelar(-se) □ *n* gelo *m*; (*culin;
finance*) congelamento *m*. **~er** *n*
congelador *m*. **~ing** *a* gélido,
glacial. **below ~ing** abaixo de
zero

freight /freit/ *n* frete *m*

French /frentʃ/ *a* francês □ *n*
(*lang*) francês *m*. **the ~** os
franceses. **~man** *n* francês *m*.
~-speaking *a* francófono. **~
window** porta *f* envidraçada.
~woman *n* francesa *f*

frenz|y /frenzi/ *n* frenesi *m*.
~ied *a* frenético

frequen|t[1] /fríːkwənt/ *a* fre-
qüente, (*P*) frequente. **~cy** *n* freqüência *f*, (*P*) frequência *f*. **~tly**
adv freqüentemente, (*P*) frequentemente

frequent[2] /frɪˈkwent/ *vt* freqüentar, (*P*) frequentar

fresh /freʃ/ *a* (**-er**, **-est**) fresco;
(*different, additional*) novo; (*colloq: cheeky*) descarado, atrevido.
~ly *adv* recentemente. **~ness**
n frescura *f*

freshen /freʃn/ *vt/i* refrescar. **~
up** refrescar-se

fret /fret/ *vt/i* (*pt* **fretted**) ralar
(-se). **~ful** *a* rabugento

friar /fraɪə(r)/ *n* frade *m*; (*before
name*) frei *m*

friction /frɪkʃn/ *n* fricção *f*

Friday /fraɪdɪ/ *n* sexta-feira *f*.
Good ~ sexta-feira *f* santa

fridge /frɪdʒ/ *n* (*colloq*) geladeira
f, (*P*) frigorífico *m*

fried /fraɪd/ *see* **fry** □ *a* frito

friend /frend/ *n* amigo *m*. **~ship**
n amizade *f*

friendl|y /frendlɪ/ *a* (**-ier**, **-iest**)
amigável, amigo, simpático.
~iness *n* simpatia *f*, gentileza *f*

frieze /friːz/ *n* friso *m*

frigate /frɪɡət/ *n* fragata *f*

fright /fraɪt/ *n* medo *m*, susto *m*.
give sb a ~ pregar um susto em
alguém. **~ful** *a* medonho, assustador

frighten /fraɪtn/ *vt* assustar. **~
off** afugentar. **~ed** *a* assustado.
be ~ed (of) ter medo (de)

frigid /frɪdʒɪd/ *a* frígido. **~ity**
/-'dʒɪdətɪ/ *n* frigidez *f*, frieza *f*;
(*psych*) frigidez *f*

frill /frɪl/ *n* babado *m*, (*P*) folho *m*

fringe /frɪndʒ/ *n* franja *f*; (*of area*)
borda *f*; (*of society*) margem *f*. **~
benefits** (*work*) regalias *fpl*
extras. **~ theatre** teatro *m* alternativo, teatro *m* de vanguarda

frisk /frɪsk/ *vi* pular, brincar □ *vt*
revistar

fritter[1] /frɪtə(r)/ *n* bolinho *m* frito, (*P*) frito *m*

fritter[2] /frɪtə(r)/ *vt* **~ away** desperdiçar

frivol|ous /frɪvələs/ *a* frívolo.
~ity /-'vɒlətɪ/ *n* frivolidade *f*

fro /frəʊ/ *see* **to and fro**

frock /frɒk/ *n* vestido *m*

frog /frɒɡ/ *n* rã *f*

frogman /frɒɡmən/ *n* (*pl* **-men**)
homem-rã *m*

frolic /frɒlɪk/ *vi* (*pt* **frolicked**)
brincar, fazer travessuras □ *n*
brincadeira *f*, travessura *f*

from /frəm/; *emphatic* /frɒm/ *prep*
de; (*with time, prices etc*) de, a
partir de; (*according to*) por, a
julgar por

front /frʌnt/ *n* (*meteo, mil, pol; of
car, train*) frente *f*; (*of shirt*) peti-
lho *m*; (*of building; fig*) fachada *f*;
(*promenade*) calçada *f* à beira-
mar □ *a* da frente; (*first*)
primeiro. **in ~ (of)** em frente
(de). **~ door** porta *f* da rua. **~-
wheel drive** tração *f*, (*P*) tracção
f dianteira. **~age** *n* frontaria *f*.
~al *a* frontal

frontier /frʌntɪə(r)/ *n* fronteira *f*

frost /frɒst/ n gelo m, temperatura f abaixo de zero; (on ground, plants etc) geada f □ vt/i cobrir (-se) de geada. ~-bite n queimadura f de frio. ~-bitten a queimado pelo frio. ~ed a (glass) fosco. ~y a glacial

froth /frɒθ/ n espuma f □ vi espumar, fazer espuma. ~y a espumoso

frown /fraʊn/ vi franzir as sobrancelhas □ n franzir m de sobrancelhas. ~ on desaprovar

froze, frozen /frəʊz, ˈfrəʊzn/ see freeze

frugal /ˈfruːgl/ a poupado; (meal) frugal. ~ly adv frugalmente

fruit /fruːt/ n fruto m; (collectively) fruta f. ~ machine n caça-níqueis ms/pl. ~ salad salada f de frutas. ~y a que tem gosto or cheiro de fruta

fruit|ful /ˈfruːtfl/ a frutífero, produtivo. ~less a infrutífero

fruition /fruːˈɪʃn/ n come to ~ realizar-se

frustrat|e /frʌˈstreɪt/ vt frustrar. ~ion /-ʃn/ n frustração f

fry /fraɪ/ vt/i (pt fried) fritar. ~ing-pan n frigideira f

fudge /fʌdʒ/ n (culin) doce m de leite, (P) doce m acaramelado □ vt/i ~ (the issue) lançar a confusão

fuel /ˈfjuːəl/ n combustível m; (for car) carburante m □ vt (pt fuelled) abastecer de combustível; (fig) atear

fugitive /ˈfjuːdʒətɪv/ a & n fugitivo (m)

fulfil /fʊlˈfɪl/ vt (pt fulfilled) cumprir, realizar; (condition) satisfazer. ~ o.s. realizar-se. ~ling a satisfatório. ~ment n realização f; (of condition) satisfação f

full /fʊl/ a (-er, -est) cheio; (meal) completo, (price) total, por inteiro; (skirt) rodado □ adv in ~ integralmente. at ~ speed a toda velocidade. to the ~ ao máximo. be ~ up (colloq: after eating) estar cheio (colloq). ~ moon lua f cheia. ~-scale a em grande. ~-size a em tamanho natural. ~ stop ponto m final. ~-time a & adv a tempo integral, full-time. ~y adv completamente

fulsome /ˈfʊlsəm/ a excessivo

fumble /ˈfʌmbl/ vi tatear, (P) tactear; (in the dark) andar tateando. ~ with estar atrapalhado com, andar às voltas com

fume /fjuːm/ vi defumar, (P) deitar fumo, fumegar; (with anger) ferver. ~s npl gases mpl

fumigate /ˈfjuːmɪgeɪt/ vt fumigar

fun /fʌn/ n divertimento m. for ~ de brincadeira. make ~ of zombar de, fazer troça de. ~-fair n parque m de diversões, (P) feira f de diversões, (P) feira f popular

function /ˈfʌŋkʃn/ n função f □ vi funcionar. ~al a funcional

fund /fʌnd/ n fundos mpl □ vt financiar

fundamental /ˌfʌndəˈmentl/ a fundamental

funeral /ˈfjuːnərəl/ n enterro m, funeral m □ a fúnebre

fungus /ˈfʌŋgəs/ n (pl -gi /-gaɪ/) fungo m

funnel /ˈfʌnl/ n funil m; (of ship) chaminé f

funn|y /ˈfʌnɪ/ a (-ier, -iest) engraçado, divertido; (odd) esquisito. ~ily adv comicamente; (oddly) estranhamente. ~ily enough por incrível que pareça

fur /fɜː(r)/ n pêlo m; (for clothing) pele f; (in kettle) depósito m, crosta f. ~ coat casaco m de pele

furious /ˈfjʊərɪəs/ a furioso. ~ly adv furiosamente

furnace /ˈfɜːnɪs/ n fornalha f

furnish /'fɜːnɪʃ/ vt mobiliar, (P) mobilar; (supply) prover (with de). ~ings npl mobiliário m e equipamento m

furniture /'fɜːnɪtʃə(r)/ n mobília f

furrow /'fʌrəʊ/ n sulco m; (wrinkle) ruga f □ vt sulcar; (wrinkle) enrugar

furry /'fɜːrɪ/ a (-ier, -iest) peludo; (toy) de pelúcia

further /'fɜːðə(r)/ a mais distante; (additional) adicional, suplementar □ adv mais longe; (more) mais □ vt promover. ~er education ensino m supletivo, cursos mpl livres, (P) educação f superior. ~est a o mais distante □ adv mais longe

furthermore /fɜːðə'mɔː(r)/ adv além disso

furtive /'fɜːtɪv/ a furtivo

fury /'fjʊərɪ/ n fúria f, furor m

fuse¹ /fjuːz/ vt/i fundir(-se); (fig) amalgamar □ n fusível m. the lights ~d os fusíveis queimaram

fuse² /fjuːz/ n (of bomb) espoleta f

fuselage /'fjuːzəlɑːʒ/ n fuselagem f

fusion /'fjuːʒn/ n fusão f

fuss /fʌs/ n história(s) f(pl), escarcéu m □ vi preocupar-se com ninharias. **make a** ~ **of** ligar demasiado para, criar caso com, fazer um aparalhafato com. ~**y** a exigente, complicado

futile /'fjuːtaɪl/ a fútil

future /'fjuːtʃə(r)/ a & n futuro (m). **in** ~ no futuro, de agora em diante

futuristic /fjuːtʃə'rɪstɪk/ a futurista, futurístico

fuzz /fʌz/ n penugem f; (hair) cabelo m frisado

fuzzy /'fʌzɪ/ a (hair) frisado; (photo) pouco nítido, desfocado

G

gab /gæb/ n (colloq) **have the gift of the** ~ ter o dom da palavra

gabble /'gæbl/ vt/i tagarelar, falar, ler muito depressa □ n tagarelice f, algaravia f

gable /'geɪbl/ n empena f, oitão m

gad /gæd/ vi (pt **gadded**) ~ **about** (colloq) badalar

gadget /'gædʒɪt/ n pequeno utensílio m; (fitting) dispositivo m; (device) engenhoca f (colloq)

Gaelic /'geɪlɪk/ n galês m

gaffe /gæf/ n gafe f

gag /gæg/ n mordaça f; (joke) gag m, piada f □ vt (pt **gagged**) amordaçar

gaiety /'geɪətɪ/ n alegria f

gaily /'geɪlɪ/ adv alegremente

gain /geɪn/ vt ganhar □ vi (of clock) adiantar-se. ~ **weight** aumentar de peso. ~ **on** (get closer to) aproximar-se de □ n ganho m; (increase) aumento m. ~**ful** a lucrativo, proveitoso

gait /geɪt/ n (modo de) andar m

gala /'gɑːlə/ n gala m; (sport) festival m

galaxy /'gæləksɪ/ n galáxia f

gale /geɪl/ n vento m forte

gall /gɔːl/ n bílis f; (fig) fel m; (sl: impudence) descaramento m, desplante m, (P) lata f (sl). ~**bladder** n vesícula f biliar. ~**stone** n cálculo m biliar

gallant /'gælənt/ a galhardo, valente; (chivalrous) galante, cortês. ~**ry** n galhardia f, valentia f; (chivalry) galanteria f, cortesia f

gallery /'gælərɪ/ n galeria f

galley /'gælɪ/ n (pl -**eys**) galera f; (ship's kitchen) cozinha f

gallivant /ˌgælɪ'vænt/ vi (colloq) vadiar, (P) andar na paródia

gallon /'gælən/ n galão m (= 4,546 litros; Amer = 3.785 litros)

gallop /'gæləp/ n galope m □ vi (pt galloped) galopar

gallows /'gæləʊz/ npl forca f

galore /gə'lɔ:(r)/ adv a beça, em abundância

galvanize /'gælvənaız/ vt galvanizar

gambit /'gæmbıt/ n gambito m

gamblle /'gæmbl/ vt/i jogar □ n jogo (de azar) m; (fig) risco m. ~e on apostar em. ~er n jogador m. ~ing n jogo m (de azar)

game /geım/ n jogo m; (football) desafio m; (animals) caça f □ a bravo. ~ for pronto para

gamekeeper /'geımki:pə(r)/ n guarda-florestal m

gammon /'gæmən/ n presunto m defumado

gamut /'gæmət/ n gama f

gang /gæŋ/ n bando m, gang m; (of workmen) turma f, (P) grupo m □ vi ~ up ligar-se (on contra)

gangling /'gæŋglıŋ/ a desengonçado

gangrene /'gæŋgri:n/ n gangrena f

gangster /'gæŋstə(r)/ n gângster m, bandido m

gangway /'gæŋweı/ n passagem f; (aisle) coxia f; (on ship) portaló m; (from ship to shore) passadiço m

gaol /dʒeıl/ n & vt = **jail**

gap /gæp/ n abertura f, brecha f; (in time) intervalo m; (deficiency) lacuna f

gaple /geıp/ vi ficar boquiaberto or embasbacado. ~ing a escancarado

garage /'gæra:ʒ/ n garagem f; (service station) posto m de gasolina, (P) estação f de serviço □ vt pôr na garagem

garbage /'ga:bıdʒ/ n lixo m. ~ can (Amer) lata f do lixo m, (P) caixote m do lixo

garble /'ga:bl/ vt deturpar

garden /'ga:dn/ n jardim m □ vi jardinar. ~er n jardineiro m. ~ing n jardinagem f

gargle /'ga:gl/ vi gargarejar □ n gargarejo m

gargoyle /'ga:gɔıl/ n gárgula f

garish /'geərıʃ/ a berrante, espalhafatoso

garland /'ga:lənd/ n grinalda f

garlic /'ga:lık/ n alho m

garment /'ga:mənt/ n peça f de vestuário, roupa f

garnish /'ga:nıʃ/ vt enfeitar, guarnecer □ n guarnição f

garrison /'gærısn/ n guarnição f □ vt guarnecer

garrulous /'gærələs/ a tagarela

garter /'ga:tə(r)/ n liga f. ~-belt (Amer) cinta f de ligas

gas /gæs/ n (pl gases) gás m; (med) anestésico m; (Amer colloq: petrol) gasolina f □ vt (pt gassed) asfixiar; (mil) gasear □ vi (collog) fazer conversa fiada. ~ fire aquecedor m a gás. ~ mask máscara f anti-gás. ~ meter medidor m do gás

gash /gæʃ/ n corte m, lanho m □ vt cortar

gasket /'gæskıt/ n junta f

gasoline /'gæsəli:n/ n (Amer) gasolina f

gasp /ga:sp/ vi arfar, arquejar; (fig: with rage, surprise) ficar sem ar □ n arquejo m

gassy /'gæsı/ a gasoso; (full of gas) cheio de gás

gastric /'gæstrık/ a gástrico

gastronomy /gæ'strɒnəmı/ n gastronomia f

gate /geıt/ n portão m, (of wood) cancela f; (barrier) barreira f; (airport) porta f

gateau /'gætəʊ/ n (pl ~x /-təʊz/) bolo m grande com creme

gatecrash /'geıtkræʃ/ vt/i entrar (numa festa) sem convite

gateway /'geıtweı/ n (porta de) entrada f

gather /'gæðə(r)/ *vt* reunir, juntar; (*pick up, collect*) apanhar; (*amass, pile up*) acumular, juntar; (*conclude*) deduzir; (*cloth*) franzir □ *vi* reunir-se; (*pile up*) acumular-se. ~ **speed** ganhar velocidade. ~**ing** *n* reunião *f*

gaudy /'gɔ:dɪ/ *a* (-**ier**, -**iest**) (*bright*) berrante; (*showy*) espalhafatoso

gauge /geɪdʒ/ *n* medida *f* padrão; (*device*) indicador *m*; (*railway*) bitola *f* □ *vt* medir, avaliar

gaunt /gɔ:nt/ *a* emagrecido, macilento; (*grim*) lúgubre, desolado

gauntlet /'gɔ:ntlɪt/ *n* **run the** ~ **of** (*fig*) expor-se a. **throw down the** ~ lançar um desafio, (*P*) atirar a luva

gauze /gɔ:z/ *n* gaze *f*

gave /geɪv/ *see* **give**

gawky /'gɔ:kɪ/ *a* (-**ier**, -**iest**) desajeitado

gay /geɪ/ *a* (-**er**, -**est**) alegre; (*colloq:homosexual*) homossexual, gay

gaze /geɪz/ *vi* ~ (**at**) olhar fixamente (para) □ *n* contemplação *f*

gazelle /gə'zel/ *n* gazela *f*

GB *abbr of* **Great Britain**

gear /gɪə(r)/ *n* equipamento *m*; (*techn*) engrenagem *f*; (*auto*) velocidade *f* □ *vt* equipar; (*adapt*) adaptar. **in** ~ engrenado. **out of** ~ em ponto morto. ~**-lever** *n* alavanca *f* de mudanças

gearbox /'gɪəbɒks/ *n* caixa *f* de mudança, caixa *f* de transmissão, (*P*) caixa *f* de velocidades

geese /gi:s/ *see* **goose**

gel /dʒel/ *n* geléia *f*, (*P*) geleia *f*

gelatine /'dʒeləti:n/ *n* gelatina *f*

gelignite /'dʒelɪgnaɪt/ *n* gelignite *f*

gem /dʒem/ *n* gema *f*, pedra *f* preciosa

Gemini /'dʒemɪnaɪ/ *n* (*astr*) Gêmeos *mpl*, (*P*) Gémeos *mpl*

gender /'dʒendə(r)/ *n* gênero *m*, (*P*) género *m*

gene /dʒi:n/ *n* gene *m*

genealogy /dʒi:nɪ'ælədʒɪ/ *n* genealogia *f*

general /'dʒenrəl/ *a* geral □ *n* general *m*. ~ **election** eleições *fpl* legislativas. ~ **practitioner** *n* clínico-geral *m*, (*P*) médico *m* de família. **in** ~ em geral. ~**ly** *adv* geralmente

generaliz|**e** /'dʒenrəlaɪz/ *vt/i* generalizar. ~**ation** /-'zeɪʃn/ *n* generalização *f*

generate /'dʒenəreɪt/ *vt* gerar, produzir

generation /dʒenə'reɪʃn/ *n* geração *f*

generator /'dʒenəreɪtə(r)/ *n* gerador *m*

gener|**ous** /'dʒenərəs/ *a* generoso; (*plentiful*) abundante. ~**osity** /-'rɒsətɪ/ *n* generosidade *f*

genetic /dʒɪ'netɪk/ *a* genético. ~**s** *n* genética *f*

genial /'dʒi:nɪəl/ *a* agradável

genital /'dʒenɪtl/ *a* genital. ~**s** *npl* órgãos *mpl* genitais

genius /'dʒi:nɪəs/ *n* (*pl* -**uses**) gênio *m*, (*P*) génio *m*

genocide /'dʒenəsaɪd/ *n* genocídio *m*

gent /dʒent/ *n* **the G**~**s** (*colloq*) banheiros *mpl* de homens, (*P*) lavabos *mpl* para homens

genteel /dʒen'ti:l/ *a* elegante, fino, refinado

gentl|**e** /'dʒentl/ *a* (~**er**, ~**est**) brando, suave. ~**ness** *n* brandura *f*, suavidade *f*. ~**y** *adv* brandamente, suavemente

gentleman /'dʒentlmən/ *n* (*pl* -**men**) senhor *m*; (*well-bred*) cavalheiro *m*

genuine /'dʒenjʊm/ *a* genuíno, verdadeiro; (*belief*) sincero

geography /dʒɪ'ɒgrəfɪ/ *n* geografia *f*. ~**er** *n* geógrafo *m*. ~**ical** /dʒɪə'græfɪkl/ *a* geográfico

geolog|**y** /dʒɪ'ɒlədʒɪ/ *n* geologia *f*. ~**ical** /dʒɪə'lɒdʒɪkl/ *a* geológico. ~**ist** *n* geólogo *m*

geometr|y /dʒɪˈɒmətrɪ/ n geometria f. **~ic(al)** /dʒɪəˈmetrɪk(l)/ a geométrico

geranium /dʒəˈreɪnɪəm/ n gerânio m

geriatric /dʒerɪˈætrɪk/ a geriátrico

germ /dʒɜːm/ n germe m, micróbio m

German /ˈdʒɜːmən/ a & n alemão (m), alemã (f); (lang) alemão (m). **~ measles** rubéola f. **~ic** /dʒəˈmænɪk/ a germânico. **~y** n Alemanha f

germinate /ˈdʒɜːmɪneɪt/ vi germinar

gestation /dʒeˈsteɪʃn/ n gestação f

gesticulate /dʒeˈstɪkjʊleɪt/ vi gesticular

gesture /ˈdʒestʃə(r)/ n gesto f

get /get/ vt (pt got, pres p getting) (have) ter; (receive) receber; (catch) apanhar; (earn, win) ganhar; (fetch) ir buscar; (find) achar; (colloq: understand) entender. **~ sth to do sth** fazer com que alguém faça alg coisa □ vi ir, chegar; (become) ficar. **~ married/ready** casar-se/aprontar-se. **~ about** andar dum lado para o outro. **~ across** atravessar. **~ along or by** (manage) ir indo. **~ along or on with** entender-se com. **~ at** (reach) chegar a; (attack) atacar; (imply) insinuar. **~ away** ir-se embora; (escape) fugir. **~ back** vi voltar □ vt recuperar. **~ by** (pass) passar, escapar; (manage) aguentar-se. **~ down** descer. **~ in** entrar. **~ off** vi descer; (leave) partir; (jur) ser absolvido □ vt (remove) tirar. **~ on** (succeed) fazer progressos, ir; (be on good terms) dar-se bem. **~ out** sair. **~ out of** (fig) fugir de. **~ over** (illness) restabelecer-se de. **~ round** (person) convencer; (rule) contornar. **~ up** vi levantar-se □ vt (mount) montar. **~-up** n (colloq) apresentação f

getaway /ˈgetəweɪ/ n fuga f

geyser /ˈgiːzə(r)/ n aquecedor m; (geol) géiser m, (P) géiser m

Ghana /ˈgɑːnə/ n Gana m

ghastly /ˈgɑːstlɪ/ a (-ier, -iest) horrível; (pale) lívido

gherkin /ˈgɜːkɪn/ n pepino m pequeno para conservas, cornichão m

ghetto /ˈgetəʊ/ n (pl -os) gueto m, ghetto m

ghost /gəʊst/ n fantasma m, espectro m. **~ly** a fantasmagórico, espectral

giant /ˈdʒaɪənt/ a & n gigante (m)

gibberish /ˈdʒɪbərɪʃ/ n algaravia f, linguagem f incompreensível

gibe /dʒaɪb/ n zombaria f □ vi **~ (at)** zombar (de)

giblets /ˈdʒɪblɪts/ npl miúdos mpl, miudezas fpl

giddy /ˈgɪdɪ/ a (-ier, -iest) estonteante, vertiginoso. **be or feel ~** ter tonturas or vertigens

gift /gɪft/ n presente m, dádiva f; (ability) dom m, dote m. **~-wrap** vt (pt -wrapped) fazer um embrulho de presente

gifted /ˈgɪftɪd/ a dotado

gig /gɪg/ n (colloq) show m, sessão f de jazz etc

gigantic /dʒaɪˈgæntɪk/ a gigantesco

giggle /ˈgɪgl/ vi dar risadinhas nervosas □ n risinho m nervoso

gild /gɪld/ vt dourar

gills /gɪlz/ npl guelras fpl

gilt /gɪlt/ a & n dourado (m). **~-edged** a de toda a confiança

gimmick /ˈgɪmɪk/ n truque m, artifício m

gin /dʒɪn/ n gin m, genebra f

ginger /ˈdʒɪndʒə(r)/ n gengibre m □ a louro-avermelhado, ruivo. **~ ale**, **~ beer** cerveja f de gengibre, (P) ginger ale m

gingerbread /'dʒɪndʒəbred/ n pão m de gengibre

gingerly /'dʒɪndʒəlɪ/ adv cautelosamente

gipsy /'dʒɪpsɪ/ n = gypsy

giraffe /dʒɪ'rɑːf/ n girafa f

girder /'gɜːdə(r)/ n trave f, viga f

girdle /'gɜːdl/ n cinto m; (corset) cinta f □ vt rodear

girl /gɜːl/ n (child) menina f; (young woman) moça f, (P) rapariga f. **~-friend** n amiga f; (of boy) namorada f. **~-hood** n (of child) meninice f; (youth) juventude f

giro /'dʒaɪrəʊ/ n sistema m de transferência de crédito entre bancos; (cheque) cheque m pago pelo governo a desempregados ou doentes

girth /gɜːθ/ n circumferência f, perímetro m

gist /dʒɪst/ n essencial m

give /gɪv/ vt/i (pt gave, pp given) dar; (bend, yield) ceder. **~ away** dar; (secret) revelar, trair. **~ back** devolver. **~ in** dar-se por vencido, render-se. **~ off** emitir. **~ out** vt anunciar □ vi esgotar-se. **~ up** vt/i desistir (de), renunciar (a). **~ o.s. up** entregar-se. **~ way** ceder; (traffic) dar prioridade; (collapse) dar de si

given /'gɪvn/ see give □ a dado. **~ name** nome m de batismo, (P) baptismo

glacier /'glæsɪə(r)/ n glaciar m, geleira f

glad /glæd/ a contente. **~ly** adv com (todo o) prazer

gladden /'glædn/ vt alegrar

glam|our /'glæmə(r)/ n fascinação f, encanto m. **~orize** vt tornar fascinante. **~orous** a fascinante, sedutor

glance /glɑːns/ n relance m, olhar m □ vi **~ at** dar uma olhada a. **at first ~** à primeira vista

gland /glænd/ n glândula f

glar|e /gleə(r)/ vi brilhar intensamente, faiscar □ n luz f crua; (fig) olhar m feroz. **~e at** olhar ferozmente para. **~ing** a brilhante; (obvious) flagrante

glass /glɑːs/ n vidro m; (vessel, its contents) copo m; (mirror) espelho m. **~es** óculos mpl. **~y** a vítreo

glaze /gleɪz/ vt (door etc) envidraçar; (pottery) vidrar □ n vidrado m

gleam /gliːm/ n raio m de luz frouxa; (fig) vislumbre m □ vi luzir, brilhar

glean /gliːn/ vt catar

glee /gliː/ n alegria f. **~ful** a cheio de alegria

glib /glɪb/ a que tem a palavra fácil, verboso. **~ly** adv fluentemente, sem hesitação. **~ness** n verbosidade f

glide /glaɪd/ vi deslizar; (bird, plane) planar. **~r** /-ə(r)/ n planador m

glimmer /'glɪmə(r)/ n luz f trêmula □ vi tremular

glimpse /glɪmps/ n vislumbre m. **catch a ~ of** entrever, ver de relance

glint /glɪnt/ n brilho m, reflexo m □ vi brilhar, cintilar

glisten /'glɪsn/ vi reluzir

glitter /'glɪtə(r)/ vi luzir, resplandecer □ n esplendor m, cintilação f

gloat /gləʊt/ vi **~ over** ter um prazer maligno em, exultar com

global /'gləʊbl/ a global

globe /gləʊb/ n globo m

gloom /gluːm/ n obscuridade f; (fig) tristeza f. **~y** a sombrio; (sad) triste; (pessimistic) pessimista

glorif|y /'glɔːrɪfaɪ/ vt glorificar. **a ~ied waitress**/etc pouco mais que uma garçonete/etc

glorious /'glɔːrɪəs/ a glorioso

glory /'glɔːrɪ/ n glória f; (beauty) esplendor m □ vi **~ in** orgulhar-se de

gloss /glɒs/ n brilho m □ a brilhante □ vt ~ over minimizar, encobrir. ~y a brilhante

glossary /'glɒsərɪ/ n (pl -ries) glossário m

glove /glʌv/ n luva f. ~d a enluvado □ ~ **compartment** porta-luvas m.

glow /gləʊ/ vi arder; (person) resplandecer □ n brasa f. ~ing a (fig) entusiástico

glucose /'glu:kəʊs/ n glucose f

glue /glu:/ n cola f □ vt (pres p gluing) colar

glum /glʌm/ a (glummer, glummest) sorumbático; (dejected) abatido

glut /glʌt/ n superabundância f

glutton /'glʌtn/ n glutão m. ~ous a glutão. ~y n gula f

GMO /dʒiː'em'əʊ/ n OGM, organismo m geneticamente modificado

gnarled /na:ld/ a nodoso

gnash /næʃ/ vt ~ one's teeth ranger os dentes

gnat /næt/ n mosquito m

gnaw /nɔ:/ vt/i roer

gnome /nəʊm/ n gnomo m

go /gəʊ/ vi (3t went, pp gone) ir; (leave) ir, ir-se; (mech) andar, funcionar; (become) ficar; (be sold) vender-se; (vanish) ir-se, desaparecer □ n (pl goes) (energy) dinamismo m; (try) tentativa f; (success) sucesso m; (turn) vez f. ~ **riding** ir andar or montar a cavalo. ~ **shopping** ir às compras. be ~**ing to do** ir fazer. ~ **ahead** ir para diante. ~ **away** ir-se embora. ~ **back** voltar atrás (on com). ~ **bad** estragar-se. ~ **by** (pass) passar. ~ **down** descer; (sun) pôr-se; (ship) afundar-se. ~ **for** ir buscar; (like) gostar de; (sl: attack) atirar-se a, ir-se a (colloq). ~ **in** entrar. ~ **in for** (exam) apresentar-se a. ~ **off** ir-se; (explode) rebentar; (sound) soar; (decay)

estragar-se. ~ **on** continuar; (happen) acontecer. ~ **out** sair; (light) apagar-se. ~ **over** or **through** verificar, examinar. ~ **round** (be enough) chegar. ~ **under** ir abaixo. ~ **up** subir. ~ **without** passar sem. on the ~ em grande atividade. ~-**ahead** n luz f verde □ a dinâmico, empreendedor. ~-**between** n intermediário m. ~-**kart** n kart m. ~-**slow** n operação f tartaruga, (P) greve f de zelo

goad /gəʊd/ n aguilhoar, espicaçar

goal /gəʊl/ n meta f; (area) baliza f; (score) gol m, (P) golo m. ~-**post** n trave f

goalkeeper /'gəʊlki:pə(r)/ n goleiro m, (P) guarda-redes m

goat /gəʊt/ n cabra f

gobble /'gɒbl/ vt comer com sofreguidão, devorar

goblet /'gɒblɪt/ n taça f, cálice m

goblin /'gɒblɪn/ n duende m

God /gɒd/ n Deus m. ~-**forsaken** a miserável, abandonado

god /gɒd/ n deus m. ~-**daughter** n afilhada f. ~-**dess** n deusa f. ~-**father** n padrinho m. ~-**ly** a devoto. ~-**mother** n madrinha f. ~-**son** n afilhado m

godsend /'gɒdsend/ n achado m, dádiva f do céu

goggles /'gɒglz/ npl óculos mpl de proteção, (P) protecção

going /'gəʊɪn/ n it is slow/hard ~ é demorado/difícil □ a (price, rate) corrente, atual, (P) actual. ~-**s-on** npl acontecimentos mpl estranhos

gold /gəʊld/ n ouro m □ a de/em ouro. ~-**mine** n mina f de ouro

golden /'gəʊldən/ a de ouro; (like gold) dourado; (opportunity) único. ~ **wedding** bodas fpl de ouro

goldfish /'gəʊldfɪʃ/ n peixe m dourado/vermelho

goldsmith /'gəʊldsmɪθ/ n ourives m inv

golf /gɒlf/ n golfe m. **~ club** clube m de golfe, associação f de golfe; (stick) taco m. **~-course** n campo m de golfe. **~er** n jogador m de golfe

gone /gɒn/ see **go** □ a ido, passado. **~ six o'clock** depois das seis

gong /gɒŋ/ n gongo m

good /gʊd/ a (**better, best**) bom □ n bem m. **as ~ as** praticamente. **for ~** para sempre. **it is no ~** não adianta. **it is no ~ shouting/etc** não adianta gritar/etc. **~ afternoon** int boa(s) tarde(s). **~ evening/night** int boa(s) noite(s). **G~ Friday** Sexta-feira f Santa. **~-looking** a bonito. **~ morning** int bom dia. **~ name** bom nome m

goodbye /gʊd'baɪ/ int & n adeus (m)

goodness /'gʊdnɪs/ n bondade f. **my ~ness!** meu Deus!

goods /gʊdz/ npl (comm) mercadorias fpl. **~ train** trem m de carga, (P) comboio m de mercadorias

goodwill /gʊd'wɪl/ n boa vontade f

goose /guːs/ n (pl **geese**) ganso m. **~-flesh**, **~-pimples** ns pele f de galinha

gooseberry /'gʊzbərɪ/ n (fruit) groselha f; (bush) groselheira f

gore[1] /gɔː(r)/ n sangue m coagulado

gore[2] /gɔː(r)/ vt perfurar

gorge /gɔːdʒ/ n desfiladeiro m, garganta f □ vt **~ o.s.** empanturrar-se

gorgeous /'gɔːdʒəs/ a magnífico, maravilhoso

gorilla /gə'rɪlə/ n gorila m

gormless /'gɔːmlɪs/ a (sl) estúpido

gorse /gɔːs/ n giesta f, tojo m, urze f

gory /'gɔːrɪ/ a (**-ier, -iest**) sangrento

gosh /gɒʃ/ int puxa!, (P) caramba!

gospel /'gɒspl/ n evangelho m

gossip /'gɒsɪp/ n bisbilhotice f, fofoca f; (person) bisbilhoteiro m, fofoqueiro m □ vi (pt **gossiped**) bisbilhotar. **~y** a bisbilhoteiro, fofoqueiro

got /gɒt/ see **get**. **have ~** ter. **have ~ to do** ter de or que fazer

Gothic /'gɒθɪk/ a gótico

gouge /gaʊdʒ/ vt **~ out** arrancar

gourmet /'gʊəmeɪ/ n gastrónomo m, (P) gastrónomo m, gourmet m

gout /gaʊt/ n gota f

govern /'gʌvn/ vt/i governar. **~ess** n preceptora f. **~or** n governador m; (of school, hospital etc) diretor m, (P) director m

government /'gʌvənmənt/ n governo m. **~al** /-'mentl/ a governamental

gown /gaʊn/ n vestido m; (of judge, teacher) toga f

GP abbr see **general practitioner**

grab /græb/ vt (pt **grabbed**) agarrar, apanhar

grace /greɪs/ n graça f □ vt honrar; (adorn) ornar. **say ~** dar graças. **~ful** a gracioso

gracious /'greɪʃəs/ a gracioso; (kind) amável, afável

grade /greɪd/ n categoria f; (of goods) classe f, qualidade f; (on scale) grau m; (school mark) nota f □ vt classificar

gradient /'greɪdɪənt/ n gradiente m, declive m

gradual /'grædʒʊəl/ a gradual, progressivo. **~ly** adv gradualmente

graduate[1] /'grædʒʊət/ n diplomado m, graduado m, licenciado m

graduat[e][2] /'grædʒʊeɪt/ vt/i formar(-se). **~ion** /-'eɪʃn/ n colação f de grau, (P) formatura f

graffiti /grə'fiːtɪ/ npl graffiti mpl

graft /grɑːft/ n (med, bot) enxerto m; (work) batalha f □ vt enxertar; (work) batalhar

grain /greɪn/ n grão m; (collectively) cereais mpl; (in paper) veio *m*. **against the ~** (*fig*) contra a maneira de ser

gram /græm/ *n* grama *m*

grammar /ˈgræmə(r)/ *n* gramática *f*. **~atical** /ɡrəˈmætɪkl/ *a* gramatical

grand /grænd/ *a* (-er, -est) grandioso, magnífico; (*duke, master*) grão. **~ piano** piano *m* de cauda.

grandchild /ˈgræntʃaɪld/ *n* (*pl* -children) neto *m*. **~daughter** *n* neta *f*. **~father** *n* avô *m*. **~mother** *n* avó *f*. **~parents** *npl* avós *mpl*. **~son** *n* neto *m*

grandeur /ˈgrændʒə(r)/ *n* grandeza *f*

grandiose /ˈgrændɪəʊs/ *a* grandioso

grandstand /ˈgrændstænd/ *n* tribuna *f* principal

granite /ˈgrænɪt/ *n* granito *m*

grant /grɑːnt/ *vt* conceder; (*a request*) ceder a; (*admit*) admitir (**that** que) □ *n* subsídio *m*; (*univ*) bolsa *f*. **take for ~ed** ter como coisa garantida, contar com

grape /greɪp/ *n* uva *f*

grapefruit /ˈgreɪpfruːt/ *n* *inv* grapefruit *m*, toronja *f*

graph /grɑːf/ *n* gráfico *m*

graphic /ˈgræfɪk/ *a* gráfico; (*fig*) vívido. **~s** *npl* (*comput*) gráficos *mpl*

grapple /ˈgræpl/ *vi* **~ with** estar engalfinhado com; (*fig*) estar às voltas com

grasp /grɑːsp/ *vt* agarrar; (*understand*) compreender □ *n* domínio *m*; (*reach*) alcance *m*; (*fig*: *understanding*) compreensão *f*

grasping /ˈgrɑːspɪŋ/ *a* ganancioso

grass /grɑːs/ *n* erva *f*; (*lawn*) grama *f*, (P) relva *f*; (*pasture*) pastagem *f*; (*sl*: *informer*) delator *m* □ *vt* cobrir com grama; (*sl*: *betray*) delatar. **~ roots** (*pol*) bases *fpl*. **~y** *a* coberto de erva

grasshopper /ˈgrɑːshɒpə(r)/ *n* gafanhoto *m*

grate[1] /greɪt/ *n* (*fireplace*) lareira *f*; (*frame*) grelha *f*

grate[2] /greɪt/ *vt* ralar □ *vi* ranger. **~ one's teeth** ranger os dentes. **~r** /-ə(r)/ *n* ralador *m*

grateful /ˈgreɪtfl/ *a* grato, agradecido. **~ly** *adv* com reconhecimento, com gratidão

gratify /ˈgrætɪfaɪ/ *vt* (*pt* -**fied**) contentar, satisfazer. **~ing** *a* gratificante

grating /ˈgreɪtɪŋ/ *n* grade *f*

gratis /ˈgreɪtɪs/ *a* & *adv* grátis (*invar*), de graça

gratitude /ˈgrætɪtjuːd/ *n* gratidão *f*, reconhecimento *m*

gratuitous /grəˈtjuːɪtəs/ *a* gratuito; (*uncalled-for*) sem motivo

gratuity /grəˈtjuːətɪ/ *n* gratificação *f*, gorjeta *f*

grave[1] /greɪv/ *n* cova *f*, sepultura *f*, túmulo *m*

grave[2] /greɪv/ *a* (-er, -est) grave, sério. **~ly** *adv* gravemente

grave[3] /grɑːv/ *a* **~ accent** acento *m* grave

gravel /ˈgrævl/ *n* cascalho *m* miúdo, saibro *m*

gravestone /ˈgreɪvstəʊn/ *n* lápide *f*, campa *f*

graveyard /ˈgreɪvjɑːd/ *n* cemitério *m*

gravity /ˈgrævətɪ/ *n* gravidade *f*

gravy /ˈgreɪvɪ/ *n* molho *m* (de carne)

graze[1] /greɪz/ *vt*/*i* pastar

graze[2] /greɪz/ *vt* roçar; (*scrape*) esfolar □ *n* esfoladura *f*, (P) esfoladela *f*

greas|**e** /griːs/ *n* gordura *f* □ *vt* engordurar; (*culin*) untar; (*mech*) lubrificar. **~e-proof paper** papel *m* vegetal. **~y** *a* gorduroso

great /greɪt/ *a* (-er, -est) grande; (*colloq*: *splendid*) esplêndido. **G~ Britain** Grã-Bretanha *f*. **~-grandfather** *n* bisavô *m*. **~-grandmother** *f* bisavó *f*. **~ly** *adv* grandemente, muito. **~ness** *n* grandeza *f*

Great Britain /greɪt'brɪtən/ n Grã-Bretanha f

Greece /gri:s/ n Grécia f

greed /gri:d/ n cobiça f, ganância f; (for food) gula f. **~y** a cobiçoso, ganancioso; (for food) guloso

Greek /gri:k/ a & n grego (m)

green /gri:n/ a (-er, -est) verde □ n verde m; (grass) gramado m, (P) relvado m. **~s** hortaliças fpl. **~ belt** zona f verde, paisagem f protegida. **~ light** luz f verde. **~ery** n verdura f

greengrocer /'gri:nɡrəʊsə(r)/ n quitandeiro m, (P) vendedor m de hortaliças

greenhouse /'gri:nhaʊs/ n estufa f. **~ effect** efeito estufa

Greenland /'gri:nlənd/ n Groenlândia f

greet /gri:t/ vt acolher. **~ing** n saudação f; (welcome) acolhimento m. **~ings** npl cumprimentos mpl; (Christmas etc) votos mpl, desejos mpl

gregarious /grɪ'ɡeərɪəs/ a gregário; (person) sociável

grenade /grɪ'neɪd/ n granada f

grew /gru:/ see **grow**

grey /greɪ/ a (-er, -est) cinzento; (of hair) grisalho □ n cinzento m

greyhound /'greɪhaʊnd/ n galgo m

grid /grɪd/ n (grating) gradeamento m, grade f; (electr) rede f

grief /gri:f/ n dor f. **come to ~** acabar mal

grievance /'gri:vns/ n razão f de queixa

grieve /gri:v/ vt sofrer, afligir □ vi sofrer. **~ for** chorar por

grill /grɪl/ n grelha f; (food) grelhado m; (place) grill m □ vt grelhar; (question) submeter a interrogatório cerrado, apertar com perguntas □ vi grelhar

grille /grɪl/ n grade f; (of car) grelha f

grim /grɪm/ a (grimmer, grimmest) sinistro; (without mercy)

implacável

grimace /grɪ'meɪs/ n careta f □ vi fazer careta(s)

grim|**e** /graɪm/ n sujeira f. **~y** a encardido, sujo

grin /grɪn/ vi (pt grinned) sorrir abertamente, dar um sorriso largo □ n sorriso m aberto

grind /graɪnd/ vt (pt ground) triturar; (coffee) moer; (sharpen) amolar, afiar. **~ one's teeth** ranger os dentes. **to a halt** parar freando lentamente

grip /grɪp/ vt (pt gripped) agarrar; (interest) prender □ n (of hands) aperto m; (control) controle m, domínio m. **come to ~s with** arcar com. **~ping** a apaixonante

grisly /'grɪzlɪ/ a (-ier, -iest) macabro, horrível

gristle /'grɪsl/ n cartilagem f

grit /grɪt/ n areia f, grão m de areia; (fig: pluck) coragem f, fortaleza f □ vt (pt gritted) (road) jogar areia em; (teeth) cerrar

groan /grəʊn/ vi gemer □ n gemido m

grocer /'grəʊsə(r)/ n dono/a m/f de mercearia. **~ies** npl artigos mpl de mercearia. **~y** n (shop) mercearia f

groggy /'grɒgɪ/ a (-ier, -iest) grogue, fraco das pernas

groin /grɔɪn/ n virilha f

groom /gru:m/ n noivo m; (for horses) moço m de estrebaria □ vt (horse) tratar de; (fig) preparar

groove /gru:v/ n ranhura f; (for door, window) calha f; (in record) estria f; (fig) rotina f

grope /grəʊp/ vi tatear. **~ for** procurar às cegas

gross /grəʊs/ a (-er, -est) (vulgar) grosseiro; (flagrant) flagrante; (of error) crasso; (of weight, figure etc) bruto □ n (pl invar) grosa f. **~ly** adv grosseiramente; (very) extremamente

grotesque /grəʊ'tesk/ a grotesco

grotty /'grɒtɪ/ a (sl) sórdido

grouch /graʊtʃ/ vi (colloq) ralhar. ~y a (colloq) rabugento

ground[1] /graʊnd/ n chão m, solo m; (area) terreno m; (reason) razão f, motivo m. ~s jardins mpl; (of coffee) borra(s) f (pl) □ vt/i (naut) encalhar; (plane) reter em terra. ~ floor térreo m, (P) rés-do-chão m. ~less a infundado, sem fundamento

ground[2] /graʊnd/ see **grind**

grounding /'graʊndɪŋ/ n bases fpl, conhecimentos mpl básicos

groundsheet /'graʊndʃiːt/ n impermeável m para o chão

groundwork /'graʊndwɜːk/ n trabalhos mpl de base or preliminares

group /gruːp/ n grupo m □ vt/i agrupar(-se)

grouse[1] /graʊs/ n (pl invar) galo m silvestre

grouse[2] /graʊs/ vi (colloq: grumble) resmungar; (colloq: complain) queixar-se

grovel /'grɒvl/ vi (pt grovelled) humilhar-se; (fig) rebaixar-se

grow /grəʊ/ vi (pt grew, pp grown) crescer; (become) tornar-se □ vt cultivar. ~ old envelhecer. ~ up crescer, tornar-se adulto. ~er n cultivador m, produtor m. ~ing a crescente

growl /graʊl/ vi rosnar □ n rosnadela f

grown /grəʊn/ see **grow** □ a ~ man homem feito. ~-up a adulto □ n pessoa f adulta

growth /grəʊθ/ n crescimento m; (increase) aumento m; (med) tumor m

grub /grʌb/ n larva f, (sl: food) bóia f, rango m, (P) comida f

grubby /'grʌbɪ/ a (-ier, -iest) sujo, porco

grudge /grʌdʒ/ vt dar/reconhecer de má vontade □ n má vontade f.

~ **doing** fazer de má vontade. ~ **sb sth** dar alg a alguém má vontade. **have a ~ against** ter ressentimento contra. **grudgingly** adv relutantemente

gruelling /'gruːəlɪŋ/ a estafante, extenuante

gruesome /'gruːsəm/ a macabro

gruff /grʌf/ a (-er, -est) carrancudo, rude

grumble /'grʌmbl/ vi resmungar (at contra, por)

grumpy /'grʌmpɪ/ a (-ier, -iest) mal-humorado, rabugento

grunt /grʌnt/ vi grunhir □ n grunhido m

guarantee /gærən'tiː/ n garantia f □ vt garantir

guard /gɑːd/ vt guardar, proteger □ vi ~ **against** precaver-se contra □ n guarda f; (person) guarda m; (on train) condutor m. ~ian n guardião m, defensor m; (of orphan) tutor m

guarded /'gɑːdɪd/ a cauteloso, circunspeto, (P) circunspecto

guerrilla /gə'rɪlə/ n guerrilheiro m, (P) guerrilha m. ~ **warfare** guerrilha f, guerra f de guerrilhas

guess /ges/ vt/i adivinhar; (suppose) supor □ n suposição f, conjetura f, (P) conjectura f

guesswork /'geswɜːk/ n suposição f, conjetura f (pl), (P) conjectura(s) f (pl)

guest /gest/ n convidado m; (in hotel) hóspede mf. ~-**house** n pensão f

guffaw /gə'fɔː/ n gargalhada f □ vi rir à(s) gargalhada(s)

guidance /'gaɪdns/ n orientação f, direção f, (P) direcção f

guide /gaɪd/ n guia mf □ vt guiar. ~d **missile** míssil m guiado; (remote-control) míssil m teleguiado. ~-**dog** n cão m de cego, cão-guia m. ~-**lines** npl diretrizes fpl, (P) directrizes fpl

Guide /gaɪd/ n Guia f

guidebook /ˈgaɪdbʊk/ n guia m (turístico)

guild /gɪld/ n corporação f

guile /gaɪl/ n astúcia f, manha f

guilt /gɪlt/ n culpa f. ~y a culpado

guinea-pig /ˈgɪnɪpɪg/ n cobaia f, porquinho-da-India m

guitar /gɪˈtɑː(r)/ n guitarra f, violão m, (P) viola f. ~ist n guitarrista mf, tocador m de violão, (P) de viola

gulf /gʌlf/ n golfo m; (hollow) abismo m

gull /gʌl/ n gaivota f

gullible /ˈgʌləbl/ a crédulo

gully /ˈgʌlɪ/ n barranco m; (drain) sarjeta f

gulp /gʌlp/ vt engulir, devorar □ vi engolir em seco □ n trago m

gum¹ /gʌm/ n (anat) gengiva f

gum² /gʌm/ n goma f; (chewing-gum) chiclete m, goma f elástica, (P) pastilha f □ vt (pt gummed) colar

gumboot /ˈgʌmbuːt/ n bota f de borracha

gumption /ˈgʌmpʃn/ n (colloq) iniciativa f e bom senso m, cabeça f, juízo m

gun /gʌn/ n (pistol) pistola f; (rifle) espingarda f; (cannon) canhão m □ vt (pt gunned) ~ down abater a tiro

gunfire /ˈgʌnfaɪə(r)/ n tiroteio m

gunman /ˈgʌnmən/ n (pl -men) bandido m armado

gunpowder /ˈgʌnpaʊdə(r)/ n pólvora f

gunshot /ˈgʌnʃɒt/ n tiro m

gurgle /ˈgɜːgl/ n gorgolejo m □ vi gorgolejar

gush /gʌʃ/ vi jorrar □ n jorro m. ~ing a efusivo, derretido

gust /gʌst/ n (of wind) rajada f; (of smoke) nuvem f. ~y a ventoso

gusto /ˈgʌstəʊ/ n gosto m, entusiasmo m

gut /gʌt/ n tripa f. ~s (belly) barriga f; (colloq: courage) coragem f □ vt (pt gutted) estripar; (fish) limpar; (fire) destruir o interior de

gutter /ˈgʌtə(r)/ n calha f, canaleta f; (in street) sarjeta f, valeta f

guy /gaɪ/ n (sl: man) cara m, (P) tipo m (colloq)

guzzle /ˈgʌzl/ vt/i comer/beber com sofreguidão, encher-se (de)

gym /dʒɪm/ n (colloq: gymnasium) ginásio m; (colloq: gymnastics) ginástica f. ~-slip n uniforme m escolar

gym|nasium /dʒɪmˈneɪzɪəm/ n ginásio m. ~nast /ˈdʒɪmnæst/ n ginasta mf. ~nastics /-ˈnæstɪks/ npl ginástica f

gynaecolog|y /gaɪnɪˈkɒlədʒɪ/ n ginecologia f. ~ist n ginecologista mf

gypsy /ˈdʒɪpsɪ/ n cigano m

gyrate /dʒaɪˈreɪt/ vi girar

H

haberdashery /ˈhæbədæʃərɪ/ n armarinho m, (P) retrosaria f

habit /ˈhæbɪt/ n hábito m, costume m; (costume) hábito m. be in/get into the ~ of ter/apanhar o hábito de

habit|able /ˈhæbɪtəbl/ a habitável. ~ation /-ˈteɪʃn/ n habitação f

habitat /ˈhæbɪtæt/ n habitat m

habitual /həˈbɪtʃʊəl/ a habitual, costumeiro; (smoker, liar) inveterado. ~ly adv habitualmente

hack¹ /hæk/ n (horse) cavalo m de aluguel; (writer) escrevinhador (pej) m. ~er (comput) micreiro m

hack² /hæk/ vt cortar, despedaçar. ~ to pieces cortar em pedaços

hackneyed /ˈhæknɪd/ a banal, batido

had /hæd/ *see* have

haddock /'hædək/ *n invar* hadoque *m*, eglefim *m*. **smoked ~** hadoque *m* fumado

haemorrhage /'hemərɪdʒ/ *n* hemorragia *f*

haemorrhoids /'hemərɔɪdz/ *npl* hemorróidas *fpl*

haggard /'hægəd/ *a* desfigurado, com o rosto desfeito, magro e macilento

haggle /'hægl/ *vi* **~ (over)** regatear

hail[1] /heɪl/ *vt* saudar; (*taxi*) fazer sinal para, chamar □ *vi* **~ from** vir de

hail[2] /heɪl/ *n* granizo *m*, (*P*) saraiva *f*, (*P*) chuva de pedra *f* □ *vi* chover granizo, (*P*) saraivar

hailstone /'heɪlstəʊn/ *n* pedra *f* de granizo

hair /heə(r)/ *n* (*on head*) cabelo(s) *m*(*pl*); (*on body*) pêlos *mpl*; (*single strand*) cabelo *m*; (*of animal*) pêlo *m*. **~-do** *n* (*colloq*) penteado *m*. **~-dryer** *n* secador *m* de cabelo. **~-raising** *a* horripilante, de pôr os cabelos em pé. **~-style** *n* estilo *m* de penteado

hairbrush /'heəbrʌʃ/ *n* escova *f* para o cabelo

haircut /'heəkʌt/ *n* corte *m* de cabelo

hairdresser /'heədresə(r)/ *n* cabeleireiro *m*, cabeleireira *f*

hairpin /'heəpɪn/ *n* grampo *m*, (*P*) gancho *m* para o cabelo. **~ bend** curva *f* fechada, quase em W

hairy /'heərɪ/ *a* (**-ier, -iest**) peludo, cabeludo; (*sl: terrifying*) de pôr os cabelos em pé, horripilante

hake /heɪk/ *n* (*pl invar*) abrótea *f*

half /hɑːf/ *n* (*pl* **halves** /hɑːvz/) metade *f*, meio *m* □ *a* meio □ *adv* ao meio. **~ a dozen** meia dúzia. **~ an hour** meia hora. **~-caste** *n* mestiço *m*. **~-hearted** *a* sem grande entusiasmo. **~-term** *n* férias *fpl* no

meio do trimestre. **~-time** *n* meio-tempo *m*. **~-way** *a* & *adv* a meio caminho. **~-wit** *n* idiota *mf*. **go halves** dividir as despesas

halibut /'hælɪbət/ *n* (*pl invar*) halibute *m*

hall /hɔːl/ *n* sala *f*; (*entrance*) vestíbulo *m*, entrada *f*; (*mansion*) solar *m*. **~ of residence** residência *f* de estudantes

hallmark /'hɔːlmɑːk/ *n* (*on gold etc*) marca *f* do contraste; (*fig*) cunho *m*, selo *m*

hallo /hə'ləʊ/ *int* & *n* (*greeting, surprise*) olá; (*on phone*) alô

hallow /'hæləʊ/ *vt* consagrar, santificar

Halloween /hæləʊ'iːn/ *n* véspera *f* do Dia de Todos os Santos

hallucination /həluːsɪ'neɪʃn/ *n* alucinação *f*

halo /'heɪləʊ/ *n* (*pl* **-oes**) halo *m*, auréola *f*

halt /hɔːlt/ *n* parada *f*, (*P*) paragem *f* □ *vt* deter, fazer parar □ *vi* fazer alto, parar

halve /hɑːv/ *vt* dividir ao meio; (*time etc*) reduzir à metade

ham /hæm/ *n* presunto *m*

hamburger /'hæmbɜːgə(r)/ *n* hambúrguer *m*, (*P*) hamburgo *m*

hamlet /'hæmlɪt/ *n* aldeola *f*, lugarejo *m*

hammer /'hæmə(r)/ *n* martelo *m* □ *vt/i* martelar; (*fig*) bater com força

hammock /'hæmək/ *n* rede *f* (de dormir)

hamper[1] /'hæmpə(r)/ *n* cesto *m*, (*P*) cabaz *m*

hamper[2] /'hæmpə(r)/ *vt* dificultar, atrapalhar

hamster /'hæmstə(r)/ *n* hamster *m*

hand /hænd/ *n* mão *f*; (*of clock*) ponteiro *m*; (*writing*) letra *f*; (*worker*) trabalhador *m*; (*cards*) mão *f*; (*measure*) palmo *m*. (**help-ing**) **~** ajuda *f*, mão *f* □ *vt* dar,

entregar. **at** ~ à mão. ~-
baggage *n* bagagem *f* de mão.
~ **in** or **over** entregar. ~ **out**
distribuir. ~-**out** *n* impresso *m*,
folheto *m*; (*money*) esmola *f*, donativo *m*. **on the one** ~... **on
the other** ~ por um lado ... por
outro. **out of** ~ incontrolável. **to**
~ à mão

handbag /'hændbæg/ *n* carteira *f*,
bolsa de mão *f*, mala de mão *f*
handbook /'hændbʊk/ *n* manual
m
handbrake /'hændbreɪk/ *n* freio
m de mão, (*P*) travão *m* de mão
handcuffs /'hændkʌfs/ *npl* algemas *fpl*
handful /'hændfʊl/ *n* mão-cheia *f*,
punhado *m*; (*a few*) punhado *m*;
(*difficult task*) mão-de-obra *f*.
she's a ~ (*colloq*) ela é danada
handicap /'hændɪkæp/ *n* (*in competition*) handicap *m*, (*disadvantage*) desvantagem *f* □ *vt* (*pt*
handicapped) prejudicar. ~**ped**
a deficiente. **mentally** ~**ped** deficiente mental
handicraft /'hændɪkrɑːft/ *n* artesanato *m*, trabalho *m* manual
handiwork /'hændɪwɜːk/ *n* obra *f*,
trabalho *m*
handkerchief /'hæŋkətʃɪf/ *n* lenço *m*
handle /'hændl/ *n* (*of door etc*) maçaneta *f*, puxador *m*; (*of cup etc*)
asa *f*; (*of implement*) cabo *m*; (*of
pan etc*) alça *f*, (*P*) pega *f* □ *vt*
(*touch*) manusear, tocar; (*operate
with hands*) manejar; (*deal in*)
negociar em; (*deal with*) tratar
de; (*person*) lidar com. **fly off
the** ~ (*colloq*) perder as estri-
beiras
handlebar /'hændlbɑː(r)/ *n* guidão *m*, (*P*) guiador *m*
handmade /'hændmeɪd/ *a* feito à
mão
handshake /'hændʃeɪk/ *n* aperto
m de mão

handsome /'hænsəm/ *a* bonito;
(*fig*) generoso
handwriting /'hændraɪtɪŋ/ *n* letra *f*, caligrafia *f*
handy /'hændɪ/ *a* (-**ier**, -**iest**)
a (*convenient*, *useful*) útil,
prático; (*person*) jeitoso; (*near*) à
mão
handyman /'hændɪmæn/ *n* (*pl
-men*) faz-tudo *m*
hang /hæŋ/ *vt* (*pt* **hung**) pendu-
rar, suspender; (*head*) baixar;
(*pt* **hanged**) (*criminal*) enforcar
□ *vi* estar dependurado, pender;
(*criminal*) ser enforcado. **get
the** ~ **of** (*colloq*) pegar o jeito
de, (*P*) apanhar. ~ **about** andar
por aí. ~ **back** hesitar. ~-
gliding *n* asa *f* delta. ~ **on**
(*wait*) aguardar. ~ **on to** (*hold
tightly*) agarrar-se a. ~ **out** (*sl:
live*) morar. ~ **up** (*phone*)
desligar. ~-**up** *n* (*sl*) complexo *m*
hangar /'hæŋə(r)/ *n* hangar *m*
hanger /'hæŋə(r)/ *n* (*for clothes*)
cabide *m*. ~-**on** *n* parasita *m*
hangover /'hæŋəʊvə(r)/ *n* (*from
drinking*) ressaca *f*
hanker /'hæŋkə(r)/ *vi* ~ **after**
ansiar por, suspirar por
haphazardly /hæp'hæzædlɪ/ *adv* ao
acaso, à sorte, a fortuito, casual
happen /'hæpən/ *vi* acontecer,
suceder. **he** ~**s to be out** por
acaso ele não está. ~**ing** *n* acontecimento *m*
happ|y /'hæpɪ/ *a* (-**ier**, -**iest**) feliz.
be ~**y with** estar contente com.
~-**y-go-lucky** *a* despreocupado.
~**ily** *adv* com satisfação; (*fortunately*) felizmente. **she smiled
** ~**ily** ela sorriu feliz. ~**iness** *n*
felicidade *f*
harass /'hærəs/ *vt* amofinar, atormentar, perseguir. ~**ment** *n*
amofinação *f*, perseguição *f*. **sexual** ~**ment** assédio *m* sexual
harbour /'hɑːbə(r)/ *n* porto *m*;
(*shelter*) abrigo *m* □ *vt* abrigar,

dar asilo a; (*fig: in the mind*) ocultar, obrigar

hard /ha:d/ *a* (**-er**, **-est**) duro; (*difficult*) difícil □ *adv* muito, intensamente; (*look*) fixamente; (*pull*) com força; (*think*) a fundo, a sério. **~back** *n* livro *m* encadernado. **~-boiled egg** ovo *m* cozido. **~ by** muito perto. **~ disk** disco *m* rígido, (P) duro. **~-headed** *a* realista, prático. **~ of hearing** meio surdo. **~ shoulder** acostamento *m*, (P) berma *f* alcatroada. **~ up** (*colloq*) sem dinheiro, teso (*sl*), liso (*sl*). **~ water** água *f* dura

hardboard /ˈhaːdbɔːd/ *n* madeira *f* compensada, madeira *f* prensada, (P) tabopan *m*

harden /ˈhaːdn/ *vt/i* endurecer. **~ed** *a* (*callous*) calejado; (*robust*) enrijado

hardly /ˈhaːdlɪ/ *adv* mal, dificilmente, a custo. **~ ever** quase nunca

hardship /ˈhaːdʃɪp/ *n* provação *f*, adversidade *f*; (*suffering*) sofrimento *m*; (*financial*) privação *f*

hardware /ˈhaːdweə(r)/ *n* ferragens *fpl*; (*comput*) hardware *m*

hardy /ˈhaːdɪ/ *a* (**-ier**, **-iest**) resistente

hare /heə(r)/ *n* lebre *f*

hark /haːk/ *vi* **~ back to** voltar a, recordar

harm /haːm/ *n* mal *m* □ *vt* prejudicar, fazer mal a. **~ful** *a* prejudicial, nocivo. **~less** *a* inofensivo. **out of ~'s way** a salvo. **there's no ~ in** não há mal em

harmonica /haːˈmɒnɪkə/ *n* gaita *f* de boca, (P) beiços

harmon|y /ˈhaːmənɪ/ *n* harmonia *f*. **~ious** /-ˈməʊnɪəs/ *a* harmonioso. **~ize** *vt/i* harmonizar(-se)

harness /ˈhaːnɪs/ *n* arreios *mpl* □ *vt* arrear; (*fig: use*) aproveitar, utilizar

harp /haːp/ *n* harpa *f* □ *vi* **~ on (about)** repisar. **~ ist** *n* harpista *mf*

harpoon /haːˈpuːn/ *n* arpão *m*

harpsichord /ˈhaːpsɪkɔːd/ *n* cravo *m*

harrowing /ˈhærəʊɪŋ/ *a* dilacerante, lancinante

harsh /haːʃ/ *a* (**-er**, **-est**) duro, severo; (*texture*, *voice*) áspero; (*light*) cru; (*colour*) gritante; (*climate*) rigoroso. **~ly** *adv* duramente. **~ness** *n* dureza *f*

harvest /ˈhaːvɪst/ *n* colheita *f*, ceifa *f* □ *vt* colher, ceifar

has /hæz/ *see* **have**

hash /hæʃ/ *n* picadinho *m*, carne *f* cozida; (*fig: jumble*) bagunça *f*. **make a ~ of** fazer uma bagunça

hashish /ˈhæʃɪʃ/ *n* haxixe *m*

hassle /ˈhæsl/ *n* (*colloq: quarrel*) discussão *f*; (*colloq: struggle*) dificuldade *f* □ *vt* (*colloq*) aborrecer

haste /heɪst/ *n* pressa *f*. **make ~** apressar-se

hasten /ˈheɪsn/ *vt/i* apressar(-se)

hast|y /ˈheɪstɪ/ *a* (**-ier**, **-iest**) apressado; (*too quick*) precipitado. **~ily** *adv* às pressas, precipitadamente

hat /hæt/ *n* chapéu *m*

hatch[1] /hætʃ/ *n* (*for food*) postigo *m*; (*naut*) escotilha *f*

hatch[2] /hætʃ/ *vt/i* chocar; (*a plot etc*) tramar, urdir

hatchback /ˈhætʃbæk/ *n* carro *m* de três ou cinco portas

hatchet /ˈhætʃɪt/ *n* machadinha *f*

hate /heɪt/ *n* ódio *m* □ *vt* odiar, detestar. **~ful** *a* odioso, detestável

hatred /ˈheɪtrɪd/ *n* ódio *m*

haughty /ˈhɔːtɪ/ *a* (**-ier**, **-iest**) altivo, soberbo, arrogante

haul /hɔːl/ *vt* arrastar, puxar; (*goods*) transportar em camião □ *n* (*booty*) presa *f*; (*fish caught*) apanha *f*; (*distance*) percurso *m*. **~age** *n* transporte *m* de cargas.

~ier n (firm) transportadora f rodoviária; (person) fretador m

haunt /hɔːnt/ vt rondar, freqüentar, (P) frequentar; (ghost) assombrar; (thought) obcecar □ n lugar m favorito. **~ed house** casa f mal-assombrada

have /hæv/ vt (3 sing pres **has**, pt **had**) ter; (bath etc) tomar; (meal) fazer; (walk) dar □ v aux ter. **~ done** ter feito. **~ it out (with)** pôr a coisa em pratos limpos, pedir uma explicação (para). **~ sth done** mandar fazer alg coisa

haven /ˈheɪvn/ n porto m; (refuge) refúgio m

haversack /ˈhævəsæk/ n mochila f

havoc /ˈhævək/ n estragos mpl. **play ~ with** causar estragos em

hawk[1] /hɔːk/ n falcão m

hawk[2] /hɔːk/ vt vender de porta em porta. **~er** n vendedor m ambulante

hawthorn /ˈhɔːθɔːn/ n pilriteiro m, estrepeiro m

hay /heɪ/ n feno m. **~ fever** febre f do feno

haystack /ˈheɪstæk/ n palheiro m, (P) meda f de feno

haywire /ˈheɪwaɪə(r)/ a **go ~** (colloq) ficar transtornado

hazard /ˈhæzəd/ n risco m □ vt arriscar. **~ warning lights** pisca-alerta m. **~ous** a arriscado

haze /heɪz/ n bruma f, neblina f, cerração f

hazel /ˈheɪzl/ n aveleira f. **~nut** n avelã f

hazy /ˈheɪzɪ/ a (-ier, -iest) brumoso, encoberto; (fig: vague) vago

he /hiː/ pron ele □ n macho m

head /hed/ n cabeça f; (chief) chefe m; (of beer) espuma f □ a principal □ vt encabeçar, estar à frente de □ vi ~ **for** dirigir-se para. **~-dress** n toucador m. **~-first** de cabeça. **~-on** a frontal □

adv de frente. **~s or tails?** cara ou coroa? **~ waiter** chefe de garçons m, (P) dos criados. **~er** n (football) cabeçada f

headache /ˈhedeɪk/ n dor f de cabeça

heading /ˈhedɪŋ/ n cabeçalho m, título m; (subject category) rubrica f

headlamp /ˈhedlæmp/ n farol m

headland /ˈhedlənd/ n promontório m

headlight /ˈhedlaɪt/ n farol m

headline /ˈhedlaɪn/ n título m, cabeçalho m

headlong /ˈhedlɒŋ/ a de cabeça; (rash) precipitado □ adv de cabeça; (rashly) precipitadamente

head|master /hedˈmɑːstə(r)/ n diretor m, (P) director m. **~mistress** n diretora f, (P) directora f

headphone /ˈhedfəʊn/ n fone m de cabeça, (P) auscultador m

headquarters /ˈhedkwɔːtəz/ npl sede f; (mil) quartel m general

headrest /ˈhedrest/ n apoio m para a cabeça

headroom /ˈhedruːm/ n (auto) espaço m para a cabeça; (bridge) limite m de altura, altura f máxima

headstrong /ˈhedstrɒŋ/ a teimoso

headway /ˈhedweɪ/ n progresso m. **make ~** fazer progressos

heady /ˈhedɪ/ a (-ier, -iest) empolgante

heal /hiːl/ vt/i curar(-se), sarar; (wound) cicatrizar

health /helθ/ n saúde f. **~ centre** posto m de saúde. **~ foods** alimentos mpl naturais, (P) a saudável, sadio

heap /hiːp/ n monte m, pilha f □ vt amontoar, empilhar. **~s of money** (colloq) dinheiro aos montes (colloq)

hear /hɪə(r)/ vt/i (pt **heard** /hɜːd/) ouvir. **~, hear!** apoiado!

from ter notícias de. **~ of** *or* **about** ouvir falar de. **I won't ~ of it** nem quero ouvir falar nisso. **~ing** *n* ouvido *m*, audição *f*; (*jur*) audiência *f*. **~ing-aid** *n* aparelho *m* de audição

hearsay /ˈhɪəseɪ/ *n* boato *m*. **it's only ~** é só por ouvir dizer

hearse /hɜːs/ *n* carro *m* funerário

heart /hɑːt/ *n* coração *m*. **~s** (*cards*) copas *fpl*. **at ~** no fundo. **by ~** de cor. **~ attack** ataque *m* de coração. **~-beat** *n* pulsação *f*, batida *f*. **~-breaking** *a* de cortar o coração. **~-broken** *a* com o coração partido, desfeito. **~-to-heart** *a* com o coração nas mãos. **lose ~** perder a coragem, desanimar

heartburn /ˈhɑːtbɜːn/ *n* azia *f*

hearten /ˈhɑːtn/ *vt* animar, encorajar

heartfelt /ˈhɑːtfelt/ *a* sincero, sentido

hearth /hɑːθ/ *n* lareira *f*

heartless /ˈhɑːtlɪs/ *a* insensível, desalmado, cruel

heart|y /ˈhɑːtɪ/ *a* (**-ier, -iest**) caloroso; (*meal*) abundante. **~ily** *adv* calorosamente; (*eat, laugh*) com vontade

heat /hiːt/ *n* calor *m*; (*fig*) ardor *m*; (*contest*) eliminatória *f* □ *vt/i* aquecer. **~-stroke** *n* insolação *f*. **~-wave** *n* onda *f* de calor. **~er** *n* aquecedor *m*. **~ing** *n* aquecimento *m*

heated /ˈhiːtɪd/ *a* (*fig*) acalorado, aceso

heathen /ˈhiːðn/ *n* pagão *m*, pagã *f*

heather /ˈheðə(r)/ *n* urze *f*

heav|e /hiːv/ *vt/i* (*lift*) içar; (*a sigh*) soltar; (*retch*) ter náuseas; (*colloq: throw*) atirar

heaven /ˈhevn/ *n* céu *m*. **~ly** *a* celestial; (*colloq*) divino

heav|y /ˈhevɪ/ *a* (**-ier, -iest**) pesado; (*blow, rain*) forte; (*cold, drinker*) grande; (*traffic*) intenso.

~ily *adv* pesadamente; (*drink, smoke etc*) inveterado

heavyweight /ˈhevɪweɪt/ *n* (*boxing*) peso-pesado *m*

Hebrew /ˈhiːbruː/ *a* hebreu, hebraico □ *n* (*lang*) hebreu *m*

heckle /ˈhekl/ *vt* interromper, interpelar

hectic /ˈhektɪk/ *a* muito agitado, febril

hedge /hedʒ/ *n* sebe *f* □ *vt* cercar □ *vi* (*in answering*) usar de evasivas. **~ one's bets** (*fig*) resguardar-se

hedgehog /ˈhedʒhɒg/ *n* ouriço-cacheiro *m*

heed /hiːd/ *vt* prestar atenção a, escutar □ *n* **pay ~ to** prestar atenção a, dar ouvidos a. **~less** *a* **~less of** indiferente a, sem prestar atenção a

heel /hiːl/ *n* calcanhar *m*; (*of shoe*) salto *m*; (*sl*) canalha *m*

hefty /ˈheftɪ/ *a* (**-ier, -iest**) robusto e corpulento

height /haɪt/ *n* altura *f*; (*of mountain, plane*) altitude *f*; (*fig*) auge *m*, cúmulo *m*

heighten /ˈhaɪtn/ *vt/i* aumentar, elevar(-se)

heir /eə(r)/ *n* herdeiro *m*. **~ess** *n* herdeira *f*

heirloom /ˈeəluːm/ *n* peça *f* de família, (*P*) relíquia *f* de família

held /held/ *see* **hold**[1]

helicopter /ˈhelɪkɒptə(r)/ *n* helicóptero *m*

hell /hel/ *n* inferno *m*. **for the ~ of it** só por gozo. **~-bent** *a* decidido a todo o custo (**on** a). **~ish** *a* infernal

hello /həˈləʊ/ *int & n* = **hallo**

helm /helm/ *n* leme *m*

helmet /ˈhelmɪt/ *n* capacete *m*

help /help/ *vt/i* ajudar □ *n* ajuda *f*. **home ~** empregada *f*, faxineira *f*, (*P*) mulher *f* a dias. **~ o.s. to** servir-se de. **he cannot ~ laughing** ele não pode conter o riso. **it can't be ~ed** não há remédio. **~er** n ajudante mf. **~ful** a útil; (serviceable) de grande ajuda. **~less** a impotente

helping /'helpɪŋ/ n porção f, dose f

hem /hem/ n bainha f □ vt (pt **hemmed**) fazer a bainha. **~ in** cercar, encurralar

hemisphere /'hemɪsfɪə(r)/ n hemisfério m

hemp /hemp/ n cânhamo m

hen /hen/ n galinha f

hence /hens/ adv (from now) a partir desta altura; (for this reason) daí, por isso. **a week ~** daqui a uma semana. **~forth** adv de agora em diante, doravante

henpecked /'henpekt/ a mandado, (P) dominado pela mulher

her /hɜ:(r)/ pron a (a ela); (after prep) ela. **(to) ~** lhe. **I know ~** conheço-a □ a seu(s), sua(s); dela

herald /'herəld/ vt anunciar

heraldry /'herəldrɪ/ n heráldica f

herb /hɜ:b/ n erva f culinária ou medicinal

herd /hɜ:d/ n manada f; (of pigs) vara f □ vi **~ together** juntar-se em rebanho

here /hɪə(r)/ adv aqui □ int tome; aqui está. **to/from ~** para aqui/daqui

hereafter /hɪər'ɑ:ftə(r)/ adv de/para o futuro, daqui em diante □ n the **~** a vida de além-túmulo, (P) a vida futura

hereby /hɪə'baɪ/ adv (jur) pelo presente ato ou decreto, etc, (P) pelo presente acto ou decreto, etc

hereditary /hɪ'redɪtrɪ/ a hereditário

heredity /hɪ'redətɪ/ n hereditariedade f

here|sy /'herəsɪ/ n heresia f. **~tic** n herege mf. **~tical** /hɪ'retɪkl/ a herético

heritage /'herɪtɪdʒ/ n herança f, patrimônio m, (P) patrimônio m

hermit /'hɜ:mɪt/ n eremita m

hernia /'hɜ:nɪə/ n hérnia f

hero /'hɪərəʊ/ n (pl -oes) herói m

heroic /hɪ'rəʊɪk/ a heróico

heroin /'herəʊɪn/ n heroína f

heroine /'herəʊɪn/ n heroína f

heroism /'herəʊɪzəm/ n heroísmo m

heron /'herən/ n garça f

herring /'herɪŋ/ n arenque m

hers /hɜ:z/ poss pron o(s) seu(s), a(s) sua(s), o(s) dela, a(s) dela. **it is ~** é (o) dela ou o seu

herself /hɜ:'self/ pron ela mesma; (reflexive) se. **by ~** sozinha. **for ~** para si mesma. **to ~** a/para si mesma. **Mary ~ said so** foi a própria Maria que o disse

hesitant /'hezɪtənt/ a hesitante

hesit|ate /'hezɪteɪt/ vt hesitar. **~ion** /-'teɪʃn/ n hesitação f

heterosexual /hetərəʊ'seksjʊəl/ a & n heterossexual (mf)

hexagon /'heksəgən/ n hexágono m. **~al** /-'ægənl/ a hexagonal

hey /heɪ/ int eh, olá

heyday /'heɪdeɪ/ n auge m, apogeu m

hi /haɪ/ int olá, viva

hibernat|e /'haɪbəneɪt/ vi hibernar. **~ion** /-'neɪʃn/ n hibernação f

hiccup /'hɪkʌp/ n soluço m □ vi soluçar, estar com soluços

hide[1] /haɪd/ vt/i (pt **hid**, pp **hidden**) esconder(-se) (**from** de). **~-and-seek** n (game) escondeesconde m. **~-out** n (colloq) esconderijo m

hide[2] /haɪd/ n pele f, couro m

hideous /'hɪdɪəs/ a horrendo, medonho

hiding /'haɪdɪŋ/ n (colloq: thrashing) sova f, surra f. **go into ~** esconder-se. **~-place** n esconderijo m

hierarchy /'haɪərɑ:kɪ/ n hierarquia f

hi-fi /'haɪfaɪ/ a & n (de) alta fidelidade (f)

high /haɪ/ a (-er, -est) alto; (price, number) elevado; (voice, pitch) agudo □ n alta f □ adv alto. **two metres** ~ com dois metros de altura. ~**chair** cadeira f alta para crianças. ~**-handed** a autoritário, prepotente. ~**jump** salto m em altura. ~**-rise building** edifício m alto, (P) torre f. ~ **school** escola f secundária. **in the** ~ **season** em plena estação. ~**-speed** a ultra-rápido. ~**-spirited** a animado, vivo. ~ **spot** (sl) ponto m culminante. ~ **street** rua f principal. ~ **tide** maré f alta. ~**er education** ensino m superior

highbrow /ˈhaɪbraʊ/ a & n (colloq) intelectual (m)

highlight /ˈhaɪlaɪt/ n (fig) ponto m alto □ vt salientar, pôr em relevo, realçar

highly /ˈhaɪlɪ/ adv altamente, extremamente. ~**-strung** a muito sensível, nervoso, tenso. **speak** ~ **of** falar bem de

Highness /ˈhaɪnɪs/ n Alteza f

highway /ˈhaɪweɪ/ n estrada f, rodovia f. **H~ Code** Código m Nacional de Trânsito

hijack /ˈhaɪdʒæk/ vt seqüestrar, (P) sequestrar □ n seqüestro m, (P) sequestro m. ~**er** n (of plane) pirata m (do ar)

hike /haɪk/ n caminhada no campo f □ vi fazer uma caminhada. ~**r** /-ə(r)/ n excursionista mf, caminhante mf

hilarious /hɪˈleərɪəs/ a divertido, despilante

hill /hɪl/ n colina f, monte m; (slope) ladeira f, subida f. ~**y** a acidentado

hillside /ˈhɪlsaɪd/ n encosta f, vertente f

hilt /hɪlt/ n punho m. **to the** ~ completamente, inteiramente

him /hɪm/ pron o (a ele); (after

prep) ele. **(to)** ~ lhe. **I know** ~ conheço-o

himself /hɪmˈself/ pron ele mesmo; (reflexive) se. **by** ~ sozinho. **for** ~ para si mesmo. **to** ~ a/ para si mesmo. **Peter** ~ **saw it** foi o próprio Pedro que o viu

hind /haɪnd/ a traseiro, posterior

hind|er /ˈhɪndə(r)/ vt empatar, estorvar; (prevent) impedir. ~**rance** n estorvo m

hindsight /ˈhaɪndsaɪt/ n with ~ em retrospecto

Hindu /hɪnˈduː/ n & a hindu (mf). ~**ism** /-ɪzəm/ n hinduísmo m

hinge /hɪndʒ/ n dobradiça f □ vi ~ **on** depender de

hint /hɪnt/ n insinuação f, indireta f, (P) indirecta f; (advice) sugestão f, dica f (colloq) □ vt dar a entender, insinuar □ vi ~ **at** fazer alusão a

hip /hɪp/ n quadril m

hippie /ˈhɪpɪ/ n hippie mf

hippopotamus /hɪpəˈpɒtəməs/ n (pl -muses) hipopótamo m

hire /ˈhaɪə(r)/ vt alugar; (person) contratar □ n aluguel m, (P) aluguer m. ~**-purchase** n compra f a prestações, (P) crediário m

hirsute /ˈhɜːsjuːt/ a hirsuto

his /hɪz/ a seu(s), sua(s), dele □ poss pron o(s) seu(s), a(s) sua(s), o(s) dele, a(s) dele. **it is** ~ é (o) dele or o seu

Hispanic /hɪsˈpænɪk/ a hispânico

hiss /hɪs/ n silvo m; (for disapproval) assobio m, vaia f □ vt/i sibilar; (for disapproval) assobiar, vaiar

historian /hɪˈstɔːrɪən/ n historiador m

histor|y /ˈhɪstərɪ/ n história f. ~**ic(al)** /hɪˈstɒrɪk(l)/ a histórico

hit /hɪt/ vt (pt hit, pres p hitting) atingir, bater em; (knock against, collide with) chocar com, ir de encontro a; (strike a target) acertar em; (find) descobrir; (affect) atingir □ *vi* ~ **on** dar com □ *n* pancada *f*; (*fig: success*) sucesso *m*. ~ **it off** dar-se bem (with com). ~**-and-run** *a* (*driver*) que foge depois do desastre. ~**-or-miss** *a* ao acaso

hitch /hɪtʃ/ *vt* atar, prender; (*to a hook*) enganchar □ *n* sacão *m*; (*snag*) problema *m*. ~ **a lift**, ~**-hike** viajar de carona, (P) boleia. ~**-hiker** *n* o que viaja de carona, boleia. ~ **up** puxar para cima

hive /haɪv/ *n* colmeia *f* □ *vt* ~ **off** separar e tornar independente

hoard /hɔːd/ *vt* juntar, açambarcar □ *n* provisão *f*; (*of valuables*) tesouro *m*

hoarding /ˈhɔːdɪŋ/ *n* tapume *m*, outdoor *m*

hoarse /hɔːs/ *a* (-**er**, -**est**) rouco. ~**ness** *n* rouquidão *f*

hoax /həʊks/ *n* (*malicious*) logro *m*, embuste *m*; (*humorous*) trote *m* □ *vt* (*malicious*) enganar; lograr; passar um trote, pregar uma peça em

hob /hɒb/ *n* placa *f* de aquecimento (do fogão)

hobble /ˈhɒbl/ *vi* coxear □ *vt* pear

hobby /ˈhɒbɪ/ *n* passatempo *m* favorito. ~**-horse** *n* (*fig*) tópico *m* favorito

hock /hɒk/ *n* vinho *m* branco do Reno

hockey /ˈhɒkɪ/ *n* hóquei *m*

hoe /həʊ/ *n* enxada *f* □ *vt* trabalhar com enxada

hog /hɒg/ *n* porco *m*; (*greedy person*) glutão *m* □ *vt* (*pt* hogged) (*colloq*) açambarcar

hoist /hɔɪst/ *vt* içar □ *n* guindaste *m*, (P) monta-cargas *m*

hold[1] /həʊld/ *vt* (*pt* held) segurar; (*contain*) levar; (*possess*) ter, possuir; (*occupy*) ocupar; (*keep, maintain*) conservar, manter; (*affirm*) manter □ *vi* (*of rope etc*) aguentar-se, (P) aguentar(-se)

□ *n* (*influence*) domínio *m*. **get** ~ **of** pôr as mãos em; (*fig*) apanhar. ~ **back** reter. ~ **on** (*colloq*) esperar. ~ **on to** guardar; (*cling to*) agarrar-se a. ~ **one's breath** suster a respiração. ~ **one's tongue** calar-se. ~ **the line** não desligar. ~ **out** resistir. ~ **up** (*support*) sustentar; (*delay*) demorar; (*rob*) assaltar. ~**-up** *n* atraso *m*; (*auto*) engarrafamento *m*; (*robbery*) assalto *m*. ~ **with** aguentar, (P) aguentar. ~ *n* detentor *m*; (*of post, title etc*) titular *mf*; (*for object*) suporte *m*

hold[2] /həʊld/ *n* (*of ship, plane*) porão *m*

holdall /ˈhəʊldɔːl/ *n* saco *m* de viagem

holding /ˈhəʊldɪŋ/ *n* (*land*) propriedade *f*; (*comm*) ações *fpl*, (P) acções *fpl*, valores *mpl*, holding *m*

hole /həʊl/ *n* buraco *m* □ *vt* abrir buraco(s) em, esburacar

holiday /ˈhɒlɪdeɪ/ *n* férias *fpl*; (*day off; public*) feriado *m* □ *vi* passar férias. ~**-maker** *n* pessoa *f* em férias; (*in summer*) veranista *mf*, (P) veraneante *mf*

holiness /ˈhəʊlɪnɪs/ *n* santidade *f*

Holland /ˈhɒlənd/ *n* Holanda *f*

hollow /ˈhɒləʊ/ *a* oco, vazio; (*fig*) falso; (*cheeks*) fundo; (*sound*) surdo □ *n* (*in the ground*) cavidade *f*; (*in the hand*) cova *f*

holly /ˈhɒlɪ/ *n* azevinho *m*

holster /ˈhəʊlstə(r)/ *n* coldre *m*

holy /ˈhəʊlɪ/ *a* (-**ier**, -**iest**) santo, sagrado; (*water*) benta. **H**~ **Ghost**, **H**~ **Spirit** Espírito *m* Santo

homage /ˈhɒmɪdʒ/ *n* homenagem *f*. **pay** ~ **to** prestar homenagem a

home /həʊm/ *n* casa *f*, lar *m*; (*institution*) lar *m*, asilo *m*; (*country*) país *m* natal □ *a* caseiro, doméstico; (*of family*) de família; (*pol*) nacional, interno; (*football match*) em casa □ *adv* (at) ~ em casa. **come/go** ~ vir/ir para casa. **make oneself at** ~ não fazer cerimónia, (*P*) cerimónia. **~-made** *a* caseiro. **H~ Office** Ministério *m* do Interior. ~ **town** cidade *f* or terra *f* natal. ~ **truth** dura verdade *f*, verdade(s) *f*(*pl*) amarga(s). **~less** *a* sem casa, desabrigado

homeland /ˈhəʊmlænd/ *n* pátria *f*

homely /ˈhəʊmlɪ/ *a* (-ier, -iest) (*simple*) simples; (*Amer: ugly*) sem graça

homesick /ˈhəʊmsɪk/ *a* **be** ~ ter saudades

homeward /ˈhəʊmwəd/ *a* (*journey*) de regresso

homework /ˈhəʊmwɜːk/ *n* trabalho *m* de casa, dever *m* de casa

homicide /ˈhɒmɪsaɪd/ *n* homicídio *m*; (*person*) homicida *mf*

homoeopath|y /ˈhəʊmɪˈɒpəθɪ/ *n* homeopatia *f*. **~ic** *a* homeopático

homosexual /həʊˈsekʃʊəl/ *a* & *n* homossexual (*mf*)

honest /ˈɒnɪst/ *a* honesto; (*frank*) franco. **~ly** *adv* honestamente; (*frankly*) francamente. **~y** *n* honestidade *f*

honey /ˈhʌnɪ/ *n* mel *m*; (*colloq: darling*) querido *m*, querida *f*, meu bem *m*

honeycomb /ˈhʌnɪkəʊm/ *n* favo *m* de mel

honeymoon /ˈhʌnɪmuːn/ *n* lua de mel *f*

honorary /ˈɒnərərɪ/ *a* honorário

honour /ˈɒnə(r)/ *n* honra *f* □ *vt* honrar. **~able** *a* honrado, honroso

hood /hʊd/ *n* capuz *m*; (*car roof*) capota *f*; (*Amer: bonnet*) capô *m*, (*P*) capot *m*

hoodwink /ˈhʊdwɪŋk/ *vt* enganar

hoof /huːf/ *n* (*pl* -fs) casco *m*

hook /hʊk/ *n* gancho *m*; (*on garment*) colchete *m*; (*for fishing*) anzol *m* □ *vt* enganchar; (*fish*) apanhar, pescar. **off the** ~ livre de dificuldades; (*phone*) desligado

hooked /hʊkt/ *a* **be** ~ **on** (*sl*) ter o vício de, estar viciado em

hookey /ˈhʊkɪ/ *n* **play** ~ (*Amer sl*) fazer gazeta

hooligan /ˈhuːlɪgən/ *n* desordeiro *m*

hoop /huːp/ *n* arco *m*; (*of cask*) cinta *f*

hooray /huːˈreɪ/ *int* & *n* = **hurrah**

hoot /huːt/ *n* (*of owl*) pio *m* de mocho; (*of horn*) buzinada *f*; (*jeer*) apupo *m* □ *vi* (*of owl*) piar; (*of horn*) buzinar; (*jeer*) apupar. **~er** *n* buzina *f*; (*of factory*) sereia *f*

Hoover /ˈhuːvə(r)/ *n* aspirador de pó *m*, (*P*) aspirador □ *vt* passar o aspirador

hop[1] /hɒp/ *vi* (*pt* hopped) saltar num pé só, (*P*) ao pé coxinho □ *n* salto *m*. ~ **in** (*colloq*) subir, saltar (*colloq*). ~ **it** (*sl*) pôr-se a andar (*colloq*). ~ **out** (*colloq*) descer, saltar (*colloq*)

hop[2] /hɒp/ *n* (*plant*) lúpulo *m*. **~s** espigas *fpl* de lúpulo

hope /həʊp/ *n* esperança *f* □ *vt/i* esperar. ~ **for** esperar (ter). **~ful** *a* esperançoso; (*promising*) promissor. **be ~ful (that)** ter esperança (que), confiar (em que). **~fully** *adv* esperançosamente; (*it is hoped that*) é de esperar que. **~less** *a* desesperado, sem esperança; (*incompetent*) incapaz

horde /hɔːd/ *n* horda *f*

horizon /həˈraɪzn/ *n* horizonte *m*

horizontal /hɒrɪˈzɒntl/ *a* horizontal

hormone /ˈhɔːməʊn/ *n* hormónio *m*, (*P*) hormona *f*

horn /hɔːn/ n chifre m, corno m; (of car) buzina f; (mus) trompa f. **∼y** a caloso, calejado

hornet /ˈhɔːnɪt/ n vespão m

horoscope /ˈhɒrəskəʊp/ n horóscopo m, (P) horoscópio m

horrible /ˈhɒrəbl/ a horrível, horroroso

horrid /ˈhɒrɪd/ a horrível, horripilante

horrific /həˈrɪfɪk/ a horrífico

horr|or /ˈhɒrə(r)/ n horror m □ a (film etc) de terror. **∼ify** vt horrorizar, horripilar

horse /hɔːs/ n cavalo m. **∼-chestnut** n castanha f da Índia. **∼-racing** n corrida f de cavalos, hipismo m. **∼-radish** n rábano m

horseback /ˈhɔːsbæk/ n **on ∼** a cavalo

horseplay /ˈhɔːspleɪ/ n brincadeira f grosseira, abrutalhada f

horsepower /ˈhɔːspaʊə(r)/ n cavalo-vapor m

horseshoe /ˈhɔːsʃuː/ n ferradura f

horticultur|e /ˈhɔːtɪkʌltʃə(r)/ n horticultura f. **∼al** /-ˈkʌltʃərəl/ a hortícola

hose /həʊz/ n **∼(-pipe)** mangueira f □ vt regar à mangueira

hospice /ˈhɒspɪs/ n hospício m; (for travellers) hospedaria f

hospit|able /həˈspɪtəbl/ a hospitaleiro. **∼ality** /-ˈtælətɪ/ n hospitalidade f

hospital /ˈhɒspɪtl/ n hospital m

host[1] /həʊst/ n anfitrião m, dono m da casa. **∼ess** n anfitriã f, dona f da casa

host[2] /həʊst/ n **a ∼ of** uma multidão de, um grande número de

host[3] /həʊst/ n (relig) hóstia f

hostage /ˈhɒstɪdʒ/ n refém m

hostel /ˈhɒstl/ n residência f de estudantes etc

hostil|e /ˈhɒstaɪl/ a hostil. **∼ity** /hɒˈstɪlətɪ/ n hostilidade f

hot /hɒt/ a (hotter, hottest) quente; (culin) picante. **be** or **feel**
∼ estar com or ter calor. **it is ∼** está or faz calor □ vt/i (pt hotted) **∼ up** (colloq) aquecer. **∼ dog** cachorro-quente m. **∼ line** linha direta f, (P) directa esp entre chefes de estado. **∼-water bottle** saco m de água quente

hotbed /ˈhɒtbed/ n (fig) foco m

hotchpotch /ˈhɒtʃpɒtʃ/ n mistura-da f, (P) salgalhada f

hotel /həʊˈtel/ n hotel m. **∼ier** /-ɪə(r)/ n hoteleiro m

hound /haʊnd/ n cão m de caça e de corrida, sabujo m □ vt acossar, perseguir

hour /ˈaʊə(r)/ n hora f. **∼ly** adv de hora em hora □ a de hora em hora. **∼ly pay** retribuição f horária. **paid ∼ly** pago por hora

house[1] /haʊs/ n (pl **∼s** /ˈhaʊzɪz/) n casa f; (pol) câmara f. **on the ∼** por conta da casa. **∼-warming** n inauguração f da casa

house[2] /haʊz/ vt alojar; (store) arrecadar, guardar

houseboat /ˈhaʊsbəʊt/ n casa f flutuante

household /ˈhaʊshəʊld/ n família f, agregado m familiar. **∼er** n ocupante mf; (owner) proprietário m

housekeep|er /ˈhaʊskiːpə(r)/ n governanta f. **∼ing** n (work) tarefas fpl domésticas

housewife /ˈhaʊswaɪf/ n (pl **-wives**) dona f de casa

housework /ˈhaʊswɜːk/ n tarefas fpl domésticas

housing /ˈhaʊzɪŋ/ n alojamento m. **∼ estate** zona f residencial

hovel /ˈhɒvl/ n casebre m, tugúrio m

hover /ˈhɒvə(r)/ vi pairar; (linger) deixar-se ficar, demorar-se

hovercraft /ˈhɒvəkrɑːft/ n invar aerobarco m, hovercraft m

how /haʊ/ adv como. **∼ long/old is...?** que comprimento/idade tem...? ~ **far?** a que distância? ~ **many?** quantos? ~ **much?** quanto? ~ **often?** com que frequência, (*P*) frequência? ~ **pretty it is** como é lindo. ~ **about a walk?** e se fôssemos dar uma volta? ~ **are you?** como vai? ~ **do you do?** muito prazer! **and** ~! oh se é!

however /haʊˈevə(r)/ *adv* de qualquer maneira; (*though*) contudo, no entanto, todavia. ~ **small it may be** por menor que seja

howl /haʊl/ *n* uivo *m* □ *vi* uivar

HP *abbr see* **hire-purchase**

hp *abbr see* **horsepower**

hub /hʌb/ *n* cubo *m* da roda; (*fig*) centro *m*. ~**-cap** *n* calota *f*, (*P*) tampão *m* da roda

hubbub /ˈhʌbʌb/ *n* chinfrim *m*

huddle /ˈhʌdl/ *vt/i* apinhar(-se). ~ **together** aconchegar-se

hue[1] /hjuː/ *n* matiz *f*, tom *m*

hue[2] /hjuː/ *n* ~ **and cry** clamor *m*, alarido *m*

huff /hʌf/ *n* em raiva, zangado

hug /hʌg/ *vt* (*pt* **hugged**) abraçar, apertar nos braços; (*keep close to*) chegar-se a □ *n* abraço *m*

huge /hjuːdʒ/ *a* enorme

hulk /hʌlk/ *n* casco (esp de navio desmantelado) *m*. ~**ing** *a* (*colloq*) desajeitadão (*colloq*)

hull /hʌl/ *n* (*of ship*) casco *m*

hullo /həˈləʊ/ *int* & *n* = **hallo**

hum /hʌm/ *vt/i* (*pt* **hummed**) cantar com a boca fechada; (*of insect, engine*) zumbir □ *n* zumbido *m*

human /ˈhjuːmən/ *a* humano □ *n* ~ **(being)** ser *m* humano

humane /hjuːˈmeɪn/ *a* humano, compassivo

humanitarian /hjuːˌmænɪˈteərɪən/ *a* humanitário

humanity /hjuːˈmænətɪ/ *n* humanidade *f*

humbl|**e** /ˈhʌmbl/ *a* (**-er, -est**) humilde □ *vt* humilhar. ~**y** *adv* humildemente

humdrum /ˈhʌmdrʌm/ *a* monótono, rotineiro

humid /ˈhjuːmɪd/ *a* úmido, (*P*) húmido. ~**ity** /-ˈmɪdətɪ/ *n* umidade *f*, (*P*) humidade *f*

humiliat|**e** /hjuːˈmɪlɪeɪt/ *vt* humilhar. ~**ion** /-ˈeɪʃn/ *n* humilhação *f*

humility /hjuːˈmɪlətɪ/ *n* humildade *f*

humorist /ˈhjuːmərɪst/ *n* humorista *mf*

hum|**our** /ˈhjuːmə(r)/ *n* humor *m* □ *vt* fazer a vontade de. ~**orous** *a* humorístico; (*person*) divertido, espirituoso

hump /hʌmp/ *n* corcova *f*; (*of the back*) corcunda *f* □ *vt* corcovar, arquear. **the** ~ (*sl*) a neura (*colloq*)

hunch[1] /hʌntʃ/ *vt* curvar. ~**ed up** curvado

hunch[2] /hʌntʃ/ *n* (*colloq*) palpite *m*

hunchback /ˈhʌntʃbæk/ *n* corcunda *mf*

hundred /ˈhʌndrəd/ *a* cem □ *n* centena *f*, cento *m*. ~**s of** centenas de. ~**fold** *a* cêntuplo □ *adv* cem vezes mais. ~**th** *a* & *n* centésimo (*m*)

hundredweight /ˈhʌndrədweɪt/ *n* quintal *m* (= *50,8 kg*; *Amer 45,36 kg*)

hung /hʌŋ/ *see* **hang**

Hungar|**y** /ˈhʌŋgərɪ/ *n* Hungria *f*. ~**ian** /-ˈgeərɪən/ *a* & *n* húngaro (*m*)

hunger /ˈhʌŋgə(r)/ *n* fome *f* □ *vi* ~ **for** ter fome de; (*fig*) desejar vivamente, ansiar por

hungr|**y** /ˈhʌŋgrɪ/ *a* (**ier, -iest**) esfomeado, .faminto. **be** ~**y** ter fome, estar com fome. ~**ily** *adv* avidamente

hunk /hʌŋk/ *n* grande naco *m*

hunt /hʌnt/ *vt/i* caçar □ *n* caça *f.*
  ~ **for** andar à caça de, andar à
procura de. ~**er** *n* caçador *m.*
~**ing** *n* caça *f*, caçada *f*

hurdle /'hɜ:dl/ *n* obstáculo *m*

hurl /hɜ:l/ *vt* arremessar, lançar
com força

hurrah, **hurray** /huˈrɑ:, huˈreɪ/
int & *n* hurra (*m*), viva (*m*)

hurricane /'hʌrɪkən/ *n* furacão *m*

hurried /'hʌrɪd/ *a* apressado.
~**ly** *adv* apressadamente, às
pressas

hurry /'hʌrɪ/ *vt/i* apressar(-se),
despachar(-se) □ *n* pressa *f.* **be
in a** ~ estar com or ter pressa.
do sth in a ~ fazer alg coisa às
pressas. ~**up!** logo

hurt /hɜ:t/ *vt* (*pt* **hurt**) fazer mal
a; (*injure*, *offend*) magoar, ferir □
vi doer □ *a* magoado, ferido □ *n*
mal *m*; (*feelings*) mágoa *f.* ~**ful**
a prejudicial; (*remark etc*) que
magoa

hurtle /'hɜ:tl/ *vi* despenhar-se;
(*move rapidly*) precipitar-se □ *vt*
arremessar

husband /'hʌzbənd/ *n* marido *m*,
esposo *m*

hush /hʌʃ/ *vt* (fazer) calar. ~! si-
lencio! □ *vi* calar-se □ *n* silêncio
m. ~**-hush** *a* (*collog*) muito em
segredo. ~ **up** abafar, encobrir

husk /hʌsk/ *n* casca *f*

husky /'hʌskɪ/ *a* (**-ier**, **-iest**)
(*hoarse*) rouco, enrouquecido;
(*burly*) corpulento □ *n* cão *m* es-
quimó

hustle /'hʌsl/ *vt* empurrar, dar encontrões a □ *n* empurrão *m.* ~
and bustle grande movimento *m*

hut /hʌt/ *n* cabana *f*, barraca *f* de
madeira

hutch /hʌtʃ/ *n* coelheira *f*

hyacinth /'haɪəsɪnθ/ *n* jacinto *m*

hybrid /'haɪbrɪd/ *a* & *n* híbrido (*m*)

hydrant /'haɪdrənt/ *n* hidrante *m*

hydraulic /haɪˈdrɔːlɪk/ *a* hidráuli-
co

hydroelectric /haɪdrəʊˈlektrɪk/ *a*
hidrelétrico, (*P*) hidroeléctrico

hydrofoil /'haɪdrəʊfɔɪl/ *n* hydrofoil *m*

hydrogen /'haɪdrədʒən/ *n* hidro-
gênio *m*, (*P*) hidrogénio *m*

hyena /haɪˈiːnə/ *n* hiena *f*

hygiene /'haɪdʒiːn/ *n* higiene *f*

hygienic /haɪˈdʒiːnɪk/ *a* higiénico,
(*P*) higiénico

hymn /hɪm/ *n* hino *m*, cântico *m*

hyper- /'haɪpə(r)/ *pref* hiper-

hypermarket /'haɪpəmɑːkɪt/ *n* hipermercado *m*

hyphen /'haɪfn/ *n* hífen *m*, traço-
de-união *m.* ~**ate** *vt* unir com
hífen

hypno|**sis** /hɪpˈnəʊsɪs/ *n* hipnose *f.*
~**tic** /-'nɒtɪk/ *a* hipnótico

hypnot|**ize** /'hɪpnətaɪz/ *vt* hipnoti-
zar. ~**ism** /-ɪzəm/ *n* hipnotismo
m

hypochondriac /haɪpəˈkɒndrɪæk/
n hipocondríaco *m*

hypocrisy /hɪˈpɒkrəsɪ/ *n* hipocrisia *f*

hypocrit|**e** /'hɪpəkrɪt/ *n* hipócrita
mf. ~**ical** /-'krɪtɪkl/ *a* hipócrita

hypodermic /haɪpəˈdɜːmɪk/ *a* hi-
podérmico □ *n* seringa *f*

hypothe|**sis** /haɪˈpɒθəsɪs/ *n* (*pl*
-theses /-siːz/) hipótese *f.*
~**tical** /-ə'θetɪkl/ *a* hipotético

hyster|**ia** /hɪˈstɪərɪə/ *n* histeria *f.*
~**ical** /hɪˈsterɪkl/ *a* histérico

I

I /aɪ/ *pron* eu

Iberian /aɪˈbɪərɪən/ *a* ibérico □ *n*
íbero *m*

ice /aɪs/ *n* gelo *m* □ *vt/i* gelar;
(*cake*) cobrir com glacê □ *vi* ~
up gelar. ~**-box** *n* (*Amer*) geladeira *f*, (*P*) frigorífico *m.* ~**-(
cream**) *n* sorvete *m*, (*P*) gelado
m. ~**-cube** *n* cubo *m* or pedra *f*

de gelo. ~ **hockey** hóquei *m* sobre o gelo. ~ **lolly** picolé *m*. ~-**pack** *n* saco *m* de gelo. ~-**rink** *n* rinque *m* de patinação, (P) patinagem *f* no gelo. ~ **skating** patinação *f*, (P) patinagem *f* no gelo

iceberg /'aɪsbɜːg/ *n* iceberg *m*; (*fig*) pedaço *m* de gelo

Iceland /'aɪslənd/ *n* Islândia *f*. ~**er** *n* islandês *m*. ~**ic** /-'lændɪk/ *a* & *n* islandês (*m*)

icicle /'aɪsɪkl/ *n* pingente *m* de gelo

icing /'aɪsɪŋ/ *n* (*culin*) cobertura *f* de açúcar, glacê *m*

icy /'aɪsɪ/ *a* (**-ier, -iest**) gelado, gélido, glacial; (*road*) com gelo

idea /aɪ'dɪə/ *n* idéia *f*, (P) ideia *f*

ideal /aɪ'dɪəl/ *a* & *n* ideal (*m*). ~**ize** *vt* idealizar. ~**ly** *adv* idealmente

idealis|t /aɪ'dɪəlɪst/ *n* idealista *mf*. ~**m** /-zəm/ *n* idealismo *m*. ~**tic** /-'lɪstɪk/ *a* idealista

identical /aɪ'dentɪkl/ *a* idêntico

identif|y /aɪ'dentɪfaɪ/ *vt* identificar □ *vi* ~**y with** identificar-se com. ~**ication** /-ɪ'keɪʃn/ *n* identificação *f*; (*papers*) documentos *mpl* de identificação

identity /aɪ'dentətɪ/ *n* identidade *f*. ~ **card** carteira *f* de identidade, (P) bilhete *m*. de identidade

ideolog|y /aɪdɪ'ɒlədʒɪ/ *n* ideologia *f*. ~**ical** /-ɪə'lɒdʒɪkl/ *a* ideológico

idiom /'ɪdɪəm/ *n* idioma *m*; (*phrase*) expressão *f* idiomática. ~**atic** /-'mætɪk/ *a* idiomático

idiosyncrasy /ɪdɪə'sɪŋkrəsɪ/ *n* idiossincrasia *f*, peculiaridade *f*

idiot /'ɪdɪət/ *n* idiota *mf*. ~**ic** /-'ɒtɪk/ *a* idiota

idl|e /'aɪdl/ *a* (**-er, -est**) (*not active; lazy*) ocioso; (*unemployed*) sem trabalho; (*of machines*) parado; (*fig: useless*) inútil □ *vt/i* (*of engine*) estar em ponto morto, P estar no ralenti. ~**eness** *n*

ociosidade *f*. ~**y** *adv* ociosamente

idol /'aɪdl/ *n* ídolo *m*. ~**ize** *vt* idolatrar

idyllic /ɪ'dɪlɪk/ *a* idílico

i.e. *abbr* isto é, quer dizer

if /ɪf/ *conj* se

igloo /'ɪɡluː/ *n* iglu *m*

ignite /ɪɡ'naɪt/ *vt/i* inflamar(-se), acender; (*catch fire*) pegar fogo; (*set fire to*) atear fogo a, (P) deitar fogo a

ignition /ɪɡ'nɪʃn/ *n* (*auto*) ignição *f*. ~ (**key**) chave *f* de ignição

ignoran|t /'ɪɡnərənt/ *a* ignorante. ~**ce** *n* ignorância *f*. **be** ~**t of** ignorar

ignore /ɪɡ'nɔː(r)/ *vt* não fazer caso de, passar por cima de; (*person in the street etc*) fingir não ver

ill /ɪl/ *a* (*sick*) doente; (*bad*) mau □ *adv* mal □ *n* mal *m*. ~-**advised** *a* pouco aconselhável. ~ **at ease** pouco à vontade. ~-**bred** *a* mal educado. ~-**fated** *a* malfadado. ~-**treat** *vt* maltratar. ~ **will** má vontade *f*, animosidade *f*

illegal /ɪ'liːɡl/ *a* ilegal

illegible /ɪ'ledʒəbl/ *a* ilegível

illegitima|te /ɪlɪ'dʒɪtɪmət/ *a* ilegítimo. ~**cy** *n* ilegitimidade *f*

illitera|te /ɪ'lɪtərət/ *a* analfabeto; (*uneducated*) iletrado. ~**cy** *n* analfabetismo *m*

illness /'ɪlnɪs/ *n* doença *f*

illogical /ɪ'lɒdʒɪkl/ *a* ilógico

illuminat|e /ɪ'luːmɪneɪt/ *vt* iluminar; (*explain*) esclarecer. ~**ion** /-'neɪʃn/ *n* iluminação *f*. ~**ions** *npl* luminárias *fpl*

illusion /ɪ'luːʒn/ *n* ilusão *f*

illusory /ɪ'luːsərɪ/ *a* ilusório

illustrat|e /'ɪləstreɪt/ *vt* ilustrar. ~**ion** /-'streɪʃn/ *n* ilustração *f*. ~**ive** /-ətɪv/ *a* ilustrativo

illustrious /ɪ'lʌstrɪəs/ *a* ilustre

image /'ɪmɪdʒ/ *n* imagem *f*. (**public**) ~ imagem *f* pública

imaginary /ɪˈmædʒɪnərɪ/ *a* imaginário

imaginat|ion /ɪˌmædʒɪˈneɪʃn/ *n* imaginação *f*. **~ive** /ɪˈmædʒɪnətɪv/ *a* imaginativo

imagin|e /ɪˈmædʒɪn/ *vt* imaginar. **~able** *a* imaginável

imbalance /ɪmˈbæləns/ *n* desequilíbrio *m*

imbecile /ˈɪmbəsiːl/ *a* & *n* imbecil (*mf*)

imbue /ɪmˈbjuː/ *vt* imbuir, impregnar

imitat|e /ˈɪmɪteɪt/ *vt* imitar. **~ion** /-ˈteɪʃn/ *n* imitação *f*

immaculate /ɪˈmækjʊlət/ *a* imaculado; (*impeccable*) impecável

immaterial /ɪməˈtɪərɪəl/ *a* (*of no importance*) irrelevante. **that's ~ to me** para mim tanto faz

immature /ɪməˈtjʊə(r)/ *a* imaturo

immediate /ɪˈmiːdɪət/ *a* imediato. **~ly** *adv* imediatamente □ *conj* logo que, assim que

immens|e /ɪˈmens/ *a* imenso. **~ely** /-slɪ/ *adv* imensamente. **~ity** *n* imensidade *f*

immers|e /ɪˈmɜːs/ *vt* mergulhar, imergir. **be ~ed in** (*fig*) estar imerso em. **~ion** /-ʃn/ *n* imersão *f*. **~ion heater** aquecedor *m* de água elétrico, (*P*) eléctrico

immigr|ate /ˈɪmɪɡreɪt/ *vi* imigrar. **~ant** *n* & *a* imigrante (*mf*), imigrado (*m*). **~ation** /-ˈɡreɪʃn/ *n* imigração *f*

imminen|t /ˈɪmɪnənt/ *a* iminente. **~ce** *n* iminência *f*

immobil|e /ɪˈməʊbaɪl/ *a* imóvel. **~ize** /-əlaɪz/ *vt* imobilizar

immoderate /ɪˈmɒdərət/ *a* imoderado, descomedido

immoral /ɪˈmɒrəl/ *a* imoral. **~ity** /ɪməˈrælətɪ/ *n* imoralidade *f*

immortal /ɪˈmɔːtl/ *a* imortal. **~ity** /-ˈtælətɪ/ *n* imortalidade *f*. **~ize** *vt* imortalizar

immun|e /ɪˈmjuːn/ *a* imune, imu-

nizado (**from**, **to** contra). **~ity** *n* imunidade *f*

imp /ɪmp/ *n* diabrete *m*

impact /ˈɪmpækt/ *n* impacto *m*

impair /ɪmˈpeə(r)/ *vt* deteriorar; (*damage*) prejudicar

impale /ɪmˈpeɪl/ *vt* empalar

impart /ɪmˈpɑːt/ *vt* comunicar, transmitir (**to** a)

impartial /ɪmˈpɑːʃl/ *a* imparcial. **~ity** /-ʃɪˈælətɪ/ *n* imparcialidade *f*

impassable /ɪmˈpɑːsəbl/ *a* (*road*, *river*) intransitável, intransitável; (*barrier etc*) intransponível

impasse /ˈæmpɑːs/ *n* impasse *m*

impatien|t /ɪmˈpeɪʃənt/ *a* impaciente. **~ce** *n* impaciência *f*. **~tly** *adv* impacientemente

impeach /ɪmˈpiːtʃ/ *vt* incriminar, acusar

impeccable /ɪmˈpekəbl/ *a* impecável

impede /ɪmˈpiːd/ *vt* impedir, estorvar

impediment /ɪmˈpedɪmənt/ *n* impedimento, obstáculo *m*. **(speech) ~** defeito *m* (na fala)

impel /ɪmˈpel/ *vt* (*pt* **impelled**) impelir, forçar (**to do** a fazer)

impending /ɪmˈpendɪŋ/ *a* iminente

impenetrable /ɪmˈpenɪtrəbl/ *a* impenetrável

imperative /ɪmˈperətɪv/ *a* imperativo; (*need etc*) imperioso □ *n* imperativo *m*

imperceptible /ɪmpəˈseptəbl/ *a* imperceptível

imperfect /ɪmˈpɜːfɪkt/ *a* imperfeito. **~ion** /-əˈfekʃn/ *n* imperfeição *f*

imperial /ɪmˈpɪərɪəl/ *a* imperial; (*of measures*) legal (*na* GB). **~ism** /-lɪzəm/ *n* imperialismo *m*

imperious /ɪmˈpɪərɪəs/ *a* imperioso

impersonal /ɪmˈpɜːsənl/ *a* impessoal

impersonat|e /ɪmˈpɜːsəneɪt/ *vt*

fazer-se passar por; (*theat*) fazer *or* representar (o papel) de. ~ion /-'neɪʃn/ *n* imitação *f*

impertinen|t /ɪm'pɜːtɪnənt/ *a* impertinente. ~ce *n* impertinência *f*. ~tly *adv* com impertinência

impervious /ɪm'pɜːvɪəs/ *a* ~ **to** (*water*) impermeável a; (*fig*) insensível a

impetuous /ɪm'petʃʊəs/ *a* impetuoso

impetus /'ɪmpɪtəs/ *n* ímpeto *m*

impinge /ɪm'pɪndʒ/ *vi* ~ **on** afetar, *P* afectar; (*encroach*) infringir

impish /'ɪmpɪʃ/ *a* travesso, malicioso

implacable /ɪm'plækəbl/ *a* implacável

implant /ɪm'plɑːnt/ *vt* implantar

implement[1] /'ɪmplɪmənt/ *n* instrumento *m*, utensílio *m*

implement[2] /'ɪmplɪment/ *vt* implementar, executar

implicat|e /'ɪmplɪkeɪt/ *vt* implicar. ~ion /-'keɪʃn/ *n* implicação *f*

implicit /ɪm'plɪsɪt/ *a* implícito; (*unquestioning*) absoluto, incondicional

implore /ɪm'plɔː(r)/ *vt* implorar, suplicar, rogar

imply /ɪm'plaɪ/ *vt* implicar; (*hint*) sugerir, dar a entender, insinuar

impolite /ɪmpə'laɪt/ *a* indelicado, incorreto, (*P*) incorrecto

import[1] /ɪm'pɔːt/ *vt* importar. ~ation /-'teɪʃn/ *n* importação *f*. ~er *n* importador *m*

import[2] /'ɪmpɔːt/ *n* importação *f*; (*meaning*) significado *m*; (*importance*) importância *f*

importan|t /ɪm'pɔːtnt/ *a* importante. ~ce *n* importância *f*

impos|e /ɪm'pəʊz/ *vt* impor; (*inflict*) infligir □ *vi* ~e **on** abusar de. ~ition /-ə'zɪʃn/ *n* imposição *f*; (*unfair burden*) abuso *m*

imposing /ɪm'pəʊzɪŋ/ *a* imponente

impossib|le /ɪm'pɒsəbl/ *a* impossível. ~ility /-'bɪlətɪ/ *n* impossibilidade *f*

impostor /ɪm'pɒstə(r)/ *n* impostor *m*

impoten|t /'ɪmpətənt/ *a* impotente. ~ce *n* impotência *f*

impound /ɪm'paʊnd/ *vt* apreender, confiscar

impoverish /ɪm'pɒvərɪʃ/ *vt* empobrecer

impracticable /ɪm'præktɪkəbl/ *a* impraticável

impractical /ɪm'præktɪkl/ *a* pouco prático

imprecise /ɪmprɪ'saɪs/ *a* impreciso

impregnable /ɪm'pregnəbl/ *a* inexpugnável; (*fig*) inabalável, irrefutável

impregnate /'ɪmpregneɪt/ *vt* impregnar (**with** de)

impresario /ɪmprɪ'sɑːrɪəʊ/ *n* (*pl* -os) empresário *m*

impress /ɪm'pres/ *vt* impressionar, causar impressão a; (*imprint*) imprimir. ~ **sth on s.o.** inculcar algo em alguém

impression /ɪm'preʃn/ *n* impressão *f*. ~able *a* impressionável. ~ist *n* impressionista *mf*

impressive /ɪm'presɪv/ *a* impressionante, imponente

imprint[1] /'ɪmprɪnt/ *n* impressão *f*, marca *f*

imprint[2] /ɪm'prɪnt/ *vt* imprimir

imprison /ɪm'prɪzn/ *vt* prender, aprisionar. ~ment *n* aprisionamento *m*, prisão *f*

improbab|le /ɪm'prɒbəbl/ *a* improvável. ~ility /-'bɪlətɪ/ *n* improbabilidade *f*

impromptu /ɪm'prɒmptjuː/ *a* & *adv* de improviso □ *n* impromptu *m*

improper /ɪm'prɒpə(r)/ *a* impróprio; (*indecent*) indecente, pouco decente; (*wrong*) incorreto, (*P*) incorrecto

improve /ɪm'pruːv/ *vt/i* melhorar.
~ **on** aperfeiçoar. ~**ment** *n*
melhoria *f*; (*in house etc*) melhoramento *m*; (*in health*) melhoras
fpl

improvise /'ɪmprəvaɪz/ *vt/i* improvisar. ~**ation** /-'zeɪʃn/ *n* improvisação *f*

imprudent /ɪm'pruːdnt/ *a* imprudente

impuden|t /'ɪmpjʊdənt/ *a* descarado, insolente. ~**ce** *n* descaramento *m*, insolência *f*

impulse /'ɪmpʌls/ *n* impulso *m*

impulsive /ɪm'pʌlsɪv/ *a* impulsivo

impur|e /ɪm'pjʊə(r)/ *a* impuro.
~**ity** *n* impureza *f*

in /ɪn/ *prep* em, dentro de □ *adv*
dentro; (*at home*) em casa; (*in fashion*) na moda. ~ **Lisbon/ English** em Lisboa/inglês. ~-**winter** no inverno. ~ **an hour**
(*at end of, within*) numa hora. ~
the rain na chuva. ~ **doing** ao
fazer. ~ **the evening** à tardinha.
the best ~ o melhor em. **we are**
~ **for** vamos ter. ~-**laws** *npl*
(*colloq*) sogros *mpl*. ~-**patient**
n doente *m* internado. **the ~s
and outs** meandros *mpl*

inability /ɪnə'bɪlətɪ/ *n* incapacidade *f* (**to do** para fazer)

inaccessible /ɪnæk'sesəbl/ *a* inacessível

inaccura|te /ɪn'ækjərət/ *a* inexato, (*P*) inexacto. ~**cy** *n* inexatidão *f*, (*P*) inexactidão *f*, falta *f* de rigor

inaction /ɪn'ækʃn/ *n* inação *f*, (*P*) inacção *f*

inactiv|e /ɪn'æktɪv/ *a* inativo, (*P*) inactivo. ~**ity** /-'tɪvətɪ/ *n* inação *f*, (*P*) inacção *f*

inadequa|te /ɪn'ædɪkwət/ *a* inadequado, impróprio; (*insufficient*)
insuficiente. ~**cy** *n* inadequação
f, (*insufficiency*) insuficiência *f*

inadmissible /ɪnəd'mɪsəbl/ *a* inadmissível

inadvertently /ɪnəd'vɜːtəntlɪ/
adv inadvertidamente; (*unintentionally*) sem querer, sem ser
por mal

inadvisable /ɪnəd'vaɪzəbl/ *a* desaconselhável, não aconselhável

inane /ɪ'neɪn/ *a* tolo, oco

inanimate /ɪn'ænɪmət/ *a* inanimado

inappropriate /ɪnə'prəʊprɪət/ *a*
impróprio, inadequado

inarticulate /ɪnɑː'tɪkjʊlət/ *a* inarticulado; (*of person*) incapaz de se
exprimir claramente

inattentive /ɪnə'tentɪv/ *a* desatento

inaugural /ɪ'nɔːgjʊrəl/ *a* inaugural

inaugurat|e /ɪ'nɔːgjʊreɪt/ *vt* inaugurar. ~**ion** /-'reɪʃn/ *n* inauguração *f*

inauspicious /ɪnɔː'spɪʃəs/ *a* pouco
auspicioso

inborn /ɪn'bɔːn/ *a* inato

inbred /ɪn'bred/ *a* inato, congênito, (*P*) congénito

incalculable /ɪn'kælkjʊləbl/ *a* incalculável

incapable /ɪn'keɪpəbl/ *a* incapaz

incapacit|y /ɪnkə'pæsətɪ/ *n* incapacidade *f*. ~**ate** *vt* incapacitar

incarnate /ɪn'kɑːneɪt/ *a* encarnado. **the devil** ~ o diabo em
pessoa. ~**ion** /-'neɪʃn/ *n* encarnação *f*

incendiary /ɪn'sendɪərɪ/ *a* incendiário □ *n* bomba *f* incendiária

incense[1] /'ɪnsens/ *n* incenso *m*

incense[2] /ɪn'sens/ *vt* exasperar,
enfurecer

incentive /ɪn'sentɪv/ *n* incentivo,
estímulo

incessant /ɪn'sesənt/ *a* incessante.
~**ly** *adv* incessantemente, sem
cessar

incest /'ɪnsest/ *n* incesto *m*.
~**uous** /ɪn'sestjʊəs/ *a* incestuoso

inch /ɪntʃ/ *n* polegada *f* (= 2.54 *cm*)
□ *vt/i* avançar palmo a palmo or

pouco a pouco. **within an ~ of** a um passo de

incidence /'ɪnsɪdəns/ n incidência f; (rate) percentagem f

incident /'ɪnsɪdənt/ n incidente m

incidental /ɪnsɪ'dentl/ a incidental, acessório; (casual) acidental; (expenses) eventuais; (music) de cena, incidental. **~ly** adv incidentalmente; (by the way) a propósito

incinerat|e /ɪn'sɪnəreɪt/ vt incinerar. **~or** n incinerador m

incision /ɪn'sɪʒn/ n incisão f

incisive /ɪn'saɪsɪv/ a incisivo

incite /ɪn'saɪt/ vt incitar, instigar. **~ment** n incitamento m

inclination /ɪnklɪ'neɪʃn/ n inclinação f, tendência f

incline[1] /ɪn'klaɪn/ vt/i inclinar (-se). **be ~d to** inclinar-se para; (have tendency) ter tendência para

incline[2] /'ɪnklaɪn/ n inclinação f, declive m

inclu|de /ɪn'kluːd/ vt incluir; (in letter) enviar junto or em anexo. **~ding** prep inclusive. **~sion** n inclusão f

inclusive /ɪn'kluːsɪv/ a & adv inclusive. **be ~ of** incluir

incognito /ɪnkɒg'niːtəʊ/ a & adv incógnito

incoherent /ɪnkəʊ'hɪərənt/ a incoerente

income /'ɪŋkʌm/ n rendimento m. **~ tax** imposto sobre a renda, (P) sobre o rendimento

incoming /'ɪnkʌmɪŋ/ a (tide) enchente; (tenant etc) novo

incomparable /ɪn'kɒmpərəbl/ a incomparável

incompatible /ɪnkəm'pætəbl/ a incompatível

incompeten|t /ɪn'kɒmpɪtənt/ a incompetente. **~ce** n incompetência f

incomplete /ɪnkəm'pliːt/ a incompleto

incomprehensible /ɪnkɒmprɪ-'hensəbl/ a incompreensível

inconceivable /ɪnkən'siːvəbl/ a inconcebível

inconclusive /ɪnkən'kluːsɪv/ a inconcludente

incongruous /ɪn'kɒŋgrʊəs/ a incongruente; (absurd) absurdo

inconsequential /ɪnkɒnsɪ'kwen-ʃl/ a sem importância

inconsiderate /ɪnkən'sɪdərət/ a impensado, inconsiderado; (lacking in regard) pouco atencioso, sem consideração (pelos sentimentos etc de outrem)

inconsisten|t /ɪnkən'sɪstənt/ a incoerente; (at variance) contraditório. **~t with** incompatível com. **~cy** n incoerência f. **~cies** npl contradições fpl

inconspicuous /ɪnkən'spɪkjʊəs/ a que não dá nas vistas, que não chama a atenção

incontinen|t /ɪn'kɒntɪnənt/ a incontinente. **~ce** n incontinência f

inconvenien|t /ɪnkən'viːnɪənt/ a inconveniente, incômodo. **~ce** n inconveniência f; (drawback) inconveniente m □ vt incomodar

incorporate /ɪn'kɔːpəreɪt/ vt incorporar; (include) incluir

incorrect /ɪnkə'rekt/ a incorreto, (P) incorrecto

incorrigible /ɪn'kɒrɪdʒəbl/ a incorrigível

increas|e[1] /ɪn'kriːs/ vt/i aumentar. **~ing** a crescente. **~ingly** adv cada vez mais

increase[2] /'ɪnkriːs/ n aumento m. **on the ~** aumentando, crescendo

incredible /ɪn'kredəbl/ a incrível

incredulous /ɪn'kredjʊləs/ a incrédulo

increment /'ɪŋkrəmənt/ n incremento m, aumento m

incriminat|e /ɪn'krɪmɪneɪt/ vt incriminar. **~ing** a comprometedor

incubat|e /'ɪnkjʊbeɪt/ vt incubar. **~ion** /-'beɪʃn/ n incubação f. **~or** n incubadora f

inculcate /'ɪnkʌlkeɪt/ vt inculcar

incumbent /ɪn'kʌmbənt/ n (pol, relig) titular mf □ a **be ~ on** incumbir a, caber a

incur /ɪn'kɜ:r/ vt (pt incurred) (displeasure, expense etc) incorrer em; (debts) contrair

incurable /ɪn'kjʊərəbl/ a incurável, que não tem cura

indebted /ɪn'detɪd/ a **~ to s.o.** em dívida (para) com alg (for por)

indecen|t /ɪn'di:snt/ a indecente. **~t assault** atentado m contra o pudor. **~cy** n indecência f

indecision /ɪndɪ'sɪʒn/ n indecisão f

indecisive /ɪndɪ'saɪsɪv/ a inconcludente, não decisivo; (hesitating) indeciso

indeed /ɪn'di:d/ adv realmente, deveras, mesmo; (in fact) de fato, (P) facto. **very much ~** muitíssimo

indefinite /ɪn'defɪnət/ a indefinido; (time) indeterminado. **~ly** adv indefinidamente

indelible /ɪn'deləbl/ a indelével

indemnify /ɪn'demnɪfaɪ/ vt indenizar, (P) indemnizar (for de); (safeguard) garantir (against contra)

indemnity /ɪn'demnəti/ n (legal exemption) isenção f; (compensation) indenização f, (P) indemnização f; (safeguard) garantia f

indent /ɪn'dent/ vt (notch) recortar; (typ) entrar. **~ation** /-'teɪʃn/ n recorte m; (typ) entrada f

independen|t /ɪndɪ'pendənt/ a independente. **~ce** n independência f. **~tly** adv independentemente

indescribable /ɪndɪ'skraɪbəbl/ a indescritível

indestructible /ɪndɪ'strʌktəbl/ a indestrutível

indeterminate /ɪndɪ'tɜ:mɪnət/ a indeterminado

index /'ɪndeks/ n (pl indexes) n (in book) índice m; (in library) catálogo m □ vt indexar. **~ card** ficha f (de fichário). **~ finger** index m, (dedo) indicador m. **~-linked** a ligado ao índice de inflação

India /'ɪndɪə/ n Índia f. **~n** a & n (of India) indiano (m); (American) índio (m)

indicat|e /'ɪndɪkeɪt/ vt indicar. **~ion** /-'keɪʃn/ n indicação f. **~or** n indicador m; (auto) pisca-pisca m; (board) quadro m

indicative /ɪn'dɪkətɪv/ a & n indicativo (m)

indict /ɪn'daɪt/ vt acusar. **~ment** n acusação f

indifferen|t /ɪn'dɪfrənt/ a indiferente; (not good) medíocre. **~ce** n indiferença f

indigenous /ɪn'dɪdʒɪnəs/ a indígena, natural, nativo (do país)

indigest|ion /ɪndɪ'dʒestʃən/ n indigestão f. **~ible** /-'təbl/ a indigesto

indign|ant /ɪn'dɪgnənt/ a indignado. **~ation** /-'neɪʃn/ n indignação f

indirect /ɪndɪ'rekt/ a indireto, (P) indirecto. **~ly** adv indiretamente, (P) indirectamente

indiscr|eet /ɪndɪ'skri:t/ a indiscreto; (not wary) imprudente. **~etion** /-'eʃn/ n indiscrição f; (action, remark etc) deslize m

indiscriminate /ɪndɪ'skrɪmɪnət/ a que tem falta de discernimento; (random) indiscriminado. **~ly** adv sem discernimento; (at random) indiscriminadamente, ao acaso

indispensable /ɪndɪ'spensəbl/ a indispensável

indispos|ed /ɪndɪ'spəʊzd/ a indisposto. **~ition** /-'zɪʃn/ n indisposição f

indisputable /ˌɪndɪˈspjuːtəbl/ a indisputável, incontestável

indistinct /ˌɪndɪˈstɪŋkt/ a indistinto

indistinguishable /ˌɪndɪˈstɪŋgwɪʃəbl/ a indistinguível, imperceptível; (*identical*) indiferenciável

individual /ˌɪndɪˈvɪdʒʊəl/ a individual □ n indivíduo m. ~ity /-ˈælətɪ/ n individualidade f. ~ly adv individualmente

indivisible /ˌɪndɪˈvɪzəbl/ a indivisível

indoctrinate /ɪnˈdɒktrɪneɪt/ vt (en)doutrinar. ~ion /-ˈneɪʃn/ n (en)doutrinação f

indolen|t /ˈɪndələnt/ a indolente. ~ce n indolência f

indoor /ˈɪndɔː(r)/ a (de) interior, interno; (*under cover*) coberto; (*games*) de salão. ~s /ɪnˈdɔːz/ adv dentro de casa, no interior

induce /ɪnˈdjuːs/ vt induzir, levar; (*cause*) causar, provocar. ~ment n incentivo m, encorajamento m

indulge /ɪnˈdʌldʒ/ vt satisfazer; (*spoil*) fazer a(s) vontade(s) de □ vi ~ in entregar-se a

indulgen|t /ɪnˈdʌldʒənt/ a indulgente. ~ce n (*leniency*) indulgência f; (*desire*) satisfação f

industrial /ɪnˈdʌstrɪəl/ a industrial; (*unrest etc*) trabalhista; (*action*) reivindicativo. ~ estate zona f industrial. ~ist n industrial m. ~ized a industrializado

industrious /ɪnˈdʌstrɪəs/ a trabalhador, aplicado

industry /ˈɪndəstrɪ/ n indústria f; (*zeal*) aplicação f, diligência f, zelo m

inebriated /ɪˈniːbrɪeɪtɪd/ a embriagado, ébrio

inedible /ɪˈnedɪbl/ a não comestível

ineffective /ˌɪnɪˈfektɪv/ a ineficaz; (*person*) ineficiente, incapaz

ineffectual /ˌɪnɪˈfektʃʊəl/ a ineficaz, improfícuo

inefficien|t /ˌɪnɪˈfɪʃnt/ a ineficiente. ~cy n ineficiência f

ineligible /ɪnˈelɪdʒəbl/ a inelegível; (*undesirable*) indesejável. **be ~ for** não ter direito a

inept /ɪˈnept/ a inepto

inequality /ˌɪnɪˈkwɒlətɪ/ n desigualdade f

inert /ɪˈnɜːt/ a inerte. ~ia /-ʃə/ n inércia f

inevitable /ɪnˈevɪtəbl/ a inevitável, fatal

inexcusable /ˌɪnɪkˈskjuːzəbl/ a indesculpável, imperdoável

inexhaustible /ˌɪnɪgˈzɔːstəbl/ a inesgotável, inexaurível

inexorable /ɪnˈeksərəbl/ a inexorável

inexpensive /ˌɪnɪkˈspensɪv/ a barato, em conta

inexperience /ˌɪnɪkˈspɪərɪəns/ n inexperiência f, falta de experiência f. ~d a inexperiente

inexplicable /ˌɪnɪkˈsplɪkəbl/ a inexplicável

inextricable /ˌɪnɪkˈstrɪkəbl/ a inextricável

infallib|le /ɪnˈfæləbl/ a infalível. ~ility /-ˈbɪlətɪ/ n infalibilidade f

infam|ous /ˈɪnfəməs/ a infame. ~y n infâmia f

infan|t /ˈɪnfənt/ n bebê m, (P) bebé m; (*child*) criança f. ~cy n infância f; (*babyhood*) primeira infância f

infantile /ˈɪnfəntaɪl/ a infantil

infantry /ˈɪnfəntrɪ/ n infantaria f

infatuat|ed /ɪnˈfætʃʊeɪtɪd/ a ~ed with cego or perdido por. ~ion /-ˈeɪʃn/ n cegueira f, paixão f

infect /ɪnˈfekt/ vt infectar. ~ s.o. with contagiar or contaminar alg com. ~ion /-ʃn/ n infecção f, contágio m. ~ious /-ʃəs/ a infeccioso, contagioso

infer /ɪnˈfɜː(r)/ vt (pt inferred) inferir, deduzir. ~ence /ˈɪnfərəns/ n inferência f

inferior /ɪnˈfɪərɪə(r)/ *a* inferior; (*work etc*) de qualidade inferior □ *n* inferior *mf*; (*in rank*) subalterno *m*. ~**ity** /-ˈɒrəti/ *n* inferioridade *f*

infernal /ɪnˈfɜːnl/ *a* infernal

infertil|e /ɪnˈfɜːtaɪl/ *a* infértil, estéril. ~**ity** /-əˈtɪləti/ *n* infertilidade *f*, esterilidade *f*

infest /ɪnˈfest/ *vt* infestar (**with** de). ~**ation** *n* infestação *f*

infidelity /ɪnfɪˈdeləti/ *n* infidelidade *f*

infiltrat|e /ˈɪnfɪltreɪt/ *vt*/*i* infiltrar (-se). ~**ion** /-ˈtreɪʃn/ *n* infiltração *f*

infinite /ˈɪnfɪnət/ *a* & *n* infinito (*m*). ~**ly** *adv* infinitamente

infinitesimal /ɪnfɪnɪˈtesɪml/ *a* infinitesimal, infinitésimo

infinitive /ɪnˈfɪnətɪv/ *n* infinitivo *m*

infinity /ɪnˈfɪnəti/ *n* infinidade *f*, infinito *m*

infirm /ɪnˈfɜːm/ *a* débil, fraco. ~**ity** *n* (*illness*) enfermidade *f*; (*weakness*) fraqueza *f*

inflam|e /ɪnˈfleɪm/ *vt* inflamar. ~**mable** /-æməbl/ *a* inflamável. ~**mation** /-əˈmeɪʃn/ *n* inflamação *f*

inflate /ɪnˈfleɪt/ *vt* (*balloon etc*) encher de ar; (*prices*) causar inflação de

inflation /ɪnˈfleɪʃn/ *n* inflação *f*. ~**ary** *a* inflacionário

inflection /ɪnˈflekʃn/ *n* inflexão *f*; (*gram*) flexão *f*, desinência *f*

inflexible /ɪnˈfleksəbl/ *a* inflexível

inflict /ɪnˈflɪkt/ *vt* infligir, impor (**on** a)

influence /ˈɪnfluəns/ *n* influência *f* □ *vt* influenciar, influir sobre

influential /ɪnfluˈenʃl/ *a* influente

influenza /ɪnfluˈenzə/ *n* gripe *f*

influx /ˈɪnflʌks/ *n* afluência *f*, influxo *m*

inform /ɪnˈfɔːm/ *vt* informar. ~ **against** *or* **on** denunciar. **keep**

~**ed** manter ao corrente *or* a par. ~**ant** *n* informante *mf*. ~**er** *n* delator *m*, denunciante *mf*

informal /ɪnˈfɔːml/ *a* informal; (*simple*) simples, sem cerimónia, (*P*) cerimónia; (*unofficial*) oficioso; (*colloquial*) familiar; (*dress*) de passeio, à vontade; (*dinner, gathering*) íntimo. ~**ity** /-ˈmæləti/ *n* informalidade *f*; (*simplicity*) simplicidade *f*; (*intimacy*) intimidade *f*. ~**ly** *adv* informalmente, sem cerimónia, (*P*) cerimónia, à vontade

information /ɪnfəˈmeɪʃn/ *n* informação *f*; (*facts, data*) informações *fpl*. ~ **technology** tecnologia *f* da informação

informative /ɪnˈfɔːmətɪv/ *a* informativo

infra-red /ɪnfrəˈred/ *a* infravermelho

infrequent /ɪnˈfriːkwənt/ *a* pouco frequente, (*P*) frequente. ~**ly** *adv* raramente

infringe /ɪnˈfrɪndʒ/ *vt* infringir. ~ **on** transgredir; (*rights*) violar. ~**ment** *n* infração *f*, (*P*) fracção *f*; (*rights*) violação *f*

infuriate /ɪnˈfjʊərɪeɪt/ *vt* enfurecer, enraivecer. ~**ing** *a* enfurecedor, de enfurecer, de dar raiva

infus|e /ɪnˈfjuːz/ *vt* infundir, incutir; (*herbs, tea*) pôr de infusão. ~**ion** /-ʒn/ *n* infusão *f*

ingen|ious /ɪnˈdʒiːnɪəs/ *a* engenhoso, bem pensado. ~**uity** /-ɪˈnjuːəti/ *n* engenho *m*, habilidade *f*, imaginação *f*

ingenuous /ɪnˈdʒenjʊəs/ *a* cândido, ingénuo, (*P*) ingénuo

ingot /ˈɪŋgət/ *n* barra *f*, lingote *m*

ingrained /ɪnˈgreɪnd/ *a* arraigado, enraizado; (*dirt*) entranhado

ingratiate /ɪnˈgreɪʃɪeɪt/ *vt* ~ **o.s. with** insinuar-se junto de, cair nas *or* ganhar as boas graças de

ingratitude /ɪnˈgrætɪtjuːd/ *n* ingratidão *f*

ingredient /ɪnˈgriːdɪənt/ n ingrediente m

inhabit /ɪnˈhæbɪt/ vt habitar. ~able a habitável. ~ant n habitante mf

inhale /ɪnˈheɪl/ vt inalar, aspirar. ~r /-ə(r)/ n inalador m

inherent /ɪnˈhɪərənt/ a inerente. ~ly adv inerentemente, em si

inherit /ɪnˈherɪt/ vt herdar (**from** de). ~ance n herança f

inhibit /ɪnˈhɪbɪt/ vt inibir; (prevent) impedir. **be ~ed** ser (um) inibido. ~ion /-ˈbɪʃn/ n inibição f

inhospitable /ɪnˈhɒspɪtəbl/ a inóspito; (of person) inospitaleiro, pouco/nada hospitaleiro

inhuman /ɪnˈhjuːmən/ a desumano. ~ity /-ˈmænətɪ/ n desumanidade f

inhumane /ɪnhjuːˈmeɪn/ a inumano, cruel

inimitable /ɪˈnɪmɪtəbl/ a inimitável

iniquitous /ɪˈnɪkwɪtəs/ a iníquo

initial /ɪˈnɪʃl/ a & n inicial f □ vt (pt **initialled**) assinar com as iniciais, rubricar. ~ly adv inicialmente

initiat|**e** /ɪˈnɪʃɪeɪt/ vt iniciar (**into** em); (scheme) lançar. ~**ion** /-ˈeɪʃn/ n iniciação f; (start) início m

initiative /ɪˈnɪʃətɪv/ n iniciativa f

inject /ɪnˈdʒekt/ vt injetar; (P) injectar; (fig) insuflar. ~**ion** /-ʃn/ n injeção f, (P) injecção f

injure /ˈɪndʒə(r)/ vt (harm) fazer mal a, prejudicar, lesar; (hurt) ferir

injury /ˈɪndʒərɪ/ n ferimento m, lesão f; (wrong) mal m

injustice /ɪnˈdʒʌstɪs/ n injustiça f

ink /ɪŋk/ n tinta f. ~**-well** n tinteiro m. ~y a sujo de tinta

inkling /ˈɪŋklɪŋ/ n idéia f, (P) ideia f, suspeita f

inlaid /ɪnˈleɪd/ see **inlay**[1]

inland /ˈɪnlənd/ a interior □ adv /ɪnˈlænd/ no interior, para o interior. **the I~ Revenue** o Fisco, a Receita Federal

inlay[1] /ɪnˈleɪ/ vt (pt **inlaid**) embutir, incrustar

inlay[2] /ˈɪnleɪ/ n incrustação f, obturação f

inlet /ˈɪnlet/ n braço m de mar, enseada f; (techn) admissão f

inmate /ˈɪnmeɪt/ n residente mf; (in hospital) internado m; (in prison) presidiário m

inn /ɪn/ n estalagem f

innards /ˈɪnədz/ npl (colloq) tripas (colloq) fpl

innate /ɪˈneɪt/ a inato

inner /ˈɪnə(r)/ a interior, interno; (fig) íntimo. ~ **city** centro m da cidade. ~**most** a mais profundo, mais íntimo. ~ **tube** n câmara f de ar

innings /ˈɪnɪŋz/ n (cricket) vez f de bater; (pol) período m no poder

innocen|**t** /ˈɪnəsnt/ a & n inocente (mf). ~**ce** n inocência f

innocuous /ɪˈnɒkjʊəs/ a inócuo, inofensivo

innovat|**e** /ˈɪnəveɪt/ vi inovar. ~**ion** /-ˈveɪʃn/ n inovação f. ~**or** n inovador m

innuendo /ɪnjuːˈendəʊ/ n (pl -oes) insinuação f, indireta f, (P) indirecta f

innumerable /ɪˈnjuːmərəbl/ a inumerável

inoculat|**e** /ɪˈnɒkjʊleɪt/ vt inocular. ~**ion** /-ˈleɪʃn/ n inoculação f, vacina f

inoffensive /ɪnəˈfensɪv/ a inofensivo

inoperative /ɪnˈɒpərətɪv/ a inoperante, ineficaz

inopportune /ɪnˈɒpətjuːn/ a inoportuno

inordinate /ɪˈnɔːdɪnət/ a excessivo, desmedido. ~**ly** adv excessivamente, desmedidamente

input /'ɪmpʊt/ n (data) dados mpl; (electr: power) energia f; (computer process) entrada f, dados mpl

inquest /'ɪnkwest/ n inquérito m

inquir|e /ɪn'kwaɪə(r)/ vi informar-se □ vt perguntar, indagar, inquirir. ~e about procurar informações sobre, indagar. ~e into inquirir, indagar. ~ing a (look) interrogativo; (mind) inquisitivo. ~y n (question) pergunta f; (jur) inquérito m; (investigation) investigação f

inquisition /ɪnkwɪ'zɪʃn/ n inquisição f

inquisitive /ɪn'kwɪzətɪv/ a curioso, inquisitivo; (prying) intrometido, bisbilhoteiro

insan|e /ɪn'seɪn/ a louco, doido. ~ity /ɪn'sænətɪ/ n loucura f, demência f

insanitary /ɪn'sænɪtrɪ/ a insalubre, anti-higiénico, (P) anti-higiénico

insatiable /ɪn'seɪʃəbl/ a insaciável

inscri|be /ɪn'skraɪb/ vt inscrever; (book) dedicar. ~ption /-ɪpʃn/ n inscrição f; (in book) dedicatória f

inscrutable /ɪn'skruːtəbl/ a impenetrável, misterioso

insect /'ɪnsekt/ n inseto m, (P) insecto m

insecur|e /ɪnsɪ'kjʊə(r)/ a (not firm) inseguro, mal seguro; (unsafe; psych) inseguro. ~ity n insegurança f, falta f de segurança

insensible /ɪn'sensəbl/ a insensível; (unconscious) inconsciente

insensitive /ɪn'sensətɪv/ a insensível

inseparable /ɪn'seprəbl/ a inseparável

insert[1] /ɪn'sɜːt/ vt inserir; (key) meter, colocar; (add) pôr, inserir. ~ion /-ʃn/ n inserção f

insert[2] /'ɪnsɜːt/ n coisa f inserida

inside /ɪn'saɪd/ n interior m. ~s (colloq) tripas fpl (colloq) □ a interior, interno □ adv no interior, dentro, por dentro □ prep dentro de; (of time) em menos de. ~ out de dentro para fora, do avesso; (thoroughly) por dentro e por fora, a fundo

insidious /ɪn'sɪdɪəs/ a insidioso

insight /'ɪnsaɪt/ n penetração f, perspicácia f; (glimpse) vislumbre m

insignificant /ɪnsɪg'nɪfɪkənt/ a insignificante

insincer|e /ɪnsɪn'sɪə(r)/ a insincero. ~ity /-'serətɪ/ n insinceridade f, falta f de sinceridade

insinuat|e /ɪn'sɪnjʊeɪt/ vt insinuar. ~ion /-'eɪʃn/ n (act) insinuação f; (hint) indireta f, (P) indirecta f, insinuação f

insipid /ɪn'sɪpɪd/ a insípido, sem sabor

insist /ɪn'sɪst/ vt/i ~ (on/that) insistir (em/em que)

insisten|t /ɪn'sɪstənt/ a insistente. ~ce n insistência f. ~tly adv insistentemente

insolen|t /'ɪnsələnt/ a insolente. ~ce n insolência f

insoluble /ɪn'sɒljʊbl/ a insolúvel

insolvent /ɪn'sɒlvənt/ a insolvente

insomnia /ɪn'sɒmnɪə/ n insónia f, (P) insónia f

inspect /ɪn'spekt/ vt inspecionar, (P) inspeccionar, examinar; (tickets) fiscalizar; (passport) controlar; (troops) passar revista a. ~ion /-ʃn/ n inspeção f, (P) inspecção f, exame m; (ticket) fiscalização f; (troops) revista f. ~or n inspetor m, (P) inspector m; (on train) fiscal m

inspir|e /ɪn'spaɪə(r)/ vt inspirar. ~ation /-ə'reɪʃn/ n inspiração f

instability /ɪnstə'bɪlətɪ/ n instabilidade f

install /ɪn'stɔːl/ vt instalar; (heater etc) montar, instalar. ~ation /-ə'leɪʃn/ n instalação f

instalment /ɪn'stɔːlmənt/ n prestação f; (of serial) episódio m

instance /'ɪnstəns/ n exemplo m, caso m. **for** ~ por exemplo. **in the first** ~ em primeiro lugar

instant /'ɪnstənt/ a imediato; (food) instantâneo □ n instante m. ~ly adv imediatamente, logo

instantaneous /ɪnstən'teɪnɪəs/ a instantâneo

instead /ɪn'sted/ adv em vez disso, em lugar disso. ~ **of** em vez de, em lugar de

instigat|e /'ɪnstɪgeɪt/ vt instigar, incitar. ~**ion** /-'geɪʃn/ n instigação f. ~**or** n instigador m

instil /ɪn'stɪl/ vt (pt instilled) instilar, insuflar

instinct /'ɪnstɪŋkt/ n instinto m. ~**ive** /ɪn'stɪŋktɪv/ a instintivo

institut|e /'ɪnstɪtjuːt/ n instituto m □ vt instituir; (legal proceedings) intentar; (inquiry) ordenar. ~**ion** /-'tjuːʃn/ n instituição f; (school) estabelecimento m de ensino; (hospital) estabelecimento m hospitalar

instruct /ɪn'strʌkt/ vt instruir; (order) mandar, ordenar; (a solicitor etc) dar instruções a. ~ **s.o. in sth** ensinar alg coisa a alguém. ~**ion** /-ʃn/ n instrução f. ~**ions** /-ʃnz/ npl instruções fpl, modo m de emprego; (orders) ordens fpl. ~**ive** a instrutivo. ~**or** n instrutor m

instrument /'ɪnstrʊmənt/ n instrumento m. ~ **panel** painel m de instrumentos

instrumental /ɪnstrʊ'mentl/ a instrumental. **be** ~ **in** ter um papel decisivo em. ~**ist** n instrumentalista m

insubordinat|e /ɪnsə'bɔːdɪnət/ a insubordinado. ~**ion** /-'neɪʃn/ n insubordinação f

insufferable /ɪn'sʌfrəbl/ a intolerável, insuportável

insufficient /ɪnsə'fɪʃnt/ a insuficiente

insular /'ɪnsjʊlə(r)/ a insular; (fig: narrow-minded) bitolado, limitado, (P) tacanho

insulat|e /'ɪnsjʊleɪt/ vt isolar. ~**ing tape** fita f isolante. ~**ion** /-'leɪʃn/ n isolamento m

insulin /'ɪnsjʊlɪn/ n insulina f

insult[1] /ɪn'sʌlt/ vt insultar, injuriar. ~**ing** a insultante, injurioso

insult[2] /'ɪnsʌlt/ n insulto m, injúria f

insur|e /ɪn'ʃʊə(r)/ vt segurar, pôr no seguro; (Amer) = ensure. ~**ance** n seguro m. ~**ance policy** apólice f de seguro

insurmountable /ɪnsə'maʊntəbl/ a insuperável

intact /ɪn'tækt/ a intato, (P) intacto

intake /'ɪnteɪk/ n admissão f; (techn) admissão f, entrada f; (of food) ingestão f

intangible /ɪn'tændʒəbl/ a intangível

integral /'ɪntɪgrəl/ a integral. **be an** ~ **part of** ser parte integrante de

integrat|e /'ɪntɪgreɪt/ vt/i integrar (-se). ~**ed circuit** circuito m integrado. ~**ion** /-'greɪʃn/ n integração f

integrity /ɪn'tegrəti/ n integridade f

intellect /'ɪntəlekt/ n intelecto m, inteligência f. ~**ual** /-'lektʃʊəl/ a & n intelectual (mf)

intelligen|t /ɪn'telɪdʒənt/ a inteligente. ~**ce** n inteligência f; (mil) informações fpl. ~**tly** adv inteligentemente

intelligible /ɪn'telɪdʒəbl/ a inteligível

intend /ɪn'tend/ vt tencionar; (destine) reservar, destinar. ~**ed** a intencional, proposital

intens|e /ɪnˈtens/ a intenso; (*person*) emotivo. **~ely** adv intensamente; (*very*) extremamente. **~ity** n intensidade f

intensif|y /ɪnˈtensɪfaɪ/ vt intensificar. **~ication** /-ˈkeɪʃn/ n intensificação f

intensive /ɪnˈtensɪv/ a intensivo. **~ care** tratamento m intensivo

intent /ɪnˈtent/ n intento m, desígnio m, propósito m □ a atento, concentrado. **~ on** absorto em; (*intending to*) decidido a. **~ly** adv atentamente

intention /ɪnˈtenʃn/ n intenção f. **~al** a intencional. **~ally** adv de propósito

inter /ɪnˈtɜː(r)/ vt (*pt* **interred**) enterrar

inter- /ˈɪntə(r)/ pref inter-

interact /ɪntərˈækt/ vi agir uns sobre os outros. **~ion** /-ʃn/ n interação f, (P) interacção f

intercede /ɪntəˈsiːd/ vi interceder

intercept /ɪntəˈsept/ vt interceptar

interchange[1] /ɪntəˈtʃeɪndʒ/ vt permutar, trocar. **~able** a permutável

interchange[2] /ˈɪntətʃeɪndʒ/ n permuta f, intercâmbio m; (*road junction*) trevo m de trânsito, (P) nó m

intercom /ˈɪntəkɒm/ n interfone m, (P) intercomunicador m

interconnected /ɪntəkəˈnektɪd/ a (*facts, events etc*) ligado

intercourse /ˈɪntəkɔːs/ n (*sexual*) relações fpl sexuais

interest /ˈɪntrəst/ n interesse m; (*legal share*) título m; (*in finance*) juro(s) m(pl). **rate of ~** taxa f de juros □ vt interessar. **~ed** a interessado. **be ~ed in** interessar-se por. **~ing** a interessante

interface /ˈɪntəfeɪs/ n interface f

interfer|e /ɪntəˈfɪə(r)/ vi interferir, intrometer-se (**in** em); (*meddle, hinder*) interferir (**with** com);

(*tamper*) mexer indevidamente (**with** em). **~ence** n interferência f

interim /ˈɪntərɪm/ n in the **~** nesse/neste ínterim m, (P) interim m □ a interino, provisório

interior /ɪnˈtɪərɪə(r)/ a & n interior (m)

interjection /ɪntəˈdʒekʃn/ n interjeição f

interlock /ɪntəˈlɒk/ vt/i entrelaçar; (*pieces of puzzle etc*) encaixar(-se); (*mech: wheels*) engrenar, engatar

interloper /ˈɪntələʊpə(r)/ n intruso m

intermarr|iage /ɪntəˈmærɪdʒ/ n casamento m entre membros de diferentes famílias, raças etc; (*between near relations*) casamento m consangüíneo, (P) consanguíneo. **~y** vi ligar-se por casamento

intermediary /ɪntəˈmiːdɪərɪ/ a & n intermediário m

intermediate /ɪntəˈmiːdɪət/ a termédio, intermediário

interminable /ɪnˈtɜːmɪnəbl/ a terminável, infindável

intermission /ɪntəˈmɪʃn/ n intervalo m

intermittent /ɪntəˈmɪtnt/ a intermitente. **~ly** adv intermitentemente

intern[1] /ɪnˈtɜːn/ vt internar. **~ee** /-ˈniː/ n internado m. **~ment** n internamento m

internal /ɪnˈtɜːnl/ a interno, interior. (*Amer.*) the **I ~** Revenue o Fisco, a Receita Federal (B). **~ly** adv internamente, interiormente

international /ɪntəˈnæʃnəl/ a & n internacional (mf)

Internet /ˈɪntənet/ n Internet f

interpret /ɪnˈtɜːprɪt/ vt/i interpretar. **~ation** /-ˈteɪʃn/ n interpretação f. **~er** n intérprete mf

interrelated /ɪntərɪ'leɪtɪd/ *a* inter-relacionado, correlacionado

interrogat|e /ɪn'terəgeɪt/ *vt* interrogar. **~ion** /-'geɪʃn/ *n* interrogação *f*; (*of police etc*) interrogatório *m*

interrogative /ɪntə'rɒgətɪv/ *a* interrogativo □ *n* (*pronoun*) pronome *m* interrogativo

interrupt /ɪntə'rʌpt/ *vt* interromper. **~ion** /-ʃn/ *n* interrupção *f*

intersect /ɪntə'sekt/ *vt/i* intersectar(-se); (*roads*) cruzar-se. **~ion** /-ʃn/ *n* intersecção *f*; (*crossroads*) cruzamento *n*

intersperse /ɪntə'spɜːs/ *vt* entremear, intercalar;(*scatter*)espalhar

interval /'ɪntəvl/ *n* intervalo *m*. at **~ s** a intervalos

interven|e /ɪntə'viːn/ *vi* (*interfere*) intervir; (*of time*) decorrer; (*occur*) sobrevir, intervir. **~tion** /-'venʃn/ *n* intervenção *f*

interview /'ɪntəvjuː/ *n* entrevista *f* □ *vt* entrevistar. **~ee** *n* entrevistado *m*. **~er** *n* entrevistador *m*

intestin|e /ɪn'testɪn/ *n* intestino *m*. **~al** *a* intestinal

intima|te¹ /'ɪntɪmət/ *a* íntimo; (*detailed*) profundo. **~cy** *n* intimidade *f*. **~tely** *adv* intimamente

intimate² /'ɪntɪmeɪt/ *vt* (*announce*) dar a conhecer, fazer saber; (*imply*) dar a entender

intimidat|e /ɪn'tɪmɪdeɪt/ *vt* intimidar. **~ion** /-'deɪʃn/ *n* intimidação *f*

into /'ɪntə/, *emphatic* /'ɪntʊ/ *prep* para dentro de. **divide ~ three** dividir em tres. **~ pieces** aos bocados. **translate ~** traduzir para

intolerable /ɪn'tɒlərəbl/ *a* intolerável, insuportável

intoleran|t /ɪn'tɒlərənt/ *a* intolerante. **~ce** *n* intolerância *f*

intonation /ɪntə'neɪʃn/ *n* entonação *f*, entoação *f*, inflexão *f*

intoxicat|ed /ɪn'tɒksɪkeɪtɪd/ *a* embriagado, etilizado. **~ion** /-'keɪ-ʃn/ *n* embriaguez *f*

intra- /ɪntrə/ *pref* intra-

intractable /ɪn'træktəbl/ *a* intratável, difícil

intranet /'ɪntrənet/ *n* rede *f* corporativa

intransigent /ɪn'trænsɪdʒənt/ *a* intransigente

intransitive /ɪn'trænsətɪv/ *a* (*verb*) intransitivo

intravenous /ɪntrə'viːnəs/ *a* intravenoso

intrepid /ɪn'trepɪd/ *a* intrépido, arrojado

intrica|te /'ɪntrɪkət/ *a* intrincado, complexo. **~cy** *n* complexidade *f*

intrigu|e /ɪn'triːg/ *vt/i* intrigar □ *n* intriga *f*. **~ing** *a* intrigante, curioso

intrinsic /ɪn'trɪnsɪk/ *a* intrínseco. **~ally** /-klɪ/ *adv* intrinsecamente

introduce /ɪntrə'djuːs/ *vt* (*programme, question*) apresentar; (*bring in, insert*) introduzir; (*initiate*) iniciar. **~ sb to sb** (*person*) apresentar alg a alguém

introduct|ion /ɪntrə'dʌkʃn/ *n* introdução *f*; (*of person*) apresentação *f*. **~ory** /-tərɪ/ *a* introdutório, de introdução; (*letter, words*) de apresentação

introspective /ɪntrə'spektɪv/ *a* introspectivo

introvert /'ɪntrəvɜːt/ *n & a* introvertido (*m*)

intru|de /ɪn'truːd/ *vi* intrometer-se, ser a mais. **~der** *n* intruso *m*. **~sion** *n* intrusão *f*. **~sive** *a* intruso

intuit|ion /ɪntjuː'ɪʃn/ *n* intuição *f*. **~ive** /ɪn'tjuːɪtɪv/ *a* intuitivo

inundate /'ɪnʌndeɪt/ *vt* inundar (**with de**)

invade /ɪn'veɪd/ *vt* invadir. **~r** /-ə(r)/ *n* invasor *m*

invalid¹ /'ɪnvəlɪd/ *n* inválido *m*

invalid² /ɪnˈvælɪd/ a inválido. ~ate vt invalidar

invaluable /ɪnˈvæljʊəbl/ a inestimável

invariabl|e /ɪnˈveərɪəbl/ a invariável. ~y adv invariavelmente

invasion /ɪnˈveɪʒn/ n invasão f

invective /ɪnˈvektɪv/ n invectiva f

invent /ɪnˈvent/ vt inventar. ~ion n invenção f. ~ive a inventivo. ~or n inventor m

inventory /ˈɪnvəntrɪ/ n inventário m

inverse /ɪnˈvɜːs/ a & n inverso (m). ~ly adv inversamente

inver|t /ɪnˈvɜːt/ vt inverter. ~ted commas aspas fpl. ~sion n inversão f

invest /ɪnˈvest/ vt investir; (time, effort) dedicar □ vi fazer um investimento. ~ in (colloq: buy) gastar dinheiro em. ~ment n investimento m. ~or n investidor m, financiador m

investigat|e /ɪnˈvestɪgeɪt/ vt investigar. ~ion n /-ˈgeɪʃn/ n investigação f. under ~ion em estudo. ~or n investigador m

inveterate /ɪnˈvetərət/ a inveterado

invidious /ɪnˈvɪdɪəs/ a antipático, odioso

invigorate /ɪnˈvɪgəreɪt/ vt revigorar; (encourage) estimular

invincible /ɪnˈvɪnsəbl/ a invencível

invisible /ɪnˈvɪzəbl/ a invisível

invit|e /ɪnˈvaɪt/ vt convidar; (bring on) pedir, provocar. ~ation /ɪnvɪˈteɪʃn/ n convite m. ~ing a (tempting) tentador; (pleasant) acolhedor, convidativo

invoice /ˈɪnvɔɪs/ n fatura f, (P) factura f □ vt faturar, (P) facturar

invoke /ɪnˈvəʊk/ vt invocar

involuntary /ɪnˈvɒləntrɪ/ a involuntário

involve /ɪnˈvɒlv/ vt implicar, envolver. ~d a (complex) compli-

cado; (at stake) em jogo; (emotionally) envolvido. ~d in implicado em. ~ment n envolvimento m, participação f

invulnerable /ɪnˈvʌlnərəbl/ a invulnerável

inward /ˈɪnwəd/ a interior; (thought etc) íntimo. ~(s) adv para dentro, para o interior. ~ly adv interiormente, intimamente

iodine /ˈaɪədiːn/ n iodo m; (antiseptic) tintura f de iodo

IOU /aɪəʊˈjuː/ n abbr vale m

IQ /aɪˈkjuː/ abbr (intelligence quotient) Q I m

Iran /ɪˈrɑːn/ n Irã m. ~ian /ɪˈreɪnɪən/ a & n iraniano (m)

Iraq /ɪˈrɑːk/ n Iraque m. ~i a & n iraquiano (m)

irascible /ɪˈræsəbl/ a irascível

irate /aɪˈreɪt/ a irado, enraivecido

Ireland /ˈaɪələnd/ n Irlanda f

iris /ˈaɪərɪs/ n (anat, bot) íris f

Irish /ˈaɪərɪʃ/ a & n (language) irlandês (m). ~man n irlandês m. ~woman n irlandesa f

irk /ɜːk/ vt aborrecer, incomodar. ~some a aborrecido

iron /ˈaɪən/ n ferro m; (appliance) ferro m de engomar □ a de ferro □ vt passar a ferro. ~ out fazer desaparecer, (fig) aplanar, resolver. ~ing n do the ~ing passar a roupa. ~ing-board n tábua f de passar roupa, (P) tábua f de engomar

ironic(al) /aɪˈrɒnɪk(l)/ a irônico, (P) irónico

ironmonger /ˈaɪənmʌŋɡə(r)/ n ferreiro m, (P) ferrageiro m. ~'s n (shop) loja f de ferragens

irony /ˈaɪərənɪ/ n ironia f

irrational /ɪˈræʃənl/ a irracional; (person) ilógico, que não raciocina

irreconcilable /ɪrekənˈsaɪləbl/ a irreconciliável

irrefutable /ɪrɪˈfjuːtəbl/ a irrefutável

irregular /ɪˈreɡjʊlə(r)/ a irregular. ~**ity** /-ˈlærətɪ/ n irregularidade f

irrelevant /ɪˈreləvənt/ a irrelevante, que não é pertinente

irreparable /ɪˈrepərəbl/ a irreparável, irremediável

irreplaceable /ɪrɪˈpleɪsəbl/ a insubstituível

irresistible /ɪrɪˈzɪstəbl/ a irresistível

irresolute /ɪˈrezəluːt/ a irresoluto

irrespective /ɪrɪˈspektɪv/ a ~ **of** sem levar em conta, independente de

irresponsible /ɪrɪˈspɒnsəbl/ a irresponsável

irretrievable /ɪrɪˈtriːvəbl/ a irreparável

irreverent /ɪˈrevərənt/ a irreverente

irreversible /ɪrɪˈvɜːsəbl/ a irreversível; (decision) irrevogável

irrigat|e /ˈɪrɪɡeɪt/ vt irrigar. ~**ion** /-ˈɡeɪʃn/ n irrigação f

irritable /ˈɪrɪtəbl/ a irritável, irascível

irritat|e /ˈɪrɪteɪt/ vt irritar. ~**ion** /-ˈteɪʃn/ n irritação f

is /ɪz/ see **be**

Islam /ˈɪzlɑːm/ n Islã m. ~**ic** /ɪzˈlæmɪk/ a islâmico

island /ˈaɪlənd/ n ilha f. traffic ~ abrigo m de pedestres, (P) placa f de refugio

isolat|e /ˈaɪsəleɪt/ vt isolar. ~**ion** /-ˈleɪʃn/ n isolamento m

Israel /ˈɪzreɪl/ n Israel m. ~**i** /ɪzˈreɪlɪ/ a & n israelense (mf), (P) israelita (mf)

issue /ˈɪʃuː/ n questão f; (outcome) resultado m; (of magazine etc) número m; (of stamps, money etc) emissão f □ vt distribuir, dar; (stamps, money etc) emitir; (orders) dar □ vi ~ **from** sair de. **at** ~ em questão. **take** ~ **with** entrar em discussão com, discutir com

it /ɪt/ pron (subject) ele, ela; (object) o, a; (non-specific) isto, isso, aquilo. ~ **is cold** está or faz frio. ~ **is the 6th of May** hoje é seis de maio. **that's** ~ é isso. **take** ~ leva isso. **who is** ~? quem é?

italic /ɪˈtælɪk/ a itálico. ~**s** npl itálico m

Ital|y /ˈɪtəlɪ/ n Itália f. ~**ian** /ɪˈtælɪən/ a & n (person, lang) italiano (m)

itch /ɪtʃ/ n coceira f, (P) comichão f, (fig: desire) desejo m ardente □ vi coçar, sentir comichão, comichar. **my arm** ~**es** estou com coceira no braço. **I am** ~**ing to** estou morto por (colloq). ~**y** a que dá coceira

item /ˈaɪtəm/ n item m, artigo m; (on programme) número m; (on agenda) ponto m. **news** ~ notícia f. ~**ize** /-aɪz/ vt discriminar, especificar

itinerant /aɪˈtɪnərənt/ a itinerante; (musician, actor) ambulante

itinerary /aɪˈtɪnərərɪ/ n itinerário m

its /ɪts/ a seu, sua, seus, suas

it's /ɪts/ = **it is, it has**

itself /ɪtˈself/ pron ele mesmo, ele próprio, ela mesma, ela própria; (reflexive) se; (after prep) si mesmo, si próprio, si mesma, si própria. **by** ~ sozinho, por si próprio

ivory /ˈaɪvərɪ/ n marfim m

ivy /ˈaɪvɪ/ n hera f

J

jab /dʒæb/ vt (pt jabbed) espetar □ n espetadela f; (colloq: injection) picada f

jabber /ˈdʒæbə(r)/ vi tagarelar; (indistinctly) falar confusamente □ n tagarelice f; (indistinct speech) algaravia f; (indistinct voices) algaraviada f

jack /dʒæk/ n (techn) macaco m; (cards) valete m □ vt ~ **up** levantar com macaco. **the Union J~** a bandeira f inglesa

jackal /'dʒækl/ n chacal m

jackdaw /'dʒækdɔː/ n gralha f

jacket /'dʒækɪt/ n casaco (curto) m; (of book) sobrecapa f; (of potato) casca f

jack-knife /'dʒæknaɪf/ vi (lorry) perder o controle

jackpot /'dʒækpɒt/ n sorte f grande. **hit the** ~ ganhar a sorte grande

Jacuzzi /dʒə'kuːzɪ/ n (P) jacuzzi m, banheira f de hidromassagem

jade /dʒeɪd/ n (stone) jade m

jaded /'dʒeɪdɪd/ a (tired) estafado; (bored) enfastiado

jagged /'dʒægɪd/ a recortado, denteado; (sharp) pontiagudo

jail /dʒeɪl/ n prisão f □ vt prender, colocar na cadeia. ~**er** n carcereiro m

jam¹ /dʒæm/ n geléia f, compota f

jam² /dʒæm/ vt/i (pt jammed) (wedge) entalar; (become wedged) entalar-se; (crowd) apinhar(-se); (mech) bloquear; (radio) provocar interferências em □ n (crush) aperto m; (traffic) engarrafamento m; (colloq: difficulty) apuro m, aperto m. ~ **one's brakes on** (colloq) pôr o pé no freio, (P) no travão subitamente, apertar o freio subitamente. ~-**packed** a (colloq) abarrotado (with de)

Jamaica /dʒə'meɪkə/ n Jamaica f

jangle /'dʒæŋgl/ n som m estridente □ vi retinir

janitor /'dʒænɪtə(r)/ n porteiro m; (caretaker) zelador m

January /'dʒænjʊərɪ/ n Janeiro m

Japan /dʒə'pæn/ n Japão m. ~**ese** /dʒæpə'niːz/ a & n japonês (m)

jar¹ /dʒɑː(r)/ n pote m. **jam-**~ n frasco m de geléia

jar² /dʒɑː(r)/ vt/i (pt jarred) ressoar, bater ruidosamente (against contra); (of colours) destoar; (disagree) discordar (with de) □ n (shock) choque m. ~**ring** a dissonante

jargon /'dʒɑːgən/ n jargão m, gíria f profissional

jaundice /'dʒɔːndɪs/ n icterícia f. ~**d** a (fig) invejoso, despeitado

jaunt /dʒɔːnt/ n (trip) passeata f

jaunty /'dʒɔːntɪ/ a (-ier, -iest) (cheerful) alegre, jovial; (sprightly) desenvolto

javelin /'dʒævlɪn/ n dardo m

jaw /dʒɔː/ n maxilar m, mandíbula f

jay /dʒeɪ/ n gaio m. ~-**walker** n pedestre m imprudente, (P) peão m indisciplinado

jazz /dʒæz/ n jazz m □ vt ~ **up** animar. ~**y** a (colloq) espalhafatoso

jealous /'dʒeləs/ a ciumento; (envious) invejoso. ~**y** n ciúme m; (envy) inveja f

jeans /dʒiːnz/ npl (blue-)jeans mpl, calça f de zuarte, (P) calças fpl de ganga

jeep /dʒiːp/ n jipe m

jeer /dʒɪə(r)/ vt/i ~ **at** (laugh) fazer troça de; (scorn) escarnecer de; (boo) vaiar □ n (mockery) troça f; (booing) vaia f

jell /dʒel/ vi tomar consistência, gelatinizar-se

jelly /'dʒelɪ/ n gelatina f.

jellyfish /'dʒelɪfɪʃ/ n água-viva f

jeopard|y /'dʒepədɪ/ n perigo m. ~**ize** vt comprometer, pôr em perigo

jerk /dʒɜːk/ n solavanco m, (P) sacão m; (sl: fool) idiota mf □ vt/i sacudir; (move jerkily) mover-se aos solavancos, (P) mover(-se) aos sacões. ~**y** a sacudido

jersey /'dʒɜːzɪ/ n (pl -eys) camisola f, pulôver m, suéter m; (fabric) jérsei m

jest /dʒest/ n gracejo m, graça f □ vi gracejar, brincar

Jesus /'dʒiːzəs/ n Jesus m

jet[1] /dʒet/ n azeviche m. **~-black** a negro de azeviche

jet[2] /dʒet/ n jato m, (P) jacto m; (plane) (avião a) jato m, (P) jacto m. **~ lag** cansaço m provocado pela diferença de fuso horário. **~-propelled** a de propulsão a jato, (P) jacto

jettison /'dʒetɪsn/ vt alijar; (discard) desfazer-se de; (fig) abandonar

jetty /'dʒetɪ/ n (breakwater) quebra-mar m; (landing-stage) desembarcadouro m, cais m

Jew /dʒuː/ n judeu m

jewel /'dʒuːəl/ n jóia f. **~ler** n joalheiro m. **~ler's (shop)** joalheria f. **~lery** n jóias fpl

Jewish /'dʒuːɪʃ/ a judeu

jib /dʒɪb/ vi (pt jibbed) recusar-se a avançar; (of a horse) empacar. **~ at** (fig) opor-se a, ter relutância em □ n (sail) bujarrona f

jig /dʒɪg/ n jiga f

jiggle /'dʒɪgl/ vt (rock) balançar; (jerk) sacolejar

jigsaw /'dʒɪgsɔː/ n **~(-puzzle)** puzzle m, quebra-cabeça m, (P) quebra-cabeças m

jilt /dʒɪlt/ vt deixar, abandonar, dar um fora em (colloq), (P) mandar passear (colloq)

jingle /'dʒɪŋgl/ vt/i tilintar, tinir □ n tilintar m, tinido m; (advertising etc) música f de anúncio

jinx /dʒɪŋks/ n (colloq) pessoa f or coisa f azarenta; (fig: spell) azar m

jitter|s /'dʒɪtəz/ npl the **~s** (colloq) nervos mpl. **~y** /-ərɪ/ a be **~y** (colloq) estar nervoso, ter os nervos à flor da pele (colloq)

job /dʒɒb/ n trabalho m; (post) emprego m. **have a ~** doing ter dificuldade em fazer. **it is a good**

~ that felizmente que. **~less** a desempregado

jobcentre /'dʒɒbsentə(r)/ n posto m de desemprego

jockey /'dʒɒkɪ/ n (pl -eys) jóquei m

jocular /'dʒɒkjʊlə(r)/ a jocoso, galhofeiro, brincalhão

jog /dʒɒg/ vt (pt jogged) dar um leve empurrão em, tocar em; (memory) refrescar □ vi (sport) fazer jogging. **~ging** n jogging m

join /dʒɔɪn/ vt juntar, unir; (become member) fazer-se sócio de, entrar para. **~** sb juntar-se a alg □ vi (of roads) juntar-se, entroncar-se; (of rivers) confluir □ n junção f, junta f, **~ in** vt/i participar (em). **~ up** alistar-se

joiner /'dʒɔɪnə(r)/ n marceneiro m

joint /dʒɔɪnt/ a comum, conjunto; (effort) conjunto □ n junta f, junção f; (anat) articulação f; (culin) quarto m; (roast meat) carne f assada; (sl: place) espelunca f. **~ author** co-autor m. **~ly** adv conjuntamente

joist /dʒɔɪst/ n trave f, barrote m

jok|e /dʒəʊk/ n piada f, gracejo m □ vi gracejar. **~er** n brincalhão m; (cards) curinga f de baralho, (P) diabo m. **~ingly** adv brincadeira

joll|y /'dʒɒlɪ/ a (-ier, -iest) alegre, bem disposto □ adv (colloq) muito. **~ity** n festança f, pândega f

jolt /dʒəʊlt/ vt sacudir, sacolejar □ vi ir aos solavancos □ n solavanco m; (shock) choque m, sobressalto m

jostle /'dʒɒsl/ vt dar um encontrão or encontrões em, empurrar □ vi empurrar, acotovelar-se

jot /dʒɒt/ n (not a) **~** nada □ vt (pt jotted) **~ (down)** apontar, tomar nota de. **~ter** n (pad) bloco m de notas

journal /'dʒɜːnl/ n diário m; (newspaper) jornal m; (periodical) periódico m, revista f. ~ism n jornalismo m. ~ist n jornalista mf

journey /'dʒɜːnɪ/ n (pl -eys) viagem f; (distance) trajeto m, (P) trajecto m □ vi viajar

jovial /'dʒəʊvɪəl/ a jovial

joy /dʒɔɪ/ n alegria f. ~-ride n passeio m em carro roubado. ~ful, ~ous adjs alegre

jubilant /'dʒuːbɪlənt/ a cheio de alegria, jubiloso. ~ation /-'leɪʃn/ n júbilo m, regozijo m

jubilee /'dʒuːbɪliː/ n jubileu m

Judaism /'dʒuːdenzəm/ n judaísmo m

judder /'dʒʌdə(r)/ vi trepidar, vibrar □ n trepidação f, vibração f

judge /dʒʌdʒ/ n juiz m □ vt julgar. ~ment n (judging) julgamento m, juízo m; (opinion) juízo m; (decision) julgamento m

judiciary /dʒuː'dɪʃərɪ/ n magistratura f; (system) judiciário m. ~ial a judiciário

judicious /dʒuː'dɪʃəs/ a judicioso

judo /'dʒuːdəʊ/ n judô m, (P) judo m

jug /dʒʌg/ n (tall) jarro m; (round) botija f, milk-~ n leiteira f

juggernaut /'dʒʌgənɔːt/ n (lorry) jainanta f, (P) camião m TIR

juggle /'dʒʌgl/ vt/i fazer malabarismos (with com). ~r /-ə(r)/ n malabarista mf

juice /dʒuːs/ n suco m, (P) sumo m. ~y a suculento; (colloq: story etc) picante

juke-box /'dʒuːkbɒks/ n juke-box m, (P) máquina f de música

July /dʒuː'laɪ/ n julho m

jumble /'dʒʌmbl/ vt misturar □ n mistura f. ~ sale venda f de caridade de objetos usados

jumbo /'dʒʌmbəʊ/ a ~ jet (avião) jumbo m

jump /dʒʌmp/ vt/i saltar; (start) sobressaltar(-se); (of prices etc) subir repentinamente □ n salto m; (start) sobressalto m; (of prices) alta f. ~ at aceitar imediatamente. ~ the gun agir prematuramente. ~ the queue furar a fila. ~ to conclusions tirar conclusões apressadas

jumper /'dʒʌmpə(r)/ n pulôver m, suéter m, (P) camisada f de lã

jumpy /'dʒʌmpɪ/ a nervoso

junction /'dʒʌŋkʃn/ n junção f; (of roads etc) entroncamento m

June /dʒuːn/ n junho m

jungle /'dʒʌŋgl/ n selva f, floresta f

junior /'dʒuːnɪə(r)/ a júnior; (in age) mais novo (to que); (in rank) subalterno; (school) primária □ n o mais novo m; (sport) júnior mf. ~ to (in rank) abaixo de

junk /dʒʌŋk/ n ferro-velho m, velharias fpl; (rubbish) lixo m. ~ food comida f sem valor nutritivo. ~ mail material m impresso, enviado por correio, sem ter sido solicitado. ~ shop loja f de ferro-velho, bricabraque m

junkie /'dʒʌŋkɪ/ n (sl) drogado m

jurisdiction /dʒʊərɪs'dɪkʃn/ n jurisdição f

juror /'dʒʊərə(r)/ n jurado m

jury /'dʒʊərɪ/ n júri m

just /dʒʌst/ a justo □ adv justamente, exatamente, (P) exactamente; (only) só. he has ~ left ele acabou de sair. ~ escuta só! ~ as assim como; (with time) assim que. ~ as tall as exatamente, (P) exactamente tão alto quanto. ~ as well than ainda bem que. ~ before um momento antes (de). ~ly adv com justiça, justamente

justice /'dʒʌstɪs/ n justiça f. J~ of the Peace juiz m de paz

justifiabl|e /'dʒʌstɪfaɪəbl/ a justificável. **~y** adv com razão, justificadamente

justif|y /'dʒʌstɪfaɪ/ vt justificar. **~ication** /-ɪ'keɪʃn/ n justificação f

jut /dʒʌt/ vi (pt **jutted**) **~ out** fazer saliência, sobressair

juvenile /'dʒuːvənaɪl/ a (youthful) juvenil; (childish) pueril; (delinquent) jovem; (court) de menores □ n jovem mf

juxtapose /dʒʌkstə'pəʊz/ vt justapor

K

kaleidoscope /kə'laɪdəskəʊp/ n caleidoscópio m

kangaroo /kæŋgə'ruː/ n canguru m

karate /kə'rɑːtɪ/ n karatê m

kebab /kɪ'bæb/ n churrasquinho m, espetinho m

keel /kiːl/ n quilha f □ vi **~ over** virar-se

keen /kiːn/ a (-er, -est) (sharp) agudo; (eager) entusiástico; (of appetite) devorador; (of intelligence) vivo; (of wind) cortante. **~ly** adv vivamente; (eagerly) com entusiasmo. **~ness** n vivacidade f; (enthusiasm) entusiasmo m

keep /kiːp/ vt (pt **kept**) vt guardar; (family) sustentar; (animals) criar; (celebrate) festejar; (conceal) esconder; (delay) demorar; (prevent) impedir (**from** de); (promise) cumprir; (shop) ter □ vi manter-se, conservar-se; (remain) ficar. **~ (on)** continuar (doing fazendo) □ n sustento m; (of castle) torre f de menagem. **~ back** vt (withhold) reter □ vi manter-se afastado. **~ in/out** impedir de entrar/de sair. **~ up** conservar. **~ up**

(with) acompanhar. **~er** n guarda mf

keeping /'kiːpɪŋ/ n guarda f, cuidado m. **in ~ with** em harmonia com, (P) de harmonia com

keepsake /'kiːpseɪk/ n (thing) lembrança f, recordação f

keg /keg/ n barril m pequeno

kennel /'kenl/ n casota f (de cão). **~s** npl canil m

kept /kept/ see **keep**

kerb /kɜːb/ n meio fio m, (P) borda f do passeio

kernel /'kɜːnl/ n (of nut) miolo m

kerosene /'kerəsiːn/ n (paraffin) querosene m, (P) petróleo m; (aviation fuel) gasolina f

ketchup /'ketʃəp/ n molho m de tomate, ketchup m

kettle /'ketl/ n chaleira f

key /kiː/ n chave f, (of piano etc) tecla f; (mus) clave f □ a chave. **~-ring** n chaveiro m, porta-chaves m invar □ vt **~ in** digitar, bater. **~ed up** tenso

keyboard /'kiːbɔːd/ n teclado m

keyhole /'kiːhəʊl/ n buraco m da fechadura

khaki /'kɑːkɪ/ a & n cáqui (invar m), (P) caqui (invar m)

kick /kɪk/ vt/i dar um pontapé or pontapés (a, em); (ball) chutar (em); (of horse) dar um coice or coices, escoicear □ n pontapé m; (of gun, horse) coice m; (colloq: thrill) excitação f, prazer m. **~-off** n chute m inicial, kick-off m. **~ out** (colloq) pôr na rua. **~ up** (colloq: fuss, racket) fazer

kid /kɪd/ n (goat) cabrito m; (sl: child) garoto m; (leather) pelica f □ vt/i (pt **kidded**) (colloq) brincar (com)

kidnap /'kɪdnæp/ vt (pt **kidnapped**) raptar. **~ping** n rapto m

kidney /'kɪdnɪ/ n rim m

kill /kɪl/ vt matar; (fig: put an end to) acabar com □ n matança f. **~er** n assassino m. **~ing**

matança f, massacre m; (of game) caçada f □ a (colloq: funny) de morrer de rir; (colloq: exhausting) de morte

killjoy /ˈkɪldʒɔɪ/ n desmancha-prazeres mf

kiln /kɪln/ n forno m

kilo /ˈkiːləʊ/ n (pl -os) quilo m

kilogram /ˈkɪləɡræm/ n quilograma m

kilometre /ˈkɪləmiːtə(r)/ n quilómetro m, (P) quilómetro m

kilowatt /ˈkɪləwɒt/ n quilowatt m, (P) quilovate m

kilt /kɪlt/ n kilt m, saiote m escocês

kin /kɪn/ n família f, parentes mpl. **next of** ~ os parentes mais próximos

kind[1] /kaɪnd/ n espécie f, género m, (P) género m, natureza f. **in** ~ em géneros, (P) géneros; (fig: in the same form) na mesma moeda. ~ **of** (colloq: somewhat) de certo modo, um pouco

kind[2] /kaɪnd/ a (-er, -est) (good) bom; (friendly) gentil, amável. ~**-hearted** a bom, bondoso. ~**ness** n bondade f

kindergarten /ˈkɪndəɡɑːtn/ n jardim de infância m, (P) infantil

kindle /ˈkɪndl/ vt/i acender(-se), atear(-se)

kindly /ˈkaɪndlɪ/ a (-ier, -iest) benévolo, bondoso □ adv bondosamente, gentilmente, com simpatia. ~ **wait** tenha a bondade de esperar

kindred /ˈkɪndrɪd/ a aparentado; (fig: connected) afim. ~ **spirit** espírito m congénere, alma f gémea

kinetic /kɪˈnetɪk/ a cinético

king /kɪŋ/ n rei m. ~**-size(d)** a de tamanho grande

kingdom /ˈkɪŋdəm/ n reino m

kingfisher /ˈkɪŋfɪʃə(r)/ n pica-peixe m, martim-pescador m

kink /kɪŋk/ n (in rope) volta f, nó m; (fig) perversão f. ~**y** a (col-

loq) excêntrico, pervertido; (of hair) encarapinhado

kiosk /ˈkiːɒsk/ n quiosque m. **telephone** ~ cabine telefónica, (P) telefónica

kip /kɪp/ n (sl) sono m □ vi (pt kipped) (sl) dormir

kipper /ˈkɪpə(r)/ n arenque m defumado

kiss /kɪs/ n beijo m □ vt/i beijar(-se)

kit /kɪt/ n equipamento m; (set of tools) ferramenta f; (for assembly) kit m □ vt (pt kitted) ~ **out** equipar

kitbag /ˈkɪtbæɡ/ n mochila f (de soldado etc); saco m de viagem

kitchen /ˈkɪtʃɪn/ n cozinha f. ~ **garden** horta f. ~ **sink** pia f, (P) lava-louças m

kite /kaɪt/ n (toy) pipa f, (P) papagaio m de papel

kith /kɪθ/ n ~ **and kin** parentes e amigos mpl

kitten /ˈkɪtn/ n gatinho m

kitty /ˈkɪtɪ/ n (fund) fundo m comum, vaquinha f; (cards) bolo m

knack /næk/ n jeito m

knapsack /ˈnæpsæk/ n mochila f

knead /niːd/ vt amassar

knee /niː/ n joelho m

kneecap /ˈniːkæp/ n rótula f

kneel /niːl/ vi (pt knelt) ~ **(down)** ajoelhar(-se)

knelt /nelt/ see **kneel**

knew /njuː/ see **know**

knickers /ˈnɪkəz/ npl calcinhas (de senhora) fpl

knife /naɪf/ n (pl knives) faca f □ vt esfaquear, apunhalar

knight /naɪt/ n cavaleiro m; (chess) cavalo m. ~**hood** n grau m de cavaleiro

knit /nɪt/ vt (pt knitted or knit) tricotar □ vi tricotar, fazer tricô; (fig: unite) unir-se; (of bones) soldar-se. ~ **one's brow** franzir as sobrancelhas. ~**ting** n malha f, tricô m

knitwear /'nɪtweə(r)/ *n* roupa *f* de malha, malhas *fpl*

knob /nɒb/ *n* (*of door*) maçaneta *f*; (*of drawer*) puxador *m*; (*of radio, TV etc*) botão *m*; (*of butter*) noz *f*. ~**bly** *a* nodoso

knock /nɒk/ *vt/i* bater (em); (*sl: criticize*) desancar (em). ~ **about** *vt* tratar mal ☐ *vi* (*wander*) andar a esmo. ~ **down** (*chair, pedestrian*) deitar no chão, derrubar; (*demolish*) jogar abaixo; (*colloq: reduce*) baixar, reduzir; (*at auction*) adjudicar (**to** a). ~**-down** *a* (*price*) muito baixo. ~**-kneed** *a* de pernas de tesoura. ~ **off** *vt* (*colloq: complete quickly*) despachar; (*sl: steal*) roubar ☐ *vi* (*colloq.*) parar de trabalhar, fechar a loja (*colloq.*). ~ **out** pôr fora de combate, eliminar; (*stun*) assombrar. ~**-out** *n* (*boxing*) nocaute *m*, KO *m*. ~ **over** entornar. ~ **up** (*meal etc*) arranjar às pressas. ~**er** *n* aldrava *f*

knot /nɒt/ *n* nó *m* ☐ *vt* (*pt* **knotted**) atar com nó, dar nó or nós em

knotty /'nɒtɪ/ *a* (**-ier, -iest**) nodoso, cheio de nós; (*difficult*) complicado, espinhoso

know /nəʊ/ *vt/i* (*pt* **knew**, *pp* **known**) saber (**that** que); (*person, place*) conhecer ☐ *n* **in the** ~ (*colloq*) por dentro. ~ **about** (*cars etc*) saber sobre, saber de. ~**-all** *n* sabe-tudo *m* (*colloq*). ~**-how** *n* know-how *m*, conhecimentos *mpl* técnicos, culturais etc. ~ **of** ter conhecimento de, ter ouvido falar de. ~**ingly** *adv* com ar conhecedor; (*consciously*) conscientemente

knowledge /'nɒlɪdʒ/ *n* conhecimento *m*; (*learning*) saber *m*. ~**able** *a* conhecedor, entendido, versado

known /nəʊn/ *see* **know** ☐ *a* conhecido

knuckle /'nʌkl/ *n* nó *m* dos dedos ☐ *vi* ~ **under** ceder, submeter-se

Koran /kə'rɑ:n/ *n* Alcorão *m*, Corão *m*

Korea /kə'rɪə/ *n* Coréia *f*

kosher /'kəʊʃə(r)/ *a* aprovado pela lei judaica; (*colloq*) como deve ser

kowtow /kaʊ'taʊ/ *vi* prosternar-se (**to** diante de); (*act obsequiously*) bajular

L

lab /læb/ *n* (*colloq*) laboratório *m*

label /'leɪbl/ *n* (*on bottle etc*) rótulo *m*; (*on clothes, luggage*) etiqueta *f* ☐ *vt* (*pt* **labelled**) rotular; etiquetar, pôr etiqueta em

laboratory /lə'bɒrətrɪ/ *n* laboratório *m*

laborious /lə'bɔ:rɪəs/ *a* laborioso, trabalhoso

labour /'leɪbə(r)/ *n* trabalho *m*, labuta *f*; (*workers*) mão-de-obra *f* ☐ *vi* trabalhar; (*try hard*) esforçar-se ☐ *vt* alongar-se sobre, insistir em. **in** ~ em trabalho de parto. ~**ed** *a* (*writing*) laborioso, sem espontaneidade; (*breathing, movement*) difícil. ~**-saving** *a* que poupa trabalho

Labour /'leɪbə(r)/ *n* (*party*) Partido *m* Trabalhista, os trabalhistas ☐ *a* trabalhista

labourer /'leɪbərə(r)/ *n* trabalhador *m*; (*on farm*) trabalhador *m* rural

labyrinth /'læbərɪnθ/ *n* labirinto *m*

lace /leɪs/ *n* renda *f*; (*of shoe*) cordão *m* de sapato, (*P*) atacador *m* ☐ *vt* atar; (*drink*) juntar um pouco (de aguardente, rum etc)

lacerate /'læsəreɪt/ *vt* lacerar, rasgar

lack /læk/ *n* falta *f* □ *vt* faltar (a), não ter. **be ~ing** faltar. **be ~ing in** carecer de

lackadaisical /lækə'deɪzɪkl/ *a* lânguido, apático, desinteressado

laconic /lə'kɒnɪk/ *a* lacónico, (P) lacónico

lacquer /'lækə(r)/ *n* laca *f*

lad /læd/ *n* rapaz *m*, moço *m*

ladder /'lædə(r)/ *n* escada de mão *f*, (P) escadote *m*; (*in stocking*) fio *m* corrido, (P) malha *f* caída □ *vi* deixar correr um fio, (P) cair uma malha □ *vt* fazer malhas em

laden /'leɪdn/ *a* carregado (**with** de)

ladle /'leɪdl/ *n* concha (de sopa) *f*

lady /'leɪdɪ/ *n* senhora *f*; (*title*) Lady *f*. **~-in-waiting** *n* dama *f* de companhia, (P) dama *f* de honor. **young ~** jovem *f*. **~like** *a* senhoril, elegante. **Ladies** *n* (*toilets*) toalete *m* das Senhoras

ladybird /'leɪdɪbɜːd/ *n* joaninha *f*

lag¹ /læg/ *vi* (*pt* **lagged**) atrasar-se, ficar para trás □ *n* atraso *m*

lag² /læg/ *vt* (*pt* **lagged**) (*pipes etc*) revestir com isolante térmico

lager /'lɑːgə(r)/ *n* cerveja *f* leve e clara, "loura" *f* (*sl*)

lagoon /lə'guːn/ *n* lagoa *f*

laid /leɪd/ *see* **lay²**

lain /leɪn/ *see* **lie²**

lair /leə(r)/ *n* toca *f*, covil *m*

laity /'leɪətɪ/ *n* leigos *mpl*

lake /leɪk/ *n* lago *m*

lamb /læm/ *n* cordeiro *m*, carneiro *m*; (*meat*) carneiro *m*

lambswool /'læmzwʊl/ *n* lã *f*

lame /leɪm/ *a* (-**er**, -**est**) coxo; (*fig: unconvincing*) fraco. **~ness** *n* claudicação *f*, coxeadura *f*

lament /lə'ment/ *n* lamento *m*, lamentação *f* □ *vt/i* lamentar(-se) (de). **~able** *a* lamentável

laminated /'læmɪneɪtɪd/ *a* laminado

lamp /læmp/ *n* lâmpada *f*

lamppost /'læmppəʊst/ *n* poste *m* (do candeeiro) (de iluminação pública)

lampshade /'læmpʃeɪd/ *n* abajur *m*, quebra-luz *m*

lance /lɑːns/ *n* lança *f* □ *vt* lancetar

lancet /'lɑːnsɪt/ *n* bisturi *m*, (P) lanceta *f*

land /lænd/ *n* terra *f*; (*country*) país *m*; (*plot*) terreno *m*; (*property*) terras *fpl* □ *a* de terra, terrestre; (*policy etc*) agrário □ *vt/i* desembarcar; (*aviat*) aterrissar, (P) aterrar; (*fall*) ir parar (**on** em); (*collog: obtain*) arranjar; (*a blow*) aplicar, mandar. **~-locked** *a* rodeado de terra

landing /'lændɪŋ/ *n* desembarque *m*; (*aviat*) aterrissagem *f*, (P) aterragem *f*; (*top of stairs*) patamar *m*. **~-stage** *n* cais *m* flutuante

land|lady /'lændleɪdɪ/ *n* (*of rented house*) senhoria *f*, proprietária *f*; (*who lets rooms*) dona *f* da casa; (*of boarding-house*) dona *f* da pensão; (*of inn etc*) proprietária *f*, estalajadeira *f*. **~lord** *n* (*of rented house*) senhorio *m*, proprietário *m*; (*of inn etc*) proprietário *m*, estalajadeiro *m*

landmark /'lændmɑːk/ *n* (*conspicuous feature*) ponto *m* de referência; (*fig*) marco *m*

landscape /'lændskeɪp/ *n* paisagem *f* □ *vt* projetar, (P) projectar paisagisticamente

landslide /'lændslaɪd/ *n* desabamento *m* or desmoronamento *m* de terras; (*fig: pol*) vitória *f* esmagadora

lane /leɪn/ *n* senda *f*, caminho *m*; (*in country*) estrada *f* pequena; (*in town*) viela *f*, ruela *f*; (*of road*) faixa *f*, pista *f*; (*of traffic*) fila *f*; (*aviat*) corredor *m*; (*naut*) rota *f*

language /'læŋgwɪdʒ/ *n* língua *f*; (*speech, style*) linguagem *f*. **bad**

~ linguagem *f* grosseira. ~ **lab** laboratório *m* de línguas

languid /'læŋgwɪd/ *a* lânguido

languish /'læŋgwɪʃ/ *vi* elanguescer

lank /læŋk/ *a* (*of hair*) escorrido, liso

lanky /'læŋkɪ/ *a* (*-ier, -iest*) desengonçado, escanifrado

lantern /'læntən/ *n* lanterna *f*

lap[1] /læp/ *n* colo *m*; (*sport*) volta *f* completa. ~**-dog** *n* cãozinho *m* de estimação

lap[2] /læp/ *vt* ~ **up** beber lambendo □ *vi* marulhar

lapel /lə'pel/ *n* lapela *f*

lapse /læps/ *vi* decair, degenerar-se; (*expire*) caducar □ *n* lapso *m*; (*jur*) prescrição *f*. ~ **into** (*thought*) mergulhar em; (*bad habit*) adquirir

larceny /'lɑːsənɪ/ *n* furto *m*

lard /lɑːd/ *n* banha de porco *f*

larder /'lɑːdə(r)/ *n* despensa *f*

large /lɑːdʒ/ *a* (*-er, -est*) grande. at ~ à solta, em liberdade. **by and ~** em geral. ~**ly** *adv* largamente, em grande parte. ~**ness** *n* grandeza *f*

lark[1] /lɑːk/ *n* (*bird*) cotovia *f*

lark[2] /lɑːk/ *n* (*colloq*) pândega *f*, brincadeira *f* □ *vi* ~ **about** (*colloq*) fazer travessuras, brincar

larva /'lɑːvə/ *n* (*pl* **-vae** /-viː/) larva *f*

laryngitis /lærɪn'dʒaɪtɪs/ *n* laringite *f*

larynx /'lærɪŋks/ *n* laringe *f*

lascivious /lə'sɪvɪəs/ *a* lascivo, sensual

laser /'leɪzə(r)/ *n* laser *m*. ~ **printer** impressora *f* a laser

lash /læʃ/ *vt* chicotear, açoitar; (*rain*) fustigar □ *n* chicote *m*; (*stroke*) chicotada *f*; (*eyelash*) pestana *f*, cílio *m*. ~ **out** atacar, atirar-se a; (*colloq: spend*) esbanjar dinheiro em algo

lashings /'læʃɪŋz/ *npl* ~ **of** (*sl*) montes de (*colloq*)

lasso /læ'suː/ *n* (*pl* **-os**) laço *m* □ *vt* laçar

last[1] /lɑːst/ *a* último □ *adv* no fim, em último lugar; (*most recently*) a última vez □ *n* último *m*. **at** (**long**) ~ por fim, finalmente. ~**-minute** *a* de última hora. ~ **night** ontem à noite, a noite passada. **the** ~ **straw** a gota d'água. **to the** ~ até o fim. ~**ly** *adv* finalmente, em último lugar

last[2] /lɑːst/ *vt/i* durar, continuar. ~**ing** *a* duradouro, durável

latch /lætʃ/ *n* trinco *m*

late /leɪt/ *a* (*-er, -est*) atrasado; (*recent*) recente; (*former*) antigo, ex-, anterior; (*hour, fruit etc*) tardio; (*deceased*) falecido □ *adv* tarde. **in** ~ **july** no fim de julho. **of** ~ ultimamente. **at the** ~**st** o mais tardar. ~**ness** *n* atraso *m*

lately /'leɪtlɪ/ *adv* nos últimos tempos, ultimamente

latent /'leɪtnt/ *a* latente

lateral /'lætərəl/ *a* lateral

lathe /leɪð/ *n* torno *m*

lather /'lɑːðə(r)/ *n* espuma *f* de sabão □ *vt* ensaboar □ *vi* fazer espuma

Latin /'lætɪn/ *n* (*lang*) latim *m* □ *a* latino. ~ **America** *n* América *f* Latina. ~ **American** *a* & *n* latino-americano (*m*)

latitude /'lætɪtjuːd/ *n* latitude *f*

latter /'lætə(r)/ *a* último, mais recente □ *n* **the** ~ este, esta. ~**ly** *adv* recentemente

lattice /'lætɪs/ *n* treliça *f*, (*P*) gradeamento *m* de ripas

laudable /'lɔːdəbl/ *a* louvável

laugh /lɑːf/ *vi* rir (**at** de). ~ **off** disfarçar com uma piada □ *n* riso *m*. ~**able** *a* irrisório, ridículo. ~**ing-stock** *n* objeto *m*, (*P*) objecto *m* de troça

laughter /'lɑːftə(r)/ *n* riso *m*, risada *f*

launch[1] /lɔ:ntʃ/ vt lançar □ n lançamento m. ~ **into** lançar-se or meter-se em. ~**ing pad** plataforma f de lançamento

launch[2] /lɔ:ntʃ/ n (boat) lancha f

launder /'lɔ:ndə(r)/ vt lavar e passar

launderette /lɔ:n'dret/ n lavanderia f automática

laundry /'lɔ:ndrɪ/ n lavandaria f; (clothes) roupa f. **do the** ~ lavar a roupa

laurel /'lɒrəl/ n loureiro m, louro m

lava /'lɑ:və/ n lava f

lavatory /'lævətrɪ/ n privada f, (P) retrete f; (room) toalete m, (P) lavabo m

lavender /'lævəndə(r)/ n alfazema f, lavanda f

lavish /'lævɪʃ/ a pródigo; (plentiful) copioso, generoso; (lush) suntuoso □ vt ser pródigoem, encher de. ~**ly** adv prodigamente; copiosamente; suntuosamente

law /lɔ:/ n lei f; (profession, study) direito m. ~-**abiding** a cumpridor da lei, respeitador da lei. ~ **and order** ordem f pública. ~-**breaker** n transgressor m da lei. ~**ful** a legal, legítimo. ~**fully** adv legalmente. ~**less** a sem lei; (act) ilegal; (person) rebelde

lawcourt /'lɔ:kɔ:t/ n tribunal m

lawn /lɔ:n/ n gramado m, (P) relvado m. ~-**mower** n cortador m de grama, (P) máquina f de cortar a relva

lawsuit /'lɔ:su:t/ n processo m, acção f, (P) acção f judicial

lawyer /'lɔ:jə(r)/ n advogado m

lax /læks/ a negligente; (discipline) frouxo; (morals) relaxado. ~**ity** n negligência f; (of discipline) frouxidão f, (of morals) relaxamento m

laxative /'læksətɪv/ n laxante m, laxativo m

lay[1] /leɪ/ a leigo. ~ **opinion** opinião f de um leigo

lay[2] /leɪ/ vt (pt laid) pôr, colocar; (trap) preparar, pôr; (eggs, table, siege) pôr; (plan) fazer □ vi pôr (ovos). ~ **aside** pôr de lado. ~ **down** pousar; (condition, law, rule) impôr; (arms) depor; (one's life) oferecer; (policy) ditar. ~ **hold of** agarrar(-se a). ~ **off** vt (worker) suspender do trabalho □ vi (colloq) parar, desistir. ~-**off** n suspensão f temporária. ~ **on** (gas, water etc) instalar, ligar; (entertainment etc) organizar, providenciar; (food) servir. ~ **out** (design) traçar, planejar; (spread out) estender, espalhar; (money) gastar. ~ **up** vt (store) juntar; (ship, car) pôr fora de serviço

lay[3] /leɪ/ see **lie**

layabout /'leɪəbaʊt/ n (sl) vadio m

lay-by /'leɪbaɪ/ n acostamento m, (P) berma f

layer /'leɪə(r)/ n camada f

layman /'leɪmən/ n (pl -men) leigo m

layout /'leɪaʊt/ n disposição f; (typ) composição f

laze /leɪz/ vi descansar, vadiar

lazy /'leɪzɪ/ a (-ier, -iest) preguiçoso. ~**iness** n preguiça f. ~**y-bones** n (colloq) vadio m, vagabundo m

lead[1] /li:d/ vt/i (pt led) conduzir, guiar, levar; (team etc) chefiar, liderar; (life) levar; (choir, band etc) dirigir □ n (distance) avanço m; (first place) dianteira f; (clue) indício m, pista f; (leash) coleira f; (electr) cabo m; (theatr) papel m principal; (example) exemplo m. **in the** ~ na frente. ~ **away** levar. ~ **on** (fig) encorajar. ~ **the way** ir na frente. ~ **up to** conduzir a

lead[2] /led/ n chumbo m; (of pencil) grafite f. ~-**en** a de chumbo; (of colour) plúmbeo

leader /'li:də(r)/ n chefe m, líder m; (of country, club, union etc) dirigente *mf*; (*pol*) líder; (*of orchestra*) regente *mf*, maestro *m*; (*in newspaper*) editorial *m*. **~ship** *n* direção *f*, (*P*) direcção *f*, liderança *f*

leading /'liːdɪŋ/ *a* principal. **~ article** artigo *m* de fundo, editorial *m*

leaf /liːf/ *n* (*pl* **leaves**) folha *f*; (*flap of table*) aba *f* □ *vi* **~ through** folhear. **~y** *a* frondoso

leaflet /'liːflɪt/ *n* prospecto *m*, folheto *m* informativo

league /liːg/ *n* liga *f*; (*sport*) campeonato *m* da Liga. **in ~ with** de coligação com, em conluio com

leak /liːk/ *n* (*escape*) fuga *f*; (*hole*) buraco *m* □ *vt/i* (*roof, container*) pingar; (*electr, gas*) ter um escapamento, (*P*) ter uma fuga; (*naut*) fazer água. **~ (out)** (*fig: divulge*) divulgar; (*fig: become known*) transpirar, divulgar-se. **~age** *n* vazamento *m*. **~y** *a* que tem um vazamento

lean[1] /liːn/ *a* (**-er, -est**) magro. **~ness** *n* magreza *f*

lean[2] /liːn/ *vt/i* (*pt* **leaned** or **leant** /lent/) encostar(-se), apoiar-se (**on** em); (*be slanting*) inclinar(-se). **~ back/forward** or **over** inclinar-se para trás/para a frente. **~ on** (*colloq*) pressionar. **~-to** *n* alpendre *m*

leaning /'liːnɪŋ/ *a* inclinado □ *n* inclinação *f*

leap /liːp/ *vt* (*pt* **leaped** or **leapt** /lept/) galgar, saltar por cima de □ *vi* saltar □ *n* salto *m*, pulo *m*. **~-frog** *n* eixo-badeixo *m*, (*P*) jogo *m* do eixo. **~ year** ano *m* bissexto

learn /lɜːn/ *vt/i* (*pt* **learned** or **learnt**) aprender; (*be told*) vir a saber, ouvir dizer. **~er** *n* principiante *mf*, aprendiz *m*

learn|**ed** /'lɜːnɪd/ *a* erudito. **~ing** *n* saber *m*, erudição *f*

lease /liːs/ *n* arrendamento *m*,

aluguel *m*, (*P*) aluguer *m* □ *vt* arrendar, (*P*) alugar

leash /liːʃ/ *n* coleira *f*

least /liːst/ *a* o menor □ *n* o mínimo *m*, o menos *m* □ *adv* o menos. **at ~** pelo menos. **not in the ~** de maneira alguma

leather /'leðə(r)/ *n* couro *m*, cabedal *m*

leave /liːv/ *vt/i* (*pt* **left**) deixar; (*depart from*) sair/partir (de), ir-se (de) □ *n* licença *f*, permissão *f*. **be left (over)** restar, sobrar. **~ alone** deixar em paz, não tocar. **~ out** omitir. **~ of absence** licença *f*. **on ~** (*mil*) de licença. **take one's ~** despedir-se (**of** de)

leavings /'liːvɪŋz/ *npl* restos *mpl*

Leban|**on** /'lebənən/ *n* Líbano *m*. **~ese** /-'niːz/ *a* & *n* libanês (*m*)

lecherous /'letʃərəs/ *a* lascivo

lectern /'lektɜːn/ *n* estante *f* (de coro de igreja)

lecture /'lektʃə(r)/ *n* conferência *f*; (*univ*) aula *f* teórica; (*fig*) sermão *m* □ *vi* dar uma conferência; (*univ*) dar aula(s) □ *vt* pregar um sermão a alg (*colloq*). **~r** /-ə(r)/ *n* conferente *m*, conferencista *mf*; (*univ*) professor *m*

led /led/ *see* **lead**[1]

ledge /ledʒ/ *n* rebordo *m*, saliência *f*; (*of window*) peitoril *m*

ledger /'ledʒə(r)/ *n* livro-mestre *m*, razão *m*

leech /liːtʃ/ *n* sanguessuga *f*

leek /liːk/ *n* alho-poró *m*, (*P*) alho-porro *m*

leer /lɪə(r)/ *vi* **~ (at)** olhar de modo malicioso or manhoso (para) □ *n* olhar *m* malicioso or manhoso

leeway /'liːweɪ/ *n* (*naut*) deriva *f*; (*fig*) liberdade *f* de ação, (*P*) acção, margem *f* (*colloq*)

left[1] /left/ *see* **leave**. **~ luggage (office)** depósito *m* de bagagens. **~-overs** *npl* restos *mpl*, sobras *fpl*

left² /left/ a esquerdo; (*pol*) de esquerda □ n esquerda f □ adv à/ para a esquerda. **~-hand** a da esquerda; (*position*) à esquerda. **~-handed** a canhoto. **~-wing** a (*pol*) de esquerda

leg /leg/ n perna f; (*of table*) pé m, perna f; (*of journey*) etapa f. **pull sb's ~** brincar or mexer com alg. **stretch one's ~s** esticar as pernas. **~-room** n espaço m para as pernas

legacy /ˈlegəsɪ/ n legado m

legal /ˈliːgl/ a legal; (*affairs etc*) jurídico. **~ adviser** advogado m. **~ity** /-ˈgælətɪ/ n legalidade f. **~ly** adv legalmente

legalize /ˈliːgəlaɪz/ vt legalizar

legend /ˈledʒənd/ n lenda f. **~ary** /ˈledʒəndrɪ/ a lendário

leggings /ˈlegɪŋz/ npl perneiras fpl; (*women's*) legging m

legib|le /ˈledʒəbl/ a legível. **~ility** /-ˈbɪlətɪ/ n legibilidade f

legion /ˈliːdʒən/ n legião f

legislat|e /ˈledʒɪsleɪt/ vi legislar. **~ion** /-ˈleɪ∫n/ n legislação f

legislat|ive /ˈledʒɪslətɪv/ a legislativo. **~ure** /-eɪt∫ə(r)/ n corpo m legislativo

legitima|te /lɪˈdʒɪtɪmət/ a legítimo. **~cy** n legitimidade f

leisure /ˈleʒə(r)/ n lazer m, tempo livre m. **at one's ~** ao bel prazer, (*P*) a seu belo prazer. **~ly** a pausado, compassado □ adv sem pressa, devagar

lemon /ˈlemən/ n limão m

lemonade /leməˈneɪd/ n limonada f

lend /lend/ vt (*pt* **lent**) emprestar; (*contribute*) dar. **~ a hand to** (*help*) ajudar. **~ itself to** prestar-se a. **~er** n pessoa f que empresta. **~ing** n empréstimo m

length /leŋθ/ n comprimento m; (*in time*) período m; (*of cloth*) corte m. **at ~** extensamente; (*at* *last*) por fim, finalmente. **~y** a longo, demorado

lengthen /ˈleŋθən/ vt/i alongar(-se)

lengthways /ˈleŋθweɪz/ adv ao comprido, em comprimento, longitudinalmente

lenien|t /ˈliːnɪənt/ a indulgente, clemente. **~cy** n indulgência f, clemência f

lens /lenz/ n (*of spectacles*) lente f; (*photo*) objetiva f, (*P*) objectiva f

lent /lent/ *see* **lend**

Lent /lent/ n Quaresma f

lentil /ˈlentl/ n lentilha f

Leo /ˈliːəʊ/ n (*astr*) Leão m

leopard /ˈlepəd/ n leopardo m

leotard /ˈliːəʊtɑːd/ n collant(s) m (*pl*), (*P*) maillot m de ginástica ou dança

leper /ˈlepə(r)/ n leproso m

leprosy /ˈleprəsɪ/ n lepra f

lesbian /ˈlezbɪən/ a lésbico □ n lésbica f

less /les/ a (*in number*) menor (*than* que); (*in quantity*) menos (*than* que) □ n, adv & prep menos. **~ and ~** cada vez menos

lessen /ˈlesn/ vt/i diminuir

lesser /ˈlesə(r)/ a menor. **to a ~ degree** em menor grau

lesson /ˈlesn/ n lição f

let /let/ vt (*pt* **let**, *pres p* **letting**) deixar, permitir; (*lease*) alugar, arrendar □ v aux **~'s go** vamos. **~ him do it** que o faça ele. **~ me know** diga-me, avise-me □ n aluguel m, (*P*) aluguer m. **~ alone** deixar em paz; (*not to mention*) sem falar em, para não falar em. **~ down** baixar; (*deflate*) esvaziar; (*disappoint*) despontar; (*fail to help*) deixar na mão. **~-down** n desapontamento m. **~ go** vt/i soltar. **~ in** deixar entrar. **~ o.s. in for** (*task, trouble*) meter-se em. **~ off** (*gun*) disparar; (*firework*) soltar, (P) deitar; (excuse) desculpar. ~ on (colloq) revelar (that que) □ vi descoser-se (colloq), (P) descair-se (colloq). ~ out deixar sair. ~ through deixar passar. ~ up (colloq) abrandar, diminuir. ~-up n (colloq) pausa f, trégua f

lethal /'li:θl/ a fatal, mortal

letharg|y /'leθədʒɪ/ n letargia f, apatia f. ~ic /lɪ'θædʒɪk/ a letárgico, apático

letter /'letə(r)/ n (symbol) letra f; (message) carta f. ~-bomb n carta-bomba f. ~-box n caixa f do correio. ~ing n letras fpl

lettuce /'letɪs/ n alface f

leukaemia /lu:'ki:mɪə/ n leucemia f

level /'levl/ a plano; (on surface) horizontal; (in height) no mesmo nível (with que); (spoonful etc) raso □ n nível m □ vt (pt levelled) nivelar; (gun, missile) apontar; (accusation) dirigir. on the ~ (colloq) franco, sincero. ~ crossing passagem f de nível. ~-headed a equilibrado, sensato

lever /'li:və(r)/ n alavanca f □ vt ~ up levantar com alavanca

leverage /'li:vərɪdʒ/ n influência f

levity /'levətɪ/ n frivolidade f, leviandade f

levy /'levɪ/ vt (tax) cobrar □ n imposto m

lewd /lu:d/ a (-er, -est) libidinoso, obsceno

liabilit|y /laɪə'bɪlətɪ/ n responsabilidade f; (colloq: handicap) desvantagem f. ~ies dívidas fpl

liable /'laɪəbl/ a ~ to do susceptível, (P) susceptível de fazer; ~ to (illness etc) susceptível, (P) susceptível a; (fine) sujeito a. ~ for responsável por

liaise /lɪ'eɪz/ vi (colloq) servir de intermediário (between entre), fazer a ligação (with com)

liaison /lɪ'eɪzn/ n ligação f

liar /'laɪə(r)/ n mentiroso m

libel /'laɪbl/ n difamação f □ vt (pt libelled) difamar

liberal /'lɪbərəl/ a liberal. ~ly adv liberalmente

Liberal /'lɪbərəl/ a & n liberal (mf)

liberat|e /'lɪbəreɪt/ vt libertar. ~ion /-'reɪʃn/ n libertação f; (of women) emancipação f

libert|y /'lɪbətɪ/ n liberdade f. at ~y to livre de. take ~ies tomar liberdades

libido /lɪ'bi:dəʊ/ n (pl -os) libido m

Libra /'li:brə/ n (astr) Balança f, Libra f

librar|y /'laɪbrərɪ/ n biblioteca f. ~ian /-'breərɪən/ n bibliotecário m

Libya /'lɪbɪə/ n Líbia f. ~n a & n líbio (m)

lice /laɪs/ n see louse

licence /'laɪsns/ n licença f; (for TV) taxa f; (for driving) carteira f, (P) carta f; (behaviour) libertinagem f

license /'laɪsns/ vt dar licença para, autorizar □ n (Amer) = licence. ~ plate placa f do carro, (P) placa f de matrícula

licentious /laɪ'senʃəs/ a licencioso

lichen /'laɪkən/ n líquen m

lick /lɪk/ vt lamber; (sl: defeat) bater (colloq), dar uma surra em (colloq) □ n lambidela f. a ~ of paint uma mão de pintura

lid /lɪd/ n tampa f

lido /'li:dəʊ/ n (pl ~os) piscina f pública ao ar livre

lie¹ /laɪ/ n mentira f □ vi (pt lied, pres p lying) mentir. give the ~ to desmentir

lie² /laɪ/ vi (pt lay, pp lain, pres p lying) estar deitado; (remain) ficar; (be situated) estar, encontrar-se; (in grave, on ground) jazer. **~ down** descansar. **~ in**, **have a ~ in** dormir até tarde. **~ low** (colloq: hide) andar escondido

lieu /lu:/ n **in ~ of** em vez de

lieutenant /lefˈtenənt/ n (army) tenente m; (navy) 1° tenente m

life /laɪf/ n (pl **lives**) vida f. **~ cycle** ciclo m vital. **~ expectancy** probabilidade f de vida. **~-guard** n salva-vidas m. **~ insurance** seguro m de vida. **~-jacket** n colete m salva-vidas. **~-size(d)** a (de) tamanho natural invar

lifebelt /ˈlaɪfbelt/ n cinto m salva-vidas, (P) cinto m de salvação

lifeboat /ˈlaɪfbəʊt/ n barco m salva-vidas

lifebuoy /ˈlaɪfbɔɪ/ n bóia f salva-vidas, (P) bóia f de salvação

lifeless /ˈlaɪflɪs/ a sem vida

lifelike /ˈlaɪflaɪk/ a natural, real; (of portrait) muito parecido

lifelong /ˈlaɪflɒŋ/ a de toda a vida, perpétuo

lifestyle /ˈlaɪfstaɪl/ n estilo m de vida

lifetime /ˈlaɪftaɪm/ n vida f. **the chance of a ~** uma oportunidade única

lift /lɪft/ vt/i levantar(-se), erguer (-se); (colloq: steal) roubar, surripiar (colloq); (of fog) levantar, dispersar-se □ n ascensor m, elevador m. **give a ~ to** dar carona, (P) boleia a (colloq). **~-off** n decolagem f, (P) descolagem f

ligament /ˈlɪgəmənt/ n ligamento m

light[1] /laɪt/ n luz f; (lamp) lâmpada f; (on vehicle) farol m; (spark) lume m □ a claro □ vt (pt **lit** or **lighted**) (ignite) acender; (illuminate) iluminar. **bring to ~** trazer à luz, revelar. **come to ~** vir à luz. **~ up** iluminar(-se), acender(-se). **~-year** n ano-luz m

light[2] /laɪt/ a & adv (-er, -est) leve.

~-headed a (dizzy) estonteado, tonto; (frivolous) leviano. **~-hearted** a alegre, despreocupado. **~ly** adv de leve, levemente, ligeiramente. **~ness** n leveza f

lighten[1] /ˈlaɪtn/ vt/i iluminar(-se); (make brighter) clarear

lighten[2] /ˈlaɪtn/ vt/i (load etc) aligeirar(-se), tornar mais leve

lighter /ˈlaɪtə(r)/ n isqueiro m

lighthouse /ˈlaɪthaʊs/ n farol m

lighting /ˈlaɪtɪŋ/ n iluminação f

lightning /ˈlaɪtnɪŋ/ n relâmpago m; (thunderbolt) raio m □ a muito rápido. **like ~** como um relâmpago

lightweight /ˈlaɪtweɪt/ a leve

like[1] /laɪk/ a semelhante (a), parecido (com) □ prep como □ conj (colloq) como □ n igual m, coisa f parecida. **~-minded** a da mesma opinião. **the ~s of you** gente como você(s).

like[2] /laɪk/ vt gostar (de). **~s** npl gostos mpl. **I would ~** gostaria (de), queria. **if you ~** se quiser. **would you ~?** gostaria?, queria? **~able** a simpático

likely /ˈlaɪklɪ/ a (-ier, -iest) provável □ adv provavelmente. **he is ~ly to come** é provável que ele venha. **not ~ly!** (colloq) nem morto, nem por sonhos. **~lihood** n probabilidade f

liken /ˈlaɪkn/ vt comparar (to com)

likeness /ˈlaɪknɪs/ n semelhança f

likewise /ˈlaɪkwaɪz/ adv também; (in the same way) da mesma maneira

liking /ˈlaɪkɪŋ/ n gosto m, inclinação f; (for person) afeição f. **take a ~ to** (thing) tomar gosto por; (person) simpatizar com

lilac /ˈlaɪlək/ n lilás m □ a lilás invar

lily /ˈlɪlɪ/ n lírio m, lis m. **~ of the valley** lírio m do vale

limb /lɪm/ n membro m

limber /'lɪmbə(r)/ vi ~ **up** fazer exercícios para desenferrujar (colloq)

lime[1] /laɪm/ n cal f

lime[2] /laɪm/ n (fruit) limão m

lime[3] /laɪm/ n ~(-tree) tília f

limelight /'laɪmlaɪt/ n **be in the** ~ estar em evidência

limerick /'lɪmərɪk/ n poema m humorístico (de cinco versos)

limit /'lɪmɪt/ n limite m □ vt limitar. ~**ation** /-'teɪʃn/ n limitação f. ~**ed company** sociedade f anónima, (P) anónima de responsabilidade limitada

limousine /'lɪməziːn/ n limusine f

limp[1] /lɪmp/ vi mancar, coxear □ n **have a** ~ coxear

limp[2] /lɪmp/ a (-er, -est) mole, frouxo

line[1] /laɪn/ n linha f; (string) fio m; (rope) corda f; (row) fila f; (of poem) verso m; (wrinkle) ruga f; (of business) ramo m; (of goods) linha f; (Amer: queue) fila f, (P) bicha f □ vt marcar com linhas; (streets etc) ladear, enfileirar-se ao longo de. ~**d paper** papel m pautado. **in** ~ **with** de acordo com. ~ **up** alinhar(-se), enfileirar(-se); (in queue) pôr(-se) em fila, (P) bicha. ~**up** n (players) formação f

line[2] /laɪn/ vt (garment) forrar (**with** de)

lineage /'lɪnɪdʒ/ n linhagem f

linear /'lɪnɪə(r)/ a linear

linen /'lɪnɪn/ n (sheets etc) roupa f (branca) de cama; (material) linho m

liner /'laɪnə(r)/ n navio m de linha regular, (P) paquete m

linesman /'laɪnzmən/ n (football, tennis) juiz m de linha

linger /'lɪŋgə(r)/ vi demorar-se, deixar-se ficar; (of smells etc) persistir

lingerie /'lænʒərɪ/ n roupa f de baixo (de senhora), lingerie f

linguist /'lɪŋgwɪst/ n lingüista mf, (P) linguista mf

linguistic /lɪŋ'gwɪstɪk/ a lingüístico, (P) linguístico. ~**s** n lingüística f, (P) linguística f

lining /'laɪnɪŋ/ n forro m

link /lɪŋk/ n laço m; (of chain; fig) elo m □ vt unir, ligar; (relate) ligar; (arm) enfiar. ~ **up** (of roads) juntar-se **with** (a). ~**age** n ligação f

lino, linoleum /'laɪnəʊ, lɪ'nəʊlɪəm/ n linóleo m

lint /lɪnt/ n (med) curativo m de fibra de algodão; (fluff) cotão m

lion /'laɪən/ n leão m. ~**ess** n leoa f

lip /lɪp/ n lábio m, beiço m; (edge) borda f; (of jug etc) bico m. ~-**read** vt/i entender pelos movimentos dos lábios. **pay** ~-**service to** fingir pena, admiração etc

lipstick /'lɪpstɪk/ n batom m, (P) báton m

liquefy /'lɪkwɪfaɪ/ vt/i liquefazer (-se)

liqueur /lɪ'kjʊə(r)/ n licor m

liquid /'lɪkwɪd/ n & a líquido (m). ~**ize** vt liquidificar, (P) liquidificar. ~**izer** n liqüidificador m, (P) liquidificador m

liquidat|e /'lɪkwɪdeɪt/ vt liquidar. ~**ion** /-'deɪʃn/ n liquidação f

liquor /'lɪkə(r)/ n bebida f alcoólica

liquorice /'lɪkərɪs/ n alcaçuz m

Lisbon /'lɪzbən/ n Lisboa f

lisp /lɪsp/ n ceceio m □ vi cecear

list[1] /lɪst/ n lista f □ vt fazer uma lista de; (enter) pôr na lista

list[2] /lɪst/ vi (of ship) adernar □ n adernamento m

listen /'lɪsn/ vi escutar, prestar atenção. ~ **to**, ~ **in** (**to**) escutar, pôr-se à escuta. ~**er** n ouvinte mf

listless /'lɪstlɪs/ a sem energia, apático

lit /lɪt/ *see* **light**[1]

literal /'lɪtərəl/ *a* literal. **~ly** *adv* literalmente

litera|te /'lɪtərət/ *a* alfabetizado. **~cy** *n* alfabetização *f*, instrução *f*

literature /'lɪtrətʃə(r)/ *n* literatura *f*; (*colloq: leaflets etc*) folhetos *mpl*

lithe /laɪð/ *a* ágil, flexível

litigation /lɪtɪ'geɪʃn/ *n* litígio *m*

litre /'liːtə(r)/ *n* litro *m*

litter /'lɪtə(r)/ *n* lixo *m*; (*animals*) ninhada *f* □ *vt* cobrir de lixo. **~ed with** coberto de. **~-bin** *n* lata *f*, (*P*) caixote *m* do lixo

little /'lɪtl/ *a* pequeno; (*not much*) pouco □ *n* pouco *m* □ *adv* pouco, mal, nem. **a ~** um pouco (de). **he ~ knows** ele mal/nem sabe. **~ by ~** pouco a pouco

liturgy /'lɪtədʒɪ/ *n* liturgia *f*

live[1] /laɪv/ *a* vivo; (*wire*) eletrizado; (*broadcast*) em direto, (*P*) direto, ao vivo

live[2] /lɪv/ *vt/i* viver; (*reside*) habitar, morar, viver. **~ down** fazer esquecer. **~ it up** cair na farra. **~ on** viver de; (*continue*) continuar a viver. **~ up to** mostrar-se à altura de; (*fulfil*) cumprir

livelihood /'laɪvlɪhʊd/ *n* modo *m* de vida

lively /'laɪvlɪ/ *a* (**-ier**, **-iest**) vivo, animado. **~iness** *n* vivacidade *f*, animação *f*

liven /'laɪvn/ *vt/i* **~ up** animar (-se)

liver /'lɪvə(r)/ *n* fígado *m*

livery /'lɪvərɪ/ *n* libré *f*

livestock /'laɪvstɒk/ *n* gado *m*

livid /'lɪvɪd/ *a* lívido; (*colloq: furious*) furioso

living /'lɪvɪŋ/ *a* vivo □ *n* vida *f*; (*livelihood*) modo de vida *m*, sustento *m*. **earn** *or* **make a ~** ganhar a vida. **standard of ~** nível *m* de vida. **~-room** *n* sala *f* de estar

lizard /'lɪzəd/ *n* lagarto *m*

llama /'laːmə/ *n* lama *m*

load /ləʊd/ *n* carga *f*; (*of lorry, ship*) carga *f*, carregamento *m*; (*weight, strain*) peso *m*. **~s of** (*colloq*) montes de (*colloq*) □ *vt* carregar. **~ed** *a* (*dice*) viciado; (*sl: rich*) cheio da nota

loaf[1] /ləʊf/ *n* (*pl* **loaves**) pão *m*

loaf[2] /ləʊf/ *vi* vadiar. **~er** *n* preguiçoso *m*, vagabundo *m*

loan /ləʊn/ *n* empréstimo *m* □ *vt* emprestar. **on ~** emprestado

loath /ləʊθ/ *a* sem vontade de, pouco disposto a, relutante em

loath|e /ləʊð/ *vt* detestar. **~ing** *n* repugnância *f*, aversão *f*.

lobby /'lɒbɪ/ *n* entrada *f*, vestíbulo *m*; (*pol*) lobby *m*, grupo *m* de pressão *f* □ *vt* fazer pressão sobre

lobe /ləʊb/ *n* lóbulo *m*

lobster /'lɒbstə(r)/ *n* lagosta *f*

local /'ləʊkl/ *a* local; (*shops etc*) do bairro □ *n* pessoa *f* do lugar; (*colloq: pub*) taberna *f*/pub *m* do bairro. **~ government** administração *f* municipal. **~ly** *adv* localmente

locale /ləʊ'kaːl/ *n* local *m*

locality /ləʊ'kælətɪ/ *n* localidade *f*; (*position*) lugar *m*

localization /ləʊəˈlaɪzeɪʃn/ *n* localização *f*

localized /'ləʊkəlaɪzd/ *a* localizado

locat|e /ləʊ'keɪt/ *vt* localizar; (*situate*) situar. **~ion** *f*-ʃn/ *n* localização *f*. **on ~ion** (*cinema*) em external, (*P*) no exterior

lock[1] /lɒk/ *n* (*hair*) mecha *f* de cabelo

lock[2] /lɒk/ *n* (*on door etc*) fecho *m*, fechadura *f*; (*on canal*) comporta *f* □ *vt/i* fechar à chave; (*auto: wheels*) imobilizar(-se). **~ in** fechar à chave, encerrar. **~ out** fechar a porta fora, deixar na rua. **~-out** *n* lockout *m*. **~ up** fechar a casa. **under ~ and key** a sete chaves

locker /'lɒkə(r)/ n compartimento m com chave

locket /'lɒkɪt/ n medalhão m

locksmith /'lɒksmɪθ/ n serralheiro m, chaveiro m

locomotion /ləʊkə'məʊʃn/ n locomoção f

locomotive /'ləʊkəməʊtɪv/ n locomotiva f

locum /'ləʊkəm/ n (med) substituto m

locust /'ləʊkəst/ n gafanhoto m

lodge /lɒdʒ/ n casa f do guarda numa propriedade; (of porter) portaria f □ vt alojar; (money) depositar. **~ a complaint** apresentar uma queixa □ vi estar alojado (**with** em casa de); (become fixed) alojar-se. **~r** /-ə(r)/ n hóspede mf

lodgings /'lɒdʒɪŋz/ n quarto m mobiliado; (flat) apartamento m

loft /lɒft/ n sótão m

lofty /'lɒftɪ/ a (-ier, -iest) elevado; (haughty) altivo

log /lɒg/ n tronco m, toro m. **~ (-book)** n (naut) diário m de bordo; (aviat) diario m de vôo. **sleep like a ~** dormir como uma pedra □ vt (pt logged) (naut/aviat) lançar no diário de bordo. **~ off** acabar de usar. **~ on** começar a usar

loggerheads /'lɒgəhedz/ npl **at ~** às turras (**with** com)

logic /'lɒdʒɪk/ a lógico. **~al** a lógico. **~ally** adv logicamente

logistics /lə'dʒɪstɪks/ n logística f

logo /'ləʊgəʊ/ n (pl -os) (colloq) emblema m, logotipo m, (P) logótipo m

loin /lɔɪn/ n (culin) lombo m, alcatra f

loiter /'lɔɪtə(r)/ vi andar vagarosamente; (stand about) rondar

loll /lɒl/ vi refestelar-se

lollipop /'lɒlɪpɒp/ n pirulito m, (P) chupa-chupa m. **~y** n (col-

loq) pirulito m, (P) chupa-chupa m; (sl: money) grana f

London /'lʌndən/ n Londres

lone /ləʊn/ a solitário. **~r** /-ə(r)/ n solitário m. **~some** a solitário

lonely /'ləʊnlɪ/ a (-ier, -iest) solitário; (person) só, solitário

long¹ /lɒŋ/ a (-er, -est) longo, comprido □ adv muito tempo, longamente. **how ~ is...?** (in size) qual é o comprimento de...? **how ~?** (in time) quanto tempo? **he will not be ~** ele não vai demorar. **a ~ time** muito tempo. **a ~ way** longe. **as or so ~ as** contanto que, desde que. **~ ago** há muito tempo. **before ~** (future) daqui a pouco, (dentro em pouco); (past) pouco (tempo) depois. **in the ~ run** no fim de contas. **~ before** muito (tempo) antes. **~-distance** a (flight) de longa distância; (phone call) interurbano. **~ face** cara f triste. **~ jump** salto m em distância. **~-playing record** LP m. **~-range** a de longo alcance; (forecast) a longo prazo. **~-sighted** a que enxerga mal à distância. **~-standing** a de longa data. **~-suffering** a com paciência exemplar/de santo. **~-term** a a longo prazo. **~ wave** ondas fpl longas. **~-winded** a prolixo. **so ~!** (colloq) até logo!

long² /lɒŋ/ vi **~ for** ansiar por, ter grande desejo de. **~ to** desejar. **~ing** n desejo m ardente

longevity /lɒn'dʒevətɪ/ n longevidade f, vida f longa

longhand /'lɒŋhænd/ n escrita f à mão

longitude /'lɒndʒɪtjuːd/ n longitude f

loo /luː/ n (colloq) banheiro m, (P) casa f de banho

look /lʊk/ vt/i olhar; (seem) parecer □ n olhar m; (appearance) m, aspecto m. **(good) ~s** beleza

f. ~ **after** tomar conta de, olhar por. ~ **at** olhar para. ~ **down on** desprezar. ~ **for** procurar. ~ **forward to** aguardar com impaciência. ~ **in on** visitar. ~ **into** examinar, investigar. ~ **like** parecer com, ter ar de. ~ **on** (*as spectator*) ver, assistir; (*regard as*) considerar. ~ **out** ter cautela. ~ **out for** procurar; (*watch*) estar à espreita de. ~ **out in** (*mil*) posto m de observação; (*watcher*) vigia m. ~ **round** olhar em redor. ~ **up** (*word*) procurar; (*visit*) ir ver. ~ **up to** respeitar

loom[1] /luːm/ n tear m

loom[2] /luːm/ vi surgir indistintamente; (*fig*) ameaçar

loony /ˈluːnɪ/ n & a (*sl*) maluco (*m*), doido (*m*)

loop /luːp/ n laçada f; (*curve*) volta f, arco m; (*aviat*) loop m □ vt dar uma laçada

loophole /ˈluːphəʊl/ n (*in rule*) saída f, furo m

loose /luːs/ a (-er, -est) (*knot etc*) frouxo; (*page etc*) solto; (*clothes*) folgado; (*not packed*) a granel; (*inexact*) vago; (*morals*) dissoluto, imoral. **at a ~ end** sem saber o que fazer, sem ocupação definida. **break ~** soltar-se. ~**ly** adv sem apertar; (*roughly*) vagamente

loosen /ˈluːsn/ vt (*slacken*) soltar, desapertar; (*untie*) desfazer, desatar

loot /luːt/ n saque m □ vt pilhar, saquear. ~**er** n assaltante mf. ~**ing** n pilhagem f, saque m

lop /lɒp/ vt (*pt* lopped) ~ **off** cortar, podar

lop-sided /lɒpˈsaɪdɪd/ a torto, inclinado para um lado

lord /lɔːd/ n senhor m; (*title*) lord m. **the L~** o Senhor. **the L~'s Prayer** o Pai-Nosso. **(good) L~!** meu Deus! ~**ly** a magnífico,

nobre; (*haughty*) altivo, arrogante

lorry /ˈlɒrɪ/ n camião m, caminhão m

lose /luːz/ vt/i (*pt* lost) perder. **get lost** perder-se. **get lost!** (*sl*) vai passear! (*colloq*). ~**r** /-ə(r)/ n perdedor m

loss /lɒs/ n perda f. **be at a ~** estar perplexo. **at a ~ for words** sem saber o que dizer

lost /lɒst/ *see* **lose** □ a perdido. ~ **property** objetos mpl, (*P*) objectos mpl perdidos (e achados)

lot[1] /lɒt/ n sorte f; (*at auction, land*) lote m. **draw ~s** tirar à sorte

lot[2] /lɒt/ n **the ~** tudo; (*people*) todos mpl. **a ~ (of)**, ~**s (of)** (*colloq*) uma porção (de) (*colloq*). **quite a ~ (of)** (*colloq*) uma boa porção (de) (*colloq*)

lotion /ˈləʊʃn/ n loção f

lottery /ˈlɒtərɪ/ n loteria f, (*P*) lotaria f

loud /laʊd/ a (-er, -est) alto, barulhento, ruidoso; (*of colours*) berrante □ adv alto. ~ **hailer** n megafone m. **out ~** em voz alta. ~**ly** adv alto

loudspeaker /laʊdˈspiːkə(r)/ n alto-falante m

lounge /laʊndʒ/ vi recostar-se preguiçosamente □ n sala f, salão m

louse /laʊs/ n (*pl* lice) piolho m

lousy /ˈlaʊzɪ/ a (-ier, -iest) piolhento; (*sl: very bad*) péssimo

lout /laʊt/ n pessoa f grosseira, arruaceiro m

lovable /ˈlʌvəbl/ a amoroso, adorável

love /lʌv/ n amor m; (*tennis*) zero m, nada m □ vt amar, estar apaixonado por; (*like greatly*) gostar muito de. **in ~** apaixonado (with por). ~ **affair** aventura f amorosa. **she sends you her ~** ela lhe manda lembranças

lovely /'lʌvlɪ/ a (-ier, -iest) lindo; (colloq: delightful) encantador, delicioso

lover /'lʌvə(r)/ n namorado m, apaixonado m; (illicit) amante m; (devotee) admirador m, apreciador m

lovesick /'lʌvsɪk/ a perdido de amor

loving /'lʌvɪŋ/ a amoroso, terno, extremoso

low /ləʊ/ a (-er, -est) baixo □ adv baixo □ n baixa f; (low pressure) área de baixa pressão f. ~ **-cut** a decotado. ~**-down** a baixo, reles □ n (colloq) a verdade autêntica, (P) a verdade nua e crua. ~**-fat** a de baixo teor de gordura. ~**-key** a (fig) moderado, discreto

lower /'ləʊə(r)/ a & adv see **low** □ vt baixar. ~ **o.s.** (re)baixar-se (to a)

lowlands /'ləʊləndz/ npl planície(s) f (pl)

lowly /'ləʊlɪ/ a (-ier, -iest) humilde, modesto

loyal /'lɔɪəl/ a leal. ~**ly** adv lealmente. ~**ty** n lealdade f

lozenge /'lɒzɪndʒ/ n (shape) losango m; (tablet) pastilha f

LP abbr see **long-playing record**

lubric|ate /'luːbrɪkeɪt/ vt lubrificar. ~**ant** n lubrificante m. ~**ation** /-'keɪʃn/ n lubrificação f

lucid /'luːsɪd/ a lúcido. ~**ity** /luː-'sɪdətɪ/ n lucidez f

luck /lʌk/ n sorte f. **bad** ~ pouca sorte f. **for** ~ para dar sorte. **good** ~! boa sorte

luck|y /'lʌkɪ/ a (-ier, -iest) sortudo, com sorte; (event etc) feliz; (number etc) que dá sorte. ~**ily** adv felizmente

lucrative /'luːkrətɪv/ a lucrativo, rentável

ludicrous /'luːdɪkrəs/ a ridículo, absurdo

lug /lʌg/ vt (pt **lugged**) arrastar

luggage /'lʌgɪdʒ/ n bagagem f. ~-

rack n porta-bagagem m. ~**-van** n furgão m

lukewarm /'luːkwɔːm/ a morno; (fig) sem entusiasmo, indiferente

lull /lʌl/ vt (send to sleep) embalar; (suspicions) acalmar □ n calmaria f, (P) acalmia f

lullaby /'lʌləbaɪ/ n canção f de embalar

lumbago /lʌm'beɪgəʊ/ n lumbago m

lumber /'lʌmbə(r)/ n trastes mpl velhos; (wood) madeira f cortada □ vt ~ **sb with** sobrecarregar alguém com

luminous /'luːmɪnəs/ a luminoso

lump /lʌmp/ n bocado m; (swelling) caroço m; (in the throat) nó m; (in liquid) grumo m; (of sugar) torrão m □ vt ~ **together** amontoar, juntar indiscriminadamente. ~ **sum** quantia f total; (payment) pagamento m de uma vez. ~**y** a grumoso, encaroçado

lunacy /'luːnəsɪ/ n loucura f

lunar /'luːnə(r)/ a lunar

lunatic /'luːnətɪk/ n lunático m. ~ **asylum** manicômio m, (P) manicómio m

lunch /lʌntʃ/ n almoço m □ vi almoçar. ~**-time** n hora f do almoço

luncheon /'lʌntʃən/ n (formal) almoço m. ~ **meat** carne f enlatada, (P) 'merenda' f. ~ **voucher** senha f de almoço

lung /lʌŋ/ n pulmão m

lunge /lʌndʒ/ n mergulho m, movimento m súbito para a frente; (thrust) arremetida f □ vi mergulhar, arremessar-se (at para cima de, contra)

lurch[1] /lɜːtʃ/ n **leave sb in the** ~ deixar alg em apuros

lurch[2] /lɜːtʃ/ vi ir aos ziguezagues, dar guinadas; (stagger) cambalear

lure /lʊə(r)/ vt atrair, tentar □ n chamariz m, engodo m. **the** ~ **of the sea** a atração, (P) atracção do mar

lurid /'luərɪd/ a berrante; (*fig: sensational*) sensacional; (*fig: shocking*) horrífico

lurk /lɜːk/ vi esconder-se à espreita; (*prowl*) rondar; (*be latent*) estar latente

luscious /'lʌʃəs/ a apetitoso; (*voluptuous*) desejável

lush /lʌʃ/ a viçoso, luxuriante

Lusitanian /lusɪˈteɪnɪən/ a & n lusitano (m)

lust /lʌst/ n luxúria f, sensualidade f; (*fig*) cobiça f, desejo m ardente □ vi — **after** cobiçar, desejar ardentemente. ~**ful** a sensual

lustre /'lʌstə(r)/ n lustre m; (*fig*) prestígio m

lusty /'lʌstɪ/ a (-ier, -iest) robusto

lute /luːt/ n alaúde m

Luxemburg /'lʌksəmbɜːɡ/ n Luxemburgo m

luxuriant /lʌɡˈzjʊərɪənt/ a luxuriante

luxurious /lʌɡˈzjʊərɪəs/ a luxuoso

luxury /'lʌkʃərɪ/ n luxo m □ a de luxo

lying /'laɪɪŋ/ see **lie**[1], **lie**[2]

lynch /lɪntʃ/ vt linchar

lynx /lɪŋks/ n lince m

lyre /'laɪə(r)/ n lira f

lyric /'lɪrɪk/ a lírico. ~**s** npl (*mus*) letra f. ~**al** a lírico

M

MA abbr see **Master of Arts**

mac /mæk/ n (*colloq*) impermeável m, gabardine f

macabre /məˈkɑːbrə/ a macabro

macaroni /mækəˈrəʊnɪ/ n macarrão m

macaroon /mækəˈruːn/ n bolinho m seco de amêndoa ralada

mace[1] /meɪs/ n (*staff*) maça f

mace[2] /meɪs/ n (*spice*) macis m

machination /mækɪˈneɪʃn/ n maquinação f

machine /məˈʃiːn/ n máquina f □ vt fazer à máquina; (*sewing*) coser à máquina. ~-**gun** n metralhadora f. ~-**readable** a em linguagem de máquina. ~ **tool** máquina-ferramenta f

machinery /məˈʃiːnərɪ/ n maquinaria f; (*working parts; fig*) mecanismo m

machinist /məˈʃiːnɪst/ n maquinista m

macho /'mætʃəʊ/ a machista

mackerel /'mækrəl/ n (*pl invar*) cavala f

mackintosh /'mækɪntɒʃ/ n impermeável m, gabardine f

mad /mæd/ a (**madder**, **maddest**) doido, louco; (*dog*) raivoso; (*colloq: angry*) furioso (*colloq*). ~ **cow disease** doença f da vaca louca. **be** ~ **about** ser doido por. **like** ~ como (um) doido. ~**ly** adv loucamente; (*frantically*) enlouquecidamente. ~**ness** n loucura f

Madagascar /mædəˈɡæskə(r)/ n Madagáscar m

madam /'mædəm/ n senhora f. **no,** ~ não senhora

madden /'mædn/ vt endoidecer, enlouquecer. **it's** ~**ing** é de enlouquecer

made /meɪd/ see **make**. ~ **to measure** feito sob medida

Madeira /məˈdɪərə/ n Madeira f; (*wine*) Madeira m

madman /'mædmən/ n (*pl* -**men**) doido m

madrigal /'mædrɪɡl/ n madrigal m

Mafia /'mæfɪə/ n Máfia f

magazine /mæɡəˈziːn/ n revista f, magazine m; (*of gun*) carregador m

magenta /məˈdʒentə/ a & n magenta (m), carmim m

maggot /'mæɡət/ n larva f. ~**y** a bichento

Magi /'meɪdʒaɪ/ *npl* the ~ os Reis *mpl* Magos

magic /'mædʒɪk/ *n* magia *f* □ *a* mágico. ~**al** *a* mágico

magician /mə'dʒɪʃn/ *n* (*conjuror*) prestidigitador *m*; (*wizard*) feiticeiro *m*

magistrate /'mædʒɪstreɪt/ *n* magistrado *m*

magnanim|ous /mæg'nænɪməs/ *a* magnânimo. ~**ity** /-ə'nɪmətɪ/ *n* magnanimidade *f*

magnate /'mægneɪt/ *n* magnata *m*

magnet /'mægnɪt/ *n* imã *m*, (*P*) íman *m*. ~**ic** /-'netɪk/ *a* magnético. ~**ism** /-tɪzəm/ *n* magnetismo *m*. ~**ize** *vt* magnetizar

magnificen|t /mæg'nɪfɪsnt/ *a* magnífico. ~**ce** *n* magnificência *f*

magnif|y /'mægnɪfaɪ/ *vt* aumentar; (*sound*) ampliar, amplificar. ~**ication** /-ɪ'keɪʃn/ *n* aumento *m*, ampliação *f*. ~**ying glass** lupa *f*

magnitude /'mægnɪtjuːd/ *n* magnitude *f*

magpie /'mægpaɪ/ *n* pega *f*

mahogany /mə'hɒgənɪ/ *n* mogno *m*

maid /meɪd/ *n* criada *f*, empregada *f*. **old** ~ solteirona *f*

maiden /'meɪdn/ *n* (*old use*) donzela *f* □ *a* (*aunt*) solteira; (*speech*, *voyage*) inaugural. ~ **name** nome *m* de solteira

mail[1] /meɪl/ *n* correio *m*; (*letters*) correio *m*, correspondência *f* □ *a* postal □ *vt* postar, no correio; (*send by mail*) mandar pelo correio. ~**bag** *n* mala *f* postal. ~**box** *n* (*Amer*) caixa *f* do correio. ~**ing-list** *n* lista *f* de endereços. ~ **order** encomenda *f* por correspondência, (*P*) por correio

mail[2] /meɪl/ *n* (*armour*) cota *f* de malha

mailman /'meɪlmæn/ *n* (*pl* -**men**) (*Amer*) carteiro *m*

maim /meɪm/ *vt* mutilar, aleijar

main[1] /meɪn/ *a* principal □ *n* in the ~ em geral, essencialmente. ~ **road** estrada *f* principal. ~**ly** *adv* principalmente, sobretudo

main[2] /meɪn/ *n* (**water/gas**) ~ cano *m* de água/gás. the ~**s** (*electr*) a rede *f* elétrica

mainland /'meɪnlənd/ *n* continente *m*

mainstay /'meɪnsteɪ/ *n* (*fig*) esteio *m*

mainstream /'meɪnstriːm/ *n* tendência *f* dominante, linha *f* principal

maintain /meɪn'teɪn/ *vt* manter, sustentar; (*rights*) defender, manter

maintenance /'meɪntənəns/ *n* (*care*, *continuation*) manutenção *f*; (*allowance*) pensão *f*

maisonette /meɪzə'net/ *n* dúplex *m*

maize /meɪz/ *n* milho *m*

majestic /mə'dʒestɪk/ *a* majestoso. ~**ally** *adv* majestosamente

majesty /'mædʒəstɪ/ *n* majestade *f*

major /'meɪdʒə(r)/ *a* maior; (*very important*) de vulto □ *n* major *m* □ *vi* ~ **in** (*Amer: univ*) especializar-se em. ~ **road** estrada *f* principal

Majorca /mə'dʒɔːkə/ *n* Maiorca *f*

majority /mə'dʒɒrətɪ/ *n* maioria *f*; (*age*) maioridade *f* □ *a* majoritário, (*P*) maioritário. the ~ **of people** a maioria *or* a maior parte das pessoas

make /meɪk/ *vt/i* (*pt* **made**) fazer; (*decision*) tomar; (*destination*) chegar a; (*cause to*) fazer (+ *inf*) *or* (com) que (+ *subj*). **you** ~ **me angry** você me aborrece □ *n* (*brand*) marca *f*. **on the** ~ (*sl*) oportunista. **be made of** ser feito de. ~ **o.s. at home** estar à vontade/como em sua casa. ~ **it** chegar; (*succeed*) triunfar. **I** ~ **it two o'clock** são duas pelo meu relógio. ~ **as if to** fazer *ou* fingir

que. ~ believe fingir. ~-believe
a fingido □ n fantasia f. ~ do
with arranjar-se com, contentar-
se com. ~ for dirigir-se para;
(contribute to) ajudar a. ~
good vi triunfar □ vt compensar;
(repair) reparar. ~ off fugir
(with com). ~ out avistar, distinguir; (understand) entender;
(claim) pretender; (a cheque) passar, emitir. ~ over ceder,
transferir. ~ up vt fazer, compor; (story) inventar; (deficit) suprir □ vi fazer as pazes. ~ up
(one's face) maquilar-se, (P)
maquilhar-se. ~-up n maquilagem f, (P) maquilhagem f; (of object) composição f; (psych)
maneira f de ser, natureza f.
~ up for compensar. ~ up
one's mind decidir-se
maker /'meɪkə(r)/ n fabricante mf
makeshift /'meɪkʃɪft/ n solução f
temporária □ a provisório
making /'meɪkɪŋ/ n be the ~ of
fazer, ser a causa do sucesso de.
in the ~ em formação. he has
the ~s of ele tem as qualidades
essenciais de
maladjusted /mælə'dʒʌstɪd/ a de-
sajustado, inadaptado
maladministration /mælədmɪnɪ-
'streɪʃn/ n mau governo m, má
gestão f
malaise /mæ'leɪz/ n mal-estar m
malaria /mə'leərɪə/ n malária f
Malay /mə'leɪ/ a & n malaio (m).
~**sia** /-ʒə/ n Malásia f
male /meɪl/ a (voice, sex) masculino; (biol, techn) macho □ n (human) homem m, indivíduo m do
sexo masculino; (arrival) macho
m
malevolen|t /mə'levələnt/ a ma-
lévolo. ~**ce** n malevolência f,
má vontade f
malform|ation /mælfɔ:'meɪʃn/ n
malformação f, deformidade f.
~**ed** a deformado

malfunction /mæl'fʌŋkʃn/ n mau
funcionamento m □ vi funcionar
mal
malice /'mælɪs/ n maldade f, malícia f. bear sb ~ guardar rancor a alg
malicious /mə'lɪʃəs/ a maldoso,
malicioso. ~**ly** adv maldosamente, maliciosamente
malign /mə'laɪn/ vt caluniar, difamar
malignan|t /mə'lɪgnənt/ a (tu-
mour) maligno; (malevolent) malévolo. ~**cy** n malignidade f;
malevolência f
malinger /mə'lɪŋgə(r)/ vi fingir-se
doente. ~**er** n pessoa f que se
finge doente
mallet /'mælɪt/ n maço m
malnutrition /mælnju:'trɪʃn/ n
desnutrição f, subalimentação f
malpractice /mæl'præktɪs/ n abuso m; (incompetence) incompetên-
cia f profissional, negligência f
malt /mɔ:lt/ n malte m
Malt|a /'mɔ:ltə/ n Malta f. ~**ese**
/-'ti:z/ a & n maltês (m)
maltreat /mæl'tri:t/ vt maltratar.
~**ment** n mau(s) trato(s) m(pl)
mammal /'mæml/ n mamífero m
mammoth /'mæməθ/ n mamute m
□ a gigantesco, colossal
man /mæn/ n (pl men) homem m;
(in sports team) jogador m;
(chess) peça f □ vt (pt manned)
prover de pessoal; (mil) guarnecer; (naut) guarnecer, equipar,
tripular; (be on duty at) estar de
serviço em. ~ in the street o
homem da rua. ~-hour n hora
f de trabalho per capita, homem-
hora f. ~-hunt n caça f ao
homem. ~-made a artificial.
~ to man de homem para
homem
manage /'mænɪdʒ/ vt (household)
governar; (tool) manejar; (boat,
affair, crowd) manobrar; (shop)
dirigir, gerir. I could ~ another

drink (*colloq*) até que tomaria mais um drinque (*colloq*) □ *vi* arranjar-se. ~**able** a manejável; (*easily controlled*) controlável. ~**ment** *n* gerência *f*, direção *f*, (*P*) direcção *f*. **managing director** diretor *m*, (*P*) director *m* geral

manager /'mænɪdʒə(r)/ *n* diretor *m*, (*P*) director *m*; (*of bank, shop*) gerente *m*; (*of actor*) empresário *m*; (*sport*) treinador *m*. ~**ess** /-'res/ *n* diretora *f*, (*P*) directora *f*; gerente *f*. ~**ial** /-'dʒɪərɪəl/ a diretivo, (*P*) directivo, administrativo. ~**ial staff** gestores *mpl*

mandarin /'mændərɪn/ *n* mandarim *m*. ~ **(orange)** mandarina *f*, tangerina *f*

mandate /'mændeɪt/ *n* mandato *m*

mandatory /'mændətrɪ/ a obrigatório

mane /meɪn/ *n* crina *f*; (*of lion*) juba *f*

mangle[1] /'mæŋgl/ *n* calandra *f* □ *vt* espremer (com a calandra)

mangle[2] /'mæŋgl/ *vt* (*mutilate*) mutilar, estropiar

mango /'mæŋgəʊ/ *n* (*pl* -oes) manga *f*

manhandle /'mænhændl/ *vt* mover à força de braço; (*treat roughly*) tratar com brutalidade

manhole /'mænhəʊl/ *n* poço *m* de inspeção, (*P*) inspecção

manhood /'mænhʊd/ *n* idade adulta *f*; (*quality*) virilidade *f*

mania /'meɪnɪə/ *n* mania *f*. ~**c** /-ɪæk/ *n* maníaco *m*

manicur|**e** /'mænɪkjʊə(r)/ *n* manicure *f* □ *vt* fazer. ~**ist** *n* manicure *m*

manifest /'mænɪfest/ a manifesto □ *vt* manifestar. ~**ation** /-'steɪʃn/ *n* manifestação *f*

manifesto /mænɪ'festəʊ/ *n* (*pl* -os) manifesto *m*

manipulat|**e** /mə'nɪpjʊleɪt/ *vt*

manipular. ~**ion** /-'leɪʃn/ *n* manipulação *f*

mankind /mæn'kaɪnd/ *n* humanidade *f*, gênero *m*, (*P*) género *m* humano

manly /'mænlɪ/ a viril, másculo

manner /'mænə(r)/ *n* maneira *f*, modo *m*; (*attitude*) modo(s) *m* (*pl*); (*kind*) espécie *f*. ~**s** *mpl* maneiras *fpl*. **bad** ~**s** má-criação *f*, falta *f* de educação. **good** ~**s** (boa) educação *f*. ~**ed** a afetado.

mannerism /'mænərɪzəm/ *n* maneirismo *m*

manoeuvre /mə'nu:və(r)/ *n* manobra *f* □ *vt/i* manobrar

manor /'mænə(r)/ *n* solar *m*

manpower /'mænpaʊə(r)/ *n* mão-de-obra *f*

mansion /'mænʃn/ *n* mansão *f*

manslaughter /'mænslɔ:tə(r)/ *n* homicídio *m* involuntário

mantelpiece /'mæntlpi:s/ *n* (*shelf*) consolo *m* da lareira, (*P*) prateleira *f* da chaminé

manual /'mænjʊəl/ a manual □ *n* manual *m*

manufacture /mænjʊ'fæktʃə(r)/ *vt* fabricar □ *n* fabrico *m*, fabricação *f*. ~**r** /-ə(r)/ *n* fabricante *m*

manure /mə'njʊə(r)/ *n* estrume *m*

manuscript /'mænjʊskrɪpt/ *n* manuscrito *m*

many /'menɪ/ a (**more**, **most**) muitos □ *n* muitos; (*many people*) muita gente *f*. **a great** ~ muitíssimos. ~ **a man/tear/***etc* muitos homens/muitas lágrimas/*etc*. **you may take as** ~ **as you want** você pode levar quantos quiser. ~ **of us/them/you** muitos de nós/deles/de vocês. **how** ~? quantos? **one too** ~ um a mais

map /mæp/ *n* mapa *m* □ *vt* (*pt* **mapped**) fazer mapa de. ~ **out** planear em pormenor; (*route*) traçar

maple /'meɪpl/ n bordo m

mar /ma:(r)/ vt (pt **marred**) estragar; (beauty) desfigurar

marathon /'mærəθən/ n maratona f

marble /'ma:bl/, n mármore m; (for game) bola f de gude, (P) berlinde m

March /ma:tʃ/ n março m

march /ma:tʃ/ vi marchar □ vt ~ **off** fazer marchar, conduzir à força. **he was ~ed off to prison** fizeram-no marchar para a prisão □ n marcha f. ~-**past** n desfile m em revista militar

mare /meə(r)/ n égua f

margarine /ma:dʒə'ri:n/ n margarina f

margin /'ma:dʒɪn/ n margem f. ~**al** a marginal. ~**al seat** (pol) lugar m ganho com pequena maioria. ~**ally** adv por uma pequena margem, muito pouco

marigold /'mærɪɡəʊld/ n cravo-de-defunto m, (P) malmequer m

marijuana /mærɪ'wa:nə/ n maconha f

marina /mə'ri:nə/ n marina f

marinade /mærɪ'neɪd/ n vinha d'alho, escalabeche m □ vt pôr na vinha d'alho

marine /mə'ri:n/ a marinho; (of ship, trade etc) marítimo □ n (shipping) marinha f; (sailor) fuzileiro m naval

marionette /mærɪə'net/ n fantoche m, marionete f

marital /'mærɪtl/ a marital, conjugal, matrimonial. ~ **status** estado m civil

maritime /'mærɪtaɪm/ a marítimo

mark[1] /ma:k/ n (currency) marco m

mark[2] /ma:k/ n marca f; (trace) marca f, sinal m; (stain) mancha f; (schol) nota f; (target) alvo m □ vt marcar; (exam etc) marcar, classificar. ~ **out** marcar. ~ **out for** escolher para, designar

para. ~ **time** marcar passo. **make one's** ~ ganhar nome. ~**er** n marcador m. ~**ing** n marcas fpl, marcação f

marked /ma:kt/ a marcado. ~**ly** /-ɪdlɪ/ adv manifestamente, visivelmente

market /'ma:kɪt/ n mercado m □ vt vender; (launch) comercializar, lançar. ~ **garden** horta f de legumes para venda. ~-**place** n mercado m. ~ **research** pesquisa f de mercado. **on the** ~ à venda. ~**ing** n marketing m

marksman /'ma:ksmən/ n (pl -men) atirador m especial

marmalade /'ma:məleɪd/ n compota f de laranja

maroon /mə'ru:n/ a & n bordô (m), (P) bordeaux (m)

marooned /mə'ru:nd/ a abandonado em ilha, costa deserta etc; (fig: stranded) encalhado (fig)

marquee /ma:'ki:/ n barraca f ou tenda f grande; (Amer: awning) toldo m

marriage /'mærɪdʒ/ n casamento m, matrimônio m, (P) matrimónio m. ~ **certificate** certidão f de casamento. ~**able** a casadouro

marrow /'mærəʊ/ n (of bone) tutano m, medula f; (vegetable) abóbora f. **chilled to the** ~ gelado até os ossos

marr|y /'mærɪ/ vt casar(-se) com; (give or unite in marriage) casar □ vi casar-se. ~**ied** a casado; (life) de casado, conjugal. **get** ~**ied** casar-se

Mars /ma:z/ n Marte m

marsh /ma:ʃ/ n pântano m. ~**y** a pantanoso

marshal /'ma:ʃl/ n (mil) marechal m; (steward) mestre m de cerimónias, (P) cerimónias □ vt (pt **marshalled**) dispor em ordem, ordenar; (usher) conduzir, escoltar

marshmallow /ma:ʃ'mæləʊ/ *n* marshmallow *m*

martial /'ma:ʃl/ *a* marcial. **~ law** lei *f* marcial

martyr /'ma:tə(r)/ *n* mártir *mf* □ *vt* martirizar. **~dom** *n* martírio *m*

marvel /'ma:vl/ *n* maravilha *f*, prodígio *m* □ *vi* (*pt* **marvelled**) (*feel wonder*) maravilhar-se (at com); (*be astonished*) pasmar (at com)

marvellous /'ma:vələs/ *a* maravilhoso

Marxis|t /'ma:ksɪst/ *a* & *n* marxista (*mf*). **~m** /-zəm/ *n* marxismo *m*

marzipan /'ma:zɪpæn/ *n* maçapão *m*

mascara /mæ'ska:rə/ *n* rímel *m*

mascot /'mæskət/ *n* mascote *f*

masculin|e /'mæskjʊlm/ *a* masculino □ *n* masculino *m*. **~ity** /-'lɪnəti/ *n* masculinidade *f*

mash /mæʃ/ *n* (*pulp*) papa *f* □ *vt* esmagar. **~ed potatoes** purê *m* de batata(s)

mask /ma:sk/ *n* máscara *f* □ *vt* mascarar

masochis|t /'mæsəkɪst/ *n* masoquista *mf*. **~m** /-zəm/ *n* masoquismo *m*

mason /'meɪsn/ *n* maçom *m*; (*building*) pedreiro *m*. **~ry** *n* maçonaria *f*; (*building*) alvenaria *f*

Mason /'meɪsn/ *n* Maçônico *m*, (*P*) Maçónico *m*. **~ic** /mə'sɒnɪk/ *a* Maçônico, (*P*) Maçónico

masquerade /mæ:skə'reɪd/ *n* mascarada *f* □ *vi* **~ as** mascarar-se de, disfarçar-se de

mass[1] /mæs/ *n* (*relig*) missa *f*

mass[2] /mæs/ *n* massa *f*; (*heap*) montão *m* □ *vt/i* aglomerar(-se), reunir(-se) em massa. **~ produce** *vt* produzir em série. **the ~es** as massas, a grande massa

massacre /'mæsəkə(r)/ *n* massacre *m* □ *vt* massacrar

massage /'mæsɑ:ʒ/ *n* massagem *f* □ *vt* massagear, fazer massagens em, (*P*) dar massagens a

masseu|r /mæ'sɜ:(r)/ *n* massagista *m*. **~se** /mæ'sɜ:z/ *n* massagista *f*

massive /'mæsɪv/ *a* (*heavy*) maciço; (*huge*) enorme

mast /mɑ:st/ *n* mastro *m*; (*for radio etc*) antena *f*

master /'mɑ:stə(r)/ *n* (*in school*) professor *m*, mestre *m*; (*expert*) mestre *m*; (*boss*) patrão *m*; (*owner*) dono *m*. **M~** (*boy*) menino *m* □ *vt* dominar. **~-key** *n* chave-mestra *f*. **~-mind** *n* (*of scheme etc*) cérebro *m* □ *vt* planejar, dirigir. **M~ of Arts/etc** Licenciado *m* em Letras/*etc.* **~stroke** *n* golpe *m* de mestre. **~y** (*knowledge*) conhecimento *m*; (*skill*) perícia *f*

masterly /'mɑ:stəlɪ/ *a* magistral

masterpiece /'mɑ:stəpi:s/ *n* obra-prima *f*

masturbat|e /'mæstəbeɪt/ *vi* masturbar-se. **~ion** /-'beɪʃn/ *n* masturbação *f*

mat /mæt/ *n* tapete *m* pequeno; (*at door*) capacho *m*. (**table-**)**~** *n* (*of cloth*) paninho *m* de mesa; (*for hot dishes*) descanso *m* para pratos

match[1] /mætʃ/ *n* fósforo *m*

match[2] /mætʃ/ *n* (*contest*) competição *f*, torneio *m*; (*game*) partida *f*; (*equal*) par *m*, parceiro *m*, igual *mf*; (*fig: marriage*) casamento *m*; (*marriage partner*) partido *m* □ *vt/i* (*set against*) contrapôr (**against** a); (*equal*) igualar; (*go with*) condizer; (*be alike*) ir com, emparceirar com. **her shoes ~ed her bag** os sapatos dela combinavam com a bolsa. **~ing** *a* condizente, a condizer

matchbox /'mætʃbɒks/ *n* caixa *f* de fósforos

mate|**e**[1] /meɪt/ n companheiro m, camarada mf; (of birds, animals) macho m, fêmea f; (assistant) ajudante mf □ vt/i acasalar(-se) (with com). ~**ing season** n época f de cio

mate[2] /meɪt/ n (chess) mate m, xeque-mate m

material /mə'tɪərɪəl/ n material m; (fabric) tecido m; (equipment) apetrechos mpl □ a material; (significant) importante

materialis|**m** /mə'tɪərɪəlɪzəm/ n materialismo m. ~**tic** /-'lɪstɪk/ a materialista

materialize /mə'tɪərɪəlaɪz/ vi realizar-se, concretizar-se; (appear) aparecer

maternal /mə'tɜːnəl/ a maternal

maternity /mə'tɜːnəti/ n maternidade f □ a (clothes) de grávida. ~ **hospital** maternidade f. ~ **leave** licença f de maternidade

mathematic|**s** /mæθə'mætɪks/ n matemática f. ~**al** a matemático. ~**ian** /-ə'tɪʃn/ n matemático m.

maths /mæθs/ n (colloq) matemática f

matinée /'mætɪneɪ/ n matinée f, (P) matinê f

matrimon|**y** /'mætrɪmənɪ/ n matrimônio m, (P) matrimónio m. ~**ial** /-'məʊnɪəl/ a matrimonial, conjugal

matrix /'meɪtrɪks/ n (pl matrices /-siːz/) matriz f

matron /'meɪtrən/ n matrona f; (in school) inspetora f; (former use: senior nursing officer) enfermeira-chefe f. ~**ly** a respeitável, muito digno

matt /mæt/ a fosco, sem brilho

matted /'mætɪd/ a emaranhado

matter /'mætə(r)/ n (substance) matéria f; (affair) assunto m, caso m, questão f; (pus) pus m □ vi importar. **as a** ~ **of fact** na verdade. **it does not** ~ não

importa. ~-**of-fact** a prosaico, terra-a-terra. **no** ~ **what happens** não importa o que acontecer. **what is the** ~? o que é que há? **what is the** ~ **with you?** o que é que você tem?

mattress /'mætrɪs/ n colchão m

matur|**e** /mə'tjʊə(r)/ a maduro, amadurecido □ vt/i amadurecer; (comm) vencer-se. ~**ity** n maturidade f, maturidade f; (comm) vencimento m

maul /mɔːl/ vt maltratar, atacar

Mauritius /mə'rɪʃəs/ n Ilha f Maurícia

mausoleum /mɔːsə'lɪəm/ n mausoléu m

mauve /məʊv/ a & n lilás (m)

maxim /'mæksɪm/ n máxima f

maxim|**um** /'mæksɪməm/ a & n (pl -**ima**) máximo (m). ~**ize** vt aumentar ao máximo, maximizar

may /meɪ/ v aux (pt **might**) poder. **he** ~/**might come** talvez venha/viesse. **you might have** podia ter. **you** ~ **leave** pode ir. ~ **I smoke?** posso fumar?, dá licença que eu fume? ~ **he be happy** que ele seja feliz. **I** ~ **or might as well go** talvez seja or fosse melhor eu ir

May /meɪ/ n maio m. ~ **Day** o primeiro de maio

maybe /'meɪbɪ/ adv talvez

mayhem /'meɪhem/ n (disorder) distúrbios mpl violentos; (havoc) estragos mpl

mayonnaise /meɪə'neɪz/ n maionese f

mayor /meə(r)/ n prefeito m. ~**ess** n prefeita f; (mayor's wife) mulher f do prefeito

maze /meɪz/ n labirinto m

me /miː/ pron me; (after prep) mim. **with** ~ comigo. **he knows** ~ ele me conhece. **it's** ~ sou eu

meadow /'medəʊ/ n prado m, campina f

meagre /'mi:gə(r)/ a (*thin*) magro; (*scanty*) escasso

meal[1] /mi:l/ n refeição f

meal[2] /mi:l/ n (*grain*) farinha f grossa

mean[1] /mi:n/ a (-er, -est) mesquinho; (*unkind*) mau. ~**ness** n mesquinhez f

mean[2] /mi:n/ a médio □ n média f. Greenwich ~ **time** tempo m médio de Greenwich

mean[3] /mi:n/ vt (pt **meant**) (*intend*) tencionar or ter (a) intenção (*to* de); (*signify*) querer dizer, significar; (*entail*) dar em resultado, resultar provavelmente em; (*refer to*) referir-se a. **be meant for** destinar-se a. **I didn't ~ it** desculpe, foi sem querer. **he ~s what he says** ele está falando sério

meander /mɪ'ændə(r)/ vi serpentear; (*wander*) perambular

meaning /'mi:nɪŋ/ n sentido m, significado m. ~**ful** a significativo. ~**less** a sem sentido

means /mi:nz/ n meio(s) m(pl) □ npl meios mpl pecuniários, recursos mpl. **by all** ~ com certeza. **by ~ of** por meio de, através de. **by no ~** de modo nenhum

meant /ment/ see **mean**[3]

mean|**time** /'mi:ntaɪm/ adv (**in the**) ~**time** entretanto. ~**while** /-waɪl/ adv entretanto

measles /'mi:zlz/ n sarampo m. **German ~** rubéola f

measly /'mi:zlɪ/ a (sl) miserável, ínfimo

measurable /'meʒərəbl/ a mensurável

measure /'meʒə(r)/ n medida f □ vt/i medir. **made to ~** feito sob medida. ~ **up to** mostrar-se à altura de. ~**d** a medido, calculado. ~**ment** n medida f

meat /mi:t/ n carne f. ~**y** a carnudo; (*fig: substantial*) substancial

mechanic /mɪ'kænɪk/ n mecânico m

mechanic|**al** /mɪ'kænɪkl/ a mecânico. ~**s** n mecânica f; npl mecanismo m

mechan|**ism** /'mekənɪzəm/ n mecanismo m. ~**ize** vt mecanizar

medal /'medl/ n medalha f. ~**list** n condecorado m. **be a gold ~list** ser medalha de ouro

medallion /mɪ'dælɪən/ n medalhão m

meddle /'medl/ vi (*interfere*) imiscuir-se, intrometer-se (*in* em); (*tinker*) mexer (*with* em). ~**some** a intrometido, abelhudo

media /'mi:dɪə/ see **medium** □ npl **the** ~ a média, os meios de comunicação social or de massa

mediat|**e** /'mi:dɪeɪt/ vi servir de intermediário, mediar. ~**ion** /-'eɪʃn/ n mediação f. ~**or** n mediador m, intermediário m

medical /'medɪkl/ a médico □ n (*colloq: examination*) exame m médico

medicat|**ed** /'medɪkeɪtɪd/ a medicinal. ~**ion** /-'keɪʃn/ n medicamentação f

medicinal /mɪ'dɪsɪnl/ a medicinal

medicine /'medsn/ n medicina f; (*substance*) remédio m, medicamento m

medieval /medɪ'i:vl/ a medieval

mediocr|**e** /mi:dɪ'əʊkə(r)/ a medíocre. ~**ity** /-'ɒkrətɪ/ n mediocridade f

meditat|**e** /'medɪteɪt/ vt/i meditar. ~**ion** /-'teɪʃn/ n meditação f

Mediterranean /medɪtə'reɪnɪən/ a mediterrâneo □ n **the** ~ o Mediterrâneo

medium /'mi:dɪəm/ n (pl **media**) meio m; (pl **mediums**) (*person*) médium mf □ a médio. ~ **wave** (*radio*) onda f média. **the happy** ~ o meio-termo

medley /'medlɪ/ n (pl **-eys**) miscelânea f

meek /miːk/ a (-er, -est) manso, submisso, sofrido

meet /miːt/ vt (pt met) encontrar; (intentionally) encontrar-se com, ir ter com; (at station etc) ir esperar, ir buscar; (make the acquaintance of) conhecer; (conform with) ir ao encontro de, satisfazer; (opponent, obligation etc) fazer face a; (bill, expenses) pagar □ vi encontrar-se; (get acquainted) familiarizar-se; (in session) reunir-se. **~ with** encontrar; (accident, misfortune) sofrer, ter

meeting /ˈmiːtɪŋ/ n reunião f, encontro m; (between two people) encontro m. **~-place** n ponto m de encontro

megalomania /meɡələʊˈmeɪnɪə/ n megalomania f, mania f de grandezas

megaphone /ˈmeɡəfəʊn/ n megafone m, porta-voz m

melancholy /ˈmelənkɒlɪ/ n melancolia f □ a melancólico

mellow /ˈmeləʊ/ a (-er, -est) (fruit, person) amadurecido, maduro; (sound, colour) quente, suave □ vt/i amadurecer; (soften) suavizar

melodious /mɪˈləʊdɪəs/ a melodioso

melodrama /ˈmelədrɑːmə/ n melodrama m. **~tic** /-əˈmætɪk/ a melodramático

melod|y /ˈmelədɪ/ n melodia f. **~ic** /mɪˈlɒdɪk/ a melódico

melon /ˈmelən/ n melão m

melt /melt/ vt/i (metals) fundir (-se); (butter, snow etc) derreter (-se); (fade away) desvanecer (-se). **~ing-pot** n cadinho m

member /ˈmembə(r)/ n membro m; (of club etc) sócio m. **M~ of Parliament** deputado m. **~ship** n qualidade f de sócio; (members) número m de sócios; (fee) cota f. **~ship**

card carteira f, (P) cartão m de sócio

membrane /ˈmembreɪn/ n membrana f

memento /mɪˈmentəʊ/ n (pl -oes) lembrança f, recordação f

memo /ˈmeməʊ/ n (pl -os) (colloq) nota f, apontamento m, lembrete m

memoir /ˈmemwɑː(r)/ n (record, essay) memória f, memorial m; **~s** npl memórias fpl

memorable /ˈmemərəbl/ a memorável

memorandum /meməˈrændəm/ n (pl -da or -dums) nota f, lembrete m; (diplomatic) memorando m

memorial /mɪˈmɔːrɪəl/ n monumento m comemorativo □ a comemorativo

memorize /ˈmeməraɪz/ vt decorar, memorizar, aprender de cor

memory /ˈmemərɪ/ n memória f. **from ~** de memória, de cor. **in ~ of** em memória de **~ stick** pente m. de memória

men /men/ see **man**

menac|e /ˈmenəs/ n ameaça f; (nuisance) praga f, chaga f □ vt ameaçar. **~ingly** adv ameaçadoramente, de modo ameaçador

menagerie /mɪˈnædʒərɪ/ n coleção f, (P) colecção f de animais ferozes em jaulas

mend /mend/ vt consertar, reparar; (darn) remendar □ n conserto m; (darn) remendo m. **~ one's ways** corrigir-se, emendar-se. **on the ~** melhorando

menial /ˈmiːnɪəl/ a humilde

meningitis /menɪnˈdʒaɪtɪs/ n meningite f

menopause /ˈmenəpɔːz/ n menopausa f

menstruation /menstrʊˈeɪʃn/ n menstruação f

mental /ˈmentl/ a mental; (hospital) de doentes mentais, psiquiátrico

mentality /men'tæləti/ n mentalidade f

mention /'menʃn/ vt mencionar □ n menção f. **don't ~ it!** não tem de quê, de nada

menu /'menju:/ n (pl **-us**) menu m, (P) ementa f

mercenary /'mɜːsɪnəri/ n (pl a mercenário (m)

merchandise /'mɜːtʃəndaɪz/ n mercadorias fpl □ vt/i negociar

merchant /'mɜːtʃənt/ n mercador m □ a (ship, navy) mercante. **~ bank** banco m comercial

merciful /'mɜːsɪfl/ a misericordioso

merciless /'mɜːsɪlɪs/ a impiedoso, sem dó

mercury /'mɜːkjʊri/ n mercúrio m

mercy /'mɜːsɪ/ n piedade f, misericórdia f. **at the ~ of** à mercê de

mere /mɪə(r)/ a mero, simples. **~ly** adv meramente, simplesmente, apenas

merge /mɜːdʒ/ vt/i fundir(-se), amalgamar(-se); (comm: companies) fundir(-se). **~r** /-ə(r)/ n fusão f

meringue /məˈræŋ/ n merengue m, suspiro m

merit /'merɪt/ n mérito m □ vt (pt **merited**) merecer

mermaid /'mɜːmeɪd/ n sereia f

merriment /'merɪmənt/ n divertimento m, alegria f, folguedo m

merry /'merɪ/ a (-ier, -iest) alegre, divertido. **~ Christmas** Feliz Natal. **~-go-round** n carrossel m. **~-making** n festa f, divertimento m. **merrily** adv alegremente

mesh /meʃ/ n malha f. **~es** npl (network; fig) malha f

mesmerize /'mezmeraɪz/ vt hipnotizar

mess /mes/ n (disorder) desordem f, trapalhada f; (trouble) embrulhada f, trapalhada f; (dirt) porcaria f; (mil: place) cantina f; (mil: food) rancho m □ vt **~ up** (make untidy) desarrumar; (make dirty) sujar; (confuse) atrapalhar, estragar □ vi **~ about** perder tempo; (behave foolishly) fazer asneiras. **~ about with** (tinker with) entreter-se com, andar às voltas com. **make a ~ of** estragar

message /'mesɪdʒ/ n mensagem f; (informal) recado m

messenger /'mesɪndʒə(r)/ n mensageiro m

Messiah /mɪ'saɪə/ n Messias m

messy /'mesɪ/ a (-ier, -iest) desarrumado, bagunçado; (dirty) sujo, porco

met /met/ see **meet**

metabolism /mɪ'tæbəlɪzm/ n metabolismo m

metal /'metl/ n metal m □ a de metal. **~lic** /mɪ'tælɪk/ a metálico; (paint, colour) metalizado

metamorphosis /metə'mɔːfəsɪs/ n (pl **-phoses** /-siːz/) metamorfose f

metaphor /'metəfə(r)/ n metáfora f. **~ical** /-'fɔrɪkl/ a metafórico

meteor /'miːtɪə(r)/ n meteoro m

meteorolog|y /miːtɪə'rɒlədʒɪ/ n meteorologia f. **~ical** /-ə'lɒdʒɪkl/ a meteorológico

meter¹ /'miːtə(r)/ n contador m

meter² /'miːtə(r)/ n (Amer) = **metre**

method /'meθəd/ n método m

methodical /mɪ'θɒdɪkl/ a metódico

Methodist /'meθədɪst/ n metodista mf

methylated /'meθɪleɪtɪd/ a **~ spirit** álcool m metílico

meticulous /mɪ'tɪkjʊləs/ a meticuloso

metre /'miːtə(r)/ n metro m

metric /'metrɪk/ a métrico. **~ation** /-'keɪʃn/ n conversão f para o sistema métrico

metropol|is /məˈtrɒpəlɪs/ n metrópole f. **~itan** /metrəˈpɒlɪtən/ a metropolitano

mettle /ˈmetl/ n têmpera f, caráter m, (P) carácter m; (spirit) brio m

mew /mjuː/ n miado m □ vi miar

Mexic|o /ˈmeksɪkəʊ/ n México m. **~an** a & n mexicano (m)

miaow /miːˈaʊ/ n & vi = **mew**

mice /maɪs/ see **mouse**

mickey /ˈmɪkɪ/ n **take the ~ out of** (sl) fazer troça de, gozar (colloq)

micro- /ˈmaɪkrəʊ/ pref micro-

microbe /ˈmaɪkrəʊb/ n micróbio m

microchip /ˈmaɪkrəʊtʃɪp/ n microchip m

microcomputer /ˈmaɪkrəʊkəmpjuːtə(r)/ n microcomputador m

microfilm /ˈmaɪkrəʊfɪlm/ n microfilme m

microlight /ˈmaɪkrəʊlaɪt/ n (aviat) ultraleve m

microphone /ˈmaɪkrəfəʊn/ n microfone m

microprocessor /maɪkrəʊˈprəʊsesə(r)/ n microprocessador m

microscop|e /ˈmaɪkrəskəʊp/ n microscópio m. **~ic** /-ˈskɒpɪk/ a microscópico

microwave /ˈmaɪkrəʊweɪv/ n microonda f. **~ oven** forno m de microondas

mid /mɪd/ a meio. **in ~-air** no ar, em pleno vôo. **in ~-March** em meados de março

midday /mɪdˈdeɪ/ n meio-dia m

middle /ˈmɪdl/ a médio, meio; (quality) médio, mediano □ n meio m. **in the ~ of** no meio de. **~-aged** a de meia idade. **M~ Ages** Idade f Média. **~-class** a burguês. **M~ East** Médio Oriente m. **~ name** segundo nome m

middleman /ˈmɪdlmæn/ n (pl -men) intermediário m

midge /mɪdʒ/ n mosquito m

midget /ˈmɪdʒɪt/ n anão m □ a minúsculo

Midlands /ˈmɪdləndz/ npl região f do centro da Inglaterra

midnight /ˈmɪdnaɪt/ n meia-noite f

midriff /ˈmɪdrɪf/ n diafragma m; (abdomen) ventre m

midst /mɪdst/ n **in the ~ of** no meio de

midsummer /mɪdˈsʌmə(r)/ n pleno verão m; (solstice) solstício m do verão

midway /mɪdˈweɪ/ adv a meio caminho

midwife /ˈmɪdwaɪf/ n (pl -wives) parteira f

might[1] /maɪt/ n potência f; (strength) força f. **~y** a poderoso; (fig: great) imenso □ adv (colloq) muito

might[2] /maɪt/ see **may**

migraine /ˈmiːgreɪn/ n enxaqueca f

migrant /ˈmaɪgrənt/ a migratório □ n (person) migrante mf, emigrante mf

migrat|e /maɪˈgreɪt/ vi migrar. **~ion** /-ʃn/ n migração f

mike /maɪk/ n (colloq) microfone m

mild /maɪld/ a (-er, -est) brando, manso; (illness, taste) leve; (climate) temperado; (weather) ameno. **~ly** adv brandamente, mansamente. **to put it ~ly** para não dizer coisa pior. **~ness** n brandura f

mildew /ˈmɪldjuː/ n bolor m, mofo m; (in plants) míldio m

mile /maɪl/ n milha f (= 1.6 km). **~s too big**/etc (colloq) grande demais. **~age** n (loosely) quilometragem f

milestone /ˈmaɪlstəʊn/ n marco m miliário; (fig) data f or acontecimento m importante

militant /ˈmɪlɪtənt/ a & n militante (mf)

military /'mɪlɪtrɪ/ a militar

militate /'mɪlɪteɪt/ vi militar. ~ **against** militar contra

milk /mɪlk/ n leite m □ a (product) lácteo □ vt ordenhar; (fig: exploit) explorar. **~-shake** n milk-shake m, leite m batido. **~y** a (like milk) leitoso; (tea etc) com muito leite. **M~ Way** Via f Láctea

milkman /'mɪlkmən/ n (pl **-men**) leiteiro m

mill /mɪl/ n moinho m; (factory) fábrica f □ vt moer □ vi ~ **around** aglomerar-se; (crowd) apinhar-se, (P) agitar-se. **~er** n moleiro m. **pepper-~** n moedor m de pimenta

millennium /mɪ'lenɪəm/ n (pl **-iums** or **-ia**) milênio m, (P) milénio m

millet /'mɪlɪt/ n painço m, milhete m

milli- /'mɪlɪ/ pref mili-

milligram /'mɪlɪgræm/ n miligrama m

millilitre /'mɪlɪliːtə(r)/ n mililitro m

millimetre /'mɪlɪmiːtə(r)/ n milímetro m

million /'mɪljən/ n milhão m. a ~ **pounds** um milhão de libras. **~aire** /-'neə(r)/ n milionário m

millstone /'mɪlstəʊn/ n mó f. a ~ **round one's neck** um peso nos ombros

mime /maɪm/ n mímica f; (actor) mímico m □ vt/i exprimir por mímica, mimar

mimic /'mɪmɪk/ vt (pt **mimicked**) imitar □ n imitador m, parodiante mf. **~ry** n imitação f.

mince /mɪns/ vt picar □ n carne f moída, (P) carne f picada. **~-pie** n pastel m recheado com massa de passas, amêndoas, especiarias etc. **~r** n máquina f de moer

mincemeat /'mɪnsmiːt/ n massa f de passas, amêndoas, especiarias

etc usada para recheio. **make ~ of** (colloq) arrasar, aniquilar

mind /maɪnd/ n espírito m, mente f; (intellect) intelecto m; (sanity) razão f □ vt (look after) tomar conta de, tratar de; (heed) prestar atenção a; (object to) importar-se com, incomodar-se com. **do you ~ if I smoke?** você se incomoda que eu fume? **do you ~ helping me?** quer fazer o favor de me ajudar? **never ~** não se importe, não tem importância. **to be out of one's ~** estar fora de si. **have a good ~ to** estar disposto a. **make up one's ~** decidir-se. **presence of ~** presença f de espírito. **to my ~** a meu ver. **~ful of** atento a, consciente de. **~less** a insensato

minder /'maɪndə(r)/ n pessoa f que toma conta mf; (bodyguard) guarda-costa mf, (P) guarda-costas mf

mine[1] /maɪn/ poss pron o(s) meu(s), a(s) minha(s). **it is ~** é (o) meu or (a) minha

mine[2] /maɪn/ n mina f □ vt escavar, explorar; (extract) extrair; (mil) minar. **~er** n mineiro m. **~ing** n exploração f mineira □ a mineiro

minefield /'maɪnfiːld/ n campo m minado

mineral /'mɪnərəl/ n mineral m; (soft drink) bebida f gasosa. **~ water** água f mineral

minesweeper /'maɪnswiːpə(r)/ n caça-minas m

mingle /'mɪŋgl/ vt/i misturar(-se) (with com)

mingy /'mɪndʒɪ/ a (-ier, -iest) (colloq) sovina, unha(s)-de-fome (colloq)

mini- /'mɪnɪ/ pref mini-

miniature /'mɪnɪtʃə(r)/ n miniatura f □ a miniatural

minibus /'mɪnɪbʌs/ n (public) microônibus m, (P) autocarro m pequeno

minim /'mmɪm/ n (mus) mínima f

minim|um /'mɪnɪməm/ a & n (pl -ma) mínimo (m). **~al** a a mínimo. **~ize** vt minimizar, dar pouca importância a

miniskirt /'mɪnɪskɜ:t/ n minissaia f

minist|er /'mɪnɪstə(r)/ n ministro m; (relig) pastor m. **~erial** /-'stɪərɪəl/ a ministerial. **~ry** n ministério m

mink /mɪŋk/ n (fur) marta f, visão m

minor /'maɪnə(r)/ a & n menor (mf)

minority /maɪ'nɒrətɪ/ n minoria f □ a minoritário

mint¹ /mɪnt/ n the M~ a Casa da Moeda. **a** ~ uma fortuna f. cunhar. **in** ~ **condition** em perfeito estado, como novo, impecável

mint² /mɪnt/ n (plant) hortelã f; (sweet) pastilha f de hortelã

minus /'maɪnəs/ prep menos; (colloq: without) sem □ n menos m

minute¹ /'mɪnɪt/ n minuto m. **~s** (of meeting) ata f, (P) acta f

minute² /maɪ'nju:t/ a diminuto, minúsculo; (detailed) minucioso

mirac|le /'mɪrəkl/ n milagre m. **~ulous** /mɪ'rækjʊləs/ a milagroso, miraculoso

mirage /'mɪrɑ:ʒ/ n miragem f

mire /maɪə(r)/ n lodo m, lama f

mirror /'mɪrə(r)/ n espelho m; (in car) retrovisor m □ vt refletir, (P) reflectir, espelhar

mirth /mɜ:θ/ n alegria f, hilaridade f

misadventure /mɪsəd'ventʃə(r)/ n desgraça f. **death by** ~ morte f acidental

misanthropist /mɪs'ænθrəpɪst/ n misantropo m

misapprehension /mɪsæprɪ'henʃn/ n mal-entendido m

misbehav|e /mɪsbɪ'heɪv/ vi portar-se mal, proceder mal. **~iour**

/-'heɪvɪə(r)/ n mau comportamento m, má conduta f

miscalculat|e /mɪs'kælkjʊleɪt/ vi calcular mal, enganar-se. **~ion** /-'leɪʃn/ n erro m de cálculo

miscarr|y /mɪs'kærɪ/ vi abortar, ter um aborto; (fail) falhar, malograr-se. **~iage** /-ɪdʒ/ n aborto m. **~iage of justice** erro m judiciário

miscellaneous /mɪsə'leɪnɪəs/ a variado, diverso

mischief /'mɪstʃɪf/ n (of children) diabrura f, travessura f; (harm) mal m, dano m. **get into** ~ fazer disparates. **make** ~ criar or semear discórdias

mischievous /'mɪstʃɪvəs/ a endiabrado, travesso

misconception /mɪskən'sepʃn/ n idéia f errada, falso conceito m

misconduct /mɪs'kɒndʌkt/ n conduta f imprópria

misconstrue /mɪskən'stru:/ vt interpretar mal

misdeed /mɪs'di:d/ n má ação f, (P) acção f; (crime) crime m

misdemeanour /mɪsdɪ'mi:nə(r)/ n delito m

miser /'maɪzə(r)/ n avarento m, sovina mf. **~ly** a avarento, sovina

miserable /'mɪzrəbl/ a infeliz; (wretched, mean) desgraçado, miserável

misery /'mɪzərɪ/ n infelicidade f

misfire /mɪs'faɪə(r)/ vi (plan, gun, engine) falhar

misfit /'mɪsfɪt/ n inadaptado m

misfortune /mɪs'fɔ:tʃən/ n desgraça f, infelicidade f, pouca sorte f

misgiving(s) /mɪs'gɪvɪŋ(z)/ n(pl) dúvida(s) f(pl), receio(s) m(pl)

misguided /mɪs'gaɪdɪd/ a (mistaken) desencaminhado; (misled) mal aconselhado, enganado

mishap /'mɪshæp/ n contratempo m, desastre m

misinform /ˌmɪsɪnˈfɔːm/ vt informar mal

misinterpret /ˌmɪsɪnˈtɜːprɪt/ vt interpretar mal

misjudge /mɪsˈdʒʌdʒ/ vt julgar mal

mislay /mɪsˈleɪ/ vt (pt **mislaid**) perder, extraviar

mislead /mɪsˈliːd/ vt (pt **misled**) induzir em erro, enganar. **~ing** a enganador

mismanage /mɪsˈmænɪdʒ/ vt dirigir mal. **~ment** n má gestão f, desgoverno m

misnomer /mɪsˈnəʊmə(r)/ n termo m impróprio

misogynist /mɪˈsɒdʒɪnɪst/ n misógino m

misprint /ˈmɪsprɪnt/ n erro m tipográfico

mispronounce /ˌmɪsprəˈnaʊns/ vt pronunciar mal

misquote /mɪsˈkwəʊt/ vt citar incorretamente

misread /mɪsˈriːd/ vt (pt **misread** /-ˈred/) ler or interpretar mal

misrepresent /ˌmɪsreprɪˈzent/ vt deturpar, desvirtuar

miss /mɪs/ vt/i (chance, bus etc) perder; (target) errar, falhar; (notice the loss of) dar pela falta de; (regret the absence of) sentir a falta de, ter saudades de. **~es her/Portugal**/etc ele sente a falta or tem saudades dela/de Portugal/etc □ n falha f. **it was a near ~** foi or escapou por um triz. **~ out** omitir. **the point** não compreender

Miss /mɪs/ n (pl **Misses**) Senhorita f, (P) Senhora f

misshapen /mɪsˈʃeɪpn/ a disforme

missile /ˈmɪsaɪl/ n míssil m; (object thrown) projétil m, (P) projéctil m

missing /ˈmɪsɪŋ/ a que falta; (lost) perdido; (person) desaparecido. **a book with a page ~** um livro com uma página a menos

mission /ˈmɪʃn/ n missão f

missionary /ˈmɪʃənrɪ/ n missionário m

misspell /mɪsˈspel/ vt (pt **misspelt** or **misspelled**) escrever mal

mist /mɪst/ n neblina f, névoa f, bruma f; (fig) névoa f □ vt/i enevoar(-se); (window) embaçar(-se)

mistake /mɪˈsteɪk/ n engano m, erro m □ vt (pt **mistook**, pp **mistaken**) compreender mal; (choose wrongly) enganar-se em. **~ for** confundir com, tomar por. **~n** /-ən/ a errado. **be ~n** enganar-se. **~nly** /-ənlɪ/ adv por engano

mistletoe /ˈmɪsltəʊ/ n visco m

mistreat /mɪsˈtriːt/ vt maltratar. **~ment** n mau trato m

mistress /ˈmɪstrɪs/ n senhora f, dona f; (teacher) professora f; (lover) amante f

mistrust /mɪsˈtrʌst/ vt desconfiar de, duvidar de □ n desconfiança f

misty /ˈmɪstɪ/ a (-ier, -iest) enevoado, brumoso; (window) embaçado; (indistinct) indistinto

misunderstand /ˌmɪsʌndəˈstænd/ vt (pt **-stood**) compreender mal. **~ing** n mal-entendido m

misuse¹ /mɪsˈjuːz/ vt empregar mal; (power etc) abusar de

misuse² /mɪsˈjuːs/ n mau uso m; (abuse) abuso m; (of funds) desvio m

mitigat|e /ˈmɪtɪgeɪt/ vt atenuar, mitigar. **~ing circumstances** circunstâncias fpl atenuantes

mitten /ˈmɪtn/ n luva f com uma única divisão entre o polegar e os dedos

mix /mɪks/ vt/i misturar(-se) □ n mistura f. **~ up** misturar bem; (fig: confuse) confundir. **~-up** m trapalhada f, confusão f. **~ with** associar-se com. **~er** n (culin) batedeira f

mixed /mɪkst/ a (*school etc*) misto; (*assorted*) sortido. **be ~ up** (*colloq*) estar confuso

mixture /ˈmɪkstʃə(r)/ n mistura f. **cough ~** xarope m para a tosse

moan /məʊn/ n gemido m □ vi gemer; (*complain*) queixar-se, lastimar-se (**about** de). **~er** n pessoa f lamurienta

moat /məʊt/ n fosso m

mob /mɒb/ n multidão f; (*tumultuous*) turba f; (*sl: gang*) bando m □ vt (*pt* **mobbed**) cercar, assediar

mobil|e /ˈməʊbaɪl/ a móvel. **~e home** caravana f, trailer m. **~e phone** telemóvel m. **~ity** /-ˈbɪlətɪ/ n mobilidade f

mobiliz|e /ˈməʊbɪlaɪz/ vt/i mobilizar. **~ation** /-ˈzeɪʃn/ n mobilização f

moccasin /ˈmɒkəsɪn/ n mocassim m

mock /mɒk/ vt/i zombar de, gozar □ a falso. **~-up** n maqueta f

mockery /ˈmɒkərɪ/ n troça f, gozação f. **a ~ of** uma gozação de

mode /məʊd/ n modo m; (*fashion*) moda f

model /ˈmɒdl/ n modelo m □ a modelo; (*exemplary*) exemplar; (*toy*) em miniatura □ vt (*pt* **modelled**) modelar; (*clothes*) apresentar □ vi ser or trabalhar como modelo

modem /ˈməʊdem/ n modem m

moderate¹ /ˈmɒdərət/ a & n moderado (m). **~ly** adv moderadamente. **~ly good** sofrível

moderat|e² /ˈmɒdəreɪt/ vt/i moderar(-se). **~ion** /-ˈreɪʃn/ n moderação f. **in ~ion** com moderação

modern /ˈmɒdn/ a moderno. **~ languages** línguas fpl vivas. **~ize** vt modernizar

modest /ˈmɒdɪst/ a modesto. **~y** n modéstia f. **~ly** adv modestamente

modicum /ˈmɒdɪkəm/ n **a ~ of** um pouco de

modif|y /ˈmɒdɪfaɪ/ vt modificar. **~ication** /-ɪˈkeɪʃn/ n modificação f

modulat|e /ˈmɒdjʊleɪt/ vt/i modular. **~ion** /-ˈleɪʃn/ n modulação f

module /ˈmɒdjuːl/ n módulo m

mohair /ˈməʊheə(r)/ n mohair m

moist /mɔɪst/ a (**-er, -est**) úmido, (P) húmido. **~ure** /ˈmɔɪstʃə(r)/ n umidade f, (P) humidade f. **~urizer** /-tʃəraɪzə(r)/ n creme m hidratante

moisten /ˈmɔɪsn/ vt/i umedecer, (P) humedecer

molasses /məˈlæsɪz/ n melaço m

mole¹ /məʊl/ n (*on skin*) sinal na pele m

mole² /məʊl/ n (*animal*) toupeira f

molecule /ˈmɒlɪkjuːl/ n molécula f

molest /məˈlest/ vt meter-se com, molestar

mollusc /ˈmɒləsk/ n molusco m

mollycoddle /ˈmɒlɪkɒdl/ vt mimar

molten /ˈməʊltən/ a fundido

moment /ˈməʊmənt/ n momento m

momentar|y /ˈməʊməntrɪ/ a momentâneo. **~ily** /ˈməʊməntrəlɪ/ adv momentaneamente

momentous /məˈmentəs/ a grave, importante

momentum /məˈmentəm/ n ímpeto m, velocidade f adquirida

Monaco /ˈmɒnəkəʊ/ n Mónaco m

monarch /ˈmɒnək/ n monarca mf. **~y** n monarquia f

monast|ery /ˈmɒnəstrɪ/ n mosteiro m, convento m. **~ic** /məˈnæstɪk/ a monástico

Monday /ˈmʌndɪ/ n segunda-feira f

monetary /ˈmʌnɪtrɪ/ a monetário

money /ˈmʌnɪ/ n dinheiro m. **~box** n cofre m. **~-lender** n agiota mf. **~ order** vale m postal

mongrel /'mʌŋgrəl/ n (cão) viralata m, (P) rafeiro m

monitor /'mɒnɪtə(r)/ n chefe m de turma; (techn) monitor m □ vt controlar; (a broadcast) monitorar (a transmissão)

monk /mʌŋk/ n monge m, frade m

monkey /'mʌŋkɪ/ n (pl -eys) macaco m. ~-nut n amendoim m. ~-wrench n chave f inglesa

mono /'mɒnəʊ/ n (pl -os) gravação f mono □ a mono invar

monocle /'mɒnəkl/ n monóculo m

monogram /'mɒnəgræm/ n monograma m

monologue /'mɒnəlɒg/ n monólogo m

monopoly /mə'nɒpəlɪ/ n monopólio m. ~ize vt monopolizar

monosyllable /'mɒnəsɪləbl/ n monossílabo m. ~ic /-'læbɪk/ a monossilábico

monotone /'mɒnətəʊn/ n tom m uniforme

monotonous /mə'nɒtənəs/ a monótono. ~y n monotonia f

monsoon /mɒn'suːn/ n monção f

monster /'mɒnstə(r)/ n monstro m. ~rous a monstruoso

monstrosity /mɒn'strɒsətɪ/ n monstruosidade f

month /mʌnθ/ n mês m

monthly /'mʌnθlɪ/ a mensal □ adv mensalmente □ n (periodical) revista f mensal

monument /'mɒnjʊmənt/ n monumento m. ~al /-'mentl/ a monumental

moo /muː/ n mugido m □ vi mugir

mood /muːd/ n humor m, disposição f. in a good/bad ~ de bom/ mau humor. ~y a de humor instável; (sullen) carrancudo

moon /muːn/ n lua f

moonlight /'muːnlaɪt/ n luar m. ~lit a iluminado pela lua, enluarado

moonlighting /'muːnlaɪtɪŋ/ n (col-

loq) segundo emprego m, esp à noite

moor[1] /mʊə(r)/ n charneca f

moor[2] /mʊə(r)/ vt amarrar, atracar. ~ings npl amarras fpl; (place) amarradouro m, fundeadouro m

moose /muːs/ n (pl invar) alce m

moot /muːt/ a discutível □ vt levantar

mop /mɒp/ n esfregão m □ vt (pt mopped) ~ (up) limpar. ~ of hair trunfa f

mope /məʊp/ vi estar or andar abatido e triste

moped /'məʊped/ n (bicicleta) motorizada f

moral /'mɒrəl/ a moral □ n moral f. ~s moral f, bons costumes mpl. ~ize vi moralizar. ~ly adv moralmente

morale /mə'raːl/ n moral m

morality /mə'rælətɪ/ n moralidade f

morass /mə'ræs/ n pântano m

morbid /'mɔːbɪd/ a mórbido

more /mɔː(r)/ a & adv mais (than (do) que) □ n mais m. (some) ~ tea/pens/etc mais chá/canetas/ etc. there is no ~ bread não há mais pão. ~ or less mais ou menos

moreover /mɔː'rəʊvə(r)/ adv além disso, de mais a mais

morgue /mɔːg/ n morgue f, necrotério m

moribund /'mɒrɪbʌnd/ a moribundo, agonizante

morning /'mɔːnɪŋ/ n manhã f. in the ~ de manhã

Morocco /mə'rɒkəʊ/ n Marrocos m. ~an a & n marroquino (m)

moron /'mɔːrɒn/ n idiota mf

morose /mə'rəʊs/ a taciturno e insociável, carrancudo

morphine /'mɔːfiːn/ n morfina f

Morse /mɔːs/ n ~ (code) (alfabeto) Morse m

morsel /'mɔːsl/ n bocado m (esp de comida)

mortal /'mɔːtl/ a & n mortal (mf). **~ity** /mɔː'tælətɪ/ n mortalidade f

mortar /'mɔːtə(r)/ n argamassa f; (bowl) almofariz m; (mil) morteiro m

mortgage /'mɔːgɪdʒ/ n hipoteca f □ vt hipotecar

mortify /'mɔːtɪfaɪ/ vt mortificar

mortuary /'mɔːtʃərɪ/ n casa f mortuária

mosaic /məʊ'zeɪk/ n mosaico m

Moscow /'mɒskəʊ/ n Moscou m, (P) Moscovo m

mosque /mɒsk/ n mesquita f

mosquito /mə'skiːtəʊ/ n (pl -oes) mosquito m

moss /mɒs/ n musgo m. **~y** a musgoso

most /məʊst/ a o mais, o maior; (majority) a maioria de, a maior parte de □ n mais m; (majority) a maioria, a maior parte, o máximo □ adv o mais; (very) muito. at **~** no máximo. for the **~** part na maior parte, na grande maioria. make the **~** of aproveitar ao máximo, tirar o melhor partido de. **~ly** adv sobretudo

motel /məʊ'tel/ n motel m

moth /mɒθ/ n mariposa f, (P) borboleta f nocturna. (clothes-) **~** n traça f. **~-ball** n bola f de naftalina. **~-eaten** a roído por traças

mother /'mʌðə(r)/ n mãe f □ vt tratar como a um filho. **~hood** n maternidade f. **~-in-law** n (pl **~s-in-law**) sogra f. **~-of-pearl** n madrepérola f. **M~'s Day** o Dia das Mães. **~-to-be** n futura mãe f. **~ly** a maternal

motif /məʊ'tiːf/ n tema m

motion /'məʊʃn/ n movimento m; (proposal) moção f □ vt/i **~ (to) sb to** fazer sinal a alg para. **~less** a imóvel

motivat|e /'məʊtɪveɪt/ vt motivar. **~ion** /-'veɪʃn/ n motivação f

motive /'məʊtɪv/ n motivo m

motor /'məʊtə(r)/ n motor m; (car) automóvel m □ a (anat) motor; (boat) a motor □ vi ir de automóvel. **~ bike** (colloq) moto f (colloq). **~ car** carro m. **~ cycle** motocicleta f. **~ cyclist** motociclista mf. **~ vehicle** veículo m automóvel. **~ing** n automobilismo m. **~ized** a motorizado

motorist /'məʊtərɪst/ n motorista mf, automobilista mf

motorway /'məʊtəweɪ/ n autoestrada f

mottled /'mɒtld/ a sarapintado, pintalgado

motto /'mɒtəʊ/ n (pl -oes) divisa f, lema m

mould¹ /məʊld/ n (container) forma f, molde m; (culin) forma f □ vt moldar. **~ing** n (archit) moldura f

mould² /məʊld/ n (fungi) bolor m, mofo m. **~y** a bolorento

moult /məʊlt/ vi estar na muda

mound /maʊnd/ n monte m de terra or de pedras; (small hill) montículo m

mount /maʊnt/ vt/i montar □ n (support) suporte m; (for gem etc) engaste m. **~ up** aumentar, subir

mountain /'maʊntɪn/ n montanha f. **~ bike** mountain bike f. **~ous** a montanhoso

mountaineer /maʊntɪ'nɪə(r)/ n alpinista mf. **~ing** n alpinismo m

mourn /mɔːn/ vt/i **~ (for)** chorar (a morte de). **~ (over)** sofrer (por). **~er** n pessoa f que acompanha o enterro. **~ing** n luto m. **in ~ing** de luto

mournful /'mɔːnfl/ a triste; (sorrowful) pesaroso

mouse /maʊs/ n (pl mice) camundongo m

mousetrap 455 multiple

mousetrap /'maustræp/ n ratoeira f

mousse /mu:s/ n mousse f

moustache /məˈstaːʃ/ n bigode m

mouth[1] /mauθ/ n boca f. **~-organ** n gaita f de boca, (P) beiços

mouth[2] /mauð/ vt/i declamar; (silently) articular sem som

mouthful /'mauθful/ n bocado m

mouthpiece /'mauθpi:s/ n (mus) bocal m, boquilha f; (fig: person) porta-voz mf

mouthwash /'mauθwɒʃ/ n líquido m para bochecho

movable /'mu:vəbl/ a móvel

move /mu:v/ vt/i mover(-se), mexer(-se), deslocar(-se); (emotionally) comover; (incite) convencer, levar a; (act) agir; (propose) propor; (depart) ir, partir; (go forward) avançar. **~ (out)** mudar-se, sair □ n movimento m; (in game) jogada f; (player's turn) vez f; (house change) mudança f. **~ back** recuar. **~ forward** avançar. **~ in** mudar-se para. **~ on!** circulem! **~ over, please** chegue-se para lá, por favor. **on the ~** em marcha

movement /'mu:vmənt/ n movimento m

movie /'mu:vɪ/ n (Amer) filme m. **the ~s** o cinema

moving /'mu:vɪŋ/ a (touching) comovente; (movable) móvil; (in motion) em movimento

mow /məu/ vt (pp mowed or mown) ceifar; (lawn) cortar a grama, (P) relva. **~ down** ceifar. **~er** n (for lawn) máquina f de cortar a grama, (P) relva

MP abbr see **Member of Parliament**

Mr /'mɪstə(r)/ n (pl **Messrs**) Senhor m. **~ Smith** o Sr Smith

Mrs /'mɪsɪz/ n Senhora f. **~ Smith** a Sra Smith. **Mr and ~ Smith** o Sr Smith e a mulher

Ms /mɪz/ n Senhora D f

much /mʌtʃ/ (more, most) a, adv & n muito (m). **very ~** muito, muitíssimo. **you may have as ~ as you need** você pode tomar o que precisar. **~ of it** muito or grande parte dele. **so ~ the better/worse** tanto melhor/pior. **how ~?** quanto? **not ~** não muito. **too ~** demasiado, demais. **he's not ~ of a gardener** não é lá grande jardineiro

muck /mʌk/ n estrume m; (colloq: dirt) porcaria f □ vi **~ about** (sl) entreter-se, perder tempo. **~ in** (sl) ajudar, dar uma mão □ vt **~ up** (sl) estragar. **~y** a sujo

mucus /'mju:kəs/ n muco m

mud /mʌd/ n lama f. **~dy** a lamacento, enlameado

muddle /'mʌdl/ vt baralhar, atrapalhar, confundir □ vi **~ through** sair-se bem, desenrascar-se (sl) □ n desordem f; (mix-up) confusão f, trapalhada f

mudguard /'mʌdgaːd/ n para-lama m

muff /mʌf/ n (for hands) regalo m

muffle /'mʌfl/ vt abafar. **~ (up)** agasalhar(-se). **~d sounds** sons mpl abafados. **~r** /-ə(r)/ n cachecol m

mug /mʌg/ n caneca f; (sl: face) cara f; (sl: fool) trouxa mf (colloq) □ vt (pt **mugged**) assaltar, agredir. **~ger** n assaltante mf. **~ging** n assalto m

muggy /'mʌgɪ/ a abafado

mule /mju:l/ n mulo m; (female) mula f

mull /mʌl/ vt **~ over** ruminar; (fig) matutar em

multi- /'mʌltɪ/ pref mult(i)-

multicoloured /'mʌltɪkʌləd/ a multicolor

multinational /mʌltɪ'næʃnəl/ a & n multinacional (f)

multiple /'mʌltɪpl/ a & n múltiplo (m)

multiply /ˈmʌltɪplaɪ/ vt/i multiplicar(-se). **~ication** /-ˈkeɪʃn/ n multiplicação f

multi-storey /mʌltɪˈstɔːrɪ/ a (car park) em vários níveis

multitude /ˈmʌltɪtjuːd/ n multidão f

mum¹ /mʌm/ a keep ~ (colloq) ficar calado

mum² /mʌm/ n (B) mamãe f (colloq) n (P) mamã

mumble /ˈmʌmbl/ vt/i resmungar, resmonear

mummy¹ /ˈmʌmɪ/ n (body) múmia f

mummy² /ˈmʌmɪ/ n (esp child's lang) mamã (B) mamãe f (colloq) (P) mãezinha f (colloq), (P)

mumps /mʌmps/ n parotidite f, papeira f

munch /mʌntʃ/ vt mastigar

mundane /mʌnˈdeɪn/ a banal; (worldly) mundano

municipal /mjuːˈnɪsɪpl/ a municipal. **~ity** /-ˈpælətɪ/ n municipalidade f

munitions /mjuːˈnɪʃnz/ npl munições fpl

mural /ˈmjʊərəl/ a & n mural (m)

murder /ˈmɜːdə(r)/ n assassínio m, assassinato m □ vt assassinar. **~er** n assassino m, assassina f. **~ous** a assassino, sanguinário; (of weapon) mortífero

murky /ˈmɜːkɪ/ a (-ier, -iest) escuro, sombrio

murmur /ˈmɜːmə(r)/ n murmúrio m □ vt/i murmurar

muscle /ˈmʌsl/ n músculo m □ vi **~ in** (colloq) impor-se, intrometer-se

muscular /ˈmʌskjʊlə(r)/ a muscular; (brawny) musculoso

muse /mjuːz/ vi meditar, cismar

museum /mjuːˈzɪəm/ n museu m

mush /mʌʃ/ n papa f de farinha de milho. **~y** a mole; (sentimental) piegas inv

mushroom /ˈmʌʃrʊm/ n cogumelo m □ vi pulular, multiplicar-se com rapidez

music /ˈmjuːzɪk/ n música f. **~al** a musical □ n (show) comédia f musical, musical m. **~al box** n caixa f de música. **~-stand** n estante f de música

musician /mjuːˈzɪʃn/ n músico m

musk /mʌsk/ n almíscar m

Muslim /ˈmʊzlɪm/ a & n muçulmano (m)

muslin /ˈmʌzlɪn/ n musselina f

mussel /ˈmʌsl/ n mexilhão m

must /mʌst/ v aux dever. **you ~ go** é necessário que você parta. **he ~ be old** ele deve ser velho. **I ~ have done it** eu devo tê-lo feito □ n **be a ~** (colloq) ser imprescindível

mustard /ˈmʌstəd/ n mostarda f

muster /ˈmʌstə(r)/ vt/i juntar(-se), reunir(-se). **pass ~** ser aceitável

musty /ˈmʌstɪ/ a (-ier, -iest) mofado, bolorento

mutation /mjuːˈteɪʃn/ n mutação f

mute /mjuːt/ a & n mudo (m)

muted /ˈmjuːtɪd/ a (sound) em surdina; (colour) suave

mutilate /ˈmjuːtɪleɪt/ vt mutilar. **~ion** /-ˈleɪʃn/ n mutilação f

mutiny /ˈmjuːtɪnɪ/ n motim f □ vi amotinar-se. **~ous** a amotinado

mutter /ˈmʌtə(r)/ vt/i resmungar

mutton /ˈmʌtn/ n (carne de) carneiro m

mutual /ˈmjuːtʃʊəl/ a mútuo; (colloq: common) comum. **~ly** adv mutuamente

muzzle /ˈmʌzl/ n focinho m; (device) focinheira f; (of gun) boca f □ vt amordaçar; (dog) pôr focinheira em

my /maɪ/ a meu(s), minha(s)

myself /maɪˈself/ pron eu mesmo, eu próprio; (reflexive) me; (after prep) mim (próprio, mesmo). **by ~** sozinho

mysterious /mɪˈstɪərɪəs/ *a* misterioso

mystery /ˈmɪstərɪ/ *n* mistério *m*

mystic /ˈmɪstɪk/ *a & n* místico (*m*). **~al** *a* místico. **~ism** /-sɪzəm/ *n* misticismo *m*

mystify /ˈmɪstɪfaɪ/ *vt* deixar perplexo

mystique /mɪˈstiːk/ *n* mística *f*

myth /mɪθ/ *n* mito *m*. **~ical** *a* mítico

mytholog|y /mɪˈθɒlədʒɪ/ *n* mitologia *f*. **~ical** /mɪθəˈlɒdʒɪkl/ *a* mitológico

N

nab /næb/ *vt* (*pt* **nabbed**) (*sl*) apanhar em flagrante, apanhar com a boca na botija (*colloq*), pilhar

nag /næg/ *vt/i* (*pt* **nagged**) implicar (com), criticar constantemente; (*pester*) apoquentar

nagging /ˈnægɪŋ/ *a* implicante; (*pain*) constante, contínuo

nail /neɪl/ *n* prego *m*; (*of finger, toe*) unha *f* □ *vt* pregar. **~-brush** *n* escova *f* de unhas. **~-file** *n* lixa *f* de unhas. **~-polish** esmalte *m*, (*P*) verniz *m* para as unhas. **hit the ~ on the head** acertar em cheio. **on the ~** sem demora

naïve /naɪˈiːv/ *a* ingênuo, (*P*) ingénuo

naked /ˈneɪkɪd/ *a* nu. **to the ~ eye** a olho nu, à vista desarmada. **~ness** *f* nudez *f*

name /neɪm/ *n* nome *m*; (*fig*) reputação *f*, fama *f* □ *vt* (*mention; appoint*) nomear; (*give a name to*) chamar, dar o nome de; (*a date*) marcar. **be ~d after** ter o nome de. **~less** *a* sem nome, anônimo, (*P*) anónimo

namely /ˈneɪmlɪ/ *adv* a saber

namesake /ˈneɪmseɪk/ *n* homônimo *m*, (*P*) homónimo *m*

nanny /ˈnænɪ/ *n* ama *f*, babá *f*

nap[1] /næp/ *n* soneca *f* □ *vi* (*pt* **napped**) dormitar, tirar um cochilo. **catch ~ping** apanhar desprevenido

nap[2] /næp/ *n* (*of material*) felpa *f*

nape /neɪp/ *n* nuca *f*

napkin /ˈnæpkɪn/ *n* guardanapo *m*; (*for baby*) fralda *f*

nappy /ˈnæpɪ/ *n* fralda *f*. **~-rash** *n* assadura *f*

narcotic /naːˈkɒtɪk/ *a & n* narcótico (*m*)

narrat|e /nəˈreɪt/ *vt* narrar. **~ion** /-ʃn/ *n* narrativa *f*. **~or** *n* narrador *m*

narrative /ˈnærətɪv/ *n* narrativa *f* □ *a* narrativo

narrow /ˈnærəʊ/ *a* (*-er, -est*) estreito; (*fig*) restrito □ *vt/i* estreitar(-se); (*limit*) limitar(-se). **~ly** *adv* (*only just*) por pouco; (*closely, carefully*) de perto, com cuidado. **~-minded** *a* bitolado, de visão limitada. **~ness** *n* estreiteza *f*

nasal /ˈneɪzl/ *a* nasal

nast|y /ˈnɑːstɪ/ *a* (*-ier, -iest*) (*malicious, of weather*) mau; (*unpleasant*) desagradável, intragável; (*rude*) grosseiro. **~ily** *adv* maldosamente; (*unpleasantly*) desagradavelmente. **~iness** *f* (*malice*) maldade *f*, (*rudeness*) grosseria *f*

nation /ˈneɪʃn/ *n* nação *f*. **~-wide** *a* em todo o país, em escala *or* a nível nacional

national /ˈnæʃnəl/ *a* nacional □ *n* natural *mf*. **~ anthem** hino *m* nacional. **~ism** *n* nacionalismo *m*. **~ize** *vt* nacionalizar. **~ly** *adv* em escala nacional

nationality /næʃəˈnælətɪ/ *n* nacionalidade *f*

native /ˈneɪtɪv/ *n* natural *mf*, nativo *m* □ *a* nativo; (*country*) natal;

(*inborn*) inato. **be a ~ of** ser natural de. **~ language** língua *f* materna. **~ speaker of Portuguese** pessoa *f* de língua portuguesa, falante *m* nativo de Português

Nativity /nə'tɪvətɪ/ *n* **the ~** a Natividade *f*

natter /'nætə(r)/ *vi* fazer conversa fiada, falar à toa, tagarelar

natural /'nætʃrəl/ *a* natural. **~ history** história *f* natural. **~ist** *n* naturalista *mf*. **~ly** *adv* naturalmente; (*by nature*) por natureza

naturaliz|e /'nætʃrəlaɪz/ *vt/i* naturalizar(-se); (*animal, plant*) aclimatar(-se). **~ation** /-'zeɪʃn/ *n* naturalização *f*

nature /'neɪtʃə(r)/ *n* natureza *f*; (*kind*) gênero *m*, (*P*) género *m*; (*of person*) índole *f*

naughty /'nɔːtɪ/ *a* (**-ier, -iest**) (*child*) levado; (*indecent*) picante

nause|a /'nɔːsɪə/ *n* náusea *f*. **~ate** /'nɔːsɪeɪt/ *vt* nausear. **~ating, ~ous** *a* nauseabundo, repugnante

nautical /'nɔːtɪkl/ *a* náutico. **~ mile** milha *f* marítima

naval /'neɪvl/ *a* naval; (*officer*) de marinha

nave /neɪv/ *n* nave *f*

navel /'neɪvl/ *n* umbigo *m*

navigable /'nævɪɡəbl/ *a* navegável

navigat|e /'nævɪɡeɪt/ *vt* (*sea etc*) navegar; (*ship*) pilotar □ *vi* navegar. **~ion** /-'ɡeɪʃn/ *n* navegação *f*. **~or** *n* navegador *m*

navy /'neɪvɪ/ *n* marinha *f* de guerra. **~ (blue)** azul-marinho *m invar*

near /nɪə(r)/ *adv* perto, quaze □ *prep* perto de □ *a* próximo □ *vt* aproximar-se de, chegar-se a. **~ draw** ~ aproximar(-se) **(to de)**. **~ by** perto, próximo. **N~ East** Oriente *m* Próximo. **~ to** perto de. **~ness** *n* proximidade *f*

nearby /'nɪəbaɪ/ *a & adv* próximo, perto

nearly /'nɪəlɪ/ *adv* quase, por pouco. **not ~ as pretty/etc as** longe de ser tão bonita/*etc* como

neat /niːt/ *a* (**-er, -est**) (bem) cuidado; (*room*) bem arrumado; (*spirits*) puro, sem gelo. **~ly** *adv* (*with care*) com cuidado; (*cleverly*) habilmente. **~ness** *n* aspecto *m* cuidado

nebulous /'nebjʊləs/ *a* nebuloso; (*vague*) vago, confuso

necessar|y /'nesəsərɪ/ *a* necessário. **~ily** *adv* necessariamente

necessitate /nɪ'sesɪteɪt/ *vt* exigir, obrigar a, tornar necessário

necessity /nɪ'sesətɪ/ *n* necessidade *f*; (*thing*) coisa *f* indispensável, artigo *m* de primeira necessidade

neck /nek/ *n* pescoço *m*; (*of dress*) gola *f*. **~ and neck** emparelhados

necklace /'neklɪs/ *n* colar *m*

neckline /'neklaɪn/ *n* decote *m*

nectarine /'nektərɪn/ *n* pêssego *m*

née /neɪ/ *a* em solteira. **Ann Jones ~ Drewe** Ann Jones cujo nome de solteira era Drewe

need /niːd/ *n* necessidade *f* □ *vt* precisar de, necessitar de. **you ~ not come** não tem de *or* não precisa vir. **~less** *a* inútil, desnecessário. **~lessly** *adv* inutilmente, sem necessidade

needle /'niːdl/ *a* agulha *f* □ *vt* (*colloq: provoke*) provocar

needlework /'niːdlwɜːk/ *n* costura *f*; (*embroidery*) bordado *m*

needy /'niːdɪ/ *a* (**-ier, -iest**) necessitado, carenciado

negation /nɪ'ɡeɪʃn/ *n* negação *f*

negative /'neɡətɪv/ *a* negativo □ *n* negativa *f*, negação *f*; (*photo*) negativo *m*. **in the ~** (*answer*) na negativa; (*gram*) na forma negativa. **~ly** *adv* negativamente

neglect /nɪ'glekt/ vt descuidar; (*opportunity*) desprezar; (*family*) não cuidar de (*duty*) não cumprir □ n falta f de cuidado(s), descuido m. **(state of)** ~ abandono m. **to** ~ (*omit to*) esquecer-se de. ~ful a negligente

negligen|t /'neglɪdʒənt/ a negligente. ~ce n negligência f, desleixo m

negligible /'neglɪdʒəbl/ a insignificante, ínfimo

negotiable /nɪ'gəʊʃəbl/ a negociável

negotiat|e /nɪ'gəʊʃɪeɪt/ vt/i negociar; (*obstacle*) transpor; (*difficulty*) vencer. ~ion /-ʃɪ'eɪʃn/ n negociação f. ~or n negociador m

Negro /'niːgrəʊ/ a & n (pl ~oes) negro (m), preto (m)

neigh /neɪ/ n relincho m □ vi relinchar

neighbour /'neɪbə(r)/ n vizinho m. ~hood n vizinhança f. ~ing a vizinho. ~ly a de boa vizinhança

neither /'naɪðə(r)/ a & pron nenhum(a) (de dois ou duas), nem um nem outro, nem uma nem outra □ adv tampouco, também não □ conj nem. ~ **big nor small** nem grande nem pequeno. ~ **am I** nem eu

neon /'niːɒn/ n néon m

nephew /'nevjuː/ n sobrinho m

nerve /nɜːv/ n nervo m; (*fig: courage*) coragem f; (*colloq: impudence*) descaramento m, (*P*) lata f (*colloq*). **get on sb's nerves** irritar, dar nos nervos de alg. ~-**racking** a de arrasar os nervos, enervante

nervous /'nɜːvəs/ a nervoso. **be or feel** ~ (*afraid*) ter receio/um certo medo. ~ **breakdown** esgotamento m nervoso. ~**ly** adv nervosamente. ~**ness** n nervosismo m; (*fear*) receio m

nest /nest/ n ninho m □ vi aninhar-se, fazer or ter ninho. ~-**egg** n pé-de-meia m

nestle /'nesl/ vi aninhar-se

net[1] /net/ n rede f □ vt (pt netted) apanhar na rede. ~**ting** n rede f. **wire** ~**ting** rede f de arame

net[2] /net/ a (*weight etc*) líquido

Netherlands /'neðələndz/ npl the ~ os Países Baixos

netsurfer /'netsɜːfə(r)/ n internauta m/f

nettle /'netl/ n urtiga f

network /'netwɜːk/ n rede f, cadeia f

neuro|sis /njʊə'rəʊsɪs/ n (pl -oses /-siːz/) neurose f. ~**tic** /-'rɒtɪk/ a & n neurótico (m)

neuter /'njuːtə(r)/ a & n neutro (m) □ vt castrar, capar

neutral /'njuːtrəl/ a neutro. ~ (**gear**) ponto m morto. ~**ity** /-'trælətɪ/ n neutralidade f

never /'nevə(r)/ adv nunca; (*colloq: not*) não. **he** ~ **refuses** ele nunca recusa. **I** ~ **saw him** (*colloq*) nunca o vi. ~ **mind** não faz mal, deixe para lá. ~-**ending** a interminável

nevertheless /nevəðə'les/ adv & conj contudo, no entanto

new /njuː/ a (-er, -est) novo. ~-**born** a recém-nascido. ~ **moon** lua f nova. ~ **year** ano m novo. **N**~ **Year's Day** dia m de Ano Novo. **N**~ **Year's Eve** véspera f de Ano Novo. **N**~ **Zealand** Nova Zelândia f. **N**~ **Zealander** neo-zelandês m. ~**ness** n novidade f

newcomer /'njuːkʌmə(r)/ n recém-chegado m, (*P*) recém-vindo m

newfangled /njuː'fæŋgld/ a (*pej*) moderno

newly /'njuːlɪ/ adv há pouco, recentemente. ~-**weds** npl recém-casados mpl

news /njuːz/ n notícia(s) f(pl); (*radio*) noticiário m; notícias fpl;

(*TV*) telejornal *m*. ~-**caster**, ~-**reader** *n* locutor *m*. ~-**flash** *n* notícia *f* de última hora

newsagent /'nju:zeɪdʒənt/ *n* jornaleiro *m*

newsletter /'nju:zletə(r)/ *n* boletim *m* informativo

newspaper /'nju:zpeɪpə(r)/ *n* jornal *m*

newsreel /'nju:zri:l/ *n* atualidades *fpl*, (*P*) actualidades *fpl*

newt /nju:t/ *n* tritão *m*

next /nekst/ *a* próximo *m*, (*adjoining*) pegado, ao lado, contíguo, (*following*) seguinte □ *adv* a seguir □ *n* seguinte *mf*. ~-**door** *a* do lado. ~ **of kin** parente *m* mais próximo. ~ **to** ao lado de. ~ **to nothing** quase nada

nib /nɪb/ *n* bico *m*, (*P*) aparo *m*

nibble /'nɪbl/ *vt* mordiscar, dar dentadinhas em

nice /naɪs/ *a* (-**er**, -**est**) agradável, bom; (*kind*) simpático, gentil; (*pretty*) bonito; (*respectable*) bem educado, correto, (*P*) correcto; (*subtle*) fino, subtil. ~**ly** *adv* agradavelmente; (*well*) bem

nicety /'naɪsətɪ/ *n* sutileza *f*, (*P*) subtileza *f*

niche /nɪtʃ/ *n* nicho *m*; (*fig*) bom lugar *m*

nick /nɪk/ *n* corte *m*, chanfradura *f*; (*sl: prison*) cadeia *f* □ *vt* dar um corte em; (*sl: steal*) roubar, limpar (*colloq*); (*sl: arrest*) apanhar, pôr a mão em (*colloq*). **in good** ~ (*colloq*) em boa forma, em bom estado. **in the** ~ **of time** mesmo a tempo

nickel /'nɪkl/ *n* níquel *m*; (*Amer*) moeda *f* de cinco cêntimos

nickname /'nɪkneɪm/ *n* apelido *m*, (*P*) alcunha *f*; (*short form*) diminutivo *m* □ *vt* apelidar de

nicotine /'nɪkəti:n/ *n* nicotina *f*

niece /ni:s/ *n* sobrinha *f*

Nigeria /naɪ'dʒɪərɪə/ *n* Nigéria *f*. ~**n** *a* & *n* nigeriano (*m*)

niggardly /'nɪgədlɪ/ *a* miserável

night /naɪt/ *n* noite *f* □ *a* de noite, nocturno, (*P*) nocturno. **at** ~ à/ de noite, (*P*) de noite. **by** ~ de noite. ~-**cap** *n* (*drink*) bebida *f* na hora de deitar. ~-**club** *n* boate *f*, (*P*) boîte *f*. ~-**dress**, ~-**gown** *ns* camisola *f* de dormir, (*P*) camisa *f* de noite. ~-**life** *n* vida *f* noturna, (*P*) nocturna. ~-**school** *n* escola *f* noturna, (*P*) nocturna. ~-**time** *n* noite *f*. ~-**watchman** *n* guarda-noturno *m*, (*P*) guarda-nocturno *m*

nightfall /'naɪtfɔ:l/ *n* anoitecer *m*

nightingale /'naɪtɪŋgeɪl/ *n* rouxinol *m*

nightly /'naɪtlɪ/ *a* noturno, (*P*) nocturno □ *adv* de noite, à noite, todas as noites

nightmare /'naɪtmeə(r)/ *n* pesadelo *m*

nil /nɪl/ *n* nada *m*; (*sport*) zero *m* □ *a* nulo

nimble /'nɪmbl/ *a* (-**er**, -**est**) ágil, ligeiro

nin|e /naɪn/ *a* & *n* nove (*m*). ~**th** *a* & *n* nono (*m*)

nineteen /naɪn'ti:n/ *a* & *n* dezenove (*m*), (*P*) dezanove (*m*). ~**th** *a* & *n* décimo nono (*m*)

ninet|y /'naɪntɪ/ *a* & *n* noventa (*m*). ~**ieth** *a* & *n* nonagésimo (*m*)

nip /nɪp/ *vt/i* (*pt* **nipped**) apertar, beliscar; (*colloq: rush*) ir correndo, ir num pulo (*colloq*) □ *n* aperto *m*, beliscão *m*; (*drink*) gole *m*, trago *m*. **a** ~ **in the air** um frio cortante. ~ **in the bud** cortar pela raiz

nipple /'nɪpl/ *n* mamilo *m*

nippy /'nɪpɪ/ *a* (-**ier**, -**iest**) (*colloq: quick*) rápido; (*colloq: chilly*) cortante

nitrogen /'naɪtrədʒən/ *n* azoto *m*, nitrogênio *m*, (*P*) nitrogénio *m*

nitwit /'nɪtwɪt/ *n* (*colloq*) imbecil *m*

no /nəʊ/ a nenhum □ adv não □ n (pl **noes**) não m. ~ **entry** entrada f proibida. ~ **money/time/** etc nenhum dinheiro/tempo/etc. ~ **man's land** terra f de ninguém. ~ **one** = **nobody**. ~ **smoking** é proibido fumar. ~ **way!** (colloq) de modo nenhum!

nob|le /'nəʊbl/ a (-er, -est) nobre. ~**ility** /-'bɪlətɪ/ n nobreza f

nobleman /'nəʊblmən/ n (pl -**men**) nobre m, fidalgo m

nobody /'nəʊbʊdɪ/ pron ninguém □ n nulidade f. **he knows** ~ ele não conhece ninguém. **is there** ~ não tem ninguém aqui

nocturnal /nɒk'tɜːnl/ a noturno, (P) nocturno

nod /nɒd/ vt/i (pt **nodded**) ~ (**one's head**) acenar (com) a cabeça; ~ (**off**) cabecear □ n aceno m com a cabeça (para dizer que sim or para cumprimentar)

noise /nɔɪz/ n ruído m, barulho m. ~**less** a silencioso

nois|y /'nɔɪzɪ/ a (-ier, -iest) ruidoso, barulhento. ~**ily** adv ruidosamente

nomad /'nəʊmæd/ n nómade m/f, (P) nómade mf. ~**ic** /-'mædɪk/ a nómade, (P) nómade

nominal /'nɒmɪnl/ a nominal, (fee, sum) simbólico

nominat|e /'nɒmɪneɪt/ vt (appoint) nomear; (put forward) propor. ~**ion** /-'neɪʃn/ n nomeação f

non- /nɒn/ pref não, sem, in-, a-, anti-, des-. ~**skid** a antiderrapante. ~**stick** a não-aderente

nonchalant /'nɒnʃələnt/ a indiferente, desinteressado

non-commissioned /nɒnkə-'mɪʃnd/ a ~ **officer** sargento m, cabo m

non-committal /nɒnkə'mɪtl/ a evasivo

nondescript /'nɒndɪskrɪpt/ a insignificante, mediocre, indefinível

none /nʌn/ pron (person) nenhum, ninguém; (thing) nenhum, nada. ~ **of us** nenhum de nós. **I have** ~ não tenho nenhum. ~ **of that!** nada disso! □ adv ~ **too** não muito. **he is** ~ **the happier** nem por isso ele é mais feliz. ~ **the less** contudo, no entanto, apesar disso

nonentity /nɒ'nentətɪ/ n nulidade f, zero m à esquerda, João Ninguém m

non-existent /nɒnɪg'zɪstənt/ a inexistente

nonplussed /nɒn'plʌst/ a perplexo, pasmado

nonsens|e /'nɒnsns/ n absurdo m, disparate m. ~**ical** /-'sensɪkl/ a absurdo, disparatado

non-smoker /nɒn'sməʊkə(r)/ n não-fumante m, (P) não-fumador m

non-stop /nɒn'stɒp/ a ininterrupto, contínuo; (train) direto, (P) directo; (flight) sem escala □ adv sem parar

noodles /'nuːdlz/ npl talharim m, (P) macaronete m

nook /nʊk/ n (re)canto m

noon /nuːn/ n meio-dia m

noose /nuːs/ n laço m corrediço

nor /nɔː(r)/ conj & adv nem, também não. ~ **do I** nem eu

norm /nɔːm/ n norma f

normal /'nɔːml/ a & n normal (m). **above/below** ~ acima/abaixo do normal. ~**ity** /nɔː'mælətɪ/ n normalidade f. ~**ly** adv normalmente

north /nɔːθ/ n norte m □ a norte, do norte; (of country, people etc) setentrional □ adv a, ao/para o norte. **N**~ **America** América f do Norte. **N**~ **American** a & n norte-americano (m). ~**-east** n nordeste m. ~**erly** /-əlɪ/ a do norte. ~**ward** a ao norte. ~**ward(s)** adv para o norte. ~**-west** n noroeste m

northern /'nɔːðən/ a do norte

Norw|ay /'nɔːweɪ/ n Noruega f. **~egian** /nɔː'wiːdʒən/ a & n norueguês (m)

nose /nəʊz/ n nariz m; (of animal) focinho m □ vi ~ about farejar. **pay through the ~** pagar um preço exorbitante

nosebleed /'nəʊzbliːd/ n hemorragia f nasal or pelo nariz

nosedive /'nəʊzdaɪv/ n vôo m picado

nostalg|ia /nɒ'stældʒə/ n nostalgia f. **~ic** a nostálgico

nostril /'nɒstrəl/ n narina f; (of horse) venta f (usually pl)

nosy /'nəʊzɪ/ a (-ier, -iest) (colloq) bisbilhoteiro

not /nɒt/ adv não. **~ at all** nada, de modo nenhum; (reply to thanks) de nada. **he is ~ at all bored** ele não está nem um pouco entediado. **~ yet** ainda não. **I suppose ~** creio que não

notable /'nəʊtəbl/ a notável □ n notabilidade f

notably /'nəʊtəblɪ/ adv notavelmente; (particularly) especialmente

notch /nɒtʃ/ n corte m em V □ vt marcar com cortes. **~ up** (score etc) marcar

note /nəʊt/ n nota f; (banknote) nota (de banco) f; (short letter) bilhete m □ vt notar

notebook /'nəʊtbʊk/ n livrinho m de notas, (P) bloco-notas m

noted /'nəʊtɪd/ a conhecido, famoso

notepaper /'nəʊtpeɪpə(r)/ n papel m de carta

noteworthy /'nəʊtwɜːðɪ/ a notável

nothing /'nʌθɪŋ/ n nada m; (person) nulidade f, zero m □ adv nada, de modo algum or nenhum, de maneira alguma or nenhuma. **he eats ~** ele não come nada. **~ big/etc** nada (de) grande/etc. **~ else** nada mais. **~ much** pouca

coisa. **for ~** (free) de graça; (in vain) em vão

notice /'nəʊtɪs/ n anúncio m, notícia f; (in street, on wall) letreiro m; (warning) aviso m; (attention) atenção f; (advance) ~ pré-aviso m □ vt notar, reparar. **at short ~** num prazo curto. **a week's ~** o prazo de uma semana. **~board** n quadro m para afixar anúncios etc. **hand in one's ~** pedir demissão. **take ~** reparar (of em). **take no ~** não fazer caso (of de)

noticeabl|e /'nəʊtɪsəbl/ a visível. **~y** adv visivelmente

notif|y /'nəʊtɪfaɪ/ vt participar, notificar. **~ication** /-ɪ'keɪʃn/ n participação f, notificação f

notion /'nəʊʃn/ n noção f

notor|ious /nəʊ'tɔːrɪəs/ a notório. **~iety** /-ə'raɪətɪ/ n fama f

notwithstanding /nɒtwɪθ'stændɪŋ/ prep apesar de, não obstante □ adv mesmo assim, ainda assim □ conj embora, conquanto, apesar de que

nougat /'nuːgɑː/ n nugá m, torrone m

nought /nɔːt/ n zero m

noun /naʊn/ n substantivo m, nome m

nourish /'nʌrɪʃ/ vt alimentar, nutrir. **~ing** a alimentício, nutritivo. **~ment** n alimento m, sustento m

novel /'nɒvl/ n romance m □ a novo, original. **~ist** n romancista mf. **~ty** n novidade f

November /nəʊ'vembə(r)/ n novembro m

novice /'nɒvɪs/ n (beginner) noviço m, novato m; (relig) noviço m

now /naʊ/ adv agora □ conj ~ (that) agora que. **by ~** a estas horas, por esta altura. **from ~ on** de agora em diante. **~ and again, ~ and then** de vez em quando. **right ~** já

nowadays /'naʊədeɪz/ *adv* hoje em dia, presentemente, atualmente, (P) actualmente

nowhere /'nəʊweə(r)/ *adv* (*position*) em lugar nenhum, em lado nenhum; (*direction*) para lado nenhum; (*parte alguma* or *nenhuma*

nozzle /'nɒzl/ *n* bico *m*, bocal *m*; (*of hose*) agulheta *f*

nuance /'nju:a:ns/ *n* nuance *f*, matiz *m*

nuclear /'nju:klɪə(r)/ *a* nuclear

nucleus /'nju:klɪəs/ *n* (*pl* **-lei** /-lɪaɪ/) núcleo *m*

nud|e /nju:d/ *a* & *n* nu (*m*). **in the** ~**e** nu. ~**ity** *n* nudez *f*

nudge /nʌdʒ/ *vt* tocar com o cotovelo, cutucar □ *n* ligeira cotovelada *f*, cutucada *f*

nudis|t /'nju:dɪst/ *n* nudista *mf*. ~**m** /-zəm/ *n* nudismo *m*

nuisance /'nju:sns/ *n* aborrecimento *m*, chatice *f* (*sl*); (*person*) chato *m* (*sl*)

null /nʌl/ *a* nulo. ~ **and void** (*jur*) írrito e nulo. ~**ify** *vt* anular, invalidar

numb /nʌm/ *a* entorpecido, dormente □ *vt* entorpecer, adormecer

number /'nʌmbə(r)/ *n* número *m*; (*numeral*) algarismo *m* □ *vt* numerar; (*amount to*) ser em número de; (*count*) contar, incluir. ~**-plate** *n* chapa (do carro) *f*

numeral /'nju:mərəl/ *n* número *m*, algarismo *m*

numerate /'nju:mərət/ *a* que tem conhecimentos básicos de matemática

numerical /nju:'merɪkl/ *a* numérico

numerous /'nju:mərəs/ *a* numeroso

nun /nʌn/ *n* freira *f*, religiosa *f*

nurs|e /nɜ:s/ *n* enfermeira *f*, enfermeiro *m*; (*nanny*) ama(-seca) *f*, babá *f* □ *vt* cuidar de, tratar de; (*hopes etc*) alimentar, aca-

lentar. ~**ing** *n* enfermagem *f*. ~**ing home** clínica *f* de repouso

nursery /'nɜ:sərɪ/ *n* quarto *m* de crianças; (*for plants*) viveiro *m*. (**day**) ~ creche *f*. ~ **rhyme** poema *m* or canção *f* infantil. ~ **school** jardim *m* de infância

nurture /'nɜ:tʃə(r)/ *vt* educar

nut /nʌt/ *n* (*bot*) noz *f*; (*techn*) porca *f* de parafuso

nutcrackers /'nʌtkrækəz/ *npl* quebra-nozes *m invar*

nutmeg /'nʌtmeg/ *n* noz-moscada *f*

nutrient /'nju:trɪənt/ *n* substância *f* nutritiva, nutriente *m*

nutrit|ion /nju:'trɪʃn/ *n* nutrição *f*. ~**ious** *a* nutritivo

nutshell /'nʌtʃel/ *n* casca *f* de noz. **in a** ~ em poucas palavras

nuzzle /'nʌzl/ *vt* esfregar com o focinho

nylon /'naɪlɒn/ *n* nylon *m*. ~**s** meias *fpl* de nylon

O

oaf /əʊf/ *n* (*pl* **oafs**) imbecil *m*, idiota *m*

oak /əʊk/ *n* carvalho *m*

OAP *abbr see* **old-age pensioner**

oar /ɔ:(r)/ *n* remo *m*

oasis /əʊ'eɪsɪs/ *n* (*pl* **oases** /-si:z/) oásis *m*

oath /əʊθ/ *n* juramento *m*; (*swear-word*) praga *f*

oatmeal /'əʊtmi:l/ *n* farinha *f* de aveia; (*porridge*) papa *f* de aveia

oats /əʊts/ *npl* aveia *f*

obedien|t /ə'bi:dɪənt/ *a* obediente. ~**ce** *n* obediência *f*. ~**tly** *adv* obedientemente

obes|e /əʊ'bi:s/ *a* obeso. ~**ity** *n* obesidade *f*

obey /ə'beɪ/ *vt/i* obedecer (a)

obituary /ə'bɪtʃʊərɪ/ *n* necrológio *m*, (P) necrologia *f*

object[1] /ˈɒbdʒɪkt/ n objeto m, (P) objecto m; (aim) objetivo m, (P) objectivo m; (gram) complemento m

object[2] /əbˈdʒekt/ vt/i objetar, (P) objectar (que). ~ **to** opor-se a, discordar de. ~**ion** /-ʃn/ n objeção f, (P) objecção f

objectionable /əbˈdʒekʃnəbl/ a censurável; (unpleasant) desagradável

objectiv|**e** /əbˈdʒektɪv/ a objetivo, (P) objectivo. ~**ity** /-ˈtɪvətɪ/ n objetividade f, (P) objectividade f

obligation /ɒblɪˈɡeɪʃn/ n obrigação f. **be under an** ~ **to sb** dever favores a alg

obligatory /əˈblɪɡətrɪ/ a obrigatório

oblig|**e** /əˈblaɪdʒ/ vt obrigar; (do a favour) fazer um favor a, obsequiar. ~**ed** a obrigado (**to** a). ~**ed to sb** em dívida (para com alg. ~**ing** a prestável, amável. ~**ingly** adv amavelmente

oblique /əˈbliːk/ a oblíquo

obliterat|**e** /əˈblɪtəreɪt/ vt obliterar. ~**ion** /-ˈreɪʃn/ n obliteração f

oblivion /əˈblɪvɪən/ n esquecimento m

oblivious /əˈblɪvɪəs/ a esquecido, sem consciência (**of/to** de)

oblong /ˈɒblɒŋ/ a oblongo □ n retângulo m, (P) rectângulo m

obnoxious /əbˈnɒkʃəs/ a ofensivo, detestável

oboe /ˈəʊbəʊ/ n oboé m

obscen|**e** /əbˈsiːn/ a obsceno. ~**ity** /-ˈenətɪ/ n obscenidade f

obscur|**e** /əbˈskjʊə(r)/ a obscuro □ vt obscurecer; (conceal) encobrir. ~**ity** n obscuridade f

obsequious /əbˈsiːkwɪəs/ a demasiado obsequioso, subserviente

observan|**t** /əbˈzɜːvənt/ a observador. ~**ce** n observância f, cumprimento m

observatory /əbˈzɜːvətrɪ/ n observatório m

observ|**e** /əbˈzɜːv/ vt observar. ~**ation** /ɒbzəˈveɪʃn/ n observação f. **keep under** ~**ation** vigiar. ~**er** n observador m

obsess /əbˈses/ vt obcecar. ~**ion** /-ʃn/ n obsessão f. ~**ive** a obsessivo

obsolete /ˈɒbsəliːt/ a obsoleto, antiguado

obstacle /ˈɒbstəkl/ n obstáculo m

obstetric|**s** /əbˈstetrɪks/ n obstetrícia f. ~**ian** /ɒbstɪˈtrɪʃn/ n obstetra mf

obstina|**te** /ˈɒbstɪnət/ a obstinado. ~**cy** n obstinação f

obstruct /əbˈstrʌkt/ vt obstruir, bloquear; (hinder) estorvar, obstruir. ~**ion** /-ʃn/ n obstrução f; (thing) obstáculo m

obtain /əbˈteɪn/ vt obter □ vi prevalecer, estar em vigor. ~**able** a que se pode obter

obtrusive /əbˈtruːsɪv/ a importuno; (thing) demasiadamente em evidência, que dá muito na vista (colloq)

obvious /ˈɒbvɪəs/ a óbvio, evidente. ~**ly** adv obviamente

occasion /əˈkeɪʒn/ n ocasião f; (event) acontecimento m □ vt ocasionar. **on** ~ de vez em quando, ocasionalmente

occasional /əˈkeɪʒənl/ a ocasional. ~**ly** adv de vez em quando, ocasionalmente

occult /ˈɒˈkʌlt/ a oculto

occupation /ɒkjʊˈpeɪʃn/ n ocupação f. ~**al** a profissional; (therapy) ocupacional

occup|**y** /ˈɒkjʊpaɪ/ vt ocupar. ~**ant**, ~**ier** ns ocupante mf

occur /əˈkɜː(r)/ vi (pt **occurred**) ocorrer, acontecer, dar-se; (arise) apresentar-se, aparecer. ~ **to sb** ocorrer a alg

occurrence /əˈkʌrəns/ n acontecimento m, ocorrência f

ocean /'əʊʃn/ n oceano m

o'clock /ə'klɒk/ adv **it is one** ~ é uma hora. **it is six** ~ são seis horas

octagon /'ɒktəgən/ n octógono m. **~al** /-'tægənl/ a octogonal

octave /'ɒktɪv/ n oitava f

October /ɒk'təʊbə(r)/ n outubro m

octopus /'ɒktəpəs/ n (pl **-puses**) polvo m

odd /ɒd/ a (**-er, -est**) estranho, singular; (number) ímpar; (left over) de sobra; (not of set) desemparelhado; (occasional) ocasional. ~ **jobs** (paid) biscates mpl; (in garden etc) trabalhos mpl diversos. **twenty** ~ vinte e tantos. ~**ity** n singularidade f; (thing) curiosidade f. ~**ly** adv de modo estranho

oddment /'ɒdmənt/ n resto m, artigo m avulso

odds /ɒdz/ npl probabilidades fpl; (in betting) ganhos mpl líquidos. **at** ~ em desacordo; (quarrelling) de mal, brigado. **it makes no** ~ não faz diferença. ~ **and ends** artigos mpl avulsos, coisas fpl pequenas

odious /'əʊdɪəs/ a odioso

odour /'əʊdə(r)/ n odor m. ~**less** a inodoro

of /əv/; emphatic /ɒv/ prep de. **a friend** ~ **mine** um amigo meu. **the fifth** ~ **June** (no dia) cinco de junho. **take six** ~ **them** leve seis deles

off /ɒf/ adv embora, fora; (switched off) apagado, desligado; (taken off) tirado, desligado; (cancelled) cancelado; (food) estragado □ prep (fora) de; (distant from) a alguma distância de. **be** ~ (depart) ir se embora, partir. **be well** ~ ser abastado. **be better/worse** ~ estar em melhor/pior situação. **a day** ~ um dia de folga. **20%** ~ redução de 20%. **on the** ~ **chance that** no caso

de. ~ **colour** indisposto, adoentado. ~**-licence** n loja f de bebidas alcoólicas. ~**-load** vt descarregar. ~**-putting** a desconcertante. ~**-stage** adv fora de cena. ~**-white** a branco-sujo

offal /'ɒfl/ n miudezas fpl, fressura f

offence /ə'fens/ n (feeling) ofensa f; (crime) delito m, transgressão f. **give** ~ **to** ofender. **take** ~ ofender-se (at com)

offend /ə'fend/ vt ofender. **be** ~**ed** ofender-se (at com). ~**er** n delinquente mf, (P) delinquente mf

offensive /ə'fensɪv/ a ofensivo; (disgusting) repugnante □ n ofensiva f

offer /'ɒfə(r)/ vt (pt **offered**) oferecer □ n oferta f. **on** ~ em promoção. ~**ing** n oferenda f

offhand /ɒf'hænd/ a espontâneo; (curt) seco □ adv de improviso, sem pensar

office /'ɒfɪs/ n escritório m; (post) cargo m; (branch) filial f. ~ **hours** horas fpl de expediente. **in** ~ no poder. **take** ~ assumir o cargo

officer /'ɒfɪsə(r)/ n oficial m; (policeman) agente m

official /ə'fɪʃl/ a oficial □ n funcionário m. ~**ly** adv oficialmente

officiate /ə'fɪʃɪeɪt/ vi (relig) oficiar. ~ **as** presidir, exercer as funções de

officious /ə'fɪʃəs/ a intrometido

offing /'ɒfɪŋ/ n **in the** ~ (fig) em perspectiva

offset /'ɒfset/ vt (pt **-set**, pres p **-setting**) compensar, contrabalançar

offshoot /'ɒfʃuːt/ n rebento m; (fig) efeito m secundário

offshore /'ɒfʃɔː(r)/ a ao largo da costa

offside /ɒf'saɪd/ a & adv offside, em impedimento, (P) fora de jogo

offspring /'ɒfsprɪŋ/ n (pl invar) descendência f, prole f

often /'ɒfn/ adv muitas vezes, freqüentemente, (P) frequentemente. **every so** ~ de vez em quando. **how** ~? quantas vezes?

oh /əʊ/ int oh, ah

oil /ɔɪl/ n óleo m; (petroleum) petróleo m □ vt lubrificar. ~-**painting** n pintura f a óleo. ~-**rig** plataforma f de poço de petróleo. ~ **well** poço m de petróleo. ~y a oleoso; (food) gorduroso

oilfield /'ɔɪlfiːld/ n campo m petrolífero

oilskins /'ɔɪlskɪnz/ npl roupa f de oleado

ointment /'ɔɪntmənt/ n pomada f

OK /əʊ'keɪ/ a & adv (colloq) (está) bem, (está) certo, (está) legal

old /əʊld/ a (-er, -est) velho; (person) velho, idoso; (former) antigo. **how** ~ **is he?** que idade tem ele? **he is eight years** ~ ele tem oito anos (de idade). **of** ~ (d)antes, antigamente. ~ **age** velhice f. ~-**age pensioner** reformado m, aposentado m, pessoa f de terceira idade. ~ **boy** antigo aluno m. ~-**fashioned** a fora de moda. ~ **girl** antiga aluna f. ~ **maid** solteirona f. ~ **man** homem m idoso, velho m. ~-**time** a antigo. ~ **woman** mulher f idosa, velha f

olive /'ɒlɪv/ n azeitona f □ a de azeitona. ~ **oil** azeite m f

Olympic /ə'lɪmpɪk/ a olímpico. ~s npl Olimpíadas fpl. ~ **Games** Jogos mpl Olímpicos

omelette /'ɒmlɪt/ n omelete f

omen /'əʊmən/ n agouro m

ominous /'ɒmɪnəs/ a agourento

omi|t /ə'mɪt/ vt (pt **omitted**) omitir. ~**ssion** /-ʃn/ n omissão f

on /ɒn/ prep sobre, em cima de, de, em □ adv para diante, para a frente; (switched on) aceso, ligado; (tap) aberto; (machine) em funcionamento; (put on) posto; (happening) em curso. ~ **arrival** na chegada, ao chegar. ~ **foot** etc a pé etc. ~ **doing** ao fazer. ~ **time** na hora, dentro do horário. ~ **Tuesday** na terça-feira. ~ **Tuesdays** às terças-feiras. **walk/**etc ~ continuar a andar/etc. **be** ~ or (film, TV) estar levando or passando. ~ **and off** de vez em quando. ~ **and** ~ sem parar

once /wʌns/ adv uma vez; (formerly) noutro(s) tempo(s) □ conj uma vez que, desde que. **all at** ~ de repente; (simultaneously) todos ao mesmo tempo. **just this** ~ só esta vez. ~ **(and) for all** duma vez para sempre. ~ **upon a time** era uma vez. ~-**over** n (colloq) vista f de olhos

oncoming /'ɒnkʌmɪŋ/ a que se aproxima, próximo. **the** ~ **traffic** o trânsito que vem do sentido oposto, (P) no sentido contrário

one /wʌn/ a um(a); (sole) único n um(a) mf □ pron um(a) mf; (impersonal) se. **by** ~ um a um. **a big/red/**etc ~ um grande/vermelho/etc. **this/that** ~ este/esse. ~ **another** um ao outro, uns aos outros. ~-**sided** a parcial. ~-**way** a (street) mão única; (ticket) simples

oneself /wʌn'self/ pron si, si mesmo/próprio; (reflexive) se. **by** ~ sozinho

onion /'ʌnɪən/ n cebola f

on-line /ɒn'laɪn/ adj conectado a (Internet)

onlooker /'ɒnlʊkə(r)/ n espectador m, circunstante mf

only /'əʊnlɪ/ a único □ adv apenas, só, somente □ conj só que. **an** ~ **child** um filho único. **he has six** ele só tem seis. **not** ~ ... **but also** não só ... mas também. ~ **too** muito, mais que

onset /'ɒnset/ n começo m; (attack) ataque m

onslaught /'ɒnslɔ:t/ n ataque m violento, assalto m

onward(s) /'ɒnwəd(z)/ adv para a frente/diante

ooze /u:z/ vt/i escorrer, verter

opal /'əʊpl/ n opala f

opaque /əʊ'peɪk/ a opaco, tosco

open /'əʊpən/ a aberto; (view) aberto, amplo; (free to all) aberto ao público; (attempt) franco □ vt/i abrir(-se); (of shop, play) abrir. **in the ~ air** ao ar livre. **keep ~ house** receber muito, abrir a porta para todos. ~ **on to** dar para. ~ **out** or **up** abrir(-se). **~-heart** a (of surgery) de coração aberto. **~-minded** a imparcial. **~-plan** a sem divisórias. ~ **secret** segredo m de polichinelo. ~ **sea** mar m alto. **~ness** n abertura f; (frankness) franqueza f

opener /'əʊpənə(r)/ n (tins) abridor m de latas; (bottles) saca-rolhas m invar

opening /'əʊpənɪŋ/ n abertura f; (beginning) começo m; (opportunity) oportunidade f; (job) vaga f

openly /'əʊpənlɪ/ adv abertamente

opera /'ɒprə/ n ópera f. **~-glasses** npl binóculo (de teatro) m, (P) binóculos mpl. **~tic** /ɒpə-'rætɪk/ a de ópera

operat|e /'ɒpəreɪt/ vt/i operar; (techn) (pôr a) funcionar. **~e on** (med) operar. **~ing-theatre** n (med) anfiteatro m, sala f de operações. **~ion** /-'reɪʃn/ n operação f. **in ~ion** em vigor; (techn) em funcionamento. **~ional** /-'reɪʃənl/ a operacional. **~or** n operador m; (telephonist) telefonista mf

operative /'ɒpərətɪv/ a (surgical) operatório; (law etc) em vigor

opinion /ə'pɪnɪən/ n opinião f, parecer m. **in my ~** a meu ver. ~ **poll** n sondagem (de opinião) f. **~ated** /-eɪtɪd/ a dogmático

opium /'əʊpɪəm/ n ópio m

Oporto /ə'pɔːtəʊ/ n Porto m

opponent /ə'pəʊnənt/ n adversário m, antagonista mf, oponente mf

opportune /'ɒpətjuːn/ a oportuno

opportunity /ɒpə'tjuːnətɪ/ n oportunidade f

oppos|e /ə'pəʊz/ vt opor-se a. **~ed** to oposto a. **~ing** a oposto

opposite /'ɒpəzɪt/ a & n oposto (m), contrário (m) □ adv em frente □ prep ~ (to) em frente de

opposition /ɒpə'zɪʃn/ n oposição f

oppress /ə'pres/ vt oprimir. **~ion** /-ʃn/ n opressão f. **~ive** a opressivo. **~or** n opressor m

opt /ɒpt/ vi ~ **for** optar por. ~ **out** recusar-se a participar (of de). ~ **to do** escolher fazer

optical /'ɒptɪkl/ a óptico. ~ **illusion** ilusão f óptica

optician /ɒp'tɪʃn/ n oculista mf

optimis|t /'ɒptɪmɪst/ n optimista mf, (P) otimista mf. **~m** /-zəm/ n optimismo m, (P) otimismo m. **~tic** /-'mɪstɪk/ a optimista, (P) otimista. **~tically** /-'mɪstɪklɪ/ adv com optimismo, (P) otimismo

optimum /'ɒptɪməm/ a & n (pl -ima) óptimo (m), (P) óptimo (m)

option /'ɒpʃn/ n escolha f, opção f. **have no ~** (but) não ter outro remédio (senão)

optional /'ɒpʃənl/ a opcional, facultativo

opulen|t /'ɒpjʊlənt/ a opulento. **~ce** n opulência f

or /ɔː(r)/ conj ou; (with negative) nem. ~ **else** senão

oracle /'ɒrəkl/ n oráculo m

oral /'ɔːrəl/ a oral

orange /'ɒrɪndʒ/ n laranja f; (colour) laranja m, cor f de laranja *a* de laranja; (*colour*) alaranjado, cor de laranja

orator /'ɒrətə(r)/ *n* orador *m*. **~y** *n* oratória *f*

orbit /'ɔ:bɪt/ *n* órbita *f* □ *vt* (*pt* **orbited**) gravitar em torno de

orchard /'ɔ:tʃəd/ *n* pomar *m*

orchestra /'ɔ:kɪstrə/ *n* orquestra *f*. **~l** /-'kestrəl/ *a* orquestral

orchestrate /'ɔ:kɪstreɪt/ *vt* orquestrar

orchid /'ɔ:kɪd/ *n* orquídea *f*

ordain /ɔ:'deɪn/ *vt* decretar; (*relig*) ordenar

ordeal /ɔ:'di:l/ *n* prova *f*, provação *f*

order /'ɔ:də(r)/ *n* ordem *f*, (*comm*) encomenda *f*, pedido *m* □ *vt* ordenar; (*goods etc*) encomendar. in **~** to para que. in **~** to para

orderly /'ɔ:dəlɪ/ *a* ordenado, em ordem; (*not unruly*) ordeiro □ *n* (*mil*) ordenança *f*; (*med*) servente *m* de hospital

ordinary /'ɔ:dɪnrɪ/ *a* normal, ordinário, vulgar. out of the **~** fora do comum

ordination /ɔ:dɪ'neɪʃn/ *n* (*relig*) ordenação *f*

ore /ɔ:(r)/ *n* minério *m*

organ /'ɔ:gən/ *n* órgão *m*. **~ist** *n* organista *m*

organic /ɔ:'gænɪk/ *a* orgânico

organism /'ɔ:gənɪzəm/ *n* organismo *m*

organize /'ɔ:gənaɪz/ *vt* organizar. **~ation** /-'zeɪʃn/ *n* organização *f*. **~er** *n* organizador *m*

orgasm /'ɔ:gæzəm/ *n* orgasmo *m*

orgy /'ɔ:dʒɪ/ *n* orgia *f*

Orient /'ɔ:rɪənt/ *n* the **~** o Oriente *m*. **~al** /-'entl/ *a* & *n* oriental (*mf*)

orientate /'ɔ:rɪənteɪt/ *vt* orientar. **~ion** /-'teɪʃn/ *n* orientação *f*

orifice /'ɒrɪfɪs/ *n* orifício *m*

origin /'ɒrɪdʒɪn/ *n* origem *f*

original /ə'rɪdʒənl/ *a* original; (*not copied*) original. **~ity**

/-'næləti/ *n* originalidade *f*. **~ly** *adv* originalmente; (*in the beginning*) originariamente

originate /ə'rɪdʒəneɪt/ *vt/i* originar(-se). **~e from** provir de. **~or** *n* iniciador *m*, criador *m*, autor *m*

ornament /'ɔ:nəmənt/ *n* ornamento *m*; (*object*) peça *f* decorativa. **~al** /-'mentl/ *a* ornamental. **~ation** /-en'teɪʃn/ *n* ornamentação *f*

ornate /ɔ:'neɪt/ *a* florido, floreado

ornithology /ɔ:nɪ'θɒlədʒɪ/ *n* ornitologia *f*. **~ist** *n* ornitólogo *m*

orphan /'ɔ:fn/ *n* órfão(ã) *f/m* □ *vt* deixar órfão. **~age** *n* orfanato *m*

orthodox /'ɔ:θədɒks/ *a* ortodoxo

orthopaedic /ɔ:θə'pi:dɪk/ *a* ortopédico

oscillate /'ɒsɪleɪt/ *vi* oscilar, vacilar

ostensibl|**e** /ɒs'tensəbl/ *a* aparente, pretenso. **~y** *adv* aparentemente, pretensamente

ostentati|**on** /ɒsten'teɪʃn/ *n* ostentação *f*. **~ous** /-'teɪʃəs/ *a* ostentoso, ostensivo

osteopath /'ɒstɪəpæθ/ *n* osteopata *mf*

ostracize /'ɒstrəsaɪz/ *vt* pôr de lado, marginalizar

ostrich /'ɒstrɪtʃ/ *n* avestruz *mf*

other /'ʌðə(r)/ *a*, *n* & *pron* outro (*m*) □ *adv* **~ than** diferente de, senão. (**some**) **~s** outros. the **~ day** no outro dia. the **~ one** o outro

otherwise /'ʌðəwaɪz/ *adv* de outro modo □ *conj* senão, caso contrário

otter /'ɒtə(r)/ *n* lontra *f*

ouch /aʊtʃ/ *int* ai!, ui!

ought /ɔ:t/ *v aux* (*pt* **ought**) dever. **you ~ to stay** você devia ficar. **he ~ to succeed** ele deve vencer. **I ~ to have done it** eu devia tê-lo feito

ounce /aʊns/ *n* onça *f* (= *28,35g*)

our /'auə(r)/ a nosso(s), nossa(s)

ours /'auəz/ *poss pron* o(s) nosso(s), a(s) nossa(s)

ourselves /auə'selvz/ *pron* nós mesmos/próprios; (*reflexive*) nos. **by** ~ sozinhos

oust /aust/ *vt* expulsar, obrigar a sair

out /aut/ *adv* fora; (*of light, fire*) apagado; (*in blossom*) aberto, desabrochado; (*of tide*) baixo. **be** ~ não estar em casa, estar fora (de casa); (*wrong*) enganar-se. **be** ~ **to** estar resolvido a. **run**/*etc* ~ sair correndo/*etc*. ~**-and**-~ *a* completo, rematado. ~ **of** fora de; (*without*) sem. ~ **of pity**/*etc* por pena/*etc*. **made** ~ **of** feito de or em. **take** ~ **of** tirar de. **5** ~ **of 6** 5 (de) entre 6. ~ **of date** fora de moda; (*not valid*) fora do prazo. ~ **of doors** ao ar livre. ~ **of one's mind** doido. ~ **of order** quebrado. ~ **of place** deslocado. ~ **of the way** afastado. ~**-patient** *n* doente *mf* de consulta externa

outboard /'autbɔːd/ *a* ~ **motor** motor *m* de popa

outbreak /'autbreik/ *n* (*of flu etc*) surto *m*, epidemia *f*; (*of war*) deflagração *f*

outburst /'autbɜːst/ *n* explosão *f*

outcast /'autkɑːst/ *n* pária *m*

outcome /'autkʌm/ *n* resultado *m*

outcry /'autkrai/ *n* clamor *m*; (*protest*) protesto *m*

outdated /aut'deitid/ *a* fora da moda, ultrapassado

outdo /aut'duː/ *vt* (*pt* **-did**, *pp* **-done**) ultrapassar, superar

outdoor /'autdɔː(r)/ *a* ao ar livre. ~**s** /-'dɔːz/ *adv* fora de casa, ao ar livre

outer /'autə(r)/ *a* exterior. ~ **space** espaço (cósmico) *m*

outfit /'autfit/ *n* equipamento *m*; (*clothes*) roupa *f*

outgoing /'autgəuɪŋ/ *a* que vai

outgrow /aut'grəu/ *vt* (*pt* **-grew**, *pp* **-grown**) crescer mais do que; (*clothes*) já não caber em

outhouse /'authaus/ *n* anexo *m*, dependência *f*

outing /'autɪŋ/ *n* saída *f*, passeio *m*

outlandish /aut'lændɪʃ/ *a* exótico, estranho

outlaw /'autlɔː/ *n* fora-da-lei *mf*, bandido *m* □ *vt* banir, proscrever

outlay /'autleɪ/ *n* despesa(s) *f*(*pl*)

outlet /'autlet/ *n* saída *f*, escoadouro *m*; (*for goods*) mercado *m*, saída *f*; (*for feelings*) escape *m*, vazão *m*; (*electr*) tomada *f*

outline /'autlaɪn/ *n* contorno *m*; (*summary*) plano *m* geral, esquema *m*, esboço *m* □ *vt* contornar; (*summarize*) descrever em linhas gerais

outlive /aut'lɪv/ *vt* sobreviver a

outlook /'autlʊk/ *n* (*view*) vista *f*; (*mental attitude*) visão *f*; (*future prospects*) perspectiva(s) *f*(*pl*)

outlying /'autlaɪŋ/ *a* afastado, remoto

outnumber /aut'nʌmbə(r)/ *vt* ultrapassar em número

outpost /'autpəust/ *n* posto *m* avançado

output /'autpʊt/ *n* rendimento *m*; (*of computer*) saída *f*, output *m*

outrage /'autreɪdʒ/ *n* atrocidade *f*, crime *m*; (*scandal*) escândalo *m* □ *vt* ultrajar

outrageous /aut'reɪdʒəs/ *a* (*shocking*) escandaloso; (*very cruel*) atroz

outright /aut'traɪt/ *adv* completamente; (*at once*) imediatamente; (*frankly*) abertamente □ *a* completo; (*refusal*) claro

outset /'autset/ *n* início *m*, começo *m*, princípio *m*

outside[1] /aut'saɪd/ *n* exterior *m* □ *adv* (lá) (por) fora □ *prep* (para) fora de, além de; (*in front of*) diante de. **at the ～** no máximo

outside[2] /aʊt'saɪd/ *a* exterior

outsider /aʊt'saɪdə(r)/ *n* estranho *m*; (*in race*) cavalo *m* com poucas probabilidades, azarão *m*

outsize /'aʊtsaɪz/ *a* tamanho extra *invar*

outskirts /'aʊtskɜːts/ *npl* arredores *mpl*, subúrbios *mpl*

outspoken /aʊt'spəʊkn/ *a* franco

outstanding /aʊt'stændɪŋ/ *a* saliente, proeminente; (*debt*) por saldar; (*very good*) notável, destacado

outstretched /aʊt'stretʃt/ *a* (*arm*) estendido, esticado

outstrip /aʊt'strɪp/ *vt* (*pt* -**stripped**) ultrapassar, passar à frente de

outward /'aʊtwəd/ *a* para o exterior; (*sign etc*) exterior; (*journey*) de ida. **～ly** *adv* exteriormente. **～s** *adv* para o exterior

outwit /aʊt'wɪt/ *vt* (*pt* -**witted**) ser mais esperto que, enganar

oval /'əʊvl/ *n & a* oval (*m*)

ovary /'əʊvərɪ/ *n* ovário *m*

ovation /əʊ'veɪʃn/ *n* ovação *f*

oven /'ʌvn/ *n* forno *m*

over /'əʊvə(r)/ *prep* sobre, acima de, por cima de; (*across*) de para o/do outro lado de; (*during*) durante, em; (*more than*) mais de □ *adv* por cima; (*too*) demais, demasiadamente; (*ended*) acabado. **the film is ～** o filme já acabou. **jump**/*etc* **～** saltar/*etc* por cima. **he has some ～** ele tem uns de sobra. **all ～ the country** em/por todo o país. **all ～ the table** por toda a mesa. **～ and above** (*besides, in addition to*) (para) além de. **～ and ～** repetidas vezes. **～ there** ali, lá, acolá

over- /'əʊvə(r)/ *pref* sobre-, super-; (*excessively*) demais, demasiado

overall[1] /'əʊvərɔːl/ *n* bata *f*. **～s** macacão *m*, (*P*) fato-macaco *m*

overall[2] /'əʊvərɔːl/ *a* global; (*length etc*) total □ *adv* globalmente

overawe /əʊvər'ɔː/ *vt* intimidar

overbalance /əʊvə'bæləns/ *vt/i* (fazer) perder o equilíbrio

overbearing /əʊvə'beərɪŋ/ *a* autoritário, despótico; (*arrogant*) arrogante

overboard /'əʊvəbɔːd/ *adv* (pela) borda fora

overcast /əʊvə'kɑːst/ *a* encoberto, nublado

overcharge /əʊvə'tʃɑːdʒ/ *vt* **～ sb** (**for**) cobrar demais a alg (por)

overcoat /'əʊvəkəʊt/ *n* casacão *m*; (*for men*) sobretudo *m*

overcome /əʊvə'kʌm/ *vt* (*pt* -**came**, *pp* -**come**) superar, vencer. **～ by** sucumbindo a, dominado or vencido por

overcrowded /əʊvə'kraʊdɪd/ *a* apinhado, superlotado; (*country*) superpovoado

overdo /əʊvə'duː/ *vt* (*pt* -**did**, *pp* -**done**) exagerar, levar longe demais. **～ne** (*culin*) cozinhado demais

overdose /'əʊvədəʊs/ *n* dose *f* excessiva

overdraft /'əʊvədrɑːft/ *n* saldo *m* negativo

overdraw /əʊvə'drɔː/ *vt* (*pt* -**drew**, *pp* -**drawn**) sacar a descoberto

overdue /əʊvə'djuː/ *a* em atraso, atrasado; (*belated*) tardio

overestimate /əʊvər'estɪmeɪt/ *vt* sobreestimar, atribuir valor excessivo a

overexpose /əʊvərɪk'spəʊz/ *vt* expor demais

overflow[1] /əʊvə'fləʊ/ *vt/i* extravasar, transbordar (**with** de)

overflow[2] /'əʊvəfləʊ/ *n* (*outlet*) descarga *f*; (*excess*) excesso *m*

overgrown /əʊvə'grəʊn/ *a* que cresceu demais; (*garden etc*) invadido pela vegetação

overhang /əʊvə'hæŋ/ *vt* (*pt* -**hung**) estar sobranceiro a, pairar sobre □ *vi* projetar-se, (*P*) projectar-se para fora □ *n* saliência *f*

overhaul[1] /əʊvəˈhɔːl/ *vt* fazer uma revisão em

overhaul[2] /ˈəʊvəhɔːl/ *n* revisão *f*

overhead[1] /əʊvəˈhed/ *adv* em or por cima, ao or no alto

overhead[2] /ˈəʊvəhed/ *a* aéreo. **~s** *npl* despesas *fpl* gerais

overhear /əʊvəˈhɪə(r)/ *vt* (*pt* **-heard**) (*eavesdrop*) ouvir sem conhecimento do falante; (*hear by chance*) ouvir por acaso

overjoyed /əʊvəˈdʒɔɪd/ *a* radiante, felicíssimo

overlap /əʊvəˈlæp/ *vt/i* (*pt* **-lapped**) sobrepor(-se) parcialmente; (*fig*) coincidir

overleaf /əʊvəˈliːf/ *adv* no verso

overload /əʊvəˈləʊd/ *vt* sobrecarregar

overlook /əʊvəˈlʊk/ *vt* deixar passar; (*of window*) dar para; (*of building*) dominar

overnight /əʊvəˈnaɪt/ *adv* durante a noite; (*fig*) dum dia para o outro □ *a* (*train*) da noite; (*stay, journey, etc*) noite, noturno; (*fig*) súbito

overpass /əʊvəˈpɑːs/ *n* passagem *f* superior

overpay /əʊvəˈpeɪ/ *vt* (*pt* **-paid**) pagar em excesso

overpower /əʊvəˈpaʊə(r)/ *vt* dominar, subjugar; (*fig*) esmagar. **~ing** *a* esmagador; (*heat*) sufocante, insuportável

overpriced /əʊvəˈpraɪst/ *a* muito caro

overrate /əʊvəˈreɪt/ *vt* sobreestimar, exagerar o valor de

overrid|e /əʊvəˈraɪd/ *vt* (*pt* **-rode**, *pp* **-ridden**) prevalecer sobre, passar por cima de. **~ing** *a* primordial, preponderante; (*importance*) maior

overripe /ˈəʊvəraɪp/ *a* demasiado maduro

overrule /əʊvəˈruːl/ *vt* anular, rejeitar; (*claim*) indeferir

overrun /əʊvəˈrʌn/ *vt* (*pt* **-ran**, *pp* **-run**, *pres p* **-running**) invadir; (*a limit*) exceder, ultrapassar

overseas /əʊvəˈsiːz/ *a* ultramarino; (*abroad*) estrangeiro □ *adv* no ultramar, no estrangeiro

oversee /əʊvəˈsiː/ *vt* (*pt* **-saw** *pp* **-seen**) supervisionar. **~r** /ˈəʊvəsɪə(r)/ *n* capataz *m*

overshadow /əʊvəˈʃædəʊ/ *vt* (*fig*) eclipsar, ofuscar

oversight /ˈəʊvəsaɪt/ *n* lapso *m*

oversleep /əʊvəˈsliːp/ *vi* (*pt* **-slept**) acordar tarde, dormir demais

overt /ˈəʊvɜːt/ *a* manifesto, claro, patente

overtake /əʊvəˈteɪk/ *vt/i* (*pt* **-took**, *pp* **-taken**) ultrapassar

overthrow /əʊvəˈθrəʊ/ *vt* (*pt* **-threw**, *pp* **-thrown**) derrubar □ *n* /ˈəʊvəθrəʊ/ (*pol*) derrubada *f*

overtime /ˈəʊvətaɪm/ *n* horas *fpl* extras

overtones /ˈəʊvətəʊnz/ *npl* (*fig*) tom *m*, implicação *f*

overture /ˈəʊvətjʊə(r)/ *n* (*mus*) abertura *f*; (*fig*) proposta *f*, abordagem *f*

overturn /əʊvəˈtɜːn/ *vt/i* virar (-se); (*car, plane*) capotar, virar-se

overweight /əʊvəˈweɪt/ *a* **be ~** ter excesso de peso

overwhelm /əʊvəˈwelm/ *vt* oprimir; (*defeat*) esmagar; (*amaze*) assoberbar. **~ing** *a* esmagador; (*urge*) irresistível

overwork /əʊvəˈwɜːk/ *vt/i* sobrecarregar(-se) com trabalho □ *n* excesso *m* de trabalho

overwrought /əʊvəˈrɔːt/ *a* muito agitado, superexcitado

ow|e /əʊ/ *vt* dever. **~ing** *a* devido. **~ing to** devido a

owl /aʊl/ *n* coruja *f*

own[1] /əʊn/ *a* próprio. **a house/etc of one's** ~ uma casa/*etc* própria. **get one's** ~ **back** (*colloq*) ir à forra, (*P*) desforrar-se. **hold one's** ~ aguentar-se, (*P*) aguentar-se. **on one's** ~ sozinho.

own[2] /əʊn/ *vt* possuir. ~ **up (to)** (*colloq*) confessar. ~**er** *n* proprietário, dono *m*. ~**ership** *n* posse *f*, propriedade *f*

ox /ɒks/ *n* (*pl* **oxen**) boi *m*

oxygen /'ɒksɪdʒən/ *n* oxigénio *m*, (*P*) oxigénio *m*

oyster /'ɔɪstə(r)/ *n* ostra *f*

ozone /'əʊzəʊn/ *n* ozónio *m*, (*P*) ozono *m*. ~ **layer** camada *f* de ozônio, (*P*) ozono *m*

P

pace /peɪs/ *n* passo *m*; (*fig*) ritmo *m* □ *vt* percorrer passo a passo □ *vi* ~ **up and down** andar de um lado para o outro. **keep** ~ **with** acompanhar, manter-se a par de

pacemaker /'peɪsmeɪkə(r)/ *n* (*med*) marcapasso *m*, (*P*) pacemaker *m*

Pacific /pə'sɪfɪk/ *a* pacífico □ *n* ~ (**Ocean**) (Oceano) Pacífico *m*

pacifist /'pæsɪfɪst/ *n* pacifista *mf*

pacify /'pæsɪfaɪ/ *vt* pacificar, apaziguar

pack /pæk/ *n* pacote *m*; (*mil*) mochila *f*; (*of hounds*) matilha *f*; (*of lies*) porção *f*, (*of cards*) baralho *m* □ *vt* empacotar; (*suitcase*) fazer; (*box, room*) encher; (*press down*) atulhar, encher até não caber mais □ *vi* fazer as malas. ~ **into** (*cram*) apinhar em, comprimir em. **send** ~**ing** pôr a andar, mandar passear. ~**ed** *a* apinhado. ~**ed lunch** merenda *f*

package /'pækɪdʒ/ *n* pacote *m*, embrulho *m* □ *vt* embalar. ~ **deal** pacote *m* de propostas. ~

holiday pacote *m* turístico, (*P*) viagem *f* organizada

packet /'pækɪt/ *n* pacote *m*; (*of cigarettes*) maço *m*

pact /pækt/ *n* pacto *m*

pad /pæd/ *n* (*in clothing*) chumaço *m*; (*for writing*) bloco *m* de papel/de notas; (*for ink*) almofada (de carimbo) *f*. (**launching**) ~ rampa *f* de lançamento □ *vt* (*pt* **padded**) enchumaçar, acolchoar; (*fig: essay etc*) encher linguiça. ~**ding** *n* chumaço *m*; (*fig*) linguiça *f*

paddle[1] /'pædl/ *n* remo *m* de canoa. ~**-steamer** *n* vapor *m* movido a rodas

paddl|**e**[2] /'pædl/ *vi* chapinhar, molhar os pés. ~**ing pool** piscina *f* de plástico para crianças

paddock /'pædək/ *n* cercado *m*; (*at racecourse*) paddock *m*

padlock /'pædlɒk/ *n* cadeado *m* □ *vt* fechar com cadeado

paediatrician /pi:dɪə'trɪʃn/ *n* pediatra *mf*

pagan /'peɪɡən/ *a* & *n* pagão (*m*), pagã (*f*)

page[1] /peɪdʒ/ *n* (*of book etc*) página *f*

page[2] /peɪdʒ/ *vt* mandar chamar

pageant /'pædʒənt/ *n* espetáculo *m*, (*P*) espectáculo *m* (histórico); (*procession*) cortejo *m*. ~**ry** *n* pompa *f*

pagoda /pə'ɡəʊdə/ *n* pagode *m*

paid /peɪd/ *see* **pay** □ *a* **put** ~ **to** (*colloq: end*) pôr fim a

pail /peɪl/ *n* balde *m*

pain /peɪn/ *n* dor *f*. ~**s** esforços *mpl* □ *vt* magoar. **be in** ~ sofrer, ter dores. ~**-killer** *n* analgésico *m*. **take** ~**s to** esforçar-se por. ~**ful** *a* doloroso; (*grievous, laborious*) penoso. ~**less** *a* sem dor, indolor

painstaking /'peɪnzteɪkɪŋ/ *a* cuidadoso, esmerado, meticuloso

paint /peɪnt/ *n* tinta *f*. ~**s** (*in box*)

tintas *fpl* □ *vt/i* pintar. ~er *n* pintor *m*. ~ing *n* pintura *f*

paintbrush /'peɪntbrʌʃ/ *n* pincel *m*

pair /peə(r)/ *n* par *m*. **a** ~ **of scissors** uma tesoura. **a** ~ **of trousers** um par de calças. **in** ~**s** aos pares □ *vi* ~ **off** formar pares

Pakistan /pɑːkɪˈstɑːn/ *n* Paquistão *m*. ~**i** *a* & *n* paquistanês (*m*)

pal /pæl/ *n* (*colloq*) colega *mf*, amigo *m*

palace /'pælɪs/ *n* palácio *m*

palat|e /'pælət/ *n* palato *m*. ~**able** *a* saboroso, gostoso; (*fig*) agradável

palatial /pəˈleɪʃl/ *a* suntuoso, (*P*) sumptuoso

pale /peɪl/ *a* (**-er, -est**) pálido; (*colour*) claro □ *vi* empalidecer. ~**ness** *n* palidez *f*

Palestin|e /'pælɪstaɪn/ *n* Palestina *f*. ~**ian** /-ˈstɪnɪən/ *a* & *n* palestino (*m*)

palette /'pælɪt/ *n* paleta *f*. ~**knife** *n* espátula *f*

pall /pɔːl/ *vi* tornar-se enfadonho, perder o interesse (**on** para)

pallid /'pælɪd/ *a* pálido

palm /pɑːm/ *n* (*of hand*) palma *f*; (*tree*) palmeira *f* □ *vt* ~ **off** impingir (**on** a). **P**~ **Sunday** Domingo *m* de Ramos

palpable /'pælpəbl/ *a* palpável

palpitat|e /'pælpɪteɪt/ *vi* palpitar. ~**ion** /-ˈteɪʃn/ *n* palpitação *f*

paltry /'pɔːltrɪ/ *a* (**-ier, -iest**) irrisório

pamper /'pæmpə(r)/ *vt* mimar, paparicar

pamphlet /'pæmflɪt/ *n* panfleto *m*, folheto *m*

pan /pæn/ *n* panela *f*; (*for frying*) frigideira *f* □ *vt* (*pt* **panned**) (*colloq*) criticar severamente

panacea /pænəˈsɪə/ *n* panacéia *f*

panache /pəˈnæʃ/ *n* brio *m*, estilo *m*, panache *m*

pancake /'pænkeɪk/ *n* crepe *m*, panqueca *f*

pancreas /'pæŋkrɪəs/ *n* pâncreas *m*

panda /'pændə/ *n* panda *m*

pandemonium /pændɪˈməʊnɪəm/ *n* pandemônio *m*, (*P*) pandemónio *m*, caos *m*

pander /'pændə(r)/ *vi* ~ **to** prestar-se a servir, ir ao encontro de, fazer concessões a

pane /peɪn/ *n* vidraça *f*

panel /'pænl/ *n* painel *m*; (*jury*) júri *m*; (*speakers*) convidados *mpl*. (**instrument**) ~ painel *m* de instrumentos, (*P*) de bordo. ~**led** *a* apainelado. ~**ling** *n* apainelamento *m*. ~**list** *n* convidado *m*

pang /pæŋ/ *n* pontada *f*, dor *f* aguda e súbita. ~**s** (*of hunger*) ataques *mpl* de fome. ~**s of conscience** remorsos *mpl*

panic /'pænɪk/ *n* pânico *m* □ *vt/i* (*pt* **panicked**) desorientar(-se), (fazer) entrar em pânico. ~**stricken** *a* tomado de pânico

panorama /pænəˈrɑːmə/ *n* panorama *m*. ~**ic** /-ˈræmɪk/ *a* panorâmico

pansy /'pænzɪ/ *n* amor-perfeito *m*

pant /pænt/ *vi* ofegar, arquejar

panther /'pænθə(r)/ *n* pantera *f*

panties /'pæntɪz/ *npl* (*colloq*) calcinhas *fpl*

pantomime /'pæntəmaɪm/ *n* pantomima *f*

pantry /'pæntrɪ/ *n* despensa *f*

pants /pænts/ *npl* (*colloq: underwear*) cuecas *fpl*; (*colloq: trousers*) calças *fpl*

papal /'peɪpl/ *a* papal

paper /'peɪpə(r)/ *n* papel *m*; (*newspaper*) jornal *m*; (*exam*) prova *f* escrita; (*essay*) comunicação *f*. ~**s** *npl* (*for identification*) documentos *mpl* □ *vt* forrar com papel. **on** ~ por escrito. ~**clip** *n* clipe *m*

paperback /'peɪpəbæk/ *a* & *n* ~ (**book**) livro *m* de capa mole

paperweight /'peɪpəweɪt/ n pesa-papéis m invar, (P) pisa-papéis m invar

paperwork /'peɪpəwɜːk/ n traba-lho m de secretária; (pej) papela-da f

paprika /'pæprɪkə/ n páprica f

par /pɑː(r)/ n **be below ~** estar abaixo do padrão desejado. **on a ~ with** em igualdade com

parable /'pærəbl/ n parábola f

parachut|e /'pærəʃuːt/ n pára-quedas m invar □ vi descer de pára-quedas. **~ist** n pára-quedista mf

parade /pə'reɪd/ n (mil) parada f militar; (procession) procissão f □ vi desfilar □ vt alardear

paradise /'pærədaɪs/ n paraíso m

paradox /'pærədɒks/ n paradoxo m. **~ical** /-'dɒksɪkl/ a paradoxal

paraffin /'pærəfɪn/ n querosene m, (P) petróleo m

paragon /'pærəgən/ n modelo de perfeição

paragraph /'pærəgrɑːf/ n pará-grafo m

parallel /'pærəlel/ a & n paralelo (m) □ vt (pt parelleled) compa-rar(-se) a

paralyse /'pærəlaɪz/ vt paralisar

paraly|sis /pə'ræləsɪs/ n paralisia f. **~tic** /-'lɪtɪk/ a & n paralítico (m)

paramedic /pærə'medɪk/ n para-médico m

parameter /pə'ræmɪtə(r)/ n parâ-metro m

paramount /'pærəmaʊnt/ a su-premo, primordial

parapet /'pærəpɪt/ n parapeito m

paraphernalia /pærəfə'neɪlɪə/ n equipamento m, tralha f (colloq)

paraphrase /'pærəfreɪz/ n pará-frase f □ vt parafrasear

paraplegic /pærə'pliːdʒɪk/ n para-plégico m

parasite /'pærəsaɪt/ n parasita mf

parasol /'pærəsɒl/ n sombrinha f;

(on table) pára-sol m, guarda-sol m

parcel /'pɑːsl/ n embrulho m; (for post) encomenda f

parch /pɑːtʃ/ vt ressecar. **be ~ed** estar com muita sede

parchment /'pɑːtʃmənt/ n perga-minho m

pardon /'pɑːdn/ n perdão m; (jur) perdão m, indulto m □ vt (pt par-doned) perdoar. **I beg your ~** perdão, desculpe. **(I beg your) ~?** como?

pare /peə(r)/ vt aparar, cortar; (peel) descascar

parent /'peərənt/ n pai m, mãe f. **~s** npl pais mpl. **~al** /pə'rentl/ a dos pais, paterno, materno

parenthesis /pə'renθəsɪs/ n (pl -theses) /-siːz/ parêntese m, pa-rêntesis m

Paris /'pærɪs/ n Paris m

parish /'pærɪʃ/ n paróquia f; (muni-cipal) freguesia f. **~ioner** /pə'rɪʃənə(r)/ n paroquiano m

parity /'pærətɪ/ n paridade f

park /pɑːk/ n parque m □ vt estacionar. **~ing** n estaciona-mento m. **no ~ing** estaciona-mento proibido. **~ing-meter** n parquímetro m

parliament /'pɑːləmənt/ n parla-mento m, assembléia f. **~ary** /-'mentrɪ/ a parlamentar

parochial /pə'rəʊkɪəl/ a paro-quial; (fig) provinciano, tacanho

parody /'pærədɪ/ n paródia f □ vt parodiar

parole /pə'rəʊl/ n **on ~** em liber-dade condicional □ vt pôr em li-berdade condicional

parquet /'pɑːkeɪ/ n parquê m, par-quete m

parrot /'pærət/ n papagaio m

parry /'pærɪ/ vt (a)parar □ n para-da f

parsimonious /pɑːsɪ'məʊnɪəs/ a parco; (mean) avarento

parsley /'pɑːslɪ/ n salsa f

parsnip /'pɑ:snɪp/ n cherovia f, pastinaga f

parson /'pɑ:sn/ n pároco m, pastor m

part /pɑ:t/ n parte f; (of serial) episódio m; (of machine) peça f; (theatre) papel m; (side in dispute) partido m □ a parcial □ adv em parte □ vt/i separar (-se) (from de). in ~ em parte. on the ~ of da parte de. ~ - exchange n troca f parcial. ~ of speech categoria f gramatical. ~time a & adv a tempo parcial, part-time. take ~ in tomar parte em. these ~s estas partes

partial /'pɑ:ʃl/ a (incomplete, biased) parcial. be ~ to gostar de. ~ity /-'ræləti/ n parcialidade f; (liking) predileção f, (P) predilecção f (for por). ~ly adv parcialmente

participate /pɑ:'tɪsɪpeɪt/ vi participar (in em). ~ant n /-ant participante mf. ~ation /-'peɪʃn/ n participação f

participle /'pɑ:tɪsɪpl/ n particípio m

particle /'pɑ:tɪkl/ n partícula f; (of dust) grão m; (fig) mínimo m

particular /pə'tɪkjʊlə(r)/ a especial, particular; (fussy) escrupuloso, (careful) escrupuloso. ~s npl pormenores mpl. in ~ adv em especial, particularmente. ~ly adv particularmente

parting /'pɑ:tɪŋ/ n separação f; (in hair) risca f □ a de despedida

partisan /pɑ:tɪ'zæn/ n partidário m; (mil) guerrilheiro m

partition /pɑ:'tɪʃn/ n (of room) tabique m, divisória f; (pol: division) partilha f, divisão f □ vt dividir, repartir. ~ off dividir por meio de tabique

partly /'pɑ:tlɪ/ adv em parte

partner /'pɑ:tnə(r)/ n sócio m; (cards, sport) parceiro m; (dan-cing) par m. ~ship n associação f; (comm) sociedade f

partridge /'pɑ:trɪdʒ/ n perdiz f

party /'pɑ:tɪ/ n festa f, reunião f; (group) grupo m; (pol) partido m; (jur) parte f. ~ line (telephone) linha f colectiva, (P) colectiva

pass /pɑ:s/ vt/i (pt passed) passar; (overtake) ultrapassar; (exam) passar; (approve) passar; (law) aprovar. ~ (by) passar por □ n (permit, sport) passe m; (geog) desfiladeiro m, garganta f; (in exam) aprovação f. make a ~ at (colloq) atirar-se para (colloq). ~ away falecer. ~ out or round distribuir. ~ out (colloq: faint) perder os sentidos, desmaiar. ~ over (disregard, overlook) passar por cima de. ~ up (colloq: forgo) deixar perder

passable /'pɑ:sbl/ a passável; (road) transitável

passage /'pæsɪdʒ/ n passagem f; (voyage) travessia f; (corridor) corredor m, passagem f

passenger /'pæsɪndʒə(r)/ n passageiro m

passer-by /pɑ:sə'baɪ/ n (pl passers-by) transeunte mf

passion /'pæʃn/ n paixão f. ~ate a apaixonado, exaltado

passive /'pæsɪv/ a passivo. ~ness n passividade f

Passover /'pɑ:səʊvə(r)/ n Páscoa f dos judeus

passport /'pɑ:spɔ:t/ n passaporte m

password /'pɑ:swɜ:d/ n senha f

past /pɑ:st/ a passado; (former) antigo □ n passado □ prep para além de; (in time) mais de; (in front of) diante de □ adv em frente. be ~ it já não ser capaz. it's five ~ eleven são onze e cinco. these ~ months estes últimos meses

pasta /'pæstə/ n prato m de massa(s)

paste /peɪst/ n cola f; (culin) massa(s) f (pl); (dough) massa f; (jewellery) strass m □ vt colar

pastel /ˈpæstl/ n pastel m □ a pastel invar

pasteurize /ˈpæstʃəraɪz/ vt pasteurizar

pastille /ˈpæstɪl/ n pastilha f

pastime /ˈpɑːstaɪm/ n passatempo m

pastoral /ˈpɑːstərəl/ a & n pastoral (f)

pastry /ˈpeɪstrɪ/ n massa f (de pastelaria); (tart) pastel m

pasture /ˈpɑːstʃə(r)/ n pastagem f

pasty[1] /ˈpæstɪ/ n empadinha f

pasty[2] /ˈpeɪstɪ/ a pastoso

pat /pæt/ vt (pt **patted**) (hit gently) dar pancadinhas em; (caress) fazer festinhas a □ n pancadinha f; (caress) festinha f □ adv a propósito; (readily) prontamente □ a preparado, pronto

patch /pætʃ/ n remendo m; (over eye) tapa-ôlho m; (spot) mancha f; (small area) pedaço m; (of vegetables) canteiro m, (P) leira f □ vt ~ **up** remendar. ~ **up a quarrel** fazer as pazes. **bad** ~ mau bocado m. **not be a** ~ **on** não chegar aos pés de. ~**work** n obra f de retalhos. ~**y** a desigual

pâté /ˈpæteɪ/ n patê m

patent /ˈpeɪtnt/ a & n patente (f) □ vt patentear. ~ **leather** verniz m, polimento m. ~**ly** adv claramente

paternal /pəˈtɜːnl/ a paternal; (relative) paterno

paternity /pəˈtɜːnətɪ/ n paternidade f

path /pɑːθ/ n (pl -s /pɑːðz/) caminho m, trilha f; (in park) aléia f; (of rocket) trajetória f, (P) trajectória f

pathetic /pəˈθetɪk/ a patético; (colloq: contemptible) desgraçado (colloq)

patholog|y /pəˈθɒlədʒɪ/ n patologia f. ~**ist** n patologista mf

pathos /ˈpeɪθɒs/ n patos m, patético m

patience /ˈpeɪʃns/ n paciência f

patient /ˈpeɪʃnt/ a paciente □ n doente mf, paciente mf. ~**ly** adv pacientemente

patio /ˈpætɪəʊ/ n (pl -os) pátio m

patriot /ˈpætrɪət/ n patriota mf. ~**ic** /-ˈɒtɪk/ a patriótico. ~**ism** /-ɪzəm/ n patriotismo m

patrol /pəˈtrəʊl/ n patrulha f □ vt/i patrulhar. ~ **car** carro m de patrulha

patron /ˈpeɪtrən/ n (of the arts etc) patrocinador m, protetor m, (P) protector m; (of charity) benfeitor m; (customer) freguês m, cliente mf. ~ **saint** padroeiro m, patrono m

patron|age /ˈpætrənɪdʒ/ n freguesia f, clientela f; (support) patrocínio m. ~**ize** vt ser cliente de; (support) patrocinar; (condescend) tratar com ares de superioridade

patter[1] /ˈpætə(r)/ n (of rain) tamborilar m, rufo m. ~ **of steps** som m leve de passos miúdos, corridinha f leve

patter[2] /ˈpætə(r)/ n (of class, profession) gíria f, jargão m; (chatter) conversa f fiada

pattern /ˈpætn/ n padrão m; (for sewing) molde m; (example) modelo m

paunch /pɔːntʃ/ n pança f

pause /pɔːz/ n pausa f □ vi pausar, fazer (uma) pausa

pav|e /peɪv/ vt pavimentar. ~**e the way** preparar o caminho (for para). ~**ing-stone** n paralelepípedo m, laje f

pavement /ˈpeɪvmənt/ n passeio m

pavilion /pəˈvɪlɪən/ n pavilhão m

paw /pɔː/ n pata f □ vt dar patadas em; (horse) escarvar; (colloq: person) pôr as patas em cima de

pawn

pawn¹ /pɔːn/ n (chess) peão m; (fig) joguete m

pawn² /pɔːn/ vt empenhar. **~-shop** casa f de penhores, prego m (colloq)

pawnbroker /'pɔːnbrəʊkə(r)/ n penhorista mf, dono m de casa de penhores, agiota mf

pay /peɪ/ vt/i (pt **paid**) pagar; (interest) render; (visit, compliment) fazer □ n pagamento m; (wages) vencimento m, ordenado m, salário m. **in the ~ of** em pagamento de. **~ attention** prestar atenção. **~ back** restituir. **~ for** pagar. **~ homage** prestar homenagem. **~ in** depositar. **~-slip** n contracheque m, (P) folha f de pagamento

payable /'peɪəbl/ a pagável

payment /'peɪmənt/ n pagamento m; (fig: reward) recompensa f

payroll /'peɪrəʊl/ n folha f de pagamentos. **be on the ~** fazer parte da folha de pagamento de uma firma

pea /piː/ n ervilha f

peace /piːs/ n paz f. **disturb the ~** perturbar a ordem pública. **~able** a pacífico

peaceful /'piːsfl/ a pacífico; (calm) calmo, sereno

peacemaker /'piːsmeɪkə(r)/ n mediador m, pacificador m

peach /piːtʃ/ n pêssego m

peacock /'piːkɒk/ n pavão m

peak /piːk/ n pico m, cume m, cimo m; (of cap) pala f; (maximum) máximo m. **~ hours** horas fpl de ponta; (electr) horas fpl de carga máxima. **~ed cap** boné m de pala

peaky /'piːki/ a com ar doentio

peal /piːl/ n (of bells) repique m; (of laughter) gargalhada f, risada f

peanut /'piːnʌt/ n amendoim m. **~s** (sl: small sum) uma bagatela f

pear /peə(r)/ n pera f

pearl /pɜːl/ n pérola f. **~y** a nacarado

peasant /'peznt/ n camponês m, aldeão m

peat /piːt/ n turfa f

pebble /'pebl/ n seixo m, calhau m

peck /pek/ vt/i bicar; (attack) dar bicadas (em) □ n bicada f; (colloq: kiss) beijo m. **~ing order** hierarquia f, ordem f de importância

peckish /'pekɪʃ/ **a be ~** (colloq) ter vontade de comer

peculiar /prˈkjuːliə(r)/ a bizarro, singular; (special) especial (to a), característico (to de). **~ity** /-ˈærətɪ/ n singularidade f; (feature) peculiaridade f

pedal /'pedl/ n pedal m □ vi (pt **pedalled**) pedalar

pedantic /prˈdæntɪk/ a pedante

peddle /'pedl/ vt vender de porta em porta; (drugs) fazer tráfico de

pedestal /'pedɪstl/ n pedestal m

pedestrian /prˈdestrɪən/ n pedestre mf, (P) peão m □ a pedestre; (fig) prosaico. **~ crossing** faixa f para pedestres, (P) passadeira f

pedigree /'pedɪgriː/ n estirpe f, linhagem f; (of animal) raça f □ a de raça

pedlar /'pedlə(r)/ n vendedor m ambulante

peek /piːk/ vi espreitar □ n espreitadela f

peel /piːl/ n casca f □ vt descascar □ vi (skin) pelar; (paint) escamar-se, descascar; (wallpaper) descolar-se. **~ings** npl cascas fpl

peep /piːp/ vi espreitar □ n espreitadela f. **~-hole** n vigia f; (in door) olho m mágico

peer¹ /pɪə(r)/ vi **~ at/into** (searchingly) perscrutar; (with difficulty) esforçar-se por ver

peer² /pɪə(r)/ n (equal, noble) par m. **~age** n pariato m

peeved /piːvd/ a (sl) irritado, chateado (sl)

peevish /ˈpiːvɪʃ/ a irritável

peg /peg/ n cavilha f; (for washing) pregador m de roupa, (P) mola f; (for coats etc) cabide m; (for tent) estaca f □ vt (pt pegged) prender com estacas. **off the ~** prêt-à-porter

pejorative /prɪˈdʒɒrətɪv/ a pejorativo

pelican /ˈpelɪkən/ n pelicano m. **~ crossing** passagem f com sinais manobrados pelos pedestres

pellet /ˈpelɪt/ n bolinha f; (for gun) grão m de chumbo

pelt[1] /pelt/ n pele f

pelt[2] /pelt/ vt bombardear (with com) □ vi chover a cântaros; (run fast) correr em disparada

pelvis /ˈpelvɪs/ n (anat) pélvis m, bacia f

pen[1] /pen/ n (enclosure) cercado m. **play-~** n cercado m, (P) parque m □ vt (pt penned) encurralar

pen[2] /pen/ n caneta f □ vt (pt penned) escrever. **~-friend** n correspondente mf. **~-name** n pseudónimo m, (P) pseudónimo m

penal /ˈpiːnl/ a penal. **~ize** vt impôr uma penalidade a; (sport) penalizar

penalty /ˈpenltɪ/ n pena f; (fine) multa f; (sport) penalidade f. **~ kick** pênalti m, (P) grande penalidade f

penance /ˈpenəns/ n penitência f

pence /pens/ see **penny**

pencil /ˈpensl/ n lápis m □ vt (pt pencilled) escrever ou desenhar a lápis. **~-sharpener** n apontador m, (P) apara-lápis m invar

pendant /ˈpendənt/ n berloque m

pending /ˈpendɪŋ/ a pendente □ prep (during) durante; (until) até

pendulum /ˈpendjʊləm/ n pêndulo m

penetrat|e /ˈpenɪtreɪt/ vt/i penetrar (em). **~ing** a penetrante. **~ion** /-ˈtreɪʃn/ n penetração f

penguin /ˈpeŋgwɪn/ n pingüim m, (P) pinguim m

penicillin /penɪˈsɪlɪn/ n penicilina f

peninsula /pəˈnɪnsjʊlə/ n península f

penis /ˈpiːnɪs/ n pênis m, (P) pénis m

peniten|t /ˈpenɪtənt/ a & n penitente (mf). **~ce** /-əns/ contrição f, penitência f

penitentiary /penɪˈtenʃərɪ/ n (Amer) penitenciária f, cadeia f

penknife /ˈpennaɪf/ n (pl -knives) canivete m

penniless /ˈpenɪlɪs/ a sem vintém, sem um tostão

penny /ˈpenɪ/ n (pl pennies or pence) pêni m, (P) péni m; (fig) centavo m, vintém m

pension /ˈpenʃn/ n pensão f; (in retirement) aposentadoria f, (P) reforma f □ vt **~ off** reformar, aposentar. **~er** n (old-age) **~er** reformado m

pensive /ˈpensɪv/ a pensativo

Pentecost /ˈpentɪkɒst/ n Pentecostes m

penthouse /ˈpenthaʊs/ n cobertura f, (P) apartamento de luxo (no último andar)

pent-up /ˈpentʌp/ a reprimido

penultimate /penˈʌltɪmət/ a penúltimo

people /ˈpiːpl/ npl pessoas fpl □ n gente f, povo m □ vt povoar. **the Portuguese ~** os portugueses mpl. **~ say** dizem, diz-se

pep /pep/ n vigor m □ vt **~ up** animar. **~ talk** discurso m de encorajamento

pepper /ˈpepə(r)/ n pimenta f; (vegetable) pimentão m, (P) pimento m □ vt apimentar. **~y** a apimentado, picante

peppermint /ˈpepəmɪnt/ n hortelã-pimenta *f*; (*sweet*) bala *f*, (P) pastilha *f* de hortelã-pimenta

per /pɜː(r)/ *prep* por. **~ annum** por ano. **~ cent** por cento. **~ kilo**/*etc* o quilo/*etc*

perceive /pə'siːv/ *vt* perceber; (*notice*) aperceber-se de

percentage /pə'sentɪdʒ/ *n* percentagem *f*

perceptible /pə'septəbl/ *a* perceptível

percept|ion /pə'sepʃn/ *n* percepção *f*. **~ive** /-tɪv/ *a* perceptivo, penetrante, perspicaz

perch[1] /pɜːtʃ/ *n* poleiro *m* □ *vi* empoleirar-se, pousar

perch[2] /pɜːtʃ/ *n* (*fish*) perca *f*

percolat|e /'pɜːkəleɪt/ *vt/i* filtrar (-se), passar. **~or** *n* máquina *f* de café com filtro, cafeteira *f*

percussion /pə'kʌʃn/ *n* percussão *f*

peremptory /pə'remptərɪ/ *a* peremptório, decisivo

perennial /pə'renɪəl/ *a* perene; (*plant*) perene

perfect[1] /'pɜːfɪkt/ *a* perfeito. **~ly** *adv* perfeitamente

perfect[2] /pə'fekt/ *vt* aperfeiçoar. **~ion** /-ʃn/ *n* perfeição *f*. **~ionist** *n* perfeccionista *mf*

perforat|e /'pɜːfəreɪt/ *vt* perfurar. **~ion** /-'reɪʃn/ *n* perfuração *f*; (*line of holes*) pontilhado *m*, picotado *m*

perform /pə'fɔːm/ *vt* (*a task*; *mus*) executar; (*a function*; *theat*) desempenhar □ *vi* representar; (*function*) funcionar. **~ance** *n* (*of task*; *mus*) execução *f*; (*of function*; *theat*) desempenho *m*; (*of car*) performance *f*, comportamento *m*, rendimento *m*; (*colloq*: *fuss*) drama *m*, cena *f*. **~er** *n* artista *mf*

perfume /'pɜːfjuːm/ *n* perfume *m*

perfunctory /pə'fʌŋktərɪ/ *a* superficial, negligente

perhaps /pə'hæps/ *adv* talvez

peril /'perəl/ *n* perigo *m*. **~ous** *a* perigoso

perimeter /pə'rɪmɪtə(r)/ *n* perímetro *m*

period /'pɪərɪəd/ *n* período *m*, época *f*; (*era*) época *f*; (*lesson*) hora *f* de aula, período *m* letivo, (P) lectivo; (*med*) período *m*; (*full stop*) ponto (final) *m* □ *a* (*of novel*) de costumes; (*of furniture*) de estilo. **~ic** /-'ɒdɪk/ *a* periódico. **~ical** /-'ɒdɪkl/ *n* periódico *m*. **~ically** /-'ɒdɪklɪ/ *adv* periodicamente

peripher|y /pə'rɪfərɪ/ *n* periferia *f*. **~al** *a* periférico; (*fig*) marginal, à margem

perish /'perɪʃ/ *vi* morrer, perecer; (*rot*) estragar-se, deteriorar-se. **~able** *a* (*of goods*) deteriorável

perjur|e /'pɜːdʒə(r)/ *vpr* **~e o.s.** jurar falso, perjurar. **~y** *n* perjúrio *m*

perk[1] /pɜːk/ *vt/i* **~ up** (*colloq*) arrebitar(-se). **~y** *a* (*colloq*) vivo, animado

perk[2] /pɜːk/ *n* (*colloq*) regalia *f*, extra *m*

perm /pɜːm/ *n* permanente *f* □ *vt* **have one's hair ~ed** fazer uma permanente

permanen|t /'pɜːmənənt/ *a* permanente. **~ce** *n* permanência *f*. **~tly** *adv* permanentemente, a título permanente

permeable /'pɜːmɪəbl/ *a* permeável

permeate /'pɜːmɪeɪt/ *vt/i* permear, penetrar

permissible /pə'mɪsəbl/ *a* permissível, admissível

permission /pə'mɪʃn/ *n* permissão *f*, licença *f*

permissive /pə'mɪsɪv/ *a* permissivo. **~ society** sociedade *f* permissiva. **~ness** *n* permissividade *f*

permit[1] /pə'mɪt/ *vt* (*pt* **permitted**) permitir, consentir (**sb to** a alguém que)

permit 480 petrify

permit[2] /'pɜːmɪt/ n licença f; (*pass*) passe m

permutation /pɜːmjuːˈteɪʃn/ n permutação f

pernicious /pəˈnɪʃəs/ a pernicioso, prejudicial

perpendicular /pɜːpənˈdɪkjʊlə(r)/ a & n perpendicular (f)

perpetrat|e /'pɜːpɪtreɪt/ vt perpetrar. **~or** n autor m

perpetual /pəˈpetʃʊəl/ a perpétuo

perpetuate /pəˈpetʃʊeɪt/ vt perpetuar

perplex /pəˈpleks/ vt deixar perplexo. **~ed** a perplexo. **~ing** a confuso. **~ity** n perplexidade f

persecut|e /'pɜːsɪkjuːt/ vt perseguir. **~ion** n /-ˈkjuːʃn/ n perseguição f

persever|e /pɜːsɪˈvɪə(r)/ vi perseverar. **~ance** n perseverança f

Persian /'pɜːʃn/ a & n (*lang*) persa (m)

persist /pəˈsɪst/ vi persistir (**in** doing em fazer). **~ence** n persistência f. **~ent** a persistente; (*obstinate*) teimoso; (*continual*) contínuo, constante. **~ently** adv persistentemente

person /'pɜːsn/ n pessoa f. **in ~** em pessoa

personal /'pɜːsənl/ a pessoal; (*secretary*) particular. **~ stereo** estereo m pessoal. **~ly** adv pessoalmente

personality /pɜːsəˈnælətɪ/ n personalidade f; (*on TV*) vedete f

personify /pəˈsɒnɪfaɪ/ vt personificar

personnel /pɜːsəˈnel/ n pessoal m

perspective /pəˈspektɪv/ n perspectiva f

perspir|e /pəˈspaɪə(r)/ vi transpirar. **~ation** /-əˈreɪʃn/ n transpiração f

persua|de /pəˈsweɪd/ vt persuadir (**to** a). **~sion** /-ˈsweɪʒn/ n persuasão f; (*belief*) crença f, convic-

ção f. **~sive** /-ˈsweɪsɪv/ a persuasivo

pert /pɜːt/ a (*saucy*) atrevido, descarado; (*lively*) vivo

pertain /pəˈteɪn/ vi **to** pertencer a; (*be relevant*) ser pertinente a, (*P*) ser próprio de

pertinent /'pɜːtɪnənt/ a pertinente

perturb /pəˈtɜːb/ vt perturbar, transtornar

Peru /pəˈruː/ n Peru m. **~vian** a & n peruano (m), (*P*) peruviano (m)

peruse /pəˈruːz/ vt ler com atenção

perva|de /pəˈveɪd/ vt espalhar-se por, invadir. **~sive** a penetrante

pervers|e /pəˈvɜːs/ a que insiste no erro; (*wicked*) perverso; (*wayward*) caprichoso. **~ity** n obstinação f; (*wickedness*) perversidade f; (*waywardness*) capricho m, birra f

pervert[1] /pəˈvɜːt/ vt perverter. **~sion** n perversão f

pervert[2] /'pɜːvɜːt/ n pervertido m

peseta /pəˈseɪtə/ n peseta f

pessimis|t /'pesɪmɪst/ n pessimista mf. **~m** /-zəm/ n pessimismo m. **~tic** /-ˈmɪstɪk/ a pessimista

pest /pest/ n inseto m, (*P*) insecto m nocivo; (*animal*) animal m daninho; (*person*) peste f

pester /'pestə(r)/ vt incomodar (*colloq*)

pesticide /'pestɪsaɪd/ n pesticida m

pet /pet/ n animal m de estimação; (*favourite*) preferido m, querido m □ a (*rabbit etc*) de estimação □ vt (*pt petted*) acariciar. **~ name** nome m usado em família

petal /'petl/ n pétala f

peter /'piːtə(r)/ vi **out** extinguir-se, acabar pouco a pouco, morrer (*fig*)

petition /pɪˈtɪʃn/ n petição f □ vt requerer

petrify /'petrɪfaɪ/ vt petrificar

petrol /'petrəl/ n gasolina f. ~ **pump** bomba f de gasolina. ~ **station** posto m de gasolina. ~ **tank** tanque m de gasolina

petroleum /pɪ'trəʊlɪəm/ n petróleo m

petticoat /'petɪkəʊt/ n combinação f, anágua f

petty /'petɪ/ a (-ier, -iest) pequeno, insignificante; (mean) mesquinho. ~ **cash** fundo m para pequenas despesas, caixa f pequena

petulan|t /'petjʊlənt/ a irritável. ~**ce** n irritabilidade f

pew /pju:/ n banco (de igreja) m

pewter /'pju:tə(r)/ n estanho m

phallic /'fælɪk/ a fálico

phantom /'fæntəm/ n fantasma m

pharmaceutical /fa:mə'sju:tɪkl/ a farmacêutico

pharmac|y /'fa:məsɪ/ n farmácia f. ~**ist** n farmacêutico m

phase /feɪz/ n fase f □ vt ~ **in/out** introduzir/retirar progressivamente

PhD abbr of **Doctor of Philosophy** n doutorado m

pheasant /'feznt/ n faisão m

phenomen|on /fɪ'nɒmɪnən/ n (pl -ena) fenômeno m, (P) fenómeno m. ~**al** a fenomenal

philanthrop|ist /fɪ'lænθrəpɪst/ n filantropo m. ~**ic** /-ən'θrɒpɪk/ a filantrópico

Philippines /'fɪlɪpi:nz/ npl the ~ as Filipinas fpl

philistine /'fɪlɪstaɪn/ n filisteu m

philosoph|y /fɪ'lɒsəfɪ/ n filosofia f. ~**er** n filósofo m. ~**ical** /-ə'sɒfɪkl/ a filosófico

phlegm /flem/ n (med) catarro m, fleuma f

phobia /'fəʊbɪə/ n fobia f

phone /fəʊn/ n (colloq) telefone m □ vt/i (colloq) telefonar (para). **on the ~** no telefone. ~ **back** voltar a telefonar, ligar de volta. ~ **book** lista f telefônica, (P) telefónica. ~ **box** cabine f telefônica, (P) telefónica. ~ **call** chamada f, telefonema m. ~**-in** n programa m de rádio ou tv com participação dos ouvintes

phonecard /'fəʊnka:d/ n cartão m para uso em telefone público

phonetic /fə'netɪk/ a fonético. ~**s** n fonética f

phoney /'fəʊnɪ/ a (-ier, -iest) (sl) falso, fingido □ n (sl: person) fingido m; (sl: thing) falso m, (P) falsificação f

phosphate /'fɒsfeɪt/ n fosfato m

phosphorus /'fɒsfərəs/ n fósforo m

photo /'fəʊtəʊ/ n (pl -os) (colloq) retrato m, foto f

photocop|y /'fəʊtəʊkɒpɪ/ n fotocópia f □ vt fotocopiar. ~**ier** n fotocopiadora f

photogenic /fəʊtəʊ'dʒenɪk/ a fotogênico, (P) fotogénico

photograph /'fəʊtəgra:f/ n fotografia f □ vt fotografar. ~**er** /fə'tɒgrəfə(r)/ n fotógrafo m. ~**ic** /-'græfɪk/ a fotográfico. ~**y** /fə'tɒgrəfɪ/ n fotografia f

phrase /freɪz/ n expressão f, frase f; (gram) locução f, frase f elíptica □ vt exprimir. ~**-book** n livro m de expressões idiomáticas

physical /'fɪzɪkl/ a físico

physician /fɪ'zɪʃn/ n médico m

physicist /'fɪzɪsɪst/ n físico m

physics /'fɪzɪks/ n física f

physiology /fɪzɪ'ɒlədʒɪ/ n fisiologia f

physiotherap|y /fɪzɪəʊ'θerəpɪ/ n fisioterapia f. ~**ist** n fisioterapeuta mf

physique /fɪ'zi:k/ n físico m

pian|o /pɪ'ænəʊ/ n (pl -os) piano m. ~**ist** /'pɪənɪst/ n pianista m

pick[1] /pɪk/ n (tool) picareta f

pick[2] /pɪk/ vt escolher; (flowers, fruit etc) colher; (lock) forçar; (teeth) palitar □ n escolha f; (best) o/a melhor f. ~ **a quarrel with** puxar uma briga com. ~ **holes in an argument** descobrir os pontos fracos dum argumento. **~ sb's pocket** bater a carteira de alg. **~ off** tirar, arrancar. **~ on** implicar com. **~ out** escolher; (*identify*) identificar, reconhecer. **~ up** *vt* apanhar; (*speed*) ganhar. **take one's ~** escolher livremente

pickaxe /'pɪkæks/ *n* picareta *f*

picket /'pɪkɪt/ *n* piquete *m*; (*single striker*) grevista *mf* de piquete □ *vt* (*pt* **picketed**) colocar um piquete em □ *vi* fazer piquete

pickings /'pɪkɪŋz/ *npl* restos *mpl*

pickle /'pɪkl/ *n* vinagre *m*. **~s** picles *mpl*, (*P*) pickles *mpl* □ *vt* conservar em vinagre. **in a ~** (*colloq*) numa encrenca (*colloq*)

pickpocket /'pɪkpɒkɪt/ *n* batedor *m* de carteiras, (*P*) carteirista *m*

picnic /'pɪknɪk/ *n* piquenique *m* □ *vi* (*pt* **picnicked**) piquenicar, (*P*) fazer um piquenique

pictorial /pɪk'tɔ:rɪəl/ *a* ilustrado

picture /'pɪktʃə(r)/ *n* imagem *f*; (*illustration*) estampa *f*, ilustração *f*; (*painting*) quadro *m*, pintura *f*; (*photo*) fotografia *f*, retrato *m*; (*drawing*) desenho *m*; (*fig*) descrição *f*, quadro *m* □ *vt* imaginar; (*describe*) pintar, descrever. **the ~s** o cinema

picturesque /pɪktʃə'resk/ *a* pitoresco

pidgin /'pɪdʒɪn/ *a* **~ English** inglês *m* estropiado

pie /paɪ/ *n* torta *f*, (*P*) tarte *f*; (*of meat*) empada *f*

piece /piːs/ *n* pedaço *m*, bocado *m*; (*of machine, in game*) peça *f*; (*of currency*) moeda *f* □ *vt* **~ together** juntar, montar. **a ~ of advice/furniture/***etc* um conselho/um móvel/*etc*. **~-work** *n* trabalho *m* por, (*P*) à peça por, (*P*) à tarefa. **take to ~s** desmontar

piecemeal /'piːsmiːl/ *a* aos poucos, pouco a pouco

pier /pɪə(r)/ *n* molhe *m*

pierce /pɪəs/ *vt* furar, penetrar. **~ing** *a* penetrante; (*of scream, pain*) lancinante

piety /'paɪətɪ/ *n* piedade *f*, devoção *f*

pig /pɪg/ *n* porco *m*. **~-headed** *a* cabeçudo, teimoso

pigeon /'pɪdʒɪn/ *n* pombo *m*. **~-hole** *n* escaninho *m*

piggy /'pɪgɪ/ *a* como um porco. **~-back** *adv* nas costas. **~ bank** cofre *m* de criança

pigment /'pɪgmənt/ *n* pigmento *m*. **~ation** /-'teɪʃn/ *n* pigmentação *f*

pigsty /'pɪgstaɪ/ *n* pocilga *f*, chiqueiro *m*

pigtail /'pɪgteɪl/ *n* trança *f*

pike /paɪk/ *n* (*pl invar*) (*fish*) lúcio *m*

pilchard /'pɪltʃəd/ *n* peixe *m* pequeno da família do arenque, sardinha *f* européia

pile /paɪl/ *n* pilha *f*; (*of carpet*) pêlo *m* □ *vt/i* amontoar(-se), empilhar(-se) (**into**). **a ~ of** (*colloq*) um monte de (*colloq*). **~ up** acumular(-se). **~-up** *n* choque *m* em cadeia

piles /paɪlz/ *npl* hemorróidas *fpl*

pilfer /'pɪlfə(r)/ *vt* furtar. **~age** *n* furto *m* (de coisas pequenas ou em pequenas quantidades)

pilgrim /'pɪlgrɪm/ *n* peregrino *m*, romeiro *m*. **~age** *n* peregrinação *f*, romaria *f*

pill /pɪl/ *n* pílula *f*, comprimido *m*

pillage /'pɪlɪdʒ/ *n* pilhagem *f*, saque *m* □ *vt* pilhar, saquear

pillar /'pɪlə(r)/ *n* pilar *m*. **~-box** *n* marco *m* do correio

pillion /'pɪlɪən/ *n* assento *m* traseiro de motorizada. **ride ~** ir no assento de trás

pillow /'pɪləʊ/ *n* travesseiro *m*

pillowcase /'pɪləʊkeɪs/ *n* fronha *f*

pilot /'paɪlət/ *n* piloto *m* □ *vt* (*pt* **piloted**) pilotar. **~-light** *n* piloto *m*; (*electr*) lâmpada *f* testemunho; (*gas*) piloto *m*

pimento /pɪˈmentəʊ/ n (pl -os) pimentão m vermelho

pimple /ˈpɪmpl/ n borbulha f, espinha f

pin /pɪn/ n alfinete m; (techn) cavilha f □ vt (pt **pinned**) pregar or prender com alfinete(s); (hold down) prender, segurar. Nas ~s and needles estar com cãibra. ~ sb down (fig) obrigar alg a definir-se, apertar alg (fig). ~point vt localizar com precisão. ~-stripe a de listras finas. ~up pregar. ~-up n (colloq) pin-up f

pinafore /ˈpɪnəfɔː(r)/ n avental m. ~ dress veste f

pincers /ˈpɪnsəz/ npl (tool) torquês f, (P) alicate m; (med) pinça f; (zool) pinça(s) f(pl), tenaz(es) f(pl)

pinch /pɪntʃ/ vt apertar; (sl: steal) surripiar (colloq) □ n aperto m; (tweak) beliscão m; (small amount) pitada f. at a ~ em caso de necessidade

pine[1] /paɪn/ n (tree) pinheiro m; (wood) pinho m

pine[2] /paɪn/ vi ~ away definhar, consumir-se. ~ for suspirar por

pineapple /ˈpaɪnæpl/ n abacaxi m, (P) ananás m

ping-pong /ˈpɪŋpɒŋ/ n pingue-pongue m

pink /pɪŋk/ a & n rosa (m)

pinnacle /ˈpɪnəkl/ n pináculo m

pint /paɪnt/ n quartilho m (= 0,57l; Amer = 0,47l)

pioneer /paɪəˈnɪə(r)/ n pioneiro m □ vt ser o pioneiro em, preparar o caminho para

pious /ˈpaɪəs/ a piedoso, devoto

pip /pɪp/ n (seed) pevide f

pipe /paɪp/ n cano m, tubo m; (of smoker) cachimbo m □ vt encanar, canalizar. ~ down calar a boca

pipeline /ˈpaɪplaɪn/ n (for oil) oleoduto m; (for gas) gaseoduto

m, (P) gasoduto m. in the ~ (fig) encaminhado

piping /ˈpaɪpɪŋ/ n tubagem f. ~ hot muito quente

piquant /ˈpiːkənt/ a picante

pirate /ˈpaɪərət/ n pirata m. ~cy n pirataria f

Pisces /ˈpaɪsiːz/ n (astr) Peixe m, (P) Pisces m

pistol /ˈpɪstl/ n pistola f

piston /ˈpɪstən/ n êmbolo m, pistão m

pit /pɪt/ n (hole) cova f, fosso m; (mine) poço m; (quarry) pedreira f □ vt (pt **pitted**) picar, esburacar; (fig) opor. ~ o.s. against (struggle) medir-se com

pitch[1] /pɪtʃ/ n breu m. ~-black a escuro como breu

pitch[2] /pɪtʃ/ vt (throw) lançar; (tent) armar □ vi cair □ n (slope) declive m; (of sound) som m; (of voice) altura f; (sport) campo m

pitchfork /ˈpɪtʃfɔːk/ n forcado m

pitfall /ˈpɪtfɔːl/ n (fig) cilada f, perigo m inesperado

pith /pɪθ/ n (of orange) parte f branca da casca, mesocarpo m; (fig: essential part) cerne m, âmago m

pithy /ˈpɪθɪ/ a (-ier, -iest) preciso, conciso

pitiful /ˈpɪtɪfl/ a lastimoso; (contemptible) miserável. ~less a impiedoso

pittance /ˈpɪtns/ n salário m miserável, miséria f

pity /ˈpɪtɪ/ n dó m, pena f, piedade f □ vt compadecer-se de. it's a ~ é uma pena. take ~ on ter pena de. what a ~! que pena!

pivot /ˈpɪvət/ n eixo m □ vt (pt **pivoted**) girar em torno de

placard /ˈplækɑːd/ n (poster) cartaz m

placate /pləˈkeɪt/ vt apaziguar, aplacar

place /pleɪs/ n lugar m, sítio m; (house) casa f; (seat, rank etc) lugar *m* □ *vt* colocar, pôr. **~ an order** fazer uma encomenda. **at/to my ~** em a *or* na minha casa. **~-mat** *n* pano *m* de mesa individual, (*P*) napperon *m* à americana

placid /ˈplæsɪd/ *a* plácido

plagiar|ize /ˈpleɪdʒəraɪz/ *vt* plagiar. **~ism** *n* plágio *m*

plague /pleɪg/ *n* peste *f*; (*of insects*) praga *f* □ *vt* atormentar, atazanar

plaice /pleɪs/ *n* (*pl invar*) solha *f*

plain /pleɪn/ *a* (**-er, -est**) claro; (*candid*) franco; (*simple*) simples; (*not pretty*) sem beleza; (*not patterned*) liso □ *adv* com franqueza □ *n* planície *f*. **in ~ clothes** à paisana. **~ly** *adv* claramente; (*candidly*) francamente

plaintiff /ˈpleɪntɪf/ *n* queixoso

plaintive /ˈpleɪntɪv/ *a* queixoso

plait /plæt/ *vt* entrançar □ *n* trança *f*

plan /plæn/ *n* plano *m*, projeto *m*, (*P*) projecto *m*, (*of a house, city etc*) plano *m*, planta *f* □ *vt* (*pt planned*) planear, planejar □ *vi* fazer planos. **~ to do** ter a intenção de fazer

plane[1] /pleɪn/ *n* (*level*) plano *m*; (*aeroplane*) avião *m* □ *a* plano

plane[2] /pleɪn/ *n* (*tool*) plaina *f* □ *vt* aplainar

planet /ˈplænɪt/ *n* planeta *m*

plank /plæŋk/ *n* prancha *f*

planning /ˈplænɪŋ/ *n* planeamento *m*, planejamento *m*. **~ permission** permissão *f* para construir

plant /plɑːnt/ *n* planta *f*; (*techn*) aparelhagem *f*; (*factory*) fábrica *f* □ *vt* plantar. **~ a bomb** colocar uma bomba. **~ation** /-ˈteɪʃn/ *n* plantação *f*

plaque /plɑːk/ *n* placa *f*; (*on teeth*) tártaro *m*, pedra *f*

plaster /ˈplɑːstə(r)/ *n* reboco *m*; (*adhesive*) esparadrapo *m*, bandaid *m* □ *vt* rebocar; (*cover*) cobrir

(*with* com, de). **in ~** engessado. **~ of Paris** gesso *m*. **~er** *n* rebocador *m*, caiador *m*

plastic /ˈplæstɪk/ *a* plástico □ *n* plástica *f*. **~ surgery** cirurgia *f* plástica

plate /pleɪt/ *n* prato *m*; (*in book*) gravura *f* □ *vt* revestir de metal

plateau /ˈplætəʊ/ *n* (*pl* **-eaux** /-əʊz/) planalto *m*, platô *m*

platform /ˈplætfɔːm/ *n* estrado *m*; (*for speaking*) tribuna *f*; (*rail*) plataforma *f*, cais *m*; (*fig*) programa *m* de partido político. **~ ticket** bilhete *m* de gare

platinum /ˈplætɪnəm/ *n* platina *f*

platitude /ˈplætɪtjuːd/ *n* banalidade *f*, lugar-comum *m*

platonic /pləˈtɒnɪk/ *a* platônico, (*P*) platónico

plausible /ˈplɔːzəbl/ *a* plausível; (*person*) convincente

play /pleɪ/ *vt/i* (*for amusement*) brincar; (*instrument*) tocar; (*cards, game*) jogar; (*opponent*) jogar contra; (*match*) disputar □ *n* jogo *m*; (*theatre*) peça *f*, (*movement*) folga *f*, margem *f*. **~ down** minimizar. **~ on** (*take advantage of*) aproveitar-se de. **~ safe** jogar pelo seguro. **~ up** (*colloq*) dar problemas (a). **~-group** *n* jardim *m* de infância, (*P*) jardim *m* infantil. **~-pen** *n* cercado *m* para crianças

playboy /ˈpleɪbɔɪ/ *n* play-boy *m*

player /ˈpleɪə(r)/ *n* jogador *m*; (*theat*) artista *mf*; (*mus*) artista *mf*, executante *mf*, instrumentista *mf*

playful /ˈpleɪfl/ *a* brincalhão *m*

playground /ˈpleɪɡraʊnd/ *n* pátio *m* de recreio

playing /ˈpleɪŋ/ *n* atuação *f*, (*P*) actuação *f*. **~-card** *n* carta *f* de jogar. **~-field** *n* campo *m* de jogos

playwright /ˈpleɪraɪt/ *n* dramaturgo *m*

plc *abbr* (*of public limited company*) SARL

plea /pli:/ *n* súplica *f*; (*reason*) pretexto *m*, desculpa *f*. (*jur*) alegação *f* da defesa

plead /pli:d/ *vt/i* pleitear; (*as excuse*) alegar. ~ **guilty** confessar-se culpado. ~ **with** implorar a

pleasant /'pleznt/ *a* agradável

please /pli:z/ *vt/i* agradar (a), dar prazer (a) □ *adv* por favor, (*P*) se faz favor. **they.** ~ **themselves, they do as they** ~ e eles fazem como bem entendem. ~**ed** *a* contente, satisfeito (**with** com). ~**ing** *a* agradável

pleasur|e /'pleʒə(r)/ *n* prazer *m*. ~**able** *a* agradável

pleat /pli:t/ *n* prega *f* □ *vt* preguear

pledge /pledʒ/ *n* penhor *m*, garantia *f*; (*fig*) promessa *f* □ *vt* prometer; (*pawn*) empenhar

plentiful /'plentifl/ *a* abundante

plenty /'plenti/ *n* abundância *f*, fartura *f*. ~ (**of**) muito (de); (*enough*) bastante (de)

pliable /'plaɪəbl/ *a* flexível

pliers /'plaɪəz/ *npl* alicate *m*

plight /plaɪt/ *n* triste situação *f*

plimsoll /'plɪmsəl/ *n* alpargata *f*, ténis *m*, (*P*) ténis *m*

plinth /plɪnθ/ *n* plinto *m*

plod /plɒd/ *vi* (*pt* **plodded**) caminhar lentamente; (*work*) trabalhar, marrar (*sl*). ~**der** *n* trabalhador *m* lento mas perseverante. ~**ding** *a* lento

plonk /plɒŋk/ *n* (*sl*) vinho *m* ordinário, (*P*) carrascão *m*

plot /plɒt/ *n* complô *m*, conspiração *f*; (*of novel etc*) trama *f*; (*of land*) lote *m* □ *vt/i* (*pt* **plotted**) conspirar; (*mark out*) traçar

plough /plaʊ/ *n* arado *m* □ *vt/i* arar. ~ **back** reinvestir. ~ **into** colidir. ~ **through** abrir caminho por

ploy /plɔɪ/ *n* (*colloq*) estratagema *m*

pluck /plʌk/ *vt* apanhar; (*bird*) depenar; (*eyebrows*) depilar; (*mus*) tanger □ *n* coragem *f*. ~ **up courage** ganhar coragem. ~**y** *a* corajoso

plug /plʌg/ *n* tampão *m*; (*electr*) tomada *f*, (*P*) ficha *f* □ *vt* (*pt* **plugged**) tapar com tampão; (*colloq: publicize*) fazer grande propaganda de □ *vi* ~ **away** (*colloq*) trabalhar com afinco. ~ **in** (*electr*) ligar. ~**hole** *n* buraco *m* do cano

plum /plʌm/ *n* ameixa *f*

plumb /plʌm/ *adv* exatamente, (*P*) exactamente, mesmo □ *vt* sondar. ~**line** *n* fio *m* de prumo

plumb|er /'plʌmə(r)/ *n* bombeiro *m*, encanador *m*, (*P*) canalizador *m*. ~**ing** *n* encanamento *m*, (*P*) canalização *f*

plummet /'plʌmɪt/ *vi* (*pt* **plummeted**) despencar

plump /plʌmp/ *a* (**-er, -est**) rechonchudo, roliço □ *vi* ~ **for** optar por. ~**ness** *n* gordura *f*

plunder /'plʌndə(r)/ *vt* pilhar, saquear □ *n* pilhagem *f*, saque *m*; (*goods*) despojo *m*

plunge /plʌndʒ/ *vt/i* mergulhar, atirar(-se), afundar(-se) □ *n* mergulho *m*. **take the** ~ (*fig*) decidir-se, dar o salto (*fig*)

plunger /'plʌndʒə(r)/ *n* (*of pump*) êmbolo *m*, pistão *m*; (*for sink etc*) desentupidor *m*

pluperfect /plu:'pɜ:fɪkt/ *n* mais-que-perfeito *m*

plural /'plʊərəl/ *a* plural; (*noun*) no plural □ *n* plural *m*

plus /plʌs/ *prep* mais □ *n* o positivo □ *n* sinal +; (*fig*) qualidade *f* positiva

plush /plʌʃ/ *n* pelúcia *f* □ *a* de pelúcia; (*colloq*) de luxo

ply /plaɪ/ *vt* (*tool*) manejar; (*trade*) exercer □ *vi* (*ship, bus*) fazer

carreira entre dois lugares. ~
sb with drink encher alguém de
bebidas

plywood /'plaɪwʊd/ n madeira f
compensada

p.m. /pi:'em/ adv da tarde, da
noite

pneumatic /nju:'mætɪk/ a pneu-
mático. ~ **drill** broca f pneu-
mática

pneumonia /nju:'məʊnɪə/ n pneumonia f

PO abbr see **Post Office**

poach /pəʊtʃ/ vt/i (steal) caçar/
pescar em propriedade alheia;
(culin) fazer pochê, (P) escalfar.
~**ed eggs** ovos mpl pochês, (P)
ovos mpl escalfados

pocket /'pɒkɪt/ n bolso m, algibeira f □ a de algibeira □
vt meter no bolso. ~**-book** n
(notebook) livro m de aponta-
mentos; (Amer: handbag) carteira f. ~**-money** n (monthly)
mesada f; (weekly) semanada f,
dinheiro m para pequenas despesas

pod /pɒd/ n vagem f

poem /'pəʊɪm/ n poema m

poet /'pəʊɪt/ n poeta m, poetisa f.
~**ic** /-'etɪk/ a poético

poetry /'pəʊɪtrɪ/ n poesia f

poignant /'pɔɪnjənt/ a pungente,
doloroso

point /pɔɪnt/ n ponto m; (tip) ponta f; (decimal point) vírgula f;
(meaning) sentido m, razão m;
(electr) tomada f. ~**s** (rail) agu-
lhas fpl □ vt/i (aim) apontar (at
para); (show) apontar, indicar
(at/to para). **on the** ~ **of** prestes a, quase a. ~**-blank** a &
adv à queima-roupa; (fig)
categórico. ~ **of view** ponto m
de vista. ~ **out** apontar, fazer
ver. **that is a good** ~ (remark)
é uma boa observação. **to the** ~
a propósito. **what is the** ~? de
que adianta?

pointed /'pɔɪntɪd/ a ponteagudo;
(of remark) intencional, contun-
dente

pointer /'pɔɪntə(r)/ n ponteiro m;
(colloq: hint) sugestão f

pointless /'pɔɪntlɪs/ a inútil, sem
sentido

poise /pɔɪz/ n equilíbrio m; (carriage) porte m; (fig: self-posses-
sion) presença f, segurança f.
~**d** a equilibrado; (person) seguro de si

poison /'pɔɪzn/ n veneno m, peço-
nha f □ vt envenenar. **blood-**
~**ing** n envenenamento m do
sangue. **food-**~**ing** n intoxica-
ção f alimentar. ~**ous** a venenoso

poke /pəʊk/ vt/i espetar; (with elbow) acotovelar; (fire) atiçar □ n
espetadela f; (with elbow) cotovelada f. ~ **about** esgaravatar, remexer, procurar. ~ **fun at** fazer
troça/pouco de. ~ **out** (head)
enfiar

poker[1] /'pəʊkə(r)/ n atiçador m

poker[2] /'pəʊkə(r)/ n (cards) pôquer m, (P) póquer f

poky /'pəʊkɪ/ a (-ier, -iest) acanhado, apertado

Poland /'pəʊlənd/ n Polónia f, (P)
Polónia f

polar /'pəʊlə(r)/ a polar. ~ **bear**
urso m branco

polarize /'pəʊləraɪz/ vt polarizar

pole[1] /pəʊl/ n vara f; (for flag)
mastro m; (post) poste m

pole[2] /pəʊl/ n (geog) pólo m

Pole /pəʊl/ n polaco m

polemic /pə'lemɪk/ n polémica f,
(P) polémica f

police /pə'li:s/ n polícia f □ vt po-
liciar. ~ **state** estado m policial.
~ **station** distrito m, delegacia
f, (P) esquadra f de polícia

police|man /pə'li:smən/ n (pl
-men) polícia m, (P) polícia m,
guarda m, agente m de polícia.
~**-woman** (pl -women) n polí-

cia f feminina, (P) mulher-polícia f

policy[1] /'pɒlɪsɪ/ n (plan of action) política f

policy[2] /'pɒlɪsɪ/ n (insurance) apólice f de seguro

polio /'pəʊlɪəʊ/ n polio f

polish /'pɒlɪʃ/ vt polir, dar lustro em; (shoes) engraxar; (floor) encerar □ n (for shoes) graxa f; (for floor) cera f; (for nails) esmalte m, (P) verniz m; (shine) polimento m; (fig) requinte m. ~ off acabar (rapidamente). ~ up (language) aperfeiçoar. ~ed a requintado, elegante

Polish /'pəʊlɪʃ/ a & n polonês (m), (P) polaco (m)

polite /pə'laɪt/ a polido, educado, delicado. ~ly adv delicadamente. ~ness n delicadeza f, cortesia f

political /pə'lɪtɪkl/ a político

politician /pɒlɪ'tɪʃn/ n político m

politics /'pɒlətɪks/ n política f

polka /'pɒlkə/ n polca f. ~ dots bolas fpl

poll /pəʊl/ n votação f; (survey) sondagem f, pesquisa f □ vt (votes) obter. **go to the ~s** votar, ir às urnas. **~ing-booth** n cabine f de voto

pollen /'pɒlən/ n pólen m

pollut|e /pə'luːt/ vt poluir. ~ion /-ʃn/ n poluição f

polo /'pəʊləʊ/ n pólo m. ~ **neck** gola f rolê

polyester /pɒlɪ'estə(r)/ n poliéster m

polytechnic /pɒlɪ'teknɪk/ n politécnica f

polythene /'pɒlɪθiːn/ n politeno m. ~ **bag** n saco m de plástico

pomegranate /'pɒmɪɡrænɪt/ n romã f

pomp /pɒmp/ n pompa f

pompon /'pɒmpɒn/ n pompom m

pomp|ous /'pɒmpəs/ a pomposo. ~osity /-'pɒsətɪ/ n imponência f

pond /pɒnd/ n lagoa f, lago m; (artificial) tanque m, lago m

ponder /'pɒndə(r)/ vt/i ponderar, meditar (over sobre)

pong /pɒŋ/ n (sl) pivete m □ vi (sl) cheirar mal, tresandar

pony /'pəʊnɪ/ n pônei m, (P) pónei m. ~-**tail** n rabo m de cavalo. ~-**trekking** n passeio m de pônei, (P) pónei

poodle /'puːdl/ n cão m de água, caniche m

pool[1] /puːl/ n (puddle) charco m, poça f; (for swimming) piscina f

pool[2] /puːl/ n (fund) fundo m comum; (econ, comm) pool m; (game) forma f de bilhar. ~s loteca f, (P) totobola m □ vt pôr num fundo comum

poor /pʊə(r)/ a (-er, -est) pobre; (not good) medíocre. ~ly adv mal □ a doente

pop[1] /pɒp/ n estalido m, ruído m seco □ vt/i (pt popped) dar um estalido, estalar; (of cork) saltar. ~ **in/out/off** entrar/sair/ir-se embora. ~ **up** aparecer de repente, saltar

pop[2] /pɒp/ n música f pop □ a pop invar

popcorn /'pɒpkɔːn/ n pipoca f

pope /pəʊp/ n papa m

poplar /'pɒplə(r)/ n choupo m, álamo m

poppy /'pɒpɪ/ n papoila f

popular /'pɒpjʊlə(r)/ a popular; (in fashion) em voga, na moda. **be ~ with** ser popular entre. ~**ity** /-'lærətɪ/ n popularidade f. ~**ize** vt popularizar, vulgarizar

populat|e /'pɒpjʊleɪt/ vt povoar. ~**ion** /-'leɪʃn/ n população f

populous /'pɒpjʊləs/ a populoso

porcelain /'pɔːslɪn/ n porcelana f

porch /pɔːtʃ/ n alpendre m; (Amer) varanda f

porcupine /'pɔːkjʊpaɪn/ n porco-espinho m

pore[1] /pɔː(r)/ n poro m

pore² /pɔː(r)/ vi ~ over examinar, estudar

pork /pɔːk/ n carne f de porco

pornography /pɔːˈnɒgrəfɪ/ n pornografia f. ~ic /-əˈgræfɪk/ a pornográfico

porous /ˈpɔːrəs/ a poroso

porpoise /ˈpɔːpəs/ n toninha f, (P) golfinho m

porridge /ˈpɒrɪdʒ/ n (papa f de) flocos mpl de aveia

port¹ /pɔːt/ n (harbour) porto m

port² /pɔːt/ n (wine) (vinho do) Porto m

portable /ˈpɔːtəbl/ a portátil

porter¹ /ˈpɔːtə(r)/ n (carrier) carregador m

porter² /ˈpɔːtə(r)/ n (doorkeeper) porteiro m

portfolio /pɔːtˈfəʊlɪəʊ/ n (pl -os) (case, post) pasta f; (securities) carteira f de investimentos

porthole /ˈpɔːthəʊl/ n vigia f

portion /ˈpɔːʃn/ n (share, helping) porção f; (part) parte f

portly /ˈpɔːtlɪ/ a (-ier, -iest) corpulento e digno

portrait /ˈpɔːtrɪt/ n retrato m

portray /pɔːˈtreɪ/ vt retratar, pintar; (fig) descrever. ~al n retrato m

Portugal /ˈpɔːtjʊgl/ n Portugal m. ~uese /-ˈgiːz/ a & n invar português (m)

pose /pəʊz/ vt/i (fazer) posar; (question) fazer □ n pose f, postura f. ~ as fazer-se passar por

poser /ˈpəʊzə(r)/ n quebra-cabeças m

posh /pɒʃ/ a (sl) chique invar

position /pəˈzɪʃn/ n posição f; (job) lugar m, colocação f; (state) situação f □ vt colocar

positive /ˈpɒzətɪv/ a positivo; (definite) categórico, definitivo; (colloq: downright) autêntico. **she's ~ that** ela tem certeza que. **~ly** adv positivamente; (absolutely) completamente

possess /pəˈzes/ vt possuir. **~ion** /-ʃn/ n posse f; (thing possessed) possessão f. **~or** n possuidor m

possessive /pəˈzesɪv/ a possessivo

possible /ˈpɒsəbl/ a possível. **~ility** /-ˈbɪlətɪ/ n possibilidade f

possibly /ˈpɒsəblɪ/ adv possivelmente, talvez. **if I ~ can** se me for possível. **I cannot ~ leave** estou impossibilitado de partir

post¹ /pəʊst/ n (pole) poste m □ vt (notice) afixar, pregar

post² /pəʊst/ n (station, job) posto m □ vt colocar; (appoint) colocar

post³ /pəʊst/ n (mail) correio m □ vt mandar pelo correio. **keep ~ed** manter informado. **~-code** n código m postal. **P~ Office** agência f dos correios, (P) estação f dos correios; (corporation) Departamento m dos Correios e Telégrafos, (P) Correios, Telégrafos e Telefones mpl (CTT)

post- /pəʊst/ pref pós-

postage /ˈpəʊstɪdʒ/ n porte m

postal /ˈpəʊstl/ a postal. **~ order** vale m postal

postcard /ˈpəʊstkɑːd/ n cartão-postal m, (P) (bilhete) postal m

poster /ˈpəʊstə(r)/ n cartaz m

posterity /pɒˈsterətɪ/ n posteridade f

postgraduate /pəʊstˈgrædʒʊət/ n pós-graduado m

posthumous /ˈpɒstjʊməs/ a póstumo. **~ly** adv a título póstumo

postman /ˈpəʊstmən/ n (pl -men) carteiro m

postmark /ˈpəʊstmɑːk/ n carimbo m do correio

post-mortem /pəʊstˈmɔːtəm/ n autópsia f

postpone /pəˈspəʊn/ vt adiar. **~ment** n adiamento m

postscript /ˈpəʊsskrɪpt/ n post scriptum m

postulate /ˈpɒstjʊleɪt/ vt postular

posture /'pɒstʃə(r)/ *n* postura *f*, posição *f* □ *vi* posar

post-war /pəʊstwɔ:(r)/ *a* de após-guerra

posy /'pəʊzɪ/ *n* raminho de flores

pot /pɒt/ *n* pote *m*; (*for cooking*) panela *f*; (*for plants*) vaso *m*; (*sl: marijuana*) maconha *f* □ *vt* plantar em vaso. **go to ~** (*sl: business*) arruinar, degringolar (*colloq*); (*sl: person*) estar arruinado *or* liquidado. **~-belly** *n* pança *f*, barriga *f*. **take ~ luck** aceitar o que houver. **take a ~-shot** dar um tiro de perto (**at** em); (*at random*) dar um tiro a esmo (**at** em)

potato /pə'teɪtəʊ/ *n* (*pl* **-oes**) batata *f*

poten|t /'pəʊtnt/ *a* potente, poderoso; (*drink*) forte. **~cy** *n* potência *f*

potential /pə'tenʃl/ *a & n* potencial (*m*). **~ly** *adv* potencialmente

pothol|e /'pɒthəʊl/ *n* caverna *f*, caldeirão *m*; (*in road*) buraco *m*. **~ing** *n* espeleologia *f*

potion /'pəʊʃn/ *n* poção *f*

potted /'pɒtɪd/ *a* (*of plant*) de vaso; (*preserved*) de conserva

potter[1] /'pɒtə(r)/ *n* oleiro *m*, ceramista *mf*. **~y** *n* olaria *f*, cerâmica *f*

potter[2] /'pɒtə(r)/ *vi* entreter-se com isto ou aquilo

potty[1] /'pɒtɪ/ *a* (**-ier**, **-iest**) (*sl*) doido, pirado (*sl*), (*P*) chanfrado (*colloq*)

potty[2] /'pɒtɪ/ *n* (**-ties**) (*colloq*) nico *m* de criança

pouch /paʊtʃ/ *n* bolsa *f*; (*for tobacco*) tabaqueira *f*

poultice /'pəʊltɪs/ *n* cataplasma *f*

poultry /'pəʊltrɪ/ *n* aves *fpl* domésticas

pounce /paʊns/ *vi* atirar-se (**on**

sobre, para cima de) □ *n* salto *m*

pound[1] /paʊnd/ *n* (*weight*) libra *f* (= *453 g*); (*money*) libra *f*

pound[2] /paʊnd/ *n* (*for dogs*) canil municipal *m*; (*for cars*) parque de viaturas rebocadas *m*

pound[3] /paʊnd/ *vt/i* (*crush*) esmagar, pisar; (*of heart*) bater com força; (*bombard*) bombardear; (*on piano etc*) martelar

pour /pɔ:(r)/ *vt* deitar □ *vi* correr; (*rain*) chover torrencialmente. **~ in/out** (*of people*) afluir/sair em massa. **~ off or out** esvaziar, vazar. **~ing rain** chuva *f* torrencial

pout /paʊt/ *vt/i* **~ (one's lips)** (*sulk*) fazer beicinho; (*in annoyance*) ficar de trombas □ *n* beicinho *m*

poverty /'pɒvətɪ/ *n* pobreza *f*, miséria *f*. **~-stricken** *a* pobre

powder /'paʊdə(r)/ *n* pó *m*; (*for face*) pó-de-arroz *m* □ *vt* polvilhar; (*face*) empoar. **~ed** *a* em pó. **~-room** *n* toalete *m*, toucador *m*. **~y** *a* como pó

power /'paʊə(r)/ *n* poder *m*; (*maths, mech*) potência *f*; (*energy*) energia *f*; (*electr*) corrente *f*. **~-cut** corte *m* de energia, blecaute *m*. **~ station** central *f* elétrica, (*P*) eléctrica. **~ed by** movido *a*; (*jet etc*) de propulsão. **~ful** *a* poderoso; (*mech*) potente. **~less** *a* impotente

practicable /'præktɪkəbl/ *a* viável

practical /'præktɪkl/ *a* prático. **~ joke** brincadeira *f* de mau gosto

practically /'præktɪklɪ/ *adv* praticamente

practice /'præktɪs/ *n* prática *f*; (*of law etc*) exercício *m*; (*sport*) treino *m*; (*clients*) clientela *f*. **in ~** (*in fact*) na prática; (*well-trained*) em forma. **out of ~** destreinado, sem prática. **put into ~** pôr em prática

practis|e /'præktɪs/ *vt/i (skill, sport)* praticar, exercitar-se em; *(profession)* exercer; *(put into practice)* pôr em prática. **~ed** *a* experimentado, experiente. **~ing** *a (Catholic etc)* praticante

practitioner /præk'tɪʃənə(r)/ *n* praticante *mf.* **general ~** médico *m* de clínica geral *or* de família

pragmatic /præg'mætɪk/ *a* pragmático

prairie /'preərɪ/ *n* pradaria *f*

praise /preɪz/ *vt* louvar, elogiar □ *n* elogio(s) *m(pl)*, louvor(es) *m(pl)*

praiseworthy /'preɪzwɜːðɪ/ *a* louvável, digno de louvor

pram /præm/ *n* carrinho *m* de bebé, *(P)* bebê

prance /prɑːns/ *vi (of horse)* curvetear, empinar-se; *(of person)* pavonear-se

prank /præŋk/ *n* brincadeira *f* de mau gosto

prattle /'prætl/ *vi* tagarelar

prawn /prɔːn/ *n* camarão *m* grande, *(P)* gamba *f*

pray /preɪ/ *vi* rezar, orar

prayer /preə(r)/ *n* oração *f.* **the Lord's P~** o Padre-Nosso. **~-book** *n* missal *m*

pre- /priː/ *pref* pré-

preach /priːtʃ/ *vt/i* pregar (**at, to** a). **~er** *n* pregador *m*

preamble /priː'æmbl/ *n* preâmbulo *m*

prearrange /priːə'reɪndʒ/ *vt* combinar *or* arranjar de antemão

precarious /prɪ'keərɪəs/ *a* precário; *(of position)* instável, inseguro

precaution /prɪ'kɔːʃn/ *n* precaução *f.* **~ary** *a* de precaução

preced|e /prɪ'siːd/ *vt* preceder. **~ing** *a* precedente

precedent /'presɪdənt/ *n* precedente *m*

precinct /'priːsɪŋkt/ *n* precinto *m*; *(Amer: district)* circunscrição *f.* **(pedestrian) ~** área *f* de pedestres, *(P)* zona *f* para peões

precious /'preʃəs/ *a* precioso

precipice /'presɪpɪs/ *n* precipício *m*

precipitat|e /prɪ'sɪpɪteɪt/ *vt* precipitar □ *a* /-ɪtət/ precipitado. **~ion** /-'teɪʃn/ *n* precipitação *f*

precis|e /prɪ'saɪs/ *a* preciso; *(careful)* meticuloso. **~ely** *adv* precisamente. **~ion** /-'sɪʒn/ *n* precisão *f*

preclude /prɪ'kluːd/ *vt* evitar, excluir, impedir

precocious /prɪ'kəʊʃəs/ *a* precoce

preconc|eived /priːkən'siːvd/ *a* preconcebido. **~eption** /priːkən'sepʃn/ *n* idéia *f* preconcebida

precursor /priː'kɜːsə(r)/ *n* precursor *m*

predator /'predətə(r)/ *n* animal *m* de rapina, predador *m.* **~y** *a* predatório

predecessor /'priːdɪsesə(r)/ *n* predecessor *m*

predicament /prɪ'dɪkəmənt/ *n* situação *f* difícil

predict /prɪ'dɪkt/ *vt* predizer, prognosticar. **~able** *a* previsível. **~ion** /-ʃn/ *n* predição *f,* prognóstico *m*

predominant /prɪ'dɒmɪnənt/ *a* predominante, preponderante. **~ly** *adv* predominantemente, preponderantemente

predominate /prɪ'dɒmɪneɪt/ *vi* predominar

pre-eminent /priː'emɪnənt/ *a* preeminente, superior

pre-empt /priː'empt/ *vt* adquirir por preempção. **~ive** *a* antecipado; *(mil)* preventivo

preen /priːn/ *vt* alisar. **~ o.s.** enfeitar-se

prefab /'priːfæb/ *n (colloq)* casa *f* pré-fabricada. **~ricated** /-'fæbrɪkeɪtɪd/ *a* pré-fabricado

preface /'prefɪs/ *n* prefácio *m*

prefect /'priːfekt/ *n* aluno *m* autorizado a disciplinar outros; (*official*) prefeito *m*

prefer /prɪ'fɜː(r)/ *vt* (*pt* **preferred**) preferir. ~**able** /'prefrəbl/ *a* preferível

preferen|ce /'prefrəns/ *n* preferência *f*. ~**tial** /-ə'renʃl/ *a* preferencial, privilegiado

prefix /'priːfɪks/ *n* (*pl* -**ixes**) prefixo *m*

pregnan|t /'pregnənt/ *a* (*woman*) grávida; (*animal*) prenhe. ~**cy** *n* gravidez *f*

prehistoric /priːhɪ'stɒrɪk/ *a* préhistórico

prejudice /'predʒudɪs/ *n* preconceito *m*, idéia *f* preconcebida, prejuízo *m*; (*harm*) prejuízo *m* □ *vt* influenciar. ~**d** *a* com preconceitos

preliminar|y /prɪ'lɪmɪnərɪ/ *a* preliminar. ~**ies** *npl* preliminares *mpl*, preâmbulos *mpl*

prelude /'preljuːd/ *n* prelúdio *m*

premarital /priː'mærɪtl/ *a* antes do casamento, pré-marital

premature /'premətjʊə(r)/ *a* prematuro

premeditated /priː'medɪteɪtɪd/ *a* premeditado

premier /'premɪə(r)/ *a* primeiro □ *n* (*pol*) primeiro-ministro *m*

premises /'premɪsɪz/ *npl* local *m*, edifício *m*. **on the** ~ neste estabelecimento, no local

premium /'priːmɪəm/ *n* prêmio *m*, (*P*) prémio *m*. **at a** ~ a peso de ouro

premonition /priːmə'nɪʃn/ *n* pressentimento *m*

preoccupation /priːɒkjʊ'peɪʃn/ *n* preocupação *f*. ~**ied** /-'ɒkjʊpaɪd/ *a* preocupado

preparation /prepə'reɪʃn/ *n* preparação *f*. ~**s** preparativos *mpl*

preparatory /prɪ'pærətrɪ/ *a* preparatório. ~ **school** escola *f* primária particular

prepare /prɪ'peə(r)/ *vt/i* preparar(-se) (**for** para). ~**d to** pronto a, preparado para

preposition /prepə'zɪʃn/ *n* preposição *f*

preposterous /prɪ'pɒstərəs/ *a* absurdo, disparatado, ridículo

prerequisite /priː'rekwɪzɪt/ *n* condição *f* prévia

prerogative /prɪ'rɒgətɪv/ *n* prerrogativa *f*

Presbyterian /prezbɪ'tɪərɪən/ *a* & *n* presbiteriano (*m*)

prescri|be /prɪ'skraɪb/ *vt* prescrever; (*med*) receitar, prescrever. ~**ption** /-ɪpʃn/ *n* prescrição *f*; (*med*) receita *f*

presence /'prezns/ *n* presença *f*. ~ **of mind** presença *f* de espírito

present[1] /'preznt/ *a* & *n* presente (*mf*). **at** ~ no momento, presentemente

present[2] /'preznt/ *n* (*gift*) presente *m*

present[3] /prɪ'zent/ *vt* apresentar; (*film etc*) dar. ~ **sb with** oferecer a alg. ~**able** *a* apresentável. ~**ation** /prezn'teɪʃn/ *n* apresentação *f*. ~**er** *n* apresentador *m*

presently /'prezntlɪ/ *adv* dentro em pouco, daqui a pouco; (*Amer: now*) neste momento

preservative /prɪ'zɜːvətɪv/ *n* preservativo *m*

preserv|e /prɪ'zɜːv/ *vt* preservar; (*maintain; culin*) conservar □ *n* reserva *f*; (*fig*) área *f*, terreno *m*; (*jam*) compota *f*. ~**ation** /prezə'veɪʃn/ *n* conservação *f*

preside /prɪ'zaɪd/ *vi* presidir (**over** a)

presiden|t /'prezɪdənt/ *n* presidente *m*. ~**cy** *n* presidência *f*. ~**tial** /-'denʃl/ *a* presidencial

press /pres/ *vt/i* carregar (**on em**); (*squeeze*) espremer; (*urge*) pressionar; (*iron*) passar a ferro □ *n* imprensa *f*; (*mech*) prensa *f*. (*for* *wine*) lagar *m*. be ~ed for estar apertado com falta de. ~ on (with) continuar (com), prosseguir (com). ~ conference entrevista *f* coletiva. ~-stud *n* mola *f*, botão *m* de pressão

pressing /'presɪŋ/ *a* premente, urgente

pressure /'preʃə(r)/ *n* pressão *f* □ *vt* fazer pressão sobre. ~-cooker *n* panela *f* de pressão. ~ group grupo *m* de pressão

pressurize /'preʃəraɪz/ *vt* pressionar, fazer pressão sobre

prestige /pre'stiːʒ/ *n* prestígio *m*

prestigious /pre'stɪdʒəs/ *a* prestigioso

presumably /prɪ'zjuːməblɪ/ *adv* provavelmente

presum|e /prɪ'zjuːm/ *vt* presumir. ~e to tomar a liberdade de, atrever-se a. ~ption /-'zʌmpʃn/ *n* presunção *f*

presumptuous /prɪ'zʌmptʃʊəs/ *a* presunçoso

pretence /prɪ'tens/ *n* fingimento *m*; (*claim*) pretensão *f*; (*pretext*) desculpa *f*, pretexto *m*

pretend /prɪ'tend/ *vt/i* fingir (to do fazer). ~ to (*lay claim to*) ter pretensões a, ser pretendente a; (*profess to have*) pretender ter

pretentious /prɪ'tenʃəs/ *a* pretencioso

pretext /'priːtekst/ *n* pretexto *m*

pretty /'prɪtɪ/ *a* (-ier, -iest) bonito, lindo □ *adv* bastante

prevail /prɪ'veɪl/ *vi* prevalecer. ~ on sb to convencer alguéma. ~ing *a* dominante

prevalen|t /'prevələnt/ *a* geral, dominante. ~ce *n* frequência *f*

prevent /prɪ'vent/ *vt* impedir (from doing de fazer). ~able *a* que se pode evitar, evitável. ~ion /-ʃn/ *n* prevenção *f*. ~ive *a* preventivo

preview /'priːvjuː/ *n* pré-estréia *f*, (*P*) ante-estréia *f*

previous /'priːvɪəs/ *a* precedente, anterior. ~ to antes de. ~ly *adv* antes, anteriormente

pre-war /priː'wɔː(r)/ *a* do pré-guerra, (*P*) de antes da guerra

prey /preɪ/ *n* presa *f* □ *vi* ~ on dar caça a; (*worry*) preocupar, atormentar. bird of ~ ave *f* de rapina, predador *m*

price /praɪs/ *n* preço *m* □ *vt* marcar o preço de. ~less *a* inestimável; (*colloq: amusing*) impagável

prick /prɪk/ *vt* picar, furar □ *n* picada *f*. ~ up one's ears arrebitar a(s) orelha(s)

prickl|e /'prɪkl/ *n* pico *m*, espinho *m*; (*sensation*) picada *f*. ~y *a* espinhoso, que pica; (*person*) irritável

pride /praɪd/ *n* orgulho *m* □ *vpr* ~ o.s. on orgulhar-se de

priest /priːst/ *n* padre *m*, sacerdote *m*. ~hood *n* sacerdócio *m*; (*clergy*) clero *m*

prim /prɪm/ *a* (primmer, primmest) formal, cheio de nove-horas; (*prudish*) pudico

primary /'praɪmərɪ/ *a* primário; (*chief, first*) primeiro. ~ school escola *f* primária

prime¹ /praɪm/ *a* primeiro, principal; (*first-rate*) de primeira qualidade. P~ Minister Primeiro-Ministro *m*. ~ number número *m* primo

prime² /praɪm/ *vt* aprontar, aprestar; (*with facts*) preparar; (*surface*) preparar, aparelhar. ~r /-ə(r)/ *n* (*paint*) aparelho *m*

primeval /praɪ'miːvl/ *a* primitivo

primitive /'prɪmɪtɪv/ *a* primitivo

primrose /'prɪmrəʊz/ *n* primavera *f*, prímula *f*

prince /prɪns/ *n* príncipe *m*

princess /prɪn'ses/ *n* princesa *f*

principal /'prɪnsəpl/ *a* principal □ *n* (*schol*) diretor *m*, (*P*) diretor *m*. ~ly *adv* principalmente

principle /'prɪnsəpl/ n princípio m. **in/on** ~ em/por princípio

print /prɪnt/ vt imprimir; (write) escrever em letra de imprensa □ n marca f, impressão f; (letters) letra f de imprensa; (photo) prova (fotográfica) f; (engraving) gravura f. **out of** ~ esgotado. ~**out** n cópia f impressa. ~**ed matter** impressos mpl

print|er /'prɪntə(r)/ n tipógrafo m; (comput) impressora f. ~**ing** n impressão f, tipografia f

prior /'praɪə(r)/ a anterior, precedente. ~ **to** antes de

priority /praɪ'ɒrətɪ/ n prioridade f

prise /praɪz/ vt forçar (com alavanca). ~ **open** arrombar

prison /'prɪzn/ n prisão f. ~**er** n prisioneiro m

pristine /'prɪstiːn/ a primitivo; (condition) perfeito, como novo

privacy /'prɪvəsɪ/ n privacidade f, intimidade f; (solitude) isolamento m

private /'praɪvət/ a privado; (confidential) confidencial; (lesson, life, house etc) particular; (ceremony) íntimo □ n soldado m raso. **in** ~ em particular; (of ceremony) na intimidade. ~**ly** adv particularmente; (inwardly) no fundo, interiormente

privet /'prɪvɪt/ n (bot) alfena f, ligustro m

privilege /'prɪvəlɪdʒ/ n privilégio m. ~**d** a privilegiado. **be** ~**d to** ter o privilégio de

prize /praɪz/ n prêmio m, (P) prémio m □ a (example) perfeito □ vt ter em grande apreço, apreciar muito. ~**-giving** n distribuição f de prêmios, (P) prémios. ~**-winner** n premiado m, vencedor m

pro /prəʊ/ n **the** ~**s and cons** os prós e os contras

pro- /prəʊ/ pref (acting for) pro-; (favouring) pró-

probab|le /'prɒbəbl/ a provável. ~**ility** /-'bɪlətɪ/ n probabilidade f. ~**ly** adv provavelmente

probation /prə'beɪʃn/ n (testing) estágio m, tirocínio m; (jur) liberdade f condicional. ~**ary** a probatório

probe /prəʊb/ n (med) sonda f; (fig: investigation) inquérito m □ vt/i ~ **(into)** sondar, investigar

problem /'prɒbləm/ n problema m □ a difícil. ~**atic** /-'mætɪk/ a problemático

procedure /prə'siːdʒə(r)/ n procedimento m, processo m, norma f

proceed /prə'siːd/ vi prosseguir, ir para diante, avançar. ~ **to do** passar a fazer. ~ **with sth** continuar or avançar com alguma coisa. ~**ing** n procedimento m

proceedings /prə'siːdɪŋz/ npl (jur) processo m; (report) ata f, (P) acta f

proceeds /'prəʊsiːdz/ npl produto m, luco m, proventos mpl

process /'prəʊses/ n processo m □ vt tratar; (photo) revelar. **in** ~ em curso. **in the** ~ **of doing** sendo feito

procession /prə'seʃn/ n procissão f, cortejo m

proclaim /prə'kleɪm/ vt proclamar. ~**amation** /prɒklə'meɪʃn/ n proclamação f

procure /prə'kjʊə(r)/ vt obter

prod /prɒd/ vt/i (pt **prodded**) (push) empurrar; (poke) espetar; (fig: urge) incitar □ n espetadela f; (fig) incitamento m

prodigal /'prɒdɪgl/ a pródigo

prodigious /prə'dɪdʒəs/ a prodigioso

prodigy /'prɒdɪdʒɪ/ n prodígio m

produce /prə'djuːs/ vt/i produzir; (bring out) tirar, extrair; (show) apresentar, mostrar; (cause) causar, provocar; (theat)

pôr em cena. ~er n produtor m.
~tion /-'dʌkʃn/ n produção f;
(theat) encenação f
produce² /'prɒdjuːs/ n produtos
(agrícolas) mpl
product /'prɒdʌkt/ n produto m
productiv|e /prə'dʌktɪv/ a pro-
dutivo. ~ity /prɒdʌk'tɪvəti/ n
produtividade f
profan|e /prə'feɪn/ a profano;
(blasphemous) blasfemo. ~ity
/-'fænəti/ n profanidade f
profess /prə'fes/ vt professar. ~
to do alegar fazer
profession /prə'feʃn/ n profissão
f. ~al a profissional; (well done)
de profissional; (person) que
exerce uma profissão liberal □ n
profissional mf
professor /prə'fesə(r)/ n professor
(universitário) m
proficien|t /prə'fɪʃnt/ a profi-
ciente, competente. ~cy n profi-
ciência f, competência f
profile /'prəʊfaɪl/ n perfil m
profit /'prɒfɪt/ n proveito m;
(money) lucro m □ vi (pt
profited) ~ by aproveitar-se
de; ~ from tirar proveito de.
~able a proveitoso; (of business)
lucrativo, rentável
profound /prə'faʊnd/ a profundo.
~ly adv profundamente
profus|e /prə'fjuːs/ a profuso.
~ely adv profusamente, em
abundância. ~ion /-ʒn/ n profusão f
program /'prəʊɡræm/ n (computer) ~ programa m □ vt (pt
programmed) programar.
~mer n programador m
programme /'prəʊɡræm/ n programa m
progress¹ /'prəʊɡres/ n progresso
m. in ~ em curso, em andamento
progress² /prə'ɡres/ vi progredir.
~ion /-ʃn/ n progressão f
progressive /prə'ɡresɪv/ a pro-

gressivo; (reforming) progres-
sista. ~ly adv progressivamente
prohibit /prə'hɪbɪt/ vt proibir (sb
from doing alg de fazer)
project¹ /prə'dʒekt/ vt projetar, (P)
projectar □ vi ressaltar, sobressair. ~ion /-ʃn/ n projeção
f, (P) projecção f; (protruding)
saliência f, ressalto m
project² /'prɒdʒekt/ n projeto m,
(P) projecto m
projectile /prə'dʒektaɪl/ n projétil
m, (P) projéctil m
projector /prə'dʒektə(r)/ n projetor m, (P) projector m
proletari|at /prəʊlɪ'teərɪət/ n pro-
letariado m. ~an a & n proletá-
rio (m)
prolifera|te /prə'lɪfəreɪt/ vi proli-
ferar. ~tion /-'reɪʃn/ n prolifera-
ção f
prolific /prə'lɪfɪk/ a prolífico
prologue /'prəʊlɒɡ/ n prólogo m
prolong /prə'lɒŋ/ vt prolongar
promenade /prɒmə'nɑːd/ n passeio m □ vt/i passear
prominen|t /'prɒmɪnənt/ a (pro-
jecting; important) proeminente;
(conspicuous) bem à vista, conspícuo. ~ce n proeminência f.
~tly adv bem à vista
promiscu|ous /prə'mɪskjʊəs/ a
promíscuo, de costumes livres.
~ity /prɒmɪs'kjuːəti/ n promis-
cuidade f, liberdade f de costumes
promis|e /'prɒmɪs/ n promessa f □
vt/i prometer. ~ing a prometedor, promissor
promot|e /prə'məʊt/ vt promover.
~ion /-'məʊʃn/ n promoção f
prompt /prɒmpt/ a pronto, rápido, imediato; (punctual) pontual
□ adv em ponto □ vt levar;
(theat) soprar, servir de ponto
para. ~er n ponto m. ~ly
adv prontamente; pontualmente.
~ness n prontidão f

prone /prəʊn/ *a* deitado (de bruços). **~ to** propenso a

prong /prɒŋ/ *n* (*of fork*) dente *m*

pronoun /ˈprəʊnaʊn/ *n* pronome *m*

pron|ounce /prəˈnaʊns/ *vt* pronunciar; (*declare*) declarar. **~ounced** *a* pronunciado. **~ouncement** *n* declaração *f*. **~unciation** /-ʌnsɪˈeɪʃn/ *n* pronúncia *f*

proof /pruːf/ *n* prova *f*; (*of liquor*) teor *m* alcoólico, graduação *f*. **~ against** à prova de

prop[1] /prɒp/ *n* suporte *m*; (*lit & fig*) apoio *m*, esteio *m* □ *vt* (*pt* **propped**) sustentar, suportar, apoiar. **~ against** apoiar contra

prop[2] /prɒp/ *n* (*colloq: theat*) acessório *m*, (*P*) adereço *m*

propaganda /prɒpəˈgændə/ *n* propaganda *f*

propagat|e /ˈprɒpəgeɪt/ *vt/i* propagar(-se). **~ion** /-ˈgeɪʃn/ *n* propagação *f*

propel /prəˈpel/ *vt* (*pt* **propelled**) propulsionar, impelir

propeller /prəˈpelə(r)/ *n* hélice *f*

proper /ˈprɒpə(r)/ *a* correto, *P* correcto; (*seemly*) conveniente; (*real*) propriamente dito; (*colloq: thorough*) belo. **~ noun** substantivo *m* próprio. **~ly** *adv* corretamente, (*P*) correctamente; (*rightly*) com razão, acertadamente; (*accurately*) propriamente

property /ˈprɒpətɪ/ *n* (*house*) imóvel *m*; (*land, quality*) propriedade *f*; (*possessions*) bens *mpl*

prophecy /ˈprɒfəsɪ/ *n* profecia *f*

prophesy /ˈprɒfɪsaɪ/ *vt/i* profetizar. **~ that** predizer que

prophet /ˈprɒfɪt/ *n* profeta *m*. **~ic** /prəˈfetɪk/ *a* profético

proportion /prəˈpɔːʃn/ *n* proporção *f*. **~al**, **~ate** *adjs* proporcional

proposal /prəˈpəʊzl/ *n* proposta *f*; (*of marriage*) pedido *m* de casamento

propos|e /prəˈpəʊz/ *vt* propor □ *vi* pedir em casamento. **~e to do** propor-se fazer. **~ition** /prɒpəˈzɪʃn/ *n* proposição *f*; (*colloq: matter*) caso *m*, questão *f*

propound /prəˈpaʊnd/ *vt* propor

proprietor /prəˈpraɪətə(r)/ *n* proprietário *m*

propriety /prəˈpraɪətɪ/ *n* propriedade *f*, correcção *f*, (*P*) correcção *f*

propulsion /prəˈpʌlʃn/ *n* propulsão *f*

prosaic /prəˈzeɪk/ *a* prosaico

prose /prəʊz/ *n* prosa *f*

prosecut|e /ˈprɒsɪkjuːt/ *vt* (*jur*) processar. **~ion** /-ˈkjuːʃn/ *n* (*jur*) acusação *f*

prospect[1] /ˈprɒspekt/ *n* perspectiva *f*

prospect[2] /prəˈspekt/ *vt/i* pesquisar, prospectar

prospective /prəˈspektɪv/ *a* futuro; (*possible*) provável

prosper /ˈprɒspə(r)/ *vi* prosperar

prosper|ous /ˈprɒspərəs/ *a* próspero. **~ity** /-ˈsperətɪ/ *n* prosperidade *f*

prostitut|e /ˈprɒstɪtjuːt/ *n* prostituta *f*. **~ion** /-ˈtjuːʃn/ *n* prostituição *f*

prostrate /ˈprɒstreɪt/ *a* prostrado

protect /prəˈtekt/ *vt* proteger. **~ion** /-ʃn/ *n* proteção *f*, (*P*) protecção *f*. **~ive** *a* protetor, (*P*) protector. **~or** *n* protetor *m*, (*P*) protector *m*

protégé /ˈprɒtɪʒeɪ/ *n* protegido *m*. **~e** *n* protegida *f*

protein /ˈprəʊtiːn/ *n* proteína *f*

protest[1] /ˈprəʊtest/ *n* protesto *m*

protest[2] /prəˈtest/ *vt/i* protestar. **~er** *n* (*pol*) manifestante *mf*

Protestant /ˈprɒtɪstənt/ *a & n* protestante (*mf*). **~ism** /-ɪzəm/ *n* protestantismo *m*

protocol /ˈprəʊtəkɒl/ *n* protocolo *m*

prototype /ˈprəʊtətaɪp/ *n* protótipo *m*

protract /prə'trækt/ vt prolongar, arrastar

protrud|e /prə'tru:d/ vi sobressair, sair do alinhamento. ~**ing** a saliente

proud /praʊd/ a (er, -est) orgulhoso. ~**ly** adv orgulhosamente

prove /pru:v/ vt prove, demonstrar □ vi ~ (to be) easy/etc verificar-se ser fácil/etc. ~o.s. dar provas de si. ~**n** /-n/ a provado

proverb /'prɒvɜ:b/ n provérbio m. ~**ial** /prə'vɜ:bɪəl/ a proverbial

provid|e /prə'vaɪd/ vt prover, munir (sb with sth alg de alguma coisa) □ vi ~ **for** providenciar para; (person) prover de, cuidar de; (allow for) levar em conta. ~**ed**, ~**ing (that)** conj desde que, contanto que

providence /'prɒvɪdəns/ n providência f

province /'prɒvɪns/ n província f; (fig) competência f

provincial /prə'vɪnʃl/ a provincial; (rustic) provinciano

provision /prə'vɪʒn/ n provisão f; (stipulation) disposição f. ~**s** (pl (food) provisões fpl

provisional /prə'vɪʒənl/ a provisório. ~**ly** adv provisoriamente

proviso /prə'vaɪzəʊ/ n (pl -os) condição f

provo|ke /prə'vəʊk/ vt provocar. ~**cation** /prɒvə'keɪʃn/ n provocação f. ~**cative** /-'vɒkətɪv/ a provocante

prowess /'praʊɪs/ n proeza f, façanha f

prowl /praʊl/ vi rondar □ n be on the ~ andar à espreita. ~**er** n pessoa f que anda à espreita

proximity /prɒk'sɪmətɪ/ n proximidade f

proxy /'prɒksɪ/ n by ~ por procuração

prude /pru:d/ n puritano m, pudico m

pruden|t /'pru:dnt/ a prudente. ~**ce** n prudência f

prune[1] /pru:n/ n ameixa f seca

prune[2] /pru:n/ vt podar

pry /praɪ/ vi bisbilhotar. ~ **into** meter o nariz em, intrometer-se em

psalm /sa:m/ n salmo m

pseudo- /'sju:dəʊ/ pref pseudo-

pseudonym /'sju:dənɪm/ n pseudônimo m, (P) pseudónimo m

psychiatr|y /saɪ'kaɪətrɪ/ n psiquiatria f. ~**ic** /-'ætrɪk/ a psiquiátrico. ~**ist** n psiquiatra mf

psychic /'saɪkɪk/ a psíquico; (person) com capacidade de telepatia

psychoanalys|e /saɪkəʊ'ænəlaɪz/ vt psicanalisar. ~**t** /-ɪst/ n psicanalista mf

psychoanalysis /saɪkəʊə'næləsɪs/ n psicanálise f

psycholog|y /saɪ'kɒlədʒɪ/ n psicologia f. ~**ical** /-ə'lɒdʒɪkl/ a psicológico. ~**ist** n psicólogo m

psychopath /'saɪkəʊpæθ/ n psicopata mf

pub /pʌb/ n pub m

puberty /'pju:bətɪ/ n puberdade f

public /'pʌblɪk/ a público; (holiday) feriado. in ~ em público. ~ **house** pub m. ~ **relations** relações fpl públicas. ~ **school** escola f particular; (Amer) escola f oficial. ~-**spirited** a de espírito cívico, patriótico. ~**ly** adv publicamente

publication /pʌblɪ'keɪʃn/ n publicação f

publicity /pʌb'lɪsətɪ/ n publicidade f

publicize /'pʌblɪsaɪz/ vt fazer publicidade de

publish /'pʌblɪʃ/ vt publicar. ~**er** n editor m. ~**ing** n publicação f. ~**ing house** editora f

pucker /'pʌkə(r)/ vt/i franzir

pudding /'pʊdɪŋ/ n pudim m; (dessert) doce m

puddle /'pʌdl/ n poça f de água, charco m

puerile /'pjʊəraɪl/ a pueril

puff /pʌf/ n baforada f □ vt/i lançar baforadas; (breathe hard) arquejar, ofegar. ~ **at** (cigar etc) dar baforadas em. ~ **out** (swell) inchar(-se). ~**pastry** n massa f folhada

puffy /'pʌfɪ/ a inchado

pugnacious /pʌg'neɪʃəs/ a belicoso, combativo

pull /pʊl/ vt/i puxar; (muscle) distender □ n puxão m; (fig: influence) influência f, empenho m. **give a** ~ dar um puxão. ~ **a face** fazer uma careta. ~ **one's weight** (fig) fazer a sua quotaparte. ~ **sb's leg** brincar com alguém, meter-se com alguém. ~ **away** ou **out** (auto) arrancar. ~ **down** puxar para baixo; (building) demolir. ~ **in** (auto) encostar-se. ~ **off** tirar; (fig) sair-se bem em, conseguir alcançar. ~ **out** partir; (extract) arrancar, tirar. ~ **through** sair-se bem. ~ **o.s. together** recompor-se, refazer-se. ~ **up** puxar para cima; (uproot) arrancar; (auto) parar

pulley /'pʊlɪ/ n roldana f

pullover /'pʊləʊvə(r)/ n pulôver m

pulp /pʌlp/ n polpa f; (for paper) pasta f de papel

pulpit /'pʊlpɪt/ n púlpito m

pulsat|e /pʌl'seɪt/ vi pulsar, bater, palpitar. ~**ion** /-'seɪʃn/ n pulsação f

pulse /pʌls/ n pulso m. **feel sb's** ~ tirar o pulso de alguém

pulverize /'pʌlvəraɪz/ vt (grind, defeat) pulverizar

pummel /'pʌml/ vt (pt pummelled) esmurrar

pump¹ /pʌmp/ n bomba f □ vt/i bombear; (person) arrancar ou extrair informações de. ~ **up** encher com bomba

pump² /pʌmp/ n (shoe) sapato m

pumpkin /'pʌmpkɪn/ n abóbora f

pun /pʌn/ n trocadilho m, jogo m de palavras

punch¹ /pʌntʃ/ vt esmurrar, dar um murro ou soco; (perforate) furar, perfurar; (a hole) fazer □ n murro m, soco m; (device) furador m. ~**line** n remate m. ~**up** n (colloq) pancadaria f

punch² /pʌntʃ/ n (drink) ponche m

punctual /'pʌŋktʃʊəl/ a pontual. ~**ity** /-'ælətɪ/ n pontualidade f

punctuat|e /'pʌŋktʃʊeɪt/ vt pontuar. ~**ion** /-'eɪʃn/ n pontuação f

puncture /'pʌŋktʃə(r)/ n (in tyre) furo m □ vt/i furar

pundit /'pʌndɪt/ n autoridade f, sumidade f

pungent /'pʌndʒənt/ a acre, pungente

punish /'pʌnɪʃ/ vt punir, castigar. ~**able** a punível. ~**ment** n punição f, castigo m

punitive /'pjuːnɪtɪv/ a (expedition, measure etc) punitivo; (taxation etc) penalizador

punt /pʌnt/ n (boat) chalana f

punter /'pʌntə(r)/ n (gambler) jogador m; (colloq: customer) freguês m

puny /'pjuːnɪ/ a (-ier, -iest) fraco, débil

pup(py) /'pʌp(ɪ)/ n cachorro m, cachorrinho m

pupil /'pjuːpl/ n aluno m; (of eye) pupila f

puppet /'pʌpɪt/ n (lit & fig) fantoche m, marionete f

purchase /'pɜːtʃəs/ vt comprar (**from sb** de alg) □ n compra f. ~**r** /-ə(r)/ n comprador m

pur|e /'pjʊə(r)/ a (-er, -est) puro. ~**ely** adv puramente. ~**ity** n pureza f

purgatory /'pɜːgətrɪ/ n purgatório m

purge /pɜːdʒ/ vt purgar; (pol) sanear □ n (med) purgante m; (pol) saneamento m

purify /'pjʊərɪfaɪ/ vt purificar. ~ication /-ɪ'keɪʃn/ n purificação f

puritan /'pjʊərɪtən/ n puritano m. ~ical /-'tænɪkl/ a puritano

purple /'pɜːpl/ a roxo, purpúreo □ n roxo m, púrpura f

purport /pə'pɔːt/ vt dizer-se, (P) dar a entender. ~ to be pretender ser

purpose /'pɜːpəs/ n propósito m; (determination) firmeza f. on ~ de propósito. to no ~ em vão. ~-built a construído especialmente.

purposely /'pɜːpəslɪ/ adv de propósito, propositadamente

purr /pɜːr/ n ronrom m □ vi ronronar

purse /pɜːs/ n carteira f; (Amer) bolsa f □ vt franzir

pursue /pə'sjuː/ vt perseguir; (go on with) prosseguir; (engage in) entregar-se a, dedicar-se a. ~r /-ə(r)/ n perseguidor m

pursuit /pə'sjuːt/ n perseguição f; (fig) atividade f, (P) actividade f

pus /pʌs/ n pus m

push /pʊʃ/ vt/i empurrar; (button) apertar; (thrust) enfiar; (colloq: recommend) insistir □ n empurrão m; (effort) esforço m; (drive) energia f. be ~ed for (time etc) estar com pouco. be ~ing thirty/etc (colloq) estar beirando os trinta/etc. give the ~ to (sl) dar o fora em alguém. ~ s.o. around fazer alguém de bobo. ~ back repelir. ~-chair n carrinho m (de criança). ~er n fornecedor m (de droga). ~ off (sl) dar o fora. ~ on continuar. ~-over n canja f, coisa f fácil. ~ up (lift) levantar; (prices) forçar o aumento de. ~-up n (Amer) fle-

xão f. ~y a (colloq) agressivo, furão

put /pʊt/ vt/i (pt put, pres p putting) colocar, pôr; (question) fazer. ~ the damage at a million estimar os danos em um milhão. I'd ~ it at a thousand eu diria mil. ~ sth tactfully dizer de maneira com tato. ~ across comunicar. ~ away guardar. ~ back repor; (delay) retardar, atrasar. ~ by pôr de lado. ~ down pôr em lugar baixo; (write) anotar; (pay) pagar; (suppress) sufocar, reprimir. ~ forward (plan) submeter. ~ in (insert) introduzir; (fix) instalar; (submit) submeter. ~ in for fazer um pedido, candidatar-se. ~ off (postpone) adiar; (disconcert) desanimar; (displease) desagradar. ~ s.o. off sth tirar o gosto de alguém por alg coisa. ~ on (clothes) pôr; (radio) ligar; (light) acender; (speed, weight) ganhar; (accent) adotar. ~ out pôr para fora; (stretch) esticar; (extinguish) extinguir, apagar; (disconcert) desconcertar; (inconvenience) incomodar. ~ up levantar; (building) erguer, construir; (notice) colocar; (price) aumentar; (guest) hospedar; (offer) oferecer. ~-up job embuste m. ~ up with suportar

putrefy /'pjuːtrɪfaɪ/ vi putrefazer-se, apodrecer

putty /'pʌtɪ/ n massa de vidraceiro f, betume m

puzzle /'pʌzl/ n puzzle m, quebra-cabeça m □ vt deixar perplexo, intrigar □ vi quebrar a cabeça. ~ing a intrigante

pygmy /'pɪgmɪ/ n pigmeu m

pyjamas /pə'dʒaːməz/ npl pijama m

pylon /'paɪlən/ n poste m

pyramid /'pɪrəmɪd/ n pirâmide f

python /'paɪθn/ n píton m

Q

quack[1] /kwæk/ n (of duck) grasnido m □ vi grasnar

quack[2] /kwæk/ n charlatão m

quadrangle /ˈkwɒdræŋgl/ n quadrângulo m; (of college) pátio m
quadrangular

quadruped /ˈkwɒdrʊped/ n quadrúpede m

quadruple /ˈkwɒdrʊpl/ a & n quádruplo (m) □ vt/i /kwɒˈdrʊpl/ quadruplicar. ~ts /-plɪts/ npl quadrigêmeos mpl; (P) quadrigémeos mpl

quagmire /ˈkwæɡmaɪə(r)/ n pântano m, lamaçal m

quail /kweɪl/ n codorniz f

quaint /kweɪnt/ a (-er, -est) pitoresco; (whimsical) estranho, bizarro

quake /kweɪk/ vi tremer □ n (colloq) tremor m de terra

Quaker /ˈkweɪkə(r)/ n quaker mf, quacre m

qualification /ˌkwɒlɪfɪˈkeɪʃn/ n qualificação f; (accomplishment) habilitação f; (diploma) diploma m, título m; (condition) requisito m, condição f; (fig) restrição f, reserva f

qualif|**y** /ˈkwɒlɪfaɪ/ vt qualificar; (fig: moderate) atenuar, moderar; (fig: limit) pôr ressalvas or restrições a □ vi (fig: be entitled to) ter os requisitos (for para); (sport) classificar-se. **he ~ied as a vet** ele formou-se em veterinária. **~ied** a formado; (able) qualificado, habilitado; (moderated) atenuado; (limited) limitado

quality /ˈkwɒlətɪ/ n qualidade f

qualm /kwɑːm/ n escrúpulo m

quandary /ˈkwɒndərɪ/ n dilema m

quantity /ˈkwɒntətɪ/ n quantidade f

quarantine /ˈkwɒrəntiːn/ n quarentena f

quarrel /ˈkwɒrəl/ n zanga f, questão f, discussão f □ vi (pt quarrelled) zangar-se, questionar, discutir. ~**some** a conflituoso, brigão

quarry[1] /ˈkwɒrɪ/ n (prey) presa f, caça f

quarry[2] /ˈkwɒrɪ/ n (excavation) pedreira f

quarter /ˈkwɔːtə(r)/ n quarto m; (of year) trimestre m; (Amer: coin) quarto m de dólar, 25 cêntimos mpl; (district) bairro m, quarteirão m. ~**s** (lodgings) alojamento m, residência f; (mil) quartel m □ vt dividir em quartos; (mil) aquartelar. **from all** ~**s** de todos os lados. ~ **of an hour** quarto m de hora. **(a)** ~ **past six** seis e quinze. **(a)** ~ **to seven** quinze para as sete. ~**-final** n (sport) quarta f de final. ~**ly** a trimestral □ adv trimestralmente

quartet /kwɔːˈtet/ n quarteto m

quartz /kwɔːts/ n quartzo m □ a (watch etc) de quartzo

quash /kwɒʃ/ vt reprimir; (jur) revogar

quaver /ˈkweɪvə(r)/ vi tremer, tremular □ n (mus) colcheia f

quay /kiː/ n cais m

queasy /ˈkwiːzɪ/ a delicado. **feel** ~ estar enjoado

queen /kwiːn/ n rainha f; (cards) dama f

queer /kwɪə(r)/ a (-er, -est) estranho; (slightly ill) indisposto; (sl: homosexual) bicha, maricas (sl); (dubious) suspeito □ n (sl) bicha m, maricas m (sl)

quell /kwel/ vt reprimir, abafar, sufocar

quench /kwentʃ/ vt (fire, flame) apagar; (thirst) matar, saciar

query /ˈkwɪərɪ/ n questão f □ vt pôr em dúvida

quest /kwest/ *n* busca *f*, procura *f*. **in ~ of** em demanda de

question /'kwestʃən/ *n* pergunta *f*, interrogação *f*; (*problem*, *affair*) questão *f* □ *vt* perguntar, interrogar; (*doubt*) pôr em dúvida *or* em causa. **in ~** em questão *or* em causa. **out of the ~** fora de toda a questão. **there's no ~ of** nem pensar em. **without ~** sem dúvida. **~ mark** ponto *m* de interrogação. **~able** *a* discutível

questionnaire /kwestʃə'neə(r)/ *n* questionário *m*

queue /kju:/ *n* fila *f*, (*P*) bicha *f* □ *vi* (*pres p* **queuing**) fazer fila, (*P*) fazer bicha

quibble /'kwɪbl/ *vi* ergueirar-se, usar de evasivas; (*raise petty objections*) discutir por coisas insignificantes

quick /kwɪk/ *a* (*-er, -est*) rápido □ *adv* depressa. **be ~** despachar-se. **have a ~ temper** exaltar-se facilmente. **~ly** *adv* rapidamente, depressa. **~ness** *n* rapidez *f*

quicken /'kwɪkən/ *vt/i* apressar (-se)

quicksand /'kwɪksænd/ *n* areia *f* movediça

quid /kwɪd/ *n invar* (*sl*) libra *f*

quiet /'kwaɪət/ *a* (*-er, -est*) quieto, sossegado, tranquilo □ *n* quietude *f*, sossego *m*, tranquilidade *f*. **keep ~** calar-se. **on the ~** às escondidas, na calada. **~ly** *adv* sossegadamente, silenciosamente. **~ness** *n* sossego *m*, tranquilidade *f*, calma *f*

quieten /'kwaɪətn/ *vt/i* sossegar, acalmar(-se)

quilt /kwɪlt/ *n* coberta *f* acolchoada. (**continental**) **~** edredão *m* de penas □ *vt* acolchoar

quince /kwɪns/ *n* marmelo *m*

quintet /kwɪn'tet/ *n* quinteto *m*

quintuplets /kwɪn'tju:plɪts/ *npl* quíntuplos *mpl*

quip /kwɪp/ *n* piada *f* □ *vt* contar piadas

quirk /kwɜ:k/ *n* mania *f*, singularidade *f*

quit /kwɪt/ *vt* (*pt* **quitted**) deixar □ *vi* ir-se embora; (*resign*) demitir-se. **~ doing** (*Amer*) parar de fazer

quite /kwaɪt/ *adv* completamente, absolutamente; (*rather*) bastante. **~ (so)!** isso mesmo!, exatamente! **~ a few** bastante, alguns/algumas. **~ a lot** bastante

quiver /'kwɪvə(r)/ *vi* tremer, estremecer □ *n* tremor *m*, estremecimento *m*

quiz /kwɪz/ *n* (*pl* **quizzes**) teste *m*; (*game*) concurso *m* □ *vt* (*pt* **quizzed**) interrogar

quizzical /'kwɪzɪkl/ *a* zombeteiro

quorum /'kwɔ:rəm/ *n* quorum *m*

quota /'kwəʊtə/ *n* cota *f*, quota *f*

quotation /kwəʊ'teɪʃn/ *n* citação *f*; (*estimate*) orçamento *m*. **~ marks** aspas *fpl*

quote /kwəʊt/ *vt* citar; (*estimate*) fazer um orçamento □ *n* (*colloq: passage*) citação *f*; (*colloq: estimate*) orçamento *m*

R

rabbi /'ræbaɪ/ *n* rabino *m*

rabbit /'ræbɪt/ *n* coelho *m*

rabble /'ræbl/ *n* turba *f*. **the ~** a ralé, a gentalha, o povinho

rabid /'ræbɪd/ *a* (*fig*) fanático, ferrenho; (*dog*) raivoso

rabies /'reɪbi:z/ *n* raiva *f*

race¹ /reɪs/ *n* corrida *f* □ *vt* (*horse*) fazer correr □ *vi* correr, dar uma corrida; (*rush*) ir em grande *or* a toda (a) velocidade. **~-track** *n* pista *f*

race² /reɪs/ *n* (*group*) raça *f* □ *a* racial

racecourse /'reɪskɔːs/ n hipódromo m

racehorse /'reɪshɔːs/ n cavalo m de corrida

racial /'reɪʃl/ a racial

racing /'reɪsɪŋ/ n corridas fpl. ~ **car** carro m de corridas

racis|t /'reɪsɪst/ a & n racista (mf). ~**m** /-zəm/ n racismo m

rack[1] /ræk/ n (for luggage) porta-bagagem m, bagageiro m; (for plates) escorredor m de prato □ vt ~ **one's brains** dar tratos à imaginação

rack[2] /ræk/ n **go to** ~ **and ruin** arruinar-se; (of buildings etc) cair em ruínas

racket[1] /'rækɪt/ n (sport) raquete f, (P) raqueta f

racket[2] /'rækɪt/ n (din) barulheira f; (swindle) roubalheira f; (sl: business) negociata f (colloq)

racy /'reɪsɪ/ a (-ier, -iest) vivo, vigoroso

radar /'reɪdɑː(r)/ n radar m □ a de radar

radian|t /'reɪdɪənt/ a radiante. ~**ce** n brilho m

radiator /'reɪdɪeɪtə(r)/ n radiador m

radical /'rædɪkl/ a & n radical (m)

radio /'reɪdɪəʊ/ n (pl -os) rádio f, (set) (aparelho de) rádio m □ vt transmitir pelo rádio. ~ **station** estação f de rádio, emissora f

radioactiv|e /reɪdɪəʊ'æktɪv/ a radioativo, (P) radioactivo. ~**ity** /-'tɪvətɪ/ n radioatividade f, (P) radioactividade f

radiograph|er /reɪdɪ'ɒɡrəfə(r)/ n radiologista mf. ~**y** n radiografia f

radish /'rædɪʃ/ n rabanete m

radius /'reɪdɪəs/ n (pl -dii /-dɪaɪ/) raio m

raffle /'ræfl/ n rifa f □ vt rifar

raft /rɑːft/ n jangada f

rafter /'rɑːftə(r)/ n trave f, viga f

rag[1] /ræg/ n farrapo m; (for wip-

ing) trapo m; (pej: newspaper) jornaleco m. ~**s** npl farrapos mpl, andrajos mpl. **in** ~**s** maltrapilho. ~ **doll** boneca f de trapos

rag[2] /ræg/ vt (pt ragged) zombar de

rage /reɪdʒ/ n raiva f, fúria f □ vi estar furioso; (of storm) rugir; (of battle) estar aceso. **be all the** ~ (colloq) fazer furor, estar na moda (colloq)

ragged /'rægɪd/ a (clothes, person) esfarrapado, roto; (edge) esfiapado, esgarçado

raid /reɪd/ n (mil) ataque m; (by police) batida f; (by criminals) assalto m □ vt fazer um ataque or uma batida or um assalto. ~**er** n atacante m, assaltante m

rail /reɪl/ n (of stairs) corrimão m; (of ship) amurada f; (on balcony) parapeito m; (for train) trilho m; (for curtain) varão m. **by** ~ por estrada, (P) caminho de ferro

railings /'reɪlɪŋz/ npl grade f

railroad /'reɪlrəʊd/ n (Amer) = railway

railway /'reɪlweɪ/ n estrada f, (P) caminho m de ferro. ~ **line** linha f do trem. ~ **station** estação f ferroviária, (P) estação f de caminho de ferro

rain /reɪn/ n chuva f □ vi chover. ~ **forest** floresta f tropical. ~**storm** n tempestade f com chuva. ~**-water** n água f da chuva

rainbow /'reɪnbəʊ/ n arco-íris m

raincoat /'reɪnkəʊt/ n impermeável m

raindrop /'reɪndrɒp/ n pingo m de chuva

rainfall /'reɪnfɔːl/ n precipitação f, pluviosidade f

rainy /'reɪnɪ/ a (-ier, -iest) chuvoso

raise /reɪz/ vt levantar, erguer; (breed) criar; (voice) levantar;

(*question*) fazer; (*price etc*) aumentar, subir; (*funds*) angariar; (*loan*) obter □ *n* (*Amer*) aumento *m*

raisin /'reɪzn/ *n* passa *f*

rake /reɪk/ *n* ancinho *m* □ *vt* juntar, alisar com ancinho; (*search*) revolver, remexer. **~ in** (*money*) ganhar a rodos. **~-off** *n* (*colloq*) percentagem *f* (*colloq*). **~ up** desenterrar, ressuscitar

rally /'ræli/ *vt/i* reunir(-se); (*reassemble*) reagrupar(-se), reorganizar(-se); (*health*) restabelecer (-se); (*strength*) recuperar as forças □ *n* (*recovery*) recuperação *f*; (*meeting*) comício *m*, assembléia *f*; (*auto*) rally *m*, rali *m*

ram /ræm/ *n* (*sheep*) carneiro *m* □ *vt* (*pt* **rammed**) (*beat down*) calcar; (*push*) meter à força; (*crash into*) bater contra

ramble /'ræmbl/ *n* caminhada *f*, perambulação *f* □ *vi* perambular, vaguear. **~e on** divagar. **~er** *n* caminhante *mf*; (*plant*) trepadeira *f*. **~ing** *a* (*speech*) desconexo

ramp /ræmp/ *n* rampa *f*

rampage /ræm'peɪdʒ/ *vi* causar distúrbios violentos

rampant /'ræmpənt/ *a* **be ~** vicejar, florescer; (*diseases etc*) grassar

rampart /'ræmpɑːt/ *n* baluarte *m*; (*fig*) defesa *f*

ramshackle /'ræmʃækl/ *a* (*car*) desconjuntado; (*house*) caindo aos pedaços

ran /ræn/ *see* **run**

ranch /rɑːntʃ/ *n* rancho *m*, estância *f*. **~er** *n* rancheiro *m*

rancid /'rænsɪd/ *a* rançoso

rancour /'ræŋkə(r)/ *n* rancor *m*

random /'rændəm/ *a* feito, tirado *etc* ao acaso □ *n* **at ~** ao acaso, a esmo, aleatoriamente

randy /'rændɪ/ *a* (**-ier**, **-iest**) lascivo, sensual

rang /ræŋ/ *see* **ring**

range /reɪndʒ/ *n* (*distance*) alcance *m*; (*scope*) âmbito *m*; (*variety*) gama *f*, variedade *f*; (*stove*) fogão *m*; (*of voice*) registro *m*, (*P*) registo *m*; (*of temperature*) variação *f* □ *vt* dispor, ordenar □ *vi* estender-se; (*vary*) variar. **~ of mountains** cordilheira *f*, serra *f*. **~r** *n* guarda *m* florestal

rank¹ /ræŋk/ *n* fila *f*, fileira *f*; (*mil*) posto *m*; (*social position*) classe *f*, categoria *f* □ *vt/i* **~ among** contar(-se) entre. **the ~ and file** a massa

rank² /ræŋk/ *a* (**-er**, **-est**) (*plants*) luxuriante; (*smell*) fétido; (*outand-out*) total

ransack /'rænsæk/ *vt* (*search*) espionar, revistar, remexer; (*pillage*) pilhar, saquear

ransom /'rænsəm/ *n* resgate *m* □ *vt* resgatar. **hold to ~** prender como refém

rant /rænt/ *vi* usar linguagem bombástica

rap /ræp/ *n* pancadinha *f* seca □ *vt/i* (*pt* **rapped**) bater, dar uma pancada seca em

rape /reɪp/ *vt* violar, estuprar □ *n* violação *f*, estupro *m*

rapid /'ræpɪd/ *a* rápido. **~ity** /rə'pɪdətɪ/ *n* rapidez *f*

rapids /'ræpɪdz/ *npl* rápidos *mpl*

rapist /'reɪpɪst/ *n* violador *m*, estuprador *m*

rapport /ræ'pɔː(r)/ *n* bom relacionamento *m*

rapt /ræpt/ *a* absorto. **~ in** mergulhado em

rapture /'ræptʃə(r)/ *n* êxtase *m*. **~ous** *a* extático; (*welcome etc*) entusiástico

rare¹ /reə(r)/ *a* (**-er**, **-est**) raro. **~ly** *adv* raramente, raras vezes. **~ity** *n* raridade *f*

rare² /reə(r)/ *a* (**-er**, **-est**) (*culin*) mal passado

rarefied /'reərɪfaɪd/ a rarefeito; (*refined*) requintado

raring /'reərɪŋ/ a ~ **to** (*colloq*) impaciente por, louco por (*colloq*)

rascal /'rɑːskl/ n (*dishonest*) patife m; (*mischievous*) maroto m

rash[1] /ræʃ/ n erupção f cutânea, irritação f na pele (*colloq*)

rash[2] /ræʃ/ a (**-er, -est**) imprudente, precipitado. ~**ly** adv imprudentemente, precipitadamente

rasher /'ræʃə(r)/ n fatia f (de presunto *or* de bacon)

rasp /rɑːsp/ n lixa f grossa, (P) lima f grossa

raspberry /'rɑːzbrɪ/ n framboesa f

rasping /'rɑːspɪŋ/ a áspero

rat /ræt/ n rato m, (P) ratazana f. ~ **race** (*fig*) luta renhida para vencer na vida, arrivismo m

rate /reɪt/ n (*ratio*) razão f; (*speed*) velocidade f; (*price*) tarifa f; (*of exchange*) (taxa m de) câmbio m; (*of interest*) taxa f. ~**s** (*taxes*) impostos mpl municipais, taxas fpl □ vt avaliar; (*fig: consider*) considerar. **at any** ~ de qualquer modo, pelo menos. **at the** ~ **of** à razão de. **at this** ~ desse jeito, desse modo

ratepayer /'reɪtpeɪə(r)/ n contribuinte mf

rather /'rɑːðə(r)/ adv (*by preference*) antes; (*fairly*) muito, bastante; (*a little*) um pouco. **I would** ~ **go** preferia ir

ratify /'rætɪfaɪ/ vt ratificar. ~**ication** /-ɪ'keɪʃn/ n ratificação f

rating /'reɪtɪŋ/ n (*comm*) rating m, (P) valor m; (*sailor*) praça f, marinheiro m; (*radio, TV*) índice m de audiência

ratio /'reɪʃɪəʊ/ n (pl **-os**) proporção f

ration /'ræʃn/ n ração f □ vt racionar

rational /'ræʃnəl/ a racional;

(*person*) sensato, razoável. ~**ize** vt racionalizar

rattle /'rætl/ vt/i matraquear; (*door, window*) bater; (*of bottles*) chocalhar; (*colloq*) agitar, mexer com os nervos de □ n (*baby's toy*) guizo m, chocalho m; (*of football fan*) matraca f; (*sound*) matraquear m, chocalhar m. ~ **off** despejar (*colloq*)

rattlesnake /'rætlsneɪk/ n cobra f cascavel

raucous /'rɔːkəs/ a áspero, rouco

ravage /'rævɪdʒ/ vt devastar, causar estragos a. ~**s** npl devastação f, estragos mpl

rave /reɪv/ vi delirar; (*in anger*) urrar. ~ **about** delirar (de entusiasmo) com

raven /'reɪvn/ n corvo m

ravenous /'rævənəs/ a esfomeado; (*greedy*) voraz

ravine /rə'viːn/ n ravina f, barranco m

raving /'reɪvɪŋ/ a ~ **lunatic** doido m varrido □ adv ~ **mad** loucamente

ravish /'rævɪʃ/ vt (*rape*) violar; (*enrapture*) arrebatar, encantar. ~**ing** a arrebatador, encantador

raw /rɔː/ a (**-er, -est**) cru; (*not processed*) bruto; (*wound*) em carne viva; (*weather*) frio e úmido, (P) húmido; (*immature*) inexperiente, verde. ~ **deal** tratamento m injusto. ~ **material** matéria-prima f

ray /reɪ/ n raio m

raze /reɪz/ vt arrasar

razor /'reɪzə(r)/ n navalha f de barba. ~**blade** n lâmina f de barbear

re /riː/ prep a respeito de, em referência a, relativo a

re- /riː/ pref re-

reach /riːtʃ/ vt chegar a atingir; (*contact*) contatar; (*pass*) passar □ vi estender-se, chegar □ n alcance m. **out of** ~ fora de alcance. ~ **for** estender a mão para agarrar. **within** ~ **of** ao alcance de; (*close to*) próximo de

react /rɪˈækt/ *vi* reagir

reaction /rɪˈækʃn/ *n* reação *f*. (P) reacção *f*. ~**ary** *a* & *n* reacionário (*m*), (P) reaccionário (*m*)

reactor /rɪˈæktə(r)/ *n* reator *m*, (P) reactor *m*

read /riːd/ *vt/i* (*pt* **read** /red/) ler; (*fig: interpret*) interpretar; (*study*) estudar; (*of instrument*) marcar, indicar □ *n* (*colloq*) leitura *f*. ~ **about** ler um artigo sobre. ~ **out** ler em voz alta. ~**able** *a* agradável e fácil de ler; (*legible*) legível. ~**er** *n* leitor *m*; (*book*) livro *m* de leitura. ~**ing** *n* leitura *f*; (*of instrument*) registro *m*, (P) registo *m*

readily /ˈredɪlɪ/ *adv* de boa vontade, prontamente; (*easily*) facilmente

readiness /ˈredɪnɪs/ *n* prontidão *f*. **in** ~ pronto (**for** para)

readjust /riːəˈdʒʌst/ *vt* reajustar □ *vi* readaptar-se

ready /ˈredɪ/ *a* (**-ier, -iest**) pronto □ *n* **at the** ~ pronto para disparar. ~**made** *a* pronto. ~**money** dinheiro *m* vivo, (P) dinheiro *m* de contado, pagamento *m* à vista. ~**-to-wear** *a* prêt-à-porter

real /rɪəl/ *a* real, verdadeiro; (*genuine*) autêntico □ *adv* (*Amer: colloq*) realmente. ~ **estate** bens *mpl* imobiliários

realis|t /ˈrɪəlɪst/ *n* realista *mf*. ~**m** /-zəm/ *n* realismo *m*. ~**tic** /-ˈlɪstɪk/ *a* realista. ~**tically** /-ˈlɪstɪklɪ/ *adv* realisticamente

reality /rɪˈælɪtɪ/ *n* realidade *f*

realize /ˈrɪəlaɪz/ *vt* dar-se conta de, aperceber-se de, perceber; (*fulfil; turn into cash*) realizar. ~**ation** /-ˈzeɪʃn/ *n* consciência *f*, noção *f*; (*fulfilment*) realização *f*

really /ˈrɪəlɪ/ *adv* realmente, na verdade

realm /relm/ *n* reino *m*; (*fig*) domínio *m*, esfera *f*

reap /riːp/ *vt* (*cut*) ceifar; (*gather, fig*) colher

reappear /riːəˈpɪə(r)/ *vi* reaparecer. ~**ance** *n* reaparição *f*

rear[1] /rɪə(r)/ *n* traseira *f*, retaguarda *f* □ *a* traseiro, de trás, posterior. **bring up the** ~ ir na retaguarda, fechar a marcha. ~**view mirror** espelho *m* retrovisor

rear[2] /rɪə(r)/ *vt* levantar, erguer; (*children, cattle*) criar □ *vi* (*of horse etc*) empinar-se. ~ **one's head** levantar a cabeça

rearrange /riːəˈreɪndʒ/ *vt* arranjar doutro modo, reorganizar

reason /ˈriːzn/ *n* razão *f* □ *vt/i* raciocinar, argumentar. ~ **with sb** procurar convencer alguém. **within** ~ razoável. ~**ing** *n* raciocínio *m*

reasonable /ˈriːznəbl/ *a* razoável

reassur|e /riːəˈʃʊə(r)/ *vt* tranquilizar, sossegar. ~**ance** *n* garantia *f*. ~**ing** *a* animador, reconfortante

rebate /ˈriːbeɪt/ *n* (*refund*) reembolso *m*; (*discount*) desconto *m*, abatimento *m*

rebel[1] /ˈrebl/ *n* rebelde *mf*

rebel[2] /rɪˈbel/ *vi* (*pt* **rebelled**) rebelar-se, revoltar-se, sublevar-se. ~**lion** *n* rebelião *f*, revolta *f*. ~**lious** *a* rebelde

rebound[1] /rɪˈbaʊnd/ *vi* repercutir, ressoar; (*fig: backfire*) recair (**on** sobre)

rebound[2] /ˈriːbaʊnd/ *n* ricochete *m*

rebuff /rɪˈbʌf/ *vt* receber mal, repelir (*colloq*) □ *n* rejeição *f*

rebuild /riːˈbɪld/ *vt* (*pt* **rebuilt**) reconstruir

rebuke /rɪˈbjuːk/ *vt* repreender □ *n* reprimenda *f*

recall /rɪˈkɔːl/ vt chamar, mandar regressar; (*remember*) lembrar-se de □ n (*summons*) ordem f de regresso

recant /rɪˈkænt/ vi retratar-se, (P) retractar-se

recap /ˈriːkæp/ vt/i (pt **recapped**) (colloq) recapitular □ n recapitulação f

recapitulate /riːkəˈpɪtʃʊleɪt/ vt/i recapitular. **~ion** /-ˈleɪʃn/ n recapitulação f

recede /rɪˈsiːd/ vi recuar, retroceder. **his hair is ~ing** ele está ficando com entradas. **~ing** a (*forehead, chin*) recuado, voltado para dentro

receipt /rɪˈsiːt/ n recibo m; (*receiving*) recepção f. **~s** (*comm*) receitas fpl

receive /rɪˈsiːv/ vt receber. **~r** /-ə(r)/ n (*of stolen goods*) receptador m; (*phone*) fone m, (P) auscultador m; (*radio/TV*) receptor m. **(official) ~r** síndico m de massa falida

recent /ˈriːsnt/ a recente. **~ly** adv recentemente

receptacle /rɪˈseptəkl/ n recipiente m, receptáculo m

reception /rɪˈsepʃn/ n recepção f; (*welcome*) acolhimento m. **~ist** n recepcionista mf

receptive /rɪˈseptɪv/ a receptivo

recess /rɪˈses/ n recesso m; (*of legislature*) recesso m; (*Amer: schol*) recreio m

recession /rɪˈseʃn/ n recessão f, depressão f

recharge /riːˈtʃɑːdʒ/ vt tornar a carregar, recarregar

recipe /ˈresəpɪ/ n (*culin*) receita f

recipient /rɪˈsɪpɪənt/ n recipiente mf; (*of letter*) destinatário m

reciprocal /rɪˈsɪprəkl/ a recíproco

reciprocate /rɪˈsɪprəkeɪt/ vt/i reciprocar(-se), retribuir, fazer o mesmo

recital /rɪˈsaɪtl/ n (*music etc*) recital m

recite /rɪˈsaɪt/ vt recitar; (*list*) enumerar

reckless /ˈreklɪs/ a inconsciente, imprudente, estouvado

reckon /ˈrekən/ vt/i calcular; (*judge*) considerar; (*think*) supor, pensar. **~ on** contar com, depender de. **~ with** contar com, levar em conta. **~ing** n conta(s) f(pl)

reclaim /rɪˈkleɪm/ vt (*demand*) reclamar; (*land*) recuperar

recline /rɪˈklaɪn/ vt/i reclinar (-se). **~ing** a (*person*) reclinado; (*chair*) reclinável

recluse /rɪˈkluːs/ n solitário m, recluso m

recognition /rekəgˈnɪʃn/ n reconhecimento m. **beyond ~** irreconhecível. **gain ~** ganhar nome, ser reconhecido

recognize /ˈrekəgnaɪz/ vt reconhecer. **~able** /ˈrekəgnaɪzəbl/ a reconhecível

recoil /rɪˈkɔɪl/ vi recuar; (*gun*) dar coice □ n recuo m; (*gun*) coice m. **~ from doing** recusar-se a fazer

recollect /rekəˈlekt/ vt recordar-se de. **~ion** /-ʃn/ n recordação f

recommend /rekəˈmend/ vt recomendar. **~ation** /-ˈdeɪʃn/ n recomendação f

recompense /ˈrekəmpens/ vt/i compensar □ n recompensa f

reconcile /ˈrekənsaɪl/ vt (*people*) reconciliar; (*facts*) conciliar. **~e o.s. to** resignar-se a, conformar-se com. **~iation** /-sɪlɪˈeɪʃn/ n reconciliação f

reconnaissance /rɪˈkɒnɪsns/ n reconhecimento m

reconnoitre /rekəˈnɔɪtə(r)/ vt/i (*pres p* **-tring**) (*mil*) reconhecer, fazer um reconhecimento (de)

reconsider /riːkənˈsɪdə(r)/ vt reconsiderar

reconstruct /riːkənˈstrʌkt/ vt

reconstruir. **~ion** /-ʃn/ n reconstrução f

record¹ /rɪ'kɔːd/ vt registar; (disc, tape etc) gravar. **~ that** referir/relatar que. **~ing** n (disc, tape etc) gravação f.

record² /'rekɔːd/ n (register) registro m, (P) registo m; (mention) menção f, nota f; (file) arquivo m; (mus) disco m; (sport) recorde m □ a a record(e) invar. **have a (criminal) ~** ter cadastro. **off the ~** (unofficial) oficioso; (secret) confidencial. **~-player** n toca-discos m invar, (P) gira-discos m invar

recorder /rɪ'kɔːdə(r)/ n (mus) flauta f de ponta; (techn) instrumento m registrador

recount /rɪ'kaʊnt/ vt narrar em pormenor, relatar

re-count /'riːkaʊnt/ n (pol) nova contagem f

recoup /rɪ'kuːp/ vt compensar; (recover) recuperar

recourse /rɪ'kɔːs/ n recurso m. **have ~ to** recorrer a

recover /rɪ'kʌvə(r)/ vt recuperar □ vi restabelecer-se. **~y** n recuperação f; (health) recuperação f, restabelecimento m

recreation /rekrɪ'eɪʃn/ n recreação f, recreio m; (pastime) passatempo m. **~al** a recreativo

recrimination /rɪkrɪmɪ'neɪʃn/ n recriminação f

recruit /rɪ'kruːt/ n recruta m □ vt recrutar. **~ment** n recrutamento m

rectangle /'rektæŋgl/ n retângulo m, (P) rectângulo m. **~ular** /-'tæŋgjʊlə(r)/ a retangular, (P) rectangular

rectify /'rektɪfaɪ/ vt retificar, (P) rectificar

recuperate /rɪ'kjuːpəreɪt/ vt/i recuperar(-se)

recur /rɪ'kɜː(r)/ vi (pt recurred) repetir-se; (come back) voltar (to a)

recurrent /rɪ'kʌrənt/ a frequente, (P) frequente, repetido, periódico. **~ce** n repetição f

recycle /riː'saɪkl/ vt reciclar

red /red/ a (redder, reddest) encarnado, vermelho; (hair) ruivo □ n encarnado m, vermelho m. **in the ~** em déficit. **~ carpet** (fig) recepção f solene, tratamento m especial. **R~ Cross** Cruz f Vermelha. **~-handed** a em flagrante (delito), com a boca na botija (colloq). **~ herring** (fig) pista f falsa. **~-hot** a escaldante, incandescente. **~ light** luz f vermelha. **~ tape** (fig) papelada f, burocracia f. **~ wine** vinho m tinto

redden /'redn/ vt/i avermelhar (-se); (blush) corar, ruborizar-se

redecorate /riː'dekəreɪt/ vt decorar/pintar de novo

redeem /rɪ'diːm/ vt (sins etc) redimir; (sth pawned) tirar do prego (colloq); (voucher etc) resgatar. **~emption** /rɪ'dempʃn/ n resgate m; (of honour) salvação f

redirect /riːdaɪ'rekt/ vt (letter) endereçar

redness /'rednɪs/ n vermelhidão f, cor f vermelha

redo /riː'duː/ vt (pt -did, pp -done) refazer

redress /rɪ'dres/ vt reparar; (set right) remediar, emendar. **~ the balance** restabelecer o equilíbrio □ n reparação f

reduce /rɪ'djuːs/ vt reduzir; (temperature etc) baixar. **~tion** /rɪ'dʌkʃn/ n redução f

redundant /rɪ'dʌndənt/ a redundante, supérfluo; (worker) desempregado. **be made ~t** ficar desempregado. **~cy** n demissão f por excesso de pessoal

reed /riːd/ n cana f, junco m; (mus) palheta f

reef /riːf/ n recife m

reek /riːk/ n mau cheiro m □ vi

cheirar mal, tresandar. **he ~s of wine** ele está com cheiro de vinho

reel /riːl/ n carretel m; (spool) bobina f □ vi cambalear, vacilar □ vt ~ **off** recitar (collog)

refectory /rɪˈfektərɪ/ n refeitório m

refer /rɪˈfɜː(r)/ vt/i (pt **referred**) ~ **to** referir-se a; (concern) aplicar-se a, dizer respeito a; (consult) consultar; (direct) remeter a

referee /refəˈriː/ n árbitro m; (for job) pessoa f que dá referências □ vt (pt **refereed**) arbitrar

reference /ˈrefrəns/ n referência f; (testimonial) referências fpl. **in** ~ or **with** ~ **to** com referência a. ~ **book** livro m de consulta

referendum /refəˈrendəm/ n (pl **-dums** or **-da**) referendo m, plebiscito m

refill[1] /riːˈfɪl/ vt encher de novo; (pen etc) pôr carga nova em

refill[2] /ˈriːfɪl/ n (pen etc) carga f nova, (P) recarga f

refine /rɪˈfaɪn/ vt refinar. ~**d** a refinado; (taste, manners etc) requintado. ~**ment** n (taste, manners etc) refinamento m, requinte m; (tech) refinação f. ~**ry** /-ərɪ/ n refinaria f

reflect /rɪˈflekt/ vt/i refletir, (P) reflectir (**on/upon** em). ~**ion** /-ʃn/ n reflexão f; (image) reflexo m. ~**or** n refletor m, (P) reflector m

reflective /rɪˈflektɪv/ a refletor, (P) reflector; (thoughtful) refletido, (P) reflectido, ponderado

reflex /ˈriːfleks/ a & n reflexo (m)

reflexive /rɪˈfleksɪv/ a (gram) reflexivo, (P) reflexo

reform /rɪˈfɔːm/ vt/i reformar(-se) □ n reforma f. ~**er** n reformador m

refract /rɪˈfrækt/ vt refratar, (P) refractar

refrain[1] /rɪˈfreɪn/ n refrão m, estribilho m

refrain[2] /rɪˈfreɪn/ vi abster-se (**from** de)

refresh /rɪˈfreʃ/ vt refrescar; (of rest etc) restaurar. ~ **one's memory** avivar or refrescar a memória. ~**ing** a refrescante; (of rest etc) reparador. ~**ments** npl refeição f leve; (drinks) refrescos mpl

refresher /rɪˈfreʃə(r)/ n ~ **course** curso m de reciclagem

refrigerat|**e** /rɪˈfrɪdʒəreɪt/ vt refrigerar. ~**or** n frigorífico m, refrigerador m, geladeira f

refuel /riːˈfjuːəl/ vt/i (pt re**fuelled**) reabastecer(-se) (de combustível)

refuge /ˈrefjuːdʒ/ n refúgio m, asilo m. **take** ~ refugiar-se

refugee /refjʊˈdʒiː/ n refugiado m

refund[1] /rɪˈfʌnd/ vt reembolsar

refund[2] /ˈriːfʌnd/ n reembolso m

refus|**e**[1] /rɪˈfjuːz/ vt/i recusar(-se). ~**al** n recusa f. **first** ~**al** preferência f, primeira opção f

refuse[2] /ˈrefjuːs/ n refugo m, lixo m. ~**-collector** n lixeiro m, (P) homem m do lixo

refute /rɪˈfjuːt/ vt refutar

regain /rɪˈgeɪn/ vt recobrar, recuperar

regal /ˈriːgl/ a real, régio

regalia /rɪˈgeɪlɪə/ npl insígnias fpl

regard /rɪˈgɑːd/ vt considerar; (gaze) olhar □ n consideração f, estima f; (gaze) olhar m. ~**s** cumprimentos mpl; (less formally) lembranças fpl, saudades fpl. **as** ~**s**, ~**ing** prep no que diz respeito a, quanto a. ~**less** adv apesar de tudo. ~**less of** apesar de

regatta /rɪˈgætə/ n regata f

regenerate /rɪˈdʒenəreɪt/ vt regenerar

regen|**t** /ˈriːdʒənt/ n regente mf. ~**cy** n regência f

regime /reɪˈʒiːm/ n regime m

regiment /ˈredʒɪmənt/ n regimento m. **∼al** /-ˈmentl/ a de regimento, regimental. **∼ation** /-enˈteɪʃn/ n arregimentação f, disciplina f excessiva

region /ˈriːdʒən/ n região f. **in the ∼ of** por volta de. **∼al** a regional

regist|er /ˈredʒɪstə(r)/ n registro m, (P) registo m □ vt (record) anotar; (notice) fixar, registar, prestar atenção a; (birth, letter) registrar, (P) registar; (vehicle) matricular; (emotions etc) exprimir □ vi inscrever-se. **∼er office** registro m, (P) registo m. **∼ration** /-ˈstreɪʃn/ n registro m, (P) registo m; (for course) inscrição f, matrícula f. **∼ration (number)** número m de placa

registrar /redʒɪˈstrɑː(r)/ n oficial m do registro, (P) registo civil; (univ) secretário m

regret /rɪˈɡret/ n pena f, pesar m; (repentance) remorso m. **I have no ∼s** não estou arrependido □ vt (pt **regretted**) lamentar, sentir (to do fazer); (feel repentance) arrepender-se de, lamentar. **∼fully** adv com pena, pesarosamente. **∼table** a lamentável. **∼tably** adv infelizmente

regular /ˈreɡjʊlə(r)/ a regular; (usual) normal; (colloq: thorough) perfeito, verdadeiro, autêntico □ n (colloq: client) cliente mf habitual. **∼ity** /-ˈlærətɪ/ n regularidade f. **∼ly** adv regularmente

regulat|e /ˈreɡjʊleɪt/ vt regular. **∼ion** /-ˈleɪʃn/ n regulação f; (rule) regulamento m, regra f

rehabilitat|e /riːəˈbɪlɪteɪt/ vt reabilitar. **∼ion** /-ˈteɪʃn/ n reabilitação f

rehash[1] /riːˈhæʃ/ vt apresentar sob nova forma, (P) cozinhar (colloq)

rehash[2] /ˈriːhæʃ/ n (fig) apanhado m, (P) cozinhado m (colloq)

rehears|e /rɪˈhɜːs/ vt ensaiar. **∼al** n ensaio m. **dress ∼al** ensaio m geral

reign /reɪn/ n reinado m □ vi reinar (over em)

reimburse /riːɪmˈbɜːs/ vt reembolsar. **∼ment** n reembolso m

rein /reɪn/ n rédea f

reincarnation /riːɪnkɑːˈneɪʃn/ n reencarnação f

reindeer /ˈreɪndɪə(r)/ n invar rena f

reinforce /riːɪnˈfɔːs/ vt reforçar. **∼ment** n reforço m. **∼ments** reforços mpl. **∼d concrete** concreto m armado, (P) cimento m or betão m armado

reinstate /riːɪnˈsteɪt/ vt reintegrar

reiterate /riːˈɪtəreɪt/ vt reiterar

reject[1] /rɪˈdʒekt/ vt rejeitar. **∼ion** /-ʃn/ n rejeição f

reject[2] /ˈriːdʒekt/ n (artigo de) refugo m

rejoic|e /rɪˈdʒɔɪs/ vi regozijar-se (at/over com). **∼ing** n regozijo m

rejuvenate /rɪˈdʒuːvəneɪt/ vt rejuvenescer

relapse /rɪˈlæps/ n recaída f □ vi recair

relate /rɪˈleɪt/ vt relatar; (associate) relacionar □ vi **∼ to** ter relação com, dizer respeito a; (get on with) entender-se com. **∼d** a aparentado; (ideas etc) afim, relacionado

relation /rɪˈleɪʃn/ n relação f; (person) parente mf. **∼ship** n parentesco m; (link) relação f; (affair) ligação f

relative /ˈrelətɪv/ n parente mf □ a relativo. **∼ly** adv relativamente

relax /rɪˈlæks/ vt/i relaxar(-se). (fig) descontrair(-se). **∼ation** /riːlækˈseɪʃn/ n relaxamento m; (fig) descontração f, (P) descon-

tracção *f*; (*recreation*) distração *f*,
(*P*) distracção *f*. ~ing *a* rela-
xante

relay¹ /'riːleɪ/ *n* turma *f*, (*P*) turno
m. ~ race corrida *f* de revezamento, (*P*) estafetas

relay² /rɪ'leɪ/ *vt* (*message*) retrans-
mitir

release /rɪ'liːs/ *vt* libertar, soltar;
(*mech*) desengatar, soltar; (*bomb,
film, record*) lançar; (*news*) dar,
publicar; (*gas, smoke*) soltar □ *n*
libertação *f*; (*mech*) desengate *m*;
(*bomb, film, record*) lançamento
m; (*news*) publicação *f*; (*gas,
smoke*) emissão *f*. new~ estréia *f*

relegate /'relɪɡeɪt/ *vt* relegar

relent /rɪ'lent/ *vi* ceder. ~less *a*
implacável, inexorável, inflexível

relevan|t /'relɪvənt/ *a* relevante,
pertinente, a propósito. be ~ to
ter a ver com. ~ce *n* pertinência
f, relevância *f*

reliab|le /rɪ'laɪəbl/ *a* de confiança,
com que se pode contar; (*source
etc*) fidedigno; (*machine etc*) seguro, confiável. ~ility /-'bɪlətɪ/
n confiabilidade *f*

reliance /rɪ'laɪəns/ *n* (*dependence*)
segurança *f*; (*trust*) confiança *f*,
fé *f* (on em)

relic /'relɪk/ *n* relíquia *f*. ~s *n* ves-
tígios *mpl*, ruínas *fpl*

relief /rɪ'liːf/ *n* alívio *m*; (*assist-
ance*) auxílio *m*, assistência *f*;
(*outline, design*) relevo *m*. ~
road estrada *f* alternativa

relieve /rɪ'liːv/ *vt* aliviar; (*help*)
socorrer; (*take over from*) reve-
zar, substituir; (*mil*) render

religion /rɪ'lɪdʒən/ *n* religião *f*

religious /rɪ'lɪdʒəs/ *a* religioso

relinquish /rɪ'lɪŋkwɪʃ/ *vt* abandonar, renunciar a

relish /'relɪʃ/ *n* prazer *m*, gosto *m*;
(*culin*) molho *m* condimentado □
vt saborear, apreciar, gostar de

relocate /riː'ləʊkeɪt/ *vt/i* transfe-
rir(-se), mudar(-se)

reluctan|t /rɪ'lʌktənt/ *a* relutante
(to em), pouco inclinado (to a).
~ce *n* relutância *f*. ~tly *adv* a
contragosto, relutantemente

rely /rɪ'laɪ/ *vi* ~ on contar com;
(*depend*) depender de

remain /rɪ'meɪn/ *vi* ficar, permanecer. ~s *npl* restos *mpl*;
(*ruins*) ruínas *fpl*. ~ing *a* res-
tante

remainder /rɪ'meɪndə(r)/ *n* res-
tante *m*, remanescente *m*

remand /rɪ'maːnd/ *vt* reconduzir
à prisão para detenção provisó-
ria □ *n* on ~ sob prisão preven-
tiva

remark /rɪ'maːk/ *n* observação *f*,
comentário *m* □ *vt* observar, comentar □ *vi* ~ on fazer observa-
ções *or* comentários sobre.
~able *a* notável

remarr|y /riː'mærɪ/ *vt/i* tornar a
casar(-se) (com). ~iage *n* novo
casamento *m*

remed|y /'remədɪ/ *n* remédio *m* □
vt remediar. ~ial /rɪ'miːdɪəl/ *a*
(*med*) corretivo, (*P*) correctivo

rememb|er /rɪ'membə(r)/ *vt* lem-
brar-se de, recordar-se de.
~rance *n* lembrança *f*, recordação *f*

remind /rɪ'maɪnd/ *vt* (fazer) lembrar (sb of sth alg coisa a
alguém). ~ sb to do lembrar a
alguém que faça. ~er *n* o que
serve para fazer lembrar; (*note*)
lembrete *m*

reminisce /remɪ'nɪs/ *vi* (re)lem-
brar (coisas passadas). ~nces
npl reminiscências *fpl*

reminiscent /remɪ'nɪsnt/ *a* ~ of
que faz lembrar, evocativo de

remiss /rɪ'mɪs/ *a* negligente, descuidado

remission /rɪ'mɪʃn/ *n* remissão *f*;
(*jur*) comutação *f* (de pena)

remit /rɪ'mɪt/ *vt* (*pt* remitted)
(*money*) remeter. ~tance *n* remessa *f* (de dinheiro)

remnant /'remnənt/ n resto m; (trace) vestígio m; (of cloth) retalho m

remorse /rɪ'mɔːs/ n remorso m. ~**ful** a arrependido, com remorsos. ~**less** a implacável

remote /rɪ'məʊt/ a remoto, distante; (person) distante; (slight) vago, leve. ~ **control** comando m à distância, telecomando m. ~**ly** adv de longe; vagamente

remov|e /rɪ'muːv/ vt tirar, remover; (lead away) levar; (dismiss) demitir; (get rid of) eliminar. ~**al** n remoção f; (dismissal) demissão f; (from house) mudança f

remunerat|e /rɪ'mjuːnəreɪt/ vt remunerar. ~**ion** /-'reɪʃn/ n remuneração f

rename /riː'neɪm/ vt rebatizar, (P) rebaptizar

render /'rendə(r)/ vt retribuir; (services) prestar; (mus) interpretar; (translate) traduzir. ~**ing** n (mus) interpretação f; (plaster) reboco m

renegade /'renɪɡeɪd/ n renegado m

renew /rɪ'njuː/ vt renovar; (resume) retomar. ~**able** a renovável. ~**al** n renovação f; (resumption) reatamento m

renounce /rɪ'naʊns/ vt renunciar a; (disown) renegar, repudiar

renovat|e /'renəveɪt/ vt renovar. ~**ion** /-'veɪʃn/ n renovação f

renown /rɪ'naʊn/ n renome m. ~**ed** a conceituado, célebre, de renome

rent /rent/ n aluguel m, (P) aluguer m, renda f □ vt alugar, arrendar. ~**al** n (charge) aluguel m, (P) aluguer m, renda f; (act of renting) aluguel m, (P) aluguer m

renunciation /rɪnʌnsɪ'eɪʃn/ n renúncia f

reopen /riː'əʊpən/ vt/i reabrir (-se). ~**ing** n reabertura f

reorganize /riːˈɔːɡənaɪz/ vt/i reorganizar(-se)

rep /rep/ n (colloq) vendedor m, caixeiro-viajante m

repair /rɪ'peə(r)/ vt reparar, consertar □ n reparo m, conserto m. **in good** ~ em bom estado (de conservação)

repartee /repɑː'tiː/ n resposta f pronta e espirituosa

repatriat|e /riː'pætrɪeɪt/ vt repatriar. ~**ion** /-'eɪʃn/ n repatriamento m

repay /riː'peɪ/ vt (pt **repaid**) pagar, devolver, reembolsar; (reward) recompensar. ~**ment** n pagamento m, reembolso m

repeal /rɪ'piːl/ vt revogar □ n revogação f

repeat /rɪ'piːt/ vt/i repetir(-se) □ n repetição f; (broadcast) retransmissão f. ~**edly** adv repetidas vezes, repetidamente

repel /rɪ'pel/ vt (pt **repelled**) repelir. ~**lent** a & n repelente (m)

repent /rɪ'pent/ vi arrepender-se (of de). ~**ance** n arrependimento m. ~**ant** a arrependido

repercussion /riːpə'kʌʃn/ n repercussão f

repertoire /'repətwɑː(r)/ n repertório m

repertory /'repətrɪ/ n repertório m

repetit|ion /repɪ'tɪʃn/ n repetição f. ~**ious** /-'tɪʃəs/, ~**ive** /-'petətɪv/ a repetitivo

replace /rɪ'pleɪs/ vt colocar no mesmo lugar, repor; (take the place of) substituir. ~**ment** n reposição f; (substitution) substituição f; (person) substituto m

replenish /rɪ'plenɪʃ/ vt voltar a encher, reabastecer; (renew) renovar

replica /'replɪkə/ n réplica f, cópia f, reprodução f

reply /rɪ'plaɪ/ vt/i responder, replicar □ n resposta f, réplica f

report /rɪ'pɔːt/ vt relatar; (notify)

informar; (*denounce*) denunciar, apresentar queixa de □ *vi* fazer um relatório. **~ (on)** (*news item*) fazer uma reportagem (sobre). **~ to** (*go*) apresentar-se a □ *n* (*in newspapers*) reportagem *f*; (*of company, doctor*) relatório *m*; (*schol*) boletim *m* escolar; (*sound*) detonação *f*; (*rumour*) rumores *mpl*. **~edly** *adv* segundo consta. **~er** *n* repórter *m*

repose /rɪˈpəʊz/ *n* repouso *m*

repossess /riːpəˈzes/ *vt* reapossar-se de, retomar se

represent /reprɪˈzent/ *vt* representar. **~ation** /-ˈteɪʃn/ *n* representação *f*

representative /reprɪˈzentətɪv/ *a* representativo □ *n* representante *mf*

repress /rɪˈpres/ *vt* reprimir. **~ion** /-ʃn/ *n* repressão *f*. **~ive** *a* repressor, repressivo

reprieve /rɪˈpriːv/ *n* suspensão *f* temporária; (*temporary relief*) tréguas *fpl* □ *vt* suspender temporariamente; (*fig*) dar tréguas a

reprimand /ˈreprɪmɑːnd/ *vt* repreender □ *n* repreensão *f*, repri- menda *f*

reprint /ˈriːprɪnt/ *n* reimpressão *f*, reedição *f* □ *vt* /riːˈprɪnt/ reimpri- mir

reprisals /rɪˈpraɪzlz/ *npl* represá- lias *fpl*

reproach /rɪˈprəʊtʃ/ *vt* censurar, repreender (**sb for sth** alguém por alg coisa, alg coisa a alguém) □ *n* censura *f*. **~ above ~** irrepreensível. **~ful** a repreen- sivo, reprovador. **~fully** *adv* re- provadoramente

reproduce /riːprəˈdjuːs/ *vt/i* re- produzir(-se). **~tion** /-ˈdʌkʃn/ *n* reprodução *f*. **~tive** /-ˈdʌktɪv/ *a* reprodutivo, reprodutor

reptile /ˈreptaɪl/ *n* réptil *m*

republic /rɪˈpʌblɪk/ *n* república *f*. **~an** *a* & *n* republicano (*m*)

repudiate /rɪˈpjuːdɪeɪt/ *vt* repu- diar, rejeitar

repugnan|t /rɪˈpʌgnənt/ *a* repug- nante. **~ce** *n* repugnância *f*

repuls|e /rɪˈpʌls/ *vt* repelir, re- pulsar. **~ion** /-ʃn/ *n* repulsa *f*. **~ive** *a* repulsivo, repelente, re- pugnante

reputable /ˈrepjʊtəbl/ *a* respeita- do, honrado; (*firm, make etc*) de renome, conceituado

reputation /repjʊˈteɪʃn/ *n* reputa- ção *f*

repute /rɪˈpjuːt/ *n* reputação *f*. **~d** /-ɪd/ *a* suposto, putativo. **~d to be** tido como, tido na con- ta de. **~dly** /-ɪdlɪ/ *adv* segundo consta, com fama de

request /rɪˈkwest/ *n* pedido *m* □ *vt* pedir, solicitar (**of, from** a)

requiem /ˈrekwɪəm/ *n* réquiem *m*; (*mass*) missa *f* de réquiem

require /rɪˈkwaɪə(r)/ *vt* requerer. **~d** a requerido; (*needed*) neces- sário, preciso. **~ment** *n* (*fig*) requi- sito *m*; (*need*) necessidade *f*; (*demand*) exigência *f*

requisite /ˈrekwɪzɪt/ *a* necessário □ *n* coisa necessária *f*, requisito *m*. **~s** (*for travel etc*) artigos *mpl*

requisition /rekwɪˈzɪʃn/ *n* requi- sição *f* □ *vt* requisitar

resale /ˈriːseɪl/ *n* revenda *f*

rescue /ˈreskjuː/ *vt* salvar, socor- rer (**from** de) □ *n* salvamento *m*; (*help*) socorro *m*, ajuda *f*. **~r** /-ə(r)/ *n* salvador *m*

research /rɪˈsɜːtʃ/ *n* pesquisa *f*, in- vestigação *f* □ *vt/i* pesquisar, fa- zer investigação (**into** sobre). **~er** *n* investigador *m*

resembl|e /rɪˈzembl/ *vt* asseme- lhar-se a, parecer-se com. **~ance** *n* semelhança *f*, simila- ridade *f* (**to** com)

resent /rɪˈzent/ *vt* ressentir(-se de), ficar ressentido com. **~ful** *a* ressentido. **~ment** *n* ressenti- mento *m*

reservation /rezə'veɪʃn/ n (booking) reserva f; (Amer) reserva f (de índios)

reserve /rɪ'zɜːv/ vt reservar □ n reserva f; (sport) suplente mf. ~ de reserva. ~d a reservado

reservoir /'rezəvwɑː(r)/ n (lake, supply etc) reservatório m; (container) depósito m

reshape /riː'ʃeɪp/ vt remodelar

reshuffle /riː'ʃʌfl/ vt (pol) remodelar □ n (pol) reforma f (do Ministério)

reside /rɪ'zaɪd/ vi residir

residen|t /'rezɪdənt/ a residente □ n morador m, habitante mf; (foreigner) residente mf; (in hotel) hóspede mf. ~ce n residência f; (of students) residência f, lar m. ~ce permit visto m de residência

residential /rezɪ'denʃl/ a residencial

residue /'rezɪdjuː/ n resíduo m

resign /rɪ'zaɪn/ vt (post) demitir-se. ~ o.s. to resignar-se a □ vi demitir-se de. ~ation /rezɪg'neɪʃn/ n resignação f; (from job) demissão f. ~ed a resignado

resilien|t /rɪ'zɪlɪənt/ a (springy) elástico; (person) resistente. ~ce n elasticidade f; (of person) resistência f

resin /'rezɪn/ n resina f

resist /rɪ'zɪst/ vt/i resistir (a). ~ance n resistência f. ~ant a resistente

resolut|e /'rezəluːt/ a resoluto. ~ion /-'luːʃn/ n resolução f

resolve /rɪ'zɒlv/ vt resolver. ~ to do resolver fazer □ n resolução f. ~d a (resolute) resoluto; (decided) resolvido (to a)

resonan|t /'rezənənt/ a ressonante. ~ce n ressonância f

resort /rɪ'zɔːt/ vi ~ to recorrer a, valer-se de □ n recurso m; (place) estância f, local m turístico. as a last ~ em último recurso. sea-

side ~ praia f, balneário m, (P) estância f balnear

resound /rɪ'zaʊnd/ vi reboar, ressoar (with com). ~ing a ressoante; (fig) retumbante

resource /rɪ'sɔːs/ n recurso m. ~s recursos mpl, riquezas fpl. ~ful a expedito, engenhoso, desembaraçado. ~fulness n expediente m, engenho m

respect /rɪ'spekt/ n respeito m □ vt respeitar. with ~ to a respeito de, com respeito a, relativamente a. ~ful a respeitoso

respectab|le /rɪ'spektəbl/ a respeitável; (passable) passável, aceitável. ~ility /-'bɪlətɪ/ n respeitabilidade f

respective /rɪ'spektɪv/ a respectivo. ~ly adv respectivamente

respiration /respə'reɪʃn/ n respiração f

respite /'respaɪt/ n pausa f, trégua f, folga f

respond /rɪ'spɒnd/ vi responder (to a); (react) reagir (to a)

response /rɪ'spɒns/ n resposta f; (reaction) reação f, (P) reacção f

responsib|le /rɪ'spɒnsəbl/ a responsável; (job) de responsabilidade. ~ility /-'bɪlətɪ/ n responsabilidade f

responsive /rɪ'spɒnsɪv/ a receptivo, que reage bem. ~ to sensível a

rest[1] /rest/ vt/i descansar, repousar; (lean) apoiar(-se) □ n descanso m, repouso m; (support) suporte m. ~-room n (Amer) banheiro m, (P) toaletes mpl

rest[2] /rest/ vi (remain) ficar □ n (remainder) resto m de (of de). the ~ (of the) (others) os outros. ~s with him cabe a ele

restaurant /'restrɒnt/ n restaurante m

restful /'restfl/ a sossegado, repousante, tranqüilo, (P) tranquilo

restitution /restɪˈtjuːʃn/ n restituição f; (for injury) indenização f, (P) indemnização f

restless /ˈrestlɪs/ a agitado, desassossegado

restor|e /rɪˈstɔː(r)/ vt restaurar; (give back) restituir, devolver. ~ation /restəˈreɪʃn/ n restauração f

restrain /rɪˈstreɪn/ vt conter, reprimir. ~ o.s. controlar-se. ~ sb from impedir alguém de. ~ed a comedido, moderado. ~t n controle m; (moderation) moderação f, comedimento m

restrict /rɪˈstrɪkt/ vt restringir, limitar. ~ion /-ʃn/ n restrição f. ~ive a restritivo

result /rɪˈzʌlt/ n resultado m □ vi resultar (from de). ~ in resultar em

resum|e /rɪˈzjuːm/ vt/i reatar, retomar; (work, travel) recomeçar. ~ption /rɪˈzʌmpʃn/ n reatamento m, retomada f, (of work) recomeço m

résumé /ˈrezjuːmeɪ/ n resumo m

resurgence /rɪˈsɜːdʒəns/ n reaparecimento m, ressurgimento m

resurrect /rezəˈrekt/ vt ressuscitar. ~ion /-ʃn/ n ressurreição f

resuscitat|e /rɪˈsʌsɪteɪt/ vt ressuscitar, reanimar. ~ion /-ˈteɪʃn/ n reanimação f

retail /ˈriːteɪl/ n retalho m □ a & adv a retalho □ vt/i vender(-se) a retalho. ~er n retalhista mf

retain /rɪˈteɪn/ vt reter; (keep) conservar, guardar

retaliat|e /rɪˈtælɪeɪt/ vi retaliar, exercer represálias, desforrar-se. ~ion /-ˈeɪʃn/ n retaliação f, represália f, desforra f

retarded /rɪˈtɑːdɪd/ a retardado, atrasado

retch /retʃ/ vi fazer esforço para vomitar, estar com ânsias de vômito

retention /rɪˈtenʃn/ n retenção f

retentive /rɪˈtentɪv/ a retentivo. ~ memory boa memória f

reticen|t /ˈretɪsnt/ a reticente. ~ce n reticência f

retina /ˈretɪnə/ n retina f

retinue /ˈretɪnjuː/ n séquito m, comitiva f

retire /rɪˈtaɪə(r)/ vi reformar-se, aposentar-se; (withdraw) retirar-se; (go to bed) ir deitar-se □ vt reformar, aposentar. ~d a reformado, aposentado. ~ment n reforma f, aposentadoria f, (P) aposentação f

retiring /rɪˈtaɪərɪŋ/ a reservado, retraído

retort /rɪˈtɔːt/ vt/i retrucar, retorquir □ n réplica f

retrace /riːˈtreɪs/ vt ~ one's steps refazer o mesmo caminho; (fig) recordar, recapitular

retract /rɪˈtrækt/ vt/i retratar (-se); (wheels) recolher; (claws) encolher, recolher

retreat /rɪˈtriːt/ vi retirar-se; (mil) retirar, bater em retirada □ n retirada f; (seclusion) retiro m

retrial /riːˈtraɪəl/ n novo julgamento m

retribution /retrɪˈbjuːʃn/ n castigo (merecido) m; (vengeance) vingança f

retriev|e /rɪˈtriːv/ vt ir buscar; (rescue) salvar; (recover) recuperar; (put right) reparar. ~al n recuperação f. **information ~al** (comput) acesso m à informação. ~er n (dog) perdigueiro m, (P) cobrador m

retrograde /ˈretrəgreɪd/ a retrógrado □ vt retroceder, recuar

retrospect /ˈretrəspekt/ n in ~ em retrospecto, (P) retrospectivamente. ~ive /-ˈspektɪv/ a retrospectivo; (of law, payment) retroativo, (P) retroactivo

return /rɪˈtɜːn/ vi voltar, regressar, retornar (to, a) □ vt devolver;

(*compliment, visit*) retribuir; (*put back*) pôr de volta □ *n* volta *f*, regresso *m*, retorno *m*; (*profit*) lucro *m*, rendimento *m*; (*restitution*) devolução *f*. **in** ~ **for** em troca de. ~ **journey** viagem *f* de volta. ~ **match** (*sport*) desafio *m* de desforra. ~ **ticket** bilhete *m* de ida e volta. **many happy** ~**s (of the day)** muitos parabéns

reunion /riːˈjuːnɪən/ *n* reunião *f*

reunite /riːjuˈnaɪt/ *vt* reunir

rev /rev/ *n* (*colloq: auto*) rotação *f* □ *vt/i* (*pt* **revved**) ~ (**up**) (*colloq: auto*) acelerar (o motor)

reveal /rɪˈviːl/ *vt* revelar; (*display*) expor. ~**ing** *a* revelador

revel /ˈrevl/ *vi* (*pt* **revelled**) divertir-se. ~ **in** deleitar-se com. ~ *ry n* festas *fpl*, festejos *mpl*

revelation /revəˈleɪʃn/ *n* revelação *f*

revenge /rɪˈvendʒ/ *n* vingança *f*; (*sport*) desforra *f* □ *vt* vingar

revenue /ˈrevənjuː/ *n* receita *f*, rendimento *m*. **Inland R**~ Fisco *m*

reverberate /rɪˈvɜːbəreɪt/ *vi* ecoar, repercutir

revere /rɪˈvɪə(r)/ *vt* reverenciar, venerar

reverend /ˈrevərənd/ *a* reverendo. **R**~ Reverendo

reverent /ˈrevərənt/ *a* reverente. ~**ce** *n* reverência *f*, veneração *f*

reverse /rɪˈvɜːs/ *a* contrário, inverso □ *n* contrário *m*; (*back*) reverso *m*; (*gear*) marcha *f* à ré (*P*) atrás □ *vt* virar ao contrário; (*order*) inverter; (*turn inside out*) virar do avesso; (*decision*) anular □ *vi* (*auto*) fazer marcha à ré, (*P*) atrás. ~**al** *n* inversão *f*, mudança *f* em sentido contrário; (*of view etc*) mudança *f*

revert /rɪˈvɜːt/ *vi* ~ **to** reverter a

review /rɪˈvjuː/ *n* (*inspection; magazine*) revista *f*; (*of a situation*)

revisão *f*; (*critique*) crítica *f* □ *vt* revistar, passar revista em; (*situation*) rever; (*book, film etc*) fazer a crítica de. ~**er** *n* crítico *m*

revis|e /rɪˈvaɪz/ *vt* rever; (*amend*) corrigir. ~**ion** /-ɪʒn/ *n* revisão *f*; (*amendment*) correção *f*

reviv|e /rɪˈvaɪv/ *vt/i* ressuscitar, reavivar; (*play*) reapresentar; (*person*) reanimar(-se). ~**al** *n* reflorescimento *m*, renascimento *m*

revoke /rɪˈvəʊk/ *vt* revogar, anular, invalidar

revolt /rɪˈvəʊlt/ *vt/i* revoltar(-se) □ *n* revolta *f*

revolting /rɪˈvəʊltɪŋ/ *a* (*disgusting*) repugnante

revolution /revəˈluːʃn/ *n* revolução *f*. ~**ary** *a & n* revolucionário (*m*). ~**ize** *vt* revolucionar

revolv|e /rɪˈvɒlv/ *vi* girar. ~**ing door** porta *f* giratória

revolver /rɪˈvɒlvə(r)/ *n* revólver *m*

revulsion /rɪˈvʌlʃn/ *n* repugnância *f*, repulsa *f*

reward /rɪˈwɔːd/ *n* prêmio *m*, (*P*) prémio *m*; (*for criminal, for lost/stolen property*) recompensa *f* □ *vt* recompensar. ~**ing** *a* compensador; (*task etc*) gratificante

rewind /riːˈwaɪnd/ *vt* (*pt* **rewound**) rebobinar

rewrite /riːˈraɪt/ *vt* (*pt* **rewrote**, *pp* **rewritten**) reescrever

rhetoric /ˈretərɪk/ *n* retórica *f*. ~**al** /rɪˈtɒrɪkl/ *a* retórico; (*question*) pro forma

rheumati|c /ruːˈmætɪk/ *a* reumático. ~**sm** /ˈruːmətɪzm/ *n* reumatismo *m*

rhinoceros /raɪˈnɒsərəs/ *n* (*pl* -oses) rinoceronte *m*

rhubarb /ˈruːbɑːb/ *n* ruibarbo *m*

rhyme /raɪm/ *n* rima *f*; (*poem*) versos *mpl* □ *vt/i* (fazer) rimar

rhythm /ˈrɪðəm/ *n* ritmo *m*. ~**ic(al)** /ˈrɪðmɪk(l)/ *a* rítmico, compassado

rib /rɪb/ *n* costela *f*.

ribbon /'rɪbən/ *n* fita *f*. **in ~s** em tiras

rice /raɪs/ *n* arroz *m*

rich /rɪtʃ/ *a* (**-er, -est**) rico; (*food*) rico em açúcar e gordura. **~es** *npl* riquezas *fpl*. **~ly** *adv* ricamente. **~ness** *n* riqueza *f*

rickety /'rɪkətɪ/ *a* (*shaky*) desconjuntado

ricochet /'rɪkəʃeɪ/ *n* ricochete *m* □ *vi* (*pt* **ricocheted** /-ʃeɪd/) fazer ricochete, ricochetear

rid /rɪd/ *vt* (*pt* **rid,** *pres p* **ridding**) desembaraçar (**of de**). **get ~ of** desembaraçar-se de, livrar-se de

riddance /'rɪdns/ *n* **good ~!** que alívio!, vai com Deus!

ridden /'rɪdn/ *see* **ride**

riddle[1] /'rɪdl/ *n* enigma *m*; (*puzzle*) charada *f*

riddle[2] /'rɪdl/ *vt* **~ with** crivar de

ride /raɪd/ *vi* (*pt* **rode,** *pp* **ridden**) andar (de bicicleta, a cavalo, de carro) □ *vt* `(horse`) montar; (*bicycle*) andar de; (*distance*) percorrer □ *n* passeio *m* or volta *f* (de carro, a cavalo etc); (*distance*) percurso *m*. **~r** /-ə(r)/ *n* cavaleiro *m*, amazona *f*; (*cyclist*) ciclista *mf*; (*in document*) aditamento *m*

ridge /rɪdʒ/ *n* aresta *f*; (*of hill*) cume *m*

ridicule /'rɪdɪkjuːl/ *n* ridículo *m* □ *vt* ridicularizar

ridiculous /rɪ'dɪkjʊləs/ *a* ridículo

riding /'raɪdɪŋ/ *n* equitação *f*

rife /raɪf/ *a* **be ~** estar espalhado; (*of illness*) grassar. **~ with** cheio de

riff-raff /'rɪfræf/ *n* gentinha *f*, povinho *m*, ralé *f*

rifle /'raɪfl/ *n* espingarda *f* □ *vt* revistar e roubar, saquear

rift /rɪft/ *n* fenda *f*, brecha *f*; (*fig: dissension*) desacordo *m*, desavença *f*, desentendimento *m*

rig[1] /rɪg/ *vt* (*pt* **rigged**) equipar □

n (*for oil*) plataforma *f* de poço de petróleo. **~ out** enfarpelar (*collog*). **~-out** *n* (*collog*) roupa *f*, farpela *f* (*collog*). **~ up** arranjar

rig[2] /rɪg/ *vt* (*pt* **rigged**) (*pej*) manipular. **~ged** *a* (*election*) fraudulento

right /raɪt/ *a* (*correct, moral*) certo, correto, (*P*) correcto; (*fair*) justo; (*not left*) direito; (*suitable*) certo, próprio □ *n* (*entitlement*) direito *m*; (*not left*) direita *f*; (*not evil*) o bem □ *vt* (*a wrong*) reparar; (*set fallen*) endireitar □ *adv* (*not left*) à direita; (*directly*) direito; (*exactly*) mesmo, bem; (*completely*) completamente. **be ~** (*person*) ter razão (to em). **be in the ~** ter razão. **on the ~** à direita. **put ~** acertar, corrigir. **~ of way** (*auto*) prioridade *f*. **~ angle** *n* ângulo reto *m*, (*P*) recto. **~ away** logo, imediatamente. **~-hand** *a* à *or* de direita. **~-handed** *a* (*person*) destro. **~-wing** *a* (*pol*) de direita

righteous /'raɪtʃəs/ *a* justo, virtuoso

rightful /'raɪtfl/ *a* legítimo. **~ly** *adv* legitimamente, legalmente

rightly /'raɪtlɪ/ *adv* devidamente, corretamente, (*P*) correctamente; (*with reason*) justificadamente

rigid /'rɪdʒɪd/ *a* rígido. **~ity** /rɪ'dʒɪdətɪ/ *n* rigidez *f*

rigmarole /'rɪgmərəʊl/ *n* (*speech: procedure*) embrulhada *f*

rig|our /'rɪgə(r)/ *n* rigor *m*. **~orous** *a* rigoroso

rile /raɪl/ *vt* (*collog*) irritar, exasperar

rim /rɪm/ *n* borda *f*; (*of wheel*) aro *m*

rind /raɪnd/ *n* (*on cheese, fruit*) casca *f*; (*on bacon*) pele *f*

ring[1] /rɪŋ/ *n* (*on finger*) anel *m*; (*for napkin, key etc*) argola *f*; (*circle*) roda *f*, círculo *m*; (*boxing*) ringue m; (arena) arena f; (of people) quadrilha f □ vt rodear, cercar. ~ road n estrada f periférica or perimetral

ring² /rɪŋ/ vt/i (pt rang, pp rung) tocar; (of words etc) soar □ n toque m; (colloq: phone call) telefonadela f (colloq). ~ the bell tocar a campainha. ~ back telefonar de volta. ~ off desligar. ~ up telefonar (a)

ringleader /'rɪŋliːdə(r)/ n cabeça m, cérebro m

rink /rɪŋk/ n rinque m de patinação

rinse /rɪns/ vt enxaguar □ n enxaguada f, (P) enxaguadela f; (hair tint) rinsagem f

riot /'raɪət/ n distúrbio m, motim m; (of colours) festival m □ vi fazer distúrbios or motins. run ~ desenfrear-se, descontrolar-se (of plants) crescer em matagal. ~er n desordeiro m

riotous /'raɪətəs/ a desenfreado, turbulento, desordeiro

rip /rɪp/ vt/i (pt ripped) rasgar (-se) □ n rasgão m. ~ off (sl: defraud) defraudar, enrolar (sl). ~-off n (sl) roubalheira f (colloq)

ripe /raɪp/ a (-er, -est) maduro. ~ness n madureza f, (P) amadurecimento m

ripen /'raɪpən/ vt/i amadurecer

ripple /'rɪpl/ n ondulação f leve; (sound) murmúrio m □ vt/i encrespar(-se), agitar(-se), ondular

rise /raɪz/ vi (pt rose, pp risen) subir, elevar-se; (stand up) erguer-se, levantar-se; (rebel) sublevar-se; (sun) nascer; (curtain, prices) subir □ n (increase) aumento m; (slope) subida f, ladeira f; (origin) origem f. give ~ to originar, causar, dar origem a. ~r /-ə(r)/ n early ~r madrugador m

rising /'raɪzɪŋ/ n (revolt) insurreição f □ a (sun) nascente

risk /rɪsk/ n risco m □ vt arriscar. at ~ em risco, em perigo. at one's own ~ por sua conta e risco. ~ doing (venture) arriscar-se a fazer. ~y a arriscado

risqué /'riːskeɪ/ a picante

rite /raɪt/ n rito m. last ~s últimos sacramentos mpl

ritual /'rɪtʃʊəl/ a & n ritual (m)

rival /'raɪvl/ n & a rival (mf); (fig) concorrente (mf), competidor (m) □ vt (pt rivalled) rivalizar com. ~ry n rivalidade f

river /'rɪvə(r)/ n rio m □ a fluvial

rivet /'rɪvɪt/ n rebite m □ vt (pt riveted) rebitar; (fig) prender, cravar. ~ing a fascinante

road /rəʊd/ n estrada f; (in town) rua f; (small; fig) caminho m. ~-block n barricada f. ~-map n mapa m das estradas. ~ sign n sinal m, placa f de sinalização. ~ tax imposto m de circulação. ~works npl obras fpl

roadside /'rəʊdsaɪd/ n beira f da estrada

roadway /'rəʊdweɪ/ n pista f de rolamento, (P) rodagem f

roadworthy /'rəʊdwɜːðɪ/ a em condições de ser utilizado na rua/estrada

roam /rəʊm/ vi errar, andar sem destino □ vt percorrer

roar /rɔː(r)/ n berro m, rugido m; (of thunder) ribombo m, troar m; (of sea, wind) bramido m □ vt/i berrar, rugir; (of lion) rugir; (of thunder) ribombar, troar; (of sea, wind) bramir. ~ with laughter rir às gargalhadas

roaring /'rɔːrɪŋ/ a (trade) florescente; (success) enorme; (fire) com grandes chamas

roast /rəʊst/ vt/i assar □ a & n assado (m)

rob /rɒb/ vt (pt robbed) roubar (sb of sth alg coisa de alguém);

(*bank*) assaltar; (*deprive*) privar (of de). **~ber** *n* ladrão *m*. **~bery** *n* roubo *m*; (*of bank*) assalto *m*

robe /rəʊb/ *n* veste *f* comprida e solta; (*dressing-gown*) robe *m*. **~s** *npl* (*of judge etc*) toga *f*

robin /'rɒbɪn/ *n* papo-roxo *m*, (P) pintarroxo *m*

robot /'rəʊbɒt/ *n* robô *m*, (P) robot *m*, autómato *m*, (P) autómato *m*

robust /rəʊ'bʌst/ *a* robusto

rock¹ /rɒk/ *n* rocha *f*; (*boulder*) penhasco *m*, rochedo *m*; (*sweet*) pirulito *m*, (P) chupa-chupa *m* comprido. **on the ~s** (*colloq: of marriage*) em crise; (*colloq: of drinks*) com gelo. **~-bottom** *n* ponto *m* mais baixo □ *a* (*of prices*) baixíssimo (*colloq*)

rock² /rɒk/ *vt/i* balouçar(-se); (*shake*) abanar, sacudir; (*child*) embalar □ *n* (*mus*) rock *m*. **~ing-chair** *n* cadeira *f* de balanço, (P) cadeira *f* de balouço. **~ing-horse** *n* cavalo *m* de balanço, (P) cavalo *m* de balouço

rocket /'rɒkɪt/ *n* foguete *m*

rocky /'rɒkɪ/ *a* (**-ier, -iest**) (*ground*) pedregoso; (*hill*) rochoso; (*colloq: unsteady*) instável; (*colloq: shaky*) tremido (*colloq*)

rod /rɒd/ *n* vara *f*, vareta *f*; (*mech*) haste *f*; (*for curtains*) bastão *m*, (P) varão *m*; (*for fishing*) vara (de pescar) *f*

rode /rəʊd/ *see* ride

rodent /'rəʊdnt/ *n* roedor *m*

rodeo /rəʊ'deɪəʊ/ *n* (*pl* **-os**) ro-de(i)o *m*

roe /rəʊ/ *n* ova(s) *f* (*pl*) de peixe

rogue /rəʊg/ *n* (*dishonest*) patife *m*, velhaco *m*; (*mischievous*) brincalhão *m*

role /rəʊl/ *n* papel *m*

roll /rəʊl/ *vt/i* (fazer) rolar; (*into ball or cylinder*) enrolar(-se) □ *n* rolo *m*; (*list*) rol *m*, lista *f*; (*bread*) pãozinho *m*; (*of ship*) ba-

lanço *m*; (*of drum*) rufar *m*; (*of thunder*) ribombo *m*. **be ~ing in money** (*colloq*) nadar em dinheiro (*colloq*). **~ over** (*turn over*) virar-se ao contrário. **~ up** *vi* (*colloq*) aparecer □ *vt* (*sleeves*) arregaçar; (*umbrella*) fechar. **~-call** *n* chamada *f*. **~ing-pin** *n* rolo *m* de pastel

roller /'rəʊlə(r)/ *n* cilindro *m*; (*wave*) vagalhão *m*; (*for hair*) rolo *m*. **~-blind** *n* estore *m*. **~-coaster** *n* montanha *f* russa. **~-skate** *n* patim *m* de rodas

rolling /'rəʊlɪŋ/ *a* ondulante

Roman /'rəʊmən/ *a* & *n* romano (*m*). **R~ Catholic** *a* & *n* católico (*m*). **~ numerals** algarismos *mpl* romanos

romance /rəʊ'mæns/ *n* (*love affair*) romance *m*; (*fig*) poesia *f*

Romania /rʊ'meɪnɪə/ *n* Roménia *f*, (P) Roménia *f*. **~n** *a* & *n* romeno (*m*)

romantic /rəʊ'mæntɪk/ *a* romântico. **~ally** *adv* românticamente. **~ism** *n* romantismo *m*. **~ize** *vi* fazer romance □ *vt* romantizar

romp /rɒmp/ *vi* brincar animadamente □ *n* brincadeira *f* animada. **~ers** *npl* macacão *m* de bebê, (P) fato *m* de bebé

roof /ruːf/ *n* (*pl* **roofs**) telhado *m*; (*of car*) teto *m*, (P) capota *f*; (*of mouth*) palato *m*, céu *m* da boca □ *vt* cobrir com telhado. **hit the ~** (*colloq*) ficar furioso. **~ing** *n* material *m* para telhados. **~-rack** *n* porta-bagagem *m*. **~-top** *n* cimo *m* do telhado

rook¹ /rʊk/ *n* (*bird*) gralha *f*

rook² /rʊk/ *n* (*chess*) torre *f*

room /ruːm/ *n* quarto *m*, divisão *f*; (*bedroom*) quarto *m* de dormir; (*large hall*) sala *f*; (*space*) espaço *m*, lugar *m*. **~s** (*lodgings*) apartamento *m*, cômodos *mpl*. **~-mate** *n* companheiro *m* de quarto. **~y** a espaçoso; (*clothes*) amplo, largo

roost /ru:st/ n poleiro m □ vi empoleirar-se. **~er** n (*Amer*) galo m

root[1] /ru:t/ n raiz f; (*fig*) origem f □ vt/i enraizar(-se), radicar(-se). **~ out** extirpar, erradicar. **take ~** criar raízes. **~less** a sem raízes, desenraizado

root[2] /ru:t/ vi **~ about** revolver, remexer. **~ for** (*Amer sl*) torcer por

rope /rəʊp/ n corda f □ vt atar. **know the ~s** estar por dentro (do assunto). **~ in** convencer a participar de

rosary /ˈrəʊzərɪ/ n rosário m

rose[1] /rəʊz/ n rosa f; (*nozzle*) ralo m (de regador). **~-bush** n roseira f

rose[2] /rəʊz/ see **rise**

rosé /ˈrəʊzeɪ/ n rosé m

rosette /rəʊˈzet/ n roseta f

rosewood /ˈrəʊzwʊd/ n pau-rosa m

roster /ˈrɒstə(r)/ n lista (de serviço) f, escala f (de serviço)

rostrum /ˈrɒstrəm/ n tribuna f; (*for conductor*) estrado m; (*sport*) podium m

rosy /ˈrəʊzɪ/ a (-ier, -iest) rosado; (*fig*) risonho

rot /rɒt/ vt/i (*pt* rotted) apodrecer □ n putrefação f, podridão f; (*sl: nonsense*) disparate m, asneiras fpl

rota /ˈrəʊtə/ n escala f de serviço

rotary /ˈrəʊtərɪ/ a rotativo, giratório

rotat|e /rəʊˈteɪt/ vt/i (fazer) girar, (fazer) revolver; (*change round*) alternar. **~ing** a rotativo. **~ion** /-ʃn/ n rotação f

rote /rəʊt/ n **by ~** de cor, maquinalmente

rotten /ˈrɒtn/ a podre; (*corrupt*) corrupto; (*colloq: bad*) mau, ruim. **~ eggs** ovos mpl podres.

feel **~** (*ill*) não se sentir nada bem

rotund /rəʊˈtʌnd/ a rotundo, redondo

rough /rʌf/ a (-er, -est) rude; (*to touch*) áspero, rugoso; (*of ground*) acidentado, irregular; (*violent*) violento; (*of sea*) agitado, encapelado; (*of weather*) tempestuoso; (*not perfect*) tosco, rudimentar; (*of estimate etc*) aproximado □ n (*ruffian*) rufia m, desordeiro m □ adv (*live*) ao relento; (*play*) bruto □ vt **~ it** viver de modo primitivo, não ter onde morar (*colloq*). **~ out** fazer um esboço preliminar de. **~-and-ready** a grosseiro mas eficiente. **~ paper** rascunho m, borrão m. **~ly** adv asperamente, rudemente; (*approximately*) aproximadamente. **~ness** n rudeza f, aspereza f; (*violence*) brutalidade f

roughage /ˈrʌfɪdʒ/ n alimentos mpl fibrosos

roulette /ru:ˈlet/ n roleta f

round /raʊnd/ a (-er, -est) redondo □ n (*circle*) círculo m; (*slice*) fatia f; (*postman's*) entrega f; (*patrol*) ronda f; (*of drinks*) rodada f; (*competition*) partida f, rodada f; (*boxing*) round m; (*of talks*) ciclo m, série f □ prep & adv em volta (de), em torno (de) □ vt arredondar; (*cape, corner*) dobrar, virar. **come ~** (*into consciousness*) voltar a si. **go or come ~ to** (*a friend etc*) dar um pulo na casa de. **~ about** (*nearby*) por aí; (*fig*) mais ou menos. **~ of applause** salva f de palmas. **~ off** terminar. **~-shouldered** a curvado. **~ the clock** noite e dia sem parar. **~ trip** viagem f de ida e volta. **~ up** (*gather*) juntar; (*a figure*) arredondar. **~-up** n (*of cattle*) rodeio m; (*of suspects*) captura f

roundabout /'raʊndəbaʊt/ n carrossel m; (for traffic) rotatória f, (P) rotunda f □ a indireto, (P) indirecto

rouse /raʊz/ vt acordar, despertar. be ~ed (angry) exaltar-se, inflamar-se, ser provocado. ~ing a (speech) inflamado, exaltado; (music) vibrante; (cheers) frenético

rout /raʊt/ n derrota f; (retreat) debandada f □ vt derrotar; (cause to retreat) pôr em debandada

route /ruːt/ n percurso m, itinerário m; (naut, aviat) rota f

routine /ruːˈtiːn/ n rotina f; (theat) número m □ a de rotina, rotineiro. **daily** ~ rotina f diária

rove /rəʊv/ vt/i errar (por), vaguear (em/por). ~ing a (life) errante

row[1] /rəʊ/ n fila f, fileira f; (in knitting) carreira f. in a ~ (consecutive) em fila

row[2] /rəʊ/ vt/i remar. ~ing n remo m. ~ing-boat n barco m a remo

row[3] /raʊ/ n (colloq: noise) barulho m, bulha f, banzé m (colloq); (colloq: quarrel) discussão f, briga f. ~ (with) vi (colloq) brigar (com), discutir (com)

rowdy /'raʊdɪ/ a (-ier, -iest) desordeiro

royal /'rɔɪəl/ a real

royalty /'rɔɪəltɪ/ n família real f; (payment) direitos mpl (de autor, de patente, etc)

rub /rʌb/ vt/i (pt rubbed) esfregar; (with ointment etc) esfregar, friccionar □ n esfrega f; (with ointment etc) fricção f. ~ in vi repisar/insistir em. ~ off on vi comunicar-se a, transmitir-se a. ~ out (with rubber) apagar

rubber /'rʌbə(r)/ n borracha f. ~band elástico m. ~ stamp carimbo m. ~-stamp vt aprovar

sem questionar. ~y a semelhante à borracha

rubbish /'rʌbɪʃ/ n (refuse) lixo m; (nonsense) disparates mpl. ~dump n lixeira f. ~y a sem valor

rubble /'rʌbl/ n entulho m

ruby /'ruːbɪ/ n rubi m

rucksack /'rʌksæk/ n mochila f

rudder /'rʌdə(r)/ n leme m

ruddy /'rʌdɪ/ a (-ier, -iest) avermelhado; (of cheeks) corado, vermelho; (sl: damned) maldito (colloq)

rude /ruːd/ a (-er, -est) mal-educado, malcriado, grosseiro. ~ly adv grosseiramente, malcriadamente. ~ness n má-educação f, má-criação f, grosseria f

rudiment /'ruːdɪmənt/ n rudimento m. ~ary /-'mentrɪ/ a rudimentar

rueful /'ruːfl/ a contrito, pesaroso

ruffian /'rʌfɪən/ n desordeiro m

ruffle /'rʌfl/ vt (feathers) eriçar; (hair) despentear; (clothes) amarrotar; (fig) perturbar □ n (frill) franzido m, (P) folho m

rug /rʌg/ n tapete m; (covering) manta f

rugged /'rʌgɪd/ a rude, irregular; (coast, landscape) acidentado; (character) forte; (features) marcado

ruin /'ruːɪn/ n ruína f □ vt arruinar; (fig) estragar. ~ous a desastroso

rule /ruːl/ n regra f; (regulation) regulamento m; (pol) governo m □ vt governar; (master) dominar; (jur) decretar; (decide) decidir □ vi governar. **as a** ~ regra geral, por via de regra. ~ **out** excluir. ~d paper papel m pautado. ~r /-ə(r)/ n (sovereign) soberano m; (leader) governante m; (measure) régua f

ruling /'ruːlɪŋ/ a (class) dirigente; (pol) no poder □ n decisão f

rum /rʌm/ n rum m

rumble /'rʌmbl/ vi ribombar, ressoar; (of stomach) roncar □ n ribombo m, estrondo m

rummage /'rʌmɪdʒ/ vt revistar, remexer

rumour /'ruːmə(r)/ n boato m, rumor m □ vt **it is ∼ed** that corre o boato de que, consta que

rump /rʌmp/ n (of horse etc) garupa f; (of fowl) mitra f. **∼ steak** n bife m de alcatra

run /rʌn/ vi (pt ran, pp run, pres p running) correr; (flow) correr; (pass) passar; (function) andar, funcionar; (melt) derreter, pingar; (bus etc) circular; (play) estar em cartaz; (colour) desbotar; (in election) candidatar-se (for a) □ vt (manage) dirigir, gerir; (a risk) correr; (a race) participar em; (water) deixar correr; (a car) ter, manter □ n corrida f; (excursion) passeio m, ida f; (rush) corrida f, correria f; (in cricket) ponto m. **be on the ∼** estar foragido. **have the ∼ of** ter à sua disposição. **in the long ∼** a longo prazo. **∼ across** encontrar por acaso, dar com. **∼ away** fugir. **∼ down** descer correndo; (of vehicle) atropelar; (belittle) dizer mal de, denegrir. **be ∼ down** estar exausto. **∼ in** (engine) ligar. **∼ into** (meet) encontrar por acaso; (hit) bater em, ir de encontro a. **∼ off** vt (copies) tirar; (water) deixar correr □ vi fugir. **∼-of-the-mill** a vulgar. **∼ out** esgotar-se; (lease) expirar. **I ran out of sugar** o açúcar acabou. **∼ over** (of vehicle) atropelar. **∼ up** deixar acumular. **the ∼-up to** o período que precede

runaway /'rʌnəweɪ/ n fugitivo m □ a fugitivo. (horse) desembestado; (vehicle) desgovernado; (success) grande

rung[1] /rʌŋ/ n (of ladder) degrace m

rung[2] /rʌŋ/ see **ring**[2]

runner /'rʌnə(r)/ n (person) corredor m; (carpet) passadeira f. **∼ bean** feijão m verde. **∼-up** n segundo classificado m

running /'rʌnɪŋ/ n corrida f; (functioning) funcionamento m □ a consecutivo, seguido; (water) corrente. **be in the ∼** (competitor) ter probabilidades de êxito. **four days ∼** quatro dias seguidos or a fio. **∼ commentary** reportagem f, comentário m

runny /'rʌnɪ/ a derretido

runway /'rʌnweɪ/ n pista f de descolagem, (P) descolagem

rupture /'rʌptʃə(r)/ n ruptura f; (med) hérnia f □ vt/i romper (-se), rebentar

rural /'rʊərəl/ a rural

ruse /ruːz/ n ardil m, estratagema m, manha f

rush[1] /rʌʃ/ n (plant) junco m

rush[2] /rʌʃ/ vi (move) precipitar-se, (be in a hurry) apressar-se □ vt fazer, mandar etc a toda a pressa; (person) pressionar; (mil) tomar de assalto □ n tropel m; (haste) pressa f. **in a ∼** as pressas. **∼ hour** rush m, (P) hora f de ponta

rusk /rʌsk/ n bolacha f, biscoito m

russet /'rʌsɪt/ a castanho avermelhado □ n maçã f reineta

Russia /'rʌʃə/ n Rússia f. **∼n** a & n russo (m)

rust /rʌst/ n (on iron, plants) ferrugem f □ vt/i enferrujar(-se). **∼-proof** a inoxidável. **∼y** a ferrugento, enferrujado; (fig) enferrujado

rustic /'rʌstɪk/ a rústico

rustle /'rʌsl/ vt/i restolhar, (fazer) farfalhar; (Amer: steal) roubar. **∼ up** (colloq: food etc) arranjar

rut /rʌt/ n sulco m; (fig) rotina f. **in a ∼** numa vida rotineira

ruthless /'ruːθlɪs/ a implacável

rye /raɪ/ n centeio m

S

sabbath /'sæbəθ/ n (Jewish) sábado m; (Christian) domingo m

sabbatical /sə'bætɪkl/ n (univ) período m de licença

sabot|age /'sæbətɑːʒ/ n sabotagem f □ vt sabotar. ~**eur** /-'tɜː(r)/ n sabotador m

sachet /'sæʃeɪ/ n sachê m

sack /sæk/ n saco m, saca f □ vt (colloq) despedir. **get the** ~ (colloq) ser despedido

sacrament /'sækrəmənt/ n sacramento m

sacred /'seɪkrɪd/ a sagrado

sacrific|e /'sækrɪfaɪs/ n sacrifício m; (fig) sacrifício m □ vt sacrificar

sacrileg|e /'sækrɪlɪdʒ/ n sacrilégio m. ~**ious** /-'lɪdʒəs/ a sacrílego

sad /sæd/ a (sadder, saddest) (person) triste; (story, news) triste. ~**ly** adv tristemente; (unfortunately) infelizmente. ~**ness** n tristeza f

sadden /'sædn/ vt entristecer

saddle /'sædl/ n sela f □ vt (horse) selar. ~ **sb with** sobrecarregar alguém com

sadis|m /'seɪdɪzəm/ n sadismo m. ~**t** /-ɪst/ n sádico m. ~**tic** /sə'dɪstɪk/ a sádico

safe /seɪf/ a (-er, -est) (not dangerous) seguro; (out of danger) fora de perigo; (reliable) confiável. ~ **from** salvo de risco de □ n cofre m, caixa-forte f. ~ **and sound** são e salvo. ~ **conduct** salvo-conduto m. ~ **keeping** custódia f, (P) protecção f. **to be on the** ~ **side** por via das dúvidas. ~**ly** adv (arrive etc) em segurança; (keep) seguro

safeguard /'seɪfgɑːd/ n salvaguarda f □ vt salvaguardar

safety /'seɪftɪ/ n segurança f. ~**-belt** n cinto m de segurança. ~**-pin** n alfinete m de fralda. ~**-valve** n válvula f de segurança

sag /sæg/ vi (pt sagged) afrouxar

saga /'sɑːgə/ n saga f

sage[1] /seɪdʒ/ n (herb) salva f

sage[2] /seɪdʒ/ a sensato, prudente □ n sábio m

Sagittarius /sædʒɪ'teərɪəs/ n (astrol) Sagitário m

said /sed/ see **say**

sail /seɪl/ n vela f; (trip) viagem f em barco à vela □ vi navegar; (leave) partir; (sport) velejar □ vt navegar. ~**ing** n navegação f à vela. ~**ing-boat** n barco m à vela

sailor /'seɪlə(r)/ n marinheiro m

saint /seɪnt/ n santo m. ~**ly** a santo, santificado

sake /seɪk/ n **for the** ~ **of** em consideração a. **for my/your/its own** ~ por mim/por você/por isso

salad /'sæləd/ n salada f. ~**-dressing** n molho m para salada

salary /'sælərɪ/ n salário m

sale /seɪl/ n venda f; (at reduced prices) liquidação f. **for** ~ "vende-se". **on** ~ à venda. ~**s assistant**, (Amer) ~**s clerk** vendedor m. ~**s department** departamento m de vendas

sales|man /'seɪlzmən/ n (pl -men) (in shop) vendedor m; (traveller) caixeiro-viajante m. ~**woman** n (pl -women) (in shop) vendedora f; (traveller) caixeira-viajante f

saline /'seɪlaɪn/ a salino □ n salina f

saliva /sə'laɪvə/ n saliva f

sallow /'sæləʊ/ a (-er, - est) amarelado

salmon /'sæmən/ n (pl invar) salmão m

saloon /sə'luːn/ n (on ship) salão m; (bar) botequim m. ~ **(car)** sedã m

salt /sɔːlt/ *n* sal *m* □ *a* salgado □ *vt* (*season*) salgar; (*cure*) pôr em salmoura. **~-cellar** *n* saleiro *m*. **~ water** água *f* salgada, água *f* do mar. **~y** *a* salgado

salutary /'sæljʊtrɪ/ *a* salutar

salute /sə'luːt/ *n* saudação *f* □ *vt/i* saudar

salvage /'sælvɪdʒ/ *n* (*naut*) salvamento *m*; (*of waste*) reciclagem *f* □ *vt* salvar

salvation /sæl'veɪʃn/ *n* salvação *f*

same /seɪm/ *a* mesmo (as que) □ *pron* the **~** o mesmo □ *adv* the **~** o mesmo. **all the ~** (*nevertheless*) mesmo assim, apesar de tudo. **at the ~ time** (*at once*) ao mesmo tempo

sample /'sɑːmpl/ *n* amostra *f* □ *vt* experimentar, provar

sanatorium /sænə'tɔːrɪəm/ *n* (*pl -iums*) sanatório *m*

sanctify /'sæŋktɪfaɪ/ *vt* santificar

sanctimonious /sæŋktɪ'məʊnɪəs/ *a* santarrão, carola

sanction /'sæŋkʃn/ *n* (*approval*) aprovação *f*; (*penalty*) pena *f*, sanção *f* □ *vt* sancionar

sanctity /'sæŋktɪtɪ/ *n* santidade *f*

sanctuary /'sæŋktʃʊərɪ/ *n* (*relig*) santuário *m*; (*refuge*) refúgio *m*; (*for animals*) reserva *f*

sand /sænd/ *n* areia *f*; (*beach*) praia *f* □ *vt* (*with sandpaper*) lixar

sandal /'sændl/ *n* sandália *f*

sandbag /'sændbæg/ *n* saco *m* de areia

sandbank /'sændbæŋk/ *n* banco *m* de areia

sandcastle /'sændkɑːsl/ *n* castelo *m* de areia

sandpaper /'sændpeɪpə(r)/ *n* lixa *f* □ *vt* lixar

sandpit /'sændpɪt/ *n* caixa *f* de areia

sandwich /'sænwɪdʒ/ *n* sanduíche *m*, (P) sandes *f invar* □ *vt* **~ed between** encaixado entre. **~**

course curso *m* profissionalizante envolvendo estudo teórico e estágio em local de trabalho

sandy /'sændɪ/ *a* (**-ier, iest**) arenoso; (*beach*) arenoso; (*hair*) ruivo

sane /seɪn/ *a* (**-er, -est**) (*not mad*) são *m*; (*sensible*) sensato, ajuizado

sang /sæŋ/ *see* **sing**

sanitary /'sænɪtrɪ/ *a* sanitário; (*system*) sanitário. **~ towel**, (*Amer*) **~ napkin** toalha *f* absorvente

sanitation /sænɪ'teɪʃn/ *n* condições *fpl* sanitárias, saneamento *m*

sanity /'sænɪtɪ/ *n* sanidade *f*

sank /sæŋk/ *see* **sink**

Santa Claus /'sæntəklɔːz/ *n* Papai Noel *m*

sap /sæp/ *n* seiva *f* □ *vt* (*pt sapped*) esgotar, minar

sapphire /'sæfaɪə(r)/ *n* safira *f*

sarcasm /'sɑːkæzəm/ *n* sarcasmo *m*. **~tic** /sɑː'kæstɪk/ *a* sarcástico

sardine /sɑː'diːn/ *n* sardinha *f*

sardonic /sɑː'dɒnɪk/ *a* sardônico

sash /sæʃ/ *n* (*around waist*) cinto *m*; (*over shoulder*) faixa *f*. **~-window** *n* janela *f* de guilhotina

sat /sæt/ *see* **sit**

satanic /sə'tænɪk/ *a* satânico

satchel /'sætʃl/ *n* sacola *f*

satellite /'sætəlaɪt/ *n* satélite *m*. **~ dish** antena *f* de satélite. **~ television** televisão *f* via satélite

satin /'sætɪn/ *n* cetim *m*

satir|e /'sætaɪə(r)/ *n* sátira *f*. **~ical** /sə'tɪrɪkl/ *a* satirical. **~ist** /'sætərɪst/ *n* satirista *mf*. **~ize** *vt* satirizar

satisfaction /sætɪs'fækʃn/ *n* satisfação *f*. **~ory** /-'fæktərɪ/ *a* satisfatório

satisfy /'sætɪsfaɪ/ *vt* satisfazer; (*convince*) convencer; (*fulfil*) atender. **~ing** *a* satisfatório

saturat|e /'sætʃəreɪt/ vt saturar; (fig) cansar. **~ed** a (wet) encharcado; (fat) saturado. **~ion** /-'reɪʃn/ n saturação f

Saturday /'sætədɪ/ n sábado m

sauce /sɔ:s/ n molho m; (colloq: cheek) atrevimento m

saucepan /'sɔ:spən/ n panela f, (P) caçarola f

saucer /'sɔ:sə(r)/ n pires m invar

saucy /'sɔ:sɪ/ a (-ier, -iest) picante

Saudi Arabia /saʊdɪə'reɪbɪə/ n Arábia f Saudita

sauna /'sɔ:nə/ n sauna f

saunter /'sɔ:ntə(r)/ vi perambular

sausage /'sɒsɪdʒ/ n salsicha f, linguiça f; (precooked) salsicha f

savage /'sævɪdʒ/ a (wild) selvagem; (fierce) cruel; (brutal) brutal □ n selvagem mf □ vt atacar ferozmente. **~ry** n selvageria f, ferocidade f

sav|e /seɪv/ vt (rescue) salvar; (keep) guardar; (collect) (P) colecionar; (money) economizar; (time) ganhar; (prevent) evitar, impedir (from de) □ n (sport) salvamento m □ prep salvo, exceto. **~er** n poupador m. **~ing** n economia f, poupança f. **~ings** npl economias fpl

saviour /'seɪvɪə(r)/ n salvador m

savour /'seɪvə(r)/ n sabor m □ vt saborear. **~y** a (tasty) saboroso; (not sweet) salgado

saw[1] /sɔ:/ see **see**[1]

saw[2] /sɔ:/ n serra f □ vt (pt sawed, pp sawn or sawed) serrar

sawdust /'sɔ:dʌst/ n serragem f

saxophone /'sæksəfəʊn/ n saxofone m

say /seɪ/ vt/i (pt said /sed/) dizer, falar □ n **have a ~** (in sth) opinar sobre alg coisa. **have one's ~** exprimir sua opinião. **I ~!** olhe! or escute! **~ing** n ditado m, provérbio m

scab /skæb/ n casca f, crosta f; (colloq: blackleg) fura-greve mf invar

scaffold /'skæfəʊld/ n cadafalso m, andaime m. **~ing** /-əldɪŋ/ n andaime m

scald /skɔ:ld/ vt escaldar, queimar □ n escaldadura f

scale[1] /skeɪl/ n (of fish etc) escama f

scale[2] /skeɪl/ n (ratio, size) escala f; (mus) escala f; (of salaries, charges) tabela f. **on a small/large/etc** ~ numa pequena/grande/etc escala □ vt (climb) escalar. **~ down** reduzir

scales /skeɪlz/ npl (for weighing) balança f

scallop /'skɒləp/ n (culin) concha f de vieira; (shape) concha f de vieira

scalp /skælp/ n couro m cabeludo □ vt escalpar

scalpel /'skælpl/ n bisturi m

scamper /'skæmpə(r)/ vi sair correndo

scampi /'skæmpɪ/ npl camarões mpl fritos

scan /skæn/ vt (pt scanned) (intently) perscrutar, esquadrinhar; (quickly) passar os olhos em; (med) examinar; (radar) explorar □ n (med) exame m

scandal /'skændl/ n (disgrace) escândalo m; (gossip) fofoca f. **~ous** a escandaloso

Scandinavia /skændɪ'neɪvɪə/ n Escandinávia f. **~n** a & n escandinavo (m)

scanty /'skæntɪ/ a (-ier, -iest) escasso; (clothing) sumário

scapegoat /'skeɪpgəʊt/ n bode m expiatório

scar /ska:(r)/ n cicatriz f □ vt (pt scarred) marcar; (fig) deixar marcas

scarc|e /skeəs/ a (-er, -est) escasso, raro. **make o.s. ~e** (colloq) sumir, dar o fora (colloq). **~ity**

n escassez *f*. **~ely** *adv* mal, apenas

scare /skeə(r)/ *vt* assustar, apavorar. **be ~d** estar com medo **(of** de) □ *n* pavor *m*, pânico *m*. **bomb ~** pânico *m* causado por suspeita de bomba num local

scarecrow /'skeəkrəʊ/ *n* espantalho *m*

scarf /skɑːf/ *n* (*pl* **scarves**) (*oblong*) cachecol *m*; (*square*) lenço *m* de cabelo

scarlet /'skɑːlət/ *a* escarlate *m*

scary /'skeərɪ/ *a* (-ier, -iest) (*colloq*) assustador, apavorante

scathing /'skeɪðɪŋ/ *a* mordaz

scatter /'skætə(r)/ *vt* (*strew*) espalhar; (*disperse*) dispersar □ *vi* espalhar-se

scavenge /'skævɪndʒ/ *vi* procurar comida *etc* no lixo. **~r** /-ə(r)/ *n* (*person*) que procura comida *etc* no lixo; (*animal*) que se alimenta de carniça

scenario /sɪ'nɑːrɪəʊ/ *n* (*pl* -os) sinopse *f*, resumo *m* detalhado

scene /siːn/ *n* cena *f*; (*of event*) cenário *m*; (*sight*) vista *f*, panorama *m*. **behind the ~s** nos bastidores. **make a ~** fazer um escândalo

scenery /'siːnərɪ/ *n* cenário *m*, paisagem *f*; (*theat*) cenário *m*

scenic /'siːnɪk/ *a* pitoresco, cênico

scent /sent/ *n* (*perfume*) perfume *m*, fragância *f*; (*trail*) rastro *m*, pista *f* □ *vt* (*discern*) sentir. **~ed** *a* perfumado

sceptic /'skeptɪk/ *n* cético *m*. **~al** *a* cético. **~ism** /-sɪzəm/ *n* ceticismo *m*

schedule /'ʃedjuːl/ *n* programa *m*; (*timetable*) horário *m* □ *vt* marcar, programar. **according to ~** conforme planejado. **behind ~** atrasado. **on ~** (*train*) na hora; (*work*) em dia. **~d flight** *n* vôo *m* regular

scheme /skiːm/ *n* esquema *m*;

(*plan of work*) plano *m*; (*plot*) conspiração *f*, maquinação *f* □ *vi* planejar, (*P*) planear; (*pej*) intrigar, maquinar, tramar

schism /'sɪzəm/ *n* cisma *f*

schizophreni|a /skɪtsəʊ'friːnɪə/ *n* esquizofrenia *f*. **~c** /-'frenɪk/ *a* esquizofrênico, (*P*) esquizofrénico

scholar /'skɒlə(r)/ *n* erudito *m*, estudioso *m*, escolar *m*. **~ly** *a* erudito. **~ship** *n* erudição *f*, saber *m*; (*grant*) bolsa *f* de estudo

school /skuːl/ *n* escola *f*; (*of university*) escola *f*, faculdade *f* □ *a* (*age, year, holidays*) escolar □ *vt* ensinar; (*train*) treinar, adestrar. **~ing** *n* instrução *f*; (*attendance*) escolaridade *f*

school|boy /'skuːlbɔɪ/ *n* aluno *m*. **~girl** *n* aluna *f*

school|master /'skuːlmɑːstə(r)/, **~mistress**, **~teacher** *ns* professor *m*, professora *f*

schooner /'skuːnə(r)/ *n* escuna *f*; (*glass*) copo *m* alto

sciatica /saɪ'ætɪkə/ *n* ciática *f*

scien|ce /'saɪəns/ *n* ciência *f*. **~ce fiction** ficção *f* científica. **~tific** /-'tɪfɪk/ *a* científico

scientist /'saɪəntɪst/ *n* cientista *mf*

scintillate /'sɪntɪleɪt/ *vi* cintilar; (*fig: person*) brilhar

scissors /'sɪzəz/ *npl* (**pair of**) **~** tesoura *f*

scoff[1] /skɒf/ *vi* **~ at** zombar de, (*P*) troçar de

scoff[2] /skɒf/ *vt* (*sl: eat*) devorar, tragar

scold /skəʊld/ *vt* ralhar com. **~ing** *n* reprensão *f*, (*P*) descompostura *f*

scone /skɒn/ *n* (*culin*) scone *m*, bolinho *m* para o chá

scoop /skuːp/ *n* (*for grain, sugar etc*) pá *f*; (*ladle*) concha *f*; (*news*) furo *m* □ *vt* **~ out** (*hollow out*) escavar, tirar com concha *or* pá. **~ up** (*lift*) apanhar

scoot /sku:t/ vi (colloq) fugir, mandar-se (colloq), (P) pôr-se a milhas (colloq)

scooter /'sku:tə(r)/ n (child's) patinete f, (P) trotinete m; (motor cycle) motoreta f, lambreta f

scope /skəup/ n âmbito m, (fig: opportunity) oportunidade f

scorch /skɔ:tʃ/ vt/i chamuscar (-se), queimar de leve. ∼ing a (colloq) escaldante, abrasador

score /skɔ:(r)/ n (sport) contagem f, escore m; (mus) partitura f □ vt marcar com corte(s), riscar; (a goal) marcar; (mus) orquestrar □ vi marcar pontos; (keep score) fazer a contagem, (football) marcar um gol, (P) golo. **a** ∼ **(of)** (twenty) uma vintena (de), vinte. ∼**s** muitos, dezenas. **on that** ∼ nesse respeito, quanto a isso. ∼**board** n marcador m. ∼**r** /-ə(r)/ n (score-keeper) marcador m; (of goals) autor m

scorn /skɔ:n/ n desprezo m □ vt desprezar. ∼**ful** a desdenhoso, escarninho. ∼**fully** adv com desdém, desdenhosamente

Scorpio /'skɔ:pɪəʊ/ n (astr) Escorpião m

scorpion /'skɔ:pɪən/ n escorpião m

Scot /skɒt/ n, ∼**tish** a escocês (m)

Scotch /skɒtʃ/ a escocês □ n uísque m

scotch /skɒtʃ/ vt pôr fim a, frustrar

scot-free /skɒt'fri:/ a impune □ adv impunemente

Scotland /'skɒtlənd/ n Escócia f

Scots /skɒts/ a escocês. ∼**man** n escocês m. ∼**woman** n escocesa f

scoundrel /'skaʊndrəl/ n patife m, canalha m

scour¹ /'skaʊə(r)/ vt (clean) esfregar, arear. ∼**er** n esfregão m de palha de aço or de nylon

scour² /'skaʊə(r)/ vt (search) percorrer, esquadrinhar

scourge /skɜ:dʒ/ n açoite m; (fig) flagelo m

scout /skaʊt/ n (mil) explorador m □ vi ∼ **about (for)** andar à procura de

Scout /skaʊt/ n escoteiro m, (P) escuteiro m. ∼**ing** n escotismo m, (P) escutismo m

scowl /skaʊl/ n carranca f, ar m carrancudo □ vi fazer um ar carrancudo

scraggy /'skrægɪ/ a (-ier, -iest) descarnado, ossudo

scramble /'skræmbl/ vi trepar; (crawl) avançar de rastros, rastejar, arrastar-se □ vt (eggs) mexer □ n luta f, confusão f

scrap¹ /skræp/ n bocadinho m. ∼**s** npl restos mpl □ vt (pt scrapped) jogar fora, (P) deitar fora; (plan etc) abandonar, pôr de lado. ∼**book** n álbum m de recortes. ∼ **heap** monte m de ferro-velho. ∼**iron** n ferro m velho, sucata f. ∼ **merchant** sucateiro m. ∼**paper** n papel m de rascunho. ∼**py** a fragmentário

scrap² /skræp/ n (colloq: fight) briga f, pancadaria f (colloq), rixa f

scrape /skreɪp/ vt raspar; (graze) esfolar, arranhar □ vi (graze, rub) roçar □ n (act of scraping) raspagem f; (mark) raspão m, esfoladura f; (fig) encrenca f, maus lençóis mpl. ∼ **through** escapar pela tangente, (P) à tangente; (exam) passar pela tangente, (P) à tangente. ∼ **together** conseguir juntar. ∼**r** /-ə(r)/ n raspadeira f

scratch /skrætʃ/ vt/i arranhar (-se); (a line) riscar; (to relieve itching) coçar(-se) □ n arranhão m; (line) risco m; (wound with claw, nail) unhada f. **start from**

~ começar do princípio. **up to** ~ à altura, ao nível requerido

scrawl /skrɔ:l/ *n* rabisco *m*, garrancho *m*, garatuja *f* □ *vt/i* rabiscar, fazer garranchos, garatujar

scrawny /'skrɔ:nɪ/ *a* (**-ier, -iest**) descarnado, ossudo, magricela

scream /skri:m/ *vt/i* gritar □ *n* grito *m* (agudo)

screech /skri:tʃ/ *vi* guinchar, gritar; (*of brakes*) chiar, guinchar □ *n* guincho *m*, grito *m* agudo

screen /skri:n/ *n* écran *m*, tela *f*; (*folding*) biombo *m*; (*fig: protection*) manto *m* (*fig*), capa *f* (*fig*) □ *vt* resguardar, tapar; (*film*) passar; (*candidates etc*) fazer a triagem de. **~ing** *n* (*med*) exame *m* médico

screw /skru:/ *n* parafuso *m* □ *vt* aparafusar, atarraxar. ~ **up** (*eyes, face*) franzir; (*sl: ruin*) estragar. ~ **up one's courage** cobrar coragem

screwdriver /'skru:draɪvə(r)/ *n* chave *f* de parafusos *or* de fenda

scribble /'skrɪbl/ *vt/i* rabiscar, garatujar □ *n* rabisco *m*, garatuja *f*

script /skrɪpt/ *n* escrita *f*; (*of film*) roteiro *m*, (P) guião *m*. **~-writer** *n* (*film*) roteirista *m*, (P) autor *m* do guião

Scriptures /'skrɪptʃəz/ *npl* the ~ a Sagrada Escritura

scroll /skrəʊl/ *n* rolo *m* (de papel ou pergaminho); (*archit*) voluta *f* □ *vt/i* (*comput*) passar na tela

scrounge /skraʊndʒ/ *vt* (*colloq: cadge*) filar (*sl*), (P) cravar (*sl*) □ *vi* (*beg*) parasitar, viver às custas de alguém. **~r** /-ə(r)/ *n* parasita *mf*, filão *m* (*sl*), (P) crava *mf* (*sl*)

scrub[1] /skrʌb/ *n* (*land*) mato *m*

scrub[2] /skrʌb/ *vt/i* (*pt* **scrubbed**) esfregar, lavar com escova e sabão; (*colloq: cancel*) cancelar □ *n* esfrega *f*

scruff /skrʌf/ *n* **by the** ~ **of the**

neck pelo cangote, (P) pelo cachaço

scruffy /'skrʌfɪ/ *a* (**-ier, -iest**) desmazelado, desleixado, mal ajambrado (*colloq*)

scrum /skrʌm/ *n* rixa *f*; (*Rugby*) placagem *f*

scruple /'skru:pl/ *n* escrúpulo *m*

scrupulous /'skru:pjʊləs/ *a* escrupuloso. **~ly** *adv* escrupulosamente. **~ly clean** impecavelmente limpo

scrutinize /'skru:tɪnɪ/ *n* averiguação *f*, escrutínio *m*. **~ize** *vt* examinar em detalhes

scuff /skʌf/ *vt* (*scrape*) esfolar, safar □ *n* esfoladura *f*

scuffle /'skʌfl/ *n* tumulto *m*, briga *f*

sculpt /skʌlpt/ *vt/i* esculpir. **~or** *n* escultor *m*. **~ure** /-tʃə(r)/ *n* escultura *f* □ *vt/i* esculpir

scum /skʌm/ *n* (*on liquid*) espuma *f*; (*pej: people*) gentinha *f*, escumalha *f*, ralé *f*

scurf /skɜ:f/ *n* películas *fpl*; (*dandruff*) caspa *f*

scurrilous /'skʌrɪləs/ *a* injurioso, insultuoso

scurry /'skʌrɪ/ *vi* dar corridinhas; (*hurry*) apressar- se. ~ **off** escapulir-se

scurvy /'skɜ:vɪ/ *n* escorbuto *m*

scuttle[1] /'skʌtl/ *n* (*bucket, box*) balde *m* para carvão

scuttle[2] /'skʌtl/ *vt* (*ship*) afundar abrindo rombos *or* as torneiras de fundo

scuttle[3] /'skʌtl/ *vi* ~ **away** *or* **off** fugir, escapulir-se

scythe /saɪð/ *n* gadanha *f*, foice *f* grande

sea /si:/ *n* mar *m* □ *a* do mar, marinho, marítimo. **at** ~ no alto mar, ao largo. **all at** ~ desnorteado. **by** ~ por mar. ~ **bird** ave *f* marinha. **~-green** *a* verde-mar. ~ **horse** cavalo-marinho *m*, hipocampo *m*. ~

level nível *m* do mar. ~ **lion**
leão-marinho *m*. ~ **shell** concha
f. ~**-shore** *n* litoral *m*; (*beach*)
praia *f*. ~ **water** água *f* do mar

seaboard /ˈsiːbɔːd/ *n* litoral *m*,
costa *f*

seafarer /ˈsiːfeərə(r)/ *n* marinheiro *m*, navegante *m*

seafood /ˈsiːfuːd/ *n* marisco(s) *m*
(*pl*)

seagull /ˈsiːɡʌl/ *n* gaivota *f*

seal[1] /siːl/ *n* (*animal*) foca *f*

seal[2] /siːl/ *n* selo *m*, sinete *m* □ *vt*
selar; (*with wax*) lacrar. ~**ing-
wax** *n* lacre *m*. ~ **off** (*area*)
vedar

seam /siːm/ *n* (*in cloth etc*) costura
f; (*of mineral*) veio *m*, filão *m*.
~**less** *a* sem costura

seaman /ˈsiːmən/ *n* (*pl* -**men**)
marinheiro *m*, marítimo *m*

seamy /ˈsiːmɪ/ *a* ~ **side** lado *m*
(do avesso); (*fig*) lado *m* sórdido

seance /ˈseɪɑːns/ *n* sessão *f* espírita

seaplane /ˈsiːpleɪn/ *n* hidroavião
m

seaport /ˈsiːpɔːt/ *n* porto *m* de
mar

search /sɜːtʃ/ *vt/i* revistar, dar
busca (a); (*one's heart, conscience
etc*) examinar □ *n* revista *f*, busca
f; (*quest*) procura *f*, busca *f*; (*official*) inquérito *m*. in ~ of à procura de. ~ **for** procurar. ~
party *n* equipe *f* de busca. ~
warrant *n* mandado *m* de
busca. ~**ing** *a* (*of look*) penetrante; (*of test etc*) minucioso

searchlight /ˈsɜːtʃlaɪt/ *n* holofote
m

seasick /ˈsiːsɪk/ *a* enjoado. ~**ness**
n enjôo *m*, P enjoo *m*

seaside /ˈsiːsaɪd/ *n* costa *f*, praia *f*,
beira-mar *f*. ~ **resort** *n* balneário *m*, praia *f*

season /ˈsiːzn/ *n* (*of year*) estação
f; (*proper time*) época *f*; (*cricket,
football etc*) temporada *f* □ *vt*

temperar; (*wood*) secar. **in** ~
na época. ~**able** *a* próprio da
estação. ~**al** *a* sazonal. ~**ed** *a*
(*of people*) experimentado. ~**ing**
n tempero *m*. ~**-ticket** *n* (*train
etc*) passe *m*; (*theatre etc*) assinatura *f*

seat /siːt/ *n* assento *m*; (*place*) lugar *m*; (*of bicycle*) selim *m*; (*of
chair*) assento *m*; (*of trousers*)
fundilho *m* □ *vt* sentar; (*have
seats for*) ter lugares sentados
para. **be** ~**ed, take a** ~ sentar-se. ~ **of learning** centro *m*
de cultura. ~**-belt** *n* cinto *m* de
segurança

seaweed /ˈsiːwiːd/ *n* alga *f* marinha

seaworthy /ˈsiːwɜːðɪ/ *a* navegável,
em condições de navegabilidade

secateurs /ˈsekətɜːz/ *npl* tesoura *f*
de poda

seclu|de /sɪˈkluːd/ *vt* isolar. ~**ded**
a isolado, retirado. ~**sion**
/sɪˈkluːʒn/ *n* isolamento *m*

second[1] /ˈsekənd/ *a* segundo □ *n*
segundo *m*; (*in duel*) testemunha
f. ~ (**gear**) (*auto*) segunda *f* (velocidade). **the** ~ **of April** dois
de Abril. ~**s** (*goods*) artigos
mpl de segunda *or* de refugo □
adv (*in race etc*) em segundo lugar □ *vt* secundar. ~**-best** *a* escolhido em segundo lugar. ~-
class *a* de segunda classe. ~-
hand *a* de segunda mão □ *n* (*on
clock*) ponteiro *m* dos segundos.
~**-rate** *a* medíocre, de segunda
ordem. ~ **thoughts** dúvidas *fpl*.
on ~ **thoughts** pensando
melhor. ~**ly** *adv* segundo, em segundo lugar

second[2] /sɪˈkɒnd/ *vt* (*transfer*)
destacar (**to** para)

secondary /ˈsekəndrɪ/ *a* secundário. ~ **school** escola *f* secundária

secrecy /ˈsiːkrəsɪ/ *n* segredo *m*

secret /ˈsiːkrɪt/ *a* secreto □ *n*

segredo *m*. **in ~** em segredo. **~ agent** *n* agente *mf* secreto. **~ly** *adv* em segredo, secretamente

secretar|y /'sekrətrɪ/ *n* secretário *m*, secretária *f*. **S~y of State** ministro *m* de Estado, (P) Secretário *m* de Estado; (*Amer*) ministro *m* dos Negócios Estrangeiros. **~ial** /-'teərɪəl/ *a* (*work, course etc*) de secretária

secret|e /sɪ'kri:t/ *vt* segregar; (*hide*) esconder. **~ion** /-ʃn/ *n* secreção *f*

secretive /'si:krətɪv/ *a* misterioso, reservado

sect /sekt/ *n* seita *f*. **~arian** /-'teərɪən/ *a* sectário

section /'sekʃn/ *n* seção *f*, (P) secção *f*; (*of country, community etc*) setor *m*, (P) sector *m*; (*district of town*) zona *f*

sector /'sektə(r)/ *n* setor *m*, (P) sector *m*

secular /'sekjʊlə(r)/ *a* secular, leigo, P laico; (*art, music etc*) profano

secure /sɪ'kjʊə(r)/ *a* seguro, em segurança; (*firm*) seguro, sólido; (*in mind*) tranquilo, P tranquilo □ *vt* prender bem *or* com segurança; (*obtain*) conseguir, arranjar; (*ensure*) assegurar; (*windows, doors*) fechar bem. **~ly** *adv* solidamente, em segurança

securit|y /sɪ'kjʊərətɪ/ *n* segurança *f*; (*for loan*) fiança *f*, caução *f*. **~ies** *npl* (*finance*) títulos *mpl*

sedate /sɪ'deɪt/ *a* sereno, comedido □ *vt* (*med*) tratar com sedativos

sedation /sɪ'deɪʃn/ *n* (*med*) sedação *f*. **under ~** sob o efeito de sedativos

sedative /'sedətɪv/ *n* (*med*) sedativo *m*

sedentary /'sedntrɪ/ *a* sedentário

sediment /'sedɪmənt/ *n* sedimento *m*, depósito *m*

seduce /sɪ'dju:s/ *vt* seduzir

seduct|ion /sɪ'dʌkʃn/ *n* sedução *f*. **~ive** /-tɪv/ *a* sedutor, aliciante

see¹ /si:/ *vt/i* (*pt* saw, *pp* seen) ver; (*escort*) acompanhar. **~ about or to** tratar de, encarregar-se de. **~ off** *vt* (*wave goodbye*) ir despedir-se de; (*chase*) acompanhar. **~ through** (*task*) levar a cabo; (*not be deceived by*) não se deixar enganar por. **~ (to it) that** assegurar que, tratar de fazer com que. **~ing that** visto que, uma vez que. **~ you later!** (*colloq*) até logo! (*colloq*)

see² /si:/ *n* sé *f*, bispado *m*

seed /si:d/ *n* semente *f*; (*fig: origin*) germe(n) *m*; (*tennis*) cabeça *f* de série; (*pip*) caroço *m*. **go to ~** produzir sementes; (*fig*) desmazelar-se (*colloq*). **~ling** *n* planta *f* brotada a partir da semente

seedy /'si:dɪ/ *a* (-ier, -iest) (com um ar) gasto, surrado; (*colloq: unwell*) abatido, deprimido, em baixo astral (*colloq*)

seek /si:k/ *vt* (*pt* sought) procurar; (*help etc*) pedir

seem /si:m/ *vi* parecer. **~ingly** *adv* aparentemente, ao que parece

seemly /'si:mlɪ/ *adv* decente, conveniente, próprio

seen /si:n/ see **see¹**

seep /si:p/ *vi* (*ooze*) filtrar-se; (*trickle*) pingar, escorrer, passar. **~age** *n* infiltração *f*

see-saw /'si:sɔ:/ *n* gangorra *f*, (P) balanço *m*

seethe /si:ð/ *vi* **~ with** (*anger*) ferver de; (*people*) fervilhar de

segment /'segmənt/ *n* segmento *m*; (*of orange*) gomo *m*

segregat|e /'segrɪgeɪt/ *vt* segregar, separar. **~ion** /-'geɪʃn/ *n* segregação *f*

seize /si:z/ *vt* agarrar, (P) deitar a mão a, apanhar; (*take possession by force*) apoderar-se de; (*by law*) apreender, confiscar, (P) apresar □ *vi* ~ **on** (*opportunity*) aproveitar. ~ **up** (*engine etc*) grimpar, emperrar. **be** ~**d with** (*fear; illness*) ter um ataque de *m*.

seizure /'si:ʒə(r)/ *n* (*med*) ataque *m*, crise *f*, (*law*) apreensão *f*, captura *f*

seldom /'seldəm/ *adv* raras vezes, raramente, raro

select /sɪ'lekt/ *vt* escolher, selecionar, (P) seleccionar □ *a* seleto, (P) selecto. ~**ion** /-ʃn/ *n* seleção *f*, (P) selecção *f*; (*comm*) sortido *m*

selective /sɪ'lektɪv/ *a* seletivo, (P) selectivo

self /self/ *n* (*pl* **selves**) **the** ~ o eu, o ego

self- /self/ *pref* ~**-assurance** *n* segurança *f*. ~**-assured** *a* seguro de si. ~**-catering** *a* em que os hóspedes tem facilidades de cozinhar. ~**-centred** *a* egocêntrico. ~**-confidence** *n* autoconfiança *f*, confiança *f* em si mesmo. ~**-confident** *a* que tem confiança em si mesmo. ~**-conscious** *a* inibido, constrangido. ~**-contained** *a* independente. ~**-control** *n* autodomínio *m*. ~**-controlled** *a* senhor de si. ~**-defence** *n* legítima defesa *f*. ~**-denial** *n* abnegação *f*. ~**-employed** *a* autónomo. ~**-esteem** *n* amor próprio. ~**-evident** *a* evidente. ~**-indulgent** *a* que não resiste a tentações; (*for ease*) comodista. ~**-interest** *n* interesse *m* pessoal. ~**-portrait** *n* auto-retrato *m*. ~**-possessed** *a* senhor de si. ~**-reliant** *a* independente, seguro de si. ~**-respect** *n* amor próprio. ~**-righteous** *a* que se tem em boa conta. ~**-sacrifice** *n* abnegação *f*, sacrifício *m*. ~**-satisfied** *a* cheio de si, convencido (*colloq*). ~**-seeking** *a* egoísta. ~**-service** *a* auto-serviço, self-

service. ~**-styled** *a* pretenso. ~**-sufficient** *a* auto-suficiente. ~**-willed** *a* voluntarioso

selfish /'selfɪʃ/ *a* egoísta; (*motive*) interesseiro. ~**ness** *n* egoísmo *m*

selfless /'selflɪs/ *a* desinteressado

sell /sel/ *vt/i* (*pt* **sold**) vender(-se). ~**-by date** vender até. ~ **off** liquidar. **be sold out** estar esgotado. ~**-out** *n* (*show*) sucesso *m*; (*colloq: betrayal*) traição *f*. ~**er** *n* vendedor *m*

Sellotape /'seləʊteɪp/ *n* fita *f* adesiva, (P) fitacola *f*

semantic /sɪ'mæntɪk/ *a* semântico. ~**s** *n* semântica *f*

semblance /'sembləns/ *n* aparência *f*

semen /'si:mən/ *n* sêmen *m*, (P) sémen *m*, esperma *m*

semester /sɪ'mestə(r)/ *n* (*Amer: univ*) semestre *m*

semi- /'semɪ/ *pref* semi-, meio

semibreve /'semɪbri:v/ *n* (*mus*) semibreve *f*

semicircle /'semɪsɜ:kl/ *n* semicírculo *m*. ~**ular** /-sɜ:kjʊlə(r)/ *a* semicircular

semicolon /semɪ'kəʊlən/ *n* ponto-e-vírgula *f*

semi-detached /semɪdɪ'tætʃt/ *a* ~ **house** casa *f* geminada

semifinal /semɪ'faɪnl/ *n* semifinal *f*, (P) meiafinal *f*

seminar /'semɪnɑ:(r)/ *n* seminário *m*

semiquaver /'semɪkweɪvə(r)/ *n* (*mus*) semicolcheia *f*

Semite /'si:maɪt/ *a* & *n* semita (*mf*). ~**ic** /sɪ'mɪtɪk/ *a* & *n* (*lang*) semítico (*m*)

semitone /'semɪtəʊn/ *n* (*mus*) semitom *m*

semolina /semə'li:nə/ *n* sêmola *f*, (P) sémola *f*, semolina *f*

senate /'senɪt/ *n* senado *m*. ~**or** /-ətə(r)/ *n* senador *m*

send /send/ *vt/i* (*pt* **sent**) enviar,

mandar. **~ back** devolver. **~ for**
(*person*) chamar, mandar vir;
(*help*) pedir. **~ (away** *or* **off)
for** encomendar, mandar vir
(por carta). **~-off** n despedida f,
bota-fora m. **~ up** (*colloq*)
parodiar. **~er** n expedidor m, re-
metente m

senil|e /'si:naɪl/ a senil. **~ity**
/sɪ'nɪlətɪ/ n senilidade f

senior /'si:nɪə(r)/ a mais velho,
mais idoso (**to** que); (*in rank*)
superior; (*in service*) mais antigo;
(*after surname*) sénior, (*P*) sénior
□ n pessoa f mais velha; (*schol*)
finalista mf. **~ citizen** pessoa f
de idade or da terceira idade.
~ity /-'ɒrətɪ/ n (*in age*) idade f,
(*in service*) antiguidade f

sensation /sen'seɪʃn/ n sensação
f. **~al** a sensacional. **~alism** n
sensacionalismo m

sense /sens/ n sentido m; (*wisdom*) bom senso m; (*sensation*)
sensação f; (*mental impression*)
sentimento m. **~s** (*sanity*) razão
f □ vt pressentir. **make ~** fazer
sentido. **make ~ of** compreender. **~less** a disparatado, sem
sentido; (*med*) sem sentidos, inconsciente

sensible /'sensəbl/ a sensato, razoável; (*clothes*) prático

sensitiv|e /'sensətɪv/ a sensível
(**to** a); (*touchy*) susceptível.
~ity /-'tɪvətɪ/ n sensibilidade f

sensory /'sensərɪ/ a sensorial

sensual /'senʃʊəl/ a sensual.
~ity /-'ælətɪ/ n sensualidade f

sensuous /'senʃʊəs/ a sensual

sent /sent/ *see* send

sentence /'sentəns/ n frase f; (*jur:
decision*) sentença f; (*punishment*) pena f □ vt **~** to condenar a

sentiment /'sentɪmənt/ n sentimento m; (*opinion*) modo m de
ver

sentimental /sentɪ'mentl/ a senti-

mental. **~ity** /-'mentælətɪ/ n
sentimentalidade f, sentimenta-
lismo m. **~ value** valor m esti-
mativo

sentry /'sentrɪ/ n sentinela f

separable /'sepərəbl/ a separável

separate[1] /'seprət/ a separado,
diferente. **~s** npl (*clothes*) conjuntos mpl. **~ly** adv separadamente, em separado

separat|e[2] /'sepəreɪt/ vt/i separar
(-se). **~ion** /-'reɪʃn/ n separação f

September /sep'tembə(r)/ n setembro m

septic /'septɪk/ a séptico, infecta-
do

sequel /'si:kwəl/ n resultado m,
seqüela f, (*P*) sequela f; (*of novel,
film*) continuação f

sequence /'si:kwəns/ n seqüência
f, (*P*) sequência f

sequin /'si:kwɪn/ n lantejoula f

serenade /serə'neɪd/ n serenata f
□ vt fazer uma serenata para

seren|e /sɪ'ri:n/ a sereno. **~ity**
/-'enətɪ/ n serenidade f

sergeant /'sɑ:dʒənt/ n sargento m

serial /'sɪərɪəl/ n folhetim m □ a
(*number*) de série. **~ize** /-laɪz/ vt
publicar em folhetim

series /'sɪərɪ:z/ n invar série f

serious /'sɪərɪəs/ a sério; (*very
bad, critical*) grave, sério. **~ly**
adv seriamente, gravemente, a
sério. **take ~ly** levar a sério.
~ness n seriedade f, gravidade
f

sermon /'sɜ:mən/ n sermão m

serpent /'sɜ:pənt/ n serpente f

serrated /sɪ'reɪtɪd/ a (*edge*) ser-
r(e)ado, com serrilha

serum /'sɪərəm/ n (*pl* -a) soro m

servant /'sɜ:vənt/ n criado m,
criada f, empregado m, empregada f

serv|e /sɜ:v/ vt/i servir; (*a sen-
tence*) cumprir; (*jur: a writ*) entregar; (*mil*) servir, prestar
serviço; (*apprenticeship*) fazer □

n (*tennis*) saque *m*, (*P*) serviço *m*. **~e as/to** servir de/para. **~e its purpose** servir para o que é (*colloq*), servir os seus fins. **it ~es you/him** *etc* **right** é bem feito. **~ing** *n* (*portion*) dose *f*, porção *f*

server /'sɜːvə(r)/ *n* (*comput*) servidor *m*

service /'sɜːvɪs/ *n* serviço *m*; (*relig*) culto *m*; (*tennis*) saque *m*, (*P*) serviço *m*; (*maintenance*) revisão *f*. **~s** (*mil*) forças *fpl* armadas □ *vt* (*car etc*) fazer a revisão de. **of ~** útil, de utilidade a. **~ area** área *f* de serviço. **~ charge** serviço *m*. **~ station** posto *m* de gasolina

serviceable /'sɜːvɪsəbl/ *a* útil, prático; (*durable*) resistente

serviceman /'sɜːvɪsmən/ *n* (*pl* -men) militar *m*

serviette /sɜːvɪ'et/ *n* guardanapo *m*

session /'seʃn/ *n* sessão *f*; (*univ*) ano *m* académico, (*P*) académico; (*Amer: univ*) semestre *m*. **in ~** (*sitting*) em sessão, reunidos

set /set/ *vt* (*pt* **set**, *pres p* **setting**) pôr, colocar; (*put down*) pousar; (*limit etc*) fixar; (*watch, clock*) regular; (*example*) dar; (*exam, task*) marcar; (*in plaster*) engessar □ *vi* (*of sun*) pôr-se; (*of jelly*) endurecer, solidificar(-se) □ *n* (*of people*) círculo *m*, roda *f*; (*of books*) colecção *f*, (*P*) colecção *f*; (*of tools, chairs etc*) jogo *m*; (*TV, radio*) aparelho *m*; (*hair*) mise *f*; (*theat*) cenário *m*; (*tennis*) partida *f*, set *m* □ *a* fixo; (*habit*) inveterado; (*jelly*) duro, sólido; (*book*) do programa, (*P*) adoptado; (*meal*) a preço fixo. **be ~ on doing** estar decidido a fazer. **~ about** *or* **to** começar a, pôr-se a. **~ back** (*plans etc*) atrasar; (*sl: cost*) custar. **~-back** *n* revés *m*, contratempo *m*, atraso *m* de vida (*colloq*). **~ fire to** atear fogo a,

(*P*) deitar fogo a. **~ free** pôr em liberdade. **~ in** (*rain etc*) pegar. **~ off** *or* **out** partir, começar a viajar. **~ off** (*mechanism*) pôr para funcionar, (*P*) pôr a funcionar; (*bomb*) explodir; (*by contrast*) realçar. **~ out** (*state*) expor; (*arrange*) dispôr. **~ sail** partir, içar as velas. **~ square** esquadro *m*. **~ the table** pôr a mesa. **~ theory** teoria *f* de conjuntos. **~-to** *n* briga *f*. **~ up** (*establish*) fundar, estabelecer. **~-up** *n* (*system*) sistema *m*, organização *f*; (*situation*) situação *f*

settee /se'tiː/ *n* sofá *m*

setting /'setɪŋ/ *n* (*framework*) quadro *m*; (*of jewel*) engaste *m*; (*typ*) composição *f*; (*mus*) arranjo *m* musical

settle /'setl/ *vt* (*arrange*) resolver; (*date*) marcar; (*nerves*) acalmar; (*doubts*) esclarecer; (*new country*) colonizar, povoar; (*bill*) pagar □ *vi* assentar; (*in country*) estabelecer-se; (*in house, chair etc*) instalar-se; (*weather*) estabilizar-se. **~ down** acalmar-se; (*become orderly*) assentar; (*sit, rest*) instalar-se. **~ for** aceitar. **~ up (with)** fazer contas (com); (*fig*) ajustar contas (com). **~r** /-ə(r)/ *n* colono *m*, colonizador *m*

settlement /'setlmənt/ *n* (*agreement*) acordo *m*; (*payment*) pagamento *m*; (*colony*) colónia *f*, (*P*) colónia *f*; (*colonization*) colonização *f*

seven /'sevn/ *a* & *n* sete (*m*). **~th** *a* & *n* sétimo (*m*)

seventeen /sevn'tiːn/ *a* & *n* dezessete (*m*), (*P*) dezassete (*m*). **~th** *a* & *n* décimo sétimo (*m*)

seventy /'sevntɪ/ *a* & *n* setenta (*m*). **~ieth** *a* & *n* septuagésimo (*m*)

sever /'sevə(r)/ *vt* cortar. **~ance** *n* corte *m*

several /'sevrəl/ *a* & *pron* vários, diversos

sever|e /sɪ'vɪə(r)/ *a* (**-er, -est**) severo; (*pain*) forte, violento; (*illness*) grave; (*winter*) rigoroso. **~ely** *adv* severamente; (*seriously*) gravemente. **~ity** /sɪ'verɪti/ *n* severidade *f*; (*seriousness*) gravidade *f*

sew /səʊ/ *vt/i* (*pt* sewed, *pp* sewn *or* sewed) coser, costurar. **~ing** *n* costura *f*. **~ing-machine** *n* máquina *f* de costura

sewage /'sjuːɪdʒ/ *n* efluentes *mpl* dos esgotos, detritos *mpl*

sewer /'sjuːə(r)/ *n* cano *m* de esgoto

sewn /səʊn/ *see* sew

sex /seks/ *n* sexo *m* □ *a* sexual. **have ~** ter relações. **~ maniac** tarado *m* sexual. **~y** *a* sexy *invar*, que tem sex-appeal

sexist /'seksɪst/ *a* & *n* sexista *mf*

sexual /'sekʃʊəl/ *a* sexual. **~ harassment** assédio *m* sexual. **~ intercourse** relações *fpl* sexuais. **~ity** /-'ælətɪ/ *n* sexualidade *f*

shabb|y /'ʃæbɪ/ *a* (**-ier, -iest**) (*clothes, object*) gasto, surrado; (*person*) maltrapilho, mal vestido; (*mean*) miserável. **~ily** *adv* miseravelmente

shack /ʃæk/ *n* cabana *f*, barraca *f*

shackles /'ʃæklz/ *npl* grilhões *mpl*, algemas *fpl*

shade /ʃeɪd/ *n* sombra *f*; (*of colour*) tom *m*, matiz *m*; (*of opinion*) matiz *m*; (*for lamp*) abat-jour *m*, quebra-luz *m*; (*Amer: blind*) estore *m* □ *vt* resguardar da luz; (*darken*) sombrear. **a ~ bigger/** *etc* ligeiramente maior/*etc*. **in the ~** à sombra

shadow /'ʃædəʊ/ *n* sombra *f* □ *vt* cobrir de sombra; (*follow*) seguir, vigiar. **S~ Cabinet** gabinete *m* formado pelo partido da oposição. **~y** *a* ensombrado,

sombreado; (*fig*) vago, indistinto

shady /'ʃeɪdɪ/ *a* (**-ier, -iest**) sombreiro, (*P*) que dá sombra; (*in shade*) à sombra; (*fig: dubious*) suspeito, duvidoso

shaft /ʃɑːft/ *n* (*of arrow, spear*) haste *f*; (*axle*) eixo *m*, veio *m*; (*of mine, lift*) poço *m*; (*of light*) raio *m*

shaggy /'ʃægɪ/ *a* (**-ier, -iest**) (*beard*) hirsuto; (*hair*) desgrenhado; (*animal*) peludo, felpudo

shake /ʃeɪk/ *vt* (*pt* shook, *pp* shaken) abanar, sacudir; (*bottle*) agitar; (*belief, house etc*) abalar □ *vi* estremecer, tremer □ *n* (*violent*) abanão *m*, safanão *m*; (*light*) sacudidela *f*. **~ hands with** apertar a mão de. **~ off** (*get rid of*) sacudir, livrar-se de. **~ one's head** (*to say no*) fazer que não com a cabeça. **~ up** agitar. **~-up** *n* (*upheaval*) reviravolta *f*

shaky /'ʃeɪkɪ/ *a* (**-ier, -iest**) (*hand, voice*) trêmulo, (*P*) trémulo; (*unsteady, unsafe*) pouco firme, inseguro; (*weak*) fraco

shall /ʃæl/; *unstressed* /ʃəl/ *v aux* **I/we ~ do** (*future*) farei/faremos. **I/you/he ~ do** (*command*) eu hei de/você há de/tu hás de/ele há de fazer

shallot /ʃə'lɒt/ *n* cebolinha *f*, (*P*) chalota *f*

shallow /'ʃæləʊ/ *a* (**-er, -est**) pouco fundo, raso; (*fig*) superficial

sham /ʃæm/ *n* fingimento *m*; (*jewel etc*) imitação *f*; (*person*) impostor *m*, fingido *m* □ *a* fingido; (*false*) falso □ *vt* (*pt* shammed) fingir

shambles /'ʃæmblz/ *npl* (*colloq: mess*) balbúrdia *f*, trapalhada *f*

shame /ʃeɪm/ *n* vergonha *f* □ *vt* (fazer) envergonhar. **it's a ~** é uma pena. **what a ~!** que pena! **~ful** *a* vergonhoso. **~less a**

sem vergonha, descarado; (*immodest*) despudorado, desavergonhado

shamefaced /'ʃeɪmfeɪst/ a envergonhado

shampoo /ʃæm'puː/ n xampu m, (P) champô m, shampoo m □ vt lavar com xampu, (P) champô or shampoo

shan't /ʃɑːnt/ = **shall not**

shanty /'ʃæntɪ/ n barraca f. ~ **town** favela f, (P) bairro(s) m(pl) da lata

shape /ʃeɪp/ n forma f □ vt moldar □ vi ~ (**up**) andar bem, fazer progressos. **take** ~ concretizar-se, avançar. ~**less** a informe, sem forma; (*of body*) deselegante, disforme

shapely /'ʃeɪplɪ/ a (-ier, -iest) (*leg, person*) bem feito, elegante

share /ʃeə(r)/ n parte f, porção f; (*comm*) ação f, (P) acção f □ vt/i partilhar (**with** com, **in** de)

shareholder /'ʃeəhəʊldə(r)/ n acionista mf, (P) accionista mf

shark /ʃɑːk/ n tubarão m

sharp /ʃɑːp/ a (-er, -est) (*knife, pencil etc*) afiado; (*pin, point etc*) pontiagudo, aguçado; (*words, reply*) áspero; (*of bend*) fechado; (*acute*) agudo; (*sudden*) brusco; (*dishonest*) pouco honesto; (*well-defined*) nítido; (*brisk*) rápido, vigoroso; (*clever*) vivo □ adv (*stop*) de repente □ n (*mus*) sustenido m. **six o'clock** ~ seis horas em ponto. ~**ly** adv (*harshly*) rispidamente; (*suddenly*) de repente

sharpen /'ʃɑːpən/ vt aguçar; (*pencil*) fazer a ponta de, (P) afiar; (*knife etc*) afiar, amolar. ~**er** n afiadeira f; (*for pencil*) apontador m, (P) apára-lápis m, (P) afia-lápis m

shatter /'ʃætə(r)/ vt/i despedaçar(-se), esmigalhar(-se); (*hopes*) destruir(-se); (*nerves*) abalar(-se);

~**ed** a (*upset*) passado; (*exhausted*) estourado (*colloq*)

shav|e /ʃeɪv/ vt/i barbear(-se), fazer a barba (de) □ n have a ~e barbear-se. **have a close** ~e (*fig*) escapar por um triz. ~**en** a raspado, barbeado. ~**er** n aparelho m de barbear, (P) máquina f de barbear. ~**ing-brush** n pincel m para a barba. ~**ing-cream** n creme m de barbear

shaving /'ʃeɪvɪŋ/ n apara f

shawl /ʃɔːl/ n xale m, (P) xaile m

she /ʃiː/ pron ela □ n fêmea f

sheaf /ʃiːf/ n (pl **sheaves**) feixe m, (*of papers*) maço m, molho m

shear /ʃɪə(r)/ vt (pp **shorn** or **sheared**) (*sheep etc*) tosquiar

shears /ʃɪəz/ npl tesoura f para jardim

sheath /ʃiːθ/ n (pl ~**s** /ʃiːðz/) bainha f; (*condom*) preservativo m, camisa-de-Vênus f

sheathe /ʃiːð/ vt embainhar

shed[1] /ʃed/ n (hut) casinhola f, (for cows) estábulo m

shed[2] /ʃed/ vt (pt **shed**, pres p **shedding**) perder, deixar cair; (*spread*) espalhar; (*blood, tears*) deitar, derramar. ~ **light on** lançar luz sobre

sheen /ʃiːn/ n brilho m, lustre m

sheep /ʃiːp/ n (pl invar) carneiro m, ovelha f. ~**-dog** n cão m de pastor

sheepish /'ʃiːpɪʃ/ a encabulado. ~**ly** adv com um ar encabulado

sheepskin /'ʃiːpskɪn/ n pele f de carneiro; (*leather*) carneira f

sheer /ʃɪə(r)/ a mero, simples; (*steep*) íngreme, a pique; (*fabric*) diáfano, transparente □ adv a pique, verticalmente

sheet /ʃiːt/ n lençol m; (*of glass, metal*) chapa f, placa f; (*of paper*) folha f

sheikh /ʃeɪk/ n xeque m, sheik m

shelf /ʃelf/ n (pl **shelves**) prateleira f

shell /ʃel/ n (of egg, nut etc) casca f; (of mollusc) concha f; (of ship, tortoise) casco m; (of building) estrutura f, armação f; (of explosive) cartucho m □ vt descascar; (mil) bombardear

shellfish /ˈʃelfɪʃ/ n (pl invar) crustáceo m; (as food) marisco m

shelter /ˈʃeltə(r)/ n abrigo m, refúgio m □ vt abrigar; (protect) proteger; (harbour) dar asilo a □ vi abrigar-se, refugiar-se. ~ed a (life etc) protegido; (spot) abrigado

shelve /ʃelv/ vt pôr em prateleiras; (fit with shelves) pôr prateleiras em; (fig) engavetar, pôr de lado

shelving /ˈʃelvɪŋ/ n (shelves) prateleiras fpl

shepherd /ˈʃepəd/ n pastor m □ vt guiar. ~'s pie empadão m de batata e carne moída

sheriff /ˈʃerɪf/ n xerife m

sherry /ˈʃerɪ/ n Xerez m

shield /ʃiːld/ n (armour, heraldry) escudo m; (screen) anteparo m □ vt proteger (from contra, de)

shift /ʃɪft/ vt/i mudar de posição, deslocar(-se); (exchange, alter) mudar de □ n mudança f; (workers; work) turno m. make ~ arranjar-se

shiftless /ˈʃɪftlɪs/ a (lazy) molengão, preguiçoso

shifty /ˈʃɪftɪ/ a (-ier, -iest) velhaco, duvidoso

shimmer /ˈʃɪmə(r)/ vi luzir suavemente □ n luzir m

shin /ʃɪn/ n perna f. ~-bone n tíbia f, canela f. ~-pad n (football) caneleira f

shin|e /ʃaɪn/ vt/i (pt shone) (polish) brilhar, (fazer) reluzir; (shoes) engraxar □ n lustro m. ~e a torch (on) iluminar com uma lanterna de mão. the sun is ~ing faz sol

shingle /ˈʃɪŋgl/ n (pebbles) seixos mpl

shingles /ˈʃɪŋglz/ npl med zona f, herpes- zóster f

shiny /ˈʃaɪnɪ/ a (-ier, -iest) brilhante; (of coat, trousers) lustroso

ship /ʃɪp/ n barco m, navio m □ vt (pt shipped) transportar; (send) mandar por via marítima; (load) embarcar. ~ment n (goods) carregamento m; (shipping) embarque m. ~per n expedidor m. ~ping n navegação f; (ships) navios mpl

shipbuilding /ˈʃɪpbɪldɪŋ/ n construção f naval

shipshape /ˈʃɪpʃeɪp/ adv & a em (perfeita) ordem, impecável

shipwreck /ˈʃɪprek/ n naufrágio m. ~ed a naufragado. be ~ed naufragar

shipyard /ˈʃɪpjaːd/ n estaleiro m

shirk /ʃɜːk/ vt fugir a, furtar-se a, (P) baldar-se a (sl). ~er n parasita mf

shirt /ʃɜːt/ n camisa f; (of woman) blusa f. in ~-sleeves em mangas de camisa

shiver /ˈʃɪvə(r)/ vi arrepiar-se, tiritar □ n arrepio m

shoal /ʃəʊl/ n (of fish) cardume m

shock /ʃɒk/ choque m, embate m; (electr) choque m elétrico, (P) eléctrico; (med) choque m □ a de choque □ vt chocar. ~ absorber (mech) amortecedor m. ~ing a chocante; (colloq: very bad) horrível

shod /ʃɒd/ see shoe

shodd|y /ˈʃɒdɪ/ a (-ier, -iest) mal feito, ordinário, de má qualidade. ~ily adv mal

shoe /ʃuː/ n sapato m; (footwear) calçado m; (horse) ferradura f; (brake) sapata f, (P) calço m (de travão) □ vt (pt shod, pres p shoeing) (horse) ferrar. ~polish n pomada f, (P) graxa f para sapatos. ~-shop n sapataria *f*. **on a ~-string** (*colloq*) com/por muito pouco dinheiro, na pindaíba (*colloq*)

shoehorn /ˈʃuːhɔːn/ *n* calçadeira *f*

shoelace /ˈʃuːleɪs/ *n* cordão *m* de sapato, (*P*) atacador *m*

shoemaker /ˈʃuːmeɪkə(r)/ *n* sapateiro *m*

shone /ʃɒn/ *see* **shine**

shoo /ʃuː/ *vt* enxotar □ *int* xô

shook /ʃʊk/ *see* **shake**

shoot /ʃuːt/ *vt* (*pt* **shot**) (*gun*) disparar; (*glance, missile*) lançar; (*kill*) matar a tiro; (*wound*) ferir a tiro; (*execute*) executar, fuzilar; (*hunt*) caçar; (*film*) filmar, rodar □ *vi* disparar, atirar (**at** contra, sobre); (*bot*) rebentar; (*football*) rematar □ *n* (*bot*) rebento *m*. **~ down** abater (a tiro). **~ in/out** (*rush*) entrar/sair correndo *ou* disparado. **~ up** (*spurt*) jorrar; (*grow quickly*) crescer a olhos vistos, dar um pulo; (*prices*) subir em disparada. **~ing** *n* (*shots*) tiroteio *m*. **~ing-range** *n* carreira *f* de tiro. **~ing star** estrela *f* cadente

shop /ʃɒp/ *n* loja *f*; (*workshop*) oficina *f* □ *vi* (*pt* **shopped**) fazer compras. **~ around** procurar, ver o que há. **~ assistant** *n* empregado *m*, caixeiro *m*; vendedor *m*. **~-floor** *n* (*workers*) trabalhadores *mpl*. **~per** *n* comprador *m*. **~-soiled**, (*Amer*) **~worn** *adjs* enxovalhado. **~ steward** delegado *m* sindical. **~ window** vitrina *f*, (*P*) montra *f*. **talk ~** falar de coisas profissionais

shopkeeper /ˈʃɒpkiːpə(r)/ *n* lojista *mf*, comerciante *mf*

shoplift|er /ˈʃɒplɪftə(r)/ *n* gatuno *m* de lojas. **~ing** *n* furto *m* em lojas

shopping /ˈʃɒpɪŋ/ *n* (*goods*) compras *fpl*. **go ~** ir às compras. **~ bag** sacola *f* de compras. **~ centre** centro *m* comercial

shore /ʃɔː(r)/ *n* (*of sea*) praia *f*, costa *f*; (*of lake*) margem *f*

shorn /ʃɔːn/ *see* **shear** □ *a* tosquiado. **~ of** despojado de

short /ʃɔːt/ *a* (**-er, -est**) curto; (*person*) baixo; (*brief*) breve, curto; (*curt*) seco, brusco. **be ~ of** (*lack*) ter falta de □ *adv* (*abruptly*) bruscamente, de repente. **cut ~** abreviar; (*interrupt*) interromper □ *n* (*electr*) curto-circuito *m*; (*film*) curta-metragem *f*, short *m*. **~s** (*trousers*) calção *m*, (*P*) calções *mpl*, short *m*, (*P*) shorts *mpl*. **a ~ time** pouco tempo. **he is called Tom for ~** o diminutivo dele é Tom. **in ~** em suma. **~-change** *vt* (*cheat*) enganar. **~ circuit** (*electr*) curto-circuito *m* **~-circuit** *vt/i* (*electr*) fazer *ou* dar um curto-circuito (em). **~ cut** atalho *m*. **~-handed** *a* com falta de pessoal. **~ list** pré-seleção *f*, (*P*) pré-selecção *f*. **~-lived** *a* de pouca duração. **~-sighted** *a* míope, (*P*) curto de vista. **~-tempered** *a* irritadiço. **~ wave** (*radio*) onda(s) *f*(*pl*) curta(s)

shortage /ˈʃɔːtɪdʒ/ *n* falta *f*, escassez *f*

shortbread /ˈʃɔːtbred/ *n* shortbread *m*, biscoito *m* de massa amanteigada

shortcoming /ˈʃɔːtkʌmɪŋ/ *n* falha *f*, imperfeição *f*

shorten /ˈʃɔːtn/ *vt/i* encurtar(-se), abreviar(-se), diminuir

shorthand /ˈʃɔːthænd/ *n* estenografia *f*, taquigrafia *f*. **~ typist** estenodactilógrafa *f*

shortly /ˈʃɔːtli/ *adv* (*soon*) em breve, dentro em pouco

shot /ʃɒt/ *see* **shoot** □ *n* (*firing, bullet*) tiro *m*; (*person*) atirador *m*; (*pellets*) chumbo *m*; (*photograph*) fotografia *f*; (*injection*) injeção *f*, (*P*) injecção *f*; (*in golf,* *billiards*) tacada *f*. **go like a ~** ir disparado. **have a ~ (at sth)** experimentar (fazer alg coisa). **~-gun** *n* espingarda *f*, caçadeira *f*

should /ʃʊd/, *unstressed* /ʃəd/ *v aux* **you ~ help me** você devia me ajudar. **I ~ have stayed** devia ter ficado. **I ~ like to** gostaria de *or* gostava de. **if he ~ come** se ele vier

shoulder /'ʃəʊldə(r)/ *n* ombro *m* □ *vt* (*responsibility*) tomar, assumir; (*burden*) carregar, arcar com. **~-blade** *n* (*anat*) omoplata *f*. **~-pad** *n* enchimento *m* de ombro, ombreira *f*

shout /ʃaʊt/ *n* grito *m*, brado *m*; (*very loud*) berro *m* □ *vt/i* gritar (**at** com); (*very loudly*) berrar (**at** com). **~ down** fazer calar com gritos. **~ing** *n* gritaria *f*, berraria *f*

shove /ʃʌv/ *n* empurrão *m* □ *vt/i* empurrar; (*colloq: put*) meter, enfiar. **~ off** (*colloq: depart*) começar a andar (*colloq*), dar o fora (*colloq*), (*P*) cavar (*colloq*)

shovel /'ʃʌvl/ *n* pá *f*; (*machine*) escavadora *f* □ *vt* (*pt* **shovelled**) remover com pá

show /ʃəʊ/ *vt* (*pt* **showed**, *pp* **shown**) mostrar; (*of dial, needle*) marcar; (*put on display*) expor; (*film*) dar, passar □ *vi* ver-se, aparecer, estar à vista □ *n* mostra *f*, demonstração *f*, manifestação *f*; (*ostentation*) alarde *m*, espalhafato *m*; (*exhibition*) mostra *f*, exposição *f*; (*theatre, cinema*) espetáculo *m*, (*P*) espectáculo *m*, show *m*. **for ~** para fazer vista. **on ~** exposto, em exposição. **~ down** *n* confrontação *f*. **~-jumping** *n* concurso *m* hípico. **~ in** mandar entrar. **~ off** *vt* exibir, ostentar □ *vi* exibir-se, querer fazer figura. **~-off** *n* exibicionista *mf*. **~ out** acompa-

nhar à porta. **~-piece** *n* peça *f* digna de se expor. **~ up** ser claramente visível, ver-se bem; (*colloq: arrive*) aparecer. **~ing** *n* (*performance*) atuação *f*, performance *f*; (*cinema*) exibição *f*

shower /'ʃaʊə(r)/ *n* (*of rain*) aguaceiro *m*, chuvarada *f*; (*of blows etc*) saraivada *f*; (*in bathroom*) chuveiro *m*, ducha *f*, (*P*) duche *m* □ *vt* **~ with** cumular de, encher de □ *vi* tomar um banho de chuveiro *or* uma ducha, (*P*) um duche. **~y** *a* chuvoso

showerproof /'ʃaʊəpru:f/ *a* impermeável

shown /ʃəʊn/ *see* **show**

showroom /'ʃəʊrʊm/ *n* espaço *m* de exposição, show-room *m*; (*for cars*) stand *m*

showy /'ʃəʊɪ/ *a* (**-ier, -iest**) vistoso; (*too bright*) berrante; (*pej*) espalhafatoso

shrank /ʃræŋk/ *see* **shrink**

shred /ʃred/ *n* tira *f*, retalho *m*, farrapo *m*; (*fig*) mínimo *m*, sombra *f* □ *vt* (*pt* **shredded**) reduzir a tiras, estraçalhar; (*culin*) desfiar. **~der** *n* trituradora *f*. (*for paper*) fragmentadora *f*

shrewd /ʃru:d/ *a* (**-er, -est**) astucioso, fino, perspicaz. **~ness** *n* astúcia *f*, perspicácia *f*

shriek /ʃri:k/ *n* grito *m* agudo, guincho *m* □ *vt/i* gritar, guinchar

shrift /ʃrɪft/ *n* **give sb short ~** tratar alguém com brusquidão, despachar alguém sem mais cerimónias, (*P*) sem cerimónias

shrill /ʃrɪl/ *a* estridente, agudo

shrimp /ʃrɪmp/ *n* camarão *m*

shrine /ʃraɪn/ *n* (*place*) santuário *m*; (*tomb*) túmulo *m*; (*casket*) relicário *m*

shrink /ʃrɪŋk/ *vt/i* (*pt* **shrank**, *pp* **shrunk**) encolher; (*recoil*) encolher-se. **~ from** esquivar-se a, fugir a (+ *inf*)/de (+ *noun*).

retrair-se de. **~age** *n* encolhimento *m*; (*comm*) contração *f*

shrivel /'ʃrɪvl/ *vt/i* (*pt* shrivelled) encarquilhar(-se)

shroud /ʃraʊd/ *n* mortalha *f* □ *vt* (*veil*) encobrir, envolver

Shrove /ʃrəʊv/ *n* ~ **Tuesday** Terça-feira *f* gorda *or* de Carnaval

shrub /ʃrʌb/ *n* arbusto *m*. **~bery** *n* arbustos *mpl*

shrug /ʃrʌɡ/ *vt* (*pt* shrugged) ~ **one's shoulders** encolher os ombros □ *n* encolher *m* de ombros. ~ **off** não dar importância a

shrunk /ʃrʌŋk/ *see* shrink. **~en** *a* encolhido; (*person*) mirrado, chupado

shudder /'ʃʌdə(r)/ *vi* arrepiar-se, estremecer, tremer □ *n* arrepio *m*, tremor *m*, estremecimento *m*. **I ~ to think** tremo só de pensar

shuffle /'ʃʌfl/ *vt* (*feet*) arrastar; (*cards*) embaralhar □ *vi* arrastar os pés □ *n* marcha *f* arrastada

shun /ʃʌn/ *vt* (*pt* shunned) evitar, fugir de

shunt /ʃʌnt/ *vt/i* (*train*) mudar de linha, manobrar

shut /ʃʌt/ *vt* (*pt* shut, *pres p* shutting) fechar □ *vi* fechar-se; (*shop, bank etc*) encerrar, fechar. ~ **down** *or* **up** fechar. **~-down** *n* encerramento *m*. ~ **in** *or* **up** trancar. ~ **up** *vi* (*colloq: stop talking*) calar-se □ *vt* (*colloq: silence*) mandar calar. ~ **up!** (*colloq*) cale-se!, cale a boca!

shutter /'ʃʌtə(r)/ *n* taipais *mpl*, (*P*) portada *f* de madeira; (*of laths*) persiana *f*, (*in shop*) taipais *mpl*; (*photo*) obturador *m*

shuttle /'ʃʌtl/ *n* (*of spaceship*) ônibus *m* espacial. ~ **service** (*plane*) ponte *f* aérea; (*bus*) navete *f*

shuttlecock /'ʃʌtlkɒk/ *n* volante *m*

shy /ʃaɪ/ *a* (-er, -est) tímido, acanhado, envergonhado □ *vi* (*horse*)

espantar-se (**at** com); (*fig*) assustar-se (**at** *or* **away from** com). **~ness** *n* timidez *f*, acanhamento *m*, vergonha *f*

Siamese /saɪə'miːz/ *a* & *n* siamês (*m*). ~ **cat** gato *m* siamês

Sicily /'sɪsɪlɪ/ *n* Sicília *f*

sick /sɪk/ *a* doente; (*humour*) negro. **be** ~ (*vomit*) vomitar. **be** ~ **of** estar farto de. **feel** ~ estar enjoado. **~-bay** *n* enfermaria *f*. **~-leave** *n* licença *f* por doença **~-room** *n* quarto *m* de doente

sicken /'sɪkn/ *vt* (*distress*) desesperar; (*disgust*) repugnar □ *vi* **be ~ing for flu** começar a pegar uma gripe (*colloq*)

sickle /'sɪkl/ *n* foice *f*

sickly /'sɪklɪ/ *a* (-ier, -iest) (*person*) doentio, achacado; (*smell*) enjoativo; (*pale*) pálido

sickness /'sɪknɪs/ *n* doença *f*, (*vomiting*) náusea *f*, vômito *m*, (*P*) vómito *m*

side /saɪd/ *n* lado *m*; (*of road, river*) beira *f*; (*of hill*) encosta *f*; (*sport*) equipe *f*, (*P*) equipa *f* □ *a* lateral □ *vi* ~ **with** tomar o partido de. **on the** ~ (*extra*) nas horas vagas; (*secretly*) pela calada. ~ **by** ~ lado a lado. **~-car** *n* sidecar *m*. **~-effect** *n* efeito *m* secundário. **~-show** *n* espetáculo *m*, (*P*) espectáculo *m* suplementar. **~-step** *vt* (*pt* -stepped) evitar. **~-track** *vt* (fazer) desviar dum propósito

sideboard /'saɪdbɔːd/ *n* aparador *m*

sideburns /'saɪdbɜːnz/ *npl* suíças *fpl*, costeletas *fpl*, (*P*) patilhas *fpl*

sidelight /'saɪdlaɪt/ *n* (*auto*) luz *f* lateral, (*P*) farolim *m*

sideline /'saɪdlaɪn/ *n* atividade *f*, (*P*) actividade *f* secundária; (*sport*) linha *f* lateral

sidelong /'saɪdlɒŋ/ *adv* & *a* de lado

sidewalk /'saɪdwɔːk/ n (Amer) passeio m

sideways /'saɪdweɪz/ adv & a de lado

siding /'saɪdɪŋ/ n desvio m, ramal m

sidle /'saɪdl/ vi ~ **up (to)** avançar furtivamente (para), chegar-se furtivamente (a)

siege /siːdʒ/ n cerco m

siesta /sɪ'estə/ n sesta f

sieve /sɪv/ n peneira f; (for liquids) coador m □ vt peneirar; (liquids) passar, coar

sift /sɪft/ vt peneirar; (sprinkle) polvilhar. ~ **through** examinar minuciosamente, esquadrinhar

sigh /saɪ/ n suspiro m □ vt/i suspirar

sight /saɪt/ n vista f; (scene) cena f; (on gun) mira f □ vt avistar, ver, divisar. **at** or **on** ~ à vista. **catch** ~ **of** avistar. **in** ~ à vista, visível. **lose** ~ **of** perder de vista. **out of** ~ longe dos olhos

sightsee|ing /'saɪtsiːɪŋ/ n visita f, turismo m. **go** ~**ing** visitar lugares turísticos. ~**r** /'saɪtsiːə(r)/ n turista m

sign /saɪn/ n sinal m; (symbol) signo m □ vt/i (in writing) assinar □ vi (make a sign) fazer sinal. ~ **on** or **up** (worker) assinar contrato. ~**-board** n tabuleta f. ~ **language** n mímica f

signal /'sɪɡnəl/ n sinal m □ vi (pt **signalled**) fazer sinal □ vt comunicar (por sinais); (person) fazer sinal para. ~**-box** n cabine f de sinalização

signature /'sɪɡnətʃə(r)/ n assinatura f. ~ **tune** indicativo m musical

signet-ring /'sɪɡnɪtrɪŋ/ n anel m de sinete

significan|t /sɪɡ'nɪfɪkənt/ a importante; (meaningful) significativo. ~**ce** n importância f; (meaning)

significado m. ~**tly** adv (much) sensivelmente

signify /'sɪɡnɪfaɪ/ vt significar

signpost /'saɪnpəʊst/ n poste m de sinalização □ vt sinalizar

silence /'saɪləns/ n silêncio m □ vt silenciar, calar. ~ **r** /-ə(r)/ n (on gun) silenciador m; (on car) silencioso m

silent /'saɪlənt/ a silencioso; (not speaking) calado; (film) mudo. ~**ly** adv silenciosamente

silhouette /sɪluː'et/ n silhueta f □ vt **be** ~**d against** estar em silhueta contra

silicon /'sɪlɪkən/ n silicone m. ~ **chip** circuito m integrado

silk /sɪlk/ n seda f. ~**en**, ~**y** adjs sedoso

sill /sɪl/ n (of window) parapeito m; (of door) soleira f, limiar m

silly /'sɪlɪ/ a (-ier, -iest) tolo, idiota. ~**iness** n tolice f, idiotice f

silo /'saɪləʊ/ n (pl -os) silo m

silt /sɪlt/ n aluvião m, sedimento m

silver /'sɪlvə(r)/ n prata f; (silverware) prataria f, pratas fpl □ a de prata. ~ **paper** papel m prateado. ~ **wedding** bodas fpl de prata. ~**y** a prateado; (sound) argentino

silversmith /'sɪlvəsmɪθ/ n ourives m

silverware /'sɪlvəweə(r)/ n prataria f, pratas fpl

similar /'sɪmɪlə(r)/ a ~ **(to)** semelhante (a), parecido (com). ~**ity** /-ə'lærətɪ/ n semelhança f. ~**ly** adv de igual modo, analogamente

simile /'sɪmɪlɪ/ n símile m, comparação f

simmer /'sɪmə(r)/ vt/i cozinhar em fogo brando; (fig: smoulder) ferver, fremir; ~ **down** acalmar(-se)

simpl|e /'sɪmpl/ a (-er, -est)

simples. **~e-minded** *a* simples; (*feeble-minded*) pobre de espírito, tolo. **~icity** /-'plɪsətɪ/ *n* simplicidade *f*. **~y** *adv* simplesmente; (*absolutely*) absolutamente, simplesmente

simpleton /'sɪmpltən/ *n* simplório *m*

simplif|y /'sɪmplɪfaɪ/ *vt* simplificar. **~ication** /-ɪ'keɪʃn/ *n* simplificação *f*. **~y** *adv* simplesmente; (*absolutely*) absolutamente, simplesmente

simulat|e /'sɪmjʊleɪt/ *vt* simular, imitar. **~ion** /-'leɪʃn/ *n* simulação *f*, imitação *f*

simultaneous /sɪml'teɪnɪəs/ *a* simultâneo, concomitante. **~ly** *adv* simultaneamente

sin /sɪn/ *n* pecado *m* ◻ *vi* (*pt* **sinned**) pecar

since /sɪns/ *prep* desde ◻ *adv* desde então ◻ *conj* desde que; (*because*) uma vez que, visto que. **~ then** desde então

sincer|e /sɪn'sɪə(r)/ *a* sincero. **~ely** *adv* sinceramente. **~ity** /-'serətɪ/ *n* sinceridade *f*

sinew /'sɪnju:/ *n* (*anat*) tendão *m*. **~s** músculos *mpl*. **~y** *a* forte, musculoso

sinful /'sɪnfl/ *a* (*wicked*) pecaminoso; (*shocking*) escandaloso

sing /sɪŋ/ *vt/i* (*pt* **sang**, *pp* **sung**) cantar. **~er** *n* cantor *m*

singe /sɪndʒ/ *vt* (*pres p* **singeing**) chamuscar

single /'sɪŋgl/ *a* único, só; (*unmarried*) solteiro; (*bed*) de solteiro; (*room*) individual; (*ticket*) de ida, simples ◻ *n* (*ticket*) bilhete *m* de ida *or* simples; (*record*) disco *m* de 45 r.p.m. **~s** (*tennis*) singulares *mpl* ◻ *vt* **~ out** escolher. **in ~ file** em fila indiana. **~-handed** *a* sem ajuda, sozinho. **~-minded** *a* decidido, aferrado à sua idéia, tenaz. **~ parent** pai *m* solteiro, mãe *f* solteira. **singly** *adv* um a um, um por um

singsong /'sɪŋsɒŋ/ *n* **have a ~**

cantar em coro ◻ *a* (*voice*) monótono, monocórdico

singular /'sɪŋgjʊlə(r)/ *n* singular *m* ◻ *a* (*uncommon*; *gram*) singular; (*noun*) no singular. **~ly** *adv* singularmente

sinister /'sɪnɪstə(r)/ *a* sinistro

sink /sɪŋk/ *vt* (*pt* **sank**, *pp* **sunk**) (*ship*) afundar, ir a pique; (*well*) abrir; (*invest money*) empatar; (*lose money*) enterrar ◻ *vi* afundar-se; (*of ground*) ceder; (*of voice*) baixar ◻ *n* pia *f*, (*P*) lavalouça *m*. **~ in** (*fig*) ficar gravado, entrar (*colloq*). **~ or swim** ou vai ou racha

sinner /'sɪnə(r)/ *n* pecador *m*

sinuous /'sɪnjʊəs/ *a* sinuoso

sinus /'saɪnəs/ *n* (*pl* **-es**) (*anat*) seio (nasal) *m*. **~itis** /-'saɪtɪs/ *n* sinusite *f*

sip /sɪp/ *n* gole *m* ◻ *vt* (*pt* **sipped**) bebericar, beber aos golinhos

siphon /'saɪfn/ *n* sifão *m* ◻ *vt* **~ off** extrair por meio de sifão

sir /sɜ:(r)/ *n* senhor *m*. **S~** (*title*) Sir *m*. **Dear S~** Exmo Senhor. **excuse me, ~** desculpe, senhor. **no, ~** não, senhor

siren /'saɪərən/ *n* sereia *f*, sirene *f*

sirloin /'sɜ:lɔɪn/ *n* lombo *m* de vaca

sissy /'sɪsɪ/ *n* maricas *m*

sister /'sɪstə(r)/ *n* irmã *f*; (*nun*) irmã *f*, freira *f*; (*nurse*) enfermeira-chefe *f*. **~-in-law** (*pl* **~s-in-law**) cunhada *f*. **~ly** *a* fraterno, fraternal

sit /sɪt/ *vt/i* (*pt* **sat**, *pres p* **sitting**) sentar(-se); (*of committee etc*) reunir-se. **~ for an exam** fazer um exame, prestar uma prova. **be ~ting** estar sentado. **~ around** não fazer nada. **~ down** sentar-se. **~ in** ocupação *f*. **~ting** *n* reunião *f*, sessão *f*; (*in restaurant*) serviço *m*. **~ting-room** *n* sala *f* de estar. **~ up**

endireitar-se na cadeira; (*not go
to bed*) passar a noite acordado
site /saɪt/ *n* local *m*. **(building)** ~
terreno *m* para construção, lote
m □ *vt* localizar, situar
situat|e /'sɪtʃʊert/ *vt* situar. **be
~ed** estar situado. **~ion**
/-'eɪʃn/ *n* (*position, condition*)
situação *f*; (*job*) emprego *m*, colocação *f*
six /sɪks/ *a* & *n* seis (*m*). **~th** *a* &
n sexto (*m*)
sixteen /sɪk'sti:n/ *a* & *n* dezesseis
m, (*P*) dezasseis (*m*). **~th** *a* & *n*
décimo sexto (*m*)
sixt|y /'sɪkstɪ/ *a* & *n* sessenta (*m*).
~ieth *a* & *n* sexagésimo (*m*)
size /saɪz/ *n* tamanho *m*; (*of person, garment etc*) tamanho *m*,
medida *f*; (*of shoes*) número *m*;
(*extent*) grandeza *f* □ *vt* ~ **up**
calcular o tamanho de; (*colloq:
judge*) formar um juízo sobre,
avaliar. **~able** *a* bastante
grande, considerável
sizzle /'sɪzl/ *vi* chiar, rechinar
skate[1] /skeɪt/ *n* (*pl invar*) (*fish*)
(ar)raia *f*
skat|e[2] /skeɪt/ *n* patim *m* □ *vi*
patinar. **~er** *n* patinador *m*.
~ing *n* patinação *f*. **~ing-rink**
n rinque *m* de patinação
skateboard /'skeɪtbɔ:d/ *n* skate *m*
skeleton /'skelɪtn/ *n* esqueleto
m; (*framework*) armação *f*.
~on crew *or* **staff** pessoal *m*
reduzido. **~on key** chave *f* mes-
tra. **~al** *a* esquelético
sketch /sketʃ/ *n* esboço *m*, cro-
qui(s) *m*; (*theat*) sketch *m*, peça *f*
curta e humorística; (*outline*)
idéia *f* geral, esboço *m* □ *vt* esbo-
çar, delinear □ *vi* fazer esboços.
~-book *n* caderno *m* de desenho
sketchy /'sketʃɪ/ *a* (-**ier**, -**iest**) incompleto, esboçado
skewer /'skjʊə(r)/ *n* espeto *m*
ski /ski:/ *n* (*pl* -**s**) esqui *m* □ *vi* (*pt*
ski'd *or* **skied**, *pres p* **skiing**) es-

quiar; (*go skiing*) fazer esqui.
~er *n* esquiador *m*. **~ing** *n* esqui *m*
skid /skɪd/ *vi* (*pt* **skidded**) derra-
par, patinar □ *n* derrapagem *f*
skilful /'skɪlfl/ *a* hábil, habilidoso.
~ly *adv* habilmente, com perícia
skill /skɪl/ *n* habilidade *f*, jeito *m*;
(*craft*) arte *f*. **~s** aptidões *fpl*.
~ed *a* hábil, habilidoso; (*worker*) especializado
skim /skɪm/ *vt* (*pt* **skimmed**) tirar a espuma de; (*milk*) desnatar,
tirar a nata de; (*pass or glide
over*) deslizar sobre, roçar □ *vi*
~ **through** ler por alto, passar
os olhos por. **~med milk** leite *m*
desnatado
skimp /skɪmp/ *vt* (*use too little*)
poupar em □ *vi* ser poupado
skimpy /'skɪmpɪ/ *a* (-**ier**, -**iest**)
(*clothes*) sumário; (*meal*) escasso,
racionado (*fig*)
skin /skɪn/ *n* (*of person, animal*)
pele *f*; (*of fruit*) casca *f* □ *vt* (*pt*
skinned) (*animal*) esfolar, tirar
a pele de; (*fruit*) descascar. **~-
diving** *n* mergulho *m*, caça *f* sub-
marina
skinny /'skɪnɪ/ *a* (-**ier**, -**iest**) magricela, escanzelado
skint /skɪnt/ *a* (*sl*) sem dinheiro,
na última lona (*sl*), (*P*) nas lonas
skip[1] /skɪp/ *vi* (*pt* **skipped**) saltar,
pular; (*jump about*) saltitar;
(*with rope*) pular corda □ *vt*
(*page*) saltar; (*class*) faltar a □
n salto *m*. **~ping rope** *n* corda
f de pular
skip[2] /skɪp/ *n* (*container*) container *m* grande para entulho
skipper /'skɪpə(r)/ *n* capitão *m*
skirmish /'skɜ:mɪʃ/ *n* escaramuça
f
skirt /skɜ:t/ *n* saia *f* □ *vt* contornar, ladear. **~ing-board** *n* rodapé *m*
skit /skɪt/ *n* (*theat*) paródia *f*,
sketch *m* satírico

skittle /'skɪtl/ n pino m. **~s** npl
boliche m, (P) jogo m de laran-
jinha

skive /skaɪv/ vi (sl) eximir-se de
um dever, evitar trabalhar (sl)

skulk /skʌlk/ vi (move) rondar
furtivamente; (hide) esconder-se

skull /skʌl/ n caveira f, crânio m

skunk /skʌŋk/ n (animal) gambá
m

sky /skaɪ/ n céu m. **~-blue** a & n
azul-celeste (m)

skylight /'skaɪlaɪt/ n clarabóia f

skyscraper /'skaɪskreɪpə(r)/ n ar-
ranha-céus m invar

slab /slæb/ n (of marble) placa f;
(of paving-stone) laje f; (of metal)
chapa f; (of cake) fatia f grossa

slack /slæk/ a (-er, -est) (rope)
bambo, frouxo; (person) descuidado, negligente; (business) parado, fraco; (period, season) morto
□ n the **~** (in rope) a parte bam-
ba □ vt/i (be lazy) estar com
preguiça, fazer cera (fig)

slacken /'slækən/ vt/i (speed, activity etc) afrouxar, abrandar

slacks /slæks/ npl calças fpl

slag /slæg/ n escória f

slain /sleɪn/ see **slay**

slam /slæm/ vt (pt slammed) bater violentamente com; (throw)
atirar; (sl: criticize) criticar, malhar □ vi (door etc) bater violentamente □ n (noise) bater m,
pancada f

slander /'slɑːndə(r)/ n calúnia f,
difamação f □ vt caluniar, difamar. **~ous** a calunioso, difama-
tório

slang /slæŋ/ n calão m, gíria f.
~y a de calão

slant /slɑːnt/ vt/i inclinar(-se);
(news) apresentar de forma ten-
denciosa □ n inclinação f; (bias)
tendência f; (point of view) ângulo m. be **~ing** ser/estar inclinado or em declive

slap /slæp/ vt (pt slapped) (strike)

bater, dar uma palmada m. (on
face) esbofetear, dar uma bofetada em; (put forcefully) atirar com
□ n palmada f, bofetada f □ adv
em cheio. **~-up** a (sl: excellent)
excelente

slapdash /'slæpdæʃ/ a descuidado; (impetuous) precipitado

slapstick /'slæpstɪk/ n farsa f com
palhaçadas

slash /slæʃ/ vt (cut) retalhar, dar
golpes em; (sever) cortar; (a garment) golpear; (fig: reduce) reduzir drasticamente, fazer um corte
radical em □ n corte m, golpe m

slat /slæt/ n (in blind) ripa f, (P)
lâmina f

slate /sleɪt/ n ardósia f □ vt (colloq: criticize) criticar severamente

slaughter /'slɔːtə(r)/ vt chacinar,
massacrar; (animals) abater □ n
chacina f, massacre m, mortan-
dade f; (animals) abate m

slaughterhouse /'slɔːtəhaʊs/ n
matadouro m

slave /sleɪv/ n escravo m □ vi
mourejar, trabalhar como um
escravo. **~-driver** n (fig) o que
obriga os outros a trabalharem
como escravos, condutor m de
escravos. **~ry** /-ərɪ/ n escravatu-
ra f

slavish /'sleɪvɪʃ/ a servil

slay /sleɪ/ vt (pt slew, pp slain)
matar

sleazy /'sliːzɪ/ a (-ier, -iest) (colloq) esquálido, sórdido

sledge /sledʒ/ n trenó m. **~-
hammer** n martelo m de forja,
marreta f

sleek /sliːk/ a (-er, -est) liso, macio e lustroso

sleep /sliːp/ n sono m □ vi (pt
slept) dormir □ vt ter lugar para,
alojar. **go to ~** ir dormir,
adormecer. **put to ~** (kill) mandar matar. **~ around** ser promíscuo. **~er** n aquele que

dorme; (*rail: beam*) dormente *m*; (*berth*) couchette *f*. **~ing-bag** *n* saco *m* de dormir. **~ing-car** *n* carro-dormitório *m*, carruagem-cama *f*, (P) vagon-lit *m*. **~less** *a* insone; (*night*) em claro, insone. **~-walker** *n* sonâmbulo *m*

sleep|y /'sli:pɪ/ *a* (**-ier, -iest**) sono-lento. **be ~y** ter or estar com sono. **~ily** *adv* meio dormindo

sleet /sli:t/ *n* geada *f* miúda □ *vi* cair geada miúda

sleeve /sli:v/ *n* manga *f*; (*of record*) capa *f*. **up one's ~** de reserva, escondido. **~less** *a* sem mangas

sleigh /sleɪ/ *n* trenó *m*

sleight /slaɪt/ *n*. **~ of hand** pres-tidigitação *f*, passe *m* de mágica

slender /'slendə(r)/ *a* esguio, es-belto; (*fig: scanty*) escasso. **~ness** *n* aspecto *m* esguio, esbelte-za *f*, elegância *f*; (*scantiness*) escassez *f*

slept /slept/ *see* **sleep**

sleuth /slu:θ/ *n* (*colloq*) detective *m*

slew[1] /slu:/ *vi* (*turn*) virar-se

slew[2] /slu:/ *see* **slay**

slice /slaɪs/ *n* fatia *f* □ *vt* cortar em fatias; (*golf, tennis*) cortar

slick /slɪk/ *a* (*slippery*) escorrega-dio; (*cunning*) astuto, habilidoso; (*unctuous*) melífluo □ *n* (oil) **~** mancha *f* de óleo

slid|e /slaɪd/ *vt/i* (*pt* **slid**) escorre-gar, deslizar □ *n* escorregadela *f*, escorregão *m*; (*in playground*) escorrega *m*; (*for hair*) prende-dor *m*, (P) travessa *f*, (*photo*) dia-positivo *m*, slide *m*. **~e-rule** *n* régua *f* de cálculo. **~ing** *a* (*door, panel*) corrediço, de correr. **~ing scale** escala *f* móvel

slight /slaɪt/ *a* (**-er, -est**) (*slender, frail*) delgado, franzino; (*inconsiderable*) leve, ligeiro □ *vt* des-considerar, desfeitear □ *n* desconsideração *f*, desfeita *f*. **the**

~est *a* o/a menor. **not in the ~est** em absoluto. **~ly** *adv* ligeiramente, um pouco

slim /slɪm/ *a* (**slimmer, slim-mest**) magro, esbelto; (*chance*) pequeno, remoto □ *vi* (*pt* **slimmed**) emagrecer. **~ness** *n* magreza *f*, esbelteza *f*

slim|e /slaɪm/ *n* lodo *m*. **~y** *a* lo-doso; (*slippery*) escorregadio; (*fig: servile*) servil, bajulador

sling /slɪŋ/ *n* (*weapon*) funda *f*, (*for arm*) tipóia *f* □ *vt* (*pt* **slung**) atirar, lançar

slip /slɪp/ *vt/i* (*pt* **slipped**) escor-regar; (*move quietly*) mover-se de mansinho □ *n* escorregadela *f*, escorregão *m*; (*mistake*) engano *m*, lapso *m*; (*petticoat*) combina-ção *f*; (*of paper*) tira *f* de papel. **give the ~ to** livrar-se de, escapar(-se) de. **~ away** esguerar-se. **~ by** passar sem se dar conta, passar despercebido. **~-cover** *n* (*Amer*) capa *f* para móveis. **~ into** (go) entrar de mansinho, enfiar-se em; (*clothes*) enfiar. **~ of the tongue** lapso *m*. **~ped disc** disco *m* deslocado. **~road** *n* acesso *m* à autoestrada. **~ sb's mind** passar pela cabeça de alguém. **~ up** (*colloq*) come-ter uma gafe. **~-up** *n* (*colloq*) gafe *f*

slipper /'slɪpə(r)/ *n* chinelo *m*

slippery /'slɪpərɪ/ *a* escorregadio; (*fig: person*) que não é de con-fiança, sem escrúpulos

slipshod /'slɪpʃɒd/ *a* (*person*) desleixado, desmazelado; (*work*) feito sem cuidado, desleixado

slit /slɪt/ *n* fenda *f*; (*cut*) corte *m* □ *vt* (*tear*) rasgão *m* □ *vt* (*pt* **slit**, *pres p* **slitting**) fender; (*cut*) fazer um corte em, cortar

slither /'slɪðə(r)/ *vi* escorregar, resvalar

sliver /'slɪvə(r)/ *n* (*of cheese etc*) fatia *f*; (*splinter*) lasca *f*

slobber /'slɒbə(r)/ vi babar-se

slog /slɒg/ vt (pt slogged) (hit) bater com força □ vi (walk) caminhar com passos pesados e firmes; (work) trabalhar duro □ n (work) trabalheira f; (walk, effort) estafa f

slogan /'sləʊgən/ n slogan m, lema m, palavra f de ordem

slop /slɒp/ vt/i (pt slopped) transbordar, entornar. **~s** npl (dirty water) água(s) f(pl) suja(s); (liquid refuse) despejos mpl

slop|e /sləʊp/ vt/i inclinar-se, formar declive □ n (of mountain) encosta f; (of street) rampa f, ladeira f. **~ing** a inclinado, em declive

sloppy /'slɒpɪ/ a (-ier, -iest) (ground) molhado, com poças de água; (food) aguado; (clothes) desleixado; (work) descuidado, feito de qualquer jeito or maneira (colloq); (person) desmazelado; (maudlin) piegas

slosh /slɒʃ/ vt entornar; (colloq: splash) esparrinhar; (sl: hit) bater em, dar (uma) sova em □ vi chapinhar

slot /slɒt/ n ranhura f; (in timetable) horário m; (TV) espaço m; (aviat) slot m □ vt/i (pt slotted) enfiar(-se), meter(-se), encaixar (-se). **~-machine** n (for stamps, tickets etc) distribuidor m automático; (for gambling) caça-níqueis m, (P) slot machine f

sloth /sləʊθ/ n preguiça f, indolência f; (zool) preguiça f

slouch /slaʊtʃ/ vi (stand, move) andar com as costas curvadas; (sit) sentar em má postura

slovenly /'slʌvnlɪ/ a desmazelado, desleixado

slow /sləʊ/ a (-er, -est) lento, vagaroso □ adv devagar, lentamente □ vt/i **~** (up or down) diminuir a velocidade, afrouxar; (auto) desacelerar. **be ~** (clock

etc) atrasar-se, estar atrasado. **in ~ motion** em câmara lenta. **~ly** adv devagar, lentamente, vagarosamente

slow|coach /'sləʊkəʊtʃ/, (Amer) **~poke** ns lesma m/f, pastelão m (fig)

sludge /slʌdʒ/ n lama f, lodo m

slug /slʌg/ n lesma f

sluggish /'slʌgɪʃ/ a (slow) lento, moroso; (lazy) indolente, preguiçoso

sluice /slu:s/ n (gate) comporta f; (channel) canal m □ vt lavar com jorros de água

slum /slʌm/ n favela f, (P) bairro m da lata; (building) cortiço m

slumber /'slʌmbə(r)/ n sono m □ vi dormir

slump /slʌmp/ n (in prices) baixa f, descida f; (in demand) quebra f na procura; (econ) depressão f □ vi (fall limply) cair, afundar-se; (of price) baixar bruscamente

slung /slʌŋ/ see **sling**

slur /slɜ:(r)/ vt/i (pt slurred) (speech) pronunciar indistintamente, mastigar □ n (in speech) som m indistinto; (discredit) nódoa f, estigma m

slush /slʌʃ/ n (snow) neve f meio derretida. **~ fund** (comm) fundo m para subornos. **~y** a (road) coberto de neve derretida, lamacento

slut /slʌt/ n (dirty woman) porca f, desmazelada f; (immoral woman) desavergonhada f

sly /slaɪ/ a (slyer, slyest) (crafty) manhoso; (secretive) sonso □ n **on the ~** na calada. **~ly** adv (craftily) astutamente; (secretively) sonsamente

smack¹ /smæk/ n palmada f, (on face) bofetada f □ vt dar uma palmada or tapa em; (on the face) esbofetear, dar uma bofetada em □ adv (colloq) em cheio, direto

smack² /smæk/ *vi* ~ **of sth** cheirar a alg coisa

small /smɔːl/ *a* (-er, -est) pequeno □ *n* ~ **of the back** zona *f* dos rins □ *adv* (*cut etc*) em pedaços pequenos, aos bocadinhos. ~ **change** trocado *m*, dinheiro *m* miúdo. ~ **talk** conversa *f* fiada, bate-papo *m*. ~ **ness** *n* pequenez *f*

smallholding /'smɔːlhəʊldɪŋ/ *n* pequena propriedade *f*

smallpox /'smɔːlpɒks/ *n* varíola *f*

smarmy /'smɑːmɪ/ *a* (-ier, -iest) (*colloq*) bajulador, puxa-saco (*colloq*)

smart /smɑːt/ *a* (-er, -est) elegante; (*clever*) esperto, vivo; (*brisk*) rápido □ *vi* (*sting*) arder, picar. ~ **ly** *adv* elegantemente, com elegância; (*cleverly*) com esperteza, vivamente; (*briskly*) rapidamente. ~ **ness** *n* elegância *f*

smarten /'smɑːtn/ *vt/i* ~ (**up**) arranjar, dar um ar mais cuidado a. ~ (**o.s.**) **up** embelezar-se, arrumar-se, (*P*) pôr-se elegante/bonito; (*tidy*) arranjar-se

smash /smæʃ/ *vt/i* ~ (*to pieces*) despedaçar(-se), estraçar(-se) (*colloq*); (*a record*) quebrar, (*opponent*) esmagar; (*ruin*) (fazer) falir; (*of vehicle*) estraçar (-se) □ *n* (*noise*) estrondo *m*; (*blow*) pancada *f* forte, golpe *m*; (*collision*) colisão *f*; (*tennis*) smash *m*

smashing /'smæʃɪŋ/ *a* (*colloq*) formidável, estupendo (*colloq*)

smattering /'smætərɪŋ/ *n* leves noções *fpl*

smear /smɪə(r)/ *vt* (*stain; discredit*) manchar; (*coat*) untar, besuntar □ *n* mancha *f*, nódoa *f*; (*med*) esfregaço *m*

smell /smel/ *n* cheiro *m*, odor *m*; (*sense*) cheiro *m*, olfato *m*, (*P*) olfacto *m* □ *vt/i* (*pt* **smelt** *or*

smelled) ~ (**of**) cheirar (a). ~ **y** *a* malcheiroso

smelt¹ /smelt/ *see* **smell**

smelt² /smelt/ *vt* (*ore*) fundir

smile /smaɪl/ *n* sorriso *m* □ *vi* sorrir. ~ **ing** *a* sorridente, risonho

smirk /smɜːk/ *n* sorriso *m* falso *or* afetado, (*P*) afectado

smithereens /smɪðə'riːnz/ *npl* **to** *or* **in** ~ em pedaços *mpl*

smock /smɒk/ *n* guarda-pó *m*

smog /smɒg/ *n* mistura *f* de nevoeiro e fumaça, smog *m*

smoke /sməʊk/ *n* fumo *m*, fumaça *f* □ *vt* fumar; (*bacon etc*) fumar, defumar □ *vi* fumar, fumegar. ~ **screen** *n* (*lit & fig*) cortina *f* de fumaça. ~ **less** *a* (*fuel*) sem fumo. ~ **r** /-ə(r)/ *n* (*person*) fumante *mf*, (*P*) fumador *m*

smoky *a* (*air*) enfumaçado, fumacento

smooth /smuːð/ *a* (-er, -est) liso; (*soft*) macio; (*movement*) regular, suave; (*manners*) lisonjeiro, conciliador, suave □ *vt* alisar. ~ **out** (*fig*) aplanar, remover. ~ **ly** *adv* suavemente, facilmente

smother /'smʌðə(r)/ *vt* (*stifle*) abafar, sufocar; (*cover, overwhelm*) cobrir (**with** de); (*suppress*) abafar, reprimir

smoulder /'sməʊldə(r)/ *vi* (*lit & fig*) arder, abrasar-se

smudge /smʌdʒ/ *n* mancha *f*, borrão *m* □ *vt/i* sujar(-se), manchar(-se), borrar(-se)

smug /smʌg/ *a* (**smugger**, **smuggest**) presunçoso, convencido (*colloq*). ~ **ly** *adv* presunçosamente. ~ **ness** *n* presunção *f*

smuggle /'smʌgl/ *vt* contrabandear, fazer contrabando de. ~ **er** *n* contrabandista *mf*. ~ **ing** *n* contrabando *m*

smut /smʌt/ *n* fuligem *f*. ~ **ty** *a* cheio de fuligem; (*colloq: obscene*) indecente, sujo (*colloq*)

snack /snæk/ n refeição f ligeira. **∼-bar** n lanchonete f, (P) snack(-bar) m

snag /snæg/ n (obstacle) obstáculo m; (drawback) problema m, contra m; (in cloth) rasgão m; (in stocking) fio m puxado

snail /sneɪl/ n caracol m. **at a ∼'s pace** em passo de tartaruga

snake /sneɪk/ n serpente f, cobra f

snap /snæp/ vt/i (pt snapped) (whip, fingers) (fazer) estalar; (break) estalar(-se), partir(-se) com um estalo, rebentar; (say) dizer irritadamente □ n estalo m; (photo) instantâneo m; (Amer: fastener) mola f □ a súbito, repentino. **∼ at** (bite) abocanhar, tentar morder; (speak angrily) retrucar asperamente. **∼ up** (buy) comprar rapidamente

snappish /ˈsnæpɪʃ/ a irritadiço

snappy /ˈsnæpɪ/ a (-ier, -iest) (colloq) vivo, animado. **make it ∼** (colloq) vai rápido!, apresse-se! (colloq)

snapshot /ˈsnæpʃɒt/ n instantâneo m

snare /sneə(r)/ n laço m, cilada f, armadilha f

snarl /snɑːl/ vi rosnar □ n rosnadela f

snatch /snætʃ/ vt (grab) agarrar, apanhar; (steal) roubar. **∼ from sb** arrancar de alguém □ n (theft) roubo m; (bit) bocado m, pedaço m

sneak /sniːk/ vi (slink) esgueirar-se furtivamente; (sl: tell tales) fazer queixa, delatar □ vt (sl: steal) rapinar (colloq) □ n (sl) dedo-duro m, queixinhas mf (sl). **∼ing** a secreto. **∼y** a sonso

sneer /snɪə(r)/ n sorriso m de desdém □ vi sorrir desdenhosamente

sneeze /sniːz/ n espirro m □ vi espirrar

snide /snaɪd/ a (colloq) sarcástico

sniff /snɪf/ vi fungar □ vt/i **∼ (at)** (smell) cheirar; (dog) farejar. **∼ at** (fig: in contempt) desprezar □ n fungadela f

snigger /ˈsnɪgə(r)/ n riso m abafado □ vi rir dissimuladamente

snip /snɪp/ vt (pt snipped) cortar com tesoura □ n pedaço m, retalho m; (sl: bargain) pechincha f

snipe /snaɪp/ vi dar tiros de emboscada. **∼r** /-ə(r)/ n franco-atirador m

snivel /ˈsnɪvl/ vi (pt snivelled) choramingar, lamuriar-se

snob /snɒb/ n esnobe mf, (P) snob mf. **∼bery** n esnobismo m, (P) snobismo m. **∼bish** a esnobe, (P) snob

snooker /ˈsnuːkə(r)/ n snooker m, sinuca f

snoop /snuːp/ vi (colloq) bisbilhotar, meter o nariz em toda a parte. **∼ on** espiar, espionar. **∼er** n bisbilhoteiro m

snooty /ˈsnuːtɪ/ a (-ier, -iest) (colloq) convencido, arrogante (colloq)

snooze /snuːz/ n (colloq) soneca f (colloq) □ vi (colloq) tirar uma soneca

snore /snɔː(r)/ n ronco m □ vi roncar

snorkel /ˈsnɔːkl/ n tubo m de respiração, snorkel m

snort /snɔːt/ n resfôlego m, bufido m □ vi resfolegar, bufar

snout /snaʊt/ n focinho m

snow /snəʊ/ n neve f □ vi nevar. **be ∼ed under** (fig: be overwhelmed) estar sobrecarregado (fig). **∼board** n snowboard m. **∼-bound** a bloqueado pela neve. **∼-drift** n banco m de neve. **∼-plough** n limpa-neve m. **∼y** a nevado, coberto de neve

snowball /ˈsnəʊbɔːl/ n bola f de neve □ vi atirar bolas de neve (em); (fig) acumular-se, ir num crescendo, aumentar rapidamente

snowdrop /'snəʊdrɒp/ n (bot) fura-neve m

snowfall /'snəʊfɔːl/ n nevada f, (P) nevão m

snowflake /'snəʊfleɪk/ n floco m de neve

snowman /'snəʊmæn/ n (pl -men) boneco m de neve

snub /snʌb/ vt (pt snubbed) desdenhar, tratar com desdém □ n desdém m

snuff[1] /snʌf/ n rapé m

snuff[2] /snʌf/ vt ~ out (candles, hopes etc) apagar, extinguir

snuffle /'snʌfl/ vi fungar

snug /snʌg/ a (snugger, snuggest) (cosy) aconchegado; (close-fitting) justo

snuggle /'snʌgl/ vt/i (nestle) aninhar-se, aconchegar-se; (cuddle) aconchegar

so /səʊ/ adv tão, de tal modo; (thus) assim, deste modo □ conj por isso, portanto, por conseguinte. ~ **am I** eu também. ~ **does he** ele também. **that is** ~ é isso. **I think** ~ acho que sim. **five or** ~ uns cinco. ~ **as to** de modo a. ~ **far** até agora, até aqui. ~ **long!** (colloq) até já! (colloq). ~ **many** tantos. ~ **much** tanto. ~ **that** para que, de modo que. ~**-and**-~ fulano m. ~**-called** a pretenso, soidisant. ~**-so** a & adv assim as sim, mais ou menos

soak /səʊk/ vt/i molhar(-se), ensopar(-se), enchacar(-se). baixei ~ **pôr de molho**. ~ **in** or **up** vt absorver, embeber. ~ **through** repassar. ~**ing** a ensopado, encharcado

soap /səʊp/ n sabão m. (toilet) ~ sabonete m □ vt ensaboar. ~ **opera** (radio) novela f radiofônica, (P) radiofónica; (TV) telenovela f. ~ **flakes** flocos mpl de

sabão. ~ **powder** sabão m em pó. ~**y** a ensaboado

soar /sɔː(r)/ vi voar alto; (go high) elevar-se; (hover) pairar

sob /sɒb/ n soluço m □ vi (pt sobbed) soluçar

sober /'səʊbə(r)/ a (not drunk, calm, of colour) sóbrio; (serious) sério, grave □ vt/i ~ **up** (fazer) ficar sóbrio, (fazer) curar a bebedeira (colloq)

soccer /'sɒkə(r)/ n (colloq) futebol m

sociable /'səʊʃəbl/ a sociável

social /'səʊʃl/ a social; (sociable) sociável; (gathering, life) de sociedade □ n reunião f social. ~**ly** adv socialmente; (meet) em sociedade. ~ **security** previdência f social; (for old age) pensão f. ~ **worker** assistente mf social

socialist /'səʊʃəlɪst/ n socialista mf. ~**m** /-zəm/ n socialismo m

socialize /'səʊʃəlaɪz/ vi socializar-se, reunir-se em sociedade. ~ **with** frequentar, (P) frequentar, conviver com

society /sə'saɪətɪ/ n sociedade f

sociology /səʊsɪ'ɒlədʒɪ/ n sociologia f. ~**ical** /-ə'lɒdʒɪkl/ a sociológico. ~**ist** n sociólogo m

sock[1] /sɒk/ n meia f curta; (men's) meia f (curta), (P) peúga f; (women's) soquete f

sock[2] /sɒk/ vt (sl: hit) esmurrar, dar um murro em (colloq)

socket /'sɒkɪt/ n cavidade f; (for lamp) suporte m; (electr) tomada f; (of tooth) alvéolo m

soda /'səʊdə/ n soda f. (baking) ~ (culin) bicarbonato m de soda. ~**(-water)** água f gasosa, soda f limonada, (P) água f gaseificada

sodden /'sɒdn/ a ensopado, empapado

sodium /'səʊdɪəm/ n sódio m

sofa /'səʊfə/ n sofá m

soft /sɒft/ a (-er, -est) (not hard, feeble) mole; (not rough, not firm) macio; (*gentle, not loud, not bright*) suave; (*tender-hearted*) sensível; (*fruit*) sem caroço; (*wood*) de coníferas; (*drink*) não alcoólico. **~-boiled** a (*egg*) quente. **~ spot** (*fig*) fraco *m*. **~ly** *adv* docemente. **~ness** *n* moleza *f*; (*to touch*) maciez *f*; (*gentleness*) suavidade *f*, brandura *f*

soften /'sɒfn/ *vt/i* amaciar, amolecer; (*tone down, lessen*) abrandar

software /'sɒftweə(r)/ *n* software *m*

soggy /'sɒgi/ a (**-ier**, **-iest**) ensopado, empapado

soil[1] /sɔɪl/ *n* solo *m*, terra *f*

soil[2] /sɔɪl/ *vt/i* sujar(-se). **~ed** a sujo

solace /'sɒlɪs/ *n* consolo *m*; (*relief*) alívio *m*

solar /'səʊlə(r)/ a solar

sold /səʊld/ *see* sell □ a **~ out** esgotado

solder /'səʊldə(r)/ *n* solda *f* □ *vt* soldar

soldier /'səʊldʒə(r)/ *n* soldado *m* □ *vi* **~ on** (*colloq*) perseverar com afinco, batalhar (*colloq*)

sole[1] /səʊl/ *n* (*of foot*) planta *f*, sola *f* do pé; (*of shoe*) sola *f*

sole[2] /səʊl/ *n* (*fish*) solha *f*

sole[3] /səʊl/ a único. **~ly** *adv* unicamente

solemn /'sɒləm/ a solene. **~ity** /sə'lemnəti/ *n* solenidade *f*. **~ly** *adv* solenemente

solicit /sə'lɪsɪt/ *vt* (*seek*) solicitar □ *vi* (*of prostitute*) aproximar-se de homens na rua

solicitor /sə'lɪsɪtə(r)/ *n* advogado *m*

solicitous /sə'lɪsɪtəs/ a solícito

solid /'sɒlɪd/ a sólido; (*not hollow*) maciço, cheio, compacto; (*gold etc*) maciço; (*meal*) substancial □ *n* sólido *m* **~s** (*food*) alimentos *mpl* sólidos. **~ity** /sə'lɪdəti/ *n* solidez *f*. **~ly** *adv* solidamente

solidarity /sɒlɪ'dærəti/ *n* solidariedade *f*

solidify /sə'lɪdɪfaɪ/ *vt/i* solidificar (-se)

soliloquy /sə'lɪləkwɪ/ *n* monólogo *m*, solilóquio *m*

solitary /'sɒlɪtrɪ/ a solitário, só; (*only one*) um único. **~ confinement** prisão *f* celular, solitária *f*

solitude /'sɒlɪtjuːd/ *n* solidão *f*

solo /'səʊləʊ/ *n* (*pl* **-os**) solo *m* □ a solo. **~ flight** vôo *m* solo. **~ist** *n* solista *mf*

soluble /'sɒljʊbl/ a solúvel

solution /sə'luːʃn/ *n* solução *f*

solve /sɒlv/ *vt* resolver, solucionar. **~able** a resolúvel, solúvel

solvent /'sɒlvənt/ a (*fin*) (dis)solvente; (*comm*) solvente □ *n* (dis)solvente *m*

sombre /'sɒmbə(r)/ a sombrio

some /sʌm/ a (*quantity*) algum(a); (*number*) algum, alguma, uns, umas; (*unspecified, some or other*) um(a)... qualquer, uns... quaisquer, umas... quaisquer; (*a little*) um pouco de, algum; (*a certain*) um certo; (*contrasted with others*) uns, umas, alguns, algumas, certos, certas □ *pron* uns, umas, algum(a), alguns, algumas; (*a little*) um pouco, algum □ *adv* (*approximately*) uns, umas. **will you have ~ coffee/***etc*? você quer café/*etc*? **~ day** algum dia. **~ of my friends** alguns dos meus amigos. **~ people say...** algumas pessoas dizem... **~ time ago** algum tempo atrás

somebody /'sʌmbədɪ/ *pron* alguém □ *n* **be a ~** ser alguém

somehow /'sʌmhaʊ/ *adv* (*in some way*) de algum modo, de alguma maneira; (*for some reason*) por alguma razão

someone /'sʌmwʌn/ *pron & n* = **somebody**

somersault /'sʌməsɔːlt/ *n* cambalhota *f*; (*in the air*) salto *m* mortal

□ *vi* dar uma cambalhota/um salto mortal

something /'sʌmθɪŋ/ *pron & n* uma/alguma/qualquer coisa *f*, algo. ~ **good**/*etc* uma coisa boa/*etc*, qualquer coisa de bom/ *etc*. ~ **like** um pouco como

sometime /'sʌmtaɪm/ *adv* a certa altura, um dia □ *a* (*former*) antigo. ~ **last summer** a certa altura no verão passado. **I'll go** ~ hei de ir um dia

sometimes /'sʌmtaɪmz/ *adv* às vezes, de vez em quando

somewhat /'sʌmwɒt/ *adv* um pouco, um tanto (ou quanto)

somewhere /'sʌmweə(r)/ *adv* (*position*) em algum lugar; (*direction*) para algum lugar

son /sʌn/ *n* filho *m*. ~-**in-law** (*pl* ~**s-in-law**) genro *m*

sonar /'səʊnɑː(r)/ *n* sonar *m*

sonata /sə'nɑːtə/ *n* (*mus*) sonata *f*

song /sɒŋ/ *n* canção *f*. ~-**bird** *n* ave *f* canora

sonic /'sɒnɪk/ *a* ~ **boom** estrondo *m* sônico, (*P*) sónico

sonnet /'sɒnɪt/ *n* soneto *m*

soon /suːn/ *adv* (-er, -est) em breve, dentro em pouco, daqui a pouco; (*early*) cedo. **as** ~ **as possible** o mais rápido possível. **I would** ~**er stay** preferia ficar. ~ **after** pouco depois. ~**er or later** mais cedo ou mais tarde

soot /sʊt/ *n* fuligem *f*. ~**y** *a* coberto de fuligem

sooth|e /suːð/ *vt* acalmar, suavizar; (*pain*) aliviar. ~**ing** *a* (*remedy*) calmante, suavizante; (*words*) confortante

sophisticated /sə'fɪstɪkeɪtɪd/ *a* sofisticado, refinado, requintado; (*machine etc*) sofisticado

soporific /sɒpə'rɪfɪk/ *a* soporífico

sopping /'sɒpɪŋ/ *a* encharcado, ensopado

soppy /'sɒpɪ/ *a* (-ier, -iest) (*colloq*:

sentimental) piegas; (*colloq*: *silly*) bobo

soprano /sə'prɑːnəʊ/ *n* (*pl* ~**s**) & *adj* soprano (*mf*)

sorbet /'sɔːbeɪ/ *n* (*water-ice*) sorvete *m* feito sem leite

sorcerer /'sɔːsərə(r)/ *n* feiticeiro *m*

sordid /'sɔːdɪd/ *a* sórdido

sore /sɔː(r)/ *a* (-er, -est) dolorido; (*vexed*) aborrecido (**at**, **with** com) □ *n* ferida *f*. **have a** ~ **throat** ter a garganta inflamada, ter dores de garganta

sorely /'sɔːlɪ/ *adv* fortemente, seriamente

sorrow /'sɒrəʊ/ *n* dor *f*, mágoa *f*, pesar *m*. ~**ful** *a* pesaroso, triste

sorry /'sɒrɪ/ *a* (-ier, -iest) (*state, sight etc*) triste. **be** ~ **to/that** (*regretful*) sentir muito/que, lamentar que; **be** ~ **about/for** (*repentant*) ter pena de, estar arrependido de. **feel** ~ **for** ter pena de. ~! desculpe!, perdão!

sort /sɔːt/ *n* gênero *m*, (*P*) género *m*, espécie *f*, qualidade *f*. **of** ~**s** (*colloq*) uma espécie de (*colloq*, *pej*). **out of** ~**s** indisposto □ *vt* separar por grupos; (*tidy*) arrumar. ~ **out** (*problem*) resolver; (*arrange, separate*) separar, distribuir

soufflé /'suːfleɪ/ *n* (*culin*) suflê *m*, (*P*) soufflé *m*

sought /sɔːt/ *see* **seek**

soul /səʊl/ *n* alma *f*. **the life and** ~ **of** (*fig*) a alma *f* de (*fig*)

soulful /'səʊlfl/ *a* emotivo, expressivo, cheio de sentimento

sound¹ /saʊnd/ *n* som *m*, barulho *m*, ruído *m* □ *vt/i* soar; (*seem*) dar a impressão de, parecer (**as if** que). ~ **a horn** tocar uma buzina, buzinar. ~ **barrier** barreira *f* de som. ~ **like** parecer ser, soar como. ~-**proof** *a* à prova de som □ *vt* fazer o isolamento sonoro de, isolar. ~-**track** *n* (*of* *film*) trilha *f* sonora, (*P*) banda *f* sonora

sound² /saʊnd/ *a* (**-er, -est**) (*healthy*) saudável, sadio; (*sensible*) sensato, acertado; (*secure*) firme, sólido. ~ **asleep** profundamente adormecido. ~**ly** *adv* solidamente

sound³ /saʊnd/ *vt* (*test*) sondar; (*med; views*) auscultar

soup /suːp/ *n* sopa *f*

sour /ˈsaʊə(r)/ *a* (**-er, -est**) azedo □ *vt/i* azedar, envinagrar

source /sɔːs/ *n* fonte *f*; (*of river*) nascente *f*

souse /saʊs/ *vt* (*throw water on*) atirar água em cima de; (*pickle*) pôr em vinagre; (*salt*) pôr em salmoura

south /saʊθ/ *n* sul *m* □ *a* sul, do sul; (*of country, people etc*) meridional □ *adv* a, ao/para o sul. **S~ Africa/America** África *f*/América *f* do Sul. **S~ African/American** *a & n* sulafricano (*m*)/sul-americano (*m*). ~**-east** *n* sudeste *m*. ~**erly** /ˈsʌðəlɪ/ *a* do sul, meridional. ~**ward** *a* ao sul. ~**ward(s)** *adv* para o sul. ~**-west** *n* sudoeste *m*

southern /ˈsʌðən/ *a* do sul, meridional, austral

souvenir /suːvəˈnɪə(r)/ *n* recordação *f*, lembrança *f*

sovereign /ˈsɒvrɪn/ *n* & *a* soberano (*m*). ~**ty** *n* soberania *f*

Soviet /ˈsəʊvɪət/ *a* soviético. **the S~ Union** a União Soviética

sow¹ /saʊ/ *vt* (*pt* **sowed**, *pp* **sowed** *or* **sown**) semear

sow² /saʊ/ *n* (*zool*) porca *f*

soy /sɔɪ/ *n* ~ **sauce** molho *m* de soja

soya /ˈsɔɪə/ *n* soja *f*. ~**-bean** semente *f* de soja

spa /spaː/ *n* termas *fpl*

space /speɪs/ *n* espaço *m*; (*room*) lugar *m*; (*period*) espaço *m*, período *m* □ *a* (*research etc*) espacial □ *vt* ~ **out** espaçar

space|craft /ˈspeɪskrɑːft/ *n* (*pl invar*), ~**ship** *n* nave espacial *f*

spacious /ˈspeɪʃəs/ *a* espaçoso

spade /speɪd/ *n* (*gardener's*) pá *f* de ferro; (*child's*) pá *f*. ~**s** (*cards*) espadas *fpl*

spadework /ˈspeɪdwɜːk/ *n* (*fig*) trabalho *m* preliminar

spaghetti /spəˈgetɪ/ *n* espaguete *m*, (*P*) esparguete *m*

Spain /speɪn/ *n* Espanha *f*

span¹ /spæn/ *n* (*of arch*) vão *m*; (*of wings*) envergadura *f*; (*of time*) espaço *m*, duração *f*; (*measure*) palmo *m* □ *vt* (*pt* **spanned**) (*extend across*) transpor; (*measure*) medir em palmos; (*in time*) abarcar, abranger, estender-se por

span² /spæn/ *see* **spick**

Spaniard /ˈspænɪəd/ *n* espanhol *m*

Spanish /ˈspænɪʃ/ *a* espanhol □ *n* (*lang*) espanhol *m*

spaniel /ˈspænɪəl/ *n* spaniel *m*, epagneul *m*

spank /spæŋk/ *vt* dar palmadas or chineladas no. ~**ing** *n* (*with hand*) palmada *f*; (*with slipper*) chinelada *f*

spanner /ˈspænə(r)/ *n* (*tool*) chave *f* de porcas; (*adjustable*) chave *f* inglesa

spar /spaː(r)/ *vi* (*pt* **sparred**) jogar boxe, esp para treino; (*fig: argue*) discutir

spare /speə(r)/ *vt* (*not hurt; use with restraint*) poupar; (*afford to give*) dispensar, ceder □ *a* (*in reserve*) de reserva, de sobra; (*tyre*) sobressalente; (*bed*) extra; (*room*) de hóspedes □ *n* (*part*) sobressalente *m*. ~ **time** horas *fpl* vagas. **have an hour to** ~ dispôr de uma hora. **have no time to** ~ não ter tempo a perder

sparing /'speərɪŋ/ a poupado. be ~ of poupar em, ser poupado com. ~ly adv frugalmente

spark /spa:k/ n centelha f, faísca f □ vt lançar faíscas. ~ off (*initiate*) desencadear, provocar. ~(ing)-plug n vela f de ignição

sparkle /'spa:kl/ vi cintilar, brilhar □ n brilho m, cintilação f

sparkling /'spa:klɪŋ/ a (*wine*) espumante

sparrow /'spærəʊ/ n pardal m

sparse /spa:s/ a esparso; (*hair*) ralo. ~ly adv (*furnished etc*) escassamente

spasm /'spæzəm/ n (*of muscle*) espasmo m; (*of coughing, anger etc*) ataque m, acesso m

spasmodic /spæz'mɒdɪk/ a espasmódico; (*at irregular intervals*) intermitente

spastic /'spæstɪk/ n deficiente mf motor

spat /spæt/ see spit¹

spate /speɪt/ n (*in river*) enxurrada f, cheia f. a ~ of (*letters etc*) uma avalanche de

spatter /'spætə(r)/ vt salpicar (with de, com)

spawn /spɔːn/ n ovas fpl □ vi desovar □ vt gerar em quantidade

speak /spi:k/ vt/i (*pt* spoke, *pp* spoken) falar (to/with sb about sth com alguém de/sobre alg coisa); (*say*) dizer. ~ out/up falar abertamente; (*louder*) falar mais alto. ~ one's mind dizer o que se pensa. so to ~ por assim dizer. English/Portuguese spoken fala-se português/inglês

speaker /'spi:kə(r)/ n (*in public*) orador m; (*loudspeaker*) altofalante m; (*of a language*) pessoa f de língua nativa

spear /spɪə(r)/ n lança f

spearhead /'spɪəhed/ n ponta f de lança □ vt (*lead*) estar à frente de, encabeçar

special /'speʃl/ a especial. ~ity

/-ɪ'ræləti/ n especialidade f. ~ly adv especialmente. ~ty n especialidade f

specialist /'speʃəlɪst/ n especialista mf

specialize /'speʃəlaɪz/ vi especializar-se (in em). ~d a especializado

species /'spi:ʃiːz/ n (*pl invar*) espécie f

specific /spə'sɪfɪk/ a específico. ~ally adv especificamente, explicitamente

specify /'spesɪfaɪ/ vt especificar. ~ication /-ɪ'keɪʃn/ n especificação f. ~ications npl (*of work etc*) caderno m de encargos

specimen /'spesɪmɪn/ n espécime(n) m, amostra f

speck /spek/ n (*stain*) mancha f pequena; (*dot*) pontinho m, pinta f; (*particle*) grão m

speckled /'spekld/ a salpicado, manchado

specs /speks/ npl (*colloq*) óculos mpl

spectacle /'spektəkl/ n espetáculo m, (P) espectáculo m. (pair of) ~s (par m de) óculos mpl

spectacular /spek'tækjʊlə(r)/ a espetacular, (P) espectacular

spectator /spek'teɪtə(r)/ n espectador m

spectre /'spektə(r)/ n espectro m, fantasma m

spectrum /'spektrəm/ n (*pl* -tra) espectro m; (*of ideas etc*) faixa f, gama f, leque m

speculat|e /'spekjʊleɪt/ vi especular, fazer especulações or conjeturas, (P) conjecturas (about sobre); (*comm*) especular, fazer especulação (in em). ~ion /-'leɪʃn/ n especulação f, conjetura f, (P) conjectura f; (*comm*) especulação f. ~or n especulador m

speech /spi:tʃ/ n (*faculty*) fala f; (*diction*) elocução f, (*dialect*)

falar *m*; (*address*) discurso *m*.
~less /a/ mudo, sem fala (**with** com, de)

speed /spi:d/ *n* velocidade *f*, rapidez *f* □ *vt/i* (*pt* **sped** /sped/) (*move*) ir depressa *or* a grande velocidade; (*send*) despedir, mandar; (*pt* **speeded**) (*drive too fast*) ultrapassar o limite de velocidade. **~ camera** radar *m*. **~ limit** limite *m* de velocidade. **~ up** acelerar (-se). **~ing** *n* excesso *m* de velocidade

speedometer /spi:'dɒmɪtə(r)/ *n* velocímetro *m*, (*P*) conta-quilómetros *m inv*

speed|**y** /'spi:dɪ/ *a* (**-ier, -iest**) rápido; (*prompt*) pronto. **~ily** *adv* rapidamente; (*promptly*) prontamente

spell[1] /spel/ *n* (*magic*) sortilégio *m*

spell[2] /spel/ *vt/i* (*pt* **spelled** *or* **spelt**) escrever; (*fig: mean*) significar, ter como resultado. **~ out** soletrar; (*fig: explain*) explicar claramente. **~ing** *n* ortografia *f*

spell[3] /spel/ *n* (*short period*) período *m* curto, breve espaço *m* de tempo; (*turn*) turno *m*

spend /spend/ *vt* (*pt* **spent**) (*money, energy*) gastar (**on** em); (*time, holiday*) passar. **~er** *n* gastador *m*

spendthrift /'spendθrɪft/ *n* perdulário *m*, esbanjador *m*

spent /spent/ *see* **spend** □ *a* gasto

sperm /spɜ:m/ *n* (*pl* **sperms** *or* **sperm**) (*semen*) esperma *m*, sémen *m*, (*P*) sémen *m*; (*cell*) espermatozóide *m*

spew /spju:/ *vt/i* vomitar, lançar

sphere /sfɪə(r)/ *n* esfera *f*

spherical /'sferɪkl/ *a* esférico

spic|**e** /spaɪs/ *n* especiaria *f*, condimento *m*; (*fig*) picante *m* □ *vt* condimentar. **~y** *a* condimentado; (*fig*) picante

spick /spɪk/ *a* **~ and span** novo em folha, impecável

spider /'spaɪdə(r)/ *n* aranha *f*

spik|**e** /spaɪk/ *n* (*of metal etc*) bico *m*, espigão *m*, ponta *f*. **~y** *a* guarnecido de bicos *or* pontas

spill /spɪl/ *vt/i* (*pt* **spilled** *or* **spilt**) derramar(-se), entornar (-se), espalhar(-se). **~ over** transbordar, extravasar

spin /spɪn/ *vt/i* (*pt* **spun**, *pres p* **spinning**) (*wool, cotton*) fiar; (*web*) tecer; (*turn*) (fazer) girar, (fazer) rodopiar. **~ out** (*money, story*) fazer durar; (*time*) (fazer) parar □ *n* volta *f*; (*aviat*) parafuso *m*. **go for a ~** dar uma volta *or* um giro. **~-drier** *n* centrifugadora *f* para a roupa, secadora *f*. **~ning-wheel** *n* roda *f* de fiar. **~-off** *n* bónus *m*, (*P*) bónus *m* inesperado; (*by-product*) derivado *m*

spinach /'spɪnɪdʒ/ *n* (*plant*) espinafre *m*; (*as food*) espinafres *mpl*

spinal /'spaɪnl/ *a* vertebral. **~ cord** espinal *f* dorsal

spindl|**e** /'spɪndl/ *n* roca *f*, fuso *m*; (*mech*) eixo *m*. **~y** *a* alto e magro; (*of plant*) espigado

spine /spaɪn/ *n* espinha *f*, coluna *f* vertebral; (*prickle*) espinho *m*, pico *m*; (*of book*) lombada *f*

spineless /'spaɪnlɪs/ *a* (*fig: cowardly*) covarde, sem fibra (*fig*)

spinster /'spɪnstə(r)/ *n* solteira *f*; (*pej*) solteirona *f*

spiral /'spaɪərəl/ *a* (em) espiral; (*staircase*) em caracol □ *n* espiral *f* □ *vi* (*pt* **spiralled**) subir em espiral

spire /'spaɪə(r)/ *n* agulha *f*, flecha *f*

spirit /'spɪrɪt/ *n* espírito *m*; (*boldness*) coragem *f*, brio *m*. **~s** (*morale*) moral *m*; (*drink*) bebidas *fpl* alcoólicas, (*P*) bebidas *fpl* espirituosas. **in high ~s** alegre

□ *vt* ~ **away** dar sumiço em, arrebatar. ~**-level** *n* nível *m* de bolha de ar

spirited /'spɪrɪtɪd/ *a* fogoso; *(attack, defence)* vigoroso, enérgico

spiritual /'spɪrɪtʃʊəl/ *a* espiritual

spiritualism /'spɪrɪtʃʊəlɪzəm/ *n* espiritismo *m*

spit¹ /spɪt/ *vt/i* (*pt* **spat** *or* **spit**, *pres p* **spitting**) cuspir; *(of rain)* chuviscar; *(of cat)* bufar □ *n* cuspe *m*, (P) cuspo *m*. **the ~ting image of** o retrato vivo de, a cara chapada de *(colloq)*

spit² /spɪt/ *n* (*for meat*) espeto *m*; *(of land)* restinga *f*, (P) língua *f* de terra

spite /spaɪt/ *n* má vontade *f*, despeito *m*, rancor *m* □ *vt* aborrecer, mortificar. **in** ~ **of** a despeito de, apesar de. ~**ful** *a* rancoroso, maldoso. ~**fully** *adv* rancorosamente, maldosamente

spittle /'spɪtl/ *n* cuspe *m*, (P) cuspo *m*, saliva *f*

splash /splæʃ/ *vt* salpicar, respingar □ *vi* esparrinhar, esparramar-se. ~ (**about**) chapinhar □ *n* (*act, mark*) salpico *m*; *(sound)* chape *m*; *(of colour)* mancha *f*. **make a ~** *(striking display)* fazer um vistão, causar furor

spleen /spliːn/ *n* (*anat*) baço *m*. **vent one's** ~ **on sb** descarregar a neura em alguém *(colloq)*

splendid /'splendɪd/ *a* esplêndido, magnífico; *(excellent)* estupendo *(colloq)*, ótimo, (P) óptimo

splendour /'splendə(r)/ *n* esplendor *m*

splint /splɪnt/ *n* (*med*) tala *f*

splinter /'splɪntə(r)/ *n* lasca *f*, estilhaço *m*; *(under the skin)* farpa *f*, lasca *f* □ *vi* estilhaçar-se, lascar-se. ~ **group** grupo *m* dissidente

split /splɪt/ *vt/i* (*pt* **split**, *pres p* **splitting**) rachar, fender(-se);

(divide, share) dividir; *(tear)* romper(-se) □ *n* racha *f*, fenda *f*; *(share)* quinhão *m*, parte *f*; *(pol)* cisão *f*. ~ **on** *(sl: inform on)* denunciar. ~ **one's sides** rebentar de risa. ~ **up** (*of couple*) separar-se. **a** ~ **second** uma fração de segundo. ~**ting headache** dor *f* de cabeça forte

splurge /splɜːdʒ/ *n* *(colloq)* espalhafato *m*, estardalhaço *m* □ *vi* *(colloq: spend)* gastar os tubos, (P) gastar à doida *(colloq)*

spool /spuːl/ *n* (*of sewing machine*) bobina *f*; (*for cotton thread*) carretel *m*, carrinho *m*; *(naut; fishing)* carretel *m*

splutter /'splʌtə(r)/ *vi* falar cuspindo; *(engine)* cuspir; *(fat)* crepitar

spoil /spɔɪl/ *vt* (*pt* **spoilt** *or* **spoiled**) estragar; *(pamper)* mimar □ *n* ~(**s**) *(plunder)* despojo(s) *m(pl)*, espólios *mpl*. ~**sport** *n* desmancha-prazeres *mf* *invar*. ~**t** *a* (*pampered*) mimado, estragado com mimos

spoke¹ /spəʊk/ *n* raio *m*

spoke², **spoken** /spəʊk, 'spəʊkən/ *see* **speak**

spokes|man /'spəʊksmən/ *n* (*pl* **-men**) ~**woman** *n* (*pl* **-women**) porta-voz *mf*

sponge /spʌndʒ/ *n* esponja *f* □ *vt* *(clean)* lavar com esponja; *(wipe)* limpar com esponja □ *vi* ~ **on** *(colloq: cadge)* viver à custa de. ~ **bag** bolsa *f* de toalete. ~ **cake** pão-de-ló *m*. ~**r** /-ə(r)/ *n* parasita *mf* *(colloq)* (*sl*). **spongy** *a* esponjoso

sponsor /'spɒnsə(r)/ *n* patrocinador *m*; (*for membership*) (sócio) proponente *m* □ *vt* patrocinar; (*for membership*) propor. ~**ship** *n* patrocínio *m*

spontaneous /spɒn'teɪnɪəs/ *a* espontâneo

spoof /spuːf/ *n* *(colloq)* paródia *f*

spooky /'spu:kɪ/ a (-ier, -iest) (colloq) fantasmagórico, que dá arrepios

spool /spu:l/ n (of sewing machine) bobina f. (for thread, line) carretel m, (P) carrinho m

spoon /spu:n/ n colher f. **~-feed** vt (pt **-fed**) alimentar de colher; (fig: help) dar na bandeja para (fig). **~ful** n (pl **~fuls**) colherada f

sporadic /spə'rædɪk/ a esporádico, acidental

sport /spɔːt/ n esporte m, (P) desporto m. (**good**) ~ (sl: person) gente f fina, (P) bom tipo m (colloq), (P) tipo m bestial □ vt (display) exibir, ostentar. **~s car/ coat** carro m/casaco m esporte, (P) de desporto. **~y** a (colloq) esportivo, (P) desportivo

sporting /'spɔːtɪŋ/ a esportivo, (P) desportivo. **a ~ chance** uma certa possibilidade de sucesso, uma boa chance

sports|man /'spɔːtsmən/ n (pl -men), **~woman** (pl -women) desportista mf. **~manship** n (spirit) espírito m desportivo; (activity) esportismo m, (P) desportismo m

spot /spɒt/ n (mark, stain) mancha f; (in pattern) pinta f, bola f; (drop) gota f; (place) lugar m, ponto m; (pimple) borbulha f, espinha f; (TV) spot m televisivo □ vt (pt **spotted**) manchar; (colloq: detect) descobrir, detectar (colloq). **a ~ of** (colloq) um pouco de. **be in a ~** (colloq) estar numa encrenca (colloq), (P) estar metido numa alhada (colloq). **on the ~** no local; (there and then) ali mesmo, logo ali. **~-on** a (colloq) certo. **~ check** inspecção f, (P) inspecção f de surpresa; (of cars) fiscalização f de surpresa. **~ted** a manchado; (with dots) de pintas, de bolas; (animal)

malhado. **~ty** a (with pimples) com borbulhas

spotless /'spɒtlɪs/ a impecável, imaculado

spotlight /'spɒtlaɪt/ n foco m; (cine, theat) refletor m, holofote m

spouse /spaʊz/ n cônjuge mf, esposo m

spout /spaʊt/ n (of vessel) bico m; (of liquid) esguicho m, jorro m; (pipe) cano m □ vi jorrar, esguichar. **up the ~** (sl: ruined) liquidado (sl)

sprain /spreɪn/ n entorse f, mau jeito m □ vt torcer, dar um mau jeito a

sprang /spræŋ/ see **spring**

sprawl /sprɔːl/ vi (sit) estirar-se, esparramar-se; (fall) estatelar-se; (town) estender-se, espraiar-se

spray[1] /spreɪ/ n (of flowers) raminho m, ramalhete m

spray[2] /spreɪ/ n (water) borrifo m, salpico m; (from sea) borrifo m de espuma; (device) bomba f, aerossol m; (for perfume) vaporizador m, atomizador m □ vt aspergir, borrifar, pulverizar; (with insecticide) pulverizar. **~-gun** n (for paint) pistola f

spread /spred/ vt/i (pt **spread**) (extend, stretch) estender(-se); (news, fear, illness etc) alastrar (-se), espalhar(-se), propagar(-se); (butter etc) passar; (wings) abrir □ n (expanse) expansão f, extensão f; (spreading) propagação f; (paste) pasta f para passar pão; (colloq: meal) banquete m. **~-eagled** a de braços e pernas abertos. **~-sheet** n (comput) folha f de cálculo

spree /spriː/ n **go on a ~** (colloq) cair na farra

sprig /sprɪg/ n raminho m

sprightly /'spraɪtlɪ/ a (-ier, -iest) vivo, animado

spring /sprɪŋ/ vi (pt **sprang**

sprung) (*arise*) nascer; (*jump*) saltar, pular □ *vt* (*produce suddenly*) sair-se com; (*a surprise*) fazer (**on sb a** alguém) □ *n* salto *m*, pulo *m*; (*device*) mola *f*; (*season*) primavera *f*, (*P*) Primavera *f*, nascente *f*. **~ from** vir de, originar-se de, provir de. **~-clean** *vt* fazer limpeza geral. **~ onion** cebolinha *f*. **~ up** surgir

springboard /ˈsprɪŋbɔːd/ *n* trampolim *m*

springtime /ˈsprɪŋtaɪm/ *n* primavera *f*

springy /ˈsprɪŋɪ/ *a* (-**ier**, -**iest**) elástico

sprinkle /ˈsprɪŋkl/ *vt* (*with liquid*) borrifar, salpicar; (*with salt, flour*) polvilhar (**with de**). **~ sand**/*etc* espalhar areia/*etc*. **~r** /-ə(r)/ *n* (*in garden*) regador *m*; (*for fires*) sprinkler *m*

sprinkling /ˈsprɪŋklɪŋ/ *n* (*amount*) pequena quantidade *f*; (*number*) pequeno número *m*

sprint /sprɪnt/ *n* (*sport*) corrida *f* de pequena distância, sprint *m* □ *vi* correr em sprint *or* a toda a velocidade; (*sport*) correr

sprout /spraʊt/ *vt/i* brotar, germinar; (*put forth*) deitar □ *n* (*on plant etc*) broto *m*. **(Brussels) ~s** couves *f* de Bruxelas

spruce /spruːs/ *a* bem arrumado □ *vt* **~ o.s. up** arrumar(-se)

sprung /sprʌŋ/ *see* **spring** □ *a* (*mattress etc*) de molas

spry /spraɪ/ *a* (**spryer**, **spryest**) vivo, ativo, (*P*) activo; (*nimble*) ágil

spud /spʌd/ *n* (*sl*) batata *f*

spun /spʌn/ *see* **spin**

spur /spɜː(r)/ *n* (*of rider*) espora *f*; (*fig: stimulus*) aguilhão *m*; (*fig*) espora *f* (*fig*) □ *vt* (*pt* **spurred**) esporear, picar com esporas; (*fig: incite*) aguilhoar, esporear. **on the ~ of the moment** impulsivamente

spurious /ˈspjʊərɪəs/ *a* falso, espúrio

spurn /spɜːn/ *vt* desdenhar, desprezar, rejeitar

spurt /spɜːt/ *vi* jorrar, esguichar; (*fig: accelerate*) acelerar subitamente, dar um arranco súbito □ *n* jorro *m*, esguicho *m*; (*of energy, speed*) arranco *m*, surto *m*

spy /spaɪ/ *n* espião *m* □ *vt* (*make out*) avistar, descortinar □ *vi* **~ (on)** espiar, espionar. **~ out** descobrir. **~ing** *n* espionagem *f*

squabble /ˈskwɒbl/ *vi* discutir, brigar □ *n* briga *f*, disputa *f*

squad /skwɒd/ *n* (*mil*) pelotão *m*; (*team*) equipe *f*, (*P*) equipa *f*. **firing ~** pelotão *m* de fuzilamento. **flying ~** brigada *f* móvel

squadron /ˈskwɒdrən/ *n* (*mil*) esquadrão *m*; (*aviat*) esquadrilha *f*; (*naut*) esquadra *f*

squalid /ˈskwɒlɪd/ *a* esquálido, sórdido. **~or** *n* sordidez *f*

squall /skwɔːl/ *n* borrasca *f*

squander /ˈskwɒndə(r)/ *vt* desperdiçar

square /skweə(r)/ *n* quadrado *m*; (*in town*) largo *m*, praça *f*; (*T-square*) régua-tê *f*; (*set-square*) esquadro *m* □ *a* (*of shape*) quadrado; (*metre, mile etc*) quadrado; (*honest*) direito, honesto; (*of meal*) abundante, substancial. **(all) ~** (*quits*) quite(s) □ *vt* (*math*) elevar ao quadrado; (*settle*) acertar □ *vi* (*agree*) concordar. **go back to ~** recomeçar tudo do princípio, voltar à estaca zero. **~ brackets** parênteses *mpl* retos, (*P*) rectos. **~ up to** enfrentar. **~ly** *adv* diretamente, (*P*) directamente; (*fairly*) honestamente

squash /skwɒʃ/ *vt* (*crush*) esmagar; (*squeeze*) espremer; (*crowd*) comprimir, apertar □ *n* (*game*) squash *m*; (*Amer: marrow*) abóbora *f*. **lemon ~** limonada *f* orange ∼ laranjada *f*. ∼y *a* mole

squat /skwɒt/ *vi* (*pt* squatted) acocorar-se, agachar-se; (*be a squatter*) ser ocupante ilegal □ *a* (*dumpy*) atarracado. ∼ter *n* ocupante *mf* ilegal de casa vazia, posseiro *m*

squawk /skwɔ:k/ *n* grasnido *m*, crocito *m* □ *vi* grasnar, crocitar

squeak /skwi:k/ *n* guincho *m*, chio *m*; (*of door, shoes etc*) rangido *m* □ *vi* guinchar, chiar; (*of door, shoes etc*) ranger. ∼y *a* (*shoe etc*) que range; (*voice*) esganiçado

squeal /skwi:l/ *vi* dar gritos agudos, guinchar □ *n* grito *m* agudo, guincho *m*. ∼ (on) (*sl: inform on*) delatar, (*P*) denunciar

squeamish /skwi:mɪʃ/ *a* (*nauseated*) que enjoa à toa

squeeze /skwi:z/ *vt* (*lemon, sponge etc*) espremer; (*hand, arm*) apertar; (*extract*) arrancar, extorquir (*from* de) □ *vi* (*force one's way*) passar à força, meter-se por □ *n* aperto *m*, apertão *m*; (*hug*) abraço *m*; (*comm*) restrições *fpl* de crédito

squelch /skweltʃ/ *vi* chapinhar or fazer chape-chape na lama

squid /skwɪd/ *n* lula *f*

squiggle /skwɪgl/ *n* rabisco *m*, floreado *m*

squint /skwɪnt/ *vi* ser estrábico or vesgo; (*with half-shut eyes*) franzir os olhos □ *n* (*med*) estrabismo *m*

squirm /skwɜ:m/ *vi* (re)torcer-se, contorcer-se

squirrel /skwɪrəl/ *n* esquilo *m*

squirt /skwɜ:t/ *vt/i* esguichar □ *n* esguicho *m*

stab /stæb/ *vt* (*pt* stabbed) apunhalar; (*knife*) esfaquear □ *n* punhalada *f*; (*with knife*) facada *f*; (*of pain*) pontada *f*; (*colloq: attempt*) tentativa *f*

stabilize /steɪbəlaɪz/ *vt* estabilizar

stable¹ /steɪbl/ *a* (-er, -est) estável. ∼ility /stəbɪlətɪ/ *n* estabilidade *f*

stable² /steɪbl/ *n* cavalariça *f*, estrebaria *f*. ∼-boy *n* moço *m* de estrebaria

stack /stæk/ *n* pilha *f*, montão *m*; (*of hay etc*) meda *f* □ *vt* ∼ (up) empilhar, amontoar

stadium /steɪdɪəm/ *n* estádio *m*

staff /sta:f/ *n* pessoal *m*; (*in school*) professores *mpl*; (*mil*) estado-maior *m*; (*stick*) bordão *m*, cajado *m*; (*mus*) (*pl* staves) pauta *f* □ *vt* prover de pessoal

stag /stæg/ *n* veado (macho) *m*, cervo *m*. ∼-party *n* (*colloq*) reunião *f* masculina; (*before wedding*) despedida *f* de solteiro

stage /steɪdʒ/ *n* (*theatre*) palco *m*; (*phase*) fase *f*, ponto *m*; (*platform in hall*) estrado *m* □ *vt* encenar, pôr em cena; (*fig: organize*) organizar. go on the ∼ seguir a carreira teatral, ir para o teatro (*colloq*). ∼ door entrada *f* dos artistas. ∼-fright *n* nervosismo *m*

stagger /stægə(r)/ *vi* vacilar, cambalear □ *vt* (*shock*) atordoar, chocar; (*holidays etc*) escalonar. ∼ing *a* atordoador, chocante

stagnant /stægnənt/ *a* estagnado, parado

stagnat|e /stægneɪt/ *vi* estagnar. ∼ion /-ʃn/ *n* estagnação *f*

staid /steɪd/ *a* sério, sensato, estável

stain /steɪn/ *vt* manchar, pôr nódoa em; (*colour*) tingir, dar cor a □ *n* mancha *f*, nódoa *f*; (*colouring*) corante *m*. ∼ed glass window vitral *m*. ∼less steel aço *m* inoxidável

stair /steə(r)/ *n* degrau *m*. ∼s escada(s) *f(pl)*

stair|case /steəkeɪs/, ∼way

/-weɪ/ ns escada(s) f(pl), escadaria f

stake /steɪk/ n (*post*) estaca f, poste m; (*wager*) parada f, aposta f □ vt (*area*) demarcar, delimitar; (*wager*) jogar, apostar. **at ~** em jogo. **have a ~ in** ter interesse em. **~ a claim to** reivindicar

stale /steɪl/ a (**-er, -est**) estragado, velho; (*bread*) duro, mofado; (*smell*) rançoso; (*air*) viciado; (*news*) velho

stalemate /ˈsteɪlmeɪt/ n (*chess*) empate m; (*fig: deadlock*) impasse m, beco-sem-saída m

stalk¹ /stɔːk/ n (*of plant*) caule m

stalk² /stɔːk/ vi andar com ar empertigado □ vt (*prey*) perseguir furtivamente, tocaiar

stall /stɔːl/ n (*in stable*) baia f; (*in market*) tenda f, barraca f. **~s** (*theat*) poltronas fpl de orquestra; (*cinema*) platéia f, (*P*) plateia f □ vt/i (*auto*) enguiçar, (*P*) ir abaixo. **~ (for time)** ganhar tempo

stalwart /ˈstɔːlwət/ a forte, rijo; (*supporter*) fiel

stamina /ˈstæmɪnə/ n resistência f

stammer /ˈstæmə(r)/ vt/i gaguejar □ n gagueira f, (*P*) gaguez f

stamp /stæmp/ vt/i ~ (**one's foot**) bater com o pé (no chão), pisar com força □ vt estampar; (*letter*) estampilhar, selar; (*with rubber stamp*) carimbar. **~ out** (*fire, rebellion etc*) esmagar; (*disease*) erradicar □ n estampa f; (*for postage*) selo m; (*fig: mark*) cunho m. **~ (rubber)** carimbo m. **~-collecting** n filatelia f

stampede /stæmˈpiːd/ n (*scattering*) debandada f; (*of horses, cattle etc*) debandada f; (*fig: rush*) corrida f □ vt/i (*fazer*) debandar; (*horses, cattle etc*) tresmalhar

stance /stæns/ n posição f, postura f

stand /stænd/ vi (*pt* **stood**) estar em pé; (*keep upright position*) ficar em pé; (*rise*) levantar-se; (*be situated*) encontrar-se, ficar, situar-se; (*pol*) candidatar-se (**for** por) □ vt pôr (de pé), colocar; (*tolerate*) suportar, agüentar, (*P*) aguentar □ n posição f; (*support*) apoio m; (*mil*) resistência f; (*at fair*) stand m, pavilhão m; (*in street*) quiosque m; (*for spectators*) arquibancada f, (*P*) bancada f; (*Amer: witness-box*) banco m das testemunhas. **~ a chance** ter uma possibilidade. **~ back** recuar. **~ by** *or* **around** estar parado sem fazer nada. **~ by** (*be ready*) estar a postos; (*promise, person*) manter-se fiel a. **~ down** desistir, retirar-se. **~ for** representar, simbolizar; (*colloq: tolerate*) aturar. **~ in for** substituir. **~ out** (*be conspicuous*) sobressair. **~ still** estar/ficar imóvel. **~ still!** não se mexa!, quieto! **~ to reason** ser lógico. **~ up** levantar-se, pôr-se em *or* de pé. **~ up for** defender, apoiar. **~ up to** enfrentar. **~-by** a (*for emergency*) de reserva; (*ticket*) de stand-by □ n (*at airport*) stand-by m. **on ~-by** (*mil*) de prontidão; (*med*) de plantão. **~-in** n substituto m, suplente mf. **~-offish** a (*colloq: aloof*) reservado, distante

standard /ˈstændəd/ n norma f, padrão m; (*level*) nível m; (*flag*) estandarte m, bandeira f. **~s** (*morals*) princípios mpl □ a regulamentar; (*average*) standard, normal. **~ lamp** abajur m de pé. **~ of living** padrão m de vida, (*P*) nível m de vida

standardize /ˈstændədaɪz/ vt padronizar

standing /'stændɪŋ/ *a* em pé, de pé *invar*; (*army, committee etc*) permanente □ *n* posição *f*; (*reputation*) prestígio *m*; (*duration*) duração *f*. **~ order** (*at bank*) ordem *f* permanente. **~-room** *n* lugares *mpl* em pé

standpoint /'stændpɔɪnt/ *n* ponto *m* de vista

standstill /'stændstɪl/ *n* paralisação *f*. **at a ~** parado, paralisado. **bring/come to a ~** (*fazer*) parar, paralisar(-se), imobilizar (-se)

stank /stæŋk/ *see* **stink**

staple[1] /'steɪpl/ *n* (*for paper*) grampo *m*, (P) agrafo *m* □ *vt* (*paper*) grampear, (P) agrafar. **~r** /-ə(r)/ *n* grampeador *m*, (P) agrafador *m*

staple[2] /'steɪpl/ *a* principal, básico □ *n* (*comm*) artigo *m* básico

star /staː(r)/ *n* estrela *f*; (*cinema*) estrela *f*, vedete *f*; (*celebrity*) celebridade *f* □ *vt* (*pt* **starred**) (*of film*) ter no papel principal, (P) ter como actor principal □ *vi* **~ in** ser a vedete ou ter o papel principal em. **~dom** *n* celebridade *f*, estrelato *m*

starch /staːtʃ/ *n* amido *m*, fécula *f*; (*for clothes*) goma *f* □ *vt* pôr em goma, engomar. **~y** *a* (*of food*) farináceo, feculento; (*fig: of person*) rígido, formal

stare /steə(r)/ *vi* **~ at** olhar fixamente □ *n* olhar *m* fixo

starfish /'staːfɪʃ/ *n* (*pl invar*) estrela-do-mar *f*

stark /staːk/ *a* (-**er**, -**est**) (*desolate*) árido, desolado; (*severe*) austero, severo; (*utter*) completo, rematado; (*fact etc*) brutal □ *adv* completamente. **~ naked** nu em pêlo, (P) em pelota (*colloq*)

starling /'staːlɪŋ/ *n* estorninho *m*

starlit /'staːlɪt/ *a* estrelado

starry /'staːrɪ/ *a* estrelado. **~-eyed** *a* (*colloq*) sonhador, idealista

start /staːt/ *vt/i* começar; (*machine*) ligar, pôr em andamento; (*fashion etc*) lançar; (*leave*) partir; (*cause*) causar, provocar; (*jump*) sobressaltar-se, estremecer; (*of car*) arrancar, partir □ *n* começo *m*, início *m*; (*of race*) largada *f*, partida *f*; (*lead*) avanço *m*; (*jump*) sobressalto *m*, estremecimento *m*. **by fits and ~s** aos arrancos, intermitentemente. **for a ~** para começar. **give sb a ~** sobressaltar alguém, pregar um susto a alguém. **~ to do** começar a *or* pôr-se a fazer. **~er** *n* (*auto*) arranque *m*; (*competitor*) corredor *m*; (*culin*) entrada *f*. **~ing-point** *n* ponto *m* de partida

startle /'staːtl/ *vt* (*make jump*) sobressaltar, pregar um susto a; (*shock*) alarmar, chocar. **~ing** *a* alarmante; (*surprising*) surpreendente

starve /staːv/ *vi* (*suffer*) passar fome; (*die*) morrer de fome. **be ~ing** (*colloq: very hungry*) ter muita fome, morrer de fome (*colloq*) □ *vt* fazer passar fome a; (*deprive*) privar. **~ation** /-'veɪʃn/ *n* fome *f*

stash /stæʃ/ *vt* (*sl*) guardar, esconder, enfurnar (*colloq*)

state /steɪt/ *n* estado *m*, condição *f*; (*pomp*) pompa *f*, gala *f*; (*pol*) Estado *m* □ *a* de Estado, do Estado; (*school*) público *m*; (*visit etc*) oficial □ *vt* afirmar (**that** que); (*views*) exprimir; (*fix*) marcar, fixar. **in a ~** muito abalado

stateless /'steɪtlɪs/ *a* apátrida

stately /'steɪtlɪ/ *a* (-**ier**, -**iest**) majestoso. **~ home** solar *m*, palácio *m*

statement /'steɪtmənt/ *n* declaração *f*; (*of account*) extrato *m*, (P) extracto *m* de conta

statesman /'steɪtsmən/ *n* (*pl* -**men**) homem *m* de estado, estadista *m*

static /'stætɪk/ *a* estático □ *n* (*radio*, *TV*) estática *f*, interferência *f*

station /'steɪʃn/ *n* (*position*) posto *m*; (*rail*, *bus*, *radio*) estação *f*; (*rank*) condição *f*, posição *f* social □ *vt* colocar. **~-wagon** *n* perua *f*, (*P*) carrinha *f*. **~ed at** *or* **in** (*mil*) estacionado em

stationary /'steɪʃnrɪ/ *a* estacionário, parado, imóvel; (*vehicle*) estacionado, parado

stationer /'steɪʃənə(r)/ *n* dono *m* de papelaria. **~'s shop** papelaria *f*. **~y** *n* artigos *mpl* de papelaria; (*writing-paper*) papel *m* de carta

statistic /stə'tɪstɪk/ *n* dado *m* estatístico. **~s** *n* (*as a science*) estatística *f*. **~al** *a* estatístico

statue /'stætʃuː/ *n* estátua *f*

stature /'stætʃə(r)/ *n* estatura *f*

status /'steɪtəs/ *n* (*pl* **-uses**) situação *f*, posição *f*, categoria *f*; (*prestige*) prestígio *m*, importância *f*, status *m*. **~ quo** status quo *m*. **~ symbol** símbolo *m* de status

statut|e /'stætʃuːt/ *n* estatuto *m*, lei *f*. **~ory** /-ʊtrɪ/ *a* estatutário, regulamentar; (*holiday*) legal

staunch /stɔːntʃ/ *a* (**-er**, **-est**) (*friend*) fiel, leal

stave /steɪv/ *n* (*mus*) pauta *f* □ *vt* **~ off** (*keep off*) conjurar, evitar; (*delay*) adiar

stay /steɪ/ *vi* estar, ficar, permanecer; (*dwell temporarily*) ficar, alojar-se, hospedar-se; (*spend time*) demorar-se □ *vt* (*hunger*) enganar □ *n* estada *f*, visita *f*, permanência *f*. **~ behind** ficar para trás. **~ in** ficar em casa. **~ put** (*colloq*) não se mexer (*colloq*). **~ up** (*late*) deitar-se tarde. **~ing-power** *n* resistência *f*

stead /sted/ *n* **in my/your/***etc* no meu/teu/*etc* lugar. **stand in good ~** ser muito útil

steadfast /'stedfɑːst/ *a* firme, constante

stead|y /'stedɪ/ *a* (**-ier**, **-iest**) (*stable*) estável, firme, seguro; (*regular*) regular, constante; (*hand*, *voice*) firme □ *vt* firmar, fixar, estabilizar; (*calm*) acalmar. **go ~y with** (*colloq*) namorar. **~ily** *adv* firmemente; (*regularly*) regularmente, de modo constante

steak /steɪk/ *n* bife *m*

steal /stiːl/ *vt*/*i* (*pt* **stole**, *pp* **stolen**) roubar (**from sb de** alguém). **~ away/in/***etc* sair/entrar/*etc* furtivamente, esgueirar-se. **~ the show** pôr os outros na sombra

stealth /stelθ/ *n* **by ~** furtivamente, na calada, às escondidas. **~y** *a* furtivo

steam /stiːm/ *n* vapor *m* de água; (*on window*) condensação *f* □ *vt* (*cook*) cozinhar a vapor. **~ up** (*window*) embaciar □ *vi* soltar vapor, fumegar; (*move*) avançar. **~-engine** *n* máquina *f* a vapor; (*locomotive*) locomotiva *f* a vapor. **~ iron** ferro *m* a vapor. **~y** *a* (*heat*) úmido, (*P*) húmido

steamer /'stiːmə(r)/ *n* (*ship*) (barco a) vapor *m*; (*culin*) utensílio *m* para cozinhar a vapor

steamroller /'stiːmrəʊlə(r)/ *n* cilindro *m* a vapor, rolo *m* compressor

steel /stiːl/ *n* aço *m* □ *a* de aço □ *vpr* **~ o.s.** endurecer-se, fortalecer-se. **~ industry** siderurgia *f*

steep[1] /stiːp/ *vt* (*soak*) mergulhar, pôr de molho; (*permeate*) passar, impregnar. **~ed in** (*fig: vice*, *misery etc*) mergulhado em; (*fig: knowledge*, *wisdom etc*) impregnado de, repassado de

steep[2] /stiːp/ *a* (**-er**, **-est**) íngreme, escarpado; (*colloq*) exagerado, exorbitante. **rise ~ly** (*slope*) subir a pique; (*price*) disparar

steeple /'sti:pl/ n campanário m, torre f

steeplechase /'sti:pltʃeɪs/ n (race) corrida f de obstáculos

steer /stɪə(r)/ vt/i guiar, conduzir, dirigir; (ship) governar; (fig) guiar, orientar. **~ clear of** evitar passar perto de. **~ing** n (auto) direcção f, (P) direcção f. **~ing-wheel** n (auto) volante f

stem[1] /stem/ n caule m, haste f; (of glass) pé m; (of pipe) boquilha f; (of word) radical m □ vi (pt stemmed) **~ from** provir de, vir de

stem[2] /stem/ vt (pt stemmed) (check) conter; (stop) estancar

stench /stentʃ/ n mau cheiro m, fedor m

stencil /'stensl/ n estênsil m, (P) stencil m □ vt (pt stencilled) (document) policopiar

step /step/ vi (pt stepped) ir andar □ vt, **~ up** aumentar □ n passo m, passada f; (of stair, train) degrau m; (action) medida f, passo m. **~s** (ladder) escada f. **in ~** no mesmo passo, a passo certo; (fig) em conformidade (with com). **~ down** (resign) demitir-se. **~ in** (intervene) intervir. **~-ladder** n escada f portátil. **~ping-stone** n (fig: means to an end) ponte f, trampolim m

stepbrother /'stepbrʌðə(r)/ n meio-irmão m. **~daughter** n nora f, (P) enteada f. **~father** n padrasto m. **~mother** n madrasta f. **~sister** n meio-irmã f. **~son** n genro m, (P) enteado m

stereo /'sterɪəʊ/ n (pl -os) estéreo m; (record-player etc) equipamento m or sistema m estéreo □ a estéreo invar. **~phonic** /-ə'fɒnɪk/ a estereofônico, (P) estereofónico

stereotype /'sterɪətaɪp/ n estereótipo m. **~d** a estereotipado

steril|e /'steraɪl/ a estéril. **~ity** /stə'rɪləti/ n esterilidade f

steriliz|e /'sterəlaɪz/ vt esterilizar. **~ation** /-'zeɪʃn/ n esterilização f

sterling /'stɜːlɪŋ/ n libra f esterlina □ a esterlino; (silver) de lei; (fig) excelente, de (primeira) qualidade

stern[1] /stɜːn/ a (-er, -est) severo

stern[2] /stɜːn/ n (of ship) popa f, ré f

stethoscope /'steθəskəʊp/ n estetoscópio m

stew /stju:/ vt/i estufar, guisar; (fruit) cozer □ n ensopado m. **~ed fruit** compota f

steward /'stjuəd/ n (of club etc) ecônomo m, (P) ecónomo m, administrador m; (on ship etc) camareiro m (de bordo), (P) criado m, (de bordo). **~ess** /-'des/ n aeromoça f, (P) hospedeira f

stick[1] /stɪk/ n pau m; (for walking) bengala f; (of celery) talo m

stick[2] /stɪk/ vt (pt stuck) (glue) colar; (thrust) cravar, espetar; (colloq: put) enfiar, meter; (sl: endure) agüentar, (P) aguentar, aturar, suportar □ vi (adhere) colar, aderir; (remain) ficar enfiado or metido; (be jammed) emperrar, ficar engatado. **~ in one's mind** ficar na memória. **be stuck with sb/sth** (colloq) não conseguir descartar-se de alguém/alg coisa (colloq). **~ out** vt (head) esticar; (tongue etc) mostrar □ vi (protrude) sobressair. **~ to** (promise) ser fiel a. **~-up** n (sl) assalto m à mão armada. **~ up for** (colloq) tomar o partido de, defender. **~ing-plaster** n esparadrapo m, (P) adesivo m

sticker /'stɪkə(r)/ n adesivo m, etiqueta f (adesiva)

stickler /'stɪklə(r)/ n **be a ~ for** fazer grande questão de, insistir em

sticky /'stɪkɪ/ a (-ier, -iest) pegajoso; (label, tape) adesivo; (weather) abafado, mormacento

stiff /stɪf/ a (-er, -est) teso, hirto, rígido; (limb, joint; hard) duro; (unbending) inflexível; (price) elevado, puxado (colloq); (penalty) severo; (drink) forte; (manner) reservado, formal. **be bored/scared ~** (colloq) estar muito aborrecido/com muito medo (colloq). **~ neck** torcicolo m. **~ness** n rigidez f

stiffen /'stɪfn/ vt/i (harden) endurecer; (limb, joint) emperrar

stifle /'staɪfl/ vt/i abafar, sufocar. **~ing** a sufocante

stigma /'stɪɡmə/ n estigma m. **~tize** vt estigmatizar

stile /staɪl/ n degrau m para passar por cima de cerca

stiletto /stɪ'letəʊ/ n (pl -os) estilete m. **~ heel** n salto m alto fino

still¹ /stɪl/ a imóvel, quieto; (quiet) sossegado □ n silêncio m, sossego m □ adv ainda; (nevertheless) apesar disso, apesar de tudo. **keep ~!** fique quieto!, não se mexa! **~ life** natureza f morta. **~ness** n calma f

still² /stɪl/ n (apparatus) alambique m

stillborn /'stɪlbɔːn/ a natimorto, (P) nado-morto

stilted /'stɪltɪd/ a afetado, (P) afectado

stilts /stɪlts/ npl pernas de pau fpl, (P) andas fpl

stimul|ate /'stɪmjʊleɪt/ vt estimular. **~ant** n estimulante m. **~ating** a estimulante. **~ation** /-'leɪʃn/ n estimulação f

stimulus /'stɪmjʊləs/ n (pl -li /-laɪ/) (spur) estímulo m

sting /stɪŋ/ n picada f; (organ) ferrão m □ vt/i (pt stung) picar □ vi picar, arder. **~ing nettle** urtiga f

stingy /'stɪndʒɪ/ a (-ier, -iest) pãoduro m, sovina (with com)

stink /stɪŋk/ n fedor m, catinga f, mau cheiro m □ vi (pt stank or stunk, pp stunk) (of-) cheirar (a), tresandar (a) □ vt **~ out** (room etc) empestar. **~ing** a malcheiroso. **~ing rich** (sl) podre de rico (colloq)

stinker /'stɪŋkə(r)/ n (sl: person) cara m horroroso (colloq); (sl: sth difficult) osso m duro de moer

stint /stɪnt/ vi □ n poupar em, apertar em □ n (work) tarefa f, parte f, quinhão m

stipulate /'stɪpjʊleɪt/ vt estipular. **~ion** /-'leɪʃn/ n condição f, estipulação f

stir /stɜː/ vt/i (pt stirred) (move) mexer(-se), mover(-se); (excite) excitar; (a liquid) mexer □ n agitação f, rebuliço m. **~ up** (trouble etc) provocar, fomentar. **~ring** a excitante

stirrup /'stɪrəp/ n estribo m

stitch /stɪtʃ/ n (in sewing; med) ponto m; (in knitting) malha f, ponto m; (pain) pontada f □ vt coser. **in ~es** (colloq) às gargalhadas (colloq)

stoat /stəʊt/ n arminho m

stock /stɒk/ n (comm) estoque m, (P) stock m, provisão f; (finance) valores mpl, fundos mpl; (family) família f, estirpe f; (culin) caldo m; (flower) goivo m □ a (goods) corrente, comum; (hackneyed) estereotipado □ vt (shop etc) abastecer, fornecer; (sell) vender □ vi **~ up with** abastecer-se de. **in ~** em estoque. **out of ~** esgotado. **take ~** (fig) fazer um balanço. **~-car** n stock-car m. **~-cube** n cubo m de caldo. **~ market** Bolsa f (de Valores). **~-still** a, adv imóvel. **~-taking** n (comm) inventário m

stockbroker /'stɒkbrəʊkə(r)/ n corretor m da Bolsa

stocking /'stɒkɪŋ/ n meia f

stockist /'stɒkɪst/ n armazenista m

stockpile /'stɒkpaɪl/ n reservas fpl □ vt acumular reservas de, estocar

stocky /'stɒkɪ/ a (-ier, -iest) atarracado

stodg|e /stɒdʒ/ n (colloq) comida f pesada (colloq). **~y** a (of food, book) pesado, maçudo

stoic /'stəʊɪk/ n estóico m. **~al** a estóico. **~ism** /-sɪzəm/ n estoicismo m

stoke /stəʊk/ vt (boiler, fire) alimentar, carregar

stole¹ /stəʊl/ n (garment) estola f

stole², **stolen** /stəʊl, 'stəʊlən/ see **steal**

stomach /'stʌmək/ n estômago m; (abdomen) barriga f, ventre m □ vt (put up with) aturar. **~-ache** n dor f de estômago; (abdomen) dores fpl de barriga

ston|e /stəʊn/ n pedra f; (pebble) seixo m; (in fruit) caroço m; (weight) 6,348 kg; (med) cálculo m, pedra f □ vt apedrejar; (fruit) tirar o caroço de. within a **~'s throw (of)** muito perto (de). **~e-cold** gelado. **~e-deaf** totalmente surdo. **~ed** a (colloq: drunk) bêbão m (colloq); (colloq: drugged) drogado. **~y** a pedregoso. **~y-broke** a (sl) duro, liso (sl)

stonemason /'stəʊnmeɪsn/ n pedreiro m

stood /stʊd/ see **stand**

stooge /stuːdʒ/ n (colloq: actor) ajudante m; (colloq: puppet) antoche m, (P) comparsa mf, parceiro m

stool /stuːl/ n banco m, tamborete m

stoop /stuːp/ vi (bend) curvar-se, baixar-se; (condescend) condescender, dignar-se. **~ to sth** rebaixar-se para (fazer) alg coisa

stop /stɒp/ vt/i (pt **stopped**) parar; (prevent) impedir (from de); (hole, leak etc) tapar, vedar; (pain, noise etc) parar; (colloq: stay) ficar □ n (of bus) parada f, (P) paragem f; (full stop) ponto m final. **put a ~ to** pôr fim a. **~ it!** acabe logo com isso! **~-over** n (break in journey) parada f, (P) paragem f; (port of call) escala f. **~press** n notícia f de última hora. **~-watch** n cronómetro m, (P) cronómetro m

stopgap /'stɒpgæp/ n substituto m provisório, tapa-buracos mpl (colloq) □ a temporário

stoppage /'stɒpɪdʒ/ n parada f, (P) paragem f; (of work) paralisação f de trabalho; (of pay) suspensão f

stopper /'stɒpə(r)/ n rolha f, tampa f

storage /'stɔːrɪdʒ/ n (of goods, food etc) armazenagem f, armazenamento m. **in cold ~** em frigorífico

store /stɔː(r)/ n reserva f, provisão f; (warehouse) armazém m, entreposto m; (shop) grande armazém m; (Amer) loja f; (in computer) memória f □ vt (for future) pôr de reserva, juntar, fazer provisão de; (in warehouse) armazenar. **be in ~** estar guardado. **have in ~ for** reservar para. **set ~ by** dar valor a. **~-room** n depósito m, almoxarifado m, (P) armazém m

storey /'stɔːrɪ/ n (pl -eys) andar m

stork /stɔːk/ n cegonha f

storm /stɔːm/ n tempestade f □ vt tomar de assalto □ vi enfurecer-se. **a ~ in a teacup** uma tempestade num copo de água. **~y** a tempestuoso

story /'stɔːrɪ/ n estória f, (P) história f; (in press) artigo m, matéria f; (Amer: storey) andar m; (colloq: lie) cascata f, (P) peta f

~-teller n contador m de estórias, (P) histórias

stout /staut/ a (-er, -est) (fat) gordo, corpulento; (strong, thick) resistente, sólido, grosso; (brave) resoluto □ n cerveja f preta forte

stove /stəuv/ n (for cooking) fogão m (de cozinha)

stow /stəu/ vt ~ (away) (put away) guardar, arrumar; (hide) esconder □ vi ~ away viajar clandestinamente

stowaway /'stəuəwei/ n passageiro m clandestino

straddle /'strædl/ vt (sit) escarranchar-se em, montar; (stand) pôr-se de pernas abertas sobre

straggle /'strægl/ vi (lag behind) desgarrar-se, ficar para trás; (spread) estender-se desordenadamente. **~r** /-ə(r)/ n retardatário m

straight /streit/ a (-er, -est) direito; (tidy) em ordem; (frank) franco, direto, (P) directo; (of hair) liso; (of drink) puro □ adv (in straight line) reto, (P) recto; (directly) direito, direto, (P) directo, diretamente, (P) directamente □ n linha f reta, (P) recta. **~ ahead** or **on** (sempre) em frente. **~ away** logo, imediatamente. **go ~** viver honestamente. **keep a ~ face** não se desmanchar, manter um ar sério

straighten /'streitn/ vt endireitar; (tidy) arrumar, pôr em ordem

straightforward /streit'fɔ:wəd/ a franco, sincero; (easy) simples

strain[1] /strein/ n (breed) raça f; (streak) tendência f, veia f

strain[2] /strein/ vt (rope) esticar, puxar; (tire) cansar; (filter) filtrar, passar; (vegetables, tea etc) coar; (med) distender, torcer; (fig) forçar, pôr à prova □ vi esforçar-se □ n tensão f; (fig: effort) esforço m; (med) distensão f. **~s** (music) melodias fpl.

one's ears apurar o ouvido. **~ed** a forçado; (relations) tenso. **~er** n coador m, (P) passador m

strait /streit/ n estreito m. **~s** estreito m; (fig) apuros mpl, dificuldades fpl. **~-jacket** n camisa-de-força f. **~-laced** a severo, puritano

strand /strænd/ n (thread) fio m; (lock of hair) mecha f, madeixa f

stranded /'strændid/ a (person) em dificuldades, deixado para trás, abandonado

strange /streindʒ/ a (-er, -est) estranho. **~ly** adv estranhamente. **~ness** n estranheza f

stranger /'streindʒə(r)/ n estranho m, desconhecido m

strangle /'strængl/ vt estrangular, sufocar

stranglehold /'strænglhəuld/ n **have a ~ on** ter domínio sobre

strangulation /strængju'leiʃn/ n estrangulamento m

strap /stræp/ n (of leather etc) correia f; (of dress) alça f; (of watch) pulseira f com correia □ vt (pt strapped) prender com correia

strapping /'stræpɪŋ/ a robusto, grande

strata /'streitə/ see stratum

stratagem /'strætədʒəm/ n estratagema m

strategic /strə'ti:dʒik/ a estratégico; (of weapons) de longo alcance

strategy /'strætədʒɪ/ n estratégia f

stratum /'strɑ:təm/ n (pl strata) estrato m, camada f

straw /strɔ:/ n palha f; (for drinking) canudo m, (P) palhinha f. **the last ~** a última gota f

strawberry /'strɔ:brɪ/ n (fruit) morango m; (plant) morangueiro m

stray /strei/ vi (deviate from path etc) extraviar-se, desencaminhar-se, afastar-se (from de); (lose one's way) perder-se; (wander) vagar, errar □ *a* perdido, extraviado; (*isolated*) isolado, raro, esporádico □ *n* animal *m* perdido *or* vadio

streak /striːk/ *n* risca *f*, lista *f*; (*strain*) veia *f*; (*period*) período *m*. **~ of lightning** relâmpago *m* □ *vt* listrar, riscar □ *vi* ir como um raio. **~er** *n* (*colloq*) pessoa *f* que corre nua em lugares públicos. **~y** *a* listrado, riscado. **~y bacon** toucinho *m* entremeado com gordura

stream /striːm/ *n* riacho *m*, córrego *m*, regato *m*; (*current*) corrente *f*; (*fig: flow*) jorro *m*, torrente *f*; (*schol*) nível *m* □ *vi* correr; (*of banner, hair*) flutuar; (*sweat*) escorrer; pingar

streamer /ˈstriːmə(r)/ *n* (*of paper*) serpentina *f*; (*flag*) flâmula *f*, bandeirola *f*

streamline /ˈstriːmlaɪn/ *vt* dar forma aerodinâmica a; (*fig*) racionalizar. **~d** *a* (*shape*) aerodinâmico

street /striːt/ *n* rua *f*. **the man in the** **~** (*fig*) o homem da rua. **~ lamp** poste *m* de iluminação

streetcar /ˈstriːtkɑː(r)/ *n* (*Amer*) bonde *m*, (*P*) carro *m* eléctrico

strength /streŋθ/ *n* força *f*; (*of wall*) solidez *f*; (*of fabric etc*) resistência *f*. **on the ~ of** à base de, em virtude de

strengthen /ˈstreŋθn/ *vt* fortificar, fortalecer, reforçar

strenuous /ˈstrenjʊəs/ *a* enérgico; (*arduous*) árduo, estrênuo, (*P*) estrénuo; (*tiring*) fatigante, esgotante. **~ly** *adv* esforçadamente, energicamente

stress /stres/ *n* acento *m*; (*pressure*) pressão *f*, tensão *f*; (*med*) stress *m* □ *vt* acentuar, sublinhar; (*sound*) acentuar. **~ful** *a* estressante

stretch /stretʃ/ *vt* (*pull taut*) esticar; (*arm, leg, neck*) estender, es-

ticar; (*clothes*) alargar; (*truth*) forçar, torcer □ *vi* estender-se; (*after sleep etc*) espreguiçar-se; (*of clothes*) alargar-se □ *n* extensão *f*, trecho *m*; (*period*) período *m*; (*of road*) troço *m* □ *a* (*of fabric*) com elasticidade. **at a ~** sem parar. **~ one's legs** esticar as pernas

stretcher /ˈstretʃə(r)/ *n* maca *f*, padiola *f*. **~-bearer** *n* padioleiro *m*, (*P*) maqueiro *m*

strew /struː/ *vt* (*pt* strewed, *pp* strewed *or* strewn) (*scatter*) espalhar; (*cover*) juncar, cobrir

stricken /ˈstrɪkən/ *a* **~ with** atacado *or* acometido de

strict /strɪkt/ *a* (-er, -est) estrito, rigoroso. **~ly** *adv* estritamente. **~ly speaking** a rigor. **~ness** *n* severidade *f*, rigor *m*

stride /straɪd/ *vi* (*pt* strode, *pp* stridden) caminhar a passos largos □ *n* passada *f*. **make great ~s** (*fig*) fazer grandes progressos. **take sth in one's ~** fazer algo coisa sem problemas

strident /ˈstraɪdnt/ *a* estridente

strife /straɪf/ *n* conflito *m* , dissensão *f*, luta *f*

strike /straɪk/ *vt* (*pt* struck) bater (em); (*blow*) dar; (*match*) riscar, acender; (*gold etc*) descobrir; (*of clock*) soar, dar, bater (horas); (*of lightning*) atingir □ *vi* fazer greve; (*attack*) atacar □ *n* (*of workers*) greve *f*; (*mil*) ataque *m*; (*find*) descoberta *f*. **on ~** em greve. **~ a bargain** fechar negócio. **~ off** *or* **out** riscar. **~ up** (*mus*) começar a tocar; (*friendship*) travar

striker /ˈstraɪkə(r)/ *n* grevista *mf*

striking /ˈstraɪkɪŋ/ *a* notável, impressionante; (*attractive*) atraente

string /strɪŋ/ *n* corda *f*, fio *m*; (*of violin, racket etc*) corda *f*; (*of pearls*) fio *m*; (*of onions, garlic*) réstia f; (of lies etc) série f; (row) fila f □ vt (pt **strung**) (thread) enfiar. **pull** ~**s** usar pistolão, (P) puxar os cordelinhos. ~ **out** espaçar-se. ~**ed** a (instrument) de cordas. ~**y** a filamentoso, fibroso; (meat) com nervos

stringent /ˈstrɪndʒənt/ a rigoroso, estrito

strip[1] /strɪp/ vt/i (pt **stripped**) (undress) despir(-se); (machine) desmontar; (deprive) despojar, privar. ~**per** n artista mf de strip-tease; (solvent) removedor m

strip[2] /strɪp/ n tira f; (of land) faixa f. ~ **comic** ~ história f em quadrinhos, (P) banda f desenhada. ~ **light** tubo m de luz fluorescente

stripe /straɪp/ n risca f, lista f, barra f. ~**d** a listrado, com listras

strive /straɪv/ vi (pt **strove**, pp **striven**) esforçar-se (**to** por)

strode /strəʊd/ see **stride**

stroke[1] /strəʊk/ n golpe m; (of pen) penada f, (P) traço m; (in swimming) braçada f; (in rowing) remada f; (med) ataque m, congestão f. ~ **of genius** rasgo m de genialidade. ~ **of luck** golpe m de sorte

stroke[2] /strəʊk/ vt (with hand) acariciar, fazer festas em

stroll /strəʊl/ vi passear, dar uma volta □ n volta f, (P) giro m. ~ **in/etc** entrar/etc tranquilamente

strong /strɒŋ/ a (-er, -est) forte; (shoes, fabric etc) resistente. **be a hundred/etc** ~ ser em número de cem/etc. ~**-box** n cofre-forte m. ~ **language** linguagem f grosseira, palavrões mpl. ~**-minded** a resoluto, firme. ~**-room** n casa-forte f. ~**ly** adv (greatly) fortemente, grandemente; (with energy) com força; (deeply) profundamente

stronghold /ˈstrɒŋhəʊld/ n fortaleza f, (fig) baluarte m, bastião m

strove /strəʊv/ see **strive**

struck /strʌk/ see **strike** □ a ~ **on** (sl) apaixonado por

structur|e /ˈstrʌktʃə(r)/ n estrutura f, (of building) edifício m, construção f. ~**al** a estrutural, de estrutura, de construção

struggle /ˈstrʌgl/ vi (to get free) debater-se; (contend) lutar; (strive) esforçar-se (**to** for por) □ n luta f; (effort) esforço m. **have a** ~ **to** ter dificuldade em. ~ **to one's feet** levantar-se a custo

strum /strʌm/ vt (pt **strummed**) (banjo etc) dedilhar

strung /strʌŋ/ see **string**

strut /strʌt/ n (support) suporte m, escora f □ vi (pt **strutted**) (walk) pavonear-se

stub /stʌb/ n (of pencil, cigarette) ponta f; (of tree) cepo m, toco m; (counterfoil) talão m, canhoto m □ vt (pt **stubbed**) ~ **one's toe** dar uma topada. ~ **out** esmagar

stubble /ˈstʌbl/ n (on chin) barba f por fazer; (of crop) restolho m

stubborn /ˈstʌbən/ a teimoso, obstinado. ~**ly** adv obstinadamente, teimosamente. ~**ness** n teimosia f, obstinação f

stubby /ˈstʌbɪ/ a (-ier, -iest) (finger) curto e grosso; (person) atarracado

stuck /stʌk/ see **stick**[2] □ a emperrado. ~**-up** a (colloq: snobbish) convencido, esnobe

stud[1] /stʌd/ n tacha f; (for collar) botão m de colarinho □ vt (pt **studded**) enfeitar com tachas. ~**ded with** salpicado de

stud[2] /stʌd/ n (horses) haras m. ~**-(-farm)** n coudelaria f. ~ **(-horse)** n garanhão m

student /ˈstjuːdnt/ n (univ) estudante mf, aluno m; (schol) aluno m □ a (life, residence) universitário

studied /'stʌdɪd/ a estudado

studio /'stju:dɪəʊ/ n (pl -os) estúdio m. ~ **flat** estúdio m

studious /'stju:dɪəs/ a (person) estudioso; (deliberate) estudado. ~**ly** adv (carefully) cuidadosamente

study /'stʌdɪ/ n estudo m; (office) escritório m □ vt/i estudar

stuff /stʌf/ n substância f, matéria f; (sl: things) coisa(s) f (pl) □ vt encher; (animal) empalhar; (cram) apinhar, encher ao máximo; (culin) rechear; (block up) entupir; (put) enfiar, meter. ~**ing** n enchimento m; (culin) recheio m

stuffy /'stʌfɪ/ a (-ier, -iest) abafado, mal arejado; (dull) enfadonho

stumble /'stʌmbl/ vi tropeçar. ~**e across** or **on** dar com, encontrar por acaso, topar com. ~**ing-block** n obstáculo m

stump /stʌmp/ n (of tree) cepo m, toco m; (of limb) coto m; (of pencil, cigar) ponta f

stumped /stʌmpt/ a (colloq: baffled) atrapalhado, perplexo

stun /stʌn/ vt (pt **stunned**) aturdir, estontear

stung /stʌŋ/ see **sting**

stunk /stʌŋk/ see **stink**

stunning /'stʌnɪŋ/ a atordoador; (colloq: delightful) fantástico, sensacional

stunt[1] /stʌnt/ vt (growth) atrofiar. ~**ed** a atrofiado

stunt[2] /stʌnt/ n (feat) façanha f, proeza f; (trick) truque m; (aviat) acrobacia f aérea. ~ **man** n dublê m, (P) duplo m

stupefy /'stju:pɪfaɪ/ vt estupefazer, (P) estupeficar

stupendous /stju:'pendəs/ a estupendo, assombroso, prodigioso

stupid /'stju:pɪd/ a estúpido, obtuso. ~**ity** /-'pɪdətɪ/ n estupidez f. ~**ly** adv estupidamente

stupor /'stju:pə(r)/ n estupor m, torpor m

sturdy /'stɜ:dɪ/ a (-ier, -iest) robusto, vigoroso, forte

stutter /'stʌtə(r)/ vi gaguejar □ n gagueira f, (P) gaguez f

sty /staɪ/ n (pigsty) pocilga f, chiqueiro m

stye /staɪ/ n (on eye) terçol m, terçolho m

styl|e /staɪl/ n estilo m; (fashion) moda f; (kind) género m, (P) gênero m, tipo m; (pattern) feitio m, modelo m □ vt (of design) desenhar, criar. **in** ~**e** (live) em grande estilo; (do things) com classe. ~**e sb's hair** fazer um penteado em alguém. ~**ist** n (of hair) cabeleireiro m

stylish /'staɪlɪʃ/ a elegante, na moda

stylized /'staɪlaɪzd/ a estilizado

stylus /'staɪləs/ n (pl -uses) (of record-player) agulha f, safira f

suave /swɑːv/ a polido, de fala mansa, (P) melifluo

sub- /sʌb/ pref sub-

subconscious /sʌb'kɒnʃəs/ a & n subconsciente (m)

subcontract /sʌbkən'trækt/ vt dar de subempreitada

subdivide /sʌbdɪ'vaɪd/ vt subdividir

subdue /səb'dju:/ vt (enemy, feeling) dominar, subjugar; (sound, voice) abrandar. ~**d** a (weak) submisso; (quiet) recolhido; (light) velado

subject[1] /'sʌbdʒɪkt/ a (state etc) dominado □ n sujeito m; (schol, univ) disciplina f, matéria f; (citizen) súdito m. ~-**matter** n conteúdo m, tema m, assunto m. ~ **to** sujeito a

subject[2] /səb'dʒekt/ vt submeter. ~**ion** /-kʃn/ n submissão f

subjective /sʌb'dʒektɪv/ a subjetivo, (P) subjectivo

subjunctive /səb'dʒʌŋktɪv/ a & n subjuntivo (m), (P) conjuntivo (m)

sublime /sə'blaɪm/ *a* sublime

submarine /sʌbmə'riːn/ *n* submarino *m*

submerge /səb'mɜːdʒ/ *vt* submergir □ *vi* submergir, mergulhar

submissive /səb'mɪsɪv/ *a* submisso

submit /səb'mɪt/ *vt/i* (*pt* **submitted**) submeter(-se) (**to** a); (*jur: argue*) alegar. **~ssion** /-'mɪʃn/ *n* submissão *f*

subnormal /sʌb'nɔːml/ *a* subnormal; (*temperature*) abaixo do normal

subordinate[1] /sə'bɔːdɪnət/ *a* subordinado, subalterno; (*gram*) subordinado □ *n* subordinado *m*, subalterno *m*

subordinate[2] /sə'bɔːdɪneɪt/ *vt* subordinar (**to** a)

subpoena /səb'piːnə/ *n* (*pl* **-as**) (*jur*) citação *f*, intimação *f*

subscribe /səb'skraɪb/ *vt/i* subscrever, contribuir (**to** para). **~ to** (*theory, opinion*) subscrever, aceitar; (*newspaper*) assinar. **~r** /-ə(r)/ *n* subscritor *m*, assinante *m*

subscription /səb'skrɪpʃn/ *n* subscrição *f*; (*to newspaper*) assinatura *f*

subsequent /'sʌbsɪkwənt/ *a* subseqüente, (*P*) subsequente, posterior. **~ly** *adv* subsequentemente, a seguir, posteriormente

subservient /səb'sɜːvɪənt/ *a* servil, subserviente

subside /səb'saɪd/ *vi* (*flood, noise etc*) baixar; (*land*) ceder, afundar; (*wind, storm, excitement*) abrandar. **~nce** /-əns/ *n* (*of land*) afundamento *m*

subsidiary /səb'sɪdɪərɪ/ *a* subsidiário □ *n* (*comm*) filial *f*, sucursal *f*

subsid|y /'sʌbsədɪ/ *n* subsídio *m*, subvenção *f*. **~ize** /-ɪdaɪz/ *vt* subsidiar, subvencionar

subsist /səb'sɪst/ *vi* subsistir.

~ on viver de. **~ence** *n* subsistência *f*. **~ence allowance** ajudas *fpl* de custo

substance /'sʌbstəns/ *n* substância *f*

substandard /sʌb'stændəd/ *a* de qualidade inferior

substantial /səb'stænʃl/ *a* substancial. **~ly** *adv* substancialmente

substantiate /səb'stænʃɪeɪt/ *vt* comprovar, fundamentar

substitut|e /'sʌbstɪtjuːt/ *n* (*person*) substituto *m*, suplente *mf* (**for** de); (*thing*) substituto *m* (**for** de) □ *vt* substituir (**for** por). **~ion** /-'tjuːʃn/ *n* substituição *f*

subterfuge /'sʌbtəfjuːdʒ/ *n* subterfúgio *m*

subtitle /'sʌbtaɪtl/ *n* subtítulo *m*

subtle /'sʌtl/ *a* (**-er**, **-est**) sutil, (*P*) subtil. **~ty** *n* sutileza *f*, (*P*) subtileza *f*

subtotal /'sʌbtəʊtl/ *n* soma *f* parcial

subtract /səb'trækt/ *vt* subtrair, diminuir. **~ion** /-kʃn/ *n* subtração *f*, diminuição *f*

suburb /'sʌbɜːb/ *n* subúrbio *m*, arredores *mpl*. **~an** /sə'bɜːbən/ *a* dos subúrbios, suburbano. **~ia** /sə'bɜːbɪə/ *n* (*pej*) os arredores

subver|t /səb'vɜːt/ *vt* subverter. **~sion** /-ʃn/ *n* subverção *f*. **~sive** /-sɪv/ *a* subversivo

subway /'sʌbweɪ/ *n* passagem *f* subterrânea; (*Amer: underground*) metropolitano *m*

succeed /sək'siːd/ *vi* ter bem sucedido, ter êxito. **~ in doing sth** conseguir fazer alg coisa □ *vt* (*follow*) suceder a. **~ing** *a* seguinte, sucessivo

success /sək'ses/ *n* sucesso *m*, êxito *m*

succession /sək'seʃn/ *n* sucessão *f*; (*series*) série *f*. **in ~** seguidos, consecutivos

successive /sək'sesɪv/ a sucessivo, consecutivo

successor /sək'sesə(r)/ n sucessor m

succinct /sək'sɪŋkt/ a sucinto

succulent /'sʌkjʊlənt/ a suculento

succumb /sə'kʌm/ vi sucumbir

such /sʌtʃ/ a & pron tal, semelhante, assim; (so much) tanto □ adv tanto. **~ a book**/etc un tal livro/etc or um livro/etc assim. **~ books**/etc tais livros/etc or livros/etc assim. **~ courage**/etc tanta coragem/etc. **~ a big house** uma casa tão grande. **as ~** como tal. **as ~ as** como, tal como. **there's no ~ thing** uma coisa dessa não existe. **~-and-such** a & pron tal e tal

suck /sʌk/ vt chupar; (breast) mamar. **~ in** or **up** (absorb) absorver, aspirar; (engulf) tragar. **~ up to** puxar o saco a (colloq). **~ one's thumb** chupar o dedo. **~er** n (sl: greenhorn) trouxa mf (collog); (bot) broto m

suckle /'sʌkl/ vt amamentar, dar de mamar a

suction /'sʌkʃn/ n sucção f

sudden /'sʌdn/ a súbito, repentino. **all of a ~** de repente, de súbito. **~ly** adv subitamente, repentinamente. **~ness** n subitaneidade f, brusquidão f

suds /sʌdz/ npl espuma f de sabão; (soapy water) água f de sabão

sue /su:/ vt (pres p **suing**) processar

suede /sweɪd/ n camurça f

suet /'su:ɪt/ n sebo m

suffer /'sʌfə(r)/ vt/i sofrer; (tolerate) tolerar, suportar. **~er** n sofredor m, o que sofre; (patient) doente mf, vítima f. **~ing** n sofrimento m

suffice /sə'faɪs/ vi bastar, chegar, ser suficiente

sufficien|t /sə'fɪʃnt/ a suficiente, bastante. **~cy** n suficiência f,

quantidade f suficiente. **~tly** adv suficientemente

suffix /'sʌfɪks/ n sufixo m

suffocat|e /'sʌfəkeɪt/ vt/i sufocar. **~ion** /-'keɪʃn/ n sufocação f, asfixia f. **~ing** a sufocante, asfixiante

sugar /'ʃʊgə(r)/ n açúcar m □ vt adoçar, pôr açúcar em. **~-bowl** n açucareiro m. **~-lump** n torrão m de açúcar, (P) quadradinho m de açúcar. **brown ~** açúcar m preto, (P) açúcar m amarelo. **~y** a açucarado; (fig: too sweet) delico-doce

suggest /sə'dʒest/ vt sugerir. **~ion** /-tʃn/ n sugestão f. **~ive** a sugestivo; (improper) brejeiro, picante. **be ~ive of** sugerir, fazer lembrar

suicid|e /'su:ɪsaɪd/ n suicídio m. **commit ~e** suicidar-se. **~al** /-'saɪdl/ a suicida

suit /su:t/ n terno m, (P) fato m; (woman's) costume m, (P) saia-casaco m; (cards) naipe m □ vt convir a; (of garment, style) ficar bem em; (adapt) adaptar. **follow ~** (fig) seguir o exemplo. **~ability** n (of action) conveniência f, oportunidade f; (of candidate) aptidão f. **~able** a conveniente, apropriado (**for** para). **~ably** adv convenientemente. **~ed a be ~ed to** ser feito para, servir para. **be well ~ed** (matched) combinar-se bem; (of people) ser o ideal

suitcase /'su:tkeɪs/ n mala f (de viagem)

suite /swi:t/ n (of rooms; mus) suite f, (P) suite f; (of furniture) mobília f

suitor /'su:tə(r)/ n pretendente m

sulk /sʌlk/ vi amuar, ficar emburrado. **~y** a amuado, emburrado (colloq)

sullen /'sʌlən/ a carrancudo

sulphur /'sʌlfə(r)/ n enxofre m.

~ic /-'fjʋərɪk/ *a* **~ic acid** ácido *m* sulfúrico

sultan /'sʌltən/ *n* sultão *m*

sultana /sʌl'ta:nə/ *n* (*fruit*) passa *f* branca, (P) sultana *f*

sultry /'sʌltrɪ/ *a,* (*-ier, -iest*) abafado, opressivo; (*fig*) sensual

sum /sʌm/ *n* soma *f*; (*amount of money*) soma *f*, quantia *f*, importância *f*; (*in arithmetic*) conta *f* □ *vt* (*pt* summed) somar. **~** up recapitular, resumir; (*assess*) avaliar, medir

summar|y /'sʌmərɪ/ *n* sumário *m*, resumo *m* □ *a* sumário. **~ize** *vt* resumir

summer /'sʌmə(r)/ *n* verão *m*, estio *m* □ *a* de verão. **~-time** *n* verão *m*, época *f* de verão. **~y** *a* estival, próprio de verão

summit /'sʌmɪt/ *n* cume *m*, cimo *m*. **~ conference** (*pol*) conferência *f* de cúpula, (P) reunião *f* de cimeira

summon /'sʌmən/ *vt* mandar chamar; (*to meeting*) convocar. **~ up** (*strength, courage etc*) chamar a si, fazer apelo a

summons /'sʌmənz/ *n* (*jur*) citação *f*, intimação *f* □ *vt* citar, intimar

sump /sʌmp/ *n* (*auto*) cárter *m*

sumptuous /'sʌmptʃʋəs/ *a* suntuoso, (P) sumptuoso, luxuoso

sun /sʌn/ *n* sol *m* □ *vt* (*pt* sunned) **~ o.s.** aquecer-se ao sol. **~glasses** *npl* óculos *mpl* de sol. **~-roof** *n* teto *m* solar. **~-tan** *n* bronzeado *m*. **~-tanned** *a* bronzeado. **~-tan oil** *n* óleo *m* de bronzear

sunbathe /'sʌnbeɪð/ *vi* tomar um banho de sol

sunburn /'sʌnbɜ:n/ *n* queimadura *f* de sol. **~t** *a* queimado pelo sol

Sunday /'sʌndɪ/ *n* domingo *m*. **~ school** catecismo *m*

sundial /'sʌndaɪəl/ *n* relógio *m* de sol

sundown /'sʌndaʊn/ *n* = **sunset**

sundr|y /'sʌndrɪ/ *a* vários, diversos. **~ies** *npl* artigos *mpl* diversos. **all ~y** todo o mundo

sunflower /'sʌnflaʊə(r)/ *n* girassol *m*

sung /sʌŋ/ *see* **sing**

sunk /sʌŋk/ *see* **sink**

sunken /'sʌŋkən/ *a* (*ship etc*) afundado; (*eyes*) fundo

sunlight /'sʌnlaɪt/ *n* luz *f* do sol, sol *m*

sunny /'sʌnɪ/ *a* (*-ier, -iest*) (*room, day etc*) ensolarado

sunrise /'sʌnraɪz/ *n* nascer *m* do sol

sunset /'sʌnset/ *n* pôr *m* do sol

sunshade /'sʌnʃeɪd/ *n* (*awning*) toldo *m*; (*parasol*) pára-sol *m*, (P) guarda-sol *m*

sunshine /'sʌnʃaɪn/ *n* sol *m*, luz *f* do sol

sunstroke /'sʌnstrəʊk/ *n* (*med*) insolação *f*

super /'su:pə(r)/ *a* (*colloq: excellent*) formidável

superb /su:'pɜ:b/ *a* soberbo, esplêndido

supercilious /su:pə'sɪlɪəs/ *a* (*haughty*) altivo; (*disdainful*) desdenhoso

superficial /su:pə'fɪʃl/ *a* superficial. **~ity** /-'ræltɪ/ *n* superficialidade *f*. **~ly** *adv* superficialmente

superfluous /su:'pɜ:flʋəs/ *a* supérfluo

superhuman /su:pə'hju:mən/ *a* sobre-humano

superimpose /su:pərɪm'pəʊz/ *vt* sobrepor (**on** a)

superintendent /su:pərɪn'tendənt/ *n* superintendente *m*; (*of police*) comissário *m*, chefe *m* de polícia

superior /su:'pɪərɪə(r)/ *a* & *n* superior (*m*). **~ity** /-'ɒrɪtɪ/ *n* superioridade *f*

superlative /suːˈpɜːlətɪv/ a supremo, superlativo □ n (gram) superlativo m

supermarket /ˈsuːpəmɑːkɪt/ n supermercado m

supernatural /suːpəˈnætʃrəl/ a sobrenatural

superpower /ˈsuːpəpaʊə(r)/ n superpotência f

supersede /suːpəˈsiːd/ vt suplantar, substituir

supersonic /suːpəˈsɒnɪk/ a supersónico, (P) supersónico

superstit|ion /suːpəˈstɪʃn/ n superstição f. **~ous** /-ˈstɪʃəs/ a supersticioso

superstore /ˈsuːpəstɔː(r)/ n hipermercado m

supertanker /ˈsuːpətæŋkə(r)/ n superpetroleiro m

supervis|e /ˈsuːpəvaɪz/ vt supervisar, fiscalizar. **~ion** /-ˈvɪʒn/ n supervisão f. **~or** n supervisor m; (shop) chefe m de secção; (firm) chefe mf de serviço. **~ory** /-ˈvaɪzəri/ a de supervisão

supper /ˈsʌpə(r)/ n jantar m; (late at night) ceia f

supple /ˈsʌpl/ a flexível, maleável

supplement[1] /ˈsʌplɪmənt/ n suplemento m. **~ary** /-ˈmentrɪ/ a suplementar

supplement[2] /ˈsʌplɪment/ vt suplementar

supplier /səˈplaɪə(r)/ n fornecedor m

suppl|y /səˈplaɪ/ vt suprir, prover; (comm) fornecer, abastecer □ n provisão f; (of goods, gas etc) fornecimento, abastecimento m □ a (teacher) substituto. **~ies** (food) víveres mpl; (mil) suprimentos mpl. **~y and demand** oferta e procura

support /səˈpɔːt/ vt (hold up, endure) suportar; (provide for) sustentar, suster; (back) apoiar, patrocinar; (sport) torcer por □

n apoio m; (techn) suporte m. **~er** n partidário m; (sport) torcedor m

suppos|e /səˈpəʊz/ vt/i supor. **~e that** supondo que, na hipótese de que. **~ed** a suposto. **he's ~ed to do** ele deve fazer; (believed to) consta que ele faz. **~edly** /-ɪdlɪ/ adv segundo dizem; (probably) supostamente, em princípio. **~ing** conj se. **~ition** /sʌpəˈzɪʃn/ n suposição f

suppress /səˈpres/ vt (put an end to) suprimir; (restrain) conter, reprimir; (stifle) abafar, sufocar; (psych) recalcar. **~ion** /-ʃn/ n supressão f; (restraint) repressão f; (psych) recalque m, (P) recalcamento m

suprem|e /suːˈpriːm/ a supremo. **~acy** /-eməsɪ/ n supremacia f

surcharge /ˈsɜːtʃɑːdʒ/ n sobretaxa f; (on stamp) sobrecarga f

sure /ʃʊə(r)/ a (-er, -est) seguro, certo □ adv (colloq: certainly) deveras, não há dúvida que, de certeza. **be ~ about** or of ter a certeza de. **be ~ to** (not fail) não deixar de. **he is ~ to find out** ele vai descobrir com certeza. **make ~** assegurar. **~ly** adv com certeza, certamente

surety /ˈʃʊərətɪ/ n (person) fiador m; (thing) garantia f

surf /sɜːf/ n (waves) ressaca f, rebentação f. **~er** n surfista mf. **~ing** n surfe m, (P) surf m, jacaré-na-praia m

surface /ˈsɜːfɪs/ n superfície f □ a superficial □ vt/i revestir; (rise, become known) emergir. **~ mail** via f marítima

surfboard /ˈsɜːfbɔːd/ n prancha f de surfe, (P) surf

surfeit /ˈsɜːfɪt/ n excesso m (of de)

surge /sɜːdʒ/ vi (waves) ondular, encapelar-se; (move forward) avançar □ n (wave) onda f, vaga f; (motion) arremetida f

surgeon /'sɜːdʒən/ n cirurgião m

surg|ery /'sɜːdʒərɪ/ n cirurgia f; (office) consultório m; (session) consulta f; (consulting hours) horas fpl de consulta. ~**ical** a cirúrgico

surly /'sɜːlɪ/ a (-ier, -iest) carrancudo, trombudo

surmise /sə'maɪz/ vt imaginar, supor, calcular □ n conjetura f, (P) conjectura f; hipótese f

surmount /sə'maʊnt/ vt sobrepujar, vencer, (P) superar

surname /'sɜːneɪm/ n sobrenome m, (P) apelido m

surpass /sə'pɑːs/ vt superar, ultrapassar, exceder

surplus /'sɜːpləs/ n excedente m, excesso m; (finance) saldo m positivo □ a excedente, em excesso

surpris|e /sə'praɪz/ n surpresa f □ vt surpreender. ~**ed** a surpreendido, admirado (**at** com). ~**ing** a surpreendente. ~**ingly** adv surpreendentemente

surrender /sə'rendə(r)/ vi render-se □ vt (hand over; mil) entregar □ n (mil) rendição f; (of rights) renúncia f

surreptitious /ˌsʌrep'tɪʃəs/ a sub-reptício, furtivo

surrogate /'sʌrəgeɪt/ n delegado m. ~ **mother** mãe f de aluguel, (P) aluguer

surround /sə'raʊnd/ vt rodear, cercar; (mil etc) cercar. ~**ing** a circundante, vizinho. ~**ings** npl arredores mpl; (setting) meio m, ambiente m

surveillance /sɜː'veɪləns/ n vigilância f

survey[1] /sə'veɪ/ vt (landscape etc) observar; (review) passar em revista; (inquire about) pesquisar; (land) fazer o levantamento de; (building) vistoriar, inspecionar, (P) inspeccionar. ~**or** n (of buildings) fiscal m; (of land) agrimensor m

survey[2] /'sɜːveɪ/ n (inspection) vistoria f, inspeção f, (P) inspecção f; (general view) panorâmica f; (inquiry) pesquisa f

survival /sə'vaɪvl/ n sobrevivência f; (relic) resíduo f, vestígio m

surviv|e /sə'vaɪv/ vt/i sobreviver (**a**). ~**or** n sobrevivente mf

susceptib|le /sə'septəbl/ a (prone) susceptível (**to** a); (sensitive, impressionable) susceptível, sensível. ~**ility** /-'bɪlətɪ/ n susceptibilidade f

suspect[1] /sə'spekt/ vt suspeitar; (doubt, distrust) desconfiar de, suspeitar de

suspect[2] /'sʌspekt/ a & n suspeito (m)

suspen|d /sə'spend/ vt (hang, stop) suspender; (from duty etc) suspender. ~**ded sentence** suspensão f de pena. ~**sion** n suspensão f. ~**sion bridge** ponte f suspensa or pênsil

suspender /sə'spendə(r)/ n (presilha de) liga f. ~ **belt** n cinta-liga f, (P) cinta f de ligas. ~**s** (Amer: braces) suspensórios mpl

suspense /sə'spens/ n ansiedade f, incerteza f; (in book etc) suspense m, tensão f

suspicion /sə'spɪʃn/ n suspeita f; (distrust) desconfiança f; (trace) vestígio m, (P) traço m

suspicious /səs'pɪʃəs/ a desconfiado; (causing suspicion) suspeito. **be ~ of** desconfiar de. ~**ly** adv de modo suspeito

sustain /sə'steɪn/ vt (support) suster, sustentar; (suffer) sofrer; (keep up) sustentar; (jur: uphold) sancionar; (interest, effort) manter. ~**ed effort** esforço m contínuo

sustenance /'sʌstɪnəns/ n (food) alimento m, sustento m

swagger /'swægə(r)/ vi pavonear-se, andar com arrogância

swallow[1] /'swɒləʊ/ vt/i engolir.

up (*absorb, engulf*) devorar, tragar

swallow[2] /'swɒləʊ/ *n* (*bird*) andorinha *f*

swam /swæm/ *see* **swim**

swamp /swɒmp/ *n* pântano *m*, brejo *m* □ *vt* (*flood, overwhelm*) inundar, submergir. **~y** *a* pantanoso

swan /swɒn/ *n* cisne *m*

swank /swæŋk/ *vi* (*colloq: show off*) gabar-se, mostrar-se (*colloq*)

swap /swɒp/ *vt/i* (*pt* **swapped**) (*colloq*) trocar (**for** por) □ *n* (*colloq*) troca *f*

swarm /swɔːm/ *n* (*of insects, people*) enxame *m* □ *vi* formigar. **~ into** *or* **round** invadir

swarthy /'swɔːðɪ/ *a* (**-ier, -iest**) moreno, trigueiro

swat /swɒt/ *vt* (*pt* **swatted**) (*fly etc*) esmagar, esborrachar

sway /sweɪ/ *vt/i* oscilar, balançar (-se); (*influence*) mover, influenciar □ *n* oscilação *f*, balanceio *m*; (*rule*) domínio *m*, poder *m*

swear /sweə(r)/ *vt/i* (*pt* **swore**, *pp* **sworn**) jurar; (*curse*) praguejar, rogar pragas (**at** contra). **~ by** jurar por; (*colloq: recommend*) ter grande fé em. **~-word** *n* palavrão *m*

sweat /swet/ *n* suor *m* □ *vi* suar. **~y** *a* suado

sweater /'swetə(r)/ *n* suéter *m*, (*P*) camisola *f*

sweatshirt /'swetʃɜːt/ *n* suéter *m* de malha *or* algodão

swede /swiːd/ *n* couve-nabo *f*

Swede /swiːd/ *n* sueco *m*. **~n** *n* Suécia *f*. **~ish** *a* & *n* sueco (*m*)

sweep /swiːp/ *vt/i* (*pt* **swept**) varrer; (*go majestically*) avançar majestosamente; (*carry away*) arrastar; (*chimney*) limpar □ *n* (*with broom*) varredela *f*; (*curve*) curva *f*; (*movement*) gesto *m* largo. (**chimney-**)**~** limpa-chaminés *m*. **~ing** *a* (*gesture*) largo;

(*action*) de grande alcance. **~ing statement** generalização *f* fácil

sweet /swiːt/ *a* (**-er, -est**) doce; (*colloq: charming*) doce, gracinha; (*colloq: pleasant*) agradável □ *n* doce *m*. **~ corn** milho *m*. **~ pea** ervilha-de-cheiro *f*. **~ shop** confeitaria *f*. **have a ~ tooth** gostar de doce. **~ly** *adv* docemente. **~ness** *n* doçura *f*

sweeten /'swiːtn/ *vt* adoçar; (*fig: mitigate*) suavizar. **~er** *n* (*for tea, coffee*) adoçante *m* (artificial); (*colloq: bribe*) agrado *m*

sweetheart /'swiːthaːt/ *n* namorado *m*, namorada *f*; (*term of endearment*) querido *m*, querida *f*, amor *m*

swell /swel/ *vt/i* (*pt* **swelled**, *pp* **swollen** *or* **swelled**) (*expand*) inchar; (*increase*) aumentar □ *n* (*of sea*) ondulação *f* □ *a* (*colloq: excellent*) excelente; (*colloq: smart*) chique. **~ing** *n* (*med*) inchação *f*, inchaço *m*

swelter /'sweltə(r)/ *vi* fazer um calor abrasador; (*person*) abafar (com calor)

swept /swept/ *see* **sweep**

swerve /swɜːv/ *vi* desviar-se, dar uma guinada

swift /swift/ *a* (**-er, -est**) rápido, veloz. **~ly** *adv* rapidamente. **~ness** *n* rapidez *f*

swig /swɪg/ *vt* (*pt* **swigged**) (*colloq: drink*) emborcar, beber em longos tragos □ *n* (*colloq*) trago *m*, gole *m*

swill /swɪl/ *vt* passar por água □ *n* (*pig-food*) lavagem *f*, (*P*) lavadura *f*

swim /swim/ *vi* (*pt* **swam**, *pp* **swum**, *pres p* **swimming**) nadar; (*room, head*) rodar □ *vt* atravessar a nado; (*distance*) nadar □ *n* banho *m*. **~mer** *n* nadador *m*. **~ming** *n* natação *f*. **~ming-bath**, **~ming-pool** *ns* piscina *f*.

~**ming-cap** n touca f de banho.
~**ming-costume**, ~**-suit** ns
maiô m, (P) fato m de banho.
~**ming-trunks** npl calção m de
banho

swindle /'swɪndl/ vt/i trapacear,
fraudar, (P) vigarizar □ n vigarice f. ~**r** /-ə(r)/ n vigarista mf

swine /swaɪn/ n (pl swine) (pigs) porcos
mpl □ n (pl invar) (colloq: person)
animal m, canalha m (colloq)

swing /swɪŋ/ vt/i (pt swung) balançar(-se); (turn round) balançar □
n (seat) balanço m; (of opinion)
reviravolta f; (mus) swing m;
(rhythm) ritmo m. in full ~ no
máximo, em plena atividade, (P)
actividade. ~ **round** (of person)
virar-se. ~**-bridge/door** ns
ponte f/porta f giratória

swipe /swaɪp/ vt (colloq: hit) bater
em, dar uma pancada em (colloq);
(colloq: steal) afanar, roubar
(colloq) □ n (colloq: hit) pancada
f (colloq). ~ **card** cartão m magnético

swirl /swɜːl/ vi rodopiar, redemoinhar □ n turbilhão m, redemoinho m

swish /swɪʃ/ vt/i sibilar, zunir, (fazer) cortar o ar; (with brushing
sound) roçar □ a (colloq) chique

Swiss /swɪs/ a & n suíço (m)

switch /swɪtʃ/ n interruptor m;
(change) mudança f □ vt (transfer) transferir; (exchange) trocar
□ vi desviar-se. ~ **off** desligar

switchboard /'swɪtʃbɔːd/ n (telephone) PBX m, mesa f telefônica

Switzerland /'swɪtsələnd/ n Suíça
f

swivel /'swɪvl/ vt/i (pt swivelled)
(fazer) girar. ~ **chair** cadeira f
giratória

swollen /'swəʊlən/ see swell □ a
inchado

swoop /swuːp/ vi (bird) lançar-se,
cair (**down on** sobre); (police) dar
uma batida policial, (P) rusga

sword /sɔːd/ n espada f

swore /swɔː(r)/ see swear

sworn /swɔːn/ see swear □ a (enemy) jurado, declarado; (ally) fiel

swot /swɒt/ vt/i (pt swotted) (colloq: study) estudar muito, (P)
marrar (sl) □ n (colloq) estudante m muito aplicado, (P) marrão m (sl)

swum /swʌm/ see swim

swung /swʌŋ/ see swing

sycamore /'sɪkəmɔː(r)/ n (maple)
sicômoro m, (P) sicómoro m;
(Amer: plane) plátano m

syllable /'sɪləbl/ n sílaba f

syllabus /'sɪləbəs/ n (pl -uses)
programa m

symbol /'sɪmbl/ n símbolo m.
~**ic(al)** /-'bɒlɪk(l)/ a simbólico.
~**ism** n simbolismo m

symbolize /'sɪmbəlaɪz/ vt simbolizar

symmetr|y /'sɪmətrɪ/ n simetria f.
~**ical** /sɪ'metrɪkl/ a simétrico

sympathize /'sɪmpəθaɪz/ vi ~
with ter pena de, condoer-se de;
(fig) compartilhar os sentimentos de. ~**r** n simpatizante mf

sympath|y /'sɪmpəθɪ/ n (pity)
pena f, compaixão f; (solidarity)
solidariedade f; (condolences) pêsames mpl, condolências fpl. be
in ~**y with** estar de acordo
com. ~**etic** /-'θetɪk/ a compreensivo, simpático; (likeable) simpático; (showing pity) compassivo.
~**etically** /-'θetɪklɪ/ adv compassivamente, (fig) compreensivamente

symphon|y /'sɪmfənɪ/ n sinfonia
f □ a sinfônico, (P) sinfónico.
~**ic** /-'fɒnɪk/ a sinfônico, (P) sinfónico

symptom /'sɪmptəm/ n sintoma
m. ~**atic** /-'mætɪk/ a sintomático (of de)

synagogue /'sɪnəgɒg/ n sinagoga f

synchronize /'sɪŋkrənaɪz/ vt sincronizar

syndicate /'sɪndɪkət/ n sindicato m

syndrome /'sɪndrəʊm/ n (med) síndrome m, (P) sindroma m

synonym /'sɪnənɪm/ n sinónimo m, (P) sinónimo m. ~ous /sɪ'nɒnɪməs/ a sinónimo, (P) sinónimo (with de)

synopsis /sɪ'nɒpsɪs/ n (pl -opses /-siːz/) sinopse f, resumo m

syntax /'sɪntæks/ n sintaxe f

synthesis /'sɪnθəsɪs/ n (pl -theses /-siːz/) síntese f

synthetic /sɪn'θetɪk/ a sintético

syphilis /'sɪfɪlɪs/ n sífilis f

Syria /'sɪrɪə/ n Síria f. ~n a & n sírio (m)

syringe /sɪ'rɪndʒ/ n seringa f □ vt seringar

syrup /'sɪrəp/ n (liquid) xarope m; (treacle) calda f de açúcar. ~y a (fig) melado, enjoativo

system /'sɪstəm/ n sistema m; (body) organismo m; (order) método m. ~atic /sɪstə'mætɪk/ a sistemático

T

tab /tæb/ n (flap) lingueta f; (for fastening, hanging) aba f; (label) etiqueta f; (loop) argola f; (Amer colloq: bill) conta f. **keep ~s on** (colloq) vigiar

table /'teɪbl/ n mesa f; (list) tabela f, lista f □ vt (submit) apresentar; (postpone) adiar. **at ~** à mesa. **lay** or **set the ~** pôr à mesa. **~ of contents** índice m (das matérias). **turn the ~s** inverter as posições. **~-cloth** n toalha de mesa f. **~-mat** n descanso m. **~ tennis** pingue-pongue m

tablespoon /'teɪblspuːn/ n colher f grande de sopa. **~ful** n (pl ~fuls) colher f de sopa cheia

tablet /'tæblɪt/ n (of stone) lápide f, placa f; (drug) comprimido m

tabloid /'tæblɔɪd/ n tablóide m. ~ **journalism** (pej) jornalismo m sensacionalista, imprensa f marron

taboo /tə'buː/ n & a tabu (m)

tacit /'tæsɪt/ a tácito

taciturn /'tæsɪtɜːn/ a taciturno

tack /tæk/ n (nail) tacha f; (stitch) ponto m de alinhavo; (naut) amura f; (fig: course of action) rumo m □ vt (nail) pregar com tachas; (stitch) alinhavar □ vi (naut) bordejar. **~ on** (add) acrescentar, juntar

tackle /'tækl/ n equipamento m, apetrechos mpl; (sport) placagem f □ vt (problem etc) atacar; (sport) placar; (a thief etc) agarrar-se a

tacky /'tækɪ/ a (-ier, -iest) pegajento, pegajoso

tact /tækt/ n tato m, (P) tacto m. ~**ful** a cheio de tato, (P) tacto, diplomático. ~**fully** adv com tato, (P) tacto. ~**less** a sem tato, (P) tacto. ~**lessly** adv sem tato, (P) tacto

tactic /'tæktɪk/ n (expedient) tática f, (P) táctica f. ~**s** n(pl) (procedure) tática f, (P) táctica f. ~**al** a tático, (P) táctico

tadpole /'tædpəʊl/ n girino m

tag /tæg/ n (label) etiqueta f; (on shoelace) agulheta f; (phrase) chavão m, clichê m □ vi (pt tagged) etiquetar; (add) juntar □ vi. **~ along** (colloq) andar atrás, seguir

Tagus /'teɪgəs/ n Tejo m

tail /teɪl/ n cauda f, rabo m; (of shirt) fralda f. ~**s!** (tossing coin) coroa! □ vt (follow) seguir, vigiar □ vi. **~ away** or **off** diminuir, baixar. **~-back** n (traffic) fila f, (P) bicha f. **~-end** n parte f traseira, cauda f. **~-light** n (auto) farolete m traseiro, (P) farolim m da rectaguarda

tailor /'teɪlə(r)/ n alfaiate m □ vt (garment) fazer; (fig: adapt) adaptar. **~-made** *a* feito sob medida, (P) por medida. **~-made for** (*fig*) feito para, talhado para

tainted /'teɪntɪd/ *a* (*infected*) contaminado; (*decayed*) estragado; (*fig*) manchado

take /teɪk/ *vt/i* (*pt* took, *pp* taken) (*get hold of*) agarrar em, pegar em; (*capture*) tomar; (*a seat, a drink; train, bus etc*) tomar; (*carry*) levar (to a, para); (*contain, escort*) levar; (*tolerate*) suportar, agüentar, (P) aguentar; (*choice, exam*) fazer; (*photo*) tirar; (*require*) exigir. **be ~n by** *or* **with** ficar encantado com. **be ~n ill** adoecer. **it ~s time** to leva tempo para. **~ after** parecer-se a. **~-away** *n* (*meal*) comida *f* para levar, take-away *m*; (*shop*) loja *f* que só vende comida para ser consumida em outro lugar. **~ away** levar. **~ away from sb/sth** tirar de alguém/ de alg coisa. **~ back** aceitar de volta; (*return*) devolver; (*accompany*) acompanhar; (*statement*) retirar, retratar. **~ down** (*object*) tirar para baixo; (*notes*) tirar, tomar. **~ in** (*garment*) meter para dentro; (*include*) incluir; (*cheat*) enganar, levar (*colloq*); (*grasp*) compreender; (*receive*) receber. **~ it that** supor que. **~ off** *vt* (*remove*) tirar; (*mimic*) imitar, macaquear □ *vi* (*aviat*) decolar, levantar vôo. **~-off** *n* imitação *f*; (*aviat*) descolagem *f*, (P) descolagem *f*. **~ on** (*task*) encarregar-se de; (*staff*) admitir, contratar. **~ out** tirar; (*on an outing*) levar para sair. **~ over** *vt* tomar conta de, assumir a direção, (P) direcção de □ *vi* tomar o poder. **~ over from** (*relieve*) render, substituir; (*succeed*) suceder a. **~-over** *n* (*pol*) tomada *f* de poder; (*comm*) take-

over *m*. **~ part** participar *or* tomar parte (**in** em). **~ place** ocorrer, suceder. **~ sides** tomar partido. **~ sides with** tomar o partido de. **~ to** gostar de, simpatizar com; (*activity*) tomar gosto por, entregar-se a. **~ up** (*object*) apanhar, pegar em; (*hobby*) dedicar-se a; (*occupy*) ocupar, tomar

takings /'teɪkɪŋz/ *npl* receita *f*

talcum /'tælkəm/ *n* talco *m*. **~ powder** pó *m* talco

tale /teɪl/ *n* conto *m*, história *f*

talent /'tælənt/ *n* talento *m*. **~ed** *a* talentoso, bem dotado

talk /tɔːk/ *vt/i* falar; (*chat*) conversar □ *n* conversa *f*; (*mode of speech*) fala *f*; (*lecture*) palestra *f*. **small ~** conversa *f* banal. **~ into doing** convencer a fazer. **~ nonsense** dizer disparates. **~ over** discutir. **~ shop** falar de assuntos profissionais. **~ to o.s.** falar sozinho, falar com os seus botões. **there's ~ of** fala-se de. **~-er** *n* conversador *m*. **~-ing-to** *n* (*colloq*) descompostura *f*

talkative /'tɔːkətɪv/ *a* falador, conversador, tagarela

tall /tɔːl/ *a* (**-er, -est**) alto. **~ story** (*colloq*) história *f* do arco-da-velha

tallboy /'tɔːlbɔɪ/ *n* cômoda *f*, (P) cómoda *f* alta

tally /'tælɪ/ *vi* corresponder (**with** a), conferir (**with** com)

tambourine /tæmbə'riːn/ *n* tamborim *m*, pandeiro *m*

tame /teɪm/ *a* (**-er, -est**) manso; (*domesticated*) domesticado; (*dull*) insípido □ *vt* amansar, domesticar

tamper /'tæmpə(r)/ *vi* **~ with** mexer indevidamente em; (*text*) alterar

tampon /'tæmpən/ *n* (*med*) tampão *m*; (*sanitary towel*) toalha *f* higiênica

tan /tæn/ *vt/i* (*pt* tanned) queimar, bronzear; (*hide*) curtir □ *n*
bronzeado *m* □ *a* castanho amarelado

tandem /'tændəm/ *n* (*bicycle*) tandem *m*. **in ~** em tandem, um
atrás do outro

tang /tæŋ/ *n* (*taste*) sabor *m* or
gosto *m* característico; (*smell*)
cheiro *m* característico

tangent /'tændʒənt/ *n* tangente *f*

tangerine /tændʒə'ri:n/ *n* tangerina *f*

tangible /'tændʒəbl/ *a* tangível

tangle /'tæŋgl/ *vt* emaranhar,
enredar □ *n* emaranhado *m*.
become ~d emaranhar-se, en-
redar-se

tank /tæŋk/ *n* tanque *m*, reservatório *m*; (*for petrol*) tanque *m*,
(*P*) depósito *m*; (*for fish*) aquário
m; (*mil*) tanque *m*

tankard /'tæŋkəd/ *n* caneca *f*
grande

tanker /'tæŋkə(r)/ *n* carro-tanque
m, camião-cisterna *m*; (*ship*) petroleiro *m*

tantaliz|e /'tæntəlaɪz/ *vt* atormen-
tar, tantalizar. **~ing** *a* tentador

tantamount /'tæntəmaʊnt/ *a* **be
~ to** equivaler a

tantrum /'tæntrəm/ *n* chilique *m*,
ataque *m* de mau génio, (*P*) génio, birra *f*

tap¹ /tæp/ *n* (*for water etc*) torneira *f* □ *vt* (*pt* tapped) (*resources*) explorar; (*telephone*)
grampear. **on ~** (*colloq: available*) disponível

tap² /tæp/ *vt/i* (*pt* tapped) bater
levemente. **~-dance** *n* sapateado
m

tape /teɪp/ *n* (*for dressmaking*)
fita *f*; (*sticky*) fita *f* adesiva. (**magnetic**) **~** fita *f* (magnética) □ *vt*
(*tie*) atar, prender; (*stick*) colar;
(*record*) gravar. **~-measure** *n*
fita *f* métrica. **~ recorder** gravador *m*

taper /'teɪpə(r)/ *n* vela *f* comprida
e fina □ *vt/i* **~ (off)** estreitar
(-se), afilar(-se). **~ed, ~ing** *adjs*
(*fingers etc*) afilado; (*trousers*)
afunilado

tapestry /'tæpɪstrɪ/ *n* tapeçaria *f*

tapioca /tæpɪ'əʊkə/ *n* tapioca *f*

tar /ta:(r)/ *n* alcatrão *m* □ *vt* (*pt
tarred*) alcatroar

target /'ta:gɪt/ *n* alvo *m* □ *vt* ter
como alvo

tariff /'tærɪf/ *n* tarifa *f*; (*on import*) direitos *mpl* aduaneiros

Tarmac /'ta:mæk/ *n* macadame
(alcatroado) *m*; (*runway*) pista *f*

tarnish /'ta:nɪʃ/ *vt/i* (fazer) perder
o brilho; (*stain*) manchar

tarpaulin /ta:'pɔ:lɪn/ *n* lona *f* impermeável (alcatroada or encera-
da) *f*

tart¹ /ta:t/ *a* (**-er, -est**) ácido; (*fig:
cutting*) mordaz, azedo

tart² /ta:t/ *n* (*culin*) torta *f* de fruta, (*P*) tarte *f*; (*sl: prostitute*) prostituta *f*, mulher *f* da vida (*sl*) □ *vt*
~ up (*collog*) embonecar(-se)

tartan /'ta:tn/ *n* tecido *m* escocês
□ *a* escocês

tartar /'ta:tə(r)/ *n* (*on teeth*) tártaro *m*, (*P*) pedra *f*. **~ sauce**
molho *m* tártaro

task /ta:sk/ *n* tarefa *f*, trabalho *m*.
take to ~ repreender, censurar.
~ force (*mil*) força-tarefa *f*

tassel /'tæsl/ *n* borla *f*

taste /teɪst/ *n* gosto *m*; (*fig: sample*) amostra *f* □ *vt* (*eat, enjoy*)
saborear; (*try*) provar; (*perceive
taste of*) sentir o gosto de □ *vi*
~ of or **like** ter o sabor de. **have
a ~ of** (*experience*) provar. **~-ful**
a de bom gosto. **~fully** *adv* com
bom gosto. **~less** *a* insípido, insosso; (*fig: not in good taste*) sem
gosto; (*fig: in bad taste*) de mau
gosto

tasty /'teɪstɪ/ *a* (**-ier, -iest**) saboroso, gostoso

tat /tæt/ *see* tit²

tatter|s /'tætəz/ npl farrapos mpl. **~ed** /-əd/ a esfarrapado

tattoo /tə'tu:/ vt tatuar □ n tatuagem f

tatty /'tætɪ/ a (-ier, -iest) (colloq) enxovalhado, em mau estado

taught /tɔ:t/ see teach

taunt /tɔ:nt/ vt escarnecer de, zombar de □ n escárnio m. **~ing** a escarninho

Taurus /'tɔ:rəs/ n (astr) Touro m, (P) Taurus m

taut /tɔ:t/ a esticado, retesado; (fig: of nerves) tenso

tawdry /'tɔ:drɪ/ a (-ier, -iest) espalhafatoso e ordinário

tawny /'tɔ:nɪ/ a fulvo

tax /tæks/ n taxa f, imposto m; (on income) imposto m de renda, (P) sobre o rendimento □ vt taxar, lançar impostos sobre, tributar; (fig: put to test) pôr à prova. **~collector** n cobrador m de impostos. **~free** a isento de imposto. **~ relief** isenção f de imposto. **~ return** declaração f do imposto de renda, (P) sobre o rendimento. **~ year** ano m fiscal. **~able** a tributável, passível de imposto. **~ation** /-'seɪʃn/ n impostos mpl, tributação f. **~ing** a penoso, difícil

taxi /'tæksɪ/ n (pl -is) táxi m □ vi (pt taxied, pres p taxiing) (aviat) rolar na pista, taxiar. **~cab** n táxi m. **~driver** n motorista mf de táxi. **~rank**, (Amer) **~ stand** ponto m de táxis, (P) praça f de táxis

taxpayer /'tækspeɪə(r)/ n contribuinte mf

tea /ti:/ n chá m. **high ~** refeição f leve à noite. **~bag** n saquinho m de chá. **~break** n intervalo m para o chá. **~cosy** n abafador m. **~leaf** n folha f de chá. **~set** n serviço m de chá. **~shop** n salão m or casa f de chá. **~-**

time n hora f do chá. **~towel** n pano m de prato

teach /ti:tʃ/ vt (pt taught) ensinar, lecionar, (P) leccionar (sb sth alg coisa a alguém) □ vi ensinar, ser professor. **~er** n professor m. **~ing** n ensino m; (doctrines) ensinamento(s) m (pl) □ a pedagógico, de ensino; (staff) docente

teacup /'ti:kʌp/ n xícara f de chá, (P) chávena f

teak /ti:k/ n teca f

team /ti:m/ n equipe f, (P) equipa f; (of oxen) junta f, (of horses) parelha f □ vi **~ up** juntar-se, associar-se (with a). **~work** n trabalho m de equipe, (P) equipa f

teapot /'ti:pɒt/ n bule m

tear¹ /teə(r)/ vt/i (pt tore, pp torn) rasgar(-se); (snatch) arrancar, puxar; (rush) lançar-se, ir numa correria; (fig) dividir □ n rasgão m. **~ o.s. away** arrancar-se (from de)

tear² /tɪə(r)/ n lágrima f. **~gas** n gases mpl lacrimogênios, (P) lacrimogéneos

tearful /'tɪəfl/ a lacrimoso, choroso. **~ly** adv choroso, com (as) lágrimas nos olhos

tease /ti:z/ vt implicar; (make fun of) caçoar de

teaspoon /'ti:spu:n/ n colher f de chá. **~ful** n (pl -fuls) colher f de chá cheia

teat /ti:t/ n (of bottle) bico m; (of animal) teta f

technical /'teknɪkl/ a técnico. **~ity** /-'kælətɪ/ n questão f de ordem técnica. **~ly** adv tecnicamente

technician /tek'nɪʃn/ n técnico m

technique /tek'ni:k/ n técnica f

technology /tek'nɒlədʒɪ/ n tecnologia f. **~ical** /-ə'lɒdʒɪkl/ a tecnológico

teddy /'tedɪ/ a **~ (bear)** ursinho m de pelúcia, (P) peluche

tedious /ˈtiːdɪəs/ a maçante

tedium /ˈtiːdɪəm/ n tédio m

tee /tiː/ n (golf) tee m

teem[1] /tiːm/ vi ~ (with) (swarm) pulular (de), fervilhar (de), abundar (em)

teem[2] /tiːm/ vi ~ (with rain) chover torrencialmente

teenage /ˈtiːneɪdʒ/ a juvenil, de/para adolescente. ~r /-ə(r)/ n jovem mf, adolescente mf

teens /tiːnz/ npl in one's ~ na adolescência, entre os 13 e os 19 anos

teeter /ˈtiːtə(r)/ vi cambalear

teeth /tiːθ/ see tooth

teeth|e /tiːð/ vi começar a ter dentes. ~ing troubles (fig) problemas mpl iniciais

teetotaller /tiːˈtəʊtlə(r)/ n abstémio m, (P) abstémio m

telecommunications /telɪkəmjuːnɪˈkeɪʃnz/ npl telecomunicações fpl

telegram /ˈtelɪɡræm/ n telegrama m

telegraph /ˈtelɪɡrɑːf/ n telégrafo m □ a telegráfico. ~ic /-ˈɡræfɪk/ a telegráfico

telepathy /tɪˈlepəθɪ/ n telepatia f. ~ic /telɪˈpæθɪk/ a telepático

telephone /ˈtelɪfəʊn/ n telefone m □ vt (person) telefonar a; (message) telefonar □ vi telefonar. ~book lista f telefónica, (P) telefónica, guia m telefónico, (P) telefónico. ~box, ~booth cabine f telefónica, (P) telefónica. ~call chamada f. ~directory lista f telefónica, (P) telefónica, guia m telefónico, (P) telefónico. ~number número m de telefone

telephonist /tɪˈlefənɪst/ n (in exchange) telefonista mf

telephoto /telɪˈfəʊtəʊ/ n ~lens teleobjetiva f, (P) teleobjectiva f

telescop|e /ˈtelɪskəʊp/ n telescópio m □ vt/i encaixar(-se). ~ic /-ˈskɒpɪk/ a telescópico

teletext /ˈtelɪtekst/ n teletexto m

televise /ˈtelɪvaɪz/ vt televisionar

television /ˈtelɪvɪʒn/ n televisão f. ~set aparelho m de televisão, televisor m

teleworking /ˈtelɪwɜːkɪŋ/ n teletrabalho m

telex /ˈteleks/ n telex m □ vt transmitir por telex, telexar

tell /tel/ vt (pt told) dizer (sb sth alg coisa a alguém); (story) contar; (distinguish) distinguir, diferençar □ vi (know) ver-se, saber. I told you so bem lhe disse. ~ off talar de. ~ off (colloq: scold) ralhar, dar uma bronca em. ~ on (have effect on) afetar, (P) afectar; (colloq: inform on) fazer queixa de (colloq). ~tale n mexeriqueiro m, fofoqueiro m □ a (revealing) revelador. ~tales mexericar, fofocar

telly /ˈtelɪ/ n (colloq) TV f (colloq)

temp /temp/ n (colloq) empregado m temporário

temper /ˈtempə(r)/ n humor m, disposição f; (anger) mau humor m □ vt temperar. keep/lose one's ~ manter a calma/perder a calma or a cabeça, zangar-se

temperament /ˈtemprəmənt/ n temperamento m. ~al /-ˈmentl/ a caprichoso

temperance /ˈtempərəns/ n (in drinking) sobriedade f

temperate /ˈtempərət/ a moderado, comedido; (climate) temperado

temperature /ˈtemprətʃə(r)/ n temperatura f. have a ~ estar com or ter febre

tempest /ˈtempɪst/ n tempestade f, temporal m

tempestuous /temˈpestʃʊəs/ a tempestuoso

template /ˈtempl(e)ɪt/ n molde m

temple[1] /ˈtempl/ n templo m

temple[2] /ˈtempl/ n (anat) têmpora f, fonte f

tempo /'tempəʊ/ n (pl -os) (mus) tempo m; (pace) ritmo m

temporar|y /'temprəri/ a temporário, provisório. **~ily** adv temporariamente, provisoriamente

tempt /tempt/ vt tentar. **~ sb to do** dar a alguém vontade de fazer, tentar alguém a fazer. **~ation** /-'teɪʃn/ n tentação f. **~ing** a tentador

ten /ten/ a & n dez (m)

tenac|ious /tɪ'neɪʃəs/ a tenaz. **~ity** /-'æsətɪ/ n tenacidade f

tenant /'tenənt/ n inquilino m, locatário m

tend[1] /tend/ vt tomar conta de, cuidar de

tend[2] /tend/ vi **~ to** (be apt to) tender a, ter tendência para

tendency /'tendənsɪ/ n tendência f

tender[1] /'tendə(r)/ a (soft, delicate) terno; (sore, painful) sensível, dolorido; (loving) terno, meigo. **~-hearted** a compassivo. **~ly** adv (lovingly) ternamente, meigamente; (delicately) delicadamente. **~ness** n (love) ternura f, meiguice f

tender[2] /'tendə(r)/ vt (money) oferecer; (apologies, resignation) apresentar □ vi **~ (for)** apresentar orçamento (para) □ n (comm) orçamento m. **legal ~** (money) moeda f corrente

tendon /'tendən/ n tendão m

tenement /'tenəmənt/ n prédio m de apartamentos de renda moderada; (Amer: slum) prédio m pobre

tenet /'tenɪt/ n princípio m, dogma m

tennis /'tenɪs/ n tênis m, (P) ténis m. **~ court** quadra f de tênis, (P) court m de ténis

tenor /'tenə(r)/ n (meaning) teor m; (mus) tenor m

tense[1] /tens/ n (gram) tempo m

tense[2] /tens/ a (-er, -est) tenso □ vt (muscles) retesar

tension /'tenʃn/ n tensão f

tent /tent/ n tenda f, barraca f. **~-peg** n estaca f

tentacle /'tentəkl/ n tentáculo m

tentative /'tentətɪv/ a provisório; (hesitant) hesitante. **~ly** adv tentativamente, a título experimental; (hesitantly) hesitantemente

tenterhooks /'tentəhʊks/ npl **on ~** em suspense

tenth /tenθ/ a & n décimo (m)

tenuous /'tenjʊəs/ a tênue, (P) ténue

tepid /'tepɪd/ a tépido, morno

term /tɜːm/ n (word) termo m; (limit) prazo m, termo m; (sch etc) período m, trimestre m; (Amer) semestre m; (of imprisonment) (duração de) pena f. **~s** (conditions) condições fpl □ vt designar, denominar, chamar. **on good/bad ~s** de boas/más relações. **not on speaking ~s** de relações cortadas. **come to ~s** with chegar a um acordo com; (become resigned to) resignar-se a. **~ of office** (pol) mandato m

terminal /'tɜːmɪnl/ a terminal, final; (illness) fatal, mortal □ n (oil, computer) terminal m; (rail) estação f terminal; (electr) borne m. **(air)** ~ terminal m (de avião)

terminat|e /'tɜːmɪnet/ vt terminar, pôr termo a □ vi terminar. **~ion** /-'neɪʃn/ n término m, (P) terminação f, termo m

terminology /tɜːmɪ'nɒlədʒɪ/ n terminologia f

terminus /'tɜːmɪnəs/ n (pl -ni /-naɪ/) (rail, coach) estação f terminal

terrace /'terəs/ n terraço m; (in cultivation) socalco m; (houses) casas fpl em fileira contínua, lance m de casas. **the ~s** (sport) arquibancada f. **~d house** casa f ladeada por outras casas

terrain /teˈreɪn/ n terreno m

terribl|e /ˈterəbl/ a terrível. ~**y**
adv terrivelmente; (colloq: very)
extremamente, espantosamente

terrific /təˈrɪfɪk/ a terrífico, tremendo; (colloq: excellent; great)
tremendo. ~**ally** adv (colloq:
very) tremendamente (colloq);
(colloq: very well) lindamente,
maravilhosamente

terrif|y /ˈterɪfaɪ/ vt aterrar,
aterrorizar. be ~**ied of** ter pavor
de

territorial /terɪˈtɔːrɪəl/ a territorial

territory /ˈterɪtərɪ/ n território m

terror /ˈterə(r)/ n terror m, pavor
m

terroris|t /ˈterərɪst/ n terrorista
mf. ~**m** /-zəm/ n terrorismo m

terrorize /ˈterəraɪz/ vt aterrorizar, aterrar

terse /tɜːs/ a conciso, lapidar;
(curt) lacônico, (P) lacónico

test /test/ n teste m, exame m, prova f; (schol) prova f, teste m; (of
goods) controle m; (of machine
etc) ensaio m; (of strength) prova
f □ vt examinar; (check) controlar; (try) ensaiar; (pupil) interrogar. **put to the** ~ pôr à
prova. ~ **match** jogo m internacional. ~-**tube** n proveta f.
~-**tube baby** bebê m de proveta

testament /ˈtestəmənt/ n testamento m. **Old/New T**~ Anti-
go/Novo Testamento m

testicle /ˈtestɪkl/ n testículo m

testify /ˈtestɪfaɪ/ vt/i testificar, testemunhar, depôr

testimonial /testɪˈməʊnɪəl/ n carta f de recomendação

testimony /ˈtestɪmənɪ/ n testemunho m

tetanus /ˈtetənəs/ n tétano m

tether /ˈteðə(r)/ vt prender com
corda □ n **be at the end of one's**
~ estar nas últimas

text /tekst/ n texto m. ~ **message**

mensagem f escrita □ vt enviar
um mensagem de texto a

textbook /ˈtekstbʊk/ n compêndio
m, manual m, livro m de texto

textile /ˈtekstaɪl/ n & a têxtil (m)

texture /ˈtekstʃə(r)/ n (of fabric)
textura f; (of paper) grão m

Thai /taɪ/ a & n tailandês (m). ~-
land n Tailândia f

Thames /temz/ n Tâmisa m

than /ðæn/; unstressed /ðən/ conj
que, do que; (with numbers) de.
more/less ~ **ten** mais/menos
de dez

thank /θæŋk/ vt agradecer. ~
you! obrigado! ~**s!** (colloq) (P)
obrigadinho! (colloq). ~**s** npl
agradecimentos mpl. ~**s to** graças a. **T**~**sgiving (Day)** (Amer)
Dia m de Ação, (P) Acção de Graças

thankful /ˈθæŋkfl/ a grato, agradecido, reconhecido (**for** por).
~**ly** adv com gratidão; (happily)
felizmente

thankless /ˈθæŋklɪs/ a ingrato

that /ðæt/; unstressed /ðət/ a &
pron (pl **those**) esse/essa, esses/
essas; (more distant) aquele/
aquela, aqueles/aquelas; (neuter)
isso invar; (more distant) aquilo
invar □ adv tão, tanto, de tal
modo □ rel pron que □ conj que.
~ **boy** esse/aquele rapaz. **what
is** ~? o que é isso? **who is** ~?
quem é? **is** ~ **you?** é você? **give
me** ~ (**one**) dá-me esse. ~ **is** (to
say) isto é, quer dizer. **after** ~
depois disso. **the day** ~ o dia em
que. ~ **much** tanto assim, tanto
como isto

thatch /θætʃ/ n colmo m. ~**ed** a
de colmo. ~**ed cottage** casa f
com telhado de colmo

thaw /θɔː/ vt/i derreter(-se), degelar; (food) descongelar □ n dege-
lo m, derretimento m

the /before vowel ðɪ, before consonant ðə, stressed ðiː/ a o, a (pl

os, as). **of** ~, **from** ~ do, da (*pl* dos, das). **at** ~, **to** ~ ao, à (*pl* aos, às), para o/a/os/as. **in** ~ no, na (*pl* nos, nas). **by** ~ **hour** a cada hora □ *adv* **all** ~ **better** tanto melhor. ~ **more...** ~ **more...** quanto mais... tanto mais...

theatre /'θɪətə(r)/ *n* teatro *m*

theatrical /θɪ'ætrɪkl/ *a* teatral

theft /θeft/ *n* roubo *m*

their /ðeə(r)/ *a* deles, delas, seu

theirs /ðeəz/ *poss pron* o(s) seu(s), a(s) sua(s), o(s) deles, a(s) delas. **it is** ~ é (o) deles/delas *or* o seu

them /ðem/; *unstressed* /ðəm/ *pron* os, as; (*after prep*) eles, elas. **(to)** ~ lhes

theme /θi:m/ *n* tema *m*. ~ **park** parque *m* temático

themselves /ðəm'selvz/ *pron* eles mesmos/próprios, elas mesmas/próprias; (*reflexive*) se; (*after prep*) si (mesmos, próprios). **by** ~ sozinhos. **with** ~ consigo

then /ðen/ *adv* (*at that time*) então, nessa altura; (*next*) depois, em seguida; (*in that case*) então, nesse caso; (*therefore*) então, portanto, por conseguinte

theology /θɪ'ɒlədʒɪ/ *n* teologia *f*. ~**ian** /θɪə'lɒdʒən/ *n* teólogo *m*

theorem /'θɪərəm/ *n* teorema *m*

theory /'θɪərɪ/ *n* teoria *f*. ~**etical** /-'retɪkl/ *a* teórico

therapeutic /θerə'pju:tɪk/ *a* terapêutico

therapy /'θerəpɪ/ *n* terapia *f*. ~**ist** *n* terapeuta *mf*

there /ðeə(r)/ *adv* aí, ali, lá; (*over there*) lá, acolá □ *int* (*triumphant*) pronto, aí está; (*consoling*) então, vamos lá. **he goes** ~ ele vai aí *or* lá. ~ **he goes** aí vai ele. ~ **is**, ~ **are** há. ~ **you are** (*giving*) toma, ~ **and then** logo ali. ~**abouts** *adv* por aí. ~**after** *adv* daí em diante, depois disso. ~**by** *adv* desse modo

therefore /'ðeəfɔ:(r)/ *adv* por isso, portanto, por conseguinte

thermal /'θɜ:ml/ *a* térmico

thermometer /θə'mɒmɪtə(r)/ *n* termômetro *m*, (*P*) termómetro *m*

Thermos /'θɜ:məs/ *n* garrafa *f* térmica, (*P*) termo *m*

thermostat /'θɜ:məstæt/ *n* termostato *m*

thesaurus /θɪ'sɔ:rəs/ *n* (*pl* -ri /-raɪ/) dicionário *m* de sinónimos, (*P*) sinónimos

these /ði:z/ *see* this

thesis /'θi:sɪs/ *n* (*pl* theses /-si:z/) tese *f*

they /ðeɪ/ *pron* eles, elas. ~ **say (that)...** diz-se *or* dizem que...

thick /θɪk/ *a* (-**er**, -**est**) espesso, grosso; (*colloq: stupid*) estúpido □ *adv* = **thickly** □ *n* **in the** ~ **of** no meio de. ~-**skinned** *a* insensível. ~**ly** *adv* espessamente; (*spread*) em camada espessa. ~**ness** *n* espessura *f*, grossura *f*

thicken /'θɪkən/ *vt/i* engrossar, espessar(-se). **the plot** ~**s** o enredo complica-se

thickset /θɪk'set/ *a* (*person*) atarracado

thief /θi:f/ *n* (*pl* thieves /θi:vz/) ladrão *m*, gatuno *m*

thigh /θaɪ/ *n* coxa *f*

thimble /'θɪmbl/ *n* dedal *m*

thin /θɪn/ *a* (**thinner**, **thinnest**) (*slender*) estreito, fino, delgado; (*lean, not plump*) magro; (*sparse*) ralo, escasso; (*flimsy*) leve, fino; (*soup*) aguado; (*hair*) ralo □ *adv* = **thinly** □ *vt/i* (*pt* **thinned**) (*of liquid*) diluir(-se); (*of fog etc*) dissipar(-se); (*of hair*) rarear. ~ **out** (*in quantity*) diminuir, reduzir; (*seedlings etc*) desbastar. ~**ly** *adv* (*sparsely*) esparsamente. ~**ness** *n* (*of board, wire etc*) finura *f*; (*of person*) magreza *f*

thing /θɪŋ/ *n* coisa *f*. ~**s** (*belongings*) pertences *mpl*. **the best** ~

is to o melhor é. **for one** ~ em primeiro lugar. **just the** ~ exatamente o que era preciso. **poor** ~ coitado

think /θɪŋk/ *vt/i* (*pt* **thought**) pensar (**about, of** em); (*carefully*) reflectir, (*P*) reflectir (**about, of** em). **I** ~ **so** eu acho que sim. ~ **better of it** (*change one's mind*) pensar melhor. ~ **nothing of** achar natural. ~ **of** (*hold opinion of*) pensar de, achar de. ~ **over** pensar bem em. ~**-tank** *n* comissão *f* de peritos. ~ **up** inventar. ~**er** *n* pensador *m*

third /θɜːd/ *a* terceiro □ *n* terceiro *m*; (*fraction*) terço *m*. ~**-party insurance** seguro *m* contra terceiros. ~**-rate** *a* inferior, medíocre. **T**~ **World** Terceiro Mundo *m*. ~**ly** *adv* em terceiro lugar

thirst /θɜːst/ *n* sede *f*. ~**y** *a* sequioso, sedento. **be** ~**y** estar com *or* ter sede. ~**ily** *adv* sofregamente

thirteen /θɜːˈtiːn/ *a & n* treze (*m*). ~**th** *a & n* décimo terceiro (*m*)

thirt|**y** /ˈθɜːtɪ/ *a & n* trinta (*m*). ~**ieth** *a & n* trigésimo (*m*)

this /ðɪs/ *a & pron* (*pl* **these**) este, esta □ *pron* isto *invar*. ~ **one** este, esta. **these ones** estes, estas. ~ **boy** este rapaz. ~ **is** isto é. **after** ~ depois disto. **like** ~ assim. ~ **is the man** este é o homem. ~ **far** até aqui. ~ **morning** esta manhã. ~ **Wednesday** esta quarta-feira

thistle /ˈθɪsl/ *n* cardo *m*

thorn /θɔːn/ *n* espinho *m*, pico *m*. ~**y** *a* espinhoso; (*fig*) bicudo, espinhoso

thorough /ˈθʌrə/ *a* consciencioso; (*deep*) completo, profundo; (*cleaning, washing*) a fundo. ~**ly** *adv* (*clean, study etc*) completo, a fundo; (*very*) perfeitamente, muito bem

thoroughbred /ˈθʌrəbred/ *n* (*horse etc*) puro-sangue *m invar*

thoroughfare /ˈθʌrəfeə(r)/ *n* artéria *f*. **no** ~ passagem *f* proibida

those /ðəʊz/ *see* **that**

though /ðəʊ/ *conj* se bem que, embora, conquanto □ *adv* (*colloq*) contudo, no entanto

thought /θɔːt/ *see* **think** □ *n* pensamento *m*; idéia *f*. **on second** ~**s** pensando bem

thoughtful /ˈθɔːtfl/ *a* pensativo; (*considerate*) atencioso, solícito. ~**ly** *adv* pensativamente; (*considerately*) com consideração, atenciosamente

thoughtless /ˈθɔːtlɪs/ *a* irrefletido, (*P*) irreflectido; (*inconsiderate*) pouco atencioso. ~**ly** *adv* sem pensar; (*inconsiderately*) sem consideração

thousand /ˈθaʊznd/ *a & n* mil (*m*). ~**s of** milhares de. ~**th** *a & n* milésimo (*m*)

thrash /θræʃ/ *vt* surrar, espancar; (*defeat*) dar uma surra *or* sova em. ~ **about** debater-se. ~ **out** debater a fundo, discutir bem

thread /θred/ *n* fio *m*; (*for sewing*) linha *f* de coser; (*of screw*) rosca *f* □ *vt* enfiar. ~ **one's way** abrir caminho, furar

threadbare /ˈθredbeə(r)/ *a* puído, surrado

threat /θret/ *n* ameaça *f*

threaten /ˈθretn/ *vt/i* ameaçar. ~**ingly** *adv* com ar ameaçador, ameaçadoramente

three /θriː/ *a & n* três (*m*)

thresh /θreʃ/ *vt* (*corn etc*) malhar, debulhar

threshold /ˈθreʃəʊld/ *n* limiar *m*, soleira *f*; (*fig*) limiar *m*

threw /θruː/ *see* **throw**

thrift /θrɪft/ *n* economia *f*, poupança *f*. ~**y** *a* econômico, (*P*) económico, poupado

thrill /θrɪl/ *n* arrepio *m* de emoção, frêmito *m*, (*P*) frémito *m* □

excitar(-se), emocionar(-se), (fazer) vibrar. **be ~ed** estar/ficar encantado. **~ing** *a* excitante, emocionante

thriller /'θrɪlə(r)/ *n* livro *m* or filme *m* de suspense

thriv|e /θraɪv/ *vi* (*pt* **thrived** *or* **throve**, *pp* **thrived** *or* **thriven**) prosperar, florescer; (*grow strong*) crescer, dar-se bem (*on* com). **~ing** *a* próspero

throat /θrəʊt/ *n* garganta *f*. **have a sore ~** ter dores de garganta

throb /θrɒb/ *vi* (*pt* **throbbed**) (*wound, head*) latejar; (*heart*) palpitar, bater; (*engine; fig*) vibrar, trepidar □ *n* (*of pain*) latejo *m*, espasmo *m*; (*of heart*) palpitação *f*, batida *f*; (*of engine*) vibração *f*, trepidação *f*. **~bing** *a* (*pain*) latejante

throes /θrəʊz/ *npl* **in the ~ of** (*fig*) às voltas com, no meio de

thrombosis /θrɒm'bəʊsɪs/ *n* trombose *f*

throne /θrəʊn/ *n* trono *m*

throng /θrɒŋ/ *n* multidão *f* □ *vt/i* apinhar(-se); (*arrive*) afluir

throttle /'θrɒtl/ *n* (*auto*) válvula-borboleta *f*, estrangulador *m*, acelerador de mão □ *vt* estrangular

through /θru:/ *prep* através de, por; (*during*) durante; (*by means or way of, out of*) por; (*by reason of*) por, por causa de □ *adv* através; (*entirely*) completamente, até o fim □ *a* (*train, traffic etc*) direto, (*P*) directo. **be ~** ter acabado (**with** com); (*telephone*) estar ligado. **come** *or* **go ~** (*cross, pierce*) atravessar. **~** (*exam*) passar. **be wet ~** estar ensopado or encharcado

throughout /θru:'aʊt/ *prep* durante, por todo. **~ the country** por todo o país afora. **~ the day** durante todo o dia, pelo dia afora

□ *adv* completamente; (*place*) por toda a parte; (*time*) durante todo o tempo

throw /θrəʊ/ *vt* (*pt* **threw**, *pp* **thrown**) atirar, jogar, lançar; (*colloq: baffle*) desconcertar □ *n* lançamento *m*; (*of dice*) lance *m*. **~ a party** (*colloq*) dar uma festa. **~ away** jogar fora, (*P*) deitar fora. **~ off** (*get rid of*) livrar-se de. **~ out** (*person*) expulsar; (*reject*) rejeitar. **~ over** (*desert*) abandonar, deixar. **~ up** (*one's arms*) levantar; (*resign from*) abandonar; (*colloq: vomit*) vomitar

thrush /θrʌʃ/ *n* (*bird*) tordo *m*

thrust /θrʌst/ *vt* (*pt* **thrust**) arremeter, empurrar, impelir □ *n* empurrão *m*, arremetida *f*. **~ into** (*put*) enfiar em, mergulhar em. **~ upon** (*force on*) impôr a

thud /θʌd/ *n* som *m* surdo, baque *m*

thug /θʌg/ *n* bandido *m*, facínora *m*, malfeitor *m*

thumb /θʌm/ *n* polegar *m* □ *vt* (*book*) manusear. **~ a lift** pedir carona, (*P*) boleia. **under sb's ~** completamente dominado por alguém. **~-index** *n* índice *m* de dedo

thumbtack /'θʌmtæk/ *n* (*Amer*) percevejo *m*

thump /θʌmp/ *vt/i* bater (em), dar pancadas (em); (*with fists*) dar murros (em); (*piano*) martelar (em); (*of heart*) bater com força □ *n* pancada *f*; (*thud*) baque *m*. **~ing** *a* (*colloq*) enorme

thunder /'θʌndə(r)/ *n* trovão *m*, trovoada *f*; (*loud noise*) estrondo *m* □ *vi* (*weather, person*) trovejar. **~ past** passar como um raio. **~y** *a* (*weather*) tempestuoso

thunderbolt /'θʌndəbəʊlt/ *n* raio *m* e ribombo *m* de trovão; (*fig*) raio *m* fulminante (*fig*)

thunderstorm /ˈθʌndəstɔːm/ n tempestade f com trovoadas, temporal m

Thursday /ˈθɜːzdɪ/ n quinta-feira f

thus /ðʌs/ adv assim, desta maneira. ~ **far** até aqui

thwart /θwɔːt/ vt frustrar, contrariar

thyme /taɪm/ n tomilho m

tiara /tɪˈɑːrə/ n tiara f, diadema m

tic /tɪk/ n tique m

tick[1] /tɪk/ n (sound) tique-taque m; (mark) sinal m; (colloq: moment) instantinho m □ vi fazer tique-taque □ vt ~ (**off**) marcar com sinal. ~ **off** (colloq: scold) dar uma bronca em (colloq). ~ **over** (engine, factory) funcionar em marcha lenta, (P) no "ralenti"

tick[2] /tɪk/ n (insect) carrapato m

ticket /ˈtɪkɪt/ n bilhete m; (label) etiqueta f; (for traffic offence) aviso m de multa. ~**collector** (railway) guarda m. ~**office** n bilheteira f

tickle /ˈtɪkl/ vt fazer cócegas; (fig: amuse) divertir □ n cócegas fpl, comichão m

ticklish /ˈtɪklɪʃ/ a coceguento, sensível a cócegas; (fig) delicado, melindroso

tidal /ˈtaɪdl/ a de marés, que tem marés. ~ **wave** onda f gigantesca; (fig) onda f de sentimento popular

tiddly-winks /ˈtɪdlɪwɪŋks/ n (game) jogo m da pulga

tide /taɪd/ n maré f; (of events) marcha f, curso m. **high** ~ maré f cheia, preia-mar f. **low** ~ maré f baixa, baixa-mar f □ vt ~ **over** (help temporarily) aguentar, (P) aguentar

tidy /ˈtaɪdɪ/ a (-ier, -iest) (room) arrumado; (appearance, work) asseado, cuidado; (methodical) bem ordenado; (colloq: amount) belo (colloq) □ vt arrumar, arranjar

~**ily** adv com cuidado. ~**iness** n arrumação f, ordem f

tie /taɪ/ vt (pres p **tying**) atar, amarrar, prender; (link) ligar, vincular; (a knot) dar, fazer □ vi (sport) empatar □ n fio m, cordel m; (necktie) gravata f; (link) laço m, vínculo m; (sport) empate m. ~ **in with** estar ligado com, relacionar-se com. ~ **up** amarrar, atar; (animal) prender; (money) imobilizar; (occupy) ocupar

tier /tɪə(r)/ n cada fila f, camada f, prateleira f etc colocada em cima de outra; (in stadium) bancada f; (of cake) andar m; (of society) camada f

tiff /tɪf/ n arrufo m

tiger /ˈtaɪgə(r)/ n tigre m

tight /taɪt/ a (-er, -est) (clothes) apertado, justo; (rope) esticado, tenso; (control) rigoroso; (knot, schedule, lid) apertado; (colloq: drunk) embriagado (colloq) □ adv = **tightly**. **be in a** ~ **corner** (fig) estar em apuros or num aperto, (P) estar entalado (colloq). ~**-fisted** a sovina, pão-duro, (P) agarrado (colloq). ~**ly** adv bem; (squeeze) com força

tighten /ˈtaɪtn/ vt/i (rope) esticar; (bolt, control) apertar. ~ **up on** apertar o cinto

tightrope /ˈtaɪtrəʊp/ n corda f (de acrobacias). ~ **walker** funâmbulo m

tights /taɪts/ npl collants mpl, meias-colant fpl

tile /taɪl/ n (on wall, floor) ladrilho m, azulejo m; (on roof) telha f □ vt ladrilhar, pôr azulejos em; (roof) telhar, cobrir com telhas

till[1] /tɪl/ vt (land) cultivar

till[2] /tɪl/ prep & conj = **until**

till[3] /tɪl/ n caixa (registadora) f

tilt /tɪlt/ vt/i inclinar(-se), pender □ n (slope) inclinação f. **(at) full** ~ a toda a velocidade

timber /'tɪmbə(r)/ n madeira f (de construção); (*trees*) árvores fpl

time /taɪm/ n tempo m; (*moment*) momento m; (*epoch*) época f, tempo m; (*by clock*) horas fpl; (*occasion*) vez f; (*rhythm*) compasso m. ~**s** (*multiplying*) vezes □ vt escolher a hora para; (*measure*) marcar o tempo de; (*sport*) cronometrar; (*regulate*) acertar. **at** ~**s** às vezes. **for the** ~ **being** por agora, por enquanto. **from** ~ **to** ~ de vez em quando. **have a good** ~ divertir-se. **have no** ~ **for** não ter paciência para. **in no** ~ num instante. **in** ~ a tempo; (*eventually*) com o tempo. **in two days'** ~ daqui a dois dias. **on** ~ na hora, (P) a horas. **take your** ~ não se apresse. **what's the** ~? que horas são? ~**-bomb** bomba-relógio f. ~**-limit** n prazo m. ~ **off** tempo m livre. ~**-sharing** n time-sharing m. ~**-zone** fuso m horário

timeless /'taɪmlɪs/ a intemporal; (*unending*) eterno

timely /'taɪmlɪ/ a oportuno

timer /'taɪmə(r)/ n (*techn*) relógio m; (*with sand*) ampulheta f

timetable /'taɪmteɪbl/ n horário m

timid /'tɪmɪd/ a tímido; (*fearful*) assustadiço, medroso. ~**ly** adv timidamente

timing /'taɪmɪŋ/ n (*measuring*) cronometragem f; (*of artist*) ritmo m; (*moment*) cálculo m do tempo, timing m. **good/bad** ~ (*moment*) momento m bem/mal escolhido

tin /tɪn/ n estanho m; (*container*) lata f □ vt (*pt* tinned) estanhar; (*food*) enlatar. ~ **foil** papel m de alumínio. ~**-opener** n abridor m de latas, (P) abre-latas m. ~**-plate** lata f, folha(-de-Flandes) f. ~**ned foods** conservas fpl. ~**ny** a (*sound*) metálico

tinge /tɪndʒ/ vt ~ (**with**) tingir (de); (*fig*) dar um toque (de) □ n tom m, matiz m; (*fig*) toque m

tingle /'tɪŋgl/ vi (*sting*) arder; (*prickle*) picar □ n ardor m; (*prickle*) picadela f

tinker /'tɪŋkə(r)/ n latoeiro m ambulante □ vi ~ (**with**) mexer (em), tentar consertar

tinkle /'tɪŋkl/ n tinido m, tilintar m □ vt/i tilintar

tinsel /'tɪnsl/ n fio m prateado/dourado, enfeites mpl metálicos de Natal; (*fig*) falso brilho m, ouropel m

tint /tɪnt/ n tom m, matiz m; (*for hair*) tintura f, tinta f □ vt tingir, colorir

tiny /'taɪnɪ/ a (-**ier**, -**iest**) minúsculo, pequenino

tip[1] /tɪp/ n ponta f. (**have sth**) **on the** ~ **of one's tongue** ter alg coisa na ponta da língua

tip[2] /tɪp/ vt/i (*pt* **tipped**) (*tilt*) inclinar(-se); (*overturn*) virar(-se); (*pour*) colocar, (P) deitar; (*empty*) despejar(-se) □ n (*money*) gorjeta f; (*advice*) sugestão f, dica f (*colloq*); (*for rubbish*) lixeira f. ~ **off** avisar, prevenir. ~**-off** n (*warning*) aviso m; (*information*) informação f

tipsy /'tɪpsɪ/ a ligeiramente embriagado, alegre, tocado

tiptoe /'tɪptəʊ/ n **on** ~ na ponta dos pés

tire[1] /'taɪə(r)/ vt/i cansar(-se (of de). ~**less** a incansável, infatigável. ~**ing** a fatigante, cansativo

tire[2] /'taɪə(r)/ n (*Amer*) pneu m

tired /'taɪəd/ a cansado, fatigado. ~ **of** (*sick of*) farto de. ~ **out** morto de cansaço

tiresome /'taɪəsəm/ a maçador, aborrecido, chato (sl)

tissue /'tɪʃuː/ n tecido m; (*handkerchief*) lenço m de papel. ~**-paper** n papel m de seda tit¹ /tɪt/ n (bird) chapim m, canário-da-terra m

tit² /tɪt/ n give ~ for tat pagar na mesma moeda

titbit /'tɪtbɪt/ n petisco m

titillate /'tɪtɪleɪt/ vt excitar, titilar, (P) dar gozo a

title /'taɪtl/ n título m. ~-deed n título m de propriedade. ~-page n página f de rosto, (P) frontispício m. ~-role n papel m principal

titter /'tɪtə(r)/ vi rir com riso abafado

to /tuː/; unstressed /tə/ prep a, para; (as far as) até; (towards) para; (of attitude) para (com) □ adv push or pull ~ (close) fechar. ~ Portugal (for a short time) a Portugal; (to stay) para Portugal. ~ the baker's para o padeiro, (P) ao padeiro. ~ do/ sit/etc (infinitive) fazer/sentar-se/etc; (expressing purpose) para fazer/para se sentar/etc. it's ten ~ six são dez para as seis, faltam dez para as seis. go ~ and fro andar de um lado para outro. husband/etc-~-be n futuro marido m/etc. ~-do n (fuss) agitação f, alvoroço m

toad /təʊd/ n sapo m

toadstool /'təʊdstuːl/ n cogumelo m venenoso

toady /'təʊdɪ/ n lambe-botas mf, puxa-saco m □ vi puxar saco

toast /təʊst/ n fatia f de pão torrado, torrada f; (drink) brinde m, saúde f □ vt (bread) torrar; (drink to) brindar, beber à saúde de. ~er n torradeira f

tobacco /tə'bækəʊ/ n tabaco m

tobacconist /tə'bækənɪst/ n vendedor m de tabaco, homem m da tabacaria (colloq). ~'s shop tabacaria f

toboggan /tə'bɒɡən/ n tobogã m, (P) toboggan m

today /tə'deɪ/ n & adv hoje (m)

toddler /'tɒdlə(r)/ n criança f que está aprendendo a andar

toe /təʊ/ n dedo m do pé; (of shoe, stocking) biqueira f □ vt ~ the line andar na linha. on one's ~s alerta, vigilante. ~-hold n apoio (precário) m. ~-nail n unha f do dedo do pé

toffee /'tɒfɪ/ n puxa-puxa m, (P) caramelo m. ~-apple n maçã f caramelizada

together /tə'ɡeðə(r)/ adv junto, juntamente, juntos; (at the same time) ao mesmo tempo. ~ with juntamente com. ~ness n camaradagem f, companheirismo m

toil /tɔɪl/ vi labutar □ n labuta f, labor m

toilet /'tɔɪlɪt/ n banheiro m, (P) casa f de banho; (grooming) toalete f. ~-paper n papel m higiênico, (P) higiénico. ~-roll n rolo m de papel higiênico, (P) higiénico. ~ water água-de-colônia f

toiletries /'tɔɪlɪtrɪz/ npl artigos mpl de toalete

token /'təʊkən/ n sinal m, prova f; (voucher) cheque m; (coin) ficha f □ a simbólico

told /təʊld/ see tell □ a all ~ (all in all) ao todo

tolerabl|e /'tɒlərəbl/ a tolerável; (not bad) sofrível, razoável. ~y adv (work, play) razoavelmente

tolerant /'tɒlərənt/ a tolerante (of para com). ~ce n tolerância f. ~tly adv com tolerância

tolerate /'tɒləreɪt/ vt tolerar

toll¹ /təʊl/ n pedágio m, (P) portagem f. death ~ número m de mortos. take its ~ (of age) fazer sentir o seu peso

toll² /təʊl/ vt/i (of bell) dobrar

tomato /tə'mɑːtəʊ/ n (pl -oes) tomate m

tomb /tuːm/ n túmulo m, sepultura f

tomboy /ˈtɒmbɔɪ/ n menina f levada (e masculinizada), (P) maria-rapaz f

tombstone /ˈtuːmstəʊn/ n lápide f, pedra f tumular

tome /təʊm/ n tomo m, volume m

tomfoolery /tɒmˈfuːlərɪ/ n disparates mpl, imbecilidades fpl

tomorrow /təˈmɒrəʊ/ n & adv amanhã (m). ~ **morning/night** amanhã de manhã/à noite

ton /tʌn/ n tonelada f (= 1016 kg). **(metric)** ~ tonelada f (= 1000 kg). ~**s of** (colloq) montes de (colloq), (P) carradas de (colloq)

tone /təʊn/ n tom m; (of radio, telephone etc) sinal m; (colour) tom m, tonalidade f; (med) tonicidade f □ vt ~ **down** atenuar □ vi ~ **in** combinar-se, harmonizar-se **(with** com). ~ **up** (muscles) tonificar. ~**-deaf** a sem ouvido musical

tongs /tɒŋz/ n tenaz f; (for sugar) pinça f; (for hair) pinça f

tongue /tʌŋ/ n língua f. ~**-in-cheek** a & adv a sério, com ironia. ~**-tied** a calado. ~**-twister** n travalíngua m

tonic /ˈtɒnɪk/ n (med) tónico m, (P) tónico m; (mus) tónica f, (P) tónica f □ a tónico, (P) tónico. ~ **up** encher; (mobiles) recarregar ~ped **with** coberto de

tonight /təˈnaɪt/ adv & n hoje à noite, logo à noite, esta noite (f)

tonne /tʌn/ n (metric) tonelada f

tonsil /ˈtɒnsl/ n amígdala f

tonsillitis /tɒnsɪˈlaɪtɪs/ n amigdalite f

too /tuː/ adv demasiado, demais; (also) também, igualmente; (colloq: very) muito. ~ **many** a demais, demasiados. ~ **much** a & adv demais, demasiado

took /tʊk/ see **take**

tool /tuːl/ n (carpenter's, plumber's etc) ferramenta f; (gardener's) utensílio m; (fig: person) joguete m. ~**-bag** n saco m de ferramenta

toot /tuːt/ n toque m de buzina □ vt/i ~ **(the horn)** buzinar

tooth /tuːθ/ n (pl **teeth**) dente m. ~**less** a desdentado

toothache /ˈtuːθeɪk/ n dor f de dentes

toothbrush /ˈtuːθbrʌʃ/ n escova f de dentes

toothpaste /ˈtuːθpeɪst/ n pasta f de dentes, dentifrício m

toothpick /ˈtuːθpɪk/ n palito m

top[1] /tɒp/ n (highest point; upper part) alto m, cimo m, topo m; (of hill; fig) cume m; (upper surface) cimo m, topo m; (surface of table) tampo m; (lid) tampa f; (of bottle) rolha f; (of list) cabeça f □ a (shelf etc) de cima, superior; (in rank) primeiro; (best) melhor; (distinguished) eminente; (maximum) máximo □ vt (pt **topped**) (exceed) ultrapassar; ir acima de. **from** ~ **to bottom** de alto a baixo. **on** ~ **of** em cima de; (fig) além de. **on** ~ **of that** ainda por cima. ~ **gear** (auto) a velocidade mais alta. ~ **hat** chapéu m alto. ~**-heavy** a mais pesado na parte de cima. ~ **secret** ultra-secreto. ~

top[2] /tɒp/ n (toy) pião m. **sleep like a** ~ dormir como uma pedra

topic /ˈtɒpɪk/ n tópico m, assunto m

topical /ˈtɒpɪkl/ a da actualidade, (P) actualidade, corrente

topless /ˈtɒplɪs/ a com o peito nu, topless

topple /ˈtɒpl/ vt/i (fazer) desabar, (fazer) tombar, (fazer) cair

torch /tɔːtʃ/ n (electric) lanterna f eléctrica, (P) eléctrica; (flaming) archote m, facho m

tore /tɔː(r)/ see **tear**[1]

torment[1] /ˈtɔːment/ n tormento m

torment[2] /tɔːˈment/ vt atormentar, torturar; (annoy) aborrecer, chatear

torn /tɔːn/ *see* **tear**[1]

tornado /tɔː'neɪdəʊ/ *n* (*pl* **-oes**) tornado *m*

torpedo /tɔː'piːdəʊ/ *n* (*pl* **-oes**) torpedo *m* □ *vt* torpedear

torrent /'tɒrənt/ *n* torrente *f*. **~ial** /tə'renʃl/ *a* torrencial

torrid /'tɒrɪd/ *a* (*climate etc*) tórrido; (*fig*) intenso, ardente

torso /'tɔːsəʊ/ *n* (*pl* **-os**) torso *m*

tortoise /'tɔːtəs/ *n* tartaruga *f*

tortoiseshell /'tɔːtəʃel/ *n* (*for ornaments etc*) tartaruga *f*

tortuous /'tɔːtʃʊəs/ *a* (*of path etc*) que dá muitas voltas, sinuoso; (*fig*) tortuoso, retorcido

torture /'tɔːtʃə(r)/ *n* tortura *f*, suplício *m* □ *vt* torturar. **~r** /-ə(r)/ *n* carrasco *m*, algoz *m*, torturador *m*

Tory /'tɔːrɪ/ *a & n* (*colloq*) conservador (*m*), (*P*) tóri (*m*)

toss /tɒs/ *vt* atirar, jogar, (*P*) deitar; (*shake*) agitar, sacudir □ *vi* agitar-se, debater-se. **~ a coin, ~ up** tirar cara ou coroa

tot[1] /tɒt/ *n* criancinha *f*; (*colloq: glass*) copinho *m*

tot[2] /tɒt/ *vt/i* (*pt* **totted**) **~ up** (*colloq*) somar

total /'təʊtl/ *a & n* total (*m*) □ *vt* (*pt* **totalled**) (*find total of*) totalizar; (*amount to*) elevar-se a, montar a. **~ity** /-'tæləti/ *n* totalidade *f*. **~ly** *adv* totalmente

totalitarian /təʊtælɪ'teərɪən/ *a* totalitário

totter /'tɒtə(r)/ *vi* cambalear, andar aos tombos; (*of tower etc*) oscilar

touch /tʌtʃ/ *vt/i* tocar; (*of ends, gardens etc*) tocar-se; (*tamper with*) mexer em; (*affect*) comover □ *n* (*sense*) tato *m*, (*P*) tacto *m*; (*contact*) toque *m*, (*P*) colour) toque *m*, retoque *m*. **a ~ of** (*small amount*) um pouco de. **get in ~ with** entrar em contato, (*P*) contacto com. **lose ~** perder conta-

to, (*P*) contacto. **~ down** (*aviat*) aterrissar, (*P*) aterrar. **~ off** disparar; (*cause*) dar início a, desencadear. **~ on** (*mention*) tocar em. **~ up** retocar. **~-and-go** *a* (*risky*) arriscado; (*uncertain*) duvidoso, incerto. **~-line** *n* linha *f* lateral

touching /'tʌtʃɪŋ/ *a* comovente, comovedor

touchy /'tʌtʃɪ/ *a* melindroso, suscetível, (*P*) susceptível, que se ofende facilmente

tough /tʌf/ *a* (**-er, -est**) (*hard, difficult; relentless*) duro; (*strong*) forte, resistente □ *n* (*guy*) valentão *m*, durão *m* (*colloq*). **~ luck!** (*colloq*) pouca sorte! **~ness** *n* dureza *f*; (*strength*) força *f*, resistência *f*

toughen /'tʌfn/ *vt/i* (*person*) endurecer; (*strengthen*) reforçar

tour /tʊə(r)/ *n* viagem *f*, (*visit*) visita *f*; (*by team etc*) tournée *f* □ *vt* visitar. **on ~** em tournée

tourism /'tʊərɪzəm/ *n* turismo *m*

tourist /'tʊərɪst/ *n* turista *mf* □ *a* turístico. **~ office** agência *f* de turismo

tournament /'tʊənəmənt/ *n* torneio *m*

tousle /'taʊzl/ *vt* despentear, esguedelhar

tout /taʊt/ *vi* angariar clientes (**for** para) □ *vt* (*try to sell*) tentar revender □ *n* (*hotel etc*) angariador *m*; (*ticket*) cambista *m*, (*P*) revendedor *m*

tow /təʊ/ *vt* rebocar □ *n* reboque *m*. **on ~** a reboque. **~ away** (*vehicle*) rebocar. **~-path** *n* caminho *m* de sirga. **~-rope** *n* cabo *m* de reboque

toward(s) /tə'wɔːd(z)/ *prep* para, em direção a, (*P*) direcção a, na direção, (*P*) direcção de; (*of attitude*) para com; (*time*) por volta de

towel /'taʊəl/ *n* toalha *f*; (*tea towel*) pano *m* de prato □ *vt* (*pt*

towelled esfregar com a toalha. **~-rail** n toalheiro m. **~ling** n atoalhado m, (P) pano m turco

tower /'taʊə(r)/ n torre f □ vi **~ above** dominar. **~ block** prédio m alto. **~ing** a muito alto; (fig: of rage etc) violento

town /taʊn/ n cidade f. **go to ~** (colloq) perder a cabeça (colloq). **~ council** município m. **~ hall** câmara f municipal. **~ planning** urbanização f

toxic /'tɒksɪk/ a tóxico

toy /tɔɪ/ n brinquedo m □ vi **~ with** (object) brincar com; (idea) considerar, cogitar

trace /treɪs/ n traço m, rastro m, sinal m; (small quantity) traço m, vestígio m □ vt seguir or encontrar a pista de; (draw) traçar; (with tracing-paper) decalcar

tracing /'treɪsɪŋ/ n decalque m, desenho m. **~-paper** n papel m vegetal

track /træk/ n (of person etc) rastro m, pista f; (race-track, of tape) pista f; (record) faixa f; (path) trilho m, carreiro m; (rail) via f □ vt seguir a pista or a trajetória, (P) trajectória de. **keep ~ of** manter-se em contato com; (keep oneself informed) seguir. **~ down** (find) encontrar, descobrir; (hunt) seguir a pista de. **~ suit** conjunto m de jogging, (P) fato m de treino

tract /trækt/ n (land) extensão f; (anat) aparelho m

tractor /'træktə(r)/ n trator m, (P) tractor m

trade /treɪd/ n comércio m; (job) ofício m, profissão f; (swap) troca f □ vt/i comerciar (em), negociar (em) □ vt (swap) trocar. **~ in** (used article) trocar. **~-in** n troca f. **~ mark** marca f de fábrica. **~ on** (exploit) tirar partido de, abusar de. **~ union** sindicato m.

~r /-ə(r)/ n negociante mf, comerciante mf

tradesman /'treɪdzmən/ n (pl -men) comerciante m

trading /'treɪdɪŋ/ n comércio m. **~ estate** zona f industrial

tradition /trə'dɪʃn/ n tradição f. **~al** a tradicional

traffic /'træfɪk/ n (trade) tráfego m, tráfico m; (on road) trânsito m, tráfego m; (aviat) tráfego m □ vi (pt trafficked) traficar (in em). **~ circle** (Amer) giratória f, (P) rotunda f. **~ island** ilha f de pedestres, (P) refúgio m para peões. **~ jam** engarrafamento m. **~-lights** npl sinal m luminoso, (P) semáforo m. **~ warden** guarda mf de trânsito. **~ker** n traficante mf

tragedy /'trædʒədɪ/ n tragédia f.

tragic /'trædʒɪk/ a trágico

trail /treɪl/ vt/i arrastar(-se), rastejar; (of plant, on ground) rastejar; (of plant, over wall) trepar; (track) seguir □ n (of powder, smoke etc) esteira f, rastro m, (P) rasto m; (track) pista f; (beaten path) trilho m

trailer /'treɪlə(r)/ n reboque m; (Amer: caravan) reboque m, caravana f, trailer m; (film) trailer m, apresentação f de filme

train /treɪn/ n (rail) trem m, (P) comboio m; (procession) fila f; (of dress) cauda f; (retinue) comitiva f □ vt (instruct, develop) educar, formar, treinar; (plant) guiar; (sportsman, animal) treinar; (aim) assestar, apontar □ vi estudar, treinar-se. **~ed** a (skilled) qualificado; (doctor etc) diplomado. **~er** n (sport) treinador m; (shoe) tênis m. **~ing** n treino m

trainee /treɪ'niː/ n estagiário m

trait /treɪ(t)/ n traço m, característica f

traitor /'treɪtə(r)/ n traidor m

tram /træm/ *n* bonde *m*, (*P*) (carro) eléctrico *m*

tramp /træmp/ *vi* marchar (com passo pesado) □ *vt* percorrer, palmilhar □ *n* som *m* de passos pesados; (*vagrant*) vagabundo *m*, andarilho *m*; (*hike*) longa caminhada *f*

trample /'træmpl/ *vt/i* ~ **(on)** pisar com força; (*fig*) menosprezar

trampoline /'træmpəli:n/ *n* (lona *f* usada como) trampolim *m*

trance /trɑ:ns/ *n* (*hypnotic*) transe *m*; (*ecstasy*) êxtase *m*, arrebatamento *m*; (*med*) estupor *m*

tranquil /'træŋkwɪl/ *a* tranquilo, (*P*) tranquilo, sossegado. ~**lity** /-'kwɪlətɪ/ *n* tranquilidade *f*, (*P*) tranquilidade *f*, sossego *m*

tranquillizer /'træŋkwɪlaɪzə(r)/ *n* (*drug*) tranquilizante *m*, (*P*) tranquilizante *m*, calmante *m*

transact /træn'zækt/ *vt* (*business*) fazer, efetuar, (*P*) efectuar. ~**ion** /-ʃn/ *n* transação *f*, (*P*) transacção *f*

transcend /træn'send/ *vt* transcender. ~**ent** *a* transcendente

transcribe /træn'skraɪb/ *vt* transcrever. ~**pt**, ~**ption** /-ɪpʃn/ *ns* transcrição *f*

transfer[1] /træns'fɜ:(r)/ *vt* (*pt* **transferred**) transferir; (*power, property*) transmitir □ *vi* mudar, ser transferido; (*change planes etc*) fazer transferência. ~ **the charges** (*telephone*) ligar a cobrar

transfer[2] /'trænsfɜ:(r)/ *n* transferência *f*; (*of power, property*) transmissão *f*; (*image*) decalcomania *f*

transfigure /træns'fɪgə(r)/ *vt* transfigurar

transform /træns'fɔ:m/ *vt* transformar. ~**ation** /-ə'meɪʃn/ *n* transformação *f*. ~**er** *n* (*electr*) transformador *m*

transfusion /træns'fju:ʒn/ *n* (*of blood*) transfusão *f*

transient /'trænzɪənt/ *a* transitório, transiente, efêmero, (*P*) efémero, passageiro

transistor /træn'zɪstə(r)/ *n* (*device, radio*) transistor *m*

transit /'trænsɪt/ *n* trânsito *m*. **in** ~ em trânsito

transition /træn'zɪʃn/ *n* transição *f*. ~**al** *a* transitório

transitive /'trænsətɪv/ *a* transitivo

transitory /'trænsɪtərɪ/ *a* transitório

translate /trænz'leɪt/ *vt* traduzir. ~**ion** /-ʃn/ *n* tradução *f*. ~**or** *n* tradutor *m*

translucent /trænz'lu:snt/ *a* translúcido

transmit /trænz'mɪt/ *vt* (*pt* **transmitted**) transmitir. ~**ssion** *n* transmissão *f*. ~**tter** *n* transmissor *m*

transparent /træns'pærənt/ *a* transparente. ~**cy** *n* transparência *f*; (*photo*) diapositivo *m*

transpire /træn'spaɪə(r)/ *vi* (*secret etc*) transpirar; (*happen*) suceder, acontecer

transplant[1] /træns'plɑ:nt/ *vt* transplantar

transplant[2] /'trænsplɑ:nt/ *n* (*med*) transplantação *f*, transplante *m*

transport[1] /træn'spɔ:t/ *vt* (*carry, delight*) transportar. ~**ation** /-'teɪʃn/ *n* transporte *m*

transport[2] /'trænspɔ:t/ *n* (*of goods, delight etc*) transporte *m*

transpose /træn'spəʊz/ *vt* transpor

transverse /'trænzvɜ:s/ *a* transversal

transvestite /trænz'vestaɪt/ *n* travesti *mf*

trap /træp/ *n* armadilha *f*, ratoeira *f*, cilada *f* □ *vt* (*pt* **trapped**) apanhar na armadilha; (*cut* *off*) prender, bloquear. **~per** *n* caçador *m* de armadilha (esp de peles)

trapdoor /'træp'dɔ:(r)/ *n* alçapão *m*

trapeze /trə'pi:z/ *n* trapézio *m*

trash /træʃ/ *n* (*worthless stuff*) porcaria *f*; (*refuse*) lixo *m*; (*nonsense*) disparates *mpl*. **~ can** *n* (*Amer*) lata *f* do lixo, (*P*) caixote *m* do lixo. **~y** *a* que não vale nada, porcaria

trauma /'trɔ:mə/ *n* trauma *m*, traumatismo *m*. **~tic** /-'mætɪk/ *a* traumático

travel /'trævl/ *vi* (*pt* **travelled**) viajar; (*of vehicle, bullet, sound*) ir □ *vt* percorrer □ *n* viagem *f*. **~ agent** agente *mf* de viagem. **~ler** *n* viajante *mf*. **~ler's cheque** cheque *m* de viagem. **~ling** *n* viagem *f*, viagens *fpl*, viajar *m*

travesty /'trævəstɪ/ *n* paródia *f*, caricatura *f*

trawler /'trɔ:lə(r)/ *n* traineira *f*, (*P*) arrastão *m*

tray /treɪ/ *n* tabuleiro *m*, bandeja *f*

treacherous /'tretʃərəs/ *a* traiçoeiro

treachery /'tretʃərɪ/ *n* traição *f*, perfídia *f*, deslealdade *f*

treacle /'tri:kl/ *n* melaço *m*

tread /tred/ *vt/i* (*pt* **trod**, *pp* **trodden**) (*step*) pisar; (*walk*) andar, caminhar; (*walk along*) seguir □ *n* passo *m*, maneira *f* de andar; (*of tyre*) trilho *m*. **~ sth into** (*carpet*) esmigalhar alg coisa sobre/em

treason /'tri:zn/ *n* traição *f*

treasure /'treʒə(r)/ *n* tesouro *m* □ *vt* ter o maior apreço por; (*store*) guardar bem guardado. **~r** *n* tesoureiro *m*

treasury /'treʒərɪ/ *n* (*building*) tesouraria *f*; (*department*) Ministério *m* das Finanças *or* da Fazenda; (*fig*) tesouro *m*

treat /tri:t/ *vt/i* tratar □ *n* (*pleasure*) prazer *m*, regalo *m*; (*present*) mimo *m*, gentileza *f*. **~ sb to sth** convidar alguém para alg coisa

treatise /'tri:tɪz/ *n* tratado *m*

treatment /'tri:tmənt/ *n* tratamento *m*

treaty /'tri:tɪ/ *n* (*pact*) tratado *m*

treble /'trebl/ *a* triplo □ *vt/i* triplicar □ *n* (*mus: voice*) soprano *m*. **~y** *adv* triplamente

tree /tri:/ *n* árvore *f*

trek /trek/ *n* viagem *f* penosa; (*walk*) caminhada *f* □ *vi* (*pt* **trekked**) viajar penosamente; (*walk*) caminhar

trellis /'trelɪs/ *n* grade *f* para trepadeiras, treliça *f*

tremble /'trembl/ *vi* tremer

tremendous /trɪ'mendəs/ *a* (*fearful, huge*) tremendo; (*colloq: excellent*) fantástico, formidável

tremor /'tremə(r)/ *n* tremor *m*, estremecimento *m*. **~ (earth)** ~ abalo (sísmico) *m*, tremor *m* de terra

trench /trentʃ/ *n* fossa *f*, vala *f*; (*mil*) trincheira *f*

trend /trend/ *n* tendência *f*; (*fashion*) moda *f*. **~y** *a* (*colloq*) na última moda, (*P*) na berra (*colloq*)

trepidation /trepɪ'deɪʃn/ *n* (*fear*) receio *m*, apreensão *f*

trespass /'trespəs/ *vi* entrar ilegalmente (**on** em). **no ~ing** entrada *f* proibida. **~er** *n* intruso *m*

trestle /'tresl/ *n* cavalete *m*, armação *f* de mesa. **~-table** *n* mesa *f* de cavaletes

trial /'traɪəl/ *n* (*jur*) julgamento *m*, processo *m*; (*test*) ensaio *m*, experiência *f*, prova *f*; (*ordeal*) provação *f*. **on ~** em julgamento. **~ and error** tentativas *fpl*

triang|le /'traɪæŋgl/ *n* triângulo *m*. **~ular** /-'æŋgjʊlə(r)/ *a* triangular

trib|**e** /traɪb/ n tribó f. **~al** a tribal

tribulation /trɪbjʊˈleɪʃn/ n tribulação f

tribunal /traɪˈbjuːnl/ n tribunal m

tributary /ˈtrɪbjʊtəri/ n afluente m, tributário m

tribute /ˈtrɪbjuːt/ n tributo m. **pay ~ to** prestar homenagem a, render tributo a

trick /trɪk/ n truque m; (prank) partida f; (habit) jeito m □ vt enganar. **do the ~** (colloq: work) dar resultado

trickery /ˈtrɪkəri/ n trapaça f

trickle /ˈtrɪkl/ vi pingar, gotejar, escorrer □ n fio m de água etc; (fig: small number) punhado m

tricky /ˈtrɪki/ a (crafty) manhoso; (problem) delicado, complicado

tricycle /ˈtraɪsɪkl/ n triciclo m

trifle /ˈtraɪfl/ n ninharia f, bagatela f; (sweet) sobremesa f feita de pão-de-ló e frutas e creme □ vi **~ with** brincar com. **a ~** um pouquinho, (P) um poucochinho

trifling /ˈtraɪflɪŋ/ a insignificante

trigger /ˈtrɪgə(r)/ n (of gun) gatilho m □ vt **~ (off)** (initiate) desencadear, despoletar

trill /trɪl/ n trinado m, gorjeio m

trilogy /ˈtrɪlədʒi/ n trilogia f

trim /trɪm/ a (trimmer, trimmest) bem arranjado, bem cuidado; (figure) elegante, esbelto □ vt (pt trimmed) (cut) aparar, (sails) orientar, marear; (ornament) enfeitar, guarnecer (with com) □ n (cut) aparadela f, corte m leve; (decoration) enfeite m; (on car) acabamento(s) m(pl), estofado m. **in ~** em ordem; (fit) em boa forma. **~ming(s)** n(pl) (dress) enfeite m; (culin) guarnição f, acompanhamento m

Trinity /ˈtrɪnəti/ n **the (Holy) ~** a Santíssima Trindade

trinket /ˈtrɪŋkɪt/ n bugiganga f; (jewel) bijuteria f, berloque m

trio /ˈtriːəʊ/ n (pl -os) trio m

trip /trɪp/ vi (pt tripped) (stumble) tropeçar, dar um passo em falso; (go or dance lightly) andar/dançar com passos leves □ vt **~ (up)** fazer tropeçar, passar uma rasteira a □ n (journey) viagem f; (outing) passeio m, excursão f; (stumble) tropeção m, passo m em falso

tripe /traɪp/ n (food) dobrada f, tripas fpl; (colloq: nonsense) disparates mpl

triple /ˈtrɪpl/ a triplo, tríplice □ vt/i triplicar. **~ts** /-plɪts/ npl trigêmeos mpl, (P) trigémeos mpl

triplicate /ˈtrɪplɪkət/ n **in ~** em triplicata

tripod /ˈtraɪpɒd/ n tripé m

trite /traɪt/ a banal, corriqueiro

triumph /ˈtraɪəmf/ n triunfo m □ vi triunfar (over sobre); (exult) exultar, rejubilar-se. **~al** /-ˈʌmfl/ a triunfal. **~ant** /-ˈʌmfənt/ a triunfante. **~antly** /-ˈʌmfəntli/ adv em triunfo, triunfantemente

trivial /ˈtrɪvɪəl/ a insignificante

trod, trodden /trɒd, ˈtrɒdn/ see tread

trolley /ˈtrɒli/ n carrinho m. **(tea-)~** carrinho m de chá

trombone /trɒmˈbəʊn/ n (mus) trombone m

troop /truːp/ n bando m, grupo m. **~s** (mil) tropas fpl □ vi **~ in/out** entrar/sair em bando or grupo. **~ing the colour** a saudação da bandeira. **~er** n soldado m de cavalaria

trophy /ˈtrəʊfi/ n troféu m

tropic /ˈtrɒpɪk/ n trópico m. **~s** trópicos mpl. **~al** a tropical

trot /trɒt/ n trote m □ vi (pt trotted) trotar; (of person) correr em passos curtos, ir num or a trote (colloq). **on the ~** (colloq) a seguir, a fio. **~ out** (colloq: produce) exibir; (colloq: state) desfiar

trouble /'trʌbl/ n (difficulty) dificuldade(s) f(pl), problema(s) m(pl); (distress) desgosto(s) m(pl), aborrecimento(s) m(pl); (pains, effort) cuidado m, trabalho m, maçada f; (inconvenience) transtorno m, incómodo m, (P) incómodo m; (med) doença f. ∼(s) (unrest) agitação f, conflito(s) m(pl) □ vt/i (bother) incomodar(-se), (P) maçar(-se); (worry) preocupar(-se); (agitate) perturbar. **be in** ∼ estar em apuros, estar em dificuldades. **get into** ∼ meter-se em encrenca/apuros. **it is not worth the** ∼ não vale a pena. ∼**-maker** n desordeiro m, provocador m. ∼**-shooter** n mediador m, negociador m. ∼**d** a agitado, perturbado; (of sleep) agitado; (of water) turvo

troublesome /'trʌblsəm/ a problemático, importuno, (P) maçador

trough /trɒf/ n (drinking) bebedouro m; (feeding) comedouro m. ∼ **(of low pressure)** depressão f, linha f de baixa pressão

trounce /traʊns/ vt (defeat) esmagar; (thrash) espancar

troupe /truːp/ n (theat) companhia f, troupe f

trousers /'traʊzəz/ npl calça f, (P) calças fpl. **short** ∼ calções mpl

trousseau /'truːsəʊ/ n (pl -s /-əʊz/) (of bride) enxoval m de noiva

trout /traʊt/ n (pl invar) truta f

trowel /'traʊəl/ n (garden) colher f de jardineiro; (for mortar) trolha f

truan|t /'truːənt/ n absentista mf, (P) absentista mf; (schol) gazeteiro m. **play** ∼**t** fazer gazeta. ∼**cy** n absenteísmo m, (P) absentismo m

truce /truːs/ n trégua(s) f(pl), armistício m

truck /trʌk/ n (lorry) camião m;

(barrow) carro m de bagageiro; (wagon) vagão m aberto. ∼**-driver** n motorista mf de camião, (P) camionista mf

truculent /'trʌkjʊlənt/ a agressivo, brigão

trudge /trʌdʒ/ vi caminhar com dificuldade, caminhar a custo, arrastar-se

true /truː/ a (-er, -est) verdadeiro; (accurate) exato, (P) exacto; (faithful) fiel. **come** ∼ (happen) realizar-se, concretizar-se. **it is** ∼ é verdade

truffle /'trʌfl/ n trufa f

truism /'truːɪzəm/ n truísmo m, verdade f evidente, (P) verdade f do Amigo Banana (colloq)

truly /'truːlɪ/ adv verdadeiramente; (faithfully) fielmente; (truthfully) sinceramente

trump /trʌmp/ n trunfo m □ vt jogar trunfo, trunfar. ∼ **up** forjar, inventar. ∼ **card** carta f de trunfo; (colloq: valuable resource) trunfo m

trumpet /'trʌmpɪt/ n trombeta f

truncheon /'trʌntʃən/ n cassetete m, (P) cassetête m

trundle /'trʌndl/ vt/i (fazer) rolar ruidosamente/pesadamente

trunk /trʌŋk/ n (of tree, body) tronco m; (of elephant) tromba f; (box) mala f grande; (Amer, auto) mala f. ∼**s** (for swimming) calção m de banho. ∼ **call** chamada f interurbana. ∼ **road** n estrada f nacional

truss /trʌs/ n (med) funda f □ vt atar, amarrar

trust /trʌst/ n confiança f; (association) truste m, (P) trust m, consórcio m; (foundation) fundação f; (responsibility) responsabilidade f; (jur) fideicomisso m □ vt (rely on) ter confiança em, confiar em; (hope) esperar □ vi ∼ **in** or **to** confiar em. **in** ∼ em fideicomisso. **on** ∼ (without

trustee · 593 · turbine

proof) sem verificação prévia; (*on credit*) a crédito. ~ **sb with** confiar em alguém. **~ed** *a* (*friend etc*) de confiança, seguro. **~ful**, **~ing** *adjs* confiante. **~y** *a* fiel

trustee /trʌs'tiː/ *n* administrador *m*; (*jur*) fideicomissório *m*

trustworthy /'trʌstwɜːðɪ/ *a* (digno) de confiança

truth /truːθ/ *n* (*pl* **-s** /truːðz/) verdade *f*. **~ful** *a* (*account etc*) verídico; (*person*) verdadeiro, que fala verdade. **~fully** *adv* sinceramente

try /traɪ/ *vt/i* (*pt* **tried**) tentar, experimentar; (*be a strain on*) cansar, pôr à prova; (*jur*) julgar □ *n* (*attempt*) tentativa *f*, experiência *f*; (*Rugby*) ensaio *m*. ~ **for** (*post, scholarship*) candidatar-se a; (*record*) tentar alcançar. ~ **on** (*clothes*) provar. ~ **out** experimentar. ~ **to do** tentar fazer. **~ing** *a* difícil

tsar /zɑː(r)/ *n* czar *m*

T-shirt /'tiː.ʃɜːt/ *n* T-shirt *f*, camiseta *f* de algodão de mangas curtas

tub /tʌb/ *n* selha *f*; (*colloq*: *bath*) tina *f*, banheira *f*

tuba /'tjuːbə/ *n* (*mus*) tuba *f*

tubby /'tʌbɪ/ *a* (**-ier**, **-iest**) baixote e gorducho

tube /tjuːb/ *n* tubo *m*; (*colloq*: *railway*) metrô *m*. **inner ~e** câmara *f* de ar. **~ing** *n* tubos *mpl*, tubagem *f*

tuber /'tjuːbə(r)/ *n* tubérculo *m*

tuberculosis /tjuːbɜːkjʊ'ləʊsɪs/ *n* tuberculose *f*

tubular /'tjuːbjʊlə(r)/ *a* tubular

tuck /tʌk/ *n* (*fold*) prega *f* cosida; (*for shortening or ornament*) refego *m* □ *vt/i* fazer pregas; (*put*) guardar, meter, enfiar; (*hide*) esconder. ~ **in** *or* **into** (*colloq*: *eat*) atacar. ~ **in** (*shirt*) meter as fraldas para dentro; (*blanket*)

prender em; (*person*) cobrir bem, aconchegar. **~-shop** *n* (*schol*) loja *f* de balas, (*P*) pastelaria *f* (*junto à escola*)

Tuesday /'tjuːzdɪ/ *n* terça-feira *f*

tuft /tʌft/ *n* tufo *m*

tug /tʌg/ *vt/i* (*pt* **tugged**) puxar com força; (*vessel*) rebocar □ *n* (*boat*) rebocador *m*; (*pull*) puxão *m*. ~ **of war** cabo-de-guerra *m*, (*P*) jogo *m* da guerra

tuition /tjuː'ɪʃn/ *n* ensino *m*

tulip /'tjuːlɪp/ *n* tulipa *f*

tumble /'tʌmbl/ *vi* tombar, baquear, dar um trambolhão □ *n* tombo *m*, trambolhão *m*. **~-drier** *n* máquina *f* de secar (roupa)

tumbledown /'tʌmbldaʊn/ *a* em ruínas

tumbler /'tʌmblə(r)/ *n* copo *m*

tummy /'tʌmɪ/ *n* (*colloq*: *stomach*) estômago *m*; (*colloq*: *abdomen*) barriga *f*. **~-ache** *n* (*colloq*) dor *f* de barriga/de estômago

tumour /'tjuːmə(r)/ *n* tumor *m*

tumult /'tjuːmʌlt/ *n* tumulto *m*. **~uous** /-'mʌltʃʊəs/ *a* tumultuado, barulhento, agitado

tuna /'tjuːnə/ *n* (*pl invar*) atum *m*

tune /tjuːn/ *n* melodia *f* □ *vt* (*engine*) regular; (*piano etc*) afinar □ *vi* ~ **in (to)** (*radio, TV*) ligar (em), (*P*) sintonizar. ~ **up** afinar. **be in ~/out of ~** (*instrument*) estar afinado/desafinado; (*singer*) cantar afinado/desafinado. **~ful** *a* melodioso, harmonioso. **~r** *n* afinador *m*; (*radio*) sintonizador *m*

tunic /'tjuːnɪk/ *n* túnica *f*

Tunisia /tjuː'nɪzɪə/ *n* Tunísia *f*. **~n** *a* & *n* tunisiano (*m*), (*P*) tunisino (*m*)

tunnel /'tʌnl/ *n* túnel *m* □ *vi* (*pt* **tunnelled**) abrir um túnel (**into** em)

turban /'tɜːbən/ *n* turbante *m*

turbine /'tɜːbaɪn/ *n* turbina *f*

turbo- /'tɜːbəʊ/ *pref* turbo-

turbot /'tɜːbət/ *n* rodovalho *m*

turbulent /'tɜːbjʊlənt/ *a* turbulento. **~ce** *n* turbulência *f*

tureen /tə'riːn/ *n* terrina *f*

turf /tɜːf/ *n* (*pl* **turfs** *or* **turves**) gramado *m*, (P) relva *f*, relvado *m* □ *vt* **~ out** (*colloq*) jogar fora, (P) deitar fora. **the ~** (*racing*) turfe *m*, hipismo *m*. **~-accountant** corretor *m* de apostas

turgid /'tɜːdʒɪd/ *a* (*speech, style*) pomposo, empolado

Turk /tɜːk/ *n* turco *m*. **~ey** *n* Turquia *f*. **~ish** *a* turco *m* □ *n* (*lang*) turco *m*

turkey /'tɜːkɪ/ *n* peru *m*

turmoil /'tɜːmɔɪl/ *n* agitação *f*, confusão *f*, desordem *f*. **in ~** em ebulição

turn /tɜːn/ *vt/i* virar(-se), voltar (-se), girar; (*change*) transformar (-se) (**into** em); (*become*) ficar, tornar-se; (*corner*) virar, dobrar; (*page*) virar, voltar □ *n* volta *f*, (*in road*) curva *f*, (*of mind, events*) mudança *f*; (*occasion, opportunity*) vez *f*; (*colloq*) ataque *m*, crise *f*; (*colloq: shock*) susto *m*. **do a good ~** prestar (um) serviço. **in ~** por sua vez, sucessivamente. **speak out of ~** dizer o que não se deve, cometer uma indiscrição. **take ~s** revezar-se. **~ of the century** virada *f* do século. **~ against** virar-se *or* voltar-se contra. **~ away** *vi* virar-se *or* voltar-se para o outro lado □ *vt* (*avert*) desviar; (*reject*) recusar; (*send away*) mandar embora. **~ back** *vi* (*return*) devolver; (*vehicle*) dar meia volta, voltar para trás □ *vt* (*fold*) dobrar para trás. **~ down** (*refuse*) baixar. **~ in** (*hand in*) entregar; (*colloq: go to bed*) deitar-se. **~ off** (*light etc*) apagar; (*tap*) fechar; (*road*) virar (para rua

transversal). **~ on** (*light etc*) acender, ligar; (*tap*) abrir. **~ out** *vt* (*light*) apagar; (*empty*) esvaziar, despejar; (*pocket*) virar do avesso; (*produce*) produzir □ *vi* (*transpire*) vir a saber-se, descobrir-se; (*colloq: come*) aparecer. **~ round** virar-se, voltar-se. **~ up** *vi* aparecer, chegar; (*be found*) aparecer □ *vt* (*find*) desenterrar; (*increase*) aumentar; (*collar*) levantar. **~-up** *n* assistência *f*. **~-up** (*of trousers*) dobra *f*

turning /'tɜːnɪŋ/ *n* rua *f* transversal; (*corner*) esquina *f*. **~-point** *n* momento *m* decisivo

turnip /'tɜːnɪp/ *n* nabo *m*

turnover /'tɜːnəʊvə(r)/ *n* (*pie, tart*) pastel *m*, empada *f*; (*money*) faturamento *m*, (P) facturação *f*; (*of staff*) rotatividade *f*

turnpike /'tɜːnpaɪk/ *n* (*Amer*) auto-estrada *f* com pedágio, (P) portagem

turnstile /'tɜːnstaɪl/ *n* (*gate*) torniquete *m*, borboleta *f*

turntable /'tɜːnteɪbl/ *n* (*for record*) prato *m* do toca-disco, (P) giradiscos; (*record-player*) tocadisco *m*, (P) giradiscos *m*

turpentine /'tɜːpəntaɪn/ *n* terebentina *f*, aguarrás *m*

turquoise /'tɜːkwɔɪz/ *a* turquesa *invar*

turret /'tʌrɪt/ *n* torreão *m*, torrinha *f*

turtle /'tɜːtl/ *n* tartaruga-do-mar *f*. **~-neck** *a* de gola alta

tusk /tʌsk/ *n* (*tooth*) presa *f*; (*elephant's*) defesa *f*, dente *m*

tussle /'tʌsl/ *n* luta *f*, briga *f*

tutor /'tjuːtə(r)/ *n* professor *m* particular; (*univ*) professor *m* universitário

tutorial /tjuː'tɔːrɪəl/ *n* (*univ*) seminário *m*

TV /tiː'viː/ *n* tevê *f*

twaddle /'twɒdl/ *n* disparates *mpl*

twang /twæŋ/ *n* (*mus*) som *m* duma corda esticada; (*in voice*) nasalação *f* □ *vt/i* (*mus*) (fazer) vibrar, dedilhar

tweet /twiːt/ *n* pio *m*, pipilo *m* □ *vi* pipilar

tweezers /ˈtwiːzəz/ *npl* pinça *f*

twel|**ve** /twelv/ *a* & *n* doze (*m*). ~ (**o'clock**) doze horas. ~**fth** *a* & *n* décimo segundo (*m*). **T**~**fth Night** véspera *f* de Reis

twent|**y** /ˈtwentɪ/ *a* & *n* vinte (*m*). ~**ieth** *a* & *n* vigésimo (*m*)

twice /twaɪs/ *adv* duas vezes

twiddle /ˈtwɪdl/ *vt/i* ~ (**with**) (*fiddle with*) torcer, brincar (com). ~ **one's thumbs** girar os polegares

twig /twɪg/ *n* galho *m*, graveto *m*

twilight /ˈtwaɪlaɪt/ *n* crepúsculo *m* □ *a* crepuscular

twin /twɪn/ *n* & *a* gêmeo (*m*), gémeo (*m*) □ *vt* (*pt* **twinned**) (*pair*) emparelhar, emparceirar. ~ **beds** par *m* de camas de solteiro. ~**ning** *n* emparelhamento *m*

twine /twaɪn/ *n* guita *f*, cordel *m* □ *vt/i* (*weave together*) entrançar; (*wind*) enroscar(-se)

twinge /twɪndʒ/ *n* dor *f* aguda e súbita, pontada *f*; (*fig*) pontada *f*, (*P*) ferroada *f*

twinkle /ˈtwɪŋkl/ *vi* cintilar, brilhar □ *n* cintilação *f*, brilho *m*

twirl /twɜːl/ *vt/i* (fazer) girar; (*moustache*) torcer

twist /twɪst/ *vt* torcer; (*weave together*) entrançar; (*roll*) enrolar; (*distort*) torcer, deturpar □ *vi* (*rope etc*) torcer-se, enrolar-se; (*road*) dar voltas ou curvas, serpentear □ *n* (*act of twisting*) torcedura *f*, (*P*) torcedela *f*; (*of rope*) nó *m*; (*of events*) reviravolta *f*. ~ **sb's arm** (*fig*) forçar alguém

twit /twɪt/ *n* (*colloq*) idiota *mf*

twitch /twɪtʃ/ *vt/i* contrair(-se) □ *n* (*tic*) tique *m*; (*jerk*) puxão *m*

two /tuː/ *a* & *n* dois (*m*). **in** *or* **of** ~ **minds** indeciso. **put** ~ **and** ~ **together** tirar conclusões. ~**-faced** *a* de duas caras, hipócrita. ~**-piece** *n* (*garment*) duas-peças *m invar*. ~**-seater** *n* (*car*) carro *m* de dois lugares. ~**-way** *a* (*of road*) mão dupla

twosome /ˈtuːsəm/ *n* par *m*

tycoon /taɪˈkuːn/ *n* magnata *m*

tying /ˈtaɪɪŋ/ *see* **tie**

type /taɪp/ *n* (*example, print*) tipo *m*; (*kind*) tipo *m*, gênero *m*, (*P*) género *m*; (*colloq: person*) cara *m*, (*P*) tipo *m* (*colloq*) □ *vt/i* (*write*) bater à máquina, datilografar, (*P*) dactilografar

typescript /ˈtaɪpskrɪpt/ *n* texto *m* datilografado, (*P*) dactilografado

typewrit|**er** /ˈtaɪpraɪtə(r)/ *n* máquina *f* de escrever. ~**ten** /-ɪtn/ *a* batido à máquina, datilografado, (*P*) dactilografado

typhoid /ˈtaɪfɔɪd/ *n* ~ (**fever**) febre *f* tifóide

typhoon /taɪˈfuːn/ *n* tufão *m*

typical /ˈtɪpɪkl/ *a* típico. ~**ly** *adv* tipicamente

typify /ˈtɪpɪfaɪ/ *vt* ser o (protó)tipo de, tipificar

typing /ˈtaɪpɪŋ/ *n* datilografia *f*, (*P*) dactilografia *f*

typist /ˈtaɪpɪst/ *n* datilógrafa *f*, (*P*) dactilógrafa *f*

tyrann|**y** /ˈtɪrənɪ/ *n* tirania *f*. ~**ical** /tɪˈrænɪkl/ *a* tirânico

tyrant /ˈtaɪərənt/ *n* tirano *m*

tyre /ˈtaɪə(r)/ *n* pneu *m*

U

ubiquitous /juːˈbɪkwɪtəs/ *a* ubíquo, onipresente

udder /ˈʌdə(r)/ *n* úbere *m*

UFO /ˈjuːfəʊ/ *n* OVNI *m*

ugl|**y** /ˈʌglɪ/ *a* (**-ier, -iest**) feio. ~**iness** *n* feiúra *f*, (*P*) fealdade *f*

UK abbr see **United Kingdom**

ulcer /ˈʌlsə(r)/ n úlcera f

ulterior /ʌlˈtɪərɪə(r)/ a ulterior. ~ **motive** razão f inconfessada, segundas intenções fpl

ultimate /ˈʌltɪmət/ a último, derradeiro; (definitive) definitivo; (maximum) supremo; (basic) fundamental. ~ly adv finalmente

ultimatum /ʌltɪˈmeɪtəm/ n (pl -ums) ultimato m

ultra- /ˈʌltrə/ pref ultra-, super-

ultraviolet /ʌltrəˈvaɪələt/ a ultravioleta

umbilical /ʌmˈbɪlɪkl/ a ~ **cord** cordão m umbilical

umbrage /ˈʌmbrɪdʒ/ n **take ~ (at sth)** ofender-se or melindrar-se (com alg coisa)

umbrella /ʌmˈbrelə/ n guarda-chuva m

umpire /ˈʌmpaɪə(r)/ n (sport) árbitro m ▫ vt arbitrar

umpteen /ˈʌmptiːn/ a (sl) sem conta, montes de (colloq). **for the ~th time** (sl) pela centésima or enésima vez

UN abbr (**United Nations**) ONU f

un- /ʌn/ pref não, pouco

unable /ʌnˈeɪbl/ a **be ~ to do ser** incapaz de/não poder fazer

unabridged /ʌnəˈbrɪdʒd/ a (text) integral

unacceptable /ʌnəkˈseptəbl/ a inaceitável, inadmissível

unaccompanied /ʌnəˈkʌmpənɪd/ a só, desacompanhado

unaccountable /ʌnəˈkaʊntəbl/ a (strange) inexplicável; (not responsible) que não tem que dar contas

unaccustomed /ʌnəˈkʌstəmd/ a desacostumado. ~ **to** não acostumado or não habituado a

unadulterated /ʌnəˈdʌltəreɪtɪd/ a (pure, sheer) puro

unaided /ʌnˈeɪdɪd/ a sem ajuda, sozinho, por si só

unanimous /juːˈnænɪməs/ a unânime. ~**ity** /-əˈnɪmətɪ/ n unanimidade f. ~**ously** adv unânimemente, por unanimidade

unarmed /ʌnˈɑːmd/ a desarmado, indefeso

unashamed /ʌnəˈʃeɪmd/ a desavergonhado, sem vergonha. ~**ly** /-ɪdlɪ/ adv sem vergonha

unassuming /ʌnəˈsjuːmɪŋ/ a modesto, despretencioso

unattached /ʌnəˈtætʃt/ a (person) livre

unattainable /ʌnəˈteɪnəbl/ a inacessível

unattended /ʌnəˈtendɪd/ a (person) desacompanhado; (car, luggage) abandonado

unattractive /ʌnəˈtræktɪv/ a sem atrativos, (P) atractivos; (offer) de pouco interesse

unauthorized /ʌnˈɔːθəraɪzd/ a não-autorizado, sem autorização

unavoidable /ʌnəˈvɔɪdəbl/ a inevitável. ~**y** adv inevitavelmente

unaware /ʌnəˈweə(r)/ a **be ~ of** desconhecer, ignorar, não ter consciência de. ~**s** /-əz/ adv (unexpectedly) inesperadamente. **catch sb ~s** apanhar alguém desprevenido

unbalanced /ʌnˈbælənst/ a (mind, person) desequilibrado

unbearable /ʌnˈbeərəbl/ a insuportável

unbeatable /ʌnˈbiːtəbl/ a imbatível. ~**en** a não vencido, invicto; (unsurpassed) insuperado

unbeknown(st) /ʌnbɪˈnəʊn(st)/ a ~ **to** (colloq) sem o conhecimento de

unbelievable /ʌnbɪˈliːvəbl/ a inacreditável, incrível

unbend /ʌnˈbend/ vi (pt **unbent**) (relax) descontrair. ~**ing** a inflexível

unbiased /ʌnˈbaɪəst/ a imparcial

unblock /ʌnˈblɒk/ vt desbloquear, desobstruir; (pipe) desentupir

unborn /ʌnˈbɔːn/ a por nascer; (*future*) vindouro, futuro

unbounded /ʌnˈbaʊndɪd/ a ilimitado

unbreakable /ʌnˈbreɪkəbl/ a inquebrável

unbridled /ʌnˈbraɪdld/ a desequilibrado, (P) desenfreado

unbroken /ʌnˈbrəʊkən/ a (*intact*) intato, (P) intacto, inteiro; (*continuous*) ininterrupto

unburden /ʌnˈbɜːdn/ vpr ~ o.s. (*open one's heart*) desabafar (to com)

unbutton /ʌnˈbʌtn/ vt desabotoar

uncalled-for /ʌnˈkɔːldfɔː(r)/ a injustificável, gratuito

uncanny /ʌnˈkænɪ/ a (-ier, -iest) estranho, misterioso

unceasing /ʌnˈsiːsɪŋ/ a incessante

unceremonious /ʌnserɪˈməʊnɪəs/ a sem cerimónia, (P) cerimônia, brusco

uncertain /ʌnˈsɜːtn/ a incerto. be ~ whether não saber ao certo se, estar indeciso quanto a. ~ty n incerteza f

unchanged /ʌnˈtʃeɪndʒd/ a inalterado, sem modificação. ~ing a inalterável, imutável

uncivilized /ʌnˈsɪvɪlaɪzd/ a não civilizado, bárbaro

uncle /ˈʌŋkl/ n tio m

uncomfortable /ʌnˈkʌmfətəbl/ a (*thing*) desconfortável, incómodo, (P) incômodo; (*unpleasant*) desagradável. feel or be ~ (*uneasy*) sentir-se or estar pouco à vontade

uncommon /ʌnˈkɒmən/ a pouco vulgar, invulgar, fora do comum. ~ly adv invulgarmente, excepcionalmente

uncompromising /ʌnˈkɒmprəmaɪzɪŋ/ a intransigente

unconcerned /ʌnkənˈsɜːnd/ a (*indifferent*) indiferente (by a)

unconditional /ʌnkənˈdɪʃənl/ a incondicional

unconscious /ʌnˈkɒnʃəs/ a in-

consciente (of de). ~ly adv inconscientemente. ~ness n inconsciência f

unconventional /ʌnkənˈvenʃənl/ a não convencional, fora do comum

uncooperative /ʌnkəʊˈɒpərətɪv/ a (*person*) pouco cooperativo, do contra (*colloq*)

uncork /ʌnˈkɔːk/ vt desarrolhar, tirar a rolha de

uncouth /ʌnˈkuːθ/ a rude, grosseiro

uncover /ʌnˈkʌvə(r)/ vt descobrir, revelar

unctuous /ˈʌŋktʃʊəs/ a untuoso, gorduroso; (*fig*) melífluo

undecided /ʌndɪˈsaɪdɪd/ a (*irresolute*) indeciso; (*not settled*) por decidir, pendente

undeniable /ʌndɪˈnaɪəbl/ a inegável, indiscutível

under /ˈʌndə(r)/ prep debaixo de, sob; (*less than*) com menos de; (*according to*) conforme, segundo □ adv por baixo, debaixo. ~ age menor de idade. ~ way em preparo

under- /ˈʌndə(r)/ pref sub-

undercarriage /ˈʌndəkærɪdʒ/ n (*aviat*) trem m de aterrissagem, (P) trem m de aterragem

underclothes /ˈʌndəkləʊðz/ npl see **underwear**

undercoat /ˈʌndəkəʊt/ n (*of paint*) primeira mão f, (P) primeira demão f

undercover /ʌndəˈkʌvə(r)/ a (*agent, operation*) secreto

undercurrent /ˈʌndəkʌrənt/ n corrente f subterrânea; (*fig*) filão m (*fig*), tendência f oculta

undercut /ʌndəˈkʌt/ vt (pt **undercut**, pres p **undercutting**) (*comm*) vender a preços mais baixos que

underdeveloped /ʌndədɪˈveləpt/ a atrofiado; (*country*) subdesenvolvido

underdog /ˈʌndədɒg/ n desprotegido m, o mais fraco (colloq)

underdone /ˈʌndədʌn/ a (of meat) mal passado

underestimate /ˈʌndərˈestɪmeɪt/ vt subestimar, não dar o devido valor a

underfed /ˈʌndəˈfed/ a subalimentado, subnutrido

underfoot /ˈʌndəˈfʊt/ adv debaixo dos pés; (on the ground) no chão

undergo /ˈʌndəˈgəʊ/ vt (pt -went, pp -gone) (be subjected to) sofrer; (treatment) ser submetido a

undergraduate /ˈʌndəˈgrædʒʊət/ n estudante mf universitário

underground¹ /ˈʌndəˈgraʊnd/ adv debaixo da terra; (fig: secretly) clandestinamente

underground² /ˈʌndəgraʊnd/ a subterrâneo; (fig: secret) clandestino □ n (rail) metro(politano) m

undergrowth /ˈʌndəgrəʊθ/ n mato m

underhand /ˈʌndəhænd/ a (deceitful) sonso, dissimulado

under|lie /ˈʌndəˈlaɪ/ vt (pt -lay, pp -lain, pres p -lying) estar por baixo de. ~**lying** a subjacente

underline /ˈʌndəˈlaɪn/ vt sublinhar

undermine /ˈʌndəˈmaɪn/ vt minar, solapar

underneath /ˈʌndəˈniːθ/ prep sob, debaixo de, por baixo de □ adv abaixo, em baixo, por baixo

underpaid /ˈʌndəˈpeɪd/ a mal pago

underpants /ˈʌndəpænts/ npl (man's) cuecas fpl

underpass /ˈʌndəpaːs/ n (for cars, people) passagem f inferior

underprivileged /ˈʌndəˈprɪvɪlɪdʒd/ a desfavorecido

underrate /ˈʌndəˈreɪt/ vt subestimar, depreciar

underside /ˈʌndəsaɪd/ n lado m inferior, base f

underskirt /ˈʌndəskəːt/ n anágua f

understand /ˈʌndəˈstænd/ vt/i (pt -stood) compreender, entender. ~**able** a compreensível. ~**ing** a compreensivo □ n compreensão f; (agreement) acordo m, entendimento m

understatement /ˈʌndəsteɪtmənt/ n versão f atenuada da verdade, litotes f

understudy /ˈʌndəstʌdɪ/ n substituto m

undertak|e /ˈʌndəˈteɪk/ vt (pt -took, pp -taken) empreender; (responsibility) assumir. ~**e to** encarregar-se de. ~**ing** n (task) empreendimento m; (promise) compromisso m

undertaker /ˈʌndəteɪkə(r)/ n agente m funerário, papa-defuntos m (colloq)

undertone /ˈʌndətəʊn/ n **in an** ~ a meia voz

undervalue /ˈʌndəˈvæljuː/ vt avaliar por baixo, subestimar

underwater /ˈʌndəˈwɔːtə(r)/ a submarino □ adv debaixo de água

underwear /ˈʌndəweə(r)/ n roupa f interior or de baixo

underweight /ˈʌndəweɪt/ a **be** ~ estar com o peso abaixo do normal, ter peso a menos

underwent /ˈʌndəˈwent/ see **undergo**

underworld /ˈʌndəwɜːld/ n (of crime) submundo m, bas-fonds mpl

underwriter /ˈʌndəraɪtə(r)/ n segurador m; (marine) underwriter m

undeserved /ˈʌndɪˈzɜːvd/ a imerecido, injusto

undesirable /ˈʌndɪˈzaɪərəbl/ a indesejável, inconveniente

undies /ˈʌndɪz/ npl (colloq) roupa f de baixo or interior

undignified /ʌnˈdɪgnɪfaɪd/ a pouco digno, sem dignidade

undisputed /ˈʌndɪˈspjuːtɪd/ a incontestado

undo /ʌnˈduː/ *vt* (*pt* **-did**, *pp* **-done** /ʌndʌn/) desfazer; (*knot*) desfazer, desatar; (*coat*, *button*) abrir. **leave** ~**ne** não fazer, deixar por fazer. ~**ing** *n* desgraça *f*, ruína *f*

undoubted /ʌnˈdaʊtɪd/ *a* indubitável. ~**ly** *adv* indubitavelmente

undress /ʌnˈdres/ *vt/i* despir(-se). **get** ~**ed** despir-se

undu|e /ʌnˈdjuː/ *a* excessivo, indevido. ~**ly** *adv* excessivamente, indevidamente

undulate /ˈʌndjʊleɪt/ *vi* ondular

undying /ʌnˈdaɪɪŋ/ *a* eterno, perene

unearth /ʌnˈɜːθ/ *vt* desenterrar; (*fig*) descobrir

unearthly /ʌnˈɜːθlɪ/ *a* sobrenatural, misterioso. ~ **hour** (*colloq*) hora *f* absurda ou inconveniente

uneasy /ʌnˈiːzɪ/ *a* (*ill at ease*) pouco à vontade; (*worried*) preocupado

uneconomic /ʌniːkəˈnɒmɪk/ *a* antieconômico. ~**al** *a* antieconômico

uneducated /ʌnˈedʒʊkeɪtɪd/ *a* (*person*) inculto, sem instrução

unemploy|ed /ʌnɪmˈplɔɪd/ *a* desempregado. ~**ment** *n* desemprego *m*. ~**ment benefit** auxílio-desemprego *m*

unending /ʌnˈendɪŋ/ *a* interminável, sem fim

unequal /ʌnˈiːkwəl/ *a* desigual. ~**led** *a* sem igual, inigualável

unequivocal /ʌnɪˈkwɪvəkl/ *a* inequívoco, claro

uneven /ʌnˈiːvn/ *a* desigual, irregular

unexpected /ʌnɪkˈspektɪd/ *a* inesperado. ~**ly** *a* inesperadamente

unfair /ʌnˈfeə(r)/ *a* injusto (**to** com). ~**ness** *n* injustiça *f*

unfaithful /ʌnˈfeɪθfl/ *a* infiel

unfamiliar /ʌnfəˈmɪliə(r)/ *a* estranho, desconhecido. **be** ~

with desconhecer, não conhecer, não estar familiarizado com

unfashionable /ʌnˈfæʃənəbl/ *a* fora de moda

unfasten /ʌnˈfɑːsn/ *vt* (*knot*) desatar, soltar; (*button*) abrir

unfavourable /ʌnˈfeɪvərəbl/ *a* desfavorável

unfeeling /ʌnˈfiːlɪŋ/ *a* insensível

unfinished /ʌnˈfɪnɪʃt/ *a* incompleto, inacabado

unfit /ʌnˈfɪt/ *a* sem preparo físico, fora de forma; (*unsuitable*) impróprio (**for** para)

unfold /ʌnˈfəʊld/ *vt* desdobrar; (*expose*) revelar □ *vi* desenrolar-se

unforeseen /ʌnfɔːˈsiːn/ *a* imprevisto, inesperado

unforgettable /ʌnfəˈgetəbl/ *a* inesquecível

unforgivable /ʌnfəˈgɪvəbl/ *a* imperdoável, indesculpável

unfortunate /ʌnˈfɔːtʃənət/ *a* (*unlucky*) infeliz; (*regrettable*) lamentável. **it was very** ~ **that** foi uma pena que ~**ly** *adv* infelizmente

unfounded /ʌnˈfaʊndɪd/ *a* (*rumour etc*) infundado, sem fundamento

unfriendly /ʌnˈfrendlɪ/ *a* pouco amável, antipático, frio

unfurnished /ʌnˈfɜːnɪʃt/ *a* sem mobília

ungainly /ʌnˈgeɪnlɪ/ *a* desajeitado, desgracioso

ungodly /ʌnˈgɒdlɪ/ *a* ímpio. ~ **hour** (*colloq*) hora *f* absurda, às altas horas (*colloq*)

ungrateful /ʌnˈgreɪtfl/ *a* ingrato

unhapp|y /ʌnˈhæpɪ/ *a* (**-ier, -iest**) infeliz, triste; (*not pleased*) descontente, pouco contente (**with** com). ~**ily** *adv* infelizmente. ~**iness** *n* infelicidade *f*, tristeza *f*

unharmed /ʌnˈhɑːmd/ *a* incólume, são e salvo, ileso

unhealthy /ʌnˈhelθɪ/ a (-ier, -iest) (*climate etc*) doentio, insalubre; (*person*) adoentado, com pouca saúde

unheard-of /ʌnˈhɜːdɒv/ a inaudito, sem precedentes

unhinge /ʌnˈhɪndʒ/ vt (*person, mind*) desequilibrar

unholy /ʌnˈhəʊlɪ/ a (-ier, -iest) (*person, act etc*) ímpio; (*colloq: great*) incrível, espantoso

unhook /ʌnˈhʊk/ vt desenganchar; (*dress*) desapertar

unhoped /ʌnˈhəʊpt/ a ~ **for** inesperado

unhurt /ʌnˈhɜːt/ a ileso, incólume

unicorn /ˈjuːnɪkɔːn/ n unicórnio m

uniform /ˈjuːnɪfɔːm/ n uniforme m □ a uniforme, sempre igual. ~**ity** /-ˈfɔːmɪtɪ/ n uniformidade f. ~**ly** adv uniformemente

unify /ˈjuːnɪfaɪ/ vt unificar. ~**ication** /-ɪˈkeɪʃn/ n unificação f

unilateral /juːnɪˈlætrəl/ a unilateral

unimaginable /ʌnɪˈmædʒɪnəbl/ a inimaginável

unimportant /ʌnɪmˈpɔːtnt/ a sem importância, insignificante

uninhabited /ʌnɪnˈhæbɪtɪd/ a desabitado

unintentional /ʌnɪnˈtenʃənl/ a involuntário, não propositado

uninterested /ʌnˈɪntrəstɪd/ a desinteressado (in em), indiferente (in a). ~**ing** a desinteressante, sem interesse

union /ˈjuːnɪən/ n união f; (*trade union*) sindicato m. ~**ist** n sindicalista mf; (*pol*) unionista mf. **U~ Jack** bandeira f britânica

unique /juːˈniːk/ a único, sem igual

unisex /ˈjuːnɪseks/ a unisexo

unison /ˈjuːnɪsn/ n **in** ~ em uníssono

unit /ˈjuːnɪt/ n unidade f; (*of furni-*ture) peça f, unidade f, (P) módulo m

unite /juːˈnaɪt/ vt/i unir(-se). **U~d Kingdom** n Reino m Unido. **U~d Nations (Organization)** n Organização f das Nações Unidas. **U~ States (of America)** Estados mpl Unidos (da América)

unity /ˈjuːnɪtɪ/ n unidade f; (*fig: harmony*) união f

universal /juːnɪˈvɜːsl/ a universal

universe /ˈjuːnɪvɜːs/ n universo m

university /juːnɪˈvɜːsətɪ/ n universidade f □ a universitário; (*student, teacher*) universitário, da universidade

unjust /ʌnˈdʒʌst/ a injusto

unkempt /ʌnˈkempt/ a desmazelado, desleixado; (*of hair*) despenteado, desgrenhado

unkind /ʌnˈkaɪnd/ a desagradável, duro. ~**ly** adv mal

unknowingly /ʌnˈnəʊɪŋlɪ/ adv sem saber, inconscientemente

unknown /ʌnˈnəʊn/ a desconhecido □ n **the** ~ o desconhecido

unleaded /ʌnˈledɪd/ a sem chumbo

unless /ʌnˈles/ conj a não ser que, a menos que, salvo se, se não

unlike /ʌnˈlaɪk/ a diferente □ prep ao contrário de

unlikely /ʌnˈlaɪklɪ/ a improvável

unlimited /ʌnˈlɪmɪtɪd/ a ilimitado

unload /ʌnˈləʊd/ vt descarregar

unlock /ʌnˈlɒk/ vt abrir (com chave)

unlucky /ʌnˈlʌkɪ/ a (-ier, -iest) infeliz, sem sorte; (*number*) que dá azar. **be** ~ **y** ter pouca sorte. ~**ily** adv infelizmente

unmarried /ʌnˈmærɪd/ a solteiro, celibatário

unmask /ʌnˈmaːsk/ vt desmascarar

unmistakable /ʌnmɪsˈteɪkəbl/ a (*voice etc*) inconfundível; (*clear*) claro, inequívoco

unmitigated /ʌnˈmɪtɪgeɪtɪd/ a (*absolute*) completo, absoluto

unmoved /ʌnˈmuːvd/ a impassível; (*indifferent*) indiferente (**by** a), insensível (**by** a)

unnatural /ʌnˈnætʃrəl/ a que não é natural; (*wicked*) desnaturado

unnecessary /ʌnˈnesəsərɪ/ a desnecessário; (*superfluous*) supérfluo, dispensável

unnerve /ʌnˈnɜːv/ vt desencorajar, desmoralizar, intimidar

unnoticed /ʌnˈnəʊtɪst/ a **go ~** passar despercebido

unobtrusive /ʌnəbˈtruːsɪv/ a discreto

unofficial /ʌnəˈfɪʃl/ a oficioso, que não é oficial; (*strike*) ilegal, inautorizado

unorthodox /ʌnˈɔːθədɒks/ a pouco ortodoxo, não ortodoxo

unpack /ʌnˈpæk/ vt (*suitcase etc*) desfazer; (*contents*) desembalar, desempacotar □ vi desfazer a mala

unpaid /ʌnˈpeɪd/ a não remunerado; (*bill*) a pagar

unpalatable /ʌnˈpælətəbl/ a (*food, fact etc*) desagradável, intragável

unparalleled /ʌnˈpærəleld/ a sem paralelo, incomparável

unpleasant /ʌnˈpleznt/ a desagradável (**to** com); (*person*) antipático

unplug /ʌnˈplʌg/ vt (*pt* **-plugged**) (*electr*) desligar a tomada, (*P*) tirar a ficha da tomada

unpopular /ʌnˈpɒpjʊlə(r)/ a impopular

unprecedented /ʌnˈpresɪdentɪd/ a sem precedentes, inaudito, nunca visto

unpredictable /ʌnprɪˈdɪktəbl/ a imprevisível

unprepared /ʌnprɪˈpeəd/ a sem preparação, improvisado; (*person*) desprevenido

unpretentious /ʌnprɪˈtenʃəs/ a despretensioso, sem pretensões

unprincipled /ʌnˈprɪnsəpld/ a sem princípios, sem escrúpulos

unprofessional /ʌnprəˈfeʃənl/ a (*work*) de amador; (*conduct*) sem consciência profissional

unprofitable /ʌnˈprɒfɪtəbl/ a não lucrativo

unqualified /ʌnˈkwɒlɪfaɪd/ a sem habilitações; (*success etc*) total, absoluto. **be ~ to** não estar habilitado para

unquestionable /ʌnˈkwestʃənəbl/ a incontestável, indiscutível

unravel /ʌnˈrævl/ vt (*pt* **unravelled**) desenredar, desemaranhar; (*knitting*) desmanchar

unreal /ʌnˈrɪəl/ a irreal

unreasonable /ʌnˈriːznəbl/ a pouco razoável, disparatado; (*excessive*) excessivo

unrecognizable /ʌnˈrekəgnaɪzəbl/ a irreconhecível

unrelated /ʌnrɪˈleɪtɪd/ a (*facts*) desconexo, sem relação (**to** com); (*people*) não aparentado (**to** com)

unreliable /ʌnrɪˈlaɪəbl/ a que não é de confiança

unremitting /ʌnrɪˈmɪtɪŋ/ a incessante, infatigável

unreservedly /ʌnrɪˈzɜːvɪdlɪ/ adv sem reservas

unrest /ʌnˈrest/ n agitação f, distúrbios mpl

unrivalled /ʌnˈraɪvld/ a sem igual, incomparável

unroll /ʌnˈrəʊl/ vt desenrolar

unruffled /ʌnˈrʌfld/ a calmo, tranquilo, imperturbável

unruly /ʌnˈruːlɪ/ a indisciplinado, turbulento

unsafe /ʌnˈseɪf/ a (*dangerous*) que não é seguro, perigoso; (*person*) em perigo

unsaid /ʌnˈsed/ a **leave ~** não mencionar, não dizer, deixar algo por dizer

unsatisfactory /ʌnsætɪsˈfæktərɪ/ a insatisfatório, pouco satisfatório

unsavoury /ʌnˈseɪvərɪ/ a desagradável, repugnante

unscathed /ʌnˈskeɪðd/ a ileso, incólume

unscrew /ʌnˈskruː/ vt desenroscar, desparafusar

unscrupulous /ʌnˈskruːpjʊləs/ a sem escrúpulos, pouco escrupuloso, sem consciência

unseemly /ʌnˈsiːmlɪ/ a inconveniente, indecoroso, impróprio

unsettle /ʌnˈsetl/ a perturbar, agitar. **~d** a perturbado; (*weather*) instável, variável; (*bill*) não saldado

unshakeable /ʌnˈʃeɪkəbl/ a (*person, belief etc*) inabalável

unshaven /ʌnˈʃeɪvn/ a com a barba por fazer, por barbear

unsightly /ʌnˈsaɪtlɪ/ a feio

unskilled /ʌnˈskɪld/ a inexperiente; (*work, worker*) não especializado; (*labour*) mão-de-obra f não especializada

unsociable /ʌnˈsəʊʃəbl/ a insociável, misantropo

unsophisticated /ʌnsəˈfɪstɪkeɪtd/ a insofisticado, simples

unsound /ʌnˈsaʊnd/ a pouco sólido. **of ~ mind** (*jur*) não estar em plena posse das suas faculdades mentais (*jur*)

unspeakable /ʌnˈspiːkəbl/ a indescritível; (*bad*) inqualificável

unspecified /ʌnˈspesɪfaɪd/ a não especificado, indeterminado

unstable /ʌnˈsteɪbl/ a instável

unsteady /ʌnˈstedɪ/ a (*step*) vacilante, incerto; (*ladder*) instável; (*hand*) pouco firme

unstuck /ʌnˈstʌk/ a (*not stuck*) descolado. **come ~** (*colloq: fail*) falhar

unsuccessful /ʌnsəkˈsesfl/ a (*candidate*) mal sucedido; (*attempt*) malogrado, fracassado. **be ~** não ter êxito. **~ly** adv em vão

unsuit|able /ʌnˈsjuːtəbl/ a impróprio, pouco apropriado, inadequado (**for** para). **~ed** a inadequado (**to** para)

unsure /ʌnˈʃʊə(r)/ a incerto

unsuspecting /ʌnsəˈspektɪŋ/ a sem desconfiar de nada, insuspeitado

untangle /ʌnˈtæŋgl/ vt desemaranhar, desenredar

unthinkable /ʌnˈθɪŋkəbl/ a impensável, inconcebível

untid|y /ʌnˈtaɪdɪ/ a (-ier, -iest) (*room, desk etc*) desarrumado; (*appearance*) desleixado, desmazelado; (*hair*) despenteado. **~ily** adv sem cuidado. **~iness** n desordem f; (*of appearance*) desmazelo m

untie /ʌnˈtaɪ/ vt (*knot, parcel*) desatar, desfazer; (*person*) desamarrar

until /ənˈtɪl/ prep até. **not ~** não antes de □ conj até que

untimely /ʌnˈtaɪmlɪ/ a inoportuno, intempestivo; (*death*) prematuro

untold /ʌnˈtəʊld/ a incalculável

untoward /ʌntəˈwɔːd/ a inconveniente, desagradável

untrue /ʌnˈtruː/ a falso

unused[1] /ʌnˈjuːzd/ a (*new*) novo, por usar; (*not in use*) não utilizado

unused[2] /ʌnˈjuːst/ a **~ to** não habituado a, não acostumado a

unusual /ʌnˈjuːʒəl/ a insólito, fora do comum. **~ly** adv excepcionalmente

unveil /ʌnˈveɪl/ vt descobrir; (*statue, portrait etc*) desvelar

unwanted /ʌnˈwɒntɪd/ a (*useless*) que já não serve; (*child*) indesejado

unwarranted /ʌnˈwɒrəntɪd/ a injustificada

unwelcome /ʌnˈwelkəm/ a desagradável; (*guest*) indesejável

unwell /ʌnˈwel/ a indisposto

unwieldy /ʌnˈwiːldɪ/ a difícil de manejar, pouco jeitoso

unwilling /ʌn'wɪlɪŋ/ a relutante (to em), pouco disposto (to a)

unwind /ʌn'waɪnd/ vt/i (pt unwound /ʌn'waʊnd/) desenrolar (-se); (colloq: relax) descontrair (-se)

unwise /ʌn'waɪz/ a imprudente, insensato

unwittingly /ʌn'wɪtɪŋlɪ/ adv sem querer

unworthy /ʌn'wɜ:ðɪ/ a indigno

unwrap /ʌn'ræp/ vt (pt unwrapped) desembrulhar, abrir, desfazer

unwritten /ʌn'rɪtn/ a (agreement) verbal, tácito

up /ʌp/ adv (to higher place) cima, para cima, para o alto; (in higher place) em cima, no alto; (out of bed) acordado, de pé; (up and dressed) pronto; (finished) acabado; (sun) alto □ prep no cima de, em cima de, no alto de. ~ the street/river/etc pela rua/pelo rio/etc acima □ vt (pt upped) (increase) aumentar. be ~ against defrontar, enfrentar. be ~ in (colloq) saber. be ~ to (do) estar fazendo; (plot) estar tramando; (task) estar à altura de. feel ~ to doing (able) sentir-se capaz de fazer. it is ~ to you depende de você. come or go ~ subir. have ~s and downs (fig) ter (os seus) altos e baixos. walk ~ and down andar dum lado para o outro or para a frente e para trás. ~-and-coming a prometedor. ~-market a requintado, fino

upbringing /'ʌpbrɪŋɪŋ/ n educação f

update /ʌp'deɪt/ vt atualizar, (P) actualizar

upheaval /ʌp'hi:vl/ n pandemónio m, (P) pandemónio m, revolução f (fig); (social, political) convulsão f

uphill /'ʌphɪl/ a ladeira acima, ascendente; (fig: difficult) árduo □ adv /ʌp'hɪl/ go ~ subir

uphold /ʌp'həʊld/ vt (pt upheld) sustentar, manter, apoiar

upholster /ʌp'həʊlstə(r)/ vt estofar. ~y n estofados mpl, (P) estofo(s) m(pl)

upkeep /'ʌpki:p/ n manutenção f

upon /ə'pɒn/ prep sobre

upper /'ʌpə(r)/ a superior □ n (of shoe) gáspea f. have the ~ hand estar por cima, estar em posição de superioridade. ~ class aristocracia f. ~most (highest) o mais alto, superior

upright /'ʌpraɪt/ a vertical; (honourable) honesto, honrado, (P) recto

uprising /'ʌpraɪzɪŋ/ n insurreição f, sublevação f, levantamento m

uproar /'ʌprɔ:(r)/ n tumulto m, alvoroço m

uproot /ʌp'ru:t/ vt desenraizar, (fig) erradicar, desarraigar

upset[1] /ʌp'set/ vt (pt upset, pres p upsetting) (overturn) entornar, virar; (plan) contrariar, transtornar; (stomach) desarranjar; (person) contrariar, transtornar, incomodar □ a aborrecido

upset[2] /'ʌpset/ n transtorno m; (of stomach) indisposição f; (distress) choque m

upshot /'ʌpʃɒt/ n resultado m

upside-down /ʌpsaɪd'daʊn/ adv (lit & fig) ao contrário, de pernas para o ar

upstairs /ʌp'steəz/ adv (at/to) em/para cima, no/para o andar de cima □ a /'ʌpsteəz/ (flat etc) de cima, do andar de cima

upstart /'ʌpstɑ:t/ n arrivista mf

upstream /ʌp'stri:m/ adv rio acima, contra a corrente

upsurge /'ʌpsɜ:dʒ/ n recrudescência f, recrudescimento m; (of anger) acesso m, ataque m

uptake /'ʌpteɪk/ n be quick on the ~ pegar rapidamente as coisas; (*fig*) ser de compreensão rápida, ser vivo

up-to-date /'ʌptədeɪt/ *a* moderno, atualizado, (P) actualizado

upturn /'ʌptɜːn/ *n* melhoria *f*

upward /'ʌpwəd/ *a* ascendente, voltado para cima. **~s** *adv* para cima

uranium /jʊˈreɪnɪəm/ *n* urânio *m*

urban /'ɜːbən/ *a* urbano

urbane /ɜːˈbeɪn/ *a* delicado, cortês, urbano

urge /ɜːdʒ/ *vt* aconselhar vivamente (**to a**) □ *n* (*strong desire*) grande vontade *f*. **~ on** (*impel*) incitar

urgen|t /'ɜːdʒənt/ *a* urgente. **be ~t** urgir. **~cy** *n* urgência *f*

urinal /jʊəˈraɪnl/ *n* urinol *m*

urin|e /'jʊərɪn/ *n* urina *f*. **~ate** *vi* urinar

urn /ɜːn/ *n* urna *f*; (*for tea, coffee*) espécie *f* de samovar

us /ʌs/, *unstressed* /əs/ *pron* nos; (*after preps*) nós. **with ~** conosco. **he knows ~** ele nos conhece

US *abbr* **United States**

USA *abbr* **United States of America**

USB port /juːesbiːpɔːt/ *n* porto *m* USB

usable /'juːzəbl/ *a* utilizável

usage /'juːzɪdʒ/ *n* uso *m*

use¹ /juːz/ *vt* usar, utilizar, servir-se de; (*exploit*) servir-se de; (*consume*) gastar, usar, consumir. **~ up** esgotar, consumir. **~r** /-ə(r)/ *n* usuário *m*, utente *mf*. **~r-friendly** *a* fácil de usar

use² /juːs/ *n* uso *m*, emprego *m*. **in ~** em uso. **it is no ~ shouting/** *etc* não serve de nada *or* não adianta gritar/*etc*. **make ~ of** servir-se de. **of ~** útil

used¹ /juːzd/ *a* (*second-hand*) usado

used² /juːst/ *pt* **he ~ to** ele costumava, ele tinha por costume *or* hábito □ *a* **~ to** acostumado a, habituado a

use|ful /'juːsfl/ *a* útil. **~less** *a* inútil; (*person*) incompetente

usher /'ʌʃə(r)/ *n* vagalume *m*, (P) arrumador *m* □ *vt* **~ in** mandar entrar. **~ette** *n* vagalume *m*, (P) arrumadora *f*

usual /'juːʒʊəl/ *a* usual, habitual, normal. **as ~** como de costume, como habitualmente. **at the ~ time** na hora de costume, (P) à(s) hora(s) de costume. **~ly** *adv* habitualmente, normalmente

USSR *abbr* URSS

usurp /juːˈzɜːp/ *vt* usurpar

utensil /juːˈtensl/ *n* utensílio *m*

uterus /'juːtərəs/ *n* útero *m*

utilitarian /juːtɪlɪˈteərɪən/ *a* utilitário

utility /juːˈtɪlətɪ/ *n* utilidade *f*. (**public**) **~** serviço *m* público. **~ room** área *f* de serviço (para as máquinas de lavar a roupa e a louça)

utilize /'juːtɪlaɪz/ *vt* utilizar

utmost /'ʌtməʊst/ *a* (*furthest*, *most intense*) extremo. **the ~ care/***etc* (*greatest*) o maior cuidado/*etc* □ *n* **do one's ~** fazer todo o possível

utter¹ /'ʌtə(r)/ *a* completo, absoluto. **~ly** *adv* completamente

utter² /'ʌtə(r)/ *vt* proferir; (*sigh, shout*) dar. **~ance** *n* expressão *f*

U-turn /'juːtɜːn/ *n* retorno *m*

V

vacan|t /'veɪkənt/ *a* (*post, room, look*) vago; (*mind*) vazio; (*seat, space, time*) desocupado, livre. **~cy** *n* (*post*) vaga *f*; (*room in hotel*) vago *m*

vacate /vəˈkeɪt/ *vt* vagar, deixar vago

vacation /vəˈkeɪʃn/ *n* férias *fpl*

vaccinate /'væksmeɪt/ vt vacinar. **~ion** /-'neɪʃn/ n vacinação f

vaccine /'væksiːn/ n vacina f

vacuum /'vækjʊəm/ n (pl -cuums or -cua) vácuo m, vazio m. ~ **flask** garrafa f térmica, (P) termo(s) m. ~ **cleaner** aspirador m de pó

vagina /və'dʒaɪnə/ n vagina f

vagrant /'veɪɡrənt/ n vadio m, vagabundo m

vague /veɪɡ/ a (-er, -est) vago; (outline) impreciso. **be ~ about** ser vago acerca de, não precisar. ~**ly** adv vagamente

vain /veɪn/ a (-er, -est) (conceited) vaidoso; (useless) vão, inútil; (fruitless) infrutífero. **in ~** em vão. ~**ly** adv em vão

valentine /'væləntaɪn/ n (card) cartão m do dia de São Valentim

valet /'vælɪt, 'væleɪ/ n (manservant) criado m de quarto; (of hotel) camareiro m □ vt (car) lavar e limpar o interior

valiant /'vælɪənt/ a corajoso, valente

valid /'vælɪd/ a válido. ~**ity** /və-'lɪdətɪ/ n validade f

validate /'vælɪdeɪt/ vt validar, confirmar, ratificar

valley /'vælɪ/ n vale m

valuable /'væljʊəbl/ a (object) valioso, de valor; (help, time etc) precioso. ~**s** npl objetos mpl, (P) objectos mpl de valor

valuation /væljʊ'eɪʃn/ n avaliação f

value /'væljuː/ n valor m □ vt avaliar; (cherish) dar valor a. ~ **added tax** imposto m de valor adicional, (P) acrescentado. ~**r** /-ə(r)/ n avaliador m

valve /vælv/ n (anat, techn, of car tyre) válvula f; (of bicycle tyre) pipo m; (of radio) lâmpada f, válvula f

vampire /'væmpaɪə(r)/ n vampiro m

van /væn/ n (large) camião m; (small) camionete f, comercial m; (milkman's, baker's etc) camionete f; (rail) bagageiro m, (P) furgão m

vandal /'vændl/ n vândalo m. ~**ism** /-əlɪzəm/ n vandalismo m

vandalize /'vændəlaɪz/ vt destruir, estragar

vanguard /'vænɡɑːd/ n vanguarda f

vanilla /və'nɪlə/ n baunilha f

vanish /'vænɪʃ/ vi desaparecer, sumir-se, desvanecer-se

vanity /'vænətɪ/ n vaidade f. ~ **case** bolsa f de maquilagem

vantage-point /'vɑːntɪdʒpɔɪnt/ n (bom) ponto m de observação

vapour /'veɪpə(r)/ n vapor m; (mist) bruma f

vari|able /'veərɪəbl/ a variável. ~**ation** /-'eɪʃn/ n variação f. ~**ed** /-ɪd/ a variado

variance /'veərɪəns/ n **at ~** em desacordo (with com)

variant /'veərɪənt/ a diverso, diferente □ n variante f

varicose /'værɪkəʊs/ a ~ **veins** varizes fpl

variety /və'raɪətɪ/ n variedade f; (entertainment) variedades fpl

various /'veərɪəs/ a vários, diversos, variados

varnish /'vɑːnɪʃ/ n verniz m □ vt envernizar; (nails) pintar

vary /'veərɪ/ vt/i variar. ~**ing** a variado

vase /vɑːz/ n vaso m, jarra f

vast /vɑːst/ a vasto, imenso. ~**ly** adv imensamente, infinitamente. ~**ness** n vastidão f, imensidão f, imensidade f

vat /væt/ n tonel m, dorna f, cuba f

VAT /viːeɪtiː, væt/ abbr ICM m, (P) IVA m

vault¹ /vɔːlt/ n (roof) abóbada f; (in bank) casa-forte f; (tomb) cripta f; (cellar) adega f

vault² /vɔːlt/ vt/i saltar □ n salto m

vaunt /vɔːnt/ vt/i gabar(-se), ufanar(-se) (de), vangloriar(-se)

VD abbr see venereal disease

VDU abbr see visual display unit

veal /viːl/ n (meat) vitela f

veer /vɪə(r)/ vi virar, mudar de direção, (P) direcção

vegan /ˈviːgən/ a & n vegetariano (m) estrito

vegetable /ˈvedʒɪtəbl/ n hortaliça f, legume m □ a vegetal

vegetarian /vedʒɪˈteərɪən/ a & n vegetariano (m)

vegetate /ˈvedʒɪteɪt/ vi vegetar

vegetation /vedʒɪˈteɪʃn/ n vegetação f

vehement /ˈviːəmənt/ a veemente. ~ly adv veementemente

vehicle /ˈviːɪkl/ n veículo m

veil /veɪl/ n véu m □ vt velar, cobrir com véu; (fig) esconder, disfarçar

vein /veɪn/ n (in body; mood) veia f; (in rock) veio m, filão m; (of leaf) nervura f

velocity /vɪˈlɒsətɪ/ n velocidade f

velvet /ˈvelvɪt/ n veludo m. ~y a aveludado

vendetta /venˈdetə/ n vendeta f

vending-machine /ˈvendɪŋməʃiːn/ n vendedora f automática, (P) máquina f de distribuição

vendor /ˈvendə(r)/ n vendedor m. **street** ~ vendedor m ambulante

veneer /vəˈnɪə(r)/ n folheado m; (fig) fachada f, máscara f

venerable /ˈvenərəbl/ a venerável

venereal /vəˈnɪərɪəl/ a venéreo. ~ **disease** doença f venérea

venetian /vəˈniːʃn/ a ~ **blinds** persiana f

Venezuela /venɪzˈweɪlə/ n Venezuela f. ~n a & n venezuelano (m)

vengeance /ˈvendʒəns/ n vingança. **with a** ~ furiosamente, em excesso, com mais força do que se pretende

venison /ˈvenɪzn/ n carne f de veado

venom /ˈvenəm/ n veneno m. ~**ous** /ˈvenəməs/ a venenoso

vent¹ /vent/ n (in coat) abertura f

vent² /vent/ n (hole) orifício m, abertura f; (for air) respiradouro m □ vt (anger) descarregar (**on** para cima de). **give** ~ **to** (fig) desabafar, dar vazão a

ventilate /ˈventɪleɪt/ vt ventilar. ~**ion** /-ˈleɪʃn/ n ventilação f. ~**or** n ventilador m

ventriloquist /venˈtrɪləkwɪst/ n ventríloquo m

venture /ˈventʃə(r)/ n empreendimento m arriscado, aventura f □ vt/i arriscar(-se)

venue /ˈvenjuː/ n porto m de encontro

veranda /vəˈrændə/ n varanda f

verb /vɜːb/ n verbo m

verbal /ˈvɜːbl/ a verbal; (literal) literal

verbatim /vɜːˈbeɪtɪm/ adv literalmente, palavra por palavra

verbose /vɜːˈbəʊs/ a palavroso, prolixo

verdict /ˈvɜːdɪkt/ n veredicto m; (opinion) opinião f

verge /vɜːdʒ/ n beira f, borda f □ vi ~ **on** estar à beira de. **on the** ~ **of doing** prestes a fazer

verify /ˈverɪfaɪ/ vt verificar

veritable /ˈverɪtəbl/ a autêntico, verdadeiro

vermicelli /vɜːmɪˈselɪ/ n aletria f

vermin /ˈvɜːmɪn/ n animais mpl nocivos; (lice, fleas etc) parasitas mpl

vermouth /ˈvɜːməθ/ n vermute m

vernacular /vəˈnækjʊlə(r)/ n vernáculo m; (dialect) dialeto m, (P) dialecto m

versatile /ˈvɜːsətaɪl/ a versátil; (tool) que serve para vários fins. ~**ity** /-ˈtɪlətɪ/ n versatilidade f

verse /vɜːs/ n (poetry) verso m,

poesia f; (*stanza*) estrofe f; (*of Bible*) versículo m

versed /vɜːst/ a ~ **in** versado em, conhecedor de

version /'vɜːʃn/ n versão f

versus /'vɜːsəs/ prep contra

vertebra /'vɜːtɪbrə/ n (pl -**brae** /-briː/) vértebra f

vertical /'vɜːtɪkl/ a vertical. ~**ly** adv verticalmente

vertigo /'vɜːtɪgəʊ/ n vertigem f

verve /vɜːv/ n verve f, vivacidade f

very /'verɪ/ adv muito □ a (*actual*) mesmo, próprio; (*exact*) preciso, exato, (P) exacto. the ~ **day**/etc o próprio or o mesmo dia/etc. at the ~ **end** mesmo or precisamente no fim. the ~ **first/best**/etc (*emph*) o primeiro/melhor/etc de todos. ~ **much** muito. ~ **well** muito bem

vessel /'vesl/ n vaso m

vest[1] /vest/ n corpete m, (P) camisola f interior; (*Amer: waistcoat*) colete m

vest[2] /vest/ vt conferir (**in** a). ~**ed interests** mpl

vestige /'vestɪdʒ/ n vestígio m

vestry /'vestrɪ/ n sacristia f

vet /vet/ n (*colloq*) veterinário m □ vt (pt **vetted**) (*candidate etc*) examinar atentamente, estudar

veteran /'vetərən/ n veterano m. (**war**) ~ veterano m de guerra

veterinary /'vetərɪnərɪ/ a veterinário. ~ **surgeon** veterinário m

veto /'viːtəʊ/ n (pl -**oes**) veto m; (*right*) direito m de veto □ vt vetar, opor o veto a

vex /veks/ vt aborrecer, irritar, contrariar. ~**ed question** questão f muito debatida, assunto m controverso

via /'vaɪə/ prep por, via

viable /'vaɪəbl/ a viável. ~**ility** /-'bɪlətɪ/ n viabilidade f

viaduct /'vaɪədʌkt/ n viaduto m

vibrant /'vaɪbrənt/ a vibrante

vibrat|**e** /vaɪ'breɪt/ vt/i (fazer) vibrar. ~**ion** /-ʃn/ n vibração f

vicar /'vɪkə(r)/ n (*Anglican*) pastor m; (*Catholic*) vigário m, pároco m. ~**age** n presbitério m

vicarious /vɪ'keərɪəs/ a vivido indiretamente, (P) indirectamente

vice[1] /vaɪs/ n (*depravity*) vício m

vice[2] /vaɪs/ n (*techn*) torno m

vice- /vaɪs/ pref vice-. ~-**chairman** vice-presidente m. ~-**chancellor** n vice-chanceler m; (*univ*) reitor m. ~-**consul** n vice-cônsul m. ~-**president** n vice-presidente mf

vice versa /vaɪsɪ'vɜːsə/ adv vice-versa

vicinity /vɪ'smətɪ/ n vizinhança f, cercania(s) fpl, arredores mpl. **in the** ~ **of** nos arredores de

vicious /'vɪʃəs/ a (*spiteful*) mau, maldoso; (*violent*) brutal, feroz. ~ **circle** círculo m vicioso. ~**ly** adv maldosamente; (*violently*) brutalmente, ferozmente

victim /'vɪktɪm/ n vítima f

victimiz|**e** /'vɪktɪmaɪz/ vt perseguir. ~**ation** /-'zeɪʃn/ n perseguição f

victor /'vɪktə(r)/ n vencedor m

victor|**y** /'vɪktərɪ/ n vitória f. ~**ious** /-'tɔːrɪəs/ a vitorioso

video /'vɪdɪəʊ/ a vídeo □ n (pl -**os**) (*colloq*) vídeo □ vt (*record*) gravar em vídeo. ~ **cassette** videocassete f. ~ **recorder** videocassete m

vie /vaɪ/ vi (pres p **vying**) rivalizar, competir (**with** com)

view /vjuː/ n vista f □ vt ver; (*examine*) examinar; (*consider*) considerar, ver; (*a house*) visitar, ver. **in my** ~ a meu ver, na minha opinião. **in** ~ **of** em vista de. **on** ~ em exposição, à mostra; (*open to the public*) aberto ao público. **with a** ~ **to** com a intenção de, com o fim de. ~**er** n (*TV*) telespectador m; (*for slides*) visor m

viewfinder /'vjuːfaɪndə(r)/ n visor m

viewpoint /'vjuːpɔɪnt/ n ponto m de vista

vigil /'vɪdʒɪl/ n vigília f; (over corpse) velório m; (relig) vigília f

vigilan|t /'vɪdʒɪlənt/ a vigilante. ~ce n vigilância f. ~te /vɪdʒɪ'læntɪ/ n vigilante m

vig|our /'vɪɡə(r)/ n vigor m. ~orous /'vɪɡərəs/ a vigoroso

vile /vaɪl/ a (base) infame, vil; (colloq: bad) horroroso, péssimo

vilify /'vɪlɪfaɪ/ vt difamar

villa /'vɪlə/ n vivenda f, vila f; (country residence) casa f de campo

village /'vɪlɪdʒ/ n aldeia f, povoado m. ~r n aldeão m, aldeã f

villain /'vɪlən/ n patife m, mau-caráter m. ~y n infâmia f, vilania f

vindicat|e /'vɪndɪkeɪt/ vt vindicar, justificar. ~ion /-'keɪʃn/ n justificação f

vindictive /vɪn'dɪktɪv/ a vingativo

vine /vaɪn/ n (plant) vinha f

vinegar /'vɪnɪɡə(r)/ n vinagre m

vineyard /'vɪnjəd/ n vinha f, vinhedo m

vintage /'vɪntɪdʒ/ n (year) ano m de colheita de qualidade excepcional □ a (wine) de colheita excepcional e de um determinado ano; (car) de museu (colloq), fabricado entre 1917 e 1930

vinyl /'vaɪnɪl/ n vinil m

viola /vɪ'əʊlə/ n (mus) viola f, violeta f

violat|e /'vaɪəleɪt/ vt violar. ~ion /-'leɪʃn/ n violação f

violen|t /'vaɪələnt/ a violento. ~ce n violência f. ~tly adv violentamente, com violência

violet /'vaɪələt/ n (bot) violeta f; (colour) violeta m □ a violeta

violin /vaɪə'lɪn/ n violino m. ~ist n violinista mf

VIP /viːaɪ'piː/ abbr (very important person) VIP m, personalidade f importante

viper /'vaɪpə(r)/ n víbora f

virgin /'vɜːdʒɪn/ a & n virgem (f); ~ity /və'dʒɪnətɪ/ n virgindade f

Virgo /'vɜːɡəʊ/ n (astr) Virgem f, (P) virgo m

viril|e /'vɪraɪl/ a viril, varonil. ~ity /vɪ'rɪlətɪ/ n virilidade f

virtual /'vɜːtʃʊəl/ a que é na prática embora não em teoria, verdadeiro. **a ~ failure**/etc. é praticamente um fracasso/etc. ~ly adv praticamente

virtue /'vɜːtʃuː/ n (goodness, chastity) virtude f; (merit) mérito m. **by** or **in** ~ **of** por or em virtude de

virtuos|o /vɜːtʃʊ'əʊsəʊ/ n (pl -si /-siː/) virtuoso m, virtuose mf. ~ity /-'ɒsɪtɪ/ n virtuosidade f, virtuosismo m

virtuous /'vɜːtʃʊəs/ a virtuoso

virulen|t /'vɪrʊlənt/ a virulento. ~ce /-ləns/ n virulência f

virus /'vaɪərəs/ n (pl -es) vírus m; (colloq: disease) virose f

visa /'viːzə/ n visto m

viscount /'vaɪkaʊnt/ n visconde m. ~ess /-ɪs/ n viscondessa f

viscous /'vɪskəs/ a viscoso

vise /vaɪs/ n (Amer: vice) torno m

visib|le /'vɪzəbl/ a visível. ~ility /-'bɪlətɪ/ n visibilidade f. ~ly adv visivelmente

vision /'vɪʒn/ n (dream, insight) visão f; (seeing, sight) vista f, visão f

visionary /'vɪʒənərɪ/ a visionário; (plan, scheme etc) fantasista, quimérico □ n visionário m

visit /'vɪzɪt/ vt (pt visited) (person) visitar, fazer uma visita a; (place) visitar □ vi estar de visita □ n (tour, call) visita f; (stay) estada f, visita f. ~or n visitante mf, (guest) visita f

visor /'vaɪzə(r)/ *n* viseira *f*; (*in vehicle*) visor *m*

vista /'vɪstə/ *n* vista *f*, panorama *m*

visual /'vɪʒʊəl/ *a* visual. ~ **display unit** terminal *m* de vídeo. ~**ly** *adv* visualmente

visualize /'vɪʒʊəlaɪz/ *vt* visualizar; (*foresee*) imaginar, prever

vital /'vaɪtl/ *a* vital. ~ **statistics** estatísticas *fpl* demográficas; (*colloq: woman*) medidas *fpl*

vitality /vaɪ'tælətɪ/ *n* vitalidade *f*

vitamin /'vɪtəmɪn/ *n* vitamina *f*

vivacious /vɪ'veɪʃəs/ *a* cheio de vida, vivo, animado. ~**ly** /-'væsətɪ/ *n* vivacidade *f*, animação *f*

vivid /'vɪvɪd/ *a* vívido; (*imagination*) vivo. ~**ly** *adv* vividamente

vivisection /vɪvɪ'sekʃn/ *n* vivissecção *f*

vixen /'vɪksn/ *n* raposa *f* fêmea

vocabulary /və'kæbjʊlərɪ/ *n* vocabulário *m*

vocal /'vəʊkl/ *a* vocal; (*fig: person*) eloquente, (*P*) eloquente. ~ **cords** cordas *fpl* vocais. ~**ist** *n* vocalista *mf*

vocation /və'keɪʃn/ *n* vocação *f*; (*trade*) profissão *f*. ~**al** *a* vocacional, profissional

vociferous /və'sɪfərəs/ *a* vociferante

vodka /'vɒdkə/ *n* vodka *m*

vogue /vəʊg/ *n* voga *f*, moda *f*, popularidade *f*. **in** ~ em voga, na moda

voice /vɔɪs/ *n* voz *f* □ *vt* (*express*) exprimir

void /vɔɪd/ *a* vazio; (*jur*) nulo, sem validade □ *n* vácuo *m*, vazio *m*. **make** ~ anular, invalidar. ~ **of** sem, destituído de

volatile /'vɒlətaɪl/ *a* (*substance*) volátil; (*fig: changeable*) instável

volcano /vɒl'keɪnəʊ/ *n* (*pl* -oes) vulcão *m*. ~**ic** /-ænɪk/ *a* vulcânico

volition /və'lɪʃn/ *n* of one's own ~ de sua própria vontade

volley /'vɒlɪ/ *n* (*of blows etc*) saraivada *f*; (*of gunfire*) salva *f*; (*tennis*) voleio *m*. ~**ball** *n* voleibol *m*, vôlei *m*

volt /vəʊlt/ *n* volt *m*. ~**age** *n* voltagem *f*

voluble /'vɒljʊbl/ *a* falante, loquaz

volume /'vɒljuːm/ *n* (*book, sound*) volume *m*; (*capacity*) capacidade *f*

voluntary /'vɒləntərɪ/ *a* voluntário; (*unpaid*) não-remunerado. ~**ily** /-trəlɪ/ *adv* voluntariamente

volunteer /vɒlən'tɪə(r)/ *n* voluntário *m* □ *vi* oferecer-se (**to do** para fazer); (*mil*) alistar-se como voluntário □ *vt* oferecer espontaneamente

voluptuous /və'lʌptʃʊəs/ *a* voluptuoso, sensual

vomit /'vɒmɪt/ *vt/i* (*pt* vomited) vomitar □ *n* vômito *m*, (*P*) vómito *m*

voodoo /'vuːduː/ *n* vodu *m*

voracious /və'reɪʃəs/ *a* voraz. ~**ously** *adv* vorazmente. ~**ty** /və'ræsətɪ/ *n* voracidade *f*

vot|e /vəʊt/ *n* voto *m*; (*right*) direito *m* de voto □ *vt/i* votar. ~**er** *n* eleitor *m*. ~**ing** *n* votação *f*; (*poll*) escrutínio *m*

vouch /vaʊtʃ/ *vi* ~ **for** responder por, garantir

voucher /'vaʊtʃə(r)/ *n* (*for meal, transport*) vale *m*; (*receipt*) comprovante *m*

vow /vaʊ/ *n* voto *m* □ *vt* (*loyalty etc*) jurar (**to** a). ~ **to do** jurar fazer

vowel /'vaʊəl/ *n* vogal *f*

voyage /'vɔɪdʒ/ *n* viagem (por mar) *f*. ~**r** /-ə(r)/ *n* viajante *m*

vulgar /'vʌlgə(r)/ *a* ordinário, grosseiro; (*in common use*) vulgar. ~**ity** /-'gærətɪ/ *n* (*behaviour*) grosseria *f*, vulgaridade *f*

vulnerab|le /'vʌlnərəbl/ *a* vulnerável. **~ility** /-'bɪlətɪ/ *n* vulnerabilidade *f*

vulture /'vʌltʃə(r)/ *n* abutre *m*, urubu *m*

vying /'vaɪɪŋ/ *see* vie

W

wad /wɒd/ *n* bucha *f*, tampão *m*; (*bundle*) maço *m*, rolo *m*

wadding /'wɒdɪŋ/ *n* enchimento *m*

waddle /'wɒdl/ *vi* bambolear-se, rebolar-se, gingar

wade /weɪd/ *vi* **~ through** (*fig*) avançar a custo por; (*mud, water*) patinhar *em*

wafer /'weɪfə(r)/ *n* (*biscuit*) bolacha *f* de baunilha; (*relig*) hóstia *f*

waffle[1] /'wɒfl/ *n* (*colloq: talk*) lengalenga *f*, papo *m*, conversa *f*; (*colloq: writing*) lenga-lenga *f* □ *vi* (*colloq*) escrever muito sem dizer nada de importante

waffle[2] /'wɒfl/ *n* (*culin*) waffle *m*

waft /wɒft/ *vi* flutuar □ *vt* espalhar, levar suavemente

wag /wæg/ *vt/i* (*pt* **wagged**) abanar, agitar, sacudir

wage[1] /weɪdʒ/ *vt* (*campaign, war*) fazer

wage[2] /weɪdʒ/ *n* **~(s)** (*weekly, daily*) salário *m*, ordenado *m*. **~-claim** *n* pedido *m* de aumento de salário. **~-earner** *n* trabalhador *m* assalariado. **~-freeze** *n* congelamento *m* de salários

wager /'weɪdʒə(r)/ *n* (*bet*) aposta *f* □ *vt* apostar (**that** que)

waggle /'wægl/ *vt/i* abanar, agitar, sacudir

wagon /'wægən/ *n* (*horse-drawn*) carroça *f*; (*rail*) vagão *m* de mercadorias

waif /weɪf/ *n* criança *f* abandonada

wail /weɪl/ *vi* lamentar-se, gemer lamentosamente □ *n* lamentação *f*, gemido *m* lamentoso

waist /weɪst/ *n* cintura *f*. **~-line** *n* cintura *f*

waistcoat /'weɪskəʊt/ *n* colete *m*

wait /weɪt/ *vt/i* esperar □ *n* espera *f*. **~ for** esperar. **~ on** servir. **lie in ~ (for)** estar escondido à espera (de), armar uma emboscada (para). **keep sb ~ing** fazer alguém esperar. **~ing-list** *n* lista *f* de espera. **~ing-room** *n* sala *f* de espera

wait|er /'weɪtə(r)/ *n* garçom *m*, (*P*) criado *m* (de mesa). **~ress** *n* garçonete *f*, (*P*) criada *f* (de mesa)

waive /weɪv/ *vt* renunciar a, desistir de

wake[1] /weɪk/ *vt/i* (*pt* **woke**, *pp* **woken**) **~ (up)** acordar, despertar □ *n* (*before burial*) velório *m*

wake[2] /weɪk/ *n* (*ship*) esteira *f* (de espuma) *f*. **in the ~ of** (*following*) atrás de, em seguida a

waken /'weɪkən/ *vt/i* acordar, despertar

Wales /weɪlz/ *n* País *m* de Gales

walk /wɔːk/ *vi* andar, caminhar; (*not ride*) andar a pé; (*stroll*) passear □ *vt* (*streets*) andar por, percorrer; (*distance*) andar, fazer a pé, percorrer; (*dog*) (levar para) passear □ *n* (*stroll*) passeio *m*, volta *f*; (*excursion*) caminhada *f*; (*gait*) passo *m*, maneira *f* de andar; (*pace*) passo *m*; (*path*) caminho *m*. **it's a 5-minute ~** são 5 minutos a pé. **~ of life** meio *m*, condição *f* social. **~ out** (*go away*) sair; (*go on strike*) fazer greve. **~ out on** abandonar. **~-over** *n* vitória *f* fácil

walker /'wɔːkə(r)/ *n* caminhante *mf*

walkie-talkie /wɔːkɪ'tɔːkɪ/ *n* walkie-talkie *m*

walking /'wɔːkɪŋ/ *n* andar (a pé)

m, marcha (a pé) □ *a* (*colloq*: *dictionary*) vivo. ~-**stick** n bengala *f*

Walkman /'wɔːkmæn/ n walkman *m*

wall /wɔːl/ n parede *f*; (*around land*) muro *m*; (*of castle, town, fig*) muralha *f*; (*of stomach etc*) parede(s) *f* (*pl*) □ *vt* (*city*) fortificar; (*property*) murar. **go to the** ~ sucumbir, falir; (*firm*) ir à falência. **up the** ~ (*colloq*) fora de si

wallet /'wɒlɪt/ n carteira *f*

wallflower /'wɔːlflaʊə(r)/ n (*bot*) goivo *m*. **be a** ~ (*fig*) tomar chá de cadeira, (*P*) levar banho de cadeira

wallop /'wɒləp/ vt (*pt* **walloped**) (*sl*) espancar (*colloq*) □ n (*sl*) pancada *f* forte

wallow /'wɒləʊ/ vi (*in mud*) chafurdar; (*fig*) regozijar-se

wallpaper /'wɔːlpeɪpə(r)/ n papel *m* de parede □ *vt* forrar com papel de parede

walnut /'wɔːlnʌt/ n (*nut*) noz *f*; (*tree*) nogueira *f*

walrus /'wɔːlrəs/ n morsa *f*

waltz /wɔːls/ n valsa *f* □ *vi* valsar

wan /wɒn/ *a* pálido

wand /wɒnd/ n (*magic*) varinha *f* mágica *or* de condão

wander /'wɒndə(r)/ vi andar ao acaso, vagar, errar; (*river*) serpentear; (*mind, speech*) divagar; (*stray*) extraviar-se. ~**er** n vagabundo *m*, andarilho *m*. ~**ing** *a* errante

wane /weɪn/ vi diminuir, minguar; (*decline*) declinar □ n **on the** ~ em declínio; (*moon*) no quarto minguante

wangle /'wæŋgl/ vt (*colloq*) conseguir algo através de pistolão

want /wɒnt/ vt querer (**to do** fazer); (*need*) precisar de; (*ask for*) exigir, requerer □ *vi* ~ **for** ter falta de □ n (*need*) necessi-

dade *f*; precisão *f*; (*desire*) desejo *m*; (*lack*) falta *f*, carência *f*. **for** ~ **of** por falta de. **I** ~ **you to go** eu quero que você vá. ~**ed** *a* (*criminal*) procurado pela polícia; (*in ad*) precisa(m)-se

wanting /'wɒntɪŋ/ *a* falho, falto (**in** de). **be found** ~ não estar à altura

wanton /'wɒntən/ *a* (*playful*) travesso, brincalhão; (*cruelty, destruction etc*) gratuito; (*woman*) despudorado

WAP /wæp/ *a* WAP

war /wɔː(r)/ n guerra *f*. **at** ~ em guerra. **on the** ~-**path** em pé de guerra

warble /'wɔːbl/ vt/i gorjear

ward /wɔːd/ n (*in hospital*) enfermaria *f*; (*jur: minor*) pupilo *m*; (*pol*) círculo *m* eleitoral □ *vt* ~ **off** (*a blow*) aparar; (*anger*) desviar; (*danger*) prevenir, evitar

warden /'wɔːdn/ n (*of institution*) diretor *m*, (*P*) director *m*; (*of park*) guarda *m*

warder /'wɔːdə(r)/ n guarda (de prisão) *m*, carcereiro *m*

wardrobe /'wɔːdrəʊb/ n (*place*) armário *m*, guarda-roupa *m*, (*P*) guarda-fato *m*; (*clothes*) guarda-roupa *m*

warehouse /'weəhaʊs/ n (*pl* -s /-haʊzɪz/) armazém *m*, depósito *m* de mercadorias

wares /weəz/ npl (*goods*) mercadorias *fpl*, artigos *mpl*

warfare /'wɔːfeə(r)/ n guerra *f*

warhead /'wɔːhed/ n ogiva (de combate) *f*

warlike /'wɔːlaɪk/ *a* marcial, guerreiro; (*bellicose*) belicoso

warm /wɔːm/ *a* (-**er**, -**est**) quente; (*hearty*) caloroso, cordial. **be or feel** ~ estar com *or* ter *or* sentir calor □ vt/i ~ (**up**) aquecer(-se). ~-**hearted** *a* afetuoso, (*P*) afectuoso, com calor humano. ~**ly** adv (*heartily*) calorosamente.

wrap up ~**ly** agasalhar-se bem. ~**th** *n* calor *m*

warn /wɔːn/ *vt* avisar, prevenir. ~ **sb off sth** (*advise against*) pôr alguém de prevenção ou de pé atrás com alg coisa; (*forbid*) proibir alg coisa a alguém. ~**ing** *n* aviso *m*. ~**ing light** lâmpada *f* de advertência. **without** ~**ing** sem aviso, sem prevenir

warp /wɔːp/ *vt/i* (*wood etc*) empenar; (*fig: pervert*) torcer, deformar, desvirtuar. ~**ed** *a* (*fig*) deturpado, pervertido

warrant /ˈwɒrənt/ *n* autorização *f*; (*for arrest*) mandato (de captura) *m*; (*comm*) título *m* de crédito, warrant *m* □ *vt* justificar; (*guarantee*) garantir

warranty /ˈwɒrənti/ *n* garantia *f*

warring /ˈwɔːriŋ/ *a* em guerra; (*rival*) contrário, antagónico, (*P*) antagónico

warrior /ˈwɒriə(r)/ *n* guerreiro *m*

warship /ˈwɔːʃip/ *n* navio *m* de guerra

wart /wɔːt/ *n* verruga *f*

wartime /ˈwɔːtaim/ *n* **in** ~ em tempo de guerra

wary /ˈweəri/ *a* (-**ier**, -**iest**) cauteloso, prudente

was /wɒz/, *unstressed* /wəz/ *see* **be**

wash /wɒʃ/ *vt/i* lavar(-se); (*flow over*) molhar, inundar □ *n* lavagem *f*; (*dirty clothes*) roupa *f* para lavar; (*of ship*) esteira *f*; (*of paint*) fina camada *f* de tinta. **have a** ~ lavar-se. ~**-basin** *n* pia *f*, (*P*) lavatório *m*. ~**-cloth** *n* (*Amer: face-cloth*) toalha *f* de rosto. **one's hands of** lavar as mãos de. ~ **out** (*cup etc*) lavar; (*stain*) tirar lavando. ~**-out** *n* (*sl*) fiasco *m*. ~**-room** *n* (*Amer*) banheiro *m*, (*P*) casa *f* de banho. ~ **up** lavar a louça; (*Amer: wash oneself*) lavar-se. ~**-able** *a* lavável. ~**ing** *n* (*dirty*) roupa *f* suja; (*clean*) roupa *f* lavada. ~**ing-**

machine *n* máquina *f* de lavar roupa. ~**ing-powder** *n* detergente *m* em pó. ~**ing-up** *n* lavagem *f* da louça

washed-out /wɒʃtˈaʊt/ *a* (*faded*) desbotado; (*exhausted*) exausto

washer /ˈwɒʃə(r)/ *n* (*machine*) máquina *f* de lavar roupa, louça *f*, (*P*) loiça *f*; (*ring*) anilha *f*

wasp /wɒsp/ *n* vespa *f*

wastage /ˈweistidʒ/ *n* desperdício *m*, perda *f*. ~ **natural** = desgaste *m* natural

waste /weist/ *vt* desperdiçar, esbanjar; (*time*) perder □ *vi* ~ **away** consumir-se □ *a* (*useless*) inútil; (*material*) de refugo □ *n* desperdício *m*, perda *f*; (*of time*) perda *f*; (*rubbish*) lixo *m*. **lay** ~ assolar, desvastar. ~ (**land**) (*desolate*) região *f* desolada, ermo *m*; (*unused*) (*terreno*) baldio *m*. ~**-disposal unit** triturador *m* de lixo. ~ **paper** papéis *mpl* velhos. ~**-paper basket** cesto *m* de papéis

wasteful /ˈweistfl/ *a* dispendioso; (*person*) esbanjador, gastador, perdulário

watch /wɒtʃ/ *vt/i* ver bem, olhar com atenção, observar; (*game, TV*) ver; (*guard, spy on*) vigiar; (*be careful about*) tomar cuidado com □ *n* vigia *f*, vigilância *f*; (*naut*) quarto *m*; (*for telling time*) relógio *m*. ~**-dog** *n* cão *m* de guarda. ~ **out** (*look out*) estar à espreita (**for** de); (*take care*) acautelar-se. ~**-strap** *n* correia *f*, pulseira *f* do relógio. ~**-tower** *n* torre *f* de observação. ~**ful** *a* atento, vigilante

watchmaker /ˈwɒtʃmeikə(r)/ *n* relojoeiro *m*

watchman /ˈwɒtʃmən/ *n* (*pl* -**men**) (*of building*) guarda *m*. **(night-)** ~ guarda-noturno *m*

watchword /ˈwɒtʃwɜːd/ *n* lema *m*, divisa *f*

water /ˈwɔːtə(r)/ n água f □ vt regar □ vi (of eyes) lacrimejar, chorar. **~ down** (milk, wine) aguar, batizar, diluir; (P) baptizar (colloq); (fig: tone down) suavizar. **~-closet** n WC m, banheiro m, (P) lavabos mpl. **~-colour** n aquarela f. **~-ice** n sorvete m. **~-lily** n nenúfar m. **~-main** n cano m principal da rede. **~-melon** n melancia f. **~-pistol** n pistola f de água. **~-polo** pólo m aquático. **~-skiing** n esqui m aquático. **~-wheel** n roda f hidráulica

watercress /ˈwɔːtəkres/ n agrião m

waterfall /ˈwɔːtəfɔːl/ n queda f de água, cascata f

watering-can /ˈwɔːtərɪŋkæn/ n regador m

waterlogged /ˈwɔːtəlɒgd/ a saturado de água; (land) empapado, alagado; (vessel) inundado, alagado

watermark /ˈwɔːtəmɑːk/ n (in paper) marca-d'água f, filigrana f

waterproof /ˈwɔːtəpruːf/ a impermeável; (watch) à prova d'água

watershed /ˈwɔːtəʃed/ n (fig) momento m decisivo; (in affairs) ponto m crítico

watertight /ˈwɔːtətaɪt/ a à prova d'água, hermético; (fig: argument etc) inequívoco, irrefutável

waterway /ˈwɔːtəweɪ/ n via f navegável

waterworks /ˈwɔːtəwɜːks/ n (place) estação f hidráulica

watery /ˈwɔːtərɪ/ a (colour) pálido; (eyes) lacrimoso; (soup) aguado; (tea) fraco

watt /wɒt/ n watt m

wav|e /weɪv/ n onda f; (in hair; radio) onda f; (sign) aceno m □ vt acenar com; (sword) brandir; (hair) ondular □ vi acenar (com a mão); (hair etc) ondular; (flag) tremular. **~eband** n faixa f de

onda. **~e goodbye** dizer adeus. **~elength** n comprimento m de onda. **~y** a ondulado

waver /ˈweɪvə(r)/ vi vacilar; (hesitate) hesitar

wax[1] /wæks/ n cera f □ vt encerar; (car) polir. **~en, ~y** adjs de cera

wax[2] /wæks/ vi (of moon) aumentar, crescer

waxwork /ˈwækswɜːk/ n (dummy) figura f de cera. **~s** npl (exhibition) museu m de figuras de cera

way /weɪ/ n (road, path) caminho m, estrada f, rua f (to para); (distance) percurso m; (direction) (P) direcção f; (manner) modo m, maneira f; (means) meios mpl; (respect) respeito m. **~s** (habits) costumes mpl □ adv (colloq) consideravelmente, de longe. **be in the ~** atrapalhar. **be on one's ~** or **the ~** estar a caminho. **by the ~** a propósito. **by ~ of** por, via, através. **get one's own ~** conseguir o que quer. **give ~** (yield) ceder; (collapse) desabar; (auto) dar a preferência. **in a ~** de certo modo. **make one's ~** ir. **that ~** dessa maneira. **this ~** desta maneira. **~ in** entrada f. **~ out** saída f. **~-out** a (colloq) excêntrico

waylay /weɪˈleɪ/ vt (pt -laid) (assail) armar uma cilada para; (stop) interceptar

wayward /ˈweɪwəd/ a (wilful) teimoso; (perverse) caprichoso, difícil

WC /dʌb(ə)ljuːˈsiː/ n WC m, banheiro m, (P) casa f de banho

we /wiː/ pron nós

weak /wiːk/ a (-er, -est) fraco; (delicate) frágil. **~en** vt/i enfraquecer; (give way) fraquejar. **~ly** adv fracamente. **~ness** n fraqueza f; (fault) ponto m fraco. **a ~ness for** (liking) um fraco por

weakling /ˈwiːklɪŋ/ n

wealth /welθ/ n riqueza f; (*riches, resources*) riquezas fpl; (*quantity*) abundância f

wealthy /'welθɪ/ a (**-ier, -iest**) rico

wean /wi:n/ vt (*baby*) desmamar; (*from habit etc*) desabituar

weapon /'wepən/ n arma f

wear /weə(r)/ vt (*pt* **wore**, *pp* **worn**) (*have on*) usar, trazer; (*put on*) pôr; (*expression*) ter; (*damage*) gastar. ~ **black/red/** *etc* vestir-se de preto/vermelho/ *etc* □ vi (*last*) durar; (*become old, damaged etc*) gastar-se □ n (*use*) uso m; (*deterioration*) gasto m, uso m; (*endurance*) resistência f; (*clothing*) roupa f. ~ **and tear** desgaste m. ~ **down** gastar; (*person*) extenuar. ~ **off** passar. ~ **on** (*time*) passar lentamente. ~ **out** gastar; (*tire*) esgotar

wear|y /'wɪərɪ/ a (**-ier, -iest**) fatigado, cansado; (*tiring*) fatigante, cansativo □ vi ~ **y of** cansar-se de. ~**ily** adv com lassidão, cansadamente. ~**iness** n fadiga f

weasel /'wi:zl/ n doninha f

weather /'weðə(r)/ n tempo m □ a meteorológico □ vt (*survive*) agüentar, (P) aguentar, resistir a. **under the** ~ (*colloq: ill*) indisposto, achacado. ~**-beaten** a curtido pelo tempo. ~**-forecast** n boletim m meteorológico. ~**-vane** n cata-vento m

weathercock /'weðəkɒk/ n (*lit & fig*) cata-vento m

weav|e[1] /wi:v/ vt (*pt* **wove**, *pp* **woven**) (*cloth etc*) tecer; (*plot*) urdir, criar □ n (*style*) tipo m de tecido. ~**er** /-ə(r)/ n tecelão m, tecelã f. ~**ing** n tecelagem f

weave[2] /wi:v/ vi (*move*) serpear; (*through traffic, obstacles*) ziguezaguear

web /web/ n (*of spider*) teia f; (*fabric*) tecido m; (*comput*) web m; (*on foot*) membrana f interdigital. ~**bed** a (*foot*) palmado.

~**bing** n (*in chair*) tira f de tecido forte. ~**-footed** a palmípede. ~ **page** página f web. ~ **site** site m

wed /wed/ vt/i (*pt* **wedded**) casar (-se)

wedding /'wedɪŋ/ n casamento m. ~**-cake** n bolo m de noiva. ~**-ring** n aliança f (de casamento) f

wedge /wedʒ/ n calço m, cunha f; (*cake*) fatia f; (*of lemon*) quarto m; (*under wheel etc*) calço m, cunha f □ vt calçar; (*push*) meter or enfiar à força; (*pack in*) entalar

Wednesday /'wenzdɪ/ n quarta-feira f

weed /wi:d/ n erva f daninha □ vt/i arrancar as ervas, capinar. ~**-killer** n herbicida m. ~ **out** suprimir, arrancar. ~**y** a (*fig: person*) fraco

week /wi:k/ n semana f. **a** ~ **to-day/tomorrow** de hoje/de amanhã a oito dias. ~**ly** a semanal □ a & n (*periodical*) (jornal) semanário (m) □ adv semanalmente, todas as semanas

weekday /'wi:kdeɪ/ n dia m de semana

weekend /'wi:kend/ n fim-de-semana m

weep /wi:p/ vt/i (*pt* **wept**) chorar (**for sb** por alguém). ~**ing willow** (salgueiro-)chorão m

weigh /weɪ/ vt/i pesar. ~ **anchor** levantar âncora or ferro, zarpar. ~ **down** (*weight*) sobrecarregar; (*bend*) envergar; (*fig*) acabrunhar. ~ **up** (*colloq: examine*) pesar

weight /weɪt/ n peso m. **lose** ~ emagrecer. **put on** ~ engordar. ~**less** a imponderável. ~**-lifter** n halterofilista m. ~**-lifting** n halterofilia f. ~**y** a pesado; (*subject etc*) de peso; (*influential*) influente

weighting /'weɪtɪŋ/ n suplemento m salarial

weir /wɪə(r)/ n represa f, açude m

weird /wɪəd/ a (-er, -est) misterioso; (strange) estranho, bizarro

welcome /'welkəm/ a agradável; (timely) oportuno □ int (seja) benvindo! □ n acolhimento m □ vt acolher, receber; (as greeting) dar as boas vindas a. **be** ~e er bem-vindo. **you're** ~e! (after thank you) não tem de quê!, de nada! ~**e to do** livre para fazer. ~**ing** a acolhedor

weld /weld/ vt soldar □ n solda f. ~**er** n soldador m. ~**ing** n soldagem f, soldadura f

welfare /'welfeə(r)/ n bem-estar m; (aid) assistência f, previdência f social. **W~ State** Estado-Providência m

well[1] /wel/ n (for water, oil) poço m; (of stairs) vão m. ~(up) vi poço m

well[2] /wel/ adv (better, best) bem □ a bem (invar) □ int bem! **as** ~ também. **we may as** ~ **go** é melhor irnos andando. **as** ~ **as** tão bem como; (in addition) assim como. **be** ~ (healthy) ir or passar bem. **do** ~ (succeed) sair-se bem, ser bem sucedido. **very** ~ muito bem. ~ **done!** bravo!, muito bem! ~**-behaved** a bem comportado, educado. ~**-being** n bem-estar m. ~**-bred** a (bem) educado. ~**-done** a (of meat) bem passado. ~**-dressed** a bem vestido. ~**-heeled** a (colloq: wealthy) rico. ~**-informed** a versado, bem informado. ~**-known** a (bem-)conhecido. ~**-meaning** a bem intencionado. ~**-off** a rico, próspero. ~**-read** a instruído. ~**-spoken** a bem-falante. ~**-timed** a oportuno. ~**-to-do** a rico. ~**-wisher** n admirador m, simpatizante mf

wellington /'welɪŋtən/ n (boot) bota f alta de borracha

Welsh /welʃ/ a galês □ n (lang)

galês m. ~**man** n galês m. ~ **woman** n galesa f

wend /wend/ vt ~ **one's way** dirigir-se, seguir o seu caminho

went /went/ see **go**

wept /wept/ see **weep**

were /wɜː(r)/; unstressed /wə(r)/ see **be**

west /west/ n oeste m. **the W~** (pol) o Oeste, o Ocidente □ a oci-dental, do oeste □ adv ao oeste, para o oeste. **W~ Indian** a & n antilhano (m). **the W~ Indies** as Antilhas. ~**erly** a ocidental, oeste. ~**ward** a para o oeste. ~**ward(s)** adv para o oeste

western /'westən/ a ocidental, do oeste; (pol) ocidental □ n (film) filme m de cowboys, bangue-bangue m

westernize /'westənaɪz/ vt ocidentalizar

wet /wet/ a (wetter, wettest) mo-lhado; (of weather) chuvoso, de chuva; (colloq: person) fraco. **get** ~ molhar-se □ vt (pt wetted) molhar. ~ **blanket** (colloq) des-mancha-prazeres mf invar (colloq). ~ **paint** pintado de fresco. ~ **suit** roupa f de mergulho

whack /wæk/ vt (colloq) bater em □ n (colloq) pancada f. ~**ed** a (colloq) morto de cansaço, reben-tado (colloq). ~**ing** a (sl) enorme, de todo o tamanho

whale /weɪl/ n baleia f

wharf /wɔːf/ n (pl wharfs) cais m

what /wɒt/ a (interr, excl) que. ~ **time is it?** que horas são? ~ **an idea!** que idéia! □ pron (interr) (o) quê, como, o que, qual, quais; (object) o que; (after prep) que; (that which) o que, aquilo que. ~? (o) quê?, como? ~ **is it?** o que é? ~ **is your address?** qual é o seu endereço? ~ **is your name?** como se chama? ~ **can you see?** o que é que você pode ver? **this is** ~ **I write with é** com isto que escrevo. **that's** ~ **I need** é disso que eu preciso. **do** ~ **you want** faça o que or aquilo que quiser. ~ **about me/him/** etc? e eu/ele/etc? ~ **about doing sth?** e se fizéssemos alg coisa? ~ **for?** para quê?

whatever /wɒtˈevə(r)/ a ~ **book/** etc qualquer livro/etc que seja □ pron (no matter what) qualquer que seja; (anything that) o que quer que, tudo o que. **nothing** ~ absolutamente nada. ~ **happens** aconteça o que acontecer. **do** ~ **you like** faça o que quiser

whatsoever /wɒtsəʊˈevə(r)/ a & pron = **whatever**

wheat /wiːt/ n trigo m

wheedle /ˈwiːdl/ vt convencer, persuadir, levar a

wheel /wiːl/ n roda f □ vt empurrar □ vi rodar, rolar. **at the** ~ (of vehicle) ao volante; (helm) ao leme

wheelbarrow /ˈwiːlbærəʊ/ n carrinho m de mão

wheelchair /ˈwiːltʃeə(r)/ n cadeira f de rodas

wheeze /wiːz/ vi respirar ruidosamente □ n respiração f difícil

when /wen/ adv, conj & pron quando. **the day/moment** ~ o dia/momento em que

whenever /wenˈevə(r)/ conj & adv (at whatever time) quando quer que, quando; (every time that) (de) cada vez que, sempre que

where /weə(r)/ adv, conj & pron onde, aonde; (in which place) em que, onde; (whereas) enquanto que, ao passo que. ~ **is he going?** aonde é que ele vai? ~**abouts** adv onde □ n paradeiro m. ~**by** adv pelo que. ~**upon** adv após o que, depois do que

whereas /weərˈæz/ conj enquanto que, ao passo que

wherever /weərˈevə(r)/ conj & adv

onde quer que. ~ **can it be?** onde pode estar?

whet /wet/ vt (pt **whetted**) (appetite, desire) aguçar, despertar

whether /ˈweðə(r)/ conj se. **not know** ~ não saber se. ~ **I go or not** caso eu vá ou não

which /wɪtʃ/ interr a & pron qual, que ~ **bag is yours?** qual das malas é a sua? ~ **is your coat?** qual é o seu casaco? **do you know** ~ **he's taken?** sabe qual/quais é que lhe levou? □ rel pron que, o qual; (referring to whole sentence) o que; (after prep) que, o qual, cujo. at ~ em qual/que. **from** ~ do qual/que. **of** ~ do qual/de que. **to** ~ para o qual/o que

whichever /wɪtʃˈevə(r)/ a ~ **book/**etc qualquer livro/etc que seja, seja que livro/etc for. **take** ~ **book you wish** leve o livro que quiser □ pron qualquer, quaisquer

whiff /wɪf/ n (of fresh air) sopro m, lufada f; (smell) baforada f

while /waɪl/ n (espaço de) tempo m, momento m. **once in a** ~ de vez em quando □ conj (when) enquanto; (although) embora; (whereas) enquanto que □ vt ~ **away** (time) passar

whim /wɪm/ n capricho m

whimper /ˈwɪmpə(r)/ vi gemer; (baby) choramingar □ n gemido m; (baby) choro m

whimsical /ˈwɪmzɪkl/ a (person) caprichoso; (odd) bizarro

whine /waɪn/ vi lamuriar-se, queixar-se; (dog) ganir □ n lamúria f, queixume m; (dog) ganido m

whip /wɪp/ n chicote m □ vt (pt whipped) chicotear; (culin) bater □ vi (move) ir a toda a pressa. ~**round** n (colloq) coleta f, vaquinha f. ~ **up** excitar; (cause) provocar; (colloq: meal) preparar

rapidamente. **~ped cream**
creme *m* chantilly

whirl /wɜːl/ *vt/i* (fazer) rodopiar, girar □ *n* rodopio *m*

whirlpool /ˈwɜːlpuːl/ *n* redemoinho *m*

whirlwind /ˈwɜːlwɪnd/ *n* redemoinho *m* de vento, turbilhão *m*

whirr /wɜː(r)/ *vi* zunir, zumbir

whisk /wɪsk/ *vt/i* levar/ tirar bruscamente; (*culin*) bater; (*flies*) sacudir □ *n* (*culin*) batedeira *f*. **~ away** (*brush away*) sacudir

whisker /ˈwɪskə(r)/ *n* fio *m* de barba. **~s** *npl* (*of animal*) bigode *m*; (*beard*) barba *f*; (*sideboards*) suíças *fpl*

whisky /ˈwɪskɪ/ *n* uísque *m*

whisper /ˈwɪspə(r)/ *vt/i* sussurrar, murmurar; (*of stream, leaves*) sussurrar □ *n* sussurro *m*, murmúrio *m*. **in a ~** baixinho, em voz baixa

whist /wɪst/ *n* uíste *m*, (*P*) whist *m*

whistle /ˈwɪsl/ *n* assobio *m*; (*instrument*) apito *m* □ *vt/i* assobiar; (*with instrument*) apitar

Whit /wɪt/ *a* **~ Sunday** domingo *m* de Pentecostes

white /waɪt/ *a* (**-er, -est**) branco, alvo; (*pale*) pálido □ *n* (*colour; of eyes; person*) branco *m*; (*of egg*) clara (de ovo) *f*. **go ~** (*turn pale*) empalidecer; (*of hair*) branquear, embranquecer. **~ coffee** café *m* com leite. **~collar worker** empregado *m* de escritório. **~ elephant** (*fig*) trambolho *m*, elefante *m* branco. **~ lie** mentirinha *f*. **~ness** *n* brancura *f*, alvura *f*

whiten /ˈwaɪtn/ *vt/i* branquear

whitewash /ˈwaɪtwɒʃ/ *n* cal *f*; (*fig*) encobrimento *m* □ *vt* caiar; (*fig*) encobrir

Whitsun /ˈwɪtsn/ *n* Pentecostes *m*

whittle /ˈwɪtl/ *vt* **~ down** aparar,

cortar aparas; (*fig*) reduzir gradualmente

whiz /wɪz/ *vi* (*pt* **whizzed**) (*through air*) zunir, sibilar; (*rush*) passar a toda a velocidade. **~-kid** *n* (*colloq*) prodígio *m*

who /huː/ *interr pron quem* □ *rel pron* que, o(a) qual, os(as) quais

whoever /huːˈevə(r)/ *pron* (*no matter who*) quem quer que, seja quem for; (*the one who*) aquele que

whole /həʊl/ *a* inteiro, todo; (*not broken*) intacto. **the ~ house/** *etc* toda a casa/*etc* □ *n* totalidade *f*; (*unit*) todo *m*. **as a ~** no conjunto, como um todo. **on the ~** de um modo geral. **~-hearted** *a* de todo o coração; (*person*) dedicado. **~-heartedly** *adv* sem reservas, sinceramente

wholefood /ˈhəʊlfuːd/ *n* comida *f* integral

wholemeal /ˈhəʊlmiːl/ *a* **~ bread** pão *m* integral

wholesale /ˈhəʊlseɪl/ *n* venda *f* por grosso *or* por atacado □ *a* (*firm*) por grosso, por atacado; (*fig*) sistemático, em massa □ *adv* (*in large quantities*) por atacado; (*fig*) em massa, em grande escala. **~r** /-ə(r)/ *n* grossista *mf*, atacadista *mf*

wholesome /ˈhəʊlsəm/ *a* sadio, saudável

wholewheat /ˈhəʊlwiːt/ *a* = **wholemeal**

wholly /ˈhəʊlɪ/ *adv* inteiramente, completamente

whom /huːm/ *interr pron quem* □ *rel pron* (*that*) que; (*after prep*) quem, que, o qual

whooping cough /ˈhuːpɪŋkɒf/ *n* coqueluche *f*

whore /hɔː(r)/ *n* prostituta *f*

whose /huːz/ *rel pron & a* cujo, de quem □ *interr pron* de quem. **~ hat is this?, ~ is this hat?** de quem é este chapéu? **~ son are**

you? de quem é que o senhor é filho?

why /waɪ/ *adv* porque, por que motivo, por que razão, porquê. **she doesn't know ~ he's here** ela não sabe porque *or* por que motivo ele está aqui. **she doesn't know ~** ela não sabe porquê. **do you know ~?** você sabe porquê? □ *int* (*protest*) ora, ora essa; (*discovery*) oh. **~ yes**/*etc* ah, sim

wick /wɪk/ *n* torcida *f*, mecha *f*, pavio *m*

wicked /'wɪkɪd/ *a* mau, malvado; (*mischievous*, *spiteful*) maldoso. **~ly** *adv* maldosamente. **~ness** *n* maldade *f*, malvadeza *f*

wicker /'wɪkə(r)/ *n* verga *f*, vime *m*. **~-work** *n* trabalho *m* de verga *or* de vime

wicket /'wɪkɪt/ *n* (*cricket*) arco *m*

wide /waɪd/ *a* (**-er**, **-est**) largo; (*extensive*) vasto, grande, extenso. **two metres ~** com dois metros de largura □ *adv* longe; (*fully*) completamente. **open ~** (*door*, *window*) abrir(-se) de par em par, escancarar(-se); (*mouth*) abrir bem. **~ awake** desperto, acordado. **far and ~** por toda a parte. **~ly** *adv* largamente; (*travel*, *spread*) muito; (*generally*) geralmente; (*extremely*) extremamente

widen /'waɪdn/ *vt/i* alargar(-se)

widespread /'waɪdspred/ *a* muito espalhado, difundido

widow /'wɪdəʊ/ *n* viúva *f*. **~ed** *a* (*man*) viúvo; (*woman*) viúva. **be ~ed** enviuvar, ficar viúvo *or* viúva. **~er** *n* viúvo *m*. **~hood** *n* viuvez *f*

width /wɪdθ/ *n* largura *f*

wield /wi:ld/ *vt* (*axe etc*) manejar; (*fig: power*) exercer

wife /waɪf/ *n* (*pl* wives) mulher *f*, esposa *f*

wig /wɪg/ *n* cabeleira (postiça) *f*; (*judge's etc*) peruca *f*

wiggle /'wɪgl/ *vt/i* remexer(-se), retorcer(-se), mexer(-se) dum lado para outro

wild /waɪld/ *a* (**-er**, **-est**) selvagem; (*of plant*) silvestre; (*mad*) louco; (*enraged*) furioso, violento □ *adv* a esmo; (*without control*) à solta. **~s** *npl* regiões *fpl* selvagens. **~goose chase** falsa pista *f*, tentativa *f* inútil. **~ly** *adv* violentamente; (*madly*) loucamente

wildcat /'waɪldkæt/ *a* **~ strike** greve *f* ilegal

wilderness /'wɪldənɪs/ *n* deserto *m*

wildlife /'waɪldlaɪf/ *n* animais *mpl* selvagens

wile /waɪl/ *n* artimanha *f*; (*cunning*) astúcia *f*, manha *f*

wilful /'wɪlfl/ *a* (*person*) voluntarioso; (*act*) intencional, propositado

will[1] /wɪl/ *v aux* you **~ sing/he ~ do**/*etc* tu cantarás/ele fará/ *etc*. (*1st person: future expressing will or intention*) **I ~ sing/we ~ do**/*etc* eu cantarei/nós faremos/*etc*. **~ you have a cup of coffee?** quer tomar um cafézinho? **~ you shut the door?** quer fazer o favor de fechar a porta?

will[2] /wɪl/ *n* vontade *f*; (*document*) testamento *m*. **at ~** à vontade, quando *or* como se quiser □ *vt* (*wish*) querer; (*bequeath*) deixar em testamento. **~-power** *n* força *f* de vontade

willing /'wɪlɪŋ/ *a* pronto, de boa vontade. **~ to** disposto a. **~ly** *adv* (*with pleasure*) de boa vontade, de bom grado; (*not forced*) voluntariamente. **~ness** *n* boa vontade *f*, disposição *f* (**to do** em fazer)

willow /'wɪləʊ/ *n* salgueiro *m*

willy-nilly /wɪlɪ'nɪlɪ/ *adv* de bom ou de mau grado, quer queira ou não

wilt /wɪlt/ vi murchar, definhar

wily /'waɪlɪ/ a (-ier, -iest) manhoso, matreiro

win /wɪn/ vt/i (pt won, pres p winning) ganhar □ n vitória f. ~ over vt convencer, conquistar

wince /wɪns/ vi estremecer, contrair-se.

winch /wɪntʃ/ n guincho m □ vt içar com guincho

wind¹ /wɪnd/ n vento m; (breath) fôlego m; (flatulence) gases mpl. get ~ of (fig) ouvir rumor de. put the ~ up (sl) assustar. in the ~ no ar. ~ farm central f eólica. ~ instrument (mus) instrumento m de sopro. ~swept a varrido pelo vento

wind² /waɪnd/ vt/i (pt wound) enrolar(-se); (wrap) envolver, pôr em volta; (of path, river) serpentear. ~ (up) (clock etc) dar corda em. ~ up (end) terminar, acabar; (fig: speech etc) concluir; (firm) liquidar. he'll ~ up in jail (colloq) vai ter a acabar na cadeia. ~ing a (path) sinuoso; (staircase) em caracol

windfall /'wɪndfɔːl/ n fruta f caída; (fig: money) sorte f grande

windmill /'wɪndmɪl/ n moinho m de vento

window /'wɪndəʊ/ n janela f; (of shop) vitrine f, (P) montra f; (counter) guichê m, (P) guichet m. ~-box n jardineira f, (P) floreira f. ~-cleaner n limpador m de janelas. ~-dressing n decoração f de vitrines; (fig) apresentação f cuidadosa. ~-ledge n peitoril m. ~-pane n vidro m, vidraça f. go ~-shopping ir ver vitrines. ~-sill n peitoril m

windpipe /'wɪndpaɪp/ n traqueia f, (P) traqueia f

windscreen /'wɪndskriːn/ n pára-brisa m, (P) pára-brisas m invar. ~-wiper /-waɪpə(r)/ n limpador m de pára-brisa

windshield /'wɪndʃiːld/ n (Amer) = windscreen

windsurf|er /'wɪndsɜːfə(r)/ n surfista mf. ~ing n surfe m

windy /'wɪndɪ/ a (-ier, -iest) ventoso. it is very ~ está ventando muito

wine /waɪn/ n vinho m. ~ bar bar m para degustação de vinhos. ~-cellar n adega f, cave f. ~-grower n vinicultor m. ~-growing n vinicultura f. ~-list n lista f de vinhos. ~-tasting n prova f or degustação f de vinhos. ~ waiter garçon m

wineglass /'waɪnɡlɑːs/ n copo m de vinho; (with stem) cálice m

wing /wɪŋ/ n asa f; (mil) flanco m; (archit) ala f; (auto) pára-lamas m invar, (P) guarda-lamas m invar. ~s (theat) bastidores mpl. under sb's ~ debaixo das asas de alguém. ~ed a alado

wink /wɪŋk/ vi piscar o olho; (light, star) cintilar, piscar □ n piscadela f. not sleep a ~ não pregar olho

winner /'wɪnə(r)/ n vencedor m

winning /'wɪnɪŋ/ see win □ a vencedor, vitorioso; (number) premiado; (smile) encantador, atraente. ~-post n meta f, poste de chegada f. ~s npl ganhos mpl

wint|er /'wɪntə(r)/ n inverno m □ vi hibernar. ~ry a de inverno, invernoso; (smile) glacial

wipe /waɪp/ vt limpar; (dry) enxugar, limpar □ n limpadela f. ~ off limpar. ~ out (destroy) aniquilar, limpar (colloq); (cancel) cancelar. ~ up enxugar

wir|e /'waɪə(r)/ n arame m; (colloq: telegram) telegrama m. ~ (electric) ~e fio eléctrico m, (P) eléctrico □ vt (a house) montar a instalação eléctrica em; (colloq: telegraph) telegrafar. ~e netting rede f de arame. ~ing n *(electr)* instalação *f* elétrica, *(P)* eléctrica

wireless /'waɪəlɪs/ *n* rádio *f*; *(set)* rádio *m*

wiry /'waɪərɪ/ *a* (**-ier, -iest**) magro e rijo

wisdom /'wɪzdəm/ *n* sagacidade *f*, sabedoria *f*; *(common sense)* bom senso *m*, sensatez *f*. ~ **tooth** dente *m* (do) sizo

wise /waɪz/ *a* (**-er, -est**) *(person)* sábio, avisado, sensato; *(look)* entendedor. ~ **guy** *(colloq)* sabichão *m* *(colloq)*, sabe-tudo *m* *(colloq)*. **none the** ~**r** sem entender nada. ~**ly** *adv* sensatamente

wisecrack /'waɪzkræk/ *n* *(colloq)* (boa) piada *f*

wish /wɪʃ/ *n* *(desire, aspiration)* desejo *m*, vontade *f*; *(request)* pedido *m*; *(greeting)* desejo *m*, voto *m*. **I have no** ~ **to go** não tenho nenhum desejo or nenhuma vontade de ir □ *vt* *(desire, bid)* desejar; *(want)* apetecer, ter vontade de, desejar *(to do* fazer*)* □ *vi* ~ **for** desejar. ~ **sb well** desejar felicidades a alguém. **I don't** ~ **to go** não me apetece ir, não tenho vontade de ir, não desejo ir. **I** ~ **he'd leave** eu gostaria que ele partisse. **with best** ~**es** *(formal: in letter)* com os melhores cumprimentos, com saudações cordiais; *(on greeting card)* com desejos or votos (**for** de)

wishful /'wɪʃfl/ *a* ~ **thinking** sonhar acordado

wishy-washy /'wɪʃɪwɒʃɪ/ *a* sem expressão, fraco, inexpressivo

wisp /wɪsp/ *n* *(of hair)* pequena mecha *f*; *(of smoke)* fio *m*

wistful /'wɪstfl/ *a* melancólico, saudoso

wit /wɪt/ *n* inteligência *f*; *(humour)* presença *f* de espírito, humor *m*; *(person)* senso *m* de humor. **be at one's** ~**'s** *or* ~**s'**

end não saber o que fazer. **keep one's** ~**s about one** estar alerta. **live by one's** ~**s** ganhar a vida de maneira suspeita. **scared out of one's** ~**s** apavorado

witch /wɪtʃ/ *n* feiticeira *f*, bruxa *f*. ~**craft** *n* feitiçaria *f*, bruxaria *f*, magia *f*

with /wɪð/ *prep* com; *(having)* de; *(because of)* de; *(at the house of)* em casa de. **the man** ~ **the beard** o homem de barbas. **fill/** *etc* ~ encher/*etc* de. **laughing/ shaking/***etc* ~ a rir/a tremer/ *etc* de. **I'm not** ~ **you** *(colloq)* não estou compreendendo-o

withdraw /wɪð'drɔː/ *vt/i* *(pt* withdrew, *pp* withdrawn*)* retirar (-se); *(money)* tirar. ~**al** *n* retirada *f*; *(med)* estado *m* de privação. ~**n** *a* *(person)* retraído, fechado

wither /'wɪðə(r)/ *vt/i* murchar, secar. ~**ed** *a* *(person)* mirrado. ~**ing** *a* *(fig: scornful)* desdenhoso

withhold /wɪð'həʊld/ *vt* *(pt* withheld*)* negar, recusar; *(retain)* reter; *(conceal, not tell)* esconder (**from** de)

within /wɪ'ðɪn/ *prep & adv* dentro (de), por dentro (de); *(in distances)* a menos de. ~ **a month** *(before)* dentro de um mês. ~ **sight** à vista

without /wɪ'ðaʊt/ *prep* sem. ~ **fail** sem falta. **go** ~ **saying** não ser preciso dizer

withstand /wɪð'stænd/ *vt* *(pt* withstood*)* resistir a, opor-se a

witness /'wɪtnɪs/ *n* testemunha *f*; *(evidence)* testemunho *m* □ *vt* testemunhar, presenciar; *(document)* assinar como testemunha. **bear** ~ **to** testemunhar, dar testemunho de. ~**-box** *n* banco *m* das testemunhas

witticism /'wɪtɪsɪzəm/ *n* dito *m* espirituoso

witty /'wɪtɪ/ a (-ier, -iest) espirituoso

wives /waɪvz/ see **wife**

wizard /'wɪzəd/ n feiticeiro m; (fig: genius) gênio m, (P) génio m

wizened /'wɪznd/ a encarquilhado

wobbl|e /'wɒbl/ vi (of jelly, voice, hand) tremer; (stagger) cambalear, vacilar; (of table, chair) balançar. **~y** a (trembling) trêmulo; (staggering) cambaleante, vacilante; (table, chair) pouco firme

woe /wəʊ/ n dor f, infortúnio m

woke, woken /wəʊk, 'wəʊkən/ see **wake**[1]

wolf /wʊlf/ n (pl wolves /wʊlvz/) lobo m □ vt (food) devorar. **cry ~** dar alarme falso. **~-whistle** n assobio m de admiração

woman /'wʊmən/ n (pl women /'wɪmɪn/) mulher f. **~hood** n as mulheres, o sexo feminino; (maturity) maturidade f. **~ly** a feminino

womb /wuːm/ n seio m, ventre m; (med) útero m; (fig) seio m

women /'wɪmɪn/ see **woman**. **~'s movement** movimento m feminista

won /wʌn/ see **win**

wonder /'wʌndə(r)/ n admiração f; (thing) maravilha f □ vt perguntar-se a si mesmo (if se) □ vi admirar-se (at de, com), ficar admirado, espantar-se (at com); (reflect) pensar (about em). **it is no ~** não admira (that que)

wonderful /'wʌndəfl/ a maravilhoso. **~ly** adv maravilhosamente. **it works ~ly** funciona às mil maravilhas

won't /wəʊnt/ = will not

wood /wʊd/ n madeira f, pau m; (for burning) lenha f. **~(s)** n (pl) (area) bosque m, mata f, floresta f. **~ed** a arborizado. **~en** a de or em madeira, de pau; (fig: stiff) rígido; (fig: inexpressive) inexpressivo, de pau

woodcut /'wʊdkʌt/ n gravura f em madeira

woodland /'wʊdlənd/ n região f arborizada, bosque m, mata f

woodlouse /'wʊdlaʊs/ n (pl -lice /laɪs/) baratinha f, tatuzinho m

woodpecker /'wʊdpekə(r)/ n (bird) pica-pau m

woodwind /'wʊdwɪnd/ n (mus) instrumentos mpl de sopro de madeira

woodwork /'wʊdwɜːk/ n (of building) madeiramento m; (carpentry) carpintaria f

woodworm /'wʊdwɜːm/ n caruncho m

woody /'wʊdɪ/ a (wooded) arborizado; (like wood) lenhoso

wool /wʊl/ n lã f. **~len** a de lã. **~lens** npl roupas fpl de lã. **~ly** a de lã; (vague) confuso □ n (colloq: garment) roupa f de lã

word /wɜːd/ n palavra f; (news) notícia(s) f(pl); (promise) palavra f □ vt exprimir, formular. **by ~ of mouth** de viva voz. **have a ~ with** dizer duas palavras a. **in other ~s** em outras palavras. **~-perfect** a que sabe de cor seu papel, a lição etc. **~ processor** processador m de textos. **~ing** n termos mpl, redação f, (P) redacção f. **~y** a prolixo

wore /wɔː(r)/ see **wear**

work /wɜːk/ n trabalho m; (product, book etc) obra f; (building etc) obras fpl. **at ~** no trabalho. **out of ~** desempregado. **~s** npl (techn) mecanismo m; (factory) fábrica f □ vt/i (of person) trabalhar; (techn) (fazer) funcionar, (fazer) andar; (of drug etc) agir, fazer efeito; (farm, mine) explorar; (land) lavrar. **~ sb** (make work) fazer alguém trabalhar. **~ in** introduzir, inserir. **~ loose** soltar-se. **~ off** (get rid of) descarregar. **~ out** vt (solve) resolver; (calculate) calcular;

(devise) planejar □ *vi (succeed)* resultar; *(sport)* treinar-se. **~-station** n estação f de trabalho. **~-to-rule** n greve f de zelo. **~-up** *vt* criar □ *vi (to climax)* ir num crescendo. **~ed up** *(person)* enervado, transtornado, agitado

workable /'wɜːkəbl/ *a* viável, praticável

workaholic /wɜːkə'hɒlɪk/ *n* be a **~** *(colloq)* trabalhar como um possesso *(colloq)*

worker /'wɜːkə(r)/ *n* trabalhador *m*, trabalhadora *f*; *(factory)* operário *m*

working /'wɜːkɪŋ/ *a (day, clothes, hypothesis, lunch etc)* de trabalho. **the ~ class(es)** a classe operária, a(s) classe(s) trabalhadora(s), o proletariado. **~-class** *a* operário, trabalhador. **~ mother** mãe f que trabalha. **~ party** comissão f consultiva, de estudo *etc*. **~s** *npl* mecanismo *m*. **in ~ order** em condições de funcionamento

workman /'wɜːkmən/ *n (pl -men)* trabalhador *m*; *(factory)* operário *m*. **~ship** *n* trabalho *m*, execução f, mão-de-obra f; *(skill)* arte f, habilidade f

workshop /'wɜːkʃɒp/ *n* oficina f

world /wɜːld/ *n* mundo *m* □ *a* mundial. **a ~ of** muito(s), grande quantidade de, um mundo de. **~-wide** *a* mundial, universal

worldly /'wɜːldlɪ/ *a* terreno; *(devoted to the affairs of life)* mundano. **~ goods** bens *mpl* materiais. **~-wise** *a* com experiência do mundo

worm /wɜːm/ *n* verme *m*; *(earthworm)* minhoca f □ *vt* **~ one's way** into insinuar-se, introduzir-se, enfiar-se. **~-eaten** *a (wood)* carunchoso; *(fruit)* bichado, bichoso

worn /wɔːn/ *see* wear □ *a* usado. **~-out** *a (thing)* completamente gasto; *(person)* esgotado

worr|y /'wʌrɪ/ *vt/i* preocupar(-se) □ *n* preocupação f. **don't ~y** fique descansado, não se preocupe. **~ied** *a* preocupado. **~ying** *a* preocupante, inquietante

worse /wɜːs/ *a & adv* pior □ *n* pior *m*. **get ~** piorar. **from bad to ~** de mal a pior. **~ luck** pouca sorte, pena

worsen /'wɜːsn/ *vt/i* piorar

worship /'wɜːʃɪp/ *n (reverence)* reverência f, veneração f; *(religious)* culto *m* □ *vt (pt* **worshipped)** adorar, venerar □ *vi* fazer as suas devoções, praticar o culto. **~per** *n (in church)* fiel *m*. **Your/His W~** Vossa/Sua Excelência f

worst /wɜːst/ *a & n* **(the) ~** (o/a) pior *(mf)* □ *adv* pior. **if the ~ comes to the ~** se o pior acontecer, na pior das hipóteses. **do one's ~** fazer todo o mal que se quiser. **get the ~ of it** ficar a perder. **the ~ (thing)** o que o pior que

worth /wɜːθ/ *a* be **~** valer; *(deserving)* merecer □ *n* valor *m*, mérito *m*. **ten pounds ~ of** dez libras de. **it's ~ it, it's ~ while** vale a pena. **it's not ~ my while** não vale a pena. **it's ~ waiting/etc** vale a pena esperar/*etc*. **for all one's ~** *(colloq)* dando tudo por tudo. **~less** *a* sem valor

worthwhile /'wɜːθwaɪl/ *a* que vale a pena; *(cause)* louvável, meritório

worthy /'wɜːðɪ/ *a* **(-ier, -iest)** *(deserving)* digno, merecedor *(of* de); *(laudable)* meritório, louvável □ *n (person)* pessoa f ilustre

would /wʊd/; *unstressed* /wəd/ *v aux* **he ~ do/you ~ sing**/*etc (conditional tense)* ele faria/você cantaria/etc. **he ~ have done** ele teria feito. **she ~ come every day** (used to) ela vinha or costumava vir aqui todos os dias. **~ you please come here?** chegue aqui por favor. **~ you like some tea?** você quer um chazinho? **he ~n't go** (refused to) ele não queria ir. **~-be author/doctor/etc** aspirante a autor/médico/etc

wound[1] /wuːnd/ n ferida f □ vt ferir. **the ~ed** os feridos mpl

wound[2] /waʊnd/ see **wind**[2]

wove, woven /waʊv, ˈwaʊvn/ see **weave**

wrangle /ˈræŋgl/ vi disputar, discutir, brigar □ n disputa f, discussão f, briga f

wrap /ræp/ vt (pt **wrapped**) **~ (up)** embrulhar (**in** em); (in cotton wool, mystery etc) envolver (**in** em) □ vi **~ up** (dress warmly) abrigar-se bem, agasalhar-se bem □ n xale m. **~ped up in** (engrossed) absorto em, mergulhado em. **~per** n (of sweet) papel m; (of book) capa f de papel. **~ing** n embalagem f

wrath /rɒθ/ n ira f. **~ful** a irado

wreak /riːk/ vt **~ havoc** (of storm etc) fazer estragos

wreath /riːθ/ n (pl -s /-ðz/) (of flowers, leaves) coroa f, grinalda f

wreck /rek/ n (sinking) naufrágio m; (ship) navio m naufragado; (remains) destroços mpl; (vehicle) veículo m destroçado □ vt destruir; (ship) fazer naufragar, afundar; (fig: hope) acabar. **be a nervous ~** estar com os nervos arrasados. **~age** n (pieces) destroços mpl

wren /ren/ n (bird) carriça f

wrench /rentʃ/ vt (pull) puxar; (twist) torcer; (snatch) arrancar (**from** a) □ n (pull) puxão m; (of ankle, wrist) torcedura f; (tool)

chave f inglesa; (fig) dor f de separação

wrest /rest/ vt arrancar (**from** a)

wrestle /ˈresl/ vi lutar, debater-se (**with com** or contra). **~er** n lutador m. **~ing** n luta f

wretch /retʃ/ n desgraçado m, miserável mf; (rascal) miserável mf

wretched /ˈretʃɪd/ a (pitiful, poor) miserável; (bad) horrível, desgraçado

wriggle /ˈrɪgl/ vt/i remexer(-se), contorcer-se

wring /rɪŋ/ vt (pt **wrung**) (twist; clothes) torcer. **~ out of** (obtain from) arrancar a. **~ing wet** encharcado; (of person) encharcado até aos ossos

wrinkle /ˈrɪŋkl/ n (on skin) ruga f; (crease) prega f □ vt/i enrugar(-se)

wrist /rɪst/ n pulso m. **~-watch** n relógio m de pulso

writ /rɪt/ n (jur) mandado m judicial

write /raɪt/ vt/i (pt **wrote**, pp **written**) escrever. **~ back** responder. **~ down** escrever, tomar nota de. **~ off** (debt) dar por liquidado; (vehicle) destinar à sucata. **~-off** n perda f total. **~ out** (in full) escrever por extenso. **~ up** (from notes) redigir. **~-up** n relato m; (review) crítica f

writer /ˈraɪtə(r)/ n escritor m, autor m

writhe /raɪð/ vi contorcer(-se)

writing /ˈraɪtɪŋ/ n escrita f. **~(s)** (works) escritos mpl, obras fpl. **in ~** por escrito. **~-paper** n papel m de carta

written /ˈrɪtn/ see **write**

wrong /rɒŋ/ a (incorrect, mistaken) mal, errado; (unfair) injusto; (wicked) mau; (amiss) que não está bem; (mus: note) falso; (clock) que não está certo □ adv mal □ n mal *m*; (*injustice*) injustiça *f* □ *vt* (*be unfair to*) ser injusto com; (*do a wrong to*) fazer mal a. what's ~? qual é o problema? what's ~ with it? (*amiss*) o que é que não vai bem?; (*morally*) que mal há nisso?, que mal tem? he's in the ~ (*his fault*) ele não tem razão. go ~ (*err*) desencaminhar-se; (*fail*) ir mal; (*vehicle*) quebrar. ~ly *adv* mal; (*blame etc*) sem razão, injustamente

wrongful /'rɒŋfl/ *a* injusto, ilegal

wrote /rəʊt/ *see* **write**

wrought /rɔːt/ *a* ~ **iron** ferro *m* forjado. ~**-up** *a* excitado

wrung /rʌŋ/ *see* **wring**

wry /raɪ/ *a* (**wryer, wryest**) torto; (*smile*) forçado. ~ **face** careta *f*

X

Xerox /'zɪərɒks/ *n* fotocópia *f*, xerox *m* □ *vt* fotocopiar, xerocar, tirar um xerox de

Xmas /'krɪsməs/ *n* **Christmas**

X-ray /'eksreɪ/ *n* raio X *m*; (*photograph*) radiografia *f* □ *vt* radiografar. **have an** ~ tirar uma radiografia

xylophone /'zaɪləfəʊn/ *n* xilofone *m*

Y

yacht /jɒt/ *n* iate *m*. ~**ing** *n* iatismo *m*, andar *m* de iate; (*racing*) regata *f* de iate

yank /jæŋk/ *vt* (*colloq*) puxar bruscamente □ *n* (*colloq*) puxão *m*

Yank /jæŋk/ *n* (*colloq*) ianque *mf*

yap /jæp/ *vi* (*pt* **yapped**) latir

yard[1] /jɑːd/ *n* (*measure*) jarda *f* (= 0,9144 m). ~**age** *n* medida *f* em jardas

yard[2] /jɑːd/ *n* (*of house*) pátio *m*; (*Amer: garden*) jardim *m*; (*for storage*) depósito *m*

yardstick /'jɑːdstɪk/ *n* jarda *f*; (*fig*) bitola *f*, craveira *f*

yarn /jɑːn/ *n* (*thread*) fio *m*; (*colloq: tale*) longa história *f*

yawn /jɔːn/ *vi* bocejar; (*be wide open*) abrir-se, escancarar-se □ *n* bocejo *m*. ~**ing** *a* escancarado

year /jɪə(r)/ *n* ano *m*. **school/tax** ~ ano *m* escolar/fiscal. **be ten/** *etc* ~**s old** ter dez/*etc* anos de idade. ~**-book** *n* anuário *m*. ~**ly** *a* anual □ *adv* anualmente

yearn /jɜːn/ *vi* ~ **for, to** desejar, ansiar por, suspirar por. ~**ing** *n* desejo *m*, anseio *m* (**for** de)

yeast /jiːst/ *n* levedura *f*

yell /jel/ *vt/i* gritar, berrar □ *n* grito *m*, berro *m*

yellow /'jeləʊ/ *a* amarelo; (*colloq: cowardly*) covarde, poltrão □ *n* amarelo *m*

yelp /jelp/ *n* (*of dog etc*) ganido *m* □ *vi* ganir

yen /jen/ *n* (*colloq: yearning*) grande vontade *f* (**for** de)

yes /jes/ *n* & *adv* sim (*m*). ~**-man** *n* (*colloq*) lambe-botas *m invar*, puxa-saco *m*

yesterday /'jestədɪ/ *n* & *adv* ontem (*m*). ~ **morning/afternoon/evening** ontem de manhã/à tarde/à noite. **the day before** ~ anteontem. **the ~ week** há oito dias, há uma semana

yet /jet/ *adv* ainda; (*already*) já □ *conj* contudo, no entanto. **as** ~ até agora, por enquanto. **his best book** ~ o seu melhor livro até agora

yew /juː/ *n* teixo *m*

Yiddish /'jɪdɪʃ/ *n* idiche *m*

yield /jiːld/ *vt* (*produce*) produzir, dar; (*profit*) render; (*surrender*) entregar □ *vi* (*give way*) ceder □ *n* produção *f*; (*comm*) rendimento *m*

yoga /'jəʊgə/ n ioga f

yoghurt /'jɒgət/ n iogurte m

yoke /jəʊk/ n jugo m, canga f; (of garment) pala f □ vt jungir; (unite) unir, ligar

yokel /'jəʊkl/ n caipira m, labrego m

yolk /jəʊk/ n gema (de ovo) f

yonder /'jɒndə(r)/ adv acolá, além

you /ju:/ pron (familiar) tu, você (pl vocês); (polite) vós, o(s) senhor(es), a(s) senhora(s); (object: familiar) te, lhe (pl vocês); (polite) o(s), a(s), lhes, vós, o(s) senhor(es), a(s) senhora(s); (after prep) ti, si, você (pl vocês); (polite) vós, o senhor, a senhora (pl os senhores, as senhoras); (indefinite) se; (after prep) si, você. **with ~** (familiar) contigo, consigo, com você (pl com vocês); (polite) com o senhor/a senhora (pl convosco, com os senhores/as senhoras). **I know ~** (familiar) eu te conheço, eu o/a conheço (pl eu os/as conheço); (polite) eu vos conheço, conheço o senhor/a senhora (pl conheço os senhores/as senhoras). **~ can see the sea** você pode ver o mar

young /jʌŋ/ a (-er, -est) jovem, novo, moço □ n (people) jovens mpl, a juventude f, a mocidade f; (of animals) crias fpl, filhotes mpl

youngster /'jʌŋstə(r)/ n jovem mf, moço m, rapaz m

your /jɔ:(r)/ a (familiar) teu, tua, seu, sua (pl teus, tuas, seus, suas); (polite) vosso, vossa, do senhor, da senhora (pl vossos, vossas, dos senhores, das senhoras)

yours /jɔ:z/ poss pron (familiar) o teu, a tua, o seu, a sua (pl os teus, as tuas, os seus, as suas); (polite) o vosso, a vossa, o/a do senhor, o/a da senhora (pl os vossos, as vossas; os/as do(s) senhor(es), os/as da(s) senhora(s)). **a book of ~** um livro seu. **~ sin-**

cerely/faithfully atenciosamente, com os cumprimentos de

yourself /jɔ:'self/ (pl **-selves** /-'selvz/) pron (familiar) tu mesmo/a, você mesmo/a (pl vocês mesmos/as); (polite) vós mesmo/a, o senhor mesmo, a senhora mesma (pl vós mesmos/as, os senhores mesmos, as senhoras mesmas); (reflexive: familiar) te, a ti mesmo/a, se, a si mesmo/a (pl a vós mesmos/as); (polite) ao senhor mesmo, à senhora mesma (pl aos senhores mesmos, às senhoras mesmas); (after prep: familiar) ti mesmo/a, si mesmo/a, você mesmo/a (pl vocês mesmos/as); (after prep: polite) vós mesmo/a, o senhor mesmo, a senhora mesma (pl vós mesmos/as, os senhores mesmos, as senhoras mesmas). **with ~** (familiar) contigo mesmo/a, consigo mesmo/a, com você (pl com vocês); (polite) convosco, com o senhor, com a senhora (pl com os senhores, com as senhoras). **by ~** sozinho

youth /ju:θ/ n (pl **-s** /-ðz/) mocidade f, juventude f; (young man) jovem m, moço m. **~ hostel** albergue m da juventude. **~ful** a juvenil, jovem

yo-yo /'jəʊjəʊ/ n (pl **-os**) ioiô m

Yugoslav /'ju:gəslɑ:v/ a & n iogoslavo (m), (P) jugoslavo (m). **~ia** /-'slɑ:vɪə/ n Iogoslávia f, (P) Jugoslávia f

Z

zany /'zeɪnɪ/ a (-ier, -iest) tolo, bobo

zeal /zi:l/ n zelo m

zealous /'zeləs/ a zeloso. **~ly** adv zelosamente

zebra /'zebrə, 'zi:brə/ *n* zebra *f*. **~ crossing** faixa *f* para pedestres, (*P*) passagem *f* para peões

zenith /'zenɪθ/ *n* zênite *m*, (*P*) zénite *m*, auge *m*

zero /'zɪərəʊ/ *n* (*pl* -os) zero *m*. **~ hour** a hora H. **below ~** abaixo de zero

zest /zest/ *n* (*gusto*) entusiasmo *m*; (*fig: spice*) sabor *m* especial; (*lemon or orange peel*) casca *f* de limão/laranja ralada

zigzag /'zɪgzæg/ *n* ziguezague *m* □ *a* & *adv* em ziguezague □ *vi* (*pt* **zigzagged**) ziguezaguear

zinc /zɪŋk/ *n* zinco *m*

zip /zɪp/ *n* (*vigour*) energia *f*, alma *f*. **~(-fastener)** fecho *m* ecler □ *vt* (*pt* **zipped**) fechar o fecho

eclerde □ *vi* ir a toda a velocidade. **Z~ code** (*Amer*) CEP de endereçamento postal *m*, (*P*) código *m* postal

zipper /'zɪpə(r)/ *n* = **zip(-fastener)**

zodiac /'zəʊdɪæk/ *n* zodíaco *m*

zombie /'zɒmbɪ/ *n* zumbi *m*; (*colloq*) zumbi *m*, (*P*) autómato *m*

zone /zəʊn/ *n* zona *f*

zoo /zu:/ *n* jardim *m* zoológico

zoolog|y /zəʊ'ɒlədʒɪ/ *n* zoologia *f*. **~ical** /-ə'lɒdʒɪkl/ *a* zoológico. **~ist** *n* zoólogo *m*

zoom /zu:m/ *vi* (*rush*) sair roando **~ lens** zum *m*, zoom *m*. **~ off** *or* **past** passar zunindo

zucchini /zu:'ki:nɪ/ *n* (*pl invar*) (*Amer*) courgette *f*

Portuguese verbs

rtuguese verbs can be divided into
ree categories: regular verbs, those
th spelling peculiarities determined by
eir sound and irregular verbs.

egular verbs:

-ar (e.g. **comprar**)

resent: compr|o, ~as, ~a, ~amos, ~ais, ~am

uture: comprar|ei, ~ás, ~á, ~emos, ~eis, ~ão

mperfect: compr|ava, ~avas, ~ava, ~ávamos, ~áveis, ~avam

eterite: compr|ei, ~aste, ~ou, ~amos (P: ~ámos), ~astes, ~aram

uperfect: compr|ara, ~aras, ~ara, ~áramos, ~áreis, ~aram

resent subjunctive: compr|e, ~es, ~e, ~emos, ~eis, ~em

mperfect subjunctive: compr|asse, ~asses, ~asse, ~ássemos, ~ásseis, ~assem

uture subjunctive: compr|ar, ~ares, ~ar, ~armos, ~ardes, ~arem

Conditional: comprar|ia, ~ias, ~ia, ~íamos, ~íeis, ~iam

Personal infinitive: comprar, ~es, ~, ~mos, ~des, ~em

Present participle: comprando
Past participle: comprado
mperative: compra, comprai

n **-er** (e.g. **bater**)

Present: bat|o, ~es, ~e, ~emos, ~eis, ~em

Future: bater|ei, ~ás, ~á, ~emos, ~eis, ~ão

mperfect: bat|ia, ~ias, ~ia, ~íamos, ~íeis, ~iam

Preterite: bat|i, ~este, ~eu, ~emos, ~estes, ~eram

Pluperfect: bat|era, ~eras, ~era, ~êramos, ~êreis, ~eram

Present subjunctive: bat|a, ~as, ~a, ~amos, ~ais, ~am

Imperfect subjunctive: bat|esse, ~esses, ~esse, ~êssemos, ~êsseis, ~essem

Future subjunctive: bat|er, ~eres, ~er, ~ermos, ~erdes, ~erem

Conditional: bater|ia, ~ias, ~ia, ~íamos, ~ieis, ~iam

Personal infinitive: bater, ~es, ~, ~mos, ~des, ~em

Present participle: batendo
Past participle: batido
Imperative: bate, batei

in **-ir** (e.g. **admitir**)

Present: admit|o, ~es, ~e, ~imos, ~is, ~em

Future: admit|ei, ~ás, ~á, ~emos, ~eis, ~ão

Imperfect: admit|ia, ~ias, ~ia, ~íamos, ~íeis, ~iam

Preterite: admit|i, ~iste, ~iu, ~imos, ~istes, ~iram

Pluperfect: admit|ira, ~iras, ~ira, ~iramos, ~íreis, ~iram

Present subjunctive: admit|a, ~as, ~a, ~amos, ~ais, ~am

Imperfect subjunctive: admit|isse, ~isses, ~isse, ~íssemos, ~ísseis, ~issem

Future subjunctive: admit|ir, ~ires, ~ir, ~irmos, ~irdes, ~irem

Conditional: admitir|ia, ~ias, ~ia, ~íamos, ~íeis, ~iam

Personal infinitive: admitir, ~es, ~, ~mos, ~des, ~em

Present participle: admitindo
Past participle: admitido
Imperative: admite, admiti

Regular verbs with spelling changes:

-ar verbs:

in -car (e.g. **ficar**)

Preterite: fiquei, ficaste, ficou, ficamos (P: ficámos), ficais, ficam
Present subjunctive: fique, fiques, fique, fiquemos, fiqueis, fiquem

in -çar (e.g. **abraçar**)

Preterite: abracei, abraçaste, abraçou, abraçamos (P: abraçámos), abraçastes, abraçaram
Present subjunctive: abrace, abraces, abrace, abracemos, abraceis, abracem

in -ear (e.g. **passear**)

Present: passeio, passeias, passeia, passeamos, passeais, passeiam
Present subjunctive: passeie, passeies, passeie, passeemos, passeeis, passeiem
Imperative: passeia, passeai

in -gar (e.g. **apagar**)

Preterite: apaguei, apagaste, apagou, apagamos (P: apagámos), apagastes, apagaram
Present subjunctive: apague, apagues, apague, apaguemos, apagueis, apaguem

in -oar (e.g. **voar**)

Present: vôo (P: voo), voas, voa, voamos, voais, voam

averiguar

Preterite: averigüei (P: averiguei), averiguaste, averiguou, averiguamos (P: averiguámos), averiguastes, averiguaram
Present subjunctive: averigüe, averigües, averigüe, averigüemos (P: averiguemos), averigüeis (P: averigueis), averigüem

enxaguar

Present: enxáguo, enxáguas, enxágua, enxaguamos, enxaguais, enxáguam
Preterite: enxagüei (P: enxaguei), enxaguaste, enxaguou, enxaguamos (P: enxaguámos), enxaguastes, enxaguaram
Present subjunctive: enxágüe, enxágües, enxágüe, enxagüemos, enxagüeis, enxágüem (P: enxágue, enxágues, enxágue, enxaguemos, enxagueis, enxáguem)
Similarly: aguar, desaguar

saudar

Present: saúdo, saúdas, saúda, saudamos, saudais, saúdam
Present subjunctive: saúde, saúdes, saúde, saudemos, saudeis, saúdem
Imperative: saúda, saudai

-er verbs:

in -cer (e.g. **tecer**)

Present: teço, teces, tece, tecemos, teceis, tecem
Present subjunctive: teça, teças, teça, teçamos, teçais, teçam

in -ger (e.g. **proteger**)

Present: protejo, proteges, protege, protegemos, protegeis, protegem
Present subjunctive: proteja, protejas, proteja, protejamos, protejais, protejam

-guer (e.g. **erguer**)

Present: ergo, ergues, ergue, erguemos, ergueis, erguem
Present subjunctive: erga, ergas, erga, ergamos, ergais, ergam

-oer (e.g. **roer**)

Present: rôo (P: roo), róis, rói, roemos, roeis, roem
Imperfect: roía, roías, roía, roíamos, roíeis, roíam
Preterite: roí, roeste, roeu, roemos, roestes, roeram
Past participle: roído
Imperative: rói, roei

ir verbs:

-ir with **-e-** in stem (e.g. **vestir**)

Present: visto, vestes, veste, vestimos, vestis, vestem
Present subjunctive: vista, vistas, vista, vistamos, vistais, vistam
Similarly: mentir, preferir, refletir, repetir, seguir, sentir, servir

-ir with **-o-** in stem (e.g. **dormir**)

Present: durmo, dormes, dorme, dormimos, dormis, dormem
Present subjunctive: durma, durmas, durma, durmamos, durmais, durmam
Similarly: cobrir, descobrir, tossir

-ir with **-u-** in stem (e.g. **subir**)

Present: subo, sobes, sobe, subimos, subis, sobem
Similarly: consumir, cuspir, fugir, sacudir, sumir

-air (e.g. **sair**)

Present: saio, sais, sai, saímos, saís, saem
Imperfect: saía, saías, saía, saíamos, saíeis, saíam

Preterite: saí, saíste, saiu, saímos, saístes, saíram
Pluperfect: saíra, saíras, saíra, saíramos, saíreis, saíram
Present subjunctive: saia, saias, saia, saiamos, saiais, saiam
Imperfect subjunctive: saísse, saísses, saísse, saíssemos, saísseis, saíssem
Future subjunctive: sair, saíres, sair, sairmos, sairdes, saírem
Personal infinitive: sair, saíres, sair, sairmos, sairdes, saírem
Present participle: saindo
Past participle: saído
Imperative: sai, saí

in -gir (e.g. **dirigir**)

Present: dirijo, diriges, dirige, dirigimos, dirigis, dirigem
Present subjunctive: dirija, dirijas, dirija, dirijamos, dirijais, dirijam

in -guir (e.g. **distinguir**)

Present: distingo, distingues, distingue, distinguimos, distinguis, distinguem
Present subjunctive: distinga, distingas, distinga, distingamos, distingais, distingam

in -uir (e.g. **atribuir**)

Present: atribuo, atribuis, atribui, atribuímos, atribuís, atribuem
Imperfect: atribuía, atribuías, atribuía, atribuíamos, atribuíeis, atribuíam
Preterite: atribuí, atribuíste, atribuiu, atribuímos, atribuístes, atribuíram
Pluperfect: atribuíra, atribuíras, atribuíra, atribuíramos, atribuíreis, atribuíram
Present subjunctive: atribua, atribuas, atribua, atribuamos, atribuais, atribuam
Imperfect subjunctive: atribuísse, atribuísses, atribuísse,

atribuíssemos, atribuísseis,
atribuíssem
Future subjunctive: atribuir, atribuíres,
atribuir, atribuirmos, atribuirdes,
atribuírem
Personal infinitive: atribuir, atribuíres,
atribuir, atribuirmos, atribuirdes,
atribuírem
Present participle: atribuindo
Past participle: atribuído
Imperative: atribui, atribuí

proibir

Present: proíbo, proíbes, proíbe,
proibimos, proibis, proíbem
Present subjunctive: proíba, proíbas,
proíba, proibamos, proibais,
proíbam
Imperative: proíbe, proibi
Similarly: coibir

reunir

Present: reúno, reúnes, reúne,
reunimos, reunis, reúnem
Present subjunctive: reúna, reúnas,
reúna, reunamos, reunais, reúnam
Imperative: reúne, reuni

in **-struir** (e.g. **construir**) - like **atribuir**
except:

Present: construo, constróis/construis,
constrói/construi, construímos,
construís, constroem/construem
Imperative: constrói/construi, construí

in **-duzir** (e.g. **produzir**)

Present: produzo, produzes, produz,
produzimos, produzis, produzem
Imperative: produz(e), produzi
Similarly: luzir, reluzir

Irregular verbs

caber

Present: caibo, cabes, cabe, cabemos,
cabeis, cabem
Preterite: coube, coubeste, coube,
coubemos, coubestes, couberam
Pluperfect: coubera, couberas,
coubera, coubéramos, coubéreis,
couberam
Present subjunctive: caiba, caibas, caiba
caibamos, caibais, caibam
Imperfect subjunctive: coubesse,
coubesses, coubesse, coubéssemos
coubésseis, coubessem
Future subjunctive: couber, couberes,
couber, coubermos, couberdes,
couberem

dar

Present: dou, dás, dá, damos, dais, dão
Preterite: dei, deste, deu, demos,
destes, deram
Pluperfect: dera, deras, dera, déramos,
déreis, deram
Present subjunctive: dê, dês, dê, demos,
deis, dêem
Imperfect subjunctive: desse, desses,
desse, déssemos, désseis, dessem
Future subjunctive: der, deres, der,
dermos, derdes, derem
Imperative: dá, dai

dizer

Present: digo, dizes, diz, dizemos,
dizeis, dizem
Future: direi, dirás, dirá, diremos,
direis, dirão
Preterite: disse, disseste, disse,
dissemos, dissestes, disseram
Pluperfect: dissera, disseras, dissera,
disséramos, disséreis, disseram
Present subjunctive: diga, digas, diga,
digamos, digais, digam

perfect subjunctive: dissesse,
dissesses, dissesse, disséssemos,
dissésseis, dissessem
Future subjunctive: disser, disseres,
disser, dissermos, disserdes,
disserem
Conditional: diria, dirias, diria,
diríamos, diríeis, diriam
Present participle: dizendo
Past participle: dito
Imperative: diz, dizei

estar

Present: estou, estás, está, estamos,
estais, estão
Preterite: estive, estiveste, esteve,
estivemos, estivestes, estiveram
Pluperfect: estivera, estiveras, estivera,
estivéramos, estivéreis, estiveram
Present subjunctive: esteja, estejas,
esteja, estejamos, estejais, estejam
Imperfect subjunctive: estivesse,
estivesses, estivesse, estivéssemos,
estivésseis, estivessem
Future subjunctive: estiver, estiveres,
estiver, estivermos, estiverdes,
estiverem
Imperative: está, estai

fazer

Present: faço, fazes, faz, fazemos,
fazeis, fazem
Future: farei, farás, fará, faremos,
fareis, farão
Preterite: fiz, fizeste, fez, fizemos,
fizestes, fizeram
Pluperfect: fizera, fizeras, fizera,
fizéramos, fizéreis, fizeram
Present subjunctive: faça, faças, faça,
façamos, façais, façam
Imperfect subjunctive: fizesse, fizesses,
fizesse, fizéssemos, fizésseis, fizessem
Future subjunctive: fizer, fizeres, fizer,
fizermos, fizerdes, fizerem

Conditional: faria, farias, faria,
faríamos, faríeis, fariam
Present participle: fazendo
Past participle: feito
Imperative: faz(e), fazei

frigir

Present: frijo, freges, frege, frigimos,
frigis, fregem
Present subjunctive: frija, frijas, frija,
frijamos, frijais, frijam
Imperative: frege, frigi

haver

Present: hei, hás, há, hemos/havemos,
haveis/heis, hão
Preterite: houve, houveste, houve,
houvemos, houvestes, houveram
Pluperfect: houvera, houveras,
houvera, houvéramos, houvéreis,
houveram
Present subjunctive: haja, hajas, haja,
hajamos, hajais, hajam
Imperfect subjunctive: houvesse,
houvesses, houvesse,
houvéssemos, houvésseis,
houvessem
Future subjunctive: houver, houveres,
houver, houvermos, houverdes,
houverem
Imperative: há, havei

ir

Present: vou, vais, vai, vamos, ides, vão
Imperfect: ia, ias, ia, íamos, íeis, iam
Preterite: fui, foste, foi, fomos, fostes,
foram
Pluperfect: fora, foras, fora, fôramos,
fôreis, foram
Present subjunctive: vá, vás, vá, vamos,
vades, vão
Imperfect subjunctive: fosse, fosses,
fosse, fôssemos, fôsseis, fossem
Future subjunctive: for, fores, for,
formos, fordes, forem

Portuguese verbs

Present participle: indo
Past participle: ido
Imperative: vai, ide

ler

Present: leio, lês, lê, lemos, ledes, lêem
Imperfect: lia, lias, lia, líamos, líeis, liam
Preterite: li, leste, leu, lemos, lestes, leram
Pluperfect: lera, leras, lera, lêramos, lêreis, leram
Present subjunctive: leia, leias, leia, leiamos, leiais, leiam
Imperfect subjunctive: lesse, lesses, lesse, lêssemos, lêsseis, lessem
Future subjunctive: ler, leres, ler, lermos, lerdes, lerem
Present participle: lendo
Past participle: lido
Imperative: lê, lede
Similarly: crer

odiar

Present: odeio, odeias, odeia, odiamos, odiais, odeiam
Present subjunctive: odeie, odeies, odeie, odiemos, odieis, odeiem
Imperative: odeia, odiai
Similarly: incendiar

ouvir

Present: ouço (P also: oiça), ouves, ouve, ouvimos, ouvis, ouvem
Present subjunctive: ouça, ouças, ouça, ouçamos, ouçais, ouçam (P also: oiça, oiças, oiça, oiçamos, oiçais, oiçam)

pedir

Present: peço, pedes, pede, pedimos, pedis, pedem
Present subjunctive: peça, peças, peça, peçamos, peçais, peçam
Similarly: despedir, impedir, medir

perder

Present: perco, perdes, perde, perdemos, perdeis, perdem
Present subjunctive: perca, percas, perca, percamos, percais, percam

poder

Present: posso, podes, pode, podemos, podeis, podem
Preterite: pude, pudeste, pôde, pudemos, pudestes, puderam
Pluperfect: pudera, puderas, pudera, pudéramos, pudéreis, puderam
Present subjunctive: possa, possas, possa, possamos, possais, possam
Imperfect subjunctive: pudesse, pudesses, pudesse, pudéssemos, pudésseis, pudessem
Future subjunctive: puder, puderes, puder, pudermos, puderdes, puderem

polir

Present: pulo, pules, pule, polimos, polis, pulem
Present subjunctive: pula, pulas, pula, pulamos, pulais, pulam
Imperative: pule, poli

pôr

Present: ponho, pões, põe, pomos, pondes, põem
Future: porei, porás, porá, poremos, poreis, porão
Imperfect: punha, punhas, punha, púnhamos, púnheis, punham
Preterite: pus, puseste, pôs, pusemos, pusestes, puseram
Pluperfect: pusera, puseras, pusera, puséramos, puséreis, puseram
Present subjunctive: ponha, ponhas, ponha, ponhamos, ponhais, ponham
Imperfect subjunctive: pusesse, pusesses, pusesse, puséssemos,

pusésseis, pusessem
Future subjunctive: puser, puseres,
 puser, pusermos, puserdes,
 puserem
Conditional: poria, porias, poria,
 poríamos, poríeis, poriam
Present participle: pondo
Past participle: posto
Imperative: põe, ponde
Similarly: compor, depor, dispor, opor,
 supor etc

prover

Present: provejo, provês, provê,
 provemos, provedes, proveem
Present subjunctive: proveja, provejas,
 proveja, provejamos, provejais,
 provejam
Imperative: provê, provede

querer

Present: quero, queres, quer,
 queremos, quereis, querem
Preterite: quis, quiseste, quis,
 quisemos, quisestes, quiseram
Pluperfect: quisera, quiseras, quisera,
 quiséramos, quiséreis, quiseram
Present subjunctive: queira, queiras,
 queira, queiramos, queirais,
 queiram
Imperfect subjunctive: quisesse,
 quisesses, quisesse, quiséssemos,
 quisésseis, quisessem
Future subjunctive: quiser, quiseres,
 quiser, quisermos, quiserdes,
 quiserem
Imperative: quer, querei

requerer

Present: requeiro, requeres, requer,
 requeremos, requereis, requerem
Present subjunctive: requeira, requeiras,
 requeira, requeiramos, requeirais,
 requeiram
Imperative: requer, requerei

rir

Present: rio, ris, ri, rimos, rides, riem
Present subjunctive: ria, rias, ria,
 riamos, riais, riam
Imperative: ri, ride
Similarly: sorrir

saber

Present: sei, sabes, sabe, sabemos,
 sabeis, sabem
Preterite: soube, soubeste, soube,
 soubemos, soubestes, souberam
Pluperfect: soubera, souberas, soubera,
 soubéramos, soubéreis, souberam
Present subjunctive: saiba, saibas, saiba,
 saibamos, saibais, saibam
Imperfect subjunctive: soubesse,
 soubesses, soubesse, soubéssemos,
 soubésseis, soubessem
Future subjunctive: souber, souberes,
 souber, soubermos, souberdes,
 souberem
Imperative: sabe, sabei

ser

Present: sou, és, é, somos, sois, são
Imperfect: era, eras, era, éramos, éreis,
 eram
Preterite: fui, foste, foi, fomos, fostes,
 foram
Pluperfect: fora, foras, fora, fôramos,
 fôreis, foram
Present subjunctive: seja, sejas, seja,
 sejamos, sejais, sejam
Imperfect subjunctive: fosse, fosses,
 fosse, fôssemos, fôsseis, fossem
Future subjunctive: for, fores, for,
 formos, fordes, forem
Present participle: sendo
Past participle: sido
Imperative: sê, sede

ter

Present: tenho, tens, tem, temos,
 tendes, têm

Portuguese verbs

Imperfect: tinha, tinhas, tinha, tínhamos, tínheis, tinham
Preterite: tive, tiveste, teve, tivemos, tivestes, tiveram
Pluperfect: tivera, tiveras, tivera, tivéramos, tivéreis, tiveram
Present subjunctive: tenha, tenhas, tenha, tenhamos, tenhais, tenham
Imperfect subjunctive: tivesse, tivesses, tivesse, tivéssemos, tivésseis, tivessem
Future subjunctive: tiver, tiveres, tiver, tivermos, tiverdes, tiverem
Present participle: tendo
Past participle: tido
Imperative: tem, tende

trazer

Present: trago, trazes, traz, trazemos, trazeis, trazem
Future: trarei, trarás, trará, traremos, trareis, trarão
Preterite: trouxe, trouxeste, trouxe, trouxemos, trouxestes, trouxeram
Pluperfect: trouxera, trouxeras, trouxera, trouxéramos, trouxéreis, trouxeram
Present subjunctive: traga, tragas, traga, tragamos, tragais, tragam
Imperfect subjunctive: trouxesse, trouxesses, trouxesse, trouxéssemos, trouxésseis, trouxessem
Future subjunctive: trouxer, trouxeres, trouxer, trouxermos, trouxerdes, trouxerem
Conditional: traria, trarias, traria, traríamos, traríeis, trariam
Imperative: traze, trazei

valer

Present: valho, vales, vale, valemos, valeis, valem
Present subjunctive: valha, valhas, valha, valhamos, valhais, valham

ver

Present: vejo, vês, vê, vemos, vedes, vêem
Imperfect: via, vias, via, víamos, víeis, viam
Preterite: vi, viste, viu, vimos, vistes, viram
Pluperfect: vira, viras, vira, víramos, víreis, viram
Present subjunctive: veja, vejas, veja, vejamos, vejais, vejam
Imperfect subjunctive: visse, visses, visse, víssemos, vísseis, vissem
Future subjunctive: vir, vires, vir, virmos, virdes, virem
Present participle: vendo
Past participle: visto
Imperative: vê, vede

vir

Present: venho, vens, vem, vimos, vindes, vêm
Imperfect: vinha, vinhas, vinha, vínhamos, vínheis, vinham
Preterite: vim, vieste, veio, viemos, viestes, vieram
Pluperfect: viera, vieras, viera, viéramos, viéreis, vieram
Present subjunctive: venha, venhas, venha, venhamos, venhais, venham
Imperfect subjunctive: viesse, viesses, viesse, viéssemos, viésseis, viessem
Future subjunctive: vier, vieres, vier, viermos, vierdes, vierem
Present participle: vindo
Past participle: vindo
Imperative: vem, vinde

Verbos irregulares ingleses

Infinitivo	Pretérito	Particípio passado		Infinitivo	Pretérito	Particípio passado
ar	was	been		**drive**	drove	driven
at	bore	borne		**eat**	ate	eaten
come	became	become		**fall**	fell	fallen
gin	began	begun		**feed**	fed	fed
nd	bent	bent		**feel**	felt	felt
t	bet, betted	bet, betted		**fight**	fought	fought
	bade, bid	bidden, bid		**find**	found	found
nd	bound	bound		**flee**	fled	fled
te	bit	bitten		**fly**	flew	flown
eed	bled	bled		**freeze**	froze	frozen
ow	blew	blown		**get**	got	got, gotten US
eak	broke	broken		**give**	gave	given
eed	bred	bred		**go**	went	gone
ing	brought	brought		**grow**	grew	grown
ild	built	built		**hang**	hung, hanged	hung, hanged
rn	burnt, burned	burnt, burned		**have**	had	had
rst	burst	burst		**hear**	heard	heard
uy	bought	bought		**hide**	hid	hidden
tch	caught	caught		**hit**	hit	hit
oose	chose	chosen		**hold**	held	held
ing	clung	clung		**hurt**	hurt	hurt
me	came	come		**keep**	kept	kept
st	cost, costed (vt)	cost, costed		**kneel**	knelt	knelt
t	cut	cut		**know**	knew	known
eal	dealt	dealt		**lay**	laid	laid
ig	dug	dug		**lead**	led	led
	did	done		**lean**	leaned, leant	leaned, leant
aw	drew	drawn		**learn**	learnt, learned	learnt, learned
eam	dreamt, dreamed	dreamt, dreamed		**leave**	left	left
rink	drank	drunk		**lend**	lent	lent
				let	let	let
				lie	lay	lain

Infinitivo	Pretérito	Particípio passado	Infinitivo	Pretérito	Particípio passado
lose	lost	lost	**spend**	spent	spent
make	made	made	**spit**	spat	spat
mean	meant	meant	**spoil**	spoilt, spoiled	spoilt, spoiled
meet	met	met			
pay	paid	paid	**spread**	spread	spread
put	put	put	**spring**	sprang	sprung
read	read	read	**stand**	stood	stood
ride	rode	ridden	**steal**	stole	stolen
ring	rang	rung	**stick**	stuck	stuck
rise	rose	risen	**sting**	stung	stung
run	ran	run	**stride**	strode	stridden
say	said	said	**strike**	struck	struck
see	saw	seen	**swear**	swore	sworn
seek	sought	sought	**sweep**	swept	swept
sell	sold	sold	**swell**	swelled	swollen, swelled
send	sent	sent			
set	set	set	**swim**	swam	swum
sew	sewed	sewn, sewed	**swing**	swung	swung
shake	shook	shaken	**take**	took	taken
shine	shone	shone	**teach**	taught	taught
shoe	shod	shod	**tear**	tore	torn
shoot	shot	shot	**tell**	told	told
show	showed	shown	**think**	thought	thought
shut	shut	shut	**throw**	threw	thrown
sing	sang	sung	**thrust**	thrust	thrust
sink	sank	sunk	**tread**	trod	trodden
sit	sat	sat	**under-stand**	under-stood	understood
sleep	slept	slept	**wake**	woke	woken
sling	slung	slung	**wear**	wore	worn
smell	smelt, smelled	smelt, smelled	**win**	won	won
			write	wrote	written
speak	spoke	spoken			
spell	spelled, spelt	spelled, spelt			

Abbreviations/Abreviaturas

adjective	*a*	adjetivo
abbreviation	*abbr/abr*	abreviatura
something	*aco*	alguma coisa
adverb	*adv*	advérbio
somebody, someone	*alg*	algúem
article	*art*	artigo
American (English)	*Amer*	(inglês) americano
anatomy	*anat*	anatomia
architecture	*arquit*	arquitetura
astrology	*astr/astrol*	astrologia
motoring	*auto*	automobilismo
aviation	*aviat*	aviação
Brazilian Portuguese	*B*	português do Brasil
biology	*biol*	biologia
botany	*bot*	botânica
Brazilian Portuguese	*Bras*	português do Brasil
cinema	*cine*	cinema
colloquial	*colloq*	coloquial
commerce	*comm/com*	comércio
computing	*comput*	computação
conjunction	*conj*	conjunção
cookery	*culin*	cozinha
electricity	*electr/eletr*	eletricidade
feminine	*f*	feminina
familiar	*fam*	familiar
figurative	*fig*	figurativo
geography	*geog*	geografia
grammar	*gramm/gram*	gramática
infinitive	*inf*	infinitivo
interjection	*int*	interjeição
interrogative	*interr*	interrogativo
invariable	*invar*	invariável
legal, law	*jur/jurid*	jurídico
language	*lang*	linguagem
literal	*lit*	literal
masculine	*m*	masculino